Great Britain
Northern Ireland
AZ Road Atlas

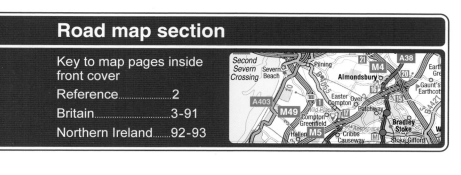
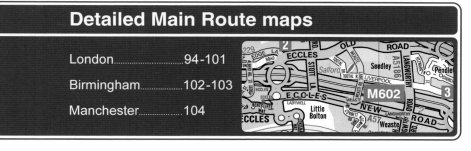

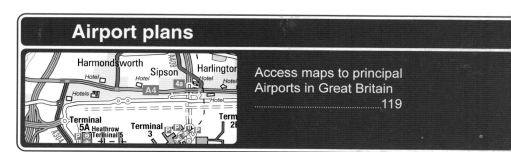
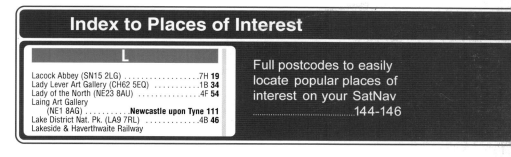

EDITION 38 2024

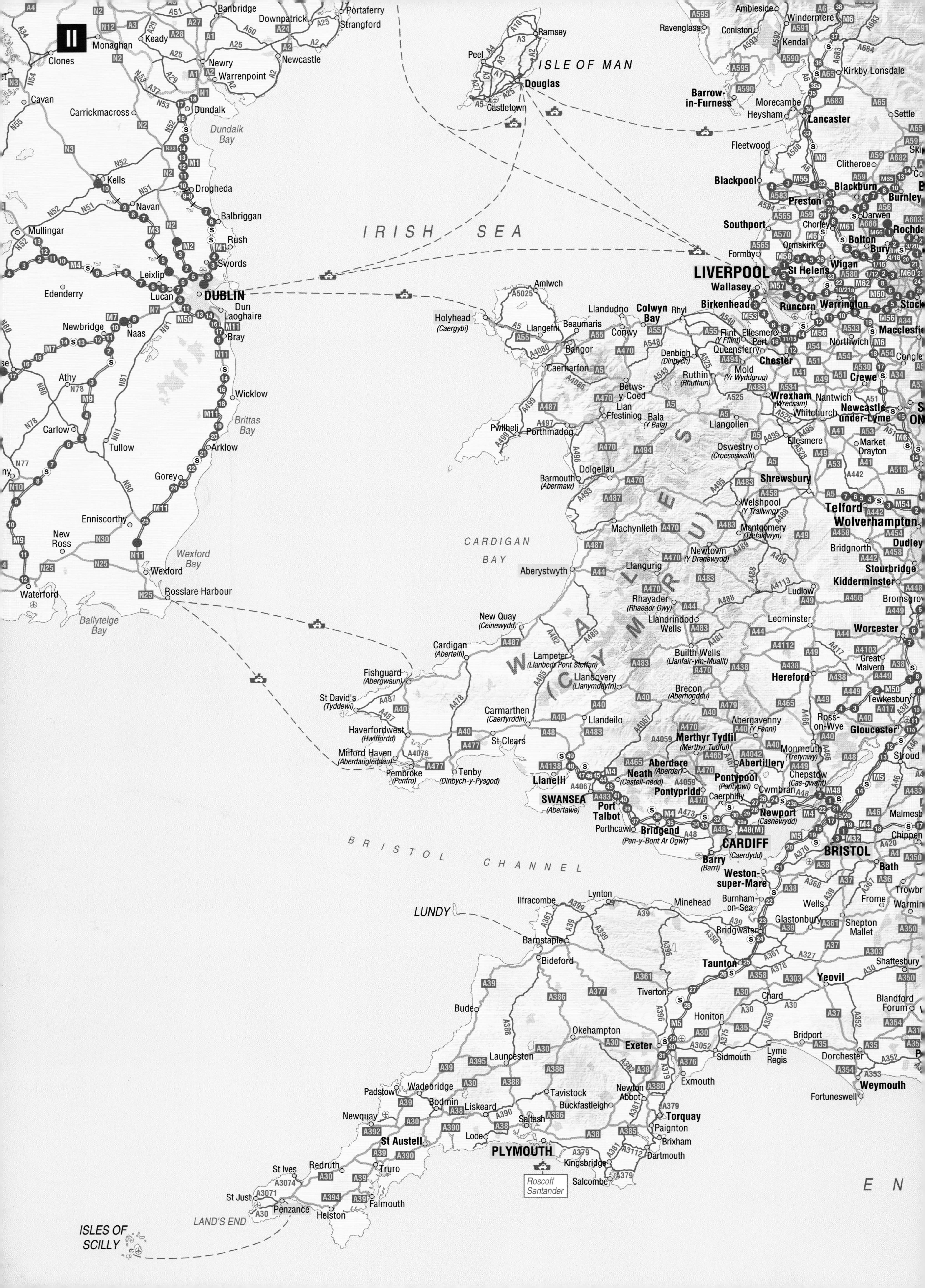

IRISH SEA
ISLE OF MAN
Ramsey
Peel
Douglas
Castletown
Banbridge
Downpatrick
Portaferry
Strangford
Newcastle
Newry
Warrenpoint
Keady
Monaghan
Clones
Cavan
Carrickmacross
Dundalk
Dundalk Bay
Kells
Navan
Drogheda
Balbriggan
Rush
Swords
Mullingar
Leixlip
Lucan
DUBLIN
Dun Laoghaire
Bray
Edenderry
Newbridge
Naas
Athy
Carlow
Tullow
Wicklow
Brittas Bay
Arklow
Gorey
Enniscorthy
New Ross
Wexford
Wexford Bay
Rosslare Harbour
Waterford
Ballyteige Bay
Ambleside
Windermere
Ravenglass
Coniston
Kendal
Kirkby Lonsdale
Barrow-in-Furness
Morecambe
Heysham
Lancaster
Settle
Fleetwood
Clitheroe
Blackpool
Blackburn
Burnley
Preston
Darwen
Southport
Chorley
Bolton
Rochdale
Ormskirk
Bury
Formby
Wigan
LIVERPOOL
St Helens
Wallasey
Birkenhead
Runcorn
Warrington
Macclesfield
Northwich
Chester
Congleton
Crewe
Nantwich
Wrexham (Wrecsam)
Whitchurch
Newcastle-under-Lyme
Ellesmere
Market Drayton
Oswestry (Croesoswallt)
Shrewsbury
Telford
Wolverhampton
Welshpool (Y Trallwng)
Montgomery (Trefaldwyn)
Newtown (Y Drenewydd)
Bridgnorth
Dudley
Stourbridge
Kidderminster
Ludlow
Bromsgrove
Leominster
Worcester
Great Malvern
Hereford
Tewkesbury
Ross-on-Wye
Gloucester
Monmouth (Trefynwy)
Stroud
Chepstow (Cas-gwent)
Amlwch
Holyhead (Caergybi)
Llangefni
Beaumaris
Llandudno
Colwyn Bay
Rhyl
Conwy
Bangor
Flint (Y Fflint)
Ellesmere Port
Queensferry
Denbigh (Dinbych)
Caernarfon
Ruthin (Rhuthun)
Mold (Yr Wyddgrug)
Betws-y-Coed
Llan Ffestiniog
Bala (Y Bala)
Llangollen
Pwllheli
Porthmadog
Barmouth (Abermaw)
Dolgellau
Machynlleth
WALES (CYMRU)
CARDIGAN BAY
Aberystwyth
Llangurig
Rhayader (Rhaeadr Gwy)
Llandrindod Wells
New Quay (Ceinewydd)
Builth Wells (Llanfair-ym-Muallt)
Cardigan (Aberteifi)
Lampeter (Llanbedr Pont Steffan)
Llandovery (Llanymddyfri)
Brecon (Aberhonddu)
Fishguard (Abergwaun)
St David's (Tyddewi)
Carmarthen (Caerfyrddin)
Llandeilo
Abergavenny (Y Fenni)
Haverfordwest (Hwlffordd)
St Clears
Merthyr Tydfil (Merthyr Tudful)
Milford Haven (Aberdaugleddau)
Aberdare (Aberdar)
Abertillery
Pembroke (Penfro)
Tenby (Dinbych-y-Pysgod)
Neath (Castell-nedd)
Pontypool (Pontypwl)
Llanelli
Pontypridd
Cwmbran
SWANSEA (Abertawe)
Port Talbot
Caerphilly
Newport (Casnewydd)
Porthcawl
Bridgend (Pen-y-Bont Ar Ogwr)
CARDIFF (Caerdydd)
BRISTOL
Malmesbury
Chippenham
Barry (Barri)
Bath
BRISTOL CHANNEL
Weston-super-Mare
LUNDY
Ilfracombe
Lynton
Minehead
Burnham-on-Sea
Frome
Wells
Barnstaple
Bridgwater
Glastonbury
Shepton Mallet
Bideford
Taunton
Shaftesbury
Yeovil
Tiverton
Chard
Bude
Honiton
Blandford Forum
Okehampton
Exeter
Sidmouth
Lyme Regis
Bridport
Dorchester
Launceston
Exmouth
Weymouth
Fortuneswell
Padstow
Wadebridge
Tavistock
Newton Abbot
Bodmin
Liskeard
Buckfastleigh
Torquay
Newquay
Saltash
Paignton
Looe
Brixham
St Austell
PLYMOUTH
Dartmouth
Kingsbridge
Roscoff Santander
Salcombe
St Ives
Redruth
Truro
St Just
Penzance
Falmouth
Helston
LAND'S END
ISLES OF SCILLY
EN

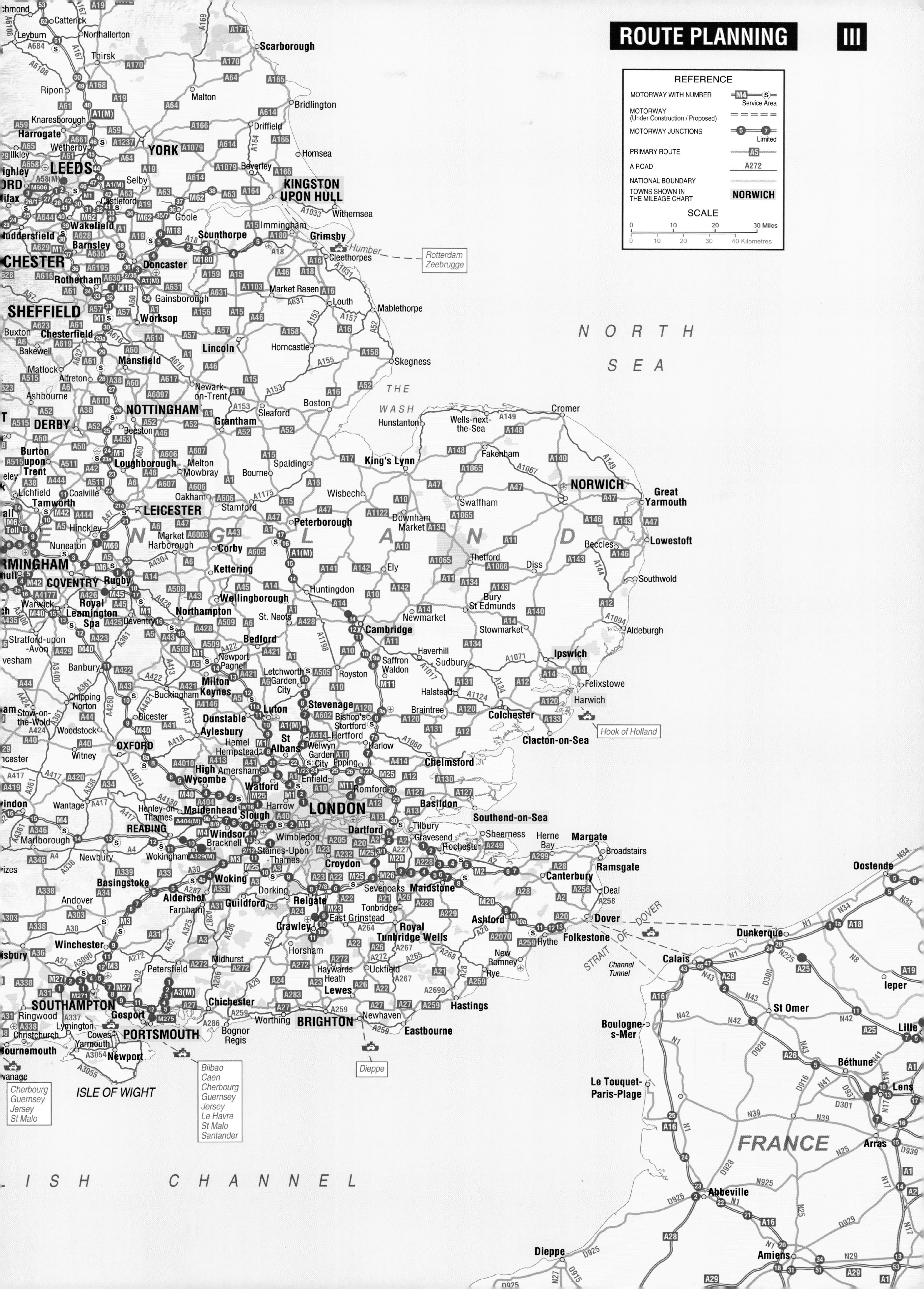

REFERENCE

MOTORWAY WITH NUMBER	M4 — s — Service Area
MOTORWAY (Under Construction / Proposed)	= = = = =
MOTORWAY JUNCTIONS	5 — 7 Limited
PRIMARY ROUTE	A5
A ROAD	A272
NATIONAL BOUNDARY	
TOWNS SHOWN IN THE MILEAGE CHART	NORWICH

SCALE

0   10   20   30 Miles
0 10 20 30 40 Kilometres

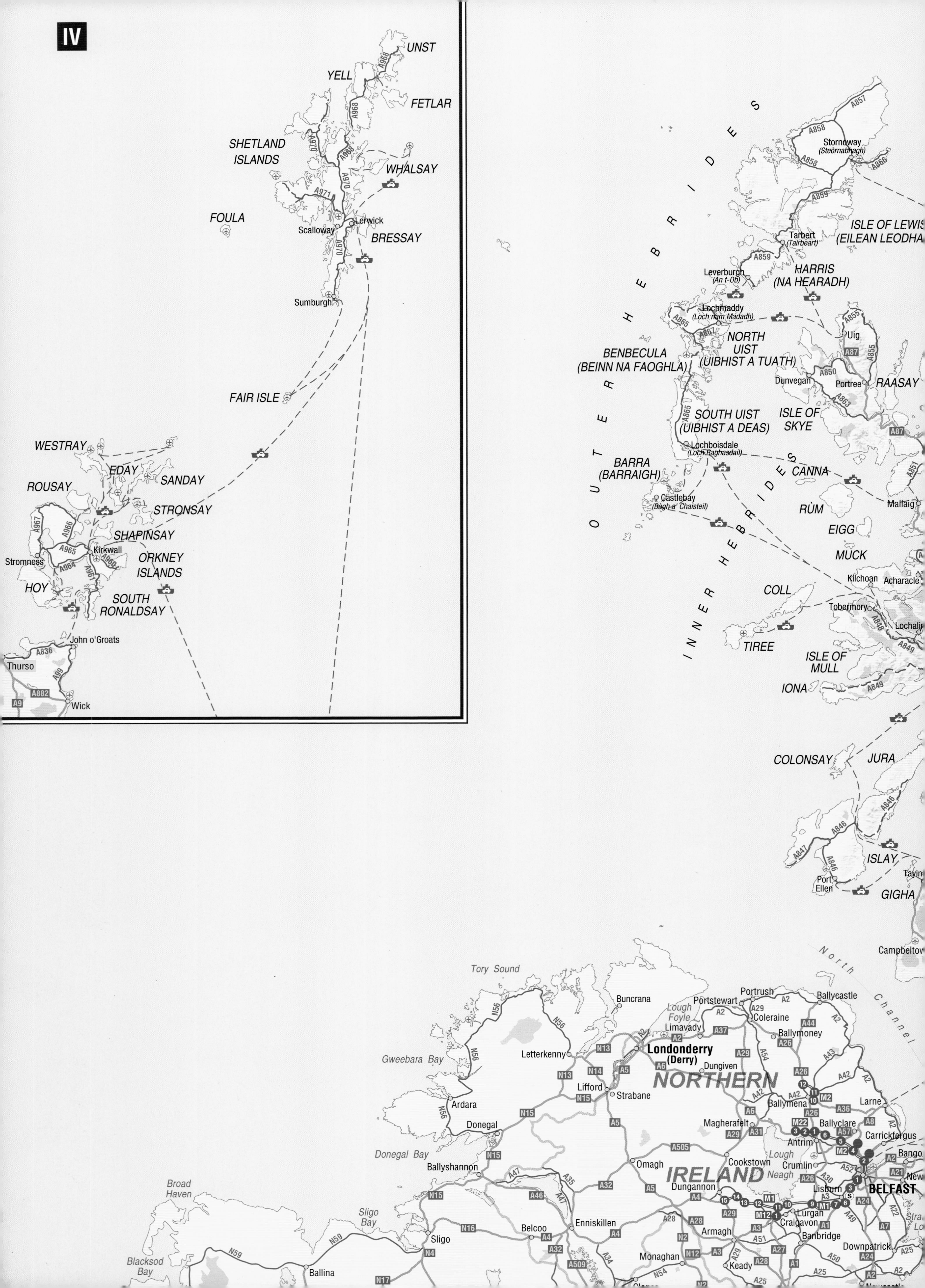

UNST
YELL
FETLAR
SHETLAND ISLANDS
WHALSAY
FOULA
Lerwick
Scalloway
BRESSAY
Sumburgh
FAIR ISLE
WESTRAY
EDAY
SANDAY
ROUSAY
STRONSAY
SHAPINSAY
Kirkwall
Stromness
ORKNEY ISLANDS
HOY
SOUTH RONALDSAY
John o'Groats
Thurso
Wick
A968
A970
A971
A967
A966
A965
A964
A961
A960
A836
A99
A882
A9
OUTER HEBRIDES
INNER HEBRIDES
Stornoway
(Steòrnabhagh)
A857
A858
A866
A859
ISLE OF LEWIS
(EILEAN LEODHAS)
Tarbert
(Tairbeart)
Leverburgh
(An t-Ob)
HARRIS
(NA HEARADH)
Lochmaddy
(Loch nam Madadh)
A865
A867
NORTH UIST
(UIBHIST A TUATH)
BENBECULA
(BEINN NA FAOGHLA)
Uig
A855
A87
A850
Dunvegan
Portree
A863
RAASAY
SOUTH UIST
(UIBHIST A DEAS)
ISLE OF SKYE
Lochboisdale
(Loch Baghasdail)
BARRA
(BARRAIGH)
CANNA
Castlebay
(Bagh a' Chaisteil)
A851
Mallaig
RÙM
EIGG
MUCK
Kilchoan
Acharacle
COLL
Tobermory
A848
Lochaline
A849
TIREE
ISLE OF MULL
IONA
COLONSAY
JURA
A846
A847
ISLAY
Port Ellen
Tayinloan
GIGHA
Campbeltown
North Channel
Tory Sound
Buncrana
Portrush
Portstewart
Ballycastle
Lough Foyle
Coleraine
Limavady
Ballymoney
Gweebara Bay
Letterkenny
Londonderry
(Derry)
Dungiven
NORTHERN
IRELAND
Lifford
Strabane
Ardara
Ballymena
Larne
Donegal
Magherafelt
Ballyclare
Carrickfergus
Antrim
Donegal Bay
Lough Neagh
Bangor
Ballyshannon
Omagh
Cookstown
Crumlin
Newtownards
Broad Haven
Dungannon
Lisburn
BELFAST
Sligo Bay
Lurgan
Craigavon
Strangford Lough
Sligo
Belcoo
Enniskillen
Armagh
Banbridge
Blacksod Bay
Downpatrick
Ballina
Monaghan
Keady
N56
N13
N14
N15
N16
N17
N4
N59
N12
N54
N2
A2
A29
A37
A54
A26
A44
A43
A42
A6
A5
A36
M2
M22
A57
A8
A31
A505
A52
A21
A30
A32
A35
A47
A46
A509
A34
A4
A28
M1
M12
A3
A51
A27
A1
A49
A24
A7
A22
A25
A50
S

NORTH SEA

Stromness
Scrabster
John o'Groats
Thurso
A836
A9
Tongue
A838
A836
A882
Wick
A9
A99
A836
A897
Scourie
A894
A838
Helmsdale
A9
Lochinver
A837
Lairg
A839
A836
Ullapool
A835
Bonar Bridge
A949
A836
Tain
Poolewe
A832
A832
Cromarty
A862
Nairn
A96
Moray Firth
Lossiemouth
A941
Elgin
Banff
Fraserburgh
A98
A98
Dingwall
A835
A862
A940
Keith
A96
A97
A95
A950
A950
Peterhead
Kinlochewe
A832
Achnasheen
A890
A896
A9
Inverness
A939
Grantown-on-Spey
A941
Dufftown
A920
Huntly
A96
A947
A952
A90
...eldaig
Strathcarron
A890
A82
Loch Ness
A95
A939
A944
Oldmeldrum
A96
A920
A920
...e of Lochalsh
(...ol Loch Ailse)
A87
Invermoriston
Aviemore
A9
A97
Inverurie
A944
A90
A87
Invergarry
Newtonmore
A9
A944
A980
A93
Petterculter
A830
A82
A86
A889
Braemar
Ballater
A93
Banchory
A93
ABERDEEN
Spean Bridge
A861
A828
A82
Fort William
Glencoe
A82
SCOTLAND
A90
A92
Stonehaven
A82
A924
Brechin
A935
Montrose
Oban
A85
A828
A85
Pitlochry
A93
A926
Forfar
A932
A933
A85
Crianlarich
A85
A822
Blairgowrie
A923
A94
Arbroath
Crieff
A85
Dunkeld
A93
A94
A90
A92
Carnoustie
Inveraray
A819
A82
A84
A9
A822
A823
Perth
A90
A930
Loch Lomond
A83
A814
A811
Doune
Dunblane
A91
A977
A824
M90
Kinross
A92
A914
St Andrews
A83
A815
A82
M9
Stirling
A91
M90
A92
Glenrothes
A915
Pittenweem
A817
Falkirk
M80
M9
Dunfermline
A985
Cowdenbeath
A921
Kirkcaldy
Firth of Forth
North Berwick
GLASGOW
EDINBURGH
A198
Dunbar
Greenock
Clydebank
Airdrie
M8
M9
Musselburgh
A1
A1107
Eyemouth
Paisley
M73
M8
Livingston
Dalkeith
A68
A1
Hamilton
Motherwell
A70
A702
Penicuik
Duns
A6105
Berwick-upon-Tweed
NORTH SEA
East Kilbride
A726
A723
A721
A701
A703
Peebles
Lauder
A68
A6105
A6112
A698
Kilmarnock
A71
M74
Biggar
A72
Galashiels
A697
A6091
A699
Coldstream
Kelso
Ayr
A70
A76
M74
A702
Selkirk
A7
A699
Jedburgh
A68
Wooler
Cumnock
A713
Sanquhar
A74(M)
Moffat
A701
Hawick
A68
Alnwick
Girvan
A714
New Galloway
A702
A712
A76
A7
Langholm
A6088
A1
Amble
A701
A76
Lockerbie
A709
A74(M)
A68
A696
Morpeth
A1068
Ashington
Newton Stewart
A712
A713
Dumfries
A75
Annan
A7
A6071
Brampton
A69
A68
A696
Blyth
NEWCASTLE UPON TYNE
A189
Whitley Bay
Amsterdam
Tynemouth
Stranraer
A75
Castle Douglas
Dalbeattie
Solway Firth
Carlisle
A595
A69
Hexham
A69
Corbridge
A68
A1(M)
South Shields
A1018
Gateshead
A692
Washington
SUNDERLAND
Cairnryan
Kirkcudbright
A711
A596
A6
Alston
A686
A689
Consett
A691
A693
A19
Seaham
A690
Whithorn
A746
A747
A755
A596
A595
M6
A689
Durham
A1(M)
A19
Peterlee
Workington
A596
A594
A595
M6
Cockermouth
Penrith
A66
A688
Bishop Auckland
A68
A690
HARTLEPOOL
Whitehaven
A595
Keswick
A66
A66
Brough
A66
A67
A688
A689
STOCKTON-ON-TEES
Egremont
A591
A592
A66
Barnard Castle
A66
A67
A1(M)
A174
Ravenglass
A595
Ambleside
A6
M6
Windermere
A685
Richmond
A66
A1(M)
MIDDLESBROUGH
Whitby
A171
Darlington
A19
A172
Coniston
A591
A683
Kendal
A684
Leyburn
A6108
Northallerton
A169
A171
ISLE OF MAN
Ramsey
A3
Scarborough

ISLE OF BUTE
Largs
A78
A737
Rothesay
A844
...nacraig
Irvine
A71
Troon
A77
Prestwick
Dunoon
Ardrossan
A841
Brodick
ISLE OF ARRAN
...rry
...ord

Mileage Chart and Journey Times

This chart shows the distance in miles and journey time between two cities or towns in Great Britain. Each route has been calculated using a combination of motorways, primary routes and other major roads. This is normally the quickest, though not always the shortest route.

Average journey times are calculated whilst driving at the maximum speed limit. These times are approximate and do not include traffic congestion or convenience breaks.

To find the distance and journey time between two cities or towns, follow a horizontal line and vertical column until they meet each other.

For example, the 285 mile journey from London to Penzance is approximately 4 hours and 59 minutes.

Thurso
Inverness
Aberdeen
Fort William
Perth
Glasgow
Edinburgh
Ayr
Coleraine
Londonderry
Antrim
Omagh
Belfast
Enniskillen
Armagh
Newry
Newcastle upon Tyne
Carlisle
Middlesbrough
Kendal
York
Bradford
Leeds
Kingston upon Hull
Liverpool
Manchester
Doncaster
Holyhead
Sheffield
Lincoln
Stoke-on-Trent
Nottingham
Derby
Shrewsbury
Leicester
Norwich
Aberystwyth
Birmingham
Coventry
Cambridge
Worcester
Ipswich
Gloucester
Oxford
Harwich
Swansea
Cardiff
London
Southend-on-Sea
Bristol
Reading
Dover
Salisbury
Southampton
Brighton
Exeter
Portsmouth
Plymouth
Penzance

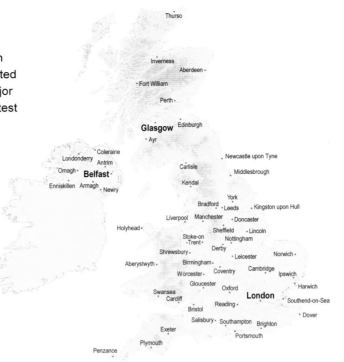

Northern Ireland

Journey times

	Armagh	Coleraine	Enniskillen	Londonderry	Newry	Omagh	Belfast
Antrim	1:01	0:53	1:41	1:14	1:07	1:13	0:30
Armagh		1:32	1:06	1:39	0:31	0:46	0:57
Coleraine			2:09	0:52	2:00	1:43	1:11
Enniskillen				1:29	1:37	0:39	1:38
Londonderry					2:09	0:54	1:33
Newry						1:15	0:51
Omagh							1:16

Distance in miles

	Antrim	Armagh	Coleraine	Enniskillen	Londonderry	Newry	Omagh
Armagh	43						
Coleraine	40	61					
Enniskillen	86	49	94				
Londonderry	55	69	31	60			
Newry	53	19	92	69	88		
Omagh	54	35	65	27	34	54	
Belfast	22	41	56	84	72	37	68

Belfast to London = 440m / 9:46h (excluding ferry)
Belfast to Glasgow = 104m / 4:46h (excluding ferry)

Great Britain

Journey times

	Aberystwyth	Ayr	Birmingham	Bradford	Brighton	Bristol	Cambridge	Cardiff	Carlisle	Coventry	Derby	Doncaster	Dover	Edinburgh	Exeter	Fort William	Glasgow	Gloucester	Harwich	Holyhead	Inverness	Ipswich	Kendal	Kingston upon Hull	Leeds	Leicester	Lincoln	Liverpool	Manchester	Middlesbrough	Newcastle upon Tyne	Norwich	Nottingham	Oxford	Penzance	Perth	Plymouth	Portsmouth	Reading	Salisbury	Sheffield	Shrewsbury	Southampton	Southend-on-Sea	Stoke-on-Trent	Swansea	Thurso	Worcester	York	London
Aberdeen	8:21	3:31	7:13	6:28	9:56	8:26	8:15	8:55	4:08	7:27	7:09	6:25	10:16	2:39	9:38	3:38	2:50	7:55	9:32	7:41	2:30	9:08	4:55	6:51	6:16	7:40	7:07	6:13	6:01	5:16	4:39	9:18	7:14	8:18	11:22	1:48	10:16	9:33	8:57	9:21	6:42	7:07	9:25	9:22	6:28	9:31	4:52	7:35	6:07	9:03
Aberystwyth		6:34	2:34	3:27	5:21	2:44	4:00	2:29	4:24	2:52	2:56	3:45	5:41	6:20	3:51	8:13	5:53	2:34	5:17	2:29	8:39	4:53	3:40	4:20	3:29	3:18	4:11	2:39	2:54	4:34	5:07	5:03	3:17	3:43	5:35	6:41	4:29	4:27	3:50	4:01	3:41	1:47	4:18	4:56	2:48	1:48	11:00	2:19	4:00	4:28
Ayr			5:28	4:28	8:11	6:42	6:31	7:10	2:24	5:43	5:25	4:41	8:32	1:48	7:54	3:03	0:48	6:11	7:48	5:56	3:51	7:24	3:10	5:06	4:32	5:55	5:22	4:29	4:16	3:56	3:28	7:34	5:29	6:34	9:37	1:53	8:31	7:49	7:13	7:37	4:57	5:23	7:40	7:37	4:43	7:46	6:12	5:50	4:22	7:16
Birmingham				2:15	3:04	1:41	1:43	2:09	3:16	0:36	1:01	1:40	3:25	5:12	2:53	7:05	4:45	1:10	3:01	2:59	7:31	2:37	2:32	2:21	2:05	1:01	1:55	1:49	1:46	2:55	3:28	2:46	1:08	1:27	4:36	5:33	3:30	2:42	2:06	2:39	1:36	0:59	2:33	2:39	1:02	2:44	9:52	0:49	2:21	2:11
Bradford					4:30	3:34	2:43	4:03	2:17	2:19	1:34	0:53	4:37	4:17	4:46	6:06	3:46	3:03	4:01	2:49	6:31	3:37	1:32	1:18	0:28	2:02	1:35	1:22	0:57	1:32	2:06	3:46	1:37	3:05	6:29	4:33	5:24	4:20	3:44	4:18	1:00	2:15	4:12	3:50	1:36	4:38	8:52	2:42	0:59	3:32
Brighton						2:49	2:09	3:26	6:00	2:42	3:15	3:53	1:53	7:53	3:41	9:49	7:29	2:47	2:19	5:39	10:14	2:20	5:15	4:35	4:19	2:57	3:43	4:32	4:29	5:08	5:42	3:05	3:21	1:58	5:24	8:16	4:18	1:14	1:39	1:54	3:49	3:45	1:35	1:41	3:45	4:01	12:35	3:07	4:35	1:27
Bristol							3:02	0:56	4:31	1:44	2:21	2:59	3:18	6:27	1:37	8:20	6:00	0:47	3:27	4:13	8:45	3:28	3:46	3:41	3:25	2:17	3:11	3:03	3:01	4:15	4:48	3:58	2:28	1:30	3:20	6:48	2:14	2:03	1:26	1:37	2:56	2:14	1:54	2:58	2:17	1:30	11:07	1:07	3:41	2:07
Cambridge								3:28	4:20	1:30	1:52	2:03	2:06	6:04	4:11	8:09	5:49	2:29	1:28	4:20	8:35	1:04	3:56	2:37	2:34	1:25	1:47	3:12	3:10	3:19	3:52	1:13	1:41	1:55	5:54	6:37	4:49	2:34	1:51	2:47	2:15	2:26	2:35	1:19	2:26	4:03	10:56	2:08	2:45	1:17
Cardiff									4:58	2:15	2:48	3:27	3:54	6:54	2:02	8:47	6:27	1:16	4:03	4:23	9:13	4:03	4:14	4:09	3:53	2:46	3:39	3:31	3:28	4:42	5:16	4:31	2:55	2:05	3:46	7:15	2:40	2:38	2:01	2:12	3:23	2:24	2:29	3:33	2:44	0:53	11:34	1:35	4:09	2:43
Carlisle										3:30	3:12	2:28	6:19	2:08	5:41	4:01	1:41	3:58	5:35	3:44	4:27	5:11	0:58	2:54	2:19	3:43	3:10	2:16	2:04	1:44	1:15	5:21	3:17	4:21	7:25	2:29	6:19	5:36	5:00	5:24	2:45	3:10	5:28	5:25	2:31	5:34	6:48	3:38	2:10	5:07
Coventry											1:03	1:41	3:05	5:29	2:55	7:22	5:02	1:12	2:49	3:13	7:48	2:21	2:49	2:23	2:06	0:45	1:39	2:06	2:03	2:56	3:30	2:31	1:09	1:04	4:38	5:50	3:32	2:19	1:43	2:17	1:37	1:18	2:11	2:20	1:19	2:49	10:09	0:56	2:22	1:53
Derby												0:57	3:33	4:58	3:31	7:02	4:42	1:48	3:09	2:52	7:27	2:45	2:28	1:39	1:23	0:49	1:24	1:45	1:42	2:13	2:46	2:55	0:33	1:51	5:14	5:29	4:08	3:06	2:30	3:04	0:54	1:21	2:58	2:48	0:53	3:22	9:49	1:27	1:39	2:19
Doncaster													3:58	4:13	4:12	6:19	3:59	2:30	3:21	3:17	6:44	2:57	2:16	0:56	0:43	1:27	0:55	1:48	1:25	1:28	2:02	3:07	1:02	2:30	5:56	4:46	4:50	3:45	3:09	3:43	0:30	2:13	3:36	3:11	1:44	4:04	9:05	2:09	0:54	2:57
Dover														7:56	4:14	10:08	7:48	3:16	2:16	5:59	10:34	2:17	5:35	4:29	4:26	3:14	3:40	4:52	4:49	5:11	5:45	3:02	3:34	2:27	5:57	8:36	4:51	2:23	2:08	2:50	4:06	4:05	2:38	1:37	4:05	4:29	12:55	3:36	4:38	1:34
Edinburgh															7:38	3:01	1:05	5:55	7:20	5:41	3:02	6:56	2:55	4:38	4:04	5:26	4:54	4:13	4:00	3:00	2:23	7:06	5:01	6:18	9:21	1:02	8:16	7:33	6:57	7:21	4:29	5:07	7:25	7:09	4:28	7:30	5:24	5:34	3:54	6:57
Exeter																9:31	7:11	1:58	4:36	5:24	9:56	4:37	4:57	4:52	4:36	3:28	4:22	4:14	4:12	5:26	5:59	5:07	3:39	2:46	1:54	7:59	0:53	2:38	2:43	1:55	4:07	3:25	2:27	4:02	3:28	2:37	12:18	2:18	4:52	3:16
Fort William																	2:26	7:49	9:26	7:35	1:32	9:02	4:49	6:44	6:10	7:34	7:00	6:07	5:54	5:34	5:06	9:12	7:07	8:12	11:15	2:09	10:10	9:27	8:51	9:15	6:35	7:01	9:19	9:16	6:22	9:24	4:04	7:28	6:01	8:56
Glasgow																		5:28	7:05	5:13	3:08	6:41	2:28	4:23	3:49	5:12	4:39	3:46	3:33	3:13	2:45	6:51	4:46	5:51	8:54	1:10	7:48	7:06	6:30	6:54	4:14	4:40	6:57	6:55	4:01	7:03	5:29	5:07	3:40	6:36
Gloucester																			3:25	3:42	8:14	3:22	3:15	3:10	2:54	1:46	2:39	2:32	2:29	3:43	4:17	3:31	1:56	1:11	3:39	6:16	2:33	2:00	1:24	1:42	2:24	1:42	1:52	2:56	1:45	1:49	10:35	0:36	3:10	2:05
Harwich																				5:38	9:53	0:42	5:13	3:55	3:52	2:43	3:05	4:30	4:28	4:37	5:10	1:32	2:59	2:26	6:20	7:55	5:14	2:49	2:17	3:12	3:33	3:44	3:01	1:09	3:44	4:38	12:14	3:26	4:03	1:42
Holyhead																					7:58	5:16	2:59	3:39	2:49	3:23	3:52	1:53	2:13	3:53	4:26	5:25	3:15	4:06	7:06	6:00	6:00	5:21	4:45	5:05	3:06	2:10	5:12	5:18	2:11	4:33	10:19	3:19	3:19	4:47
Inverness																						9:27	5:14	7:10	6:35	7:59	7:26	6:32	6:20	5:41	5:04	9:37	7:33	8:37	11:41	2:10	10:35	9:52	9:16	9:40	7:01	7:26	9:44	9:41	6:47	9:50	2:31	7:54	6:26	9:21
Ipswich																							4:50	3:31	3:28	2:20	2:41	4:06	4:04	4:13	4:46	1:08	2:35	2:27	6:21	7:31	5:15	2:50	2:18	3:13	3:09	3:20	3:02	1:10	3:20	4:39	11:50	3:02	3:39	1:43
Kendal																								2:44	1:53	3:02	3:00	1:36	1:23	1:38	1:59	5:00	2:54	3:41	6:44	3:13	5:38	4:56	4:20	4:44	2:22	2:30	4:47	4:53	1:50	4:53	7:32	2:57	2:04	4:22
Kingston upon Hull																									1:08	2:08	0:58	2:13	1:49	1:54	2:27	3:18	1:43	3:10	6:36	5:12	5:30	4:25	3:49	4:23	1:11	2:53	4:17	3:43	2:25	4:44	9:31	2:49	1:02	3:39
Leeds																										1:53	1:25	1:23	0:58	1:20	1:53	3:37	1:27	2:55	6:21	4:38	5:15	4:10	3:34	4:08	0:50	2:16	4:02	3:40	1:37	4:29	8:57	2:34	0:46	3:23
Leicester																											1:16	2:17	2:14	2:42	3:15	2:27	0:46	1:32	5:11	6:01	4:05	2:47	2:11	2:45	1:23	1:43	2:39	2:29	1:24	3:20	10:20	1:25	2:08	2:01
Lincoln																												2:31	2:02	2:11	2:44	2:20	0:59	2:28	6:07	5:29	5:01	3:43	3:07	3:41	1:07	2:33	3:34	2:54	2:10	4:16	9:48	2:21	1:35	2:51
Liverpool																													0:48	2:28	3:01	4:16	2:10	2:56	6:00	4:33	4:54	4:11	3:35	3:59	1:52	1:25	4:03	4:09	1:06	3:48	8:53	2:13	1:54	3:39
Manchester																														2:03	2:36	4:12	1:51	2:52	5:55	4:22	4:49	4:07	3:30	3:55	1:14	1:41	3:58	4:04	1:01	4:04	8:41	2:08	1:29	3:37
Middlesbrough																															0:55	4:20	2:15	3:43	7:09	3:40	6:03	4:58	4:22	4:56	1:43	3:20	4:50	4:24	2:40	5:17	8:02	3:22	1:05	4:12
Newcastle upon Tyne																																4:54	2:49	4:17	7:43	3:03	6:37	5:32	4:56	5:30	2:17	3:54	5:24	4:58	3:14	5:51	7:25	3:56	1:43	4:46
Norwich																																	2:44	2:58	6:51	7:40	5:45	3:31	2:48	3:43	3:18	3:29	3:32	2:00	3:28	5:06	11:59	3:10	3:48	2:13
Nottingham																																		1:57	5:23	5:34	4:17	3:12	2:36	3:10	0:57	1:44	3:04	2:49	1:18	3:31	9:53	1:36	1:42	2:25
Oxford																																			4:30	6:40	3:24	1:28	0:45	1:25	2:25	2:08	1:19	1:56	2:09	2:40	10:59	1:31	3:10	1:15
Penzance																																				9:43	1:41	4:22	4:27	3:39	5:51	5:09	4:11	5:46	5:12	4:20	14:02	4:02	6:36	4:59
Perth																																					8:37	7:54	7:18	7:42	5:03	5:28	7:46	7:43	4:49	7:52	4:30	5:55	4:28	7:24
Plymouth																																						3:16	3:20	2:32	4:44	4:02	3:04	4:39	4:05	3:14	12:55	2:55	5:29	3:54
Portsmouth																																							1:18	0:52	3:39	3:23	0:32	2:11	3:23	3:13	12:13	2:20	4:25	1:39
Reading																																								1:22	3:01	2:45	1:09	1:46	2:45	2:37	11:35	1:44	3:47	0:56
Salisbury																																									3:37	3:09	0:40	2:37	3:12	2:47	12:02	2:02	4:22	1:52
Sheffield																																										2:08	3:32	3:22	1:40	3:59	9:22	2:04	1:11	2:53
Shrewsbury																																											3:16	3:22	1:04	2:45	9:46	1:23	2:46	2:53
Southampton																																												2:26	3:15	3:05	12:05	2:12	4:16	1:40
Southend-on-Sea																																													3:21	4:09	12:02	3:03	3:51	1:07
Stoke-on-Trent																																														3:18	9:08	1:23	2:09	2:53
Swansea																																															12:11	2:10	4:44	3:18
Thurso																																																10:15	8:47	11:43
Worcester																																																	2:49	2:24
York																																																		3:39

Distance in miles

	Aberdeen	Aberystwyth	Ayr	Birmingham	Bradford	Brighton	Bristol	Cambridge	Cardiff	Carlisle	Coventry	Derby	Doncaster	Dover	Edinburgh	Exeter	Fort William	Glasgow	Gloucester	Harwich	Holyhead	Inverness	Ipswich	Kendal	Kingston upon Hull	Leeds	Leicester	Lincoln	Liverpool	Manchester	Middlesbrough	Newcastle upon Tyne	Norwich	Nottingham	Oxford	Penzance	Perth	Plymouth	Portsmouth	Reading	Salisbury	Sheffield	Shrewsbury	Southampton	Southend-on-Sea	Stoke-on-Trent	Swansea	Thurso	Worcester	York
Aberystwyth	471																																																	
Ayr	181	324																																																
Birmingham	423	114	272																																															
Bradford	377	159	196	124																																														
Brighton	596	258	441	169	263																																													
Bristol	505	122	375	88	215	129																																												
Cambridge	487	198	366	102	156	117	167																																											
Cardiff	525	106	377	106	233	168	42	201																																										
Carlisle	229	232	89	183	107	345	286	256	288																																									
Coventry	442	134	297	18	124	157	102	84	129	200																																								
Derby	418	137	269	41	88	188	134	99	159	180	43																																							
Doncaster	371	192	239	95	40	232	184	117	210	150	94	57																																						
Dover	620	315	477	195	284	81	194	118	233	393	180	208	244																																					
Edinburgh	126	340	75	284	198	466	377	326	379	91	303	266	212	444																																				
Exeter	581	199	425	161	282	170	75	323	107	336	166	213	257	244	439																																			
Fort William	159	430	136	391	305	568	478	456	486	198	415	387	345	591	131	549																																		
Glasgow	146	322	36	291	203	468	378	355	384	96	313	282	245	491	46	449	100																																	
Gloucester	473	109	317	53	171	152	35	132	53	228	59	93	149	189	331	107	435	324																																
Harwich	568	258	411	170	224	130	203	64	234	323	152	167	185	129	397	262	524	419	171																															
Holyhead	452	96	315	151	158	330	204	252	209	226	167	156	169	358	316	279	423	323	189	331																														
Inverness	105	492	198	449	353	620	536	490	558	260	458	421	369	601	157	607	63	162	496	554	481																													
Ipswich	538	268	420	156	210	125	206	54	240	311	138	155	171	127	381	264	510	409	177	21	307	538																												
Kendal	280	182	139	151	62	324	235	215	232	50	170	136	99	344	141	307	248	146	200	279	180	310	268																											
Kingston upon Hull	398	235	255	139	68	243	228	134	239	165	123	94	37	254	230	290	367	255	195	204	218	387	189	127																										
Leeds	359	171	198	119	9	256	209	144	226	111	117	74	32	275	190	279	309	208	167	217	162	345	197	72	60																									
Leicester	445	155	294	43	99	163	118	70	140	214	24	30	73	183	282	189	412	312	83	146	182	431	125	166	98	97																								
Lincoln	411	208	249	87	80	207	170	88	192	178	76	53	41	206	247	241	376	274	135	152	204	402	124	140	46	72	52																							
Liverpool	354	120	199	99	67	267	180	179	169	110	113	90	89	294	201	240	308	213	142	265	95	370	236	75	126	73	110	118																						
Manchester	349	128	204	87	37	252	167	159	188	117	99	58	51	273	208	239	315	215	132	230	120	363	211	72	96	42	95	87	34																					
Middlesbrough	289	233	181	174	69	316	265	196	287	92	175	130	84	316	147	337	279	192	230	266	226	306	253	77	88	64	154	127	134	106																				
Newcastle upon Tyne	252	266	146	209	98	345	300	232	312	58	209	165	115	350	104	369	237	153	263	297	257	263	287	88	130	96	188	153	167	136	40																			
Norwich	536	270	348	163	185	174	234	62	256	280	142	146	142	169	351	284	478	378	193	72	289	505	44	249	145	178	112	103	222	177	221	252																		
Nottingham	416	155	267	54	78	191	140	84	165	188	52	15	48	210	256	218	386	286	108	165	177	410	140	141	92	72	27	37	107	68	128	159	118																	
Oxford	497	151	335	68	167	106	73	92	106	267	57	101	138	142	358	151	465	365	47	134	208	515	128	223	175	162	76	123	168	157	218	253	159	104																
Penzance	688	301	552	269	394	279	184	343	218	463	278	316	369	355	551	109	663	561	217	374	388	715	375	419	412	391	310	359	353	344	449	481	393	323	261															
Perth	86	366	85	336	245	509	412	370	422	134	346	309	254	485	43	487	103	59	362	439	360	113	424	184	273	233	326	290	244	254	191	148	394	299	404	598														
Plymouth	619	232	461	203	325	206	111	274	159	372	209	254	300	286	485	43	592	490	150	305	322	648	305	348	326	323	231	284	299	281	379	412	327	255	193	75	529													
Portsmouth	579	231	440	147	274	50	95	132	138	357	132	184	231	137	448	127	555	455	114	161	303	603	158	308	268	245	166	209	254	237	315	360	200	191	83	235	486	170												
Reading	538	180	399	103	213	79	77	90	112	309	90	138	184	115	402	141	506	406	75	129	264	554	126	263	209	207	113	168	193	197	264	295	152	129	25	251	445	184	60											
Salisbury	538	178	383	121	245	82	53	140	101	312	113	159	207	158	400	91	510	408	73	177	262	569	177	265	251	230	132	187	213	208	287	318	200	162	65	201	443	132	43	57										
Sheffield	390	173	235	79	40	225	163	121	193	154	75	35	21	268	230	245	352	250	139	185	164	387	176	102	66	33	68	46	74	40	102	133	144	37	137	361	273	293	228	160	203									
Shrewsbury	419	73	260	47	100	216	116	140	107	171	64	67	114	249	262	175	369	267	77	215	104	424	195	125	163	102	79	123	59	67	166	203	196	86	105	286	309	218	195	147	150	85								
Southampton	564	213	401	128	235	64	75	129	122	330	114	167	201	150	433	106	528	426	98	157	287	590	162	276	249	230	136	189	235	215	288	320	190	162	66	217	476	149	20	47	23	206	175							
Southend-on-Sea	549	258	431	152	220	85	177	64	211	342	129	168	185	89	395	226	548	438	152	57	303	549	57	283	200	213	139	156	255	225	262	299	99	160	105	337	439	269	117	98	132	197	173	126						
Stoke-on-Trent	381	108	243	47	75	217	127	137	140	150	64	36	74	236	241	202	348	248	95	201	122	410	179	121	117	78	55	87	56	36	142	173	171	55	118	311	287	241	201	147	168	50	35	183	199					
Swansea	529	76	368	124	220	209	80	236	41	279	150	184	244	264	370	154	477	375	91	279	172	578	279	249	262	229	174	226	168	187	293	323	286	178	144	266	446	196	175	147	136	202	124	159	245	159				
Thurso	212	584	304	557	461	728	644	589	640	352	552	529	475	706	262	715	169	268	604	657	589	108	654	402	492	453	544	510	463	471	410	367	613	519	621	823	220	758	709	662	664	506	523	682	659	502	631			
Worcester	448	96	309	29	135	162	62	119	73	220	46	68	124	197	306	136	418	311	28	168	151	480	174	169	166	146	72	118	108	101	203	229	180	85	57	244	350	177	146	95	101	103	49	124	150	65	97	572		
York	345	193	201	129	34	269	227	151	237	116	129	84	33	269	187	289	314	214	181	232	185	344	200	81	38	24	108	76	96	65	48	83	176	84	174	400	230	331	257	217	244	54	132	244	214	114	268	450	164	
London	537	228	440	118	203	53	118	61	151	309	97	129	171	76	403	179	511	404	116	86	277	562	82	263	214	195	103	155	211	209	251	283	117	128	59	285	451	216	84	41	92	166	161	82	43	161	187	669	136	211

Scales to Map Pages

BRITAIN
1:221,760 = 3.5 miles to 1 inch (2.54 cm)
2.2 km to 1 cm

0 1 2 3 4 5 10 15 20 25 Miles
0 1 2 3 4 5 10 15 20 25 30 35 40 Kilometres

NORTHERN IRELAND
1:380,160 = 6 miles to 1 inch (2.54 cm)
3.8 km to 1 cm

0 1 2 3 4 5 10 15 20 25 Miles
0 1 2 3 4 5 10 15 20 25 30 35 40 Kilometres

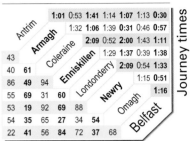

Limited Interchange Motorway Junctions

Limited Interchange Motorway Junctions are shown on the mapping pages by red junction indicators 2

M1

Junction		
2	Northbound Southbound	No exit, access from A1 only No access, exit to A1 only
4	Northbound Southbound	No exit, access from A41 only No access, exit to A41 only
6a	Northbound Southbound	No exit, access from M25 only No access, exit to M25 only
17	Northbound Southbound	No access, exit to M45 only No exit, access from M45 only
19	Northbound Southbound	Exit to M6 only, access from A14 only Access from M6 only, exit to A14 only
21a	Northbound Southbound	No access, exit to A46 only No exit, access from A46 only
24a	Northbound Southbound	No exit Access from A50 only
35a	Northbound Southbound	No access, exit to A616 only No exit, access from A616 only
43	Northbound Southbound	Exit to M621 only Access from M621 only
48	Eastbound Westbound	Exit to A1(M) northbound only Access from A1(M) southbound only

M2

Junction		
1	Eastbound Westbound	Access from A2 eastbound only Exit to A2 westbound only

M3

Junction		
8	Eastbound Westbound	No exit, access from A303 only No access, exit to A303 only
10	Northbound Southbound	No access from A31 No exit to A31
13	Southbound	No access from A335 to M3 leading to M27 Eastbound

M4

Junction		
1	Eastbound Westbound	Exit to A4 eastbound only Access from A4 westbound only
21	Eastbound Westbound	No exit to M48 No access from M48
23	Eastbound Westbound	No access from M48 No exit to M48
25	Eastbound Westbound	No exit No access
25a	Eastbound Westbound	No exit No access
29	Eastbound Westbound	No exit, access from A48(M) only No access, exit to A48(M) only
38	Westbound	No access, exit to A48 only
39	Eastbound Westbound	No access or exit No exit, access from A48 only
42	Eastbound Westbound	No access from A48 No exit to A48

M5

Junction		
10	Northbound Southbound	No exit, access from A4019 only No access, exit to A4019 only
11a	Southbound	No exit to A417 westbound
18a	Northbound Southbound	No access from M49 No exit to M49

M6

Junction		
3a	Eastbound Westbound	No exit to M6 Toll No access from M6 Toll
4	Northbound Southbound	No exit to M42 northbound No access from M42 southbound No exit to M42 No access from M42 southbound
4a	Northbound Southbound	No exit, access from M42 S'bound only No access, exit to M42 only
5	Northbound Southbound	No access, exit to A452 only No exit, access from A452 only
10a	Northbound Southbound	No access, exit to M54 only No exit, access from M54 only
11a	Northbound Southbound	No exit to M6 Toll No access from M6 Toll
20	Northbound Southbound	No exit to M56 eastbound No access from M56 westbound
24	Northbound Southbound	No exit, access from A58 only No access, exit to A58 only
25	Northbound Southbound	No access, exit to A49 only No exit, access from A49 only
30	Northbound Southbound	No exit, access from M61 N'bound only No access, exit to M61 S'bound only
31a	Northbound Southbound	No access, exit to B6242 only No exit, access from B6242 only
45	Northbound Southbound	No access onto A74(M) No exit from A74(M)

M6 Toll

Junction		
T1	Northbound Southbound	No exit No access
T2	Northbound Southbound	No access or exit No access
T5	Northbound Southbound	No exit No access
T7	Northbound Southbound	No access from A5 No exit
T8	Northbound Southbound	No exit to A460 northbound No exit

M8

Junction		
6	Eastbound Westbound	No exit, access only No access, exit only
6a	Eastbound Westbound	No access, exit only No exit, access only
7	Eastbound Westbound	No access, exit only No exit, access only
7a	Eastbound Westbound	No exit, access from A725 Northbound only No access, exit to A725 Southbound only
8	Eastbound Westbound	No exit to M73 northbound No access from M73 southbound
9	Eastbound Westbound	No access, exit only No exit, access only
13	Eastbound Westbound	No access from M80 southbound No exit to M80 northbound
14	Eastbound Westbound	No access, exit only No exit, access only
16	Eastbound Westbound	No exit, access only No access, exit only
17	Eastbound Westbound	No exit, access from A82 only No access, exit to A82 only
18	Westbound	No exit, access only
19	Eastbound Westbound	No exit to A814 eastbound No access from A814 westbound
20	Eastbound Westbound	No exit, access only No access, exit only
21	Eastbound Westbound	No access, exit only No exit, access only
22	Eastbound Westbound	No exit, access from M77 only No access, exit to M77 only
23	Eastbound Westbound	No exit, access from B768 only No access, exit to B768 only
25	Eastbound & Westbound	Access from A739 southbound only Exit to A739 northbound only
25a	Eastbound Westbound	Access only Exit only
28	Eastbound Westbound	No exit, access from airport only No access, exit to airport only
29a	Eastbound Westbound	No exit, access only No access, exit only

M9

Junction		
2	Northbound Southbound	No exit, access from B8046 only No access, exit to B8046 only
3	Northbound Southbound	No access, exit to A803 only No exit, access from A803 only
6	Northbound Southbound	No exit, access only No access, exit to A905 only
8	Northbound Southbound	No access, exit to M876 only No exit, access from M876 only

M11

Junction		
4	Northbound Southbound	No exit, access from A406 E'bound only No access, exit to A406 W'bound only
5	Northbound Southbound	No access, exit to A1168 only No exit, access from A1168 only
8a	Northbound Southbound	No access, exit only No exit, access only
9	Northbound Southbound	No access, exit only No exit, access only
13	Northbound Southbound	No access, exit only No exit, access only
14	Northbound Southbound	No access from A428 eastbound No exit to A428 westbound No exit, access from A428 E'bound only

M20

Junction		
2	Eastbound Westbound	No access, exit to A20 only (access via M26 Junction 2a) No exit, access only (exit via M26 J2a)
3	Eastbound Westbound	No exit, access from M26 E'bound only No access, exit to M26 W'bound only
10	Eastbound Westbound	No access, exit only No exit, access only
11a	Eastbound Westbound	No access from Channel Tunnel No exit to Channel Tunnel

M23

Junction		
7	Northbound Southbound	No exit to A23 southbound No access from A23 northbound

M25

Junction		
5	Clockwise Anti-clockwise	No exit to M26 eastbound No access from M26 westbound
Spur to A21	Northbound Southbound	No exit to M26 eastbound No access from M26 westbound
19	Clockwise Anti-clockwise	No access, exit only No exit, access only
21	Clockwise & Anti-clockwise	No exit to M1 southbound No access from M1 northbound
31	Northbound Southbound	No access, exit only (access via J.30) No exit, access only (exit via J.30)

M26

Junction with M25 (M25 Jun.5)

Eastbound	No access from M25 clockwise or spur from A21 northbound
Westbound	No exit to M25 anti-clockwise or spur to A21 southbound

Junction with M20 (M20 Jun.3)

Eastbound	No exit to M20 westbound
Westbound	No access from M20 eastbound

M27

Junction		
4	Eastbound & Westbound	No exit to A33 S'bound (Southampton) No access from A33 northbound
10	Eastbound Westbound	No exit, access from A32 only No access, exit to A32 only

M40

Junction		
3	North-Westbound South-Eastbound	No access, exit to A40 only No exit, access from A40 only
7	N.W bound S.E bound	No access, exit only No exit, access only
13	N.W bound S.E bound	No access, exit only No exit, access only
14	N.W bound S.E bound	No exit, access only No access, exit only
16	N.W bound S.E bound	No exit, access only No access, exit only

M42

Junction		
1	Eastbound Westbound	No exit No access
7	Northbound Southbound	No access, exit to M6 only No exit, access from M6 N'bound only
8	Northbound Southbound	No exit, access from M6 S'bound only Exit to M6 nothbound only Access from M6 southbound only

M45

Junction with M1 (M1 Jun.17)

Eastbound	No exit to M1 northbound
Westbound	No access from M1 southbound

Junction with A45 east of Dunchurch

Eastbound	No access, exit to A45 only
Westbound	No exit, access from A45 N'bound only

M48

Junction with M4 (M4 Jun.21)

Eastbound	No exit to M4 westbound
Westbound	No access from M4 eastbound

Junction with M4 (M4 Jun.23)

Eastbound	No access from M4 westbound
Westbound	No exit to M4 eastbound

M53

Junction		
11	Northbound & Southbound	No access from M56 eastbound, no exit to M56 westbound

M56

Junction		
1	Eastbound S.E bound Westbound	No exit to M60 N.W bound No exit to A34 southbound No access from A34 northbound No access from M60
2	Eastbound Westbound	No exit, access from A560 only No access, exit to A560 only
3	Eastbound Westbound	No access, exit only No exit, access only
4	Eastbound Westbound	No exit, access only No access, exit only
7	Westbound	No access, exit only
8	Eastbound Westbound	No access or exit No exit, access from A556 only
9	Eastbound Westbound	No access from M6 northbound No exit to M60 southbound
10a	Northbound Southbound	No exit, access only No access, exit only
15	Eastbound Westbound	No exit to M53 No access from M53

M57

Junction		
3	Northbound Southbound	No exit, access only No access, exit only
5	Northbound Southbound	No exit, access from A580 W'bound only No access, exit to A580 E'bound only

M60

Junction		
2	N.E bound S.W bound	No access, exit to A560 only No exit, access from A560 only
3	Eastbound Westbound	No access from A34 southbound No exit to A34 northbound
4	Eastbound Westbound	No exit to M56 S.W bound No exit to A34 northbound No access from A34 southbound No access from M56 eastbound
5	N.W bound S.E bound	No access from or exit to A5103 S'bound No access from or exit to A5103 N'bound
14	Eastbound Westbound	No exit to A580 No access from A580 westbound No exit to A580 eastbound No access from A580
16	Eastbound Westbound	No exit, access from A666 only No access, exit to A666 only
20	Eastbound Westbound	No access from A664 No exit to A664
22	Westbound	No access from A62
25	S.W bound	No access from A560 / A6017
26	N.E bound	No access or exit
27	N.E bound S.W bound	No access, exit only No exit, access only

M61

Junction		
2&3	N.W bound S.E bound	No access from A580 eastbound No exit to A580 westbound

Junction with M6 (M6 Jun.30)

N.W bound	No exit to M6 southbound
S.E bound	No access from M6 northbound

M62

Junction		
23	Eastbound Westbound	No access, exit to A640 only No exit, access from A640 only

M65

Junction		
9	N.E bound S.W bound	No access, exit to A679 only No exit, access from A679 only
11	N.E bound S.W bound	No exit, access only No access, exit only

M66

Junction		
1	Northbound Southbound	No access, exit to A56 only No exit, access from A56 only

M67

Junction		
1	Eastbound Westbound	Access from A57 eastbound only Exit to A57 westbound only
1a	Eastbound Westbound	No access, exit to A6017 only No exit, access from A6017 only
2	Eastbound Westbound	No exit, access from A57 only No access, exit to A57 only

M69

Junction		
2	N.E bound S.W bound	No exit, access from B4669 only No access, exit to B4669 only

M73

Junction		
1	Southbound	No exit to A721 eastbound
2	Northbound Southbound	No access from M8 eastbound No exit to A89 eastbound No exit to M8 westbound No access from A89 westbound
3	Northbound Southbound	No exit to A80 S.W bound No access from A80 N.E bound

M74

Junction		
1	Eastbound Westbound	No access from M8 Westbound No exit to M8 Westbound
3	Eastbound Westbound	No exit No access
7	Northbound Southbound	No exit, access from A72 only No access, exit to A72 only
9	Northbound Southbound	No access or exit No access, exit to B7078 only
10	Southbound	No exit, access from B7078 only
11	Northbound Southbound	No exit, access from B7078 only No access, exit to B7078 only
12	Northbound Southbound	No access, exit to A70 only No exit, access from A70 only

M77

Junction with M8 (M8 Jun.22)

Northbound	No exit to M8 westbound
Southbound	No access from M8 eastbound

Junction		
4	Northbound Southbound	No exit No access
6	Northbound Southbound	No exit to A77 No access from A77
7	Northbound	No access from A77 No exit to A77

M80

Junction		
1	Northbound Southbound	No access from M8 westbound No exit to M8 eastbound
4a	Northbound Southbound	No access No exit
6a	Northbound Southbound	No exit No access
8	Northbound Southbound	No access from M876 No exit to M876

M90

Junction		
1	Northbound Southbound	No exit No Access from A90
2a	Northbound Southbound	No access, exit to A92 only No exit, access from A92 only
7	Northbound Southbound	No exit, access from A91 only No access, exit to A91 only
8	Northbound Southbound	No access, exit to A91 only No exit, access from A91 only
10	Northbound Southbound	No access from A912 Exit to A912 northbound only No exit to A912 Access from A912 southbound only

M180

Junction		
1	Eastbound Westbound	No access, exit only No exit, access from A18 only

M606

Junction		
2	Northbound	No access, exit only

M621

Junction		
2a	Eastbound Westbound	No exit, access only No access, exit only
4	Southbound	No exit
5	Northbound Southbound	No access, exit to A61 only No exit, access from A61 only
6	Northbound Southbound	No exit, access only No access, exit only
7	Eastbound Westbound	No access, exit only No exit, access only
8	Northbound Southbound	No access, exit only No exit, access only

M876

Junction with M80 (M80 Jun.5)

N.E bound	No access from M80 southbound
S.W bound	No exit to M80 northbound

Junction with M9 (M9 Jun.8)

N.E bound	No exit to M9 northbound
S.W bound	No access from M9 southbound

A1(M)

Hertfordshire Section

Junction		
2	Northbound Southbound	No access, exit only No exit, access from A1001 only
3	Southbound	No access, exit only
5	Northbound Southbound	No exit, access only No access or exit

Cambridgeshire Section

Junction		
14	Northbound Southbound	No exit, access only No access, exit only

Leeds Section

Junction		
40	Southbound	Exit to A1 southbound only
43	Northbound Southbound	Access from M1 eastbound only Exit to M1 westbound only

Durham Section

Junction		
57	Northbound Southbound	No access, exit to A66(M) only No exit, access from A66(M)
65	Northbound Southbound	Exit to A1 N.W bound and to A194(M) only Access from A1 S.E bound and from A194(M) only

A3(M)

Junction		
4	Northbound Southbound	No access, exit only No exit, access only

Aston Expressway A38(M)

Junction with Victoria Road, Aston

Northbound	No exit, access only
Southbound	No access, exit only

A48(M)

Junction with M4 (M4 Jun.29)

N.E bound	Exit to M4 eastbound only
S.W bound	Access from M4 westbound only

Junction		
29a	N.E bound S.W bound	Access from A48 eastbound only Exit to A48 westbound only

Mancunian Way A57(M)

Junction with A34 Brook Street, Manchester

Eastbound	No access, exit to A34 Brook Street, southbound only
Westbound	No exit, access only

Leeds Inner Ring Road A58(M)

Junction with Park Lane / Westgate

Southbound	No access, exit only

Leeds Inner Ring Road A64(M) (continuation of A58(M))

Junction with A58 Clay Pit Lane

Eastbound	No access
Westbound	No exit

A66(M)

Junction with A1(M) (A1(M) Jun.57)

N.E bound	Access from A1(M) N'bound only
S.W bound	Exit to A1(M) southbound only

A74(M)

Junction		
18	Northbound Southbound	No access No exit

Newcastle Central Motorway A167(M)

Junction with Camden Street

Northbound	No exit, access only
Southbound	No access or exit

A194(M)

Junction with A1(M) (A1(M) Jun.65) **and A1 Gateshead Western By-Pass**

Northbound	Access from A1(M) only
Southbound	Exit to A1(M) only

Northern Ireland

M1

Junction		
3	Northbound Southbound	No exit, access only No access, exit only
7	Westbound	No access, exit only

M2

Junction		
2	Eastbound Westbound	No access to M5 northbound No exit to M5 southbound

M5

Junction		
2	Northbound Southbound	No access from M2 eastbound No exit to M2 westbound

Motorway
Autoroute
Autobahn
`M1`

Motorway Under Construction
Autoroute en construction
Autobahn im Bau

Motorway Proposed
Autoroute prévue
Geplante Autobahn

Motorway Junctions with Numbers
Unlimited Interchange **4**
Limited Interchange **5**
Autoroute échangeur numéroté
Echangeur complet
Echangeur partiel
Autobahnanschlußstelle mit Nummer
Unbeschränkter Fahrtrichtungswechsel
Beschränkter Fahrtrichtungswechsel

Motorway Service Area (with fuel station)
with access from one carriageway only
Aire de services d'autoroute (avec station service)
accessible d'un seul côté
Rastplatz oder Raststätte (mit tankstelle)
Einbahn

Major Road Service Area (with fuel station) with 24 hour facilities
Primary Route Class A Road
Aire de services sur route prioritaire (avec station service) Ouverte 24h sur 24
Route à grande circulation Route de type A
Raststätte (mit tankstelle) Durchgehend geöffnet
Hauptverkehrsstraße A- Straße

Major Road Junctions Detailed **4**
Jonctions grands routiers Détaillé
Hauptverkehrsstraße Kreuzungen Ausführlich
 Other Autre Andere

Truckstop (selection of)
Sélection d'aire pour poids lourds
Auswahl von Fernfahrerrastplatz

Primary Route
Route à grande circulation
Hauptverkehrsstraße
`A41`

Primary Route Junction with Number
Echangeur numéroté
Hauptverkehrsstraßenkreuzung mit Nummer
5

Primary Route Destination
Route prioritaire, direction
Hauptverkehrsstraße Richtung
DOVER

Dual Carriageways (A & B roads)
Route à double chaussées séparées (route A & B)
Zweispurige Schnellstraße (A- und B- Straßen)

Class A Road
Route de type A
A-Straße
`A129`

Class B Road
Route de type B
B-Straße
`B177`

Narrow Major Road (passing places)
Route prioritaire étroite (possibilité de dépassement)
Schmale Hauptverkehrsstraße (mit Überholmöglichkeit)

Major Roads Under Construction
Route prioritaire en construction
Hauptverkehrsstaße im Bau

Major Roads Proposed
Route prioritaire prévue
Geplante Hauptverkehrsstaße

Gradient 1:7 (14%) **& steeper**
(descent in direction of arrow)
Pente égale ou supérieure à 14% (dans le sens de la descente)
14% Steigung und steiler (in Pfeilrichtung)
»»

Toll
Barrière de péage
Gebührenpflichtig
Toll

Dart Charge
www.gov.uk/pay-dartford-crossing-charge

Park & Ride
Parking avec Service Navette
Parken und Reisen
`P+R`

Mileage between markers
Distence en miles entre les flèches
Strecke zwischen Markierungen in Meilen
8

Airport
Aéroport
Flughafen

Airfield
Terrain d'aviation
Flugplatz

Heliport
Héliport
Hubschrauberlandeplatz

Ferry Bac Fähre
(vehicular, sea) (véhicules, mer) (auto, meer)
(vehicular, river) (véhicules, rivière) (auto, fluß)
(foot only) (piétons) (nur für Personen)

Railway and Station
Voie ferrée et gare
Eisenbahnlinie und Bahnhof

Level Crossing and Tunnel
Passage à niveau et tunnel
Bahnübergang und Tunnel

River or Canal
Rivière ou canal
Fluß oder Kanal

County or Unitary Authority Boundary
Limite de comté ou de division administrative
Grafschafts- oder Verwaltungsbezirksgrenze

National Boundary
Frontière nationale
Landesgrenze

Built-up Area
Agglomération
Geschloßene Ortschaft

Town, Village or Hamlet
Ville, Village ou hameau
Stadt, Dorf oder Weiler

Wooded Area
Zone boisée
Waldgebiet

Spot Height in Feet
Altitude (en pieds)
Höhe in Fuß
· *813*

Relief above 400' (122m)
Relief par estompage au-dessus de 400' (122m)
Reliefschattierung über 400' (122m)

National Grid Reference (kilometres)
Coordonnées géographiques nationales (Kilomètres)
Nationale geographische Koordinaten (Kilometer)
¹00

Page Continuation
Suite à la page indiquée
Seitenfortsetzung
48

Area covered by Main Route map
Repartition des cartes des principaux axes routiers
Von Karten mit Hauptverkehrsstrecken
`MAIN ROUTE 94`

Area covered by Town Plan
Ville ayant un plan à la page indiquée
Von Karten mit Stadtplänen erfaßter Bereich
`PAGE 109`

Abbey, Church, Friary, Priory †
Abbaye, église, monastère, prieuré
Abtei, Kirche, Mönchskloster, Kloster

Animal Collection
Ménagerie
Tiersammlung

Aquarium
Aquarium
Aquarium

Arboretum, Botanical Garden
Jardin Botanique
Botanischer Garten

Aviary, Bird Garden
Volière
Voliere

Battle Site and Date
Champ de bataille et date *1066*
Schlachtfeld und Datum

Blue Flag Beach
Plage Pavillon Bleu
Blaue Flagge Strand

Bridge
Pont
Brücke

Butterfly Farm
Ferme aux Papillons
Schmetterlingsfarm

Castle (open to public)
Château (ouvert au public)
Schloß / Burg (für die Öffentlichkeit zugänglich)

Castle with Garden (open to public)
Château avec parc (ouvert au public)
Schloß mit Garten (für die Öffentlichkeit zugänglich)

Cathedral ✝
Cathédrale
Kathedrale

Cidermaker
Cidrerie (fabrication)
Apfelwein Hersteller

Country Park
Parc régional
Landschaftspark

Distillery
Distillerie
Brennerei

Farm Park, Open Farm
Park Animalier
Bauernhof Park

Fortress, Hill Fort ※
Château Fort
Festung

Garden (open to public) ✳
Jardin (ouvert au public)
Garten (für die Öffentlichkeit zugänglich)

Golf Course ⚑
Terrain de golf
Golfplatz

Historic Building (open to public)
Monument historique (ouvert au public)
Historisches Gebäude (für die Öffentlichkeit zugänglich)

Historic Building with Garden (open to public)
Monument historique avec jardin (ouvert au public)
Historisches Gebäude mit Garten (für die Öffentlichkeit zugänglich)

Horse Racecourse
Hippodrome
Pferderennbahn

Industrial Monument ✲
Monument Industrielle
Industriedenkmal

Leisure Park, Leisure Pool
Parc d'Attraction, Loisirs Piscine
Freizeitpark, Freizeit pool

Lighthouse
Phare
Leuchtturm

Mine, Cave
Mine, Grotte
Bergwerk, Höhle

Monument
Monument
Denkmal

Motor Racing Circuit
Circuit Automobile
Automobilrennbahn

Museum, Art Gallery `M`
Musée
Museum, Galerie

National Park
Parc national
Nationalpark

National Trail
Sentier national
Nationaler Weg

National Trust Property
National Trust Property
National Trust- Eigentum

Natural Attraction ★
Attraction Naturelle
Natürliche Anziehung

Nature Reserve or Bird Sanctuary
Réserve naturelle botanique ou ornithologique
Natur- oder Vogelschutzgebiet

Nature Trail or Forest Walk
Chemin forestier, piste verte
Naturpfad oder Waldweg

Picnic Site
Lieu pour pique-nique
Picknickplatz

Place of Interest *Craft Centre* •
Site, curiosité
Sehenswürdigkeit

Prehistoric Monument
Monument Préhistorique
Prähistorische Denkmal

Railway, Steam or Narrow Gauge
Chemin de fer, à vapeur ou à voie étroite
Eisenbahn, Dampf- oder Schmalspurbahn

Roman Remains
Vestiges Romains
Römischen Ruinen

Theme Park
Centre de loisirs
Vergnügungspark

Tourist Information Centre `i`
Office de Tourisme
Touristeninformationen

Viewpoint (360 degrees) (180 degrees)
Vue panoramique (360 degrés) (180 degrés)
Aussichtspunkt (360 Grade) (180 Grade)

Vineyard
Vignoble
Weinberg

Visitor Information Centre `V`
Centre d'information touristique
Besucherzentrum

Wildlife Park
Réserve de faune
Wildpark

Windmill
Moulin à vent
Windmühle

Zoo or Safari Park
Parc ou réserve zoologique
Zoo oder Safari-Park

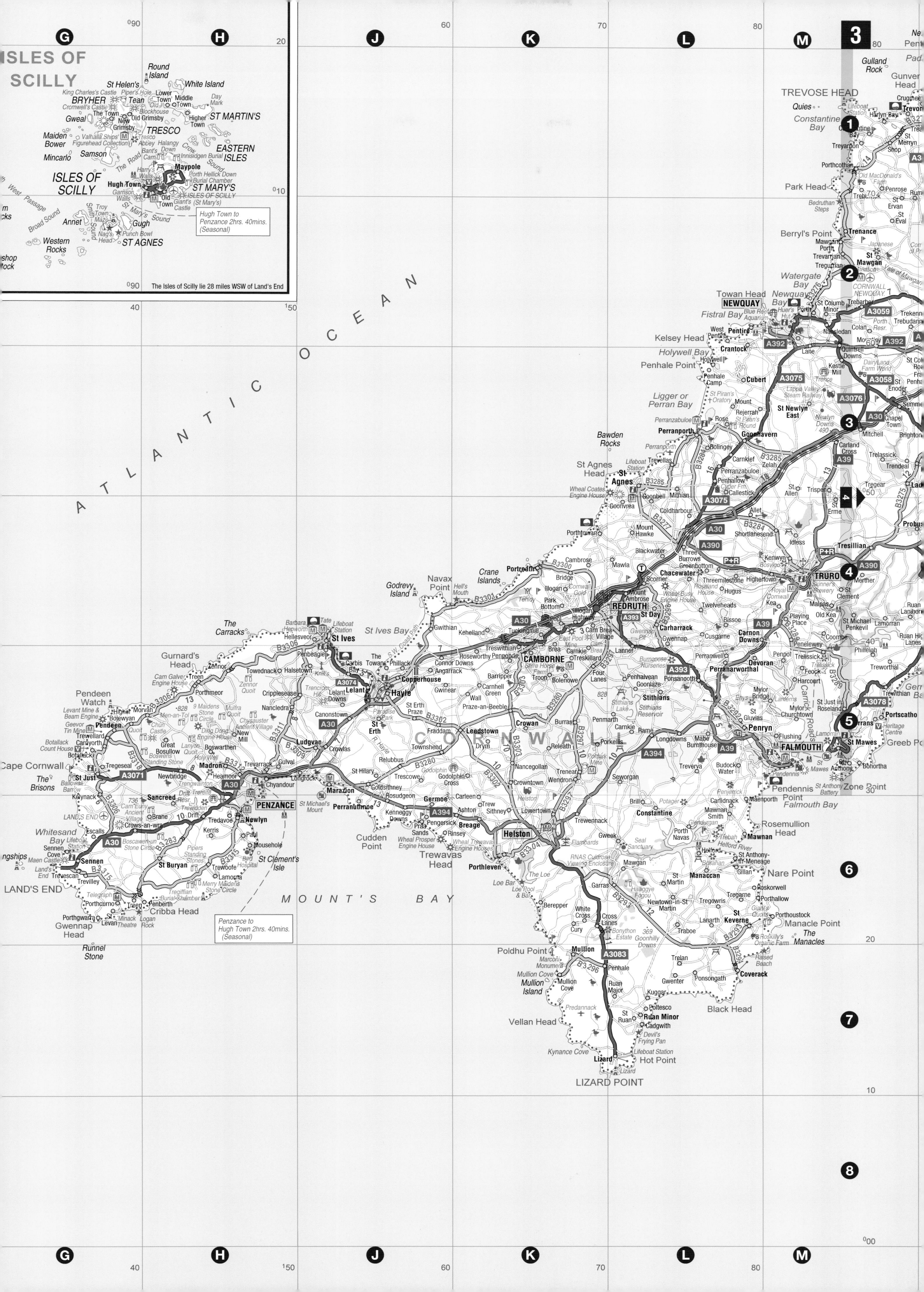
ISLES OF SCILLY
Round Island
St Helen's
White Island
BRYHER
Tean
Lower Town
Middle Town
ST MARTIN'S
Higher Town
Gweal
The Town
Old Grimsby
New Grimsby
TRESCO
Maiden Bower
EASTERN ISLES
Samson
Mincarlo
ISLES OF SCILLY
Maypole
Hugh Town
ST MARY'S
Old Town
Annet
Gugh
ST AGNES
Western Rocks
Hugh Town to Penzance 2hrs. 40mins. (Seasonal)
The Isles of Scilly lie 28 miles WSW of Land's End
ATLANTIC OCEAN
TREVOSE HEAD
Gulland Rock
Gunver Head
Quies
Constantine Bay
Treyarnon
Porthcothan
Park Head
Bedruthan Steps
Berryl's Point
Trenance
Mawgan Porth
St Mawgan
Watergate Bay
Towan Head
NEWQUAY
Newquay Bay
Fistral Bay
Kelsey Head
West Pentire
Pentire
Crantock
Holywell Bay
Holywell
Penhale Point
Penhale Camp
Cubert
A3059
A392
A3075
A3058
A3076
St Newlyn East
Ligger or Perran Bay
Perranporth
Goonhavern
Mitchell
Bawden Rocks
St Agnes Head
St Agnes
Mithian
Zelah
Carland Cross
A39
A30
Porthtowan
Mount Hawke
Blackwater
Shortlanesend
Chacewater
Kenwyn
TRURO
A390
Tresillian
Probus
Crane Islands
Portreath
Illogan
Navax Point
Godrevy Island
REDRUTH
St Day
Mount Ambrose
Scorrier
Carharrack
Threemilestone
Kea
Malpas
The Carracks
St Ives Bay
St Ives
Gwithian
Kehelland
Tuckingmill
Pool
Lanner
Carnon Downs
Devoran
Perranarworthal
Gurnard's Head
Zennor
Carbis Bay
Lelant
Hayle
Copperhouse
CAMBORNE
Troon
Four Lanes
Stithians
Pendeen Watch
Pendeen
Morvah
Porthmeor
St Erth
Connor Downs
Leedstown
Crowan
Penryn
Mylor Bridge
FALMOUTH
St Mawes
St Just in Roseland
Portscatho
Cape Cornwall
St Just
A3071
Madron
Heamoor
Gulval
Ludgvan
Crowlas
Townshend
Praze-an-Beeble
Nancegollan
Constantine
Mawnan
Mawnan Smith
Rosemullion Head
Pendennis Point
Falmouth Bay
Zone Point
St Anthony
The Brisons
Sancreed
Drift
PENZANCE
Newlyn
Mousehole
Marazion
Perranuthnoe
Germoe
Breage
Helston
Porthleven
Loe Bar
Whitesand Bay
Sennen
Sennen Cove
LAND'S END
St Buryan
Treen
Porthcurno
Penberth
Cribba Head
Gwennap Head
Runnel Stone
Lamorna
Cudden Point
Trewavas Head
Mount's Bay
Penzance to Hugh Town 2hrs. 40mins. (Seasonal)
St Clement's Isle
St Michael's Mount
CORNWALL
Manaccan
Nare Point
St Keverne
Manacle Point
The Manacles
Porthoustock
Coverack
Black Head
Mullion
Poldhu Point
Mullion Island
Cury
A3083
Ruan Major
Ruan Minor
Cadgwith
Vellan Head
Kynance Cove
Lizard
Hot Point
LIZARD POINT
G
H
J
K
L
M
1
2
3
4
5
6
7
8
40
50
60
70
80
20
10
00

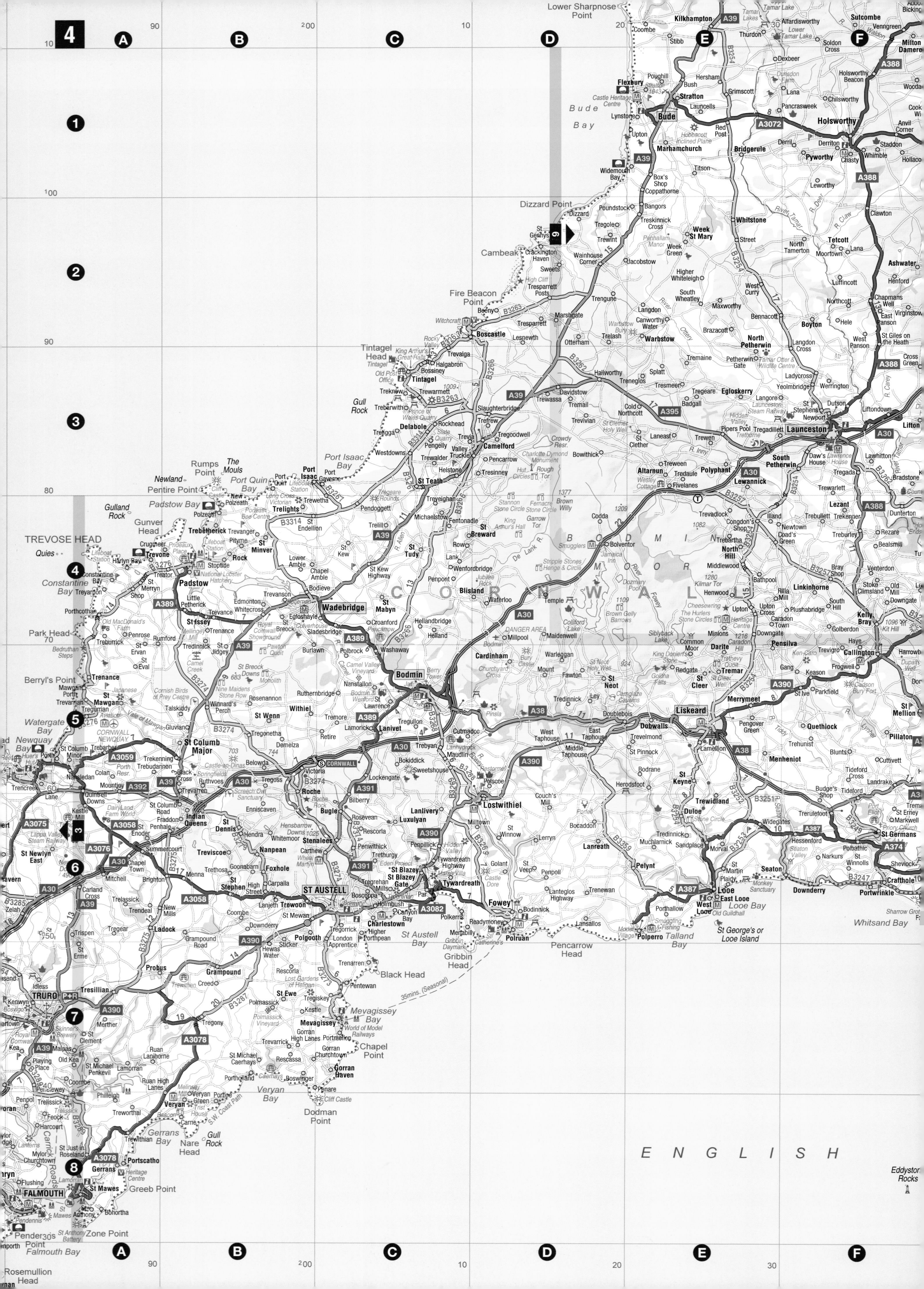
A
B
C
D
E
F
1
2
3
4
5
6
7
8
90
200
10
20
30
100
80
70
ENGLISH
CORNWALL
BODMIN MOOR
Lower Sharpnose Point
Kilkhampton
Bude
Bude Bay
Stratton
Holsworthy
Marhamchurch
Bridgerule
Widemouth Bay
Dizzard Point
Cambeak
Crackington Haven
Fire Beacon Point
Boscastle
Tintagel Head
Tintagel
Gull Rock
Delabole
Camelford
Port Isaac
Port Isaac Bay
Port Quin Bay
Rumps Point
The Mouls
Newland
Pentire Point
Padstow Bay
Gulland Rock
Gunver Head
TREVOSE HEAD
Quies
Trevone
Padstow
Rock
Constantine Bay
Wadebridge
St Teath
Launceston
Whitstone
Week St Mary
Altarnun
Polyphant
South Petherwin
Lewannick
North Hill
Callington
Bodmin
Lostwithiel
Liskeard
Dobwalls
St Neot
St Cleer
Park Head
Berryl's Point
Watergate Bay
Newquay
Newquay Bay
St Columb Major
Indian Queens
Roche
Bugle
ST AUSTELL
St Austell Bay
Charlestown
Par
Fowey
Polruan
Gribbin Head
Polperro
Talland Bay
Looe
Looe Bay
St George's or Looe Island
Whitsand Bay
Saltash
St Germans
Torpoint
Pencarrow Head
Mevagissey
Mevagissey Bay
Black Head
Chapel Point
Gorran Haven
Dodman Point
Veryan Bay
Veryan
Gerrans Bay
Nare Head
Gull Rock
Grampound
Probus
Tresillian
TRURO
Falmouth Bay
FALMOUTH
St Mawes
Portscatho
Gerrans
Greeb Point
Zone Point
Pendennis Point
Rosemullion Head
Eddystone Rocks
A39
A30
A38
A388
A3072
A395
A389
A390
A391
A3058
A3059
A392
A3075
A3076
A3078
A3082
A387
A374
B3263
B3266
B3314
B3274
B3254
B3257
B3359
B3269
B3273
B3287

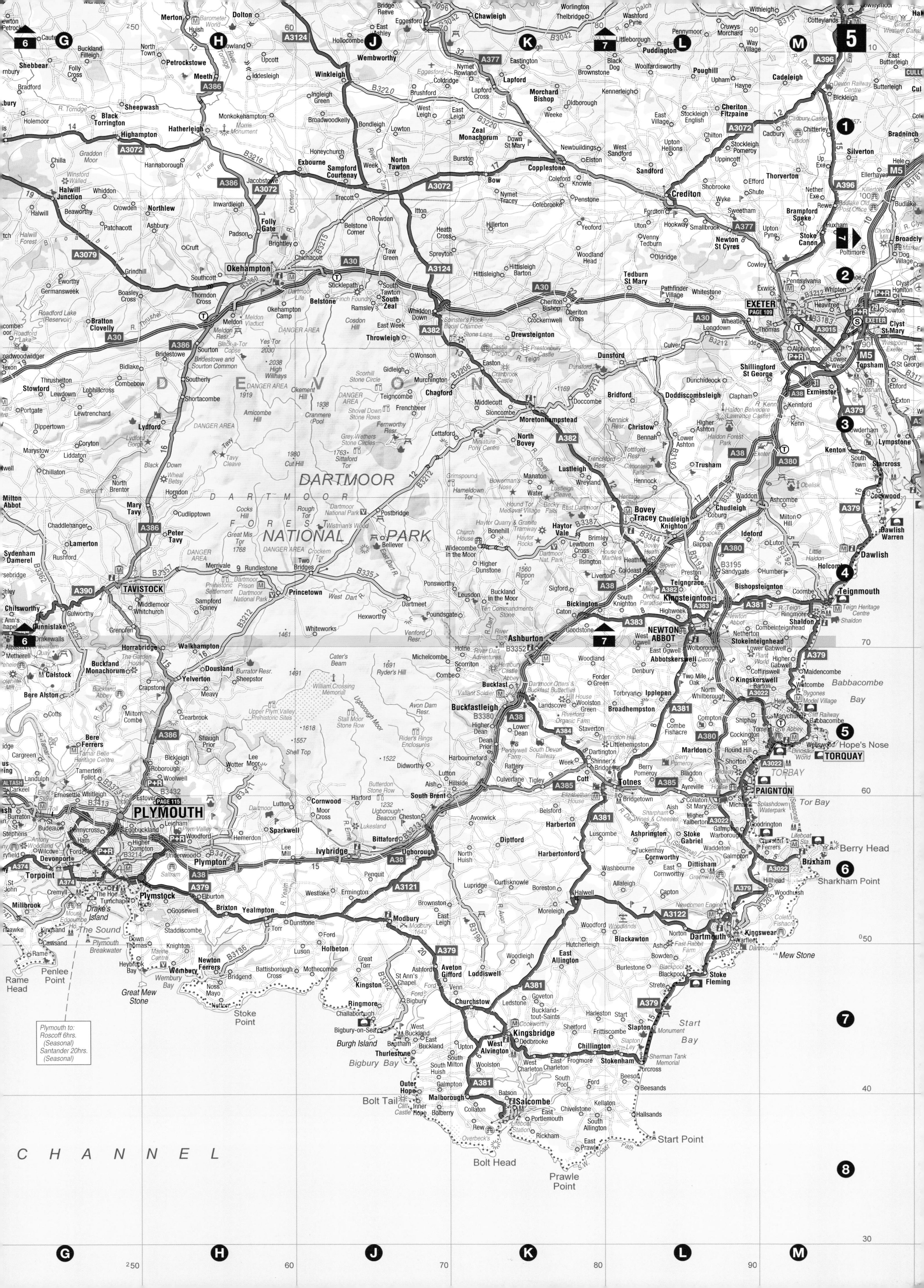
5
6
7
G
H
J
K
L
M
1
2
3
4
5
6
7
8
DEVON
DARTMOOR
DARTMOOR FOREST
NATIONAL PARK
PLYMOUTH
PAGE 115
EXETER
PAGE 109
TORQUAY
PAIGNTON
TORBAY
NEWTON ABBOT
TAVISTOCK
Okehampton
Crediton
Tiverton
Kingsteignton
Teignmouth
Dawlish
Exmouth
Topsham
Exminster
Starcross
Kenton
Chudleigh
Bovey Tracey
Ashburton
Buckfastleigh
Totnes
Dartmouth
Kingswear
Brixham
Kingsbridge
Salcombe
Ivybridge
Plympton
Plymstock
Yelverton
Princetown
Moretonhampstead
Chagford
Lydford
Hatherleigh
Winkleigh
Copplestone
Tedburn St Mary
Dunsford
Modbury
Yealmpton
Torpoint
Devonport
Saltash
Cadeleigh
Silverton
Thorverton
Bradninch
Babbacombe Bay
Hope's Nose
Tor Bay
Berry Head
Sharkham Point
Mew Stone
Start Bay
Start Point
Prawle Point
Bolt Head
Bolt Tail
Bigbury Bay
Burgh Island
Great Mew Stone
Stoke Point
Rame Head
Penlee Point
The Sound
CHANNEL
Plymouth to:
Roscoff 6hrs. (Seasonal)
Santander 20hrs. (Seasonal)
A30
A38
A380
A381
A382
A383
A385
A386
A379
A3022
A3072
A3121
A3122
A3124
A377
A396
A390
A374
M5
250
60
70
80
90
50
40
30

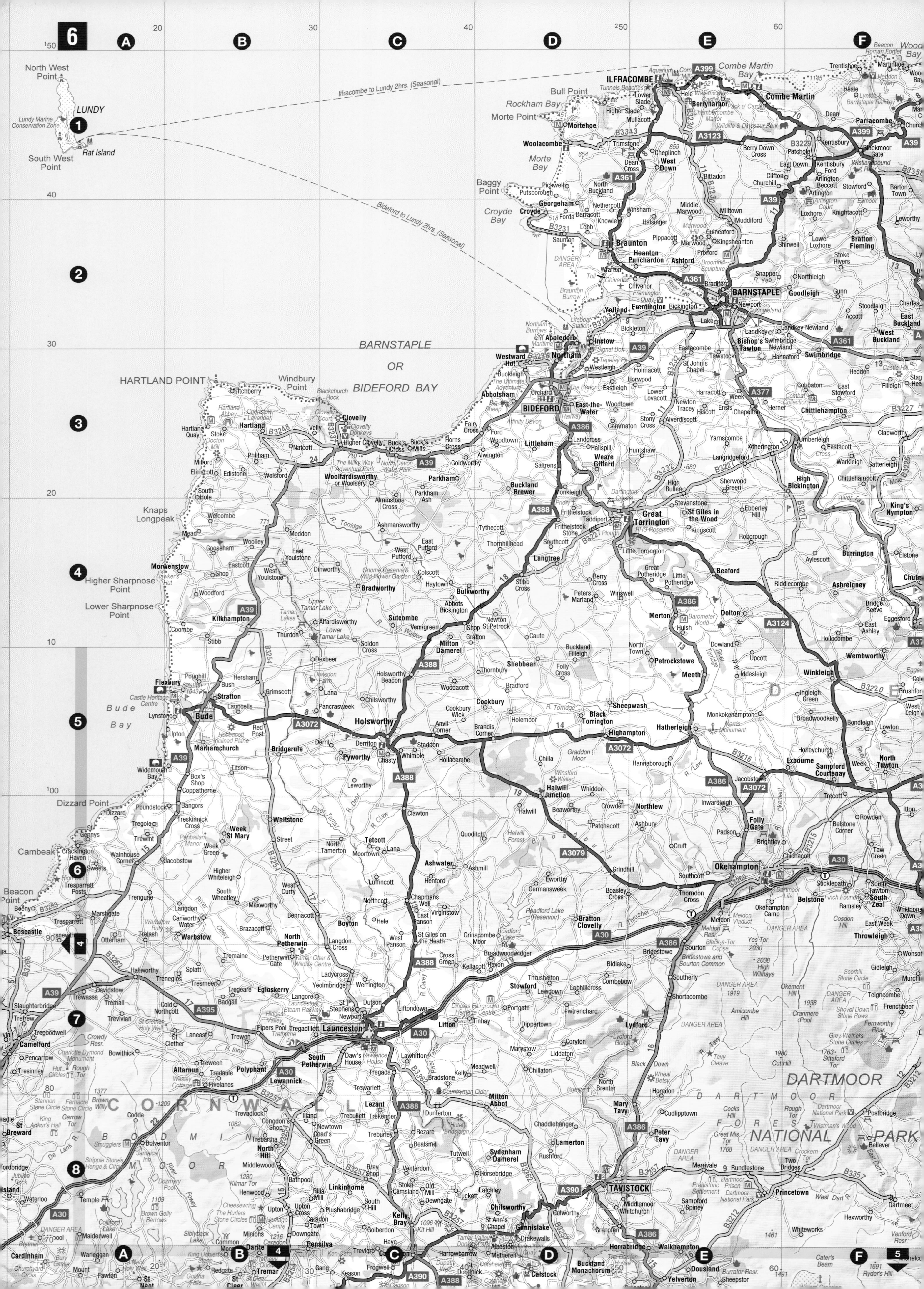

LUNDY
North West Point
South West Point
Rat Island
Lundy Marine Conservation Zone
Ilfracombe to Lundy 2hrs. (Seasonal)
Bideford to Lundy 2hrs. (Seasonal)
BARNSTAPLE
OR
BIDEFORD BAY
HARTLAND POINT
Windbury Point
Knaps Longpeak
Higher Sharpnose Point
Lower Sharpnose Point
Bude
Bay
Dizzard Point
Cambeak
Beacon Point
Bull Point
Rockham Bay
Morte Point
Morte Bay
Baggy Point
Croyde Bay
Combe Martin Bay
ILFRACOMBE
Combe Martin
Mortehoe
Woolacombe
Georgeham
Croyde
Braunton
BARNSTAPLE
Bishop's Tawton
Swimbridge
Chittlehampton
Instow
Appledore
Northam
Westward Ho!
BIDEFORD
Abbotsham
Clovelly
Hartland
Great Torrington
Weare Giffard
Woolfardisworthy or Woolsery
Parkham
Bradworthy
Kilkhampton
Morwenstow
Holsworthy
Bude
Stratton
Flexbury
Marhamchurch
Bridgerule
Pyworthy
Milton Damerel
Shebbear
Black Torrington
Highampton
Hatherleigh
Halwill Junction
Northlew
Okehampton
Belstone
South Zeal
Winkleigh
Dolton
Merton
Beaford
Chulmleigh
High Bickington
Sampford Courtenay
North Tawton
Exbourne
Folly Gate
Boscastle
Camelford
Launceston
Lifton
Lydford
Mary Tavy
Peter Tavy
TAVISTOCK
Princetown
Gunnislake
Calstock
Callington
Kelly Bray
Milton Abbot
Lewannick
Altarnun
Polyphant
Egloskerry
Week St Mary
Whitstone
North Petherwin
South Petherwin
Stoke Climsland
North Hill
Linkinhorne
Pensilva
Darite
Tremar
Bolventor
St Breward
Cardinham
Yelverton
Buckland Monachorum
Horrabridge
Walkhampton
Bridestowe
Sourton
Lamerton
Sydenham Damerel
CORNWALL
BODMIN MOOR
DARTMOOR
DARTMOOR FOREST
NATIONAL PARK
DANGER AREA

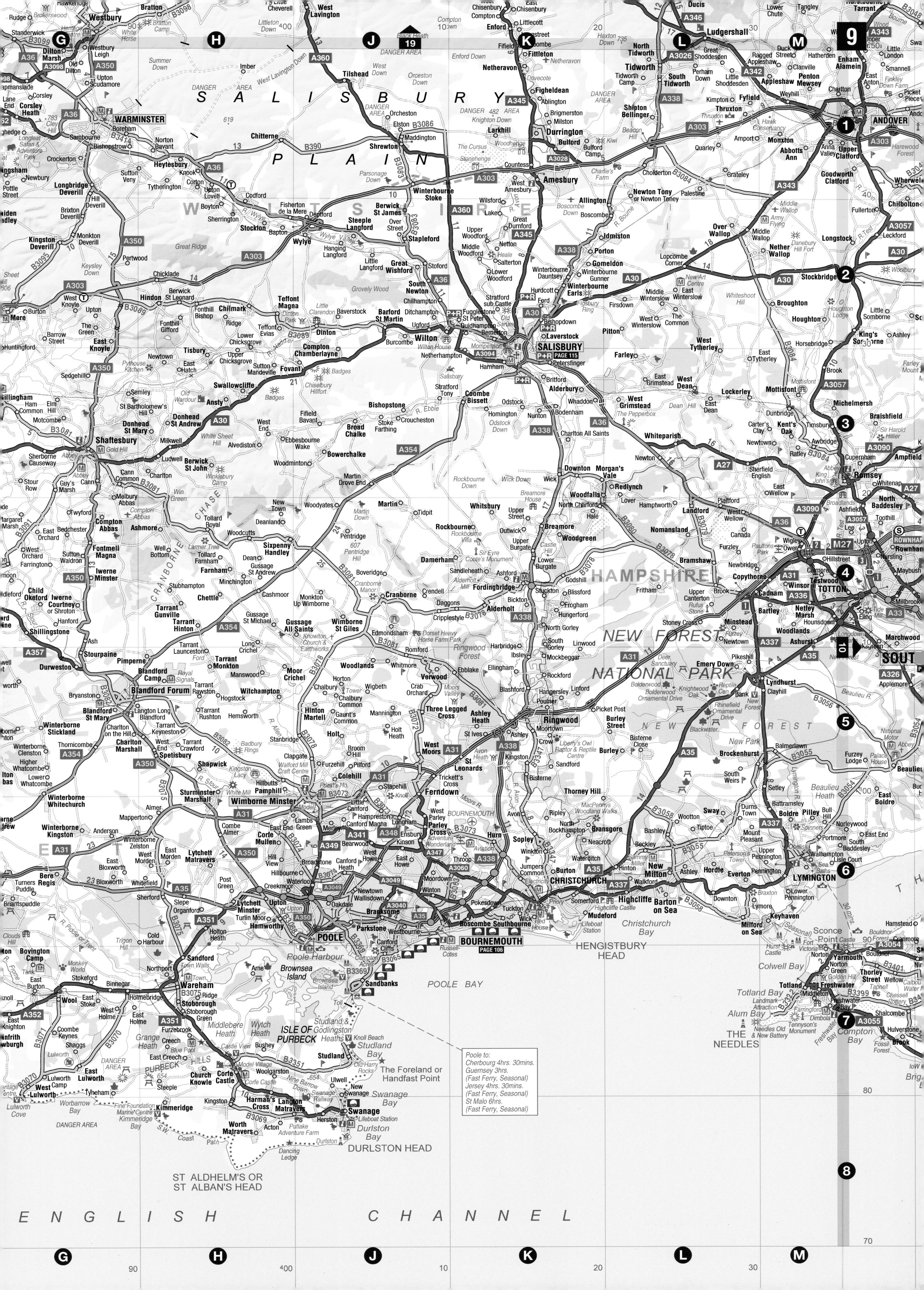
9
SALISBURY PLAIN
WILTSHIRE
HAMPSHIRE
NEW FOREST NATIONAL PARK
ENGLISH CHANNEL
POOLE BAY
Christchurch Bay
HENGISTBURY HEAD
DURLSTON HEAD
ST ALDHELM'S OR ST ALBAN'S HEAD
THE NEEDLES
ISLE OF PURBECK
Brownsea Island
Poole Harbour
Studland Bay
Swanage Bay
Durlston Bay
Worbarrow Bay
Kimmeridge Bay
Colwell Bay
Totland Bay
Alum Bay
Compton Bay
The Foreland or Handfast Point
Poole to:
Cherbourg 4hrs. 30mins.
Guernsey 3hrs.
(Fast Ferry, Seasonal)
Jersey 4hrs. 30mins.
(Fast Ferry, Seasonal)
St Malo 6hrs.
(Fast Ferry, Seasonal)
WARMINSTER
SALISBURY
PAGE 115
BOURNEMOUTH
PAGE 106
POOLE
ANDOVER
ROMSEY
TOTTON
LYMINGTON
CHRISTCHURCH
Ringwood
Fordingbridge
Wimborne Minster
Blandford Forum
Shaftesbury
Amesbury
Wilton
Tidworth
Ludgershall
Westbury
Wareham
Swanage
Lyndhurst
Yarmouth
Ferndown
Highcliffe
Milford on Sea
Barton on Sea
New Milton
Stockbridge
Durrington
Warminster
Mere
Tisbury
Hamworthy
Sandbanks
Corfe Castle
A36
A303
A338
A354
A350
A30
A31
A35
A27
A36
A337
A345
A360
A3057
M27
G
H
J
K
L
M
1
2
3
4
5
6
7
8
10
DANGER AREA
90
400
10
20
30
70
80

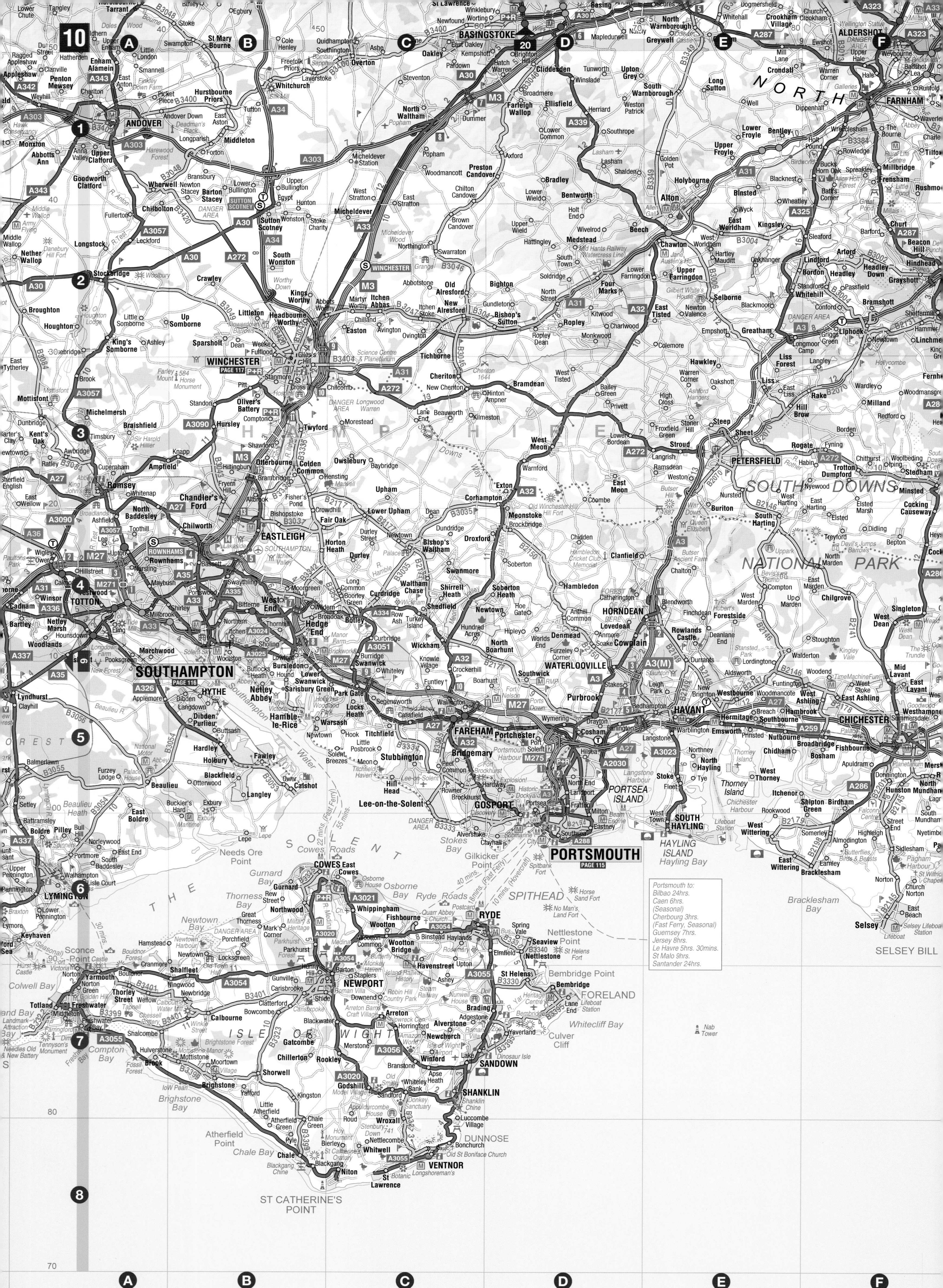
ANDOVER
BASINGSTOKE
ALDERSHOT
FARNHAM
WINCHESTER
PAGE 117
ALTON
PETERSFIELD
EASTLEIGH
ROMSEY
TOTTON
SOUTHAMPTON
PAGE 118
HYTHE
FAREHAM
GOSPORT
PORTSMOUTH
PAGE 115
HAVANT
WATERLOOVILLE
HORNDEAN
CHICHESTER
LYMINGTON
COWES
NEWPORT
RYDE
SANDOWN
SHANKLIN
VENTNOR
HAMPSHIRE
SOUTH DOWNS
NATIONAL PARK
NORTH
THE SOLENT
SPITHEAD
ISLE OF WIGHT
PORTSEA ISLAND
HAYLING ISLAND
SOUTH HAYLING
Hayling Bay
SELSEY BILL
ST CATHERINE'S POINT
DUNNOSE
FORELAND
Bembridge Point
Culver Cliff
Whitecliff Bay
Nab Tower
Compton Bay
Brighstone Bay
Chale Bay
Atherfield Point
Colwell Bay
Needs Ore Point
Gurnard Bay
Thorness Bay
Newtown Bay
Osborne Bay
Ryde Roads
Cowes Roads
Stokes Bay
Gilkicker Point
Bracklesham Bay
Southampton Water
Lee-on-the-Solent
Stubbington
Titchfield
Hamble-le-Rice
Fawley
Beaulieu
Lyndhurst
Stockbridge
Whitchurch
Overton
Alresford
Bishop's Waltham
Wickham
Emsworth
Selsey
Yarmouth
Freshwater
Bembridge
Portsmouth to:
Bilbao 24hrs.
Caen 6hrs.
(Seasonal)
Cherbourg 3hrs.
(Fast Ferry, Seasonal)
Guernsey 7hrs.
Jersey 8hrs.
Le Havre 5hrs. 30mins.
St Malo 9hrs.
Santander 24hrs.

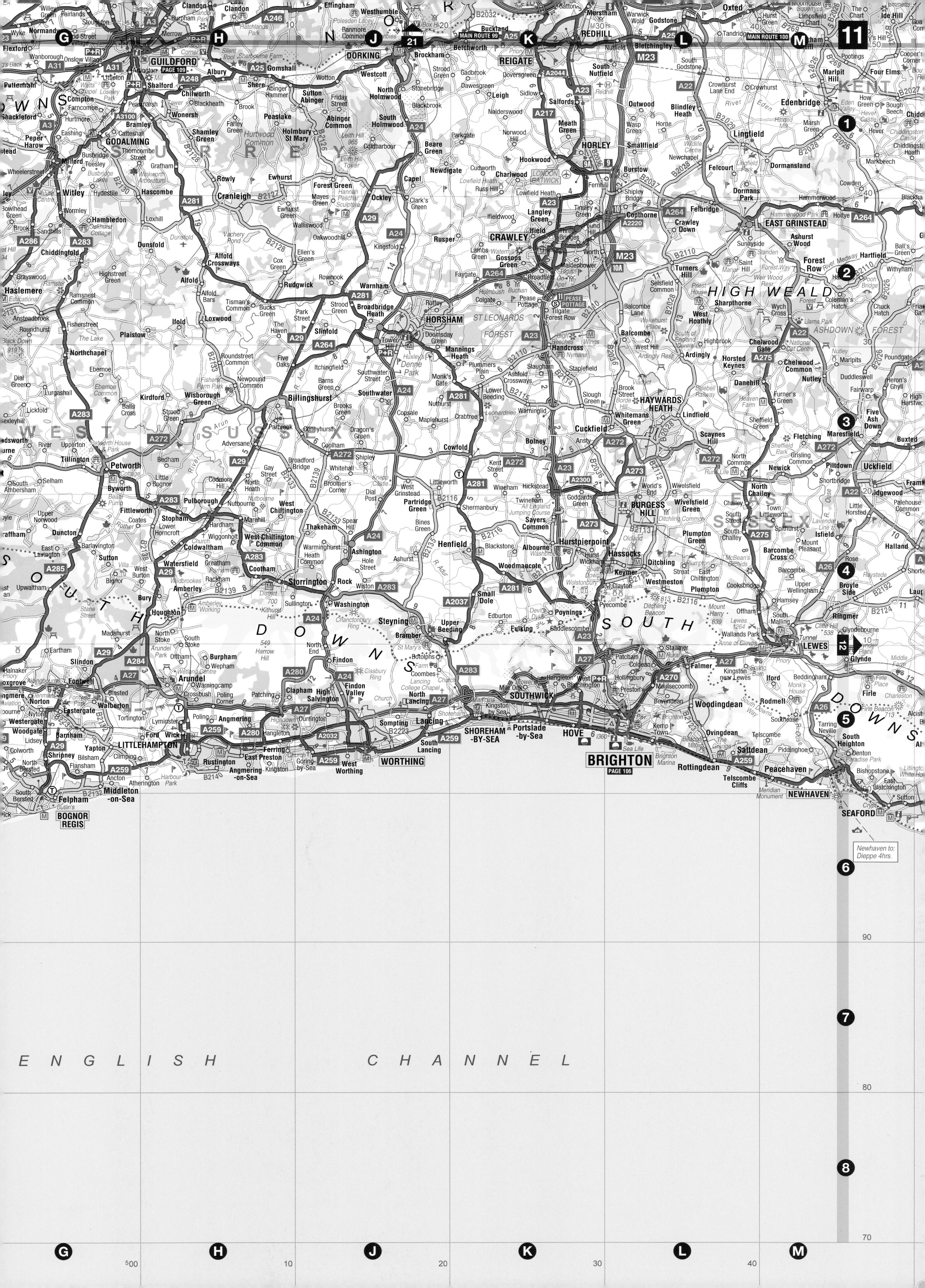

11
MAIN ROUTE 99
MAIN ROUTE 100
21
12
G
H
J
K
L
M
GUILDFORD
PAGE 109
DORKING
REIGATE
REDHILL
Oxted
Godstone
KENT
Edenbridge
GODALMING
SURREY
Haslemere
Cranleigh
HORLEY
LONDON GATWICK
CRAWLEY
EAST GRINSTEAD
HIGH WEALD
ASHDOWN FOREST
HORSHAM
ST LEONARDS FOREST
HAYWARDS HEATH
WEST SUSSEX
EAST SUSSEX
Uckfield
BURGESS HILL
Petworth
Billingshurst
Storrington
Steyning
LEWES
SOUTH DOWNS
Arundel
LITTLEHAMPTON
WORTHING
SHOREHAM-BY-SEA
Portslade-by-Sea
HOVE
BRIGHTON
PAGE 106
Rottingdean
Peacehaven
NEWHAVEN
SEAFORD
BOGNOR REGIS
Felpham
Middleton-on-Sea
Newhaven to: Dieppe 4hrs.
ENGLISH CHANNEL
1
2
3
4
5
6
7
8
500
10
20
30
40
70
80
90

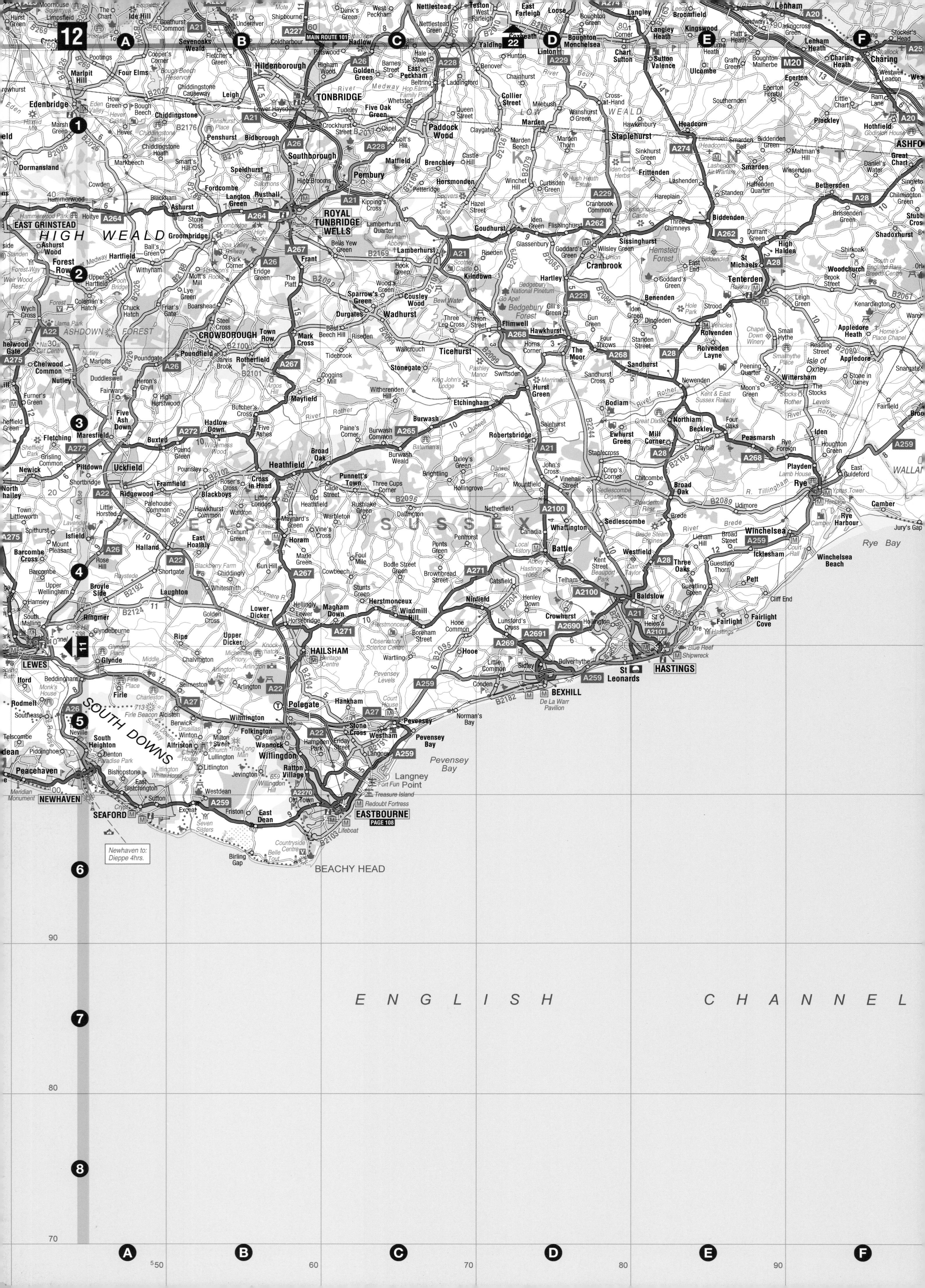
12
MAIN ROUTE 101
22
11
EAST GRINSTEAD
HIGH WEALD
ASHDOWN FOREST
ROYAL TUNBRIDGE WELLS
TONBRIDGE
Southborough
Hildenborough
Edenbridge
Paddock Wood
Pembury
CROWBOROUGH
Uckfield
Heathfield
Mayfield
Wadhurst
Ticehurst
Hawkhurst
Cranbrook
Staplehurst
Marden
Headcorn
Tenterden
Rye
Winchelsea
Battle
Bexhill
St Leonards
HASTINGS
HAILSHAM
Polegate
EASTBOURNE
PAGE 108
LEWES
NEWHAVEN
SEAFORD
Peacehaven
SOUTH DOWNS
EAST SUSSEX
KENT
BEACHY HEAD
Pevensey Bay
Langney Point
Rye Bay
Newhaven to: Dieppe 4hrs.
ENGLISH CHANNEL
Charing
Lenham
ASHFORD

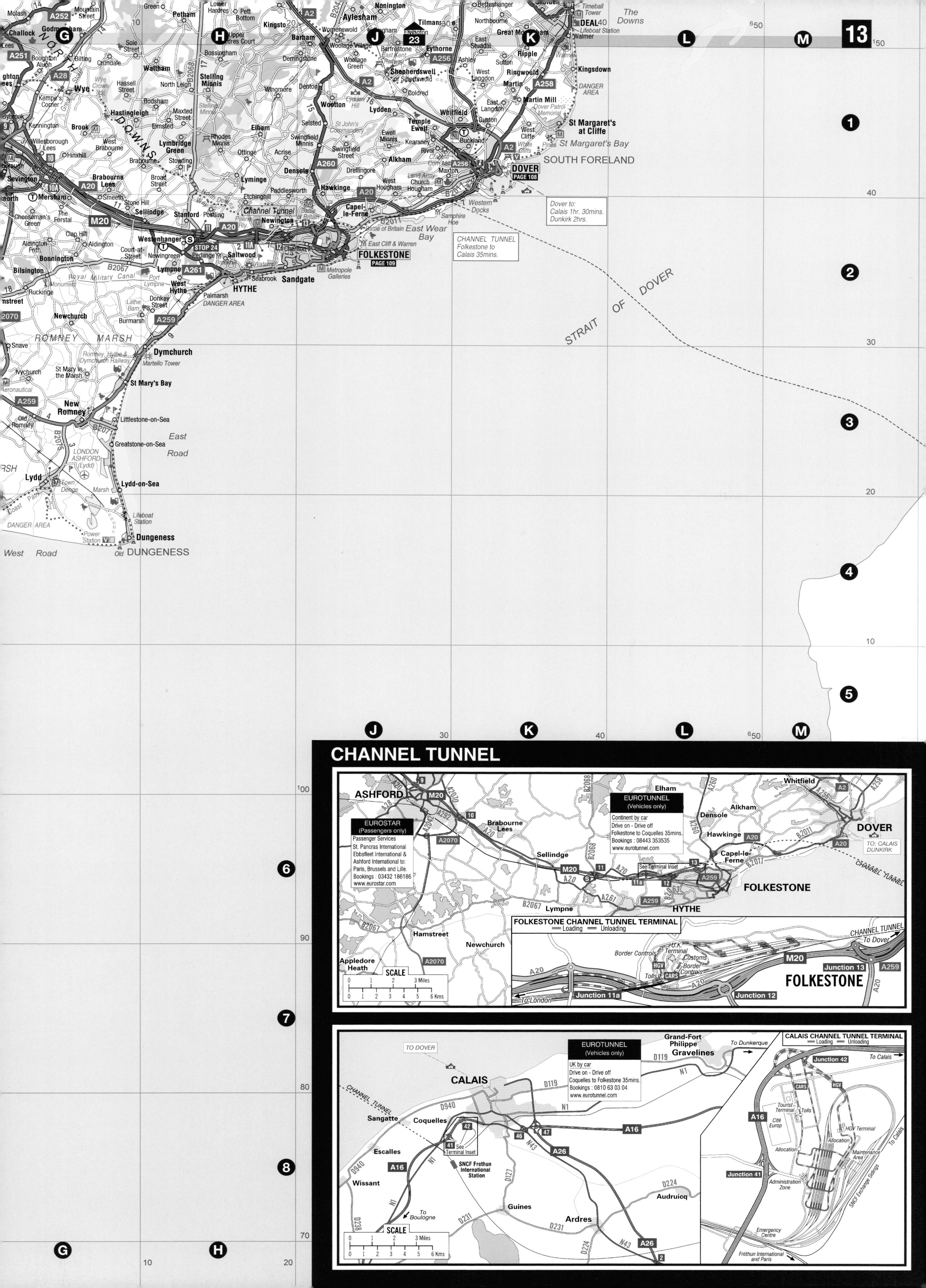
DEAL
DOVER
PAGE 108
FOLKESTONE
PAGE 109
HYTHE
Sandgate
SOUTH FORELAND
St Margaret's at Cliffe
St Margaret's Bay
Kingsdown
Walmer
The Downs
Dover to:
Calais 1hr. 30mins.
Dunkirk 2hrs.
CHANNEL TUNNEL
Folkestone to
Calais 35mins.
STRAIT OF DOVER
East Wear Bay
Dymchurch
St Mary's Bay
New Romney
Littlestone-on-Sea
Greatstone-on-Sea
East Road
Lydd
Lydd-on-Sea
Dungeness
DUNGENESS
West Road
ROMNEY MARSH
NORTH DOWNS
Wye
Aylesham
Nonington
Tilmanstone
Eythorne
Shepherdswell
Lydden
Temple Ewell
Whitfield
River
Alkham
Hawkinge
Capel-le-Ferne
Densole
Elham
Lyminge
Sellindge
Newington
Saltwood
Lympne
West Hythe
Bilsington
Newchurch
Burmarsh
Brabourne Lees
Mersham
Stanford
Westenhanger
STOP 24
M20
A20
A2
A256
A258
A260
A259
A261
CHANNEL TUNNEL
ASHFORD
EUROSTAR
(Passengers only)
Passenger Services
St. Pancras International
Ebbsfleet International &
Ashford International to:
Paris, Brussels and Lille.
Bookings : 03432 186186
www.eurostar.com
EUROTUNNEL
(Vehicles only)
Continent by car
Drive on - Drive off
Folkestone to Coquelles 35mins.
Bookings : 08443 353535
www.eurotunnel.com
FOLKESTONE CHANNEL TUNNEL TERMINAL
Loading
Unloading
Border Controls
U.K. Terminal
Customs
Border Controls
Junction 11a
Junction 12
Junction 13
To London
To Dover
FOLKESTONE
SCALE
3 Miles
6 Kms
TO: CALAIS DUNKIRK
TO DOVER
CALAIS
EUROTUNNEL
(Vehicles only)
UK by car
Drive on - Drive off
Coquelles to Folkestone 35mins.
Bookings : 0810 63 03 04
www.eurotunnel.com
Grand-Fort Philippe
Gravelines
To Dunkerque
Sangatte
Coquelles
Escalles
Wissant
SNCF Frethun International Station
Guines
Ardres
Audruicq
To Boulogne
CALAIS CHANNEL TUNNEL TERMINAL
Junction 42
Junction 41
To Calais
Tourist Terminal
Tolls
Cité Europ
HGV Terminal
Allocation
Maintenance Area
Administration Zone
Emergency Centre
Fréthun International and Paris
SNCF Exchange Sidings

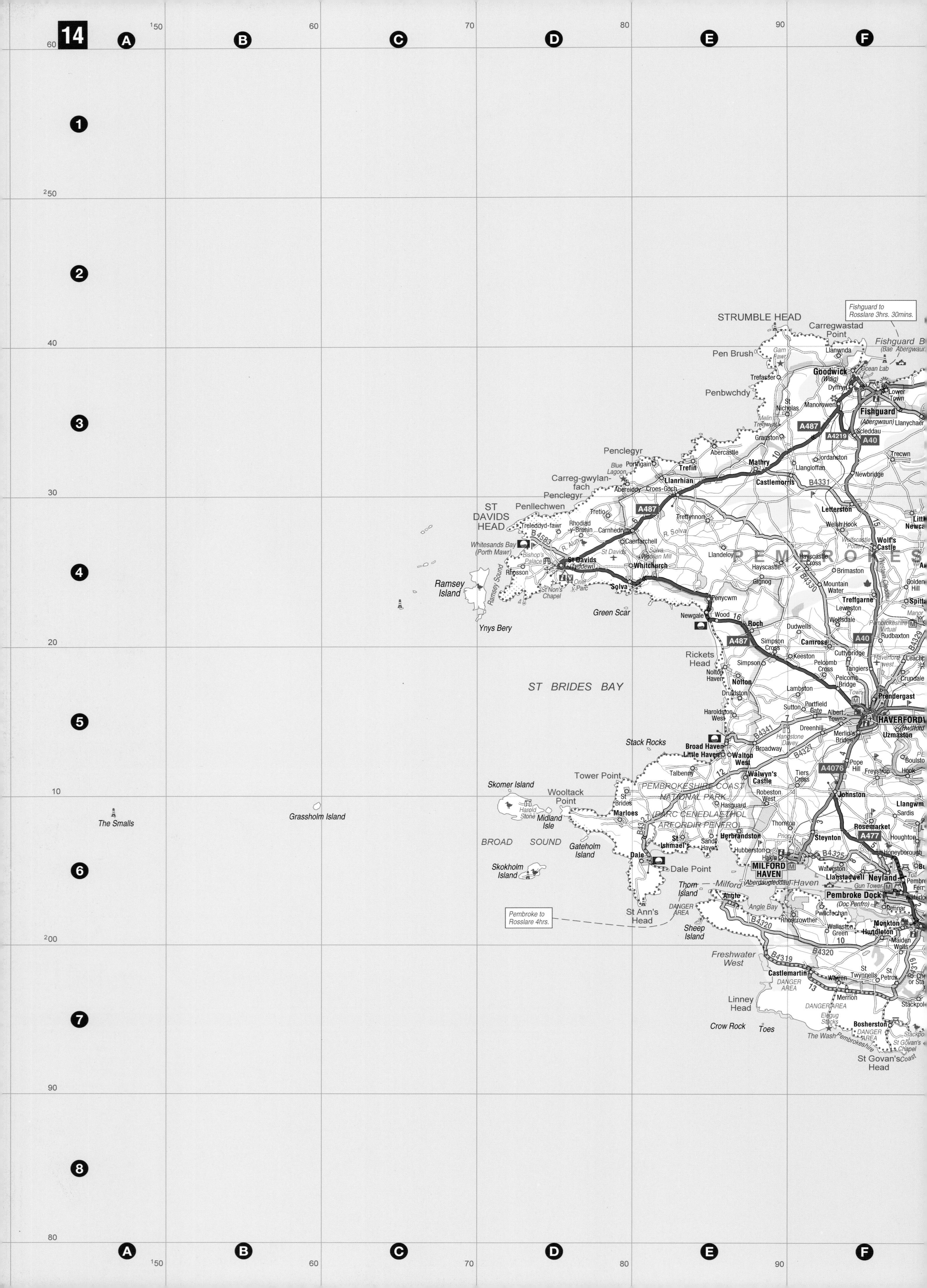

14

A **¹50** B 60 C 70 D 80 E 90 F

60

1

²50

2

40

STRUMBLE HEAD
Carregwastad
Point
Fishguard B
(Bae Abergwaun)
Fishguard to
Rosslare 3hrs. 30mins.
Pen Brush
Gam
Fawr
Llanwnda
Ocean Lab
Goodwick
(Wdig)
Dyffryn
Lower
Town
Trefasser
St Nicholas
Penbwchdy
Manorowen
Fishguard
(Abergwaun)
Llanychaer

3

A487
A4219
A40
Scleddau
Gramston
Jordanston
Newbridge
Trecwn
Penclegyr
Portingain
Blue
Lagoon
Trefin
Abercastle
Mathry
Llangloffan
Carreg-gwylan-
fach
Llanrhian
Croes-Goch
Castlemorris
B4331
Penclegyr
Aberreiddy
Tretio
A487
Letterston
Welsh Hook
Littl
Newca

30

ST
DAVIDS
HEAD
Penllechwen
Treleddyd-fawr
Rhodiad
y-Brenin
Carnhedryn
Treffynnon
R. Solva
Whitchurch
Wolfscastle
Pottery
Wolf's
Castle
Brimaston
Hayscastle
Cross
PEMBROKES

4

Whitesands Bay
(Porth Mawr)
Bishop's
Palace
B4583
St Davids
(Tyddewi)
St Davids
Solva
Wooden Mill
Llandeloy
Hayscastle
Gignog
Mountain
Water
14 B4330
Treffgarne
Spitt
Manor
Ramsey
Island
St Non's
Chapel
Ynys Bery
Whitchurch
Solva
Penycwm
Leweston
Wolfsdale
Pembrokeshire
Virtual
Rudbaxton
A40
Golden
Hill
Green Scar
Newgale
Wood 16
Roch
Dudwells
A487
Camrose
Cuttybridge
A40
B4320

20

Rickets
Head
A487
Roch
Simpson
Cross
Keeston
Pelcomb
Cross
Tangiers
Haverford
west
Leach
Simpson
Notton
Pelcomb
Bridge
Crundale
Nolton
Haven
Lambston
Druidston
Portfield
Gate
Prendergast
Sutton
Albert
Town
Town

5

ST BRIDES BAY
Haroldston
West
7
Dreenhill
Merlin's
Bridge
HAVERFORD
(Hwilford)
Uzmaston
Stack Rocks
Handstone
Dave
B4341
Broadway
B4321
Broad Haven
Little Haven
Walton
West
Walwyn's
Castle
Tiers
Cross
A4076
Pope
Hill
Freystrop
Boulsto
Hook
PE
Tower Point
Talbenny
12
Robeston
West
Johnston
Langwm
Sardis

Skomer Island
Wooltack
Point
St
Brides
Hasguard
Thornton
Priory
Rosemarket
Houghton
Llangwm
The Smalls
Grassholm Island
Harold
Stone
Midland
Isle
Marloes
Herbrandston
Steynton
A477
Honeyborough
BROAD SOUND
Gateholm
Island
St
Ishmael's
Sandy
Haven
Hubberston
Hakin
MILFORD
HAVEN
(Aberdaugleddau)
B4325
Waterston
Llanstadwell
Neyland
Toll
Pembre
Ferr

6

Skokholm
Island
Dale
Dale Point
Thorn
Island
Milford
Haven
Pembroke Dock
(Doc Penfro)
Gun Tower
M
Monkton
Pennar
Pembroke to
Rosslare 4hrs.
St Ann's
Head
Thorn
Milford
DANGER
AREA
Angle
Angle Bay
Rhoscrowther
Pwllcrochan
B4320
Huntleton

²00

DANGER
AREA
Sheep
Island
Wallaston
Green 10
Maiden
Wells
Freshwater
West
B4319
B4320
Warren
St
Twynnells
St
Petrox
Ch
or Sta

7

Castlemartin
DANGER
AREA
Linney
Head
DANGER AREA
Merrion
13
Elegug
Stacks
Crow Rock
Toes
Bosherston
St Govan's
Chapel
The Wash
Pembrokeshire
Stackpol
DANGER
AREA

90

St Govan's
Head
Coast

8

80

A **¹50** B 60 C 70 D 80 E 90 F

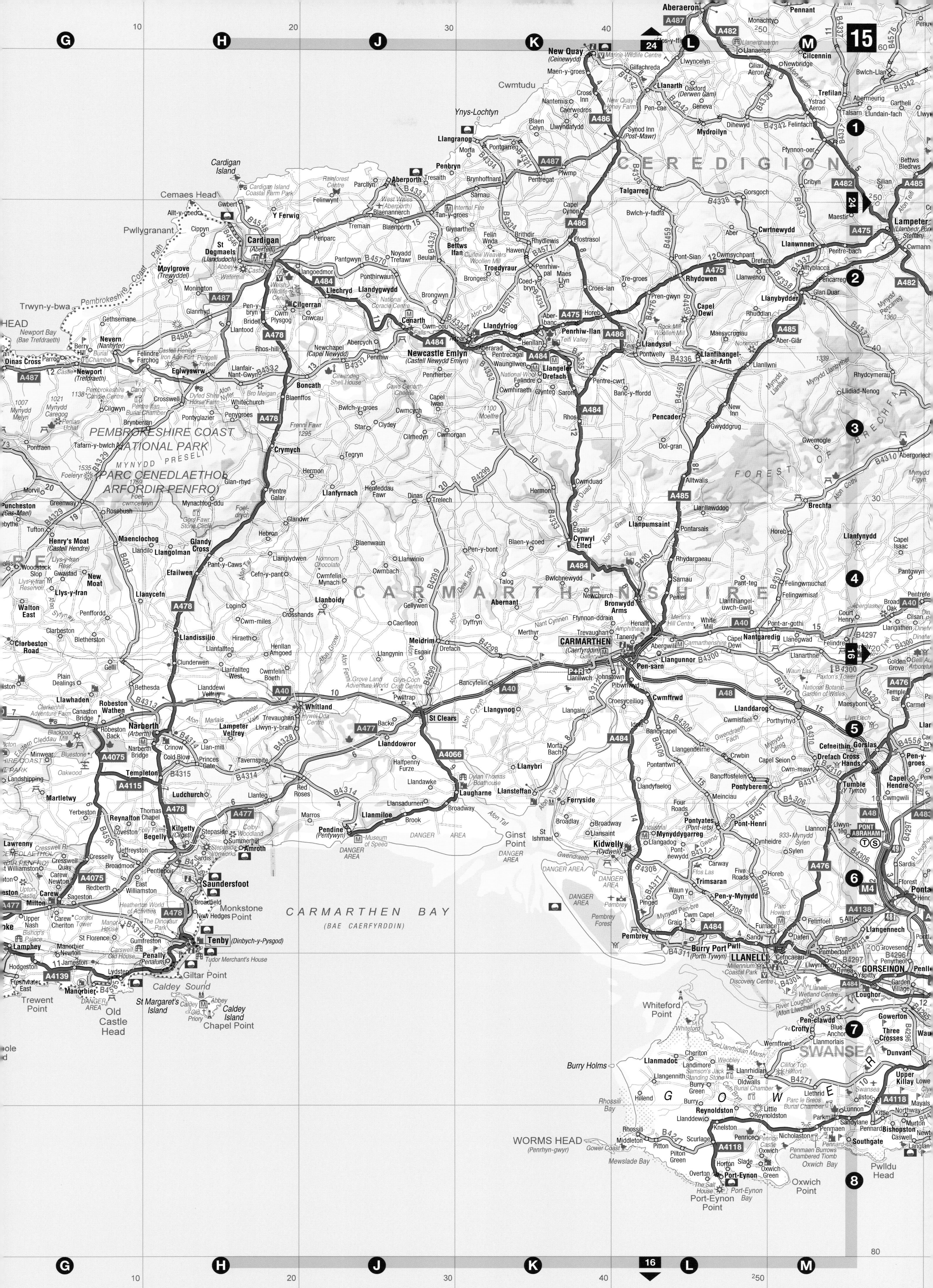

G
H
J
K
L
M
10
20
30
40
50
60
24
16
1
2
3
4
5
6
7
8
CEREDIGION
CARMARTHENSHIRE
PEMBROKESHIRE COAST NATIONAL PARK
PARC CENEDLAETHOL ARFORDIR PENFRO
MYNYDD PRESELI
FOREST OF BRECHFA
CARMARTHEN BAY
(BAE CAERFYRDDIN)
GOWER
SWANSEA
Aberaeron
New Quay
(Ceinewydd)
Cwmtudu
Ynys-Lochtyn
Llangranog
Penbryn
Aberporth
Cardigan Island
Cemaes Head
Pwllygranant
Cardigan
(Aberteifi)
St Dogmaels
(Llandudoch)
Moylgrove
(Trewyddel)
Trwyn-y-bwa
Pembrokeshire Coast Path
Newport Bay
(Bae Trefdraeth)
Nevern
(Nanhyfer)
Dinas Cross
Newport
(Trefdraeth)
Eglwyswrw
Cilgerran
Llechryd
Llandygwydd
Cenarth
Newcastle Emlyn
(Castell Newydd Emlyn)
Llandyfriog
Penrhiw-llan
Llandysul
Llanybydder
Lampeter
(Llanbedr Pont Steffan)
Talgarreg
Synod Inn
(Post-Mawr)
Llanarth
Mydroilyn
Trefilan
Cilcennin
Pennant
Crymych
Boncath
Rhydowen
Capel Dewi
Llanfihangel-ar-Arth
Pencader
Alltwalis
Brechfa
Llanpumsaint
Cynwyl Elfed
Bronwydd Arms
CARMARTHEN
(Caerfyrddin)
Nantgaredig
Llanfynydd
Abernant
Meidrim
Llanboidy
Llanfyrnach
Maenclochog
Glandy Cross
Llangolman
Efailwen
Henry's Moat
(Castell Hendre)
New Moat
Llys-y-fran
Walton East
Clarbeston Road
Llandissilio
Llawhaden
Robeston Wathen
Narberth
(Arberth)
Whitland
St Clears
Llangynog
Llanddowror
Laugharne
Llansteffan
Ferryside
Kidwelly
(Cydweli)
Pendine
(Pentywyn)
Llanmiloe
Templeton
Ludchurch
Kilgetty
(Cilgeti)
Begelly
Saundersfoot
Amroth
Tenby
(Dinbych-y-Pysgod)
Penally
(Penalum)
Manorbier
Lamphey
Caldey Island
Giltar Point
Monkstone Point
Old Castle Head
Trewent Point
Caldey Sound
St Margaret's Island
Chapel Point
Martletwy
Carew
Milton
Pembrey
Burry Port
(Porth Tywyn)
LLANELLI
Pen-sarn
Cwmffrwd
Llanddarog
Cross Hands
Tumble
(Y Tymbl)
Gorslas
Cefneithin
Pontyberem
Pontyates
(Pont-iets)
Mynyddygarreg
Pont-Henri
Trimsaran
Pen-y-Mynydd
Llanon
PONT ABRAHAM
GORSEINON
Loughor
Penclawdd
Crofty
Gowerton
Three Crosses
Dunvant
Upper Killay
Whiteford Point
Burry Holms
Rhossili Bay
Llanmadoc
Llangennith
Llanrhidian
Reynoldston
Knelston
Scurlage
Port-Eynon
Port-Eynon Point
Oxwich Point
Pwlldu Head
Bishopston
Southgate
WORMS HEAD
(Penrhyn-gwyr)
Mewslade Bay
Ginst Point
St Ishmael
DANGER AREA
A40
A48
A475
A476
A477
A478
A482
A484
A485
A486
A487
A4066
A4075
A4115
A4118
A4138
A4139
M4

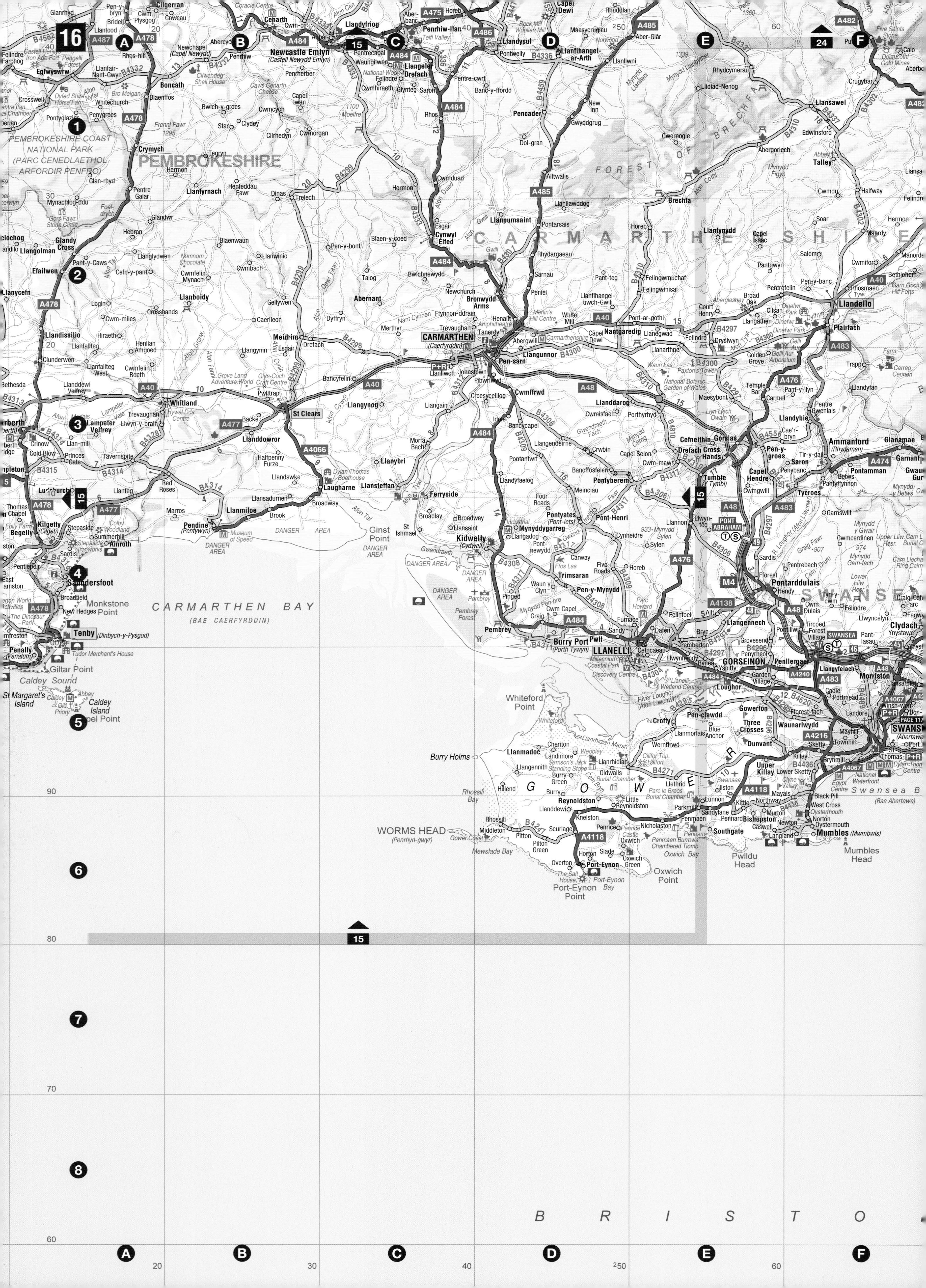
PEMBROKESHIRE
PEMBROKESHIRE COAST NATIONAL PARK (PARC CENEDLAETHOL ARFORDIR PENFRO)
CARMARTHENSHIRE
FOREST OF BRECHFA
CARMARTHEN BAY (BAE CAERFYRDDIN)
GOWER
SWANSEA
BRISTO
Newcastle Emlyn (Castell Newydd Emlyn)
Cenarth
Llandyfriog
Penrhiw-llan
Llandysul
Llanfihangel-ar-Arth
Capel Dewi
Crymych
Boncath
Eglwyswrw
Whitland
St Clears
Laugharne
Llansteffan
Pendine (Pentywyn)
Llanmiloe
CARMARTHEN (Caerfyrddin)
Pen-sarn
Cwmffrwd
Kidwelly (Cydweli)
Ferryside
Pembrey
Burry Port (Porth Tywyn)
Pwll
LLANELLI
Pontyberem
Pontyates (Pont-iets)
Trimsaran
Llandeilo
Ammanford (Rhydaman)
Llandybie
Cross Hands
Tumble (Y Tymbl)
Pontarddulais
Gorseinon
Loughor
Llangennech
Penllergaer
Morriston
Clydach
Mumbles (Mwmbwls)
Port-Eynon
Reynoldston
Rhossili
Worms Head (Penrhyn-gwyr)
Llanmadoc
Burry Holms
Whiteford Point
Tenby (Dinbych-y-Pysgod)
Saundersfoot
Kilgetty
Amroth
Narberth
Caldey Island
Giltar Point
Monkstone Point
St Margaret's Island
Talley
Llansawel
Brechfa
Abergorlech
Pencader
Alltwalis
Cynwyl Elfed
Llanpumsaint
Nantgaredig
Llanddarog
Llangunnor
Meidrim
Llanboidy
Efailwen
Glandy Cross
Lampeter Velfrey
Pontamman
Garnant
Glanaman
Tycroes
Pen-clawdd
Gowerton
Three Crosses
Dunvant
Upper Killay
Bishopston
Southgate
Oxwich Point
Pwlldu Head
Mumbles Head
Port-Eynon Point
A B C D E F
20 30 40 250 60
90 80 70 60

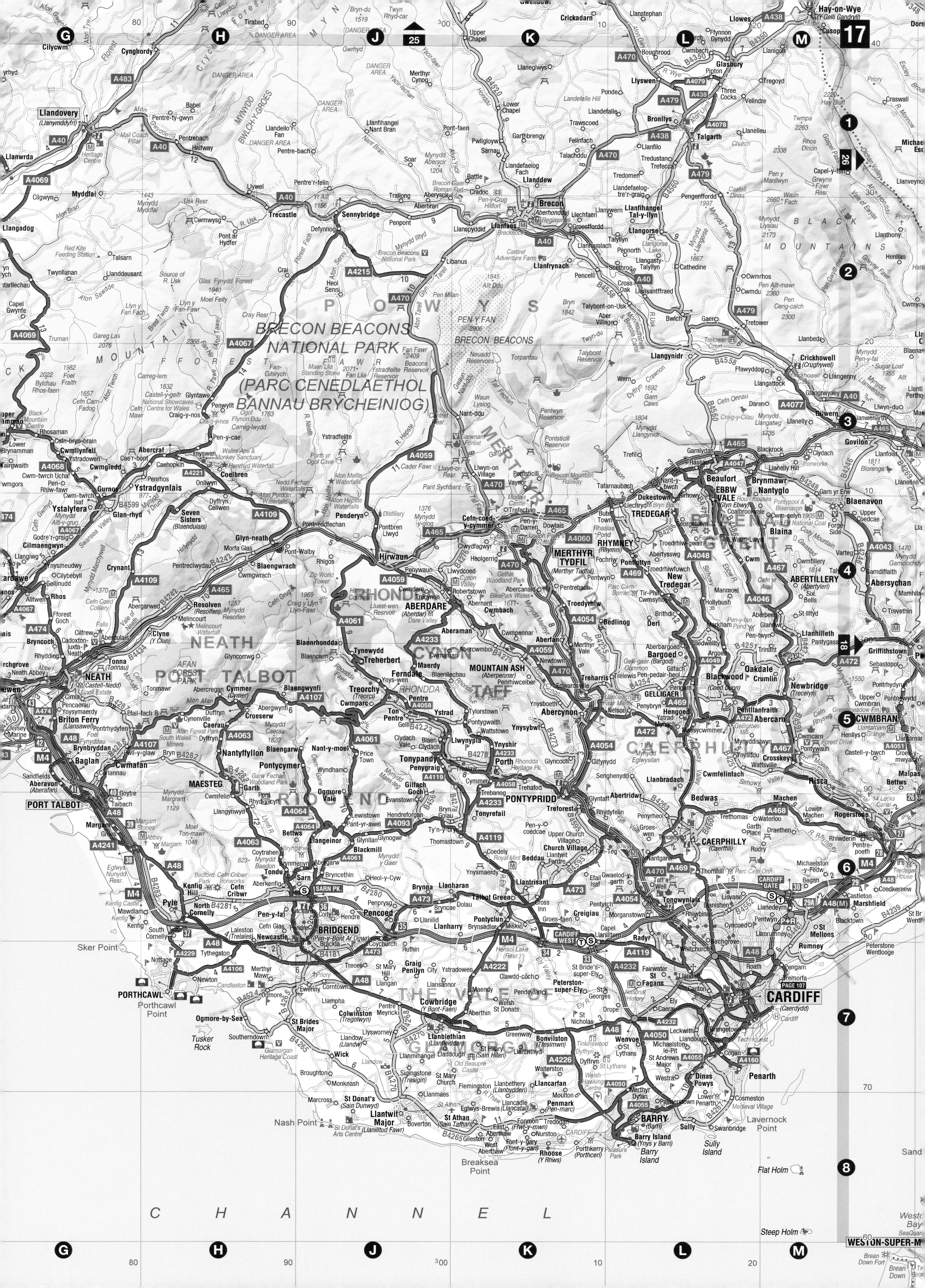
G
H
J
K
L
M
25
26
18
Hay-on-Wye
(Y Gelli Gandryll)
Llandovery
(Llanymddyfri)
Brecon
(Aberhonddu)
Talgarth
Crickhowell
(Crughywel)
POWYS
BRECON BEACONS
NATIONAL PARK
(PARC CENEDLAETHOL
BANNAU BRYCHEINIOG)
PEN Y FAN
2906
BRECON BEACONS
BLACK
MOUNTAINS
Sennybridge
Trecastle
Llangadog
Myddfai
Ystradgynlais
Ystalyfera
Glyn-neath
Hirwaun
Merthyr Tydfil
(Merthyr Tudful)
Ebbw Vale
(Glyn Ebwy)
Tredegar
Rhymney
(Rhymni)
Blaenavon
Abertillery
(Abertyleri)
Abersychan
Aberdare
(Aberdâr)
RHONDDA
CYNON
TAFF
Mountain Ash
(Aberpennar)
Treherbert
Treorchy
(Treorci)
Tonypandy
Porth
Pontypridd
Abercynon
Caerphilly
(Caerffili)
Cwmbran
Newbridge
(Trecelyn)
Blackwood
(Coed Duon)
Risca
Neath
(Castell-Nedd)
NEATH
PORT TALBOT
Port Talbot
Aberavon
(Aberafan)
Maesteg
BRIDGEND
Bridgend
(Pen-y-Bont Ar Ogwr)
Porthcawl
Porthcawl Point
Pyle
Pencoed
Llantrisant
Cowbridge
(Y Bont-Faen)
THE VALE OF GLAMORGAN
Llantwit Major
(Llanilltud Fawr)
Barry
(Barri)
Barry Island
(Ynys y Barri)
Penarth
Cardiff
(Caerdydd)
Sully Island
Lavernock Point
Flat Holm
Steep Holm
Nash Point
Breaksea Point
Sker Point
Tusker Rock
Ogmore-by-Sea
Rhoose
(Y Rhws)
CHANNEL
WESTON-SUPER-MARE
A40
A470
A465
A4059
A4061
A4063
A4067
A4109
A4119
A4232
A48
M4
A469
A4042
A467
A472
A4043
A479
A438
A4069
A483
PAGE 107
1
2
3
4
5
6
7
8
80
90
300
10
20

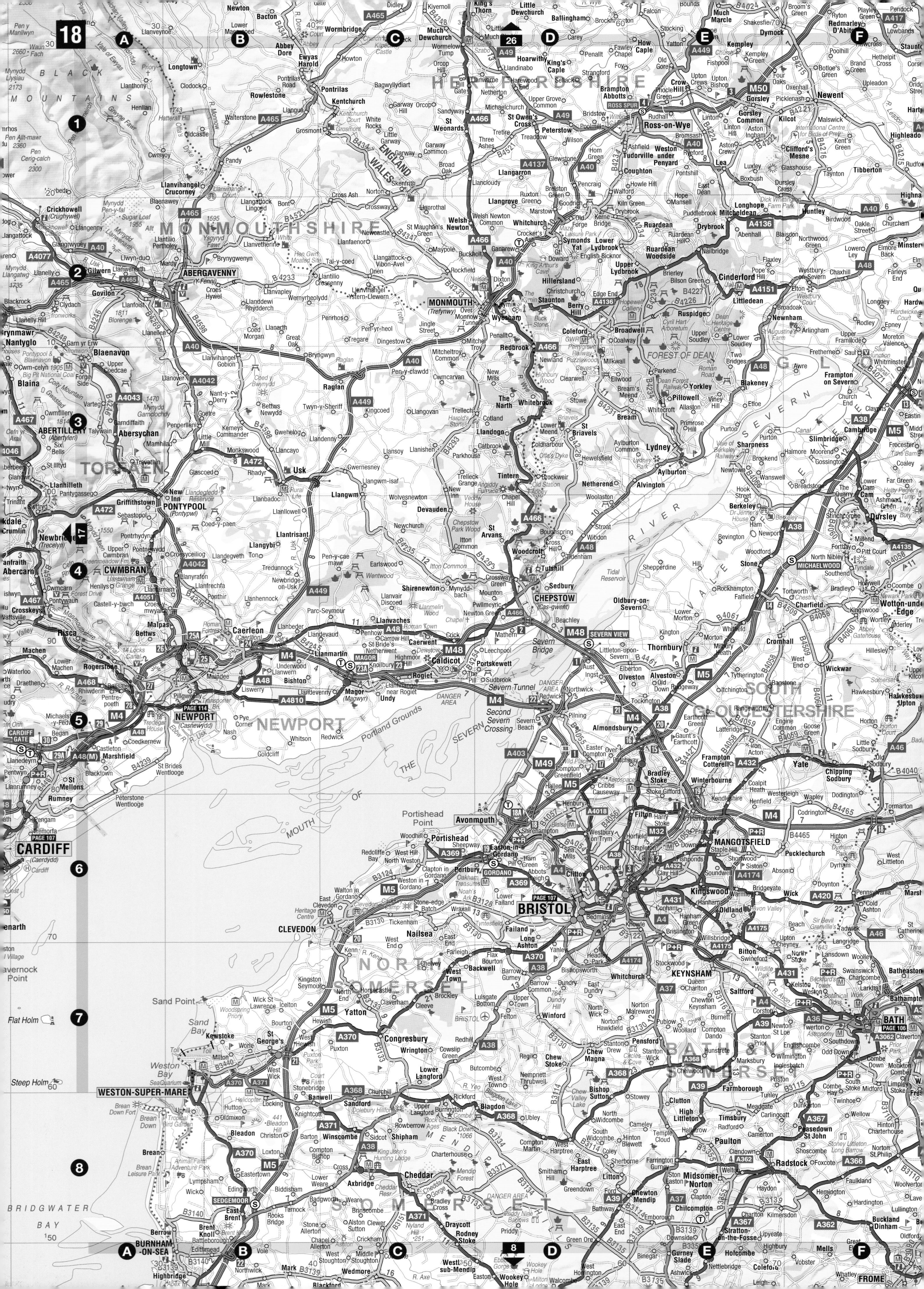
BLACK MOUNTAINS
HEREFORDSHIRE
MONMOUTHSHIRE
TORFAEN
NEWPORT
NORTH SOMERSET
SOUTH GLOUCESTERSHIRE
BATH & N. E. SOMERSET
SOMERSET
ENGLAND
WALES
FOREST OF DEAN
RIVER SEVERN
MOUTH OF THE SEVERN
BRIDGWATER BAY
Abergavenny
(Y Fenni)
Monmouth
(Trefynwy)
Ross-on-Wye
Newent
Pontypool
(Pontypŵl)
Cwmbran
Newport
(Casnewydd)
Cardiff
(Caerdydd)
Chepstow
(Cas-gwent)
Caerleon
Usk
Raglan
Lydney
Cinderford
Coleford
Bristol
Avonmouth
Portishead
Clevedon
Nailsea
Weston-super-Mare
Burnham-on-Sea
Cheddar
Keynsham
Bath
Midsomer Norton
Radstock
Frome
Yate
Thornbury
Kingswood
Mangotsfield
Dursley
Wotton-under-Edge
Abertillery
(Abertyleri)
Blaenavon
Crickhowell
(Crughywel)
Caldicot
Magor
(Magwyr)
M4
M5
M48
M49
M50
M32
Severn Bridge
Second Severn Crossing
Severn Tunnel
PAGE 107
PAGE 114
PAGE 106
26
8
17

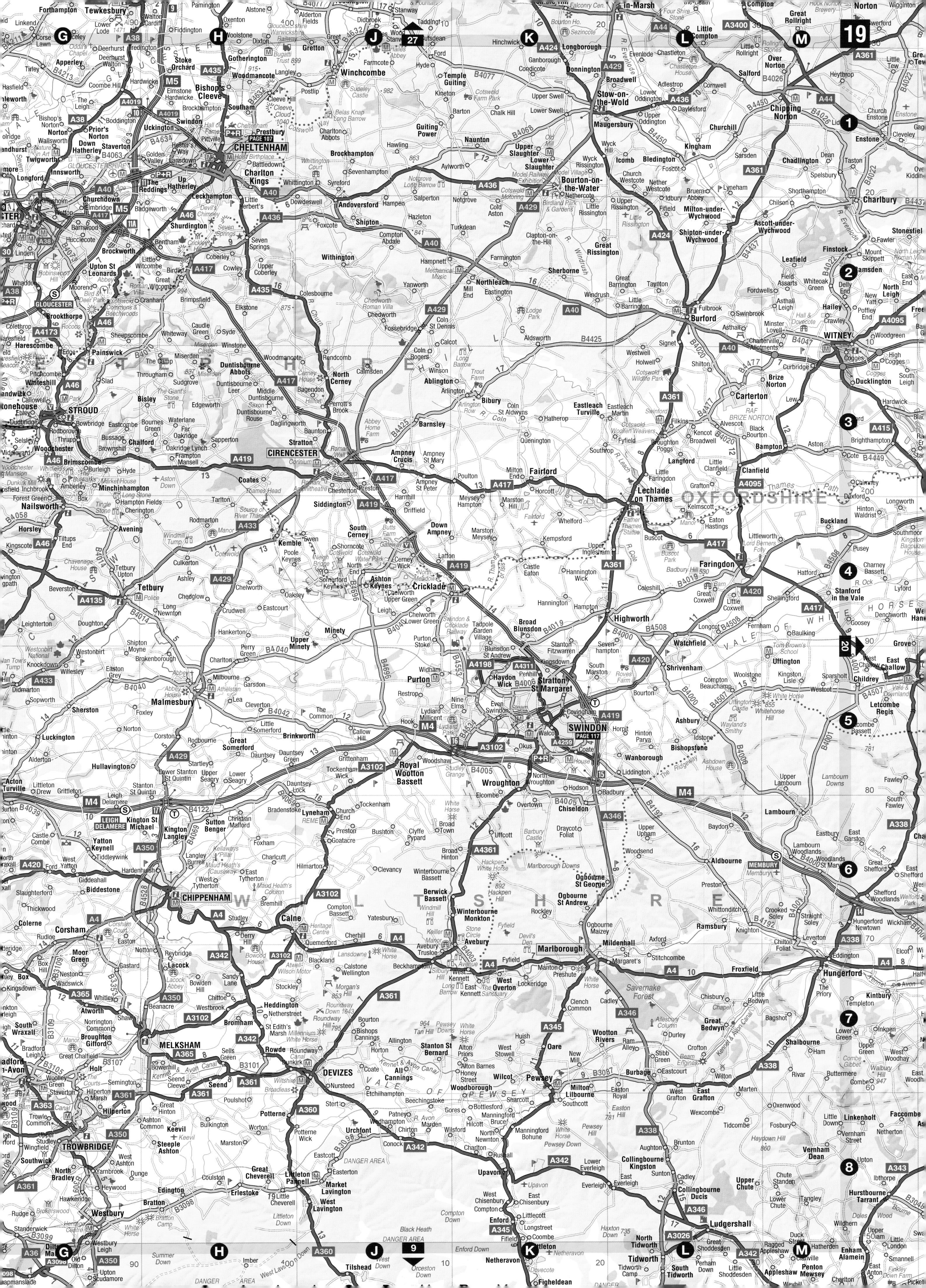

19
20
27
9
G
H
J
K
L
M
1
2
3
4
5
6
7
8
PAGE 107
PAGE 117
CHELTENHAM
GLOUCESTER
STROUD
CIRENCESTER
SWINDON
CHIPPENHAM
MELKSHAM
TROWBRIDGE
DEVIZES
Marlborough
Hungerford
WITNEY
OXFORDSHIRE
WILTSHIRE
Tewkesbury
Winchcombe
Stow-on-the-Wold
Chipping Norton
Charlbury
Burford
Bourton-on-the-Water
Northleach
Fairford
Lechlade on Thames
Faringdon
Highworth
Cricklade
Malmesbury
Tetbury
Nailsworth
Royal Wootton Bassett
Calne
Wroughton
Pewsey
Ludgershall
Tidworth
Westbury
Corsham
Carterton
Stratton St Margaret
Bishop's Cleeve
Minchinhampton
Lambourn

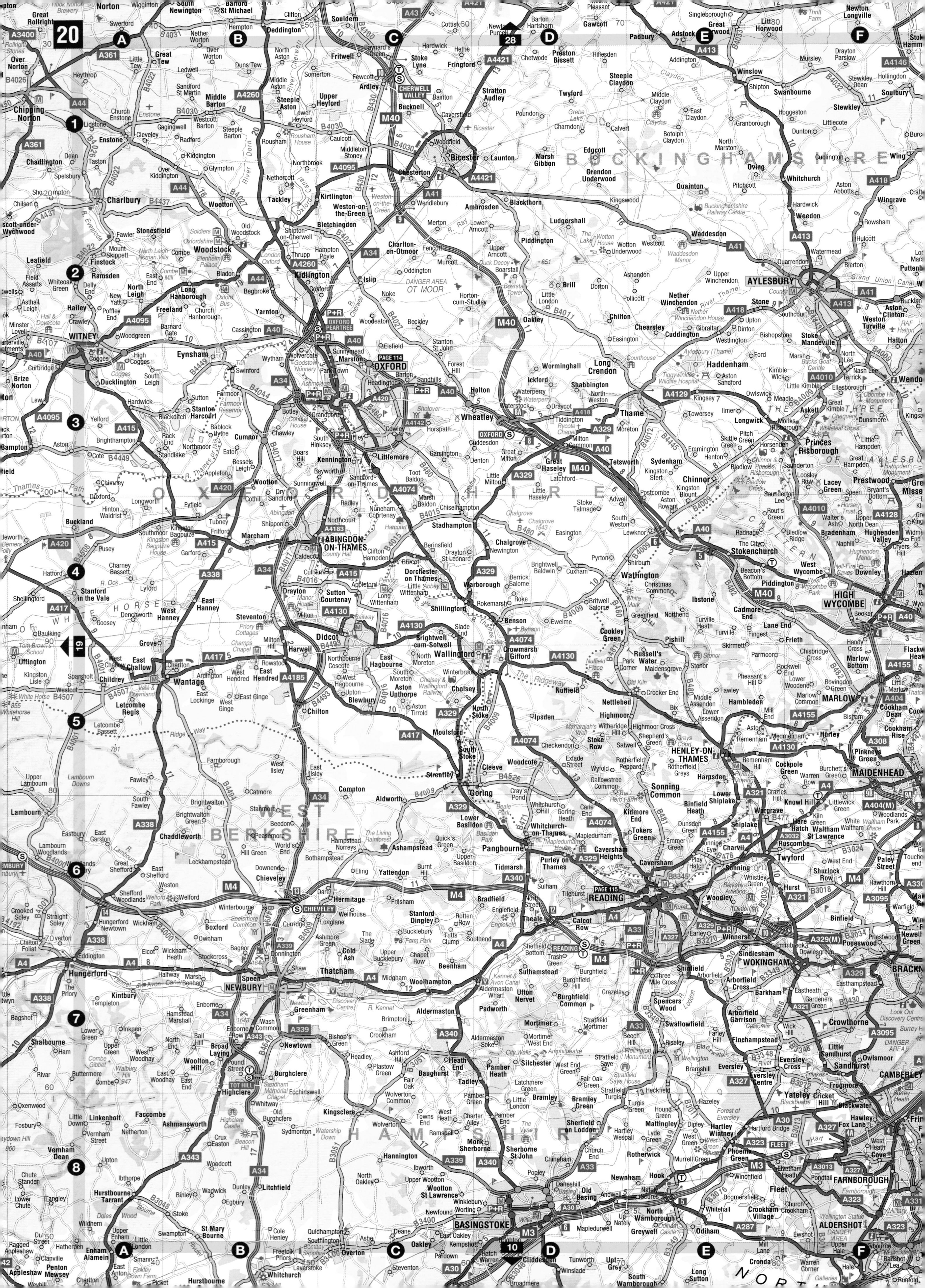

20
A
B
C
D
E
F
28
19
10
1
2
3
4
5
6
7
8
BUCKINGHAMSHIRE
OXFORDSHIRE
WEST BERKSHIRE
HAMPSHIRE
CHILTERN
Chipping Norton
Bicester
Aylesbury
Witney
Kidlington
Woodstock
Charlbury
OXFORD
PAGE 114
Abingdon-on-Thames
Thame
Wheatley
Didcot
Wallingford
Wantage
Henley-on-Thames
High Wycombe
Marlow
Maidenhead
READING
PAGE 115
Wokingham
Newbury
Hungerford
Thatcham
Basingstoke
Fleet
Farnborough
Aldershot
Camberley
Princes Risborough
M40
M4
M3
A34
A40
A41
A4
A33
A339
A338
OXFORD
CHERWELL VALLEY
CHIEVELEY
READING
FLEET

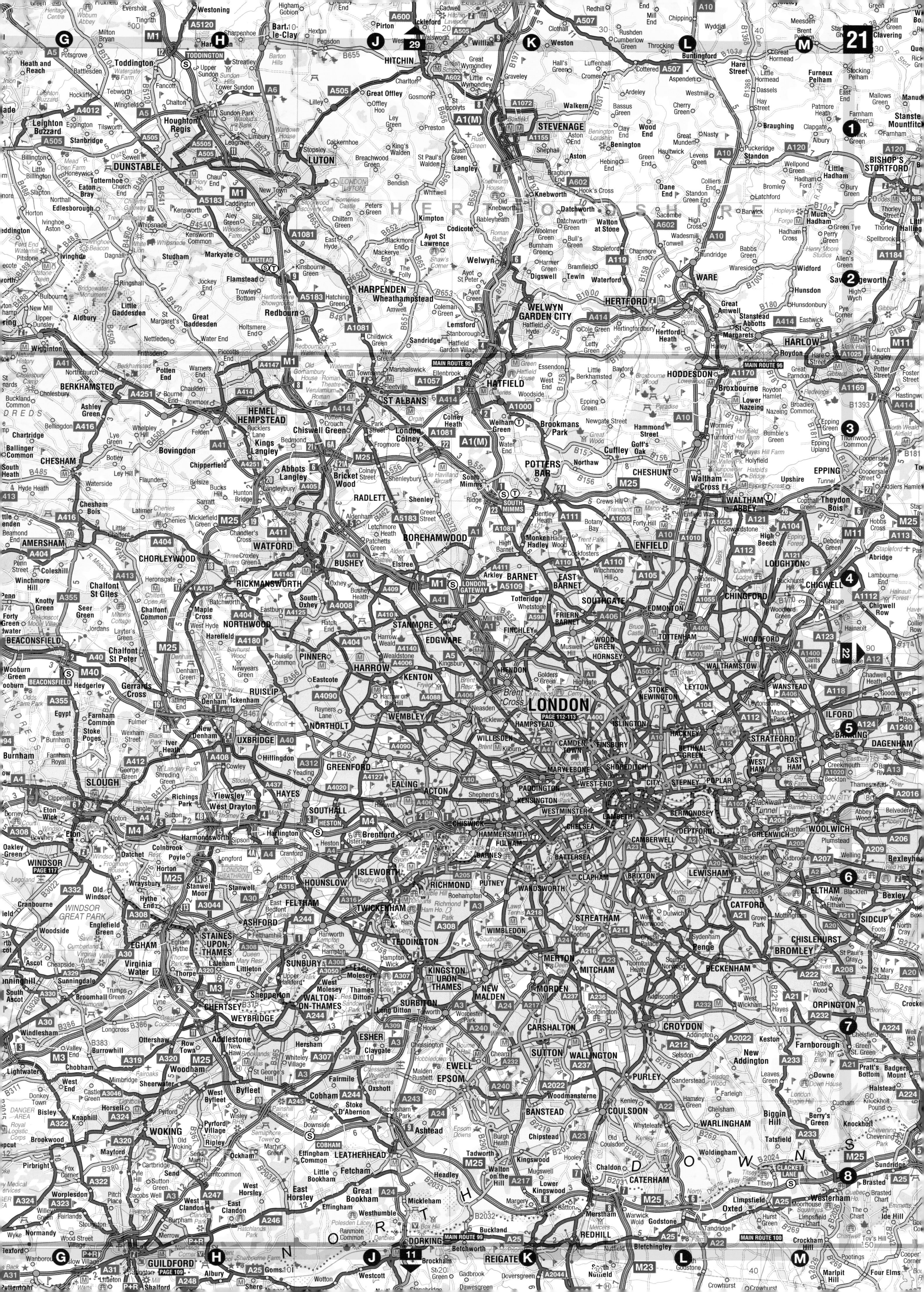
HITCHIN
STEVENAGE
LUTON
DUNSTABLE
Leighton Buzzard
Houghton Regis
HARPENDEN
WELWYN GARDEN CITY
HERTFORD
WARE
BISHOP'S STORTFORD
HARLOW
HERTFORDSHIRE
ST ALBANS
HATFIELD
HEMEL HEMPSTEAD
BERKHAMSTED
CHESHAM
AMERSHAM
HODDESDON
EPPING
WATFORD
BOREHAMWOOD
ENFIELD
POTTERS BAR
CHESHUNT
WALTHAM ABBEY
RICKMANSWORTH
CHORLEYWOOD
BARNET
LOUGHTON
CHIGWELL
BEACONSFIELD
HARROW
EDGWARE
STANMORE
PINNER
RUISLIP
UXBRIDGE
SLOUGH
WEMBLEY
LONDON
PAGE 112-113
HAMPSTEAD
ISLINGTON
WALTHAMSTOW
ILFORD
DAGENHAM
STRATFORD
HACKNEY
WESTMINSTER
CITY
ACTON
EALING
SOUTHALL
HAYES
HOUNSLOW
RICHMOND
TWICKENHAM
WIMBLEDON
WOOLWICH
GREENWICH
LEWISHAM
BROMLEY
CROYDON
SUTTON
EPSOM
KINGSTON UPON THAMES
STAINES-UPON-THAMES
WINDSOR
PAGE 117
EGHAM
WEYBRIDGE
WOKING
LEATHERHEAD
DORKING
REIGATE
REDHILL
GUILDFORD
PAGE 109
CATERHAM
ORPINGTON
SIDCUP
Bexley
M1
M4
M11
M25
M40
M3
M23
A1(M)
MAIN ROUTE 95
MAIN ROUTE 96
MAIN ROUTE 99
MAIN ROUTE 100
NORTH DOWNS
SURREY
29
11
22

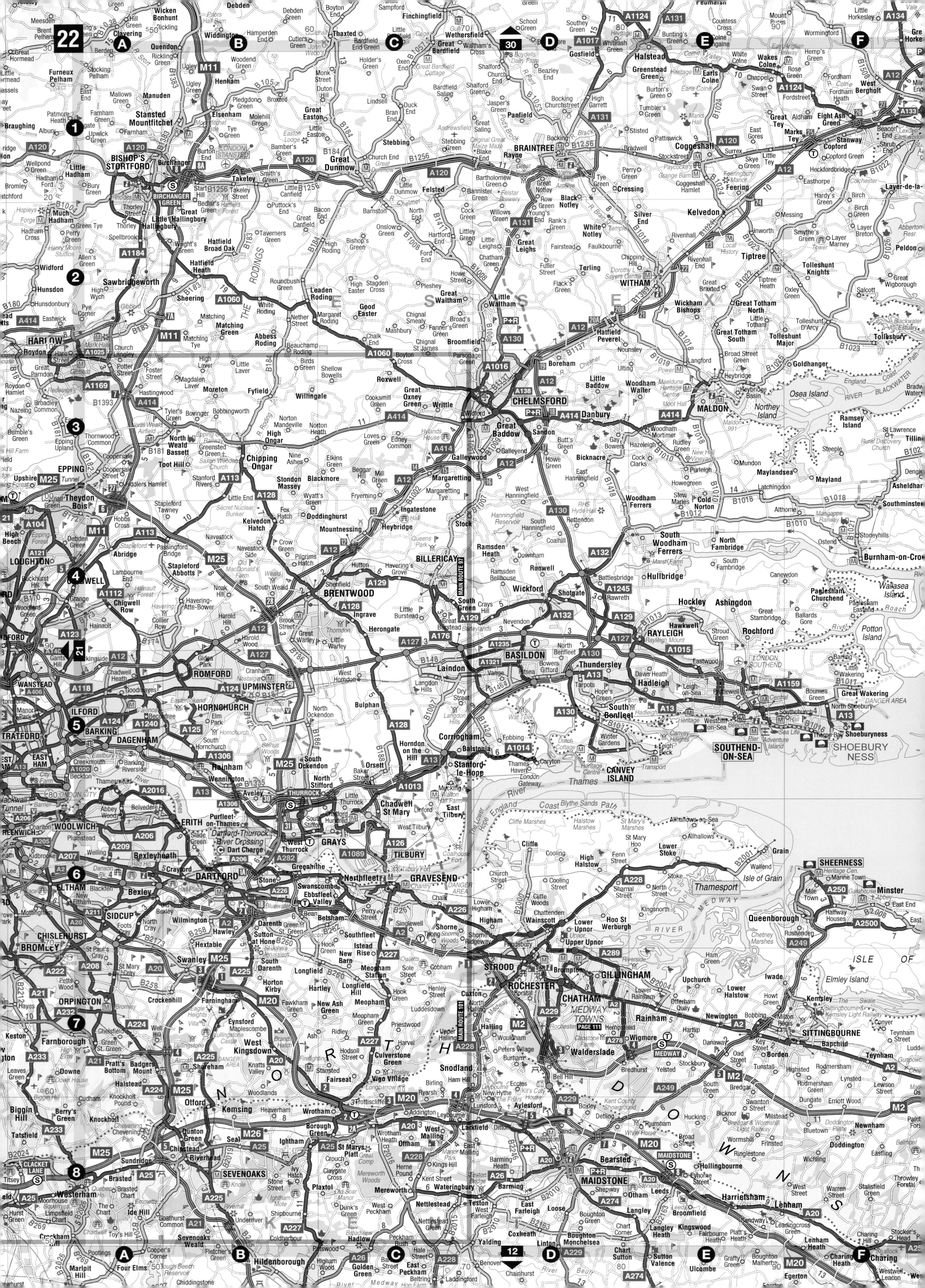
22
A
B
C
D
E
F
30
21
12
Bishop's Stortford
Stansted Mountfitchet
Sawbridgeworth
Harlow
Epping
Loughton
Chigwell
Romford
Ilford
Barking
Dagenham
Hornchurch
Upminster
Wanstead
Stratford
East Ham
Woolwich
Eltham
Bexleyheath
Bexley
Sidcup
Chislehurst
Bromley
Orpington
Farnborough
Westerham
Sevenoaks
Hildenborough
Swanley
Dartford
Crayford
Erith
Gravesend
Northfleet
Tilbury
Grays
Thurrock
Stanford-le-Hope
Corringham
Basildon
Laindon
Billericay
Brentwood
Ingatestone
Chipping Ongar
Chelmsford
Great Baddow
Danbury
Maldon
Witham
Braintree
Halstead
Coggeshall
Kelvedon
Tiptree
Great Dunmow
Thaxted
Wickford
Rayleigh
Hockley
Rochford
Southend-on-Sea
Shoeburyness
Canvey Island
Benfleet
Hadleigh
Thundersley
Burnham-on-Crouch
Southminster
Rochester
Strood
Chatham
Gillingham
Rainham
Walderslade
Snodland
Maidstone
West Malling
Sittingbourne
Sheerness
Minster
Queenborough
Isle of Grain
Isle of Sheppey
Lenham
Harrietsham
Charing
Hollingbourne
Bearsted
Kingswood
Mereworth
Borough Green
Wrotham
Kemsing
Otford
Shoreham
Biggin Hill
Tatsfield
Chelmer
Thames
Medway
Essex
North Downs
Kent
Northey Island
Osea Island
Wallasea Island
Potton Island
The Rodings
Main Route 97
Main Route 101
Page 111
M11
M25
M20
M2
M26
A12
A13
A120
A127
A130
A414
A2
A20
A228
A229
A249
A1060

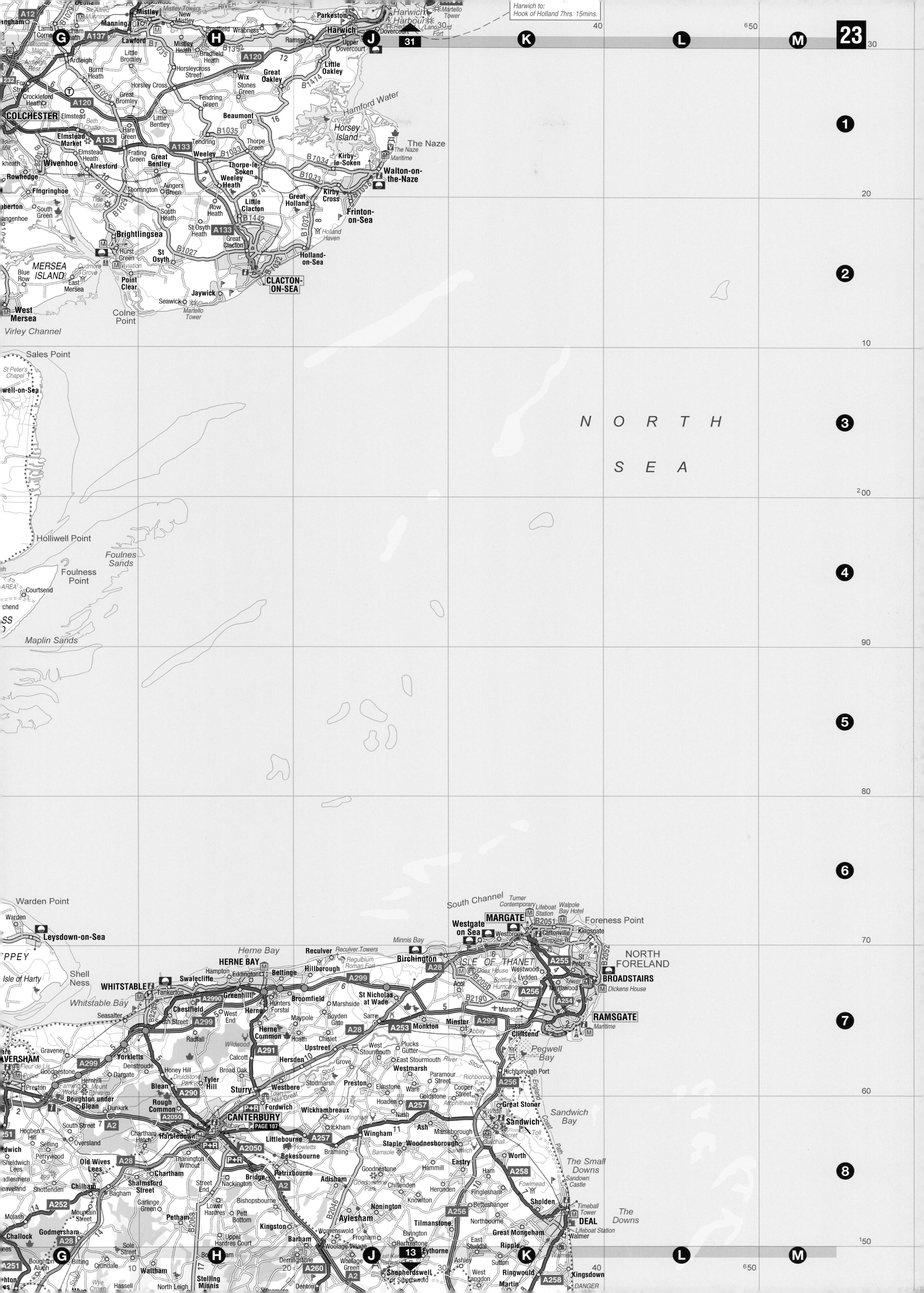
Harwich to:
Hook of Holland 7hrs. 15mins.
NORTH SEA
COLCHESTER
Wivenhoe
Brightlingsea
MERSEA ISLAND
West Mersea
Colne Point
Virley Channel
Harwich
Dovercourt
Mistley
Manningtree
Lawford
Hamford Water
Horsey Island
The Naze
Walton-on-the-Naze
Frinton-on-Sea
Holland-on-Sea
CLACTON-ON-SEA
Jaywick
St Osyth
Point Clear
Sales Point
Holliwell Point
Foulness Sands
Foulness Point
Courtsend
Maplin Sands
Warden Point
Leysdown-on-Sea
Isle of Harty
Shell Ness
Whitstable Bay
Herne Bay
WHITSTABLE
HERNE BAY
Reculver
Minnis Bay
Birchington
South Channel
Westgate on Sea
MARGATE
Foreness Point
NORTH FORELAND
BROADSTAIRS
RAMSGATE
ISLE OF THANET
Pegwell Bay
Sandwich Bay
Sandwich
CANTERBURY
PAGE 107
FAVERSHAM
The Small Downs
The Downs
DEAL
Walmer
Kingsdown
Wingham
Aylesham
Chartham
Chilham
Shepherdswell or Sibertswold
31
13
G
H
J
K
L
M
1
2
3
4
5
6
7
8
650
200
150
30
20
10
90
80
70
60
40

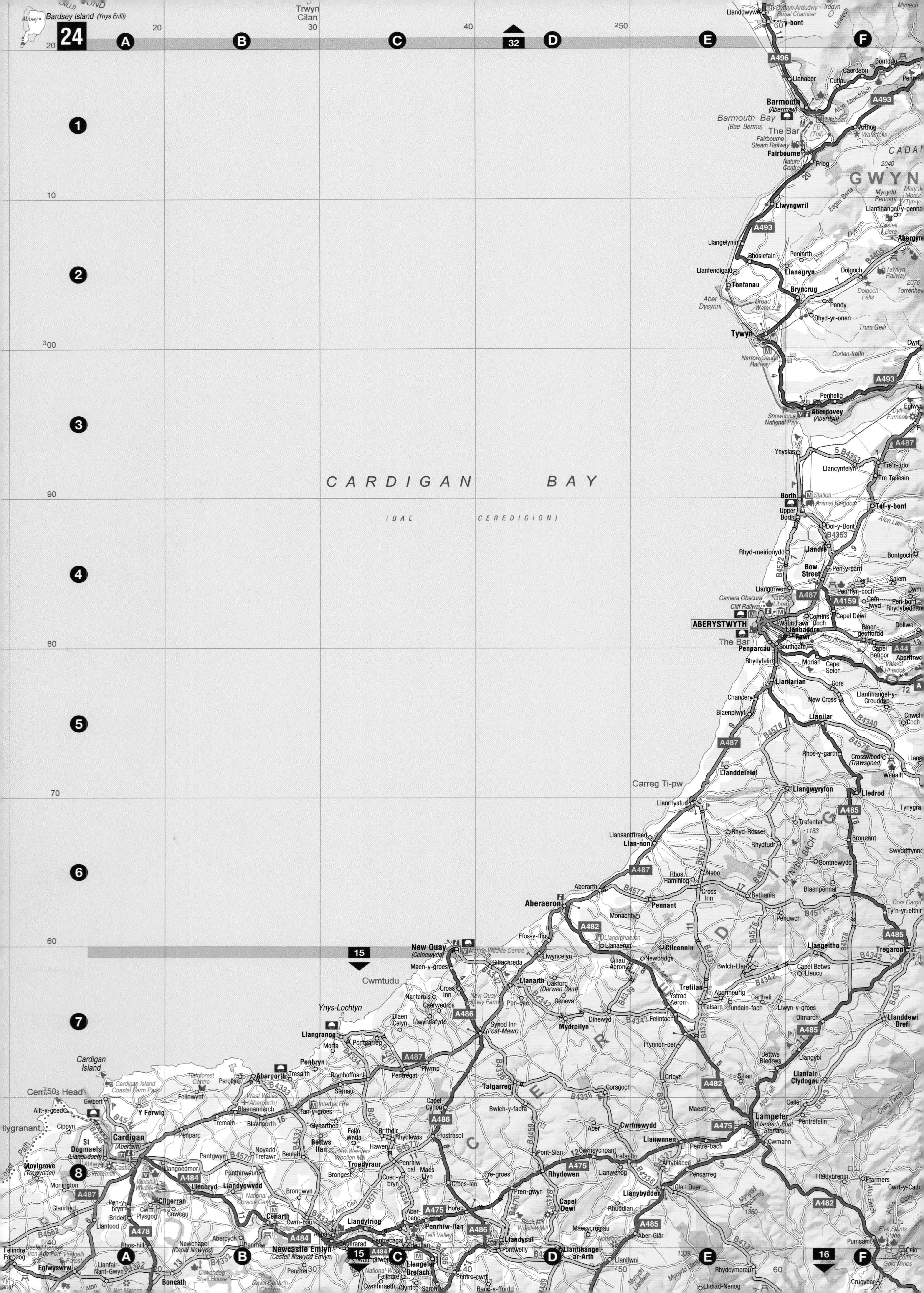

CARDIGAN BAY
(BAE CEREDIGION)
Bardsey Island (Ynys Enlli)
Trwyn Cilan
Barmouth (Abermaw)
Barmouth Bay (Bae Bermo)
The Bar
Fairbourne Steam Railway
Fairbourne
Friog
Llwyngwril
Llangelynin
Rhoslefain
Llanfendigaid
Tonfanau
Llanegryn
Bryncrug
Aber Dysynni
Broad Water
Tywyn
Narrow Gauge Railway
Penhelig
Aberdovey (Aberdyfi)
Snowdonia National Park
Ynyslas
Borth
Upper Borth
Tal-y-bont
Llandre
Bow Street
Llangorwen
Camera Obscura
Cliff Railway
ABERYSTWYTH
The Bar
Penparcau
Llanbadarn Fawr
Rhydyfelin
Llanfarian
Chancery
Blaenplwyf
Llanilar
Llanddeiniol
Carreg Ti-pw
Llanrhystud
Llangwyryfon
Lledrod
Llansantffraed
Llan-non
Aberarth
Aberaeron
Pennant
Tregaron
Cilcennin
Llanarth
New Quay (Ceinewydd)
Cwmtudu
Ynys-Lochtyn
Llangranog
Penbryn
Aberporth
Cardigan Island
Cemaes Head
Gwbert
Y Ferwig
St Dogmaels (Llandudoch)
Cardigan (Aberteifi)
Moylgrove (Trewyddel)
Cilgerran
Llechryd
Cenarth
Newcastle Emlyn (Castell Newydd Emlyn)
Llandysul
Lampeter (Llanbedr Pont Steffan)
Llanybydder
Talgarreg
Mydroilyn
Synod Inn (Post-Mawr)
Llanfihangel-ar-Arth
Pencader
Boncath
Eglwyswrw
A487
A493
A496
A482
A485
A486
A475
A484
A478
32
15
16
1
2
3
4
5
6
7
8
A
B
C
D
E
F

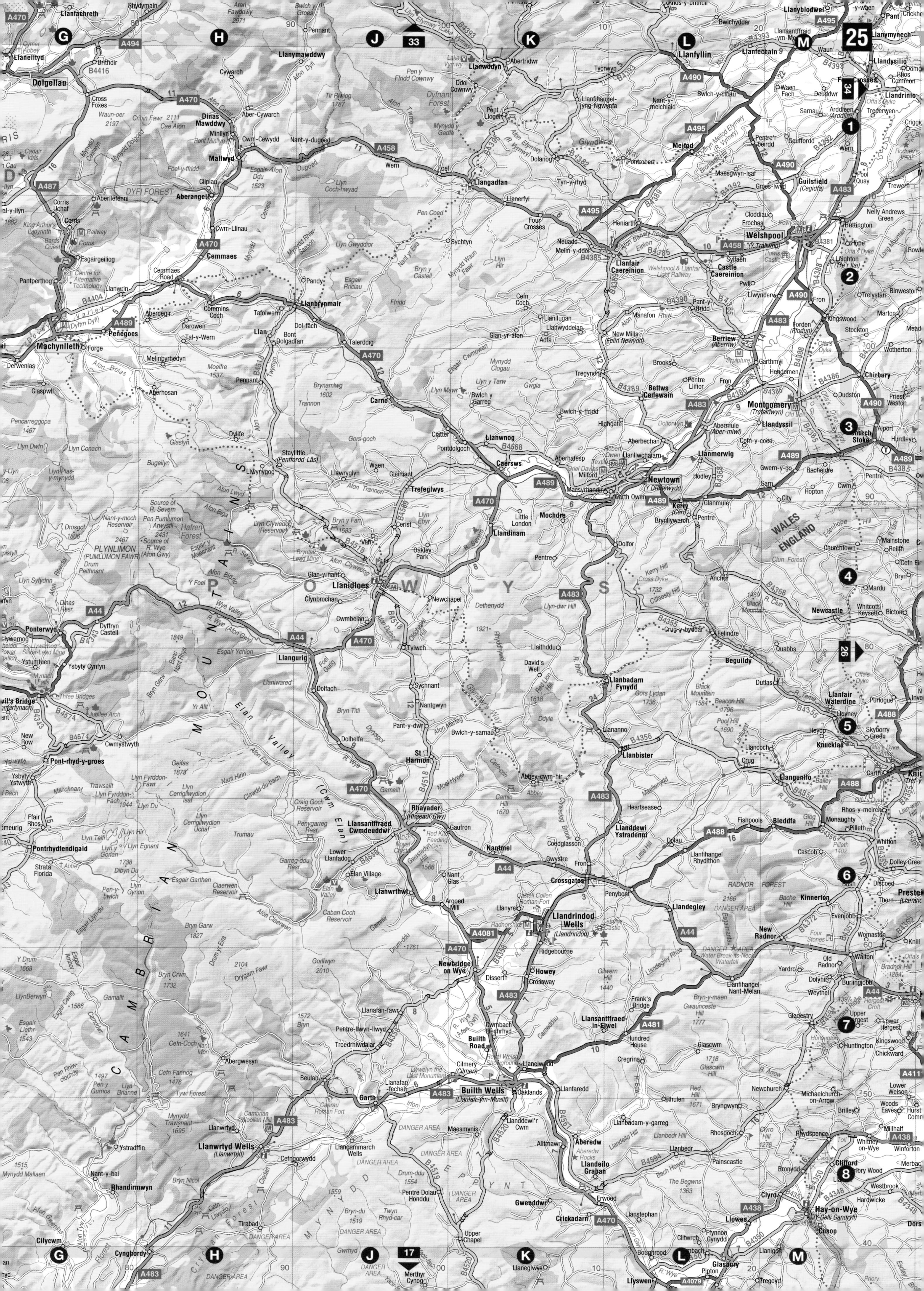
33
34
26
17
G
H
J
K
L
M
1
2
3
4
5
6
7
8
Dolgellau
Llanelltyd
Llanfachreth
Brithdir
Cross Foxes
Dinas Mawddwy
Mallwyd
Llanymawddwy
Llanwddyn
Lake Vyrnwy
Abertridwr
Llanfyllin
Llansantffraid-ym-Mechain
Llanymynech
Llandysilio
Four Crosses
Ardd-lin (Arddlin)
Meifod
Guilsfield (Cegidfa)
Pool Quay
Llangadfan
Foel
Aberangell
DYFI FOREST
Corris
Cemmaes
Cemmaes Road
Machynlleth
Penegoes
Forge
Derwenlas
Llanbrynmair
Talerddig
Carno
Pennant
Dylife
Staylittle (Penffordd-Lâs)
Llanidloes
Llyn Clywedog (Reservoir)
Trefeglwys
Caersws
Llanwnog
Pontdolgoch
Llanfair Caereinion
Castle Caereinion
Welshpool (Y Trallwng)
Welshpool & Llanfair Light Railway
Buttington
Forden (Ffodun)
Kingswood
Berriew (Aberriw)
Bettws Cedewain
Montgomery (Trefaldwyn)
Chirbury
Churchstoke
Abermule (Aber-miwl)
Llandyssil
Newtown (Y Drenewydd)
Kerry (Ceri)
WALES
ENGLAND
Llandinam
Mochdre
Dolfor
PLYNLIMON (PUMLUMON FAWR)
2467
Nant-y-moch Reservoir
Ponterwyd
Devil's Bridge (Pontarfynach)
Ystumtuen
Pont-rhyd-y-groes
Pontrhydfendigaid
Strata Florida
Llangurig
POWYS
CAMBRIAN MOUNTAINS
Elan Valley
St Harmon
Rhayader (Rhaeadr Gwy)
Llansantffraed Cwmdeuddwr
Elan Village
Claerwen Reservoir
Caban Coch Reservoir
Nantmel
Crossgates
Llandrindod Wells (Llandrindod)
Newbridge on Wye
Howey
Llanbadarn Fynydd
Llanbister
Beguildy
Felindre
Knucklas
Llangunllo
Bleddfa
Llanfair Waterdine
Newcastle
RADNOR FOREST
New Radnor
Kinnerton
Old Radnor
Gladestry
Kington
Llandegley
Penybont
Llanfihangel-Nant-Melan
Llansantffraed-in-Elwel
Builth Wells (Llanfair-ym-Muallt)
Builth Road
Cilmery (Cilmeri)
Garth
Beulah
Abergwesyn
Llanwrtyd Wells (Llanwrtud)
Llangammarch Wells
Rhandirmwyn
Cilycwm
Cynghordy
Erwood
Aberedw
Crickadarn
Gwenddwr
Upper Chapel
Merthyr Cynog
Glasbury
Clyro
Hay-on-Wye (Y Gelli Gandryll)
Clifford
Cusop
Llyswen
Boughrood
Painscastle
Glascwm
Hundred House
MYNYDD EPPYNT
A470
A494
A487
A458
A495
A490
A483
A489
A44
A4081
A481
A488
A438
A4079
B4518
B4574
B4343
B4385
B4386
B4356
B4355
B4594
B4520
B4519
B4350
B4348
B4358

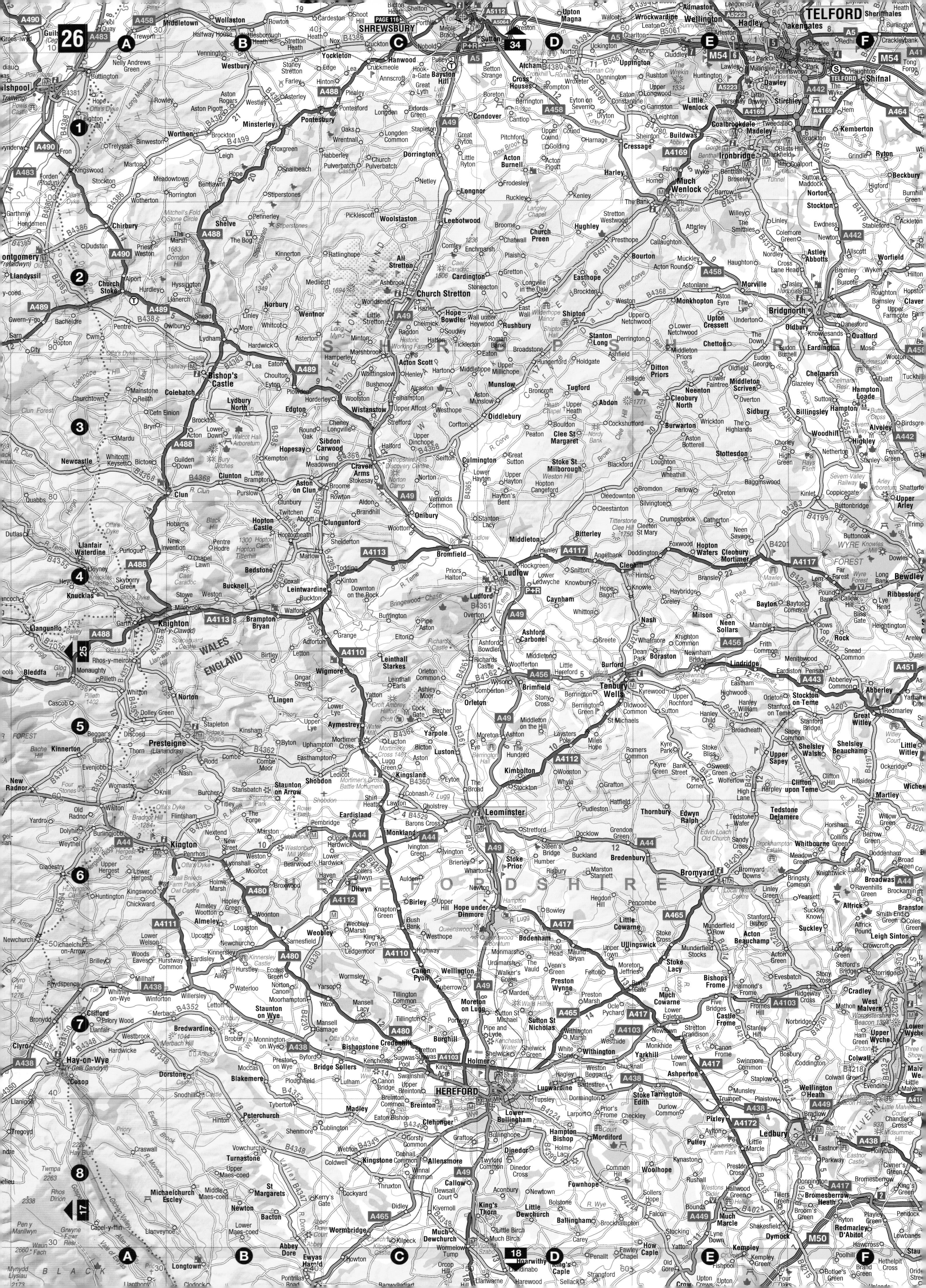
26
A
B
C
D
E
F
TELFORD
SHREWSBURY
PAGE 116
34
25
17
18
Wellington
Shifnal
Welshpool
Church Stretton
Bishop's Castle
Bridgnorth
Much Wenlock
Ironbridge
Ludlow
Knighton
Presteigne
Kington
Leominster
Tenbury Wells
Bromyard
HEREFORD
Ledbury
Hay-on-Wye
Cleobury Mortimer
Bewdley
Great Witley
Craven Arms
Clun
Montgomery
SHROPSHIRE
HEREFORDSHIRE
WALES
ENGLAND
A49
A458
A488
A489
A4117
A4113
A44
A438
A465
A4103
A480
A417
A456
M54
M50

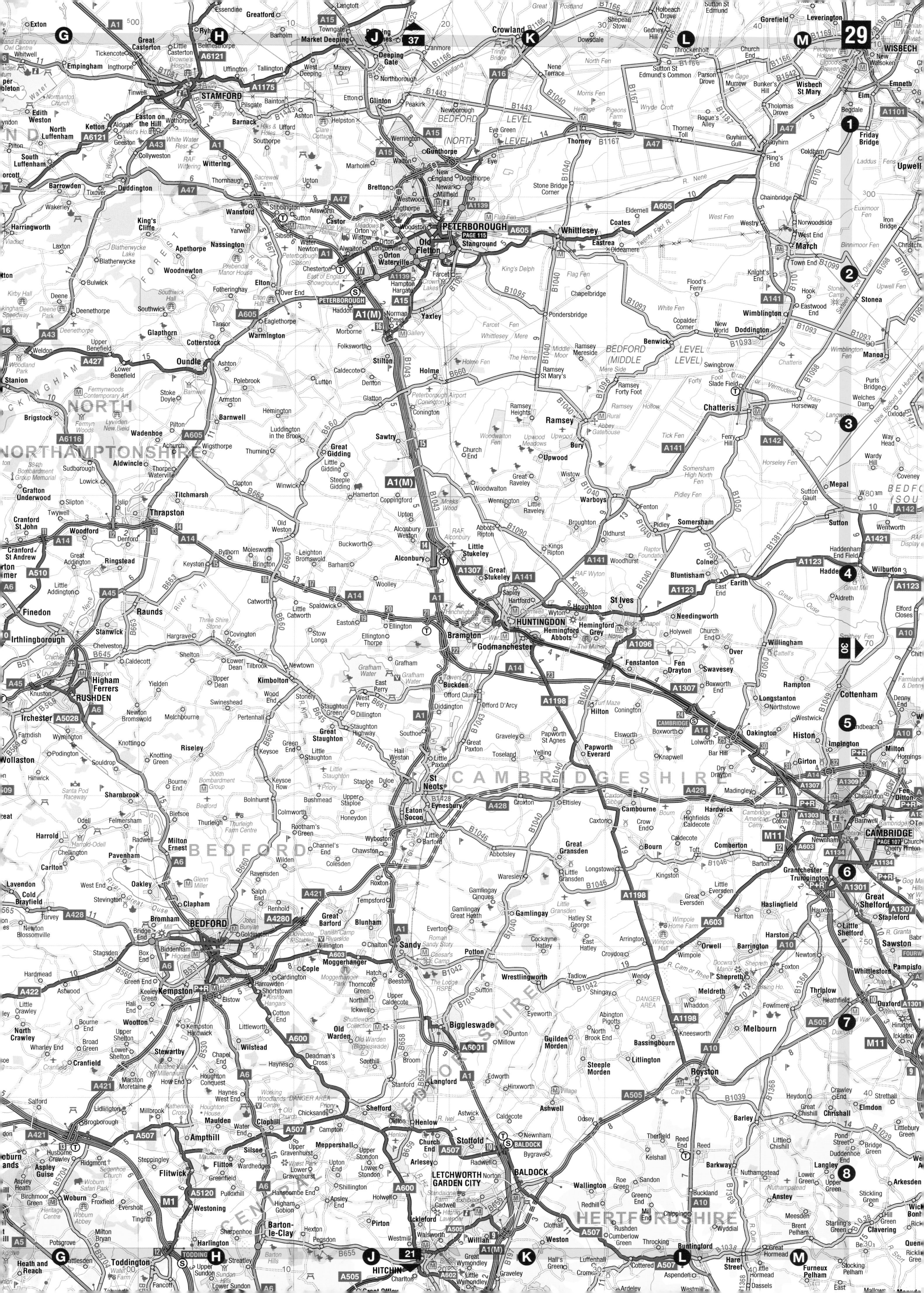

29
37
30
21
PAGE 115
PAGE 107
G
H
J
K
L
M
1
2
3
4
5
6
7
8
NORTHAMPTONSHIRE
CAMBRIDGESHIRE
BEDFORD
HERTFORDSHIRE
BEDFORD LEVEL (NORTH LEVEL)
BEDFORD (MIDDLE LEVEL)
STAMFORD
PETERBOROUGH
WISBECH
March
Chatteris
Ramsey
Whittlesey
Thorney
Crowland
Market Deeping
Oundle
Thrapston
Raunds
Higham Ferrers
RUSHDEN
Irthlingborough
Wollaston
Kimbolton
HUNTINGDON
Godmanchester
St Ives
St Neots
Eaton Socon
Sandy
Biggleswade
Potton
BEDFORD
Kempston
Ampthill
Flitwick
Shefford
Stotfold
BALDOCK
LETCHWORTH GARDEN CITY
HITCHIN
Royston
Melbourn
CAMBRIDGE
Histon
Cottenham
Somersham
Warboys
Sawtry
Yaxley
Brampton
Stilton
A1
A1(M)
A14
A15
A16
A47
A141
A142
A428
A421
A603
A605
A1198
A1307
A505
A507
A600
A6
M1
M11
A10

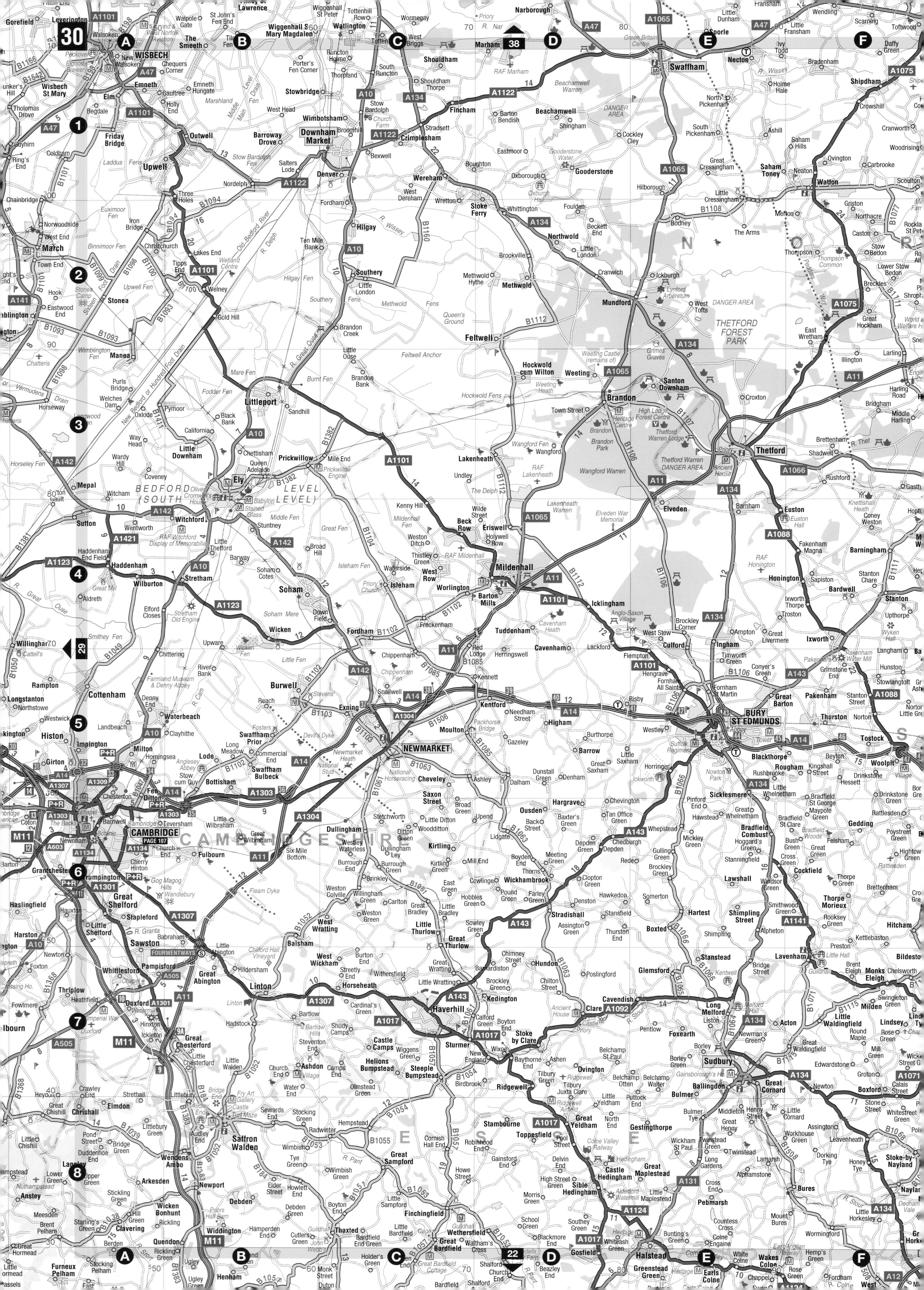

30
A
B
C
D
E
F
1
2
3
4
5
6
7
8
38
29
22
WISBECH
March
Upwell
Outwell
Downham Market
Denver
Swaffham
Narborough
Marham
Shouldham
Fincham
Crimplesham
Wereham
Stoke Ferry
Methwold
Feltwell
Mundford
Hilgay
Southery
Littleport
Ely
Chatteris
Manea
Stonea
Sutton
Haddenham
Wilburton
Stretham
Soham
Fordham
Wicken
Mildenhall
Lakenheath
Brandon
Thetford
THETFORD FOREST PARK
Watton
Shipdham
Elveden
Euston
Barnham
Honington
Ixworth
Icklingham
Kentford
NEWMARKET
Burwell
Cottenham
Histon
Girton
CAMBRIDGE
PAGE 107
CAMBRIDGESHIRE
BEDFORD (SOUTH LEVEL)
Fulbourn
Great Shelford
Sawston
Linton
Haverhill
Clare
Cavendish
Long Melford
Lavenham
Sudbury
BURY ST EDMUNDS
Great Barton
Woolpit
Boxford
Nayland
Bures
Halstead
Castle Hedingham
Sible Hedingham
Great Yeldham
Ridgewell
Steeple Bumpstead
Saffron Walden
Thaxted
Great Bardfield
Finchingfield
Great Sampford
Newport
Clavering
Duxford
Great Chesterford
Whittlesford
Royston
Earls Colne
A10
A11
A14
A47
A134
A142
A143
A1065
A1066
A1075
A1088
A1101
A1122
A1123
A1303
A1304
A1307
A1017
A1092
A505
M11

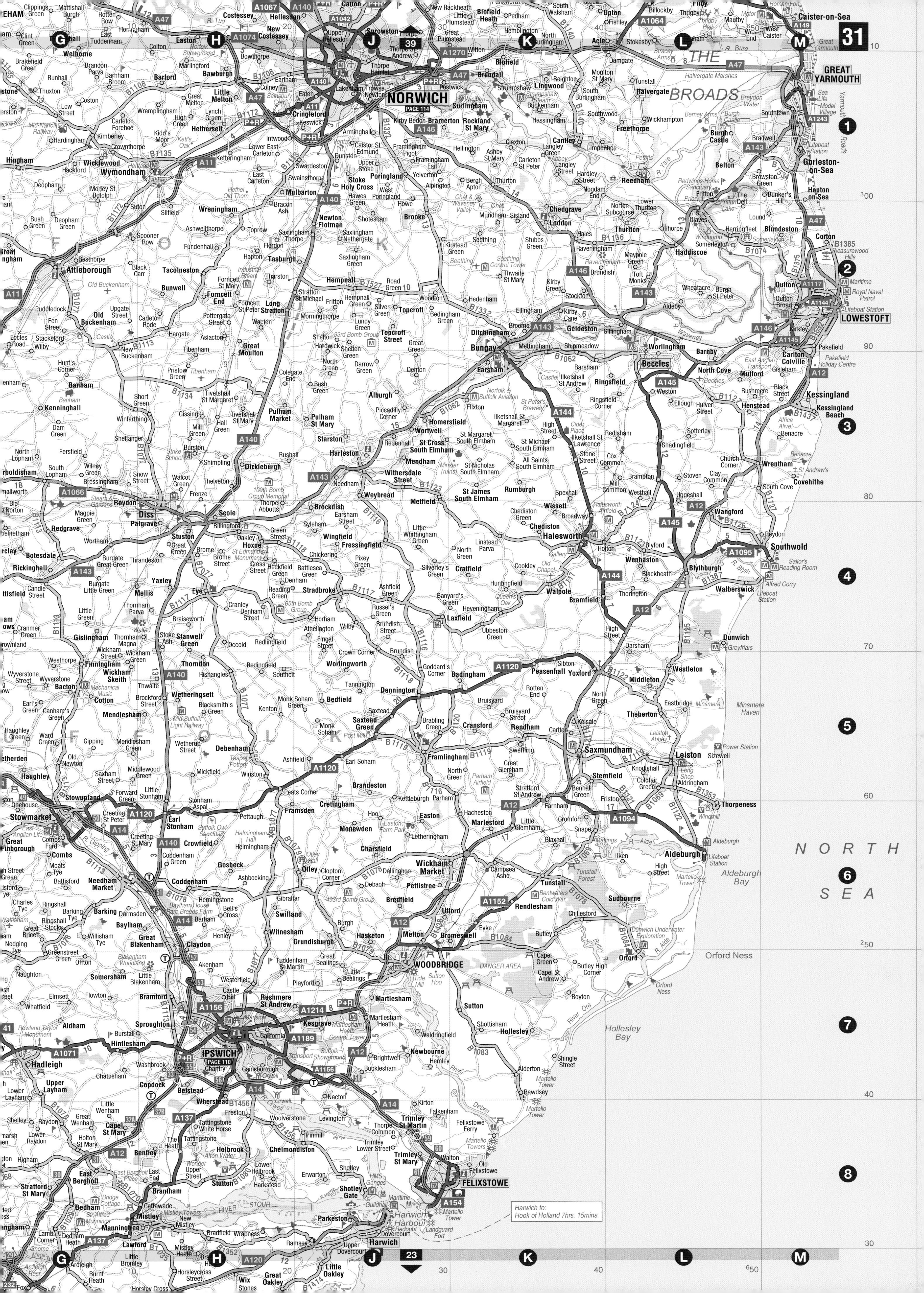

31
G
H
J
K
L
M
1
2
3
4
5
6
7
8
39
23
NORWICH
PAGE 114
IPSWICH
PAGE 110
GREAT YARMOUTH
LOWESTOFT
FELIXSTOWE
WOODBRIDGE
THE BROADS
NORTH SEA
Caister-on-Sea
Gorleston-on-Sea
Hopton on Sea
Corton
Oulton Broad
Kessingland
Southwold
Walberswick
Dunwich
Westleton
Minsmere Haven
Leiston
Sizewell
Thorpeness
Aldeburgh
Aldeburgh Bay
Orford
Orford Ness
Hollesley Bay
Harwich
Dovercourt
Harwich Harbour
Harwich to:
Hook of Holland 7hrs. 15mins.
Costessey
Hellesdon
Sprowston
Wymondham
Attleborough
Diss
Eye
Harleston
Bungay
Beccles
Halesworth
Wangford
Wrentham
Blythburgh
Saxmundham
Framlingham
Wickham Market
Debenham
Stowmarket
Needham Market
Hadleigh
Manningtree
Mistley
Dedham
Loddon
Acle
Reedham
Yoxford
Peasenhall
Stradbroke
Hoxne
Scole
Long Stratton
Wickham Skeith
Bacton
Mendlesham
Claydon
Kesgrave
Martlesham
Melton
Rendlesham
Tunstall
Snape
Sudbourne
Holbrook
Shotley Gate
Trimley St Martin
Trimley St Mary
Walton
DANGER AREA
RIVER STOUR
A11
A12
A14
A47
A140
A143
A144
A145
A146
A120
A137
A1120
A1094
A1152
A1156
A1189
A1214
A1071
A1066
A1095
A154

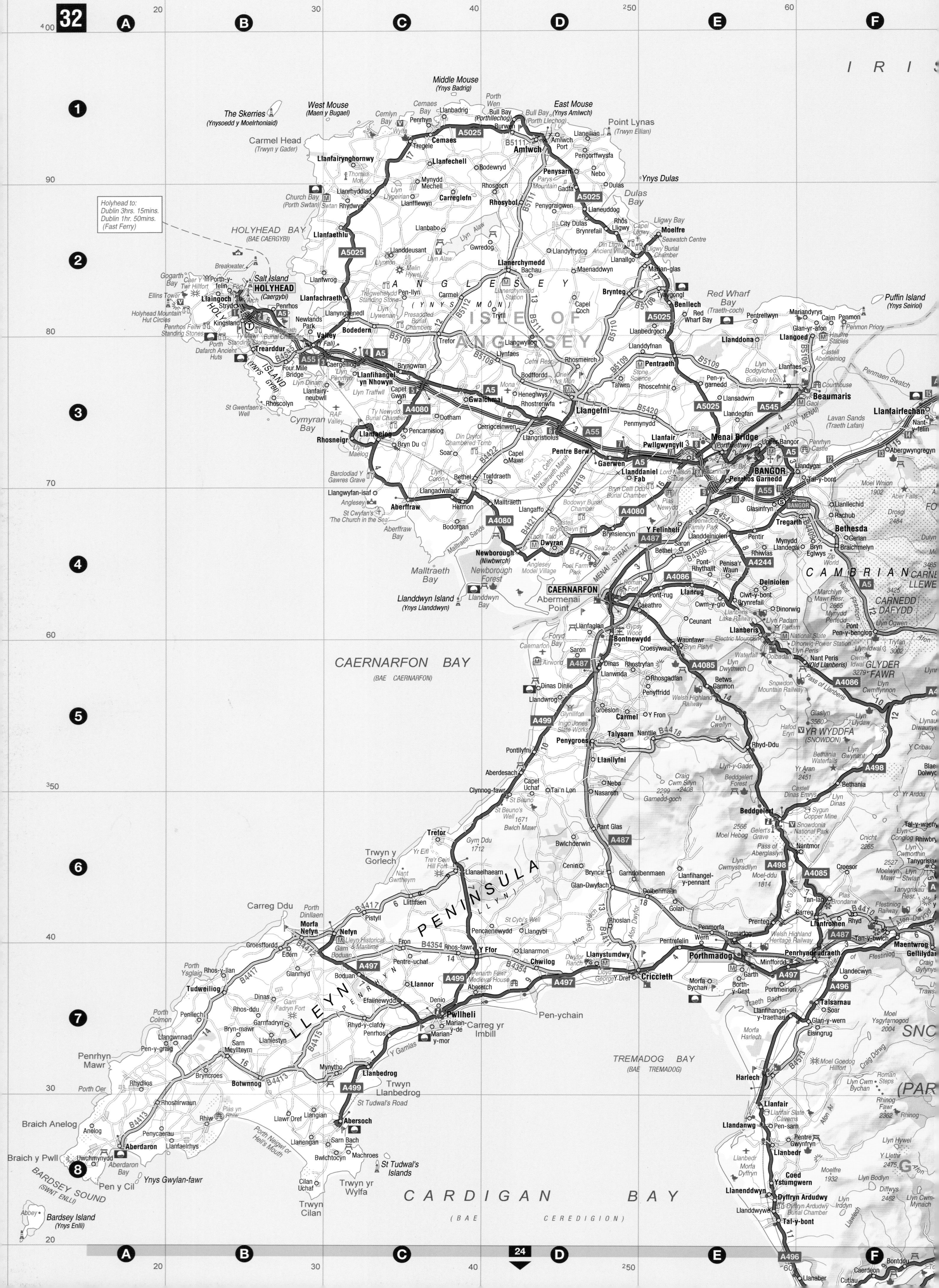
A
B
C
D
E
F
1
2
3
4
5
6
7
8
IRIS
Middle Mouse
(Ynys Badrig)
West Mouse
(Maen y Bugael)
The Skerries
(Ynysoedd y Moelrhoniaid)
East Mouse
(Ynys Amlwch)
Point Lynas
(Trwyn Eilian)
Carmel Head
(Trwyn y Gader)
Cemaes Bay
Bull Bay
(Porth Llechog)
Amlwch
Amlwch Port
Cemaes
Llanfechell
Llanfairynghornwy
Ynys Dulas
Dulas Bay
Holyhead to:
Dublin 3hrs. 15mins.
Dublin 1hr. 50mins.
(Fast Ferry)
HOLYHEAD BAY
(BAE CAERGYBI)
HOLYHEAD
(Caergybi)
Salt Island
Breakwater
Gogarth Bay
Ellins Tower
Holyhead Mountain Hut Circles
Penrhos Feilw Standing Stones
Porth Dafarch Ancient Huts
HOLY ISLAND
(YNYS GYBI)
Trearddur
Valley
Rhoscolyn
St Gwenfaen's Well
Church Bay
(Porth Swtan)
Llanfaethlu
Llanfachraeth
Llanrhyddlad
Rhydwyn
Carreglefn
Rhosybol
Penysarn
Moelfre
Lligwy Bay
Llanallgo
Marian-glas
Benllech
Red Wharf Bay
(Traeth-coch)
Brynteg
Llannerch-y-medd
ANGLESEY
(YNYS MÔN)
ISLE OF ANGLESEY
Llangefni
Gwalchmai
Bodedern
Llanfihangel yn Nhowyn
Rhosneigr
Llanfaelog
Cymyran Bay
Aberffraw
Bodorgan
Malltraeth
Newborough
(Niwbwrch)
Newborough Forest
Malltraeth Bay
Llanddwyn Island
(Ynys Llanddwyn)
Dwyran
Brynsiencyn
Llanfair Pwllgwyngyll
Menai Bridge
(Porthaethwy)
Pentraeth
Beaumaris
Llangoed
Penmon
Puffin Island
(Ynys Seiriol)
Lavan Sands
(Traeth Lafan)
Llanfairfechan
BANGOR
Upper Bangor
Tregarth
Bethesda
Y Felinheli
CAERNARFON
Abermenai Point
Llanrug
Llanberis
Deiniolen
CAMBRIAN
CARNEDD DAFYDD
GLYDER FAWR
YR WYDDFA
(SNOWDON)
CAERNARFON BAY
(BAE CAERNARFON)
Dinas Dinlle
Bontnewydd
Groeslon
Penygroes
Talysarn
Carmel
Rhyd-Ddu
Beddgelert
Clynnog-fawr
Trefor
Llanaelhaearn
Trwyn y Gorlech
LLEYN PENINSULA
(LLYN)
Carreg Ddu
Morfa Nefyn
Nefyn
Pistyll
Llanystumdwy
Criccieth
Porthmadog
Tremadog
Penrhyndeudraeth
Minffordd
Portmeirion
Maentwrog
Tan-y-bwlch
Pwllheli
Llanbedrog
Abersoch
St Tudwal's Islands
Tudweiliog
Botwnnog
Aberdaron
Braich Anelog
Braich y Pwll
Aberdaron Bay
Ynys Gwylan-fawr
Pen y Cil
BARDSEY SOUND
(SWNT ENLLI)
Bardsey Island
(Ynys Enlli)
CARDIGAN BAY
(BAE CEREDIGION)
TREMADOG BAY
(BAE TREMADOG)
Harlech
Talsarnau
Llanfair
Llandanwg
Llanbedr
Dyffryn Ardudwy
Tal-y-bont
Barmouth
A5
A55
A5025
A4080
A487
A499
A497
A4085
A498
A4086
A4244
A496
A545
B5109
B4366
B4417
B4413
B4354
B4418
B4415
B4411
20
30
40
250
60
400
90
80
70
60
350
40
30
20

24

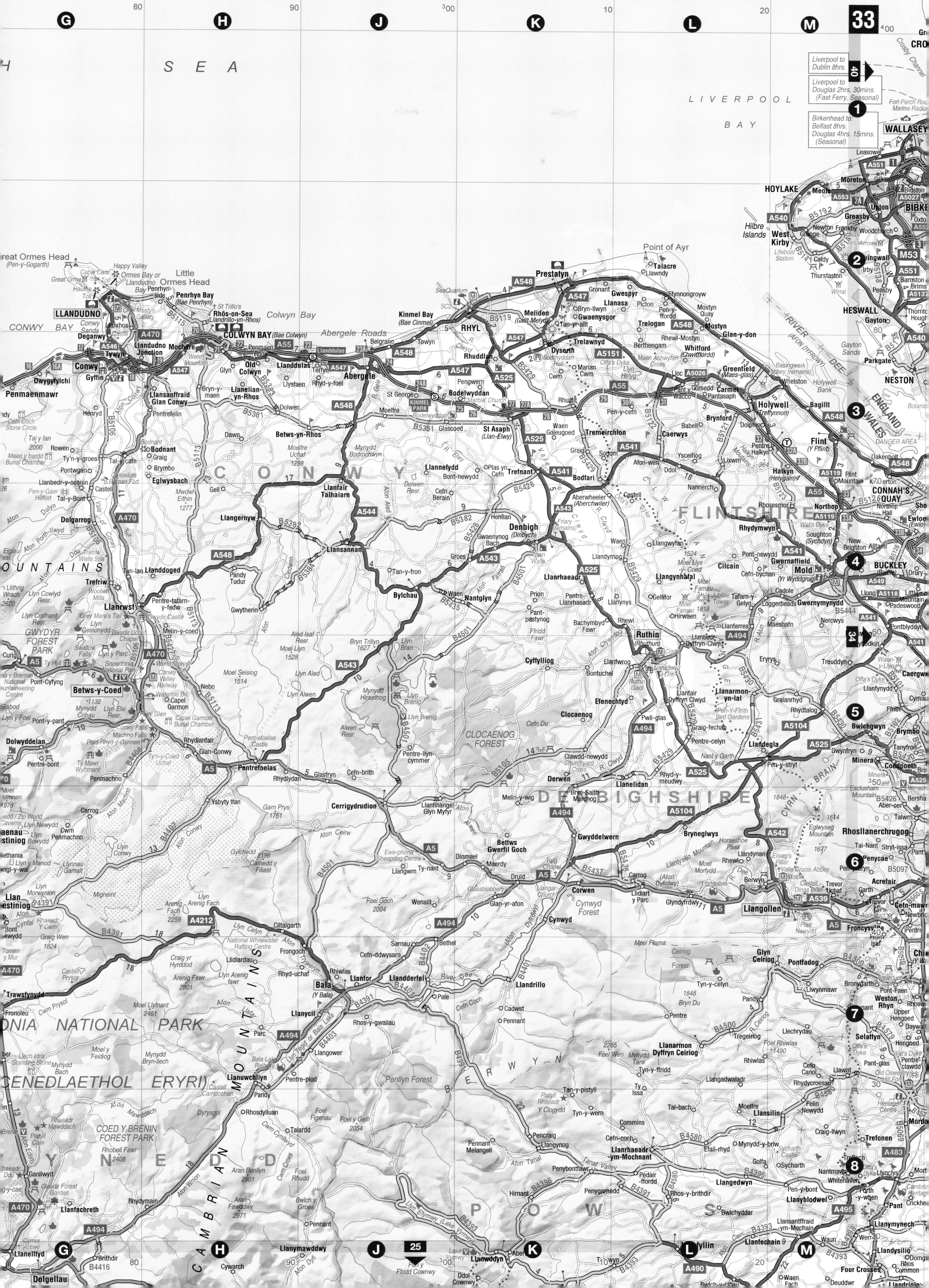
G
H
J
K
L
M
80
90
300
10
20
400
SEA
LIVERPOOL
BAY
Liverpool to Dublin 8hrs.
Liverpool to Douglas 2hrs. 30mins. (Fast Ferry, Seasonal)
Birkenhead to: Belfast 8hrs. Douglas 4hrs. 15mins. (Seasonal)
40
1
2
3
4
5
6
7
8
WALLASEY
HOYLAKE
Meols
Moreton
West Kirby
Hilbre Islands
HESWALL
NESTON
Point of Ayr
Talacre
Prestatyn
Gronant
Gwespyr
Llanasa
Mostyn
RHYL
Meliden
Dyserth
Rhuddlan
Trelawnyd
Whitford
Greenfield
Holywell
Bagillt
Flint (Y Fflint)
CONNAH'S QUAY
Northop
BUCKLEY
Mold (Yr Wyddgrug)
Great Ormes Head
Little Ormes Head
LLANDUDNO
Deganwy
Conwy
CONWY BAY
Penrhyn Bay
Rhôs-on-Sea
COLWYN BAY (Bae Colwyn)
Colwyn Bay
Abergele Roads
Kinmel Bay
Towyn
Llandudno Junction
Mochdre
Old Colwyn
Llanddulas
Abergele
Bodelwyddan
St Asaph (Llan-Elwy)
Dwygyfylchi
Penmaenmawr
Llansanffraid Glan Conwy
Betws-yn-Rhos
Trefnant
Tremeirchion
Caerwys
Bodfari
Halkyn
CONWY
FLINTSHIRE
Llanfair Talhaiarn
Llangernyw
Llansannan
Denbigh (Dinbych)
Dolgarrog
Trefriw
Llanddoged
Llanrwst
Bylchau
Nantglyn
Llanrhaeadr
Ruthin (Rhuthun)
Cilcain
Loggerheads
Llanferres
GWYDYR FOREST PARK
Betws-y-Coed
Pont-y-pant
Dolwyddelan
Cyffylliog
Efenechtyd
Clocaenog
CLOCAENOG FOREST
Llanarmon-yn-Ial
Llandegla
Pentrefoelas
Cerrigydrudion
Derwen
Llanelidan
DENBIGHSHIRE
Gwyddelwern
Bettws Gwerfil Goch
Corwen
Llangollen
Rhosllanerchrugog
Penycae
Acrefair
Trawsfynydd
SNOWDONIA NATIONAL PARK
PARC CENEDLAETHOL ERYRI
Bala (Y Bala)
Llanfor
Llandderfel
Llandrillo
Llanycil
Llanuwchllyn
Glyn Ceiriog
Pontfadog
Llanarmon Dyffryn Ceiriog
Selattyn
Llansilin
Trefonen
Llanrhaeadr-ym-Mochnant
Llangedwyn
Llanfyllin
Llanwddyn
Lake Vyrnwy
BERWYN
CAMBRIAN MOUNTAINS
COED Y BRENIN FOREST PARK
GWYNEDD
POWYS
Llanfachreth
Dolgellau
Llanelltyd
Llanymawddwy
25

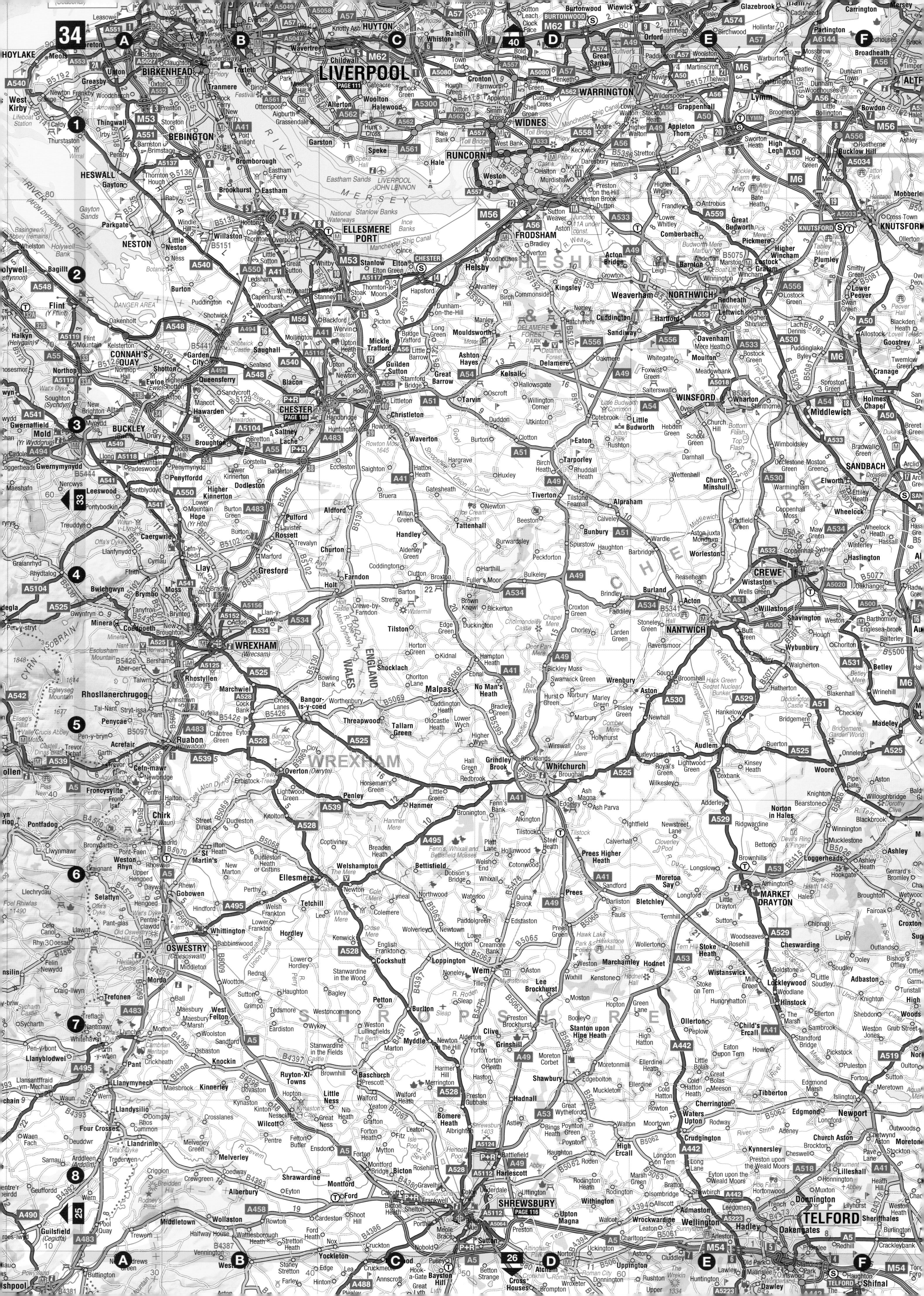
LIVERPOOL
PAGE 111
BIRKENHEAD
HOYLAKE
West Kirby
BEBINGTON
HESWALL
NESTON
ELLESMERE PORT
HUYTON
WIDNES
RUNCORN
WARRINGTON
FRODSHAM
NORTHWICH
KNUTSFORD
WINSFORD
MIDDLEWICH
SANDBACH
CREWE
NANTWICH
CHESTER
PAGE 108
CONNAH'S QUAY
BUCKLEY
Mold
Flint
WREXHAM
Ruabon
Chirk
OSWESTRY
Whitchurch
Ellesmere
Wem
MARKET DRAYTON
SHREWSBURY
PAGE 116
TELFORD
Newport
Wellington
Donnington
CHESHIRE
SHROPSHIRE
WREXHAM
WALES
ENGLAND
RIVER MERSEY
RIVER DEE
LIVERPOOL JOHN LENNON
Manchester Ship Canal
DELAMERE FOREST PARK
M6
M53
M56
M62
M54
A41
A49
A51
A525
A534
A483
A5
A530
A529
A442
40
33
25
26
A
B
C
D
E
F
1
2
3
4
5
6
7
8

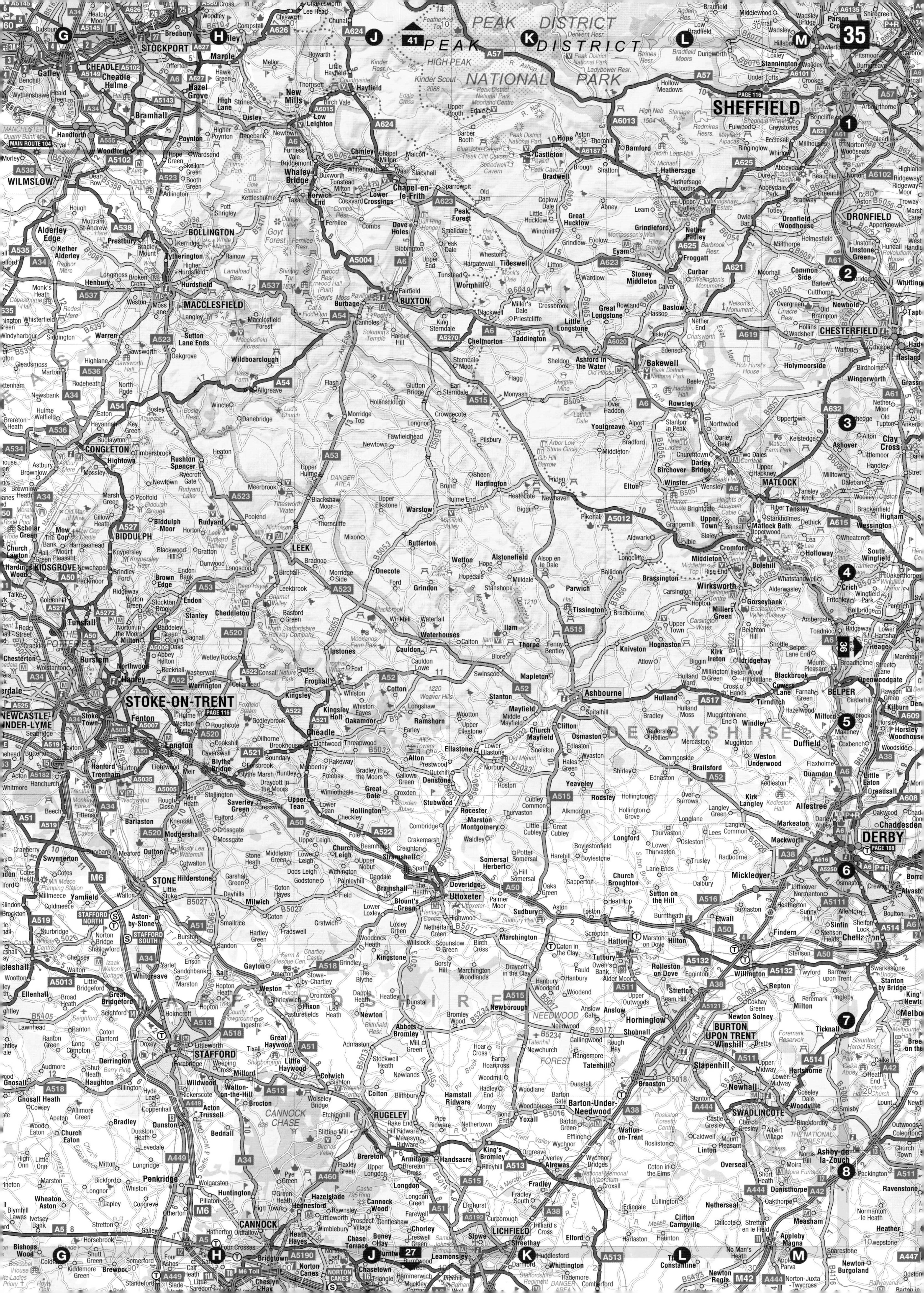
35
41
36
27
60
PEAK DISTRICT
PEAK DISTRICT NATIONAL PARK
SHEFFIELD
STOCKPORT
CHEADLE
MACCLESFIELD
BUXTON
CHESTERFIELD
DRONFIELD
MATLOCK
BELPER
DERBY
CONGLETON
BIDDULPH
KIDSGROVE
LEEK
STOKE-ON-TRENT
NEWCASTLE-UNDER-LYME
STONE
STAFFORD
CANNOCK
RUGELEY
LICHFIELD
BURTON UPON TRENT
SWADLINCOTE
Ashbourne
Uttoxeter
Bakewell
Cheadle
DERBYSHIRE
STAFFORDSHIRE
CANNOCK CHASE
NEEDWOOD FOREST
MAIN ROUTE 104
PAGE 116
PAGE 108
M6
M42
A50
A38
A6
A515
A52
A53
A54
A57
A61
A623
A5012
A516
A514
A444
A513
A5
G
H
J
K
L
M
1
2
3
4
5
6
7
8

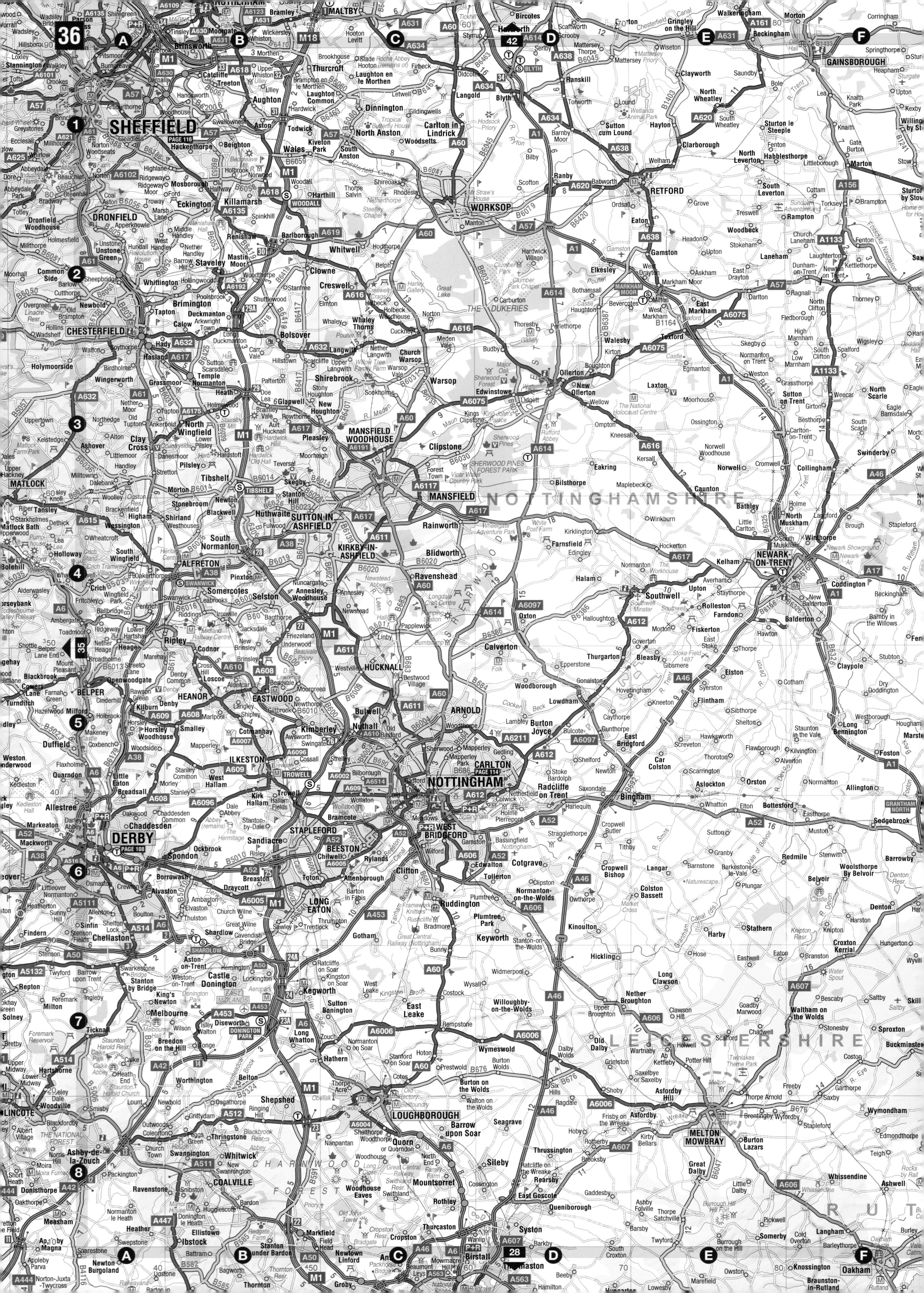
36
42
35
28
SHEFFIELD
PAGE 118
NOTTINGHAM
PAGE 114
DERBY
PAGE 108
NOTTINGHAMSHIRE
LEICESTERSHIRE
GAINSBOROUGH
RETFORD
WORKSOP
CHESTERFIELD
DRONFIELD
MATLOCK
MANSFIELD
MANSFIELD WOODHOUSE
SUTTON IN ASHFIELD
KIRKBY-IN-ASHFIELD
ALFRETON
BELPER
HUCKNALL
ARNOLD
CARLTON
WEST BRIDGFORD
BEESTON
STAPLEFORD
ILKESTON
HEANOR
EASTWOOD
LONG EATON
NEWARK-ON-TRENT
LOUGHBOROUGH
MELTON MOWBRAY
COALVILLE
Ashby-de-la-Zouch
Oakham
M1
A1
A46
A60
A6

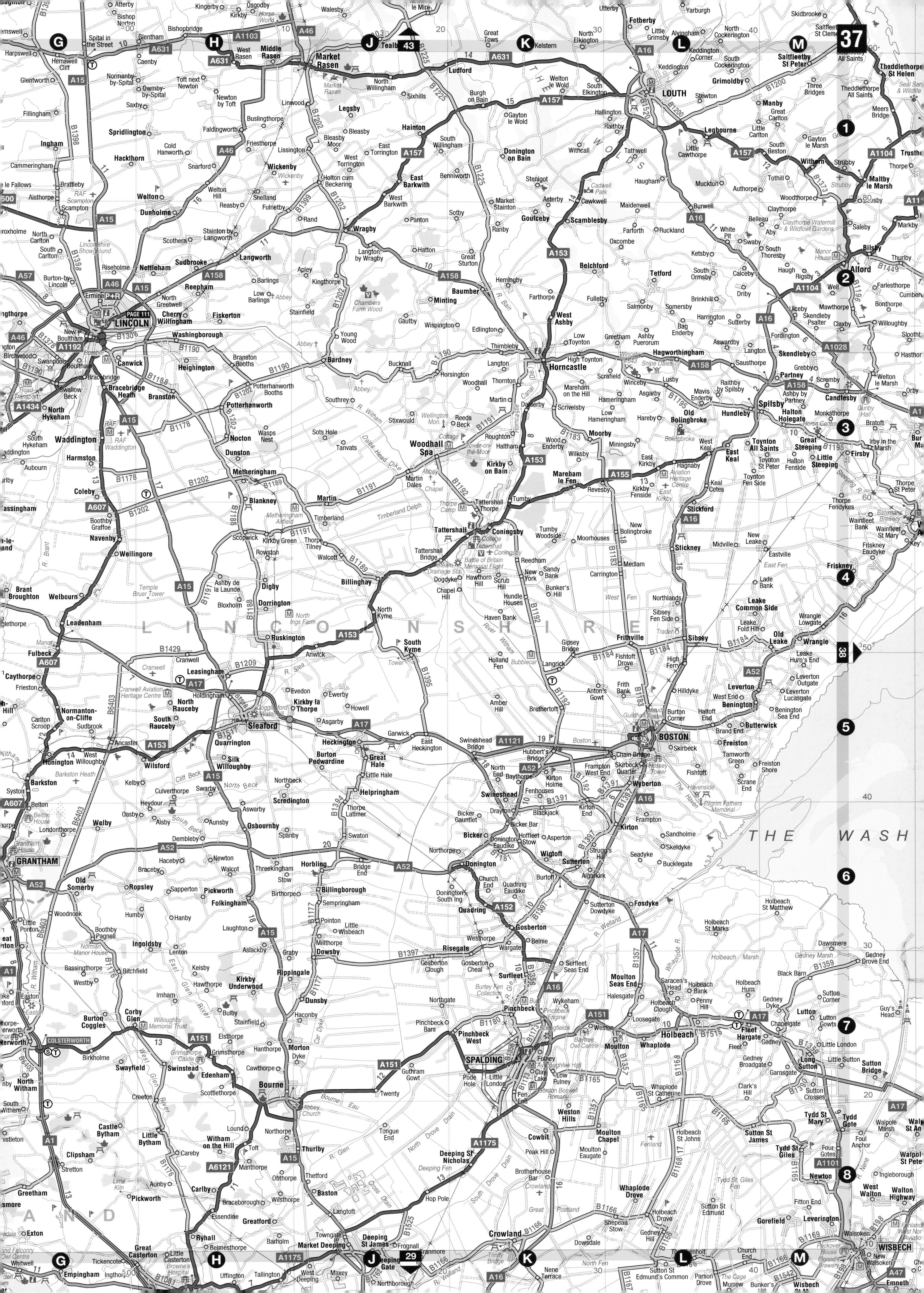

37
38
43
29
PAGE 111
G
H
J
K
L
M
1
2
3
4
5
6
7
8
LINCOLN
LOUTH
Market Rasen
Horncastle
Spilsby
Alford
Woodhall Spa
Coningsby
Tattershall
Sleaford
BOSTON
GRANTHAM
SPALDING
Holbeach
Bourne
Market Deeping
Crowland
WISBECH
Long Sutton
L I N C O L N S H I R E
THE WASH
Skegness
Wainfleet
Friskney
Wrangle
Sibsey
Stickney
Kirton
Donington
Gosberton
Pinchbeck
Sutton Bridge
Colsterworth
Ancaster
Navenby
Waddington
Bracebridge Heath
North Hykeham
Welton
Wragby
Ludford
Legbourne
Saltfleetby St Peter
Burgh on Bain
Tetford
Heckington
Billinghay
Ruskington
Folkingham
Billingborough
Morton
Deeping St Nicholas
Fleet Hargate
Whaplode
Moulton
Cowbit
A15
A16
A17
A46
A52
A57
A151
A153
A155
A157
A158
A607
A631
A1
A1104
A1121
A1175

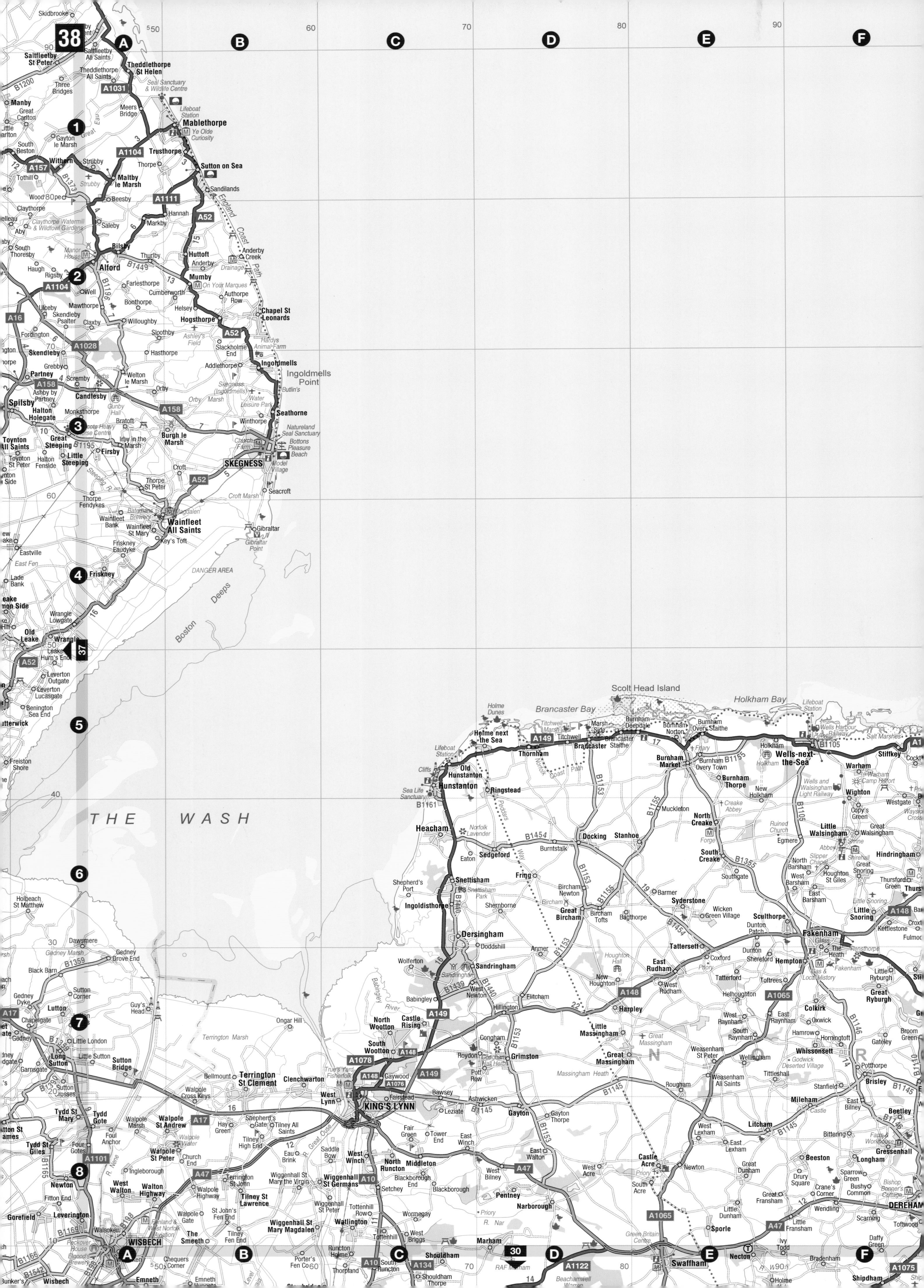
A
B
C
D
E
F
50
60
70
80
90
Skidbrooke
Saltfleetby St Peter
Saltfleetby All Saints
Theddlethorpe St Helen
Theddlethorpe All Saints
Three Bridges
A1031
Seal Sanctuary & Wildlife Centre
Manby
Great Carlton
Meers Bridge
Lifeboat Station
Mablethorpe
Ye Olde Curiosity
Gayton le Marsh
South Reston
A1104
Trusthorpe
A157
Withern
Strubby
Thorpe
Sutton on Sea
Tothill
Maltby le Marsh
Sandilands
Beesby
A1111
Claythorpe
Claythorpe Watermill & Wildfowl Gardens
Hannah
A52
Aby
Saleby
Markby
South Thoresby
Manor House
Bilsby
Thurlby
Huttoft
Anderby
Anderby Creek
Alford
B1449
Haugh
Rigsby
Farlesthorpe
Mumby
On Your Marques
A1104
Well
Bonthorpe
Cumberworth
Authorpe Row
Mawthorpe
Ulceby
Skendleby Psalter
Claxby
Helsey
Chapel St Leonards
Hogsthorpe
A16
Willoughby
Sloothby
Fordington
Ashley's Field
A52
Slackholme End
Hardys Animal Farm
A1028
Skendleby
Hasthorpe
Grebby
Ingoldmells
Addlethorpe
Ingoldmells Point
Partney
Scremby
Welton le Marsh
Candlesby
Orby
Butlin's
A158
Ashby by Partney
Gunby Hall
Skegness (Ingoldmells)
Orby Marsh
Spilsby
Water Leisure Park
Halton Holegate
Monksthorpe
A158
Seathorne
Bratoft
Winthorpe
Toynton All Saints
Great Steeping
Irby in the Marsh
Burgh le Marsh
Natureland Seal Sanctuary
Church Farm
Bottons Pleasure Beach
Little Steeping
Firsby
Toynton St Peter
Halton Fenside
SKEGNESS
Model Village
Croft
Thorpe St Peter
A52
Seacroft
Thorpe Fendykes
Croft Marsh
Wainfleet Bank
Batemans Brewery
Magdalen
Wainfleet All Saints
Wainfleet St Mary
Gibraltar
Friskney Eaudyke
Key's Toft
Gibraltar Point
Eastville
East Fen
DANGER AREA
Friskney
Lade Bank
Boston
Deeps
Wrangle Lowgate
Old Leake
Wrangle
37
A52
Leake Hurn's End
Leverton Outgate
Leverton Lucasgate
Benington Sea End
Freiston Shore
THE WASH
Holbeach St Matthew
Dawsmere
Gedney Marsh
Gedney Drove End
Black Barn
B1359
Sutton Corner
Gedney Dyke
Lutton
Guy's Head
A17
Chapelgate
Little London
Long Sutton
Little Sutton
Sutton Bridge
Ongar Hill
Terrington Marsh
Garnsgate
Bellmount
Terrington St Clement
Clenchwarton
Sutton Crosses
Walpole Cross Keys
Tydd St Mary
Tydd Gote
Walpole Marsh
Walpole St Andrew
A17
Hay Green
Shepherd's Gate
Tilney All Saints
Tydd St Giles
Four Gotes
Foul Anchor
Walpole Water
Tilney High End
A1101
Walpole St Peter
Church End
Ingleborough
A47
Terrington St John
Newton
West Walton
Walton Highway
Walpole Highway
Tilney St Lawrence
Fitton End
Gorefield
Leverington
Walpole Gate
St John's Fen End
Walsoken
Fenland & West Norfolk Aviation
The Smeeth
Tilney Fen End
WISBECH
Peckover House
Elgood's Brewery
Chequers Corner
Emneth
Wisbech
A
B
Scolt Head Island
Brancaster Bay
Holkham Bay
Holme Dunes
Titchwell Marsh
Lifeboat Station
Holme next the Sea
A149
Titchwell
Brancaster
Brancaster Staithe
Burnham Deepdale
Burnham Norton
Burnham Overy Staithe
Wells Harbour Railway
Salt Marshes
Lifeboat Station
Thornham
Friary
Burnham Market
Burnham Overy Town
B1155
Holkham
Wells-next-the-Sea
B1105
Stiffkey
Cliffs
Old Hunstanton
Norfolk Coast Path
Hunstanton
Ringstead
Burnham Thorpe
New Holkham
Wells and Walsingham Light Railway
Warham
Warham Camp Hillfort
Sea Life Sanctuary
B1161
B1153
B1155
Muckleton
Wighton
Creake Abbey
North Creake
Copy's Green
Westgate
Heacham
Norfolk Lavender
B1454
Docking
Stanhoe
Forge
Ruined Church
Egmere
Little Walsingham
Great Walsingham
Abbey
Eaton
Sedgeford
Burntstalk
South Creake
Hindringham
Fring
B1355
North Barsham
Slipper Chapel
Shirehall
Great Snoring
Snettisham
Snettisham Park
Bircham Newton
Southgate
West Barsham
Houghton St Giles
Thursford Green
Shepherd's Port
Barmer
East Barsham
Ingoldisthorpe
Shernborne
Birchams
Great Bircham
Bircham Tofts
Syderstone
Wicken Green Village
Little Snoring
Bagthorpe
Sculthorpe
Little Snoring
A148
Dunton Patch
Dersingham
Fakenham
Kettlestone
Doddshill
Anmer
Tattersett
Dunton
Pensthorpe
Wolferton
Sandringham
Houghton Hall
Coxford
Shereford
Hempton
East Rudham
Fakenham
Little Ryburgh
Babingley River
Priory
New Houghton
West Rudham
Tatterford
Gas & Local History
Toftrees
Great Ryburgh
Babingley
West Newton
Flitcham
A148
Helhoughton
A1065
A149
Hillington
Harpley
Colkirk
Oxwick
North Wootton
Castle Rising
East Raynham
West Raynham
Little Massingham
Great Massingham
South Raynham
Horningtoft
South Wootton
Congham
Grimston
Hamrow
Whissonsett
A1078
A148
Roydon
Weasenham St Peter
Wellingham
Godwick Deserted Village
Great Massingham
Pott Row
Massingham Heath
Tittleshall
True's Yard Fisherfolk
A149
Gaywood
Weasenham All Saints
Stanfield
Brisley
West Lynn
Fairstead
Bawsey
Ashwicken
Rougham
KING'S LYNN
Leziate
Mileham
B1145
Gayton
Gayton Thorpe
Castle
East Bilney
Beetley
Fair Green
Tower End
East Winch
Litcham
West Winch
West Lexham
East Lexham
Bittering
Saddle Bow
Gressenhall
Eau Brink
East Walton
Castle Acre
Beeston
North Runcton
Middleton
West Acre
Newton
Longham
A47
West Bilney
Great Dunham
Drury Square
Wiggenhall St Mary the Virgin
Wiggenhall St Germans
A10
Blackborough End
Setchey
Blackborough
Pentney
Priory
South Acre
Great Fransham
Crane's Corner
Bushy Common
DEREHAM
Wiggenhall St Peter
Tottenhill Row
Narborough
Little Dunham
Wendling
Watlington
Wormegay
R. Nar
A1065
Little Fransham
Scarning
Wiggenhall St Mary Magdalen
Tottenhill
West Briggs
Marham
Green Britain Centre
Sporle
A47
Ivy Todd
Daffy Green
Runcton Holme
Shouldham
30
Swaffham
Necton
Bradenham
Porter's Fen Co
Thorpland
South Runcton
A134
Shouldham Thorpe
RAF Marham
A1122
Beachamwell
Holme
Shipdham
A1075
C
D
E
F

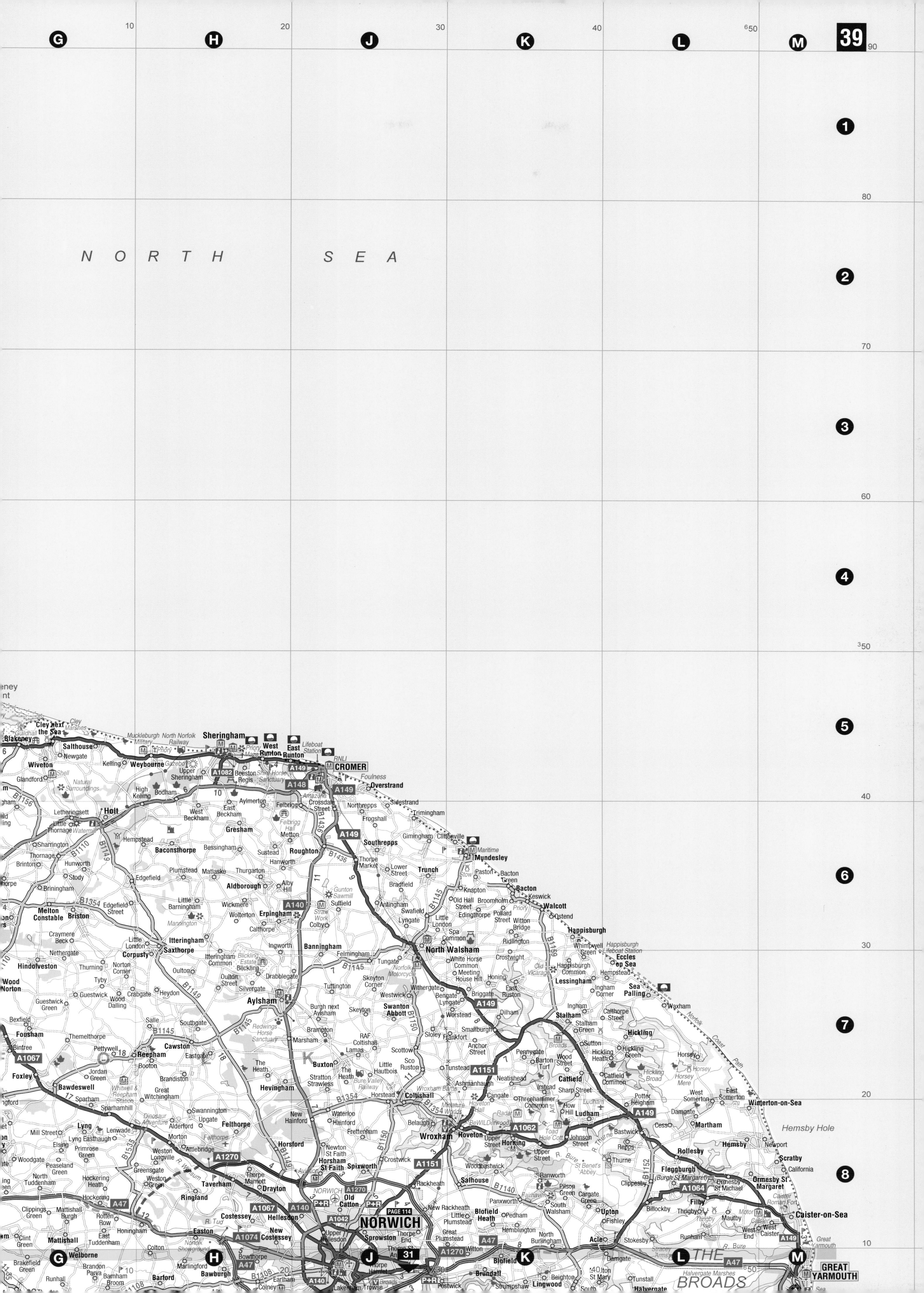
G
H
J
K
L
M
1
2
3
4
5
6
7
8
N O R T H S E A
Hemsby Hole
Sheringham
West Runton
East Runton
CROMER
Overstrand
Sidestrand
Trimingham
Mundesley
Bacton
Walcott
Happisburgh
Eccles on Sea
Sea Palling
Waxham
Horsey
Winterton-on-Sea
Hemsby
Scratby
California
Ormesby St Margaret
Caister-on-Sea
GREAT YARMOUTH
Cley next the Sea
Blakeney
Salthouse
Weybourne
Holt
Aylsham
North Walsham
Stalham
Hickling
Catfield
Ludham
Potter Heigham
Martham
Rollesby
Fleggburgh
Filby
Acle
Wroxham
Hoveton
Horning
Coltishall
Horstead
Reepham
Cawston
Foulsham
Foxley
Bawdeswell
Lyng
Taverham
Drayton
Horsford
Hellesdon
Costessey
New Costessey
Easton
Sprowston
Old Catton
NORWICH
PAGE 114
Thorpe End
Blofield
Brundall
Lingwood
Upton
South Walsham
Ranworth
Salhouse
Rackheath
Spixworth
Horsham St Faith
Hevingham
Buxton
Marsham
Banningham
Erpingham
Itteringham
Saxthorpe
Corpusty
Melton Constable
Briston
Hindolveston
Wood Norton
Guestwick
Mattishall
Welborne
Hockering
Ringland
Barford
Bawburgh
Marlingford
Roughton
Southrepps
Trunch
Knapton
Swanton Abbott
Worstead
Smallburgh
Dilham
Ingham
Lessingham
Gresham
Baconsthorpe
Aldborough
Suffield
Antingham
THE BROADS
A149
A148
A1082
A140
A1067
A1270
A47
A1151
A1062
A1064
A1042
A1074
B1145
B1149
B1354
B1150
B1159
B1152
B1436
B1110
B1156
B1140
B1108
B1535
10
20
30
40
650
90
80
70
60
350
40
30
20
10

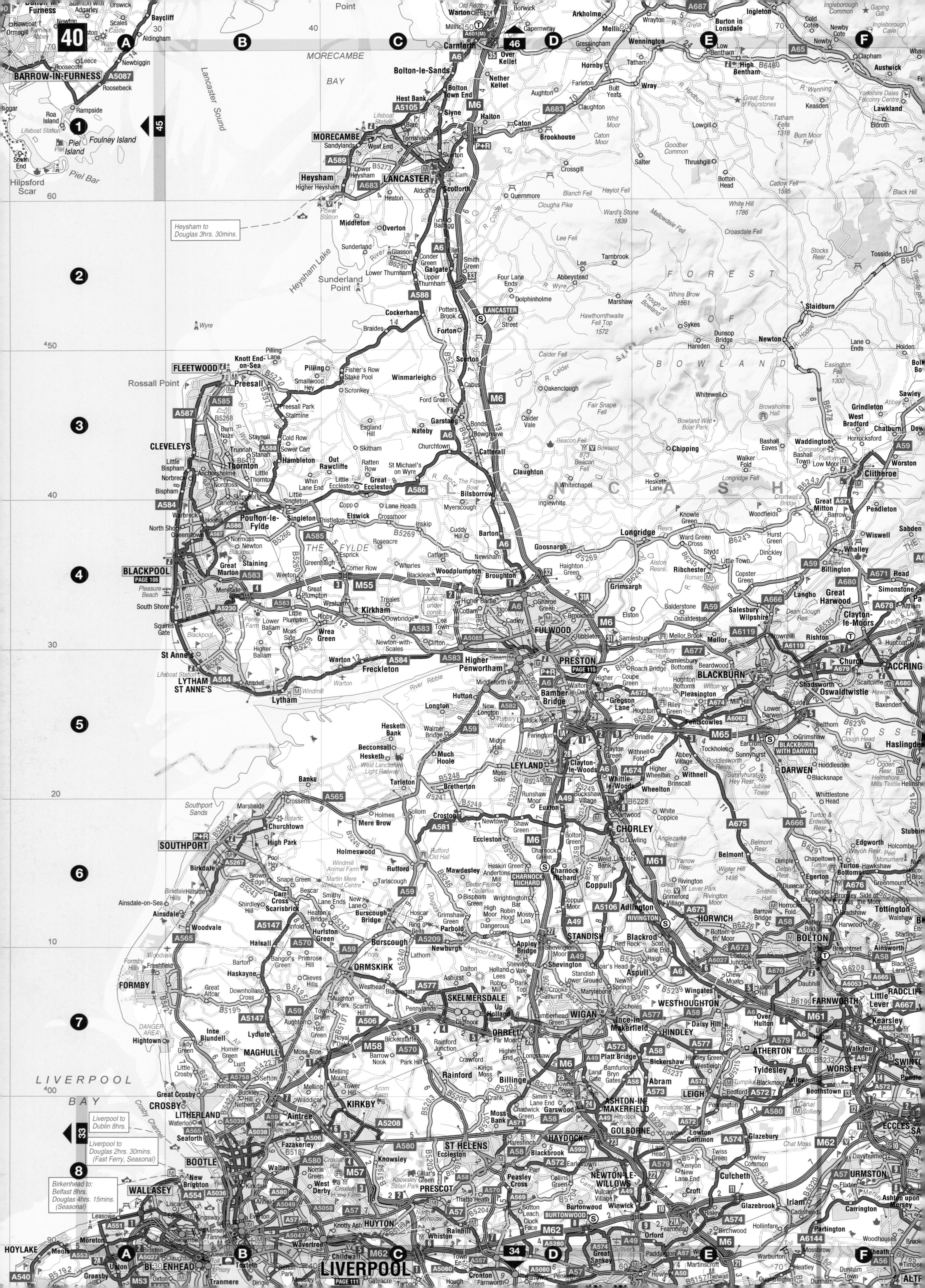
MORECAMBE BAY
BARROW-IN-FURNESS
Lancaster Sound
MORECAMBE
Heysham
LANCASTER
Carnforth
Bolton-le-Sands
Galgate
FOREST OF BOWLAND
FLEETWOOD
Rossall Point
Preesall
CLEVELEYS
Thornton
Poulton-le-Fylde
BLACKPOOL
PAGE 106
THE FYLDE
Kirkham
St Anne's
LYTHAM ST ANNE'S
Lytham
Freckleton
PRESTON
PAGE 115
FULWOOD
Longridge
Ribchester
Clitheroe
Whalley
BLACKBURN
DARWEN
LEYLAND
CHORLEY
SOUTHPORT
Formby
ORMSKIRK
SKELMERSDALE
WIGAN
BOLTON
MAGHULL
KIRKBY
CROSBY
LITHERLAND
BOOTLE
WALLASEY
BIRKENHEAD
LIVERPOOL
PAGE 111
ST HELENS
HUYTON
PRESCOT
NEWTON-LE-WILLOWS
LEIGH
ATHERTON
ASHTON-IN-MAKERFIELD
ECCLES
URMSTON
LIVERPOOL BAY
Heysham to Douglas 3hrs. 30mins.
Liverpool to Dublin 8hrs.
Liverpool to Douglas 2hrs. 30mins. (Fast Ferry, Seasonal)
Birkenhead to: Belfast 8hrs. Douglas 4hrs. 15mins. (Seasonal)
M6
M55
M65
M61
M58
M57
M62
45
46
33
34

47

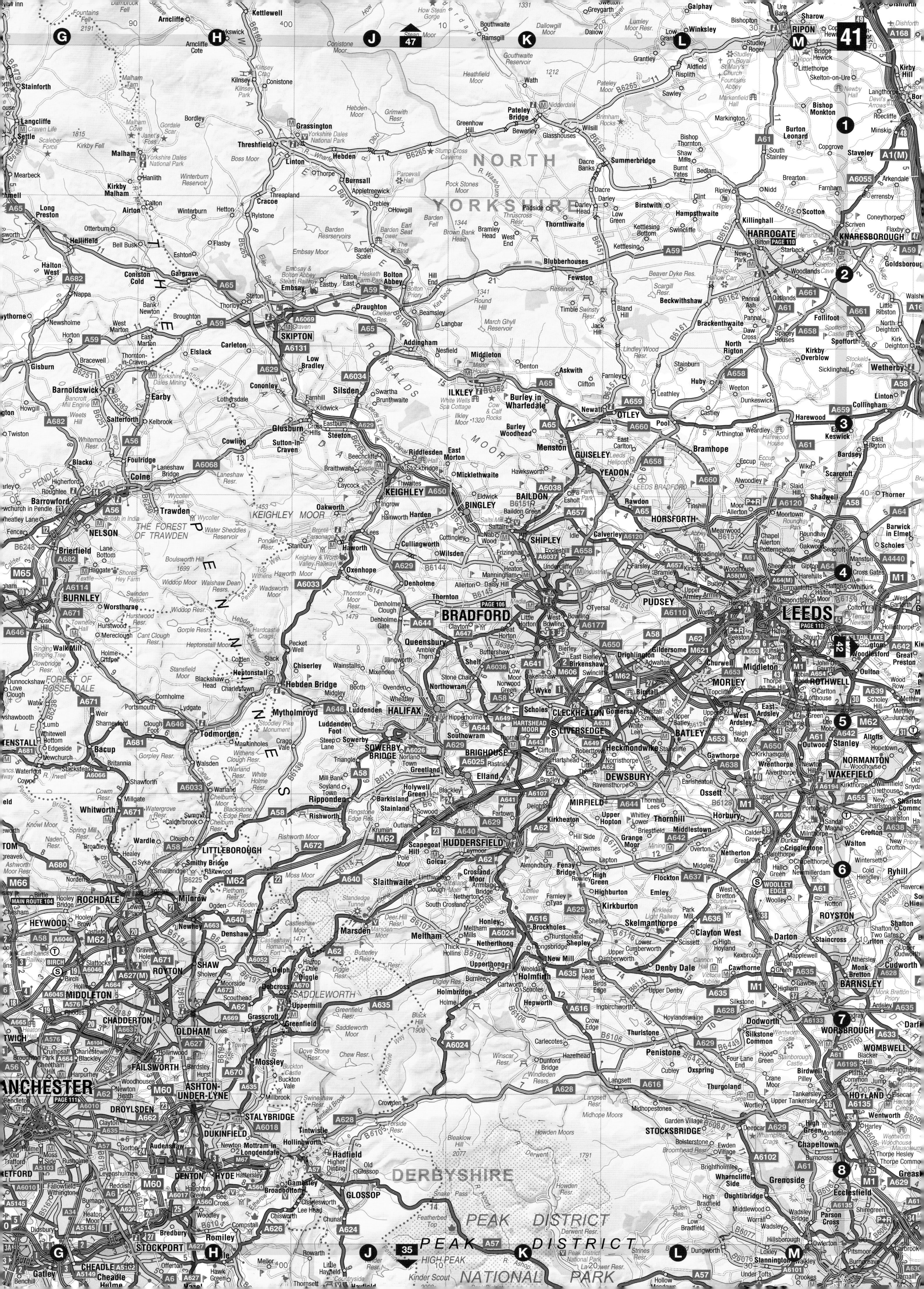
NORTH YORKSHIRE
RIPON
HARROGATE
KNARESBOROUGH
SKIPTON
ILKLEY
OTLEY
KEIGHLEY
BINGLEY
SHIPLEY
BRADFORD
LEEDS
HALIFAX
HUDDERSFIELD
DEWSBURY
WAKEFIELD
BARNSLEY
OLDHAM
ROCHDALE
BURNLEY
NELSON
MANCHESTER
STOCKPORT
GLOSSOP
DERBYSHIRE
PEAK DISTRICT
PEAK DISTRICT NATIONAL PARK
THE PENNINES
THE FOREST OF TRAWDEN
FOREST OF ROSSENDALE
SADDLEWORTH
KEIGHLEY MOOR
ROMBALDS MOOR
YORKSHIRE DALES
PUDSEY
MORLEY
BATLEY
ROTHWELL
NORMANTON
ROYSTON
PENISTONE
STOCKSBRIDGE
HOYLAND
WOMBWELL
WORSBOROUGH
CLECKHEATON
LIVERSEDGE
BRIGHOUSE
ELLAND
SOWERBY BRIDGE
TODMORDEN
LITTLEBOROUGH
MIDDLETON
CHADDERTON
ROYTON
SHAW
HEYWOOD
FAILSWORTH
ASHTON-UNDER-LYNE
STALYBRIDGE
DUKINFIELD
DROYLSDEN
DENTON
HYDE
CHEADLE
HIGH PEAK
M62
M1
M60
M65
M66
M606
M621
A1(M)

35

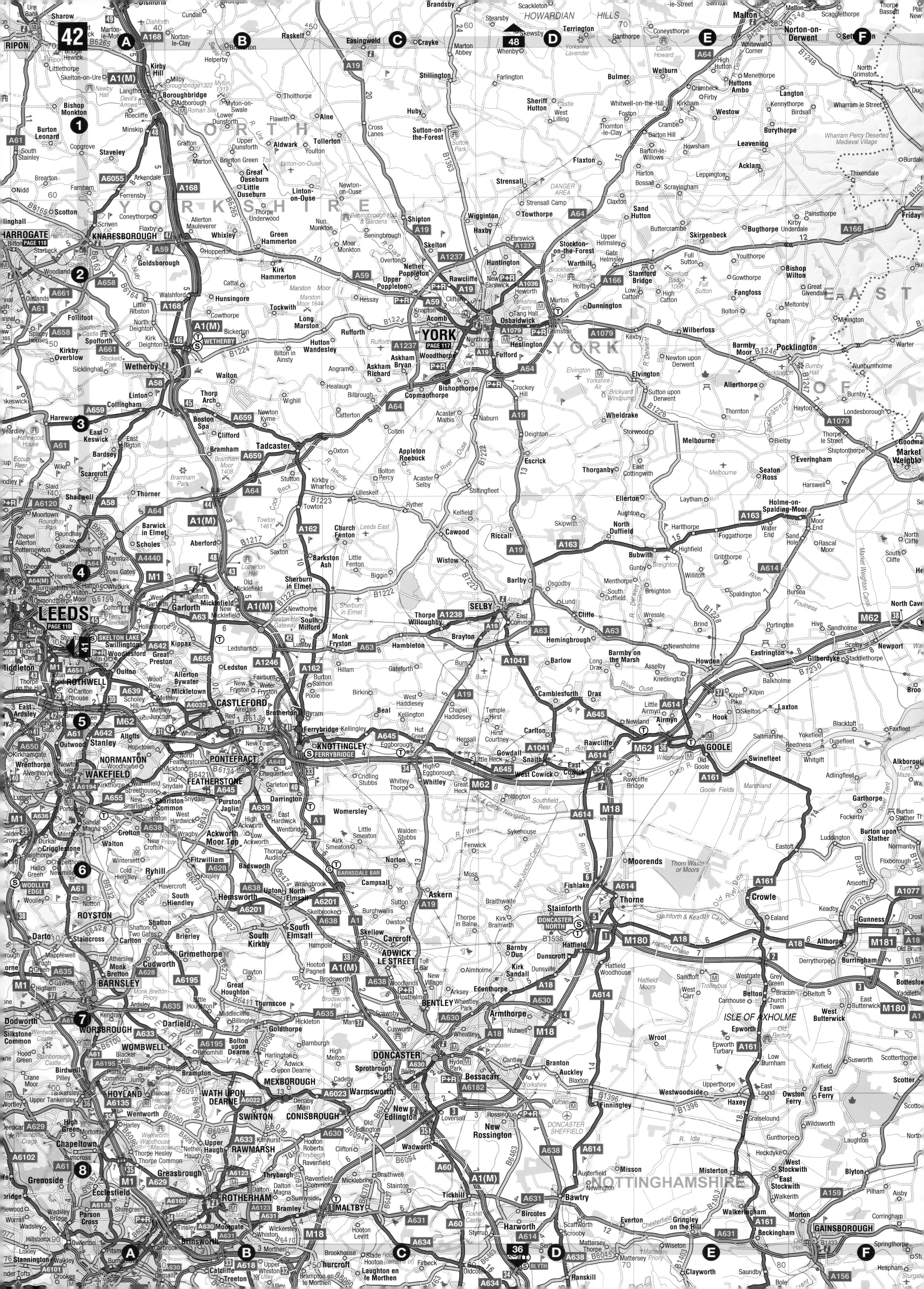

48
RIPON
Easingwold
Malton
Norton-on-Derwent
Terrington
HOWARDIAN HILLS
NORTH YORKSHIRE
HARROGATE
KNARESBOROUGH
Boroughbridge
Wetherby
WETHERBY
YORK
PAGE 117
Strensall
Haxby
Stamford Bridge
Pocklington
EAST YORK
Tadcaster
Selby
SELBY
Howden
Goole
GOOLE
LEEDS
PAGE 110
CASTLEFORD
PONTEFRACT
KNOTTINGLEY
FERRYBRIDGE
WAKEFIELD
NORMANTON
FEATHERSTONE
SKELTON LAKE
41
ROTHWELL
BARNSLEY
ROYSTON
WOOLLEY EDGE
DONCASTER
ADWICK LE STREET
BENTLEY
MEXBOROUGH
CONISBROUGH
WATH UPON DEARNE
SWINTON
ROTHERHAM
RAWMARSH
MALTBY
WOMBWELL
HOYLAND
WORSBROUGH
Thorne
Crowle
ISLE OF AXHOLME
Epworth
Haxey
Bawtry
Tickhill
Harworth
BLYTH
36
NOTTINGHAMSHIRE
GAINSBOROUGH
DONCASTER SHEFFIELD
DONCASTER NORTH
BARNSDALE BAR
A1(M)
M1
M62
M18
M180
M181
A1
A19
A64
A63
A614
A161
A18
A630
A631
A638
1
2
3
4
5
6
7
8
A
B
C
D
E
F

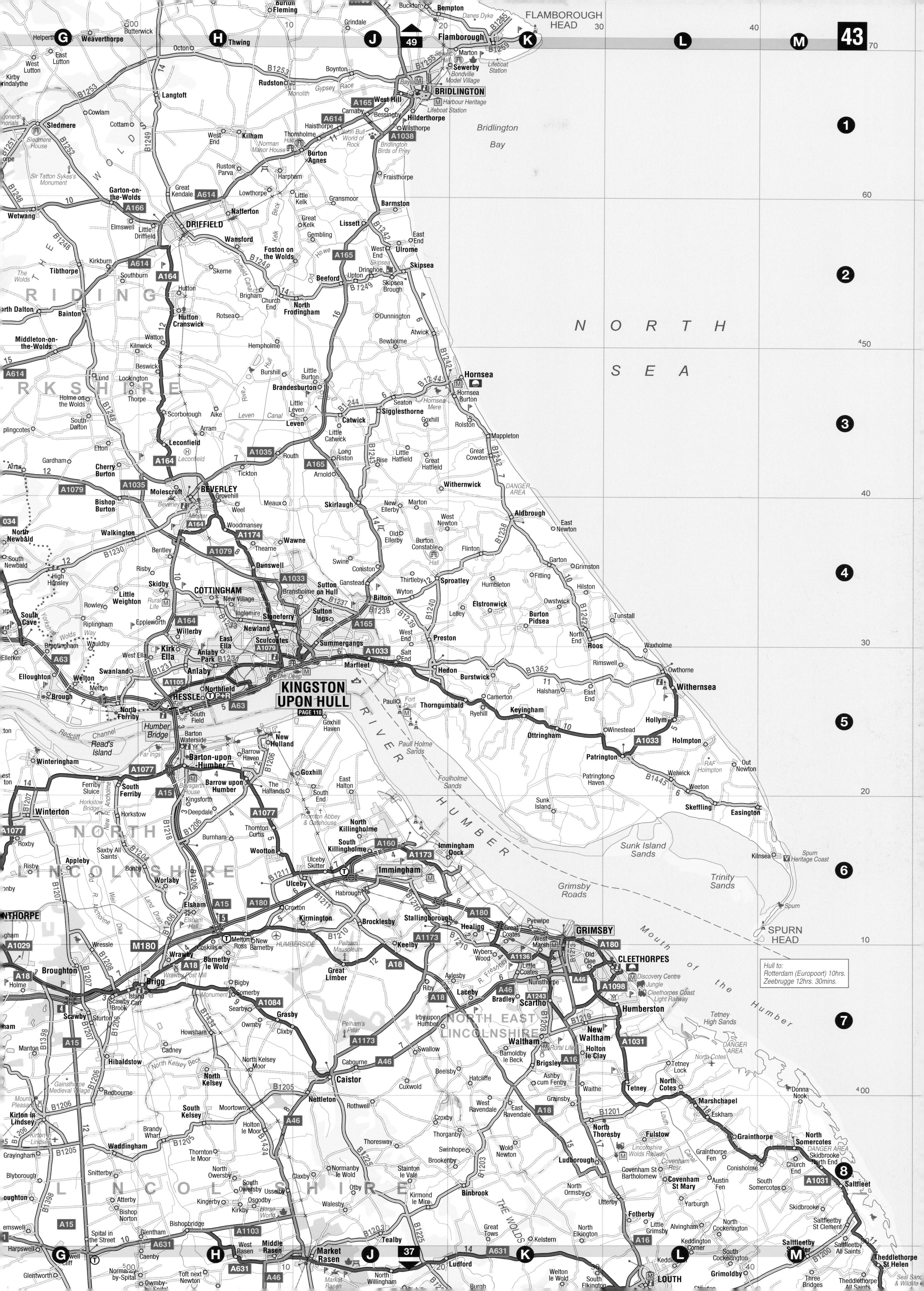
FLAMBOROUGH HEAD
Flamborough
Bempton
Buckton
Danes Dyke
Bridlington Bay
BRIDLINGTON
Sewerby
Marton
Lifeboat Station
Harbour Heritage
Hilderthorpe
Wilsthorpe
Fraisthorpe
Burton Agnes
Kilham
Rudston
Boynton
Grindale
Thwing
Octon
Weaverthorpe
Helperthorpe
Sledmere
Langtoft
Cowlam
Cottam
Garton-on-the-Wolds
DRIFFIELD
Nafferton
Wansford
Lowthorpe
Harpham
Great Kendale
Little Driffield
Elmswell
Wetwang
Tibthorpe
Kirkburn
Southburn
Skerne
Foston on the Wolds
Beeford
Lissett
Barmston
Ulrome
Skipsea
Brigham
North Frodingham
Hutton Cranswick
Rotsea
Bainton
Middleton-on-the-Wolds
Watton
Kilnwick
Beswick
Lockington
Dunnington
Atwick
Bewholme
Hornsea
Hornsea Mere
Hornsea Burton
Seaton
Sigglesthorne
Brandesburton
Burshill
Hempholme
Leven
Catwick
Goxhill
Rolston
Mappleton
Great Cowden
Leconfield
Arram
Scorborough
Cherry Burton
Etton
South Dalton
Holme on the Wolds
BEVERLEY
Molescroft
Tickton
Routh
Long Riston
Rise
Little Hatfield
Great Hatfield
Withernwick
Skirlaugh
Meaux
Weel
Woodmansey
Wawne
Bishop Burton
Walkington
North Newbald
South Newbald
Bentley
Risby
Skidby
Thearne
Dunswell
COTTINGHAM
Little Weighton
Rowley
Riplingham
Sutton on Hull
Ganstead
Swine
Coniston
Bilton
Wyton
Thirtleby
Sprotley
Humbleton
Flinton
Aldbrough
East Newton
Garton
Grimston
Fitling
Hilston
Elstronwick
Owstwick
Burton Pidsea
Tunstall
Roos
North End
Lelley
Preston
Hedon
Burstwick
Rimswell
Waxholme
Owthorne
Withernsea
Halsham
Camerton
Ryehill
Thorngumbald
Paull
Keyingham
Ottringham
Winestead
Hollym
Holmpton
Patrington
Patrington Haven
Welwick
Weeton
Out Newton
Skeffling
Easington
Kilnsea
Spurn Heritage Coast
SPURN HEAD
Sunk Island
Sunk Island Sands
Trinity Sands
Grimsby Roads
Mouth of the Humber
KINGSTON UPON HULL
PAGE 110
Marfleet
Summergangs
Sculcoates
Newland
Stoneferry
Sutton Ings
Anlaby
Anlaby Park
Kirk Ella
West Ella
East Ella
Willerby
Swanland
HESSLE
North Ferriby
Welton
Melton
Elloughton
Brough
South Cave
Humber Bridge
Barton Waterside
Barton-upon-Humber
Barrow upon Humber
Barrow Haven
New Holland
Goxhill
Goxhill Haven
The Hallands
South End
East Halton
North Killingholme
South Killingholme
Immingham
Immingham Dock
Thornton Curtis
Wootton
Ulceby
Ulceby Skitter
Croxton
Kirmington
Brocklesby
Habrough
Stallingborough
Healing
Great Coates
Pywipe
GRIMSBY
CLEETHORPES
Old Clee
Humberston
Scartho
Bradley
Laceby
Waltham
New Waltham
Holton le Clay
Tetney
North Cotes
Marshchapel
Grainthorpe
Donna Nook
North Somercotes
Saltfleet
Reads Island
Winteringham
Ferriby Sluice
South Ferriby
Horkstow
Winterton
Roxby
Appleby
Saxby All Saints
Bonby
Worlaby
Elsham
Wrawby
Brigg
Barnetby le Wold
Melton Ross
New Barnetby
Keelby
Great Limber
Broughton
Scawby
Bigby
Searby
Owmby
Grasby
Clixby
Caistor
Cabourne
Swallow
Irby upon Humber
Barnoldby le Beck
Brigsley
Ashby cum Fenby
Waithe
North Thoresby
Fulstow
Ludborough
Covenham St Mary
Covenham St Bartholomew
Utterby
Fotherby
Little Grimsby
North Elkington
Kelstern
Binbrook
Thoresway
Rothwell
Nettleton
Hibaldstow
North Kelsey
South Kelsey
Kirton in Lindsey
Waddingham
Snitterby
Atterby
Bishop Norton
Glentham
Bishopbridge
Spital in the Street
Harpswell
Middle Rasen
West Rasen
Market Rasen
Tealby
Ludford
Walesby
Osgodby
Kingerby
Normanby le Wold
Claxby
Usselby
South Owersby
North Owersby
Thornton le Moor
Holton le Moor
Moortown
LOUTH
Keddington Corner
Grimoldby
Alvingham
North Cockerington
South Cockerington
Saltfleetby St Clement
Saltfleetby All Saints
Theddlethorpe St Helen
NORTH SEA
RIVER HUMBER
NORTH EAST LINCOLNSHIRE
NORTH LINCOLNSHIRE
LINCOLNSHIRE
EAST RIDING OF YORKSHIRE
THE WOLDS
HUMBERSIDE
Hull to: Rotterdam (Europoort) 10hrs. Zeebrugge 12hrs. 30mins.
A165
A614
A1038
A166
A164
A1035
A1079
A1174
A1033
A63
A1105
A15
A1077
A160
A1173
A180
A18
M180
A1084
A46
A16
A1031
A1136
A1098
A1243
A631
A1103
B1253
B1249
B1242
B1244
B1238
B1362
B1445
B1230
B1206
B1211
B1210
B1201
B1225
B1205
B1434
49
37

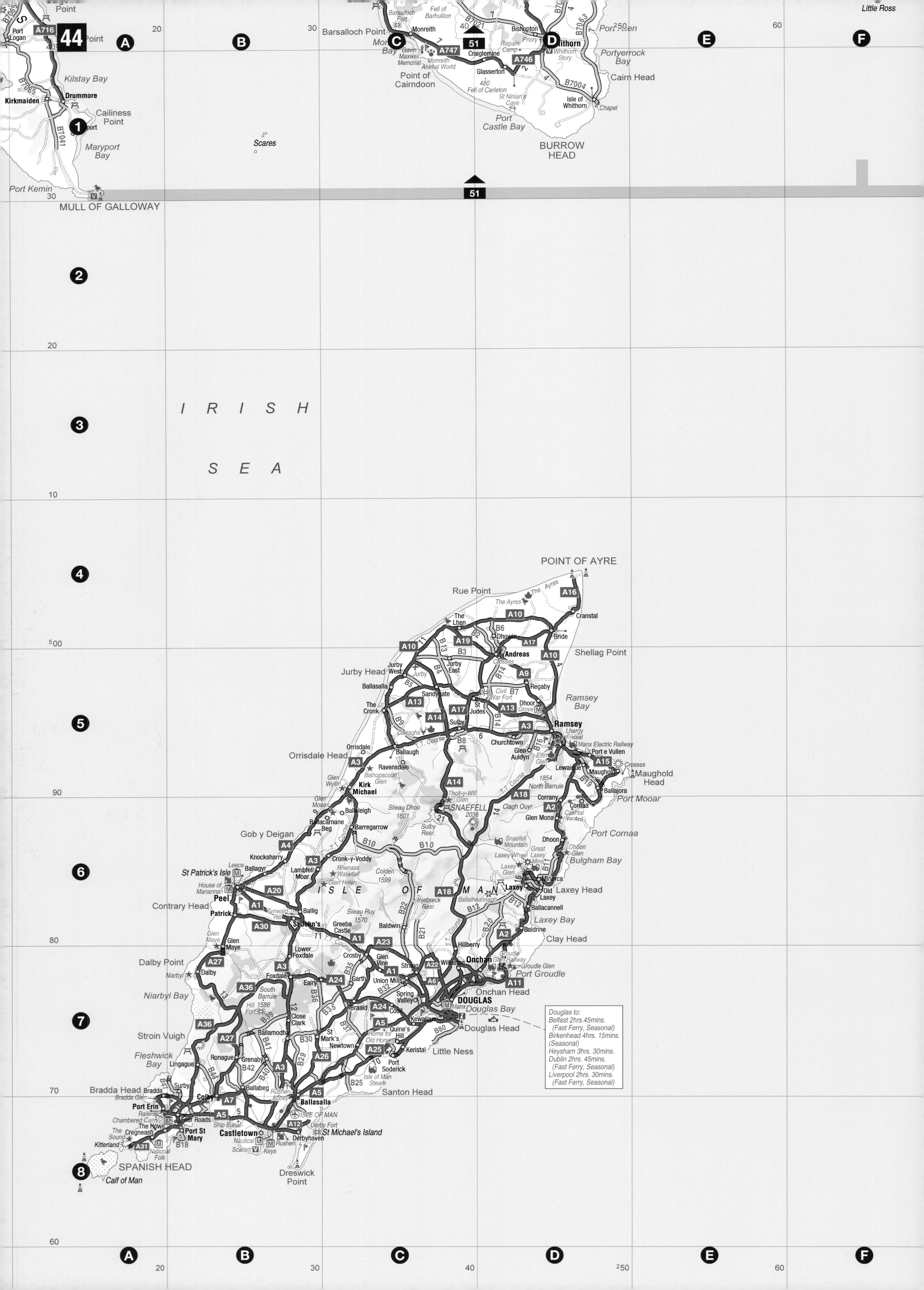

44
A
B
C
D
E
F
1
2
3
4
5
6
7
8
20
30
40
250
60
10
500
90
80
70
Little Ross
Point
Port Logan
A716
Kilstay Bay
Drummore
Kirkmaiden
Cailiness Point
B7041
B7065
Maryport Bay
Port Kemin
MULL OF GALLOWAY
Scares
Barsalloch Point
Monreith
Gavin Maxwell Memorial
Monreith Animal World
Fell of Barhullion
A747
Craiglemine
Point of Cairndoon
B7021
51
Bishopton
Priory
Whithorn
Whithorn Story
Rispain Camp
A746
Glasserton
480 Fell of Carleton
St Ninian's Cave
Port Castle Bay
BURROW HEAD
B7063
Port Allen
Portyerrock Bay
Cairn Head
B7004
Isle of Whithorn
Chapel
I R I S H
S E A
POINT OF AYRE
Rue Point
The Ayres
A16
Cranstal
A10
The Lhen
B6
Dhowin
A17
Bride
Andreas
Shellag Point
Jurby Head
Jurby West
Jurby East
Ballasalla
The Cronk
Sandygate
A13
A14
A17
St Judes
Civil War Fort
A9
Regaby
Dhoor
Grove
Ramsey Bay
Ramsey
Sulby
Churchtown
A3
Lhergy Frissel
Manx Electric Railway
Orrisdale
Orrisdale Head
Ballaugh
Glen Auldyn
Port e Vullen
A15
Lewaigue
Maughold
Crosses
Maughold Head
Ravensdale
Bishopscourt Glen
Glen Wyllin
Kirk Michael
A14
Tholt-y-Will Glen
SNAEFELL 2036
North Barrule
1854
A18
Ballajora
Port Mooar
Corrany
A2
Cornaa
Cashtal Yn Ard
Glen Mona
Clagh Ouyr
Slieau Dhoo 1601
Glen Mooar
Ballaleigh
Ballacarnane Beg
Barregarrow
Sulby Resr.
Gob y Deigan
A4
B10
Snaefell Mountain
Dhoon
Port Cornaa
Dhoon Glen
Bulgham Bay
Knocksharry
Ballagyr
A3
Cronk-y-Voddy
Lambfell Moar
Rhenass Waterfall
Glen Helen
Colden 1599
Laxey Wheel
Great Laxey Mine
Laxey Glen
St Patrick's Isle
Leece
House of Manannan
Peel
A20
ISLE OF MAN
A18
Laxey
Minorca
Old Laxey
Laxey Head
Ballacannell
Contrary Head
Patrick
A1
Ballig
Tynwald Hill
Injebreck Resr.
Ballalheannagh
B12
B22
Laxey Bay
A30
St John's
Greeba Castle
Slieau Ruy 1570
Baldwin
B21
B20
A2
Baldrine
Clay Head
Glen Maye
Glen Maye
A1
A23
Hillberry
Dalby Point
A27
Lower Foxdale
Crosby
Glen Vine
Strang
A22
Willaston
Onchan
Groudle Glen Railway
Groudle Glen
Port Groudle
Niarbyl
Dalby
A3
Foxdale
Eairy
A24
Garth
Union Mills
A6
A11
Onchan Head
Niarbyl Bay
A36
South Barrule 1586
Hill Fort
B36
Spring Valley
DOUGLAS
Manx
Douglas Bay
Close Clark
B35
Braaid
A24
Cooil
Kewaigue
Douglas Head
Stroin Vuigh
A36
Ballamodha
A5
Quine's Hill
B80
A27
B41
St Mark's
Newtown
Home for Old Horses
Little Ness
Fleshwick Bay
Lingague
Ronague
Grenaby
B30
A25
Keristal
B29
A26
Port Soderick
B42
A3
Isle of Man Steam
B25
Bradda Head
Bradda
Surby
Ballabeg
Rushen Abbey
A5
Santon Head
Bradda Glen
Colby
A7
Ballasalla
Port Erin
Railway
Chambered Cairn
A5
ISLE OF MAN
Four Roads
Ship Burial
The Howe
Cregneash
The Sound
Port St Mary
Castletown
A12
Derby Fort
Derbyhaven
St Michael's Island
Kitterland
A31
National Folk
B18
Nautical
Scarlett
Rushen Keys
SPANISH HEAD
Calf of Man
Dreswick Point
Douglas to:
Belfast 2hrs.45mins. (Fast Ferry, Seasonal)
Birkenhead 4hrs. 15mins. (Seasonal)
Heysham 3hrs. 30mins.
Dublin 2hrs. 45mins. (Fast Ferry, Seasonal)
Liverpool 2hrs. 30mins. (Fast Ferry, Seasonal)

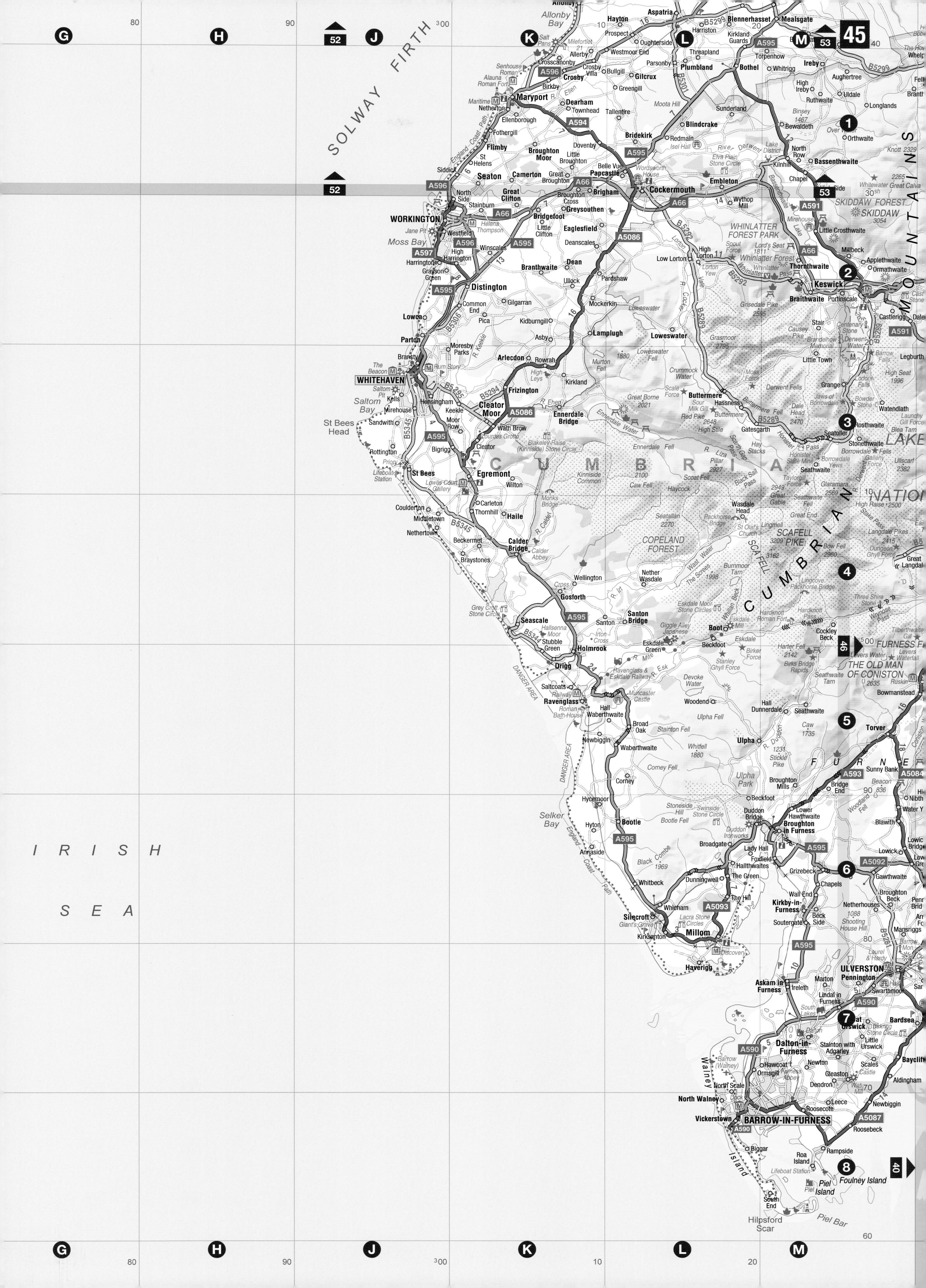
SOLWAY FIRTH
IRISH SEA
CUMBRIA
CUMBRIAN MOUNTAINS
LAKE
NATIO
FURNESS FELLS
FURNE
WORKINGTON
WHITEHAVEN
BARROW-IN-FURNESS
ULVERSTON
Maryport
Cockermouth
Keswick
Aspatria
Allonby Bay
Allonby
Hayton
Prospect
Oughterside
Harriston
Blennerhasset
Mealsgate
Kirkland Guards
Ireby
Torpenhow
Whitrigg
Aughertree
Uldale
Longlands
Westmoor End
Threapland
Plumbland
Bothel
Parsonby
Crosscanonby
Allerby
Crosby
Crosby Villa
Bullgill
Gilcrux
Greengill
Birkby
Senhouse Roman
Alauna Roman Fort
Netherton
Ellenborough
Dearham
Townhead
Tallentire
Moota Hill
Sunderland
Binsey 1467
Bewaldeth
Over Water
Orthwaite
Fothergill
Flimby
Broughton Moor
Dovenby
Little Broughton
Bridekirk
Blindcrake
Redmain
Isel Hall
North Row
Bassenthwaite
Knott 2329
St Helens
Siddick
Seaton
Camerton
Great Broughton
Belle Vue
Papcastle
Wordsworth House
Elva Plain Stone Circle
Kilnhill
Chapel
Whitewater Great Calva
Embleton
Wythop Mill
SKIDDAW FOREST
SKIDDAW 3054
North Side
Stainburn
Great Clifton
Brigham
Broughton Cross
Greysouthen
Bridgefoot
Little Clifton
Eaglesfield
Helena Thompson
Jane Pit
Westfield
Moss Bay
High Harrington
Harrington
Winscales
Deanscales
Whinlatter Forest Park
Lord's Seat 1811
Spout Force
Whinlatter Forest
Whinlatter Pass
High Lorton
Low Lorton
Lorton Yew
Mirehouse
Little Crosthwaite
Millbeck
Applethwaite
Ormathwaite
Thornthwaite
Braithwaite
Portinscale
Grayson Green
Distington
Branthwaite
Dean
Ullock
Pardshaw
Gilgarran
Lowca
Common End
Pica
Mockerkin
Loweswater
Grisedale Pike 2595
Castlerigg
Kidburngill
Asby
Lamplugh
Loweswater
Stair
Causey Pike
Centenary Stone
Derwent Water
Parton
Moresby Parks
Arlecdon
Rowrah
Loweswater Fell
Grasmoor 2795
Brandelhow Memorial
Little Town
Barrow Falls
Legburth
Bransty
The Beacon
Haig Pit
High Leys
Kirkland
Murton Fell
Crummock Water
Scale Force
Moss Force
Derwent Fells
Grange
Lodore Falls
High Seat 1996
Frizington
Buttermere
Hassness
Jaws of Borrowdale
Bowder Stone
Watendlath
Saltom Pit
Kells
Saltom Bay
Mirehouse
Hensingham
Keekle
Cleator Moor
Ennerdale Bridge
Great Borne 2021
Sour Milk Gill
Red Pike 2648
Buttermere Fell
Dale Head 2470
Launchy Gill Force
St Bees Head
Sandwith
Moor Row
Wath Brow
Lourdes Grotto
Blakeley Raise (Kinniside) Stone Circle
Ennerdale Water
High Stile
Gatesgarth
Seatoller
Rosthwaite
Blea Tarn
Rottington
Bigrigg
Cleator
Ennerdale Fell
Liza Pillar 2927
Hay Stacks
Honister Pass
Honister Slate Mine
Stonethwaite
Borrowdale Fells
Ullscarf 2382
Priory
Lifeboat Station
St Bees
Egremont
Kinniside Common
2100
Caw Fell
Scoat Fell
Black Sail Pass
Seathwaite
Taylorgill Force
Glaramara 2569
Lowes Court Gallery
Wilton
Haycock
2949 Great Gable
Seathwaite Fell
High Raise 2500
Carleton
Thornhill
Haile
Monks Bridge
Coulderton
Middletown
Nethertown
Beckermet
Calder Bridge
Calder Abbey
Seatallan 2270
Copeland Forest
Wasdale Head
Packhorse Bridge
St Olaf's Church
Lingmell
Scafell Pike 3209
Sca Fell 3162
Great End
Stake Pass
Langdale Pikes 2415
Dungeon Ghyll Force
Bow Fell 2960
Great Langdal
Braystones
Wellington
Nether Wasdale
Wast Water
The Screes 1998
Burnmoor Tarn
Lingcove Packhorse Bridge
Cross
Gosforth
Whillan Beck
Three Shire Stone
Wrynose Pass
Grey Croft Stone Circle
Seascale
Hallsenna Moor
Stubble Green
Santon
Santon Bridge
Irton Cross
Eskdale Moor Stone Circles
Hardknott Roman Fort
Hardknott Pass
Cockley Beck
Tilberthwaite Gill
Giggle Alley Japanese
Eskdale Green
Boot
Eskdale Mill
Beckfoot
Eskdale
Birker Force
Harter Fell 2142
Birks Bridge Rapids
Lovers Waterfall
THE OLD MAN OF CONISTON 2635
Holmrook
Drigg
Mite
Ravenglass & Eskdale Railway
Esk
Stanley Ghyll Force
Devoke Water
Seathwaite Tarn
Ruskin
Bowmanstead
Danger Area
Saltcoats
Ravenglass
Roman Bath House
Muncaster Castle
Hall Waberthwaite
Woodend
Hall Dunnerdale
Seathwaite
Broad Oak
Stainton Fell
Ulpha Fell
Caw 1735
Torver
Newbiggin
Waberthwaite
Whitfell 1880
Ulpha
Duddon
Stickle Pike 1231
Sunny Bank
Beacon 836
Corney Fell
Corney
Ulpha Park
Broughton Mills
Bridge End
Nibthwaite
Water Yeat
Woodland Fell
Hycemoor
Selker Bay
Hyton
Bootle
Stoneside Hill
Bootle Fell
Swinside Stone Circle
Beckfoot
Duddon Bridge
Lower Hawthwaite
Broughton in Furness
Duddon Ironworks
Blawith
Broadgate
Lady Hall
Foxfield
Hallthwaites
Annaside
Black Combe 1969
Lowick
Lowick Bridge
Grizebeck
Gawthwaite
Whitbeck
Dunningwell
The Green
Chapels
Wall End
Broughton Beck
The Hill
Kirkby-in-Furness
Netherhouses
Whicham
Beck Side
Silecroft
Giant's Grave
Kirksanton
Lacra Stone Circles
Millom
Soutergate
1088 Shooting House Hill
Mansriggs
Laurel & Hardy
Discovery
Haverigg
Askam in Furness
Ireleth
Marton
Lindal in Furness
Pennington
Swarthmoor
South Lakes
Great Urswick
Birkrigg Stone Circle
Bardsea
Little Urswick
Dalton-in-Furness
Stainton with Adgarley
Walney
Barrow (Walney)
Hawcoat
Ormsgill
Furness Abbey
Newton
Scales
Baycliff
Gleaston Castle
Aldingham
Dendron
North Scale
North Walney
Leece
Roosecote
Newbiggin
Vickerstown
Roosebeck
Biggar
Rampside
Walney Island
Roa Island
Lifeboat Station
Piel Island
Foulney Island
South End
Hilpsford Scar
Piel Bar
A595
A596
A594
A66
A5086
A597
A591
A593
A5084
A5092
A5093
A590
A5087
B5299
B5301
B5292
B5289
B5306
B5295
B5294
B5345
B5344
52
53
46
40

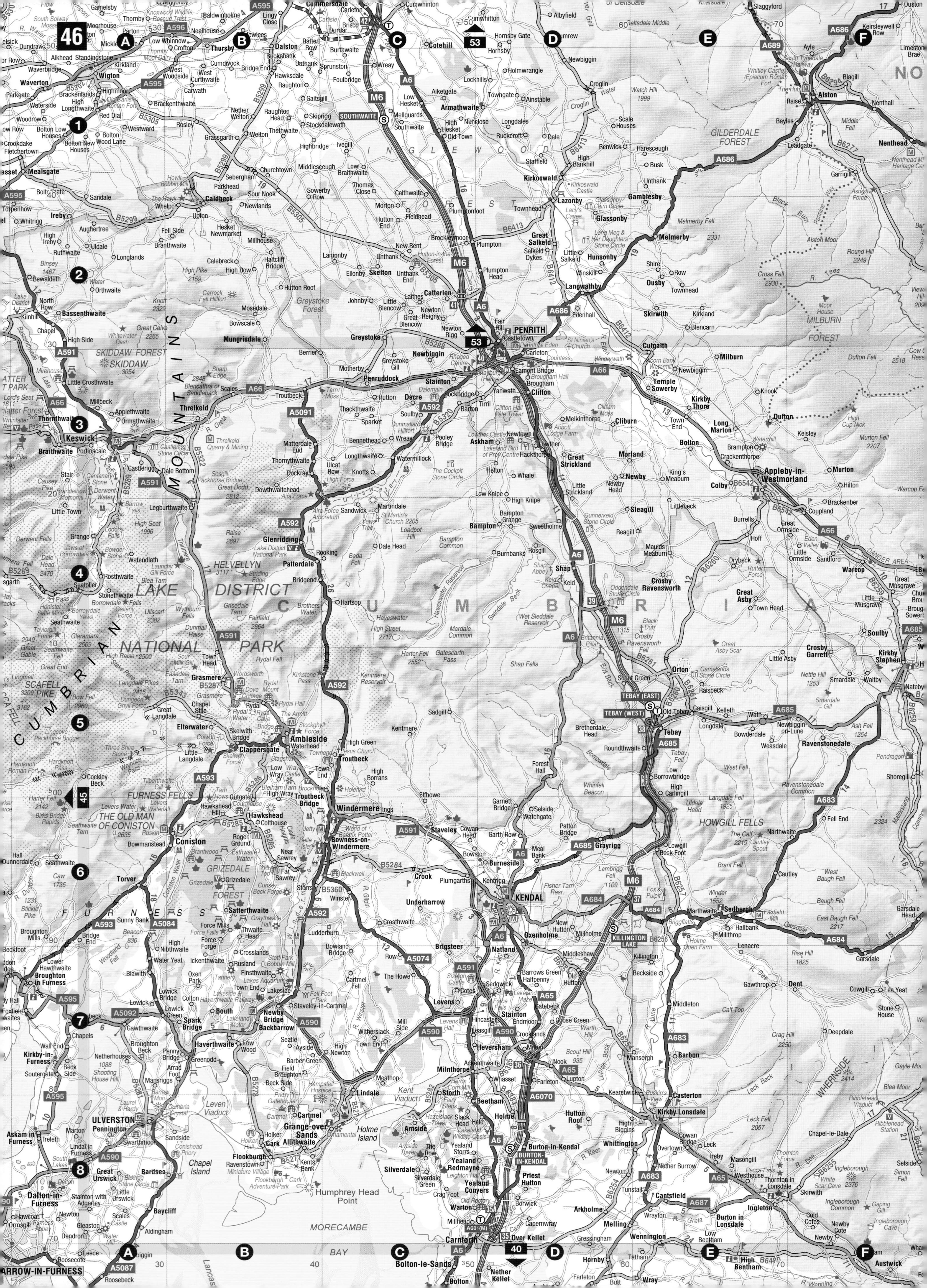
46
A
B
C
D
E
F
1
2
3
4
5
6
7
8
53
45
40
CUMBRIAN MOUNTAINS
LAKE DISTRICT NATIONAL PARK
C U M B R I A
SKIDDAW FOREST
SKIDDAW 3054
HELVELLYN 3117
SCAFELL PIKE 3209
THE OLD MAN OF CONISTON 2635
FURNESS FELLS
GRIZEDALE FOREST
F U R N E S S
HOWGILL FELLS
GILDERDALE FOREST
MILBURN FOREST
INGLEWOOD FOREST
WHERNSIDE 2414
MORECAMBE BAY
Humphrey Head Point
Chapel Island
Holme Island
PENRITH
KENDAL
Keswick
Ambleside
Windermere
Bowness-on-Windermere
Coniston
Hawkshead
Grasmere
Ulverston
Dalton-in-Furness
Grange-over-Sands
Carnforth
Kirkby Lonsdale
Sedbergh
Appleby-in-Westmorland
Kirkby Stephen
Alston
Wigton
Caldbeck
Shap
Tebay
Orton
Milnthorpe
Ingleton
Dent
Kirkoswald
Lazonby
Glenridding
Patterdale
Staveley
BARROW-IN-FURNESS
M6
A6
A66
A591
A592
A590
A595
A683
A684
A685
A686
A65
SOUTHWAITE
TEBAY (EAST)
TEBAY (WEST)
KILLINGTON LAKE
BURTON-IN-KENDAL

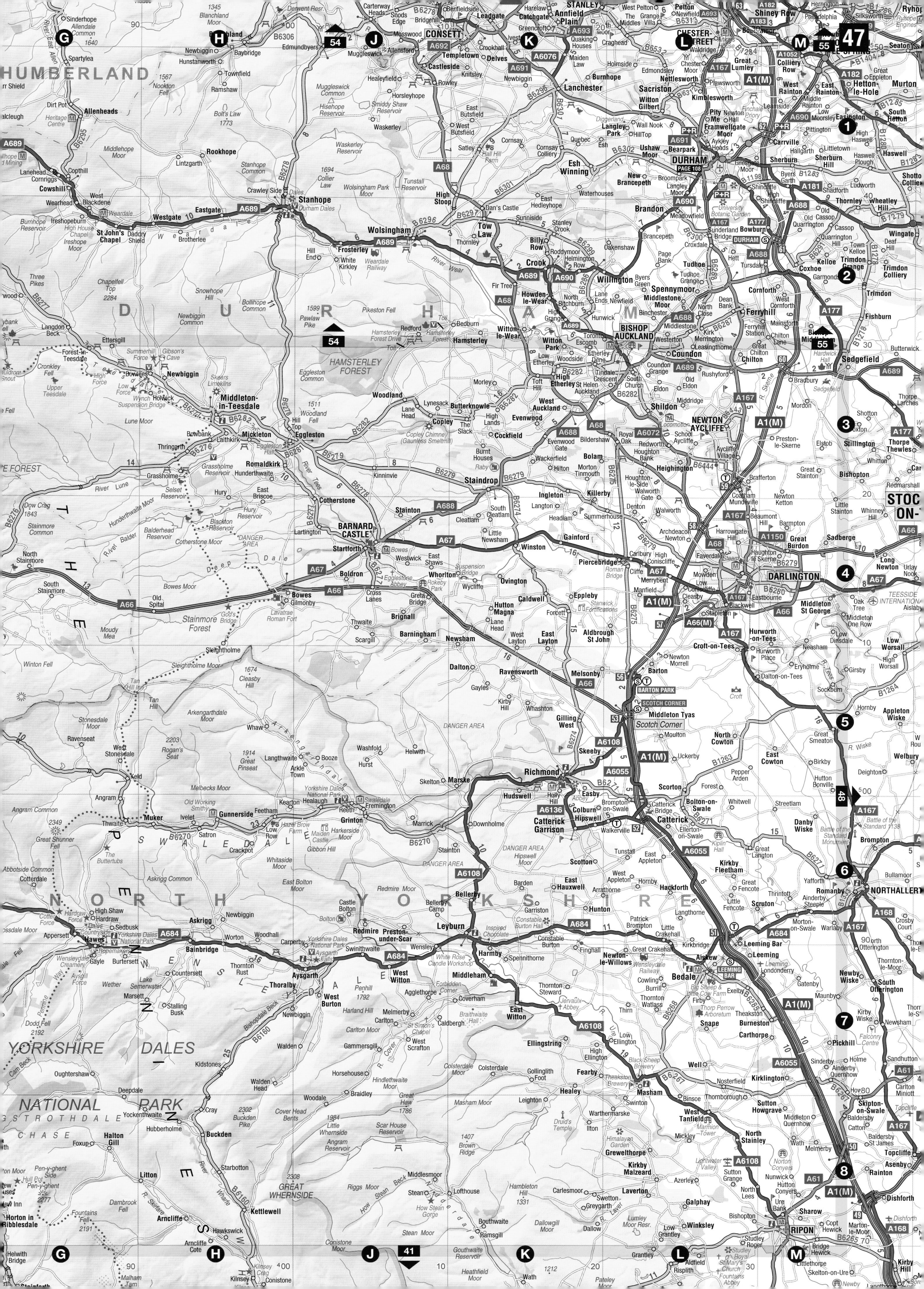

G
H
J
K
L
M
54
55
48
41
HUMBERLAND
D U R H A M
N O R T H   Y O R K S H I R E
YORKSHIRE DALES
NATIONAL PARK
HAMSTERLEY FOREST
CONSETT
STANLEY
CHESTER-LE-STREET
DURHAM
BISHOP AUCKLAND
NEWTON AYCLIFFE
DARLINGTON
BARNARD CASTLE
Middleton-in-Teesdale
Stanhope
Wolsingham
Crook
Spennymoor
Ferryhill
Sedgefield
Shildon
Staindrop
Richmond
Scotch Corner
Catterick Garrison
Catterick
Leyburn
Hawes
Askrigg
Aysgarth
Middleham
Masham
Bedale
Northallerton
Thirsk
RIPON
Kettlewell
Stainmore Forest
Weardale
Swaledale
Wensleydale
A1(M)
A66
A67
A68
A684
A689
A6108
A167

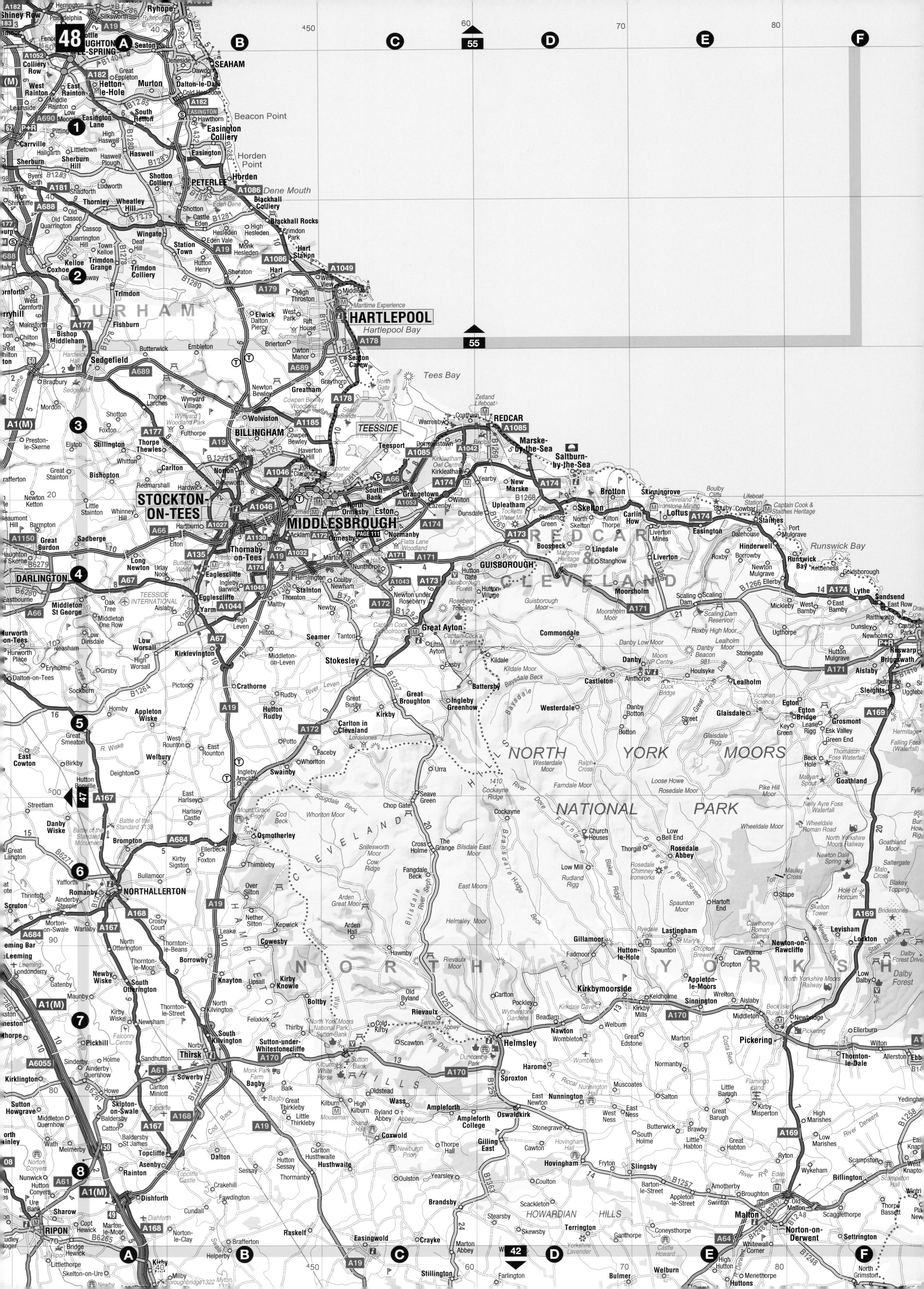

55
HARTLEPOOL
Hartlepool Bay
DURHAM
Tees Bay
TEESSIDE
STOCKTON-ON-TEES
MIDDLESBROUGH
PAGE 111
BILLINGHAM
REDCAR
Marske-by-the-Sea
Saltburn-by-the-Sea
REDCAR & CLEVELAND
GUISBOROUGH
DARLINGTON
NORTHALLERTON
Thirsk
RIPON
Helmsley
Pickering
Malton
Norton-on-Derwent
Kirkbymoorside
Great Ayton
Stokesley
Yarm
SEAHAM
PETERLEE
Sedgefield
Easington
Loftus
Whitby
Runswick Bay
Beacon Point
Horden Point
Dene Mouth
NORTH YORK MOORS NATIONAL PARK
CLEVELAND HILLS
HAMBLETON HILLS
HOWARDIAN HILLS
NORTH YORKSHIRE
Osmotherley
Easingwold
Hovingham
Ampleforth
Goathland
Lythe
Sandsend
Grosmont
Castleton
Danby
Lealholm
Glaisdale
Rosedale Abbey
Hutton-le-Hole
Lastingham
A1(M)
A19
A66
A67
A167
A168
A169
A170
A171
A172
A173
A174
A178
A179
A181
A182
A684
A688
A689
A1085
A1086
47
42

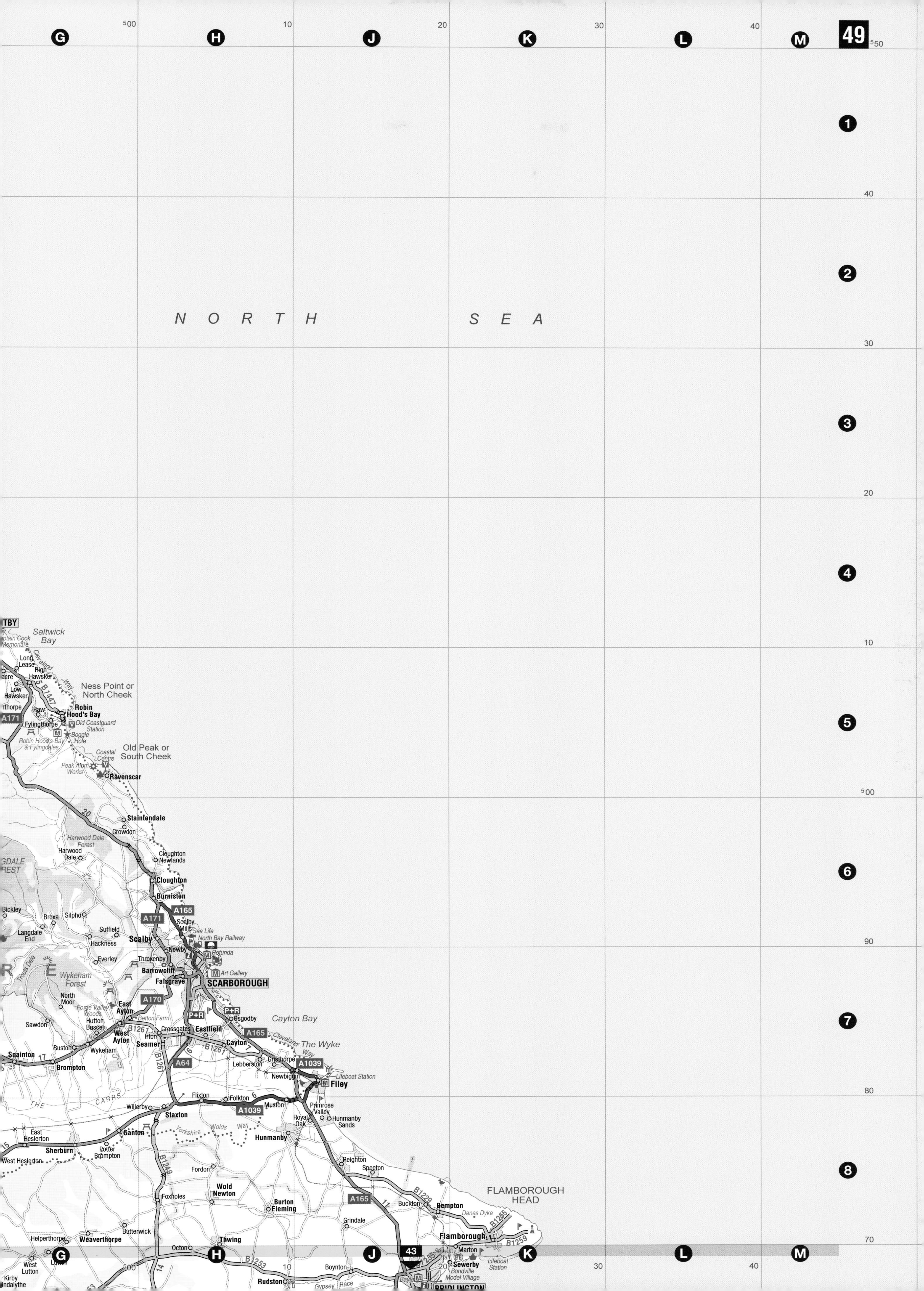
NORTH SEA
Saltwick Bay
Ness Point or North Cheek
Robin Hood's Bay
Fylingthorpe
Old Coastguard Station
Boggle Hole
Old Peak or South Cheek
Coastal Centre
Peak Alum Works
Ravenscar
Staintondale
Crowdon
Harwood Dale Forest
Harwood Dale
Cloughton Newlands
Cloughton
Burniston
Scalby Mills
Sea Life
North Bay Railway
Rotunda
Art Gallery
Bickley
Broxa
Silpho
Langdale End
Suffield
Hackness
Scalby
Newby
Everley
Throxenby
Barrowcliff
Falsgrave
SCARBOROUGH
Wykeham Forest
Troutsdale
North Moor
Forge Valley Woods
East Ayton
Betton Farm
Hutton Buscel
West Ayton
Sawdon
Osgodby
Cayton Bay
Crossgates
Eastfield
Irton
Seamer
Cayton
Cleveland Way
The Wyke
Ruston
Wykeham
Snainton
Brompton
Lebberston
Gristhorpe
Newbiggin
Lifeboat Station
Filey
THE CARRS
Flixton
Folkton
Muston
Willerby
Staxton
Primrose Valley
Royal Oak
Hunmanby Sands
Yorkshire Wolds Way
Ganton
East Heslerton
Hunmanby
Sherburn
Potter Brompton
West Heslerton
Reighton
Speeton
Fordon
Wold Newton
Foxholes
Burton Fleming
Buckton
Bempton
Danes Dyke
FLAMBOROUGH HEAD
Grindale
Flamborough
Butterwick
Helperthorpe
Weaverthorpe
Thwing
Octon
Marton
Sewerby
Bondville Model Village
Lifeboat Station
West Lutton
Boynton
Rudston
Gypsey Race
BRIDLINGTON
A171
A165
A170
A64
A1039
B1261
B1447
B1249
B1229
B1255
B1259
B1253
G H J K L M
43

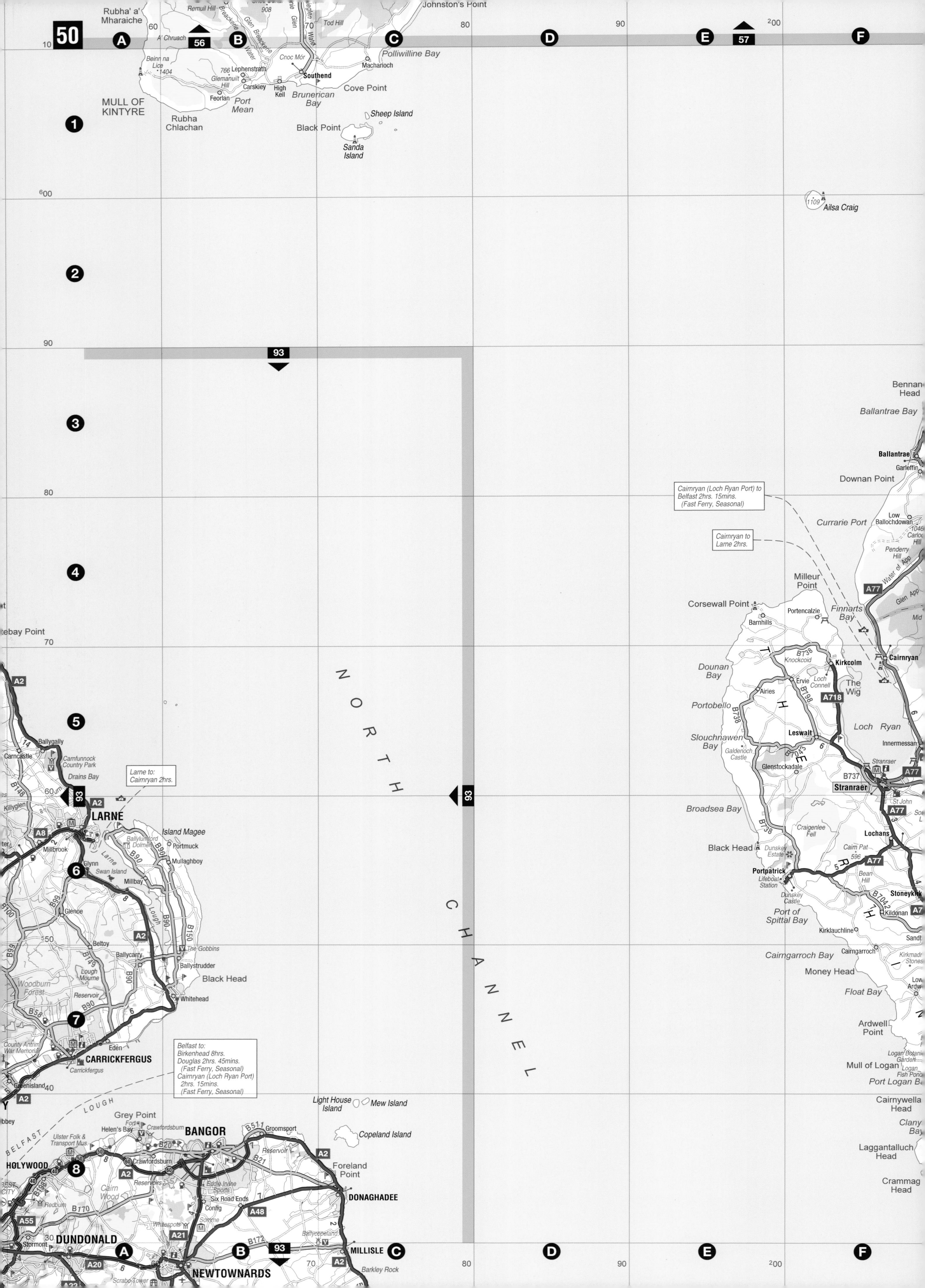
Rubha' a' Mharaiche
Remuil Hill
Johnston's Point
A' Chruach
56
57
Glen Breackerie
Breackerie Water
Conieglen Water
Tod Hill
Polliwilline Bay
Beinn na Lice
Glemanuilt Hill
Lephenstrath
Cnoc Mór
Southend
Machribeg
Macharioch
Carskiey
High Keil
Cove Point
Feorlan
MULL OF KINTYRE
Port Mean
Brunerican Bay
Sheep Island
Rubha Chlachan
Black Point
Sanda Island
Ailsa Craig
Bennane Head
Ballantrae Bay
Ballantrae
Garleffin
Downan Point
Cairnryan (Loch Ryan Port) to Belfast 2hrs. 15mins. (Fast Ferry, Seasonal)
Currarie Port
Low Ballochdowan
Cairnryan to Larne 2hrs.
Pennery Hill
Water of App
Glen App
Milleur Point
Corsewall Point
Portencalzie
Finnarts Bay
Barnhills
Cairnryan
Kirkcolm
Dounan Bay
Knockcoid
Ervie
Loch Connell
The Wig
Airies
Portobello
A718
Loch Ryan
Leswalt
Slouchnawen Bay
Galdenoch Castle
Innermessan
Glenstockadale
Stranraer
B737
A77
Broadsea Bay
Craigenlee Fell
Lochans
Black Head
Dunskey Estate
Cairn Pat
Portpatrick
Lifeboat Station
Bean Hill
Dunskey Castle
Stoneykirk
Port of Spittal Bay
Kildonan
Kirklauchline
Cairngarroch Bay
Cairngarroch
Money Head
Float Bay
Ardwell Point
Mull of Logan
Port Logan Bay
Cairnywellan Head
Clanyard Bay
Laggantalluch Head
Crammag Head
NORTH CHANNEL
RHINNS
93
Ballygally
Carncastle
Carnfunnock Country Park
Drains Bay
Larne to: Cairnryan 2hrs.
LARNE
A2
A8
Island Magee
Ballylumford Dolmen
Portmuck
Millbrook
Mullaghboy
Glynn
Swan Island
Millbay
Larne Lough
Glenoe
Beltoy
Ballycarry
The Gobbins
Ballystrudder
Black Head
Lough Mourne
Woodburn Forest
Reservoir
Whitehead
County Antrim War Memorial
Eden
CARRICKFERGUS
Carrickfergus
Greenisland
Belfast to: Birkenhead 8hrs. Douglas 2hrs. 45mins. (Fast Ferry, Seasonal) Cairnryan (Loch Ryan Port) 2hrs. 15mins. (Fast Ferry, Seasonal)
BELFAST LOUGH
Grey Point
Helen's Bay
Crawfordsburn
BANGOR
Groomsport
Light House Island
Mew Island
Copeland Island
Ulster Folk & Transport Mus.
HOLYWOOD
Crawfordsburn
Reservoir
Foreland Point
Cairn Wood
Redburn
Six Road Ends
Conlig
DONAGHADEE
A48
A55
A21
DUNDONALD
Stormont
Ballycopeland
MILLISLE
Barkley Rock
A20
NEWTOWNARDS
Scrabo Tower

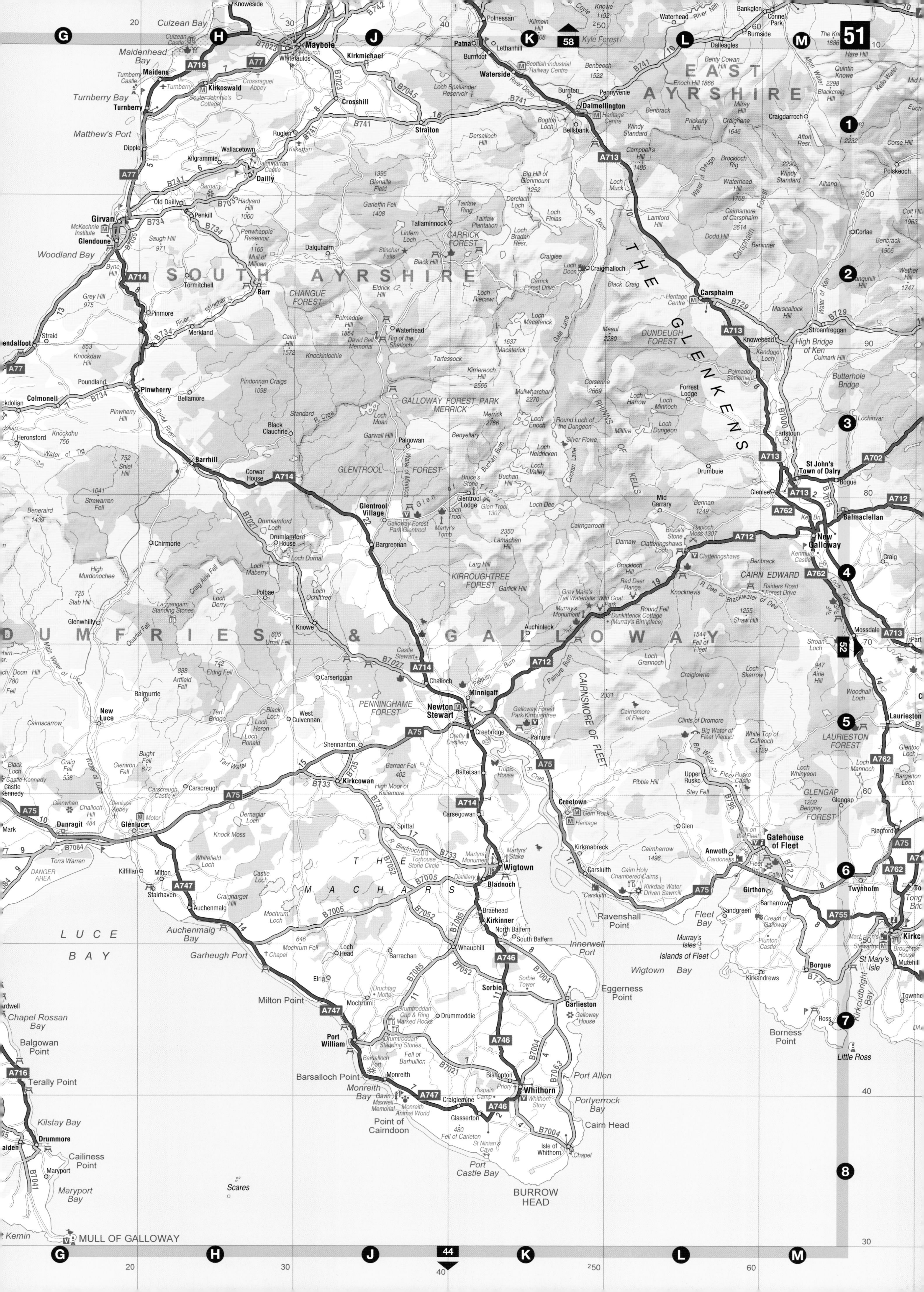

Culzean Bay
Maidenhead Bay
Turnberry Bay
Matthew's Port
Woodland Bay
Maybole
Kirkmichael
Maidens
Kirkoswald
Turnberry
Crosshill
Straiton
Dailly
Girvan
Glendoune
Barr
Pinmore
Pinwherry
Colmonell
Barrhill
New Luce
Glenluce
Dunragit
Patna
Waterside
Dalmellington
Carsphairn
EAST AYRSHIRE
SOUTH AYRSHIRE
DUMFRIES & GALLOWAY
THE GLENKENS
RHINNS OF KELLS
CARRICK FOREST
GALLOWAY FOREST PARK
MERRICK
GLENTROOL FOREST
KIRROUGHTREE FOREST
PENNINGHAME FOREST
DUNDEUGH FOREST
LAURIESTON FOREST
GLENGAP FOREST
CAIRNSMORE OF FLEET
Glentrool Village
Bargrennan
St John's Town of Dalry
New Galloway
Balmaclellan
Mossdale
Laurieston
Newton Stewart
Minnigaff
Creebridge
Kirkcowan
Creetown
Wigtown
Bladnoch
Kirkinner
Whauphill
Sorbie
Garlieston
Port William
Monreith
Whithorn
Isle of Whithorn
Gatehouse of Fleet
Twynholm
Borgue
LUCE BAY
Wigtown Bay
Fleet Bay
Burrow Head
Mull of Galloway
Drummore
Scares
Little Ross
THE MACHARS
A77
A719
A714
A713
A712
A702
A762
A75
A747
A746
A716
A755

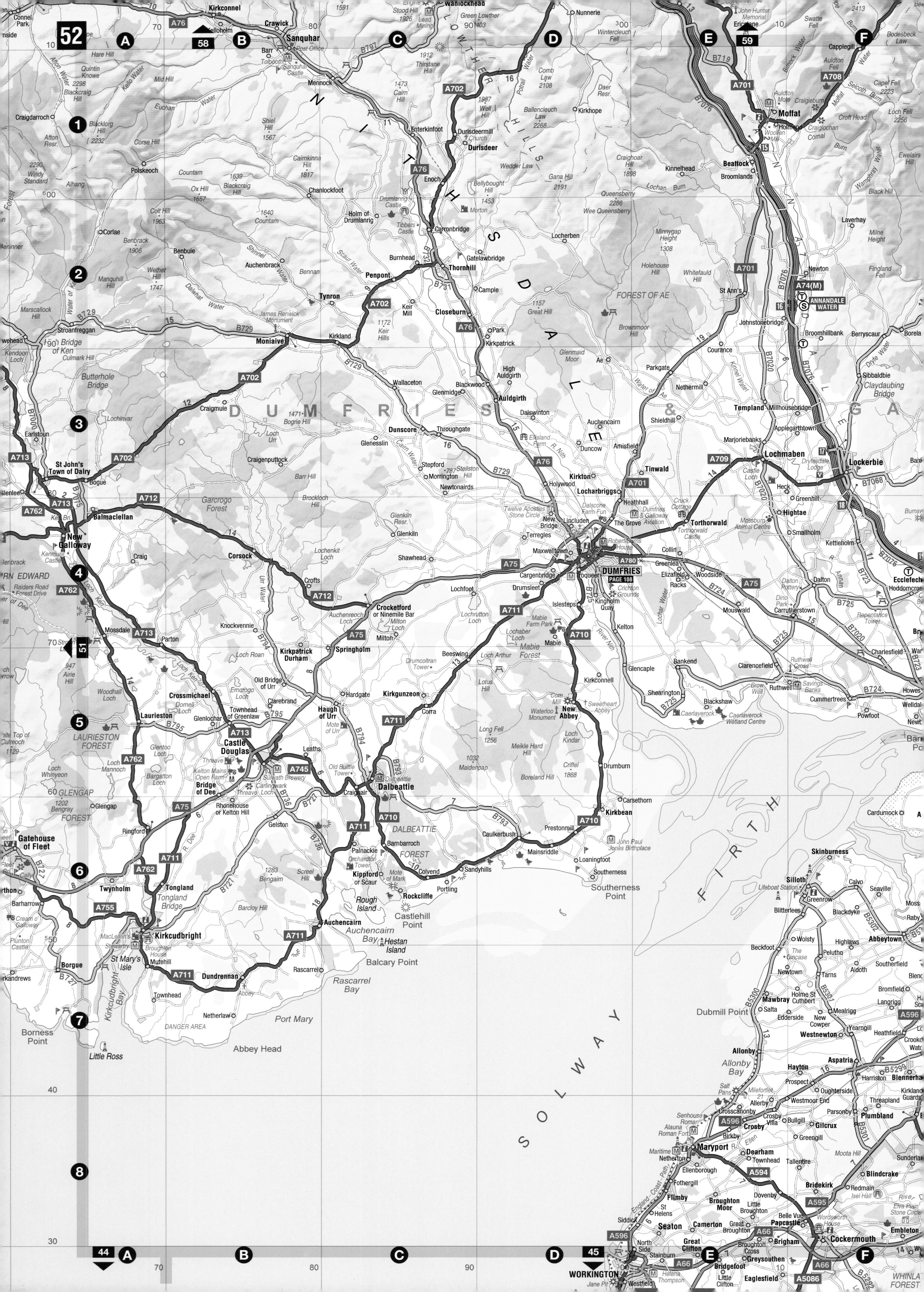

Kirkconnel
Kelloholm
Crawick
Sanquhar
Post Office
Barr
Tolbooth
Sanquhar Castle
Mennock
Wanlockhead
Stood Hill 1926
Lead Mining
Green Lowther
Nunnerie
Wintercleuch Fell
Erickstane
John Hunter Memorial
Swatte Fell
Bodesbeck Law
Capplegill
Connel Park
Hare Hill
Quintin Knowe
Blackcraig Hill 2298
Afton Water
Kello Water
Mid Hill
Euchan Water
Craigdarroch
Blacklorg Hill 2232
Afton Resr.
Corse Hill
Windy Standard 2290
Polskeoch
Alhang
Countam
1912 Thirstane Hill
1473 Cairn Hill
Shiel Hill 1567
Cairnkinna Hill 1817
Enterkinfoot
Durisdeermill
Church
Durisdeer
Enoch
Comb Law 2108
Daer Resr.
Ballencleuch Law 2268
Kirkhope
Craighoar Hill 1898
Wedder Law
Gana Hill 2191
Kinnelhead
Queensberry 2286
Wee Queensberry
Lochan Burn
Moffat
Holmend
Woollen Mill
Craigieburn
Craiglochan
Comal
Auldton Fell
Capel Fell 2223
Loch Fell 2256
Croft Head
Selcoth Burn
Beattock
Broomlands
Ewelairs Hill
Wamphray Water
Black Hill
Laverhay
Milne Height
Finngland Fell
Newton
ANNANDALE WATER
Johnstonebridge
Broomhillbank
Berryscaur
Chanlockfoot
Blackcraig Hill 1639
Ox Hill 1657
Bellybought Hill 1453
Morton
Drumlanrig Castle
Holm of Drumlanrig
Tibbers Castle
Carronbridge
Locherben
Minnygap Height 1308
Colt Hill 1963
Countam 1640
Corlae
Benbrack 1906
Benbuie
Auchenbrack
Shinnel Water
Scaur Water
Bennan
Burnhead
Thornhill
Gatelawbridge
Penpont
Tynron
Keir Mill
Closeburn
Cample
Holehouse Hill
Whitefauld Hill
FOREST OF AE
St Ann's
Manquhill Hill
Wether Hill 1747
Dalwhat Water
Marscallock Hill
Water of Ken
Stroanfreggan
James Renwick Monument
Moniaive
Kirkland
Keir Hills 1172
Park
Kirkpatrick
Great Hill 1157
Brownmoor Hill
Bridge of Ken
Culmark Hill
Kendoon Loch
Butterhole Bridge
Glenmaid Moor
Ae
Courance
Parkgate
Kinnel Water
Sibbaldbie
Claydaubing Bridge
Wallaceton
Glenmidge
Blackwood
High Auldgirth
Auldgirth
Nethermill
Lochinvar
Earlstoun
Craigmuie
Bogrie Hill 1471
DUMFRIES & GALLOWAY
NITHSDALE
NITHS HILLS
LOWTHER HILLS
Dalswinton
Auchencairn
Shieldhill
Templand
Millhousebridge
Applegarthtown
Marjoriebanks
Lochmaben
Lockerbie
Dryfesdale Lodge
Dunscore
Throughgate
Glenesslin
Loch Urr
Ellisland Farm
Duncow
Amisfield
Tinwald
St John's Town of Dalry
Craigenputtock
Stepford
Morrington
Steilston Hill
Newtonairds
Kirkton
Holywood
Locharbriggs
Heathhall
Castle Loch
Heck
Greenhill
Hightae
Bogue
Barr Hill
Brockloch Hill
Garcrogo Forest
Twelve Apostles Stone Circle
New Bridge
Lincluden
Dalscone Farm Fun
Dumfries & Galloway Aviation
The Grove
Cruck Cottage
Torthorwald
Torthorwald Castle
Mossburn Animal Centre
Smallholm
Kettleholm
Balmaclellan
Ken Bri.
New Galloway
Glenkiln Resr.
Glenkiln
Terregles
Robert Burns House
Maxwelltown
Collin
Greenlea
Craig
Kenmure Castle
Corsock
Lochenkit Loch
Shawhead
Cargenbridge
DUMFRIES
PAGE 108
Troqueer
Crichton Grounds
Kingholm Quay
Elizafield
Racks
Woodside
Dalton
Ecclefechan
Hoddomcross
Dalton Pottery
Dino Park
Carrutherstown
Mouswald
Repentance Tower
Raiders Road Forest Drive
Crofts
Lochfoot
Drumsleet
Islesteps
Kelton
Crocketford or Ninemile Bar
Auchenreoch Loch
Milton Loch
Milton
Lochrutton Loch
Mabie Farm Park
Lochaber Loch
Mabie
Mabie Forest
Mossdale
Parton
Knockvennie
Urr Water
Loch Roan
Kirkpatrick Durham
Springholm
Drumcoltran Tower
Beeswing
Loch Arthur
Lotus Hill
Glencaple
Bankend
Clarencefield
Ruthwell Cross
Ruthwell
Savings Banks
Brow Well
Cummertrees
Charlesfield
Airie Hill 947
Woodhall Loch
Crossmichael
Ernarogo Loch
Old Bridge of Urr
Clarebrand
Hardgate
Kirkgunzeon
Corra
Kirkconnell
Corn Mill
Sweetheart Abbey
New Abbey
Waterloo Monument
Shearington
Blackshaw
Caerlaverock
Caerlaverock Wetland Centre
Powfoot
Laurieston
LAURIESTON FOREST
Dornell Loch
Glenlochar
Townhead of Greenlaw
Haugh of Urr
Mote of Urr
Long Fell 1256
Meikle Hard Hill
Loch Kindar
Criffel 1868
Glentoo Loch
Castle Douglas
Threave
Kelton Mains Open Farm
Sulwath Brewery
Carlingwark Loch
Leaths
Old Buittle Tower
Dalbeattie
Maidenpap 1032
Boreland Hill
Drumburn
Loch Mannoch
Loch Whinyeon
Bargatton Loch
Bridge of Dee
Rhonehouse or Kelton Hill
GLENGAP FOREST
Bengray 1202
Glengap
Craignair
Carsethorn
Kirkbean
Ringford
R. Dee
Gelston
DALBEATTIE FOREST
Barnbarroch
Palnackie
Orchardton Tower
Caulkerbush
Prestonmill
John Paul Jones Birthplace
Mainsriddle
Loaningfoot
Southerness
Southerness Point
Gatehouse of Fleet
Twynholm
Tongland
Tongland Bridge
Bengairn 1283
Screel Hill
Kippford or Scaur
Mote of Mark
Colvend
Sandyhills
Portling
Rockcliffe
Rough Island
Castlehill Point
Barharrow
Cream o' Galloway
Barcloy Hill
Auchencairn
Auchencairn Bay
Hestan Island
Kirkcudbright
MacLellan's Castle
Stewartry Museum
Broughton House
Plunton Castle
St Mary's Isle
Mutehill
Dundrennan
Abbey
Rascarrel
Balcary Point
Rascarrel Bay
Borgue
Kirkandrews
Kirkcudbright Bay
Townhead
Netherlaw
DANGER AREA
Port Mary
Borness Point
Little Ross
Abbey Head
SOLWAY FIRTH
Skinburness
Silloth
Lifeboat Station
Greenrow
Calvo
Seaville
Blitterlees
Blackdyke
Wolsty
Highlaws
Abbeytown
The Gincase
Pelutho
Newtown
Aldoth
Southerfield
Beckfoot
Tarns
Bromfield
Mawbray
Holme St Cuthbert
Langrigg
Salta
Edderside
Mealrigg
Dubmill Point
New Cowper
Westnewton
Yearngill
Heathfield
Allonby
Allonby Bay
Hayton
Aspatria
Prospect
Harriston
Blennerhasset
Oughterside
Salt Pans
Milefortlet 21
Allerby
Westmoor End
Parsonby
Threapland
Senhouse Roman Museum
Crosscanonby
Crosby
Crosby Villa
Bullgill
Gilcrux
Plumbland
Alauna Roman Fort
Birkby
Greengill
Maritime Museum
Maryport
Netherton
Dearham
Townhead
Tallentire
Moota Hill
Ellenborough
England Coast Path
Fothergill
Blindcrake
Dovenby
Bridekirk
Redmain
Isel Hall
Flimby
St Helens
Broughton Moor
Little Broughton
Belle Vue
Papcastle
Wordsworth House
Cockermouth
Embleton
Siddick
Seaton
Camerton
Great Broughton
Brigham
North Side
Stainburn
Great Clifton
Broughton Cross
Greysouthen
WORKINGTON
Helena Thompson
Jane Pit
Westfield
Bridgefoot
Little Clifton
Eaglesfield
WHINLATTER FOREST
A76 A702 A701 A708 A74(M) A709 A75 A780 A711 A710 A712 A713 A762 A745 A755 A596 A594 A595 A66 A5086
B797 B719 B7076 B729 B732 B731 B7020 B7068 B723 B725 B724 B7000 B795 B794 B793 B736 B727 B721 B5300 B5302 B5301 B5299
58
59
51
44
45
A B C D E F
1 2 3 4 5 6 7 8
70 80 90 10

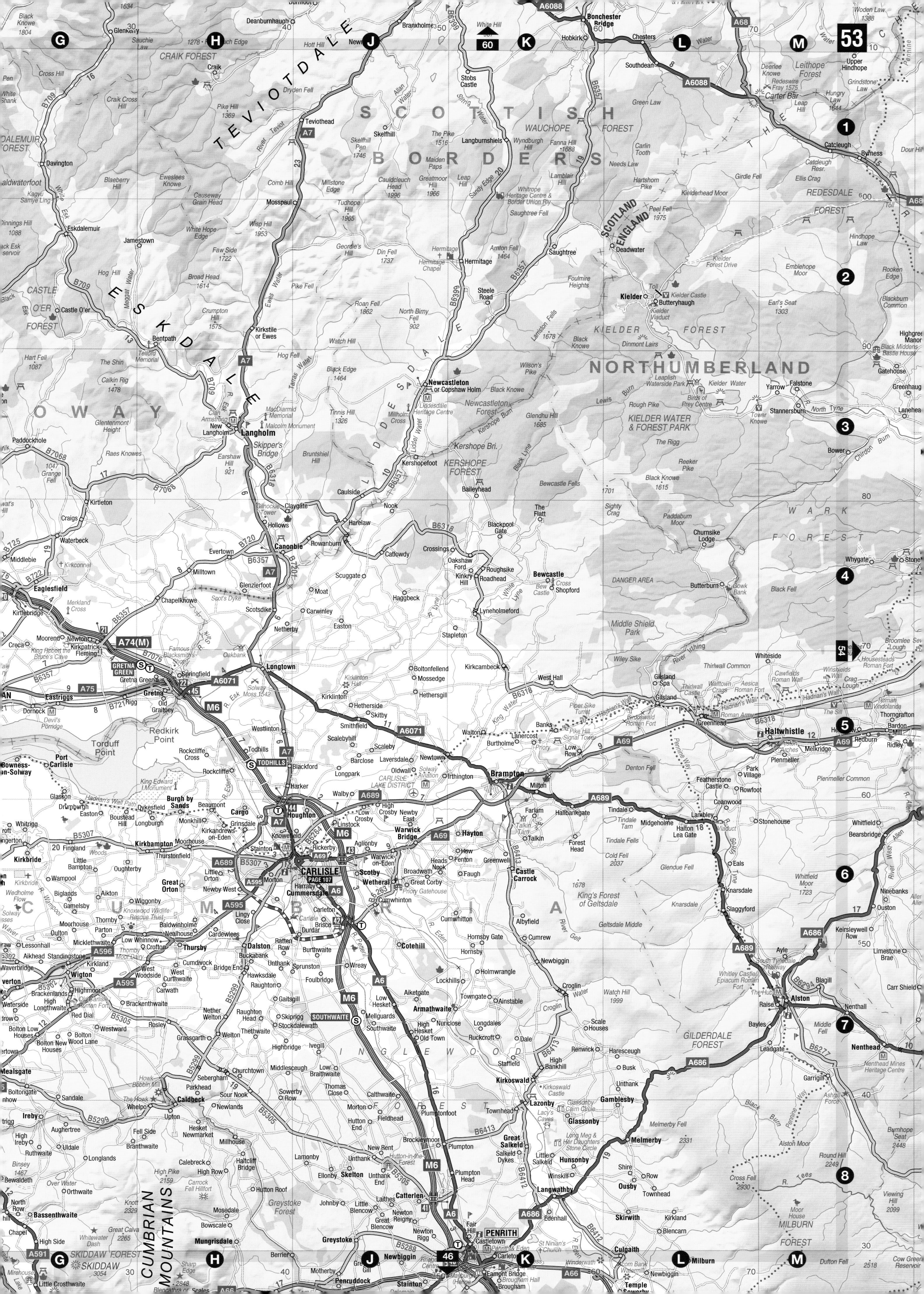
G
H
J
K
L
M
60
54
46
TEVIOTDALE
SCOTTISH BORDERS
WAUCHOPE FOREST
CRAIK FOREST
ESKDALE
LIDDESDALE
CASTLE O'ER FOREST
KIELDER FOREST
NORTHUMBERLAND
SCOTLAND
ENGLAND
REDESDALE FOREST
KIELDER WATER & FOREST PARK
KERSHOPE FOREST
Newcastleton Forest
WARK FOREST
DANGER AREA
Middle Shield Park
King's Forest of Geltsdale
CUMBRIA
INGLEWOOD FOREST
GILDERDALE FOREST
MILBURN FOREST
CUMBRIAN MOUNTAINS
SKIDDAW FOREST
SKIDDAW 3054
Greystoke Forest
Bonchester Bridge
Chesters
Southdean
Carter Bar
Catcleugh
Byrness
Teviothead
Skelfhill
Stobs Castle
Langburnshiels
Mosspaul
Eskdalemuir
Davington
Jamestown
Bentpath
Hermitage
Saughtree
Deadwater
Kielder
Kielder Castle
Butteryhaugh
Newcastleton or Copshaw Holm
Kershopefoot
Langholm
New Langholm
Canonbie
Rowanburn
Falstone
Stannersburn
Bower
Whygate
Butterburn
Bewcastle
Roadhead
Kirtleton
Waterbeck
Eaglesfield
Kirtlebridge
Gretna
Gretna Green
Springfield
Eastriggs
Longtown
Gilsland
Greenhead
Haltwhistle
Brampton
Milton
Walton
Lanercost
Irthington
Carlisle
Harraby
Houghton
Stanwix
Dalston
Wigton
Thursby
Warwick Bridge
Wetheral
Hayton
Castle Carrock
Cumwhitton
Hallbankgate
Lambley
Slaggyford
Knarsdale
Alston
Nenthall
Nenthead
Garrigill
Southwaite
Armathwaite
Lazonby
Kirkoswald
Glassonby
Melmerby
Langwathby
Culgaith
Milburn
Plumpton
Penrith
Eamont Bridge
Caldbeck
Sebergham
Ireby
Bassenthwaite
Mungrisdale
Greystoke
Newbiggin
Penruddock
Stainton
Little Crosthwaite
A7
A74(M)
A75
A6071
A69
A689
A595
A596
A591
A6
A66
A686
A6088
A68
M6
B709
B7068
B6357
B6399
B6318
B5307
B5299
B5305
B6413
B6412
B6277
B6294
B5288
B720
B722
B725
B6263
B6264
B6412
B7076
B721
PAGE 107
SOUTHWAITE
TODHILLS
GRETNA GREEN
KIELDER WATER
Hadrian's Wall
Pennine Way
South Tynedale Railway
Peel Fell 1975
Carter Fell
Cross Fell 2930
Knott 2329
Great Calva 2265
High Pike 2159

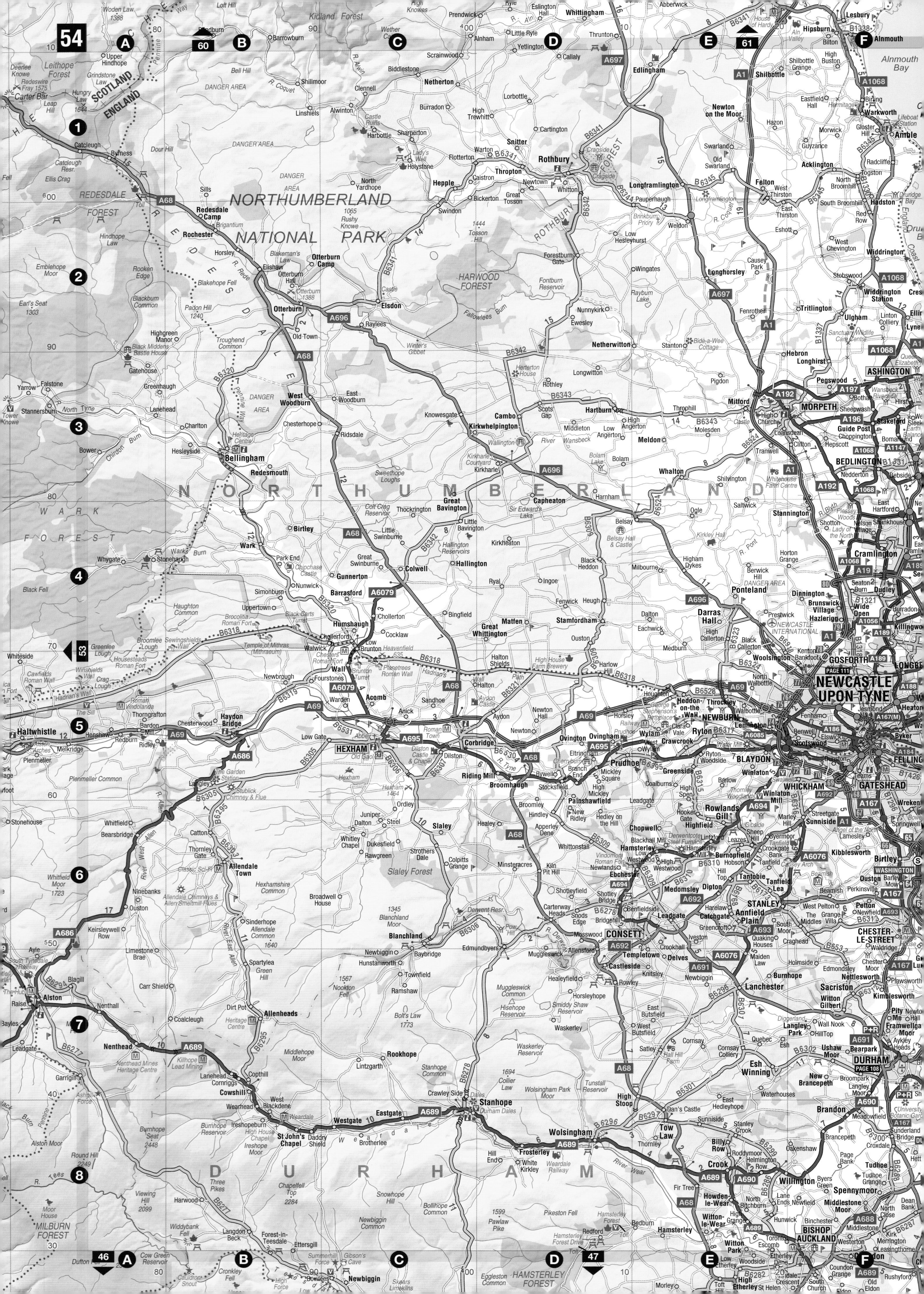
60
61
53
46
47
SCOTLAND
ENGLAND
Carter Bar
NORTHUMBERLAND NATIONAL PARK
NORTHUMBERLAND
DURHAM
REDESDALE FOREST
WARK FOREST
KIELDER
Kidland Forest
HARWOOD FOREST
Slaley Forest
MILBURN FOREST
HAMSTERLEY FOREST
Alnmouth Bay
Alnmouth
Alnwick
Warkworth
Amble
Rothbury
Otterburn
Elsdon
Bellingham
Wark
Morpeth
Ashington
Bedlington
Cramlington
Ponteland
NEWCASTLE UPON TYNE
GATESHEAD
Gosforth
Whickham
Blaydon
Ryton
Prudhoe
Corbridge
Hexham
Haydon Bridge
Haltwhistle
Allendale Town
Allenheads
Alston
Nenthead
Blanchland
Consett
Stanley
Chester-le-Street
Lanchester
DURHAM
Stanhope
Wolsingham
Tow Law
Crook
Willington
Spennymoor
Brandon
BISHOP AUCKLAND
Middleton-in-Teesdale
Byrness
Catcleugh
Rochester
Redesdale Camp
Otterburn Camp
Falstone
Kielder
Hadrian's Wall
Chesters Roman Fort
Housesteads Roman Fort
Vindolanda
NEWCASTLE INTERNATIONAL
PAGE 111
PAGE 108
A1
A68
A69
A696
A697
A1068
A189
A19
A167
A686
A689
A691
A692
A693
A694
A695
A6076
A6079
Durham Dales
Weardale
River Wear
R. Tyne
R. Tees
R. Derwent
R. Coquet
R. Rede
North Tyne
DANGER AREA

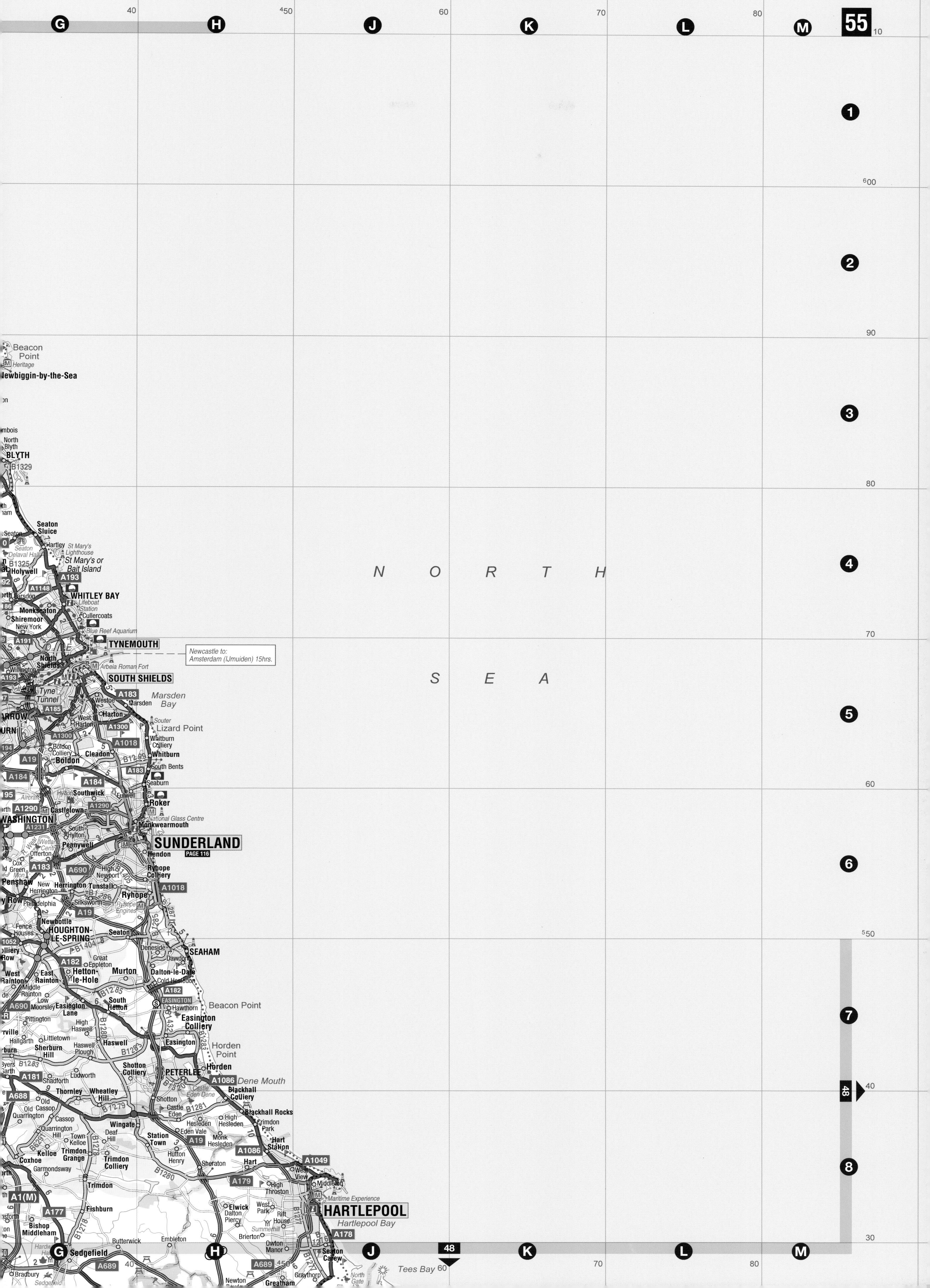
N O R T H
S E A
Beacon Point
Newbiggin-by-the-Sea
North Blyth
BLYTH
B1329
Seaton Sluice
Hartley
St Mary's Lighthouse
St Mary's or Bait Island
Seaton Delaval Hall
B1325
Holywell
A193
A1148
WHITLEY BAY
Lifeboat Station
Monkseaton
Shiremoor
New York
Cullercoats
Blue Reef Aquarium
A191
TYNEMOUTH
Newcastle to: Amsterdam (IJmuiden) 15hrs.
North Shields
Willington
Arbeia Roman Fort
SOUTH SHIELDS
Tyne Tunnel
A183
Westoe
Marsden
Marsden Bay
A185
Harton
West Harton
A1300
Souter Lizard Point
Whitburn Colliery
Whitburn
A1018
South Bents
Boldon Colliery
Boldon
Cleadon
A19
A184
Seaburn
Southwick
Fulwell
Roker
A1290
Castletown
National Glass Centre
Monkwearmouth
WASHINGTON
A1231
South Hylton
Pennywell
SUNDERLAND
PAGE 116
Hendon
Offerton
Cox Green
A183
A690
High Newport
Ryhope Colliery
Penshaw
New Herrington
Herrington
Tunstall
Ryhope
Philadelphia
Silksworth
Ryhope Engines
Newbottle
HOUGHTON-LE-SPRING
Fence Houses
Seaton
Deneside
Dawdon
SEAHAM
A182
Great Eppleton
West Rainton
East Rainton
Hetton-le-Hole
Murton
Dalton-le-Dale
Cold Hesledon
Middle Rainton
Low Moorsley
Easington Lane
South Hetton
EASINGTON
Hawthorn
Beacon Point
Easington Colliery
Pittington
High Haswell
Easington
Littletown
Hallgarth
Sherburn Hill
Haswell Plough
Haswell
Horden Point
Horden
Shotton Colliery
PETERLEE
A181
Shadforth
Ludworth
A1086
Dene Mouth
Castle Eden Dene
Blackhall Colliery
Thornley
Wheatley Hill
A688
Old Cassop
Quarrington
Cassop
Shotton
Castle Eden
Blackhall Rocks
High Hesleden
Crimdon Park
Wingate
Hesleden
Quarrington Hill
Deaf Hill
Station Town
Eden Vale
Monk Hesleden
Hart Station
Town Kelloe
Kelloe
Trimdon Grange
Coxhoe
Trimdon Colliery
Hutton Henry
Sheraton
Hart
A1049
West View
Garmondsway
Trimdon
B1280
A179
High Throston
Middleton
Maritime Experience
A1(M)
A177
Fishburn
Elwick
Dalton Piercy
West Park
Rift House
HARTLEPOOL
Hartlepool Bay
Bishop Middleham
Summerhill
Brierton
A178
Sedgefield
Butterwick
Embleton
Owton Manor
Seaton Carew
A689
Bradbury
Newton
Greatham
Graythorp
Tees Bay
North Gare
48

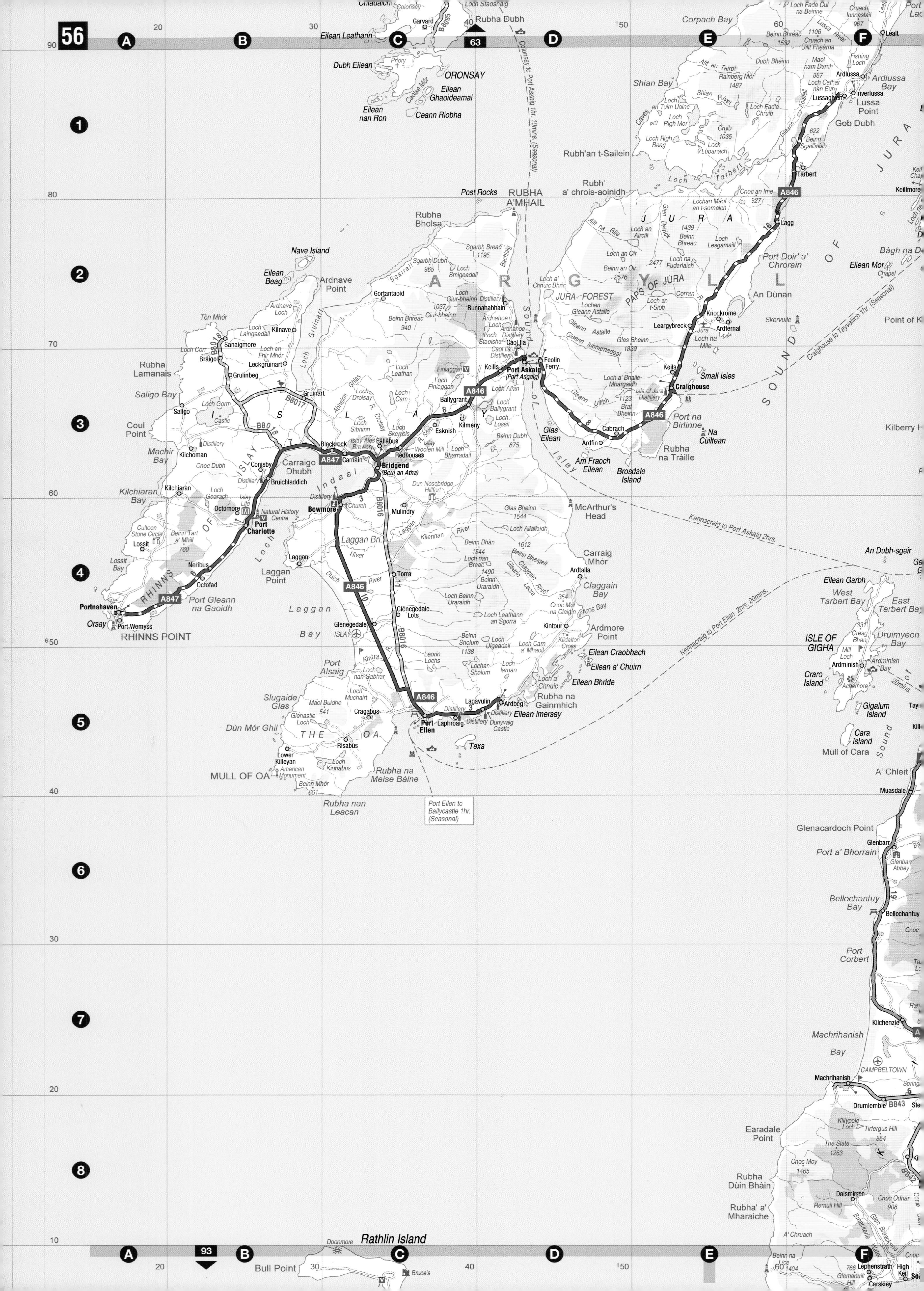

Colonsay
Garvard
B8085
Loch Staosnaig
Rubha Dubh
63
Eilean Leathann
Corpach Bay
Loch Fada Cul na Beinne
Cruach Ionnastail 967
Lealt
Beinn Bhreac 1532
Cruach an Uillt Fhearna
Lussa River
Fishing Loch
Dubh Eilean
Priory
ORONSAY
Eilean Ghaoideamal
Eilean nan Ron
Cadas Mòr
Ceann Riobha
Colonsay to Port Askaig 1hr. 10mins. (Seasonal)
Allt an Tairbh
Rainberg Mòr 1487
Dubh Bheinn
Maol nam Damh 887
Loch Cathar nan Eun
Ardlussa
Ardlussa Bay
Inverlussa
Lussagiven
Lussa Point
Gob Dubh
Shian Bay
Shian River
Loch an Tuim Uaine
Loch Righ Mòr
Caves
Loch Fad'a Chruib
Cruib 1036
Loch Righ Beag
Loch Lùbanach
Gleann Aoistail
Beinn Sgaillinish 622
Rubh'an t-Sailein
Tarbert
Loch Tarbert
Post Rocks
RUBHA A'MHAIL
Rubh' a' chrois-aoinidh
Cnoc an Ime 927
A846
Keillmore
Lochan Maol an t-sornaich
JURA
Lagg
Rubha Bholsa
Allt na Gile
Glen Batrick
Loch an Aircill
1439 Beinn Bhreac
Loch Lesgamaill
Port Doir' a' Chrorain
Nave Island
Sgarbh Breac 1195
Bachlaig
Loch an Oir
Beinn an Oir 2576
2477
Loch na Fudarlaich
Bàgh na D
Eilean Mor
Chapel
Eilean Beag
Ardnave Point
Sgarbh Dubh 965
Loch Smigeadail
Sgairail
ARGYLL
Loch a' Chnuic Bhric
PAPS OF JURA
JURA FOREST
Lochan Gleann Astaile
Corran
Loch an t-Siob
An Dùnan
Gortantaoid
Loch Giur-bheinn
Distillery
Bunnahabhain
1037 Giur-bheinn
Ardnave Loch
Tòn Mhór
Loch Gruinart
Beinn Bhreac 940
Ardnahoe Loch
Ardnahoe Distillery
Loch Staoisha
Caol Ila
Caol Ila Distillery
Sound of Islay
Gleann Astaile
Gleann Iubharnadeal
Glas Bheinn 1839
Knockrome
Leargybreck
Jura
Ardfernal
Loch na Mile
Skervuile
Point of K
Craighouse to Tayvallich 1hr. (Seasonal)
Kilnave
Loch Laingeadail
B8018
Sanaigmore
Loch Corr
Braigo
Loch an Fhir Mhóir
Leckgruinart
Rubha Lamanais
Grulinbeg
Saligo Bay
Gruinart
B8017
Abhainn Ghlas
Loch Leathan
Finlaggan
Loch Finlaggan
Keills
Port Askaig (Port Asgaig)
Feolin Ferry
Loch Allan
Loch a' Bhaile-Mhargaidh
Keils
Small Isles
Isle of Jura Distillery
Craighouse
SOUND OF JURA
Saligo
Loch Gorm
Castle
ISLAY
Loch Drolsay
Loch Cam
Ballygrant
Loch Ballygrant
Gleann Ullibh
1123 Brat Bheinn
Cabrach
Port na Birlinne
A846
Kilberry H
Coul Point
Machir Bay
Kilchoman
Distillery
B8018
Blackrock
Carnain
A847
Loch Sibhinn
Islay Ales Brewery
Eallabus
Loch Skerrols
R. Drolsay
R. Sorn
Esknish
Kilmeny
Loch Lossit
Glas Eilean
Ardfin
Na Cùiltean
Rubha na Tràille
Carraigo Dhubh
Conisby
Islay Woolen Mill
Redhouses
Loch Bharradail
Beinn Dubh 875
Am Fraoch Eilean
Brosdale Island
Cnoc Dubh
Distillery
Bruichladdich
Bridgend (Beul an Atha)
Loch Indaal
Kilchiaran Bay
Kilchiaran
Loch Gearach
Dun Nosebridge Hillfort
McArthur's Head
Distillery
Bowmore
Church
Octomore
Islay Life
Natural History Centre
Port Charlotte
Mulindry
B8016
Glas Bheinn 1544
Loch Allallaidh
Kennacraig to Port Askaig 2hrs.
Cultoon Stone Circle
Beinn Tart a' Mhill 760
Laggan Bri.
Laggan
Kilennan River
Beinn Bhàn 1544
Loch nan Breac
1612 Beinn Bheigeir
Carraig Mhór
Lossit
RHINNS OF ISLAY
Laggan River
Ardtalla
An Dubh-sgeir
Lossit Bay
Neribus
Laggan Point
Torra
Claggain River
Gleann Leora
Claggain Bay
Eilean Garbh
West Tarbert Bay
Octofad
Duich River
A846
Beinn Uraraidh 1490
Loch Beinn Uaraidh
354 Cnoc Mòr na Claigin
Aros Bay
East Tarbert Bay
Portnahaven
A847
Port Gleann na Gaoidh
Laggan Bay
Glenegedale Lots
Kintour
Ardmore Point
Creag Bhàn 331
Druimyeon Bay
Orsay
Port Wemyss
RHINNS POINT
Glenegedale
ISLAY
Loch Leathann an Sgorra
Beinn Sholum 1138
Loch Uigeadail
Loch Cam a' Mhaoil
Kildalton Cross
Eilean Craobhach
Eilean a' Chuirn
Kennacraig to Port Ellen 2hrs. 20mins.
ISLE OF GIGHA
Mill Loch
Ardminish
Ardminish Bay
Port Alsaig
Kintra
Loch nan Gabhar
Leorin Lochs
Lochan Sholum
Loch Iarnan
Loch a' Chnuic
Eilean Bhride
Craro Island
Achamore
Slugaide Glas
Loch Muchairt
A846
Rubha na Gainmhich
Gigalum Island
Màol Buidhe 541
Glenastle Loch
Cragabus
Lagavulin
Ardbeg
Distillery
Eilean Imersay
Dùn Mór Ghil
THE OA
Port Ellen
Laphroaig
Distillery
Dunyvaig Castle
Cara Island
Risabus
Texa
Mull of Cara
Lower Killeyan
American Monument
Loch Kinnabus
Rubha na Meise Bàine
MULL OF OA
A' Chleit
Beinn Mhór 661
Muasdale
Rubha nan Leacan
Port Ellen to Ballycastle 1hr. (Seasonal)
Glenacardoch Point
Glenbarr
Port a' Bhorrain
Glenbarr Abbey
Bellochantuy Bay
Bellochantuy
Port Corbert
Kilchenzie
Machrihanish Bay
CAMPBELTOWN
Machrihanish
Drumlemble
B843
Killypole Loch
Tirfergus Hill 854
Earadale Point
The Slate 1263
Cnoc Moy 1465
B842
Rubha Dùin Bhàin
Dalsmirren
Remuil Hill
Cnoc Odhar 908
Rubha' a' Mharaiche
Glen Breackerie
Breackerie Water
A' Chruach
Rathlin Island
Doonmore
93
Bull Point
Bruce's
Beinn na Lice 1404
766 Glemanuilt Hill
Lephenstrath
High Keil
Carskiey
A B C D E F
1 2 3 4 5 6 7 8

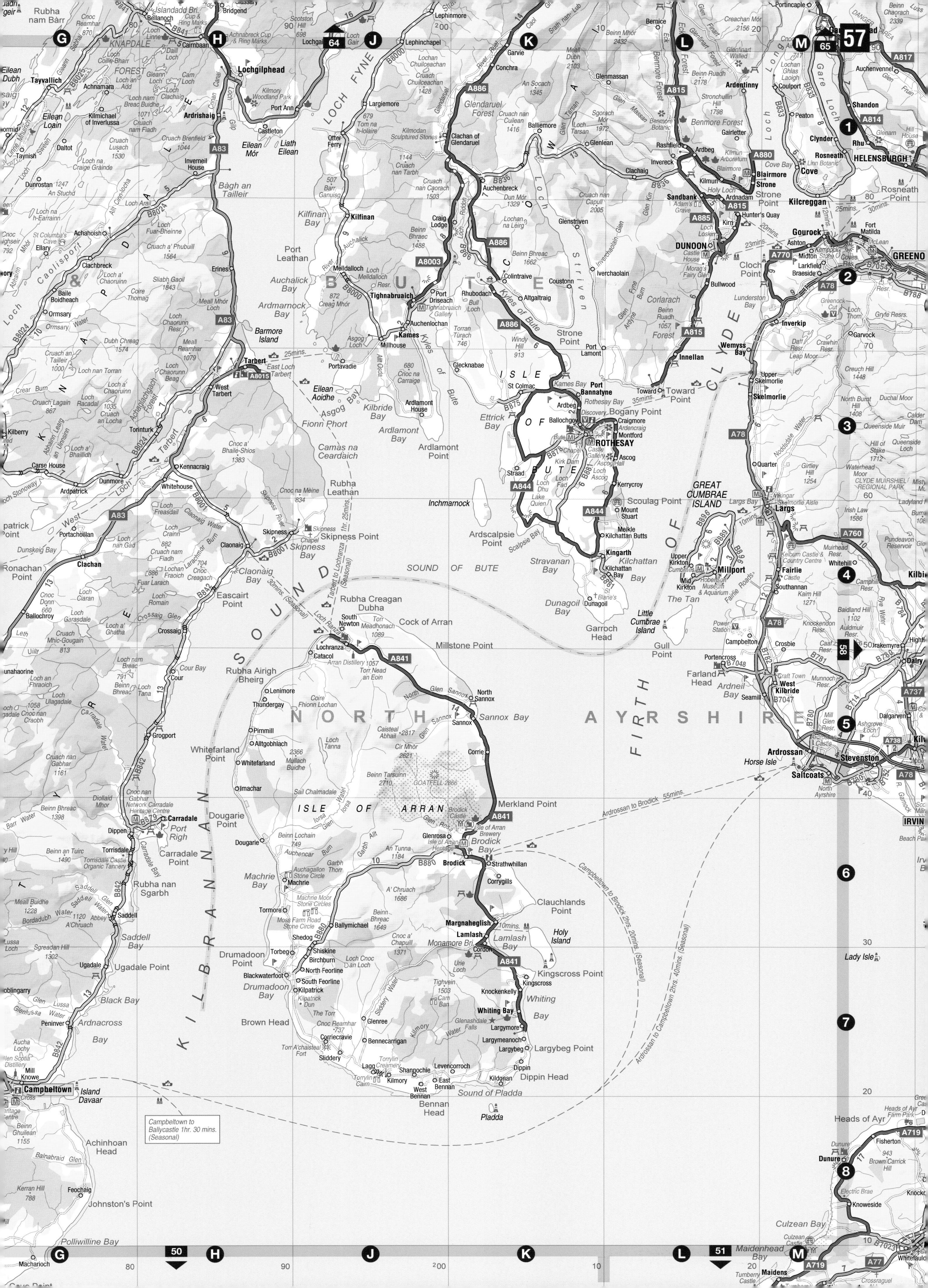

Lochgilphead
Ardrishaig
Tayvallich
Knapdale Forest
Loch Fyne
Lochgair
Lephinchapel
Garvie
Conchra
Glendaruel Forest
Clachan of Glendaruel
Otter Ferry
Largiemore
Castleton
Eilean Mòr
Liath Eilean
Inverneil House
Kilfinan
Kilfinan Bay
Port Leathan
Auchalick Bay
Ardmarnock Bay
Tighnabruaich
Kames
Millhouse
Portavadie
Tarbert
West Tarbert
Barmore Island
Kennacraig
Whitehouse
Dunmore
Ardpatrick
Skipness
Skipness Point
Skipness Bay
Claonaig
Claonaig Bay
Eascairt Point
Crossaig
Cour
Cour Bay
Grogport
Carradale
Carradale Point
Port Righ
Dippen
Torrisdale
Saddell
Saddell Bay
Ugadale
Ugadale Point
Black Bay
Peninver
Ardnacross Bay
Campbeltown
Island Davaar
Achinhoan Head
Feochaig
Johnston's Point
Polliwilline Bay
Macharioch
Clachan
Ronachan Point
Ballochroy
Isle of Bute
Rothesay
Port Bannatyne
Ardbeg
Ballochgoy
Craigmore
Montford
Ascog
Kerrycroy
Scoulag Point
Mount Stuart
Kilchattan Bay
Kingarth
Dunagoil Bay
Garroch Head
Ettrick Bay
St Colmac
Straad
Inchmarnock
Ardscalpsie Point
Stravanan Bay
Colintraive
Rhubodach
Kyles of Bute
Strone Point
Port Lamont
Toward
Toward Point
Innellan
Dunoon
Kirn
Hunter's Quay
Sandbank
Kilmun
Strone
Blairmore
Ardentinny
Benmore Forest
Cove
Kilcreggan
Rosneath Point
Helensburgh
Rhu
Shandon
Gourock
Greenock
Cloch Point
Lunderston Bay
Inverkip
Wemyss Bay
Skelmorlie
Largs
Great Cumbrae Island
Millport
Little Cumbrae Island
Fairlie
Southannan
West Kilbride
Seamill
Ardneil Bay
Farland Head
Portencross
Ardrossan
Saltcoats
Stevenston
Horse Isle
North Ayrshire
Firth of Clyde
Sound of Bute
Kilbrannan Sound
Isle of Arran
Lochranza
Catacol
Cock of Arran
Millstone Point
North Sannox
Sannox
Sannox Bay
Corrie
Goatfell 2866
Merkland Point
Brodick
Brodick Bay
Strathwhillan
Corrygills
Clauchlands Point
Lamlash
Lamlash Bay
Holy Island
Kingscross Point
Whiting Bay
Largybeg Point
Dippin Head
Kildonan
Pladda
Sound of Pladda
Bennan Head
Kilmory
Lagg
Sliddery
Blackwaterfoot
Drumadoon Point
Drumadoon Bay
Machrie Bay
Machrie
Dougarie Point
Whitefarland Point
Pirnmill
Lenimore
Thundergay
Rubha Airigh Bheirg
Shiskine
Kilpatrick
Lady Isle
Heads of Ayr
Dunure
Culzean Bay
Maidenhead Bay
Maidens
Ardrossan to Brodick 55mins.
Campbeltown to Ballycastle 1hr. 30 mins. (Seasonal)
Tarbert to Lochranza 1hr. 25mins. (Seasonal)
G H J K L M
50 51 58 64 65

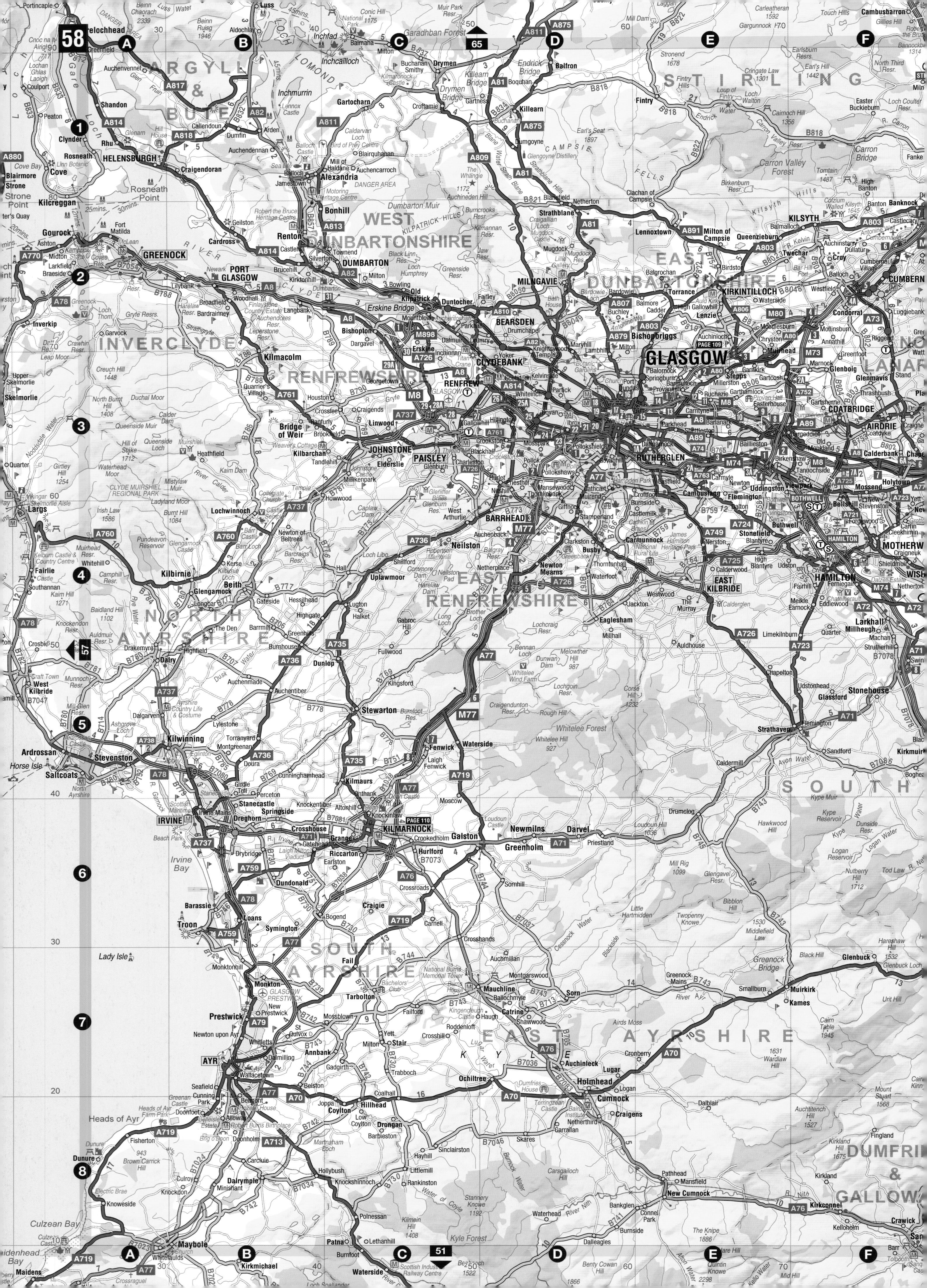
ARGYLL & BUTE
STIRLING
WEST DUNBARTONSHIRE
EAST DUNBARTONSHIRE
INVERCLYDE
RENFREWSHIRE
EAST RENFREWSHIRE
NORTH AYRSHIRE
SOUTH AYRSHIRE
EAST AYRSHIRE
SOUTH
LANAR
DUMFRI & GALLOW
GLASGOW
PAGE 109
PAGE 110
65
57
51
Garelochhead
Greenfield
Auchenvennel
Shandon
Clynder
Rosneath
Rhu
HELENSBURGH
Craigendoran
Cove
Kilcreggan
Rosneath Point
Blairmore
Strone
Gourock
Fort Matilda
Ashton
GREENOCK
Larkfield
Braeside
PORT GLASGOW
Inverkip
Kilmacolm
Quarrier's Village
Bridge of Weir
Houston
Linwood
Johnstone
Elderslie
PAISLEY
RENFREW
Erskine Bridge
Bishopton
Erskine
Inchinnan
CLYDEBANK
Old Kilpatrick
Duntocher
Bowling
DUMBARTON
Renton
Alexandria
Bonhill
Balloch
Jamestown
Cardross
Arden
Luss
Aldochlay
Balmaha
Milton
Drymen
Croftamie
Gartocharn
Killearn
Balfron
Fintry
Strathblane
Blanefield
Milngavie
BEARSDEN
Torrance
Lennoxtown
Milton of Campsie
Kirkintilloch
Lenzie
Bishopbriggs
Stepps
Muirhead
Chryston
Condorrat
Cumbernauld
Kilsyth
Queenzieburn
Banton
Croy
Carron Valley Forest
Coatbridge
Airdrie
Bellshill
Motherwell
Hamilton
Uddingston
Bothwell
Blantyre
Rutherglen
Cambuslang
East Kilbride
Strathaven
Stonehouse
Glassford
Larkhall
Barrhead
Neilston
Newton Mearns
Busby
Clarkston
Giffnock
Eaglesham
Uplawmoor
Lochwinnoch
Kilbirnie
Beith
Dalry
Kilwinning
Stevenston
Saltcoats
Ardrossan
West Kilbride
Fairlie
Largs
Skelmorlie
Stewarton
Dunlop
Fenwick
Kilmaurs
KILMARNOCK
Galston
Newmilns
Darvel
Hurlford
Irvine
Dreghorn
Springside
Dundonald
Troon
Loans
Symington
Barassie
Monkton
Prestwick
Tarbolton
Mauchline
Catrine
Sorn
Muirkirk
Glenbuck
AYR
Alloway
Dalmilling
Annbank
Stair
Coylton
Drongan
Ochiltree
Auchinleck
Cumnock
Lugar
New Cumnock
Kirkconnel
Dalrymple
Maybole
Dunure
Heads of Ayr
Culzean Bay
Maidens
Kirkmichael
Patna
Waterside
Dalmellington
Lady Isle
Horse Isle
Irvine Bay
Whitelee Forest
Kyle Forest
A
B
C
D
E
F
1
2
3
4
5
6
7
8
M8
M73
M74
M77
M80
M898
A8
A70
A71
A76
A77
A78
A719
A736
A737
A760
A761
A81
A809
A811
A814
A82

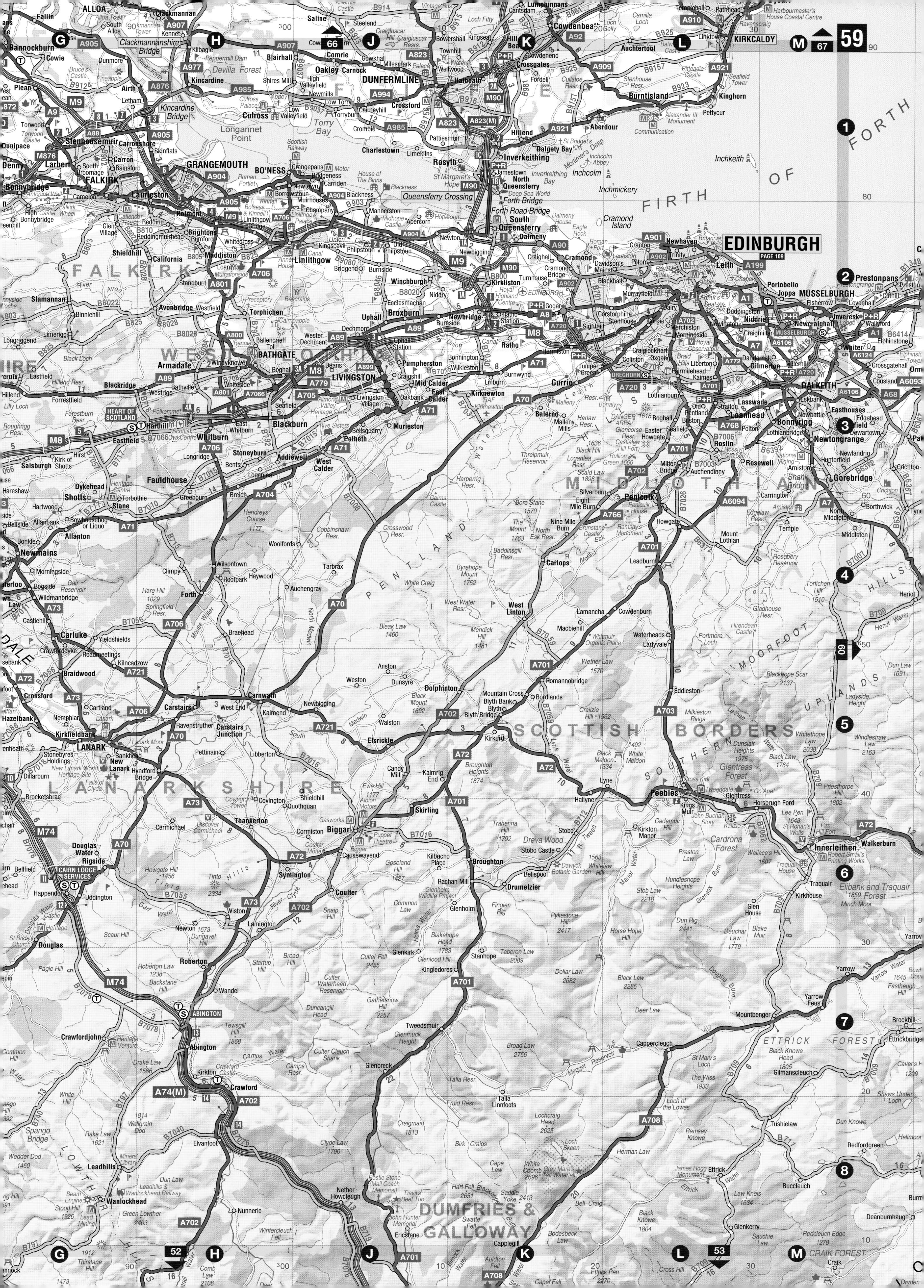
59
66
67
52
53
60
G
H
J
K
L
M
1
2
3
4
5
6
7
8
FIRTH OF FORTH
EDINBURGH
PAGE 109
FALKIRK
WEST LOTHIAN
MIDLOTHIAN
LANARKSHIRE
SCOTTISH BORDERS
DUMFRIES & GALLOWAY
FIFE
PENTLAND HILLS
MOORFOOT HILLS
SOUTHERN UPLANDS
ETTRICK FOREST
CRAIK FOREST
ALLOA
Clackmannan
Bannockburn
Cowie
DUNFERMLINE
KIRKCALDY
Cowdenbeath
Burntisland
Kinghorn
Inverkeithing
Rosyth
GRANGEMOUTH
BO'NESS
FALKIRK
Stenhousemuir
Larbert
Denny
Bonnybridge
Polmont
Linlithgow
Queensferry Crossing
Forth Bridge
Forth Road Bridge
South Queensferry
Kirkliston
Broxburn
Uphall
Livingston
BATHGATE
Armadale
Whitburn
Blackburn
West Calder
Mid Calder
Currie
Balerno
Penicuik
Dalkeith
Bonnyrigg
Newtongrange
Gorebridge
Loanhead
Lasswade
Leith
Portobello
Musselburgh
Prestonpans
Shotts
Newmains
Carluke
LANARK
Carstairs
Carnwath
Biggar
Peebles
Innerleithen
Walkerburn
West Linton
Abington
Crawford
Douglas
Leadhills
Wanlockhead
Tweedsmuir
HEART OF SCOTLAND
CAIRN LODGE SERVICES
ABINGTON
M8
M9
M74
A74(M)
A70
A71
A72
A701
A702
A703
A708
A720

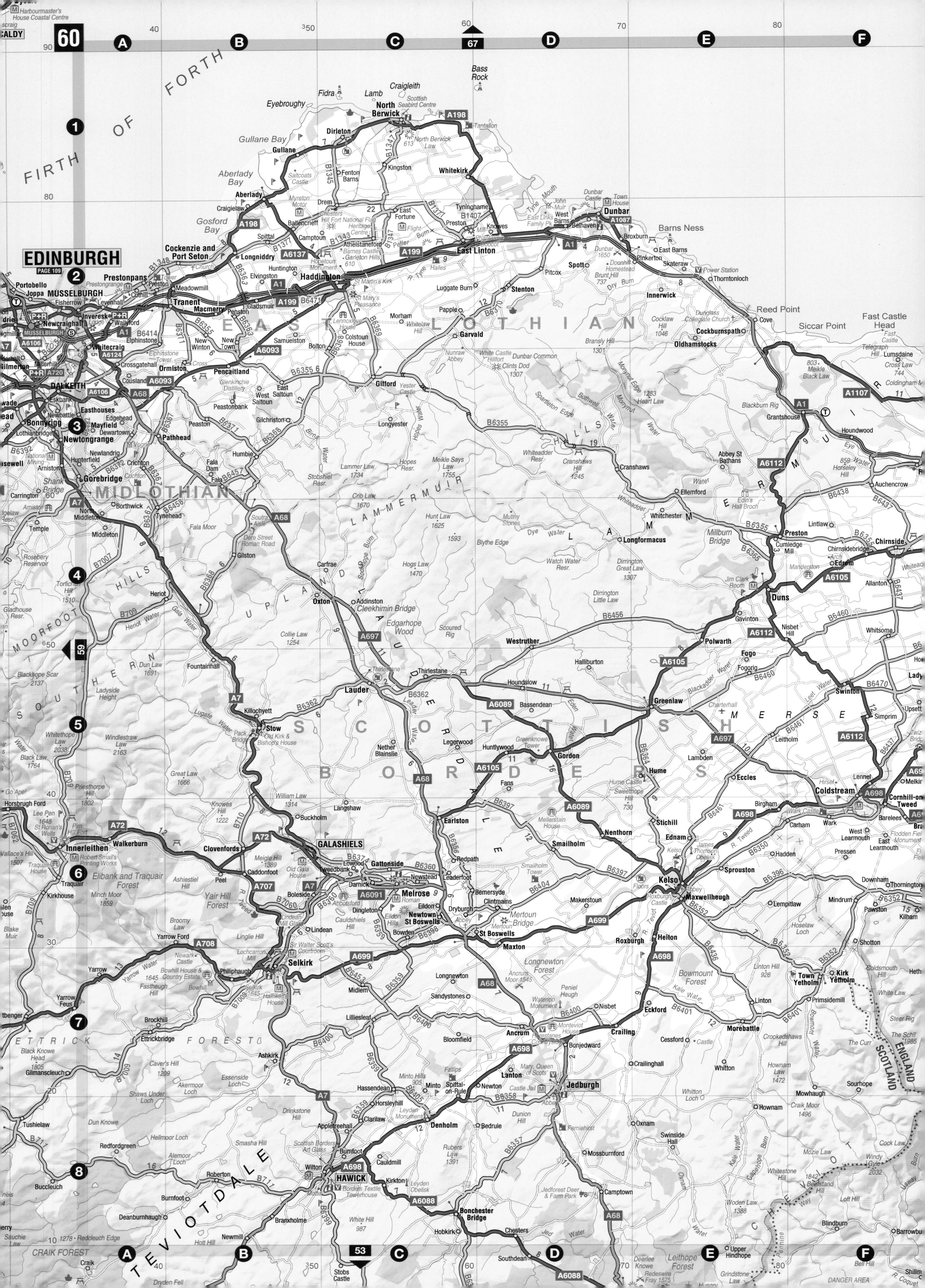
FIRTH OF FORTH
EDINBURGH
PAGE 109
North Berwick
Bass Rock
Fidra
Lamb
Craigleith
Eyebroughy
Tantallon
Dirleton
Gullane Bay
Gullane
North Berwick Law
Kingston
Whitekirk
Fenton Barns
Aberlady Bay
Aberlady
Craigielaw
Gosford Bay
Drem
East Fortune
Tyninghame
Preston
East Linton
Dunbar
Dunbar Castle
Town House
West Barns
Belhaven
Barns Ness
Broxburn
East Barns
Pinkerton
Skateraw
Power Station
Thorntonloch
Cockenzie and Port Seton
Longniddry
Prestonpans
Spittal
Camptoun
Athelstaneford
Haddington
Huntington
Elvington
Portobello
Joppa
MUSSELBURGH
Tranent
Meadowmill
Gladsmuir
Macmerry
Penston
Inveresk
Wallyford
Newcraighall
Whitecraig
Elphinstone
New Winton
New Town
Samuelston
Bolton
Colstoun House
Ormiston
Pencaitland
Crossgatehall
Cousland
DALKEITH
Eskbank
Easthouses
Bonnyrigg
Mayfield
Newtongrange
Dewartown
Pathhead
Peaston
East Saltoun
West Saltoun
Peastonbank
Gilchriston
Gifford
Longyester
Garvald
Stenton
Pitcox
Spott
Luggate Burn
Papple
Morham
Innerwick
Cove
Reed Point
Cockburnspath
Oldhamstocks
Fast Castle Head
Siccar Point
EAST LOTHIAN
LAMMERMUIR HILLS
Humbie
Fala
Fala Dam
Crichton
Gorebridge
Arniston
Hunterfield
Newlandrig
MIDLOTHIAN
Carrington
Borthwick
North Middleton
Middleton
Temple
Tynehead
Gilston
Heriot
Oxton
Carfrae
Addinston
Cleekhimin Bridge
Edgarhope Wood
MOORFOOT HILLS
Fountainhall
Lauder
Thirlestane
Westruther
Houndslow
Bassendean
Cranshaws
Ellemford
Abbey St Bathans
Whitchester
Longformacus
Preston
Cumledge Mill
Chirnside
Chirnsidebridge
Edrom
Allanton
Duns
Gavinton
Nisbet Hill
Whitsome
Polwarth
Fogo
Greenlaw
Swinton
Simprim
Leitholm
Gordon
Legerwood
Hume
Eccles
Coldstream
Cornhill-on-Tweed
Lennel
Birgham
Carham
Wark
Stichill
Ednam
Kelso
Maxwellheugh
Sprouston
Nenthorn
Smailholm
Earlston
Redpath
Leaderfoot
Bemersyde
Clintmains
Makerstoun
Roxburgh
Heiton
St Boswells
Newtown St Boswells
Maxton
Dryburgh
Melrose
Newstead
Gattonside
Darnick
Tweedbank
Lowood
GALASHIELS
Clovenfords
Caddonfoot
Peel
Stow
Killochyett
Innerleithen
Walkerburn
Traquair
Kirkhouse
Selkirk
Philiphaugh
Lindean
Yarrow
Yarrow Feus
Yarrow Ford
Midlem
Lilliesleaf
Longnewton
Sandystones
Ancrum
Nisbet
Crailing
Eckford
Morebattle
Cessford
Linton
Town Yetholm
Kirk Yetholm
Primsidemill
Jedburgh
Lanton
Bonjedward
Crailinghall
Minto
Spittal-on-Rule
Newton
Denholm
Bedrule
Hassendean
Horsleyhill
Clarilaw
Appletreehall
Burnfoot
Wilton
HAWICK
Cauldmill
Kirkton
Bonchester Bridge
Hobkirk
Chesters
Southdean
Camptown
Oxnam
Swinside Hall
Mossburnford
Hownam
Whitton
Ashkirk
Brockhill
Ettrickbridge
ETTRICK FOREST
TEVIOTDALE
Tushielaw
Redfordgreen
Buccleuch
Roberton
Burnfoot
Deanburnhaugh
Branxholme
Newmill
CRAIK FOREST
Craik
Stobs Castle
Upper Hindhope
SCOTLAND
ENGLAND
CHEVIOT
A1
A68
A7
A697
A698
A699
A6105
A6112
A6089
A6088
A6091
A6093
A6137
A199
A198
A1087
A1107
A72
A707
A708
A720
A6106
A6124
59
67
53

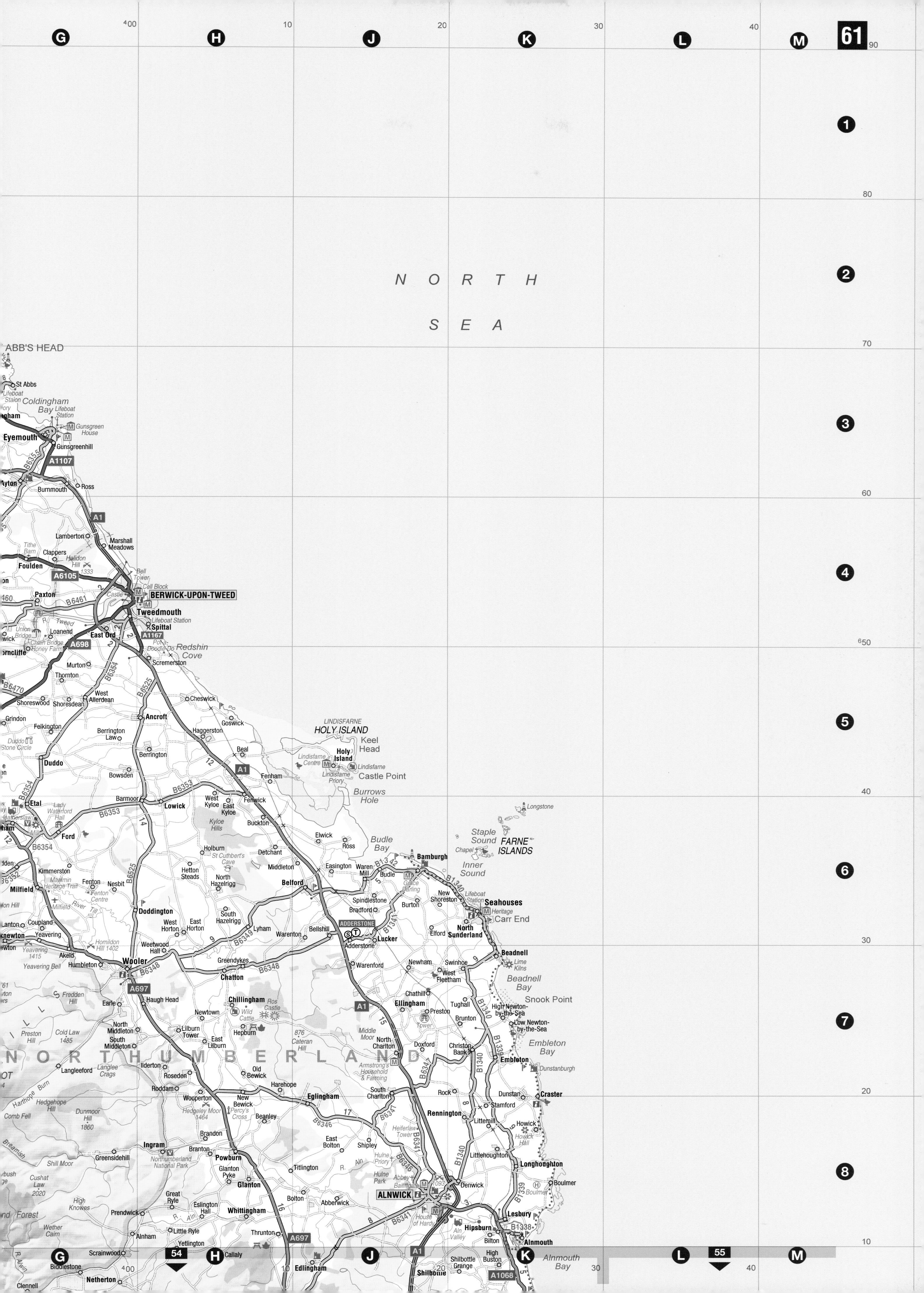

NORTH

SEA

ABB'S HEAD

St Abbs
Lifeboat
Station
Coldingham
Bay Lifeboat
Station
Eyemouth
Gunsgreen
House
Gunsgreenhill

Burnmouth
Ross
Ayton

Lamberton
Marshall
Meadows
Tithe
Barn
Clappers
Halidon
Hill
1333
Foulden
Paxton
Bell
Tower
Cell Block
BERWICK-UPON-TWEED
Tweedmouth
Spittal
Lifeboat Station
Murton
East Ord
Redshin
Thornton
Screnerston
Cove

West
Allerdean
Shoreswood
Shoresdean
Cheswick
Ancroft
Goswick
Grindon
Felkington
Berrington
Law
Haggerston
Duddo
Berrington
Beal
Duddo
Stone Circle
Bowsden
LINDISFARNE
HOLY ISLAND
Keel
Head
Lindisfarne
Fenham
Holy
Island
Lindisfarne
Centre
Etal
Barmoor
West
Kyloe
East
Kyloe
Lindisfarne
Priory
Castle Point
Lady
Waterford
Hall
Lowick
Fenwick
Burrows
Hole
Ford
Buckton
Longstone
Kyloe
Hills
Holburn
Elwick
Budle
Staple
Sound
FARNE
Milfield
Kimmerston
Fenton
Nesbit
St Cuthbert's
Cave
Detchant
Ross
Bay
Chapel
ISLANDS
Heatherslaw
Heritage Trail
Fenton
Centre
Hetton
Steads
North
Hazelrigg
Middleton
Easington
Waren
Mill
Bamburgh
Inner
Sound
Milfield
River Till
Doddington
Belford
Budle
Grace
Darling
Lifeboat
Station
Coupland
West
Horton
East
Horton
South
Hazelrigg
Bradford
Spindlestone
Burton
New
Shoreston
Seahouses
Heritage
Carr End
Yeavering
Akeld
Homildon
Hill 1402
Weetwood
Hall
Lyham
Warenton
ADDERSTONE
Elford
North
Sunderland
Humbleton
Wooler
Greendykes
Lucker
Adderstone
Beadnell
Lime
Kilns
Fredden
Hill
Chatton
Warenford
Newham
Swinhoe
West
Fleetham
Beadnell
Bay
Earle
Haugh Head
Chillingham
Ros
Castle
Wild
Cattle
Chathill
Snook Point
Preston
Hill
Cold Law
1485
North
Middleton
Lilburn
Tower
Newtown
East
Lilburn
Hepburn
Ellingham
Preston
Tughall
High Newton-
by-the-Sea
Low Newton-
by-the-Sea
Langleeford
Langlee
Crags
Ilderton
Roseden
Old
Bewick
876
Cateran
Hill
Middle
Moor
North
Charlton
Doxford
Brunton
Embleton
Bay
Hedgehope
Hill
1860
Dunmoor
Hill
Wooperton
New
Bewick
Harehope
Eglingham
South
Charlton
Rock
Armstrong's
Household
& Farming
Christon
Bank
Stamford
Embleton
Dunstanburgh
Comb Fell
Percy's
Cross
Beanley
Rennington
Littlemill
Howick
Dunstan
Craster
Brandon
Shipley
Heiferlaw
Tower
Howick
Hall
Ingram
Branton
East
Bolton
Howick
Northumberland
National Park
Powburn
Glanton
Pyke
Titlington
Hulne
Priory
Littlehoughton
Longhoughton
Boulmer
Great
Ryle
Glanton
Bolton
Abberwick
Hulne
Park
Abbey
Bailiffgate
ALNWICK
Denwick
Prendwick
Eslington
Hall
Whittingham
Alnham
Little Ryle
Yetlington
Thrunton
House
of Hardy
B1338
Lesbury
Shill Moor
Hipsburn
Bilton
Alnmouth
Cushat
Law
2020
High
Knowes
NORTHUMBERLAND
Scrainwood
Callaly
Edlingham
Shilbottle
Grange
High
Buston
Alnmouth
Bay
Bluddleston
Netherton
Shilbottle
A1068
Clennell

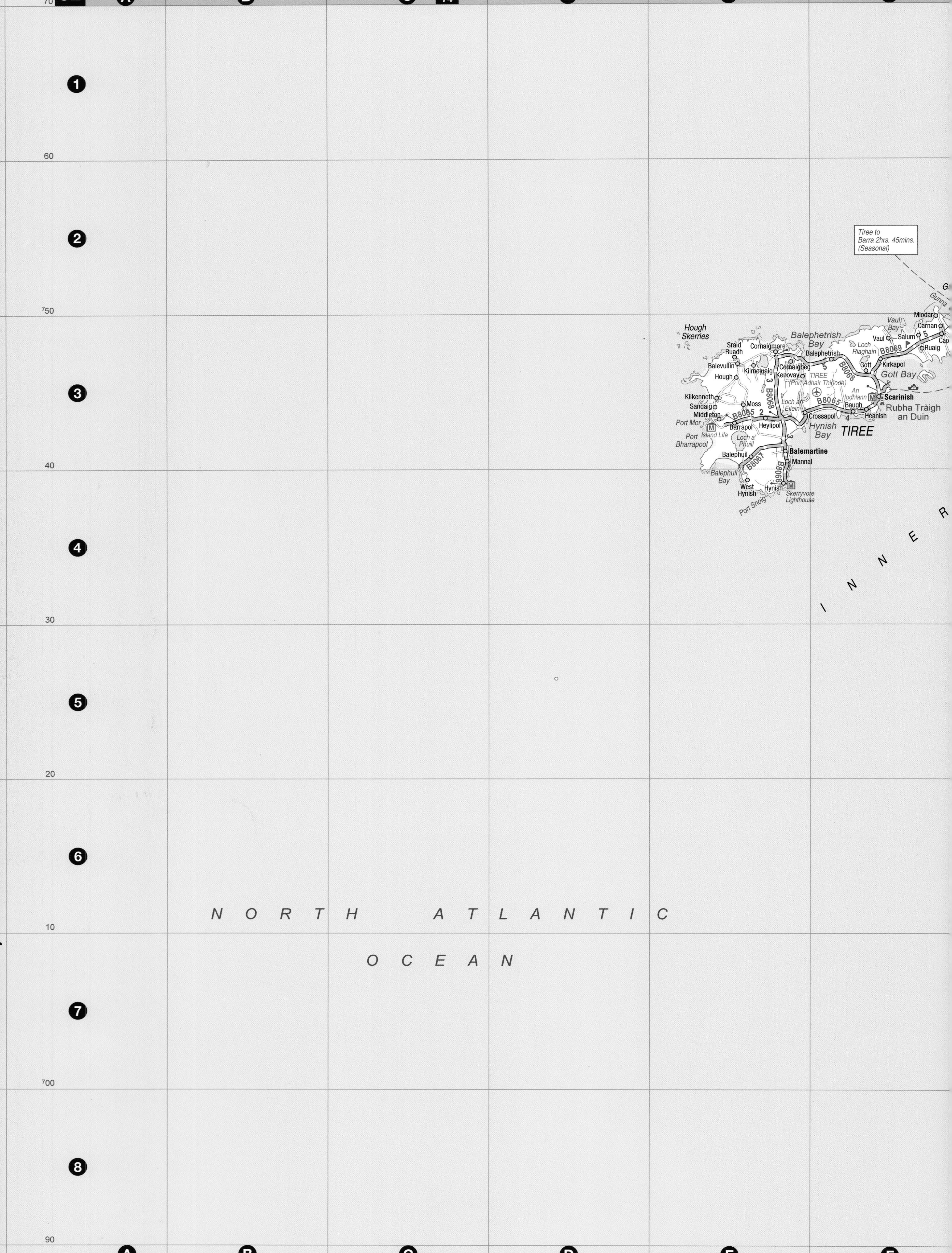

60

2

⁷50

⁷50

Tiree to
Barra 2hrs. 45mins.
(Seasonal)

Gu

40

30

20

10

N O R T H   A T L A N T I C

O C E A N

⁷00

90

**Hough
Skerries**

Sraid
Ruadh   Cornaigmore   *Balephetrish
Bay*
Balevullin   Kilmoluaig   Balephetrish
Cornaigbeg   *Loch
Riaghain*
Hough   Kenovay   5
  TIREE   Gott   Kirkapol
(Port Adhair Thiriodh)   *Gott Bay*
Kilkenneth   *An
Iodhlann*   M   **Scarinish**
Sandaig   *Loch an
Eilein*   Baugh
Middleton   2   *Rubha Tràigh
an Duin*
Port Mor   Barrapol   Crossapol   Heanish
*Port
Bharrapool*   *Island Life*   Heylipol   *Hynish
Bay*
*Loch a'
Phuill*   *TIREE*
Balephuil   **Balemartine**
  Mannal
*Balephuil
Bay*   West   Hynish
Hynish
Port Snoig   *Skerryvore
Lighthouse*

Vaul
Bay   Miodaro
Carnan
Vaul   Salum   5
Cao   Ruaig

B8069

B8068

B8065

B8065

B8068

B8055

B8067

B8066

I N N E R   R

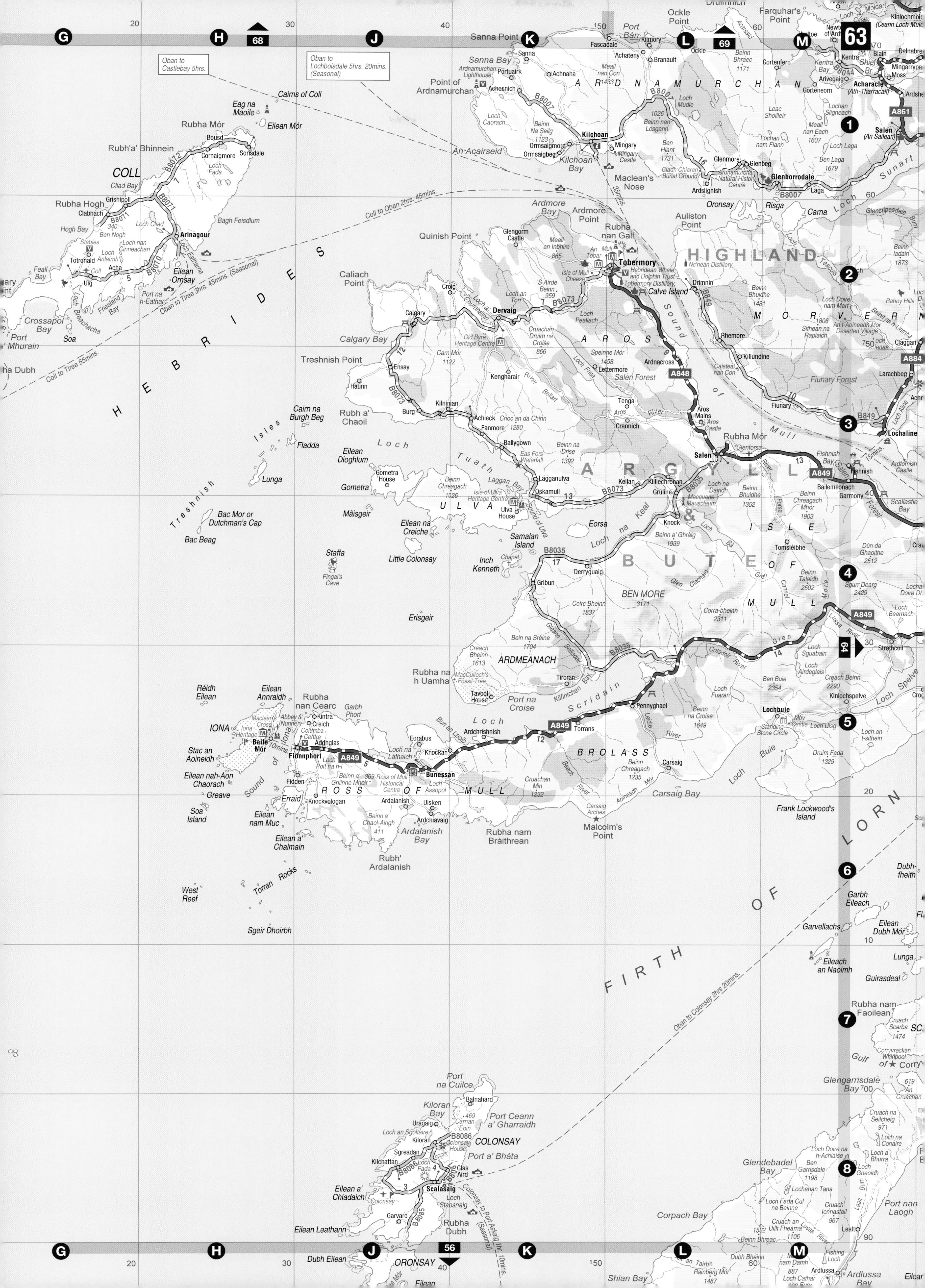

63
G
H
J
K
L
M
68
69
56
64
Oban to Castlebay 5hrs.
Oban to Lochboisdale 5hrs. 20mins. (Seasonal)
Coll to Oban 2hrs. 45mins.
Oban to Tiree 3hrs. 45mins. (Seasonal)
Coll to Tiree 55mins.
Oban to Colonsay 2hrs 20mins.
Colonsay to Port Askaig thr. 10mins. (Seasonal)
Sanna Point
Sanna Bay
Sanna
Portuairk
Achnaha
Achosnich
Point of Ardnamurchan
Ardnamurchan Lighthouse
Fascadale
Port Bàn
Kilmory
Achateny
Branault
Ockle Point
Ockle
Farquhar's Point
Gortenfern
Kentra Bay
Kentra
Arivegaig
Gorteneorn
Acharacle (Àth-Tharracail)
Salen (An Sàilean)
Glenborrodale
Glenmore
Glenbeg
Ardslignish
Laga
Oronsay
Risga
Carna
Loch Sunart
A R D N A M U R C H A N
Kilchoan
Kilchoan Bay
Ormsaigmore
Ormsaigbeg
Mingary
Mingary Castle
Maclean's Nose
An Acairseid
Beinn na Seilg 1123
Loch Caorach
Cairns of Coll
Eag na Maoile
Eilean Mór
Rubha Mór
Rubh'a' Bhinnein
COLL
Cliad Bay
Bousd
Cornaigmore
Sorisdale
Loch Fada
Grishipoll
Rubha Hogh
Clabhach
Hogh Bay
Ben Hogh
Bagh Feisdlum
Arinagour
Loch Eatharna
Eilean Ornsay
Totronald
Acha
Uig
Feall Bay
Crossapol Bay
Port na h-Eathar
Friesland Bay
Loch Breachacha
Soa
Port a' Mhurain
H E B R I D E S
Ardmore Bay
Ardmore Point
Rubha nan Gall
Quinish Point
Glengorm Castle
Tobermory
Hebridean Whale and Dolphin Trust
Tobermory Distillery
Calve Island
Auliston Point
HIGHLAND
Drimnin
M O R V E R N
Rhemore
Killundine
Fiunary
Fiunary Forest
Larachbeg
Lochaline
Caliach Point
Croig
Dervaig
Calgary
Calgary Bay
Treshnish Point
Ensay
Haunn
Burg
Kilninian
Achleck
Fanmore
Ballygown
Eas Fors Waterfall
Lagganulva
Oskamull
Kellan
Killiechronan
Gruline
A R O S
Salen Forest
Sound of Mull
Ardnacross
Aros Mains
Aros Castle
Tenga
Crannich
Salen
Rubha Mór
Fishnish
Fishnish Bay
Bailemeonach
Garmony
A R G Y L L & I S L E O F M U L L
B U T E
Cairn na Burgh Beg
Fladda
Lunga
Treshnish Isles
Rubh a' Chaoil
Loch Tuath
Eilean Dioghlum
Gometra House
Gometra
Màisgeir
U L V A
Ulva House
Sound of Ulva
Eilean na Creiche
Little Colonsay
Staffa
Fingal's Cave
Bac Mor or Dutchman's Cap
Bac Beag
Samalan Island
Eorsa
Loch na Keal
Inch Kenneth
Gribun
Derryguaig
Knock
BEN MORE 3171
Erisgeir
ARDMEANACH
Rubha na h Uamha
Tiroran
Tavool House
Port na Croise
Loch Scridain
Pennyghael
Strathcoil
Kinlochspelve
Loch Spelve
Lochbuie
Loch Buie
Carsaig
Carsaig Bay
Carsaig Arches
Malcolm's Point
B R O L A S S
Réidh Eilean
Eilean Annraidh
Rubha nan Cearc
IONA
Baile Mór
Stac an Aoineidh
Sound of Iona
Fionnphort
Kintra
Creich
Ardtun
Eilean nah-Aon Chaorach
Greave
Soa Island
Fidden
Erraid
Knockvologan
Eilean nam Muc
Eilean a' Chalmain
Bunessan
Ardchrishnish
Eorabus
Knockan
Uisken
Ardchiavaig
Ardalanish
Ardalanish Bay
Rubh' Ardalanish
R O S S O F M U L L
Rubha nam Bràithrean
Torran Rocks
West Reef
Sgeir Dhoirbh
Frank Lockwood's Island
FIRTH OF LORN
Garbh Eileach
Garvellachs
Eilean Dubh Mór
Eileach an Naoimh
Lunga
Rubha nam Faoilean
Gulf of Corryvreckan
Glengarrisdale Bay
Glendebadel Bay
Corpach Bay
Port nan Laogh
Port na Cuilce
Kiloran Bay
Balnahard
Port Ceann a' Gharraidh
COLONSAY
Uragaig
Kiloran
Port a' Bhàta
Kilchattan
Scalasaig
Glas Aird
Eilean a' Chladaich
Garvard
Eilean Leathann
Rubha Dubh
Dubh Eilean
ORONSAY
Shian Bay
A848
A849
A861
A884
B8007
B8072
B8071
B8070
B8073
B8035
B849
B8086
B8085
B8044
1
2
3
4
5
6
7
8

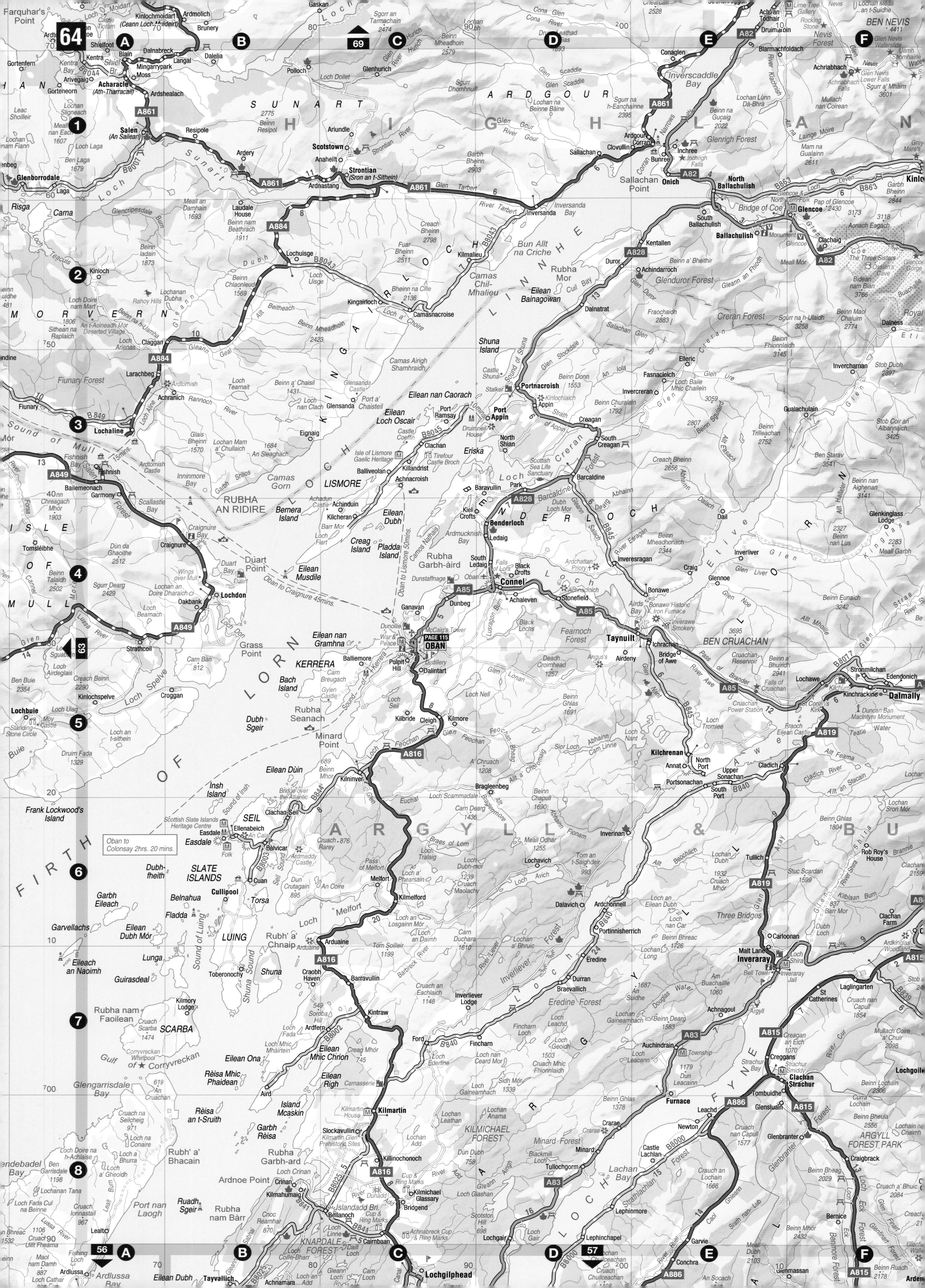
Farquhar's Point
Kinlochmoidart
Ardmolich
Brunery
Shielfoot
Blain
Dalnabreck
Langal
Dalelia
Kentra
Kentra Bay
Mingarrypark
Moss
Arivegaig
Gortenfern
Gorteneorn
Acharacle
(Ath-Tharracail)
Ardshealach
A861
Salen
(An Sailean)
Resipole
Ardery
Glenborrodale
Laga
Loch Sunart
Risga
Carna
S U N A R T
H I G H L A N D
Polloch
Loch Doilet
Glenhurich
Ariundle
Scotstown
Anaheilt
Strontian
(Sron an t-Sithein)
Ardnastang
Glen Tarbert
A R D G O U R
Glen Scaddle
Conaglen
Inverscaddle Bay
Ardgour
Clovullin
Corran
Sallachan
Sallachan Point
Onich
Bunree
Inchree
Glenrigh Forest
A82
North Ballachulish
South Ballachulish
Ballachulish
Bridge of Coe
Glencoe
Clachaig
The Three Sisters
Ossian's Cave
Bidean nam Bian
Aonach Eagach
Pap of Glencoe
BEN NEVIS
Nevis Forest
Achriabhach
Glen Nevis
Kinloch
Laudale House
A884
Lochuisge
B8043
Kilmalieu
Inversanda
Inversanda Bay
River Tarbert
Kentallen
Duror
Achindarroch
Glenduror Forest
Kingairloch
Camasnacroise
Loch a' Choire
Camas Chil-Mhalieu
Rubha Mor
Cuil Bay
Eilean Bainagowan
Dalnatrat
Creran Forest
Kinloch
M O R V E R N
Rahoy Hills
Claggan
Larachbeg
Ardtornish
Achranich
Fiunary Forest
Fiunary
B849
Lochaline
Sound of Mull
Fishnish
Fishnish Bay
A849
Bailemeonach
Garmony
Scallastle Bay
ISLE OF MULL
Craignure
Craignure Bay
Duart Bay
Duart Point
Lochdon
Oakbank
Strathcoil
Lussa River
Glensanda
Glensanda Castle
Port a' Chaisteil
Eignaig
Camas Gorn
RUBHA AN RIDIRE
Innimore Bay
LOCH LINNHE
Eilean nan Caorach
Shuna Island
Eilean Loch Oscair
Port Ramsay
Castle Coeffin
Clachan
Balliveolan
Killandrist
Achnacroish
LISMORE
Achinduin
Kilcheran
Bernera Island
Eilean Dubh
Creag Island
Pladda Island
Eilean Musdile
Port Appin
North Shian
Eriska
Portnacroish
Castle Stalker
Appin
Strath of Appin
Creagan
South Creagan
Barcaldine
A828
Baravullin
Benderloch
Ledaig
South Ledaig
Connel
Black Crofts
Achaleven
Stonefield
A85
Dunstaffnage
Dunbeg
Ganavan
Dunollie
OBAN
PAGE 115
Pulpit Hill
Dalintart
KERRERA
Balliemore
Gylen Castle
Bach Island
Rubha Seanach
Dubh Sgeir
Minard Point
Grass Point
Carn Bàn
Croggan
Loch Spelve
Lochbuie
Kinlochspelve
Loch Uisg
FIRTH OF LORN
Oban to Craignure 45mins.
Oban to Lismore 50mins.
Kilbride
Cleigh
Kilmore
Glen Feochan
Loch Nell
Loch Feochan
A816
Kilninver
Eilean Dùin
Insh Island
SEIL
Clachan-Seil
Ellenabeich
Easdale
Balvicar
B8003
Cuan
Oban to Colonsay 2hrs. 20 mins.
Frank Lockwood's Island
Dubh-fheith
SLATE ISLANDS
Cullipool
Belnahua
Fladda
Torsa
LUING
Garbh Eileach
Garvellachs
Eilean Dubh Mór
Eileach an Naoimh
Lunga
Guirasdeal
Toberonochy
Shuna
Kilmory Lodge
Rubha nam Faoilean
SCARBA
Gulf of Corryvreckan
Glengarrisdale Bay
Melfort
Kilmelford
Loch Melfort
Pass of Melfort
Arduaine
Rubh' a' Chnaip
Craobh Haven
Barravullin
Kintraw
Ardfern
B8002
Eilean Righ
Eilean Mhic Chrion
Eilean Ona
Rèisa Mhic Phaidean
Rèisa an t-Sruith
Aird
Island Macaskin
Garbh Rèisa
Rubh' a' Bhacain
Rubha Garbh-ard
Ardnoe Point
Crinan
Kilmahumaig
Bellanoch
Islandadd Bri.
Rubha nam Bàrr
Ruadh Sgeir
Port nan Laogh
KNAPDALE FOREST
Cairnbaan
Lochgilphead
Tayvallich
Eilean Dubh
Ardlussa
Lealt
Kilmartin
Slockavullin
Killinochonoch
Kilmichael Glassary
Bridgend
Ford
Fincharn
B840
Carnasserie
KILMICHAEL FOREST
Minard Forest
Minard
Tullochgorm
Lochgair
Loch Gair
Lachan Bay
A83
A R G Y L L & B U T E
Braes of Lorn
Loch Scammadale
Bragleenbeg
Lochavich
Loch Avich
Dalavich
Ardchonnell
Portinnisherrich
Eredine
Eredine Forest
Inverliever Forest
Durran
Braevallich
Inverliever Lodge
Kilchrenan
Annat
North Port
Portsonachan
South Port
Inverinan
LOCH AWE
Taynuilt
Airdeny
Ichrachan
Bridge of Awe
Pass of Brander
BEN CRUACHAN
Cruachan Reservoir
Lochawe
Kilchurn
Kinchrackine
Dalmally
Stronmilchan
Edendonich
A819
Cladich
Tullich
Carloonan
Malt Land
Inveraray
Inveraray Jail
Three Bridges
Rob Roy's House
Clachan Farm
A815
St Catherines
Laglingarten
Achnagoul
Auchindrain
Furnace
Leachd
Newton
Crarae
Castle Lachlan
Lephinmore
Lephinchapel
Garvie
Conchra
Creggans
Strachur Bay
Clachan Strachur
Tombuidhe
Glenbranter
A886
ARGYLL FOREST PARK
Craigbrack
Bernice
Lochgoilhead
Glenmassan
Bonawe
Inveresragan
Glennoe
Craig
Glen Etive
Inverliever
Dail
Elleric
Fasnacloich
Invercreran
Glen Creran
Gualachulain
Glenkinglass Lodge
Invercharnan
Dalness
Ardchattan Priory
Fearnoch Forest
Black Lochs
Dubh Loch Mór
B845
Loch Creran
Loch Etive
Falls of Lora
Benderloch
56
57
63
69

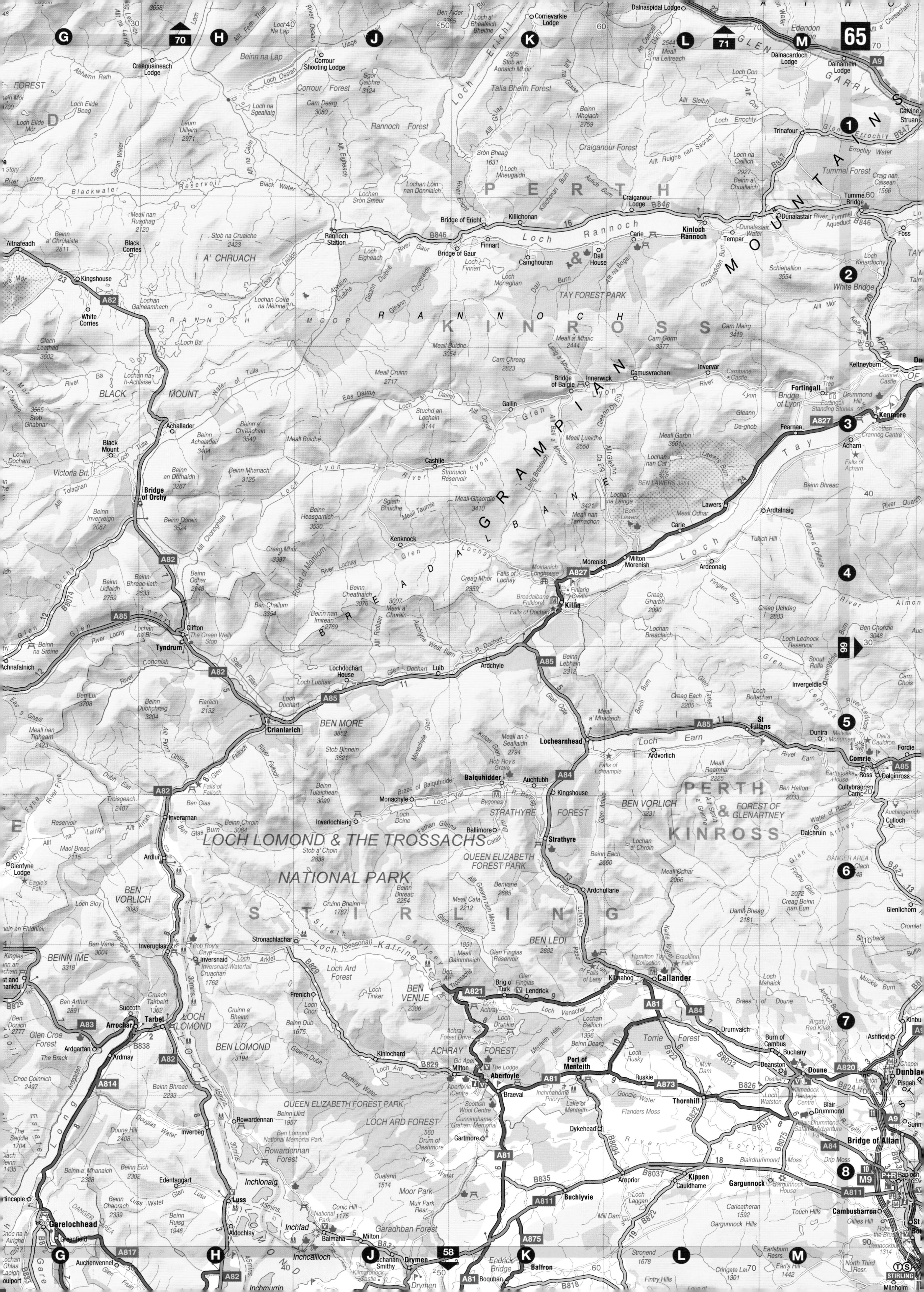
PERTH
KINROSS
GRAMPIAN
MOUNTAINS
RANNOCH
MOOR
BREADALBANE
LOCH LOMOND & THE TROSSACHS
NATIONAL PARK
STIRLING
PERTH & KINROSS
Corrour Shooting Lodge
Corrour Forest
Rannoch Forest
Talla Bheith Forest
Craiganour Forest
Loch Rannoch
Rannoch Station
Bridge of Gaur
Bridge of Ericht
Killichonan
Kinloch Rannoch
Dunalastair Water
Tummel Bridge
Trinafour
Dalnaspidal Lodge
Dalnacardoch Lodge
Schiehallion 3554
TAY FOREST PARK
White Bridge
Kingshouse
White Corries
Loch Ba'
BLACK MOUNT
Achallader
Bridge of Orchy
Tyndrum
Clifton
Crianlarich
Fortingall
Kenmore
Fearnan
Loch Tay
BEN LAWERS 3984
Lawers
Carie
Milton Morenish
Ardtalnaig
Ardeonaig
Killin
Glen Lochay
Glen Dochart
Luib
Ardchyle
Lochearnhead
Loch Earn
St Fillans
Comrie
Balquhidder
Kingshouse
Strathyre
BEN VORLICH
BEN MORE 3852
Stob Binnein 3821
Ardlui
Inverarnan
Inveruglas
Inversnaid
Loch Katrine
Stronachlachar
BEN VENUE
BEN LEDI 2882
Callander
Kilmahog
Loch Venachar
Brig o' Turk
Aberfoyle
Port of Menteith
Thornhill
Doune
Dunblane
Bridge of Allan
Kippen
Gargunnock
Cambusbarron
STIRLING
Buchlyvie
Balfron
Drymen
Balmaha
Luss
Tarbet
Arrochar
Succoth
Ardgartan
BEN LOMOND
Rowardennan
Inverbeg
Garelochhead
Gartmore
QUEEN ELIZABETH FOREST PARK
LOCH ARD FOREST
A82
A85
A84
A81
A821
A827
A811
A873
A9
B846
M9
Inchcailloch
Inchmurrin

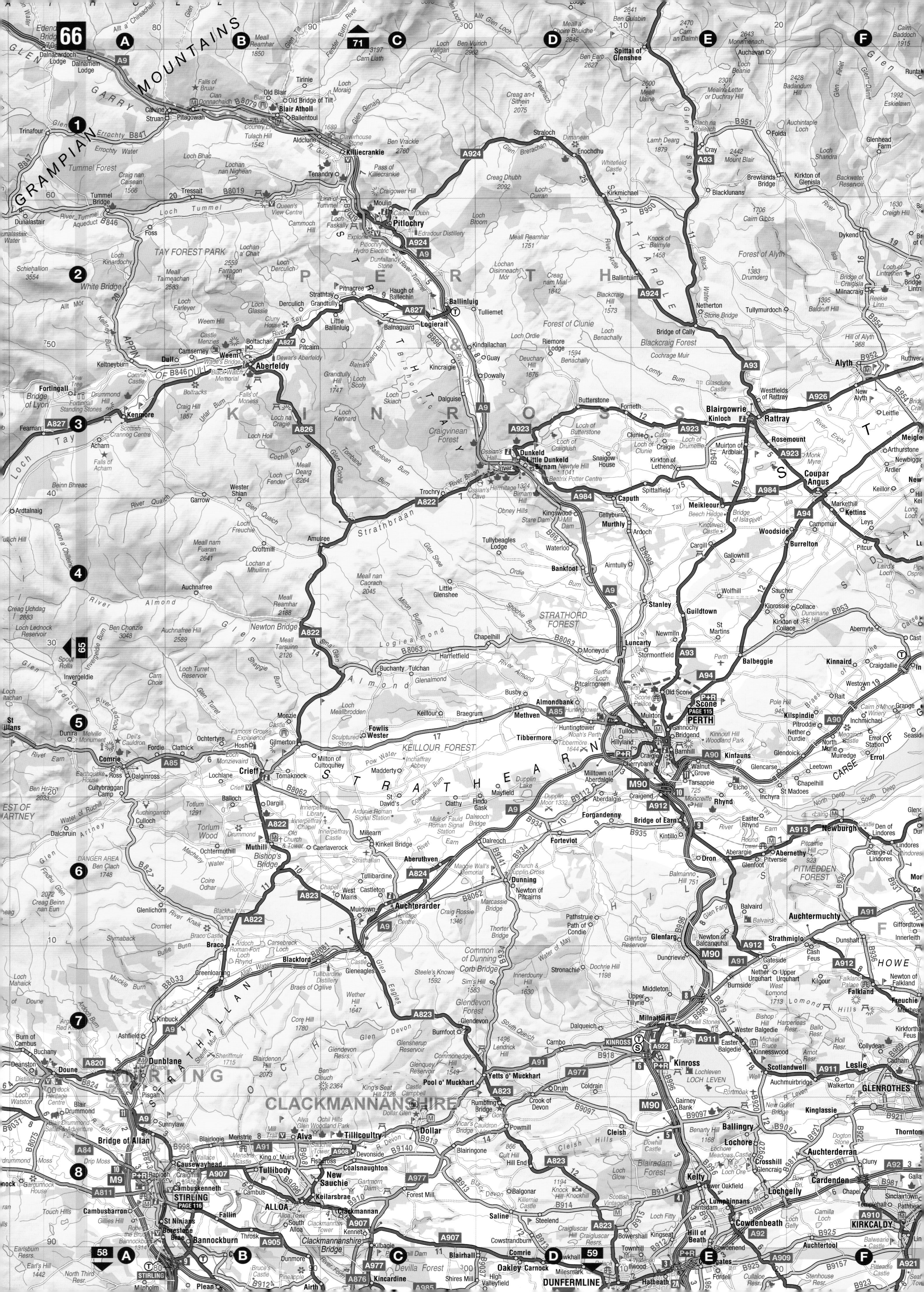
66
71
65
58
59
PAGE 115
PAGE 116
GRAMPIAN MOUNTAINS
PERTH & KINROSS
STIRLING
CLACKMANNANSHIRE
STRATHEARN
STRATHALLAN
TAY FOREST PARK
Blair Atholl
Killiecrankie
Pitlochry
Ballinluig
Logierait
Aberfeldy
Kenmore
Dunkeld
Little Dunkeld
Birnam
Blairgowrie
Rattray
Coupar Angus
Alyth
Spittal of Glenshee
Bridge of Cally
Meikleour
Caputh
Murthly
Bankfoot
Stanley
Luncarty
Guildtown
Balbeggie
Scone
PERTH
Almondbank
Methven
Tibbermore
Crieff
Comrie
Muthill
Auchterarder
Blackford
Dunblane
Doune
Bridge of Allan
STIRLING
Bannockburn
Alloa
Tullibody
Alva
Tillicoultry
Dollar
Yetts o' Muckhart
Pool o' Muckhart
Kinross
Milnathort
Glenfarg
Bridge of Earn
Abernethy
Newburgh
Auchtermuchty
Strathmiglo
Falkland
Leslie
GLENROTHES
Kinglassie
Ballingry
Lochore
Kelty
Lochgelly
Cardenden
Cowdenbeath
Auchterderran
KIRKCALDY
DUNFERMLINE
Kincardine
Oakley
Carnock
Saline
Clackmannan
New Sauchie
Kinnaird
Errol
Kinfauns
Glencarse
Rhynd
Forgandenny
Dunning
Forteviot
Aberuthven
Kettins
Woodside
Burrelton
Kirkton of Glenisla
A9
A93
A94
A85
A822
A823
A824
A826
A827
A923
A924
A926
A984
A90
A91
A92
A911
A912
A913
A907
A908
A977
A820
A811
A84
A905
M9
M90

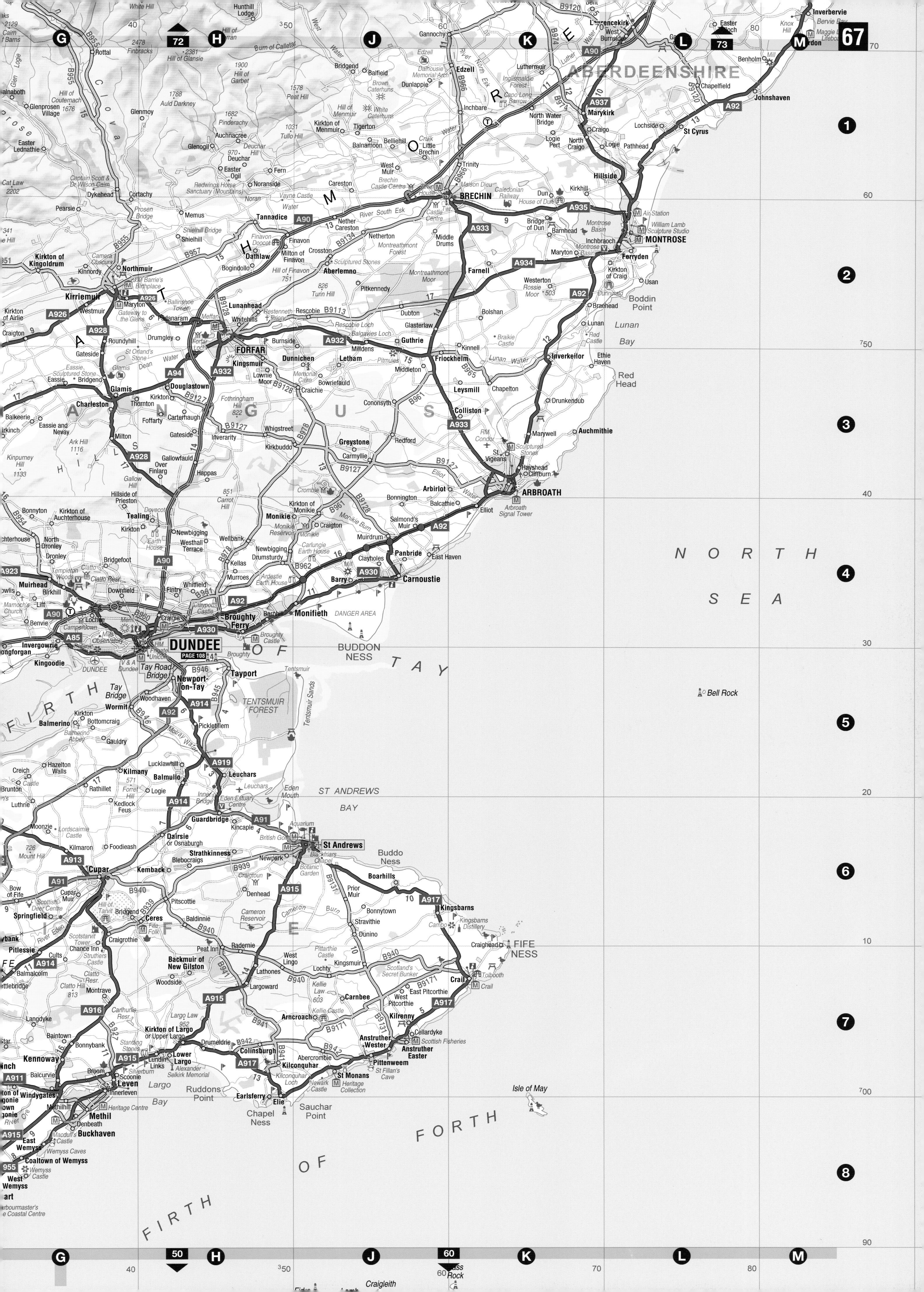
ABERDEENSHIRE
ANGUS
FIFE
NORTH SEA
FIRTH OF TAY
FIRTH OF FORTH
ST ANDREWS BAY
Lunan Bay
Largo Bay
Inverbervie
Gourdon
Johnshaven
St Cyrus
Marykirk
Laurencekirk
Edzell
Brechin
Montrose
Ferryden
Kirriemuir
Forfar
Glamis
Letham
Friockheim
Inverkeilor
Arbroath
Carnoustie
Monifieth
Broughty Ferry
DUNDEE
PAGE 108
Tayport
Newport-on-Tay
Leuchars
Guardbridge
St Andrews
Cupar
Kingsbarns
FIFE NESS
Crail
Anstruther Wester
Anstruther Easter
Pittenweem
St Monans
Elie
Kilconquhar
Colinsburgh
Lower Largo
Leven
Methil
Buckhaven
Kennoway
BUDDON NESS
TENTSMUIR FOREST
Bell Rock
Isle of May
Red Head
Boddin Point
Buddo Ness
Ruddons Point
Chapel Ness
Sauchar Point
Tay Road Bridge
Tay Bridge
A90
A92
A94
A91
A915
A917
A933
A934
A935
A937
A914
A916
A919
A926
A928
A930
A932
72
73
50
60
G
H
J
K
L
M
1
2
3
4
5
6
7
8

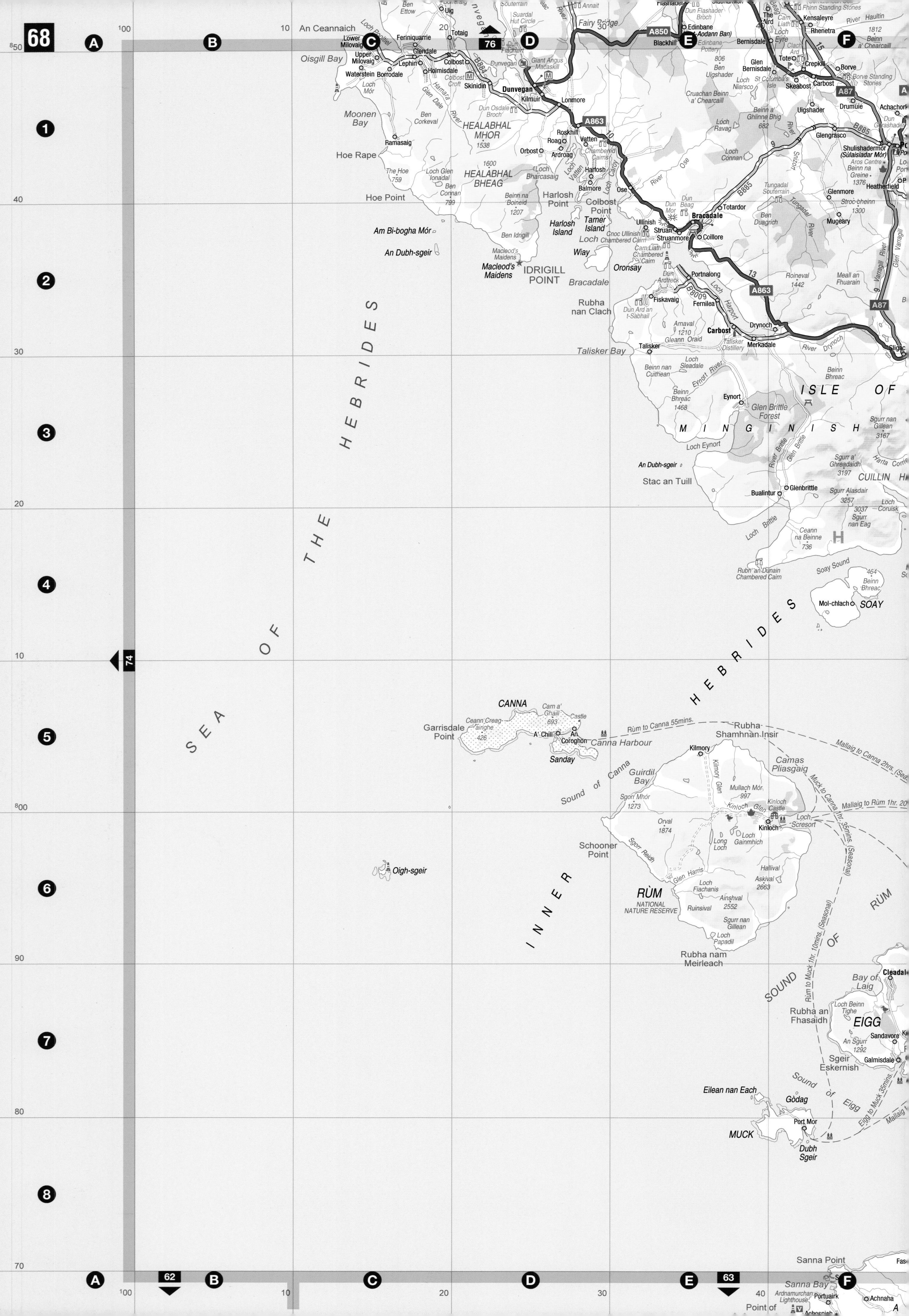

SEA OF THE HEBRIDES
INNER HEBRIDES
ISLE OF
MINGINISH
An Ceannaich
Loch Pooltiel
Lower Milovaig
Upper Milovaig
Feriniquarrie
Glendale
Totaig
Oisgill Bay
Waterstein
Borrodale
Lephin
Holmisdale
Colbost
Skinidin
Dunvegan
Kilmuir
Lonmore
Moonen Bay
Ben Corkeval
HEALABHAL MHOR
1538
HEALABHAL BHEAG
1600
Ramasaig
Hoe Rape
The Hoe
759
Hoe Point
Am Bi-bogha Mór
An Dubh-sgeir
Macleod's Maidens
IDRIGILL POINT
Orbost
Roskhill
Roag
Ardroag
Vatten
Harlosh
Balmore
Harlosh Point
Harlosh Island
Tarner Island
Colbost Point
Wiay
Oronsay
Bracadale
Rubha nan Clach
Ullinish
Struan
Struanmore
Coillore
Portnalong
Fiskavaig
Fernilea
Carbost
Drynoch
Talisker
Talisker Bay
Merkadale
Eynort
Glen Brittle Forest
Loch Eynort
An Dubh-sgeir
Stac an Tuill
Bualintur
Glenbrittle
Loch Brittle
Rubh' an Dùnain Chambered Cairn
Soay Sound
Mol-chlach
SOAY
CUILLIN HILLS
Sgurr nan Gillean
3167
Sgurr Alasdair
3257
Fairy Bridge
Edinbane
Blackhill
Bernisdale
Kensaleyre
Rhenetra
Tote
Crepkill
Skeabost
Carbost
Borve
Uigshader
Drumuie
Achachork
Glengrasco
Shulishadermor
Heatherfield
Glenmore
Mugeary
Totardor
Bracadale
A863
A850
A87
B885
B884
CANNA
Garrisdale Point
A' Chill
An Coroghon
Sanday
Canna Harbour
Rùm to Canna 55mins.
Rubha Shamhnan Insir
Sound of Canna
Kilmory
Guirdil Bay
Camas Pliasgaig
Mullach Mór
997
Kinloch
Kinloch Castle
Loch Scresort
Orval
1874
Schooner Point
Sgorr Reidh
Glen Harris
Loch Fiachanis
Hallival
Askival
2663
Ainshval
2552
RÙM
NATIONAL NATURE RESERVE
Ruinsival
Sgurr nan Gillean
Loch Papadil
Rubha nam Meirleach
Mallaig to Rùm 1hr. 20
Muck to Canna 1hr. 35mins. (Seasonal)
Rùm to Muck 1hr. 10mins. (Seasonal)
Oigh-sgeir
SOUND OF RÙM
Bay of Laig
Cleadale
Rubha an Fhasaidh
EIGG
An Sgurr
1292
Sandavore
Galmisdale
Sgeir Eskernish
Sound of Eigg
Eilean nan Each
Gòdag
Port Mor
MUCK
Dubh Sgeir
Sanna Point
Sanna Bay
Portuairk
Achnaha

76
74
62
63

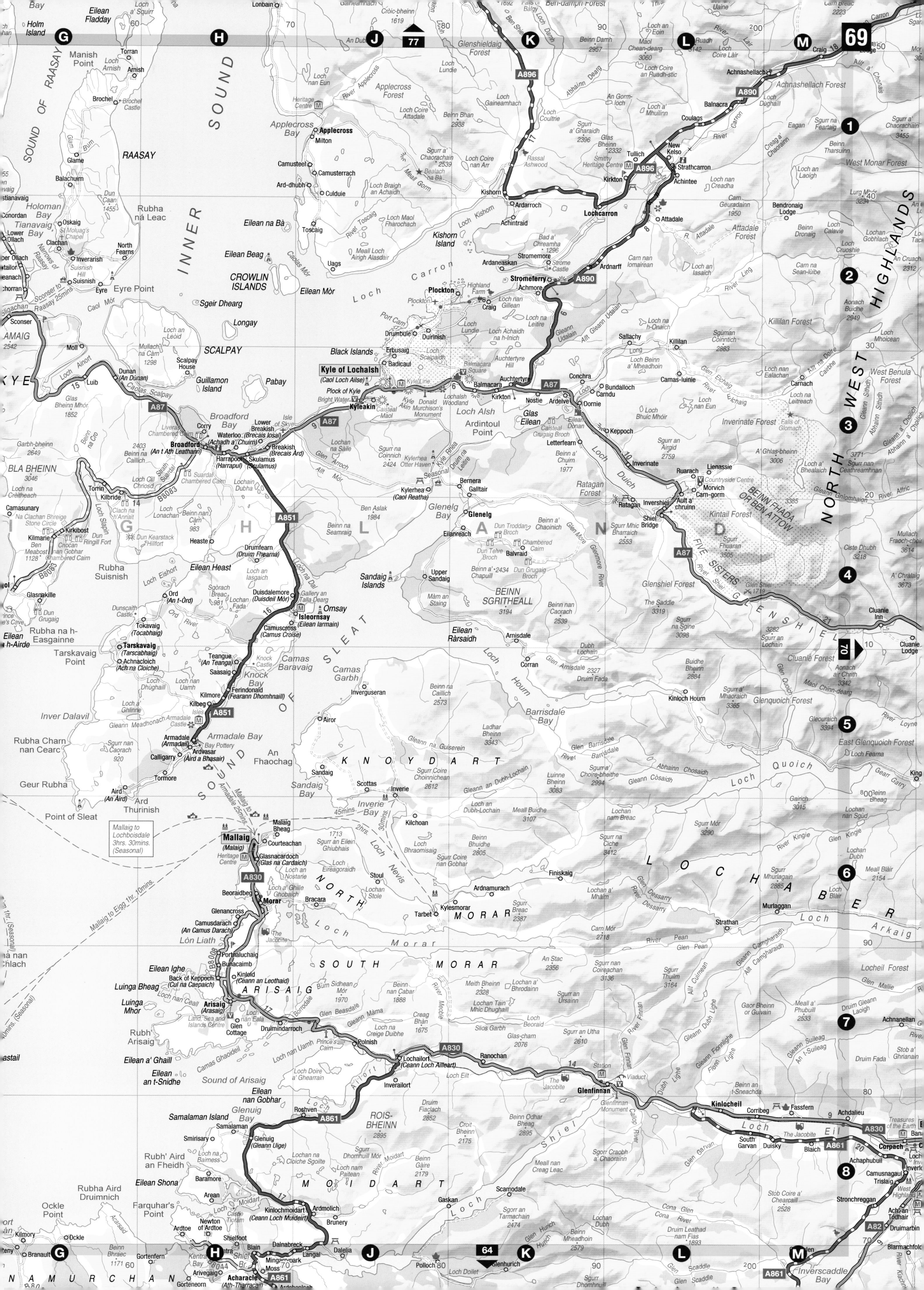
77
64
70
SOUND OF RAASAY
INNER SOUND
RAASAY
Holm Island
Eilean Fladday
Manish Point
Brochel
Applecross
Applecross Bay
Applecross Forest
Glenshieldaig Forest
Achnashellach Forest
Achnashellach
Balnacra
Coulags
New Kelso
Strathcarron
Tullich
Kirkton
Achintee
Kishorn
Ardarroch
Lochcarron
Attadale
Attadale Forest
West Monar Forest
Bendronaig Lodge
Kishorn Island
Loch Carron
Stromeferry
Achmore
Plockton
Craig
Duirinish
Drumbuie
Erbusaig
Badicaul
Black Islands
Kyle of Lochalsh
(Caol Loch Ailse)
Plock of Kyle
Kyleakin
Balmacara
Auchtertyre
Kirkton
Nostie
Ardelve
Dornie
Eilean Donan
Conchra
Bundalloch
Carndu
Sallachy
Killilan
Camas-luinie
Killilan Forest
Inverinate Forest
West Benula Forest
Carnach
Falls of Glomach
NORTH WEST HIGHLANDS
Loch Alsh
Ardintoul Point
Glas Eilean
Keppoch
Letterfearn
Inverinate
Loch Duich
Ratagan Forest
Ratagan
Ruarach
Morvich
Carn-gorm
Lienassie
Inverhiel
Ault a' chruinn
Shiel Bridge
Kintail Forest
BEINN FHADA OR BEN ATTOW
FIVE SISTERS
Glenshiel Forest
GLEN SHIEL
Cluanie Inn
Cluanie Lodge
Cluanie Forest
Eilean na Bà
Eilean Beag
CROWLIN ISLANDS
Eilean Mòr
Sgeir Dhearg
Longay
SCALPAY
Scalpay House
Guillamon Island
Pabay
Broadford
Broadford Bay
Corry
Waterloo
Lower Breakish
Breakish
Harrapool
Skulamus
Luib
Dunan
Moll
Sconser
Loch Ainort
Caolas Scalpay
BLA BHEINN
Torrin
Kilbride
Camasunary
Kilmarie
Kirkibost
Heaste
Rubha Suisnish
Eilean Heast
Ord
Tokavaig
Tarskavaig
Tarskavaig Point
Achnacloich
Inver Dalavil
Rubha Chàrn nan Cearc
Geur Rubha
Point of Sleat
Aird
Ard Thurinish
Calligarry
Tormore
Ardvasar
Armadale
Armadale Bay
Kilmore
Kilbeg
Ferindonald
Saasaig
Teangue
Knock Bay
Camuscross
Isleornsay
Ornsay
Duisdalemore
Drumfearn
Kylerhea
Glenelg Bay
Glenelg
Bernera
Galltair
Eilanreach
Balvraid
Upper Sandaig
Sandaig Islands
BEINN SGRITHEALL
Eilean Ràrsaidh
Arnisdale
Corran
Loch Hourn
Kinloch Hourn
Barrisdale Bay
Glenquoich Forest
East Glenquoich Forest
Loch Quoich
SOUND OF SLEAT
Camas Baravaig
Camas Garbh
Inverguseran
Airor
An Fhaochag
KNOYDART
Sandaig
Sandaig Bay
Scottas
Inverie
Inverie Bay
Kilchoan
Loch Nevis
Mallaig
Mallaig Bheag
Courteachan
Glasnacardoch
Mallaig to Lochboisdale 3hrs. 30mins. (Seasonal)
Mallaig to Armadale 25mins.
Mallaig to Eigg 1hr. 10mins.
Beoraidbeg
Morar
Bracara
Stoul
Tarbet
Kylesmorar
NORTH MORAR
Ardnamurach
Finiskaig
LOCHABER
Strathan
Loch Arkaig
Murlaggan
Locheil Forest
Glencancross
Camusdarach
Lòn Liath
Portnaluchaig
Bunacaimb
Eilean Ighe
Back of Keppoch
Kinloid
Luinga Bheag
Luinga Mhor
Arisaig
ARISAIG
Rubh' Arisaig
SOUTH MORAR
Loch Morar
Drumindarroch
Polnish
Lochailort
Inverailort
Ranochan
Glenfinnan
Kinlocheil
Corribeg
Fassfern
Achdalieu
Loch Eil
South Garvan
Duisky
Blaich
Corpach
Achaphubuil
Camusnagaul
Trislaig
Stronchreggan
Achnanellan
Eilean a' Ghaill
Eilean an t-Snidhe
Sound of Arisaig
Eilean nan Gobhar
Glenuig Bay
Samalaman Island
Samalaman
Roshven
Smirisary
Glenuig
Rubh' Aird an Fheidh
ROIS-BHEINN
Eilean Shona
Rubha Aird Druimnich
Farquhar's Point
Ockle Point
Ockle
Kilmory
Branault
Ardtoe
Newton of Ardtoe
Shielfoot
Arevegaig
Acharacle
Blain
Mingarrypark
Moss
Dalnabreck
Langal
Dalelia
Polloch
Glenhurich
Loch Shiel
Kinlochmoidart
Ardmolich
Brunery
Gaskan
Scamodale
MOIDART
Inverscaddle Bay
Blarmachfoldach
Druimarbin
Achintodhair
A87
A851
A830
A861
A890
A896
A82
B8083
B8008

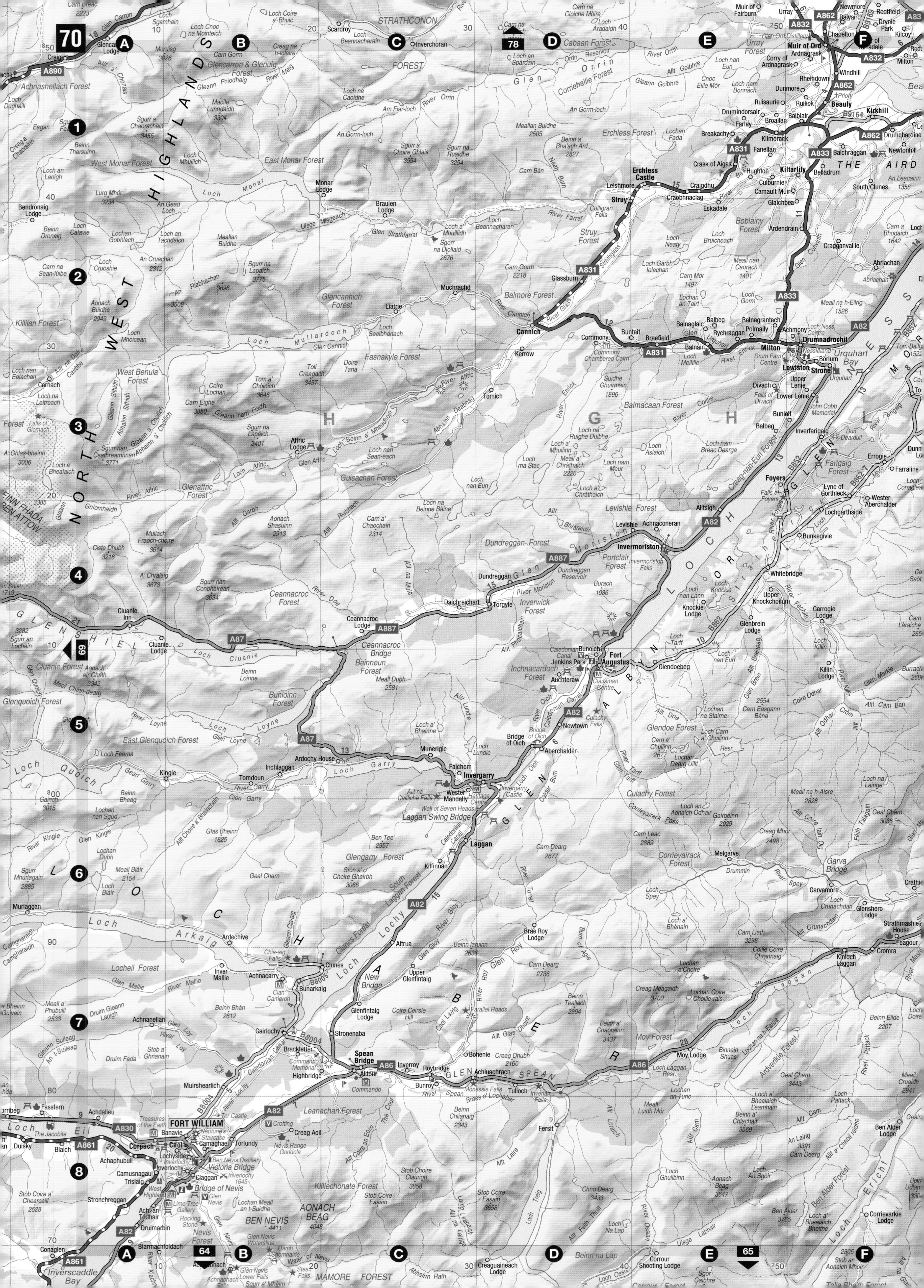
NORTH WEST HIGHLANDS
STRATHCONON
FOREST
Glen Carron
Glencarron Lodge
Craig
Achnashellach Forest
A890
Loch Sgamhain
Moruisg 3026
Carn Gorm
Glencarron & Glenuig Forest
River Meig
Scardroy
Loch Beannacharain
Inverchoran
Cabaan Forest
Orrin Reservoir
Corriehallie Forest
Glen Orrin
Urray Forest
Muir of Ord
A832
A862
Beauly
Kirkhill
Kilmorack
Kiltarlity
Belladrum
THE AIRD
A833
A831
Erchless Castle
Struy
Struy Forest
River Farrar
Glen Strathfarrar
Monar Lodge
Loch Monar
Braulen Lodge
West Monar Forest
East Monar Forest
Sgurr a' Choire Ghlais 3554
Sgurr na Ruaidhe 3254
Erchless Forest
Boblainy Forest
Sgurr na Lapaich 3775
Riabhachan 3696
Glencannich Forest
Muchrachd
Liatrie
Loch Mullardoch
Glen Cannich
Cannich
Balmore Forest
Glassburn
Strathglass
River Glass
Corrimony
Buntait
Braefield
Balnain
Glen Urquhart
Milton
Drumnadrochit
Urquhart Bay
Lewiston
Strone
A82
Fasnakyle Forest
Toll Creagach 3457
Tomich
West Benula Forest
Carn Eighe 3880
Gleann nam Fiadh
Affric Lodge
Loch Affric
Loch Beinn a' Mheadhoin
Guisachan Forest
Glenaffric Forest
Balmacaan Forest
Levishie Forest
Sgurr nan Ceathreamhnan 3771
Falls of Glomach
Killilan Forest
Carnach
Loch Ness
Foyers
Inverfarigaig
Creag-nan-Eun Forest
Glen Moriston
Invermoriston
Dundreggan Forest
A887
Dundreggan
Portclair Forest
Inverwick Forest
Torgyle
Dalchreichart
Ceannacroc Lodge
Ceannacroc Forest
Ceannacroc Bridge
Beinneun Forest
Glen Shiel
Cluanie Inn
Cluanie Lodge
Loch Cluanie
A87
Cluanie Forest
Glenquoich Forest
Loch Quoich
Loch Loyne
East Glenquoich Forest
Bunloinn Forest
Inchnacardoch Forest
Fort Augustus
Jenkins Park
Auchteraw
Glendoebeg
Whitebridge
Knockie Lodge
Glenbrein Lodge
Garrogie Lodge
Stratherrick
Loch Tarff
Glendoe Forest
Bridge of Oich
Aberchalder
Newtown
Culachy Forest
Corrieyairack Pass
Invergarry
Ardochy House
Tomdoun
Kingie
Glen Garry
Loch Garry
Inchlaggan
Munerigie
Faichem
Wester Mandally
Laggan Swing Bridge
Laggan
Glengarry Forest
Kilfinnan
Corrieyairack Forest
Melgarve
Garva Bridge
Garvamore
Glenshero Lodge
Strathmashie House
Kinloch Laggan
Loch Laggan
Moy Forest
Moy Lodge
Loch Lochy
South Laggan Forest
Clunes Forest
Altrua
Loch Arkaig
Ardechive
Murlaggan
Locheil Forest
Clunes
Achnacarry
Bunarkaig
Glen Gloy
Upper Glenfintaig
Glen Roy
Brae Roy Lodge
Parallel Roads
Glenfintaig Lodge
Gairlochy
Stronenaba
Spean Bridge
Achnanellan
Glen Loy
Commando Memorial
Highbridge
Inverroy
Roybridge
Glen Spean
Achluachrach
Tulloch
Bunroy
A86
Muirshearlich
Fassfern
Achdalieu
Loch Eil
A830
FORT WILLIAM
Banavie
Corpach
Caol
A861
Lochyside
Inverlochy
Claggan
Victoria Bridge
Bridge of Nevis
Torlundy
Camusnagaul
Trislaig
Stronchreggan
Achintore
Glen Nevis
BEN NEVIS 4411
AONACH BEAG 4048
Killiechonate Forest
Leanachan Forest
Fersit
Loch Treig
Beinn na Lap
Corrour Shooting Lodge
MAMORE FOREST
Blarmachfoldach
Conaglen
Inverscaddle Bay
Creag Meagaidh 3700
Ardverikie Forest
Ben Alder Forest
Ben Alder 3765
Ben Alder Lodge
Loch Ericht
Corrievarkie Lodge
64
65
69
78

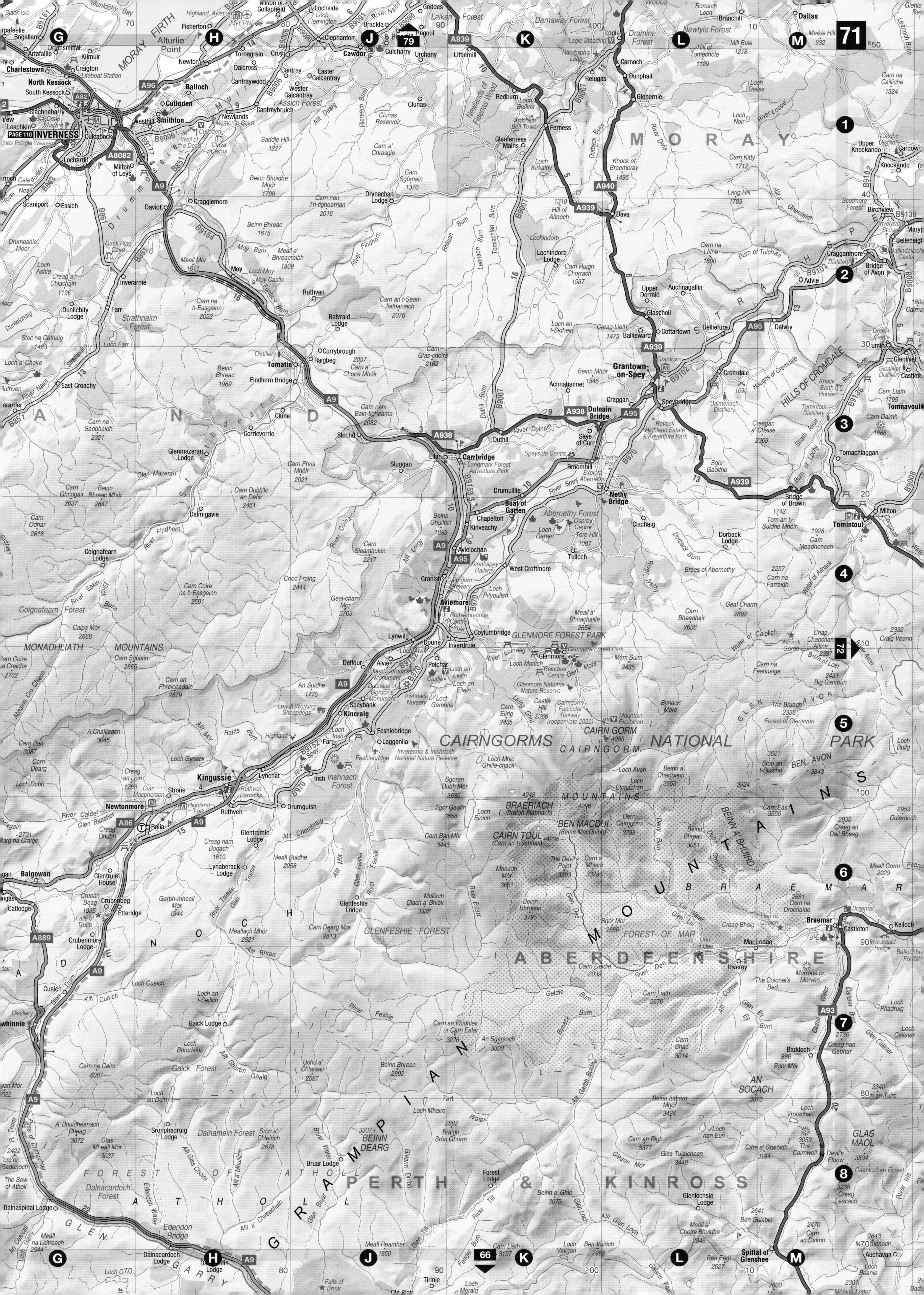

MORAY FIRTH
Inverness
Culloden
Cawdor
Nairn
Fisherton
Balloch
Smithton
Daviot
Moy
Tomatin
Carrbridge
Boat of Garten
Nethy Bridge
Aviemore
Kincraig
Kingussie
Newtonmore
Grantown-on-Spey
Dulnain Bridge
Tomintoul
Braemar
Dava
Ferness
MORAY
CAIRNGORMS NATIONAL PARK
CAIRNGORM MOUNTAINS
MONADHLIATH MOUNTAINS
GLENMORE FOREST PARK
BRAERIACH
BEN MACDUI
CAIRN TOUL
CAIRN GORM
BEN AVON
BEINN A' BHUIRD
FOREST OF MAR
ABERDEENSHIRE
PERTH & KINROSS
GRAMPIAN
GLENFESHIE FOREST
FOREST OF ATHOLL
GLAS MAOL
HILLS OF CROMDALE
Spittal of Glenshee
Dalnaspidal Lodge
A9
A96
A939
A938
A95
A86
A889
A93
A940
G
H
J
K
L
M
79
72
66

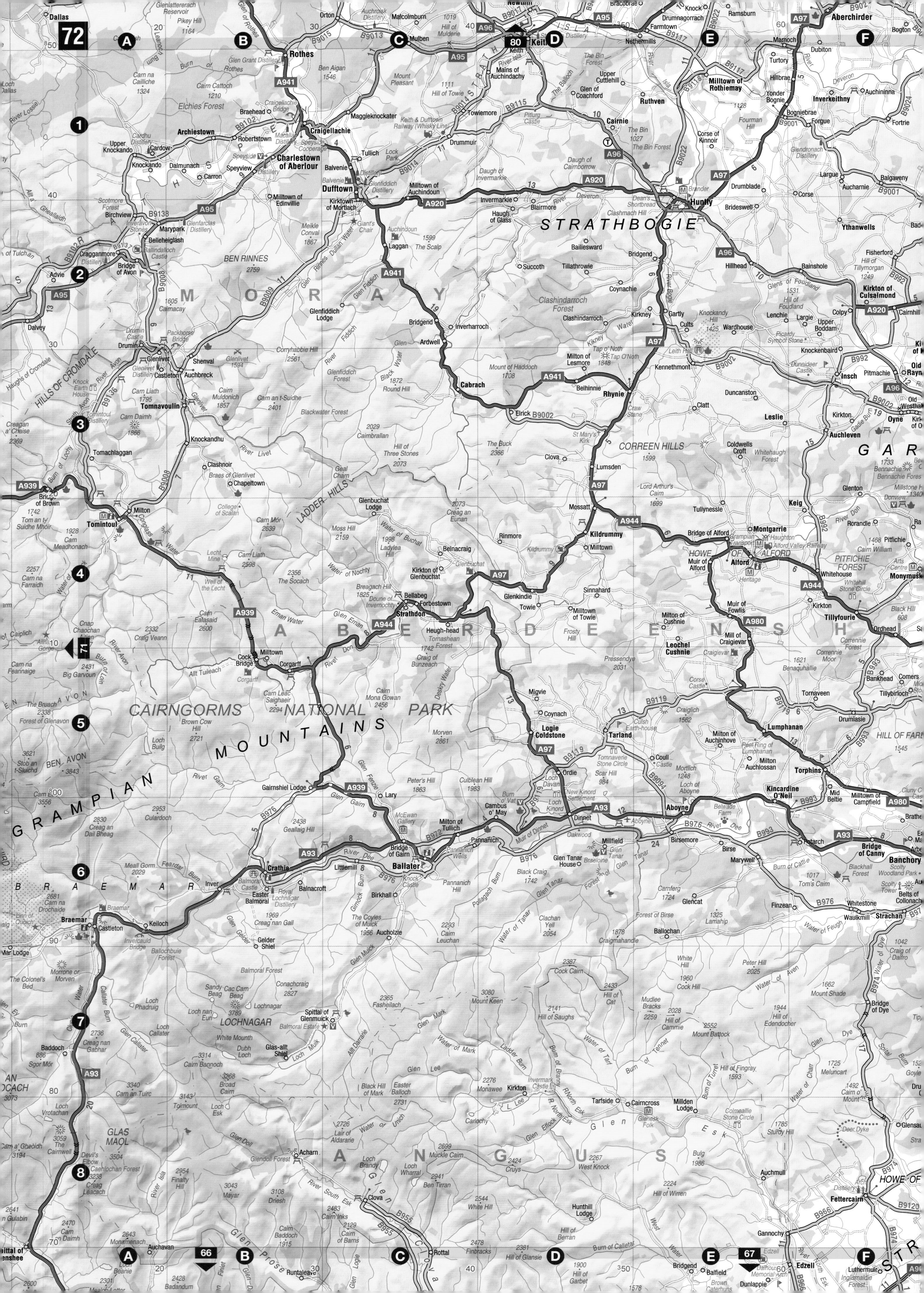
A
B
C
D
E
F
1
2
3
4
5
6
7
8
Dallas
Rothes
Mulben
Keith
Aberchirder
Craigellachie
Archiestown
Charlestown of Aberlour
Dufftown
Kirktown of Mortlach
Huntly
STRATHBOGIE
Milltown of Rothiemay
Inverkeithny
Ruthven
Cairnie
Elchies Forest
Knockando
Upper Knockando
Cardow
Dalmunach
Carron
Speyview
Marypark
Birchview
Belleheiglash
Bridge of Avon
Cragganmore
Advie
Dalvey
Glenlivet
Drumin
Castleton
Auchbreck
Shenval
Tomnavoulin
Knockandhu
Clashnoir
Chapeltown
Tomachlaggan
Bridge of Brown
Tomintoul
Milton
MORAY
BEN RINNES
2759
HILLS OF CROMDALE
LADDER HILLS
Glenfiddich Lodge
Laggan
Bridgend
Inverharroch
Ardwell
Cabrach
Blackwater Forest
Glenbuchat Lodge
Kirkton of Glenbuchat
Bellabeg
Forbestown
Strathdon
Heugh-head
Corgarff
Cock Bridge
Milltown
Rhynie
Lumsden
Mossatt
Kildrummy
Milltown
Glenkindie
Towie
Milltown of Towie
Bridge of Alford
Montgarrie
Alford
Muir of Alford
HOWE OF ALFORD
Muir of Fowlis
Mill of Craigievar
Leochel Cushnie
Insch
Leslie
Auchleven
Oyne
Clatt
Kennethmont
Gartly
Cults
Tillyfourie
Whitehouse
Monymusk
Kirkton
Ordhead
Lumphanan
Torphins
Tarland
Logie Coldstone
Coynach
Migvie
Ordie
Dinnet
Aboyne
Kincardine O'Neil
Banchory
Bridge of Canny
Potarch
Birsemore
Ballater
Bridge of Gairn
Crathie
Balmoral Castle
Easter Balmoral
Inver
Braemar
Keiloch
Castleton
Mar Lodge
Gairnshiel Lodge
CAIRNGORMS NATIONAL PARK
GRAMPIAN MOUNTAINS
BRAEMAR
BEN AVON
3843
ABERDEENSHIRE
LOCHNAGAR
3789
Spittal of Glenmuick
Glas-allt Shiel
Mount Keen
3080
Kirkton
Tarfside
Millden Lodge
Glen Esk
ANGUS
Clova
Acharn
GLAS MAOL
Devil's Elbow
Cairnwell
Gannochy
Edzell
Fettercairn
Strachan
Bridge of Dye
Finzean
Whitestone
Rottal
Bridgend
Balfield
Dunlappie
Auchavan
Spittal of Glenshee
Runtaleave
Glen Prosen
Glen Clova
A95
A96
A941
A920
A97
A939
A944
A980
A93
B976
B9002
66
67
71
80

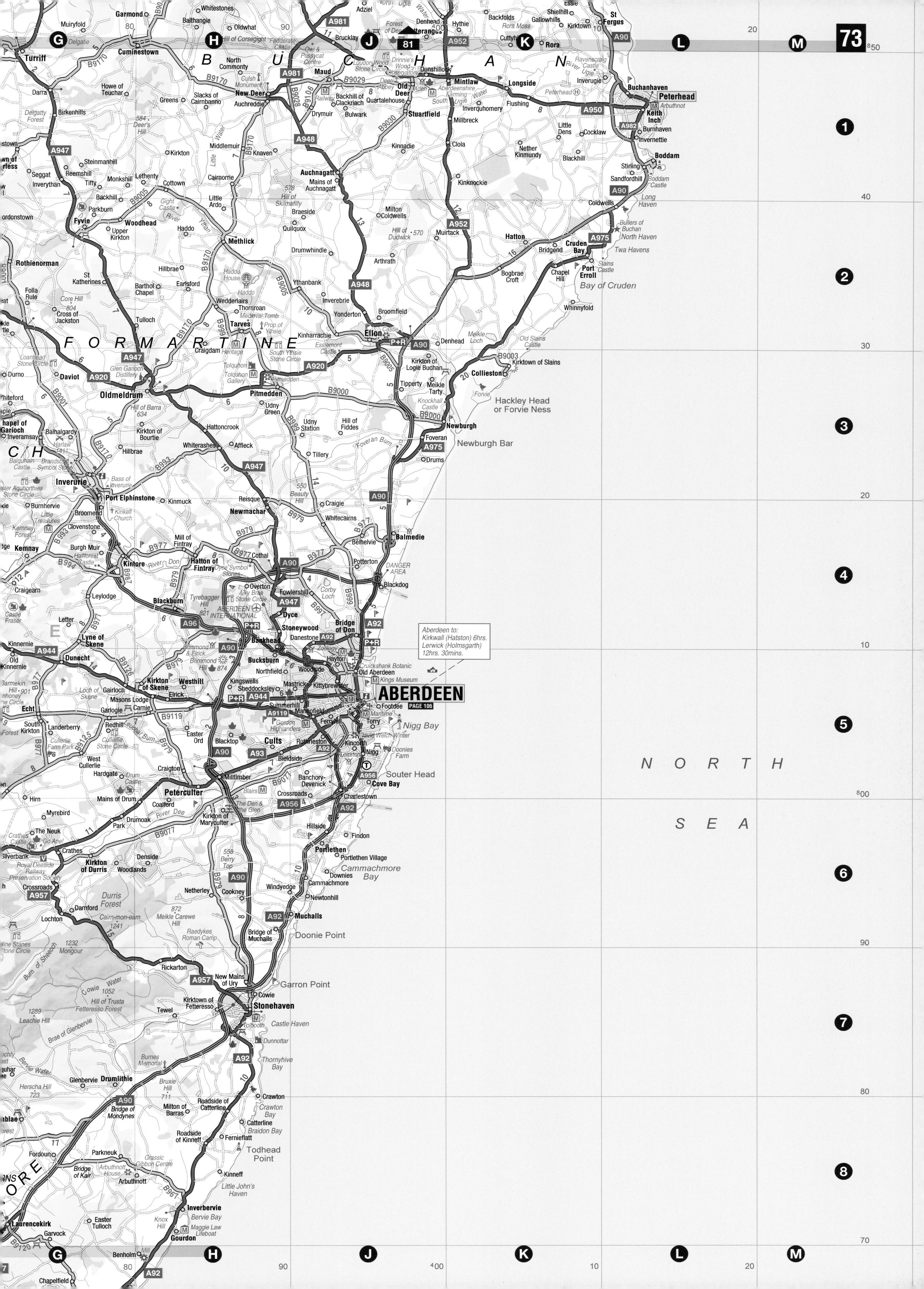
BUCHAN
FORMARTINE
NORTH SEA
ABERDEEN
PAGE 106
Aberdeen to:
Kirkwall (Hatston) 6hrs.
Lerwick (Holmsgarth) 12hrs. 30mins.
Peterhead
Fraserburgh
Turriff
Cuminestown
New Deer
Maud
Mintlaw
Longside
Old Deer
Stuartfield
Buchanhaven
Keith Inch
Boddam
Cruden Bay
Port Erroll
Bay of Cruden
Hatton
Auchnagatt
Fyvie
Methlick
Tarves
Ellon
Collieston
Hackley Head or Forvie Ness
Newburgh
Newburgh Bar
Oldmeldrum
Pitmedden
Inverurie
Port Elphinstone
Newmachar
Balmedie
Kintore
Hatton of Fintray
Blackburn
Dyce
Bridge of Don
Bankhead
Bucksburn
Westhill
Kirkton of Skene
Cults
Peterculter
Nigg Bay
Souter Head
Cove Bay
Portlethen
Cammachmore Bay
Newtonhill
Muchalls
Doonie Point
Garron Point
Stonehaven
Castle Haven
Dunnottar
Crawton
Todhead Point
Kinneff
Inverbervie
Gourdon
Laurencekirk
Drumlithie
Glenbervie
Durris Forest
Crathes
Banchory-Devenick
Rothienorman
Daviot
Echt
Dunecht
Kemnay
Lyne of Skene
A90
A92
A93
A96
A947
A948
A950
A952
A956
A957
A975
A981
A982
A920
A944
A9119
G
H
J
K
L
M
1
2
3
4
5
6
7
8
81

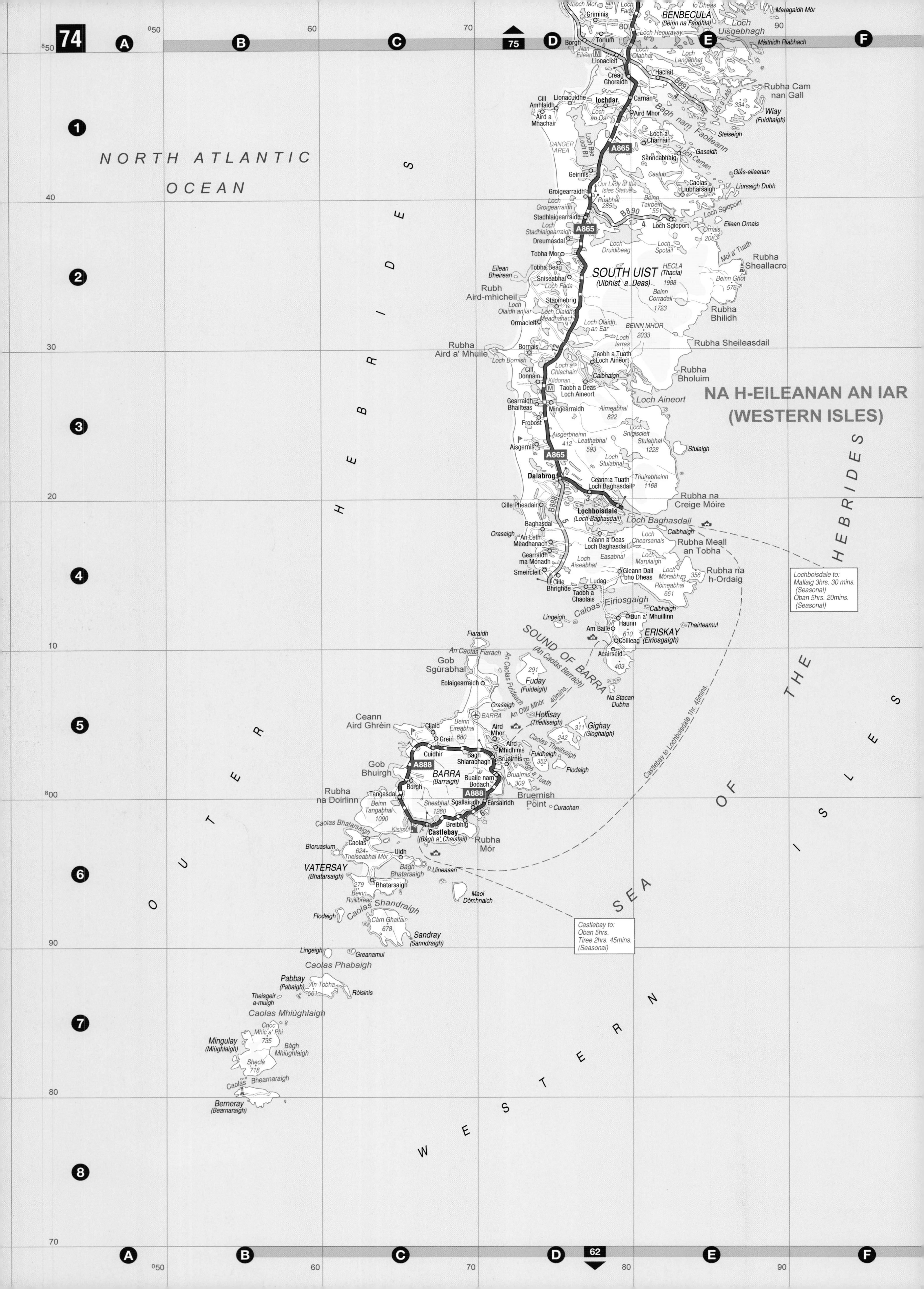
NORTH ATLANTIC
OCEAN
OUTER HEBRIDES
SEA OF THE HEBRIDES
THE SEA OF THE HEBRIDES
WESTERN ISLES
NA H-EILEANAN AN IAR
(WESTERN ISLES)
BENBECULA
(Beinn na Faoghla)
Loch Uisgebhagh
Màithidh Riabhach
Maragaidh Mòr
Griminis
Borgh
Torlum
Lionacleit
Haclait
Creag Ghoraidh
B891
Rubha Cam nan Gall
Wiay
(Fuidhaigh)
Cill Amhlaidh
Lionacuidhe
Iochdar
Carnan
Aird a Mhachair
Aird Mhor
Bagh nam Faoileann
Steiseigh
Loch a Charnain
Gasaidh
DANGER AREA
A865
Sanndabhaig
Glas-eileanan
Liursaigh Dubh
Geirinis
Caolas Liubharsaigh
Groigearraidh
Our Lady of the Isles Statue
Rueabhal 285
Beinn Tairbeirt 551
Loch Sgioport
B890
Stadhlaigearraidh
Eilean Ornais
Dreumasdal
Loch Druidibeag
Tobha Mor
Eilean Bheirean
Tobha Beag
SOUTH UIST
(Uibhist a Deas)
HECLA
(Thacla)
1988
Rubha Sheallacro
Beinn Ghot 576
Sniseabhal
Rubh Aird-mhicheil
Staoinebrig
Beinn Corradail 1723
Rubha Bhilidh
Ormacleit
BEINN MHOR 2033
Rubha Aird a' Mhuile
Bornais
Rubha Sheileasdail
Taobh a Tuath Loch Aineort
Cill Donnain
Rubha Bholuim
Taobh a Deas Loch Aineort
Gearraidh Bhailteas
Mingearraidh
Loch Aineort
Frobost
Airneabhal 822
Aisgerbheinn 412
Leathabhal 593
Stulabhal 1228
Aisgernis
Stulaigh
Dalabrog
Loch Stulabhal
Ceann a Tuath Loch Baghasdail
Triuirebheinn 1168
Cille Pheadair
Rubha na Creige Móire
Lochboisdale
(Loch Baghasdail)
B888
Loch Baghasdail
Baghasdal
Calbhaigh
Orasaigh
An Leth Meadhanach
Ceann a Deas Loch Baghasdail
Rubha Meall an Tobha
Gearraidh ma Monadh
Easabhal
Gleann Dail bho Dheas
Rubha na h-Ordaig
Smeircleit
Cille Bhrighde
Ludag
Taobh a Chaolais
Roineabhal 661
356
Lochboisdale to:
Mallaig 3hrs. 30 mins.
(Seasonal)
Oban 5hrs. 20mins.
(Seasonal)
Eiriosgaigh
Lingeigh
Caolas
Calbhaigh
Bun a' Mhuillinn
Haunn
Am Baile
Thairteamul
610
Coilleag
ERISKAY
(Eiriosgaigh)
Fiaraidh
SOUND OF BARRA
(An Caolas Barrach)
An Caolas Fiarach
Acairseid
403
Gob Sgùrabhal
291
Fuday
(Fuideigh)
Eolaigearraidh
Na Stacan Dubha
Orasaigh
An Oitir Mhòr
40mins.
Castlebay to Lochboisdale 1hr. 45mins.
Ceann Aird Ghrèin
BARRA
Hellisay
(Theiliseigh)
311
Gighay
(Gioghaigh)
Cliaid
Beinn Eireabhal 680
Aird Mhor
Grein
242
Caolas Theiliseigh
Cuidhir
Aird Mhidhinis
Bagh Shiarabhagh
Bruairnis
Fuidheigh 352
Gob Bhuirgh
A888
BARRA
(Barraigh)
Buaile nam Bodach
Bruairnis 309
Bàgh a Tuath
Flodaigh
Borgh
Rubha na Doirlinn
Tangasdal
Beinn Tangabhal 1090
Sheabhal 1260
Sgallairidh
Earsairidh
Bruernish Point
Curachan
Caolas Bhatarsaigh
Kisimul
Breibhig
Castlebay
(Bàgh a' Chaisteil)
Rubha Mór
Bioruaslum
Caolas
624
Theiseabhal Mòr
Uidh
VATERSAY
(Bhatarsaigh)
Bàgh Bhatarsaigh
Uineasan
279
Bhatarsaigh
Beinn Ruilibreac
Maol Dòmhnaich
Caolas Shandraigh
Flodaigh
Càrn Ghaltair 678
Sandray
(Sanndraigh)
Castlebay to:
Oban 5hrs.
Tiree 2hrs. 45mins.
(Seasonal)
Lingeigh
Greanamul
Caolas Phabaigh
Pabbay
(Pabaigh)
An Tobha 561
Ròisinis
Theisgeir a-muigh
Caolas Mhiùghlaigh
Mingulay
(Miùghlaigh)
Cnoc Mhic a' Phi 735
Bàgh Mhiùghlaigh
Shecla 718
Bhearnaraigh
Caolas
Berneray
(Bearnaraigh)
75
62

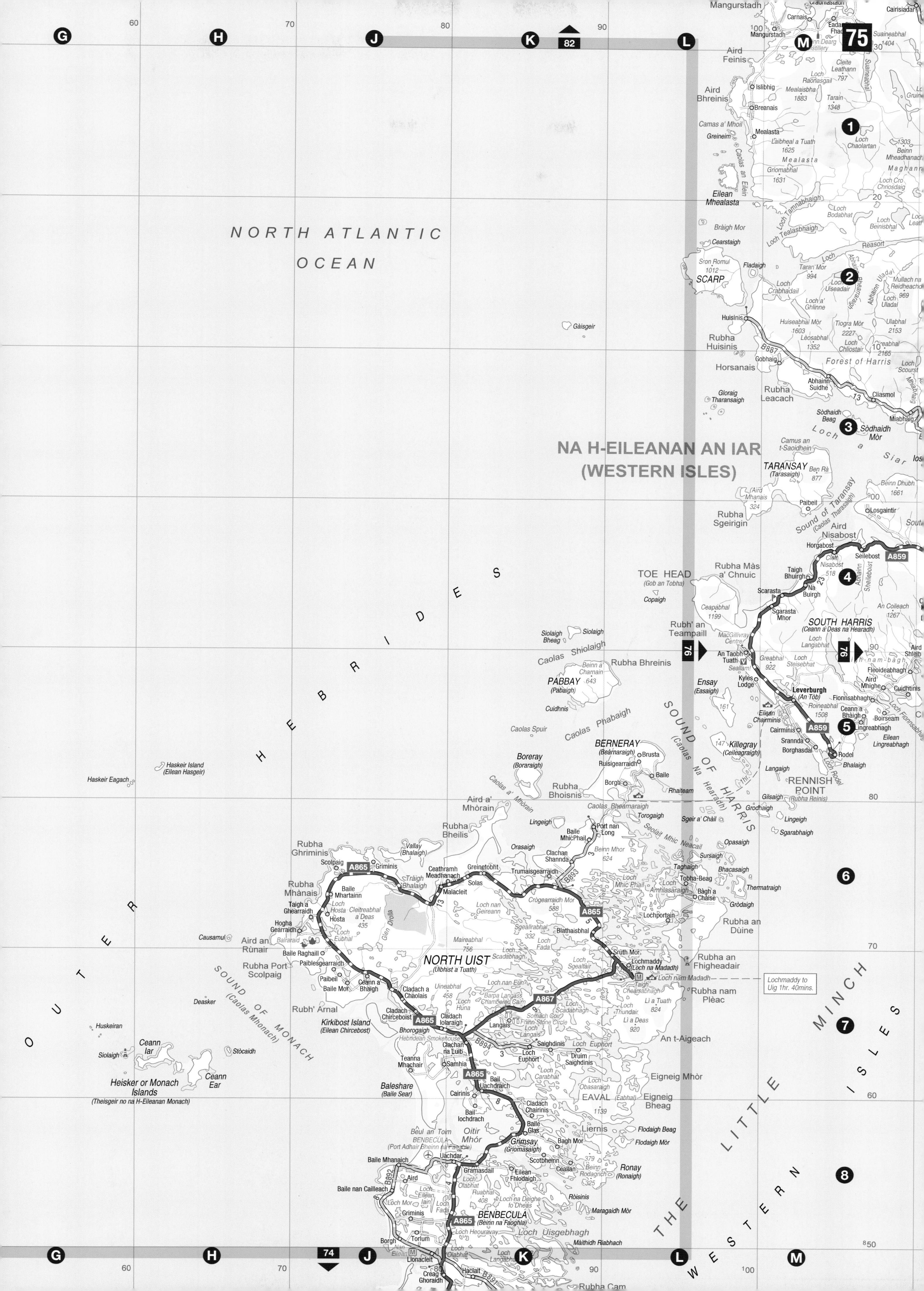
75
82
74
76
NORTH ATLANTIC OCEAN
NA H-EILEANAN AN IAR (WESTERN ISLES)
OUTER HEBRIDES
THE LITTLE MINCH
WESTERN ISLES
SOUND OF HARRIS (Caolas na Hearadh)
SOUND OF MONACH (Caolas Mhonach)
Mangurstadh
Carnais
Aird Feinis
Islibhig
Aird Bhreinis
Breanais
Camas a' Mhoil
Greineim
Mealasta
Caolas an Eilein
Eilean Mhealasta
Bràigh Mor
Cearstaigh
Sron Romul 1012
SCARP
Fladaigh
Huisinis
Rubha Huisinis
B887
Gobhaig
Horsanais
Rubha Leacach
Gloraig Tharansaigh
Abhainn Suidhe
Cliasmol
Forest of Harris
Sòdhaidh Beag
Sòdhaidh Mòr
Loch a Siar
Camus an t-Saoidhein
TARANSAY (Tarasaigh)
Ben Rà 877
Rubha Sgeirigin
Paibeil
Sound of Taransay (Caolas Tharasaigh)
Aird Nisabost
Horgabost
Seilebost
A859
TOE HEAD (Gob an Tobha)
Copaigh
Rubha Màs a' Chnuic
Taigh Bhuirgh
Na Buirgh
Scarasta
Ceapabhal 1199
Sgarasta Mhor
SOUTH HARRIS (Ceann a Deas na Hearadh)
Rubh' an Teampaill
An Taobh Tuath
Kyles Lodge
Leverburgh (An Tòb)
Ensay (Easaigh)
Killegray (Ceileagraigh)
Siolaigh Bheag
Siolaigh
Caolas Shiolaigh
Rubha Bhreinis
PABBAY (Pabaigh)
Beinn a' Charnain 643
Cuidhnis
Caolas Spuir
Caolas Phabaigh
BERNERAY (Beàrnaraigh)
Brusta
Ruisigearraidh
Baile
Borgh
Boreray (Boraraigh)
Rubha Bhoisnis
Caolas a' Mhòrain
Aird a' Mhòrain
Caolas Bheàrnaraigh
Rodel
RENNISH POINT (Rubha Reinis)
Gàisgeir
Haskeir Island (Eilean Hasgeir)
Haskeir Eagach
Rubha Bheilis
Rubha Ghriminis
Vallay (Bhalaigh)
Scolpaig
A865
Griminis
Ceathramh Meadhanach
Greinetobht
Solas
Tràigh Bhalaigh
Malacleit
Trumaisgearraidh
Clachan Shannda
Lingeigh
Orasaigh
Baile MhicPhail
Port nan Long
Beinn Mhor 624
Seolait Mhic Neacail
Rubha Mhànais
Taigh a Ghearraidh
Hogha Gearraidh
Causamul
Aird an Rùnair
Baile Raghaill
Rubha Port Scolpaig
Paiblesgearraidh
Paibeil
Baile Mor
Ceann a Bhàigh
NORTH UIST (Uibhist a Tuath)
Crògearraidh Mòr 588
Blathaisbhal
Lochportain
Sruth Mor
Lochmaddy (Loch na Madadh)
Loch nam Madadh
Lochmaddy to Uig 1hr. 40mins.
Rubha an Fhigheadair
Rubha nam Plèac
Rubha an Dùine
Deasker
Rubh' Arnal
Kirkibost Island (Eilean Chircebost)
Cladach a Chaolais
Cladach Chircebost
Cladach Iolaraigh
A867
Langais
Bhoragaigh
Clachan na Luib
Saighdinis
Loch Euphort
Druim Saighdinis
An t-Aigeach
Li a Tuath 824
Li a Deas 920
Huskeiran
Siolaigh
Ceann Iar
Ceann Ear
Stòcaidh
Heisker or Monach Islands (Theisgeir no na H-Eileanan Monach)
Teanna Mhachair
Samhla
Baleshare (Baile Sear)
Cairinis
Bail Uachdraich
EAVAL (Ebhal) 1139
Eigneig Mhòr
Eigneig Bheag
Cladach Chairinis
Baile Glas
Liernis
Flodaigh Beag
Flodaigh Mòr
Oitir Mhór
Grimsay (Griomasaigh)
Bagh Mor
Scotbheinn
Ceallan
Ronay (Ronaigh)
Baile Mhanaich
Uachdar
Gramasdail
Eilean Fhlodaigh
Ròisinis
Maragaidh Mòr
Baile nan Cailleach
Aird
Griminis
BENBECULA (Beinn na Faoghla)
A865
Torlum
Loch Uisgebhagh
Màithidh Riabhach
Borgh
Lionacleit
Creag Ghoraidh
Haclait
Rubha Cam
G
H
J
K
L
M
1
2
3
4
5
6
7
8
60
70
80
90
100

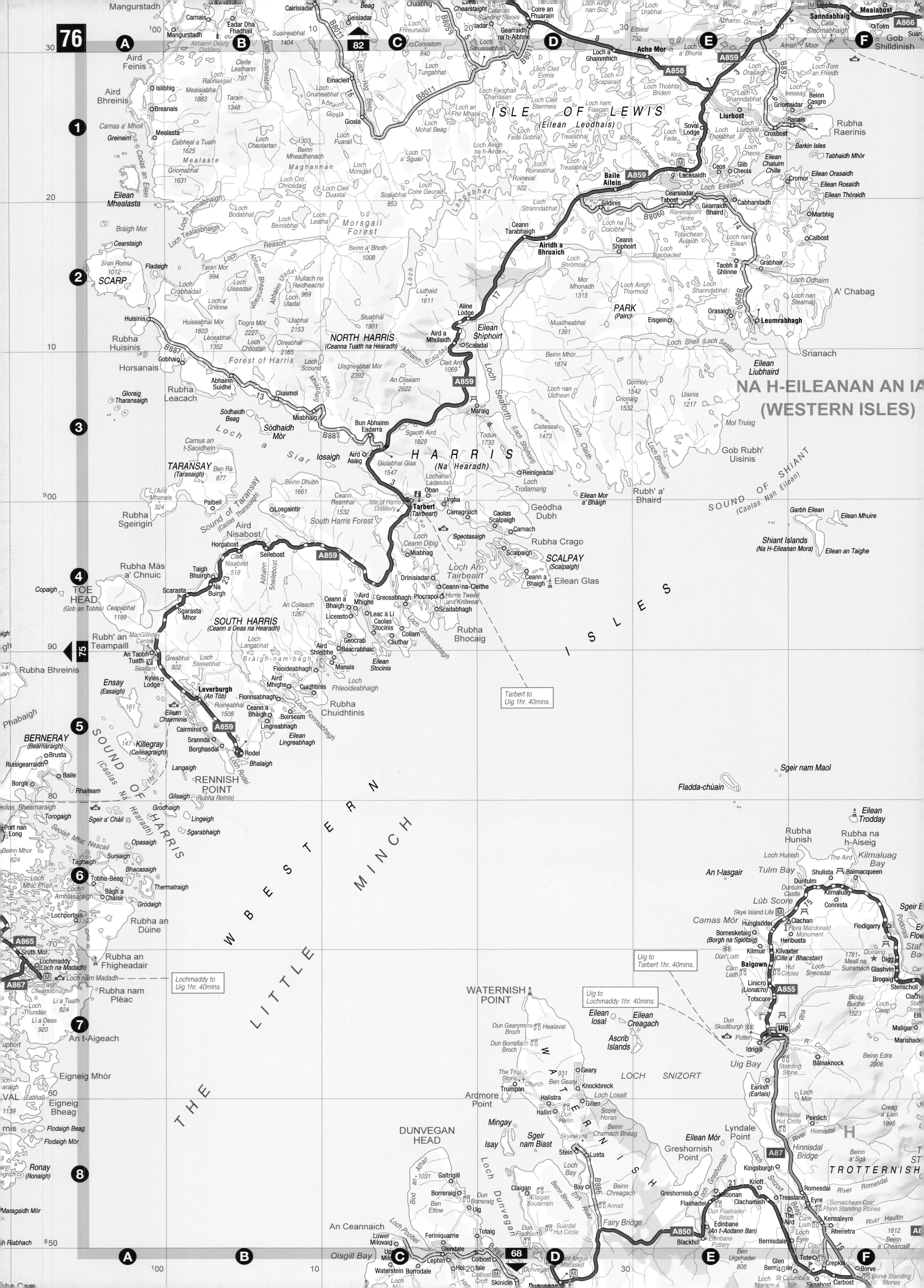
ISLE OF LEWIS
(Eilean Leodhais)
NORTH HARRIS
(Ceanna Tuath na Hearadh)
HARRIS
(Na Hearadh)
SOUTH HARRIS
(Ceann a Deas na Hearadh)
NA H-EILEANAN AN IA
(WESTERN ISLES)
PARK
(Pairc)
THE LITTLE MINCH
WESTERN ISLES
SOUND OF HARRIS
(Caolas Na Hearadh)
SOUND OF SHIANT
(Caolas Nan Eilean)
Sound of Taransay
(Caolas Tharansaigh)
Loch a Siar
Loch Seaforth
Morsgail Forest
Forest of Harris
South Harris Forest
TARANSAY
(Tarasaigh)
SCARP
SCALPAY
(Scalpaigh)
Eilean Glas
Shiant Islands
(Na H-Eileanan Mora)
Garbh Eilean
Eilean Mhuire
Eilean an Taighe
Sgeir nam Maol
Fladda-chùain
Eilean Trodday
BERNERAY
(Bearnaraigh)
Killegray
(Ceileagraigh)
Ensay
(Easaigh)
TOE HEAD
(Gob an Tobha)
RENNISH POINT
(Rubha Reinis)
Mangurstadh
Aird Feinis
Aird Bhreinis
Eilean Mhealasta
Huisinis
Rubha Huisinis
Horsanais
Tarbert
(Tairbeart)
Leverburgh
(An Tòb)
Rodel
Acha Mor
Baile Ailein
Liurbost
Leumrabhagh
Lochmaddy
(Loch nam Madadh)
Tarbert to Uig 1hr. 40mins.
Uig to Tarbert 1hr. 40mins.
Uig to Lochmaddy 1hr. 40mins.
Lochmaddy to Uig 1hr. 40mins.
WATERNISH POINT
WATERNISH
LOCH SNIZORT
DUNVEGAN HEAD
TROTTERNISH
Uig
Uig Bay
Kilmaluag Bay
Tulm Bay
Rubha Hunish
Ascrib Islands
Isay
Mingay
Ardmore Point
Lyndale Point
Greshornish Point
Fairy Bridge
A859
A858
A866
A865
A867
A855
A850
A87
B887
B8011
B8060
B886
A B C D E F
1 2 3 4 5 6 7 8
82
75
68

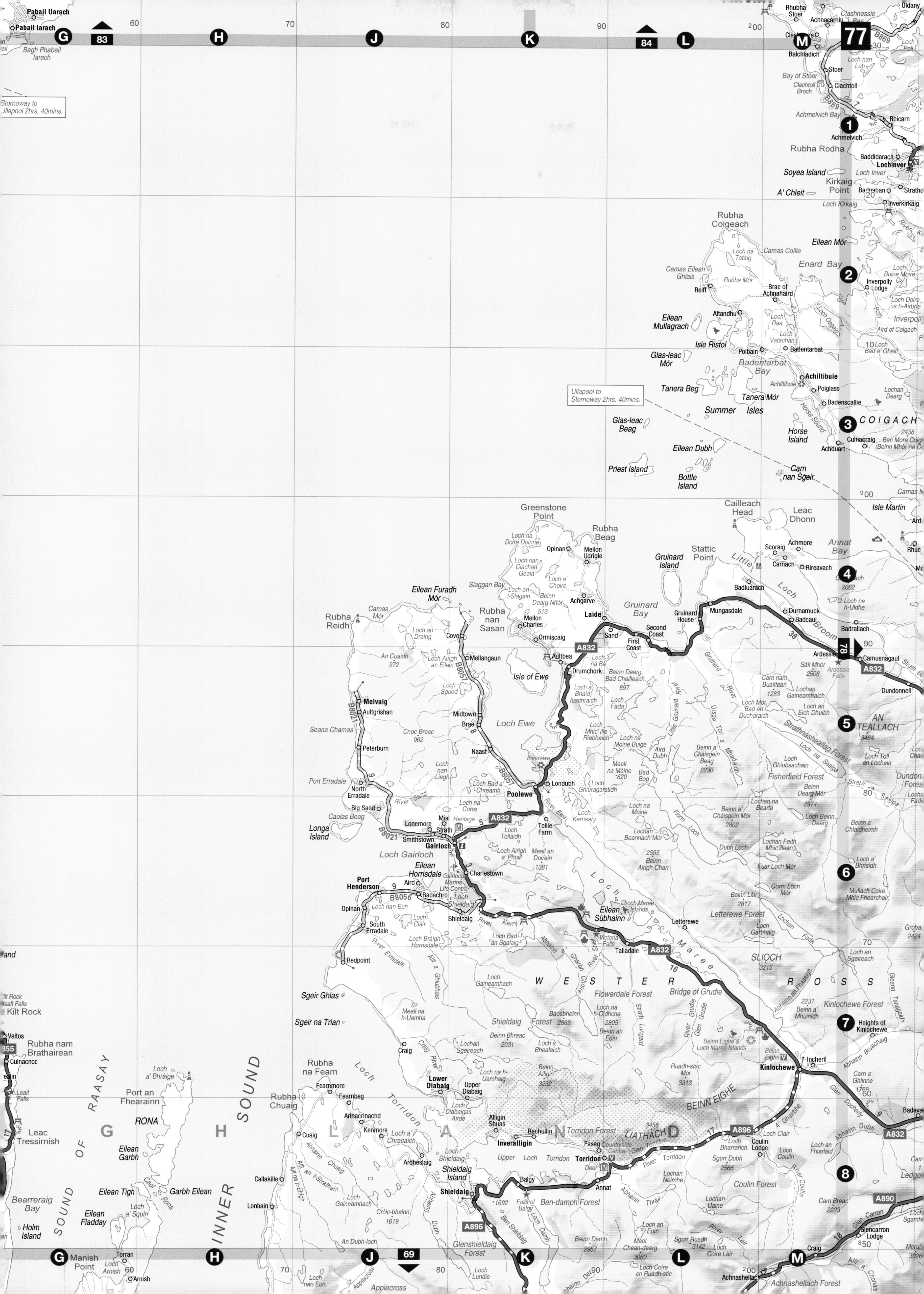

Pabail Uarach
Pabail Iarach
Bagh Phabail Iarach
Stornoway to Ullapool 2hrs. 40mins.
G
H
J
K
L
M
83
84
60
70
80
90
200
Rhubha Stoer
Achnacarnin
Clashnessie Bay
Clashmore
Balchladich
B869
Loch nan Lub
Stoer
Bay of Stoer
Clachtoll Broch
Clachtoll
Achmelvich Bay
Achmelvich
Rhicarn
Rubha Rodha
Baddidarach
Lochinver
Soyea Island
Loch Inver
Kirkaig Point
A' Chleit
Badnaban
Strathan
Loch Kirkaig
Inverkirkaig
Rubha Coigeach
Eilean Mór
Camas Coille
Loch na Totaig
Enard Bay
Camas Eilean Ghlais
Rubha Mór
Brae of Achnahaird
Reiff
Inverpolly Lodge
Loch Buine Moire
Loch Doire na h-Airbhe
Eilean Mullagrach
Altandhu
Loch Raa
Loch Osgaig
Inverpolly
Aird of Coigach
Loch Vatachan
Isle Ristol
Polbain
Badentarbat
Glas-leac Mór
Badentarbat Bay
Loch Bad a' Ghaill
Achiltibuie
Tanera Beg
Polglass
Ullapool to Stornoway 2hrs. 40mins.
Tanera Mór
Summer Isles
Badenscallie
Lochan Dearg
Horse Sound
COIGACH
Glas-leac Beag
Horse Island
2438
Culnacraig
Ben More Coigach (Beinn Mhòr na Coigich)
Achduart
Eilean Dubh
Priest Island
Carn nan Sgeir
Bottle Island
Camas M
Isle Martin
Greenstone Point
Cailleach Head
Leac Dhonn
Loch na Doire Duinne
Rubha Beag
Opinan
Mellon Udrigle
Gruinard Island
Static Point
Scoraig
Achmore
Annat Bay
Carnach
Rireavach
Rhue
Loch nan Clachan Geala
Loch a' Choire
Little Loch Broom
Badluarach
Slaggan Bay
Loch an t-Slagain
Beinn Dearg Nhòr 513
Achgarve
Gruinard Bay
Loch na h-Uidhe
Eilean Furadh Mór
Rubha nan Sasan
Laide
Gruinard House
Mungasdale
Dundonnell
Dumamuck
Badcaul
Rubha Reidh
Camas Mór
Mellon Charles
Sand
Second Coast
First Coast
Badrallach
Loch an Draing
Cove
Ormiscaig
A832
Ardessie
Ardessie Falls
Camusnagaul
An Cuaidh 972
Loch Airigh an Eilein
Mellangaun
Aultbea
Loch a' Bhaid-luachraich
Sàil Mhòr 2508
Isle of Ewe
Drumchork
Beinn Dearg Bad Chailleach 897
Carn nam Buailtean 1283
Lochan Gaineamhaich
Loch Sguod
Loch Fada
Gruinard River
Loch Mór Bad an Ducharaich
Loch an Eich Dhuibh
Melvaig
B8021
Aultgrishan
B8057
Midtown
Brae
Loch Ewe
Loch Mhic' ille Riabhaich
Little Gruinard River
Uisge Toll a' Mhadaidh
Strathnasheallag Forest
AN TEALLACH 3484
Seana Chamas
Cnoc Breac 962
Loch na Moine Buige
Aird Dubh
Loch Toll an Lochain
Peterburn
Naast
Inverewe
Meall na Mèine 820
Beinn a' Chàisgein Beag 2230
Loch Ghiubsachain
Loch na Sealga
Loch nan Liagh
Bad Bog
Fisherfield Forest
Port Erradale
North Erradale
Loch Bad a' Chreamh
Poolewe
Londubh
Loch Ghiuragarstidh
Beinn Dearg Mór 2974
Big Sand
River Sand
Loch na Curra
Heritage
A832
Tollie Farm
Loch Kernsary
Loch na Moine
Lochan na Bearta
Beinn a' Chàisgein Mór 2802
Loch Beinn Dearg
Caolas Beag
Lonemore
Mial
Strath
Smithstown
Gairloch
River Ewe
Beinn a' Chlaidheimh
Longa Island
Loch Tollaidh
Lochan Beannach Mór
Lochan Feith Mhic'illean
Loch Gairloch
Loch Airigh a' Phuill
Meall an Doirein 1381
2595 Beinn Airigh Charr
Dubh Loch
Fionn Loch
Loch a' Bhrisidh
Eilean Horrisdale
Charlestown
Fuar Loch Mór
Port Henderson
Aird
Gairloch Marine Life Centre
Gorm Loch Mór
Mullach Coire Mhic Fhearchair
B8056
Badachro
Loch Shieldaig
Eilean Sùbhainn
Loch Maree Islands
Beinn Lair 2817
Opinan
Loch nan Eun
Shieldaig
Letterewe
Letterewe Forest
South Erradale
Loch Clàir
River Kerry
Loch Garbhaig
Victoria Falls
Loch Bad an Sgalaig
Loch Braigh Horrisdale
Talladale
Groba 2424
Redpoint
River Erradale
Allt a' Ghiubhais
Abhainn Gharbh Choire
Loch Maree
SLIOCH 3215
Loch an Sgeireach
Loch Gaineamhach
WESTER ROSS
Flowerdale Forest
Bridge of Grudie
Abhainn an Fhasaigh
Sgeir Ghlas
Kilt Rock
Mealt Falls
Meall na h-Uamha
Shieldaig Forest
Baosbheinn 2869
Loch na h-Oidhche
Beinn an Eòin 2805
Strath Lungard
River Grudie
Glen Grudie
2231 Beinn a' Mhùinidh
Kinlochewe Forest
Gleann Tanagaidh
Sgeir na Trian
Beinn Bhreac 2031
Beinn Eighe & Loch Maree Islands
Heights of Kinlochewe
Valtos
Rubha nam Brathairean
A855
Culnacnoc
Craig
Lochan Sgeireach
Loch a' Bhealaich
Ruadh-stac Mor 3313
Beinn Eighe
Incheril
Kinlochewe
Abhainn Bruachaig
Loch a' Bhràige
Rubha na Fearn
Loch Torridon
Craig River
Lower Diabaig
Upper Diabaig
Loch na h-Uamhaig
Beinn Alligin 3232
BEINN EIGHE
Carn a' Ghlinne 1760
Port an Fhearainn
Fearnmore
Fearnbeg
Lealt Falls
RONA
SOUND OF RAASAY
Rubha Chuaig
Loch Diabaigas Airde
Glen Docherty
Arrinacrinachd
Alligin Shuas
Torridon Forest
3456
LIATHACH
A896
A' Ghairbhe
Badavanich
Leac Tressirnish
Kenmore
Inveralligin
Rechullin
Fasag
Countryside Centre
Glen Torridon
Loch Clair
Abhainn Dubh
A832
Eilean Garbh
Cuaig
Loch a' Chracaich
Upper Loch Torridon
Torridon
Loch Bharranch
Coulin Lodge
Loch an Fhìarlaid
Loch Coulin
Caol Rona
Abhainn Chuaig
Ardheslaig
Loch Shieldaig
Deer
River Torridon
Sgurr Dubh 2566
Shieldaig Island
Lochan Neimhe
River Coulin
Garbh Eilean
Eilean Tigh
Callakille
Allt an t-Strathain
Balgy
Annat
Coulin Forest
Bearreraig Bay
Allt na h-Eirgh
Loch Gaineamhach
Shieldaig
Abhainn Dubh
Falls of Balgy
Ben-damph Forest
Abhainn Thrail
Lochan Uaine
A890
Carn Breac 2223
Eilean Fladday
Loch a' Squirr
Lonbain
Croic-bheinn 1619
1692
Loch Damh
River Lair
Glen Carron
Holm Island
INNER SOUND
A896
Ben Shieldaig
Loch an Eoin
Glencarron Lodge
An Dubh-loch
Glenshieldaig Forest
Beinn Damh 2957
Maol Chean-dearg 3060
Sgorr Ruadh 3142
Loch Coire Làir
Craig
Manish Point
Torran
69
Loch Arnish
Arnish
Applecross
Loch nan Eun
Loch Lundie
Loch Coire an Ruadh-stac
Achnashellach
Achnashellach Forest
Allt a' Chonais

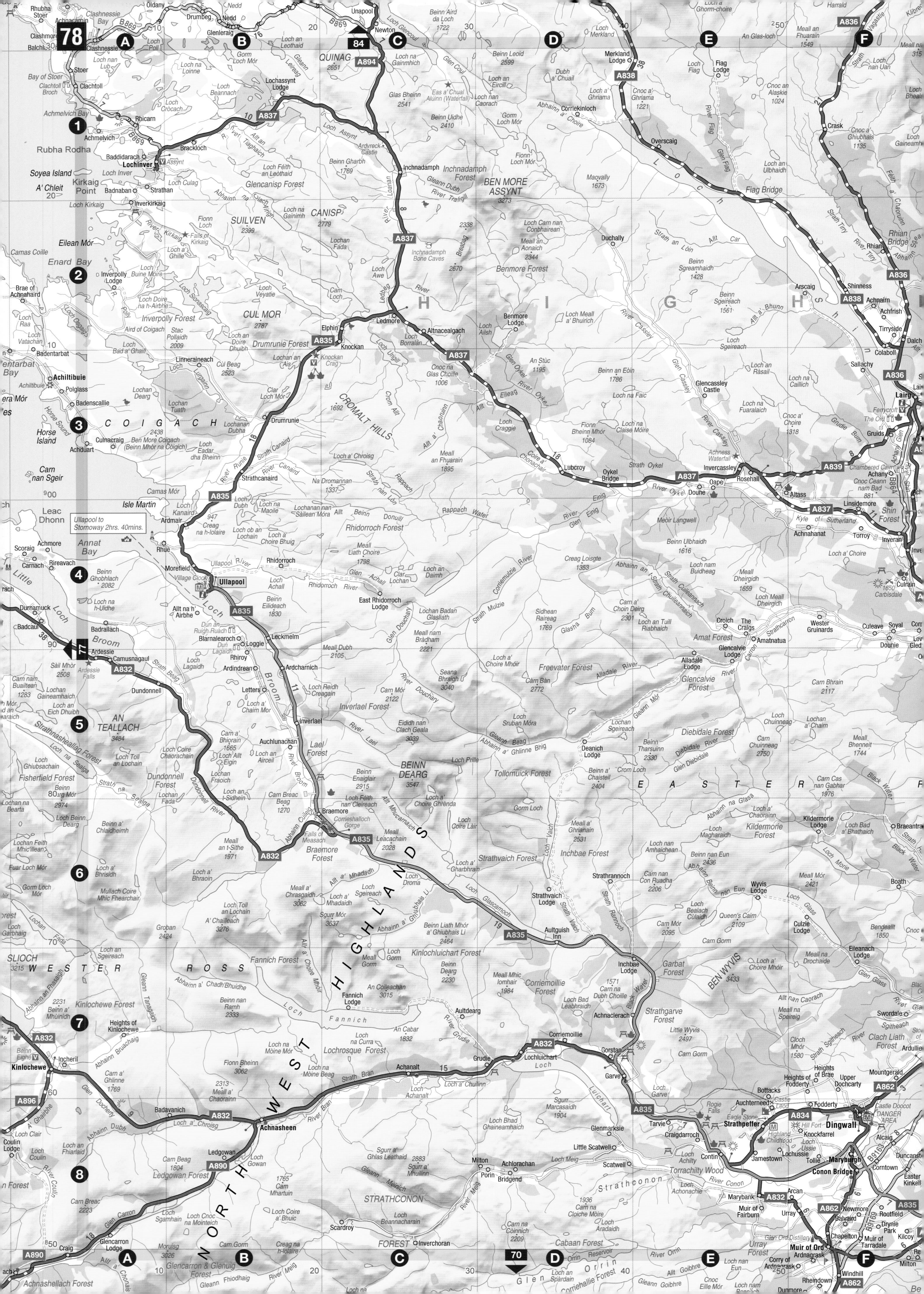
78
84
77
70
A
B
C
D
E
F
1
2
3
4
5
6
7
8
Rhubha Stoer
Clashnessie Bay
Oldany
Drumbeg
Nedd
Glenleraig
Unapool
Newton
Loch Glencoul
Beinn Aird da Loch 1722
Loch Merkland
Harrald
Loch a' Ghorm-choire
Meall an Fhuarain 1549
Clashmore
Balchladich
Achnacarnin
Clashnessie
Loch Poll
Loch an Leothaid
QUINAG 2651
A894
Loch na Gainmhich
Beinn Leoid 2599
Dubh a' Chuail
Merkland Lodge
A838
An Glas-loch
Flag Lodge
Loch Flag
A836
Stoer
Clachtoll
Bay of Stoer
Clachtoll Broch
Loch nan Lub
Loch na Loinne
Gorm Loch Mór
Lochassynt Lodge
Glas Bheinn 2541
Eas a' Chual Aluinn (Waterfall)
Loch an Eircill
Loch nan Caorach
Glen Coul
Loch a' Ghriama
Cnoc a' Ghriama 1221
Cnoc an Alaskie 1024
Corriekinloch
Abhainn a' Choire
Achmelvich Bay
Rhicarn
Achmelvich
Rubha Rodha
Baddidarach
Lochinver
Assynt
Brackloch
A837
Loch Assynt
Ardvreck Castle
Beinn Uidhe 2410
Gorm Loch Mór
Fionn Loch Mór
Overscaig
Crask
Cnoc a' Ghiubhais 1135
Soyea Island
Loch Inver
Kirkaig Point
A' Chleit
Badnaban
Strathan
Loch Culag
Glencanisp Forest
Loch Fèith an Leòthaid
Beinn Gharbh 1769
Inchnadamph
Inchnadamph Forest
Gleann Dubh
BEN MORE ASSYNT 3273
Maovally 1673
Flag Bridge
Loch an Ulbhaidh
Loch Kirkaig
Inverkirkaig
Loch na Gainimh
CANISP 2779
SUILVEN 2399
Fionn Loch
Falls of Kirkaig
River Kirkaig
Loch a' Ghille
Lochan Fada
Inchnadamph Bone Caves
Breabag
2338
2670
Loch Carn nan Conbhairean
Meall an Aonaich 2344
Benmore Forest
Duchally
Strath an Lòin
Ben Sgreamhaidh 1428
Rhian
Rhian Bridge
Eilean Mór
Camas Coille
Enard Bay
Inverpolly Lodge
Loch Buine Moire
Loch Veyatie
Cam Loch
Loch Awe
Ledbeg
Ledmore
Altnacealgach
Elphin
Brae of Achnahaird
Loch Doire na h-Airbhe
Loch Sionascaig
Inverpolly Forest
CUL MOR 2787
Stac Pollaidh 2009
Aird of Coigach
Knockan
Knockan Crag
A835
Loch Borralan
Loch Urigill
Loch Ailsh
Benmore Lodge
Loch Meall a' Bhuirich
Arscaig
Ben Sgeireach 1561
Shinness
A838
Achnairn
Achfrish
Tirryside
Loch Raa
Loch Vatachan
Badentarbat
Achiltibuie
Polglass
Badenscallie
Loch Bad a' Ghaill
Linneraineach
Cùl Beag 2523
Loch an Doire Dhuibh
Drumrunie Forest
Lochan an Ais
Cnoc na Glas Choille 1006
An Stùc 1195
Loch Sgeireach
Glencassley Castle
Loch an Ràsail
Loch na Caillich
Sallachy
Colaboll
Dalchork
Lochan Dearg
Lochan Tuath
Clar Loch Mór
CROMALT HILLS
Glen Oykel
River Oykel
Beinn an Eòin 1786
Loch na Faic
Loch na Fuaralaich
Cnoc a' Choire 1318
Lairg
Ferrycroft
The Ord
Horse Island
Horse Sound
COIGACH
Lochanan Dubha
Drumrunie
Ben More Coigach (Beinn Mhòr na Coigich)
Culnacraig
Achduart
Loch Eadar dha Bheinn
Loch a' Chroisg
Allt a' Chaorainn
Loch Craggie
Fionn Bheinn Mhór 1084
Loch na Claise Mòire
River Cassley
Gruids
Achany Glen
Carn nan Sgeir
Camas Mór
Isle Martin
Strathcanaird
Na Dromannan 1337
Meall an Fhuarain 1895
Coire a' Chonachair
Lubcroy
Oykel Bridge
Strath Oykel
Achness Waterfall
Invercassley
Rosehall
A839
Chambered Cairn
Achany
Cnoc Ceann nam Bad 881
Leac Dhonn
Ullapool to Stornoway 2hrs. 40mins.
Loch Kanaird
Ardmair
Loch Dubh
Loch na Maoile
Lochanan nan Sàilean Mòra
Beinn Donuill
Rappach Water
River Einig
Glen Einig
Oape
Doune
Altass
Linsidemore
Shin Forest
Meòir Langwell
Kyle of Sutherland
Achnahanat
Torroy
Inveran
Scoraig
Achmore
Annat Bay
Carnach
Rireavach
Rhue
Loch ob an Lochain
Loch a' Choire Bhuig
Rhidorroch Forest
Meall Liath Choire 1798
Creag Loisgte 1353
Abhainn an t-Strath Chuileannaich
Beinn Ulbhaidh 1616
Loch a' Choire
Morefield
Village Clock
Ullapool
Ullapool River
Rhidorroch
Loch Achall
Glen Achall
Clar Lochan
Loch an Daimh
Corriemulzie River
Loch nam Buidheag
Meall Dheirgidh 1659
Culrain
Carbisdale
Little Loch Broom
Beinn Ghobhlach 2082
Loch na h-Uidhe
Allt na h' Airbhe
Beinn Eilideach 1830
East Rhidorroch Lodge
Lochan Badan Glasliath
Strath Mulzie
Sidhean Raireag 1769
Carn a' Choin Deirg 2301
Loch an Tuill Riabhaich
Loch Meall Dheirgidh
Durnamuck
Badcaul
Badrallach
Dùn an Ruigh-Ruadh
Blarnalearoch
Dùn Lagaidh
Loggie
Leckmelm
Meall nam Bràdham 2221
Croich
The Craigs
Western Gruinards
Culeave
Soyal
Ardessie
Camusnagaul
Sàil Mhór 2508
Ardessie Falls
A832
Rhiroy
Ardindrean
Loch Broom
Ardcharnich
Meall Dubh 2105
Glen Douchary
Loch a' Choire Mhóir
Glasha Burn
Amat Forest
Glencalvie Lodge
Strathcarron
Amatnatua
Dounie
Carn nam Buailtean 1283
Lochan Gaineamhaich
Loch an Eich Dhuibh
Dundonnell
Strath Beag
Loch Lagaidh
Letters
Loch a' Chairn Mor
Loch Reidh Creagain
Carn Mór 2122
Seana Bhraigh 3040
Carn Bàn 2772
Freevater Forest
Alladale Lodge
Alladale River
Glencalvie Forest
Carn Bhrain 2117
AN TEALLACH 3484
Strathnasealiag Forest
Loch na Sealga
Loch Toll an Lochain
Loch Coire Chaorachain
Carn a' Bhiorain 1665
Loch 'Allt Eigin
Auchlunachan
Inverlael
Inverlael Forest
River Lael
Lael Forest
Eididh nan Clach Geala 3039
Loch Sruban Mòra
Gleann Beag
Lochan Sgeireach
Gleann Mór
Diebidale Forest
Loch Chuinneag
Lochan a' Chairn
Carn Chuinneag 2750
Meall Bhenneit 1744
Loch Ghiubhsachain
Fisherfield Forest
Beinn Dearg Mór 2974
Dundonnell Forest
Lochan Fraoich
Loch an Airceil
Loch an t-Sidhein
Lochan Fada
Carn Breac Beag 1270
Beinn Enaiglair 2915
Loch Fèith nan Cleireach
BEINN DEARG 3547
Loch Prille
Abhainn a' Ghlinne Bhig
Tollomuick Forest
Deanich Lodge
Crom Loch
Beinn Tharsuinn 2330
Glen Diebidale
Beinn a' Chaisteil 2404
EASTER ROSS
Carn Cas nan Gabhar 1976
Black Water
Lochan na Bearta
Loch Beinn Dearg
Beinn a' Chlaidheimh
Braemore
Corrieshalloch Gorge
Falls of Measach
Abhainn Cuileig
Loch a' Choire Ghrànda
Allt Mhucarnaich
Meall Leacachain 2028
Loch Coire Làir
Gorm Loch
Meall a' Ghrianain 2531
Abhainn na Glasa
Loch a' Chaorainn
Kildermorie Lodge
Kildermorie Forest
Loch Bad a' Bhathaich
Braeantra
Lochan Feith Mhic'illean
Carn Loch Mór
Meall an t-Sithe 1971
Braemore Forest
Loch Droma
Loch a' Gharbhrain
Strathvaich Forest
Loch Vaich
Inchbae Forest
Loch nan Amhaichean
Beinn nan Eun 2436
Loch Magharaidh
Loch Morie
Fuar Loch Mór
Loch a' Bhrisidh
Mullach Coire Mhic Fhearchair
Loch a' Bhraoin
Allt a' Mhadaidh
Loch Sgeireach
Meall a' Chrasgaidh 3062
Loch a' Mhadaidh
Sgurr Mór 3637
Abhainn a' Ghiubhais Li
Loch Glascarnoch
Strathrannoch
Strathvaich Lodge
Strath Vaich
Strath Rannoch
Carn nan Con Ruadha 2206
Wyvis Lodge
Loch Glass
Meall Mór 2421
Boath
Gorm Loch Mór
Loch Toll an Lochain
A' Chailleach 3276
Groban 2424
Beinn Liath Mhór a' Ghiubhais Li 2464
Aultguish Inn
Loch Bealach Culaidh
Carn Mór 2095
Queen's Cairn 2109
Culzie Lodge
Bendeallt 1850
Lochan Fada
SLIOCH 3215
WESTER ROSS
Loch an Sgeireach
Fannich Forest
Meall Gorm
Loch Gorm
Kinlochluichart Forest
Inchbae Lodge
Garbat Forest
BEN WYVIS 3433
Carn Gorm
Loch a' Choire Mhóir
Meall na Drochaide
Eileanach Lodge
Glen Glass
Abhainn an Fhasaigh
Beinn a' Mhùinidh 2231
Kinlochewe Forest
Gleann Tanagaidh
Abhainn a' Chadh'Bhuidhe
Beinn nan Ramh 2333
Fannich Lodge
An Coileachan 3015
Beinn Dearg 2230
Meall Mhic Iomhair 1984
Corriemoillie Forest
Carn na Dubh Choille 1571
Black Water
Loch Bad Leabhraidh
Achnaclerach
Strathgarve Forest
Allt nan Caorach
Meall na Speireig
Swordale
NORTH WEST HIGHLANDS
Heights of Kinlochewe
Loch Fannich
Aultdearg
River Grudie
An Cabar 1832
Little Wyvis 2497
Sgitheach
Clach Liath Forest
Beinn Eighe
Kinlochewe
Incheril
Abhainn Bruachaig
Carn a' Ghlinne 1769
Loch na Mòine Mór
Loch na Curra
Lochrosque Forest
Corriemoillie
Lochluichart
Gorstan
Carn Gorm
Clach Mhór 1580
Strath Sgitheach
Ardullie
Fionn Bheinn 3062
Loch na Mòine Beag
Achanalt
Grudie
Loch Luichart
Loch a' Chuilinn
Garve
Heights of Fodderty
Heights of Brae
Upper Dochcarty
Mountgerald
A896
Glen Docherty
2313 Meall a' Chaorainn
Strath Bran
River Bran
Loch Achanalt
Loch Garve
Rogie Falls
Eagle Stone
Auchterneed
Bottacks
Castle Leod
Fodderty
Castle Doocot
A862
Badavanich
Loch a' Chroisg
Achnasheen
Sgurr Marcasaidh 1904
Glenmarksie
Loch Bhad Ghaineamhaich
A835
Tarvie
Strathpeffer
A834
Hill Fort
Dingwall
DANGER AREA
Abhainn Dubh
Loch Clair
Coulin Lodge
Loch an Fhiarlaid
Loch Coulin
Ledgowan
Loch Gowan
Carn Beag 1604
Ledgowan Forest
A890
Sgurr a' Ghlas Leathaid 2883
Sgurr a' Mhuilinn
Milton
Porin
Achlorachan
Bridgend
Loch Meig
Little Scatwell
Scatwell
Craigdarroch
Contin
Loch Achilty
Highland Childhood
Loch Ussie
Knockfarrel
Lochussie
Jamestown
Tollie
Maryburgh
Conon Bridge
Alcaig
Duncanston
Corntown
Torrachilty Wood
River Conon
Strathconon
Loch Achonachie
Coulin Forest
River Coulin
Cam Breac 2223
1765 Carn Mhartuin
Gleann Meinich
STRATHCONON
River Meig
Loch Coire a' Bhuic
Loch Beannacharain
1936 Carn na Cloiche Mòire
Loch Aradaidh
Marybank
Muir of Fairburn
Arcan
Urray
A832
A862
Newmore
Balvaird
Rootfield
Drynie Park
Easter Kinkell
Loch Sgamhain
Loch Cnoc na Mointeich
Scardroy
Carn na Coinnich 2209
Glen Carron
Glencarron Lodge
Craig
A890
Moruisg 3026
Carn Gorm
Creag na h-Iolaire
Cabaan Forest
Glen Ord Distillery
Urray Forest
Chapelton
Muir of Tarradale
Kilcoy
Muir of Ord
Ardnagrask
FOREST
Invercharon
River Orrin
Reservoir
Corry of Ardnagrask
Windhill
Rheindown
Milton
Achnashellach Forest
Allt a' Chonais
Glencarron & Glenuig Forest
Gleann Fhiodhaig
River Meig
Glen Orrin
Loch an Spàrdain
Corriehallie Forest
Allt Goibhre
Gleann Goibhre
Cnoc Eille Mòr
Loch nan Eun
Loch nam Bonnach
Dunmore

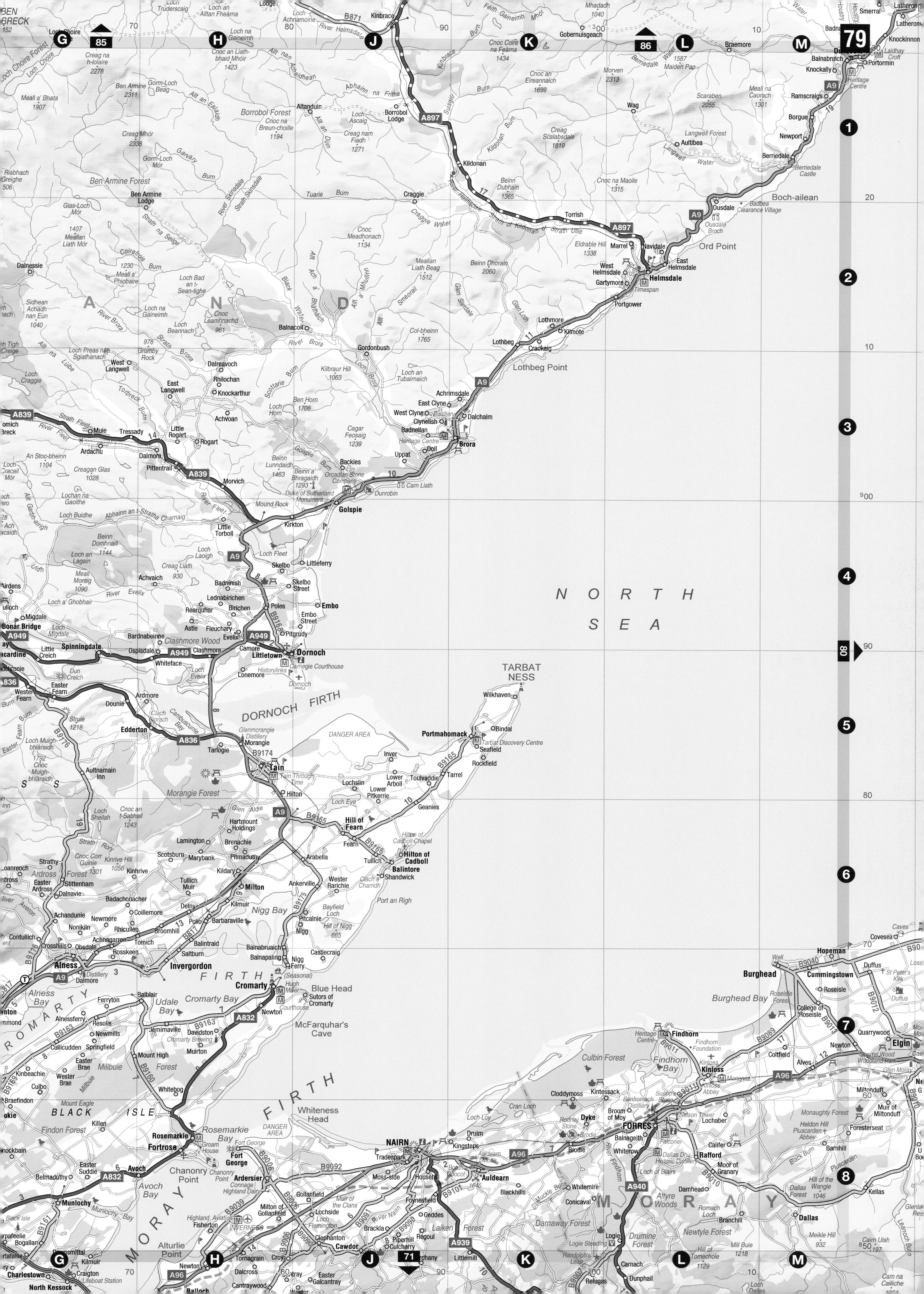
85
86
80
71
NORTH SEA
DORNOCH FIRTH
MORAY FIRTH
CROMARTY FIRTH
BLACK ISLE
MORAY
TARBAT NESS
Helmsdale
Brora
Golspie
Dornoch
Embo
Tain
Portmahomack
Invergordon
Alness
Cromarty
Fortrose
Rosemarkie
Avoch
Munlochy
Fort George
Ardersier
Nairn
Auldearn
Forres
Kinloss
Findhorn
Burghead
Hopeman
Elgin
Rafford
Dallas
Cawdor
Berriedale
Dunbeath
Kildonan
Kinbrace
Bonar Bridge
Spinningdale
Edderton
Balintore
Hill of Fearn
Dalmore
Charlestown
North Kessock
Ord Point
Lothbeg Point
Burghead Bay
Nigg Bay
Udale Bay
Cromarty Bay
Rosemarkie Bay
Avoch Bay
Chanonry Point
Alturlie Point
Whiteness Head
Culbin Forest
Findhorn Bay
Borrobol Forest
Ben Armine Forest
Morangie Forest
A9
A9
A897
A839
A949
A836
A832
A96
A939
A940
B9174
B9165
B9166
B9175
B817
B9163
B9160
B9161
B9006
B9092
B9090
B9101
B9010
B9089
B9011
B9040
B9012
B9013
G
H
J
K
L
M
1
2
3
4
5
6
7
8

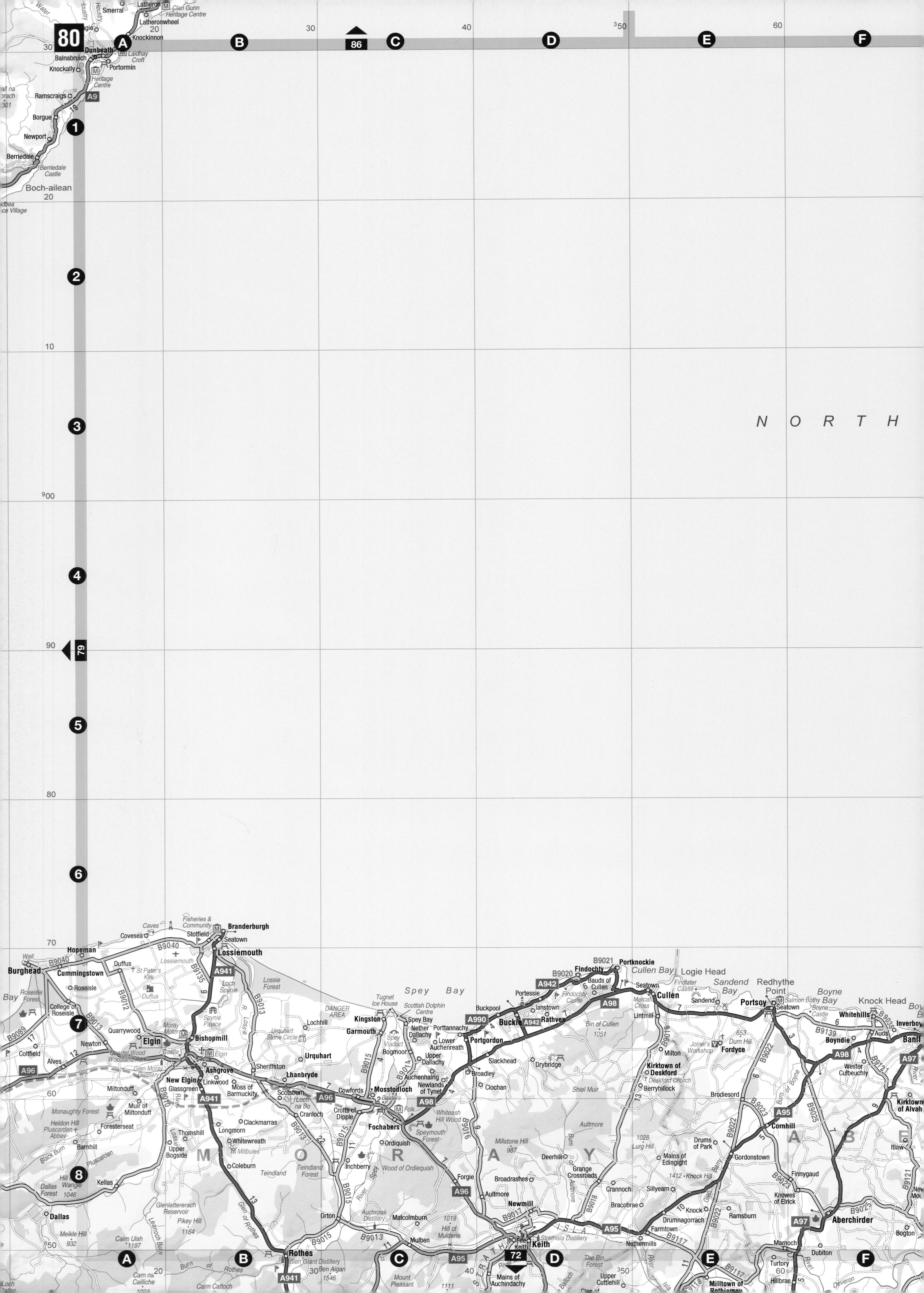
A
B
C
D
E
F
86
79
72
1
2
3
4
5
6
7
8
N O R T H
Dunbeath
Latheron
Latheronwheel
Knockinnon
Smerral
Clan Gunn Heritage Centre
Balnabruich
Knockally
Portormin
Laidhay Croft
Heritage Centre
Ramscraigs
Borgue
Newport
Berriedale
Berriedale Castle
Boch-ailean
A9
Spey Bay
Cullen Bay
Logie Head
Sandend Bay
Redhythe Point
Boyne Bay
Knock Head
Burghead
Hopeman
Cummingstown
Roseisle
College of Roseisle
Duffus
Covesea
Stotfield
Branderburgh
Seatown
Lossiemouth
Fisheries & Community
Elgin
Bishopmill
Ashgrove
New Elgin
Quarrywood
Newton
Alves
Coltfield
Miltonduff
Muir of Miltonduff
Glassgreen
Linkwood
Moss of Barmuckity
Lhanbryde
Urquhart
Sheriffston
Lochhill
Garmouth
Kingston
Mosstodloch
Cowfords
Fochabers
Spey Bay
Portgordon
Buckie
Buckpool
Portessie
Ianstown
Rathven
Findochty
Portknockie
Bauds of Cullen
Cullen
Seatown
Sandend
Portsoy
Fordyce
Whitehills
Banff
Boyndie
Inverboyndie
Cornhill
Aberchirder
Keith
Newmill
Rothes
Dallas
Kellas
Thornhill
Longmorn
Clackmarras
Whitewreath
Coleburn
Ordiquish
Inchberry
Mulben
Orton
Malcolmburn
Forgie
Aultmore
Broadrashes
Deerhill
Grange Crossroads
Crannoch
Bracobrae
Sillyearn
Knock
Drummagorrach
Farmtown
Nethermills
Ramsburn
Knowes of Elrick
Finnygaud
Gordonstown
Drums of Park
Kirktown of Deskford
Berryhillock
Milton
Lintmill
Brodiesord
Drybridge
Clochan
Broadley
Slackhead
Kirktown of Alvah
Marnoch
Dubiton
Turtory
Hillbrae
Mains of Auchindachy
Upper Cuttlehill
Milltown of Rothiemay
Bogton
Itlaw
A96
A941
A98
A990
A942
A95
A97
B9040
B9012
B9013
B9135
B9015
B9014
B9016
B9017
B9018
B9020
B9021
B9022
B9023
B9025
B9139
B9121
B9117
B9010
B9089
M O R A Y
Glen of Rothes
Teindland Forest
Monaughty Forest
Wood of Ordiequish
Speymouth Forest
Whiteash Hill Wood
Bin of Cullen 1051
Knock Hill 1412
Hill of Mulderie 1019
Millstone Hill 987
Lurg Hill 1028
Cairn Uish 1197
Meikle Hill 932
Pikey Hill 1164
Ben Aigan 1546
Glenlatterach Reservoir
Glen Grant Distillery
Strathisla Distillery
Auchroisk Distillery
Tugnet Ice House
Scottish Dolphin Centre
Spey Viaduct
Baxters
Spynie Palace
Duffus Castle
Urquhart Stone Circle
Moray Motor Museum
Glen Moray Distillery
Quarrel Wood Woodland Park
Findlater Castle
Salmon Bothy
Boyne Castle
Deskford Church
Joiner's Workshop
Dallas Forest
Hill of Wangie 1046
Loch Spynie
Lossie Forest
Heldon Hill
Pluscarden Abbey
Foresterseat
Barnhill
Upper Bogside
Tynet
Nether Dallachy
Upper Dallachy
Newlands of Tynet
Auchenhalrig
Porttannachy
Lower Auchenreath
Bogmoor
Crofts of Dipple
Cranloch
Scotsburn
Mains of Auchindachy
Edingight
Mains of Edingight
Western Culbeuchly
Auds
Carn na Cailliche
Cairn Cattoch
Mount Pleasant
The Bin Forest
Danger Area
20
30
40
50
60
10
900
90
80
70

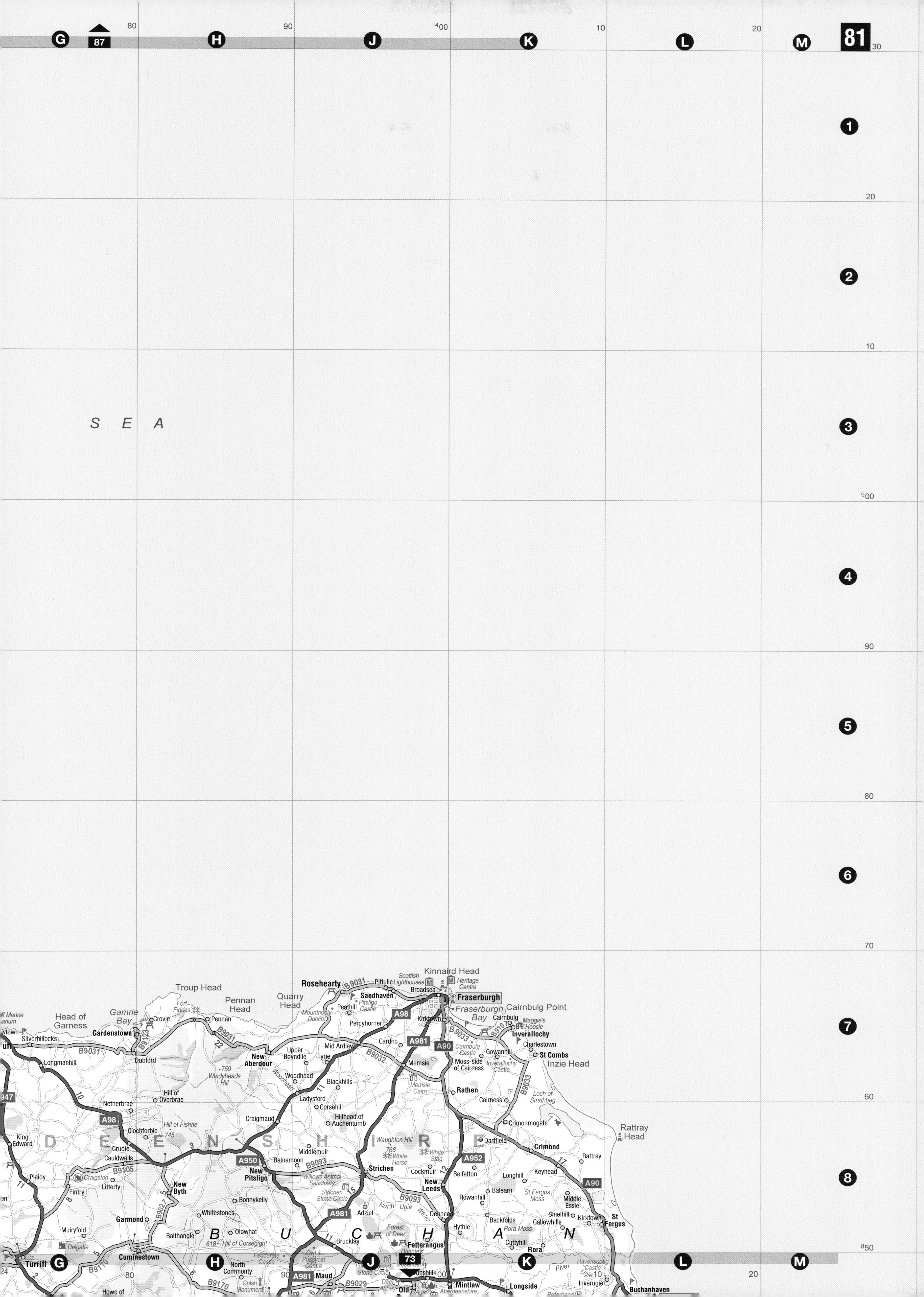

G
87
H
J
K
L
M
80
90
400
10
20
30
1
2
3
4
5
6
7
8
20
10
900
90
80
70
60
850
S E A
Troup Head
Pennan Head
Quarry Head
Rosehearty
Pittulie
Scottish Lighthouses
Kinnaird Head
Heritage Centre
Sandhaven
Broadsea
Fraserburgh
Fraserburgh Bay
Cairnbulg Point
Head of Garness
Gamrie Bay
Fort Fiddes
Crovie
Pennan
Gardenstown
Silverhillocks
Mounthooly Doocot
Peathill
Pitsligo Castle
Percyhorner
Kirktown
Cairnbulg
Maggie's Hoosie
Inverallochy
Charlestown
St Combs
Inzie Head
Longmanhill
Dubford
Upper Boyndlie
Tyrie
Mid Ardlaw
Cardno
Memsie
Cairnbulg Castle
Gowanhill
Moss-side of Cairness
Inverallochy Castle
New Aberdour
Windyheads Hill
Woodhead
Blackhills
Memsie Cairn
Rathen
Loch of Strathbeg
Cairness
Hill of Overbrae
Netherbrae
Ladysford
Corsehill
Hillhead of Auchentumb
Craigmaud
Crimonmogate
Rattray Head
King Edward
Clochforbie
Hill of Fishrie
Waughton Hill
White Horse
White Stag
Dartfield
Crimond
Rattray
Cauldwells
Crudie
Middlemuir
Balnamoon
New Pitsligo
Strichen
Cockmuir
Belfatton
Longhill
Keyhead
Plaidy
Craigston
Fintry
Litterty
New Byth
Willows Animal Sanctuary
Strichen Stone Circle
New Leeds
Balearn
St Fergus Moss
Rowanhill
Middle Essie
Bonnykelly
Whitestones
Adziel
North Ugie Water
Denhead
Backfolds
Gallowhills
Shielhill
Kirktown
St Fergus
Garmond
Muiryfold
Delgatie
Balthangie
Oldwhat
Hill of Corsegight
Forest of Deer
Hythie
Rora Moss
Brucklay
Fetterangus
Cuttyhill
Rora
Turriff
Cuminestown
Fedderate Castle
Owl & Pussycat Centre
North Commonty
73
Maud
Stone Circle
Mintlaw
Longside
Ravenscraig Castle
Inverugie
Buchanhaven
Howe of
Culsh Monument
Old Deer
Aberdeenshire
River Ugie
B U C H A N
D E E N S H I R E
A98
A981
A90
A950
A952
B9031
B9032
B9033
B9093
B9105
B9107
B9170
B9029
B9123
B9027

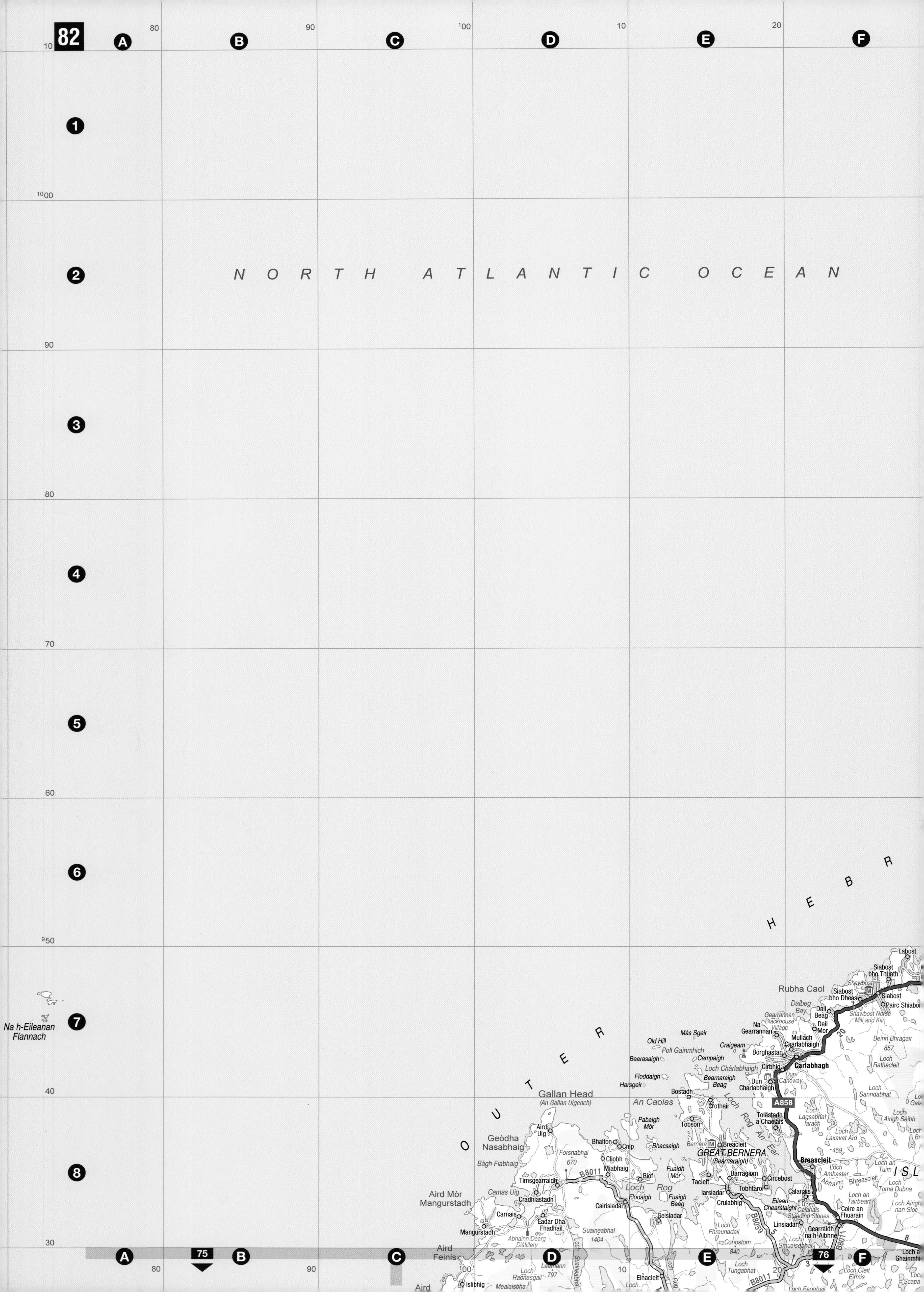

A   80   B   90   C   100   D   10   E   20   F

1

1000

N O R T H   A T L A N T I C   O C E A N

2

90

3

80

4

70

5

60

6

H   E   B   R

950

Labost

Siabost
bho Thuath
Rubha Caol   Shawbost M   Siabost
bho Dheas   Siabost
Dalbeg   Dail   Pairc Shiabost
Beag
Gearrannan   Dalbeg   Dail
Bay   Blackhouse   Mòr   Shawbost Norse
Village   Mill and Kiln
7   Na   Mullach   Beinn Bhragair
Old Hill   Màs Sgeir   Gearrannan   Charlabhaigh   857
Na h-Eileanan   Poll Gainmhich   Craigeam   Borghastan
Flannach   Bearasaigh   Loch
Campaigh   Bearnaraigh   Rathacleit
Floddaigh   Loch Chàrlabhaigh   Beag   Dun   Carlabhagh
Harsgeir   Cirbhig   Charlabhaigh
40   Bostadh   Dun
Gallan Head   An Caolas   Carloway   A858   Loch
(An Gallan Uigeach)   Pabaigh   Tolàstadh   Lagsabhat   Sanndabhat
Mòr   Tobson   a Chaolais   Iarach   Loch
Crothair   Loch   Airigh Sèibh
Aird   Bhacsaigh   Loch   Laxavat Ard   Loch
Uig   Bhalton   Cnip   Bernera M   Breacleit   Rog   ·459
Geòdha   Breascleit   Loch
Nasabhaig   Forsnabhaigh   Cliobh   GREAT BERNERA   An   Amhaster   Bhreascleit   Loch
8   Bàgh Fiabhaig   670   Miabhaig   Biof   (Bearnaraigh)   Barraglom   Circebost   Loch an   Tuim   Toma Dubha
Timsgearraidh   Fuaidh   Tacleit   Tairbeart   ISL
Aird Mòr   Camas Uig   Mòr   Iarsiadar   Calanais   Loch Airigh
Mangurstadh   Cradhlastadh   B8011   Loch   Rog   Tobhtarol   Coire an   nan Sloc
Carnais   Crulabhig   Eilean   Fhuarain
Cairisiadar   Flodaigh   Fuaigh   Chearstaight   Gearraidh
Eadar Dha   Beag   Calanais   na h-Aibhne
Mangurstadh   Fhadhail   Geisiadar   Standing Stones
30   Loch   Linsiadar   Loch
Aird   Suaineabhal   Fhreunadail   840   Loch
Feinis   A   75   B   1404   Abhainn Dearg   C   Leumrabhal   797   D   Conostom   E   76   F
80   Distillery   90   100   Loch   10   20   3   Loch Cleit
Aird   Raonasgail   Eirmis
Islibhig   Loch   Eiñacleit   Loch   B8011
Mealaisbha   Loch   Tungabhat   Loch Faoghail

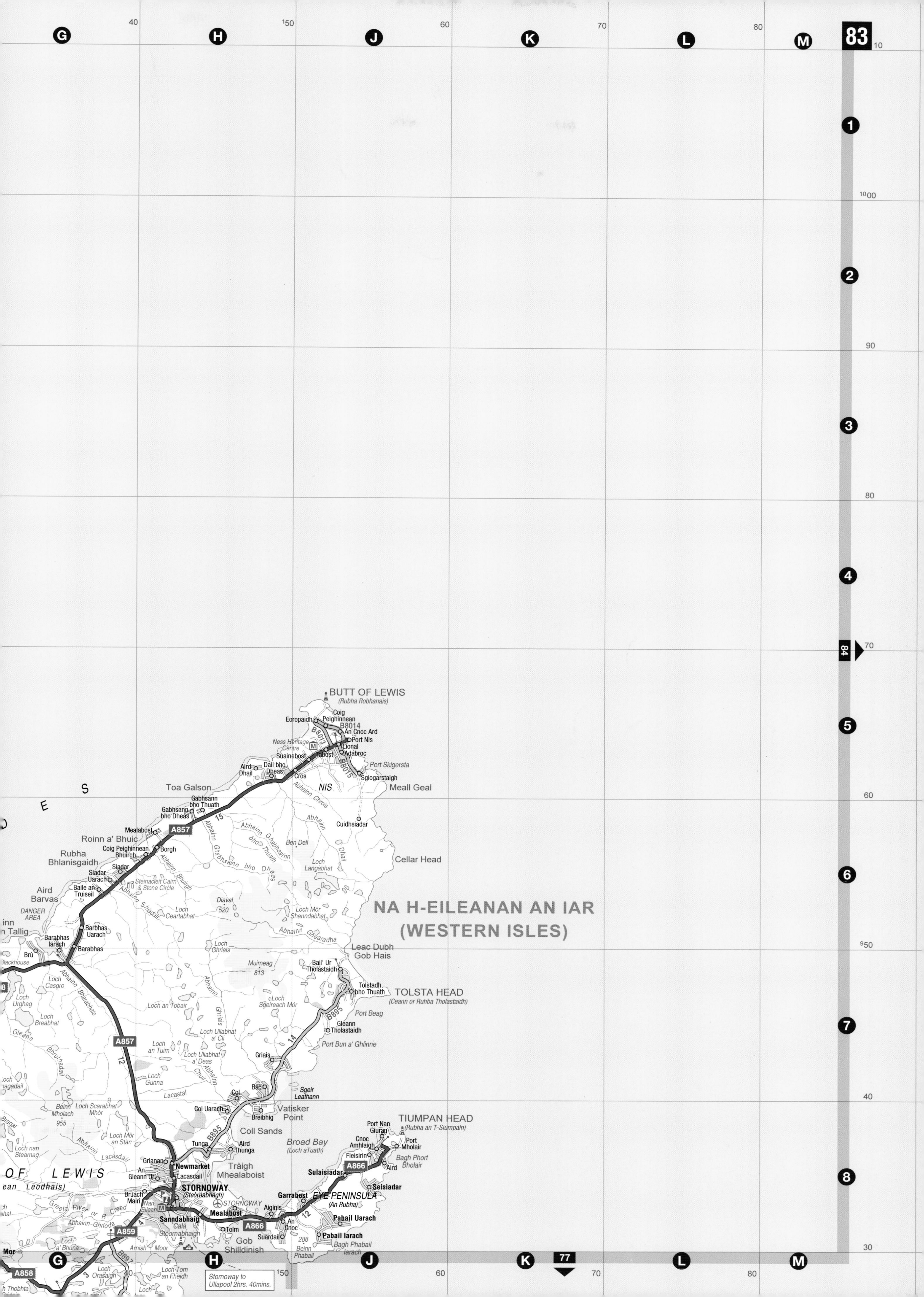

1

10'00

2

90

3

80

4

84 70

5

60

6

950

7

40

8

30

BUTT OF LEWIS
(Rubha Robhanais)

Eoropaidh
Coig
Peighinnean
B8014
An Cnoc Ard
Port Nis
Lional
Adabroc
Ness Heritage
Centre
Suainebost
Habost
Dail bho
Aird
Dhail
Dheas
Cros
NIS
Port Skigersta
Sgiogarstaigh
Cuidhsiadar
Meall Geal

Toa Galson
Gabhsann
bho Thuath
Gabhsann
bho Dheas
Mealabost
A857
Roinn a' Bhuic
Coig Peighinnean
Bhuirgh
Borgh
15
Ben Dell
Abhainn Chrois
Cellar Head
Rubha
Bhlanisgaidh
Siadar
Uarach
Siadar
Loch
Langabhat
Aird
Barvas
Baile an
Truiseil
Steinacleit Cairn
& Stone Circle
Diaval
520
Loch Mòr
Shanndabhat
Abhainn Gheàradha

DANGER
AREA

inn
n Tallig
Barbhas
Uarach
Barbhas
Iarach
Barbhas
Blackhouse
Bru
Loch
Casgro
Loch
Ghriais
Leac Dubh
Gob Hais

**NA H-EILEANAN AN IAR
(WESTERN ISLES)**

Loch
Urghag
Loch
Breabhat
Muirneag
813
Bail' Ur
Tholastaidh
Gleann
8
A857
12
Loch
Sgeireach Mòr
Loch an Tobair
Tolstadh
bho Thuath
TOLSTA HEAD
(Ceann or Ruhba Tholastaidh)
Port Beag
Gleann
Tholastaidh
B895
Port Bun a' Ghlinne
Loch an Tuim
Loch Ullabhat
a' Cli
14
Loch Ullabhat
a' Deas
Griais
Loch
Gunna
Lacastal
Loch
nagadail
Sgeir
Leathann
Col
Bac
Col Uarach
TIUMPAN HEAD
(Rubha an T-Siumpain)
Beinn
Mholach
955
Loch Mòr
an Starr
Breibhig
Vatisker
Point
Port Nan
Giuran
Cnoc
Amhlaigh
Port
Mholair
Loch nan
Stearnag
Coll Sands
Aird
Thunga
*Broad Bay
(Loch aTuath)*
Fleisirin
Aird
Tunga
B895
A866
OF LEWIS
(ean Leodhais)
Grianan
An
Gleann Ur
Lacasdail
Newmarket
Tràigh
Mhealaboist
Sulaisiadar
Seisiadar
Bruach
Mairi
STORNOWAY
(Steòrnabhagh)
Mealabost
EYE PENINSULA
(An Rubha)
Greeta River or
R Creed
Nan
Eilean
STORNOWAY
Aiginis
Garrabost
Pabail Uarach
Abhainn Ghrioda
Sanndabhaig
Cala
Steòrnabhaig
An
Cnoc
12
Mor
A859
A866
Tolm
Suardail
288
Beinn
Phabail
Pabail Iarach
Bagh Phabail
iarach
Loch
a' Bhùna
Gob
Shilldinish
h Thobhta
A858
Loch
Orasaigh
B897
Loch Tom
an Fheidh
Stornoway to
Ullapool 2hrs. 40mins.

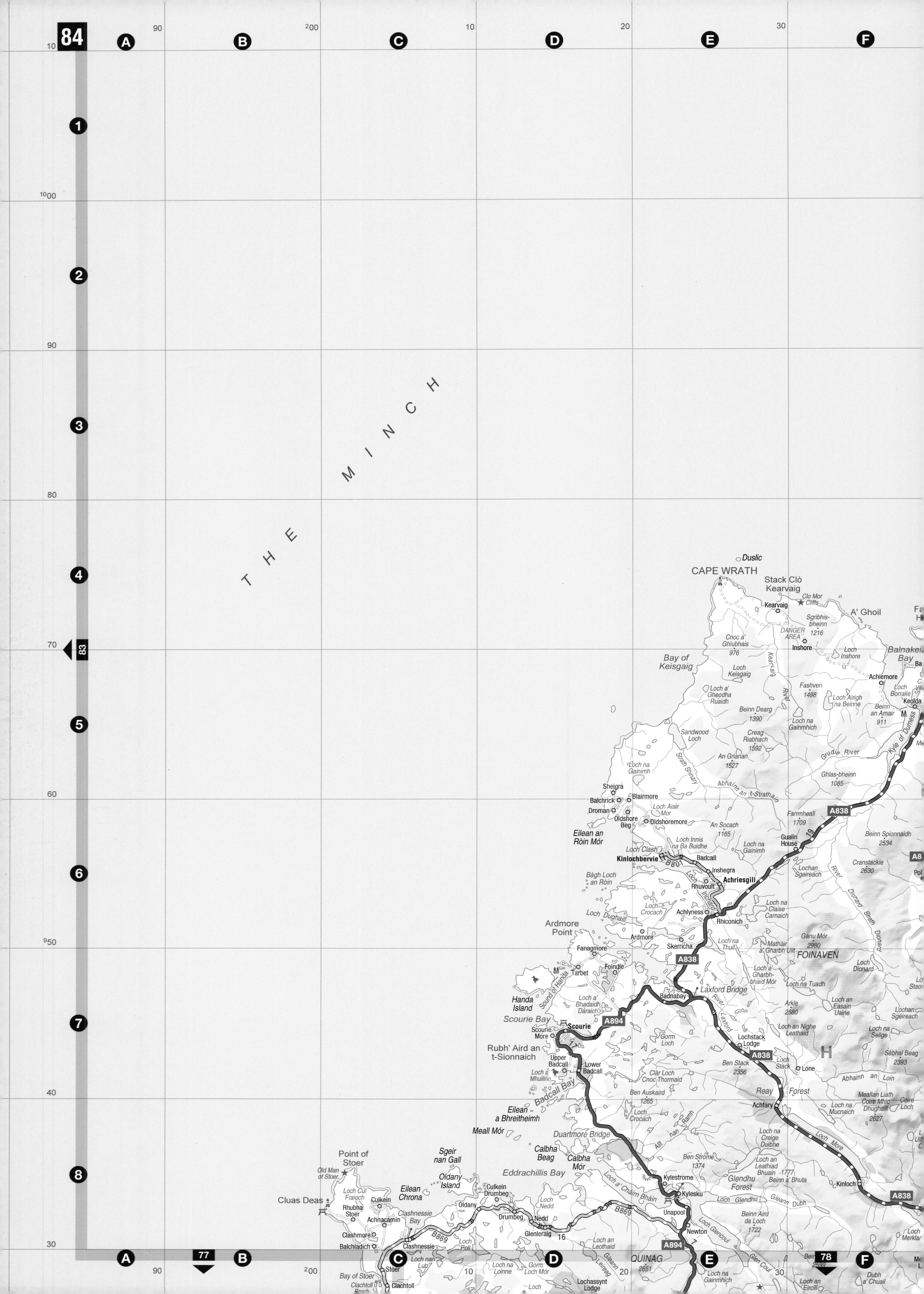
THE MINCH
CAPE WRATH
Duslic
Stack Clò Kearvaig
Kearvaig
Clo Mor Cliffs
A' Ghoil
Sgribhis-bheinn 1216
DANGER AREA
Inshore
Cnoc a' Ghiubhais 976
Loch Inshore
Balnakeil Bay
Bay of Keisgaig
Loch Keisgaig
Kearvaig River
Achiemore
Loch Borralie
Fashven 1498
Loch Airigh na Beinne
Loch a' Gheodha Ruaidh
Beinn an Amair 911
Keoldale
Kyle of Durness
Beinn Dearg 1390
Loch na Gainmhich
Sandwood Loch
Creag Riabhach 1592
Strath Shinary
Grudie River
An Grianan 1527
Loch na Gainimh
Ghlas-bheinn 1085
Abhainn an t-Strathain
Sheigra
Balchrick
Blairmore
Droman
Loch Aisir Mor
Oldshore Beg
Oldshoremore
Farmheall 1709
A838
Eilean an Ròin Mór
An Socach 1165
Beinn Spionnaidh 2534
Loch Clash
Loch Innis na Ba Buidhe
Loch na Gainimh
Gualin House
Kinlochbervie
B801
Badcall
Inshegra
Cranstackie 2630
Bàgh Loch an Ròin
Rhuvoult
Achriesgill
Lochan Sgeireach
River Dionard
Loch Inchard
Loch Crocach
Loch Dughaill
Achlyness
Rhiconich
Loch na Claise Carnaich
Strath Dionard
Ardmore Point
Ardmore
Loch na Thull
Ganu Mór 2980
Skerricha
Mathair a' Gharbh Uilt
FOINAVEN
Fanagmore
A838
Loch Dionard
Foindle
Tarbet
Loch a' Gharbh-bhaid Mór
Sound of Handa
Loch na Tuadh
Laxford Bridge
Badnabay
Handa Island
Loch a' Bhadaidh Daraich
River Laxford
Arkle 2580
Loch an Easain Uaine
Lochan Sgeireach
Scourie Bay
A894
Scourie
Scourie More
Loch an Nighe Leathaid
Gorm Loch
Lochstack Lodge
Loch na Seilge
Rubh' Aird an t-Sionnaich
A838
Sàbhal Beag 2393
Upper Badcall
Lower Badcall
Ben Stack 2356
Loch Stack
Lone
Loch a' Mhuilinn
Clàr Loch
Cnoc Thormaid
Abhainn an Loin
Badcall Bay
Ben Auskaird 1265
Reay Forest
Meallan Liath Coire Mhic Dhughaill 2627
Eilean a Bhreitheimh
Achfary
Loch Crocach
Loch na Mucnaich
Coire Loch
Meall Mór
Duartmore Bridge
Allt nan Ramh
Loch na Creige Duibhe
Loch More
Calbha Beag
Calbha Mór
Point of Stoer
Sgeir nan Gall
Ben Strome 1374
Old Man of Stoer
Eddrachillis Bay
Loch an Leathiad Bhuain
Beinn a' Bhuta 1777
Oldany Island
Kylestrome
Kinloch
A838
Loch Cùl Fraioch
Eilean Chrona
Culkein Drumbeg
Glendhu Forest
Cluas Deas
Culkein
Kylesku
Loch a' Chàirn Bhàin
Loch Glendhu
Gleann Dubh
Rhubha Stoer
Achnacarnin
Clashnessie Bay
Oldany
Loch Nedd
B869
Unapool
Drumbeg
Nedd
Beinn Aird da Loch 1722
Clashmore
B869
Glenleraig
Loch Glencoul
Loch Poll
Newton
Balchladich
Clashnessie
Loch an Leothaid
A894
QUINAG 2651
Glen Coul
Stoer
Loch nan Lub
Loch na Loinne
Gorm Loch Mór
Gleann Leireag
Loch na Gainmhich
Dubh a' Chuail
Bay of Stoer
Clachtoll Broch
Clachtoll
Loch
Lochassynt Lodge
Loch an Eircill
83
77
78

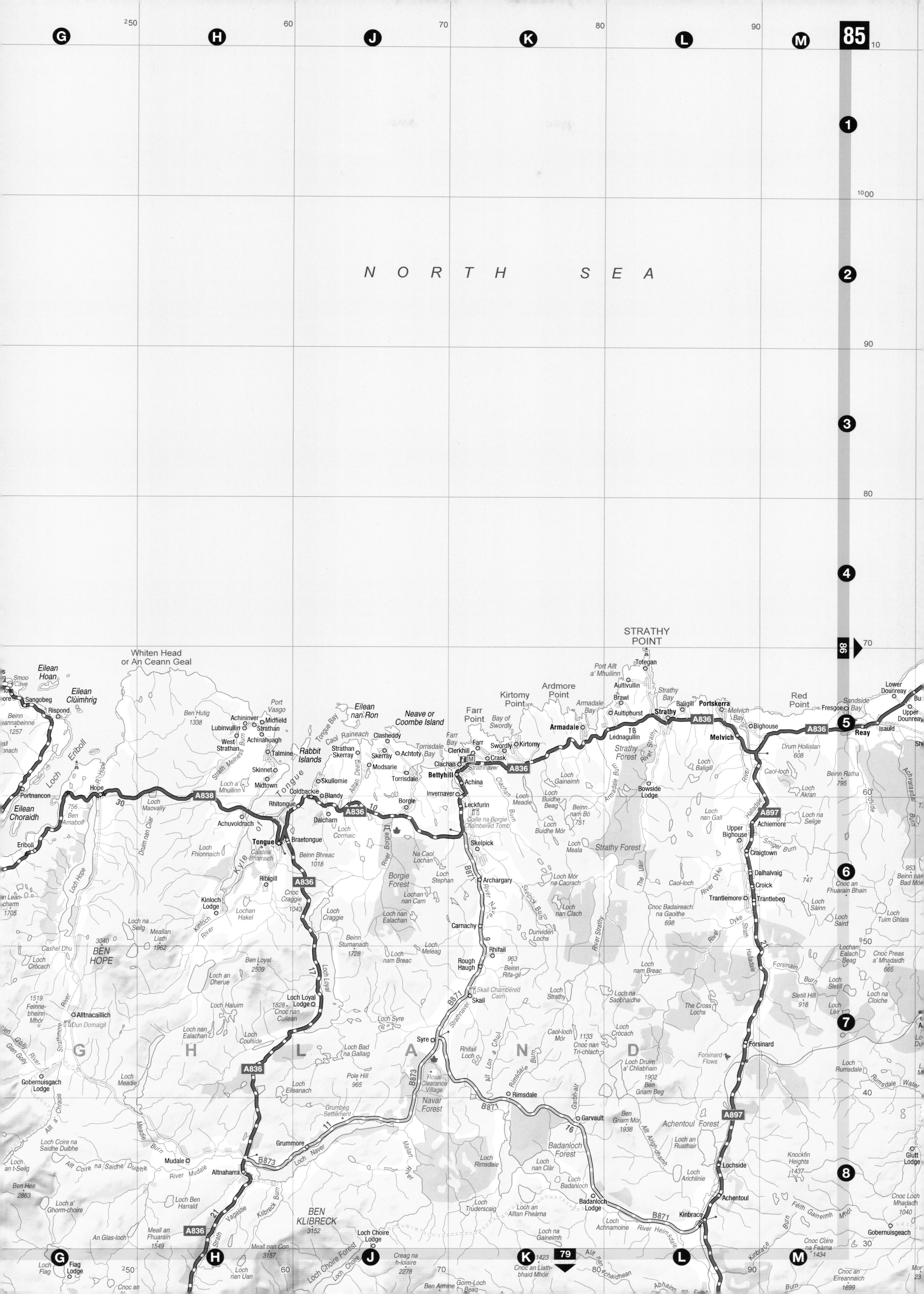
NORTH SEA
STRATHY POINT
Whiten Head or An Ceann Geal
Eilean Hoan
Eilean Clùimhrig
Sangobeg
Rispond
Loch Eriboll
Portnancon
Eilean Choraidh
Eriboll
Hope
A838
Ben Hutig 1338
Achininver
Midfield
Lubinvullin
Strathan
West Strathan
Achinahuagh
Talmine
Skinnet
Midtown
Port Vasgo
Rabbit Islands
Eilean nan Ron
Neave or Coombe Island
Tongue Bay
Kyle of Tongue
Rhitongue
Coldbackie
Achuvoldrach
Tongue
Braetongue
Castle Bharraich
Beinn Bhreac 1018
Ribigill
A836
Cnoc Craggie 1043
Kinloch Lodge
Loch Hakel
Skullomie
Blandy
Dalcharn
Strathan Skerray
Clashaddy
Skerray
Achtoty
Modsarie
Torrisdale
Borgie
Borgie Forest
Farr Point
Farr Bay
Farr
Clerkhill
Clachan
Bettyhill
Achina
Invernaver
Leckfurin
Skelpick
Archargary
Carnachy
Rhifail
Rough Haugh
Skail
Syre
Kirtomy Point
Kirtomy
Swordly
Crask
Bay of Swordly
Ardmore Point
Armadale
Armadale Bay
Port Allt a' Mhuilinn
Totegan
Aultivullin
Brawl
Aultiphurst
Strathy
Strathy Bay
Baligill
Portskerra
Melvich
Melvich Bay
Lednagullin
Strathy Forest
Bowside Lodge
Bighouse
Red Point
Fresgoe
Sandside Bay
Reay
Isauld
Lower Dounreay
Upper Dounreay
Drum Hollistan 608
Beinn Ratha 795
Achiemore
Upper Bighouse
Craigtown
Dalhalvaig
Croick
Trantlemore
Trantlebeg
A897
Forsinard
Forsinard Flows
Strath Halladale
Cnoc Badaireach na Gaoithe 698
The Cross Lochs
Loch nam Breac
Loch na Saobhaidhe
Loch Druim a' Chliabhain
Ben Griam Beg 1902
Ben Griam Mòr 1938
Achentoul Forest
Garvault
Rimsdale
Badanloch Forest
Badanloch Lodge
Lochside
Achentoul
Kinbrace
Knockfin Heights 1437
Loch Rimsdale
Gobernuisgeach
Sletill Hill 918
Cnoc Preas a' Mhadaidh 665
B871
B873
Rosal Clearance Village
Navar Forest
Grummore
Loch Naver
Altnaharra
Mudale
Loch Loyal
Loch Loyal Lodge
Ben Loyal 2509
Meallan Liath 1962
BEN HOPE 3040
Cashel Dhu
Alltnacaillich
Dun Domaigil
Gobernuisgach Lodge
Strathmore River
Ben Hee 2863
BEN KLIBRECK 3152
Loch Choire Lodge
Loch Choire Forest
Meall nan Con 3157
Creag na h-Iolaire 2278
Beinn Stumanadh 1728
Pole Hill 965
G H L A N D
Fiag Lodge
Loch Fiag
A836
79
86

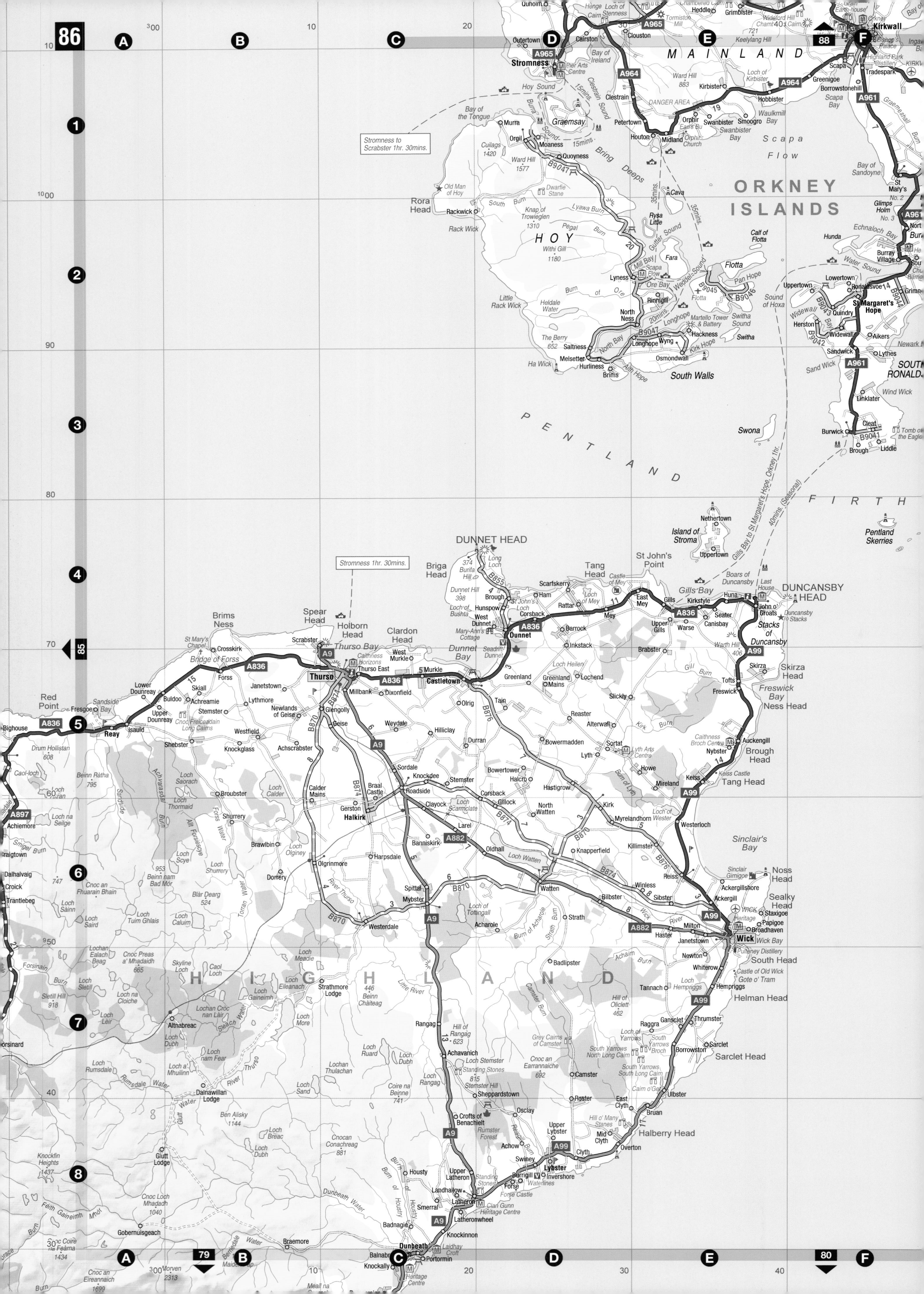
ORKNEY ISLANDS
MAINLAND
Kirkwall
Stromness
HOY
Graemsay
Hoy Sound
Scapa Flow
Flotta
South Walls
SOUTH RONALDSAY
St Margaret's Hope
Burray Village
Swona
Island of Stroma
Pentland Skerries
PENTLAND FIRTH
Stromness to Scrabster 1hr. 30mins.
Stromness 1hr. 30mins.
Gills Bay to St Margaret's Hope, Orkney 1hr.
40mins. (Seasonal)
Old Man of Hoy
Rora Head
Rackwick
Ward Hill 1577
Cuilags 1420
Withi Gill 1180
Knap of Trowieglen 1310
Lyness
Longhope
Melsetter
Orphir
Houton
Clestrain
Ward Hill 883
A965
A964
A961
B9047
B9045
B9046
B9043
B9042
B9041
DUNNET HEAD
Dunnet
Dunnet Bay
Brough
Ham
Scarfskerry
Tang Head
St John's Point
Castle of Mey
East Mey
Gills
Gills Bay
Huna
John o' Groats
DUNCANSBY HEAD
Duncansby Stacks
Stacks of Duncansby
Skirza Head
Freswick Bay
Ness Head
Brough Head
Keiss
Tang Head
Sinclair's Bay
Noss Head
Sealky Head
Wick
Wick Bay
South Head
Helman Head
Sarclet Head
Halberry Head
Lybster
Latheron
Dunbeath
Thurso
Thurso Bay
Scrabster
Holborn Head
Clardon Head
Castletown
Murkle
Dunnet Head
Brims Ness
Crosskirk
Forss
Reay
Red Point
Sandside Bay
Bighouse
Halkirk
Georgemas
Watten
Mybster
Spittal
Westerdale
Altnabreac
Dalnawillan Lodge
Strathmore Lodge
Rangag
Achavanich
Camster
Ulbster
Thrumster
Clyth
Forse
Borrowston
Houstry
Braemore
Gobernuisgeach
Morven 2313
Knockfin Heights 1437
Ben Alisky 1144
Loch Watten
Loch Calder
Loch More
Loch Rangag
Loch Stemster
Loch of Yarrows
Grey Cairns of Camster
Hill of Yarrows
Hill o' Many Stanes
Scaraben
H I G H L A N D
A9
A99
A836
A882
A897
B870
B874
B876
B855
A
B
C
D
E
F
1
2
3
4
5
6
7
8
85
79
80
88

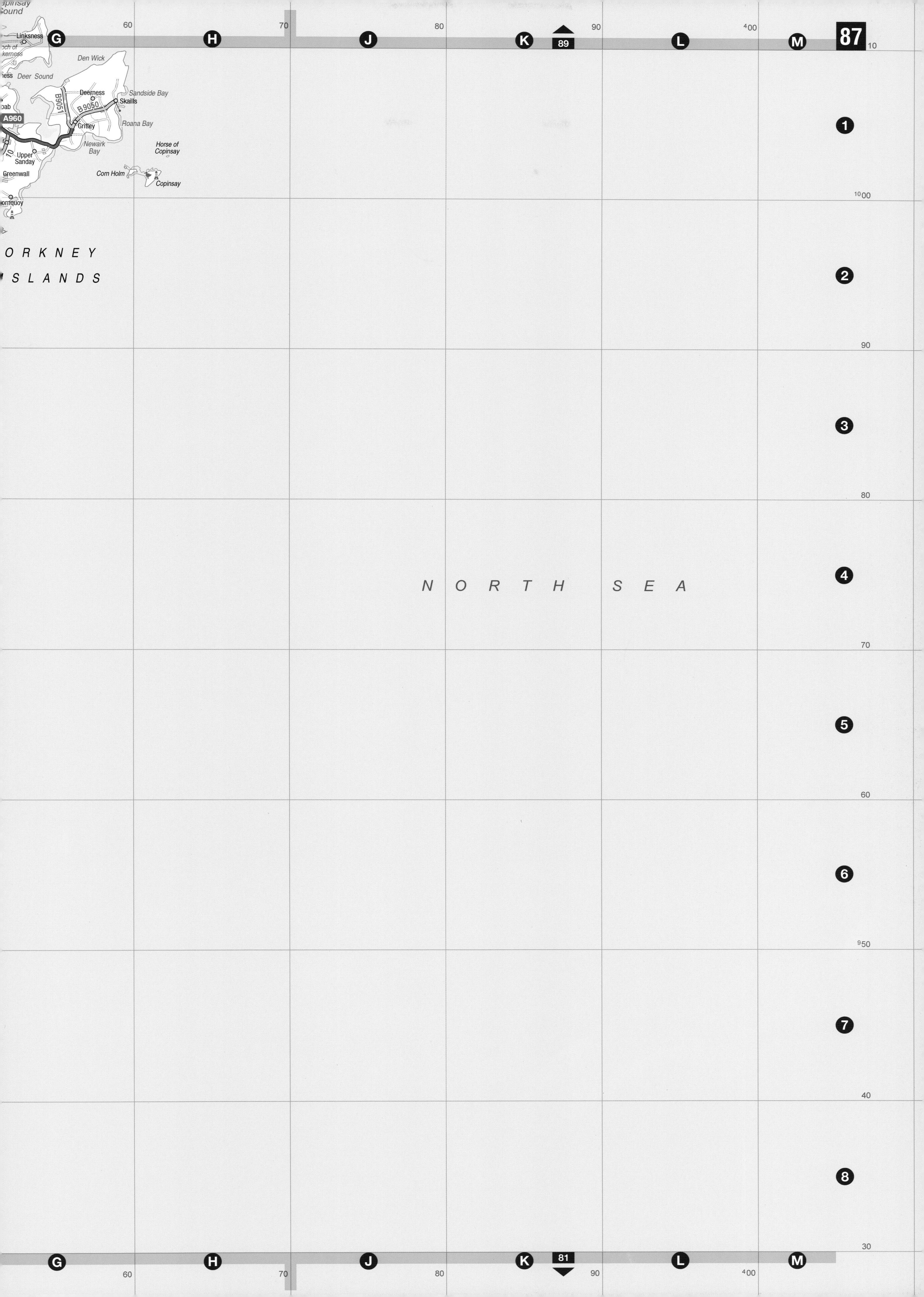

ORKNEY

ISLANDS

Copinsay Sound
Linksness

Den Wick
Deerness
Sandside Bay
B9051 *Skaills*
B9050 *Gritley* *Roana Bay*
A960
Newark
Bay
Upper
Sanday *Horse of*
Copinsay
Greenwall
Corn Holm
Copinsay
ornquoy

Deer Sound

N O R T H   S E A

1

2

3

4

5

6

7

8

90

80

70

60

950

40

30

1000

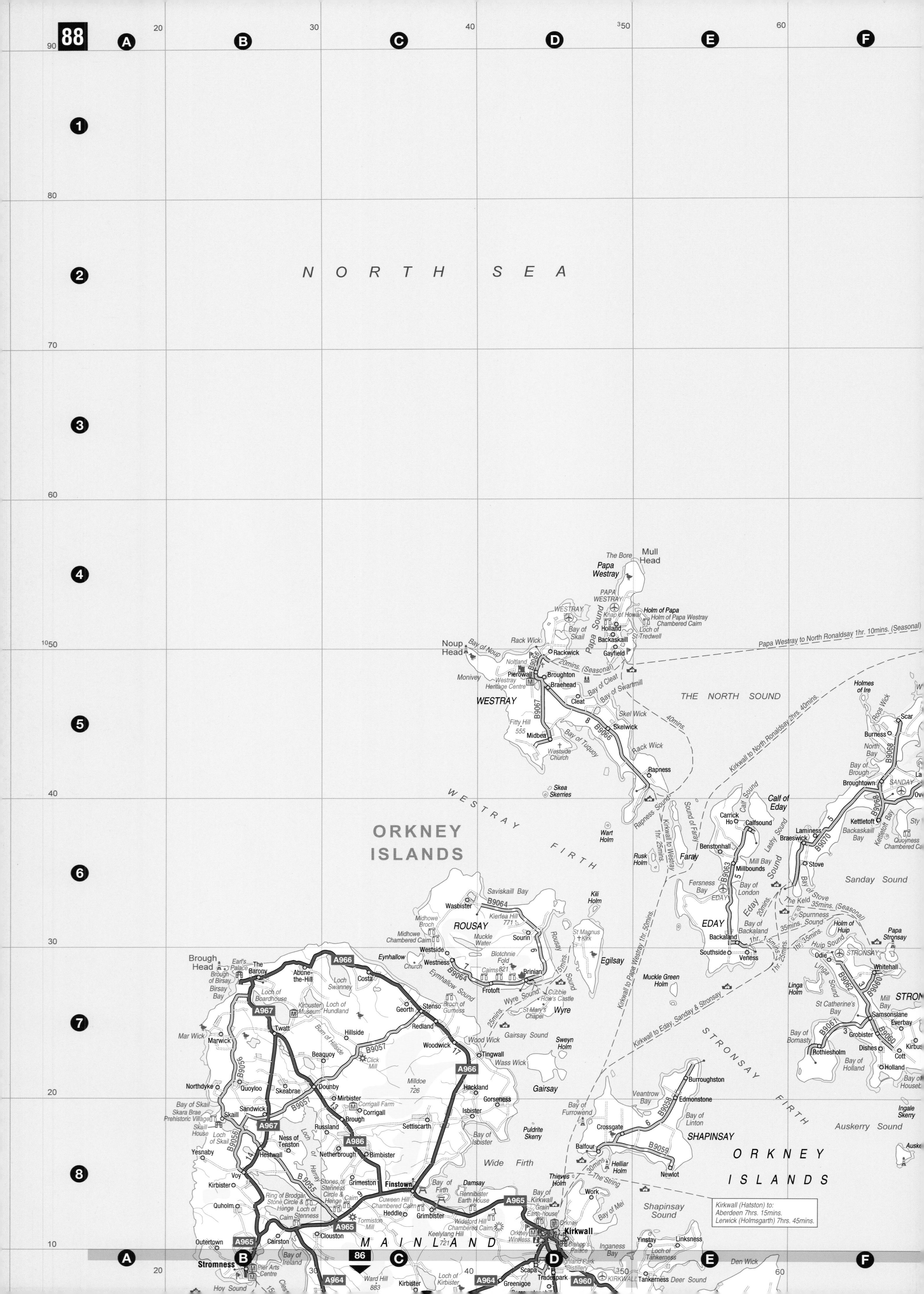
NORTH SEA
ORKNEY ISLANDS
Papa Westray
Mull Head
Westray
Noup Head
Pierowall
Rackwick
Broughton
Braehead
Cleat
Skelwick
Midbea
Rapness
THE NORTH SOUND
WESTRAY FIRTH
Rousay
Wasbister
Sourin
Westside
Westness
Brinian
Frotoft
Egilsay
Wyre
Gairsay
Eday
Calf of Eday
Faray
Backaland
Southside
Veness
Sanday
Scar
Burness
Broughtown
Kettletoft
Laminess
Braeswick
Stove
Sanday Sound
Stronsay
Whitehall
Rothiesholm
Shapinsay
Balfour
Burroughston
Edmonstone
Crossgate
Newlot
STRONSAY FIRTH
Brough Head
The Barony
Marwick
Skaill
Bay of Skaill
Skara Brae Prehistoric Village
Yesnaby
Voy
Stromness
Hestwall
Quoyloo
Dounby
Evie
Costa
Twatt
Russland
Finstown
Grimeston
Heddle
Grimbister
Stenso
Tingwall
Rendall
Gorseness
Isbister
Settiscarth
Kirkwall
Scapa
Tradespark
Clouston
Cairston
MAINLAND
Wide Firth
Shapinsay Sound
Auskerry Sound
Kirkwall (Hatston) to:
Aberdeen 7hrs. 15mins.
Lerwick (Holmsgarth) 7hrs. 45mins.
Papa Westray to North Ronaldsay 1hr. 10mins. (Seasonal)
Kirkwall to North Ronaldsay 2hrs. 40mins.
Kirkwall to Papa Westray 1hr. 50mins.
Kirkwall to Eday, Sanday & Stronsay
A965
A966
A967
A986
A964
A960
B9055
B9056
B9057
B9064
B9066
B9067
B9059
B9060
B9062
B9063
B9068
B9069
B9070
86

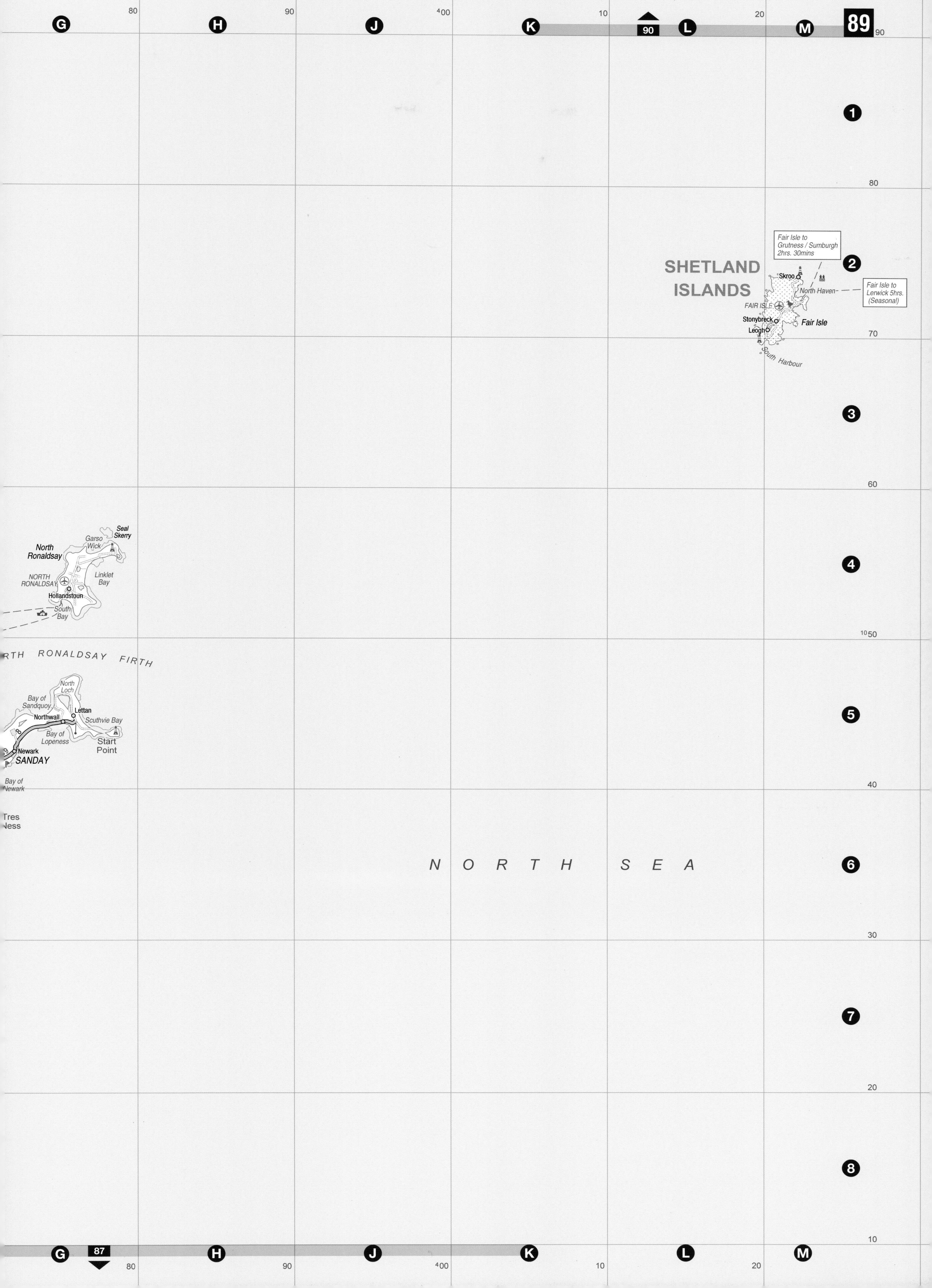

1

80

Fair Isle to Grutness / Sumburgh 2hrs. 30mins	

SHETLAND ISLANDS

Skroo

North Haven

Fair Isle to Lerwick 5hrs. (Seasonal)

2

FAIR ISLE

Stonybreck

Leogh

Fair Isle

70

South Harbour

3

60

Seal Skerry

Garso Wick

North Ronaldsay

NORTH RONALDSAY

Linklet Bay

Hollandstoun

South Bay

4

¹⁰50

RTH RONALDSAY FIRTH

North Loch

Bay of Sandquoy

Lettan

Northwall

Scuthvie Bay

Bay of Lopeness

Start Point

Newark

SANDAY

5

Bay of Newark

40

Tres Ness

N O R T H   S E A

6

30

7

20

8

10

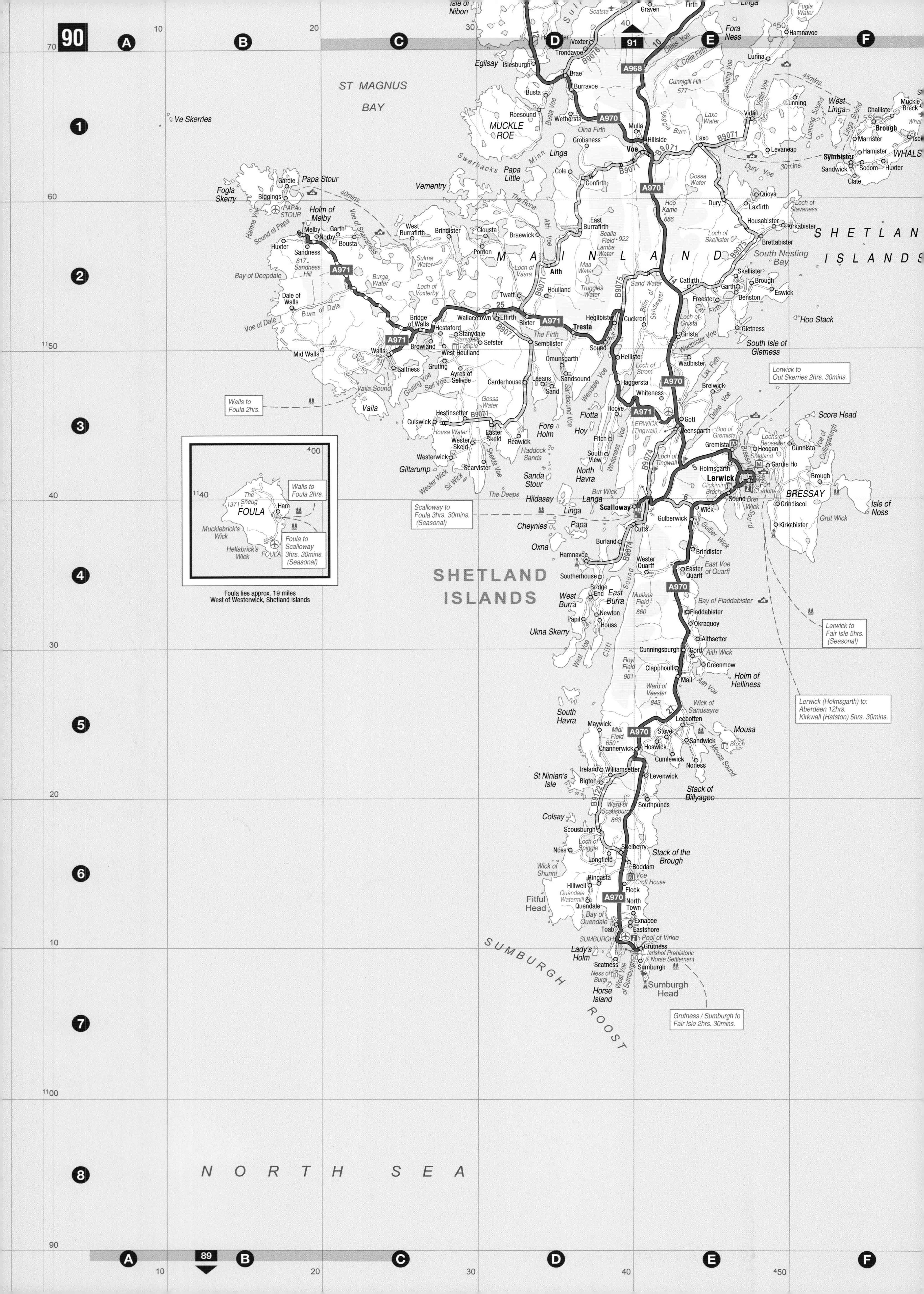

A   10   B   20   C   30   D   40   91   10   E   450   F

70

ST MAGNUS
BAY

Isle of
Nibon

Scatsta

Graven   Firth

Linga

Fugla
Water

Hamnavoe

Voxter
Egilsay   Islesburgh
Trondavoe

Dales Voe   Fora
Ness

West
Linga

Challister   Muckle
Breck

1   Ve Skerries   Brae   Busta
Burravoe

Roesound

Busta Voe

Wetherstra

Cunnigill Hill
577

Colla Firth

Swining Voe

Tidlin Voe

Lunning

Lunning Sound

Isbi

Brough

MUCKLE
ROE   Olna Firth   A970   Mulla

Hillside   Laxo   B9071

Laxo
Water

Vidlin   Levaneap

Quoys

45mins   WHALS

Symbister   Hamister

60   Fogla
Skerry   Gardie   Papa Stour

Biggings

Melby   Norby
Garth   Bousta   Grobsness

Swarbacks
Minn   Linga

Voe   B9071

Vementry   Papa
Little   Cole   Gonfirth   A970

Gossa
Water

Dury Voe   30mins.

Sandwick   Sodom   Huxter   Clate

Dury   Laxfirth   Loch of
Stavaness

Huxter
Holm of
Melby

Sandness   PAPA
STOUR   West
Burrafirth   Brindister   Clousta
Braewick   MAINLAND   East
Burrafirth   Scalla
Field   922   Hoo Kame
686

Housabister   Kirkabister

SHETLAND
ISLANDS

2   Hamna Voe   817
Sandness
Hill   A971   Sulma
Water   Loch of
Vaara   Aith   Maa
Water   Lamba
Water   Sand Water   Catfirth   Brettabister

Dale of
Walls   Bay of Deepdale   Burga
Water   Twatt   Houlland   Freester   Garth   Brough   South Nesting
Bay

Hoo Stack

Voe of Dale   25   Loch of
Voxterby   Bridge
of Walls   Wallacetown   Effirth   Bixter   A971   B9075   Whiteness   Girlsta   Gletness

Burn of Dale   A971   Hestaford   Stanydale
Temple   Stanydale   Sefster   Tresta   Cuckron   Sound   Hellister   Wadbister   South Isle of
Gletness

50   Mid Walls   Walls   Browland   West Houlland   Semblister   The Firth   Heglibister   Haggersta   Loch of
Strom   Lerwick to
Out Skerries 2hrs. 30mins.

Saltness   Gruting   Ayres of
Selivoe   Garderhouse   Leeans
Sand   Sandsound   Omunsgarth   A970   Breiwick

Vaila Sound   Gruting Voe   Seli Voe   Gossa
Water   Flotta   Hoove   A971   Gott   Score Head

Walls to
Foula 2hrs.   Culswick   B9071   Easter
Skeld   Hoy   Fitch   Bod of
Gremista   Gunnista

Vaila   Hestinsetter   Reawick   LERWICK
(Tingwall)   Jeensgarth   Lochs of
Beosetter   Heogan   Voe of
Cullingsburgh

3   400   Wester
Skeld   Haddock
Sands   South
View   B9074   Gremista   Gardie Ho   Brough

Westerwick   Scarvister   North
Havra   Loch of
Tingwall   Holmsgarth   Lerwick   Clickimin
Broch   Fort
Charlotte   BRESSAY

1140   The
Sheug   1371   Walls to
Foula 2hrs.   Giltarump   Sanda
Stour   Scalloway   Grindiscol   Kirkabister   Isle of
Noss

40   FOULA   Ham   Hildasay   Langa   Sound Brei
Wick   Grut Wick

Mucklebrick's
Wick   Foula to
Scalloway
3hrs. 30mins.
(Seasonal)   The Deeps   Bur Wick   Scalloway to
Foula 3hrs. 30mins.
(Seasonal)   Cutts   Wick   Lerwick to
Fair Isle 5hrs.
(Seasonal)

Hellabrick's
Wick   FOULA   Cheynies   Linga   Papa   Gulberwick

4   Foula lies approx. 19 miles
West of Westerwick, Shetland Islands   Oxna   Burland   Brindister

Hamnavoe   Wester
Quarff   Easter
Quarff   East Voe
of Quarff

SHETLAND
ISLANDS   West
Burra   Bridge
End   East
Burra   A970   Bay of Fladdabister   Lerwick to
Fair Isle 5hrs.
(Seasonal)

Papil   Newton
Houss   Muskna
Field
860   Fladdabister

Ukna Skerry   Okraquoy   Aithsetter

30

Cunningsburgh   Gord   Aith Wick

Roy
Field
961   Clapphoull   Greenmow   Holm of
Helliness

5   South
Havra   Ward of
Veester
843   Mail   Aith Voe

Lerwick (Holmsgarth) to:
Aberdeen 12hrs.
Kirkwall (Hatston) 5hrs. 30mins.

Maywick   Midi
Field
650   A970   Stove   Wick of
Sandsayre   Mousa

Channerwick   Hoswick   Sandwick   Broch

Ireland   Williamsetter   Cumlewick   Noness

St Ninian's
Isle   Bigton   Levenwick   Mousa Sound   Stack of
Billyageo

20   Colsay   Ward of
Scousburgh
863   Southpunds

B9122   Scousburgh   Skelberry

6   Noss   Loch of
Spiggie   Boddam   Stack of the
Brough

Wick of
Shunni   Longfield   Ringasta   Voe
Croft House

Hillwell   Fleck

Fitful
Head   Quendale
Watermill   Quendale   A970   North
Town   Exnaboe

10   Bay of
Quendale   Toab   Eastshore
Pool of Virkie

SUMBURGH   Grutness

SUMBURGH   Jarlshof Prehistoric
& Norse Settlement

Lady's
Holm   Scatness   Sumburgh

Ness of
Burgi   West
Voe
of
Sumburgh   Sumburgh
Head

7   Horse
Island   SUMBURGH
ROOST   Grutness / Sumburgh to
Fair Isle 2hrs. 30mins.

1100

8   NORTH   SEA

90   A   10   89   B   20   C   30   D   40   450   E   F

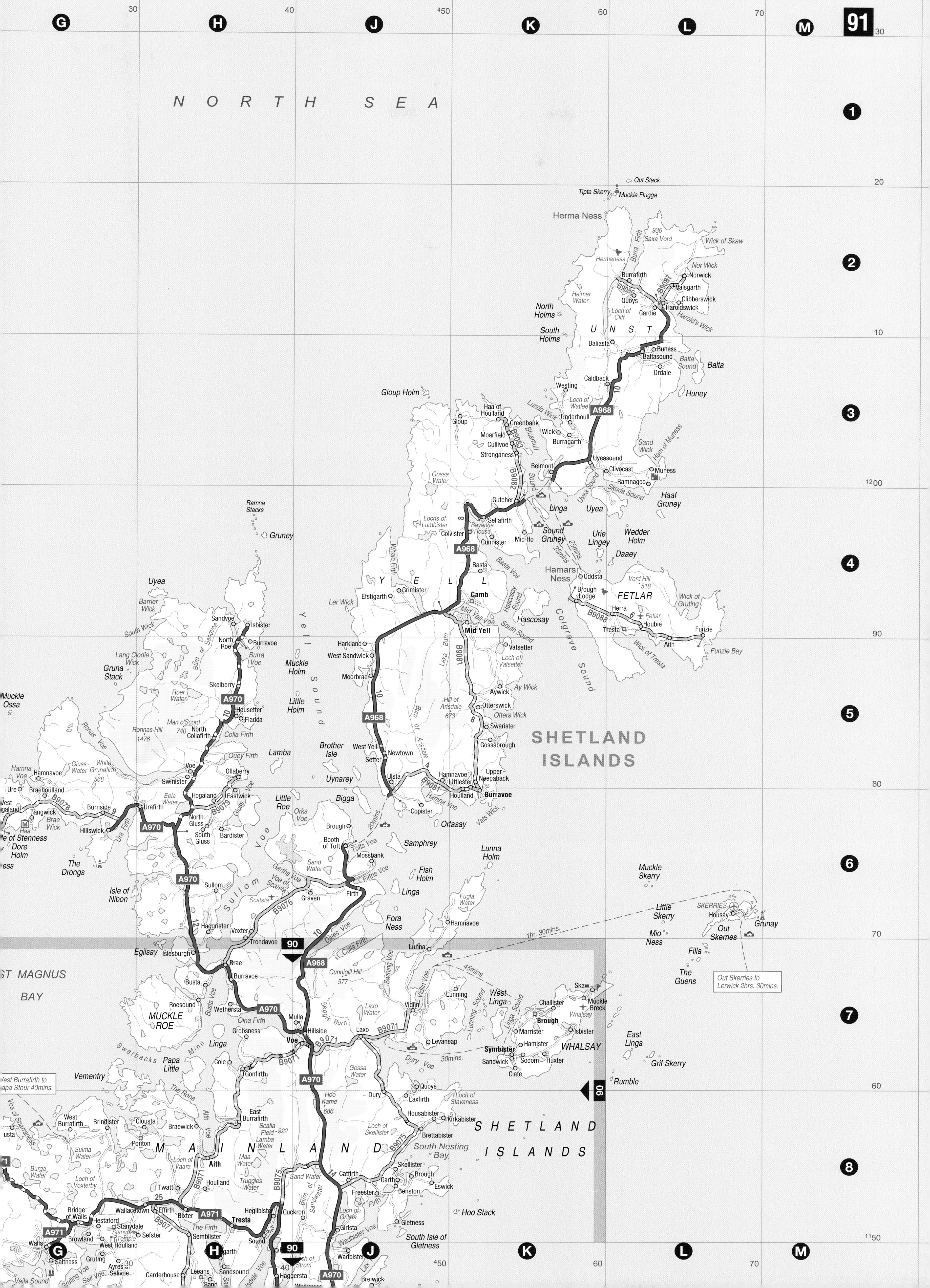

N O R T H S E A
Out Stack
Tipta Skerry
Muckle Flugga
Herma Ness
Hermaness
936 Saxa Vord
Wick of Skaw
Burra Firth
Burrafirth
Nor Wick
Norwick
Valsgarth
Clibberswick
Haroldswick
Harold's Wick
Heimar Water
Quoys
Loch of Cliff
Gardie
North Holms
South Holms
U N S T
Baliasta
Buness
Baltasound
Balta Sound
Balta
Ordale
Caldback
Huney
Westing
Loch of Watlee
Lunda Wick
Underhoull
Wick
Burragarth
Sand Wick
Ham of Muness
Uyeasound
Clivocast
Muness
Ramnageo
Skuda Sound
Haaf Gruney
Belmont
Linga
Uyea
Uyea Sound
Gloup Holm
Haa of Houlland
Gloup
Greenbank
Moarfield
Cullivoe
Stronganess
Bluemull Sound
Gossa Water
Gutcher
Sellafirth
Bayanne House
Lochs of Lumbister
Colvister
Cunnister
Mid Ho
Sound Gruney
25mins.
Urie Lingey
Wedder Holm
Daaey
Hamars Ness
Oddsta
Brough Lodge
Vord Hill 518
FETLAR
Wick of Gruting
Herra
Fetlar
Houbie
Tresta
Aith
Funzie
Funzie Bay
Wick of Tresta
Colgrave Sound
Basta
Basta Voe
Camb
Y E L L
Whale Firth
Grimister
Efstigarth
Ler Wick
Mid Yell Voe
Mid Yell
Hascosay Sound
Hascosay
South Sound
Vatsetter
Loch of Vatsetter
Harkland
West Sandwick
Moorbrae
Laxa Burn
Ay Wick
Aywick
Hill of Arisdale 673
Otterswick
Otters Wick
Swarister
Gossabrough
Burn of Arisdale
West Yell
Setter
Newtown
Ulsta
Hamnavoe
Littlester
Upper Neepaback
Houlland
Burravoe
Copister
Hamna Voe
Orfasay
Vats Wick
SHETLAND ISLANDS
Ramna Stacks
Gruney
Uyea
Barrier Wick
South Wick
Sandvoe
Burn of Sandvoe
Isbister
North Roe
Burravoe
Burra Voe
Lang Clodie Wick
Gruna Stack
Skelberry
Roer Water
Muckle Holm
Little Holm
Yell Sound
Muckle Ossa
Housetter
Fladda
Man o'Scord 740
North Collafirth
Colla Firth
Ronnas Hill 1476
Ronas Voe
Quey Firth
Lamba
Brother Isle
Uynarey
Hamna Voe
Hamnavoe
Gluss Water
White Grunafirth 568
Voe
Swinister
Ollaberry
Ure
Braehoulland
Eela Water
Hogaland
Eastwick
Gluss Voe
Little Roe
Orka Voe
Bigga
Tangwick
Burnside
Urafirth
North Gluss
South Gluss
Bardister
Haa
Brae Wick
Hillswick
Ura Firth
Brough
Booth of Toft
Tofts Voe
Samphrey
Dore Holm
The Drongs
Mossbank
Lunna Holm
Sand Water
Garths Voe
Voe of Scatsta
Fish Holm
Muckle Skerry
Isle of Nibon
Sullom
Sullom Voe
Firths Voe
Linga
Scatsta
Graven
Firth
Fugla Water
Little Skerry
SKERRIES
Housay
Out Skerries
Grunay
Haggrister
Voxter
Fora Ness
Hamnavoe
Mio Ness
Egilsay
Islesburgh
Trondavoe
Dales Voe
Lunna
1hr. 30mins.
Filla
ST MAGNUS BAY
Brae
Colla Firth
Cunnigill Hill 577
45mins.
The Guens
Out Skerries to Lerwick 2hrs. 30mins.
Busta
Burravoe
Busta Voe
Swining Voe
Vidlin Voe
Lunning
Skaw
West Linga
Challister
Muckle Breck
Roesound
Wethersta
Segie Burn
Laxo Water
Vidlin
Lunning Sound
Linga Sound
Brough
Whalsay
MUCKLE ROE
Olna Firth
Mulla
Grobsness
Hillside
Laxo
Marrister
Isbister
East Linga
Voe
Levaneap
Hamister
Swarbacks Minn
Linga
Symbister
WHALSAY
Papa Little
Cole
Dury Voe
Sandwick
Sodom
Huxter
Grif Skerry
Vementry
Gonfirth
Gossa Water
30mins.
Ciate
Rumble
West Burrafirth to Papa Stour 40mins.
The Rona
Hoo Kame 686
Dury
Quoys
Laxfirth
Loch of Stavaness
Voe of Snarraness
West Burrafirth
Brindister
Clousta
Braewick
East Burrafirth
Aith Voe
Scalla Field 922
Housabister
Kirkabister
Loch of Skellister
Brettabister
S H E T L A N D
Ponton
Lamba Water
South Nesting Bay
I S L A N D S
Sulma Water
M A I N L A N D
Burga Water
Loch of Vaara
Aith
Maa Water
Skellister
Catfirth
Loch of Voxterby
Houlland
Truggles Water
Sand Water
Brough
Garth
Eswick
Twatt
Burn of Sandwater
Freester
Benston
Cat Firth
Bridge of Walls
Wallacetown
Effirth
Bixter
Tresta
Heglibister
Cuckron
Hoo Stack
Hestaford
Stanydale
Stanydale Temple
The Firth
Loch of Girlsta
Gletness
Browland
Sefster
Semblister
Sound
Girlsta
South Isle of Gletness
Walls
West Houlland
Wadbister Voe
Saltness
Gruting
Ayres
Garth
Loch of Strom
Wadbister
Gruting Voe
Seli Voe
Selivoe
Garderhouse
Leeans
Sandsound
Haggersta
Lax Firth
Breiwick
Vaila Sound
Sand
A970
A968
A971
B9086
B9087
B9082
B9088
B9081
B9078
B9079
B9076
B9071
B9075
90

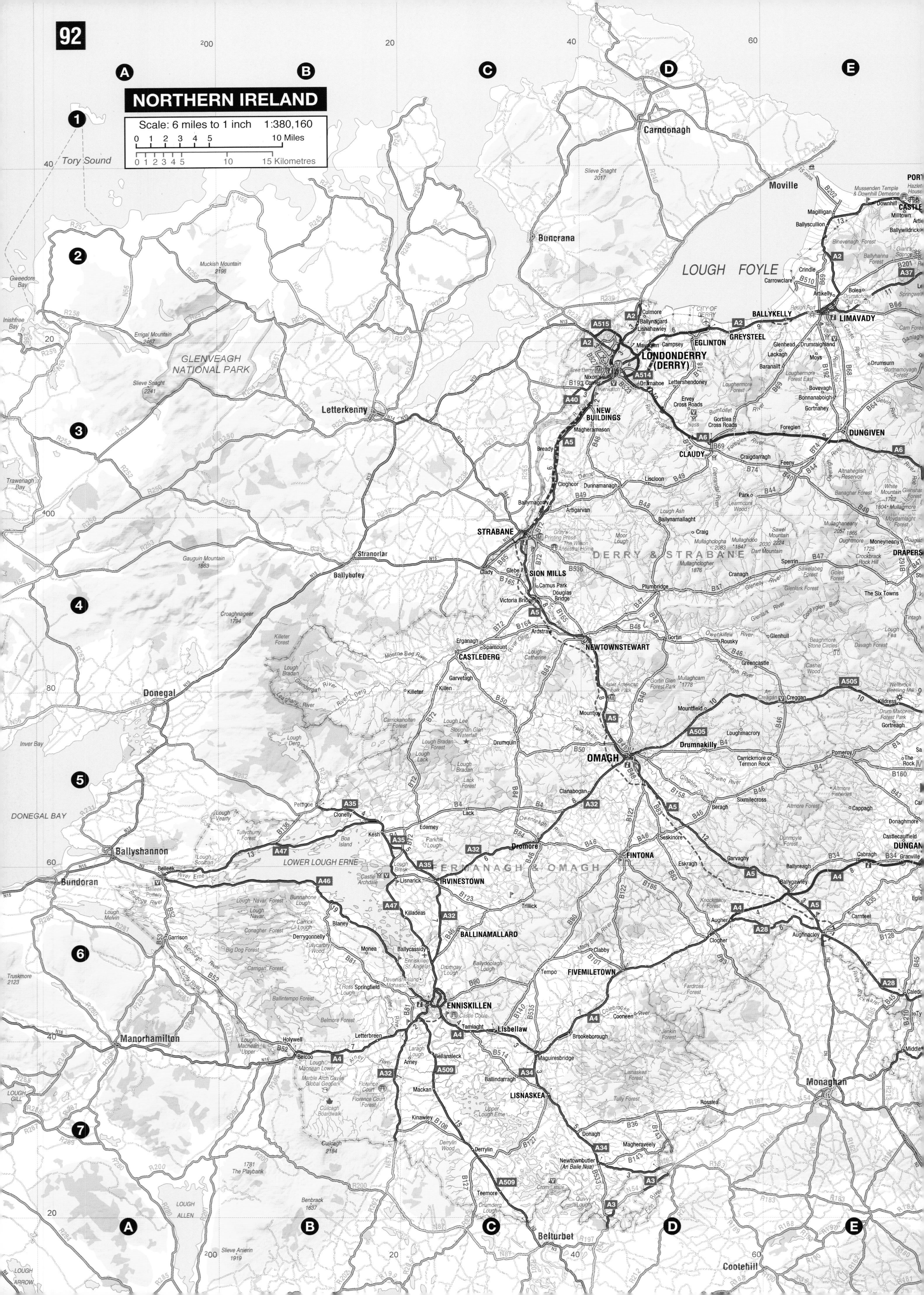
NORTHERN IRELAND
Scale: 6 miles to 1 inch 1:380,160
0 1 2 3 4 5 10 Miles
0 1 2 3 4 5 10 15 Kilometres
Tory Sound
Carndonagh
Moville
Buncrana
LOUGH FOYLE
Gweedore Bay
Muckish Mountain 2198
Errigal Mountain 2467
GLENVEAGH NATIONAL PARK
Slieve Snaght 2241
Slieve Snaght 2017
Letterkenny
LONDONDERRY (DERRY)
CITY OF DERRY
EGLINTON
GREYSTEEL
BALLYKELLY
LIMAVADY
DUNGIVEN
CLAUDY
NEW BUILDINGS
Trawenagh Bay
STRABANE
SION MILLS
Stranorlar
Ballybofey
Gauguin Mountain 1863
DERRY & STRABANE
Plumbridge
Croaghnageer 1794
Victoria Bridge
NEWTOWNSTEWART
CASTLEDERG
Gortin
Donegal
Inver Bay
OMAGH
Drumquin
DONEGAL BAY
Ballyshannon
Bundoran
LOWER LOUGH ERNE
IRVINESTOWN
Dromore
FINTONA
FERMANAGH & OMAGH
BALLINAMALLARD
FIVEMILETOWN
Ballygawley
Aughnacloy
Augher
Clogher
DUNGANNON
ENNISKILLEN
Lisbellaw
Manorhamilton
LISNASKEA
Monaghan
Truskmore 2123
LOUGH GILL
Cuilcagh 2184
Newtownbutler (An Baile Nua)
Belturbet
Cootehill
LOUGH ALLEN
Slieve Anierin 1919
Benbrack 1637
LOUGH ARROW
A
B
C
D
E
1
2
3
4
5
6
7

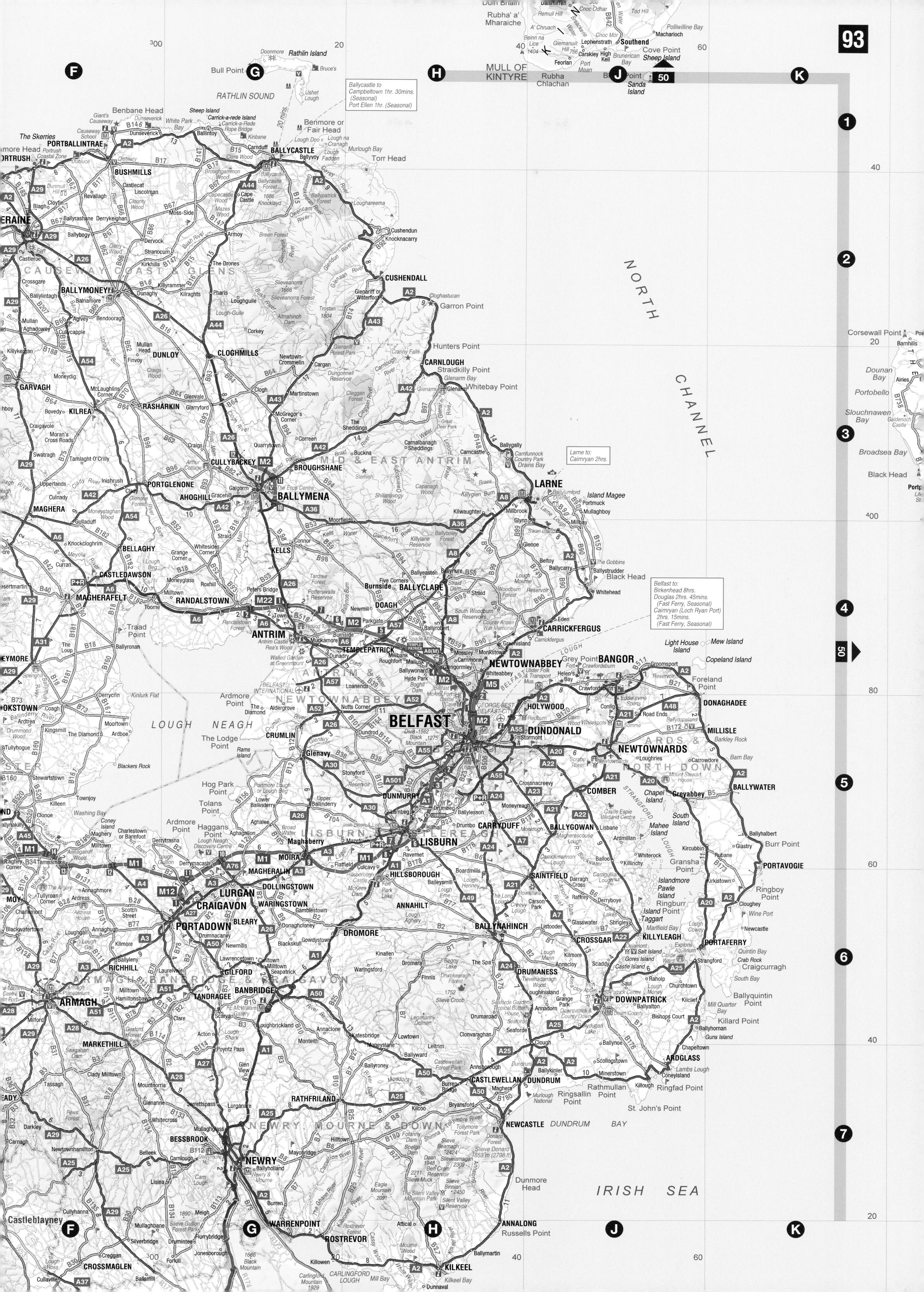
Rathlin Island
Bull Point
RATHLIN SOUND
Ballycastle to Campbeltown 1hr. 30mins. (Seasonal) Port Ellen 1hr. (Seasonal)
MULL OF KINTYRE
Southend
Sanda Island
Benbane Head
Giant's Causeway
The Skerries
PORTBALLINTRAE
BUSHMILLS
BALLYCASTLE
Fair Head
Torr Head
COLERAINE
CAUSEWAY COAST & GLENS
BALLYMONEY
CUSHENDALL
Garron Point
NORTH CHANNEL
Corsewall Point
DUNLOY
CLOGHMILLS
Hunters Point
CARNLOUGH
Straidkilly Point
Whitebay Point
GARVAGH
KILREA
RASHARKIN
MID & EAST ANTRIM
CULLYBACKEY
BROUGHSHANE
Larne to: Cairnryan 2hrs.
PORTGLENONE
AHOGHILL
BALLYMENA
LARNE
Island Magee
MAGHERA
Black Head
BELLAGHY
CASTLEDAWSON
MAGHERAFELT
KELLS
BALLYCLARE
DOAGH
RANDALSTOWN
ANTRIM
Belfast to: Birkenhead 8hrs. Douglas 2hrs. 45mins. (Fast Ferry, Seasonal) Cairnryan (Loch Ryan Port) 2hrs. 15mins. (Fast Ferry, Seasonal)
CARRICKFERGUS
TEMPLEPATRICK
NEWTOWNABBEY
BANGOR
Copeland Island
Mew Island
ANTRIM & NEWTOWNABBEY
LOUGH NEAGH
BELFAST
HOLYWOOD
DONAGHADEE
CRUMLIN
DUNDONALD
MILLISLE
NEWTOWNARDS
ARDS & NORTH DOWN
BALLYWATER
DUNMURRY
COMBER
Greyabbey
LISBURN & CASTLEREAGH
CARRYDUFF
BALLYGOWAN
LISBURN
Burr Point
MOIRA
HILLSBOROUGH
SAINTFIELD
PORTAVOGIE
MAGHERALIN
DOLLINGSTOWN
LURGAN
CRAIGAVON
WARINGSTOWN
PORTADOWN
BLEARY
DROMORE
ANNAHILT
BALLYNAHINCH
CROSSGAR
KILLYLEAGH
PORTAFERRY
RICHHILL
GILFORD
ARMAGH BANBRIDGE & CRAIGAVON
DRUMANESS
TANDRAGEE
BANBRIDGE
DOWNPATRICK
ARMAGH
MARKETHILL
ARDGLASS
CASTLEWELLAN
DUNDRUM
Ringfad Point
RATHFRILAND
St. John's Point
NEWCASTLE
DUNDRUM BAY
NEWRY MOURNE & DOWN
BESSBROOK
NEWRY
Slieve Donard 853m (2798ft)
IRISH SEA
Castleblayney
WARRENPOINT
ROSTREVOR
ANNALONG
CROSSMAGLEN
KILKEEL
CARLINGFORD LOUGH
F
G
H
J
K
1
2
3
4
5
6
7
50

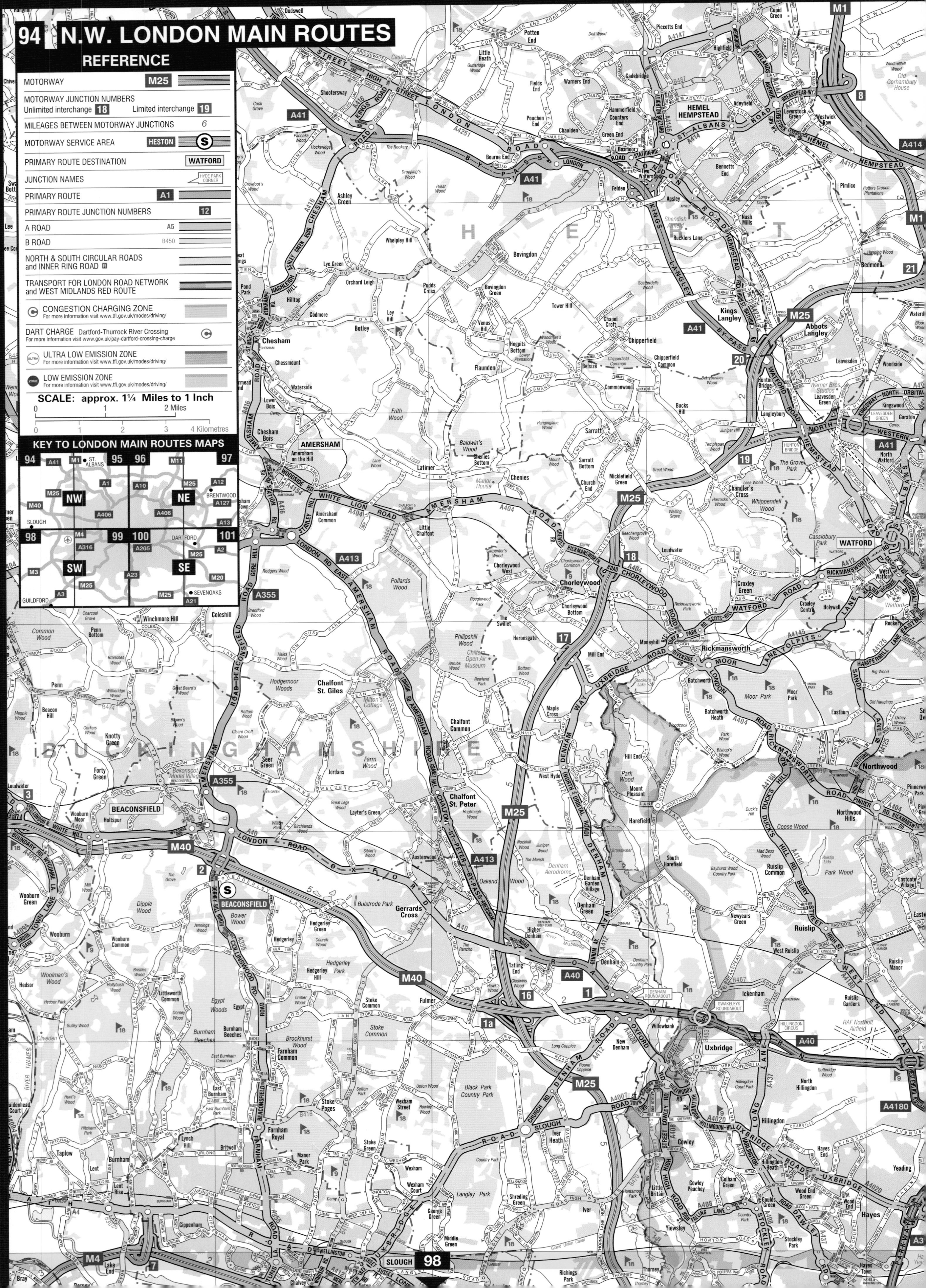

REFERENCE

MOTORWAY	M25
MOTORWAY JUNCTION NUMBERS	
Unlimited interchange **18** Limited interchange **19**	
MILEAGES BETWEEN MOTORWAY JUNCTIONS	6
MOTORWAY SERVICE AREA	HESTON Ⓢ
PRIMARY ROUTE DESTINATION	WATFORD
JUNCTION NAMES	HYDE PARK CORNER
PRIMARY ROUTE	A1
PRIMARY ROUTE JUNCTION NUMBERS	12
A ROAD	A5
B ROAD	B450
NORTH & SOUTH CIRCULAR ROADS and INNER RING ROAD	Ⓑ
TRANSPORT FOR LONDON ROAD NETWORK and WEST MIDLANDS RED ROUTE	

Ⓒ CONGESTION CHARGING ZONE
For more information visit www.tfl.gov.uk/modes/driving/

DART CHARGE   Dartford-Thurrock River Crossing   Ⓒ
For more information visit www.gov.uk/pay-dartford-crossing-charge

ULEZ ULTRA LOW EMISSION ZONE
For more information visit www.tfl.gov.uk/modes/driving/

ZONE LOW EMISSION ZONE
For more information visit www.tfl.gov.uk/modes/driving/

SCALE: approx. 1¼ Miles to 1 Inch

0 — 1 — 2 Miles

0 — 1 — 2 — 3 — 4 Kilometres

KEY TO LONDON MAIN ROUTES MAPS

94	95	96	97
NW		NE	
98	99	100	101
SW		SE	

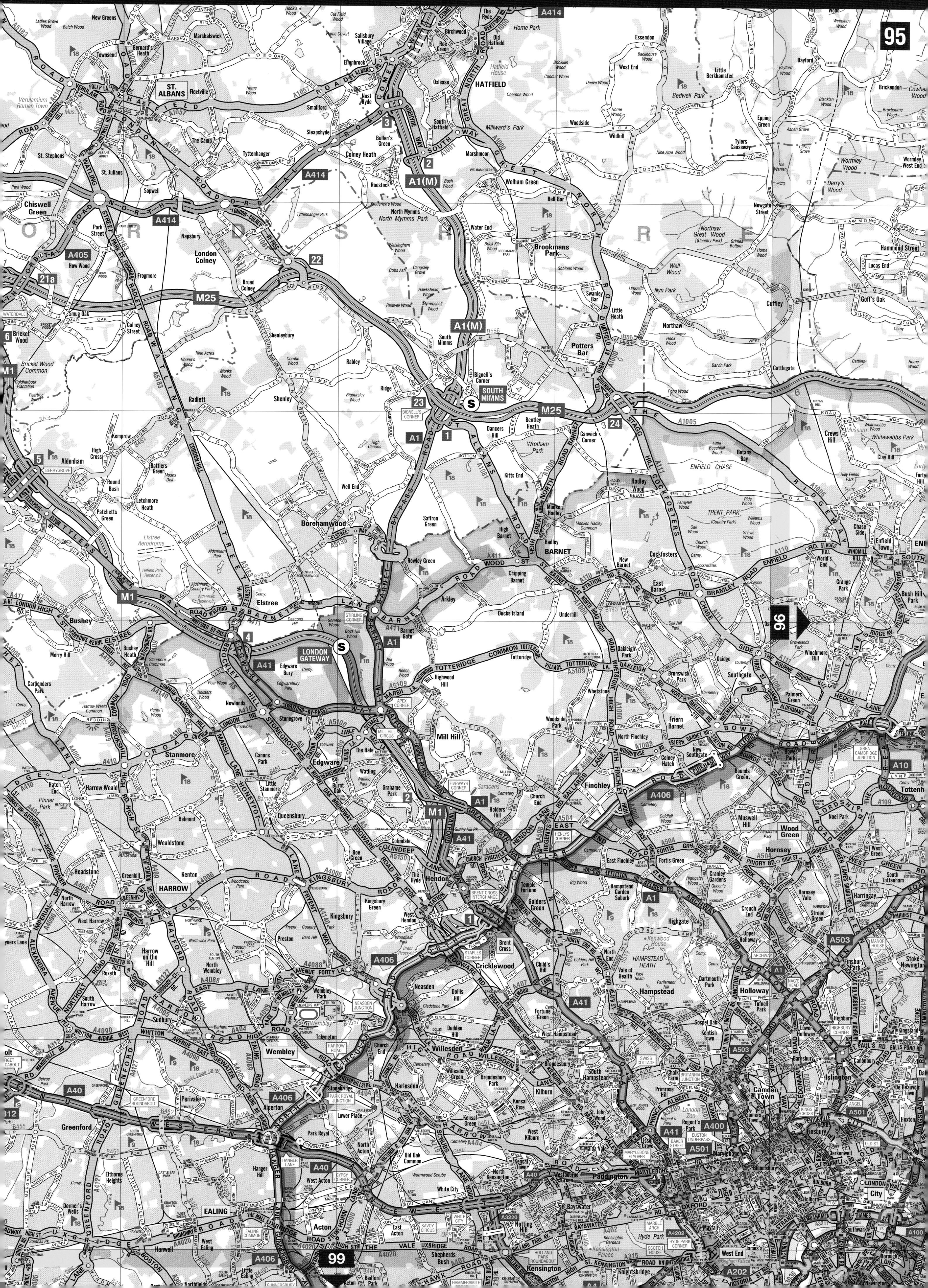
ST. ALBANS
HATFIELD
London Colney
Welham Green
Brookmans Park
Potters Bar
South Mimms
SOUTH MIMMS
Shenley
Radlett
Borehamwood
Elstree
Bushey
BARNET
Cockfosters
Enfield Chase
Stanmore
Edgware
Mill Hill
Finchley
HARROW
Wembley
Kingsbury
Hendon
Cricklewood
Hampstead
Highgate
Holloway
Islington
Camden Town
Willesden
Harlesden
Kilburn
Paddington
Marylebone
Kensington
Acton
EALING
Greenford
Perivale
Alperton
Bayswater
Notting Hill
Shepherds Bush
Oxford
M25
M1
A1(M)
A406
A40
A41
A414
A405
LONDON GATEWAY
STIRLING CORNER
HERTFORDSHIRE
Hatfield House
Whitewebbs Park
Trent Park
Northaw
Cuffley
Goff's Oak
Crews Hill
Enfield Town
Southgate
Wood Green
Hornsey
Harringay
Stoke Newington
Finsbury Park
City

96

99

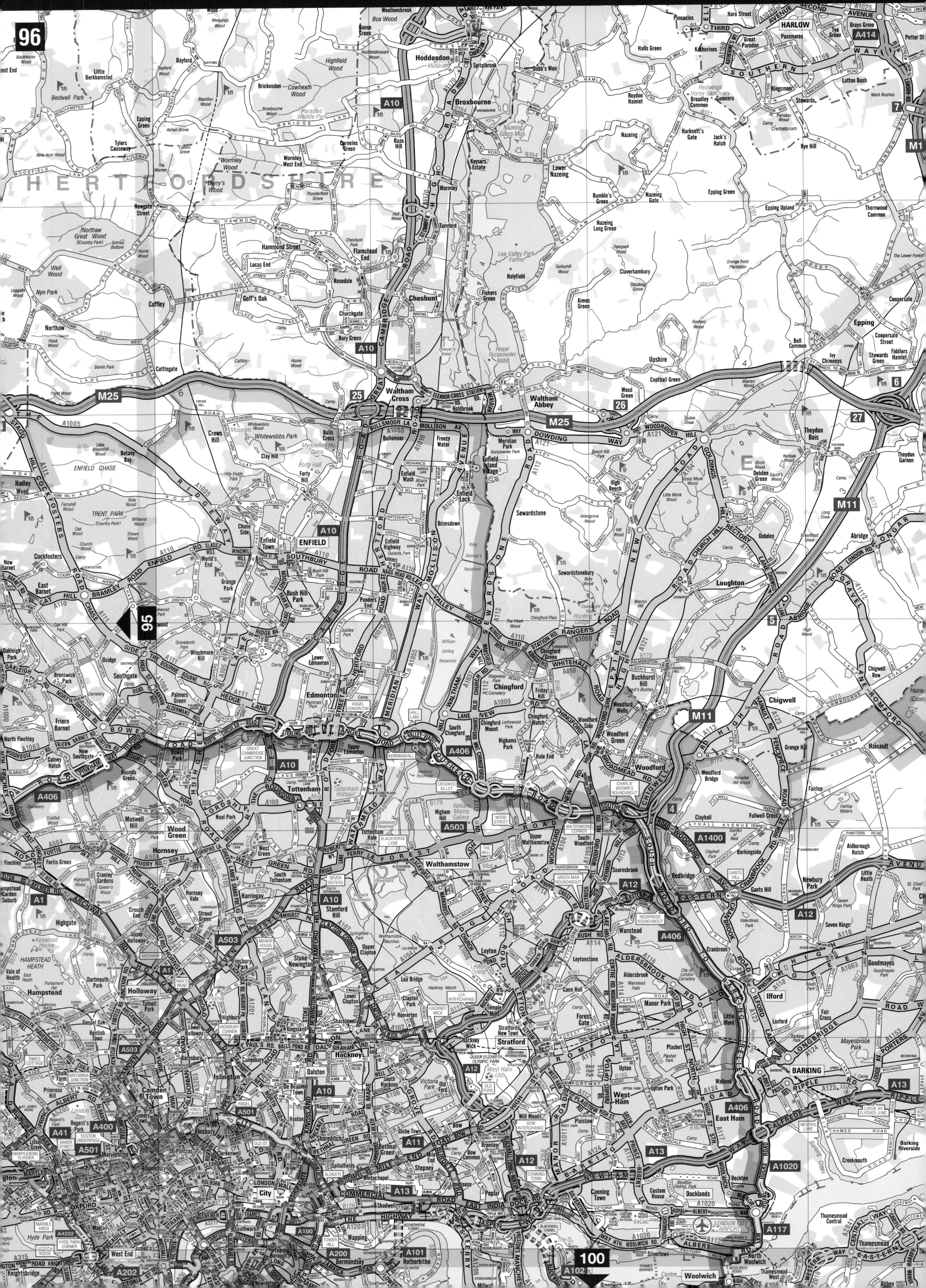
HERTFORDSHIRE
Hoddesdon
Broxbourne
HARLOW
Cheshunt
Waltham Cross
Waltham Abbey
Epping
Theydon Bois
Enfield
Southgate
Edmonton
Chingford
Loughton
Chigwell
Woodford
Walthamstow
Tottenham
Hornsey
Highgate
Hampstead
Holloway
Islington
Camden Town
Hackney
Leyton
Leytonstone
Wanstead
Stratford
Ilford
Barking
West Ham
East Ham
Dalston
Stoke Newington
Bow
Poplar
Stepney
Whitechapel
City
Bermondsey
Rotherhithe
Canning Town
Silvertown
Woolwich
North Woolwich
Thamesmead
Hainault
Fairlop
Goodmayes
Seven Kings
M25
M11
M1
A10
A406
A12
A13
A11
A1
A503
A1400
A1020
A117
A102

95
100

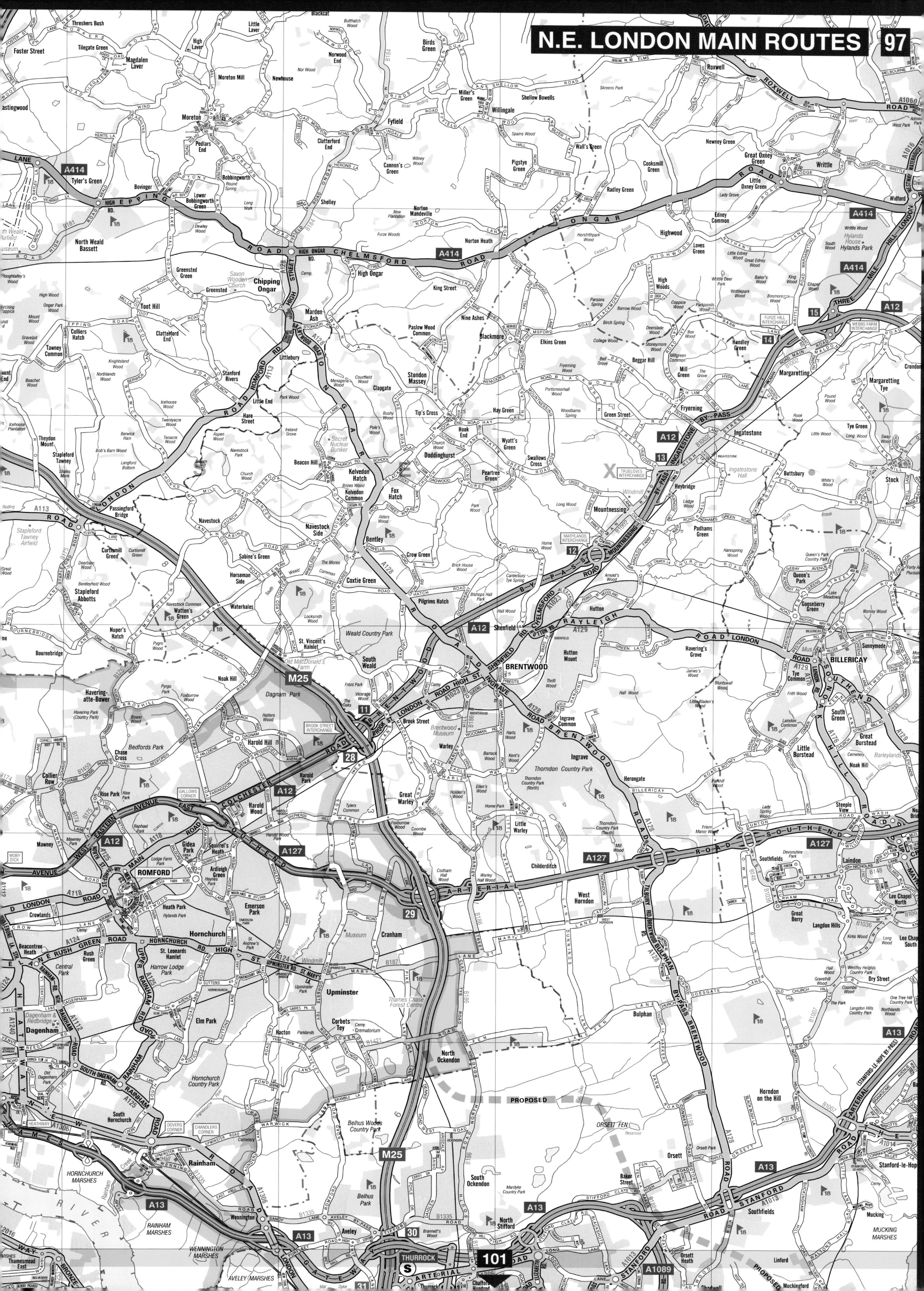
Threshers Bush
Foster Street
Tilegate Green
Magdalen Laver
Little Laver
High Laver
Birds Green
Norwood End
Moreton
Moreton Mill
Newhouse
Fyfield
Miller's Green
Willingale
Shellow Bowells
Roxwell
Writtle
Great Oxney Green
Little Oxney Green
Newney Green
Cooksmill Green
Radley Green
Wall's Green
Pigstye Green
Cannon's Green
Clatterford End
Pedlars End
Bobbingworth
Lower Bobbingworth Green
Bovinger
Tyler's Green
North Weald Bassett
Shelley
Norton Mandeville
Norton Heath
A414
HIGH ONGAR
ONGAR ROAD
CHELMSFORD ROAD
High Ongar
Chipping Ongar
Greensted Green
Greensted
Toot Hill
Clatterford End
Marden Ash
King Street
Nine Ashes
Blackmore
Elkins Green
Highwood
Loves Green
Edney Common
Widford
Hylands Park
High Woods
Handley Green
Margaretting
Margaretting Tye
FURZE HILL INTERCHANGE
WEBBS FARM INTERCHANGE
Colliers Hatch
Tawney Common
Stanford Rivers
Littlebury
Little End
Hare Street
Paslow Wood Common
Stondon Massey
Clapgate
Tip's Cross
Hay Green
Beggar Hill
Mill Green
Fryerning
INGATESTONE BY-PASS
Ingatestone
Green Street
Hook End
Wyatt's Green
Doddinghurst
Swallows Cross
Peartree Green
Kelvedon Hatch
Kelvedon Common
Fox Hatch
Beacon Hill
Secret Nuclear Bunker
Theydon Mount
Stapleford Tawney
Passingford Bridge
Navestock
Navestock Side
Bentley
Crow Green
Mountnessing
Heybridge
Buttsbury
Stock
TRUELOVES INTERCHANGE
MARYLANDS INTERCHANGE
Padhams Green
Curtismill Green
Stapleford Abbotts
Sabine's Green
Horseman Side
Coxtie Green
Pilgrims Hatch
Watton's Green
Waterhales
Nuper's Hatch
Bournebridge
Weald Country Park
St. Vincent's Hamlet
South Weald
Shenfield
BRENTWOOD
Hutton
Hutton Mount
RAYLEIGH ROAD
Havering's Grove
Queen's Park
Gooseberry Green
Sunnymede
BILLERICAY
Tye Common
South Green
Great Burstead
Little Burstead
Noak Hill
Havering-atte-Bower
Noak Hill
Dagnam Park
M25
BROOK STREET INTERCHANGE
Brook Street
Brentwood Museum
Warley
Ingrave
Ingrave Common
Thorndon Country Park
Herongate
Harold Hill
Chase Cross
Collier Row
Rise Park
Harold Park
Harold Wood
GALLOWS CORNER
A12
A127
Great Warley
Little Warley
Childerditch
West Horndon
Steeple View
Laindon
Langdon Hills
Lee Chapel North
Great Berry
Dunton
Mawney
Gidea Park
Squirrel's Heath
Ardleigh Green
ROMFORD
Heath Park
Emerson Park
Hornchurch
Crowlands
Beacontree Heath
Rush Green
Central Park
St. Leonards Hamlet
Harrow Lodge Park
Upminster
Cranham
Elm Park
Dagenham
Corbets Tey
Hacton
Thames Chase Forest Centre
North Ockendon
Bulphan
Hornchurch Country Park
South Hornchurch
Rainham
Wennington
PROPOSED
Belhus Woods Country Park
Belhus Park
South Ockendon
Orsett Fen
Orsett
Baker Street
Horndon on the Hill
Stanford-le-Hope
Southfields
Mucking
North Stifford
Aveley
A13
A1089
THURROCK
Linford
Orsett Heath
Muckingford
HORNCHURCH MARSHES
RAINHAM MARSHES
WENNINGTON MARSHES
AVELEY MARSHES
Thamesmead East
RIVER THAMES
101
11
12
13
14
15
28
29
30
31

94

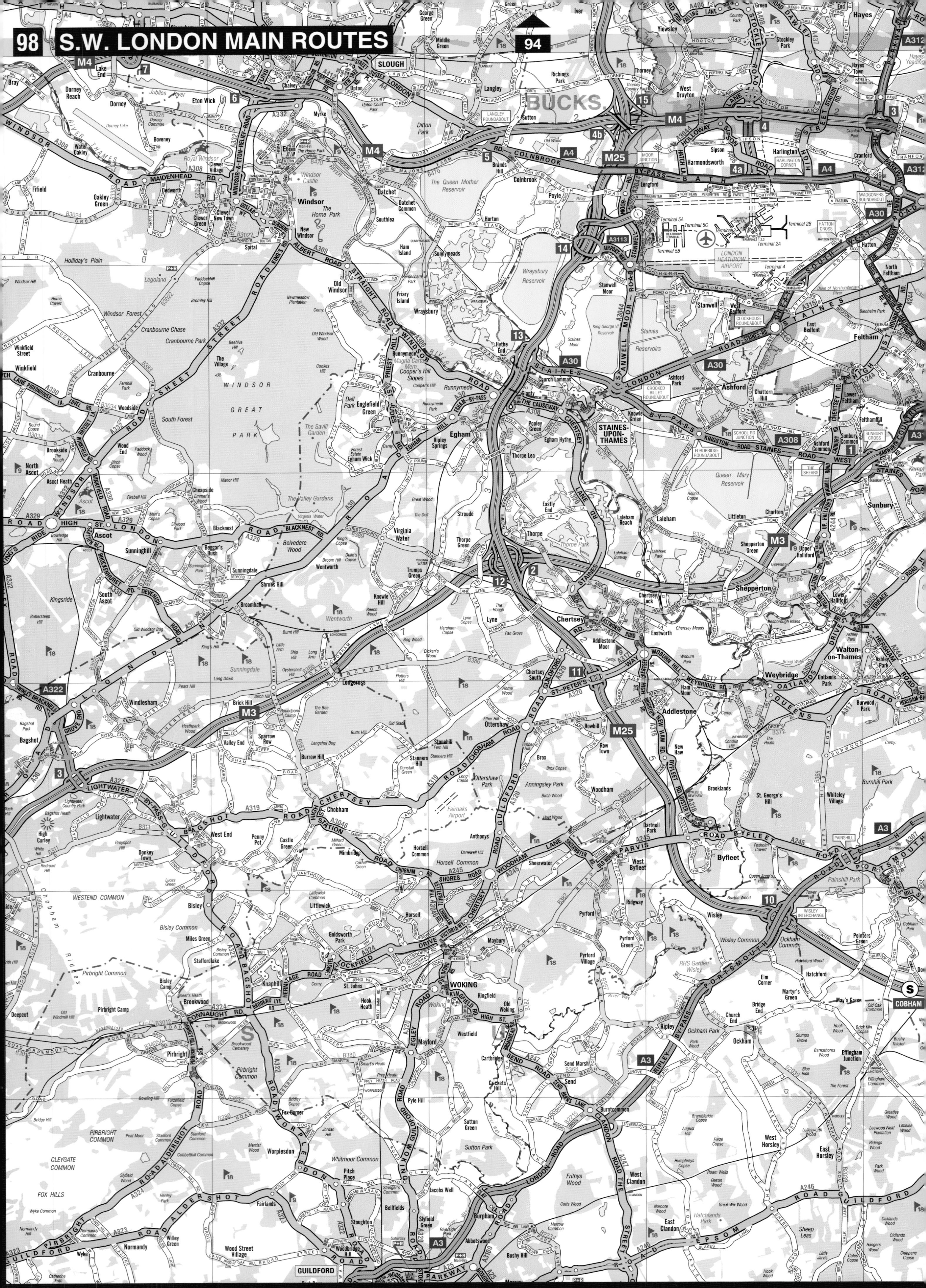
SLOUGH
BUCKS.
Windsor
Eton
Datchet
Colnbrook
Langley
Iver
Yiewsley
West Drayton
Harmondsworth
Harlington
Hayes
Sipson
Longford
LONDON HEATHROW AIRPORT
Stanwell
Stanwell Moor
Bedfont
East Bedfont
Feltham
North Feltham
Hatton
Ashford
Staines
STAINES-UPON-THAMES
Egham
Englefield Green
Old Windsor
Wraysbury
Runnymede
WINDSOR GREAT PARK
Sunbury
Shepperton
Laleham
Littleton
Chertsey
Thorpe
Virginia Water
Sunningdale
Sunninghill
Ascot
South Ascot
Windlesham
Bagshot
Lightwater
Chobham
West End
Bisley
Knaphill
Woking
Horsell
Pyrford
Byfleet
West Byfleet
Addlestone
New Haw
Weybridge
Walton-on-Thames
Ottershaw
Lyne
Longcross
Wisley
Ockham
Ripley
Send
Send Marsh
Old Woking
Mayford
Westfield
Worplesdon
Jacobs Well
Burpham
Merrow
East Clandon
West Clandon
East Horsley
West Horsley
Effingham Junction
COBHAM
Pirbright
Brookwood
Normandy
Wyke
GUILDFORD
Dorney
Bray
Cranbourne
Winkfield
Fifield
Oakley Green
M4
M25
M3
A3
A30
A4
A308
A322
A319
A320
A245
A246
A323
A324

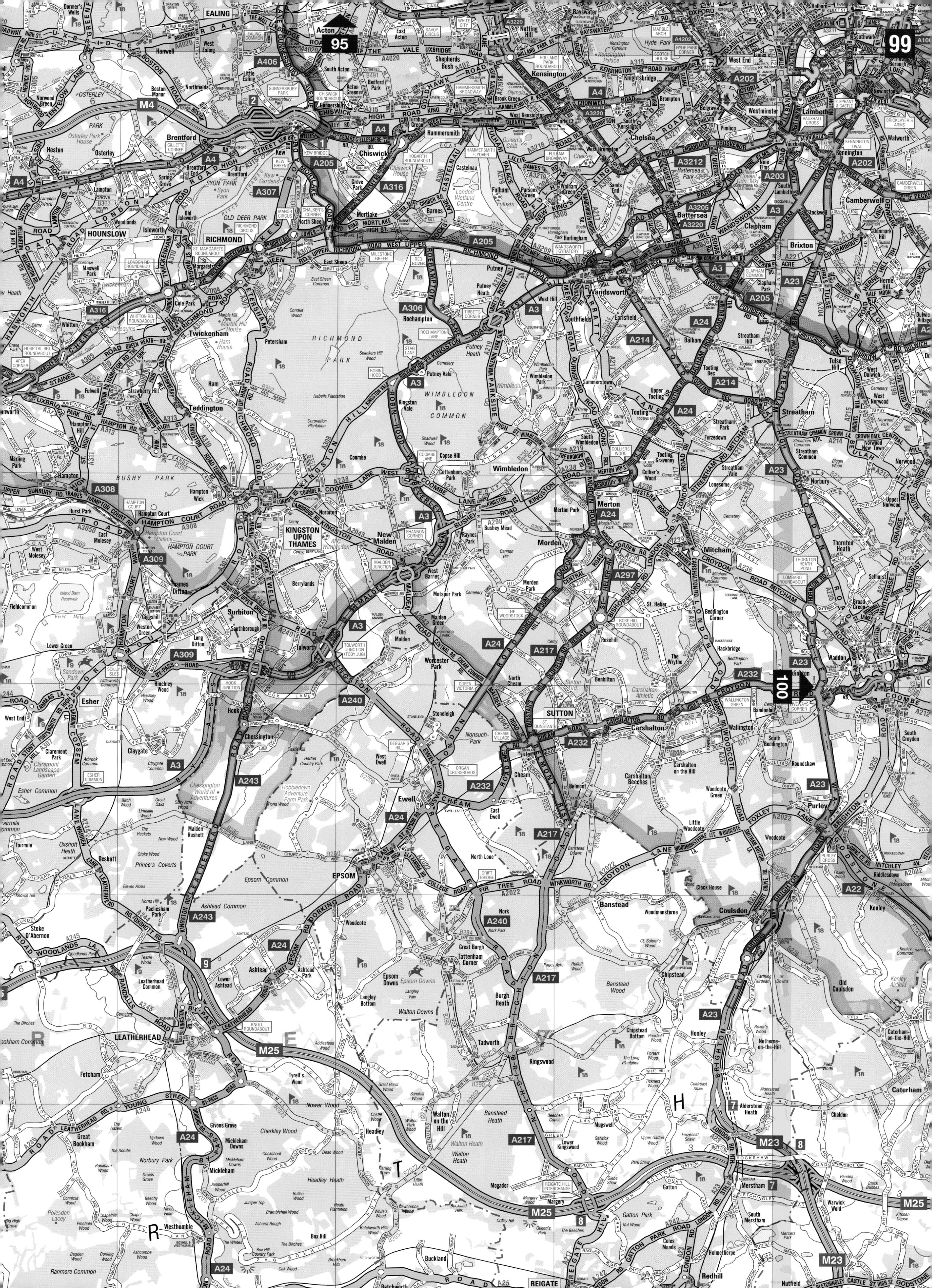
95
99
100
EALING
Acton
Hanwell
West Ealing
Kensington
Bayswater
Hyde Park
Knightsbridge
Chelsea
Hammersmith
Chiswick
Brentford
Osterley
Heston
HOUNSLOW
RICHMOND
Isleworth
Twickenham
Teddington
Fulham
Putney
Barnes
Mortlake
Wandsworth
Battersea
Clapham
Brixton
Lambeth
Westminster
Camberwell
Balham
Streatham
Tooting
Wimbledon
RICHMOND PARK
WIMBLEDON COMMON
BUSHY PARK
HAMPTON COURT PARK
Hampton
Hampton Court
KINGSTON UPON THAMES
New Malden
Surbiton
Merton
Morden
Mitcham
Norbury
Thornton Heath
Tolworth
Worcester Park
Esher
Chessington
Epsom
Ewell
SUTTON
Cheam
Carshalton
Wallington
Purley
Coulsdon
Banstead
Kenley
Caterham
Leatherhead
Ashtead
Fetcham
Great Bookham
Mickleham
Tadworth
Kingswood
Chipstead
Merstham
Redhill
REIGATE
M4
M25
M23
A3
A4
A23
A24
A205
A217
A232
A240
A243
A308
A309

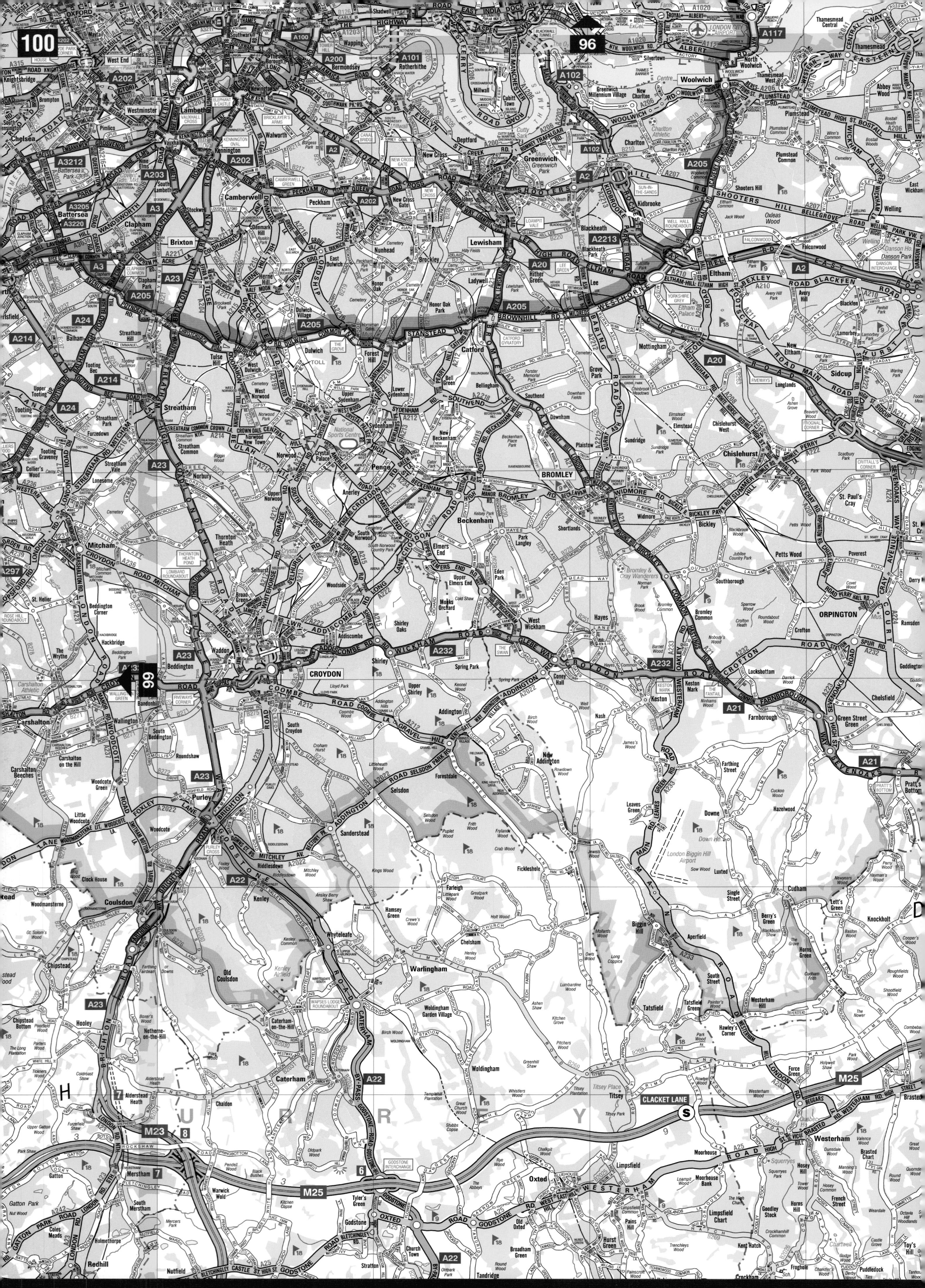
100
96
99
Westminster
Lambeth
Chelsea
Battersea
Clapham
Brixton
Camberwell
Peckham
Deptford
Greenwich
Lewisham
Woolwich
Eltham
Catford
Dulwich
Streatham
Mitcham
Norbury
Sydenham
Penge
Beckenham
BROMLEY
Chislehurst
Sidcup
ORPINGTON
CROYDON
Addiscombe
Shirley
Purley
Coulsdon
Caterham
Warlingham
Biggin Hill
Westerham
Oxted
Godstone
Redhill
Merstham
Carshalton
Wallington
Sutton
M25
M23
A23
A22
A21
A20
A2
A205
A232
CLACKET LANE
S U R R E Y
London Biggin Hill Airport
LONDON CITY AIRPORT

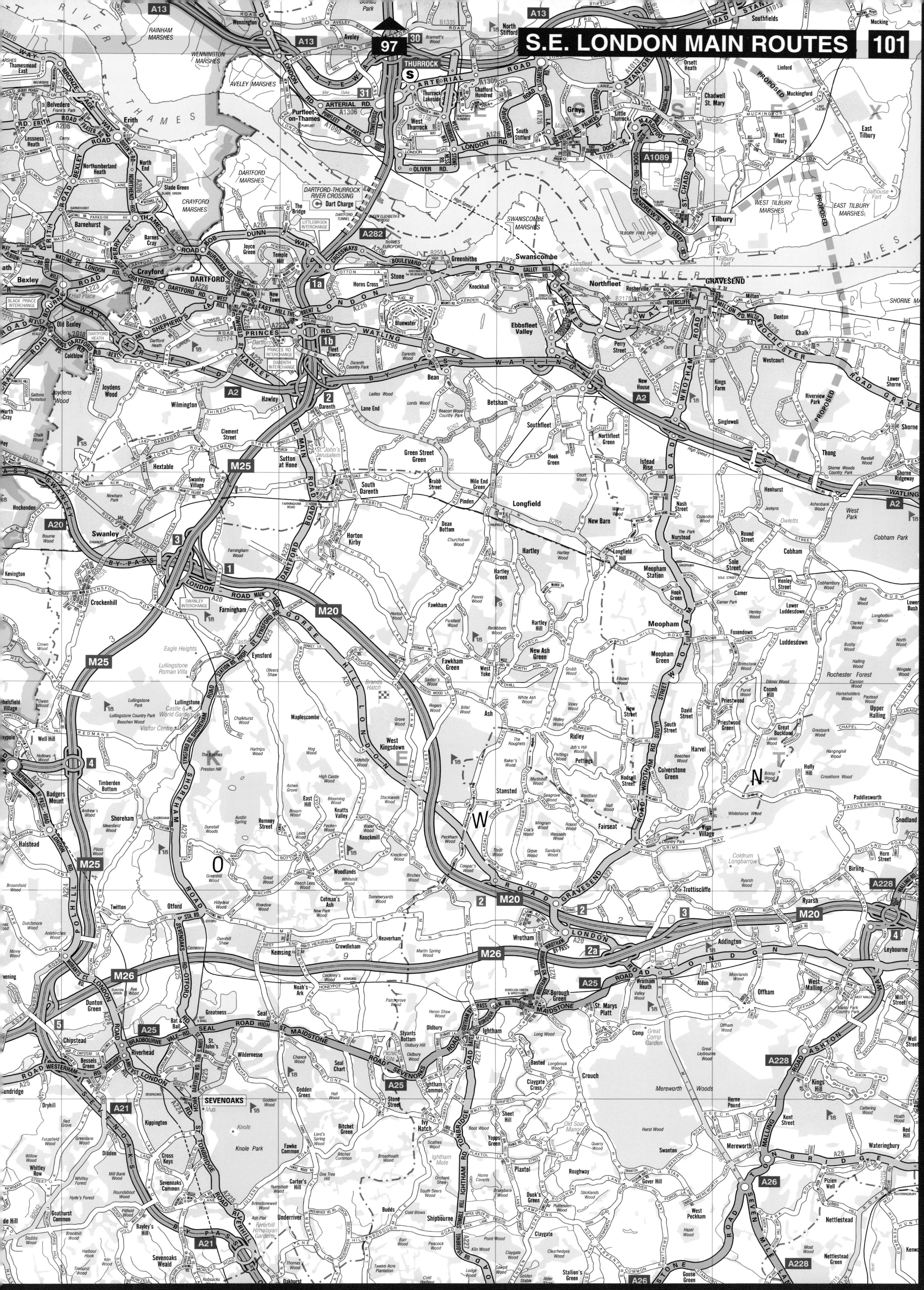
97
30
31
THURROCK
Wennington
Aveley
North Stifford
RAINHAM MARSHES
WENNINGTON MARSHES
AVELEY MARSHES
Purfleet-on-Thames
West Thurrock
Thurrock Lakeside
Chafford Hundred
South Stifford
Grays
Little Thurrock
Orsett Heath
Chadwell St. Mary
Southfields
Mucking
Linford
Muckingford
West Tilbury
East Tilbury
Tilbury
WEST TILBURY MARSHES
EAST TILBURY MARSHES
TILBURY FREE PORT
A1089
A13
A282
DARTFORD MARSHES
CRAYFORD MARSHES
DARTFORD-THURROCK RIVER CROSSING
Dart Charge
The Bridge
LITTLEBROOK INTERCHANGE
SWANSCOMBE MARSHES
RIVER THAMES
Thamesmead East
Belvedere
Erith
Lessness Heath
Northumberland Heath
North End
Slade Green
Barnehurst
Barnes Cray
Crayford
Bexley
DARTFORD
Joyce Green
Temple Hill
Stone
Greenhithe
Swanscombe
Knockhall
Bluewater
Horns Cross
Northfleet
Rosherville
GRAVESEND
Milton
Denton
Chalk
Shorne
Old Bexley
Dartford Heath
Coldblow
Fleet Downs
Darenth
Ebbsfleet Valley
Perry Street
Westcourt
New House
Kings Farm
Riverview Park
Lower Shorne
Joydens Wood
Wilmington
Hawley
Lane End
Bean
Betsham
Southfleet
Northfleet Green
Istead Rise
Singlewell
Thong
Clement Street
Hextable
Swanley Village
Sutton at Hone
South Darenth
Green Street Green
Mile End Green
Longfield
Hook Green
Nash Street
New Barn
Henhurst
West Park
Cobham Park
Hockenden
Swanley
Horton Kirby
Dean Bottom
Hartley
Longfield Hill
Meopham Station
Round Street
Cobham
Sole Street
Henley Street
Kevington
Crockenhill
Farningham
Fawkham
Hartley Green
Hook Green
Camer
Lower Luddesdown
Meopham
Meopham Green
Luddesdown
Foxendown
Eynsford
Lullingstone Roman Villa
Lullingstone Castle
Fawkham Green
West Yoke
New Ash Green
Ash
Brands Hatch
Maplescombe
West Kingsdown
Rochester Forest
Upper Halling
Well Hill
Timberden Bottom
Badgers Mount
Shoreham
Halstead
Preston Hill
Romney Street
East Hill
Knatts Valley
Knockmill
Stansted
Ridley
Pettings
Hodsell Street
Culverstone Green
Harvel
Great Buckland
Holly Hill
Fairseat
Vigo Village
Trosley Country Park
Snodland
Paddlesworth
Twitton
Otford
Woodlands
Cotman's Ash
Heaverham
Kemsing
Wrotham
Trottiscliffe
Addington
Ryarsh
Birling
Leybourne
Crowdleham
Noah's Ark
Dunton Green
Chipstead
Bat & Ball
Greatness
Seal
St. John's
Wildernesse
Riverhead
Bessels Green
Borough Green
Wrotham Heath
St. Marys Platt
Aldon
Offham
West Malling
Styants Bottom
Oldbury
Ightham
Basted
Crouch
Comp
Great Comp Garden
Mereworth Woods
Kings Hill
SEVENOAKS
Knole Park
Kippington
Seal Chart
Godden Green
Stone Street
Ivy Hatch
Ightham Common
Claygate Cross
Sheet Hill
Herne Pound
Kent Street
Yopps Green
Ightham Mote
Plaxtol
Roughway
Fawke Common
Bitchet Green
Dibden
Cross Keys
Sevenoaks Common
Carter's Hill
Underriver
Budds
Shipbourne
Dunk's Green
Claygate
Mereworth
Wateringbury
Swanton
Gover Hill
West Peckham
Pizien Well
Nettlestead
Goathurst Common
Bayley's Hill
Sevenoaks Weald
Riverhill Himalayan Gardens
Stallion's Green
Goose Green
Golden Green
Nettlestead Green
M25
M20
M26
A2
A20
A25
A21
A26
A227
A228

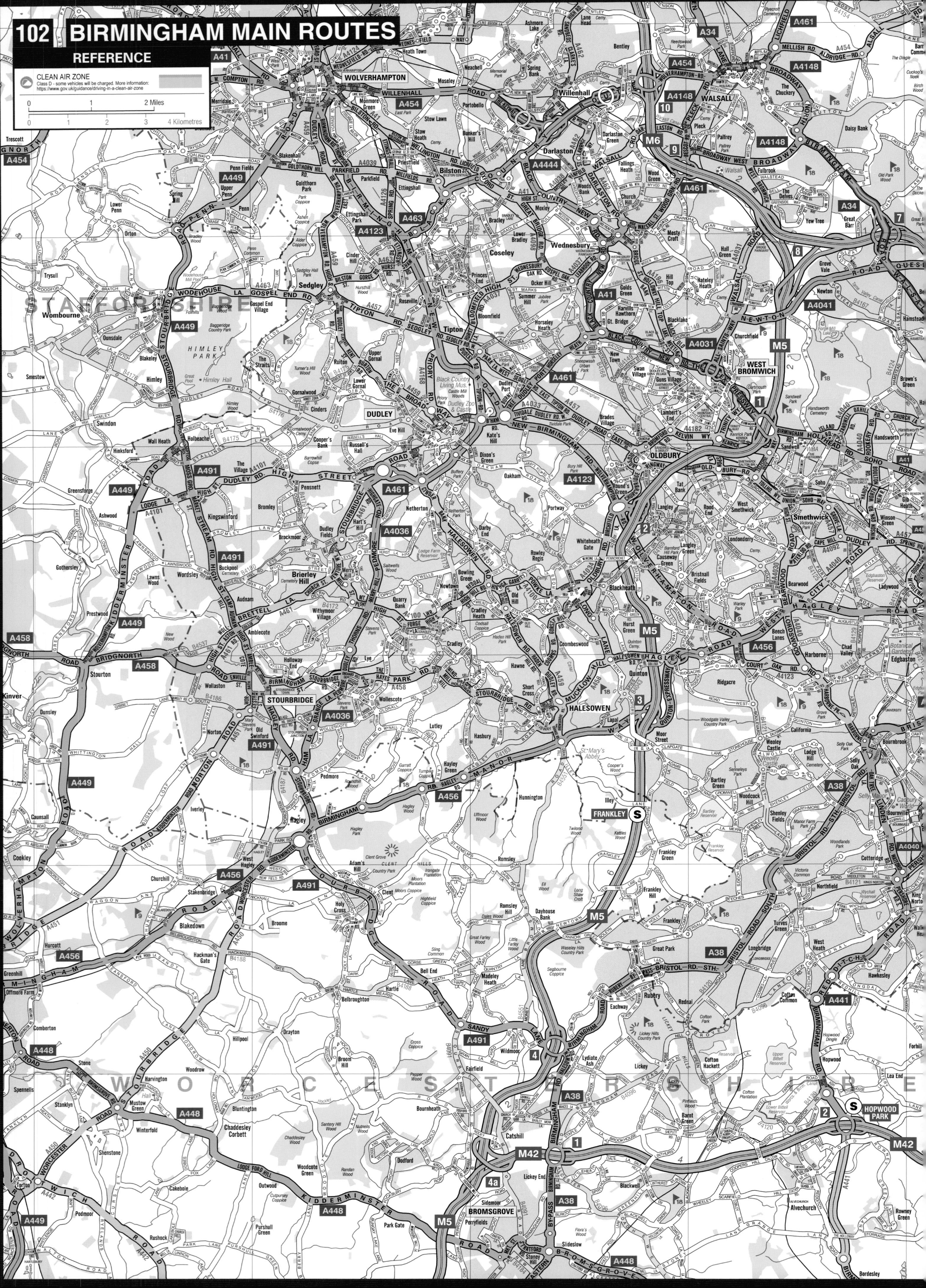

CLEAN AIR ZONE
Class D - some vehicles will be charged. More information:
https://www.gov.uk/guidance/driving-in-a-clean-air-zone

0   1   2 Miles
0   1   2   3   4 Kilometres

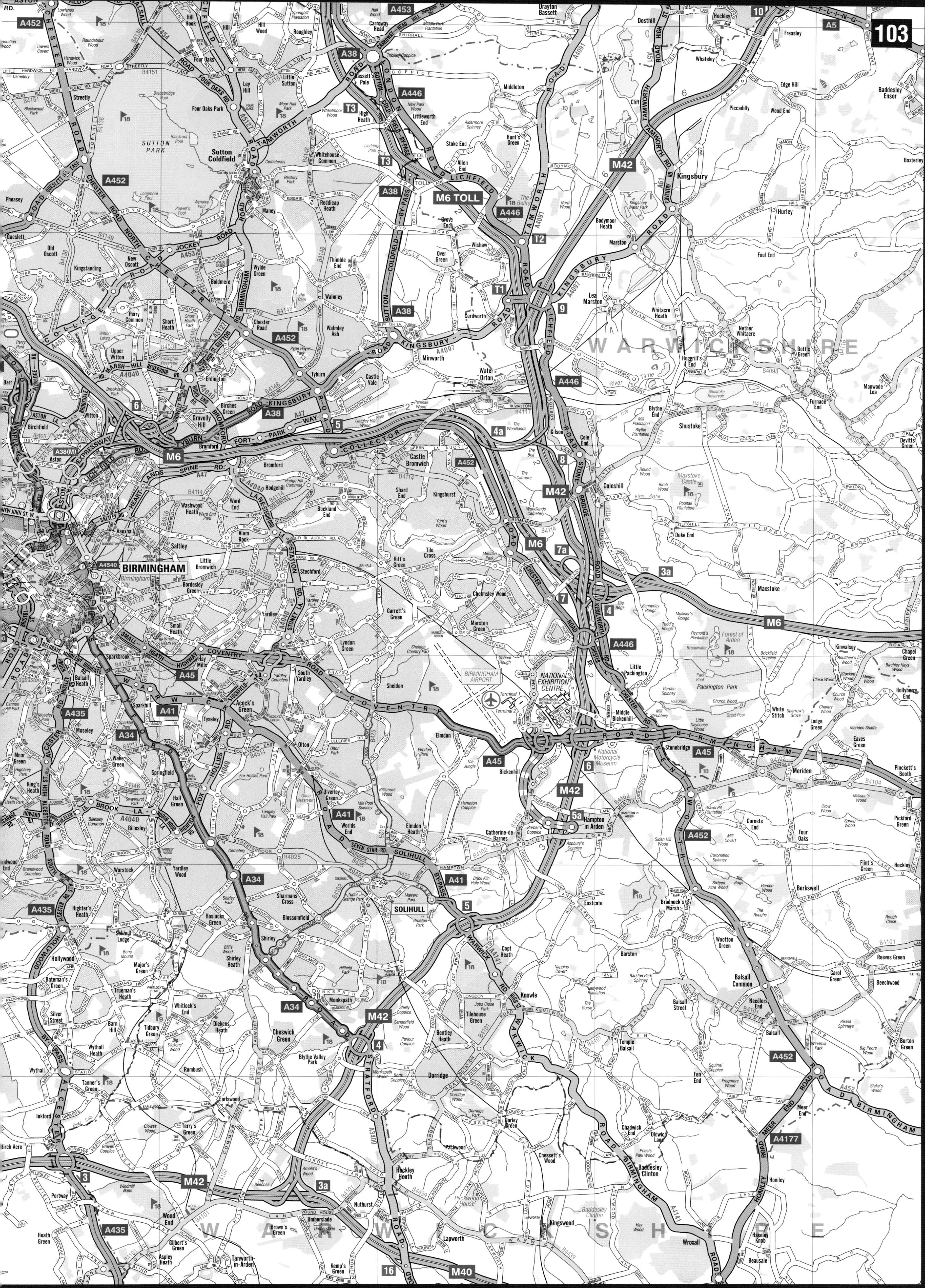
BIRMINGHAM
WARWICKSHIRE
WARWICKSHIRE
SUTTON PARK
Sutton Coldfield
SOLIHULL
BIRMINGHAM AIRPORT
NATIONAL EXHIBITION CENTRE
National Motorcycle Museum
Forest of Arden
Packington Park
Maxstoke Castle
M6 TOLL
M6
M42
M40
A38(M)
A452
A453
A38
A446
A5
A4097
A47
A45
A41
A34
A435
A4040
A4177
T1
T2
T3
Four Oaks
Streetly
Kingstanding
Erdington
Tyburn
Castle Vale
Minworth
Water Orton
Coleshill
Kingsbury
Hurley
Shustoke
Maxstoke
Castle Bromwich
Kingshurst
Chelmsley Wood
Marston Green
Stechford
Saltley
Aston
Yardley
Sheldon
Elmdon
Bickenhill
Hampton in Arden
Meriden
Berkswell
Balsall Common
Knowle
Dorridge
Shirley
Olton
Acock's Green
Sparkhill
Moseley
Hall Green
Yardley Wood
Hollywood
Wythall
Earlswood
Hockley Heath
Lapworth
Kingswood
Baddesley Clinton
Wroxall
Honiley
Haseley Knob
Beausale
Tanworth-in-Arden
Wood End
Portway
Drayton Bassett
Middleton
Curdworth
Wishaw
Lea Marston
Nether Whitacre
Whitacre Heath
Fillongley
Little Packington
Stonebridge
Tile Cross
Garrett's Green
Little Bromwich
Solihull Lodge
Cheswick Green
Blythe Valley Park
Catherine-de-Barnes
Temple Balsall
Eastcote
Barston
Chadwick End
Copt Heath

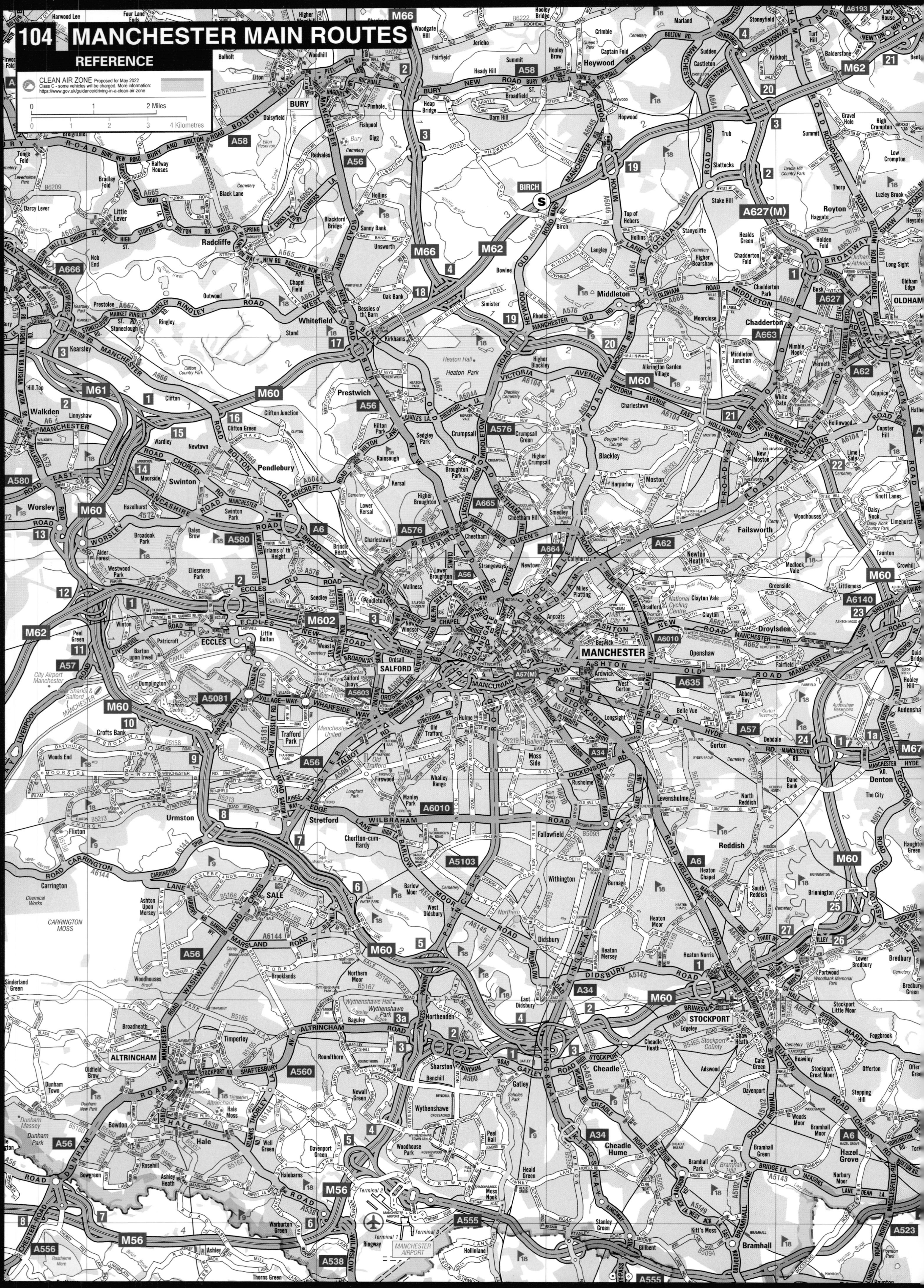

REFERENCE

CLEAN AIR ZONE Proposed for May 2022
Class C - some vehicles will be charged. More information:
https://www.gov.uk/guidance/driving-in-a-clean-air-zone

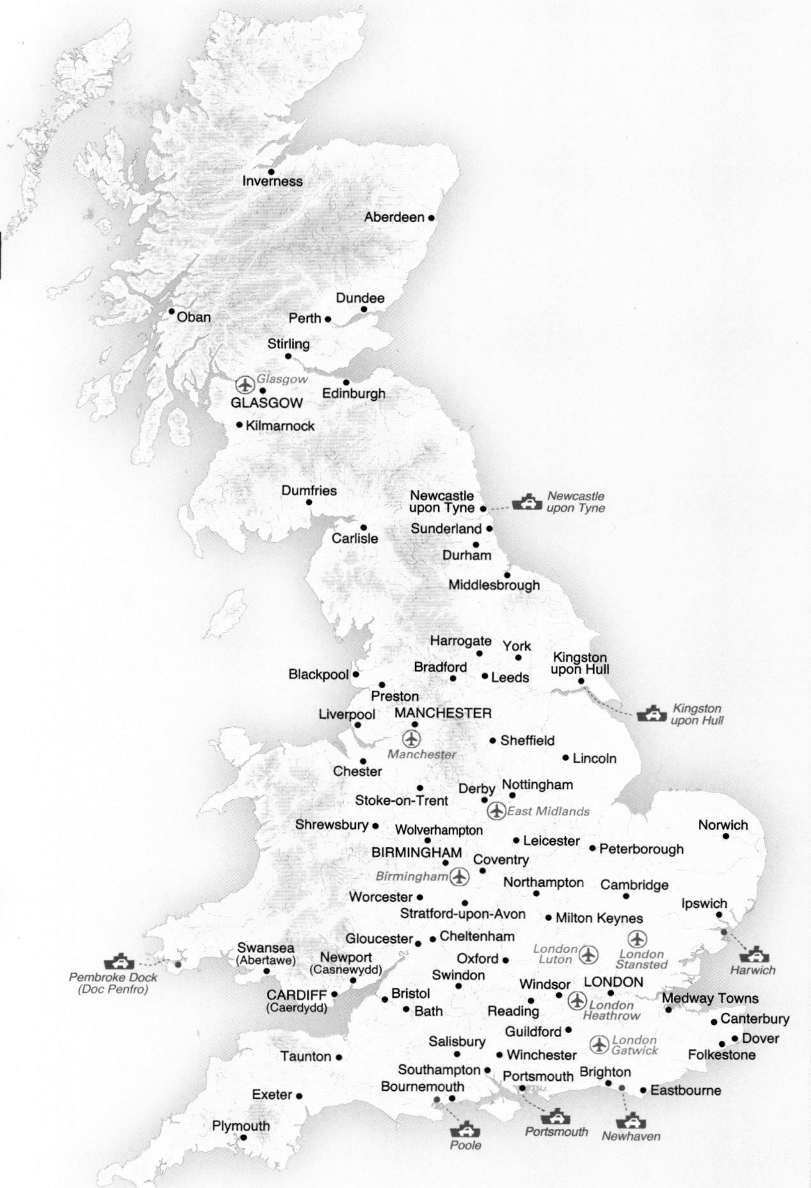

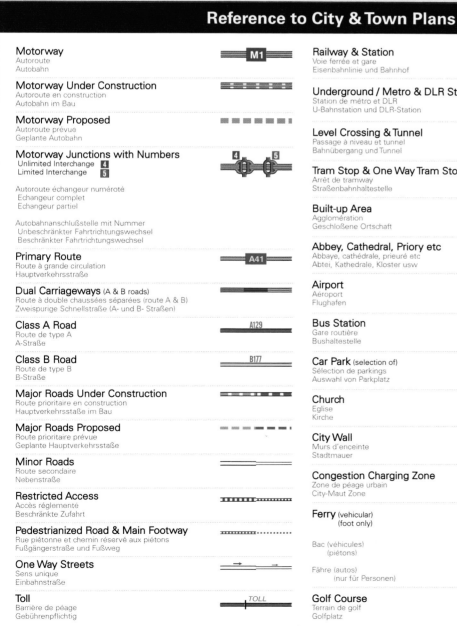

Reference to City & Town Plans   Légende   Zeichenerklärung

Motorway / Autoroute / Autobahn	M1
Motorway Under Construction / Autoroute en construction / Autobahn im Bau	
Motorway Proposed / Autoroute prévue / Geplante Autobahn	
Motorway Junctions with Numbers — Unlimited Interchange 4, Limited Interchange 5 / Autoroute échangeur numéroté, Échangeur complet, Échangeur partiel / Autobahnanschlußstelle mit Nummer, Unbeschränkter Fahrtrichtungswechsel, Beschränkter Fahrtrichtungswechsel	4 5
Primary Route / Route à grande circulation / Hauptverkehrsstraße	A41
Dual Carriageways (A & B roads) / Route à double chaussées séparées (route A & B) / Zweispurige Schnellstraße (A- und B- Straßen)	
Class A Road / Route de type A / A-Straße	A129
Class B Road / Route de type B / B-Straße	B177
Major Roads Under Construction / Route prioritaire en construction / Hauptverkehrsstaße im Bau	
Major Roads Proposed / Route prioritaire prévue / Geplante Hauptverkehrsstraße	
Minor Roads / Route secondaire / Nebenstraße	
Restricted Access / Accès réglementée / Beschränkte Zufahrt	
Pedestrianized Road & Main Footway / Rue piétonne et chemin réservé aux piétons / Fußgängerstraße und Fußweg	
One Way Streets / Sens unique / Einbahnstraße	
Toll / Barrière de péage / Gebührenpflichtig	TOLL

Railway & Station / Voie ferrée et gare / Eisenbahnlinie und Bahnhof	
Underground / Metro & DLR Station / Station de métro et DLR / U-Bahnstation und DLR-Station	DLR
Level Crossing & Tunnel / Passage à niveau et tunnel / Bahnübergang und Tunnel	
Tram Stop & One Way Tram Stop / Arrêt de tramway / Straßenbahnhaltestelle	
Built-up Area / Agglomération / Geschloßene Ortschaft	
Abbey, Cathedral, Priory etc / Abbaye, cathédrale, prieuré etc / Abtei, Kathedrale, Kloster usw	†
Airport / Aéroport / Flughafen	✈
Bus Station / Gare routière / Bushaltestelle	
Car Park (selection of) / Sélection de parkings / Auswahl von Parkplatz	P
Church / Eglise / Kirche	†
City Wall / Murs d'enceinte / Stadtmauer	
Congestion Charging Zone / Zone de péage urbain / City-Maut Zone	
Ferry (vehicular) (foot only) / Bac (véhicules) (piétons) / Fähre (autos) (nur für Personen)	
Golf Course / Terrain de golf / Golfplatz	

Heliport / Héliport / Hubschrauberlandeplatz	
Hospital / Hôpital / Krankenhaus	H
Lighthouse / Phare / Leuchtturm	
Market / Marché / Markt	
National Trust Property (open) (restricted opening) (National Trust for Scotland) / National Trust Property (ouvert) (heures d'ouverture) (National Trust for Scotland) / National Trust- Eigentum (geöffnet) (beschränkte Öffnungszeit) (National Trust for Scotland)	NT NT NTS NTS
Park & Ride / Parking relais / Auswahl von Parkplatz	
Place of Interest / Curiosité / Sehenswürdigkeit	
Police Station / Commissariat de police / Polizeirevier	▲
Post Office / Bureau de poste / Postamt	★
Shopping Area (main street & precinct) / Quartier commerçant (rue et zone principales) / Einkaufsviertel (hauptgeschäftsstraße, fußgängerzone)	
Shopmobility / Shopmobility / Shopmobility	
Toilet / Toilettes / Toilette	
Tourist Information Centre / Syndicat d'initiative / Information	i
Viewpoint / Vue panoramique / Aussichtspunkt	
Visitor Information Centre / Centre d'information touristique / Besucherzentrum	V

ABERDEEN

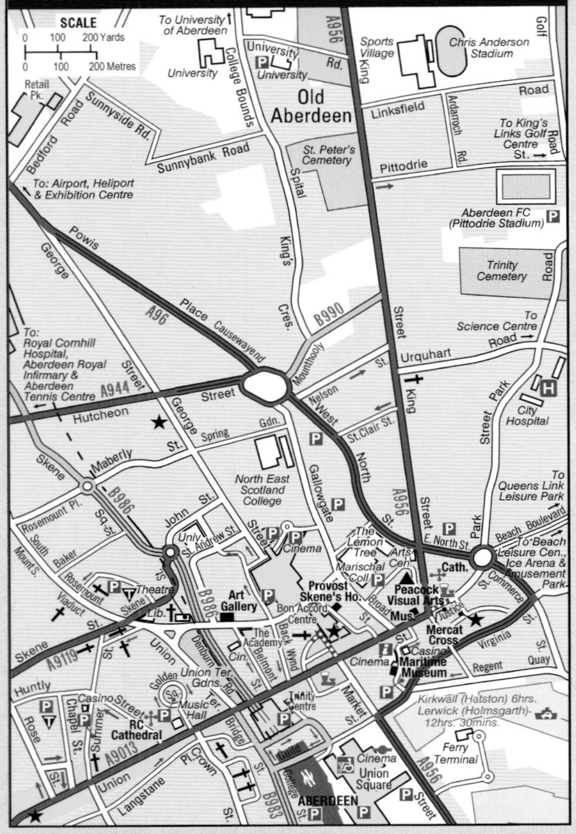

BATH

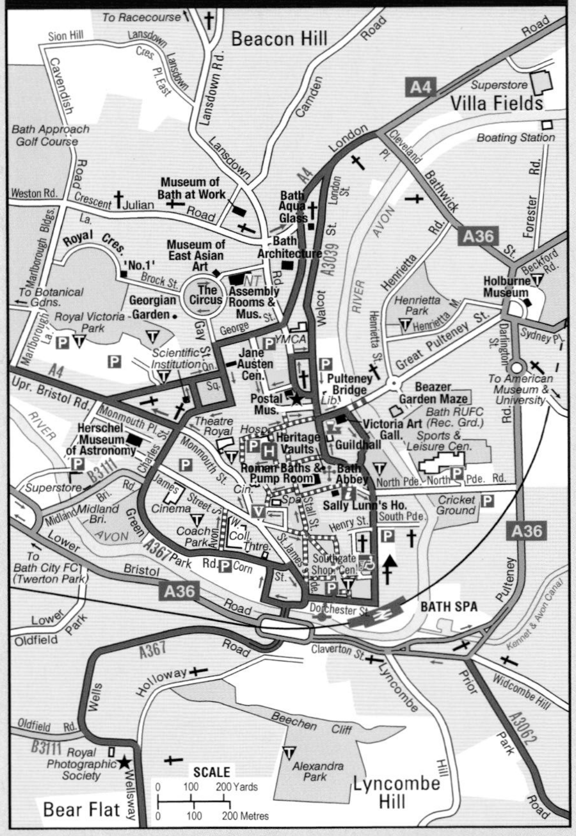

BLACKPOOL

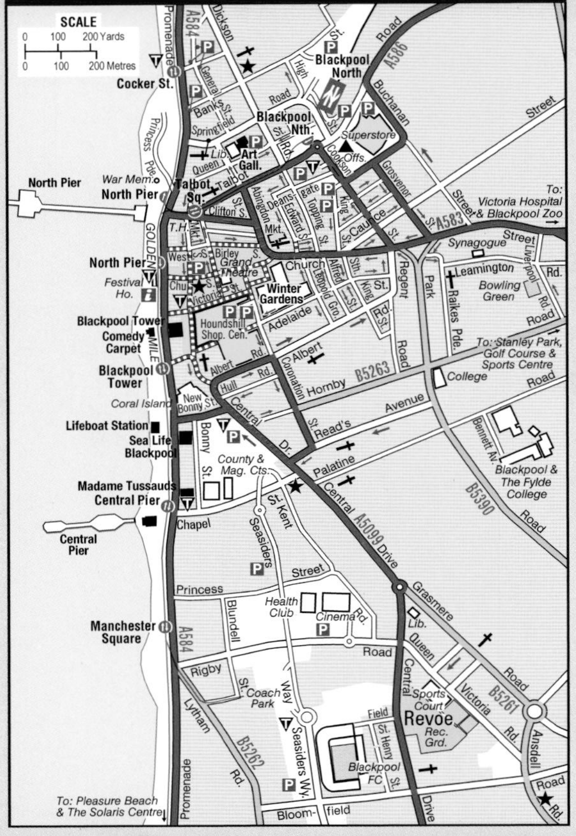

BIRMINGHAM (CITY CENTRE)

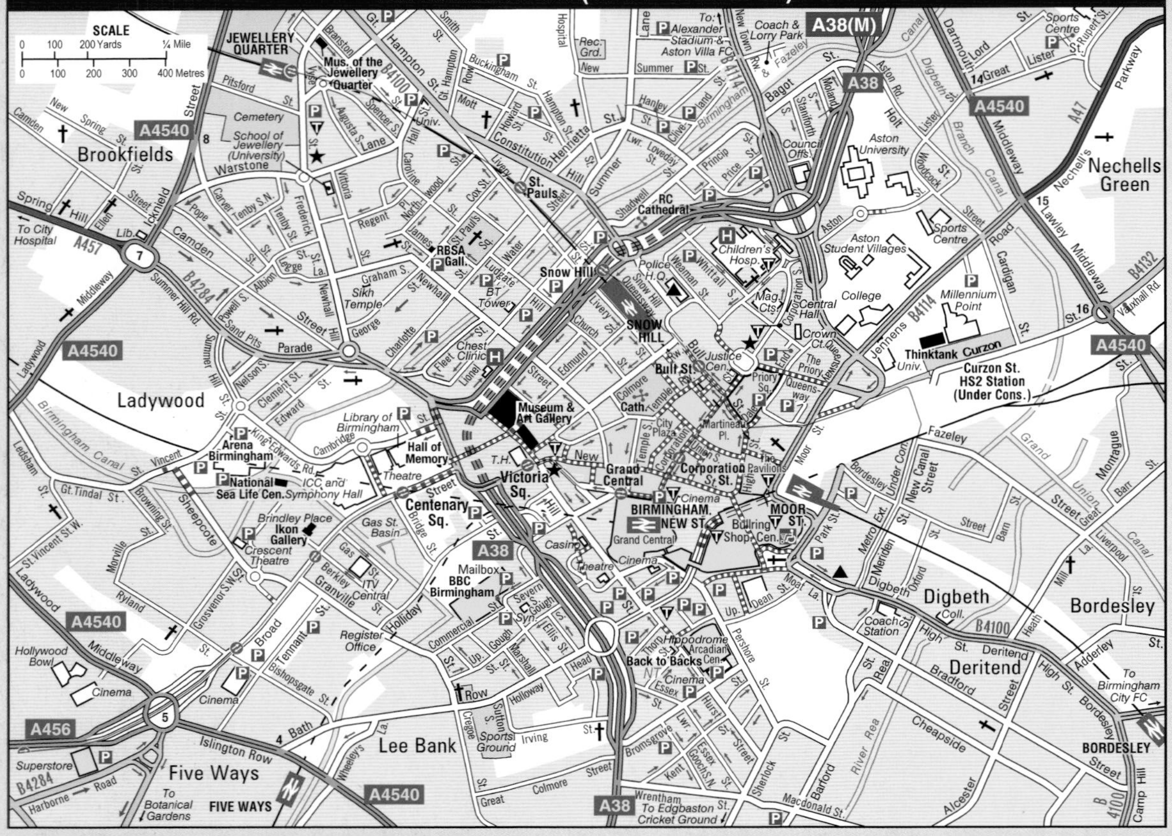

BOURNEMOUTH

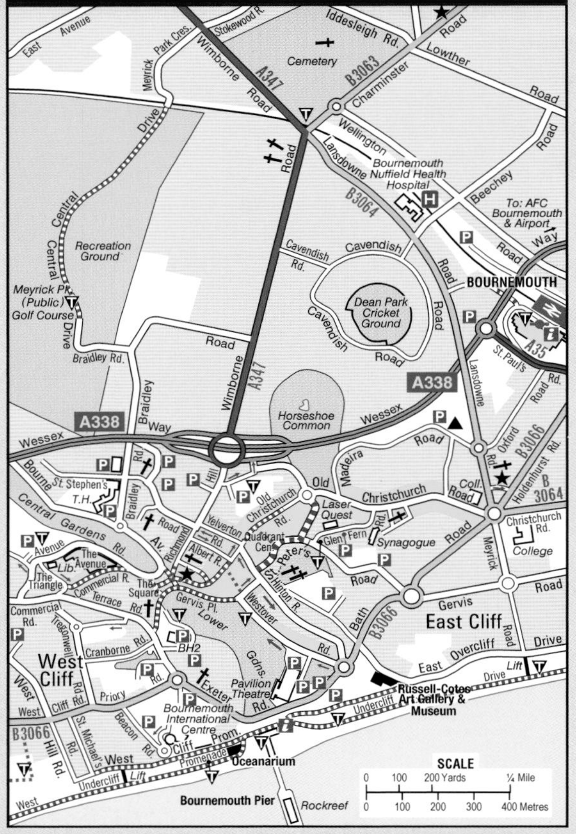

BRADFORD

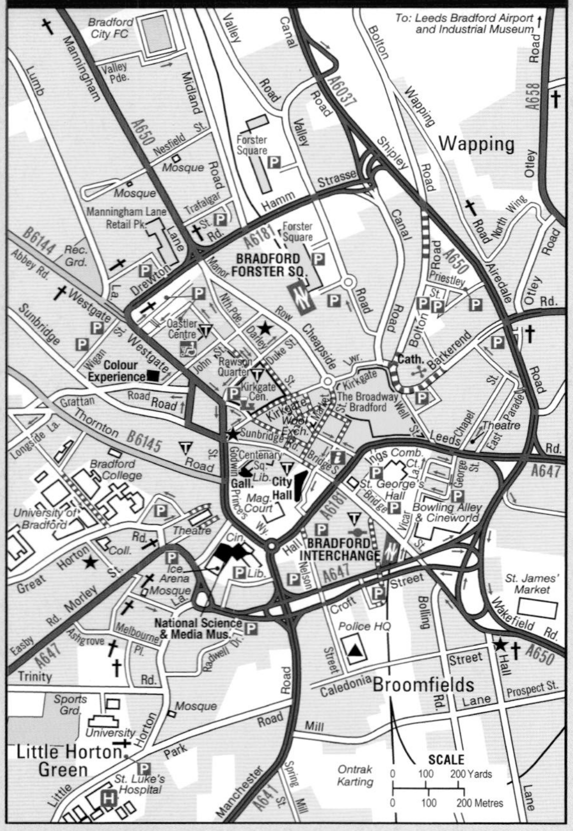

BRIGHTON and HOVE

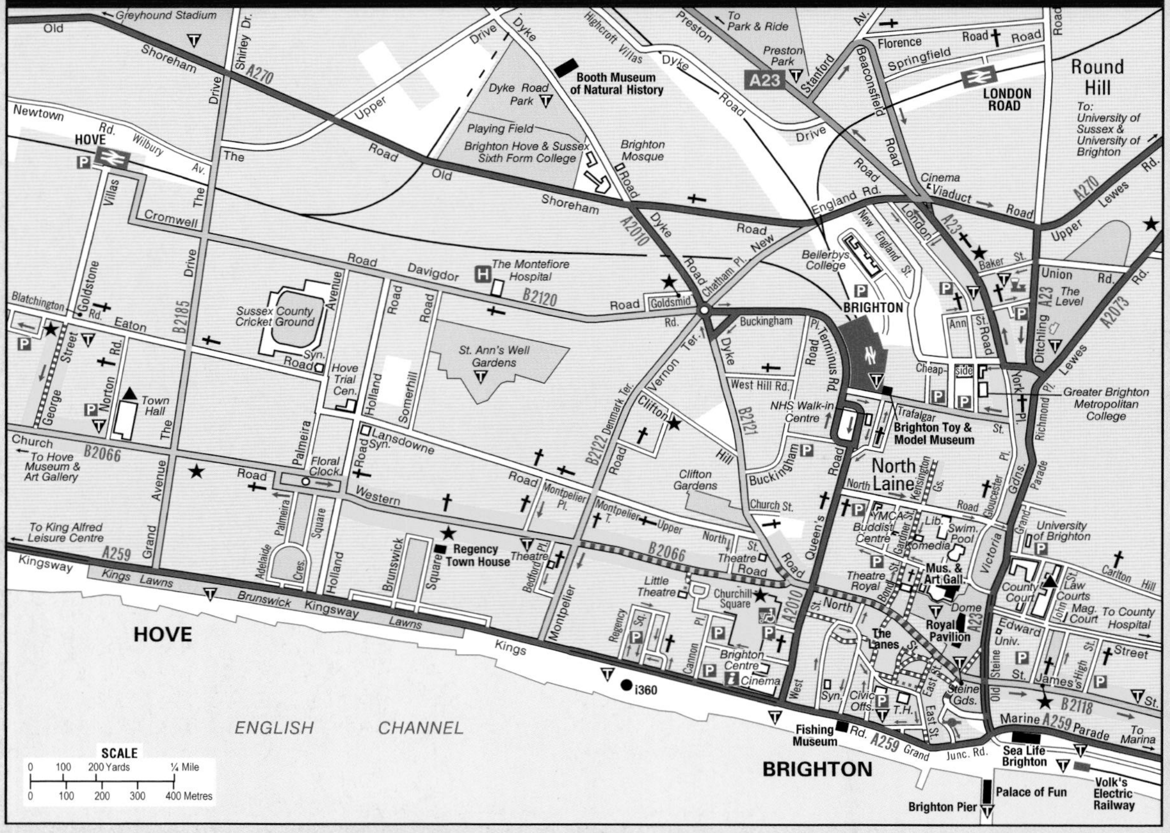

BRISTOL

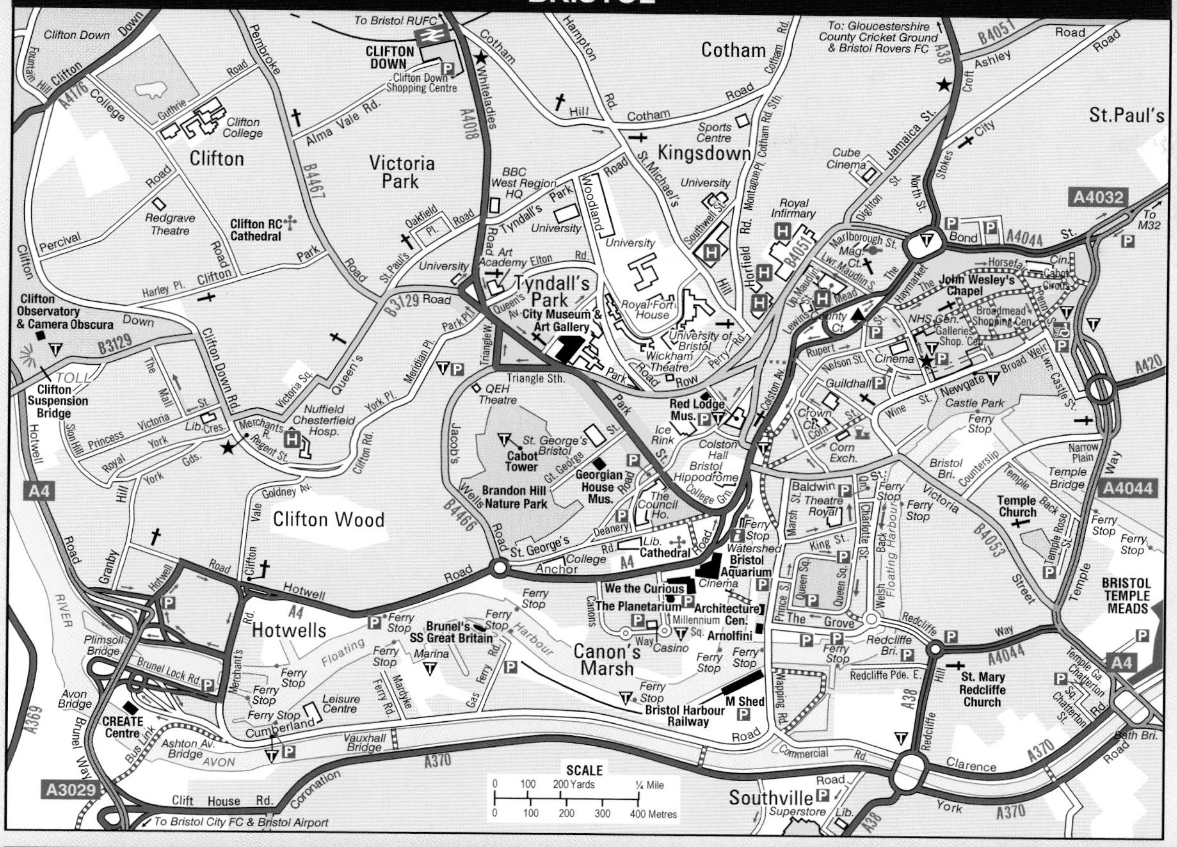

CANTERBURY

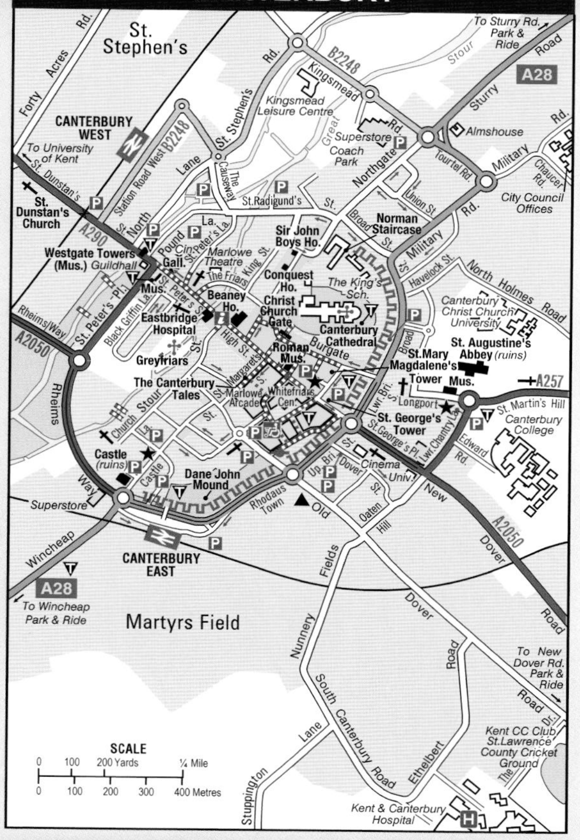

CAMBRIDGE

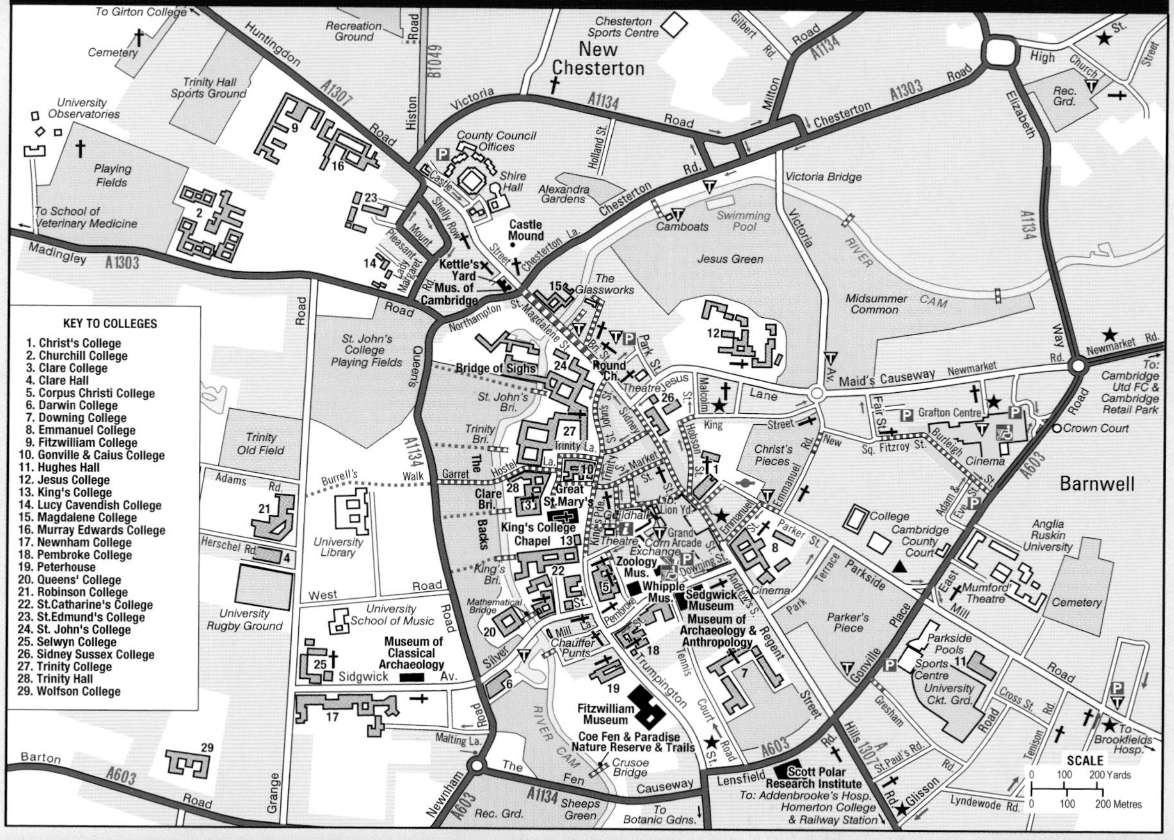

KEY TO COLLEGES
1. Christ's College
2. Churchill College
3. Clare College
4. Clare Hall
5. Corpus Christi College
6. Darwin College
7. Downing College
8. Emmanuel College
9. Fitzwilliam College
10. Gonville & Caius College
11. Hughes Hall
12. Jesus College
13. King's College
14. Lucy Cavendish College
15. Magdalene College
16. Murray Edwards College
17. Newnham College
18. Pembroke College
19. Peterhouse
20. Queens' College
21. Robinson College
22. St.Catharine's College
23. St.Edmund's College
24. St. John's College
25. Selwyn College
26. Sidney Sussex College
27. Trinity College
28. Trinity Hall
29. Wolfson College

CARLISLE

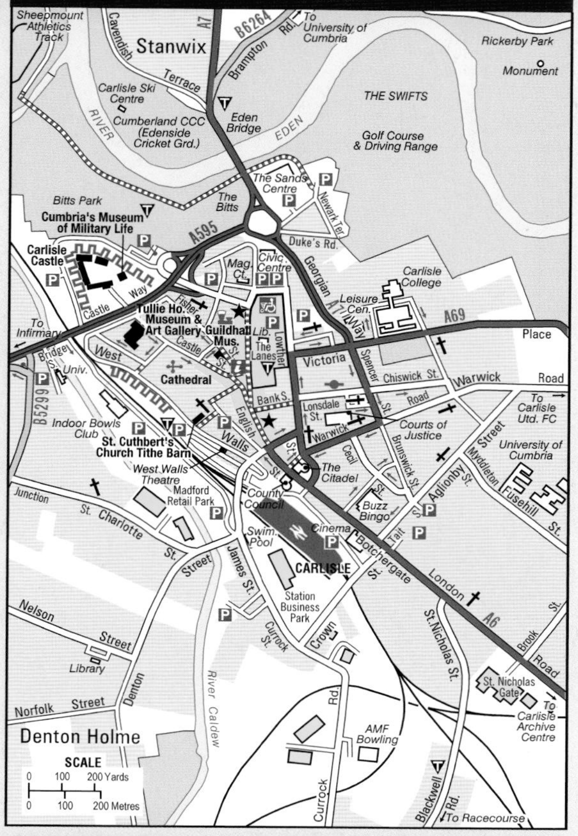

CARDIFF (CAERDYDD)

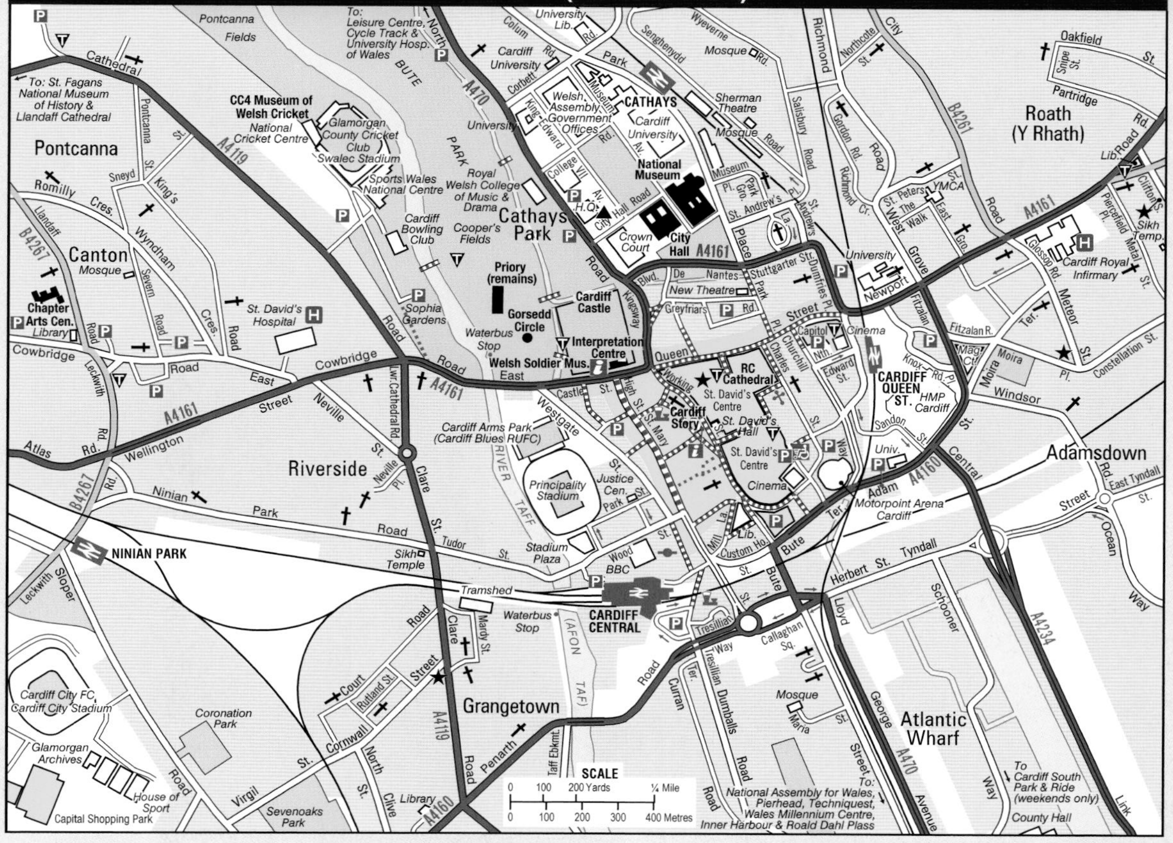

CHELTENHAM

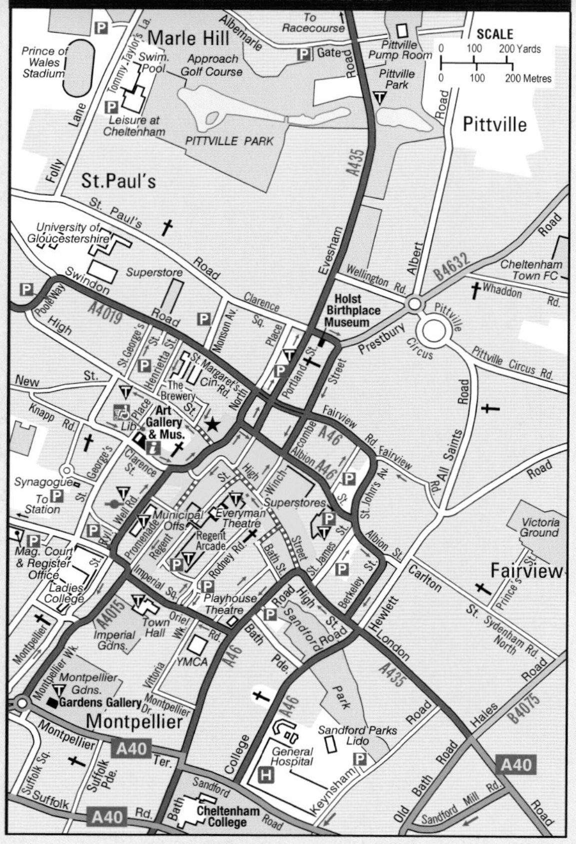

CHESTER

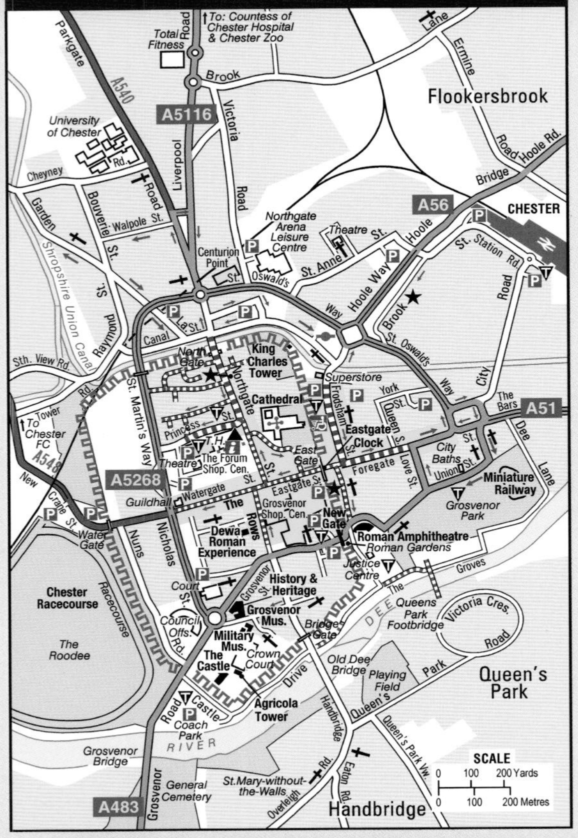

COVENTRY

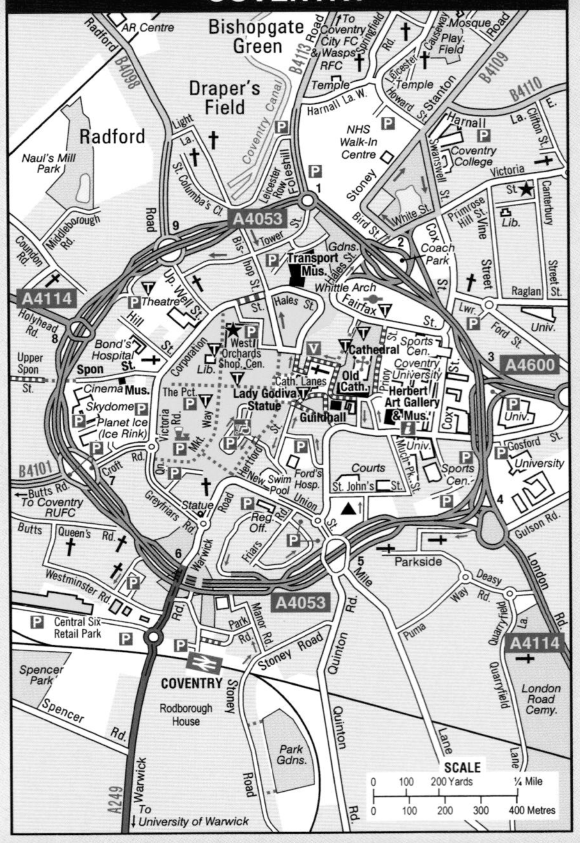

DERBY

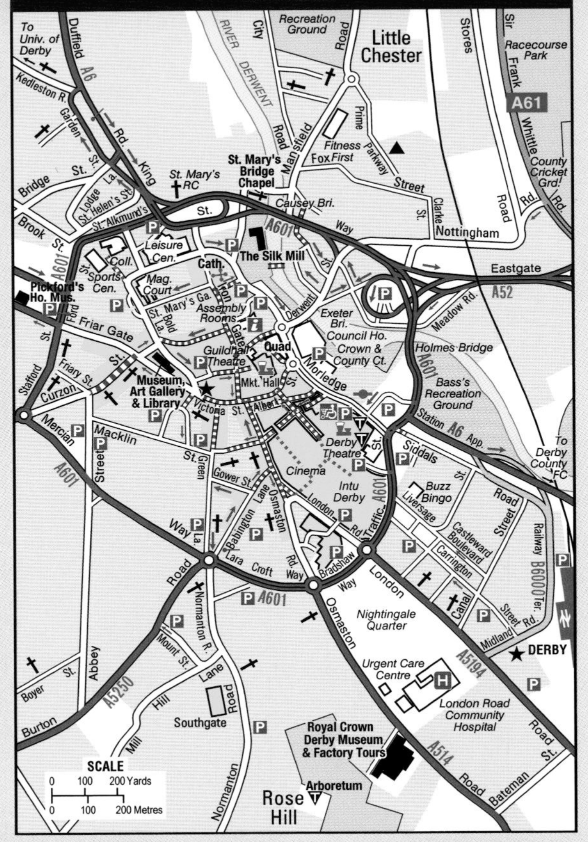

DOVER

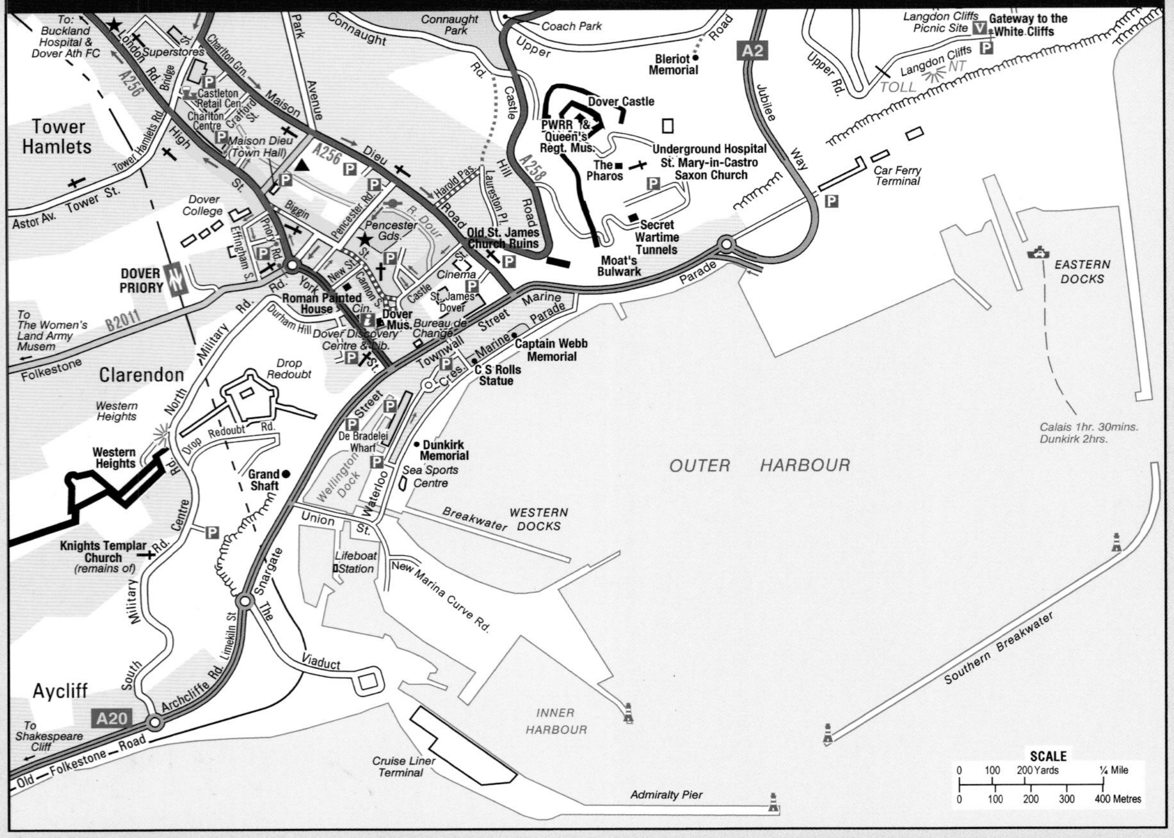

DUMFRIES

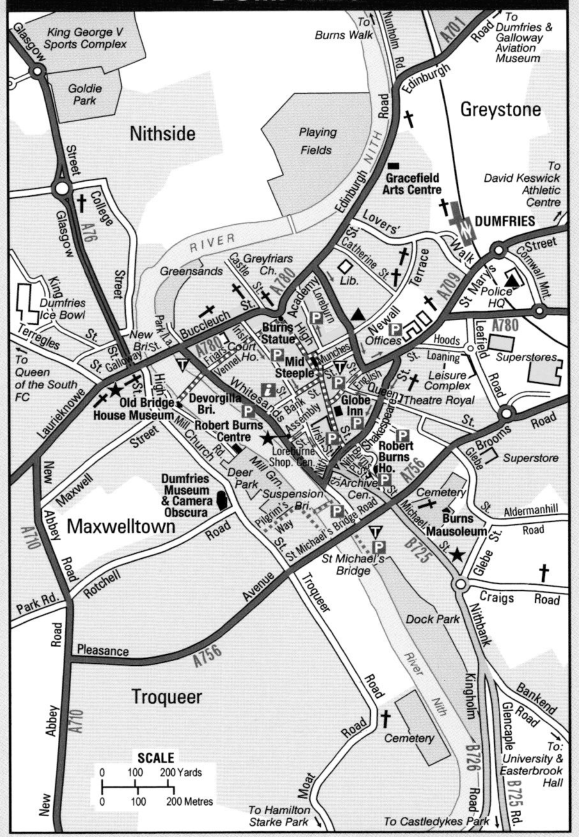

DUNDEE

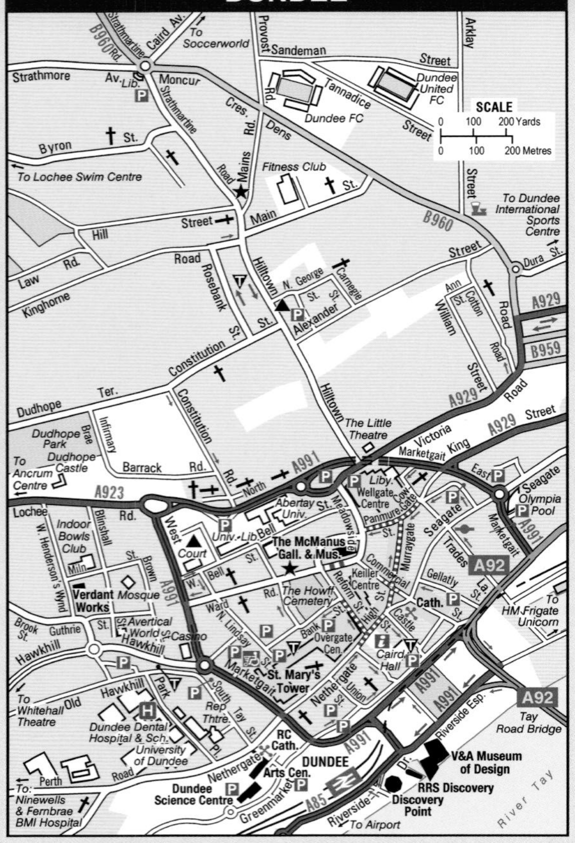

DURHAM

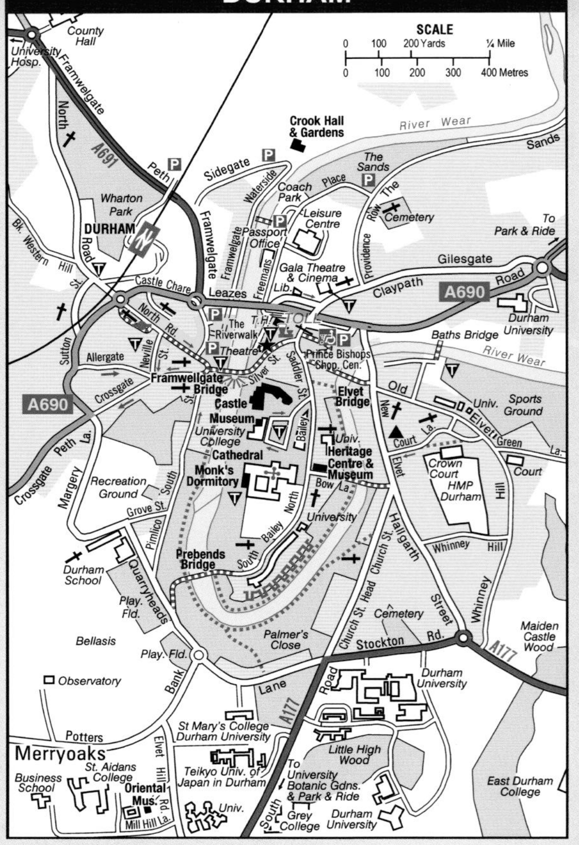

EASTBOURNE

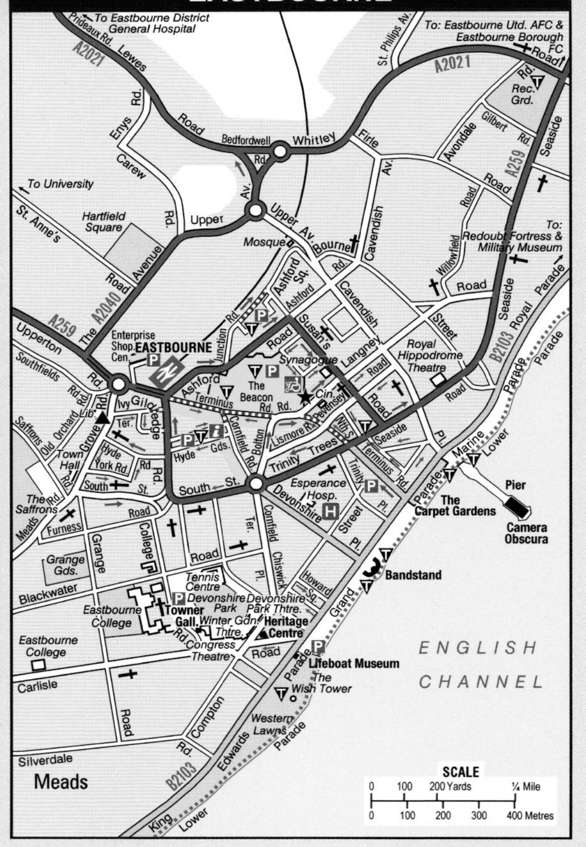

EDINBURGH

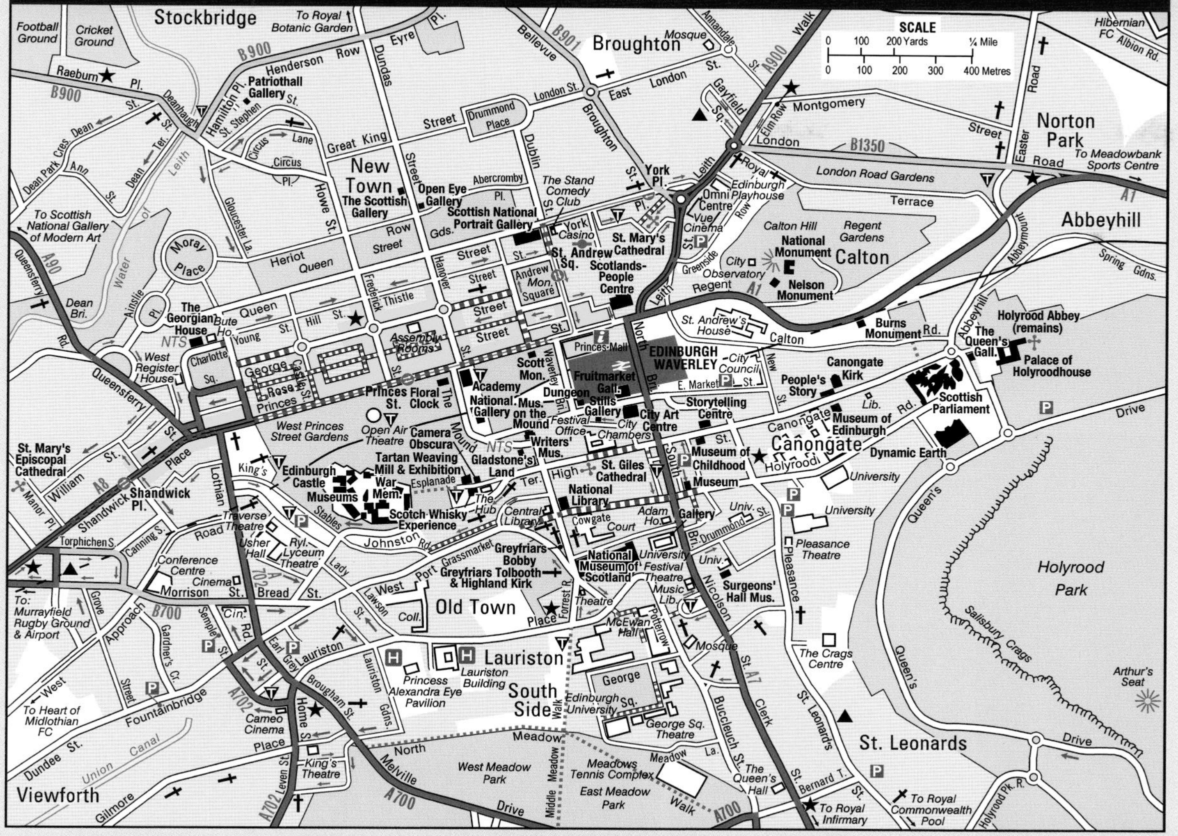

FOLKESTONE

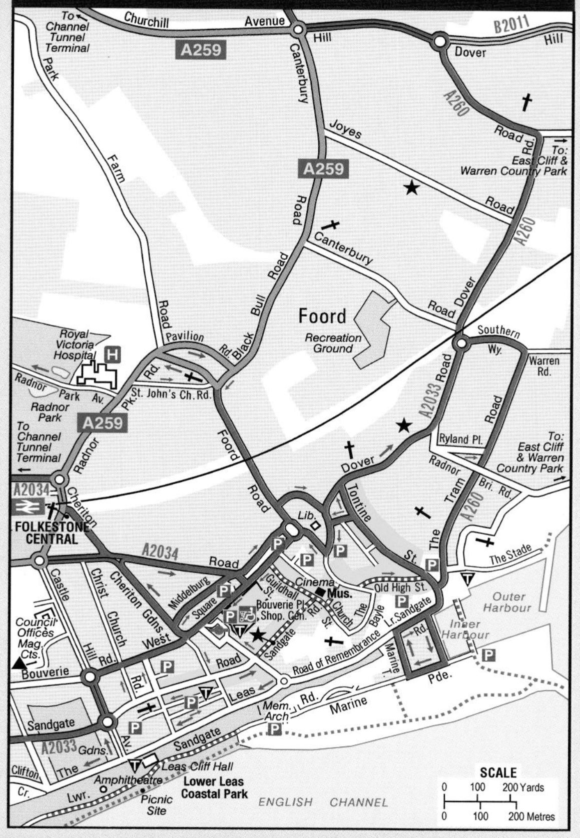

EXETER

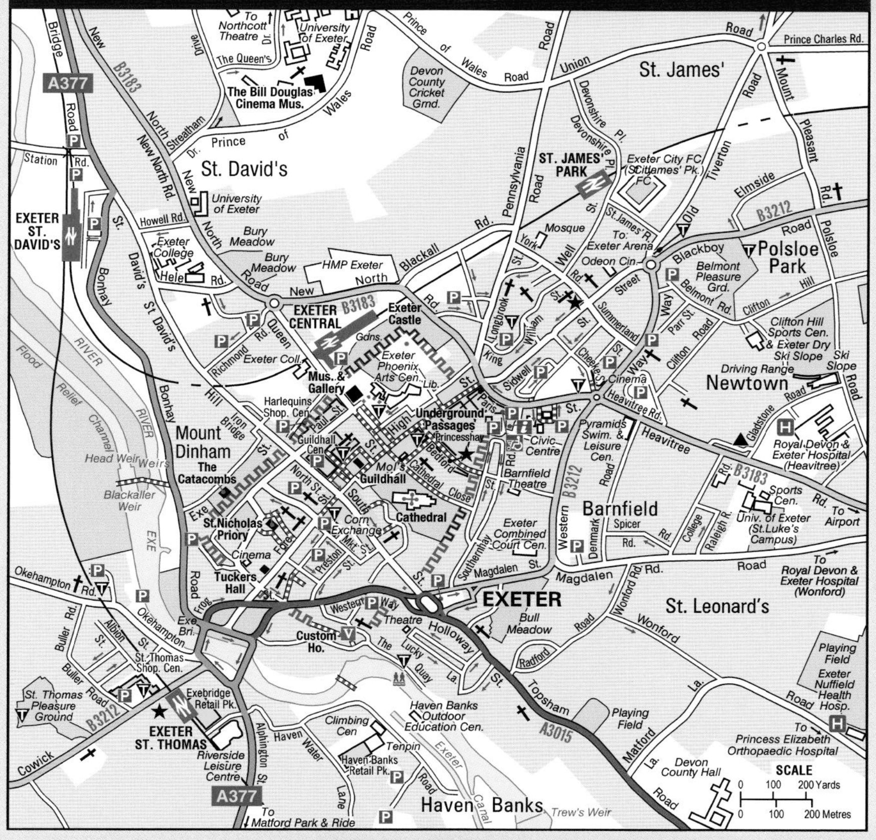

GUILDFORD

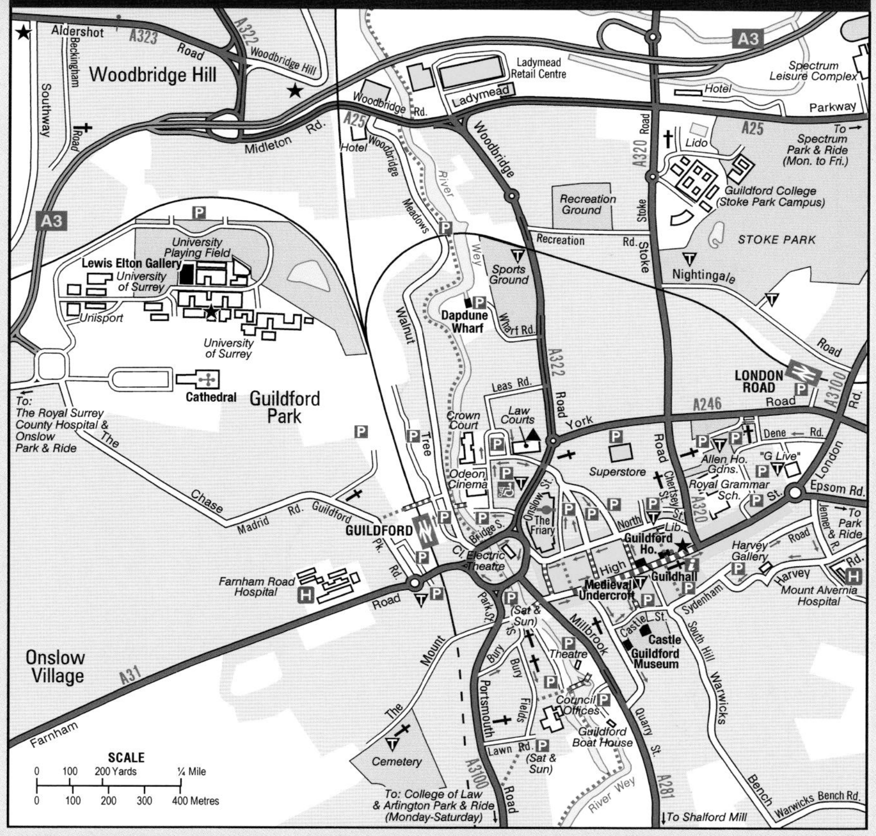

GLASGOW

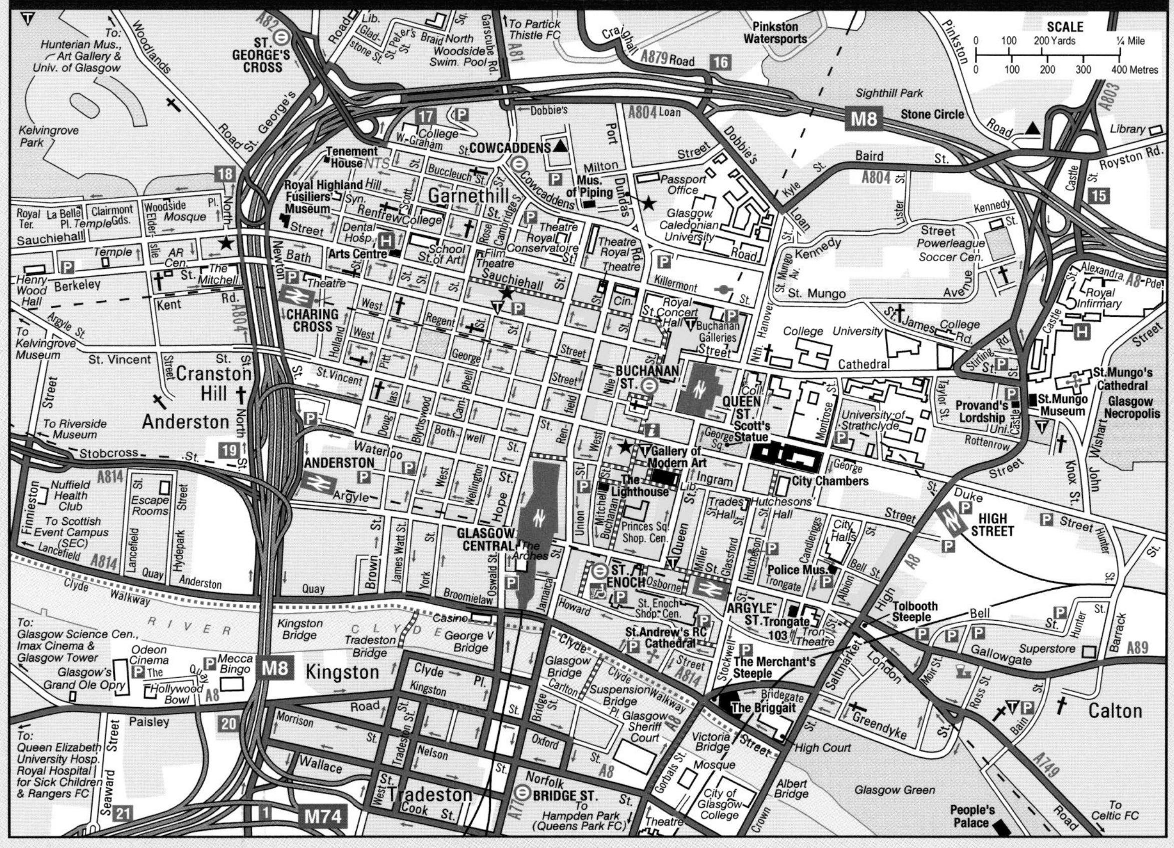

GLOUCESTER

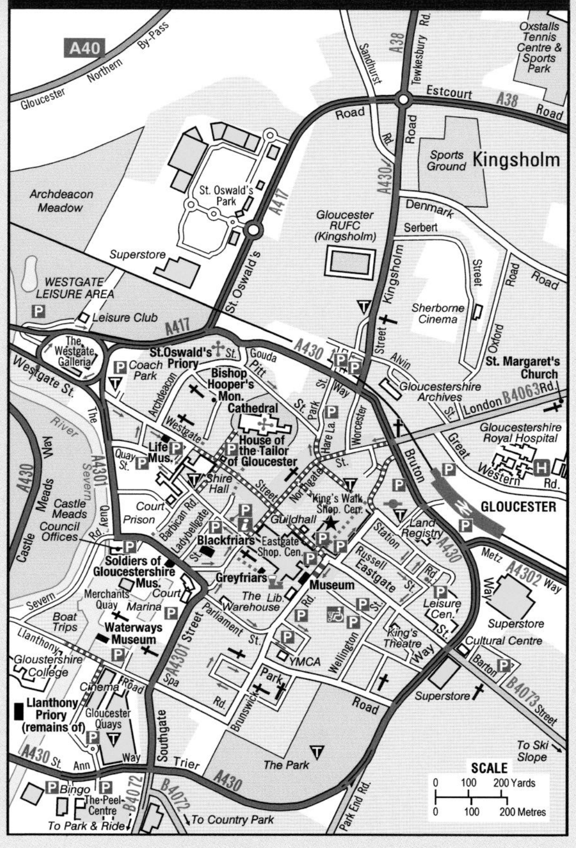

HARROGATE

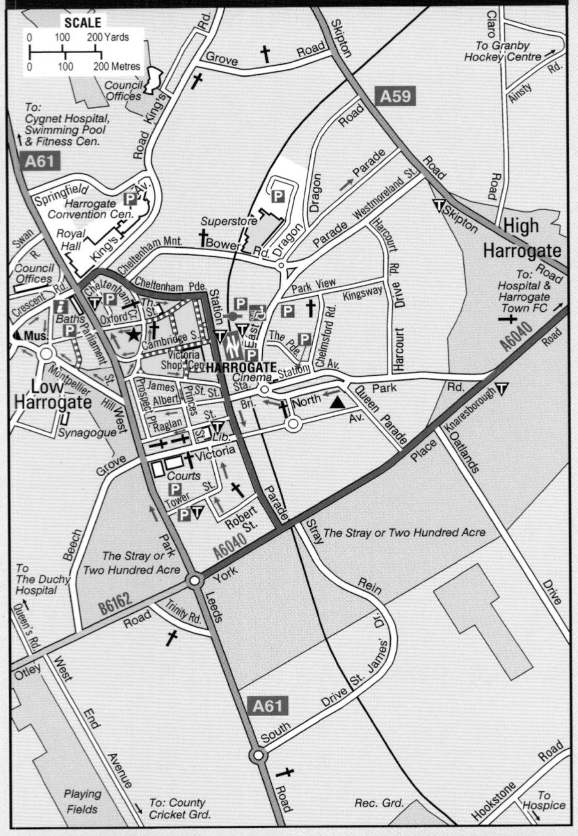

INVERNESS

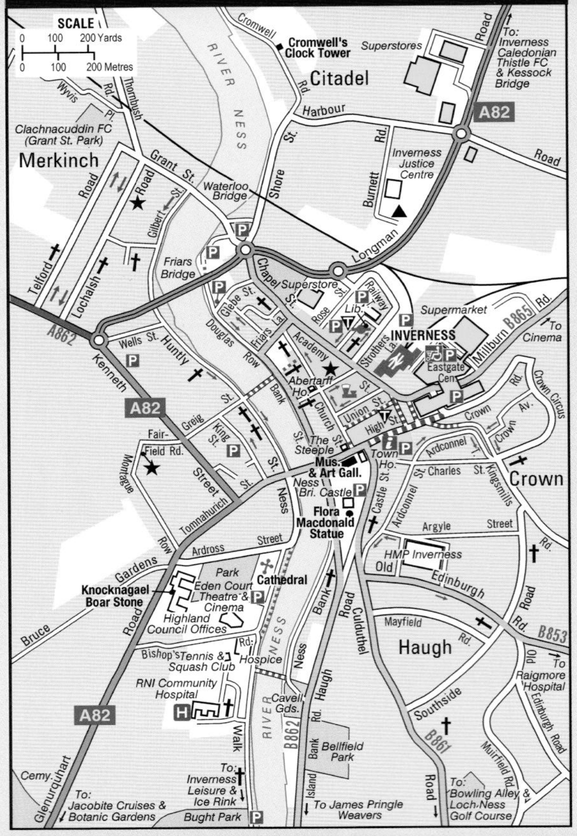

IPSWICH

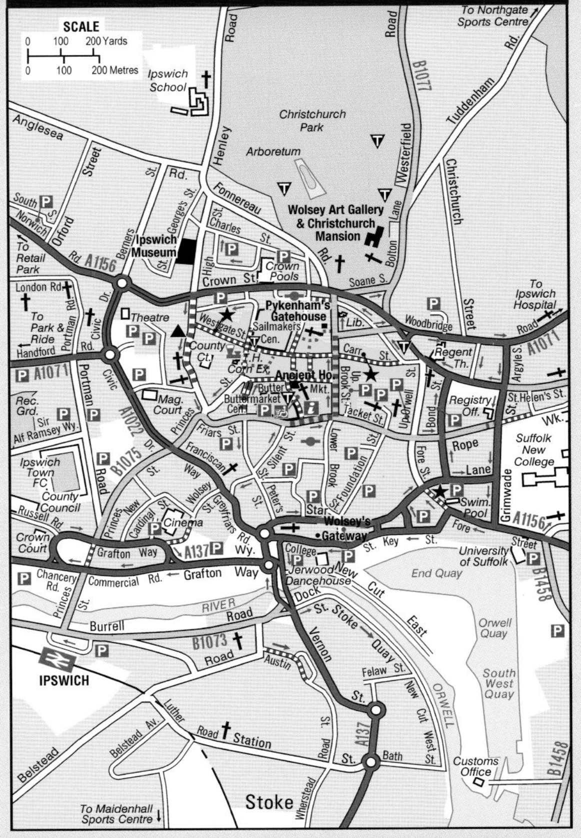

KILMARNOCK

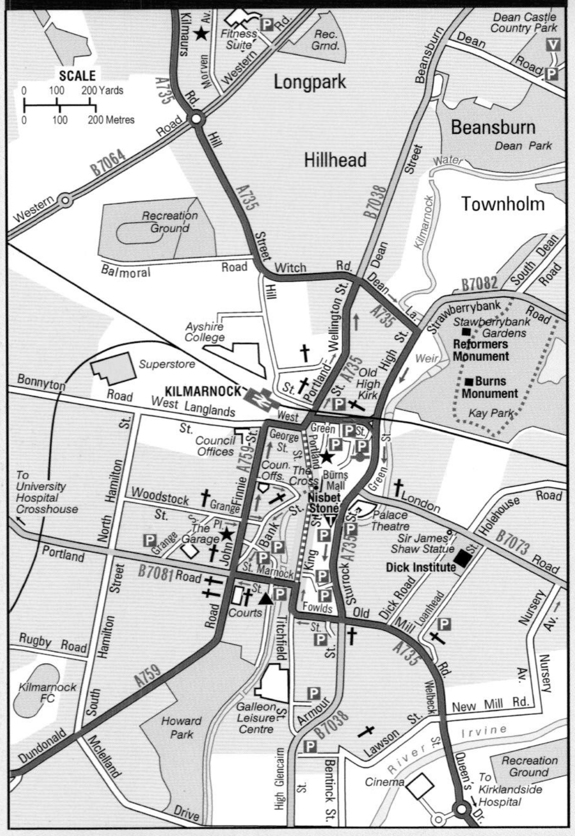

LEEDS

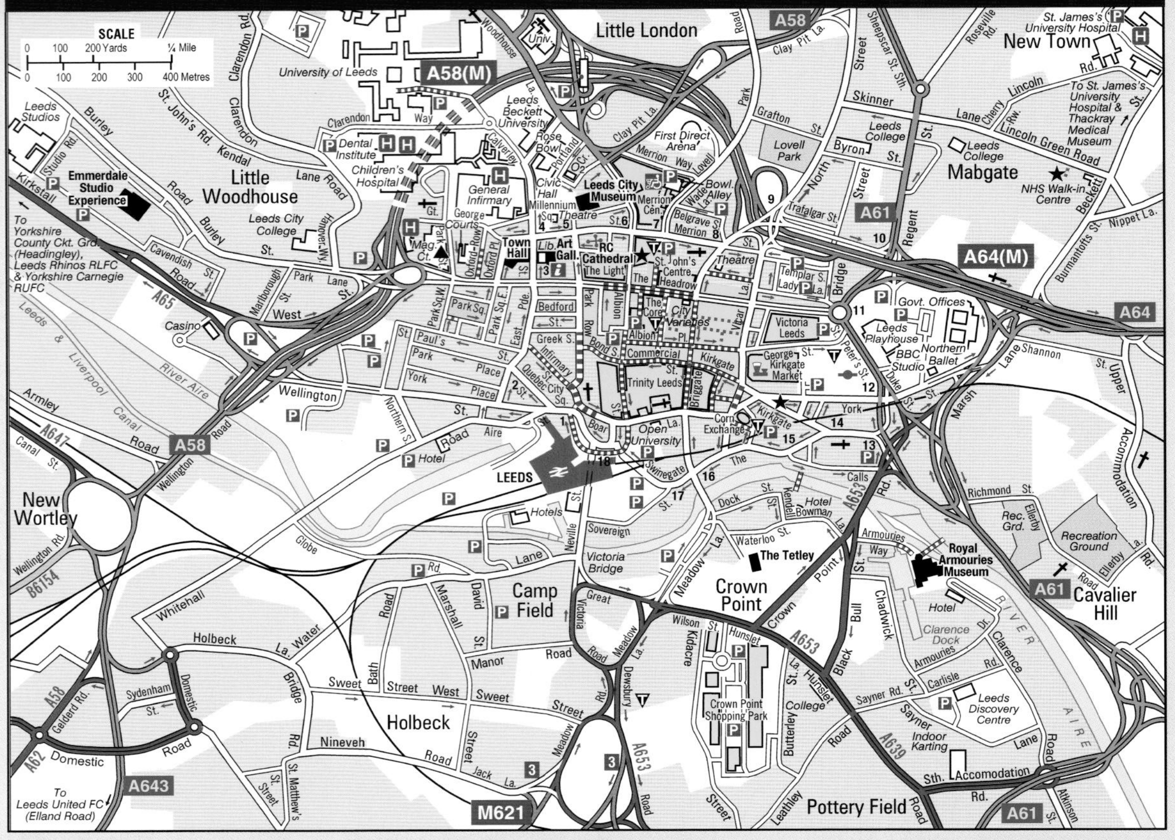

KINGSTON UPON HULL

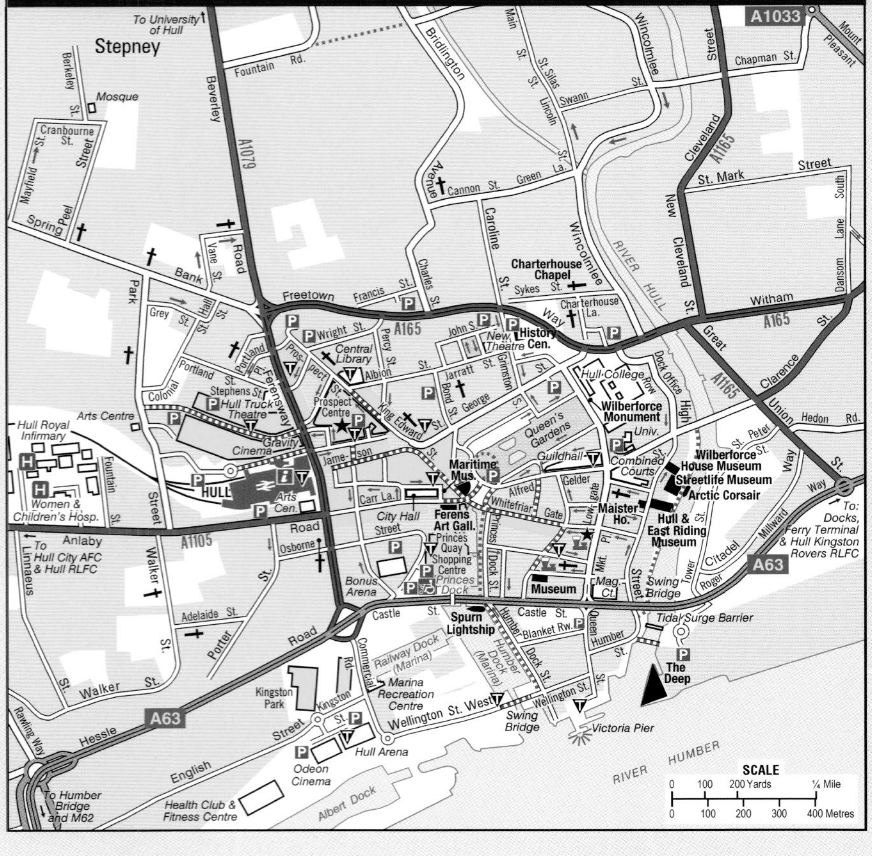

LEICESTER

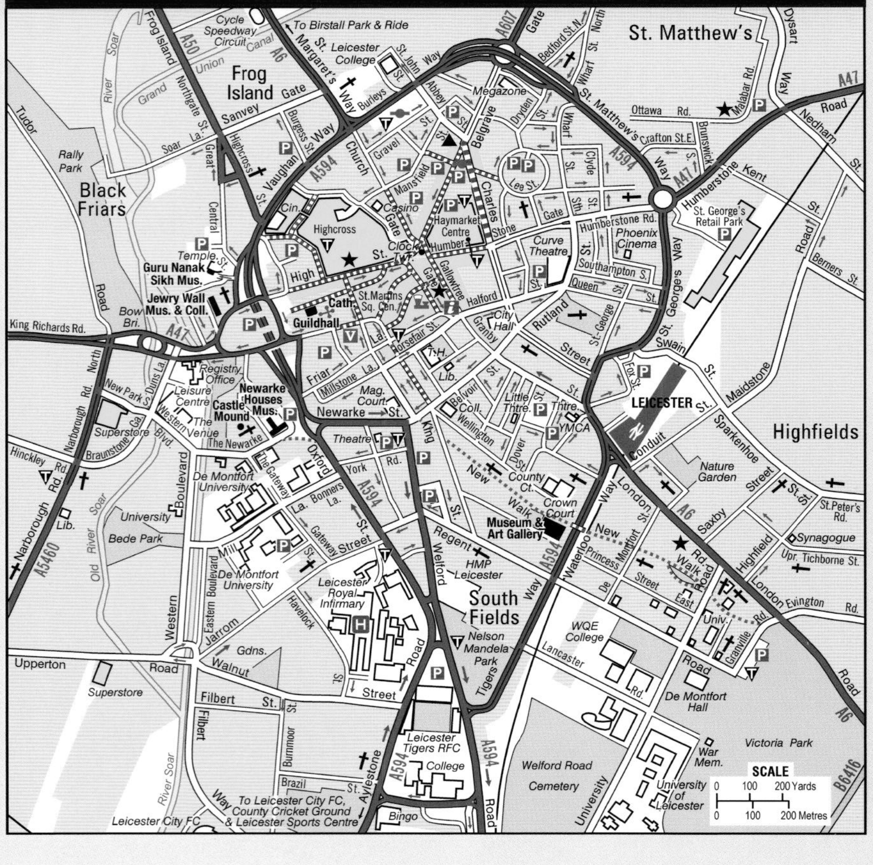

LINCOLN
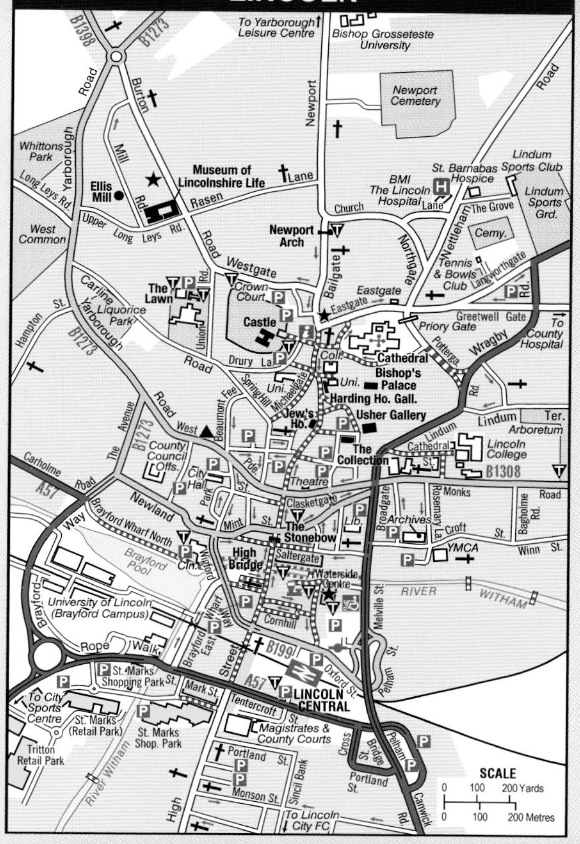

LIVERPOOL
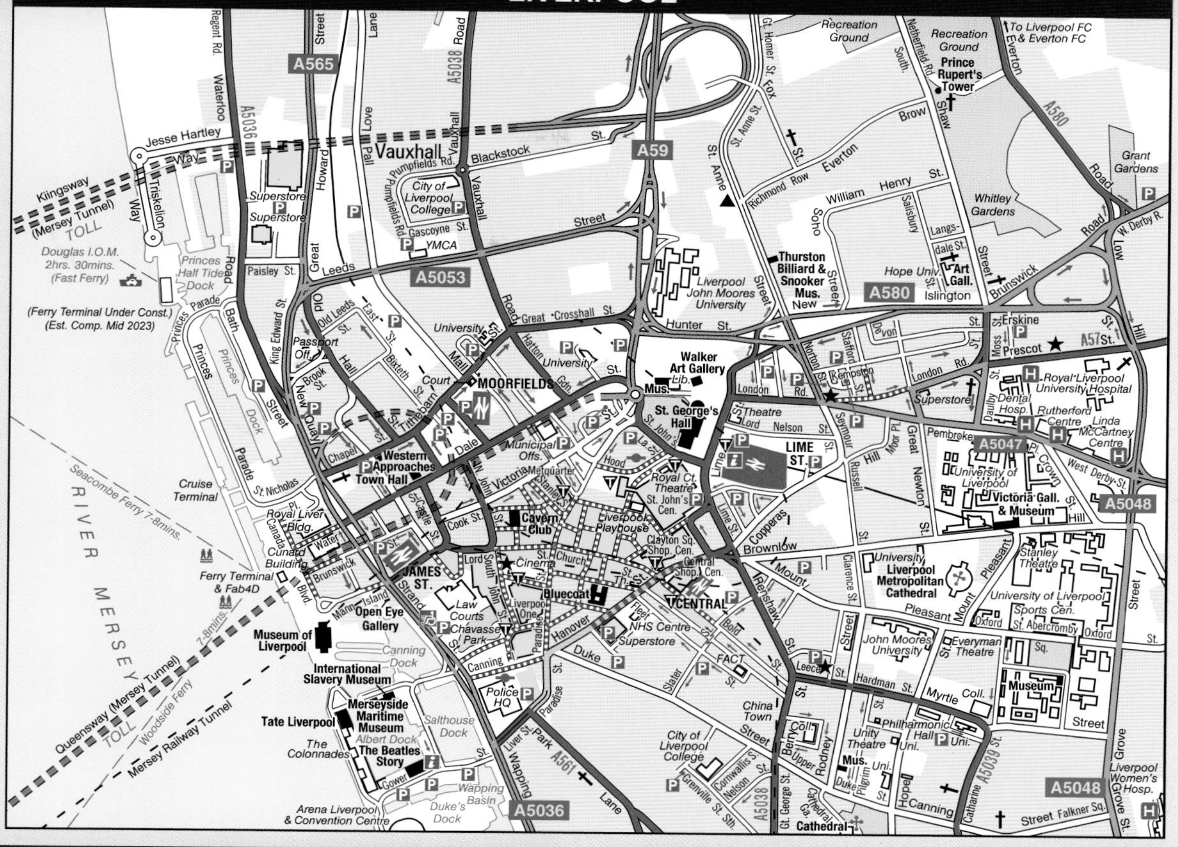

MANCHESTER (CITY CENTRE)
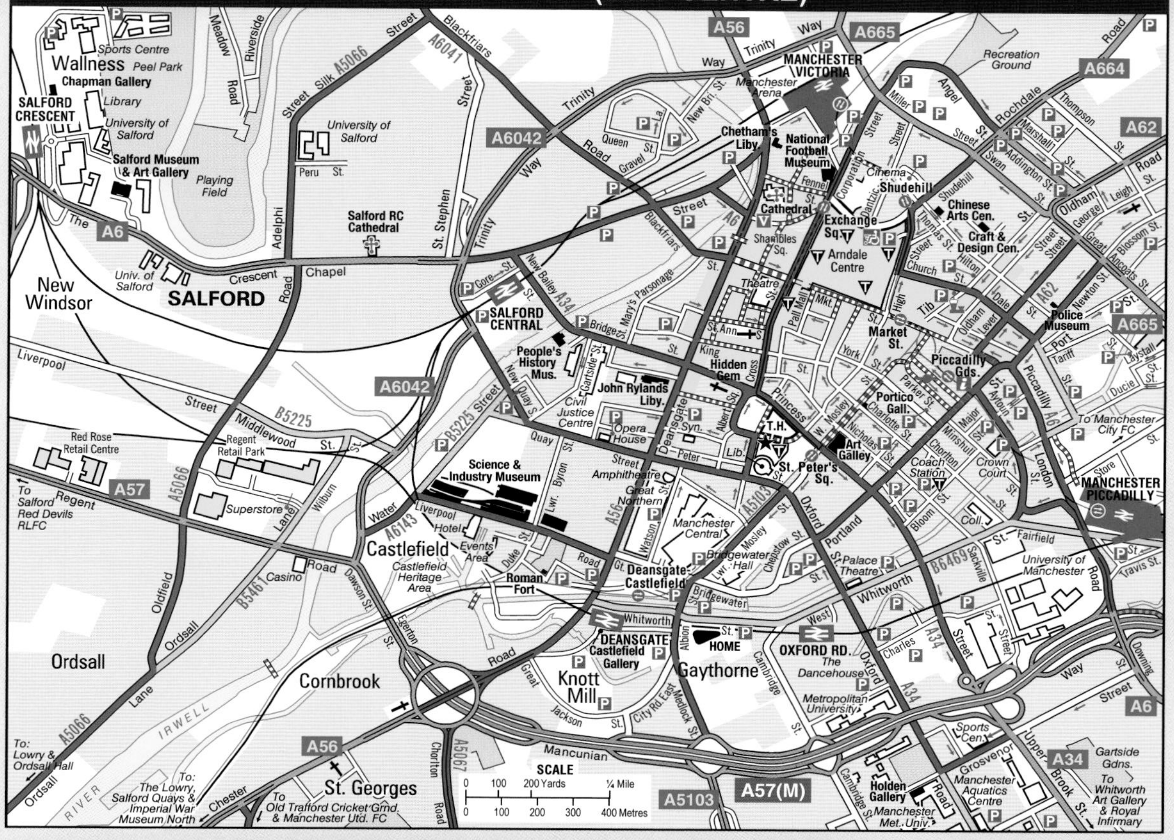

MIDDLESBROUGH
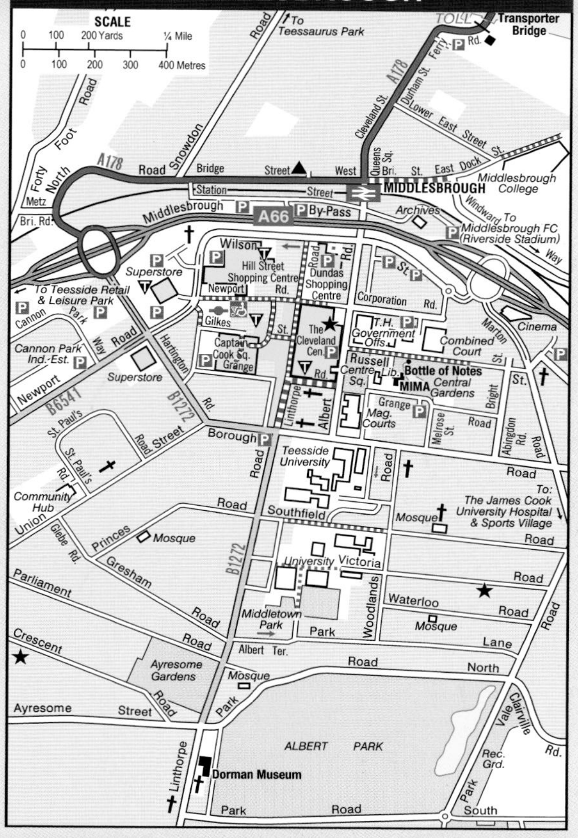

MEDWAY TOWNS
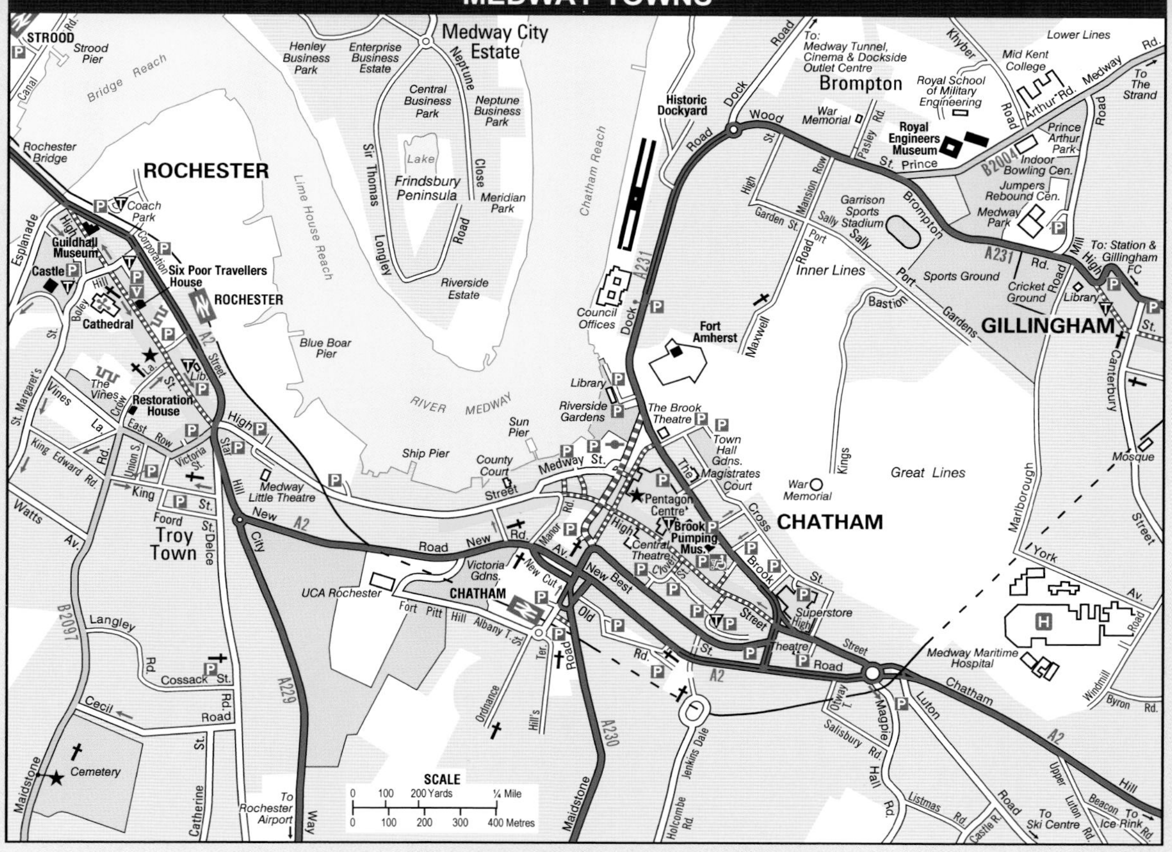

NEWCASTLE UPON TYNE
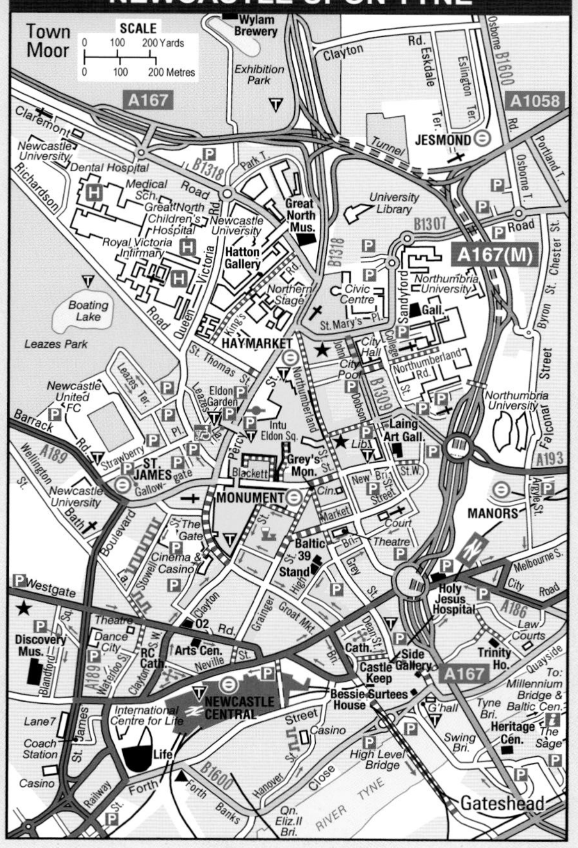

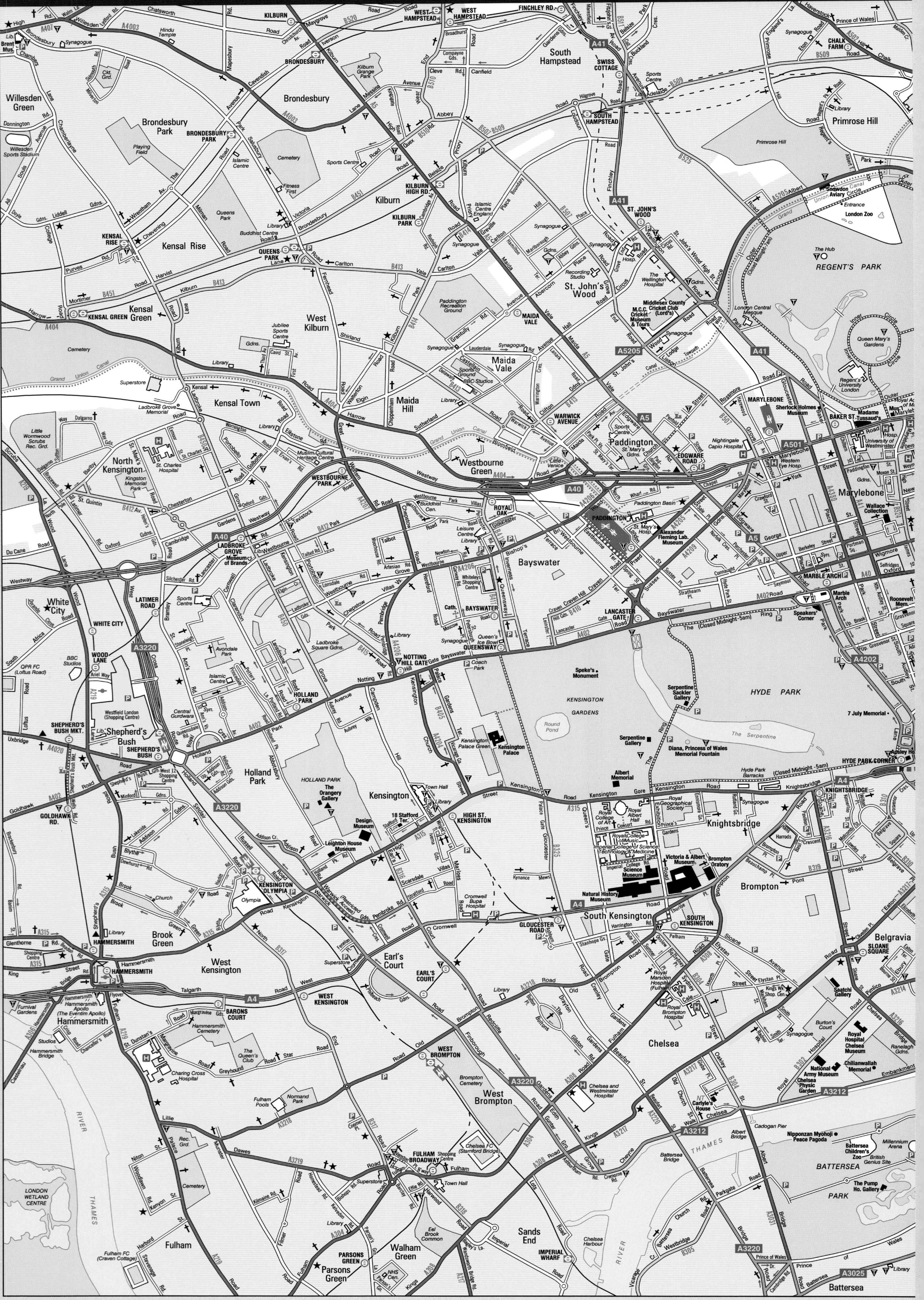
Willesden Green
Brondesbury Park
Brondesbury
Kilburn
Kensal Rise
Kensal Green
West Kilburn
South Hampstead
St. John's Wood
Primrose Hill
REGENT'S PARK
London Zoo
Maida Vale
Maida Hill
Kensal Town
North Kensington
Westbourne Green
Paddington
Marylebone
Bayswater
White City
Shepherd's Bush
Holland Park
Kensington
KENSINGTON GARDENS
HYDE PARK
The Serpentine
Knightsbridge
Brompton
South Kensington
Belgravia
Brook Green
West Kensington
Earl's Court
Hammersmith
Chelsea
West Brompton
Fulham
Walham Green
Parsons Green
Sands End
BATTERSEA PARK
Battersea
RIVER THAMES
LONDON WETLAND CENTRE

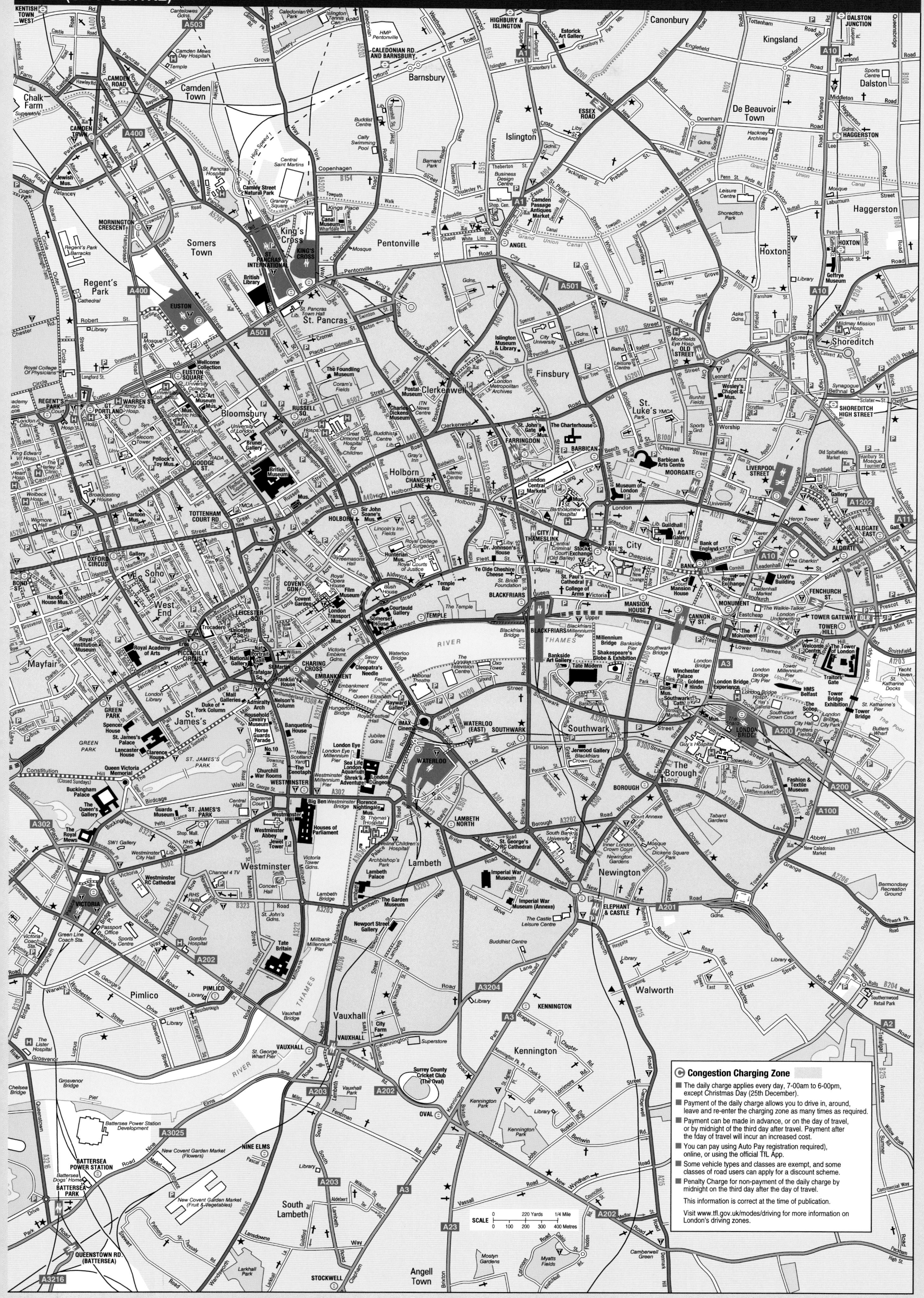

(CITY CENTRE)

Congestion Charging Zone

- The daily charge applies every day, 7-00am to 6-00pm, except Christmas Day (25th December).
- Payment of the daily charge allows you to drive in, around, leave and re-enter the charging zone as many times as required.
- Payment can be made in advance, or on the day of travel, or by midnight of the third day after travel. Payment after the fday of travel will incur an increased cost.
- You can pay using Auto Pay (registration required), online, or using the official TfL App.
- Some vehicle types and classes are exempt, and some classes of road users can apply for a discount scheme.
- Penalty Charge for non-payment of the daily charge by midnight on the third day after the day of travel.

This information is correct at the time of publication.

Visit www.tfl.gov.uk/modes/driving for more information on London's driving zones.

SCALE 0   220 Yards   1/4 Mile
       0   100 200 300 400 Metres

MILTON KEYNES

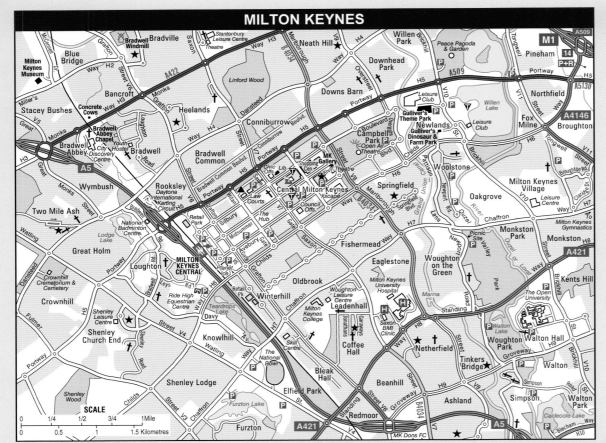

NEWPORT (CASNEWYDD)

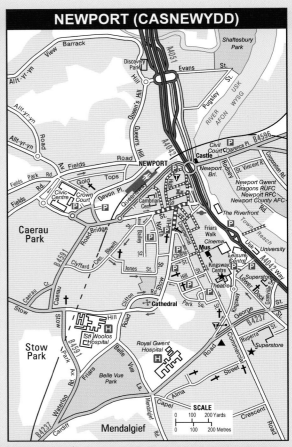

NORWICH

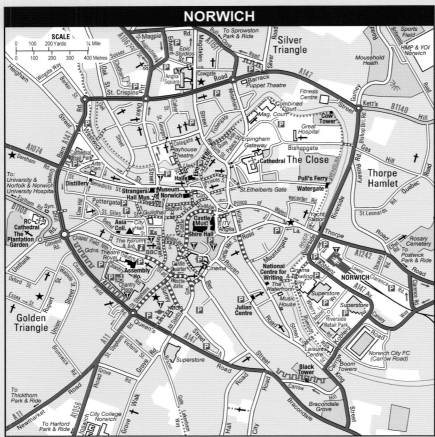

NOTTINGHAM

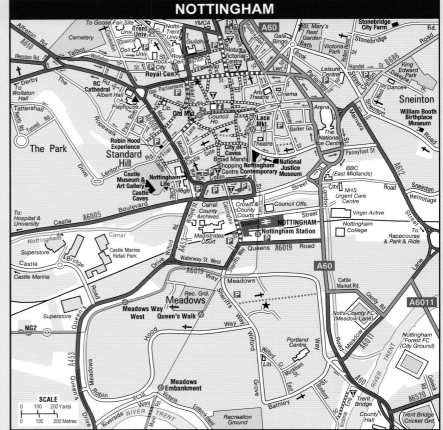

NORTHAMPTON

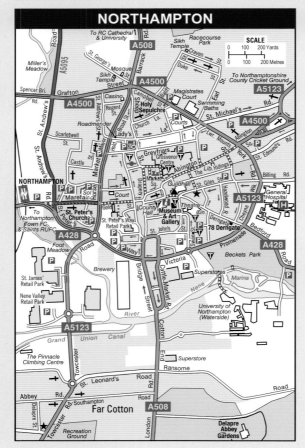

OXFORD

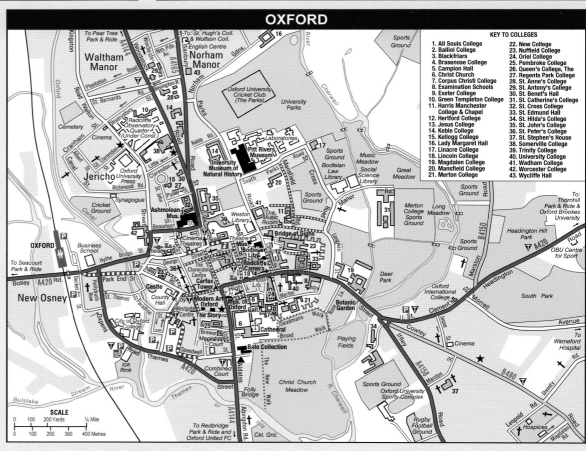

KEY TO COLLEGES

1. All Souls College
2. Balliol College
3. Blackfriars
4. Brasenose College
5. Campion Hall
6. Christ Church
7. Corpus Christi College
8. Examination Schools
9. Exeter College
10. Green Templeton College
11. Harris Manchester College & Chapel
12. Hertford College
13. Jesus College
14. Keble College
15. Kellogg College
16. Lady Margaret Hall
17. Linacre College
18. Lincoln College
19. Magdalen College
20. Mansfield College
21. Merton College
22. New College
23. Nuffield College
24. Oriel College
25. Pembroke College
26. Queen's College, The
27. Regents Park College
28. St. Anne's College
29. St. Antony's College
30. St. Benet's Hall
31. St. Catherine's College
32. St. Cross College
33. St. Edmund Hall
34. St. Hilda's College
35. St. John's College
36. St. Peter's College
37. St. Stephen's House
38. Somerville College
39. Trinity College
40. University College
41. Wadham College
42. Worcester College
43. Wycliffe Hall

OBAN

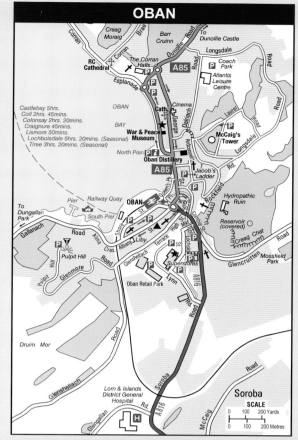

PERTH

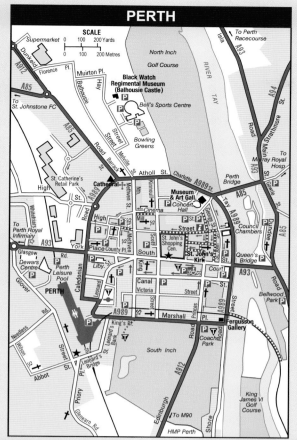

PETERBOROUGH

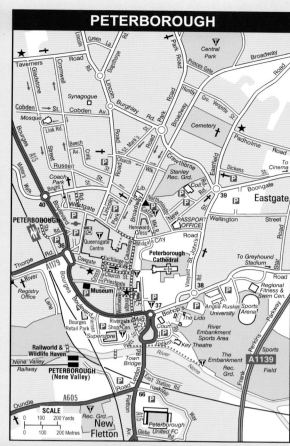

PLYMOUTH

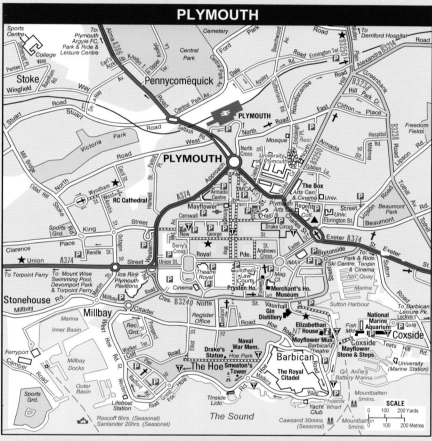

PORTSMOUTH

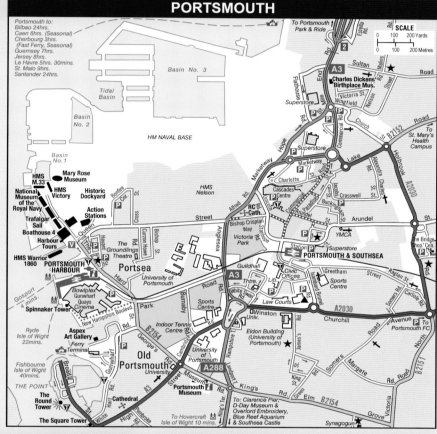

PRESTON

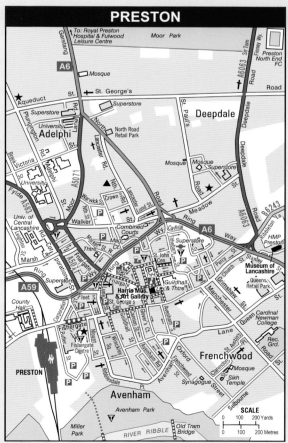

READING

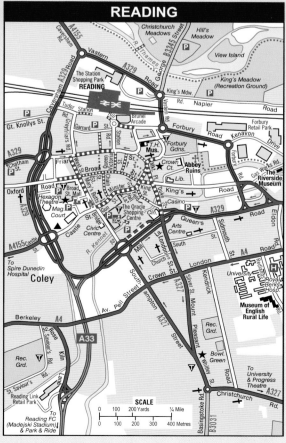

SALISBURY

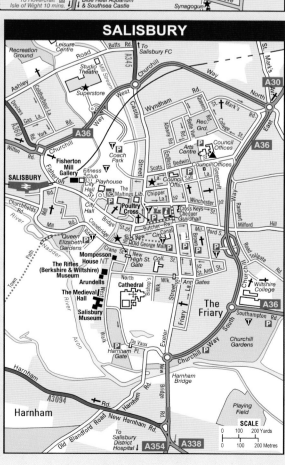

SHEFFIELD

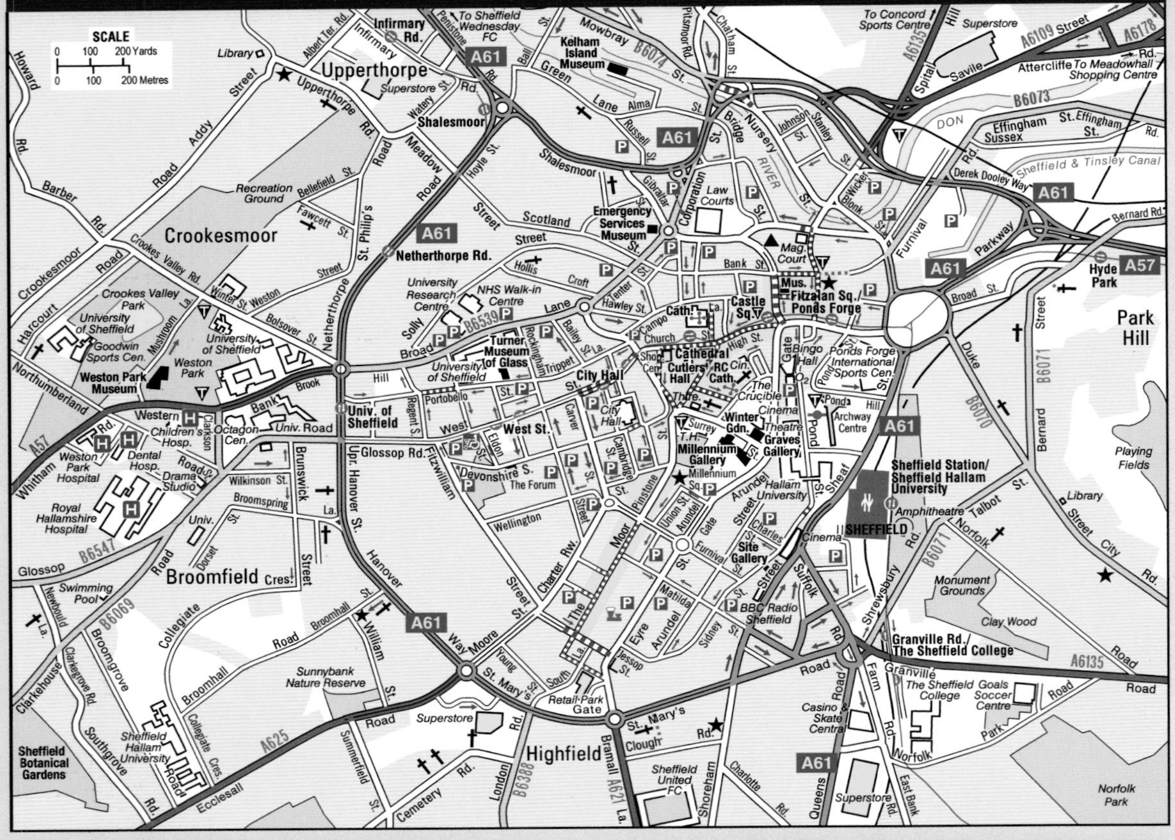

SHREWSBURY

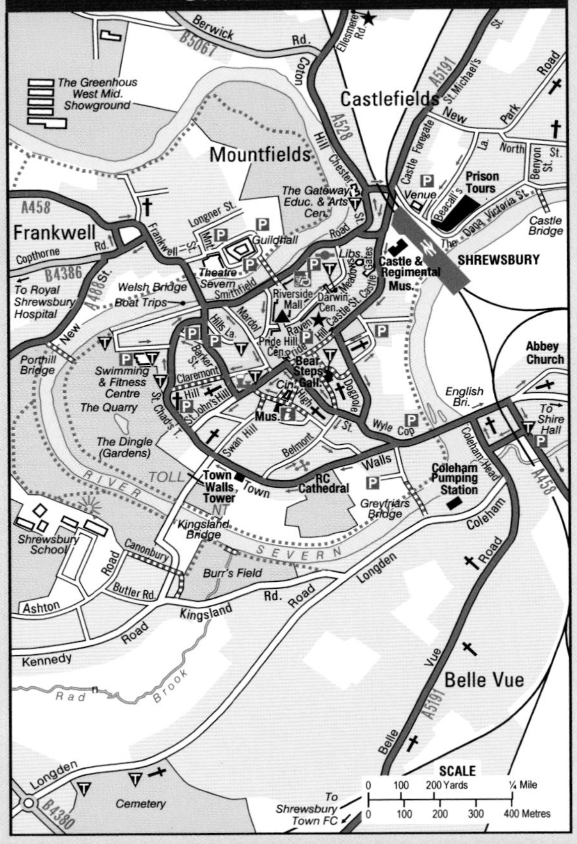

SOUTHAMPTON

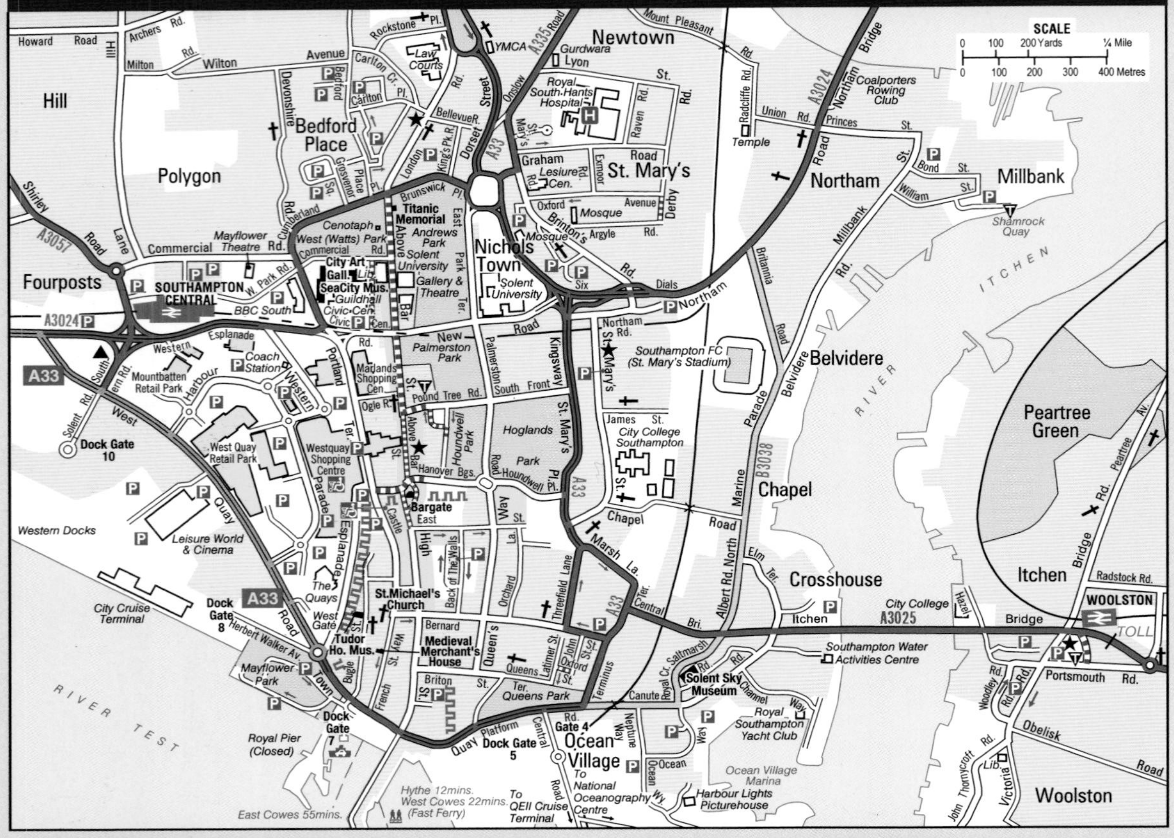

STIRLING

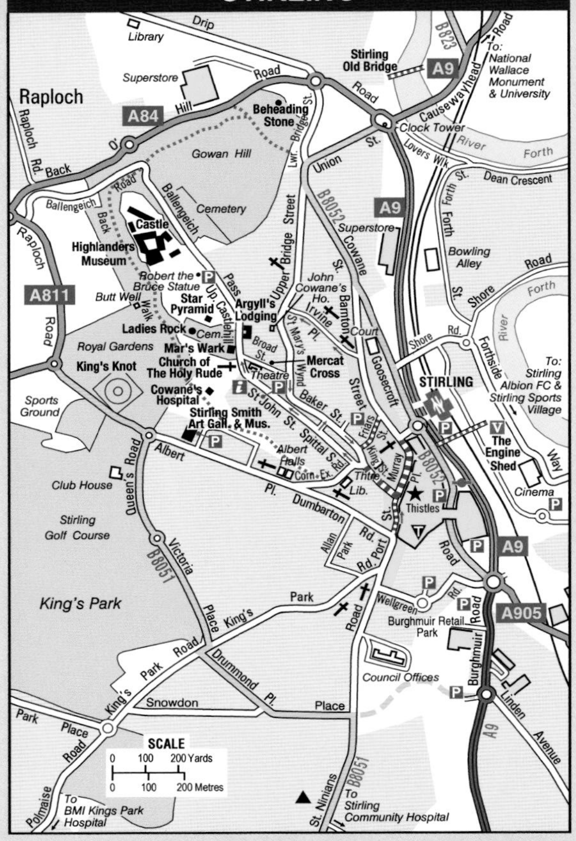

STOKE-ON-TRENT

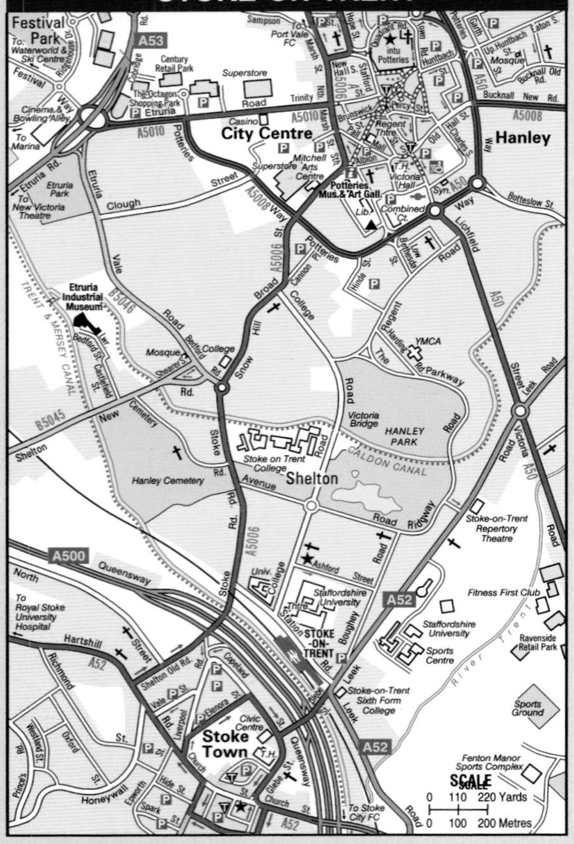

STRATFORD UPON AVON

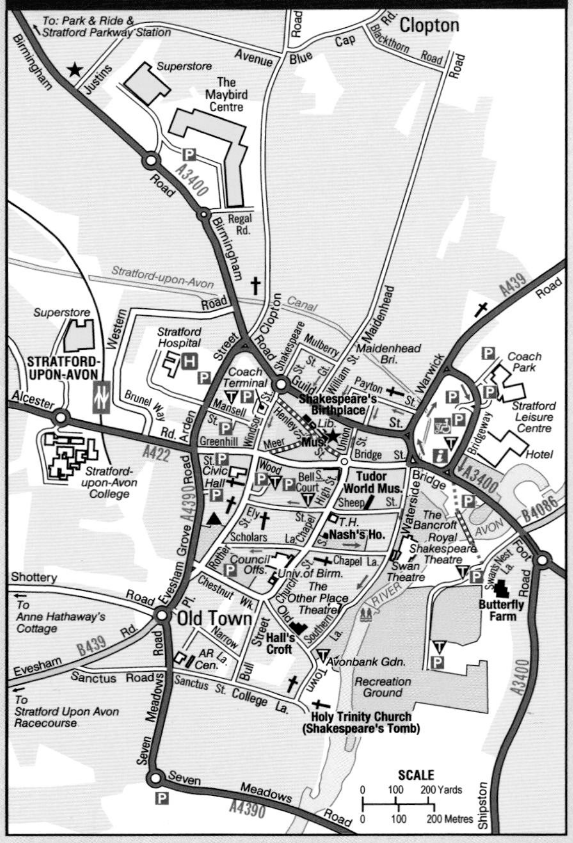

SUNDERLAND

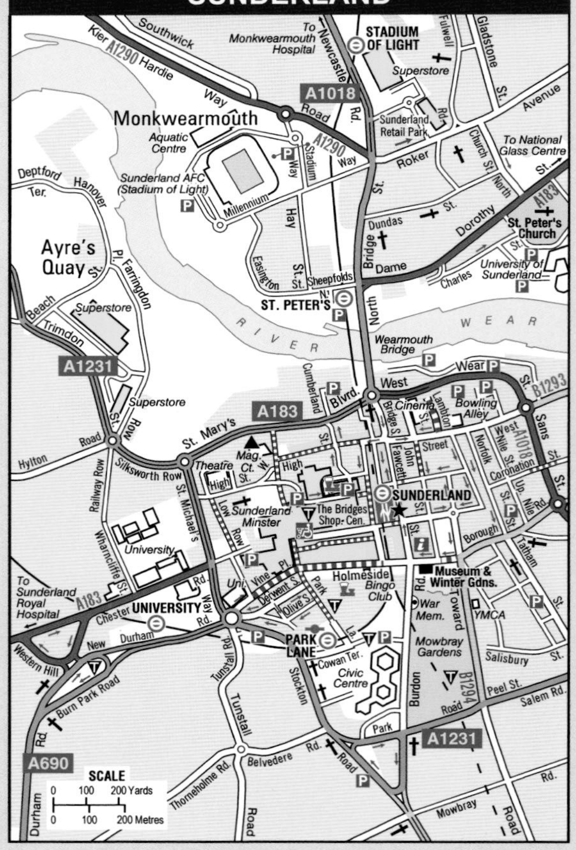

SWANSEA (ABERTAWE)

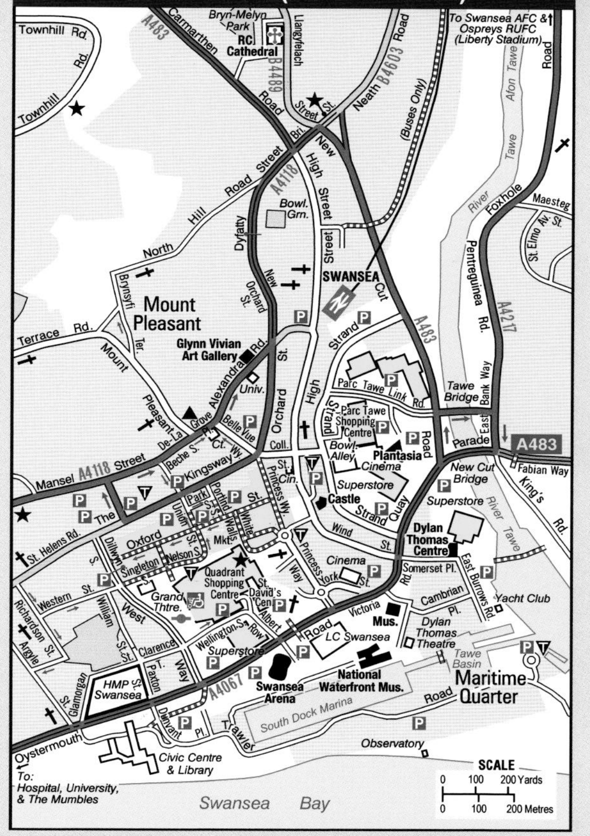

SWINDON

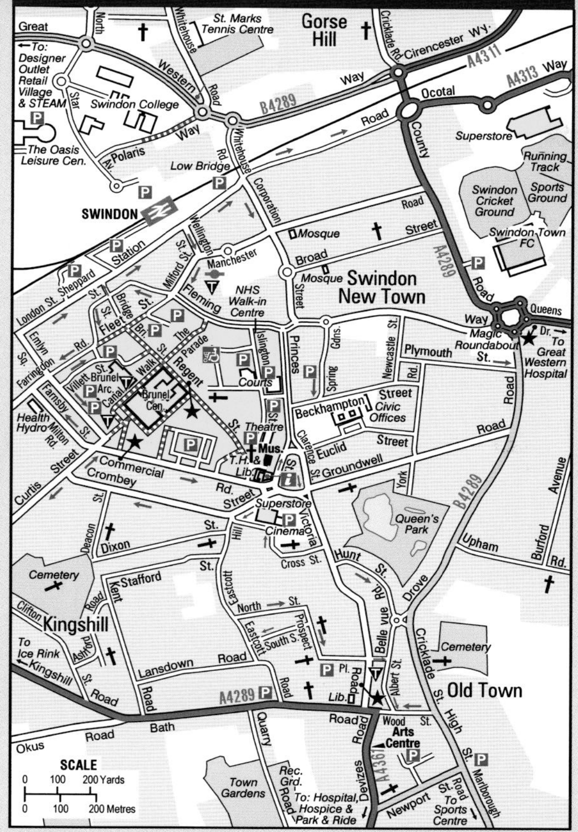

TAUNTON

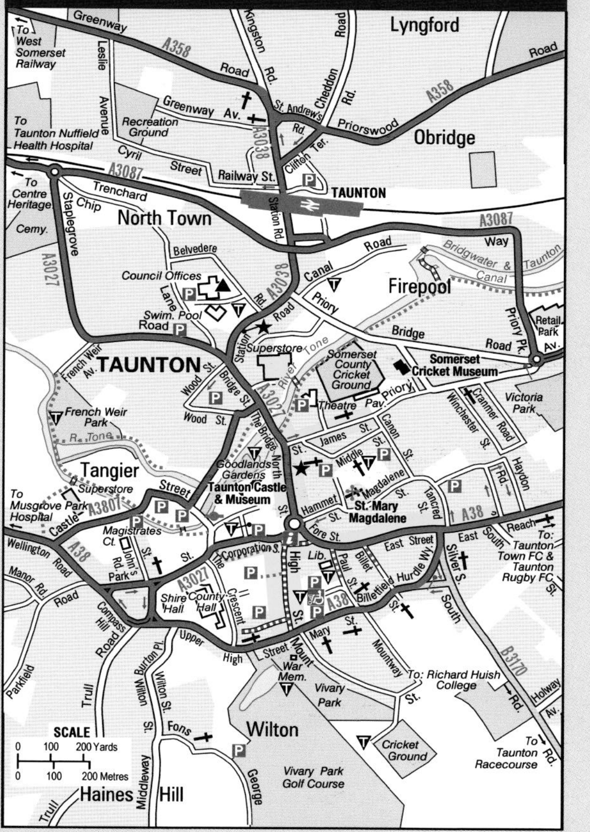

WINCHESTER

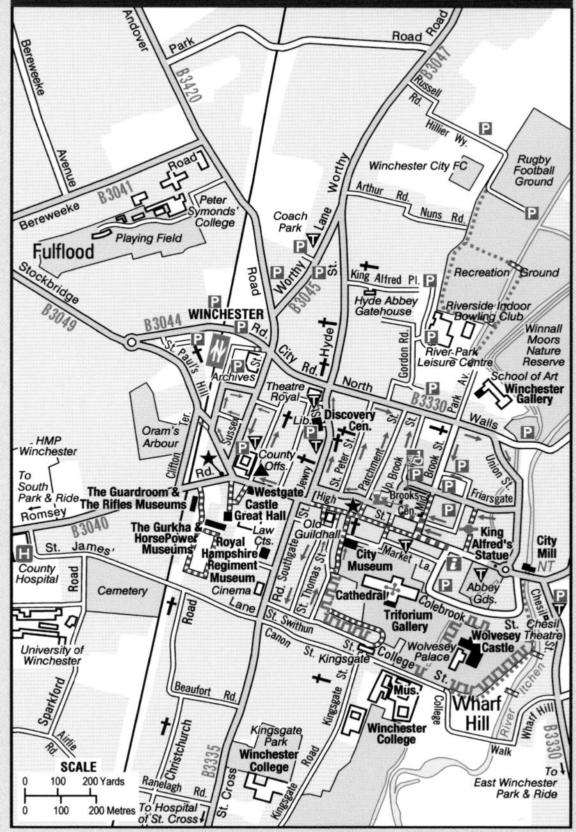

WINDSOR

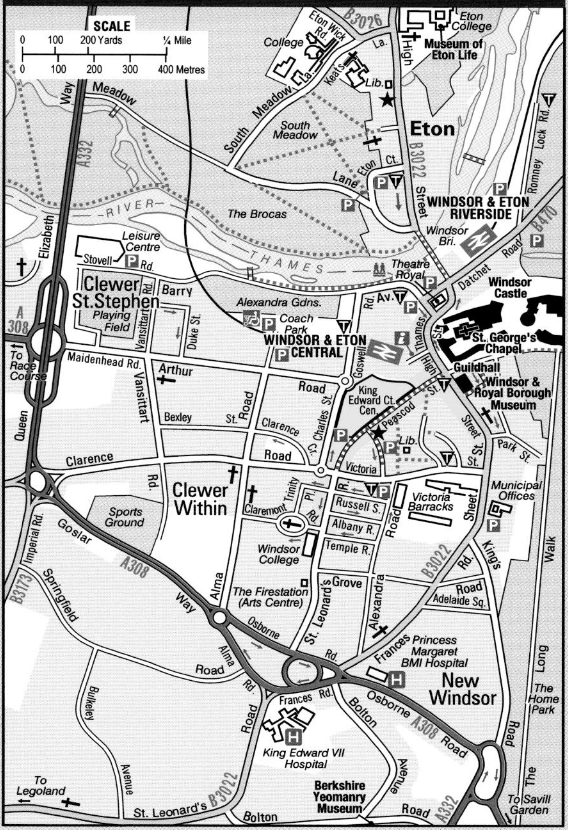

WOLVERHAMPTON

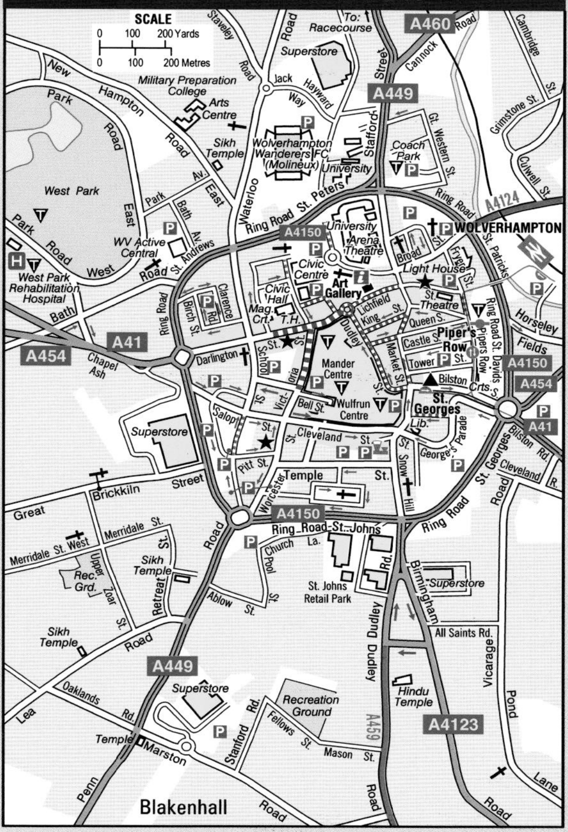

WORCESTER

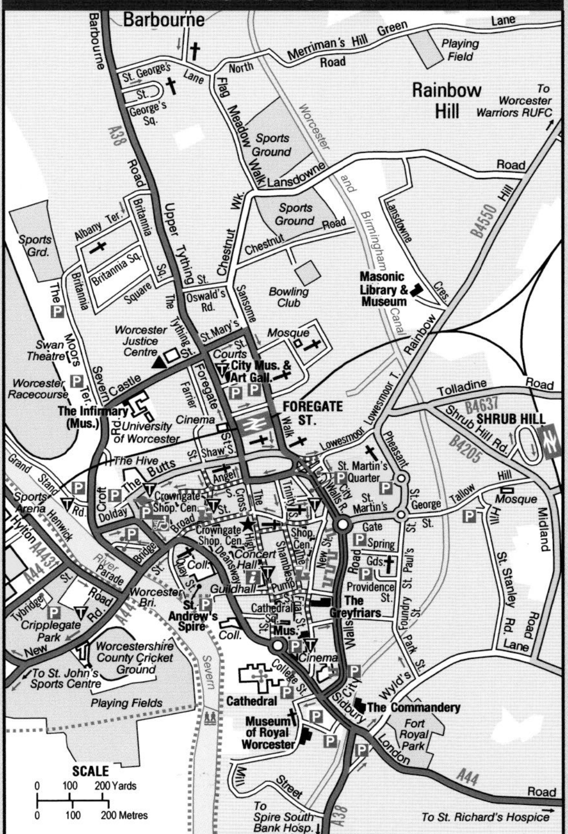

YORK

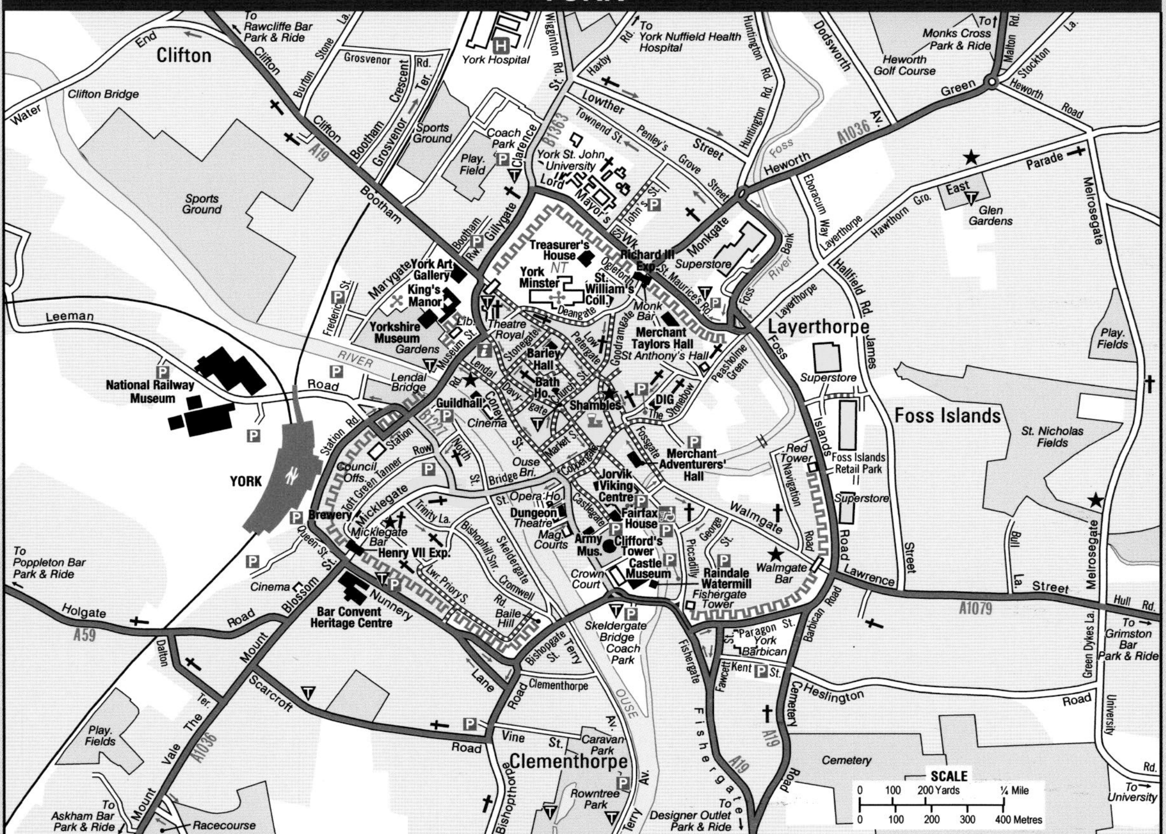

PORT PLANS

HARWICH

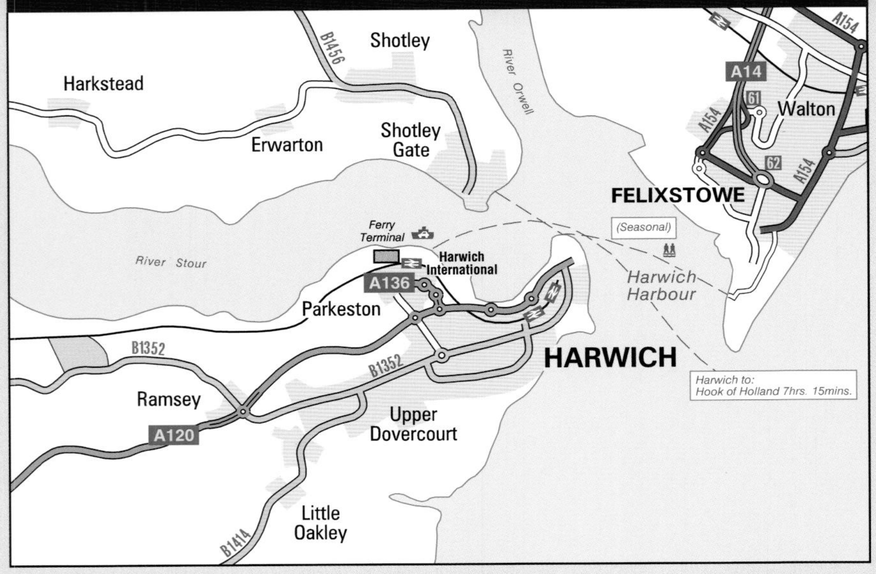

KINGSTON UPON HULL

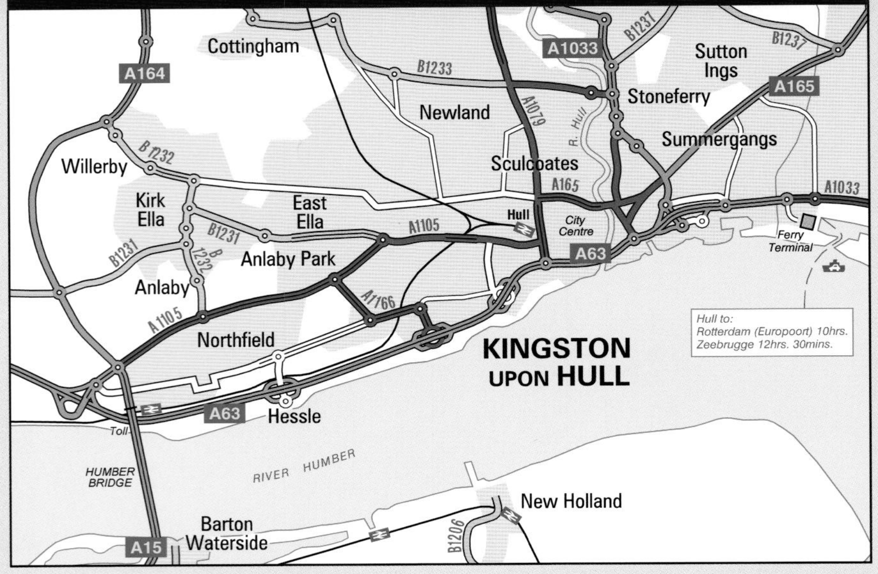

NEWCASTLE UPON TYNE

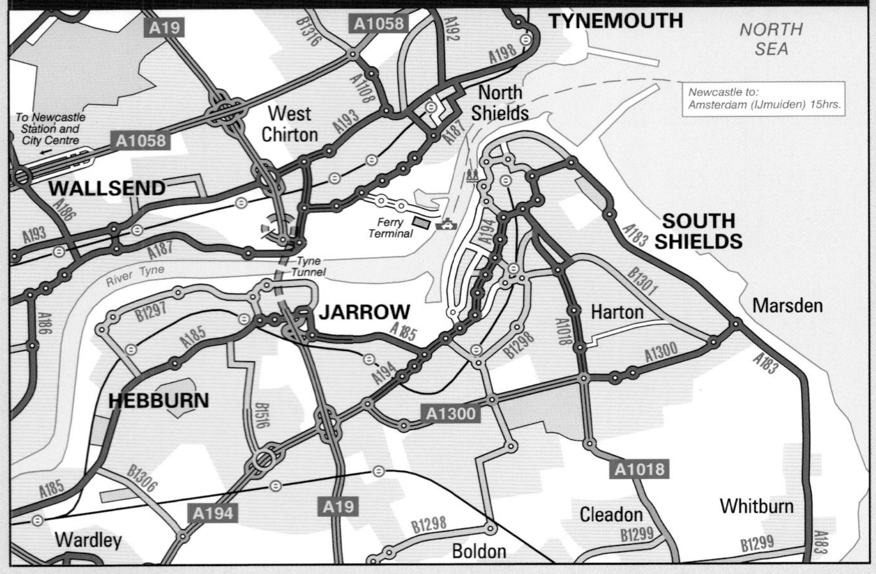

NEWHAVEN

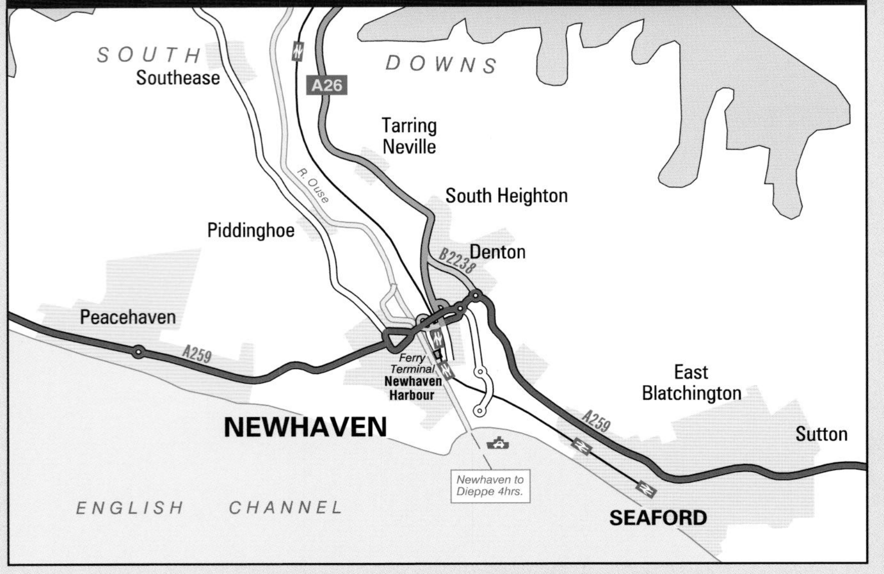

PEMBROKE DOCK (DOC PENFRO)

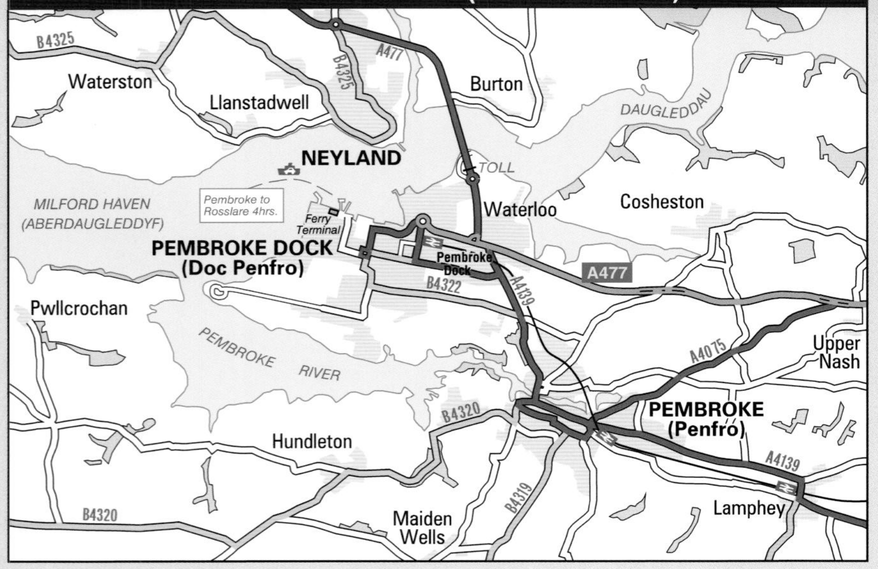

POOLE

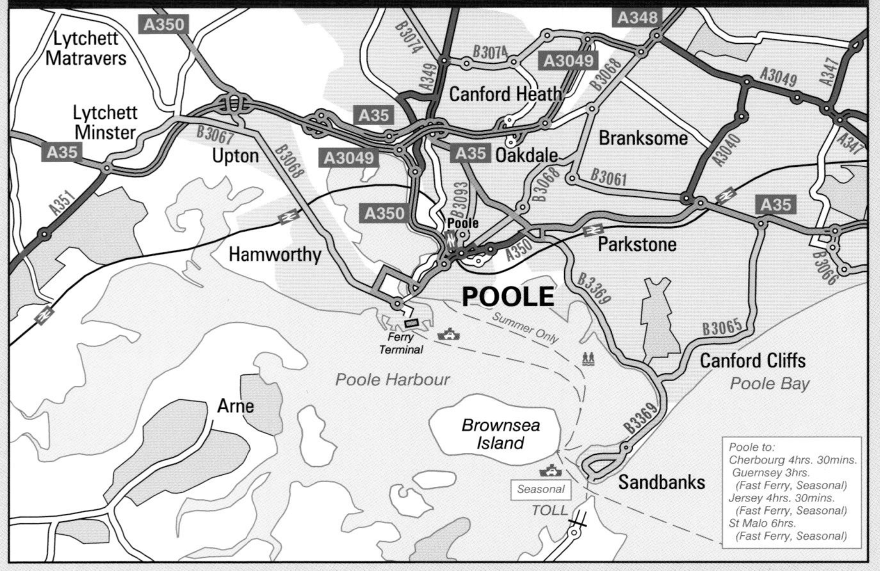

PORTSMOUTH

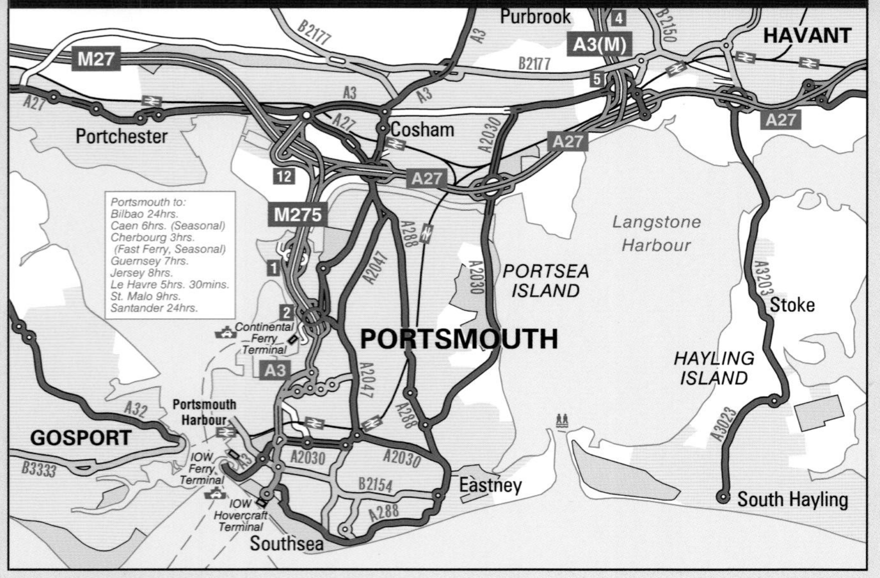

Other Port Plans

Please refer to Town Plans for detailed plans of the following Ports:

Dover - page 108

Plymouth - page 115

Southampton - page 116

AIRPORT PLANS

BIRMINGHAM

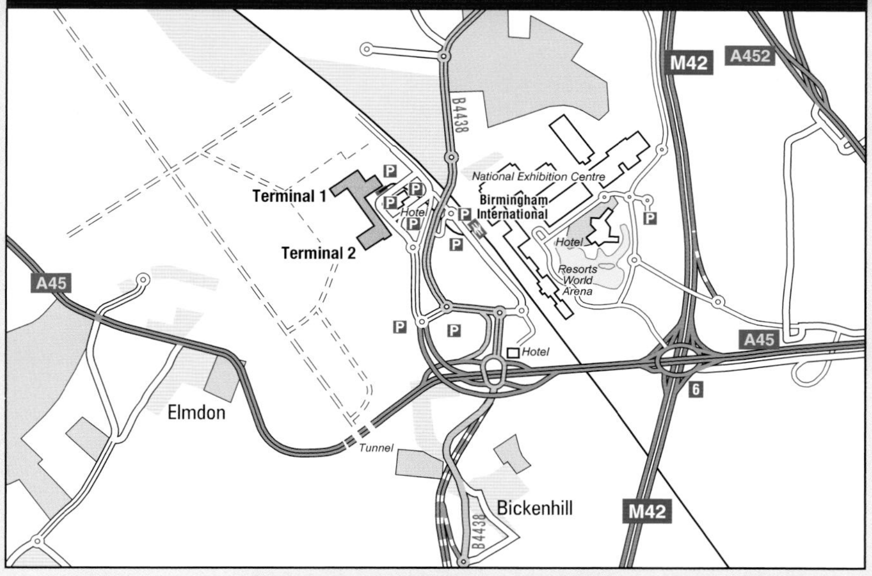

EAST MIDLANDS

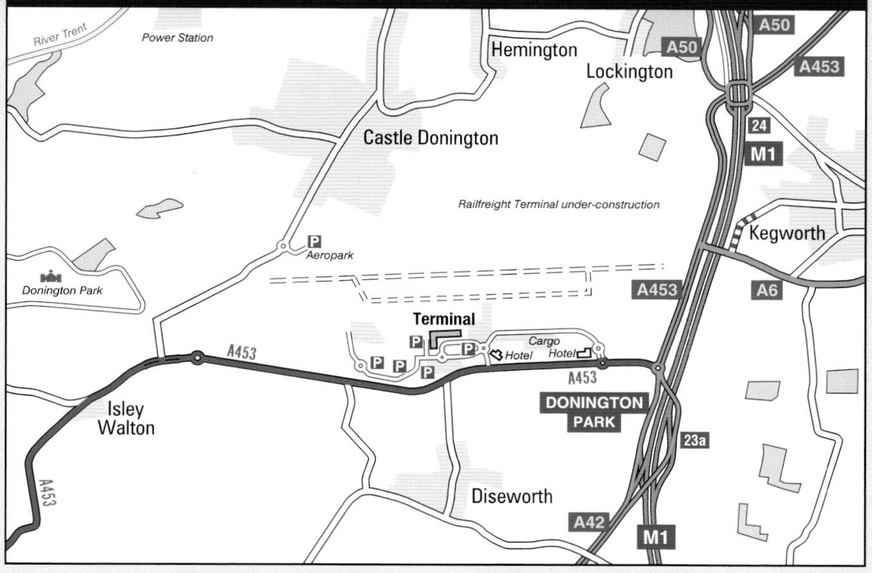

GLASGOW

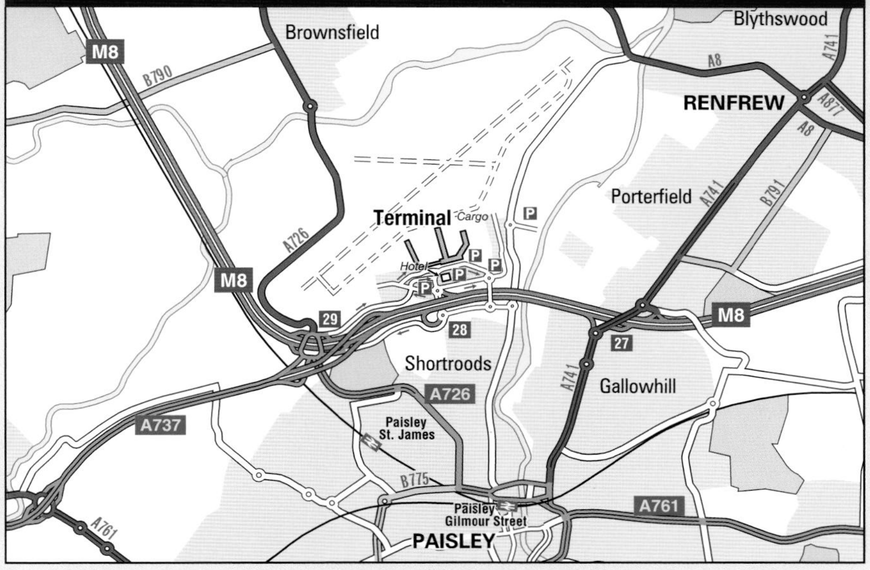

LONDON GATWICK

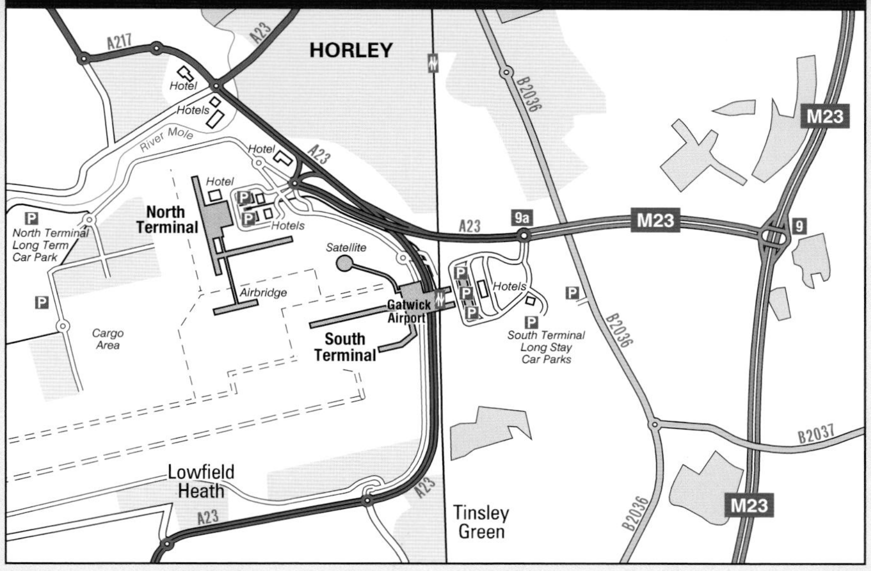

LONDON HEATHROW

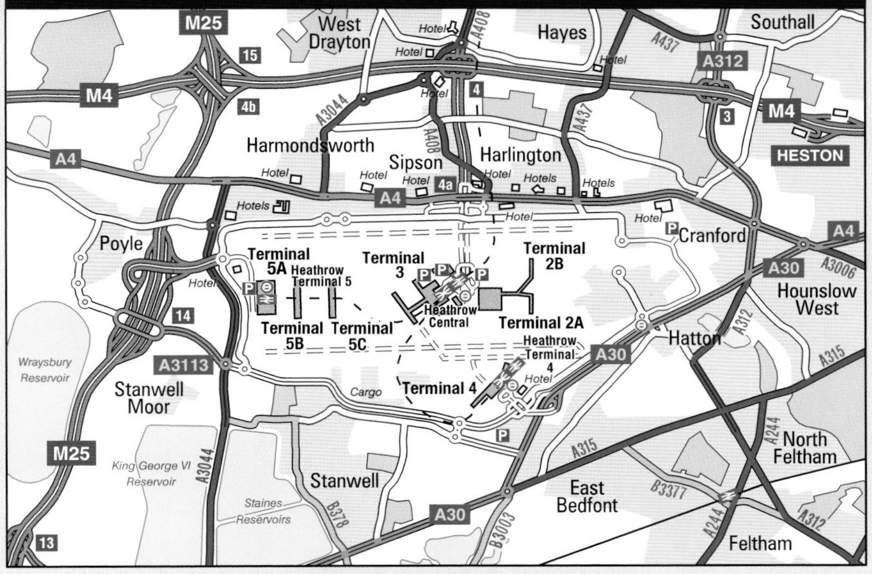

LONDON LUTON

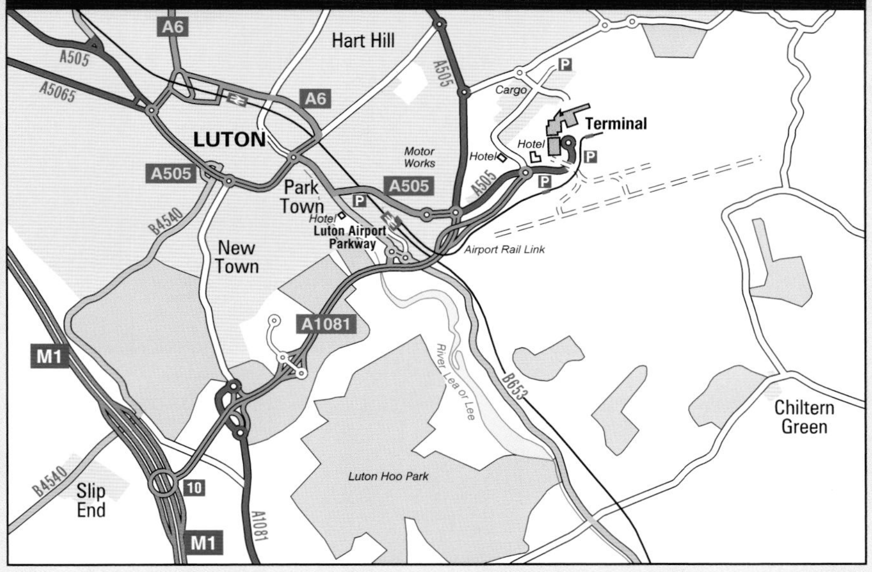

LONDON STANSTED

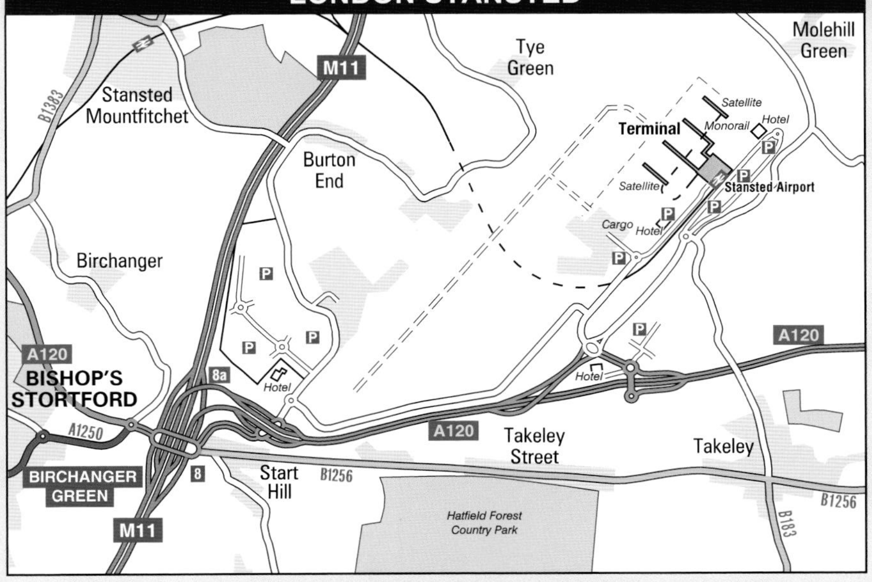

MANCHESTER

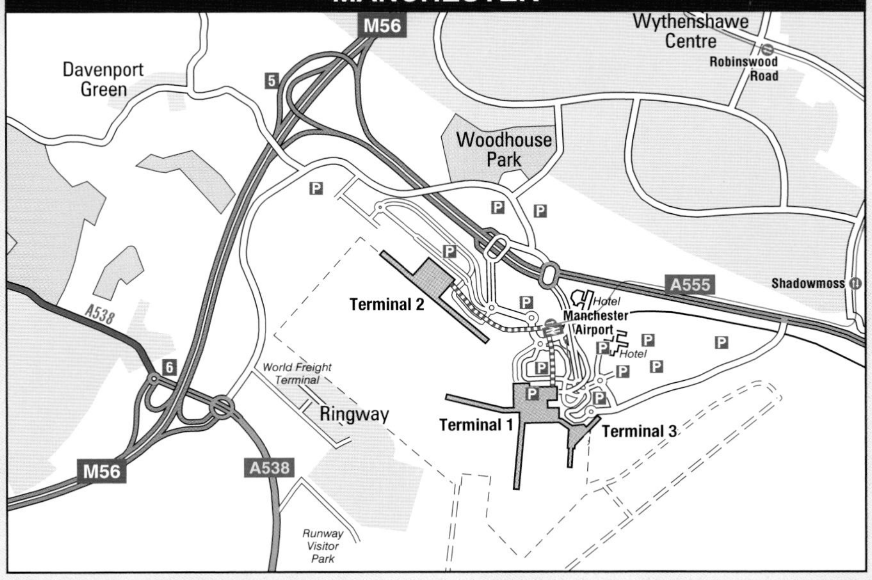

INDEX TO CITIES, TOWNS, VILLAGES, HAMLETS, LOCATIONS, AIRPORTS & PORTS

(1) A strict alphabetical order is used e.g. An Dùnan follows Andreas but precedes Andwell.

(2) The map reference given refers to the actual map square in which the town spot or built-up area is located and not to the place name.

(3) Major towns and destinations are shown in bold, i.e. **Aberdeen**. *Aber* **106** (5J **73**)
Page references for Town Plan entries are shown first.

(4) Where two or more places of the same name occur in the same County or Unitary Authority, the nearest large town is also given; e.g. Achiemore. *High* nr. Durness . . . . 5F **84** indicates that Achiemore is located in square 5F on page **84** and is situated near Durness in the Unitary Authority of Highland.

(5) Only one reference is given although due to page overlaps the place may appear on more than one page.

COUNTIES and UNITARY AUTHORITIES with the abbreviations used in this index

Aberdeen : *Aber*
Aberdeenshire : *Abers*
Angus : *Ang*
Antrim & Newtownabbey : *Ant*
Ards & North Down : *Ards*
Argyll & Bute : *Arg*
Armagh, Banbridge & Craigavon : *Arm*
Bath & N E Somerset : *Bath*
Bedford : *Bed*
Belfast : *Bel*
Blackburn with Darwen : *Bkbn*
Blackpool : *Bkpl*
Blaenau Gwent : *Blae*
Bournemouth : *Bour*
Bracknell Forest : *Brac*
Bridgend : *B'end*
Brighton & Hove : *Brig*
Bristol : *Bris*
Buckinghamshire : *Buck*
Caerphilly : *Cphy*
Cambridgeshire : *Cambs*
Cardiff : *Card*
Carmarthenshire : *Carm*
Causeway Coast & Glens : *Caus*
Central Bedfordshire : *C Beds*
Ceredigion : *Cdgn*
Cheshire East : *Ches E*
Cheshire West & Chester : *Ches W*
Clackmannanshire : *Clac*
Conwy : *Cnwy*
Cornwall : *Corn*
Cumbria : *Cumb*
Darlington : *Darl*
Denbighshire : *Den*
Derby : *Derb*
Derbyshire : *Derbs*
Derry & Strabane : *Derr*
Devon : *Devn*
Dorset : *Dors*
Dumfries & Galloway : *Dum*
Dundee : *D'dee*
Durham : *Dur*
East Ayrshire : *E Ayr*
East Dunbartonshire : *E Dun*
East Lothian : *E Lot*
East Renfrewshire : *E Ren*
East Riding of Yorkshire : *E Yor*
East Sussex : *E Sus*
Edinburgh : *Edin*
Essex : *Essx*
Falkirk : *Falk*
Fermanagh & Omagh : *Ferm*
Fife : *Fife*
Flintshire : *Flin*
Glasgow : *Glas*
Gloucestershire : *Glos*
Greater London : *G Lon*
Greater Manchester : *G Man*
Gwynedd : *Gwyn*
Halton : *Hal*
Hampshire : *Hants*
Hartlepool : *Hart*
Herefordshire : *Here*
Hertfordshire : *Herts*
Highland : *High*
Inverclyde : *Inv*
Isle of Anglesey : *IOA*
Isle of Man : *IOM*
Isle of Wight : *IOW*
Isles of Scilly : *IOS*
Kent : *Kent*
Kingston upon Hull : *Hull*
Lancashire : *Lanc*
Leicester : *Leic*
Leicestershire : *Leics*
Lincolnshire : *Linc*
Lisburn & Castlereagh : *Lis*
Luton : *Lutn*
Medway : *Medw*
Merseyside : *Mers*
Merthyr Tydfil : *Mer T*
Mid & East Antrim : *ME Ant*
Middlesbrough : *Midd*
Midlothian : *Midl*
Mid Ulster : *M Ulst*
Milton Keynes : *Mil*
Monmouthshire : *Mon*
Moray : *Mor*
Neath Port Talbot : *Neat*
Newport : *Newp*
Newry, Mourne & Down : *New M*
Norfolk : *Norf*
Northamptonshire : *Nptn*
North Ayrshire : *N Ayr*
North East Lincolnshire : *NE Lin*
North Lanarkshire : *N Lan*
North Lincolnshire : *N Lin*
North Somerset : *N Som*
Northumberland : *Nmbd*
North Yorkshire : *N Yor*
Nottingham : *Nott*
Nottinghamshire : *Notts*
Orkney : *Orkn*
Oxfordshire : *Oxon*
Pembrokeshire : *Pemb*
Perth & Kinross : *Per*
Peterborough : *Pet*
Plymouth : *Plym*
Poole : *Pool*
Portsmouth : *Port*
Powys : *Powy*
Reading : *Read*
Redcar & Cleveland : *Red C*
Renfrewshire : *Ren*
Rhondda Cynon Taff : *Rhon*
Rutland : *Rut*
Scottish Borders : *Bord*
Shetland : *Shet*
Shropshire : *Shrp*
Slough : *Slo*
Somerset : *Som*
Southampton : *Sotn*
South Ayrshire : *S Ayr*
Southend-on-Sea : *S'end*
South Gloucestershire : *S Glo*
South Lanarkshire : *S Lan*
South Yorkshire : *S Yor*
Staffordshire : *Staf*
Stirling : *Stir*
Stockton-on-Tees : *Stoc T*
Stoke-on-Trent : *Stoke*
Suffolk : *Suff*
Surrey : *Surr*
Swansea : *Swan*
Swindon : *Swin*
Telford & Wrekin : *Telf*
Thurrock : *Thur*
Torbay : *Torb*
Torfaen : *Torf*
Tyne & Wear : *Tyne*
Vale of Glamorgan, The : *V Glam*
Warrington : *Warr*
Warwickshire : *Warw*
West Berkshire : *W Ber*
West Dunbartonshire : *W Dun*
Western Isles : *W Isl*
West Lothian : *W Lot*
West Midlands : *W Mid*
West Sussex : *W Sus*
West Yorkshire : *W Yor*
Wiltshire : *Wilts*
Windsor & Maidenhead : *Wind*
Wokingham : *Wok*
Worcestershire : *Worc*
Wrexham : *Wrex*
York : *York*

INDEX

A

Abbas Combe. *Som* 3F 8
Abberley. *Worc* 5F 26
Abberley Common. *Worc* 5F 26
Abberton. *Essx* 2G 23
Abberton. *Worc* 6H 27
Abberwick. *Nmbd* 8J 61
Abbess Roding. *Essx* 2B 22
Abbey. *Devn* 4L 7
Abbey-cwm-hir. *Powy* 5K 25
Abbeydale. *S Yor* 1M 35
Abbeydale Park. *S Yor* 1M 35
Abbey Dore. *Here* 8B 26
Abbey Gate. *Devn* 6A 8
Abbey Hulton. *Stoke* 5H 35
Abbey St Bathans. *Bord* 3E 60
Abbeystead. *Lanc* 2D 40
Abbeytown. *Cumb* 6F 52
Abbey Village. *Lanc* 5E 40
Abbey Wood. *G Lon* 6A 22
Abbots Bickington. *Devn* 4C 6
Abbots Bromley. *Staf* 7J 35
Abbotsbury. *Dors* 7D 8
Abbotsham. *Devn* 3D 6
Abbotskerswell. *Devn* 5L 5
Abbots Langley. *Herts* 3H 21
Abbots Leigh. *N Som* 6D 18
Abbotsley. *Cambs* 6K 29
Abbots Morton. *Worc* 6J 27
Abbots Ripton. *Cambs* 4K 29
Abbot's Salford. *Warw* 6J 27
Abbotstone. *Hants* 2C 10
Abbots Worthy. *Hants* 2B 10
Abbotts Ann. *Hants* 1M 9
Abcott. *Shrp* 4B 26
Abdon. *Shrp* 3D 26
Abenhall. *Glos* 2E 18
Aber. *Cdgn* 2L 15
Aberaeron. *Cdgn* 6D 24
Aberafan. *Neat* 8A 10
Aberaman. *Rhon* 5K 17
Aberangell. *Gwyn* 1H 25
Aberarad. *Carm* 3K 15
Aberarder. *High* 3G 71
Aberargie. *Per* 6E 66
Aberarth. *Cdgn* 6D 24
Aberavon. *Neat* 5G 17
Aber-banc. *Cdgn* 2K 15
Aberbargoed. *Cphy* 5L 17
Aberbechan. *Powy* 3L 25
Aberbeeg. *Blae* 4M 17
Aberbowlan. *Carm* 1F 16
Aberbran. *Powy* 2J 17
Abercanaid. *Mer T* 4K 17
Abercarn. *Cphy* 5M 17
Abercastle. *Pemb* 3E 14
Abercegir. *Powy* 2H 25
Aberchalder. *High* 5D 70
Aberchirder. *Abers* 8F 80
Aberchwiler. *Den* 4K 33
Abercorn. *W Lot* 2J 59
Abercraf. *Powy* 3H 17
Abercregan. *Neat* 5H 17
Abercrombie. *Fife* 7J 67
Abercwmboi. *Rhon* 5K 17
Abercych. *Pemb* 2J 15
Abercynon. *Rhon* 5K 17
Aber-Cywarch. *Gwyn* 1H 25
Aberdalgie. *Per* 5D 66
Aberdar. *Rhon* 4J 17
Aberdare. *Rhon* 4J 17
Aberdaron. *Gwyn* 8A 32
Aberdaugleddau. *Pemb* 6F 14
Aberdeen. *Aber* **106** (5J **73**)
Aberdeen International Airport. *Aber* 4H 73
Aberdesach. *Gwyn* 5D 32
Aberdour. *Fife* 1K 59
Aberdovey. *Gwyn* 3F 24
Aberdulais. *Neat* 4G 17
Aberdyfi. *Gwyn* 3F 24
Aberedw. *Powy* 8K 25
Abereiddy. *Pemb* 3D 14
Abererch. *Gwyn* 7C 32
Aberfan. *Mer T* 4K 17
Aberfeldy. *Per* 3B 66
Aberffraw. *IOA* 4C 32
Aberffrwd. *Cdgn* 5F 24
Aberford. *W Yor* 4B 42
Aberfoyle. *Stir* 7K 65
Abergarw. *B'end* 6J 17
Abergarwed. *Neat* 4H 17
Abergavenny. *Mon* 3B 18
Abergele. *Cnwy* 3J 33
Aber-Giâr. *Carm* 2M 15
Abergorlech. *Carm* 1E 16
Abergwaun. *Pemb* 3F 14
Abergwesyn. *Powy* 7H 25
Abergwili. *Carm* 4L 15
Abergwynfi. *Neat* 5H 17
Abergwyngregyn. *Gwyn* 3F 32
Abergynolwyn. *Gwyn* 2F 24
Aberhafesp. *Powy* 3K 25
Aberhonddu. *Powy* 2K 17
Aberhosan. *Powy* 3H 25
Aberkenfig. *B'end* 6H 17
Aberlady. *E Lot* 1B 60
Aberlemno. *Ang* 2J 67
Aberllefenni. *Gwyn* 2G 25
Abermaw. *Gwyn* 1F 24
Abermeurig. *Cdgn* 7E 24
Aber-miwl. *Powy* 3L 25
Abermule. *Powy* 3L 25
Abernant. *Carm* 4K 15
Abernant. *Rhon* 4K 17
Abernethy. *Per* 6E 66
Abernyte. *Per* 4F 66
Aber-oer. *Wrex* 5A 34
Aberpennar. *Rhon* 5K 17
Aberporth. *Cdgn* 1J 15
Aberriw. *Powy* 2L 25
Abersoch. *Gwyn* 8C 32
Abersychan. *Torf* 3A 18
Abertawe. *Swan* **117** (5F **16**)
Aberteifi. *Cdgn* 2H 15
Aberthin. *V Glam* 7K 17
Abertillery. *Blae* 4M 17
Abertridwr. *Cphy* 6L 17
Abertyleri. *Blae* 4M 17
Abertysswg. *Cphy* 4L 17
Aberuthven. *Per* 6C 66
Aber Village. *Powy* 2L 17
Aberwheeler. *Den* 4K 33
Aberyscir. *Powy* 2J 17
Aberystwyth. *Cdgn* 4E 24
Abhainn Suidhe. *W Isl* 3B 76
Abingdon-on-Thames. *Oxon* 4B 20
Abinger Common. *Surr* 1J 11
Abinger Hammer. *Surr* 1H 11
Abington. *S Lan* 7H 59
Abington Pigotts. *Cambs* 7L 29
Ab Kettleby. *Leics* 7E 36
Ab Lench. *Worc* 6J 27
Ablington. *Glos* 3K 19
Ablington. *Wilts* 1K 9
Abney. *Derbs* 2K 35
Aboyne. *Abers* 6E 72
Abram. *G Man* 7E 40
Abriachan. *High* 2F 70
Abridge. *Essx* 4A 22
Abronhill. *N Lan* 2F 58
Abson. *S Glo* 6F 18
Abthorpe. *Nptn* 7D 28
Abune-the-Hill. *Orkn* 7B 88
Aby. *Linc* 2M 37
Acairseid. *W Isl* 5D 74
Acaster Malbis. *York* 3C 42
Acaster Selby. *N Yor* 3C 42
Accott. *Devn* 2F 6
Accrington. *Lanc* 5F 40
Acha. *Arg* 2G 63
Achachork. *High* 1F 68
Achadh a' Chuirn. *High* 3H 69
Achahoish. *Arg* 2G 57
Achaleven. *Arg* 4D 64
Achallader. *Arg* 3H 65
Acha Mor. *W Isl* 1E 76
Achanalt. *High* 7C 78
Achandunie. *High* 6G 79
Ach' an Todhair. *High* 8A 70
Achany. *High* 3F 78
Achaphubuil. *High* 8A 70
Acharacle. *High* 1A 64
Acharn. *Ang* 8B 72
Acharn. *Per* 3A 66
Acharole. *High* 6D 86
Achateny. *High* 1L 63
Achavanich. *High* 8C 86
Achdalieu. *High* 7J 69
Achduart. *High* 3M 77
Achentoul. *High* 8L 85
Achfary. *High* 8E 84
Achfrish. *High* 2F 78
Achgarve. *High* 4K 77
Achiemore. *High*
  nr. Durness 5F 84
  nr. Thurso 6L 85
A' Chill. *High* 5B 68
Achiltibuie. *High* 3M 77
Achina. *High* 5K 85
Achinahuagh. *High* 5H 85
Achindarroch. *High* 2E 64
Achinduich. *High* 3F 78
Achinduin. *Arg* 4C 64
Achininver. *High* 5H 85
Achintee. *High* 1L 69
Achintraid. *High* 2K 69
Achleck. *Arg* 3K 63
Achlorachan. *High* 8D 78
Achluachrach. *High* 7C 70
Achlyness. *High* 6E 84
Achmelvich. *High* 1A 78
Achmony. *High* 2F 70
Achmore. *High*
  nr. Stromeferry 2K 69
  nr. Ullapool 4M 77
Achnacarnin. *High* 8C 84
Achnacarry. *High* 7B 70
Achnaclerach. *High* 7E 78
Achnacloich. *High* 5G 69
Ach na Cloiche. *High* 5G 69
Achnaconeran. *High* 4E 70
Achnacroish. *Arg* 3C 64
Achnafalnich. *Arg* 5G 65
Achnagarron. *High* 6G 79
Achnagoul. *Arg* 7E 64
Achnaha. *High* 1K 63
Achnahanat. *High* 4F 78
Achnahannet. *High* 3K 71
Achnairn. *High* 2F 78
Achnamara. *Arg* 1G 57
Achnanellan. *High* 7A 70
Achnasheen. *High* 8A 78
Achnashellach. *High* 1M 69
Achosnich. *High* 1K 63
Achow. *High* 8D 86
Achranich. *High* 3B 64
Achreamie. *High* 5B 86
Achriabhach. *High* 8B 70
Achriesgill. *High* 6E 84
Achrimsdale. *High* 3K 79
Achscrabster. *High* 5B 86
Achtoty. *High* 5J 85
Achurch. *Nptn* 3H 29
Achuvoldrach. *High* 6H 85
Achvaich. *High* 4H 79
Achvoan. *High* 3H 79
Ackenthwaite. *Cumb* 7D 46
Ackergill. *High* 6E 86
Ackergillshore. *High* 6E 86
Acklam. *Midd* 4B 48
Acklam. *N Yor* 1E 42
Ackleton. *Shrp* 2F 26
Acklington. *Nmbd* 1F 54
Ackton. *W Yor* 5B 42
Ackworth Moor Top. *W Yor* 6B 42
Acle. *Norf* 8L 39
Acocks Green. *W Mid* 3K 27
Acol. *Kent* 7K 23
Acomb. *Nmbd* 5C 54
Acomb. *York* 2C 42
Aconbury. *Here* 8D 26
Acre. *G Man* 7H 41
Acre. *Lanc* 5F 40
Acrefair. *Wrex* 5A 34
Acrise. *Kent* 1H 13
Acton. *Arm* 6G 93
Acton. *Ches E* 4E 34
Acton. *Dors* 8H 9
Acton. *G Lon* 5J 21
Acton. *Shrp* 3B 26
Acton. *Staf* 5G 35
Acton. *Suff* 7E 30
Acton. *Worc* 5G 27
Acton. *Wrex* 4B 34
Acton Beauchamp. *Here* 6E 26
Acton Bridge. *Ches W* 2D 34
Acton Burnell. *Shrp* 1D 26
Acton Green. *Here* 6E 26
Acton Pigott. *Shrp* 1D 26
Acton Round. *Shrp* 2E 26
Acton Scott. *Shrp* 3C 26
Acton Trussell. *Staf* 8H 35
Acton Turville. *S Glo* 5G 19
Adabroc. *W Isl* 4J 83
Adam's Hill. *Worc* 4H 27
Adbaston. *Staf* 7F 34
Adber. *Dors* 3E 8
Adderbury. *Oxon* 8B 28
Adderley. *Shrp* 6E 34
Adderstone. *Nmbd* 6J 61
Addiewell. *W Lot* 3H 59
Addingham. *W Yor* 3J 41
Addington. *Buck* 1E 20
Addington. *G Lon* 7L 21
Addington. *Kent* 8C 22
Addinston. *Bord* 4C 60
Addiscombe. *G Lon* 7L 21
Addlestone. *Surr* 7H 21
Addlethorpe. *Linc* 3B 38
Adeney. *Telf* 8F 34
Adfa. *Powy* 2K 25
Adforton. *Here* 4C 26
Adgestone. *IOW* 7C 10
Adisham. *Kent* 8J 23
Adlestrop. *Glos* 1L 19
Adlingfleet. *E Yor* 5F 42
Adlington. *Ches E* 1H 35
Adlington. *Lanc* 6E 40
Admaston. *Staf* 7J 35
Admaston. *Telf* 8E 34
Admington. *Warw* 7L 27
Adpar. *Cdgn* 2K 15
Adsborough. *Som* 3A 8
Adstock. *Buck* 8E 28
Adstone. *Nptn* 6C 28
Adversane. *W Sus* 3H 11
Advie. *High* 2M 71
Adwalton. *W Yor* 5L 41
Adwell. *Oxon* 4D 20
Adwick le Street. *S Yor* 7C 42
Adwick upon Dearne. *S Yor* 7B 42
Adziel. *Abers* 8J 81
Ae. *Dum* 3D 52
Affleck. *Abers* 3H 73
Affpuddle. *Dors* 6G 9
Affric Lodge. *High* 3B 70
Afon-wen. *Flin* 3L 33
Agglethorpe. *N Yor* 7J 47
Aghagallon. *Arm* 5G 93
Aghalee. *Lis* 5G 93
Aglionby. *Cumb* 6J 53
Aghadowey. *ME Ant* 3G 93
Aigburth. *Mers* 1B 34
Aiginis. *W Isl* 8H 83
Aike. *E Yor* 3H 43
Aikers. *Orkn* 2F 86
Aiketgate. *Cumb* 7J 53
Aikhead. *Cumb* 7G 53
Aikton. *Cumb* 6G 53
Ailey. *Here* 7B 26
Ailsworth. *Pet* 2J 29
Ainderby Quernhow. *N Yor* 7M 47
Ainderby Steeple. *N Yor* 6M 47
Aingers Green. *Essx* 1H 23
Ainsdale. *Mers* 6B 40
Ainsdale-on-Sea. *Mers* 6B 40
Ainstable. *Cumb* 7K 53
Ainsworth. *G Man* 6F 40
Ainthorpe. *N Yor* 5E 48
Aintree. *Mers* 8B 40
Aird. *Arg* 7B 64
Aird. *Dum* 5F 50
Aird. *High*
  nr. Port Henderson 6J 77
  nr. Tarskavaig 5G 69
Aird. *W Isl*
  on Benbecula 8J 75
  on Isle of Lewis 8J 83
The Aird. *High* 8F 76
Àird a Bhasair. *High* 5H 69
Aird a Mhachair. *W Isl* 1D 74
Aird a Mhulaidh. *W Isl* 2C 76
Aird Asaig. *W Isl* 3C 76
Aird Dhail. *W Isl* 5H 83
Airdens. *High* 4G 79
Airdeny. *Arg* 5E 64
Aird Mhidhinis. *W Isl* 5D 74
Aird Mhighe. *W Isl*
  nr. Ceann a Bhaigh 4C 76
  nr. Fionnsabhagh 5B 76
Aird Mhor. *W Isl*
  on Barra 5D 74
  on South Uist 1E 74
Airdrie. *N Lan* 3F 58
Aird Shleibhe. *W Isl* 5C 76
Aird Thunga. *W Isl* 8H 83
Aird Uig. *W Isl* 8D 82
Airedale. *W Yor* 5B 42
Airidh a Bhruaich. *W Isl* 2D 76
Airies. *Dum* 5E 50
Airmyn. *E Yor* 5E 42
Airntully. *Per* 4D 66
Airor. *High* 5J 69
Airth. *Falk* 1H 59
Airton. *N Yor* 2H 41
Aisby. *Linc*
  nr. Gainsborough 8F 42
  nr. Grantham 6H 37
Aisgernis. *W Isl* 3D 74
Aish. *Devn*
  nr. Buckfastleigh 5J 5
  nr. Totnes 6L 5
Aisholt. *Som* 2L 7
Aiskew. *N Yor* 7L 47
Aislaby. *N Yor*
  nr. Pickering 7E 48
  nr. Whitby 5F 48
Aislaby. *Stoc T* 4B 48
Aisthorpe. *Linc* 1G 37
Aith. *Shet*
  on Fetlar 5L 91
  on Mainland 2D 90
Aithsetter. *Shet* 4E 90
Akeld. *Nmbd* 7G 61
Akeley. *Buck* 8E 28
Albaston. *Corn* 8D 6
Alberbury. *Shrp* 8B 34
Albert Town. *Pemb* 5F 14
Albert Village. *Leics* 8M 35
Albourne. *W Sus* 4K 11
Albrighton. *Shrp*
  nr. Shrewsbury 8C 34
  nr. Telford 1G 27
Alburgh. *Norf* 3J 31
Albury. *Herts* 1M 21
Albury. *Surr* 1H 11
Albyfield. *Cumb* 6K 53
Alby Hill. *Norf* 6H 39
Alcaig. *High* 8F 78
Alcaston. *Shrp* 3C 26
Alcester. *Warw* 6J 27
Alciston. *E Sus* 5B 12
Alcombe. *Som* 1J 7
Alconbury. *Cambs* 4J 29
Alconbury Weston. *Cambs* 4J 29
Aldborough. *Norf* 6H 39
Aldborough. *N Yor* 1B 42
Aldbourne. *Wilts* 6L 19
Aldbrough. *E Yor* 4K 43
Aldbrough St John. *N Yor* 4L 47
Aldbury. *Herts* 2G 21
Aldcliffe. *Lanc* 1C 40
Aldclune. *Per* 1C 66
Aldeburgh. *Suff* 6L 31
Aldeby. *Norf* 2L 31
Aldenham. *Herts* 4J 21
Alderbury. *Wilts* 3K 9
Aldercar. *Derbs* 5B 36
Alderford. *Norf* 8H 39
Alderholt. *Dors* 4K 9
Alderley. *Glos* 4F 18
Alderley Edge. *Ches E* 2G 35
Aldermaston. *W Ber* 7C 20
Aldermaston Soke. *Hants* 7D 20
Aldermaston Wharf. *W Ber* 7D 20
Alderminster. *Warw* 7L 27
Alder Moor. *Staf* 7L 35
Aldersey Green. *Ches W* 4C 34
Aldershot. *Hants* 8F 20
Alderton. *Glos* 8J 27
Alderton. *Nptn* 7E 28
Alderton. *Shrp* 7C 34
Alderton. *Suff* 7K 31
Alderton. *Wilts* 5G 19
Alderton Fields. *Glos* 8J 27
Alderwasley. *Derbs* 4M 35
Aldfield. *N Yor* 1L 41
Aldford. *Ches W* 4C 34
Aldgate. *Rut* 1G 29
Aldham. *Essx* 1F 22
Aldham. *Suff* 7G 31
Aldingbourne. *W Sus* 5G 11
Aldingham. *Cumb* 8A 46
Aldington. *Kent* 2G 13
Aldington. *Worc* 7J 27
Aldington Frith. *Kent* 2G 13
Aldochlay. *Arg* 8H 65
Aldon. *Shrp* 4C 26
Aldoth. *Cumb* 7F 52
Aldreth. *Cambs* 4M 29
Aldridge. *W Mid* 1J 27
Aldringham. *Suff* 5L 31
Aldsworth. *Glos* 2K 19
Aldsworth. *W Sus* 5E 10
Aldwark. *Derbs* 4L 35
Aldwark. *N Yor* 1B 42
Aldwick. *W Sus* 6G 11
Aldwincle. *Nptn* 3H 29
Aldworth. *W Ber* 6C 20
Alexandria. *W Dun* 2C 58
Aley. *Som* 2L 7
Aley Green. *C Beds* 2H 21
Alfardisworthy. *Devn* 4B 6
Alfington. *Devn* 6L 7
Alfold. *Surr* 2H 11
Alfold Bars. *W Sus* 2H 11
Alfold Crossways. *Surr* 2H 11
Alford. *Abers* 4E 72
Alford. *Linc* 2A 38
Alford. *Som* 2E 8
Alfreton. *Derbs* 4B 36
Alfrick. *Worc* 6F 26
Alfrick Pound. *Worc* 6F 26
Alfriston. *E Sus* 5B 12
Algarkirk. *Linc* 6K 37
Alhampton. *Som* 2E 8
Aline Lodge. *W Isl* 2C 76
Alkborough. *N Lin* 5F 42
Alkerton. *Oxon* 7A 28
Alkham. *Kent* 1J 13
Alkington. *Shrp* 6D 34
Alkmonton. *Derbs* 6K 35
Alladale Lodge. *High* 5E 78
Allaleigh. *Devn* 6L 5
Allanbank. *N Lan* 4G 59
Allanton. *N Lan* 4G 59
Allanton. *Bord* 4F 60
Allaston. *Glos* 4E 18
Allbrook. *Hants* 3B 10
All Cannings. *Wilts* 7J 19
Allendale Town. *Nmbd* 6B 54
Allen End. *Warw* 2K 27
Allenheads. *Nmbd* 7B 54
Allensford. *Dur* 7D 54
Allen's Green. *Herts* 2A 22
Allensmore. *Here* 8C 26
Allenton. *Derb* 6A 36
Aller. *Som* 3C 8
Allerby. *Cumb* 8E 52
Allercombe. *Devn* 6K 7
Allerford. *Som* 1J 7
Allerston. *N Yor* 7F 48
Allerthorpe. *E Yor* 3E 42
Allerton. *Mers* 1C 34
Allerton. *W Yor* 4K 41
Allerton Bywater. *W Yor* 5B 42
Allerton Mauleverer. *N Yor* 2B 42
Allesley. *W Mid* 3L 27
Allestree. *Derb* 6M 35
Allet. *Corn* 4L 3
Allexton. *Leics* 1F 28
Allgreave. *Ches E* 3H 35
Allhallows. *Medw* 6E 22
Allhallows-on-Sea. *Medw* 6E 22
Alligin Shuas. *High* 8K 77
Allimore Green. *Staf* 8G 35
Allington. *Kent* 8D 22
Allington. *Linc* 5F 36
Allington. *Wilts*
  nr. Amesbury 2L 9
  nr. Devizes 7J 19
Allithwaite. *Cumb* 8B 46
Alloa. *Clac* 8B 66
Allonby. *Cumb* 7E 52
Allostock. *Ches W* 3F 34
Alloway. *S Ayr* 8B 58
Allowenshay. *Som* 4B 8
All Saints South Elmham. *Suff* 3K 31
Allscott. *Shrp* 2F 26
Allscott. *Telf* 8E 34
All Stretton. *Shrp* 2C 26
Allt. *Carm* 4E 16
Alltami. *Flin* 3A 34
Alltgobhlach. *N Ayr* 5H 57
Alltmawr. *Powy* 8K 25
Alltnacaillich. *High* 7G 85
Allt na h' Airbhe. *High* 4A 78
Alltour. *High* 7C 70
Alltsigh. *High* 4E 70
Alltwalis. *Carm* 3L 15
Alltwen. *Neat* 4G 17
Alltyblacca. *Cdgn* 2M 15
Allt-y-goed. *Pemb* 2H 15
Almeley. *Here* 6B 26
Almeley Wootton. *Here* 6B 26
Almer. *Dors* 6H 9
Almholme. *S Yor* 7C 42
Almington. *Staf* 6F 34
Alminstone Cross. *Devn* 3C 6
Almodington. *W Sus* 6F 10
Almondbank. *Per* 5D 66
Almondbury. *W Yor* 6K 41
Almondsbury. *S Glo* 5E 18
Alne. *N Yor* 1B 42
Alness. *High* 7G 79
Alnessferry. *High* 7G 79
Alnham. *Nmbd* 8G 61
Alnmouth. *Nmbd* 8K 61
Alnwick. *Nmbd* 8J 61
Alphamstone. *Essx* 8E 30
Alpheton. *Suff* 6E 30
Alphington. *Devn* 6J 7
Alpington. *Norf* 1J 31
Alport. *Derbs* 3L 35
Alport. *Powy* 2A 26
Alpraham. *Ches E* 4D 34
Alresford. *Essx* 1G 23
Alrewas. *Staf* 8K 35
Alsager. *Ches E* 4F 34
Alsagers Bank. *Staf* 5G 35
Alsop en le Dale. *Derbs* 4K 35
Alston. *Cumb* 7M 53
Alston. *Devn* 5B 8
Alstone. *Glos* 8H 27
Alstone. *Som* 1B 8
Alstonefield. *Staf* 4K 35
Alston Sutton. *Som* 8C 18
Alswear. *Devn* 3G 7
Altandhu. *High* 2L 77
Altanduin. *High* 1J 79
Altarnun. *Corn* 7B 6
Altass. *High* 3E 78
Alterwall. *High* 5D 86
Altgaltraig. *Arg* 2K 57
Altham. *Lanc* 4F 40
Althorne. *Essx* 4F 22
Althorpe. *N Lin* 7F 42
Altnabreac. *High* 7B 86
Altnacealgach. *High* 2C 78
Altnafeadh. *High* 2G 65
Altnaharra. *High* 8H 85
Altofts. *W Yor* 5A 42
Alton. *Derbs* 3A 36
Alton. *Hants* 2E 10
Alton. *Staf* 5J 35
Alton Barnes. *Wilts* 7K 19
Altonhill. *E Ayr* 6C 58
Alton Pancras. *Dors* 5F 8
Alton Priors. *Wilts* 7K 19
Altrincham. *G Man* 1F 34
Altrua. *High* 7C 70
Alva. *Clac* 8B 66
Alvanley. *Ches W* 1C 34
Alvaston. *Derb* 6A 36
Alvechurch. *Worc* 4J 27
Alvecote. *Warw* 1L 27
Alvediston. *Wilts* 3H 9
Alveley. *Shrp* 3F 26
Alverdiscott. *Devn* 3E 6
Alverstoke. *Hants* 6C 10
Alverstone. *IOW* 7C 10
Alverthorpe. *W Yor* 5M 41
Alverton. *Notts* 5E 36
Alves. *Mor* 7M 79
Alvescot. *Oxon* 3L 19
Alveston. *S Glo* 5E 18
Alveston. *Warw* 6L 27
Alvie. *High* 5J 71
Alvingham. *Linc* 8L 43
Alvington. *Glos* 3E 18
Alwalton. *Cambs* 2J 29
Alweston. *Dors* 4E 8
Alwington. *Devn* 3D 6
Alwinton. *Nmbd* 1C 54
Alwoodley. *W Yor* 3L 41
Alyth. *Per* 3F 66
Amatnatua. *High* 4E 78
Am Baile. *W Isl* 4D 74
Ambaston. *Derbs* 6B 36
Ambergate. *Derbs* 4M 35
Amber Hill. *Linc* 5K 37
Amberley. *Glos* 3G 19
Amberley. *W Sus* 4H 11
Amble. *Nmbd* 1F 54
Amblecote. *W Mid* 3G 27
Ambler Thorn. *W Yor* 5J 41
Ambleside. *Cumb* 5B 46
Ambleston. *Pemb* 4G 15
Ambrosden. *Oxon* 2D 20
Amcotts. *N Lin* 6F 42
Amersham. *Buck* 4G 21
Amerton. *Staf* 7H 35
Amesbury. *Wilts* 1K 9
Amisfield. *Dum* 3D 52
Amlwch. *IOA* 1D 32
Amlwch Port. *IOA* 1D 32
Ammanford. *Carm* 3F 16
Amotherby. *N Yor* 8E 48
Ampfield. *Hants* 3B 10
Ampleforth. *N Yor* 8C 48
Ampleforth College. *N Yor* 8C 48
Ampney Crucis. *Glos* 3J 19
Ampney St Mary. *Glos* 3J 19
Ampney St Peter. *Glos* 3J 19
Amport. *Hants* 1L 9
Ampthill. *C Beds* 8H 29
Ampton. *Suff* 4E 30
Amroth. *Pemb* 6J 15
Amulree. *Per* 4C 66
Amwell. *Herts* 2J 21
Anaheilt. *High* 1C 64
An Àird. *High* 5H 69
An Baile Nua. *Ferm* 7D 92
An Camus Darach. *High* 6H 69
Ancaster. *Linc* 5G 37
Anchor. *Shrp* 3L 25
Anchorsholme. *Lanc* 3B 40
An Cnoc. *W Isl* 8H 83
An Cnoc Ard. *W Isl* 5J 83
An Coroghon. *High* 4D 68
Ancroft. *Nmbd* 5H 61
Ancrum. *Bord* 7D 60
Ancton. *W Sus* 5G 11
Anderby. *Linc* 2B 38
Anderby Creek. *Linc* 2B 38
Anderson. *Dors* 6G 9
Anderton. *Ches W* 2E 34
Andertons Mill. *Lanc* 6D 40
Andover. *Hants* 1A 10
Andover Down. *Hants* 1A 10
Andoversford. *Glos* 2J 19
Andreas. *IOM* 5D 44
An Dùnan. *High* 3G 69
Andwell. *Hants* 8D 20
Anelog. *Gwyn* 8A 32
Anfield. *Mers* 8B 40
Angarrack. *Corn* 5J 3
Angersleigh. *Som* 4L 7
Angelbank. *Shrp* 4D 26
Angerton. *Cumb* 6G 53
Angle. *Pemb* 6E 14
An Gleann Ur. *W Isl* 8H 83
Angmering. *W Sus* 5H 11
Angmering-on-Sea. *W Sus* 5H 11
Angram. *N Yor*
  nr. Keld 6G 47
  nr. York 3C 42
Anick. *Nmbd* 5C 54
Ankerbold. *Derbs* 3A 36
Ankerville. *High* 6J 79
Anlaby. *E Yor* 5H 43
Anlaby Park. *Hull* 5H 43
An Leth Meadhanach. *W Isl* 4D 74
Anmer. *Norf* 7D 38
Anmore. *Hants* 4D 10
Annacloy. *New M* 6J 93
Annadorn. *New M* 6J 93
Annaghmore. *Arm* 6F 93
Annaghugh. *Arm* 6F 93
Annahilt. *Lis* 6H 93
Annalong. *New M* 7H 93
Annan. *Dum* 5F 52
Annaside. *Cumb* 6K 45
Annat. *Arg* 5E 64
Annat. *High* 8K 77
Annathill. *N Lan* 2F 58
Anna Valley. *Hants* 1M 9
Annbank. *S Ayr* 7C 58
Annesley. *Notts* 4C 36
Annesley Woodhouse. *Notts* 4C 36
Annfield Plain. *Dur* 6E 54
Annsborough. *New M* 7H 93
Annscroft. *Shrp* 1C 26
An Sailean. *High* 1A 64
Ansdell. *Lanc* 5B 40
Ansford. *Som* 2E 8
Ansley. *Warw* 2L 27
Anslow. *Staf* 7L 35
Anslow Gate. *Staf* 7K 35
Ansteadbrook. *Surr* 2G 11
Anstey. *Herts* 8M 29
Anstey. *Leics* 1C 28
Anston. *S Lan* 5J 59
Anstruther Easter. *Fife* 7J 67
Anstruther Wester. *Fife* 7J 67
Ansty. *Warw* 3A 28
Ansty. *W Sus* 3K 11
Ansty. *Wilts* 3H 9
An Taobh Tuath. *W Isl* 5A 76
An t-Aodann Ban. *High* 8E 76
An t Ath Leathann. *High* 3H 69
An Teanga. *High* 5H 69
Anthill Common. *Hants* 4D 10
Anthorn. *Cumb* 6F 52
Antingham. *Norf* 6J 39
An t-Ob. *W Isl* 5B 76
Anton's Gowt. *Linc* 5K 37
Antony. *Corn* 6G 5
An t-Òrd. *High* 4H 69
Antrim. *Ant* 4G 93
Antrobus. *Ches W* 2E 34
Anvil Corner. *Devn* 5C 6
Anwick. *Linc* 4J 37
Anwoth. *Dum* 6L 51
Apethorpe. *Nptn* 2H 29
Apeton. *Staf* 8G 35
Apley. *Linc* 2J 37
Apperknowle. *Derbs* 2A 36
Apperley. *Glos* 1G 19
Apperley Dene. *Nmbd* 6D 54
Appersett. *N Yor* 6G 47
Appin. *Arg* 3D 64
Appleby. *N Lin* 6G 43
Appleby-in-Westmorland. *Cumb* 3E 46
Appleby Magna. *Leics* 1M 27
Appleby Parva. *Leics* 1M 27
Applecross. *High* 1J 69
Appledore. *Devn*
  nr. Bideford 2D 6
  nr. Tiverton 4K 7
Appledore. *Kent* 3F 12
Appledore Heath. *Kent* 2F 12
Appleford. *Oxon* 4C 20
Applegarthtown. *Dum* 3F 52
Applemore. *Hants* 5A 10
Appleshaw. *Hants* 1M 9
Applethwaite. *Cumb* 3A 46
Appleton. *Hal* 1D 34
Appleton. *Oxon* 3B 20
Appleton-le-Moors. *N Yor* 7E 48
Appleton-le-Street. *N Yor* 8E 48
Appleton Roebuck. *N Yor* 3C 42
Appleton Thorn. *Warr* 1E 34
Appleton Wiske. *N Yor* 5A 48
Appletree. *Nptn* 7B 28
Appletreehall. *Bord* 8C 60
Appletreewick. *N Yor* 1J 41
Appley. *Som* 3K 7
Appley Bridge. *Lanc* 7D 40
Apse Heath. *IOW* 7C 10
Apsley End. *C Beds* 8J 29
Apuldram. *W Sus* 5F 10
Arabella. *High* 6J 79
Arasaig. *High* 7H 69
Arbeadie. *Abers* 6F 72
Arberth. *Pemb* 5H 15
Arbirlot. *Ang* 3K 67
Arborfield. *Wok* 7E 20
Arborfield Cross. *Wok* 7E 20
Arborfield Garrison. *Wok* 7E 20
Arbourthorne. *S Yor* 1A 36
Arbroath. *Ang* 3K 67
Arbuthnott. *Abers* 8H 73
Arcan. *High* 8F 78
Archargary. *High* 6K 85
Archdeacon Newton. *Darl* 4L 47
Archiestown. *Mor* 1B 72
Arclid. *Ches E* 3F 34
Arclid Green. *Ches E* 3F 34
Ardachu. *High* 3G 79
Ardalanish. *Arg* 6J 63
Ardaneaskan. *High* 2K 69
Ardarroch. *High* 2K 69
Ardbeg. *Arg*
  nr. Dunoon 1L 57
  on Islay 5D 56
  on Isle of Bute 3K 57
Ardboe. *M Ulst* 5F 93
Ardcharnich. *High* 5B 78
Ardchiavaig. *Arg* 6J 63
Ardchonnell. *Arg* 6D 64
Ardchrishnish. *Arg* 5K 63
Ardchronie. *High* 5G 79
Ardchullarie. *Stir* 6K 65
Ardchyle. *Stir* 5K 65
Ard-dhubh. *High* 1J 69
Arddleen. *Powy* 8A 34
Arddlîn. *Powy* 8A 34
Ardechive. *High* 6B 70
Ardeley. *Herts* 1L 21
Ardelve. *High* 3K 69
Arden. *Arg* 1B 58
Ardendrain. *High* 2F 70
Arden Hall. *N Yor* 6C 48
Ardens Grafton. *Warw* 6K 27
Ardentinny. *Arg* 1L 57
Ardeonaig. *Stir* 4L 65
Ardersier. *High* 8H 79
Ardery. *High* 1B 64
Ardessie. *High* 5A 78
Ardfern. *Arg* 7C 64
Ardfernal. *Arg* 2E 56
Ardfin. *Arg* 3D 56
Ardgartan. *Arg* 7G 65
Ardgay. *High* 4G 79
Ardglass. *New M* 7J 93
Ardgour. *High* 1E 64
Ardheslaig. *High* 8J 77
Ardindrean. *High* 5B 78
Ardingly. *W Sus* 3L 11
Ardington. *Oxon* 5B 20
Ardlamont House. *Arg* 3J 57
Ardleigh. *Essx* 1G 23
Ardler. *Per* 3F 66
Ardley. *Oxon* 1C 20
Ardlui. *Arg* 6H 65
Ardlussa. *Arg* 1F 56
Ardmair. *High* 4B 78
Ardmay. *Arg* 7G 65
Ardmillan. *Ards* 5J 93
Ardminish. *Arg* 6F 56
Ardmolich. *High* 8J 69
Ardmore. *High*
  nr. Kinlochbervie 6E 84
  nr. Tain 5H 79
Ardnacross. *Arg* 3L 63
Ardnadam. *Arg* 1L 57
Ardnagrask. *High* 1F 70
Ardnamurach. *High* 6K 69
Ardnarff. *High* 2K 69
Ardnastang. *High* 1C 64
Ardoch. *Per* 4D 66
Ardochy House. *High* 5C 70
Ardpatrick. *Arg* 3G 57
Ardrishaig. *Arg* 1H 57
Ardroag. *High* 1D 68
Ardross. *High* 6G 79
Ardrossan. *N Ayr* 5M 57
Ardshealach. *High* 1A 64
Ardsley. *S Yor* 7A 42
Ardslignish. *High* 1L 63
Ardstraw. *Derr* 4C 92
Ardtalla. *Arg* 4D 56
Ardtalnaig. *Per* 4M 65
Ardtoe. *High* 8H 69
Arduaine. *Arg* 6B 64
Ardullie. *High* 7F 78
Ardvasar. *High* 5H 69
Ardvorlich. *Per* 5L 65
Ardwell. *Dum* 7G 51
Ardwell. *Mor* 2C 72
Arean. *High* 8H 69
Areley Common. *Worc* 4G 27
Areley Kings. *Worc* 4G 27
Arford. *Hants* 2F 10
Argoed. *Cphy* 5L 17
Argoed Mill. *Powy* 6J 25
Aridhglas. *Arg* 5J 63
Arinacrinachd. *High* 8J 77
Arinagour. *Arg* 2H 63
Arisaig. *High* 7H 69
Ariundle. *High* 1C 64
Arivegaig. *High* 1A 64
Arkendale. *N Yor* 1A 42
Arkesden. *Essx* 8A 30
Arkholme. *Lanc* 8D 46
Arkle Town. *N Yor* 5J 47
Arkley. *G Lon* 4K 21
Arksey. *S Yor* 7C 42
Arkwright Town. *Derbs* 2B 36
Arlecdon. *Cumb* 3K 45
Arlescote. *Warw* 7A 28
Arlesey. *C Beds* 8J 29
Arleston. *Telf* 8E 34
Arley. *Ches E* 1E 34
Arlingham. *Glos* 2F 18
Arlington. *Devn* 1F 6
Arlington. *E Sus* 5B 12
Arlington. *Glos* 3K 19
Arlington Beccott. *Devn* 1F 6
Armadail. *High* 5H 69
Armadale. *High*
  nr. Isleornsay 5H 69
  nr. Strathy 5K 85
Armadale. *W Lot* 3H 59
Armagh. *Arm* 6F 93
Armathwaite. *Cumb* 7K 53
Arminghall. *Norf* 1J 31
Armitage. *Staf* 8J 35
Armitage Bridge. *W Yor* 6K 41
Armoy. *Caus* 2G 93
The Arms. *Norf* 2E 30
Armscote. *Warw* 7L 27
Armston. *Nptn* 3H 29
Armthorpe. *S Yor* 7D 42
Arncliffe. *N Yor* 8H 47
Arncliffe Cote. *N Yor* 8H 47
Arncroach. *Fife* 7J 67
Arne. *Dors* 7H 9
Arnesby. *Leics* 2D 28
Arnicle. *Arg* 6G 57
Arnisdale. *High* 4K 69
Arnish. *High* 1G 69
Arniston. *Midl* 3M 59
Arnol. *W Isl* 7F 82
Arnold. *E Yor* 3J 43
Arnold. *Notts* 5C 36
Arnprior. *Stir* 8L 65
Arnside. *Cumb* 8C 46
Aros Mains. *Arg* 3L 63
Arpafeelie. *High* 8G 79
Arrad Foot. *Cumb* 7B 46
Arram. *E Yor* 3H 43
Arras. *E Yor* 3G 43
Arrathorne. *N Yor* 6K 47
Arreton. *IOW* 7C 10
Arrington. *Cambs* 6L 29
Arrochar. *Arg* 7G 65
Arrow. *Warw* 6J 27
Arscaig. *High* 2F 78
Artafallie. *High* 1G 71
Arthington. *W Yor* 3L 41
Arthingworth. *Nptn* 3E 28
Arthog. *Gwyn* 1F 24
Arthrath. *Abers* 2J 73
Arthurstone. *Per* 3F 66
Articlave. *Caus* 2E 92
Artigarvan. *Derr* 3C 92
Artikelly. *Caus* 2E 92
Artington. *Surr* 1G 11
Arundel. *W Sus* 5H 11
Asby. *Cumb* 2K 45
Ascog. *Arg* 3L 57
Ascot. *Wind* 7G 21
Ascott-under-Wychwood. *Oxon* 2M 19
Asenby. *N Yor* 8A 48
Asfordby. *Leics* 8E 36
Asfordby Hill. *Leics* 8E 36
Asgarby. *Linc*
  nr. Horncastle 3L 37
  nr. Sleaford 5J 37
Ash. *Devn* 7L 5
Ash. *Dors* 4G 9
Ash. *Kent*
  nr. Sandwich 8J 23
  nr. Swanley 7C 22
Ash. *Som* 3C 8
Ash. *Surr* 8F 20
Ashampstead. *W Ber* 6C 20
Ashbocking. *Suff* 6H 31
Ashbourne. *Derbs* 5K 35
Ashbrittle. *Som* 3K 7
Ashbrook. *Shrp* 2C 26
Ashburton. *Devn* 5K 5
Ashbury. *Devn* 6E 6
Ashbury. *Oxon* 5L 19
Ashby. *N Lin* 7F 42
Ashby by Partney. *Linc* 3M 37
Ashby cum Fenby. *NE Lin* 7K 43
Ashby de la Launde. *Linc* 4H 37
Ashby-de-la-Zouch. *Leics* 8A 36
Ashby Folville. *Leics* 8E 36
Ashby Magna. *Leics* 2C 28
Ashby Parva. *Leics* 3C 28
Ashby Puerorum. *Linc* 2L 37
Ashby St Ledgars. *Nptn* 5C 28
Ashby St Mary. *Norf* 1K 31
Ashchurch. *Glos* 8H 27
Ashcombe. *Devn* 8J 7
Ashcott. *Som* 2C 8
Ashdon. *Essx* 7B 30
Ashe. *Hants* 1C 10
Asheldham. *Essx* 3F 22
Ashen. *Essx* 7D 30
Ashendon. *Buck* 2E 20
Ashey. *IOW* 7C 10
Ashfield. *Hants* 4A 10
Ashfield. *Here* 1D 18
Ashfield. *Shrp* 3D 26
Ashfield. *Stir* 7A 66
Ashfield. *Suff* 5J 31
Ashfield Green. *Suff* 4J 31
Ashfold Crossways. *W Sus* 3K 11
Ashford. *Devn*
  nr. Barnstaple 2E 6
  nr. Kingsbridge 7J 5
Ashford. *Hants* 4K 9
Ashford. *Kent* 1G 13
Ashford. *Surr* 6H 21
Ashford Bowdler. *Shrp* 4D 26
Ashford Carbonel. *Shrp* 4D 26
Ashford Hill. *Hants* 7C 20
Ashford in the Water. *Derbs* 3K 35
Ashgill. *S Lan* 5F 58
Ash Green. *Warw* 3M 27
Ashgrove. *Mor* 7B 80
Ashill. *Devn* 4K 7
Ashill. *Norf* 1E 30
Ashill. *Som* 4B 8
Ashingdon. *Essx* 4E 22
Ashington. *Nmbd* 3F 54
Ashington. *W Sus* 4J 11
Ashkirk. *Bord* 7B 60
Ashleworth. *Glos* 1G 19
Ashley. *Cambs* 5C 30
Ashley. *Ches E* 1G 35
Ashley. *Dors* 5K 9
Ashley. *Glos* 4H 19
Ashley. *Hants*
  nr. New Milton 6L 9
  nr. Winchester 2A 10
Ashley. *Kent* 1K 13
Ashley. *Nptn* 2E 28
Ashley. *Staf* 6F 34
Ashley. *Wilts* 7G 19
Ashley Green. *Buck* 3G 21
Ashley Heath. *Dors* 5K 9
Ashley Heath. *Staf* 6F 34
Ashley Moor. *Here* 5C 26
Ash Magna. *Shrp* 6D 34
Ashmanhaugh. *Norf* 7K 39
Ashmansworth. *Hants* 8B 20
Ashmansworthy. *Devn* 4C 6
Ashmead Green. *Glos* 4F 18
Ashmill. *Devn* 6C 6
Ash Mill. *Devn* 3G 7
Ashmore. *Dors* 4H 9
Ashmore Green. *W Ber* 7C 20
Ashorne. *Warw* 6M 27
Ashover. *Derbs* 3A 36
Ashow. *Warw* 4M 27
Ash Parva. *Shrp* 6D 34
Ashperton. *Here* 7E 26
Ashprington. *Devn* 6L 5
Ash Priors. *Som* 3L 7
Ashreigney. *Devn* 4F 6
Ash Street. *Suff* 7G 31
Ashstead. *Surr* 8J 21
Ash Thomas. *Devn* 4K 7
Ashton. *Corn* 6K 3
Ashton. *Here* 5D 26
Ashton. *Inv* 2M 57
Ashton. *Nptn*
  nr. Oundle 3H 29
  nr. Roade 7E 28
Ashton. *Pet* 1J 29
Ashton Common. *Wilts* 8G 19
Ashton Hayes. *Ches W* 3D 34
Ashton-in-Makerfield. *G Man* 8D 40
Ashton Keynes. *Wilts* 4J 19
Ashton under Hill. *Worc* 8H 27
Ashton-under-Lyne. *G Man* 8H 41
Ashton upon Mersey. *G Man* 8F 40
Ashurst. *Hants* 4M 9

Ashurst – Bewaldeth

Ashurst. Kent 2B 12
Ashurst. Lanc 7C 40
Ashurst. W Sus 4J 11
Ashurst Wood. W Sus 2M 11
Ash Vale. Surr 8F 20
Ashwater. Devn 6C 6
Ashwell. Herts 8K 29
Ashwell. Rut 8F 36
Ashwellthorpe. Norf 2H 31
Ashwick. Som 1E 8
Ashwicken. Norf 8D 38
Ashwood. Staf 3G 27
Askam in Furness. Cumb 7M 45
Askern. S Yor 6C 42
Askerswell. Dors 6D 8
Askett. Buck 3F 20
Askham. Cumb 3D 46
Askham. Notts 2E 36
Askham Bryan. York 3C 42
Askham Richard. York 3C 42
Askrigg. N Yor 6H 47
Askwith. N Yor 3K 41
Aslackby. Linc 6H 37
Aslacton. Norf 2H 31
Aslockton. Notts 5E 36
Aspatria. Cumb 7F 52
Aspenden. Herts 1L 21
Asperton. Linc 6K 37
Aspley Guise. C Beds 8G 29
Aspley Heath. C Beds 8G 29
Aspull. G Man 7E 40
Asselby. E Yor 5E 42
Assington. Suff 8F 30
Assington Green. Suff 6D 30
Astbury. Ches E 3G 35
Astcote. Nptn 6D 28
Asterby. Linc 2K 37
Asterley. Shrp 1B 26
Asterton. Shrp 2B 26
Asthall. Oxon 2L 19
Asthall Leigh. Oxon 2M 19
Astle. High 4H 79
Astley. G Man 7F 40
Astley. Shrp 8D 34
Astley. Warw 3M 27
Astley. Worc 5F 26
Astley Abbotts. Shrp 2F 26
Astley Bridge. G Man 6F 40
Astley Cross. Worc 5G 27
Aston. Ches E 5E 34
Aston. Ches W 2D 34
Aston. Derbs
nr. Hope 1K 35
nr. Sudbury 6K 35
Aston. Flin 3B 34
Aston. Here 5C 26
Aston. Herts 1K 21
Aston. Oxon 3M 19
Aston. Shrp
nr. Bridgnorth 2G 27
nr. Wem 7D 34
Aston. S Yor 1B 36
Aston. Staf 5F 34
Aston. Telf 1E 26
Aston. W Mid 2J 27
Aston. Wok 5E 20
Aston Abbotts. Buck 1F 20
Aston Botterell. Shrp 3E 26
Aston-by-Stone. Staf 6H 35
Aston Cantlow. Warw 6K 27
Aston Clinton. Buck 2F 20
Aston Crews. Here 1E 18
Aston Cross. Glos 8H 27
Aston End. Herts 1K 21
Aston Eyre. Shrp 2E 26
Aston Fields. Worc 5H 27
Aston Flamville. Leics 2B 28
Aston Ingham. Here 1E 18
Aston juxta Mondrum.
Ches E 4E 34
Astonlane. Shrp 2E 26
Aston le Walls. Nptn 6B 28
Aston Magna. Glos 8K 27
Aston Munslow. Shrp 3D 26
Aston on Carrant. Glos 8H 27
Aston on Clun. Shrp 3B 26
Aston-on-Trent. Derbs 7B 36
Aston Pigott. Shrp 1B 26
Aston Rogers. Shrp 1B 26
Aston Rowant. Oxon 4E 20
Aston Sandford. Buck 3E 20
Aston Somerville. Worc 8J 27
Aston Subedge. Glos 7K 27
Aston Tirrold. Oxon 5C 20
Aston Upthorpe. Oxon 5C 20
Astrop. Nptn 8C 28
Astwick. C Beds 8K 29
Astwood. Mil 7G 29
Astwood Bank. Worc 5J 27
Aswarby. Linc 6H 37
Aswardby. Linc 2L 37
Atcham. Shrp 1D 26
Atch Lench. Worc 6J 27
Athelhampton. Dors 6F 8
Athelington. Suff 4J 31
Athelney. Som 3B 8
Athelstaneford. E Lot 2C 60
Atherfield Green. IOW 8B 10
Atherington. Devn 3E 6
Atherington. W Sus 5H 11
Athersley. S Yor 7A 42
Atherstone. Warw 2M 27
Atherstone on Stour. Warw 6L 27
Atherton. G Man 7E 40
Ath-Tharracail. High 1A 64
Atlow. Derbs 5L 35
Attadale. High 2L 69
Attenborough. Notts 6C 36
Atterby. Linc 8G 43
Atterley. Shrp 2E 26
Atterton. Leics 2A 28
Attical. New M 7H 93
Attleborough. Norf 2G 31
Attleborough. Warw 2A 28
Attlebridge. Norf 8H 39
Atwick. E Yor 2J 43
Atworth. Wilts 7G 19
Auberrow. Here 7C 26
Aubourn. Linc 3G 37
Aucharnie. Abers 1F 72
Auchattie. Abers 6F 72
Auchavan. Ang 1E 66
Auchbreck. Mor 3B 72
Auchenback. E Ren 4D 58
Auchenblae. Abers 8G 73
Auchenbrack. Dum 2B 52
Auchenbreck. Arg 1K 57
Auchencairn. Dum
nr. Dalbeattie 6B 52
nr. Dumfries 3D 52
Auchencarroch. W Dun 1C 58
Auchencrow. Bord 3F 60
Auchendennan. Arg 1B 58
Auchendinny. Midl 3L 59
Auchengray. S Lan 4H 59
Auchenhalrig. Mor 7C 80
Auchenheath. S Lan 5G 59
Auchenlochan. Arg 2J 57
Auchenmade. N Ayr 5B 58
Auchenmalg. Dum 6H 51
Auchentiber. N Ayr 5B 58
Auchenvennel. Arg 1A 58
Auchindrain. Arg 7E 64
Auchininna. Abers 1F 72
Auchinleck. Dum 4K 51
Auchinleck. E Ayr 7D 58
Auchinloch. N Lan 2E 58
Auchinstarry. N Lan 2F 58
Auchleven. Abers 3F 72
Auchlochan. S Lan 6G 59
Auchlunachan. High 5B 78
Auchmillan. E Ayr 7D 58
Auchmithie. Ang 3K 67
Auchmuirbridge. Fife 7F 66
Auchmull. Ang 8E 72
Auchnacree. Ang 1H 67
Auchnafree. Per 4B 66
Auchnagallin. High 2L 71
Auchnagatt. Abers 1J 73
Aucholzie. Abers 6D 72
Auchreddie. Abers 1H 73
Auchterarder. Per 6C 66
Auchteraw. High 5D 70
Auchterderran. Fife 8F 66
Auchterhouse. Ang 4G 67
Auchtermuchty. Fife 6F 66
Auchterneed. High 8E 78
Auchtertool. Fife 8F 66
Auchtertyre. High 3K 69
Auchtubh. Stir 5K 65
Auckengill. High 5E 86
Auckley. S Yor 7D 42
Audenshaw. G Man 8H 41
Audlem. Ches E 5E 34
Audley. Staf 4F 34
Audley End. Essx 8B 30
Audmore. Staf 7G 35
Auds. Abers 7F 80
Augher. M Ulst 6D 92
Aughertree. Cumb 8G 53
Aughnacloy. M Ulst 6E 92
Aughton. E Yor 4E 42
Aughton. Lanc
nr. Lancaster 1D 40
nr. Ormskirk 7B 40
Aughton. S Yor 1B 36
Aughton. Wilts 8L 19
Aughton Park. Lanc 7C 40
Auldearn. High 8K 79
Aulden. Here 6C 26
Auldgirth. Dum 3D 52
Auldhouse. S Lan 4E 58
Ault a' chruinn. High 3L 69
Aultbea. High 5K 77
Aultdearg. High 7C 78
Aultgrishan. High 5J 77
Aultguish Inn. High 6D 78
Ault Hucknall. Derbs 3B 36
Aultibea. High 1L 79
Aultiphurst. High 5L 85
Aultivullin. High 5L 85
Aultmore. Mor 8D 80
Aultnamain Inn. High 5G 79
Aunby. Linc 8H 37
Aunsby. Linc 6H 37
Aust. S Glo 5D 18
Austerfield. S Yor 8D 42
Austin Fen. Linc 8L 43
Austrey. Warw 1L 27
Austwick. N Yor 1F 40
Authorpe. Linc 1M 37
Authorpe Row. Linc 2B 38
Avebury. Wilts 7K 19
Avebury Trusloe. Wilts 7J 19
Aveley. Thur 5B 22
Avening. Glos 4G 19
Averham. Notts 4E 36
Aveton Gifford. Devn 7J 5
Avielochan. High 4K 71
Aviemore. High 4J 71
Avington. Hants 2C 10
Avoch. High 8H 79
Avon. Hants 6K 9
Avonbridge. Falk 2H 59
Avon Dassett. Warw 6B 28
Avonmouth. Bris 6D 18
Avonwick. Devn 6K 5
Awbridge. Hants 3M 9
Awliscombe. Devn 5L 7
Awre. Glos 3F 18
Awsworth. Notts 5B 36
Axbridge. Som 8C 18
Axford. Hants 1D 10
Axford. Wilts 7L 19
Axminster. Devn 6B 8
Axmouth. Devn 6A 8
Aycliffe Village. Dur 3L 47
Aydon. Nmbd 5D 54
Aykley Heads. Dur 7F 54
Aylburton. Glos 3E 18
Aylburton Common. Glos 3E 18
Ayle. Nmbd 7M 53
Aylesbeare. Devn 6K 7
Aylesbury. Buck 2F 20
Aylesby. NE Lin 7K 43
Aylescott. Devn 4F 6
Aylesford. Kent 8D 22
Aylesham. Kent 8J 23
Aylestone. Leic 1C 28
Aylmerton. Norf 6H 39
Aylsham. Norf 7H 39
Aylton. Here 8E 26
Aylworth. Glos 1K 19
Aymestrey. Here 5C 26
Aynho. Nptn 8C 28
Ayot Green. Herts 2K 21
Ayot St Lawrence. Herts 2J 21
Ayot St Peter. Herts 2K 21
Ayr. S Ayr 7B 58
Ayres of Selivoe. Shet 3C 90
Ayreville. Torb 5L 5
Aysgarth. N Yor 7J 47
Ayshford. Devn 4K 7
Ayside. Cumb 7B 46
Ayston. Rut 1F 28
Ayton. Bord 3G 61
Aywick. Shet 5K 91
Azerley. N Yor 8L 47

B

Babbacombe. Torb 5M 5
Babbinswood. Shrp 6B 34
Babbs Green. Herts 2L 21
Babcary. Som 3D 8
Babel. Carm 1H 17
Babell. Flin 3L 33
Babingley. Norf 7C 38
Bablock Hythe. Oxon 3B 20
Babraham. Cambs 6B 30
Babworth. Notts 1D 36
Bac. W Isl 7H 83
Bachau. IOA 2D 32
Bacheldre. Powy 3M 25
Bachymbyd Fawr. Den 4K 33
Backaland. Orkn 6E 88
Backaskaill. Orkn 4D 88
Backbarrow. Cumb 7B 46
Backe. Carm 5J 15
Backfolds. Abers 8K 81
Backford. Ches W 2C 34
Backhill. Abers 2G 73
Backhill of Clackriach.
Abers 1J 73
Backies. High 3J 79
Backmuir of New Gilston.
Fife 7H 67
Back of Keppoch. High 7H 69
Back Street. Suff 6D 30
Backwell. N Som 7C 18
Backworth. Tyne 4G 55
Bacon End. Essx 2C 22
Baconsthorpe. Norf 6H 39
Bacton. Here 8B 26
Bacton. Norf 6K 39
Bacton. Suff 5G 31
Bacton Green. Norf 6K 39
Bacup. Lanc 5G 41
Badachonacher. High 6G 79
Badachro. High 6J 77
Badanloch Lodge. High 8K 85
Badavanich. High 8B 78
Badbury. Swin 5K 19
Badby. Nptn 6C 28
Badcall. High 6E 84
Badcaul. High 4M 77
Baddeley Green. Stoke 4H 35
Baddesley Clinton. W Mid 4L 27
Baddesley Ensor. Warw 2L 27
Baddidarach. High 1A 78
Baddoch. Abers 7M 71
Badenscallie. High 3M 77
Badenscoth. Abers 2G 73
Badentarbat. High 2M 77
Badgall. Corn 7B 6
Badgers Mount. Kent 7A 22
Badgeworth. Glos 2H 19
Badgworth. Som 8B 18
Badicaul. High 3J 69
Badingham. Suff 5K 31
Badlesmere. Kent 8G 23
Badlipster. High 7D 86
Badluarach. High 4L 77
Badminton. S Glo 5G 19
Badnaban. High 1A 78
Badnabay. High 7E 84
Badnagie. High 8C 86
Badnellan. High 3J 79
Badninish. High 4H 79
Badrallach. High 4A 78
Badsey. Worc 7J 27
Badshot Lea. Surr 1F 10
Badsworth. W Yor 6B 42
Badwell Ash. Suff 5F 30
Bae Cinmel. Cnwy 2J 33
Bae Colwyn. Cnwy 3H 33
Bae Penrhyn. Cnwy 2H 33
Bagby. N Yor 7B 48
Bag Enderby. Linc 2L 37
Bagendon. Glos 3J 19
Bagginswood. Shrp 3E 26
Bàgh a Chàise. W Isl 6A 76
Bàgh a' Chaisteil. W Isl 6C 74
Bagham. Kent 8G 23
Baghasdal. W Isl 4D 74
Bagh Mor. W Isl 8K 75
Bagh Shiarabhagh. W Isl 5D 74
Bagillt. Flin 3M 33
Baginton. Warw 4M 27
Baglan. Neat 5G 17
Bagley. Shrp 7C 34
Bagley. Som 1C 8
Bagnall. Staf 4H 35
Bagnor. W Ber 7B 20
Bagshot. Surr 7G 21
Bagshot. Wilts 7M 19
Bagstone. S Glo 5E 18
Bagthorpe. Norf 6D 38
Bagthorpe. Notts 4B 36
Bagworth. Leics 1B 28
Bagwy Llydiart. Here 1C 18
Baildon. W Yor 4K 41
Baildon Green. W Yor 4K 41
Baile. W Isl 5L 75
Baile Ailein. W Isl 1D 76
Baile an Truiseil. W Isl 6G 83
Baile Boidheach. Arg 2G 57
Baile Glas. W Isl 8K 75
Bailemeonach. Arg 3A 64
Baile Mhanaich. W Isl 8J 75
Baile Mhartainn. W Isl 6J 75
Baile MhicPhail. W Isl 6K 75
Baile Mor. W Isl 7J 75
Baile Mór. Arg 5H 63
Baile nan Cailleach. W Isl 8J 75
Baile Raghaill. W Isl 7J 75
Bailey Green. Hants 3D 10
Baileyhead. Cumb 3K 53
Baileysmill. Lis 6H 93
Bailiesward. Abers 2D 72
Bail' lochdrach. W Isl 8K 75
Baillieston. Glas 3E 58
Bailrigg. Lanc 2C 40
Bail Uachdraich. W Isl 7K 75
Bail' Ur Tholastaidh. W Isl 7J 83
Bainbridge. N Yor 6H 47
Bainsford. Falk 1G 59
Bainshole. Abers 2F 72
Bainton. E Yor 2G 43
Bainton. Oxon 1C 20
Bainton. Pet 1H 29
Baintown. Fife 7G 67
Baker Street. Thur 5C 22
Bakewell. Derbs 3L 35
Bala. Gwyn 7J 33
Y Bala. Gwyn 7J 33
Balachuirn. High 1G 69
Balbeg. High
nr. Cannich 2E 70
nr. Loch Ness 3E 70
Balbeggie. Per 5E 66
Balblair. High
nr. Bonar Bridge 4F 78
nr. Invergordon 7H 79
nr. Inverness 1F 70
Balby. S Yor 7C 42
Balcathie. Ang 4K 67
Balchladich. High 8C 84
Balchraggan. High 1F 70
Balchrick. High 6D 84
Balcombe. W Sus 2L 11
Balcombe Lane. W Sus 2L 11
Balcurvie. Fife 7G 67
Baldersby. N Yor 8A 48
Baldersby St James. N Yor 8A 48
Balderstone. Lanc 4E 40
Balderton. Ches W 3B 34
Balderton. Notts 4F 36
Baldinnie. Fife 6H 67
Baldock. Herts 8K 29
Baldrine. IOM 6D 44
Baldslow. E Sus 4E 12
Baldwin. IOM 6C 44
Baldwinholme. Cumb 6H 53
Baldwin's Gate. Staf 6F 34
Bale. Norf 6G 39
Balearn. Abers 8K 81
Balemartine. Arg 3E 62
Balephetrish. Arg 3F 62
Balephuil. Arg 3E 62
Balerno. Edin 3K 59
Balevullin. Arg 3E 62
Balfield. Ang 1J 67
Balfour. Orkn 8D 88
Balfron. Stir 1D 58
Balgaveny. Abers 1F 72
Balgonar. Fife 8D 66
Balgowan. High 6G 71
Balgown. High 7E 76
Balgrochan. E Dun 2E 58
Balgy. High 8K 77
Balhalgardy. Abers 3G 73
Baliasta. Shet 3L 91
Baligill. High 5L 85
Balintore. Ang 2F 66
Balintore. High 6J 79
Balintraid. High 6H 79
Balk. N Yor 7B 48
Balkeerie. Ang 3G 67
Balkholme. E Yor 5E 42
Ball. Shrp 7B 34
Ballabeg. IOM 7B 44
Ballacannell. IOM 6D 44
Ballacarnane Beg. IOM 6C 44
Ballachulish. High 2E 64
Ballagyr. IOM 6B 44
Ballajora. IOM 5D 44
Ballaleigh. IOM 6C 44
Ballamodha. IOM 7B 44
Ballantrae. S Ayr 3F 50
Ballards Gore. Essx 4F 22
Ballasalla. IOM
nr. Castletown 7B 44
nr. Kirk Michael 5C 44
Ballater. Abers 6C 72
Ballaugh. IOM 5C 44
Ballencrieff. E Lot 2B 60
Ballencrieff Toll. W Lot 2H 59
Ballentoul. Per 1B 66
Ball Hill. Hants 7B 20
Ballidon. Derbs 4L 35
Balliemore. Arg
nr. Dunoon 1K 57
nr. Oban 5C 64
Ballieward. High 2L 71
Ballig. IOM 6B 44
Ballimore. Stir 6K 65
Ballinamallard. Ferm 6C 92
Ballindarragh. Ferm 7C 92
Ballingdon. Suff 7E 30
Ballinger Common. Buck 3G 21
Ballingham. Here 8D 26
Ballingry. Fife 8E 66
Ballinluig. Per 2C 66
Ballintoy. Caus 1G 93
Ballintuim. Per 2E 66
Balliveolan. Arg 3C 64
Balloan. High 3F 78
Balloch. High 1H 71
Balloch. N Lan 2F 58
Balloch. Per 6B 66
Balloch. W Dun 1B 58
Ballochan. Abers 6E 72
Ballochgoy. Arg 3K 57
Ballochmyle. E Ayr 7D 58
Ballochroy. Arg 4G 57
Balloo. Ards 5J 93
Balls Cross. W Sus 3G 11
Ball's Green. E Sus 2A 12
Ballsmill. New M 7F 93
Ballyalton. New M 6J 93
Ballybogy. Caus 2F 93
Ballycarry. ME Ant 4J 93
Ballycassidy. Ferm 6C 92
Ballycastle. Caus 1G 93
Ballyclare. Ant 4H 93
Ballyeaston. Ant 4H 93
Ballygally. ME Ant 3H 93
Ballygawley. M Ulst 6E 92
Ballygowan. Ards 5J 93
Ballygown. Arg 3K 63
Ballygrant. Arg 3C 56
Ballyhalbert. Ards 5K 93
Ballyholland. New M 7G 93
Ballyhornan. New M 6J 93
Ballykelly. Caus 2E 92
Ballykinler. New M 7J 93
Ballylesson. Lis 5H 93
Ballymagorry. Derr 3C 92
Ballymartin. New M 7H 93
Ballymena. ME Ant 3G 93
Ballymichael. N Ayr 6J 57
Ballymoney. Caus 2F 93
Ballynagard. Derr 2D 92
Ballynahinch. New M 6H 93
Ballynakilly. M Ulst 5F 93
Ballynoe. New M 6J 93
Ballynure. Ant 4H 93
Ballyrashane. Caus 2F 93
Ballyrobert. Ant 4H 93
Ballyronan. M Ulst 4F 93
Ballyroney. Arm 7H 93
Ballyscullion. Caus 2E 92
Ballystrudder. ME Ant 4J 93
Ballyvoy. Caus 1G 93
Ballyward. New M 7H 93
Ballywater. Ards 5K 93
Ballywonard. Ant 4H 93
Balmacara. High 3K 69
Balmaclellan. Dum 4A 52
Balmacqueen. High 6F 76
Balmaha. Stir 8J 65
Balmalcolm. Fife 7G 67
Balmalloch. N Lan 2F 58
Balmeanach. High 2G 69
Balmedie. Abers 4J 73
Balmerino. Fife 5G 67
Balmerlawn. Hants 5M 9
Balmore. E Dun 2E 58
Balmore. High 1D 68
Balmullo. Fife 5H 67
Balmurrie. Dum 5H 51
Balnaboth. Ang 1G 67
Balnabruaich. High 6H 79
Balnabruich. High 1A 80
Balnacoil. High 2J 79
Balnacra. High 1L 69
Balnacroft. Abers 6B 72
Balnageith. Mor 8L 79
Balnaglaic. High 2E 70
Balnagrantach. High 2E 70
Balnaguard. Per 2C 66
Balnahard. Arg 8K 63
Balnain. High 2E 70
Balnakeil. High 5F 84
Balnaknock. High 7F 76
Balnamoon. Abers 8J 81
Balnamoon. Ang 1J 67
Balnamore. Caus 2F 93
Balnapaling. High 7H 79
Balornock. Glas 3E 58
Balquhidder. Stir 5K 65
Balsall. W Mid 4L 27
Balsall Common. W Mid 4L 27
Balscote. Oxon 7A 28
Balsham. Cambs 6B 30
Balstonia. Thur 5C 22
Baltasound. Shet 3L 91
Balterley. Staf 4F 34
Baltersan. Dum 5K 51
Balthangie. Abers 8H 81
Baltonsborough. Som 2D 8
Balvaird. High 8F 78
Balvaird. Per 6E 66
Balvenie. Mor 1C 72
Balvicar. Arg 6B 64
Balvraid. High 4K 69
Balvraid Lodge. High 2J 71
Bamber Bridge. Lanc 5D 40
Bamber's Green. Essx 1B 22
Bamburgh. Nmbd 6J 61
Bamford. Derbs 1L 35
Bamfurlong. G Man 7D 40
Bampton. Cumb 4D 46
Bampton. Devn 3J 7
Bampton. Oxon 3M 19
Bampton Grange. Cumb 4D 46
Banavie. High 8B 70
Banbridge. Arm 6G 93
Banbury. Oxon 7B 28
Bancffosfelen. Carm 5L 15
Banchory. Abers 6F 72
Banchory-Devenick. Abers 5J 73
Bancycapel. Carm 5L 15
Bancyfelin. Carm 5K 15
Banc-y-ffordd. Carm 3L 15
Banff. Abers 7F 80
Bangor. Ards 4J 93
Bangor. Gwyn 3E 32
Bangor-is-y-coed. Wrex 5B 34
Bangors. Corn 6B 6
Bangor's Green. Lanc 7B 40
Banham. Norf 3G 31
Bank. Hants 5L 9
The Bank. Ches E 4G 35
The Bank. Shrp 2E 26
Bankend. Dum 5E 52
Bankfoot. Per 4D 66
Bankglen. E Ayr 8E 58
Bankhead. Aber 4H 73
Bankhead. Abers 5F 72
Bankhead. S Lan 5G 59
Bankland. Som 3B 8
Bank Newton. N Yor 2H 41
Banknock. Falk 2F 58
Banks. Cumb 5K 53
Banks. Lanc 5B 40
Bankshill. Dum 3F 52
Bank Street. Worc 5E 26
Bank Top. Lanc 7D 40
Banners Gate. W Mid 2J 27
Banningham. Norf 7J 39
Banniskirk. High 6C 86
Bannister Green. Essx 1C 22
Bannockburn. Stir 8B 66
Banstead. Surr 8K 21
Bantham. Devn 7J 5
Banton. N Lan 2F 58
Banwell. N Som 8B 18
Banyard's Green. Suff 4K 31
Bapchild. Kent 7F 22
Bapton. Wilts 2H 9
Barabhas. W Isl 6G 83
Barabhas Iarach. W Isl 7G 83
Baramore. High 8H 69
Barassie. S Ayr 6B 58
Baravullin. Arg 3D 64
Barbaraville. High 6H 79
Barber Booth. Derbs 1K 35
Barber Green. Cumb 7B 46
Barbhas Uarach. W Isl 6G 83
Barbieston. S Ayr 8C 58
Barbon. Cumb 7E 46
Barbourne. Worc 6G 27
Barbridge. Ches E 4E 34
Barbrook. Devn 1G 7
Barby. Nptn 4C 28
Barby Nortoft. Nptn 4C 28
Barcaldine. Arg 3D 64
Barcheston. Warw 8L 27
Barclose. Cumb 5J 53
Barcombe. E Sus 4M 11
Barcombe Cross. E Sus 4M 11
Barden. N Yor 6K 47
Barden Scale. N Yor 2J 41
Bardfield End Green. Essx 8C 30
Bardfield Saling. Essx 1C 22
Bardister. Shet 6H 91
Bardnabeinne. High 4H 79
Bardney. Linc 3J 37
Bardon. Leics 8B 36
Bardon Mill. Nmbd 5A 54
Bardowie. E Dun 2D 58
Bardrainney. Inv 2B 58
Bardsea. Cumb 8B 46
Bardsey. W Yor 3A 42
Bardsley. G Man 7H 41
Bardwell. Suff 4F 30
Bare. Lanc 1C 40
Barelees. Nmbd 6F 60
Barewood. Here 6B 26
Barford. Hants 2F 10
Barford. Norf 1H 31
Barford. Warw 5L 27
Barford St John. Oxon 8B 28
Barford St Martin. Wilts 2J 9
Barford St Michael. Oxon 8B 28
Barfrestone. Kent 8J 23
Bargeddie. N Lan 3E 58
Bargod. Cphy 5L 17
Bargoed. Cphy 5L 17
Bargrennan. Dum 4J 51
Barham. Cambs 4J 29
Barham. Kent 8J 23
Barham. Suff 6H 31
Barharrow. Dum 6M 51
Bar Hill. Cambs 5L 29
Barholm. Linc 8H 37
Barkby. Leics 1D 28
Barkestone-le-Vale. Leics 6E 36
Barkham. Wok 7E 20
Barking. G Lon 5M 21
Barking. Suff 6G 31
Barking Riverside. G Lon 5A 22
Barkingside. G Lon 5A 22
Barking Tye. Suff 6G 31
Barkisland. W Yor 6J 41
Barkston. Linc 5G 37
Barkston Ash. N Yor 4B 42
Barkway. Herts 8L 29
Barlanark. Glas 3E 58
Barlaston. Staf 6G 35
Barlavington. W Sus 4G 11
Barlborough. Derbs 2B 36
Barlby. N Yor 4D 42
Barlestone. Leics 1B 28
Barley. Herts 8L 29
Barley. Lanc 3G 41
Barley Mow. Tyne 6F 54
Barleythorpe. Rut 1F 28
Barling. Essx 5F 22
Barlings. Linc 2H 37
Barlow. Derbs 2M 35
Barlow. N Yor 5D 42
Barlow. Tyne 5E 54
Barmby Moor. E Yor 3E 42
Barmby on the Marsh. E Yor 5D 42
Barmer. Norf 6E 38
Barming. Kent 8D 22
Barming Heath. Kent 8D 22
Barmoor. Nmbd 6H 61
Barmouth. Gwyn 1F 24
Barmpton. Darl 4M 47
Barmston. E Yor 2J 43
Barmulloch. Glas 3E 58
Barnack. Pet 1H 29
Barnacle. Warw 3A 28
Barnard Castle. Dur 4J 47
Barnard Gate. Oxon 2B 20
Barnardiston. Suff 7D 30
Barnbarroch. Dum 6C 52
Barnburgh. S Yor 7B 42
Barnby. Suff 3L 31
Barnby Dun. S Yor 7D 42
Barnby in the Willows.
Notts 4F 36
Barnby Moor. Notts 1D 36
Barnes. G Lon 6K 21
Barnes Street. Kent 1C 12
Barnet. G Lon 4K 21
Barnetby le Wold. N Lin 7H 43
Barney. Norf 6F 38
Barnham. Suff 4E 30
Barnham. W Sus 5G 11
Barnham Broom. Norf 1G 31
Barnhead. Ang 2K 67
Barnhill. D'dee 4H 67
Barnhill. Mor 8M 79
Barnhill. Per 5E 66
Barnhills. Dum 4E 50
Barningham. Dur 4J 47
Barningham. Suff 4F 30
Barnoldby le Beck. NE Lin 7K 43
Barnoldswick. Lanc 3G 41
Barns Green. W Sus 3J 11
Barnsley. Glos 3J 19
Barnsley. Shrp 2F 26
Barnsley. S Yor 7M 41
Barnstaple. Devn 2E 6
Barnston. Essx 2C 22
Barnston. Mers 1A 34
Barnstone. Notts 6E 36
Barnt Green. Worc 4J 27
Barnton. Ches W 2E 34
Barnwell. Cambs 6A 30
Barnwell. Nptn 3H 29
Barnwood. Glos 2G 19
Barons Cross. Here 6C 26
The Barony. Orkn 7B 88
Barr. Dum 1B 52
Barr. S Ayr 2H 51
Barra Airport. W Isl 5C 74
Barrachan. Dum 7J 51
Barraglom. W Isl 8E 82
Barrahormid. Arg 1G 57
Barrapol. Arg 3E 62
Barrasford. Nmbd 4C 54
Barravullin. Arg 7C 64
Barregarrow. IOM 6C 44
Barrhead. E Ren 4D 58
Barrhill. S Ayr 3H 51
Barri. V Glam 8L 17
Barrington. Cambs 7L 29
Barrington. Som 4B 8
Barripper. Corn 5K 3
Barrmill. N Ayr 4B 58
Barrock. High 4D 86
Barrow. Lanc 4F 40
Barrow. Rut 8F 36
Barrow. Shrp 1E 26
Barrow. Som 2F 8
Barrow. Suff 5D 30
Barroway Drove. Norf 1B 30
Barrow Bridge. G Man 6E 40
Barrowburn. Nmbd 8F 60
Barrowby. Linc 6F 36
Barrowcliff. N Yor 7H 49
Barrow Common. N Som 7D 18
Barrowden. Rut 1G 29
Barrowford. Lanc 4G 41
Barrow Gurney. N Som 7D 18
Barrow Haven. N Lin 5H 43
Barrow Hill. Derbs 2B 36
Barrow-in-Furness. Cumb 8M 45
Barrow Nook. Lanc 7C 40
Barrow's Green. Hal 1D 34
Barrows Green. Cumb 7D 46
Barrow Street. Wilts 2G 9
Barrow upon Humber.
N Lin 5H 43
Barrow upon Soar. Leics 8C 36
Barrow upon Trent. Derbs 7A 36
Barry. Ang 4J 67
Barry. V Glam 8L 17
Barry Island. V Glam 8L 17
Barsby. Leics 8D 36
Barsham. Suff 3K 31
Barston. W Mid 4L 27
Bartestree. Here 7D 26
Barthol Chapel. Abers 2H 73
Bartholomew Green. Essx 1D 22
Barthomley. Ches E 4F 34
Bartley. Hants 4M 9
Bartley Green. W Mid 3J 27
Bartlow. Cambs 7B 30
Barton. Cambs 6M 29
Barton. Ches W 4C 34
Barton. Cumb 3C 46
Barton. Glos 1K 19
Barton. IOW 7C 10
Barton. Lanc
nr. Ormskirk 7B 40
nr. Preston 4D 40
Barton. N Som 8B 18
Barton. N Yor 5L 47
Barton. Oxon 3C 20
Barton. Torb 5M 5
Barton. Warw 6K 27
Barton Bendish. Norf 1D 30
Barton Gate. Staf 8K 35
Barton Green. Staf 8K 35
Barton Hartsthorn. Buck 8D 28
Barton Hill. N Yor 1E 42
Barton in Fabis. Notts 6C 36
Barton in the Beans. Leics 1A 28
Barton-le-Clay. C Beds 8H 29
Barton-le-Street. N Yor 8E 48
Barton-le-Willows. N Yor 1E 42
Barton Mills. Suff 4D 30
Barton on Sea. Hants 6L 9
Barton-on-the-Heath. Warw 8L 27
Barton St David. Som 2D 8
Barton Seagrave. Nptn 4F 28
Barton Stacey. Hants 1B 10
Barton Town. Devn 1F 6
Barton Turf. Norf 7K 39
Barton-Under-Needwood.
Staf 8K 35
Barton-upon-Humber.
N Lin 5H 43
Barton Waterside. N Lin 5H 43
Barugh Green. S Yor 7M 41
Barway. Cambs 4B 30
Barwell. Leics 2B 28
Barwick. Herts 2L 21
Barwick. Som 4D 8
Barwick in Elmet. W Yor 4A 42
Baschurch. Shrp 7C 34
Bascote. Warw 5B 28
Basford Green. Staf 4H 35
Bashall Eaves. Lanc 3E 40
Bashall Town. Lanc 3F 40
Bashley. Hants 6L 9
Basildon. Essx 5D 22
Basingstoke. Hants 8D 20
Baslow. Derbs 2L 35
Bason Bridge. Som 1B 8
Bassaleg. Newp 5A 18
Bassendean. Bord 5D 60
Bassenthwaite. Cumb 8G 53
Bassett. Sotn 4B 10
Bassingbourn. Cambs 7L 29
Bassingfield. Notts 6D 36
Bassingham. Linc 3G 37
Bassingthorpe. Linc 7G 37
Bassus Green. Herts 1L 21
Basta. Shet 4K 91
Baston. Linc 8J 37
Bastonford. Worc 6G 27
Bastwick. Norf 8L 39
Batchley. Worc 5J 27
Batchworth. Herts 4H 21
Batcombe. Dors 5E 8
Batcombe. Som 2E 8
Bate Heath. Ches E 2E 34
Bath. Bath 106 (7F 18)
Bathampton. Bath 7F 18
Bathealton. Som 3K 7
Batheaston. Bath 7F 18
Bathford. Bath 7F 18
Bathgate. W Lot 3H 59
Bathley. Notts 4E 36
Bathpool. Corn 8B 6
Bathpool. Som 3A 8
Bathville. W Lot 3H 59
Bathway. Som 8D 18
Batley. W Yor 5L 41
Batsford. Glos 8K 27
Batson. Devn 8K 5
Battersby. N Yor 5C 48
Battersea. G Lon 6K 21
Battisborough Cross. Devn 7J 5
Battisford. Suff 6G 31
Battisford Tye. Suff 6G 31
Battle. E Sus 4D 12
Battle. Powy 1K 17
Battleborough. Som 8B 18
Battledown. Glos 1H 19
Battlefield. Shrp 8D 34
Battlesbridge. Essx 4D 22
Battlesden. C Beds 1G 21
Battlesea Green. Suff 4J 31
Battleton. Som 3J 7
Battram. Leics 1B 28
Battramsley. Hants 6M 9
Batt's Corner. Surr 1F 10
Bauds of Cullen. Mor 7D 80
Baugh. Arg 3F 62
Baughton. Worc 7G 27
Baughurst. Hants 7C 20
Baulking. Oxon 4M 19
Baumber. Linc 2K 37
Baunton. Glos 3J 19
Baverstock. Wilts 2J 9
Bawburgh. Norf 1H 31
Bawdeswell. Norf 7G 39
Bawdrip. Som 2B 8
Bawdsey. Suff 7K 31
Bawsey. Norf 8C 38
Bawtry. S Yor 8D 42
Baxenden. Lanc 5F 40
Baxterley. Warw 2L 27
Baxter's Green. Suff 6D 30
Bay. High 8D 76
Baybridge. Hants 3C 10
Baybridge. Nmbd 6C 54
Baycliff. Cumb 8A 46
Baydon. Wilts 6L 19
Bayford. Herts 3L 21
Bayford. Som 3F 8
Bayles. Cumb 7M 53
Baylham. Suff 6H 31
Baynard's Green. Oxon 1C 20
Bayston Hill. Shrp 1C 26
Baythorne End. Essx 7D 30
Baythorpe. Linc 5K 37
Bayton. Worc 4E 26
Bayton Common. Worc 4F 26
Bayworth. Oxon 3C 20
Beach. S Glo 6F 18
Beachampton. Buck 8E 28
Beachamwell. Norf 1D 30
Beachley. Glos 4D 18
Beacon. Devn 5L 7
Beacon End. Essx 1F 22
Beacon Hill. Surr 2F 10
Beacon's Bottom. Buck 4E 20
Beaconsfield. Buck 4G 21
Beacrabhaic. W Isl 4C 76
Beadlam. N Yor 7D 48
Beadnell. Nmbd 7K 61
Beaford. Devn 4E 6
Beal. Nmbd 5H 61
Beal. N Yor 5C 42
Bealsmill. Corn 8C 6
Beam Hill. Staf 7L 35
Beamhurst. Staf 6J 35
Beaminster. Dors 5C 8
Beamish. Dur 6F 54
Beamond End. Buck 4G 21
Beamsley. N Yor 2J 41
Bean. Kent 6B 22
Beanacre. Wilts 7H 19
Beanley. Nmbd 8H 61
Beaquoy. Orkn 7C 88
Beardwood. Bkbn 5E 40
Beare Green. Surr 1J 11
Bearley. Warw 5K 27
Bearpark. Dur 7F 54
Bearsbridge. Nmbd 6A 54
Bearsden. E Dun 2D 58
Bearsted. Kent 8D 22
Bearstone. Shrp 6F 34
Bearwood. Pool 6J 9
Bearwood. W Mid 3J 27
Beattock. Dum 1E 52
Beauchamp Roding. Essx 2B 22
Beauchief. S Yor 1M 35
Beaufort. Blae 3L 17
Beaulieu. Hants 5A 10
Beauly. High 1F 70
Beaumaris. IOA 3F 32
Beaumont. Cumb 6H 53
Beaumont. Essx 1H 23
Beaumont Hill. Darl 4L 47
Beaumont Leys. Leic 1C 28
Beausale. Warw 4L 27
Beauvale. Notts 5B 36
Beauworth. Hants 3C 10
Beaworthy. Devn 6D 6
Beazley End. Essx 1D 22
Bebington. Mers 1B 34
Bebside. Nmbd 3F 54
Beccles. Suff 3L 31
Becconsall. Lanc 5C 40
Beckbury. Shrp 1F 26
Beckenham. G Lon 7L 21
Beckermet. Cumb 4K 45
Beckett End. Norf 2D 30
Beck Foot. Cumb 6E 46
Beckfoot. Cumb
nr. Broughton in Furness 6L 45
nr. Seascale 4L 45
nr. Silloth 7E 52
Beckford. Worc 8H 27
Beckhampton. Wilts 7J 19
Beck Hole. N Yor 5F 48
Beckingham. Linc 4F 36
Beckingham. Notts 8E 42
Beckington. Som 8G 19
Beckley. E Sus 3E 12
Beckley. Hants 6L 9
Beckley. Oxon 2C 20
Beck Row. Suff 4C 30
Beck Side. Cumb
nr. Cartmel 7B 46
nr. Ulverston 6M 45
Beckside. Cumb 7E 46
Beckton. G Lon 5M 21
Beckwithshaw. N Yor 2L 41
Becontree. G Lon 5A 22
Bedale. N Yor 7L 47
Bedburn. Dur 8E 54
Bedchester. Dors 4G 9
Beddau. Rhon 6K 17
Beddgelert. Gwyn 6E 32
Beddingham. E Sus 5M 11
Beddington. G Lon 7L 21
Bedfield. Suff 5J 31
Bedford. Bed 7H 29
Bedford. G Man 8E 40
Bedham. W Sus 3H 11
Bedhampton. Hants 5E 10
Bedingfield. Suff 5H 31
Bedingham Green. Norf 2J 31
Bedlam. N Yor 1L 41
Bedlar's Green. Essx 1B 22
Bedlington. Nmbd 3F 54
Bedlinog. Mer T 4K 17
Bedminster. Bris 6D 18
Bedmond. Herts 3H 21
Bednall. Staf 8H 35
Bedrule. Bord 8D 60
Bedstone. Shrp 4B 26
Bedwas. Cphy 6L 17
Bedwellty. Cphy 4L 17
Bedworth. Warw 3A 28
Beeby. Leics 1D 28
Beech. Hants 2D 10
Beech. Staf 6G 35
Beechcliffe. W Yor 3J 41
Beech Hill. W Ber 7D 20
Beechingstoke. Wilts 8J 19
Beedon. W Ber 6B 20
Beeford. E Yor 2J 43
Beeley. Derbs 3L 35
Beelsby. NE Lin 7K 43
Beenham. W Ber 7C 20
Beeny. Corn 2D 4
Beer. Devn 7M 7
Beer. Som 2C 8
Beercrocombe. Som 3B 8
Beer Hackett. Dors 4E 8
Beesands. Devn 7L 5
Beesby. Linc 1A 38
Beeson. Devn 7L 5
Beeston. C Beds 7J 29
Beeston. Ches W 4D 34
Beeston. Norf 8F 38
Beeston. Notts 6C 36
Beeston. W Yor 4L 41
Beeston Regis. Norf 5H 39
Beeswing. Dum 5C 52
Beetham. Cumb 8C 46
Beetham. Som 4A 8
Beetley. Norf 8F 38
Beffcote. Staf 8G 35
Began. Card 6M 17
Begbroke. Oxon 2B 20
Begdale. Cambs 1A 30
Begelly. Pemb 6H 15
Beggar Hill. Essx 3C 22
Beggar's Bush. Powy 5A 26
Beggearn Huish. Som 2K 7
Beguildy. Powy 5L 25
Beighton. Norf 1K 31
Beighton. S Yor 1B 36
Beighton Hill. Derbs 4L 35
Beinn Casgro. W Isl 1F 76
Beith. N Ayr 4B 58
Bekesbourne. Kent 8H 23
Belaugh. Norf 8J 39
Belbroughton. Worc 4H 27
Belchalwell. Dors 5F 8
Belchalwell Street. Dors 5F 8
Belchamp Otten. Essx 7E 30
Belchamp St Paul. Essx 7D 30
Belchamp Walter. Essx 7E 30
Belchford. Linc 2K 37
Belcoo. Ferm 7B 92
Belfast. Bel 5H 93
Belfast City George Best Airport.
Bel 5H 93
Belfast International Airport.
Ant 4G 93
Belfatton. Abers 8K 81
Belford. Nmbd 6J 61
Belgrano. Cnwy 3J 33
Belhaven. E Lot 2D 60
Belhelvie. Abers 4J 73
Belhinnie. Abers 3D 72
Bellabeg. Abers 4C 72
Belladrum. High 1F 70
Bellaghy. M Ulst 4F 93
Bellamore. S Ayr 3H 51
Bellanaleck. Ferm 7C 92
Bellanoch. Arg 8C 64
Bell Busk. N Yor 2H 41
Belleau. Linc 2M 37
Belleek. Ferm 6A 92
Belleek. New M 7F 93
Belleheiglash. Mor 2A 72
Bell End. Worc 4H 27
Bellerby. N Yor 6K 47
Bellerby Camp. N Yor 6J 47
Bellever. Devn 8F 6
Belle Vue. Cumb 8F 52
Belle Vue. Shrp 8C 34
Bellfield. S Lan 6G 59
Belliehill. Ang 1J 67
Bellingdon. Buck 3G 21
Bellingham. Nmbd 3B 54
Bellmount. Norf 7B 38
Bellochantuy. Arg 6F 56
Bellsbank. E Ayr 1K 51
Bell's Cross. Suff 6H 31
Bellshill. N Lan 4F 58
Bellshill. Nmbd 6J 61
Bellside. N Lan 4G 59
Bellspool. Bord 6K 59
Bellsquarry. W Lot 3J 59
Bells Yew Green. E Sus 2C 12
Belmaduthy. High 8G 79
Belmesthorpe. Rut 8H 37
Belmont. Bkbn 6E 40
Belmont. Shet 3K 91
Belmont. S Ayr 7B 58
Belnacraig. Abers 4C 72
Belnie. Linc 6K 37
Belowda. Corn 5B 4
Belper. Derbs 5A 36
Belper Lane End. Derbs 5M 35
Belph. Derbs 2C 36
Belsay. Nmbd 4E 54
Belsford. Devn 6K 5
Belsize. Herts 3H 21
Belstead. Suff 7H 31
Belston. S Ayr 7B 58
Belstone. Devn 6F 6
Belstone Corner. Devn 6F 6
Belthorn. Lanc 5F 40
Beltinge. Kent 7H 23
Beltoft. N Lin 7F 42
Belton. Leics 7B 36
Belton. Linc 6G 37
Belton. Norf 1L 31
Belton. N Lin 7E 42
Belton-in-Rutland. Rut 1F 28
Beltring. Kent 1C 12
Belts of Collonach. Abers 6F 72
Belvedere. G Lon 6A 22
Belvoir. Leics 6F 36
Bembridge. IOW 7D 10
Bemersyde. Bord 6C 60
Bemerton. Wilts 2K 9
Bempton. E Yor 8J 49
Benacre. Suff 3M 31
Ben Alder Lodge. High 8F 70
Ben Armine Lodge. High 2H 79
Benbecula Airport. W Isl 8J 75
Benbuie. Dum 2B 52
Benburb. M Ulst 6F 93
Benchill. G Man 1G 35
Benderloch. Arg 4D 64
Bendish. Herts 1J 21
Bendooragh. Caus 2F 93
Bendronaig Lodge. High 2M 69
Benenden. Kent 2E 12
Benfieldside. Dur 6D 54
Bengate. Norf 7K 39
Bengeworth. Worc 7J 27
Benhall Green. Suff 5K 31
Benholm. Abers 1M 67
Beningbrough. N Yor 2C 42
Benington. Herts 1K 21
Benington. Linc 5L 37
Benington Sea End. Linc 5M 37
Benllech. IOA 2E 32
Benmore Lodge. High 2D 78
Bennacott. Corn 6B 6
Bennah. Devn 7H 7
Bennecarrigan. N Ayr 7J 57
Bennethead. Cumb 3C 46
Benniworth. Linc 1K 37
Benover. Kent 1D 12
Benson. Oxon 4D 20
Benston. Shet 2E 90
Benstonhall. Orkn 6E 88
Bent. Abers 8F 72
Benthall. Shrp 1E 26
Bentham. Glos 2H 19
Bentlawnt. Shrp 1B 26
Bentley. E Yor 4H 43
Bentley. Hants 1E 10
Bentley. S Yor 7C 42
Bentley. Suff 8H 31
Bentley. Warw 2L 27
Bentley. W Mid 2H 27
Bentley Heath. Herts 4K 21
Bentley Heath. W Mid 4K 27
Bentpath. Dum 2H 53
Bents. W Lot 3H 59
Bentworth. Hants 1D 10
Benvie. D'dee 4G 67
Benville. Dors 5D 8
Benwell. Tyne 5F 54
Benwick. Cambs 2L 29
Beoley. Worc 5J 27
Beoraidbeg. High 6H 69
Bepton. W Sus 4F 10
Beragh. Ferm 5D 92
Berden. Essx 1A 22
Bere Alston. Devn 5G 5
Bere Ferrers. Devn 5G 5
Berepper. Corn 6K 3
Bere Regis. Dors 6G 9
Bergh Apton. Norf 1K 31
Berinsfield. Oxon 4C 20
Berkeley. Glos 4E 18
Berkhamsted. Herts 3G 21
Berkley. Som 1G 9
Berkswell. W Mid 4L 27
Bermondsey. G Lon 6L 21
Bernera. High 3K 69
Bernice. Arg 8F 64
Bernisdale. High 8F 76
Berrick Salome. Oxon 4D 20
Berriedale. High 1M 79
Berrier. Cumb 3B 46
Berriew. Powy 2L 25
Berrington. Nmbd 5H 61
Berrington. Shrp 1D 26
Berrington. Worc 5D 26
Berrington Green. Worc 5D 26
Berrington Law. Nmbd 5G 61
Berrow. Som 8B 18
Berrow Green. Worc 6F 26
Berry Cross. Devn 4D 6
Berry Down Cross. Devn 1E 6
Berry Hill. Glos 2D 18
Berry Hill. Pemb 2G 15
Berryhillock. Mor 7E 80
Berrynarbor. Devn 1E 6
Berry Pomeroy. Devn 5L 5
Berryscaur. Dum 2F 52
Berry's Green. G Lon 8M 21
Bersham. Wrex 5B 34
Berthengam. Flin 3L 33
Berwick. E Sus 5B 12
Berwick Bassett. Wilts 6K 19
Berwick Hill. Nmbd 4E 54
Berwick St James. Wilts 2J 9
Berwick St John. Wilts 3H 9
Berwick St Leonard. Wilts 2H 9
Berwick-upon-Tweed.
Nmbd 4G 61
Berwyn. Den 6L 33
Bescaby. Leics 7F 36
Bescar. Lanc 6B 40
Besford. Worc 7H 27
Bessacarr. S Yor 7D 42
Bessbrook. New M 7G 93
Bessels Leigh. Oxon 3B 20
Bessingby. E Yor 1J 43
Bessingham. Norf 6H 39
Best Beech Hill. E Sus 2C 12
Besthorpe. Norf 2G 31
Besthorpe. Notts 3F 36
Bestwood Village. Notts 5C 36
Beswick. E Yor 3H 43
Betchworth. Surr 8K 21
Bethania. Cdgn 6E 24
Bethania. Gwyn
nr. Blaenau Ffestiniog 6G 33
nr. Caernarfon 5F 32
Bethel. Gwyn
nr. Bala 7J 33
nr. Caernarfon 4E 32
Bethel. IOA 3C 32
Bethersden. Kent 1F 12
Bethesda. Gwyn 4F 32
Bethesda. Pemb 5G 15
Bethlehem. Carm 2F 16
Bethnal Green. G Lon 5L 21
Betley. Staf 5F 34
Betsham. Kent 6C 22
Betteshanger. Kent 8K 23
Bettiscombe. Dors 6C 8
Bettisfield. Wrex 6C 34
Betton. Shrp 6E 34
Betton Strange. Shrp 1D 26
Bettws. B'end 6J 17
Bettws. Newp 4A 18
Bettws Bledrws. Cdgn 7E 24
Bettws Cedewain. Powy 3L 25
Bettws Gwerfil Goch. Den 6K 33
Bettws Ifan. Cdgn 2K 15
Bettws Newydd. Mon 3B 18
Bettyhill. High 5K 85
Betws. Carm 3F 16
Betws Garmon. Gwyn 5E 32
Betws-y-Coed. Cnwy 5G 33
Betws-yn-Rhos. Cnwy 3J 33
Beulah. Cdgn 2J 15
Beulah. Powy 7J 25
Beul an Atha. Arg 3C 56
Bevendean. Brig 5L 11
Bevercotes. Notts 2E 36
Beverley. E Yor 4H 43
Beverston. Glos 4G 19
Bevington. Glos 4E 18
Bewaldeth. Cumb 8G 53

Bewcastle – Bridlington

Bewcastle. Cumb 4K 53
Bewdley. Worc 4F 26
Bewerley. N Yor 1K 41
Bewholme. E Yor 2J 43
Bexfield. Norf 7G 39
Bexhill. E Sus 5D 12
Bexley. G Lon 6A 22
Bexleyheath. G Lon 6A 22
Bexleyhill. W Sus 3G 11
Bexwell. Norf 1C 30
Beyton. Suff 5F 30
Bhalton. W Isl 8D 82
Bhatarsaigh. W Isl 6C 74
Bibbington. Derbs 2J 35
Bibury. Glos 3K 19
Bicester. Oxon 1C 20
Bickenhall. Som 4A 8
Bickenhill. W Mid 3K 27
Bicker. Linc 6K 37
Bicker Bar. Linc 6K 37
Bicker Gauntlet. Linc 6K 37
Bickershaw. G Man 7E 40
Bickerstaffe. Lanc 7C 40
Bickerton. Ches E 4D 34
Bickerton. Nmbd 1C 54
Bickerton. N Yor 2B 42
Bickford. Staf 8G 35
Bickington. Devn
nr. Barnstaple 2E 6
nr. Newton Abbot 8G 7
Bickleigh. Devn
nr. Plymouth 5H 5
nr. Tiverton 5J 7
Bickleton. Devn 2E 6
Bickley. N Yor 6G 49
Bickley Moss. Ches W 5D 34
Bickmarsh. Worc 7K 27
Bicknacre. Essx 3D 22
Bicknoller. Som 2L 7
Bicknor. Kent 8E 22
Bickton. Hants 4K 9
Bicton. Here 5C 26
Bicton. Shrp
nr. Bishop's Castle 3A 26
nr. Shrewsbury 8C 34
Bicton Heath. Shrp 8C 34
Bidborough. Kent 1B 12
Biddenden. Kent 2E 12
Biddenden Green. Kent 1E 12
Biddenham. Bed 6H 29
Biddestone. Wilts 6G 19
Biddisham. Som 8B 18
Biddlesden. Buck 7D 28
Biddlestone. Nmbd 1C 54
Biddulph. Staf 4G 35
Biddulph Moor. Staf 4H 35
Bideford. Devn 3D 6
Bidford-on-Avon. Warw 6J 27
Bidlake. Devn 7E 6
Bidston. Mers 1A 34
Bielby. E Yor 3E 42
Bieldside. Aber 5H 73
Bierley. IOW 8C 10
Bierley. W Yor 4K 41
Bierton. Buck 2F 20
Bigbury. Devn 7J 5
Bigbury-on-Sea. Devn 7J 5
Bigby. Linc 7H 43
Biggar. Cumb 8L 45
Biggar. S Lan 6J 59
Biggin. Derbs
nr. Hartington 4K 35
nr. Hulland 5L 35
Biggin. N Yor 4C 42
Biggings. Shet 1B 90
Biggin Hill. G Lon 8M 21
Biggleswade. C Beds 7J 29
Bighouse. High 5L 85
Bighton. Hants 2D 10
Biglands. Cumb 6G 53
Bignall End. Staf 4G 35
Bignor. W Sus 4G 11
Bigrigg. Cumb 3K 45
Big Sand. High 6J 77
Bigton. Shet 5D 90
Bilberry. Corn 6C 4
Bilborough. Nott 5C 36
Bilbrook. Som 1K 7
Bilbrook. Staf 1G 27
Bilbrough. N Yor 3C 42
Bilbster. High 6D 86
Bilby. Notts 1D 36
Bildershaw. Dur 3L 47
Bildeston. Suff 7F 30
Billericay. Essx 4C 22
Billesdon. Leics 1E 28
Billesley. Warw 6K 27
Billingborough. Linc 6J 37
Billinge. Mers 7D 40
Billingford. Norf
nr. Dereham 7G 39
nr. Diss 4H 31
Billingham. Stoc T 3B 48
Billinghay. Linc 4J 37
Billingley. S Yor 7B 42
Billingshurst. W Sus 3H 11
Billingsley. Shrp 3F 26
Billington. C Beds 1G 21
Billington. Lanc 4F 40
Billington. Staf 7G 35
Billockby. Norf 8L 39
Billy Row. Dur 8E 54
Bilsborrow. Lanc 3D 40
Bilsby. Linc 2A 38
Bilsham. W Sus 5G 11
Bilsington. Kent 2G 13
Bilson Green. Glos 2E 18
Bilsthorpe. Notts 3D 36
Bilston. Midl 3L 59
Bilston. W Mid 2H 27
Bilstone. Leics 1A 28
Bilting. Kent 1G 13
Bilton. E Yor 4J 43
Bilton. Nmbd 8K 61
Bilton. N Yor 2M 41
Bilton. Warw 4B 28
Bilton in Ainsty. N Yor 3B 42
Bimbister. Orkn 8C 88
Binbrook. Linc 8K 43
Binchester. Dur 8F 54
Bincombe. Dors 7E 8
Bindal. High 5K 79
Binegar. Som 1E 8
Bines Green. W Sus 4J 11
Binfield. Brac 6F 20
Binfield Heath. Oxon 6E 20
Bingfield. Nmbd 4C 54
Bingham. Notts 6E 36
Bingham's Melcombe. Dors 5F 8
Bingley. W Yor 4K 41
Bings Heath. Shrp 8D 34
Binham. Norf 6F 38
Binley. Hants 8B 20
Binley. W Mid 4A 28
Binnegar. Dors 7G 9
Binniehill. Falk 2G 59
Binsoe. N Yor 8L 47
Binstead. IOW 6C 10
Binsted. Hants 1E 10
Binsted. W Sus 5G 11
Binton. Warw 6K 27
Bintree. Norf 7G 39
Binweston. Shrp 1B 26
Birch. Essx 2F 22
Birch. G Man 7G 41
Birchall. Staf 4H 35
Bircham Newton. Norf 6D 38
Bircham Tofts. Norf 6D 38
Birchanger. Essx 1B 22
Birchburn. N Ayr 7J 57
Birch Cross. Staf 6K 35
Bircher. Here 5C 26
Birch Green. Essx 2F 22
Birchgrove. Card 6L 17
Birchgrove. Swan 5G 17
Birch Heath. Ches W 3D 34
Birch Hill. Ches W 2D 34
Birchill. Devn 5B 8
Birchington. Kent 7J 23
Birchley Heath. Warw 2L 27
Birchmoor. Warw 1L 27
Birchmoor Green. C Beds 8G 29
Birchover. Derbs 3L 35
Birch Vale. Derbs 1J 35
Birchview. Mor 2A 72
Birchwood. Linc 3G 37
Birchwood. Som 4M 7
Birchwood. Warr 8E 40
Bircotes. Notts 8D 42
Birdbrook. Essx 7D 30
Birdham. W Sus 5F 10
Birdholme. Derbs 3A 36
Birdingbury. Warw 5B 28
Birdlip. Glos 2H 19
Birdsall. N Yor 1F 42
Birds Edge. W Yor 7L 41
Birds Green. Essx 3B 22
Birdsgreen. Shrp 3F 26
Birdsmoorgate. Dors 5B 8
Birdston. E Dun 2E 58
Birdwell. S Yor 7M 41
Birdwood. Glos 2F 18
Birgham. Bord 6E 60
Birichen. High 4H 79
Birkby. Cumb 8E 52
Birkby. N Yor 5M 47
Birkdale. Mers 6B 40
Birkenhead. Mers 1B 34
Birkenhills. Abers 1G 73
Birkenshaw. N Lan 3E 58
Birkenshaw. W Yor 5L 41
Birkhall. Abers 6C 72
Birkhill. Ang 4G 67
Birkholme. Linc 7G 37
Birkin. N Yor 5C 42
Birley. Here 6C 26
Birling. Kent 7C 22
Birling. Nmbd 1F 54
Birling Gap. E Sus 6B 12
Birlingham. Worc 7H 27
Birmingham. W Mid 106 (3J 27)
Birmingham Airport.
W Mid 119 (3K 27)
Birnam. Per 3D 66
Birse. Abers 6E 72
Birsemore. Abers 6E 72
Birstall. Leics 1C 28
Birstall. W Yor 5L 41
Birstall Smithies. W Yor 5L 41
Birstwith. N Yor 2L 41
Birthorpe. Linc 6J 37
Birtle. G Man 6G 41
Birtley. Here 5B 26
Birtley. Nmbd 4B 54
Birtley. Tyne 6F 54
Birtsmorton. Worc 8G 27
Birts Street. Worc 8F 26
Bisbrooke. Rut 2F 28
Bisham. Wind 5F 20
Bishampton. Worc 6H 27
Bish Mill. Devn 3G 7
Bishop Auckland. Dur 3L 47
Bishopbridge. Linc 8H 43
Bishopbriggs. E Dun 2E 58
Bishop Burton. E Yor 4G 43
Bishopdown. Wilts 2K 9
Bishop Middleham. Dur 8G 55
Bishopmill. Mor 7B 80
Bishop Monkton. N Yor 1M 41
Bishop Norton. Linc 8G 43
Bishopsbourne. Kent 8H 23
Bishops Cannings. Wilts 7J 19
Bishop's Castle. Shrp 3B 26
Bishop's Caundle. Dors 4E 8
Bishop's Cleeve. Glos 1H 19
Bishops Court. New M 6J 93
Bishop's Down. Dors 4E 8
Bishop's Frome. Here 7E 26
Bishop's Green. Essx 2C 22
Bishop's Green. Hants 7C 20
Bishop's Hull. Som 3M 7
Bishop's Itchington. Warw 6A 28
Bishops Lydeard. Som 3L 7
Bishop's Norton. Glos 1G 19
Bishop's Nympton. Devn 3G 7
Bishop's Offley. Staf 7F 34
Bishop's Stortford. Herts 1A 22
Bishop's Sutton. Hants 2D 10
Bishop's Tachbrook. Warw 5M 27
Bishop's Tawton. Devn 2E 6
Bishopsteignton. Devn 8J 7
Bishopstoke. Hants 4B 10
Bishopston. Swan 6E 16
Bishopstone. Buck 2F 20
Bishopstone. E Sus 5A 12
Bishopstone. Here 7C 26
Bishopstone. Swin 5L 19
Bishopstone. Wilts 3J 9
Bishopstrow. Wilts 1G 9
Bishop Sutton. Bath 8D 18
Bishop's Waltham. Hants 4C 10
Bishops Wood. Staf 1G 27
Bishopswood. Som 4A 8
Bishopsworth. Bris 7D 18
Bishop Thornton. N Yor 1L 41
Bishopthorpe. York 3C 42
Bishopton. Darl 3A 48
Bishopton. Dum 7K 51
Bishopton. N Yor 8L 47
Bishopton. Ren 2C 58
Bishopton. Warw 6K 27
Bishop Wilton. E Yor 2E 42
Bishton. Newp 5B 18
Bishton. Staf 7J 35
Bisley. Glos 3H 19
Bisley. Surr 8G 21
Bispham. Bkpl 3B 40
Bispham Green. Lanc 6C 40
Bissoe. Corn 4L 3
Bisterne. Hants 5K 9
Bisterne Close. Hants 5L 9
Bitchfield. Linc 7G 37
Bittadon. Devn 1E 6
Bittaford. Devn 6J 5
Bittering. Norf 8F 38
Bitterley. Shrp 4D 26
Bitterne. Sotn 4B 10
Bitteswell. Leics 3C 28
Bitton. S Glo 7E 18
Bix. Oxon 5E 20
Bixter. Shet 2D 90
Blaby. Leics 2C 28
Blackawton. Devn 6L 5
Black Bank. Cambs 3B 30
Black Barn. Linc 7M 37
Blackborough. Devn 5K 7
Blackborough. Norf 8C 38
Blackborough End. Norf 8C 38
Black Bourton. Oxon 3L 19
Blackboys. E Sus 3B 12
Blackbrook. Derbs 5M 35
Blackbrook. Mers 8D 40
Blackbrook. Staf 6F 34
Blackbrook. Surr 1J 11
Blackburn. Abers 4H 73
Blackburn. Bkbn 5E 40
Blackburn. W Lot 3H 59
Black Callerton. Tyne 5E 54
Black Carr. Norf 2G 31
Black Clauchrie. S Ayr 3H 51
Black Corries. High 2G 65
Black Crofts. Arg 4D 64
Black Cross. Corn 5B 4
Blackden Heath. Ches E 2F 34
Blackditch. Oxon 3B 20
Black Dog. Devn 5H 7
Blackdog. Abers 4J 73
Blackdown. Dors 5B 8
Blackdyke. Cumb 6F 52
Blacker Hill. S Yor 7A 42
Blackfen. G Lon 6A 22
Blackfield. Hants 5B 10
Blackford. Cumb 5H 53
Blackford. Per 7B 66
Blackford. Shrp 3D 26
Blackford. Som
nr. Burnham-on-Sea 1C 8
nr. Wincanton 3E 8
Blackfordby. Leics 8M 35
Blackgang. IOW 8B 10
Blackhall. Edin 2L 59
Blackhall. Ren 3C 58
Blackhall Colliery. Dur 8H 55
Blackhall Mill. Tyne 6E 54
Blackhall Rocks. Dur 8H 55
Blackham. E Sus 2A 12
Blackheath. Essx 1G 23
Blackheath. G Lon 6L 21
Blackheath. Suff 4L 31
Blackheath. Surr 1H 11
Blackheath. W Mid 3H 27
Black Heddon. Nmbd 4D 54
Black Hill. Warw 6L 27
Blackhill. Abers 1K 73
Blackhill. High 8E 76
Blackhills. Abers 7J 81
Blackhills. High 8K 79
Blackjack. Linc 6K 37
Blackland. Wilts 7J 19
Black Lane. G Man 7F 40
Blackleach. Lanc 4C 40
Blackley. G Man 7G 41
Blackley. W Yor 6K 41
Blacklunans. Per 1E 66
Blackmill. B'end 6J 17
Blackmoor. G Man 7E 40
Blackmoor. Hants 2E 10
Blackmoor Gate. Devn 1F 6
Blackmore. Essx 3C 22
Blackmore End. Essx 8D 30
Blackmore End. Herts 2J 21
Black Mount. Arg 3G 65
Blackness. Falk 2J 59
Blacknest. Hants 1E 10
Blackney. Dors 6C 8
Blacknoll. Dors 7G 9
Black Notley. Essx 1D 22
Blacko. Lanc 3G 41
Black Pill. Swan 5F 16
Blackpool. Bkpl 106 (4B 40)
Blackpool. Devn 7L 5
Blackpool Corner. Dors 6B 8
Blackpool Gate. Cumb 4K 53
Blackridge. W Lot 3G 59
Blackrock. Arg 3C 56
Blackrock. Mon 3M 17
Blackrod. G Man 6E 40
Blackshaw. Dum 5E 52
Blackshaw Head. W Yor 5H 41
Blackshaw Moor. Staf 4J 35
Blackskull. Arm 6G 93
Blacksmith's Green. Suff 5H 31
Blacksnape. Bkbn 5F 40
Blackstone. W Sus 4K 11
Black Street. Suff 3M 31
Black Tar. Pemb 6F 14
Blackthorn. Oxon 2D 20
Blackthorpe. Suff 5F 30
Blacktoft. E Yor 5F 42
Blacktop. Aber 5H 73
Black Torrington. Devn 5D 6
Blacktown. Newp 5A 18
Blackwall Tunnel. G Lon 5L 21
Blackwater. Corn 4L 3
Blackwater. Hants 8F 20
Blackwater. IOW 7C 10
Blackwater. Som 4A 8
Blackwaterfoot. N Ayr 7H 57
Blackwatertown. Arm 6F 93
Blackwell. Darl 4L 47
Blackwell. Derbs
nr. Alfreton 4B 36
nr. Buxton 2K 35
Blackwell. Som 3K 7
Blackwell. Warw 7L 27
Blackwell. Worc 4H 27
Blackwood. Cphy 5L 17
Blackwood. Dum 3D 52
Blackwood. S Lan 5F 58
Blackwood Hill. Staf 4H 35
Blacon. Ches W 3B 34
Bladnoch. Dum 6K 51
Bladon. Oxon 2B 20
Blaenannerch. Cdgn 2J 15
Blaenau Dolwyddelan.
Cnwy 5F 32
Blaenau Ffestiniog. Gwyn 6G 33
Blaenavon. Torf 3A 18
Blaenawey. Mon 2A 18
Blaen Celyn. Cdgn 1K 15
Blaen Clydach. Rhon 5J 17
Blaencwm. Rhon 5J 17
Blaendulais. Neat 4H 17
Blaenffos. Pemb 3H 15
Blaengarw. B'end 5J 17
Blaen-geuffordd. Cdgn 4F 24
Blaengwrach. Neat 4H 17
Blaengwynfi. Neat 5H 17
Blaenllechau. Rhon 5J 17
Blaenpennal. Cdgn 6F 24
Blaenplwyf. Cdgn 5E 24
Blaenporth. Cdgn 2J 15
Blaenrhondda. Rhon 4J 17
Blaenwaun. Carm 4J 15
Blaen-y-coed. Carm 4K 15
Blagdon. N Som 8D 18
Blagdon. Torb 5L 5
Blagdon Hill. Som 4M 7
Blagill. Cumb 7M 53
Blaguegate. Lanc 7C 40
Blaich. High 8M 69
Blain. High 1A 64
Blaina. Blae 4M 17
Blair Atholl. Per 1B 66
Blair Drummond. Stir 8M 65
Blairgowrie. Per 3E 66
Blairhall. Fife 1J 59
Blairingone. Per 8C 66
Blairlogie. Stir 8B 66
Blairmore. Abers 2D 72
Blairmore. Arg 1L 57
Blairmore. High 6D 84
Blairquhanan. W Dun 1C 58
Blaisdon. Glos 2F 18
Blakebrook. Worc 4G 27
Blakedown. Worc 4G 27
Blake End. Essx 1D 22
Blakemere. Here 7B 26
Blakeney. Glos 3E 18
Blakeney. Norf 5G 39
Blakenhall. Ches E 5F 34
Blakeshall. Worc 3G 27
Blakesley. Nptn 6D 28
Blanchland. Nmbd 6C 54
Blandford Camp. Dors 5H 9
Blandford Forum. Dors 5G 9
Blandford St Mary. Dors 5G 9
Bland Hill. N Yor 2L 41
Blandy. High 5J 85
Blanefield. Stir 2D 58
Blaney. Ferm 6B 92
Blankney. Linc 3H 37
Blantyre. S Lan 4E 58
Blarmachfoldach. High 1E 64
Blarnalearoch. High 4B 78
Blashford. Hants 5K 9
Blaston. Leics 2F 28
Blatchbridge. Som 1F 8
Blathaisbhal. W Isl 6K 75
Blatherwycke. Nptn 2G 29
Blawith. Cumb 7A 46
Blaxhall. Suff 6K 31
Blaxton. S Yor 7D 42
Blaydon. Tyne 5E 54
Bleadney. Som 1C 8
Bleadon. N Som 8B 18
Blean. Kent 7H 23
Bleary. Arm 6G 93
Bleasby. Linc 1J 37
Bleasby. Notts 5E 36
Bleasby Moor. Linc 1J 37
Blebocraigs. Fife 6H 67
Bleddfa. Powy 6M 25
Bledington. Glos 1L 19
Bledlow. Buck 3E 20
Bledlow Ridge. Buck 4E 20
Blencarn. Cumb 8L 53
Blencogo. Cumb 7F 52
Blendworth. Hants 4E 10
Blennerhasset. Cumb 7F 52
Bletchingdon. Oxon 2C 20
Bletchingley. Surr 8L 21
Bletchley. Mil 8F 28
Bletchley. Shrp 6E 34
Bletherston. Pemb 4G 15
Bletsoe. Bed 6H 29
Blewbury. Oxon 5C 20
Blickling. Norf 7H 39
Blidworth. Notts 4C 36
Blindburn. Nmbd 8F 60
Blindcrake. Cumb 8F 52
Blindley Heath. Surr 1L 11
Blindmoor. Som 4A 8
Blisland. Corn 4D 4
Blissford. Hants 4K 9
Bliss Gate. Worc 4F 26
Blists Hill. Telf 1E 26
Blisworth. Nptn 6E 28
Blithbury. Staf 7J 35
Blitterlees. Cumb 6F 52
Blockley. Glos 8K 27
Blofield. Norf 1K 31
Blofield Heath. Norf 8K 39
Blo' Norton. Norf 4G 31
Bloomfield. Bord 7C 60
Blore. Staf 5K 35
Blount's Green. Staf 6J 35
Bloxham. Oxon 8B 28
Bloxholm. Linc 4H 37
Bloxwich. W Mid 1H 27
Bloxworth. Dors 6G 9
Blubberhouses. N Yor 2K 41
Blue Anchor. Som 1K 7
Blue Anchor. Swan 5E 16
Blue Bell Hill. Kent 7D 22
Blue Row. Essx 2G 23
Bluetown. Kent 8F 22
Blundeston. Suff 2M 31
Blunham. C Beds 6J 29
Blunsdon St Andrew. Swin 5K 19
Bluntington. Worc 4G 27
Bluntisham. Cambs 4L 29
Blunts. Corn 5F 4
Blurton. Stoke 5G 35
Blyborough. Linc 8G 43
Blyford. Suff 4L 31
Blymhill. Staf 8G 35
Blymhill Lawns. Staf 8G 35
Blyth. Nmbd 3G 55
Blyth. Notts 1D 36
Blyth. Bord 5K 59
Blyth Bank. Bord 5K 59
Blyth Bridge. Bord 5K 59
Blythburgh. Suff 4L 31
The Blythe. Staf 7J 35
Blythe Bridge. Staf 5H 35
Blythe Marsh. Staf 5H 35
Blyton. Linc 8F 42
Boardmills. Lis 6H 93
Boarhills. Fife 6J 67
Boarhunt. Hants 5D 10
Boar's Head. G Man 7D 40
Boarshead. E Sus 2B 12
Boars Hill. Oxon 3B 20
Boarstall. Buck 2D 20
Boasley Cross. Devn 6E 6
Boath. High 6F 78
Boat of Garten. High 4K 71
Bobbing. Kent 7E 22
Bobbington. Staf 2G 27
Bobbingworth. Essx 3B 22
Bocaddon. Corn 6D 4
Bocking. Essx 1D 22
Bocking Churchstreet. Essx 1D 22
Boddam. Abers 1L 73
Boddam. Shet 6D 90
Boddington. Glos 1G 19
Bodedern. IOA 2C 32
Bodelwyddan. Den 3K 33
Bodenham. Here 6D 26
Bodenham. Wilts 3K 9
Bodewryd. IOA 1C 32
Bodfari. Den 3K 33
Bodffordd. IOA 3D 32
Bodham. Norf 5H 39
Bodiam. E Sus 3D 12
Bodicote. Oxon 8B 28
Bodieve. Corn 4B 4
Bodinnick. Corn 6D 4
Bodle Street Green. E Sus 4C 12
Bodmin. Corn 5C 4
Bodnant. Cnwy 3H 33
Bodney. Norf 2E 30
Bodorgan. IOA 4C 32
Bodrane. Corn 5E 4
Bodsham. Kent 1H 13
Boduan. Gwyn 7C 32
Bodymoor Heath. Warw 2K 27
The Bog. Shrp 2B 26
Bogallan. High 8G 79
Bogbrae Croft. Abers 2K 73
Bogend. S Ayr 6B 58
Boghall. Midl 3L 59
Boghall. W Lot 3H 59
Boghead. S Lan 5F 58
Bogindollo. Ang 2H 67
Bogmoor. Mor 7C 80
Bogniebrae. Abers 1E 72
Bognor Regis. W Sus 6G 11
Bograxie. Abers 4G 73
Bogside. N Lan 4G 59
Bogton. Abers 8F 80
Bogue. Dum 3M 51
Bohenie. High 7C 70
Bohortha. Corn 8A 4
Boirseam. W Isl 5B 76
Bokiddick. Corn 5C 4
Bolam. Dur 3K 47
Bolam. Nmbd 3D 54
Bolberry. Devn 8J 5
Bold Heath. Mers 1D 34
Boldon. Tyne 5G 55
Boldon Colliery. Tyne 5G 55
Boldre. Hants 6M 9
Boldron. Dur 4J 47
Bole. Notts 1E 36
Bolehall. Staf 1L 27
Bolehill. Derbs 4L 35
Bolenowe. Corn 5K 3
Boleside. Bord 6B 60
Bolham. Devn 4J 7
Bolham Water. Devn 4L 7
Bolingey. Corn 3L 3
Bollington. Ches E 2H 35
Bolney. W Sus 3K 11
Bolnhurst. Bed 6H 29
Bolshan. Ang 2K 67
Bolsover. Derbs 2B 36
Bolsterstone. S Yor 8L 41
Bolstone. Here 8D 26
Boltachan. Per 2B 66
Boltby. N Yor 7B 48
Bolton. Cumb 3E 46
Bolton. E Lot 2C 60
Bolton. E Yor 2E 42
Bolton. G Man 7F 40
Bolton. Nmbd 8J 61
Bolton Abbey. N Yor 2J 41
Bolton-by-Bowland. Lanc 3F 40
Boltonfellend. Cumb 5J 53
Boltongate. Cumb 7G 53
Bolton Green. Lanc 6D 40
Bolton-le-Sands. Lanc 1C 40
Bolton Low Houses. Cumb 7G 53
Bolton New Houses. Cumb 7G 53
Bolton-on-Swale. N Yor 6L 47
Bolton Percy. N Yor 3C 42
Bolton Town End. Lanc 1C 40
Bolton upon Dearne. S Yor 7B 42
Bolton Wood Lane. Cumb 7G 53
Bolventor. Corn 8A 6
Bomarsund. Nmbd 3F 54
Bomere Heath. Shrp 8C 34
Bonar Bridge. High 4G 79
Bonawe. Arg 4E 64
Bonby. N Lin 6H 43
Boncath. Pemb 3J 15
Bonchester Bridge. Bord 8C 60
Bonchurch. IOW 8C 10
Bond End. Staf 8K 35
Bondleigh. Devn 5F 6
Bonds. Lanc 3C 40
Bonehill. Devn 8G 7
Bonehill. Staf 1K 27
Bo'ness. Falk 1H 59
Boney Hay. Staf 8J 35
Bonham. Wilts 2F 8
Bonhill. W Dun 2B 58
Boningale. Shrp 1G 27
Bonjedward. Bord 7D 60
Bonkle. N Lan 4G 59
Bonnanaboigh. Caus 3E 92
Bonnington. Ang 4J 67
Bonnington. Edin 3K 59
Bonnington. Kent 2G 13
Bonnybank. Fife 7G 67
Bonnybridge. Falk 1G 59
Bonnykelly. Abers 8H 81
Bonnyrigg. Midl 3M 59
Bonnyton. Ang 4G 67
Bonnytown. Fife 6J 67
Bonsall. Derbs 4L 35
Bont. Mon 2B 18
Bontddu. Gwyn 1F 24
Bont Dolgadfan. Powy 2H 25
Y Bont-Faen. V Glam 7J 17
Bontgoch. Cdgn 4F 24
Bonthorpe. Linc 2A 38
Bont Newydd. Gwyn 6G 33
Bont-newydd. Cnwy 3K 33
Bontnewydd. Cdgn 6F 24
Bontnewydd. Gwyn 4D 32
Bontuchel. Den 5K 33
Bonvilston. V Glam 7K 17
Bon-y-maen. Swan 5F 16
Booker. Buck 4F 20
Booley. Shrp 7D 34
Boorley Green. Hants 4C 10
Boosbeck. Red C 4D 48
Boot. Cumb 4L 45
Booth. W Yor 5J 41
Boothby Graffoe. Linc 4G 37
Boothby Pagnell. Linc 6G 37
Booth Green. Ches E 1H 35
Booth of Toft. Shet 6J 91
Boothstown. G Man 7F 40
Boothville. Nptn 5E 28
Bootle. Cumb 6L 45
Bootle. Mers 8B 40
Booton. Norf 7H 39
Booze. N Yor 5J 47
Boquhan. Stir 1D 58
Boraston. Shrp 4E 26
Borden. Kent 7E 22
Borden. W Sus 3F 10
Bordlands. Bord 5K 59
Bordley. N Yor 1H 41
Bordon. Hants 2E 10
Boreham. Essx 3D 22
Boreham. Wilts 1G 9
Boreham Street. E Sus 4C 12
Borehamwood. Herts 4J 21
Boreland. Dum 2F 52
Boreston. Devn 6K 5
Borestone Brae. Stir 8A 66
Boreton. Shrp 1D 26
Borgh. W Isl
on Barra 5C 74
on Benbecula 8J 75
on Berneray 5L 75
on Isle of Lewis 6H 83
Borghasdal. W Isl 5B 76
Borghastan. W Isl 7E 82
Borgh na Sgiotaig. High 6E 76
Borgie. High 6J 85
Borgue. Dum 7M 51
Borgue. High 1M 79
Borley. Essx 7E 30
Borley Green. Essx 7E 30
Borley Green. Suff 5F 30
Borlum. High 3F 70
Bornais. W Isl 3D 74
Bornesketaig. High 6E 76
Boroughbridge. N Yor 1A 42
Borough Green. Kent 8C 22
Borreraig. High 8C 76
Borrobol Lodge. High 1J 79
Borrodale. High 1C 68
Borrowash. Derbs 6B 36
Borrowby. N Yor
nr. Northallerton 7B 48
nr. Whitby 4E 48
Borrowston. High 7E 86
Borrowstonehill. Orkn 1F 86
Borrowstoun. Falk 1H 59
Borstal. Medw 7D 22
Borth. Cdgn 4F 24
Borthwick. Midl 4A 60
Borth-y-Gest. Gwyn 7E 32
Borve. High 1F 68
Borwick. Lanc 8D 46
Bosbury. Here 7E 26
Boscastle. Corn 2C 4
Boscombe. Bour 6K 9
Boscombe. Wilts 2L 9
Boscoppa. Corn 6C 4
Bosham. W Sus 5F 10
Bosherston. Pemb 7F 14
Bosley. Ches E 3H 35
Bossall. N Yor 1E 42
Bossiney. Corn 3C 4
Bossingham. Kent 1H 13
Bossington. Som 1H 7
Bostadh. W Isl 7E 82
Bostock Green. Ches W 3E 34
Boston. Linc 5L 37
Boston Spa. W Yor 3B 42
Boswarthen. Corn 5H 3
Boswinger. Corn 7B 4
Botallack. Corn 5G 3
Botany Bay. G Lon 4K 21
Botcheston. Leics 1B 28
Botesdale. Suff 4G 31
Bothal. Nmbd 3F 54
Bothampstead. W Ber 6C 20
Bothamsall. Notts 2D 36
Bothel. Cumb 8F 52
Bothenhampton. Dors 6C 8
Bothwell. S Lan 4F 58
Botley. Buck 3G 21
Botley. Hants 4C 10
Botley. Oxon 3B 20
Botloe's Green. Glos 1F 18
Botolph Claydon. Buck 1E 20
Botolphs. W Sus 5J 11
Bottacks. High 7E 78
Bottesford. Leics 6F 36
Bottesford. N Lin 7F 42
Bottisham. Cambs 5B 30
Bottlesford. Wilts 8K 19
Bottomcraig. Fife 5G 67
Bottom o' th' Moor. G Man 6E 40
Botton. N Yor 5D 48
Botton Head. Lanc 1E 40
Bottreaux Mill. Devn 3H 7
Botus Fleming. Corn 5G 5
Botwnnog. Gwyn 7B 32
Bough Beech. Kent 1A 12
Boughrood. Powy 1L 17
Boughspring. Glos 4D 18
Boughton. Norf 1C 30
Boughton. Nptn 5E 28
Boughton. Notts 3D 36
Boughton Aluph. Kent 1G 13
Boughton Green. Kent 8D 22
Boughton Lees. Kent 1G 13
Boughton Malherbe. Kent 1E 12
Boughton Monchelsea.
Kent 8D 22
Boughton under Blean.
Kent 8G 23
Boulby. Red C 4E 48
Bouldnor. IOW 7A 10
Bouldon. Shrp 3D 26
Boulmer. Nmbd 8K 61
Boulston. Pemb 5F 14
Boultham. Linc 3G 37
Boulton. Derb 6A 36
Boundary. Staf 5H 35
Bounds. Here 8E 26
Bourn. Cambs 6L 29
Bournbrook. W Mid 3J 27
Bourne. Linc 7H 37
The Bourne. Surr 1F 10
Bourne End. Bed 5H 29
Bourne End. Buck 5F 20
Bourne End. C Beds 7G 29
Bourne End. Herts 3H 21
Bournemouth. Bour 106 (6J 9)
Bournemouth Airport. Dors 6K 9
Bournes Green. Glos 3H 19
Bournes Green. S'end 5F 22
Bournheath. Worc 4H 27
Bournmoor. Dur 6G 55
Bournville. W Mid 3J 27
Bourton. Dors 2F 8
Bourton. N Som 7B 18
Bourton. Oxon 5L 19
Bourton. Shrp 2D 26
Bourton. Wilts 7J 19
Bourton on Dunsmore.
Warw 4B 28
Bourton-on-the-Hill. Glos 8K 27
Bourton-on-the-Water. Glos 1K 19
Bousd. Arg 1H 63
Bousta. Shet 2C 90
Boustead Hill. Cumb 6G 53
Bouth. Cumb 7B 46
Bouthwaite. N Yor 8K 47
Boveney. Buck 6G 21
Boveridge. Dors 4J 9
Boverton. V Glam 8J 17
Bovey Tracey. Devn 8H 7
Bovingdon. Herts 3H 21
Bovingdon Green. Buck 5F 20
Bovinger. Essx 3B 22
Bovington Camp. Dors 7G 9
Bow. Devn 5G 7
Bowbank. Dur 3H 47
Bow Brickhill. Mil 8G 29
Bowbridge. Glos 3G 19
Bowburn. Dur 8G 55
Bowcombe. IOW 7B 10
Bowd. Devn 7L 7
Bowden. Devn 7L 5
Bowden. Bord 6C 60
Bowden Hill. Wilts 7H 19
Bowdens. Som 3C 8
Bowderdale. Cumb 5E 46
Bowdon. G Man 1F 34
Bower. Nmbd 3A 54
Bowerchalke. Wilts 3J 9
Bowerhill. Wilts 7H 19
Bower Hinton. Som 4C 8
Bowermadden. High 5D 86
Bowers. Staf 6G 35
Bowers Gifford. Essx 5D 22
Bowershall. Fife 8D 66
Bowertower. High 5D 86
Bowes. Dur 4H 47
Bowgreave. Lanc 3C 40
Bowhousebog. N Lan 4G 59
Bowithick. Corn 7A 6
Bowland Bridge. Cumb 7C 46
Bowlees. Dur 3H 47
Bowley. Here 6D 26
Bowlhead Green. Surr 2G 11
Bowling. W Dun 2C 58
Bowling. W Yor 4K 41
Bowling Bank. Wrex 5B 34
Bowling Green. Worc 6G 27
Bowlish. Som 1E 8
Bowmanstead. Cumb 6B 46
Bowmore. Arg 4C 56
Bowness-on-Solway.
Cumb 5G 53
Bowness-on-Windermere.
Cumb 6C 46
Bow of Fife. Fife 6G 67
Bowriefauld. Ang 3J 67
Bowscale. Cumb 8H 53
Bowsden. Nmbd 5G 61
Bowside Lodge. High 5L 85
Bowston. Cumb 6C 46
Bow Street. Cdgn 4F 24
Bowthorpe. Norf 1H 31
Box. Glos 3G 19
Box. Wilts 7G 19
Boxbush. Glos 1E 18
Box End. Bed 7H 29
Boxford. Suff 7F 30
Boxford. W Ber 6B 20
Boxgrove. W Sus 5G 11
Box Hill. Wilts 7G 19
Boxley. Kent 8D 22
Boxmoor. Herts 3H 21
Box's Shop. Corn 5B 6
Boxted. Essx 8F 30
Boxted. Suff 6E 30
Boxted Cross. Essx 8G 31
Boxworth. Cambs 5L 29
Boxworth End. Cambs 5L 29
Boyden End. Suff 6D 30
Boyden Gate. Kent 7J 23
Boylestone. Derbs 6K 35
Boylestonfield. Derbs 6K 35
Boyndie. Abers 7F 80
Boynton. E Yor 1J 43
Boys Hill. Dors 4E 8
Boythorpe. Derbs 3A 36
Boyton. Corn 6C 6
Boyton. Suff 7K 31
Boyton. Wilts 2H 9
Boyton Cross. Essx 3C 22
Boyton End. Essx 8C 30
Boyton End. Suff 7D 30
Bozeat. Nptn 6G 29
Braaid. IOM 7C 44
Braal Castle. High 6C 86
Brabling Green. Suff 5J 31
Brabourne. Kent 1H 13
Brabourne Lees. Kent 1G 13
Brabster. High 5E 86
Bracadale. High 2E 68
Bracara. High 6J 69
Braceborough. Linc 8H 37
Bracebridge. Linc 3G 37
Bracebridge Heath. Linc 3G 37
Braceby. Linc 6H 37
Bracewell. Lanc 3G 41
Brackenber. Cumb 4F 46
Brackenfield. Derbs 4A 36
Brackenlands. Cumb 7G 53
Brackenthwaite. Cumb 7G 53
Brackenthwaite. N Yor 2L 41
Brackla. B'end 7J 17
Brackla. High 8J 79
Bracklesham. W Sus 6F 10
Brackletter. High 7B 70
Brackley. Nptn 8C 28
Brackley Hatch. Nptn 7D 28
Brackloch. High 1B 78
Bracknell. Brac 7F 20
Braco. Per 7B 66
Bracobrae. Mor 8E 80
Bracon. N Lin 7E 42
Bracon Ash. Norf 2H 31
Bradbourne. Derbs 4L 35
Bradbury. Dur 3M 47
Bradda. IOM 7A 44
Bradden. Nptn 7D 28
Bradenham. Buck 4F 20
Bradenham. Norf 1F 30
Bradenstoke. Wilts 6J 19
Bradfield. Essx 8H 31
Bradfield. Norf 6J 39
Bradfield. W Ber 6D 20
Bradfield Combust. Suff 6E 30
Bradfield Green. Ches E 4E 34
Bradfield Heath. Essx 1H 23
Bradfield St Clare. Suff 6F 30
Bradfield St George. Suff 5F 30
Bradford. Derbs 3L 35
Bradford. Devn 5D 6
Bradford. Nmbd 6J 61
Bradford. W Yor 106 (4K 41)
Bradford Abbas. Dors 4D 8
Bradford Barton. Devn 4H 7
Bradford Leigh. Wilts 7G 19
Bradford-on-Avon. Wilts 7G 19
Bradford-on-Tone. Som 3L 7
Bradford Peverell. Dors 6E 8
Bradiford. Devn 2E 6
Brading. IOW 7D 10
Bradley. Ches W 2D 34
Bradley. Derbs 5L 35
Bradley. Glos 4F 18
Bradley. Hants 1D 10
Bradley. NE Lin 7K 43
Bradley. N Yor 7J 47
Bradley. Staf 8G 35
Bradley. W Mid 2H 27
Bradley. W Yor 5K 41
Bradley. Wrex 4B 34
Bradley Cross. Som 8C 18
Bradley Green. Ches W 5D 34
Bradley Green. Som 2A 8
Bradley Green. Warw 1L 27
Bradley Green. Worc 5H 27
Bradley in the Moors. Staf 5J 35
Bradley Mount. Ches E 2H 35
Bradley Stoke. S Glo 5E 18
Bradlow. Here 8F 26
Bradmore. Notts 6C 36
Bradmore. W Mid 2G 27
Bradninch. Devn 5K 7
Bradnop. Staf 4J 35
Bradpole. Dors 6C 8
Bradshaw. G Man 6F 40
Bradstone. Devn 7C 6
Bradwall Green. Ches E 3F 34
Bradway. S Yor 1M 35
Bradwell. Derbs 1K 35
Bradwell. Essx 1E 22
Bradwell. Mil 8F 28
Bradwell. Norf 1M 31
Bradwell-on-Sea. Essx 3G 23
Bradwell Waterside. Essx 3F 22
Bradworthy. Devn 4C 6
Brae. High 5K 77
Brae. Shet 1D 90
Braeantra. High 6F 78
Braefield. High 2E 70
Braefindon. High 8G 79
Braegrum. Per 5D 66
Braehead. Ang 2K 67
Braehead. Dum 6K 51
Braehead. Mor 1B 72
Braehead. Orkn 5D 88
Braehead. S Lan
nr. Coalburn 6G 59
nr. Forth 4H 59
Braehoulland. Shet 6G 91
Braemar. Abers 6A 72
Braemore. High
nr. Dunbeath 8B 86
nr. Ullapool 6B 78
Brae of Achnahaird. High 2M 77
Brae Roy Lodge. High 6D 70
Braeside. Abers 2J 73
Braeside. Inv 2M 57
Braes of Coul. Ang 2F 66
Braeswick. Orkn 6F 88
Braetongue. High 6H 85
Braeval. Stir 7K 65
Braevallich. Arg 7D 64
Braewick. Shet 2D 90
Brafferton. Darl 3L 47
Brafferton. N Yor 8B 48
Brafield-on-the-Green. Nptn 6F 28
Bragar. W Isl 7F 82
Bragbury End. Herts 1K 21
Bragleenbeg. Arg 5D 64
Braichmelyn. Gwyn 4F 32
Braides. Lanc 2C 40
Braidwood. S Lan 5G 59
Braigo. Arg 3B 56
Brailsford. Derbs 5L 35
Braintree. Essx 1D 22
Braiseworth. Suff 4H 31
Braishfield. Hants 3A 10
Braithwaite. Cumb 2M 45
Braithwaite. S Yor 6D 42
Braithwaite. W Yor 3J 41
Braithwell. S Yor 8C 42
Brakefield Green. Norf 1G 31
Bramber. W Sus 4J 11
Brambridge. Hants 3B 10
Bramcote. Notts 6C 36
Bramcote. Warw 3B 28
Bramdean. Hants 3D 10
Bramerton. Norf 1J 31
Bramfield. Herts 2K 21
Bramfield. Suff 4K 31
Bramford. Suff 7H 31
Bramhall. G Man 1G 35
Bramham. W Yor 3B 42
Bramhope. W Yor 3L 41
Bramley. Hants 8D 20
Bramley. S Yor 8B 42
Bramley. Surr 1H 11
Bramley. W Yor 4L 41
Bramley Green. Hants 8D 20
Bramley Head. N Yor 2K 41
Bramley Vale. Derbs 3B 36
Bramling. Kent 8J 23
Brampford Speke. Devn 6J 7
Brampton. Cambs 4K 29
Brampton. Cumb
nr. Appleby-in-Westmorland 3E 46
nr. Carlisle 5K 53
Brampton. Linc 2F 36
Brampton. Norf 7J 39
Brampton. S Yor 7B 42
Brampton. Suff 3L 31
Brampton Abbotts. Here 1E 18
Brampton Ash. Nptn 3E 28
Brampton Bryan. Here 4B 26
Brampton en le Morthen.
S Yor 1B 36
Bramshall. Staf 6J 35
Bramshaw. Hants 4L 9
Bramshill. Hants 7E 20
Bramshott. Hants 2F 10
Branault. High 1L 63
Brancaster. Norf 5D 38
Brancaster Staithe. Norf 5D 38
Brancepeth. Dur 8F 54
Branch End. Nmbd 5D 54
Branchill. Mor 8L 79
Brand End. Linc 5L 37
Branderburgh. Mor 6B 80
Brandesburton. E Yor 3J 43
Brandeston. Suff 5J 31
Brand Green. Glos 1F 18
Brandhill. Shrp 4C 26
Brandis Corner. Devn 5D 6
Brandish Street. Som 1J 7
Brandiston. Norf 7H 39
Brandon. Dur 8F 54
Brandon. Linc 5G 37
Brandon. Nmbd 8H 61
Brandon. Suff 3D 30
Brandon. Warw 4B 28
Brandon Bank. Cambs 3C 30
Brandon Creek. Norf 2C 30
Brandon Parva. Norf 1G 31
Brandsby. N Yor 8C 48
Brandy Wharf. Linc 8H 43
Brane. Corn 6H 3
Bran End. Essx 1C 22
Branksome. Pool 6J 9
Bransbury. Hants 1B 10
Bransby. Linc 2F 36
Branscombe. Devn 7L 7
Bransford. Worc 6F 26
Bransgore. Hants 6K 9
Bransholme. Hull 4J 43
Bransley. Shrp 4E 26
Branston. Leics 7F 36
Branston. Linc 3H 37
Branston. Staf 7L 35
Branston Booths. Linc 3H 37
Branstone. IOW 7C 10
Bransty. Cumb 3J 45
Brant Broughton. Linc 4G 37
Brantham. Suff 8H 31
Branthwaite. Cumb
nr. Caldbeck 8G 53
nr. Workington 2K 45
Brantingham. E Yor 5G 43
Branton. Nmbd 8H 61
Branton. S Yor 7D 42
Branton Green. N Yor 1B 42
Branxholme. Bord 8B 60
Branxton. Nmbd 6F 60
Brassington. Derbs 4L 35
Brasted. Kent 8A 22
Brasted Chart. Kent 8A 22
The Bratch. Staf 2G 27
Brathens. Abers 6F 72
Bratoft. Linc 3A 38
Brattleby. Linc 1G 37
Bratton. Som 1J 7
Bratton. Telf 8E 34
Bratton. Wilts 8H 19
Bratton Clovelly. Devn 6D 6
Bratton Fleming. Devn 2F 6
Bratton Seymour. Som 3E 8
Braughing. Herts 1L 21
Braulen Lodge. High 2C 70
Braunston. Nptn 5C 28
Braunstone Town. Leics 1C 28
Braunston-in-Rutland. Rut 1F 28
Braunton. Devn 2D 6
Brawby. N Yor 8E 48
Brawl. High 5L 85
Brawlbin. High 6B 86
Bray. Wind 6G 21
Braybrooke. Nptn 3E 28
Brayford. Devn 2F 6
Bray Shop. Corn 8C 6
Braystones. Cumb 4K 45
Brayton. N Yor 4D 42
Bray Wick. Wind 6F 20
Brazacott. Corn 6B 6
Brea. Corn 4K 3
Breach. W Sus 5E 10
Breachwood Green. Herts 1J 21
Breacleit. W Isl 8E 82
Breaden Heath. Shrp 6C 34
Breadsall. Derbs 5A 36
Breadstone. Glos 3F 18
Breage. Corn 6K 3
Breakachy. High 1E 70
Breakish. High 3H 69
Bream. Glos 3E 18
Breamore. Hants 4K 9
Bream's Meend. Glos 3E 18
Brean. Som 8A 18
Breanais. W Isl 1A 76
Brearton. N Yor 1M 41
Breascleit. W Isl 8F 82
Breaston. Derbs 6B 36
Brecais Àrd. High 3H 69
Brecais Iosal. High 3H 69
Brechfa. Carm 3M 15
Brechin. Ang 2K 67
Breckles. Norf 2F 30
Brecon. Powy 2K 17
Bredbury. G Man 8H 41
Brede. E Sus 4E 12
Bredenbury. Here 6E 26
Bredfield. Suff 6J 31
Bredgar. Kent 7E 22
Bredhurst. Kent 7D 22
Bredicot. Worc 6H 27
Bredon. Worc 8H 27
Bredon's Norton. Worc 8H 27
Bredwardine. Here 7B 26
Breedon on the Hill. Leics 7B 36
Breibhig. W Isl
on Barra 6C 74
on Isle of Lewis 8H 83
Breich. W Lot 3H 59
Breightmet. G Man 7F 40
Breighton. E Yor 4E 42
Breinton. Here 8C 26
Breinton Common. Here 8C 26
Breiwick. Shet 3E 90
Brelston Green. Here 1D 18
Bremhill. Wilts 6H 19
Brenachie. High 6H 79
Brenchley. Kent 1C 12
Brendon. Devn 1G 7
Brent Cross. G Lon 5K 21
Brent Eleigh. Suff 7F 30
Brentford. G Lon 6J 21
Brentingby. Leics 8E 36
Brent Knoll. Som 8B 18
Brent Pelham. Herts 8M 29
Brentwood. Essx 4B 22
Brenzett. Kent 3G 13
Brereton. Staf 8J 35
Brereton Cross. Staf 8J 35
Brereton Green. Ches E 3F 34
Brereton Heath. Ches E 3G 35
Bressingham. Norf 3G 31
Bretby. Derbs 7L 35
Bretford. Warw 4B 28
Bretforton. Worc 7J 27
Bretherdale Head. Cumb 5D 46
Bretherton. Lanc 5C 40
Brettabister. Shet 2E 90
Brettenham. Norf 3F 30
Brettenham. Suff 6F 30
Bretton. Flin 3B 34
Bretton. Pet 1J 29
Brewlands Bridge. Ang 1E 66
Brewood. Staf 1G 27
Briantspuddle. Dors 6G 9
Bricket Wood. Herts 3J 21
Bricklehampton. Worc 7H 27
Bride. IOM 4D 44
Bridekirk. Cumb 8F 52
Bridell. Pemb 2H 15
Bridestowe. Devn 7E 6
Brideswell. Abers 2E 72
Bridford. Devn 7H 7
Bridge. Corn 4K 3
Bridge. Kent 8H 23
Bridge. Som 5B 8
Bridge End. Bed 6H 29
Bridge End. Cumb
nr. Broughton in Furness 5M 45
nr. Dalston 7H 53
Bridge End. Linc 6J 37
Bridge End. Shet 4D 90
Bridgefoot. Ang 4G 67
Bridgefoot. Cumb 2K 45
Bridge Green. Essx 8A 30
Bridgehampton. Som 3D 8
Bridge Hewick. N Yor 8M 47
Bridgehill. Dur 6D 54
Bridgemary. Hants 5C 10
Bridgemere. Ches E 5F 34
Bridgemont. Derbs 1J 35
Bridgend. Abers
nr. Huntly 2E 72
nr. Peterhead 2K 73
Bridgend. Ang
nr. Brechin 1J 67
nr. Kirriemuir 3G 67
Bridgend. Arg
nr. Lochgilphead 8C 64
on Islay 3C 56
Bridgend. B'end 6J 17
Bridgend. Cumb 4B 46
Bridgend. Devn 7H 5
Bridgend. Fife 6G 67
Bridgend. High 8D 78
Bridgend. Mor 2C 72
Bridgend. Per 5E 66
Bridgend. W Lot 2J 59
Bridgend of Lintrathen. Ang 2F 66
Bridgeness. Falk 1J 59
Bridge of Alford. Abers 4E 72
Bridge of Allan. Stir 8A 66
Bridge of Avon. Mor 2A 72
Bridge of Awe. Arg 5E 64
Bridge of Balgie. Per 3K 65
Bridge of Brown. High 3M 71
Bridge of Cally. Per 2E 66
Bridge of Canny. Abers 6F 72
Bridge of Dee. Dum 5B 52
Bridge of Don. Aber 4J 73
Bridge of Dun. Ang 2K 67
Bridge of Dye. Abers 7F 72
Bridge of Earn. Per 6E 66
Bridge of Ericht. Per 2K 65
Bridge of Feugh. Abers 6G 73
Bridge of Gairn. Abers 6C 72
Bridge of Gaur. Per 2K 65
Bridge of Muchalls. Abers 6H 73
Bridge of Oich. High 5D 70
Bridge of Orchy. Arg 4H 65
Bridge of Walls. Shet 2C 90
Bridge of Weir. Ren 3B 58
Bridge Reeve. Devn 4F 6
Bridgerule. Devn 5B 6
Bridge Sollers. Here 7C 26
Bridge Street. Suff 7E 30
Bridge Town. Warw 6L 27
Bridgetown. Devn 5L 5
Bridgetown. Som 2J 7
Bridge Trafford. Ches W 2C 34
Bridgeyate. S Glo 6E 18
Bridgham. Norf 3F 30
Bridgnorth. Shrp 2F 26
Bridgtown. Staf 1H 27
Bridgwater. Som 2B 8
Bridlington. E Yor 1J 43

Bridport – Carlton-on-Trent

Bridport. Dors 6C 8
Bridstow. Here 1D 18
Brierfield. Lanc 4G 41
Brierley. Glos 2E 18
Brierley. Here 6C 26
Brierley. S Yor 6B 42
Brierley Hill. W Mid 3H 27
Brierton. Hart 8H 55
Briestfield. W Yor 6L 41
Brigg. N Lin 7H 43
Briggate. Norf 7K 39
Briggswath. N Yor 5F 48
Brigham. Cumb 8E 52
Brigham. E Yor 2H 43
Brighouse. W Yor 5K 41
Brighstone. IOW 7B 10
Brightgate. Derbs 4L 35
Brighthampton. Oxon 3A 20
Brightholmlee. S Yor 8L 41
Brightley. Devn 6F 6
Brightling. E Sus 3C 12
Brightlingsea. Essx 2G 23
Brighton. Brig 106 (5L 11)
Brighton. Corn 6B 4
Brighton Hill. Hants 1D 10
Brightons. Falk 2H 59
Brightwalton. W Ber 6B 20
Brightwalton Green. W Ber 6B 20
Brightwell. Suff 7J 31
Brightwell Baldwin. Oxon 4D 20
Brightwell-cum-Sotwell.
Oxon 4C 20
Brigmerston. Wilts 1K 9
Brignall. Dur 4J 47
Brig o' Turk. Stir 7K 65
Brigsley. NE Lin 7K 43
Brigsteer. Cumb 7C 46
Brigstock. Nptn 3G 29
Brill. Buck 2D 20
Brill. Corn 6L 3
Brilley. Here 7A 26
Brimaston. Pemb 4F 14
Brimfield. Here 5D 26
Brimington. Derbs 2B 36
Brimley. Devn 8H 7
Brimpsfield. Glos 2H 19
Brimpton. W Ber 7C 20
Brims. Orkn 3D 86
Brimscombe. Glos 3G 19
Brimstage. Mers 1B 34
Brincliffe. S Yor 1M 35
Brind. E Yor 4E 42
Brindister. Shet
nr. West Burrafirth 2C 90
nr. West Lerwick 4E 90
Brindle. Lanc 5D 40
Brindley. Ches E 4D 34
Brindley Ford. Stoke 4G 35
Brineton. Staf 8G 35
Bringhurst. Leics 2F 28
Bringsty Common. Here 6E 26
Brington. Cambs 4H 29
Brinian. Orkn 7D 88
Briningham. Norf 6G 39
Brinkhill. Linc 2L 37
Brinkley. Cambs 6C 30
Brinklow. Warw 4B 28
Brinkworth. Wilts 5J 19
Brinscall. Lanc 5E 40
Brinscombe. Som 8C 18
Brinsley. Notts 5B 36
Brinsworth. S Yor 1B 36
Brinton. Norf 6G 39
Brisco. Cumb 6J 53
Brisley. Norf 7F 38
Brislington. Bris 6E 18
Brissenden Green. Kent 2F 12
Bristol. Bris 107 (6D 18)
Bristol Airport. N Som 7D 18
Briston. Norf 6G 39
Britannia. Lanc 5G 41
Britford. Wilts 3K 9
Brithdir. Cphy 4L 17
Brithdir. Cdgn 2K 15
Brithdir. Gwyn 1G 25
Briton Ferry. Neat 5G 17
Britwell Salome. Oxon 4D 20
Brixham. Torb 6M 5
Brixton. Devn 6H 5
Brixton. G Lon 6L 21
Brixton Deverill. Wilts 2G 9
Brixworth. Nptn 4E 28
Brize Norton. Oxon 3M 19
The Broad. Here 5C 26
Broad Alley. Worc 5G 27
Broad Blunsdon. Swin 4K 19
Broadbottom. G Man 8H 41
Broadbridge. W Sus 5F 10
Broadbridge Heath. W Sus 2J 11
Broad Campden. Glos 8K 27
Broad Chalke. Wilts 3J 9
Broadclyst. Devn 6J 7
Broadfield. Inv 2B 58
Broadfield. Pemb 6H 15
Broadfield. W Sus 2K 11
Broadford. High 3H 69
Broadford Bridge. W Sus 3H 11
Broadgate. Cumb 6L 45
Broad Green. Cambs 6C 30
Broad Green. C Beds 7G 29
Broad Green. Worc
nr. Bromsgrove 4H 27
nr. Worcester 6F 26
Broad Haven. Pemb 5E 14
Broadhaven. High 6E 86
Broad Heath. Staf 7G 35
Broadheath. G Man 1F 34
Broadheath. Worc 5E 26
Broadheath Common.
Worc 6G 27
Broadhembury. Devn 5L 7
Broadhempston. Devn 5L 5
Broad Hill. Cambs 4B 30
Broad Hinton. Wilts 6K 19
Broadholme. Derbs 5A 36
Broadholme. Linc 2F 36
Broadlay. Carm 6K 15
Broad Laying. Hants 7B 20
Broadley. Lanc 6G 41
Broadley. Mor 7C 80
Broadley Common. Essx 3M 21
Broad Marston. Worc 7K 27
Broadmayne. Dors 7F 8
Broadmere. Hants 1D 10
Broadmoor. Pemb 6G 15
Broad Oak. Carm 2E 16
Broad Oak. Cumb 5L 45
Broad Oak. Devn 6K 7
Broad Oak. Dors 4F 8
Broad Oak. E Sus
nr. Hastings 4E 12
nr. Heathfield 3C 12
Broad Oak. Here 1C 18
Broad Oak. Kent 7H 23
Broadoak. Dors 6C 8
Broadoak. Glos 2E 18
Broadoak. Hants 4C 10
Broadrashes. Mor 8D 80
Broadsea. Abers 7J 81
Broad's Green. Essx 2C 22
Broadshard. Som 4C 8
Broadstairs. Kent 7K 23
Broadstone. Pool 6J 9
Broadstone. Shrp 3D 26
Broad Street. E Sus 4E 12
Broad Street. Kent
nr. Ashford 1H 13
nr. Maidstone 8E 22
Broad Street Green. Essx 3E 22
Broad Town. Wilts 6J 19
Broadwas. Worc 6F 26
Broadwath. Cumb 6J 53
Broadway. Carm
nr. Kidwelly 6K 15
nr. Laugharne 6J 15
Broadway. Pemb 5E 14
Broadway. Som 4B 8
Broadway. Suff 4K 31
Broadway. Worc 8J 27
Broadwell. Glos
nr. Cinderford 2D 18
nr. Stow-on-the-Wold 1L 19
Broadwell. Oxon 3L 19
Broadwell. Warw 5B 28
Broadwell House. Nmbd 6C 54
Broadwey. Dors 7E 8
Broadwindsor. Dors 5C 8
Broadwoodkelly. Devn 5F 6
Broadwoodwidger. Devn 7D 6
Broallan. High 1E 70
Brobury. Here 7B 26
Brochel. High 1G 69
Brockaghboy. Caus 3F 93
Brockamin. Worc 6F 26
Brockbridge. Hants 4D 10
Brockdish. Norf 4J 31
Brockencote. Worc 4G 27
Brockenhurst. Hants 5L 9
Brocketsbrae. S Lan 6G 59
Brockford Street. Suff 5H 31
Brockhall. Nptn 5D 28
Brockham. Surr 1J 11
Brockhampton. Glos
nr. Bishop's Cleeve 1H 19
nr. Sevenhampton 1J 19
Brockhampton. Here 8D 26
Brockhill. Bord 7A 60
Brockholes. W Yor 6K 41
Brockhurst. Hants 5C 10
Brocklesby. Linc 6J 43
Brockley. N Som 7C 18
Brockley Corner. Suff 4E 30
Brockley Green. Suff
nr. Bury St Edmunds 7D 30
nr. Haverhill 6E 30
Brockleymoor. Cumb 8J 53
Brockmoor. W Mid 3H 27
Brockton. Shrp
nr. Bishop's Castle 3B 26
nr. Madeley 1F 26
nr. Much Wenlock 2D 26
nr. Pontesbury 1B 26
Brockton. Staf 6G 35
Brockton. Telf 8F 34
Brockweir. Glos 3D 18
Brockworth. Glos 2G 19
Brocton. Staf 8H 35
Brodick. N Ayr 6K 57
Brodie. Mor 8K 79
Brodiesord. Abers 8E 80
Brodsworth. S Yor 7C 42
Brogaig. High 7F 76
Brogborough. C Beds 8G 29
Brokenborough. Wilts 5H 19
Broken Cross. Ches E 2G 35
Bromborough. Mers 1B 34
Bromdon. Shrp 3E 26
Brome. Suff 4H 31
Brome Street. Suff 4H 31
Bromeswell. Suff 6K 31
Bromfield. Cumb 7F 52
Bromfield. Shrp 4C 26
Bromford. W Mid 2K 27
Bromham. Bed 6H 29
Bromham. Wilts 7H 19
Bromley. G Lon 7M 21
Bromley. Herts 1M 21
Bromley. Shrp 2F 26
Bromley Cross. G Man 6F 40
Bromley Green. Kent 2F 12
Bromley Wood. Staf 7K 35
Brompton. Medw 7D 22
Brompton. N Yor
nr. Northallerton 6A 48
nr. Scarborough 7G 49
Brompton. Shrp 1D 26
Brompton-on-Swale. N Yor 6L 47
Brompton Ralph. Som 2K 7
Brompton Regis. Som 2J 7
Bromsash. Here 1E 18
Bromsberrow. Glos 8F 26
Bromsberrow Heath. Glos 8F 26
Bromsgrove. Worc 4H 27
Bromstead Heath. Staf 8F 34
Bromyard. Here 6E 26
Bromyard Downs. Here 6E 26
Bronaber. Gwyn 7G 33
Broncroft. Shrp 3D 26
Brongest. Cdgn 2K 15
Brongwyn. Cdgn 2J 15
Bronington. Wrex 6C 34
Bronllys. Powy 1L 17
Bronnant. Cdgn 6F 24
Bronwydd Arms. Carm 4L 15
Bronydd. Powy 8M 25
Bronygarth. Shrp 6A 34
Brook. Carm 6J 15
Brook. Hants
nr. Cadnam 4L 9
nr. Romsey 3M 9
Brook. IOW 7A 10
Brook. Kent 1G 13
Brook. Surr
nr. Guildford 1H 11
nr. Haslemere 2G 11
Brooke. Norf 2J 31
Brooke. Rut 1F 28
Brookeborough. Ferm 6C 92
Brookenby. Linc 8K 43
Brook End. Worc 7G 27
Brookend. Glos 3E 18
Brookfield. Lanc 4D 40
Brookfield. Ren 3C 58
Brookhouse. Lanc 1D 40
Brookhouse. S Yor 1C 36
Brookhouse Green. Ches E 3G 35
Brookhouses. Staf 5H 35
Brookhurst. Mers 1B 34
Brookland. Kent 3F 12
Brooklands. G Man 8F 40
Brooklands. Shrp 5D 34
Brookmans Park. Herts 3K 21
Brooks. Powy 3L 25
Brooksby. Leics 8D 36
Brooks Green. W Sus 3J 11
Brook Street. Essx 4B 22
Brook Street. Kent 2F 12
Brook Street. W Sus 3L 11
Brookthorpe. Glos 2G 19
Brookville. Norf 2D 30
Brookwood. Surr 8G 21
Broom. C Beds 7J 29
Broom. Fife 7G 67
Broom. Warw 6J 27
Broome. Norf 2K 31
Broome. Shrp
nr. Cardington 2D 26
nr. Craven Arms 3C 26
Broome. Worc 4H 27
Broomedge. Warr 1F 34
Broomend. Abers 4G 73
Broomer's Corner. W Sus 3J 11
Broomfield. Abers 2J 73
Broomfield. Essx 2D 22
Broomfield. Kent
nr. Herne Bay 7H 23
nr. Maidstone 8E 22
Broomfield. Som 2M 7
Broomfleet. E Yor 5F 42
Broom Green. Norf 7F 38
Broomhall. Ches E 5E 34
Broomhall. Wind 7G 21
Broomhaugh. Nmbd 5D 54
Broom Hill. Dors 5J 9
Broom Hill. Worc 4H 27
Broomhill. High
nr. Grantown-on-Spey 3K 71
nr. Invergordon 6H 79
Broomhill. Norf 1C 30
Broomhill. S Yor 7B 42
Broomhillbank. Dum 2F 52
Broomholm. Norf 6K 39
Broomlands. Dum 1E 52
Broomley. Nmbd 5D 54
Broom of Moy. Mor 8L 79
Broompark. Dur 7F 54
Broom's Green. Glos 8F 26
Brora. High 3K 79
Broseley. Shrp 1E 26
Brotherhouse Bar. Linc 8K 37
Brotheridge Green. Worc 7G 27
Brotherlee. Dur 8C 54
Brothertoft. Linc 5K 37
Brotherton. N Yor 5B 42
Brotton. Red C 4D 48
Broubster. High 5B 86
Brough. Cumb 4F 46
Brough. Derbs 1K 35
Brough. E Yor 5G 43
Brough. High 4D 86
Brough. Notts 4F 36
Brough. Orkn
nr. Finstown 8C 88
nr. St Margaret's Hope 3F 86
Brough. Shet
nr. Benston 2E 90
nr. Booth of Toft 6J 91
on Bressay 3F 90
on Whalsay 1F 90
Broughall. Shrp 5D 34
Brougham. Cumb 3D 46
Brough Lodge. Shet 4K 91
Broughshane. ME Ant 3G 93
Brough Sowerby. Cumb 4F 46
Broughton. Cambs 4K 29
Broughton. Flin 3B 34
Broughton. Hants 2M 9
Broughton. Lanc 4D 40
Broughton. Mil 8F 28
Broughton. Nptn 4F 28
Broughton. N Lin 7G 43
Broughton. N Yor
nr. Malton 8E 48
nr. Skipton 2H 41
Broughton. Orkn 5D 88
Broughton. Oxon 8B 28
Broughton. Bord 6K 59
Broughton. Staf 6F 34
Broughton. V Glam 7J 17
Broughton Astley. Leics 2C 28
Broughton Beck. Cumb 7A 46
Broughton Cross. Cumb 8E 52
Broughton Gifford. Wilts 7G 19
Broughton Green. Worc 5H 27
Broughton Hackett. Worc 6H 27
Broughton in Furness.
Cumb 6M 45
Broughton Mills. Cumb 5M 45
Broughton Moor. Cumb 8E 52
Broughton Park. G Man 7G 41
Broughton Poggs. Oxon 3L 19
Broughtown. Orkn 5F 88
Broughty Ferry. D'dee 4H 67
Browland. Shet 2C 90
Brownbread Street. E Sus 4C 12
Brown Candover. Hants 2C 10
Brown Edge. Lanc 6B 40
Brown Edge. Staf 4H 35
Brownhill. Bkbn 4E 40
Brownhill. Shrp 7C 34
Brownhills. Shrp 6E 34
Brownhills. W Mid 1J 27
Brown Knowl. Ches W 4C 34
Brownlow. Ches E 3G 35
Brownlow Heath. Ches E 3G 35
Brown's Green. W Mid 2J 27
Brownshill. Glos 3G 19
Brownston. Devn 6J 5
Brownstone. Devn 5G 7
Browston Green. Norf 1L 31
Broxa. N Yor 6G 49
Broxbourne. Herts 3L 21
Broxburn. E Lot 2D 60
Broxburn. W Lot 2J 59
Broxholme. Linc 2G 37
Broxted. Essx 1B 22
Broxton. Ches W 4C 34
Broxwood. Here 6B 26
Broyle Side. E Sus 4A 12
Brù. W Isl 7G 83
Bruach Mairi. W Isl 8H 83
Bruairnis. W Isl 5D 74
Bruan. High 8E 86
Bruar Lodge. Per 8J 71
Brucehill. W Dun 2B 58
Brucklay. Abers 8J 81
Bruera. Ches W 3C 34
Bruern Abbey. Oxon 1L 19
Bruichladdich. Arg 3B 56
Bruisyard. Suff 5K 31
Bruisyard Street. Suff 5K 31
Brund. Staf 3K 35
Brundall. Norf 1K 31
Brundish. Norf 2K 31
Brundish. Suff 5J 31
Brundish Street. Suff 4J 31
Brunery. High 8J 69
Brunswick Village. Tyne 4F 54
Brunthwaite. W Yor 3J 41
Bruntingthorpe. Leics 2D 28
Brunton. Fife 5G 67
Brunton. Nmbd 7K 61
Brunton. Wilts 8L 19
Brushford. Devn 5F 6
Brushford. Som 3J 7
Brusta. W Isl 5L 75
Bruton. Som 2E 8
Bryansford. New M 7H 93
Bryanston. Dors 5G 9
Bryant's Bottom. Buck 4F 20
Brydekirk. Dum 4F 52
Brymbo. Cnwy 3H 33
Brymbo. Wrex 4A 34
Brympton D'Evercy. Som 4D 8
Bryn. Carm 6M 15
Bryn. G Man 7D 40
Bryn. Neat 5H 17
Bryn. Shrp 3A 26
Brynamman. Carm 3G 17
Brynberian. Pemb 3H 15
Brynbryddan. Neat 5G 17
Bryncae. Rhon 6J 17
Bryncethin. B'end 6J 17
Bryncir. Gwyn 6D 32
Bryncoch. Neat 5G 17
Bryncroes. Gwyn 7B 32
Bryncrug. Gwyn 2F 24
Bryn Du. IOA 3C 32
Bryn Eden. Gwyn 8G 33
Bryn Eglwys. Gwyn 4F 32
Bryneglwys. Den 6L 33
Brynford. Flin 3L 33
Bryn Gates. G Man 7D 40
Bryn Golau. Rhon 6K 17
Bryngwran. IOA 3C 32
Bryngwyn. Mon 3B 18
Bryngwyn. Powy 8L 25
Bryn-henllan. Pemb 3G 15
Brynhoffnant. Cdgn 1K 15
Bryn-llwyn. Den 2K 33
Brynllywarch. Powy 4L 25
Bryn-mawr. Gwyn 7B 32
Brynmawr. Blae 3L 17
Brynmenyn. B'end 6J 17
Brynmill. Swan 5F 16
Brynna. Rhon 6J 17
Brynrefail. Gwyn 4E 32
Brynrefail. IOA 2D 32
Brynsadler. Rhon 6K 17
Bryn-Saith Marchog. Den 5K 33
Brynsiencyn. IOA 4D 32
Brynteg. IOA 2D 32
Brynteg. Wrex 4B 34
Brynygwenyn. Mon 2B 18
Bryn-y-maen. Cnwy 3H 33
Buaile nam Bodach. W Isl 5D 74
Bualintur. High 3F 68
Bubbenhall. Warw 4A 28
Bubwith. E Yor 4E 42
Buccleuch. Bord 8M 59
Buchanan Smithy. Stir 1C 58
Buchanhaven. Abers 1L 73
Buchanty. Per 5C 66
Buchany. Stir 7M 65
Buchley. E Dun 2D 58
Buchlyvie. Stir 8K 65
Buckabank. Cumb 7H 53
Buckden. Cambs 5J 29
Buckden. N Yor 8H 47
Buckenham. Norf 1K 31
Buckerell. Devn 5L 7
Buckfast. Devn 5K 5
Buckfastleigh. Devn 5K 5
Buckhaven. Fife 8G 67
Buckholm. Bord 6B 60
Buckholt. Here 2D 18
Buckhorn Weston. Dors 3F 8
Buckhurst Hill. Essx 4M 21
Buckie. Mor 7D 80
Buckingham. Buck 8D 28
Buckland. Buck 2F 20
Buckland. Glos 8J 27
Buckland. Here 6D 26
Buckland. Herts 8L 29
Buckland. Kent 1K 13
Buckland. Oxon 4M 19
Buckland. Surr 8K 21
Buckland Brewer. Devn 3D 6
Buckland Common. Buck 3G 21
Buckland Dinham. Som 8F 18
Buckland Filleigh. Devn 5D 6
Buckland in the Moor. Devn 8G 7
Buckland Monachorum.
Devn 5G 5
Buckland Newton. Dors 5E 8
Buckland Ripers. Dors 7E 8
Buckland St Mary. Som 4A 8
Buckland-tout-Saints. Devn 7K 5
Bucklebury. W Ber 6C 20
Bucklegate. Linc 6L 37
Bucklegh. Devn 3D 6
Buckler's Hard. Hants 6B 10
Bucklesham. Suff 7J 31
Buckley. Flin 3A 34
Buckley Green. Warw 5K 27
Buckley Hill. Mers 8B 40
Bucklow Hill. Ches E 1F 34
Buckminster. Leics 7F 36
Bucknall. Linc 3J 37
Bucknall. Stoke 5H 35
Bucknell. Oxon 1C 20
Bucknell. Shrp 4B 26
Buckpool. Mor 7D 80
Bucksburn. Aber 5H 73
Buck's Cross. Devn 3C 6
Bucks Green. W Sus 2H 11
Buckshaw Village. Lanc 5D 40
Bucks Hill. Herts 3H 21
Bucks Horn Oak. Hants 1F 10
Buck's Mills. Devn 3C 6
Buckton. E Yor 8J 49
Buckton. Here 4B 26
Buckton. Nmbd 6H 61
Buckton Vale. G Man 7H 41
Buckworth. Cambs 4J 29
Budby. Notts 3D 36
Bude. Corn 5B 6
Budge's Shop. Corn 6F 4
Budlake. Devn 5J 7
Budle. Nmbd 6J 61
Budleigh Salterton. Devn 7K 7
Budock Water. Corn 5L 3
Buerton. Ches E 5E 34
Buffler's Holt. Buck 8D 28
Bugbrooke. Nptn 6D 28
Buglawton. Ches E 3G 35
Bugle. Corn 6C 4
Bugthorpe. E Yor 2E 42
Buildwas. Shrp 1E 26
Builth Road. Powy 7K 25
Builth Wells. Powy 7K 25
Bulbourne. Herts 2G 21
Bulby. Linc 7H 37
Bulcote. Notts 5D 36
Buldoo. High 5A 86
Bulford. Wilts 1K 9
Bulford Camp. Wilts 1K 9
Bulkeley. Ches E 4D 34
Bulkington. Warw 3A 28
Bulkington. Wilts 8H 19
Bulkworthy. Devn 4C 6
Bullamoor. N Yor 6A 48
Bull Bay. IOA 1D 32
Bullbridge. Derbs 4A 36
Bullgill. Cumb 8E 52
Bull Hill. Hants 6M 9
Bullinghope. Here 8D 26
Bull's Green. Herts 2K 21
Bullwood. Arg 2L 57
Bulmer. Essx 7E 30
Bulmer. N Yor 1D 42
Bulmer Tye. Essx 8E 30
Bulphan. Thur 5C 22
Bulverhythe. E Sus 5D 12
Bulwark. Abers 1J 73
Bulwell. Nott 5C 36
Bulwick. Nptn 2G 29
Bumble's Green. Essx 3M 21
Bun Abhainn Eadarra. W Isl 3C 76
Bunacaimb. High 7H 69
Bun a' Mhuillinn. W Isl 4D 74
Bunarkaig. High 7B 70
Bunbury. Ches E 4D 34
Bunchrew. High 1G 71
Bundalloch. High 3K 69
Buness. Shet 3L 91
Bunessan. Arg 5J 63
Bungay. Suff 3K 31
Bunkegivie. High 4F 70
Bunker's Hill. Cambs 1M 29
Bunker's Hill. Suff 1M 31
Bunkers Hill. Linc 4K 37
Bunloit. High 3F 70
Bunnahabhain. Arg 2D 56
Bunny. Notts 7C 36
Bunoich. High 5D 70
Bunree. High 1E 64
Bunroy. High 7C 70
Buntait. High 2E 70
Buntingford. Herts 1L 21
Bunting's Green. Essx 8E 30
Bunwell. Norf 2H 31
Burbage. Derbs 2J 35
Burbage. Leics 2B 28
Burbage. Wilts 7L 19
Burcher. Here 5B 26
Burchett's Green. Wind 5F 20
Burcombe. Wilts 2J 9
Burcot. Oxon 4C 20
Burcot. Worc 4H 27
Burcote. Shrp 2F 26
Burcott. Buck 1F 20
Burcott. Som 1D 8
Burdale. N Yor 1F 42
Burdrop. Oxon 8A 28
Bures. Suff 8F 30
The Burf. Worc 5G 27
Burford. Oxon 2L 19
Burford. Shrp 5D 26
Burg. Arg 3J 63
Burgate Great Green. Suff 4G 31
Burgate Little Green. Suff 4G 31
Burgess Hill. W Sus 4L 11
Burgh. Suff 6J 31
Burgh by Sands. Cumb 6H 53
Burgh Castle. Norf 1L 31
Burghclere. Hants 7B 20
Burghead. Mor 7M 79
Burghfield. W Ber 7D 20
Burghfield Common.
W Ber 7D 20
Burghfield Hill. W Ber 7D 20
Burgh Heath. Surr 8K 21
Burghill. Here 7C 26
Burgh le Marsh. Linc 3B 38
Burgh Muir. Abers 4G 73
Burgh next Aylsham. Norf 7J 39
Burgh on Bain. Linc 1K 37
Burgh St Margaret. Norf 8L 39
Burgh St Peter. Norf 2L 31
Burghwallis. S Yor 6C 42
Burham. Kent 7D 22
Buriton. Hants 3E 10
Burland. Ches E 4E 34
Burland. Shet 4D 90
Burlawn. Corn 5B 4
Burleigh. Glos 3G 19
Burleigh. Wind 6F 20
Burlescombe. Devn 4K 7
Burleston. Dors 6F 8
Burlestone. Devn 7L 5
Burley. Hants 5L 9
Burley. Rut 8F 36
Burley. W Yor 4L 41
Burleydam. Ches E 5E 34
Burley Gate. Here 7D 26
Burley in Wharfedale.
W Yor 3K 41
Burley Street. Hants 5L 9
Burley Woodhead. W Yor 3K 41
Burlingjobb. Powy 6A 26
Burlington. Shrp 8F 34
Burlton. Shrp 7C 34
Burmantofts. W Yor 4M 41
Burmarsh. Kent 2H 13
Burmington. Warw 8L 27
Burn. N Yor 5C 42
Burnage. G Man 8G 41
Burnaston. Derbs 6L 35
Burnbanks. Cumb 4D 46
Burnby. E Yor 3F 42
Burncross. S Yor 8M 41
Burneside. Cumb 6D 46
Burness. Orkn 5F 88
Burneston. N Yor 7M 47
Burnett. Bath 7E 18
Burnfoot. E Ayr 1K 51
Burnfoot. Per 7C 66
Burnfoot. Bord
nr. Hawick 8C 60
nr. Roberton 8B 60
Burngreave. S Yor 1A 36
Burnham. Buck 5G 21
Burnham. N Lin 6H 43
Burnham Deepdale. Norf 5E 38
Burnham Green. Herts 2K 21
Burnham Market. Norf 5E 38
Burnham Norton. Norf 5E 38
Burnham-on-Crouch. Essx 4F 22
Burnham-on-Sea. Som 1B 8
Burnham Overy Staithe.
Norf 5E 38
Burnham Overy Town. Norf 5E 38
Burnham Thorpe. Norf 5E 38
Burnhaven. Abers 1L 73
Burnhead. Dum 2C 52
Burnhervie. Abers 4G 73
Burnhill Green. Staf 1F 26
Burnhope. Dur 7E 54
Burnhouse. N Ayr 4B 58
Burniston. N Yor 6H 49
Burnlee. W Yor 7K 41
Burnley. Lanc 4G 41
Burnmouth. Bord 3G 61
Burn Naze. Lanc 3B 40
Burn of Cambus. Stir 7M 65
Burnopfield. Dur 6E 54
Burnsall. N Yor 1J 41
Burnside. Ang 2J 67
Burnside. Ant
nr. Antrim 4G 93
nr. Ballyclare 4H 93
Burnside. E Ayr 8D 58
Burnside. Per 7E 66
Burnside. Shet 6G 91
Burnside. S Lan 4E 58
Burnside. W Lot
nr. Broxburn 2J 59
nr. Winchburgh 2J 59
Burntcommon. Surr 8H 21
Burnt Heath. Essx 1G 23
Burntheath. Derbs 6L 35
Burnt Hill. W Ber 6C 20
Burnt Houses. Dur 3K 47
Burntisland. Fife 1L 59
Burnt Oak. G Lon 4K 21
Burnton. E Ayr 1K 51
Burntstalk. Norf 6D 38
Burntwood. Staf 1J 27
Burntwood Green. Staf 1J 27
Burnt Yates. N Yor 1L 41
Burnwynd. Edin 3K 59
Burpham. Surr 8H 21
Burpham. W Sus 5H 11
Burradon. Nmbd 1C 54
Burradon. Tyne 4F 54
Burrafirth. Shet 2L 91
Burragarth. Shet 3K 91
Burras. Corn 5K 3
Burraton. Corn 6G 5
Burravoe. Shet
nr. North Roe 5H 91
on Mainland 1D 90
on Yell 6K 91
Burray Village. Orkn 2F 86
Burrells. Cumb 4E 46
Burrelton. Per 4F 66
Burren. New M 7G 93
Burren Bridge. New M 7H 93
Burridge. Hants 4C 10
Burridge. Som 5B 8
Burrigill. High 8D 86
Burrill. N Yor 7L 47
Burringham. N Lin 7F 42
Burrington. Devn 4F 6
Burrington. Here 4C 26
Burrington. N Som 8C 18
Burrough End. Cambs 6C 30
Burrough Green. Cambs 6C 30
Burrough on the Hill. Leics 8E 36
Burroughston. Orkn 7E 88
Burrow. Devn 7K 7
Burrow. Som 1J 7
Burrowbridge. Som 3B 8
Burrowhill. Surr 7G 21
Burry. Swan 7L 15
Burry Green. Swan 7L 15
Burry Port. Carm 6L 15
Burscough. Lanc 6C 40
Burscough Bridge. Lanc 6C 40
Bursea. E Yor 4F 42
Burshill. E Yor 3H 43
Bursledon. Hants 5B 10
Burslem. Stoke 5G 35
Burstall. Suff 7G 31
Burstock. Dors 5C 8
Burston. Devn 5G 7
Burston. Norf 3H 31
Burston. Staf 6H 35
Burstow. Surr 1L 11
Burstwick. E Yor 5K 43
Burtersett. N Yor 7G 47
Burtholme. Cumb 5K 53
Burthorpe. Suff 5D 30
Burthwaite. Cumb 7J 53
Burtle. Som 1C 8
Burtoft. Linc 6K 37
Burton. Ches W
nr. Kelsall 3D 34
nr. Neston 2B 34
Burton. Dors
nr. Christchurch 6K 9
nr. Dorchester 6E 8
Burton. Nmbd 6J 61
Burton. Pemb 6F 14
Burton. Som 1L 7
Burton. Wilts
nr. Chippenham 6G 19
nr. Warminster 2G 9
Burton. Wrex 4B 34
Burton Agnes. E Yor 1J 43
Burton Bradstock. Dors 7C 8
Burton-by-Lincoln. Linc 2G 37
Burton Coggles. Linc 7G 37
Burton Constable. E Yor 4J 43
Burton Corner. Linc 5L 37
Burton End. Cambs 7C 30
Burton End. Essx 1B 22
Burton Fleming. E Yor 8H 49
Burton Green. Warw 4L 27
Burton Green. Wrex 4B 34
Burton Hastings. Warw 3B 28
Burton-in-Kendal. Cumb 8D 46
Burton in Lonsdale. N Yor 8E 46
Burton Joyce. Notts 5D 36
Burton Latimer. Nptn 4G 29
Burton Lazars. Leics 8E 36
Burton Leonard. N Yor 1M 41
Burton on the Wolds. Leics 7C 36
Burton Overy. Leics 2D 28
Burton Pedwardine. Linc 5J 37
Burton Pidsea. E Yor 4K 43
Burton Salmon. N Yor 5B 42
Burton's Green. Essx 1E 22
Burton Stather. N Lin 6F 42
Burton upon Stather. N Lin 6F 42
Burton upon Trent. Staf 7L 35
Burton Wolds. Leics 7D 36
Burtonwood. Warr 8D 40
Burwardsley. Ches W 4D 34
Burwarton. Shrp 3E 26
Burwash. E Sus 3C 12
Burwash Common. E Sus 3C 12
Burwash Weald. E Sus 3C 12
Burwell. Cambs 5B 30
Burwell. Linc 2L 37
Burwen. IOA 1D 32
Burwick. Orkn 3F 86
Bury. Cambs 3K 29
Bury. G Man 6G 41
Bury. Som 3J 7
Bury. W Sus 4H 11
Burybank. Staf 6G 35
Bury End. Worc 8J 27
Bury Green. Herts 1A 22
Bury St Edmunds. Suff 5E 30
Burythorpe. N Yor 1E 42
Busbridge. Surr 1G 11
Busby. E Ren 4D 58
Busby. Per 5D 66
Buscot. Oxon 4L 19
Bush. Corn 5B 6
The Bush. M Ulst 5F 93
Bush Bank. Here 6C 26
Bushbury. W Mid 1H 27
Bushby. Leics 1D 28
Bushey. Dors 7H 9
Bushey. Herts 4J 21
Bushey Heath. Herts 4J 21
Bush Green. Norf
nr. Attleborough 2G 31
nr. Harleston 3J 31
Bush Green. Suff 6F 30
Bushley. Worc 8G 27
Bushley Green. Worc 8G 27
Bushmead. Bed 5J 29
Bushmills. Caus 1F 93
Bushmoor. Shrp 3C 26
Bushton. Wilts 6J 19
Bushy Common. Norf 8F 38
Busk. Cumb 7L 53
Buslingthorpe. Linc 1H 37
Bussage. Glos 3G 19
Bussex. Som 2B 8
Busta. Shet 1D 90
Butcher's Cross. E Sus 3B 12
Butcombe. N Som 7D 18
Bute Town. Cphy 4L 17
Butleigh. Som 2D 8
Butleigh Wootton. Som 2D 8
Butlers Marston. Warw 7M 27
Butley. Suff 6K 31
Butley High Corner. Suff 7K 31
Butlocks Heath. Hants 5B 10
Butterburn. Cumb 4L 53
Buttercrambe. N Yor 2E 42
Butterknowle. Dur 3K 47
Butterleigh. Devn 5J 7
Buttermere. Cumb 3L 45
Buttermere. Wilts 7M 19
Buttershaw. W Yor 5K 41
Butterstone. Per 3D 66
Butterton. Staf
nr. Leek 4J 35
nr. Stoke-on-Trent 5G 35
Butterwick. Dur 3A 48
Butterwick. Linc 5L 37
Butterwick. N Yor
nr. Malton 8E 48
nr. Weaverthorpe 8G 49
Butteryhaugh. Nmbd 2L 53
Butt Green. Ches E 4E 34
Buttington. Powy 1A 26
Buttonbridge. Shrp 4F 26
Buttonoak. Shrp 4F 26
Buttsash. Hants 5B 10
Butt's Green. Essx 3D 22
Butt Yeats. Lanc 1D 40
Buxhall. Suff 6G 31
Buxted. E Sus 3A 12
Buxton. Derbs 2J 35
Buxton. Norf 7J 39
Buxworth. Derbs 1J 35
Bwcle. Flin 3A 34
Bwlch. Powy 2L 17
Bwlchderwin. Gwyn 6D 32
Bwlchgwyn. Wrex 4A 34
Bwlch-Llan. Cdgn 7E 24
Bwlchnewydd. Carm 4K 15
Bwlchtocyn. Gwyn 8C 32
Bwlch-y-cibau. Powy 1L 25
Bwlchyddar. Powy 8L 33
Bwlch-y-fadfa. Cdgn 2L 15
Bwlch-y-ffridd. Powy 3K 25
Bwlch y Garreg. Powy 3K 25
Bwlch-y-groes. Pemb 3J 15
Bwlch-y-sarnau. Powy 5K 25
Bybrook. Kent 1G 13
Byermoor. Tyne 6E 54
Byers Garth. Dur 7G 55
Byers Green. Dur 8F 54
Byfield. Nptn 6C 28
Byfleet. Surr 7H 21
Byford. Here 7B 26
Bygrave. Herts 8K 29
Byker. Tyne 5F 54
Byland Abbey. N Yor 8C 48
Bylchau. Cnwy 4J 33
Byley. Ches W 3F 34
Bynea. Carm 7M 15
Byram. N Yor 5B 42
Byrness. Nmbd 1A 54
Bystock. Devn 7K 7
Bythorn. Cambs 4H 29
Byton. Here 5B 26
Bywell. Nmbd 5D 54
Byworth. W Sus 3G 11

C

Cabharstadh. W Isl 2E 76
Cabourne. Linc 7J 43
Cabrach. Arg 3D 56
Cabrach. Mor 3C 72
Cabragh. M Ulst 5E 92
Cabus. Lanc 3C 40
Cadbury. Devn 5J 7
Cadder. E Dun 2E 58
Caddington. C Beds 2H 21
Caddonfoot. Bord 6B 60
Cadeby. Leics 1B 28
Cadeby. S Yor 7C 42
Cadeleigh. Devn 5J 7
Cade Street. E Sus 3C 12
Cadgwith. Corn 7L 3
Cadham. Fife 7F 66
Cadishead. G Man 8F 40
Cadle. Swan 5F 16
Cadley. Lanc 4D 40
Cadley. Wilts
nr. Ludgershall 8L 19
nr. Marlborough 7L 19
Cadmore End. Buck 4E 20
Cadnam. Hants 4L 9
Cadney. N Lin 7H 43
Cadole. Flin 4M 33
Cadoxton-juxta-Neath. Neat 5G 17
Cadwell. Herts 8J 29
Cadwst. Den 7K 33
Caeathro. Gwyn 4E 32
Caehopkin. Powy 3H 17
Caenby. Linc 1H 37
Caerau. B'end 5H 17
Caerau. Card 7L 17
Cae'r-bont. Powy 3H 17
Cae'r-bryn. Carm 3E 16
Caerdeon. Gwyn 1F 24
Caerdydd. Card 107 (7L 17)
Caerfarchell. Pemb 4D 14
Caerffili. Cphy 6L 17
Caerfyrddin. Carm 5L 15
Caergeiliog. IOA 3C 32
Caergwrle. Flin 4B 34
Caergybi. IOA 2B 32
Caerlaverock. Per 6B 66
Caerleon. Carm 4B 18
Caerleon. Newp 4B 18
Caerllion. Newp 4B 18
Caernarfon. Gwyn 4D 32
Caerphilly. Cphy 6L 17
Caersws. Powy 3K 25
Caerwedros. Cdgn 1K 15
Caerwent. Mon 4C 18
Caerwys. Flin 3L 33
Caim. IOA 2F 32
Caio. Carm 1F 16
Cairinis. W Isl 7K 75
Cairisiadar. W Isl 8D 82
Cairminis. W Isl 5B 76
Cairnbaan. Arg 8C 64
Cairnbulg. Abers 7K 81
Cairncross. Ang 8D 72
Cairndow. Arg 6F 64
Cairness. Abers 7K 81
Cairneyhill. Fife 1J 59
Cairngarroch. Dum 7F 50
Cairnhill. Abers 2F 72
Cairnie. Abers 1D 72
Cairnorrie. Abers 1H 73
Cairnryan. Dum 5F 50
Cairston. Orkn 8B 88
Caister-on-Sea. Norf 8M 39
Caistor. Linc 7J 43
Caistor St Edmund. Norf 1J 31
Caistron. Nmbd 1C 54
Cakebole. Worc 4G 27
Calais Street. Suff 7F 30
Calanais. W Isl 8F 82
Calbost. W Isl 2F 76
Calbourne. IOW 7B 10
Calceby. Linc 2L 37
Calcot. Glos 2J 19
Calcot Row. W Ber 6D 20
Calcott. Kent 7H 23
Calcott. Shrp 8C 34
Caldback. Shet 3L 91
Caldbeck. Cumb 8H 53
Caldbergh. N Yor 7J 47
Caldecote. Cambs
nr. Cambridge 6L 29
nr. Peterborough 3J 29
Caldecote. Herts 8K 29
Caldecote. Nptn 6D 28
Caldecote. Warw 2A 28
Caldecott. Nptn 5G 29
Caldecott. Oxon 4B 20
Caldecott. Rut 2F 28
Calderbank. N Lan 3F 58
Calder Bridge. Cumb 4K 45
Calderbrook. G Man 6H 41
Caldercruix. N Lan 3G 59
Calder Grove. W Yor 6M 41
Calder Mains. High 6B 86
Caldermill. S Lan 5E 58
Calder Vale. Lanc 3D 40
Calderwood. S Lan 4E 58
Caldicot. Mon 5C 18
Caldwell. Derbs 8L 35
Caldwell. N Yor 4K 47
Caldy. Mers 2M 33
Calebrack. Cumb 8H 53
Caledon. M Ulst 6E 92
Calf Heath. Staf 1H 27
Calford Green. Suff 7C 30
Calfsound. Orkn 6E 88
Calgary. Arg 2J 63
Califer. Mor 8L 79
California. Cambs 3B 30
California. Falk 2H 59
California. Norf 8M 39
California. Suff 7H 31
Calke. Derbs 7A 36
Callakille. High 8H 77
Callaly. Nmbd 1D 54
Callander. Stir 7L 65
Callaughton. Shrp 2E 26
Callendoun. Arg 1B 58
Callestick. Corn 3L 3
Calligarry. High 5H 69
Callington. Corn 5F 4
Callingwood. Staf 7K 35
Callow. Here 8C 26
Callowell. Glos 3G 19
Callow End. Worc 7G 27
Callow Hill. Wilts 5J 19
Callow Hill. Worc
nr. Bewdley 4F 26
nr. Redditch 5J 27
Calmore. Hants 4M 9
Calmsden. Glos 3J 19
Calne. Wilts 6H 19
Calow. Derbs 2B 36
Calshot. Hants 5B 10
Calstock. Corn 5G 5
Calstone Wellington. Wilts 7J 19
Calthorpe. Norf 6H 39
Calthorpe Street. Norf 7L 39
Calthwaite. Cumb 7J 53
Calton. N Yor 2H 41
Calton. Staf 4K 35
Calveley. Ches E 4D 34
Calver. Derbs 2L 35
Calverhall. Shrp 6E 34
Calverleigh. Devn 4J 7
Calverley. W Yor 4L 41
Calvert. Buck 1D 20
Calverton. Mil 8E 28
Calverton. Notts 5D 36
Calvine. Per 1B 66
Calvo. Cumb 6F 52
Cam. Glos 4F 18
Camaghael. High 8B 70
Camas-luinie. High 3L 69
Camasnacroise. High 2C 64
Camastianavaig. High 2G 69
Camasunary. High 4G 69
Camault Muir. High 1F 70
Camb. Shet 4K 91
Camber. E Sus 4F 12
Camberley. Surr 7F 20
Camberwell. G Lon 6L 21
Camblesforth. N Yor 5D 42
Cambo. Nmbd 3D 54
Cambois. Nmbd 3G 55
Camborne. Corn 5K 3
Cambourne. Cambs 6L 29
Cambridge. Cambs 107 (6A 30)
Cambridge. Glos 3F 18
Cambrose. Corn 4K 3
Cambus. Clac 8B 66
Cambusbarron. Stir 8A 66
Cambuskenneth. Stir 8B 66
Cambuslang. S Lan 3E 58
Cambusnethan. N Lan 4G 59
Cambus o' May. Abers 6D 72
Camden Town. G Lon 5K 21
Cameley. Bath 8E 18
Camelford. Corn 3D 4
Camelon. Falk 1G 59
Camelsdale. W Sus 2F 10
Camer's Green. Worc 8F 26
Camerton. Bath 8E 18
Camerton. Cumb 8E 52
Camerton. E Yor 5K 43
Camghouran. Per 2K 65
Camlough. New M 7G 93
Cammachmore. Abers 6J 73
Cammeringham. Linc 1G 37
Camore. High 4H 79
The Camp. Glos 3H 19
Campbelton. N Ayr 4L 57
Campbeltown. Arg 7G 57
Campbeltown Airport. Arg 7F 56
Cample. Dum 2C 52
Campmuir. Per 4F 66
Campsall. S Yor 6C 42
Campsea Ashe. Suff 6K 31
Camps End. Cambs 7C 30
Campsey. Derr 2D 92
Campton. C Beds 8J 29
Camptoun. E Lot 2C 60
Camptown. Bord 8D 60
Camrose. Pemb 4F 14
Camserney. Per 3B 66
Camster. High 7D 86
Camus Croise. High 4H 69
Camuscross. High 4H 69
Camusdarach. High 6H 69
Camusnagaul. High
nr. Fort William 8A 70
nr. Little Loch Broom 5A 78
Camus Park. Derr 4C 92
Camusteel. High 1J 69
Camusterrach. High 1J 69
Camusvrachan. Per 3L 65
Canada. Hants 4L 9
Canadia. E Sus 4D 12
Canaston Bridge. Pemb 5G 15
Candlesby. Linc 3A 38
Candle Street. Suff 4G 31
Candy Mill. S Lan 5J 59
Cane End. Oxon 6D 20
Canewdon. Essx 4F 22
Canford Cliffs. Pool 7J 9
Canford Heath. Pool 6J 9
Canford Magna. Pool 6J 9
Cangate. Norf 8K 39
Canham's Green. Suff 5G 31
Canholes. Derbs 2J 35
Canisbay. High 4E 86
Canley. W Mid 4M 27
Cann. Dors 3G 9
Cann Common. Dors 3G 9
Cannich. High 2D 70
Cannington. Som 2A 8
Cannock. Staf 8H 35
Cannock Wood. Staf 8J 35
Canonbie. Dum 4H 53
Canon Bridge. Here 7C 26
Canon Frome. Here 7E 26
Canon Pyon. Here 7C 26
Canons Ashby. Nptn 6C 28
Canonstown. Corn 5J 3
Canterbury. Kent 107 (8H 23)
Cantley. Norf 1K 31
Cantley. S Yor 7D 42
Cantlop. Shrp 1D 26
Canton. Card 7L 17
Cantray. High 1H 71
Cantraybruich. High 1H 71
Cantraywood. High 1H 71
Cantsdam. Fife 8E 66
Cantsfield. Lanc 8E 46
Canvey Island. Essx 5D 22
Canwick. Linc 3G 37
Canworthy Water. Corn 6B 6
Caol. High 8B 70
Caolas. Arg 3F 62
Caolas. W Isl 6C 74
Caolas Liubharsaigh. W Isl 1E 74
Caolas Scalpaigh. W Isl 4D 76
Caolas Stocinis. W Isl 4C 76
Caol Ila. Arg 2D 56
Caol Loch Ailse. High 3J 69
Caol Reatha. High 3J 69
Capel. Kent 1C 12
Capel. Surr 1J 11
Capel Bangor. Cdgn 4F 24
Capel Betws Lleucu. Cdgn 7F 24
Capel Coch. IOA 2D 32
Capel Curig. Cnwy 5G 33
Capel Cynon. Cdgn 2K 15
Capel Dewi. Carm 4L 15
Capel Dewi. Cdgn
nr. Aberystwyth 4F 24
nr. Llandysul 2L 15
Capel Garmon. Cnwy 5H 33
Capel Green. Suff 7K 31
Capel Gwyn. IOA 3C 32
Capel Gwynfe. Carm 2G 17
Capel Hendre. Carm 3E 16
Capel Isaac. Carm 2E 16
Capel Iwan. Carm 3J 15
Capel-le-Ferne. Kent 2J 13
Capel Llanilltern. Card 7K 17
Capel Mawr. IOA 3D 32
Capel Newydd. Pemb 3J 15
Capel St Andrew. Suff 7K 31
Capel St Mary. Suff 8G 31
Capel Seion. Carm 5M 15
Capel Seion. Cdgn 5F 24
Capel Uchaf. Gwyn 6D 32
Capel-y-ffin. Powy 8A 26
Capenhurst. Ches W 2B 34
Capernwray. Lanc 8D 46
Capheaton. Nmbd 3D 54
Cappagh. M Ulst 5E 92
Cappercleuch. Bord 7L 59
Capplegill. Dum 1F 52
Capton. Devn 6L 5
Capton. Som 2K 7
Caputh. Per 4D 66
Caradon Town. Corn 8B 6
Carbis Bay. Corn 5J 3
Carbost. High
nr. Loch Harport 2E 68
nr. Portree 1F 68
Carbrook. S Yor 1A 36
Carbrooke. Norf 1F 30
Carburton. Notts 2D 36
Carcluie. S Ayr 8B 58
Car Colston. Notts 5E 36
Carcroft. S Yor 7C 42
Cardenden. Fife 8F 66
Cardeston. Shrp 8B 34
Cardewlees. Cumb 6H 53
Cardiff. Card 107 (7L 17)
Cardiff Airport. V Glam 8K 17
Cardigan. Cdgn 2H 15
Cardinal's Green. Cambs 7C 30
Cardington. Bed 7H 29
Cardington. Shrp 2D 26
Cardinham. Corn 5D 4
Cardno. Abers 7J 81
Cardow. Mor 1A 72
Cardross. Arg 2B 58
Cardurnock. Cumb 6F 52
Careby. Linc 8H 37
Careston. Ang 1J 67
Carew. Pemb 6G 15
Carew Cheriton. Pemb 6G 15
Carew Newton. Pemb 6G 15
Carey. Here 8D 26
Carfin. N Lan 4F 58
Carfrae. Bord 4C 60
Cargan. ME Ant 3G 93
Cargate Green. Norf 8K 39
Cargenbridge. Dum 4D 52
Cargill. Per 4E 66
Cargo. Cumb 6H 53
Cargreen. Corn 5G 5
Carham. Nmbd 6F 60
Carhampton. Som 1K 7
Carharrack. Corn 4L 3
Carie. Per
nr. Loch Rannah 2L 65
nr. Loch Tay 4L 65
Carisbrooke. IOW 7B 10
Cark. Cumb 8B 46
Carkeel. Corn 5G 5
Carlabhagh. W Isl 7F 82
Carland Cross. Corn 3M 3
Carlbury. Darl 4L 47
Carlby. Linc 8H 37
Carlecotes. S Yor 7K 41
Carleen. Corn 6K 3
Carlesmoor. N Yor 8K 47
Carleton. Cumb
nr. Carlisle 6J 53
nr. Egremont 4K 45
nr. Penrith 3D 46
Carleton. Lanc 3B 40
Carleton. N Yor 3H 41
Carleton. W Yor 5B 42
Carleton Forehoe. Norf 1G 31
Carleton Rode. Norf 2H 31
Carleton St Peter. Norf 1K 31
Carlidnack. Corn 6L 3
Carlingcott. Bath 8E 18
Carlin How. Red C 4E 48
Carlisle. Cumb 107 (6J 53)
Carloonan. Arg 6E 64
Carlops. Bord 4K 59
Carlton. Bed 6G 29
Carlton. Cambs 6C 30
Carlton. Leics 1A 28
Carlton. N Yor
nr. Helmsley 7D 48
nr. Middleham 7J 47
nr. Selby 5D 42
Carlton. Notts 5D 36
Carlton. S Yor 6A 42
Carlton. Stoc T 3A 48
Carlton. Suff 5K 31
Carlton. W Yor 5M 41
Carlton Colville. Suff 2M 31
Carlton Curlieu. Leics 2D 28
Carlton Husthwaite. N Yor 8B 48
Carlton in Cleveland. N Yor 5C 48
Carlton in Lindrick. Notts 1C 36
Carlton-le-Moorland. Linc 4G 37
Carlton Miniott. N Yor 7A 48
Carlton-on-Trent. Notts 3F 36

A-Z Great Britain Road Atlas 123

Cwm-twrch Isaf. *Powy*	4G 17
Cwm-twrch Uchaf. *Powy*	3G 17
Cwmwysg. *Powy*	2H 17
Cwm-y-glo. *Gwyn*	4E 32
Cwmyoy. *Mon*	1B 18
Cwmystwyth. *Cdgn*	5G 25
Cwrt. *Gwyn*	2F 24
Cwrtnewydd. *Cdgn*	2L 15
Cwrt-y-Cadno. *Carm*	8F 24
Cydweli. *Carm*	6L 15
Cyffylliog. *Den*	5K 33
Cymau. *Flin*	4A 34
Cymer. *Neat*	5H 17
Cymmer. *Neat*	5H 17
Cymmer. *Rhon*	5K 17
Cyncoed. *Card*	6L 17
Cynghordy. *Carm*	1H 17
Cynheidre. *Carm*	6L 15
Cynonville. *Neat*	5H 17
Cynwyd. *Den*	6K 33
Cynwyl Elfed. *Carm*	4K 15
Cywarch. *Gwyn*	1H 25

East Halton – Ford

East Halton. N Lin 5J 43
East Ham. G Lon 5M 21
Eastham. Mers 1B 34
Eastham. Worc 5E 26
Eastham Ferry. Mers 1B 34
Easthampstead. Brac 7F 20
Easthampton. Here 5C 26
East Hanney. Oxon 4B 20
East Hanningfield. Essx 3D 22
East Hardwick. W Yor 6B 42
East Harling. Norf 3F 30
East Harlsey. N Yor 6B 48
East Harptree. Bath 8D 18
East Hartford. Nmbd 4F 54
East Harting. W Sus 4F 10
East Hatch. Wilts 3H 9
East Hatley. Cambs 6K 29
Easthaugh. Norf 8G 39
East Hauxwell. N Yor 6K 47
East Haven. Ang 4J 67
Eastheath. Wok 7F 20
East Heckington. Linc 5J 37
East Hedleyhope. Dur 7E 54
East Helmsdale. High 2L 79
East Hendred. Oxon 5B 20
East Heslerton. N Yor 8G 49
East Hoathly. E Sus 4B 12
East Holme. Dors 7G 9
Easthope. Shrp 2D 26
Easthorpe. Essx 1F 22
Easthorpe. Leics 6F 36
East Horrington. Som 1D 8
East Horsley. Surr 8H 21
East Horton. Nmbd 6H 61
Easthouses. Midl 3M 59
East Howe. Bour 6J 9
East Huntspill. Som 1B 8
East Hyde. C Beds 2J 21
East Ilsley. W Ber 5B 20
Eastington. Devn 5G 7
Eastington. Glos
nr. Northleach 2K 19
nr. Stonehouse 3F 18
East Keal. Linc 3L 37
East Kennett. Wilts 7K 19
East Keswick. W Yor 3A 42
East Kilbride. S Lan 4E 58
East Kirkby. Linc 3L 37
East Knapton. N Yor 8F 48
East Knighton. Dors 7G 9
East Knowstone. Devn 3H 7
East Knoyle. Wilts 2G 9
East Kyloe. Nmbd 6H 61
East Lambrook. Som 4C 8
East Langdon. Kent 1K 13
East Langton. Leics 2E 28
East Langwell. High 3H 79
East Lavant. W Sus 5F 10
East Lavington. W Sus 4G 11
East Layton. N Yor 5K 47
Eastleach Martin. Glos 3L 19
Eastleach Turville. Glos 3K 19
East Leake. Notts 7C 36
East Learmouth. Nmbd 6F 60
East Leigh. Devn
nr. Crediton 5F 6
nr. Modbury 6J 5
Eastleigh. Devn 3D 6
Eastleigh. Hants 4B 10
East Lexham. Norf 8E 38
East Lilburn. Nmbd 7H 61
Eastling. Kent 8F 22
East Linton. E Lot 2C 60
East Liss. Hants 3E 10
East Lockinge. Oxon 5B 20
East Looe. Corn 6E 4
East Lound. N Lin 8E 42
East Lulworth. Dors 7G 9
East Lutton. N Yor 1G 43
East Lydford. Som 2D 8
East Lyng. Som 3B 8
East Mains. Abers 6F 72
East Malling. Kent 8D 22
East Marden. W Sus 4F 10
East Markham. Notts 2E 36
East Marton. N Yor 2H 41
East Meon. Hants 3D 10
East Mersea. Essx 2G 23
East Mey. High 4E 86
East Midlands Airport.
Leics 119 (7B 36)
East Molesey. Surr 7J 21
Eastmoor. Norf 1D 30
East Morden. Dors 6H 9
East Morton. W Yor 3K 41
East Ness. N Yor 8D 48
East Newton. E Yor 4K 43
East Newton. N Yor 8D 48
Eastney. Port 6D 10
Eastnor. Here 8F 26
East Norton. Leics 1E 28
East Nynehead. Som 3L 7
East Oakley. Hants 8C 20
Eastoft. N Lin 6F 42
East Ogwell. Devn 8H 7
Easton. Cambs 4J 29
Easton. Cumb
nr. Burgh by Sands 6G 53
nr. Longtown 4J 53
Easton. Devn 7G 7
Easton. Dors 8E 8
Easton. Hants 2C 10
Easton. Linc 7G 37
Easton. Norf 8H 39
Easton. Som 1D 8
Easton. Suff 6J 31
Easton. Wilts 6G 19
Easton Grey. Wilts 5G 19
Easton-in-Gordano. N Som 6D 18
Easton Maudit. Nptn 6F 28
Easton on the Hill. Nptn 1H 29
Easton Royal. Wilts 7L 19
East Orchard. Dors 4G 9
East Ord. Nmbd 4G 61
East Panson. Devn 6C 6
East Peckham. Kent 1C 12
East Pennard. Som 2D 8
East Perry. Cambs 5J 29
East Pitcorthie. Fife 7J 67
East Portlemouth. Devn 8K 5
East Prawle. Devn 8K 5
East Preston. W Sus 5H 11
East Putford. Devn 4C 6
East Quantoxhead. Som 1L 7
East Rainton. Tyne 7G 55
East Ravendale. NE Lin 8K 43
East Raynham. Norf 7E 38
Eastrea. Cambs 2K 29
East Rhidorroch Lodge. High 4C 78
Eastriggs. Dum 5G 53
East Rigton. W Yor 3A 42
Eastrington. E Yor 5E 42
East Rounton. N Yor 5B 48
East Row. N Yor 4F 48
East Rudham. Norf 7E 38
East Runton. Norf 5H 39
East Ruston. Norf 7K 39
Eastry. Kent 8K 23
East Saltoun. E Lot 3B 60
East Shaws. Dur 4J 47
East Shefford. W Ber 6A 20
Eastshore. Shet 6D 90
East Sleekburn. Nmbd 3F 54
East Somerton. Norf 8L 39
East Stockwith. Linc 8E 42
East Stoke. Dors 7G 9
East Stoke. Notts 5E 36
East Stoke. Som 4C 8
East Stour. Dors 3G 9
East Stourmouth. Kent 7J 23
East Stowford. Devn 3F 6
East Stratton. Hants 1C 10
East Studdal. Kent 1K 13
East Taphouse. Corn 5D 4
East-the-Water. Devn 3D 6
East Thirston. Nmbd 2E 54
East Tilbury. Thur 6C 22
East Tisted. Hants 2E 10
East Torrington. Linc 1J 37
East Tuddenham. Norf 8G 39
East Tytherley. Hants 3L 9
East Tytherton. Wilts 6H 19
East Village. Devn 5H 7
Eastville. Linc 4M 37
East Wall. Shrp 2D 26
East Walton. Norf 8D 38
East Week. Devn 6F 6
Eastwell. Leics 7E 36
East Wellow. Hants 3M 9
East Wemyss. Fife 8G 67
East Whitburn. W Lot 3H 59
Eastwick. Herts 2M 21
Eastwick. Shet 6H 91
East Williamston. Pemb 6G 15
East Winch. Norf 8C 38
East Winterslow. Wilts 2L 9
East Wittering. W Sus 6E 10
East Witton. N Yor 7K 47
Eastwood. Notts 5B 36
Eastwood. S'end 5E 22
East Woodburn. Nmbd 3C 54
Eastwood End. Cambs 2M 29
East Woodhay. Hants 7B 20
East Woodlands. Som 1F 8
East Worldham. Hants 2E 10
East Worlington. Devn 4G 7
East Wretham. Norf 2F 30
East Youlstone. Devn 4B 6
Eathorpe. Warw 5A 28
Eaton. Ches E 3G 35
Eaton. Ches W 3D 34
Eaton. Leics 7E 36
Eaton. Norf
nr. Heacham 6C 38
nr. Norwich 1J 31
Eaton. Notts 2E 36
Eaton. Oxon 3B 20
Eaton. Shrp
nr. Bishop's Castle 3B 26
nr. Church Stretton 3D 26
Eaton Bishop. Here 8C 26
Eaton Bray. C Beds 1G 21
Eaton Constantine. Shrp 1D 26
Eaton Hastings. Oxon 4L 19
Eaton Socon. Cambs 6J 29
Eaton upon Tern. Shrp 7E 34
Eau Brink. Norf 8B 38
Eaves Green. W Mid 3L 27
Ebberley Hill. Devn 4E 6
Ebberston. N Yor 7F 48
Ebbesbourne Wake. Wilts 3H 9
Ebblake. Dors 5K 9
Ebbsfleet. Kent 6C 22
Ebbsfleet Valley. Kent 6C 22
Ebbw Vale. Blae 4L 17
Ebchester. Dur 6E 54
Ebernoe. W Sus 3G 11
Ebford. Devn 7J 7
Ebley. Glos 3G 19
Ebnal. Ches W 5C 34
Ebrington. Glos 7K 27
Ecchinswell. Hants 8C 20
Ecclefechan. Dum 4F 52
Eccles. G Man 8F 40
Eccles. Kent 7D 22
Eccles. Bord 5E 60
Ecclesall. S Yor 1M 35
Ecclesfield. S Yor 8A 42
Eccles Green. Here 7B 26
Eccleshall. Staf 7G 35
Eccleshill. W Yor 4K 41
Ecclesmachan. W Lot 2J 59
Eccles on Sea. Norf 7L 39
Eccles Road. Norf 2G 31
Eccleston. Ches W 3C 34
Eccleston. Lanc 6D 40
Eccleston. Mers 8C 40
Eccup. W Yor 3L 41
Echt. Abers 5G 73
Eckford. Bord 7E 60
Eckington. Derbs 2B 36
Eckington. Worc 7H 27
Ecton. Nptn 5F 28
Edale. Derbs 1K 35
Eday Airport. Orkn 6E 88
Edburton. W Sus 4K 11
Edderside. Cumb 7F 52
Edderton. High 5H 79
Eddington. Kent 7H 23
Eddington. W Ber 7M 19
Eddleston. Bord 5L 59
Eddlewood. S Lan 4F 58
Eden. ME Ant 4J 93
Edenbridge. Kent 1M 11
Edendonich. Arg 5F 64
Edenfield. Lanc 6F 40
Edenhall. Cumb 8K 53
Edenham. Linc 7H 37
Edensor. Derbs 2L 35
Edentaggart. Arg 8H 65
Edenthorpe. S Yor 7D 42
Eden Vale. Dur 8H 55
Edern. Gwyn 7B 32
Ederney. Ferm 5C 92
Edgarley. Som 2D 8
Edgbaston. W Mid 3J 27
Edgcott. Buck 1D 20
Edgcott. Som 2H 7
Edge. Glos 3G 19
Edge. Shrp 1B 26
Edgebolton. Shrp 7D 34
Edge End. Glos 2D 18
Edgefield. Norf 6G 39
Edgefield Street. Norf 6G 39
Edge Green. Ches W 4C 34
Edgehead. Midl 3A 60
Edgeley. Shrp 5D 34
Edgeside. Lanc 5G 41
Edgeworth. Glos 3H 19
Edgiock. Worc 5J 27
Edgmond. Telf 8F 34
Edgmond Marsh. Telf 7F 34
Edgton. Shrp 3B 26
Edgware. G Lon 4J 21
Edgworth. Bkbn 6F 40
Edinbane. High 8E 76
Edinburgh. Edin 109 (2L 59)
Edinburgh Airport. Edin 2K 59
Edingale. Staf 8L 35
Edingley. Notts 4D 36
Edingthorpe. Norf 6K 39
Edington. Som 2B 8
Edington. Wilts 8H 19
Edingworth. Som 8B 18
Edistone. Devn 3B 6
Edithmead. Som 1B 8
Edith Weston. Rut 1G 29
Edlaston. Derbs 5K 35
Edlesborough. Buck 2G 21
Edlingham. Nmbd 1E 54
Edlington. Linc 2K 37
Edmondsham. Dors 4J 9
Edmondsley. Dur 7F 54
Edmondthorpe. Leics 8F 36
Edmonstone. Orkn 7E 88
Edmonton. Corn 4B 4
Edmonton. G Lon 4L 21
Edmundbyers. Dur 6D 54
Ednam. Bord 6E 60
Ednaston. Derbs 5L 35
Edney Common. Essx 3C 22
Edrom. Bord 4F 60
Edstaston. Shrp 6D 34
Edstone. Warw 5K 27
Edwalton. Notts 6C 36
Edwardstone. Suff 7F 30
Edwardsville. Mer T 5K 17
Edwinsford. Carm 1F 16
Edwinstowe. Notts 3D 36
Edworth. C Beds 7K 29
Edwyn Ralph. Here 6E 26
Edzell. Ang 1K 67
Efail-fach. Neat 5G 17
Efail Isaf. Rhon 6K 17
Efailnewydd. Gwyn 7C 32
Efail-rhyd. Powy 8L 33
Efailwen. Carm 4H 15
Efenechtyd. Den 5L 33
Effingham. Surr 8J 21
Effingham Common. Surr 8J 21
Effirth. Shet 2D 90
Efflinch. Staf 8K 35
Efford. Devn 5H 7
Efstigarth. Shet 4J 91
Egbury. Hants 8B 20
Egdon. Worc 6H 27
Egerton. G Man 6F 40
Egerton. Kent 1F 12
Egerton Forstal. Kent 1E 12
Eggborough. N Yor 5C 42
Eggbuckland. Plym 6G 5
Eggesford. Devn 4F 6
Eggington. C Beds 1G 21
Egginton. Derbs 7L 35
Egglescliffe. Stoc T 4B 48
Eggleston. Dur 3H 47
Egham. Surr 6H 21
Egham Hythe. Surr 6H 21
Egleton. Rut 1F 28
Eglingham. Nmbd 8J 61
Eglinton. Derr 2D 92
Eglish. M Ulst 6E 92
Egloshayle. Corn 4C 4
Egloskerry. Corn 7B 6
Eglwysbach. Cnwy 3H 33
Eglwys-Brewis. V Glam 8K 17
Eglwys Fach. Cdgn 3F 24
Eglwyswrw. Pemb 3H 15
Egmanton. Notts 3E 36
Egmere. Norf 6F 38
Egremont. Cumb 3K 45
Egremont. Mers 8B 40
Egton. N Yor 5F 48
Egton Bridge. N Yor 5F 48
Egypt. Buck 5G 21
Egypt. Hants 1B 10
Eight Ash Green. Essx 1F 22
Eight Mile Burn. Midl 4K 59
Eignaig. High 3B 64
Eilanreach. High 4K 69
Eildon. Bord 6C 60
Eileanach Lodge. High 7F 78
Eilean Fhlodaigh. W Isl 8K 75
Eilean Iarmain. High 4J 69
Einacleit. W Isl 1C 76
Eisgein. W Isl 2E 76
Eisingrug. Gwyn 7F 32
Elan Village. Powy 6J 25
Elberton. S Glo 5E 18
Elbridge. W Sus 5G 11
Elburton. Plym 6H 5
Elcho. Per 5E 66
Elcombe. Swin 5K 19
Elcot. W Ber 7A 20
Eldernell. Cambs 2L 29
Eldersfield. Worc 8G 27
Elderslie. Ren 3C 58
Elder Street. Essx 8B 30
Eldon. Dur 3L 47
Eldroth. N Yor 1F 40
Eldwick. W Yor 3K 41
Elfhowe. Cumb 6C 46
Elford. Nmbd 6J 61
Elford. Staf 8K 35
Elford Closes. Cambs 4A 30
Elgin. Mor 7B 80
Elgol. High 4G 69
Elham. Kent 1H 13
Elie. Fife 7H 67
Eling. Hants 4A 10
Eling. W Ber 6C 20
Elishaw. Nmbd 2B 54
Elizafield. Dum 4E 52
Elkesley. Notts 2D 36
Elkington. Nptn 4D 28
Elkins Green. Essx 3C 22
Elkstone. Glos 2H 19
Ellan. High 3J 71
Elland. W Yor 5K 41
Ellary. Arg 2G 57
Ellastone. Staf 5K 35
Ellbridge. Corn 5G 5
Ellel. Lanc 2C 40
Ellemford. Bord 3E 60
Ellenabeich. Arg 6B 64
Ellenborough. Cumb 8E 52
Ellenbrook. Herts 3K 21
Ellenhall. Staf 7G 35
Ellen's Green. Surr 2H 11
Ellerbeck. N Yor 6B 48
Ellerburn. N Yor 7F 48
Ellerby. N Yor 4E 48
Ellerdine. Telf 7E 34
Ellerdine Heath. Telf 7E 34
Ellerhayes. Devn 5J 7
Elleric. Arg 3E 64
Ellerker. E Yor 5G 43
Ellerton. E Yor 4E 42
Ellerton. Shrp 7F 34
Ellerton-on-Swale. N Yor 6L 47
Ellesborough. Buck 3F 20
Ellesmere. Shrp 6C 34
Ellesmere Port. Ches W 2C 34
Ellingham. Hants 5K 9
Ellingham. Norf 2K 31
Ellingham. Nmbd 7J 61
Ellingstring. N Yor 7K 47
Ellington. Cambs 4J 29
Ellington. Nmbd 2F 54
Ellington Thorpe. Cambs 4J 29
Elliot. Ang 4K 67
Ellisfield. Hants 1D 10
Ellishadder. High 7G 77
Ellistown. Leics 8B 36
Ellon. Abers 2J 73
Ellonby. Cumb 8J 53
Ellough. Suff 3L 31
Elloughton. E Yor 5G 43
Ellwood. Glos 3D 18
Elm. Cambs 1A 30
Elmbridge. Glos 2G 19
Elmbridge. Worc 5H 27
Elmdon. Essx 8A 30
Elmdon. W Mid 3K 27
Elmdon Heath. W Mid 3K 27
Elmesthorpe. Leics 2B 28
Elmfield. IOW 6D 10
Elm Hill. Dors 3G 9
Elmhurst. Staf 8K 35
Elmley Castle. Worc 7H 27
Elmley Lovett. Worc 5G 27
Elmore. Glos 2F 18
Elmore Back. Glos 2F 18
Elm Park. G Lon 5B 22
Elmscott. Devn 3B 6
Elmsett. Suff 7G 31
Elmstead. Essx 1G 23
Elmstead Heath. Essx 1G 23
Elmstead Market. Essx 1G 23
Elmsted. Kent 1H 13
Elmstone. Kent 7J 23
Elmstone Hardwicke. Glos 1H 19
Elmswell. E Yor 2G 43
Elmswell. Suff 5F 30
Elmton. Derbs 2C 36
Elphin. High 2C 78
Elphinstone. E Lot 2A 60
Elrick. Abers 5H 73
Elrick. Mor 3D 72
Elrig. Dum 7J 51
Elsdon. Nmbd 2C 54
Elsecar. S Yor 8A 42
Elsenham. Essx 1B 22
Elsfield. Oxon 2C 20
Elsham. N Lin 6H 43
Elsing. Norf 8G 39
Elslack. N Yor 3H 41
Elsrickle. S Lan 5J 59
Elstead. Surr 1G 11
Elsted. W Sus 4F 10
Elsted Marsh. W Sus 3F 10
Elsthorpe. Linc 7H 37
Elstob. Dur 3M 47
Elston. Devn 5G 7
Elston. Lanc 4E 40
Elston. Notts 5E 36
Elston. Wilts 1J 9
Elstone. Devn 4F 6
Elstow. Bed 7H 29
Elstree. Herts 4J 21
Elstronwick. E Yor 4K 43
Elswick. Lanc 4C 40
Elswick. Tyne 5F 54
Elsworth. Cambs 5L 29
Elterwater. Cumb 5B 46
Eltham. G Lon 6M 21
Eltisley. Cambs 6K 29
Elton. Cambs 2H 29
Elton. Ches W 2C 34
Elton. Derbs 3L 35
Elton. Glos 2F 18
Elton. G Man 6F 40
Elton. Here 4C 26
Elton. Notts 6E 36
Elton. Stoc T 4B 48
Elton Green. Ches W 2C 34
Eltringham. Nmbd 5D 54
Elvanfoot. S Lan 8H 59
Elvaston. Derbs 6B 36
Elveden. Suff 4E 30
Elvetham Heath. Hants 8E 20
Elvingston. E Lot 2B 60
Elvington. Kent 8J 23
Elvington. York 3E 42
Elwick. Hart 8H 55
Elwick. Nmbd 6J 61
Elworth. Ches E 3F 34
Elworth. Dors 7D 8
Elworthy. Som 2K 7
Ely. Cambs 3B 30
Ely. Card 7L 17
Emberton. Mil 7F 28
Embleton. Cumb 8F 52
Embleton. Hart 3B 48
Embleton. Nmbd 7K 61
Embo. High 4J 79
Emborough. Som 8E 18
Embo Street. High 4J 79
Embsay. N Yor 2J 41
Emery Down. Hants 5L 9
Emley. W Yor 6L 41
Emmbrook. Wok 7E 20
Emmer Green. Read 6E 20
Emmington. Oxon 3E 20
Emneth. Norf 1A 30
Emneth Hungate. Norf 1B 30
Empingham. Rut 1G 29
Empshott. Hants 2E 10
Emsworth. Hants 5E 10
Enborne. W Ber 7B 20
Enborne Row. W Ber 7B 20
Enchmarsh. Shrp 2D 26
Enderby. Leics 2C 28
Endmoor. Cumb 7D 46
Endon. Staf 4H 35
Endon Bank. Staf 4H 35
Enfield. G Lon 4L 21
Enfield Wash. G Lon 4L 21
Enford. Wilts 8K 19
Engine Common. S Glo 5E 18
Englefield. W Ber 6D 20
Englefield Green. Surr 6G 21
Englesea-brook. Ches E 4F 34
English Bicknor. Glos 2D 18
Englishcombe. Bath 7F 18
English Frankton. Shrp 7C 34
Enham Alamein. Hants 1A 10
Enmore. Som 2M 7
Ennerdale Bridge. Cumb 3K 45
Enniscaven. Corn 6B 4
Enniskillen. Ferm 6C 92
Enoch. Dum 1C 52
Enochdhu. Per 1D 66
Ensay. Arg 3J 63
Ensbury. Bour 6J 9
Ensdon. Shrp 8C 34
Ensis. Devn 3E 6
Enson. Staf 7H 35
Enstone. Oxon 1A 20
Enterkinfoot. Dum 1C 52
Enville. Staf 3G 27
Eolaigearraidh. W Isl 5D 74
Eorabus. Arg 5J 63
Eoropaidh. W Isl 5J 83
Epney. Glos 2F 18
Epperstone. Notts 5D 36
Epping. Essx 3A 22
Epping Green. Essx 3M 21
Epping Green. Herts 3K 21
Epping Upland. Essx 3M 21
Eppleby. N Yor 4K 47
Eppleworth. E Yor 4H 43
Epsom. Surr 7K 21
Epwell. Oxon 7A 28
Epworth. N Lin 7E 42
Epworth Turbary. N Lin 7E 42
Erbistock. Wrex 5B 34
Erbusaig. High 3J 69
Erchless Castle. High 1E 70
Erdington. W Mid 2K 27
Eredine. Arg 7D 64
Erganagh. Derr 4C 92
Eriboll. High 6G 85
Ericstane. Dum 8J 59
Eridge Green. E Sus 2B 12
Erines. Arg 2H 57
Eriswell. Suff 4D 30
Erith. G Lon 6B 22
Erlestoke. Wilts 8H 19
Ermine. Linc 2G 37
Ermington. Devn 6J 5
Ernesettle. Plym 6G 5
Erpingham. Norf 6H 39
Erriott Wood. Kent 8F 22
Errogie. High 3F 70
Errol. Per 5F 66
Errol Station. Per 5F 66
Erskine. Ren 2C 58
Erskine Bridge. Ren 2C 58
Ervie. Dum 5F 50
Erwarton. Suff 8J 31
Erwood. Powy 8K 25
Eryholme. N Yor 5M 47
Eryrys. Den 5M 33
Escalls. Corn 6G 3
Escomb. Dur 8E 54
Escrick. N Yor 3D 42
Esgair. Carm
nr. Carmarthen 4K 15
nr. St Clears 5J 15
Esgairgeiliog. Powy 2G 25
Esh. Dur 7E 54
Esher. Surr 7J 21
Esholt. W Yor 3K 41
Eshott. Nmbd 2F 54
Eshton. N Yor 2H 41
Esh Winning. Dur 7E 54
Eskadale. High 2E 70
Eskbank. Midl 3M 59
Eskdale Green. Cumb 4L 45
Eskdalemuir. Dum 2G 53
Eskham. Linc 8L 43
Esknish. Arg 3C 56
Esk Valley. N Yor 5F 48
Eslington Hall. Nmbd 8H 61
Esprick. Lanc 4C 40
Essendine. Rut 8H 37
Essendon. Herts 3K 21
Essich. High 2G 71
Essington. Staf 1H 27
Eston. Red C 4C 48
Estover. Plym 6H 5
Eswick. Shet 2E 90
Etal. Nmbd 6G 61
Etchilhampton. Wilts 7J 19
Etchingham. E Sus 3D 12
Etchinghill. Kent 2H 13
Etchinghill. Staf 8J 35
Etherley Dene. Dur 3K 47
Ethie Haven. Ang 3K 67
Etling Green. Norf 8G 39
Etloe. Glos 3E 18
Eton. Wind 6G 21
Eton Wick. Wind 6G 21
Etteridge. High 6G 71
Ettersgill. Dur 3G 47
Ettiley Heath. Ches E 3F 34
Ettington. Warw 7L 27
Etton. E Yor 3G 43
Etton. Pet 1J 29
Ettrick. Bord 8L 59
Ettrickbridge. Bord 7A 60
Etwall. Derbs 6L 35
Eudon Burnell. Shrp 3F 26
Eudon George. Shrp 3E 26
Euston. Suff 4E 30
Euxton. Lanc 6D 40
Evanstown. B'end 6J 17
Evanton. High 7G 79
Evedon. Linc 5H 37
Evelix. High 4H 79
Evendine. Here 7F 26
Evenjobb. Powy 5A 26
Evenley. Nptn 8C 28
Evenlode. Glos 1L 19
Even Swindon. Swin 5K 19
Evenwood. Dur 3K 47
Evenwood Gate. Dur 3K 47
Everbay. Orkn 7F 88
Evercreech. Som 2E 8
Everdon. Nptn 6C 28
Everingham. E Yor 3F 42
Everleigh. Wilts 8L 19
Everley. N Yor 7G 49
Eversholt. C Beds 8G 29
Evershot. Dors 5D 8
Eversley. Hants 7E 20
Eversley Centre. Hants 7E 20
Eversley Cross. Hants 7E 20
Everthorpe. E Yor 4G 43
Everton. C Beds 6K 29
Everton. Hants 6L 9
Everton. Mers 8B 40
Everton. Notts 8D 42
Evertown. Dum 4H 53
Evesbatch. Here 7E 26
Evesham. Worc 7J 27
Evington. Leic 1D 28
Ewden Village. S Yor 8L 41
Ewdness. Shrp 2F 26
Ewell. Surr 7K 21
Ewell Minnis. Kent 1J 13
Ewelme. Oxon 4D 20
Ewen. Glos 4J 19
Ewenny. V Glam 7J 17
Ewerby. Linc 5J 37
Ewes. Dum 2H 53
Ewesley. Nmbd 2D 54
Ewhurst. Surr 1H 11
Ewhurst Green. E Sus 3D 12
Ewhurst Green. Surr 2H 11
Ewlo. Flin 3A 34
Ewloe. Flin 3A 34
Ewood Bridge. Lanc 5F 40
Eworthy. Devn 6D 6
Ewshot. Hants 8F 20
Ewyas Harold. Here 1B 18
Exbourne. Devn 5F 6
Exbury. Hants 5B 10
Exceat. E Sus 6B 12
Exebridge. Som 3J 7
Exelby. N Yor 7L 47
Exeter. Devn 109 (6J 7)
Exeter Airport. Devn 6K 7
Exford. Som 2H 7
Exfords Green. Shrp 1C 26
Exhall. Warw 6K 27
Exlade Street. Oxon 5D 20
Exminster. Devn 7J 7
Exmouth. Devn 7K 7
Exnaboe. Shet 6D 90
Exning. Suff 5C 30
Exton. Devn 7J 7
Exton. Hants 3D 10
Exton. Rut 8G 37
Exton. Som 2J 7
Exwick. Devn 6J 7
Eyam. Derbs 2L 35
Eydon. Nptn 6C 28
Eye. Here 5C 26
Eye. Pet 1K 29
Eye. Suff 4H 31
Eye Green. Pet 1K 29
Eyemouth. Bord 3G 61
Eyeworth. C Beds 7K 29
Eyhorne Street. Kent 8E 22
Eyke. Suff 6K 31
Eynesbury. Cambs 6J 29
Eynort. High 3E 68
Eynsford. Kent 7B 22
Eynsham. Oxon 3B 20
Eyre. High
on Isle of Skye 8F 76
on Raasay 2G 69
Eythorne. Kent 1J 13
Eyton. Here 5C 26
Eyton. Shrp
nr. Bishop's Castle 3B 26
nr. Shrewsbury 8B 34
Eyton. Wrex 5B 34
Eyton on Severn. Shrp 1D 26
Eyton upon the Weald Moors.
Telf 8E 34

F

Faccombe. Hants 8A 20
Faceby. N Yor 5B 48
Faddiley. Ches E 4D 34
Fadmoor. N Yor 7D 48
Fagwyr. Swan 4F 16
Faichem. High 5C 70
Faifley. W Dun 2D 58
Fail. S Ayr 7C 58
Failand. N Som 6D 18
Failford. S Ayr 7C 58
Failsworth. G Man 7H 41
Fairbourne. Gwyn 1F 24
Fairbourne Heath. Kent 8E 22
Fairburn. N Yor 5B 42
Fairfield. Derbs 2J 35
Fairfield. Kent 3F 12
Fairfield. Worc
nr. Bromsgrove 4H 27
nr. Evesham 7J 27
Fairford. Glos 3K 19
Fair Green. Norf 8C 38
Fair Hill. Cumb 8K 53
Fairhill. S Lan 4F 58
Fair Isle Airport. Shet 2M 89
Fairlands. Surr 8G 21
Fairlie. N Ayr 4M 57
Fairlight. E Sus 4E 12
Fairlight Cove. E Sus 4E 12
Fairmile. Devn 6K 7
Fairmile. Surr 7J 21
Fairmilehead. Edin 3L 59
Fair Oak. Devn 4K 7
Fair Oak. Hants
nr. Eastleigh 4B 10
nr. Kingsclere 7C 20
Fairoak. Staf 6F 34
Fair Oak Green. Hants 7D 20
Fairseat. Kent 7C 22
Fairstead. Essx 2D 22
Fairstead. Norf 8C 38
Fairwarp. E Sus 3A 12
Fairwater. Card 7L 17
Fairy Cross. Devn 3D 6
Fakenham. Norf 6F 38
Fakenham Magna. Suff 4F 30
Fala. Midl 3B 60
Fala Dam. Midl 3B 60
Falcon. Here 8E 26
Faldingworth. Linc 1H 37
Falfield. S Glo 4E 18
Y Fali. IOA 3B 32
Falkenham. Suff 8J 31
Falkirk. Falk 1G 59
Falkland. Fife 7F 66
Fallin. Stir 8B 66
Fallowfield. G Man 8G 41
Falmer. E Sus 5L 11
Falmouth. Corn 5M 3
Falsgrave. N Yor 7H 49
Falstone. Nmbd 3M 53
Fanagmore. High 7D 84
Fancott. C Beds 1H 21
Fanellan. High 1E 70
Fangdale Beck. N Yor 6C 48
Fangfoss. E Yor 2E 42
Fankerton. Falk 1F 58
Fanmore. Arg 3K 63
Fanner's Green. Essx 2C 22
Fannich Lodge. High 7C 78
Fans. Bord 5D 60
Farcet. Cambs 2K 29
Far Cotton. Nptn 6E 28
Fareham. Hants 5C 10
Farewell. Staf 8J 35
Far Forest. Worc 4F 26
Farforth. Linc 2L 37
Far Green. Glos 3F 18
Far Hoarcross. Staf 7K 35
Faringdon. Oxon 4L 19
Farington. Lanc 5D 40
Farlam. Cumb 6K 53
Farleigh. N Som 7C 18
Farleigh. Surr 7L 21
Farleigh Hungerford. Som 8G 19
Farleigh Wallop. Hants 1D 10
Farleigh Wick. Wilts 7G 19
Farlesthorpe. Linc 2A 38
Farleton. Cumb 7D 46
Farleton. Lanc 1D 40
Farley. High 1E 70
Farley. Shrp
nr. Shrewsbury 1B 26
nr. Telford 1E 26
Farley. Staf 5J 35
Farley. Wilts 3L 9
Farley Green. Suff 6D 30
Farley Green. Surr 1H 11
Farley Hill. Wok 7E 20
Farley's End. Glos 2F 18
Farlington. N Yor 1D 42
Farlington. Port 5D 10
Farlow. Shrp 3E 26
Farmborough. Bath 7E 18
Farmcote. Glos 1J 19
Farmcote. Shrp 2F 26
Farmington. Glos 2K 19
Far Moor. G Man 7D 40
Farmoor. Oxon 3B 20
Farmtown. Mor 8E 80
Farnah Green. Derbs 5M 35
Farnborough. G Lon 7M 21
Farnborough. Hants 8F 20
Farnborough. Warw 7B 28
Farnborough. W Ber 5B 20
Farncombe. Surr 1G 11
Farndish. Bed 5G 29
Farndon. Ches W 4C 34
Farndon. Notts 4E 36
Farnell. Ang 2K 67
Farnham. Dors 4H 9
Farnham. Essx 1A 22
Farnham. N Yor 1A 42
Farnham. Suff 5K 31
Farnham. Surr 1F 10
Farnham Common. Buck 5G 21
Farnham Green. Essx 1A 22
Farnham Royal. Buck 5G 21
Farnhill. N Yor 3J 41
Farningham. Kent 7B 22
Farnley. N Yor 3L 41
Farnley Tyas. W Yor 6K 41
Farnsfield. Notts 4D 36
Farnworth. G Man 7F 40
Farnworth. Hal 1D 34
Far Oakridge. Glos 3H 19
Farr. High
nr. Bettyhill 5K 85
nr. Inverness 2G 71
nr. Kingussie 5J 71
Farraline. High 3F 70
Farringdon. Devn 6K 7
Farrington. Dors 4G 9
Farrington Gurney. Bath 8E 18
Far Sawrey. Cumb 6B 46
Farsley. W Yor 4L 41
Farthinghoe. Nptn 8C 28
Farthingstone. Nptn 6D 28
Farthorpe. Linc 2K 37
Fartown. W Yor 6K 41
Farway. Devn 6L 7
Fasag. High 8K 77
Fascadale. High 8G 69
Fasnacloich. Arg 3E 64
Fassfern. High 8M 69
Fatfield. Tyne 6G 55
Faugh. Cumb 6K 53
Fauld. Staf 7K 35
Fauldhouse. W Lot 3H 59
Faulkbourne. Essx 2D 22
Faulkland. Som 8F 18
Fauls. Shrp 6D 34
Faverdale. Darl 4L 47
Faversham. Kent 7G 23
Fawdington. N Yor 8B 48
Fawfieldhead. Staf 3J 35
Fawkham Green. Kent 7B 22
Fawler. Oxon 2A 20
Fawley. Buck 5E 20
Fawley. Hants 5B 10
Fawley. W Ber 5A 20
Fawley Chapel. Here 1D 18
Fawton. Corn 5D 4
Faxfleet. E Yor 5F 42
Faygate. W Sus 2K 11
Fazakerley. Mers 8B 40
Fazeley. Staf 1K 27
Feagour. High 6F 70
Fearann Dhomhnaill. High 5H 69
Fearby. N Yor 7K 47
Fearn. High 6J 79
Fearnan. Per 3M 65
Fearnbeg. High 8J 77
Fearnhead. Warr 8E 40
Fearnmore. High 7J 77
Featherstone. Staf 1H 27
Featherstone. W Yor 5B 42
Featherstone Castle. Nmbd 5L 53
Feckenham. Worc 5J 27
Feeny. Caus 3E 92
Feering. Essx 1E 22
Feetham. N Yor 6H 47
Feizor. N Yor 1F 40
Felbridge. Surr 2L 11
Felbrigg. Norf 6J 39
Felcourt. Surr 1L 11
Felden. Herts 3H 21
Felhampton. Shrp 3C 26
Felindre. Carm
nr. Llandeilo 2E 16
nr. Llandovery 1F 16
nr. Newcastle Emlyn 3K 15
Felindre. Powy 4L 25
Felindre. Swan 4F 16
Felindre Farchog. Pemb 3H 15
Felinfach. Cdgn 1M 15
Felinfach. Powy 1K 17
Felinfoel. Carm 6M 15
Felingwmisaf. Carm 4M 15
Felingwmuchaf. Carm 4M 15
Y Felinheli. Gwyn 4E 32
Felin Newydd. Powy
nr. Newtown 2K 25
nr. Oswestry 8M 33
Felin Wnda. Cdgn 2K 15
Felinwynt. Cdgn 1J 15
Felixkirk. N Yor 7B 48
Felixstowe. Suff 8J 31
Felixstowe Ferry. Suff 8K 31
Felkington. Nmbd 5G 61
Fell End. Cumb 6F 46
Felling. Tyne 5F 54
Fell Side. Cumb 8H 53
Felmersham. Bed 6G 29
Felmingham. Norf 7J 39
Felpham. W Sus 6G 11
Felsham. Suff 6F 30
Felsted. Essx 1C 22
Feltham. G Lon 6J 21
Felthamhill. Surr 6H 21
Felthorpe. Norf 8H 39
Felton. Here 7D 26
Felton. N Som 7D 18
Felton. Nmbd 1E 54
Felton Butler. Shrp 8B 34
Feltwell. Norf 2D 30
Fenay Bridge. W Yor 6K 41
Fence. Lanc 4G 41
Fence Houses. Tyne 6G 55
Fencott. Oxon 2C 20
Fen Ditton. Cambs 5A 30
Fen Drayton. Cambs 5L 29
Fen End. Linc 7K 37
Fen End. W Mid 4L 27
Fenham. Nmbd 5H 61
Fenham. Tyne 5F 54
Fenhouses. Linc 5K 37
Feniscowles. Bkbn 5E 40
Feniton. Devn 6K 7
Fenn Green. Shrp 3F 26
Y Fenni. Mon 2B 18
Fenn's Bank. Wrex 6D 34
Fenn Street. Medw 6D 22
Fenny Bentley. Derbs 4K 35
Fenny Bridges. Devn 6L 7
Fenny Compton. Warw 6B 28
Fenny Drayton. Leics 2M 27
Fenny Stratford. Mil 8F 28
Fenrother. Nmbd 2E 54
Fenstanton. Cambs 5L 29
Fen Street. Norf 2G 31
Fenton. Cambs 4L 29
Fenton. Cumb 6K 53
Fenton. Linc
nr. Caythorpe 4F 36
nr. Saxilby 2F 36
Fenton. Nmbd 6G 61
Fenton. Notts 1E 36
Fenton. Stoke 5G 35
Fentonadle. Corn 4C 4
Fenton Barns. E Lot 1C 60
Fenwick. E Ayr 5C 58
Fenwick. Nmbd
nr. Berwick-upon-Tweed 5H 61
nr. Hexham 4D 54
Fenwick. S Yor 6C 42
Feochaig. Arg 8G 57
Feock. Corn 5M 3
Feolin Ferry. Arg 3D 56
Feorlan. Arg 1B 50
Ferindonald. High 5H 69
Feriniquarrie. High 8C 76
Fern. Ang 1H 67
Ferndale. Rhon 5J 17
Ferndown. Dors 5J 9
Ferness. High 1K 71
Fernham. Oxon 4L 19
Fernhill. W Sus 1L 11
Fernhill Heath. Worc 6G 27
Fernhurst. W Sus 3F 10
Fernieflatt. Abers 8H 73
Ferniegair. S Lan 4F 58
Fernilea. High 2E 68
Fernilee. Derbs 2J 35
Ferrensby. N Yor 1A 42
Ferriby Sluice. N Lin 5G 43
Ferring. W Sus 5H 11
Ferrybridge. W Yor 5B 42
Ferryden. Ang 2L 67
Ferry Hill. Cambs 3L 29
Ferryhill. Aber 5J 73
Ferryhill. Dur 8F 54
Ferryhill Station. Dur 8G 55
Ferryside. Carm 5K 15
Ferryton. High 7G 79
Fersfield. Norf 3G 31
Fersit. High 8D 70
Y Ferwig. Cdgn 2H 15
Feshiebridge. High 5J 71
Fetcham. Surr 8J 21
Fetterangus. Abers 8J 81
Fettercairn. Abers 8F 72
Fewcott. Oxon 1C 20
Fewston. N Yor 2K 41
Ffairfach. Carm 2F 16
Ffair Rhos. Cdgn 6G 25
Ffaldybrenin. Carm 8F 24
Ffarmers. Carm 8F 24
Ffawyddog. Powy 3M 17
Y Fflint. Flin 3M 33
Ffodun. Powy 2M 25
Ffont-y-gari. V Glam 8K 17
Y Ffor. Gwyn 7C 32
Fforest. Carm 4E 16
Fforest-fach. Swan 5F 16
Fforest Goch. Neat 4G 17
Ffostrasol. Cdgn 2K 15
Ffos-y-ffin. Cdgn 6D 24
Ffrith. Flin 4A 34
Ffwl-y-mwn. V Glam 8K 17
Ffynnon-ddrain. Carm 4L 15
Ffynnongroyw. Flin 2L 33
Ffynnon Gynydd. Powy 8L 25
Ffynnon-oer. Cdgn 1M 15
Fiag Lodge. High 1E 78
Fidden. Arg 5J 63
Fiddington. Glos 8H 27
Fiddington. Som 1M 7
Fiddleford. Dors 4G 9
Fiddlers Hamlet. Essx 3A 22
Field. Staf 6J 35
Field Assarts. Oxon 2M 19
Field Broughton. Cumb 7B 46
Field Dalling. Norf 6G 39
Field Head. Leics 1B 28
Fieldhead. Cumb 8J 53
Fifehead Magdalen. Dors 3F 8
Fifehead Neville. Dors 4F 8
Fifehead St Quintin. Dors 4F 8
Fife Keith. Mor 8D 80
Fifield. Oxon 2L 19
Fifield. Wilts 8K 19
Fifield. Wind 6G 21
Fifield Bavant. Wilts 3J 9
Figheldean. Wilts 1K 9
Filby. Norf 8L 39
Filey. N Yor 7J 49
Filford. Dors 6C 8
Filgrave. Mil 7F 28
Filkins. Oxon 3L 19
Filleigh. Devn
nr. Crediton 4G 7
nr. South Molton 3F 6
Fillingham. Linc 1G 37
Fillongley. Warw 3L 27
Filton. S Glo 6E 18
Fimber. E Yor 1F 42
Finavon. Ang 2H 67
Fincham. Norf 1C 30
Finchampstead. Wok 7E 20
Fincharn. Arg 7D 64
Finchdean. Hants 4E 10
Finchingfield. Essx 8C 30
Finchley. G Lon 4K 21
Findern. Derbs 6M 35
Findhorn. Mor 7L 79
Findhorn Bridge. High 3J 71
Findochty. Mor 7D 80
Findo Gask. Per 5D 66
Findon. Abers 6J 73
Findon. W Sus 5J 11
Findon Mains. High 7G 79
Findon Valley. W Sus 5J 11
Finedon. Nptn 4G 29
Fingal Street. Suff 4J 31
Fingest. Buck 4E 20
Finghall. N Yor 7K 47
Fingland. Cumb 6G 53
Fingland. Dum 8F 58
Finglesham. Kent 8K 23
Fingringhoe. Essx 1G 23
Finiskaig. High 6K 69
Finmere. Oxon 8D 28
Finnart. Per 2K 65
Finningham. Suff 5G 31
Finningley. S Yor 8D 42
Finnygaud. Abers 8F 80
Finsbury. G Lon 5L 21
Finstall. Worc 5H 27
Finsthwaite. Cumb 7B 46
Finstock. Oxon 2A 20
Finstown. Orkn 8C 88
Fintona. Ferm 5D 92
Fintry. Abers 8G 81
Fintry. D'dee 4H 67
Fintry. Stir 1E 58
Finvoy. Caus 3F 93
Finwood. Warw 5K 27
Finzean. Abers 6F 72
Fionnphort. Arg 5J 63
Fionnsabhagh. W Isl 5B 76
Firbeck. S Yor 1C 36
Firby. N Yor
nr. Bedale 7L 47
nr. Malton 1E 42
Firgrove. G Man 6H 41
Firle. E Sus 5A 12
Firsby. Linc 3A 38
Firsdown. Wilts 2L 9
First Coast. High 4L 77
Firth. Shet 6J 91
Fir Tree. Dur 8E 54
Fishbourne. IOW 6C 10
Fishbourne. W Sus 5F 10
Fishburn. Dur 8G 55
Fishcross. Clac 8B 66
Fisherford. Abers 2F 72
Fisherrow. E Lot 2M 59
Fisher's Pond. Hants 3B 10
Fisher's Row. Lanc 3C 40
Fisherstreet. W Sus 2G 11
Fisherton. High 8H 79
Fisherton. S Ayr 8A 58
Fisherton de la Mere. Wilts 2H 9
Fishguard. Pemb 3F 14
Fishlake. S Yor 6D 42
Fishley. Norf 8L 39
Fishnish. Arg 3A 64
Fishpond Bottom. Dors 6B 8
Fishponds. Bris 6E 18
Fishpool. Glos 1E 18
Fishpool. G Man 6G 41
Fishpools. Powy 6L 25
Fishtoft. Linc 5L 37
Fishtoft Drove. Linc 5L 37
Fishwick. Bord 4G 61
Fiskavaig. High 2E 68
Fiskerton. Linc 2H 37
Fiskerton. Notts 4E 36
Fitch. Shet 3D 90
Fitling. E Yor 4K 43
Fittleton. Wilts 1K 9
Fittleworth. W Sus 4H 11
Fitton End. Cambs 8M 37
Fitz. Shrp 8C 34
Fitzhead. Som 3L 7
Fitzwilliam. W Yor 6B 42
Fiunary. High 3M 63
Five Ash Down. E Sus 3A 12
Five Ashes. E Sus 3B 12
Five Bells. Som 1K 7
Five Bridges. Here 7E 26
Fivehead. Som 3B 8
Fivelanes. Corn 7B 6
Fivemiletown. M Ulst 6D 92
Five Oak Green. Kent 1C 12
Five Oaks. W Sus 3H 11
Five Roads. Carm 6L 15
Five Ways. Warw 4L 27
Flack's Green. Essx 2D 22
Flackwell Heath. Buck 5F 20
Fladbury. Worc 7H 27
Fladda. Shet 5H 91
Fladdabister. Shet 4E 90
Flagg. Derbs 3K 35
Flamborough. E Yor 8K 49
Flamstead. Herts 2H 21
Flansham. W Sus 5G 11
Flasby. N Yor 2H 41
Flash. Staf 3J 35
Flashader. High 8E 76
The Flatt. Cumb 4K 53
Flaunden. Herts 3H 21
Flawborough. Notts 5E 36
Flawith. N Yor 1B 42
Flax Bourton. N Som 7D 18
Flaxby. N Yor 2A 42
Flaxholme. Derbs 5M 35
Flaxley. Glos 2E 18
Flaxley Green. Staf 8J 35
Flaxpool. Som 2L 7
Flaxton. N Yor 1D 42
Fleck. Shet 6D 90
Fleckney. Leics 2D 28
Flecknoe. Warw 5C 28
Fledborough. Notts 2F 36
Fleet. Dors 7E 8
Fleet. Hants
nr. Farnborough 8F 20
Fleet. Hants
nr. South Hayling 5E 10
Fleet. Linc 7L 37
Fleet Hargate. Linc 7L 37
Fleetville. Herts 3J 21
Fleetwood. Lanc 3B 40
Fleggburgh. Norf 8L 39
Fleisirin. W Isl 8J 83
Flemingston. V Glam 8K 17
Flemington. S Lan
nr. Glasgow 3E 58
nr. Strathaven 5F 58
Flempton. Suff 5E 30
Fleoideabhagh. W Isl 5B 76
Fletcher's Green. Kent 1B 12
Fletchertown. Cumb 7G 53
Fletching. E Sus 3M 11
Fleuchary. High 4H 79
Flexbury. Corn 5B 6
Flexford. Surr 1G 11
Flimby. Cumb 8E 52
Flimwell. E Sus 2D 12
Flint. Flin 3M 33
Flintham. Notts 5E 36
Flint Mountain. Flin 3M 33
Flinton. E Yor 4K 43
Flintsham. Here 6B 26
Flishinghurst. Kent 2D 12
Flitcham. Norf 7D 38
Flitton. C Beds 8H 29
Flitwick. C Beds 8H 29
Flixborough. N Lin 6F 42
Flixton. G Man 8F 40
Flixton. N Yor 8H 49
Flixton. Suff 3K 31
Flockton. W Yor 6L 41
Flodden. Nmbd 6G 61
Flodigarry. High 6F 76
Flood's Ferry. Cambs 2L 29
Flookburgh. Cumb 8B 46
Flordon. Norf 2H 31
Flore. Nptn 5D 28
Flotterton. Nmbd 1C 54
Flowton. Suff 7G 31
Flushing. Abers 1K 73
Flushing. Corn 5M 3
Fluxton. Devn 6K 7
Flyford Flavell. Worc 6H 27
Fobbing. Thur 5D 22
Fochabers. Mor 8C 80
Fochriw. Cphy 4L 17
Fockerby. N Lin 6F 42
Fodderty. High 8F 78
Foddington. Som 3D 8
Foel. Powy 1J 25
Foffarty. Ang 3H 67
Foggathorpe. E Yor 4E 42
Fogo. Bord 5E 60
Fogorig. Bord 5E 60
Foindle. High 7D 84
Folda. Ang 1E 66
Fole. Staf 6J 35
Foleshill. W Mid 3A 28
Foley Park. Worc 4G 27
Folke. Dors 4E 8
Folkestone. Kent 109 (2J 13)
Folkingham. Linc 6H 37
Folkington. E Sus 5B 12
Folksworth. Cambs 3J 29
Folkton. N Yor 8H 49
Folla Rule. Abers 2G 73
Follifoot. N Yor 2M 41
The Folly. Herts 2J 21
Folly Cross. Devn 5D 6
Folly Gate. Devn 6E 6
Fonmon. V Glam 8K 17
Fonthill Bishop. Wilts 2H 9
Fonthill Gifford. Wilts 2H 9
Fontmell Magna. Dors 4G 9
Fontwell. W Sus 5G 11
Font-y-gary. V Glam 8K 17
Foodieash. Fife 6G 67
Foolow. Derbs 2K 35
Footdee. Aber 5J 73
Footherley. Staf 1K 27
Foots Cray. G Lon 6A 22
Forbestown. Abers 4C 72
Force Forge. Cumb 6B 46
Force Mills. Cumb 6B 46
Forcett. N Yor 4K 47
Ford. Arg 7C 64
Ford. Buck 3E 20
Ford. Derbs 1B 36
Ford. Devn
nr. Bideford 3D 6
nr. Holbeton 6J 5
nr. Salcombe 7K 5
Ford. Glos 1J 19

A-Z Great Britain Road Atlas 127

Ford – Great Hockham

Ford. Nmbd 6G 61
Ford. Plym 6G 5
Ford. Shrp 8C 34
Ford. Som
nr. Wells 8D 18
nr. Wiveliscombe 3K 7
Ford. Staf 4J 35
Ford. W Sus 5H 11
Ford. Wilts
nr. Chippenham 6G 19
nr. Salisbury 2K 9
Forda. Devn 2D 6
Ford Barton. Devn 4J 7
Fordcombe. Kent 1B 12
Fordell. Fife 1K 59
Forden. Powy 2M 25
Ford End. Essx 2C 22
Forder Green. Devn 5K 5
Ford Green. Lanc 3C 40
Fordham. Cambs 4C 30
Fordham. Essx 1F 22
Fordham. Norf 2C 30
Fordham Heath. Essx 1F 22
Ford Heath. Shrp 8C 34
Fordhouses. W Mid 1H 27
Fordie. Per 5A 66
Fordingbridge. Hants 4K 9
Fordington. Linc 2M 37
Fordon. E Yor 8H 49
Fordoun. Abers 8G 73
Ford Street. Essx 1F 22
Ford Street. Som 4L 7
Fordton. Devn 6H 7
Fordwells. Oxon 2M 19
Fordwich. Kent 8H 23
Fordyce. Abers 7E 80
Forebridge. Staf 7H 35
Foreglen. Caus 3E 92
Foremark. Derbs 7M 35
Forest. N Yor 5L 47
Forestburn Gate. Nmbd 2D 54
Foresterseat. Mor 8A 80
Forest Green. Glos 4G 19
Forest Green. Surr 1J 11
Forest Hall. Cumb 5D 46
Forest Head. Cumb 6K 53
Forest Hill. Oxon 3C 20
Forest-in-Teesdale. Dur 3G 47
Forest Lodge. Per 8K 71
Forest Mill. Clac 8C 66
Forest Row. E Sus 2M 11
Forestside. W Sus 4E 10
Forest Town. Notts 3C 36
Forfar. Ang 2H 67
Forgandenny. Per 6D 66
Forge. Powy 3G 25
The Forge. Here 6B 26
Forge Side. Torf 4M 17
Forgewood. N Lan 4F 58
Forgie. Mor 8C 80
Forgue. Abers 1F 72
Forkill. New M 7G 93
Formby. Mers 7B 40
Forncett End. Norf 2H 31
Forncett St Mary. Norf 2H 31
Forncett St Peter. Norf 2H 31
Forneth. Per 3D 66
Fornham All Saints. Suff 5E 30
Fornham St Martin. Suff 5E 30
Forres. Mor 8L 79
Forrestfield. N Lan 3G 59
Forrest Lodge. Dum 3L 51
Forsbrook. Staf 5H 35
Forse. High 8D 86
Forsinard. High 7L 85
Forss. High 5B 86
The Forstal. Kent 2G 13
Forston. Dors 6E 8
Fort Augustus. High 5D 70
Forteviot. Per 6D 66
Fort George. High 8H 79
Forth. S Lan 4H 59
Forthampton. Glos 8G 27
Forthay. Glos 4F 18
Fortingall. Per 3M 65
Fort Matilda. Inv 2A 58
Forton. Hants 1B 10
Forton. Lanc 2C 40
Forton. Shrp 8C 34
Forton. Som 5B 8
Forton. Staf 7F 34
Forton Heath. Shrp 8C 34
Fortrie. Abers 1F 72
Fortrose. High 8H 79
Fortuneswell. Dors 8E 8
Fort William. High 8B 70
Forty Green. Buck 4G 21
Forty Hill. G Lon 4L 21
Forward Green. Suff 6G 31
Fosbury. Wilts 8M 19
Foscot. Oxon 1L 19
Fosdyke. Linc 6L 37
Foss. Per 2A 66
Fossebridge. Glos 2J 19
Foster Street. Essx 3A 22
Foston. Derbs 6K 35
Foston. Leics 2D 28
Foston. Linc 5F 36
Foston. N Yor 1D 42
Foston on the Wolds. E Yor 2J 43
Fotherby. Linc 8L 43
Fothergill. Cumb 8E 52
Fotheringhay. Nptn 2H 29
Foubister. Orkn 1G 87
Foula Airport. Shet 4B 90
Foul Anchor. Cambs 8A 38
Foulbridge. Cumb 7J 53
Foulden. Norf 2D 30
Foulden. Bord 4G 61
Foul Mile. E Sus 4C 12
Foulridge. Lanc 3G 41
Foulsham. Norf 7G 39
Fountainhall. Bord 5B 60
The Four Alls. Shrp 6E 34
Four Ashes. Staf
nr. Cannock 1H 27
nr. Kinver 3G 27
Four Ashes. Suff 4G 31
Four Crosses. Powy
nr. Llanerfyl 2K 25
nr. Llanymynech 8A 34
Four Crosses. Staf 1H 27
Four Elms. Kent 1A 12
Four Forks. Som 2M 7
Four Gotes. Cambs 8A 38
Four Lane End. S Yor 7L 41
Four Lane Ends. Lanc 2D 40
Four Lanes. Corn 5K 3
Fourlanes End. Ches E 4G 35
Four Marks. Hants 2D 10
Four Mile Bridge. IOA 3B 32
Four Oaks. E Sus 3E 12
Four Oaks. Glos 1E 18
Four Oaks. W Mid 3L 27
Four Roads. Carm 6L 15
Four Roads. IOM 8B 44
Fourstones. Nmbd 5B 54
Four Throws. Kent 3D 12
Fovant. Wilts 3J 9
Foveran. Abers 3J 73
Fowey. Corn 6D 4
Fowlershill. Aber 4J 73
Fowley Common. Warr 8E 40
Fowlis. Ang 4G 67
Fowlis Wester. Per 5C 66
Fowlmere. Cambs 7M 29
Fownhope. Here 8D 26
Fox Corner. Surr 8G 21
Foxcote. Glos 2J 19
Foxcote. Som 8F 18
Foxdale. IOM 7B 44
Foxearth. Essx 7E 30
Foxfield. Cumb 6M 45
Foxham. Wilts 6H 19
Fox Hatch. Essx 4B 22
Foxhole. Corn 6B 4
Foxholes. N Yor 8H 49
Foxhunt Green. E Sus 4B 12
Fox Lane. Hants 8F 20
Foxley. Norf 7G 39
Foxley. Nptn 6D 28
Foxley. Wilts 5G 19
Foxlydiate. Worc 5J 27
Fox Street. Essx 1G 23
Foxt. Staf 5J 35
Foxton. Cambs 7M 29
Foxton. Dur 3A 48
Foxton. Leics 3D 28
Foxton. N Yor 6B 48
Foxup. N Yor 8G 47
Foxwist Green. Ches W 3E 34
Foxwood. Shrp 4E 26
Foy. Here 1D 18
Foyers. High 3E 70
Foynesfield. High 8J 79
Fraddam. Corn 5J 3
Fraddon. Corn 6B 4
Fradley. Staf 8K 35
Fradley South. Staf 8K 35
Fradswell. Staf 6H 35
Fraisthorpe. E Yor 1J 43
Framfield. E Sus 3A 12
Framingham Earl. Norf 1J 31
Framingham Pigot. Norf 1J 31
Framlingham. Suff 5J 31
Frampton. Dors 6E 8
Frampton. Linc 6L 37
Frampton Cotterell. S Glo 5E 18
Frampton Mansell. Glos 3H 19
Frampton on Severn. Glos 3F 18
Frampton West End. Linc 5K 37
Framsden. Suff 6H 31
Framwellgate Moor. Dur 7F 54
Franche. Worc 4G 27
Frandley. Ches W 2E 34
Frankby. Mers 2M 33
Frankfort. Norf 7K 39
Frankley. Worc 3H 27
Frank's Bridge. Powy 7L 25
Frankton. Warw 4B 28
Frankwell. Shrp 8C 34
Frant. E Sus 2B 12
Fraserburgh. Abers 7J 81
Frating Green. Essx 1G 23
Fratton. Port 5D 10
Freathy. Corn 6G 5
Freckenham. Suff 4C 30
Freckleton. Lanc 5C 40
Freeby. Leics 7F 36
Freefolk Priors. Hants 1B 10
Freehay. Staf 5J 35
Freeland. Oxon 2B 20
Freester. Shet 2E 90
Freethorpe. Norf 1L 31
Freiston. Linc 5L 37
Freiston Shore. Linc 5L 37
Fremington. Devn 2E 6
Fremington. N Yor 6J 47
Frenchay. S Glo 6E 18
Frenchbeer. Devn 7F 6
Frenich. Stir 7J 65
Frensham. Surr 1F 10
Frenze. Norf 3H 31
Fresgoe. High 5A 86
Freshfield. Mers 7A 40
Freshford. Bath 7F 18
Freshwater. IOW 7M 9
Freshwater Bay. IOW 7M 9
Freshwater East. Pemb 7G 15
Fressingfield. Suff 4J 31
Freston. Suff 8H 31
Freswick. High 5E 86
Fretherne. Glos 3F 18
Frettenham. Norf 8J 39
Freuchie. Fife 7F 66
Freystrop. Pemb 5F 14
Friar's Gate. E Sus 2A 12
Friar Waddon. Dors 7E 8
Friday Bridge. Cambs 1A 30
Friday Street. E Sus 5C 12
Friday Street. Surr 1J 11
Fridaythorpe. E Yor 2F 42
Friden. Derbs 3K 35
Friern Barnet. G Lon 4K 21
Friesthorpe. Linc 1H 37
Frieston. Linc 5G 37
Frieth. Buck 4E 20
Friezeland. Notts 4B 36
Frilford. Oxon 4B 20
Frilsham. W Ber 6C 20
Frimley. Surr 8F 20
Frimley Green. Surr 8F 20
Frindsbury. Medw 7D 22
Fring. Norf 6D 38
Fringford. Oxon 1D 20
Frinsted. Kent 8E 22
Frinton-on-Sea. Essx 2J 23
Friockheim. Ang 3J 67
Friog. Gwyn 1F 24
Frisby. Leics 1E 28
Frisby on the Wreake.
Leics 8D 36
Friskney. Linc 4A 38
Friskney Eaudyke. Linc 4A 38
Friston. E Sus 6B 12
Friston. Suff 5L 31
Fritchley. Derbs 4A 36
Fritham. Hants 4L 9
Frith Bank. Linc 5L 37
Frith Common. Worc 5E 26
Frithelstock. Devn 4D 6
Frithelstock Stone. Devn 4D 6
Frithsden. Herts 3H 21
Frithville. Linc 4L 37
Frittenden. Kent 1E 12
Frittiscombe. Devn 7L 5
Fritton. Norf
nr. Great Yarmouth 1L 31
nr. Long Stratton 2J 31
Fritwell. Oxon 1C 20
Frizinghall. W Yor 4K 41
Frizington. Cumb 3K 45
Frobost. W Isl 3D 74
Frocester. Glos 3F 18
Frochas. Powy 2L 25
Frodesley. Shrp 1D 26
Frodingham. N Lin 6G 43
Frodsham. Ches W 2D 34
Froggatt. Derbs 2L 35
Froghall. Staf 5J 35
Frogham. Hants 4K 9
Frogham. Kent 8J 23
Frogmore. Devn 7K 5
Frogmore. Hants 7F 20
Frogmore. Herts 3J 21
Frognall. Linc 8J 37
Frogshall. Norf 6J 39
Frogwell. Corn 5F 4
Frolesworth. Leics 2C 28
Frome. Som 1F 8
Fromefield. Som 1F 8
Frome St Quintin. Dors 5D 8
Fromes Hill. Here 7E 26
Fron. Gwyn 7C 32
Fron. Powy
nr. Llandrindod Wells 6K 25
nr. Newtown 3L 25
nr. Welshpool 2M 25
Y Fron. Gwyn 5E 32
Froncysyllte. Wrex 5A 34
Frongoch. Gwyn 7J 33
Fron Isaf. Wrex 5A 34
Fronoleu. Gwyn 7G 33
Frosterley. Dur 8D 54
Frotoft. Orkn 7D 88
Froxfield. C Beds 8G 29
Froxfield. Wilts 7L 19
Froxfield Green. Hants 3E 10
Fryern Hill. Hants 3B 10
Fryerning. Essx 3C 22
Fryton. N Yor 8D 48
Fugglestone St Peter. Wilts 2K 9
Fulbeck. Linc 4G 37
Fulbourn. Cambs 6B 30
Fulbrook. Oxon 2L 19
Fulflood. Hants 2B 10
Fulford. Som 3M 7
Fulford. Staf 6H 35
Fulford. York 3D 42
Fulham. G Lon 6K 21
Fulking. W Sus 4K 11
Fuller's Moor. Ches W 4C 34
Fuller Street. Essx 2D 22
Fullerton. Hants 2A 10
Fulletby. Linc 2K 37
Full Sutton. E Yor 2E 42
Fullwood. E Ayr 4C 58
Fulmer. Buck 5G 21
Fulmodestone. Norf 6F 38
Fulnetby. Linc 2H 37
Fulney. Linc 7K 37
Fulstow. Linc 8L 43
Fulthorpe. Stoc T 3B 48
Fulwell. Tyne 6G 55
Fulwood. Lanc 4D 40
Fulwood. Notts 4B 36
Fulwood. Som 4M 7
Fulwood. S Yor 1L 35
Fundenhall. Norf 2H 31
Funtington. W Sus 5F 10
Funtley. Hants 5C 10
Funzie. Shet 4L 91
Furley. Devn 5A 8
Furnace. Arg 7E 64
Furnace. Carm 6M 15
Furnace. Cdgn 3F 24
Furner's Green. E Sus 3M 11
Furness Vale. Derbs 1J 35
Furneux Pelham. Herts 1M 21
Furzebrook. Dors 7H 9
Furzehill. Devn 1G 7
Furzehill. Dors 5J 9
Furzeley Corner. Hants 4D 10
Furzey Lodge. Hants 5A 10
Furzley. Hants 4L 9
Fyfield. Essx 3B 22
Fyfield. Glos 3L 19
Fyfield. Hants 1L 9
Fyfield. Oxon 4B 20
Fyfield. Wilts 7K 19
The Fylde. Lanc 4B 40
Fylingthorpe. N Yor 5G 49
Fyning. W Sus 3F 10
Fyvie. Abers 2G 73

G

Gabhsann bho Dheas.
W Isl 6H 83
Gabhsann bho Thuath.
W Isl 6H 83
Gabroc Hill. E Ayr 4C 58
Gadbrook. Surr 1K 11
Gaddesby. Leics 8D 36
Gadfa. IOA 2D 32
Gadgirth. S Ayr 7C 58
Gaer. Powy 2L 17
Gaerwen. IOA 3D 32
Gagingwell. Oxon 1B 20
Gaick Lodge. High 7H 71
Gailey. Staf 8H 35
Gainford. Dur 4K 47
Gainsborough. Linc 8F 42
Gainsborough. Suff 7H 31
Gainsford End. Essx 8D 30
Gairletter. Arg 1L 57
Gairloch. Abers 5G 73
Gairloch. High 6K 77
Gairlochy. High 7B 70
Gairney Bank. Per 8E 66
Gairnshiel Lodge. Abers 5B 72
Gaisgill. Cumb 5E 46
Gaitsgill. Cumb 7H 53
Galashiels. Bord 6B 60
Galgate. Lanc 2C 40
Galgorm. ME Ant 3G 93
Galhampton. Som 3E 8
Gallatown. Fife 8F 66
Galley Common. Warw 2M 27
Galleyend. Essx 3D 22
Galleywood. Essx 3D 22
Gallin. Per 3K 65
Gallowfauld. Ang 3H 67
Gallowhill. Per 4E 66
Gallowhill. Ren 3C 58
Gallowhills. Abers 8K 81
Gallows Green. Staf 5J 35
Gallows Green. Worc 5H 27
Gallowstree Common.
Oxon 5D 20
Galltair. High 3K 69
Gallt Melyd. Den 2K 33
Galmington. Som 3M 7
Galmisdale. High 7F 68
Galmpton. Devn 7J 5
Galmpton. Torb 6L 5
Galmpton Warborough. Torb 6L 5
Galphay. N Yor 8L 47
Galston. E Ayr 6C 58
Galton. Dors 7F 8
Galtrigill. High 8C 76
Gamblesby. Cumb 8L 53
Gamblestown. Arm 6G 93
Gamelsby. Cumb 6G 53
Gamesley. Derbs 8J 41
Gamlingay. Cambs 6K 29
Gamlingay Cinques. Cambs 6K 29
Gamlingay Great Heath.
Cambs 6K 29
Gammaton. Devn 3D 6
Gammersgill. N Yor 7J 47
Gamston. Notts
nr. Nottingham 6D 36
nr. Retford 2E 36
Ganarew. Here 2D 18
Ganavan. Arg 4C 64
Ganborough. Glos 1K 19
Gang. Corn 5F 4
Ganllwyd. Gwyn 8G 33
Gannochy. Ang 8E 72
Gannochy. Per 5E 66
Gansclet. High 7E 86
Ganstead. E Yor 4J 43
Ganthorpe. N Yor 8D 48
Ganton. N Yor 8G 49
Gants Hill. G Lon 5M 21
Gappah. Devn 8H 7
Garafad. High 7F 76
Garboldisham. Norf 3G 31
Garden City. Flin 3B 34
Gardeners Green. Wok 7F 20
Gardenstown. Abers 7H 81
Garden Village. S Yor 8L 41
Garden Village. Swan 5E 16
Garderhouse. Shet 3D 90
Gardham. E Yor 3G 43
Gardie. Shet
on Papa Stour 1B 90
on Unst 2L 91
Gardie Ho. Shet 3E 90
Gare Hill. Wilts 1F 8
Garelochhead. Arg 8G 65
Garford. Oxon 4B 20
Garforth. W Yor 4B 42
Gargrave. N Yor 2H 41
Gargunnock. Stir 8M 65
Garleffin. S Ayr 3F 50
Garlieston. Dum 7K 51
Garlinge Green. Kent 8H 23
Garlogie. Abers 5G 73
Garmelow. Staf 7F 34
Garmond. Abers 8H 81
Garmondsway. Dur 8G 55
Garmony. Arg 3A 64
Garmouth. Mor 7C 80
Garmston. Shrp 1E 26
Garnant. Carm 3F 16
Garndiffaith. Torf 3A 18
Garndolbenmaen. Gwyn 6D 32
Garnett Bridge. Cumb 6D 46
Garnfadryn. Gwyn 7B 32
Garnkirk. N Lan 3E 58
Garnlydan. Blae 3L 17
Garnsgate. Linc 7M 37
Garnswllt. Swan 4F 16
Garn yr Erw. Torf 3M 17
Garrabost. W Isl 8J 83
Garrallan. E Ayr 8D 58
Garras. Corn 6L 3
Garreg. Gwyn 6F 32
Garrigill. Cumb 7M 53
Garrison. Ferm 6A 92
Garriston. N Yor 6K 47
Garrogie Lodge. High 4F 70
Garros. High 7F 76
Garrow. Per 3B 66
Garsdale. Cumb 7F 46
Garsdale Head. Cumb 6F 46
Garsdon. Wilts 5H 19
Garshall Green. Staf 6H 35
Garsington. Oxon 3C 20
Garstang. Lanc 3C 40
Garston. Mers 1C 34
Garswood. Mers 8D 40
Gartcosh. N Lan 3E 58
Garth. B'end 5H 17
Garth. Cdgn 4F 24
Garth. Gwyn 7E 32
Garth. IOM 7C 44
Garth. Powy
nr. Builth Wells 8J 25
nr. Knighton 4A 26
Garth. Shet
nr. Sandness 2C 90
nr. Skellister 2E 90
Garth. Wrex 5A 34
Garthamlock. Glas 3E 58
Garthbrengy. Powy 1K 17
Gartheli. Cdgn 7E 24
Garthmyl. Powy 3L 25
Garthorpe. Leics 7F 36
Garthorpe. N Lin 6F 42
Garth Owen. Powy 3L 25
Garth Place. Cphy 6L 17
Garth Row. Cumb 6D 46
Gartly. Abers 2E 72
Gartmore. Stir 8K 65
Gartness. N Lan 3F 58
Gartness. Stir 1D 58
Gartocharn. W Dun 1C 58
Garton. E Yor 4K 43
Garton-on-the-Wolds.
E Yor 2G 43
Gartsherrie. N Lan 3F 58
Gartymore. High 2L 79
Garvagh. Caus 3F 93
Garvaghy. Ferm 5D 92
Garvald. E Lot 2C 60
Garvamore. High 6F 70
Garvard. Arg 8J 63
Garvault. High 8K 85
Garve. High 7D 78
Garvestone. Norf 1G 31
Garvetagh. Derr 4C 92
Garvie. Arg 8E 64
Garvock. Abers 8G 73
Garvock. Inv 2A 58
Garway. Here 1C 18
Garway Common. Here 1C 18
Garway Hill. Here 1C 18
Garwick. Linc 5J 37
Gaskan. High 8K 69
Gasper. Wilts 2F 8
Gastard. Wilts 7G 19
Gasthorpe. Norf 3F 30
Gatcombe. IOW 7B 10
Gateacre. Mers 1C 34
Gatebeck. Cumb 7D 46
Gate Burton. Linc 1F 36
Gateforth. N Yor 5C 42
Gatehead. E Ayr 6B 58
Gate Helmsley. N Yor 2D 42
Gatehouse. Nmbd 3A 54
Gatehouse of Fleet. Dum 6M 51
Gatelawbridge. Dum 2D 52
Gateley. Norf 7F 38
Gatenby. N Yor 7M 47
Gatesgarth. Cumb 3L 45
Gateshead. Tyne 5F 54
Gatesheath. Ches W 3C 34
Gateside. Ang
nr. Forfar 3H 67
nr. Kirriemuir 3G 67
Gateside. Fife 7E 66
Gateside. N Ayr 4B 58
Gathurst. G Man 7D 40
Gatley. G Man 1G 35
Gatton. Surr 8K 21
Gattonside. Bord 6C 60
Gatwick Airport.
W Sus 119 (1K 11)
Gaufron. Powy 6J 25
Gaulby. Leics 1D 28
Gauldry. Fife 5G 67
Gaultree. Norf 1A 30
Gaunt's Common. Dors 5J 9
Gaunt's Earthcott. S Glo 5E 18
Gautby. Linc 2J 37
Gavinton. Bord 4E 60
Gawber. S Yor 7M 41
Gawcott. Buck 8D 28
Gawsworth. Ches E 3G 35
Gawthorpe. W Yor 5L 41
Gawthrop. Cumb 7E 46
Gawthwaite. Cumb 7A 46
Gay Bowers. Essx 3D 22
Gaydon. Warw 6A 28
Gayfield. Orkn 4D 88
Gayhurst. Mil 7F 28
Gayle. N Yor 7G 47
Gayles. N Yor 5K 47
Gay Street. W Sus 3H 11
Gayton. Mers 1A 34
Gayton. Norf 8D 38
Gayton. Nptn 6E 28
Gayton. Staf 7H 35
Gayton le Marsh. Linc 1M 37
Gayton le Wold. Linc 1K 37
Gayton Thorpe. Norf 8D 38
Gaywood. Norf 7C 38
Gazeley. Suff 5D 30
Geanies. High 6J 79
Gearraidh Bhailteas. W Isl 3D 74
Gearraidh Bhaird. W Isl 2E 76
Gearraidh ma Monadh.
W Isl 4D 74
Gearraidh na h-Aibhne.
W Isl 8F 82
Geary. High 7D 76
Geddes. High 8J 79
Gedding. Suff 6F 30
Geddington. Nptn 3F 28
Gedintailor. High 2G 69
Gedling. Notts 5D 36
Gedney. Linc 7M 37
Gedney Broadgate. Linc 7M 37
Gedney Drove End. Linc 7A 38
Gedney Dyke. Linc 7M 37
Gedney Hill. Linc 8L 37
Gee Cross. G Man 8H 41
Geeston. Rut 1G 29
Geilston. Arg 2B 58
Geirinis. W Isl 1D 74
Geise. High 5C 86
Geisiadar. W Isl 8E 82
Gelder Shiel. Abers 7B 72
Geldeston. Norf 2K 31
Gell. Cnwy 4H 33
Gelli. Pemb 5G 15
Gelli. Rhon 5J 17
Gellifor. Den 4L 33
Gelligaer. Cphy 5L 17
Y Gelli Gandryll. Powy 8M 25
Gellilydan. Gwyn 7F 32
Gellinudd. Neat 4G 17
Gellyburn. Per 4D 66
Gellywen. Carm 4J 15
Gelston. Dum 6B 52
Gelston. Linc 5G 37
Gembling. E Yor 2J 43
Geneva. Cdgn 1L 15
Gentleshaw. Staf 8J 35
Geocrab. W Isl 4C 76
George Best Belfast City Airport.
Bel 5H 93
George Green. Buck 5G 21
Georgeham. Devn 2D 6
George Nympton. Devn 3G 7
Georgetown. Blae 4L 17
Georgetown. Ren 3C 58
Georth. Orkn 7C 88
Gerlan. Gwyn 4F 32
Germansweek. Devn 6D 6
Germoe. Corn 6J 3
Gerrans. Corn 8A 4
Gerrard's Bromley. Staf 6F 34
Gerrards Cross. Buck 5G 21
Gerston. High 6C 86
Gestingthorpe. Essx 8E 30
Gethsemane. Pemb 2G 15
Geuffordd. Powy 1M 25
Gibraltar. Buck 2E 20
Gibraltar. Linc 4B 38
Gibraltar. Suff 6H 31
Gibsmere. Notts 5E 36
Giddeahall. Wilts 6G 19
Gidea Park. G Lon 5B 22
Gidleigh. Devn 7F 6
Giffnock. E Ren 4D 58
Gifford. E Lot 3C 60
Giffordtown. Fife 6F 66
Giggetty. Staf 2G 27
Giggleswick. N Yor 1G 41
Gignog. Pemb 4E 14
Gilberdyke. E Yor 5F 42
Gilbert's End. Worc 7G 27
Gilbert's Green. Warw 4K 27
Gilchriston. E Lot 3B 60
Gilcrux. Cumb 8F 52
Gildersome. W Yor 5L 41
Gildingwells. S Yor 1C 36
Gilesgate Moor. Dur 7F 54
Gileston. V Glam 8K 17
Gilfach. Cphy 5L 17
Gilfach Goch. Rhon 6J 17
Gilfachreda. Cdgn 1L 15
Gilford. Arm 6G 93
Gilgarran. Cumb 2K 45
Gillamoor. N Yor 6D 48
Gillan. Corn 6L 3
Gillar's Green. Mers 8C 40
Gillen. High 8D 76
Gilling East. N Yor 8D 48
Gillingham. Dors 3G 9
Gillingham. Medw
Medway Towns 111 (7D 22)
Gillingham. Norf 2L 31
Gilling West. N Yor 5K 47
Gillock. High 6D 86
Gillow Heath. Staf 4G 35
Gills. High 4E 86
Gill's Green. Kent 2D 12
Gilmanscleuch. Bord 7M 59
Gilmerton. Edin 3L 59
Gilmerton. Per 5B 66
Gilmonby. Dur 4H 47
Gilmorton. Leics 3C 28
Gilsland. Nmbd 5L 53
Gilsland Spa. Cumb 5L 53
Gilston. Bord 4B 60
Giltbrook. Notts 5B 36
Gilwern. Mon 3M 17
Gimingham. Norf 6J 39
Giosla. W Isl 1C 76
Gipping. Suff 5G 31
Gipsey Bridge. Linc 5K 37
Gipton. W Yor 4M 41
Girdle Toll. N Ayr 5B 58
Girlsta. Shet 2E 90
Girsby. N Yor 5A 48
Girthon. Dum 6M 51
Girton. Cambs 5M 29
Girton. Notts 3F 36
Girvan. S Ayr 2G 51
Gisburn. Lanc 3G 41
Gisleham. Suff 3M 31
Gislingham. Suff 4G 31
Gissing. Norf 3H 31
Gittisham. Devn 6L 7
Gladestry. Powy 7M 25
Gladsmuir. E Lot 2B 60
Glaichbea. High 2F 70
Glais. Swan 4G 17
Glaisdale. N Yor 5E 48
Glame. High 1G 69
Glamis. Ang 3G 67
Glanaman. Carm 3F 16
Glan-Conwy. Cnwy 5H 33
Glandford. Norf 5G 39
Glan Duar. Carm 2M 15
Glandwr. Blae 4M 17
Glandwr. Pemb 4H 15
Glan-Dwyfach. Gwyn 6D 32
Glandy Cross. Carm 4H 15
Glandyfi. Cdgn 3F 24
Glangrwyney. Powy 3M 17
Glanmule. Powy 3L 25
Glan-rhyd. Pemb 3H 15
Glan-rhyd. Powy 4G 17
Glanrhyd. Gwyn 7B 32
Glanrhyd. Pemb 2H 15
Glanton. Nmbd 8H 61
Glanton Pyke. Nmbd 8H 61
Glanvilles Wootton. Dors 5E 8
Glan-y-don. Flin 3L 33
Glan-y-nant. Powy 4J 25
Glan-yr-afon. Gwyn 6K 33
Glan-yr-afon. IOA 2F 32
Glan-yr-afon. Powy 2K 25
Glan-y-wern. Gwyn 7F 32
Glapthorn. Nptn 2H 29
Glapwell. Derbs 3B 36
Glarryford. ME Ant 3G 93
Glas Aird. Arg 8J 63
Glas-allt Shiel. Abers 7B 72
Glasbury. Powy 1L 17
Glaschoil. High 2L 71
Glascoed. Den 3J 33
Glascoed. Mon 3B 18
Glascote. Staf 1L 27
Glascwm. Powy 7L 25
Glasfryn. Cnwy 5J 33
Glasgow. Glas 109 (3D 58)
Glasgow Airport. Ren 119 (3C 58)
Glasgow Prestwick Airport.
S Ayr 7B 58
Glashvin. High 7F 76
Glasinfryn. Gwyn 4E 32
Glas na Cardaich. High 6H 69
Glasnacardoch. High 6H 69
Glasnakille. High 4G 69
Glaspwll. Cdgn 3G 25
Glassburn. High 2D 70
Glassenbury. Kent 2D 12
Glasserton. Dum 8K 51
Glassford. S Lan 5F 58
Glassgreen. Mor 7B 80
Glasshouse. Glos 1F 18
Glasshouses. N Yor 1K 41
Glasson. Cumb 5G 53
Glasson. Lanc 2C 40
Glassonby. Cumb 8K 53
Glasswater. New M 6J 93
Glasterlaw. Ang 2J 67
Glaston. Rut 1F 28
Glastonbury. Som 2C 8
Glatton. Cambs 3J 29
Glazebrook. Warr 8E 40
Glazebury. Warr 8E 40
Glazeley. Shrp 3F 26
Gleadless. S Yor 1A 36
Gleadsmoss. Ches E 3G 35
Gleann Dail bho Dheas.
W Isl 4D 74
Gleann Tholastaidh. W Isl 7J 83
Gleann Uige. High 8H 69
Gleaston. Cumb 8A 46
Glebe. Derr 4C 92
Glecknabae. Arg 3K 57
Gledrid. Shrp 6A 34
Gleiniant. Powy 3J 25
Glemsford. Suff 7E 30
Glen. Dum 6L 51
Glenancross. High 6H 69
Glenanne. Arm 7F 93
Glenariff. Caus 2H 93
Glenarm. ME Ant 3H 93
Glen Auldyn. IOM 5D 44
Glenavy. Lis 5G 93
Glenbarr. Arg 6F 56
Glenbeg. High 1L 63
Glen Bernisdale. High 1F 68
Glenbervie. Abers 7G 73
Glenboig. N Lan 3F 58
Glenborrodale. High 1M 63
Glenbranter. Arg 8F 64
Glenbreck. Bord 7J 59
Glenbrein Lodge. High 4E 70
Glenbrittle. High 3F 68
Glenbuchat Lodge. Abers 4C 72
Glenbuck. E Ayr 7F 58
Glenburn. Ren 3C 58
Glencalvie Lodge. High 5E 78
Glencaple. Dum 5D 52
Glencarron Lodge. High 8A 78
Glencarse. Per 5E 66
Glencassley Castle. High 3E 78
Glencat. Abers 6E 72
Glencoe. High 2F 64
Glen Cottage. High 7H 69
Glencraig. Fife 8E 66
Glendale. High 1C 68
Glendevon. Per 7C 66
Glendoebeg. High 5E 70
Glendoick. Per 5F 66
Glendoune. S Ayr 2G 51
Glenduckie. Fife 6F 66
Gleneagles. Per 7C 66
Glenegedale. Arg 4C 56
Glenegedale Lots. Arg 4C 56
Glenelg. High 4K 69
Glenernie. Mor 1L 71
Glenesslin. Dum 3C 52
Glenfarg. Per 6E 66
Glenfarquhar Lodge. Abers 7G 73
Glenferness Mains. High 1K 71
Glenfeshie Lodge. High 6J 71
Glenfiddich Lodge. Mor 2C 72
Glenfield. Leics 1C 28
Glenfinnan. High 7L 69
Glenfintaig Lodge. High 7C 70
Glenfoot. Per 6E 66
Glenfyne Lodge. Arg 6G 65
Glengap. Dum 6A 52
Glengarnock. N Ayr 4B 58
Glengolly. High 5C 86
Glengorm Castle. Arg 2K 63
Glengormley. Ant 4H 93
Glengrasco. High 1F 68
Glenhead Farm. Ang 1F 66
Glenholm. Bord 6K 59
Glen House. Bord 6L 59
Glenhurich. High 1C 64
Glenkerry. Bord 8L 59
Glenkiln. Dum 4C 52
Glenkindie. Abers 4D 72
Glenkinglass Lodge. Arg 4F 64
Glenkirk. Bord 7J 59
Glenlean. Arg 1K 57
Glenlee. Dum 3M 51
Glenleraig. High 8D 84
Glenlichorn. Per 6A 66
Glenlivet. Mor 3A 72
Glenlochar. Dum 5B 52
Glenlochsie Lodge. Per 8L 71
Glenluce. Dum 6G 51
Glenmarksie. High 8D 78
Glenmassan. Arg 1L 57
Glenmavis. N Lan 3F 58
Glen Maye. IOM 7B 44
Glenmazeran Lodge. High 3H 71
Glenmidge. Dum 3C 52
Glen Mona. IOM 6D 44
Glenmore. High
nr. Glenborrodale 1L 63
nr. Kingussie 5K 71
on Isle of Skye 1F 68
Glenmoy. Ang 1H 67
Glennoe. Arg 4E 64
Glen of Coachford. Abers 1D 72
Glenogil. Ang 1H 67
Glen Parva. Leics 2C 28
Glenprosen Village. Ang 1G 67
Glenree. N Ayr 7J 57
Glenridding. Cumb 4B 46
Glenrosa. N Ayr 6K 57
Glenrothes. Fife 7F 66
Glensanda. High 3C 64
Glensaugh. Abers 8F 72
Glenshero Lodge. High 6F 70
Glensluain. Arg 8E 64
Glenstockadale. Dum 5F 50
Glenstriven. Arg 2K 57
Glen Tanar House. Abers 6D 72
Glentham. Linc 8H 43
Glenton. Abers 3F 72
Glentress. Bord 6L 59
Glentromie Lodge. High 6H 71
Glentrool Lodge. Dum 3K 51
Glentrool Village. Dum 4J 51
Glentruim House. High 6G 71
Glentworth. Linc 1G 37
Glenuig. High 8H 69
Glen View. New M 7G 93
Glen Village. Falk 2G 59
Glen Vine. IOM 7C 44
Glenwhilly. Dum 4G 51
Glenzierfoot. Dum 4H 53
Glespin. S Lan 7G 59
Gletness. Shet 2E 90
Glewstone. Here 1D 18
Glib Cheois. W Isl 1E 76
Glinton. Pet 1J 29
Glooston. Leics 2E 28
Glossop. Derbs 8J 41
Gloster Hill. Nmbd 1F 54
Gloucester. Glos 109 (2G 19)
Gloucestershire Airport.
Glos 1G 19
Gloup. Shet 3K 91
Glusburn. N Yor 3J 41
Glutt Lodge. High 8A 86
Glutton Bridge. Derbs 3J 35
Gluvian. Corn 5B 4
Glympton. Oxon 1B 20
Glyn. Cnwy 3H 33
Glynarthen. Cdgn 2K 15
Glynbrochan. Powy 4J 25
Glyn Ceiriog. Wrex 7M 33
Glyncoch. Rhon 5K 17
Glyncorrwg. Neat 5H 17
Glynde. E Sus 5A 12
Glyndebourne. E Sus 4A 12
Glyndyfrdwy. Den 6L 33
Glyn Ebwy. Blae 4L 17
Glynllan. B'end 6J 17
Glynn. ME Ant 4J 93
Glyn-neath. Neat 4H 17
Glynogwr. B'end 6J 17
Glyntaff. Rhon 6K 17
Glyntawe. Powy 3H 17
Glynteg. Carm 3K 15
Gnosall. Staf 7G 35
Gnosall Heath. Staf 7G 35
Goadby. Leics 2E 28
Goadby Marwood. Leics 7E 36
Goatacre. Wilts 6J 19
Goathill. Dors 4E 8
Goathland. N Yor 5F 48
Goathurst. Som 2A 8
Goathurst Common. Kent 8A 22
Goat Lees. Kent 1G 13
Gobernuisgach Lodge. High 7G 85
Gobernuisgeach. High 8A 86
Gobhaig. W Isl 3B 76
Gobowen. Shrp 6B 34
Godalming. Surr 1G 11
Goddard's Corner. Suff 5J 31
Goddard's Green. Kent
nr. Benenden 2E 12
nr. Cranbrook 2D 12
Goddards' Green. W Sus 3K 11
Godford Cross. Devn 5L 7
Godleybrook. Staf 5H 35
Godmanchester. Cambs 4K 29
Godmanstone. Dors 6E 8
Godmersham. Kent 8G 23
Godolphin Cross. Corn 5K 3
Godre'r-graig. Neat 4G 17
Godshill. Hants 4K 9
Godshill. IOW 7C 10
Godstone. Staf 6J 35
Godstone. Surr 8L 21
Goetre. Mon 3B 18
Goff's Oak. Herts 3L 21
Gogar. Edin 2K 59
Goginan. Cdgn 4F 24
Golan. Gwyn 6E 32
Golant. Corn 6D 4
Golberdon. Corn 8C 6
Golborne. G Man 8E 40
Golcar. W Yor 6J 41
Goldcliff. Newp 5B 18
Golden Cross. E Sus 4B 12
Golden Green. Kent 1C 12
Golden Grove. Carm 3E 16
Golden Grove. N Yor 5F 48
Golden Hill. Pemb 4F 14
Goldenhill. Stoke 4G 35
Golden Pot. Hants 1E 10
Golden Valley. Glos 1H 19
Golders Green. G Lon 5K 21
Goldhanger. Essx 3F 22
Gold Hill. Norf 2B 30
Golding. Shrp 1D 26
Goldington. Bed 6H 29
Goldsborough. N Yor
nr. Harrogate 2A 42
nr. Whitby 4F 48
Goldsithney. Corn 5J 3
Goldstone. Kent 7J 23
Goldstone. Shrp 7F 34
Goldthorpe. S Yor 7B 42
Goldworthy. Devn 3C 6
Golfa. Powy 8L 33
Gollanfield. High 8J 79
Gollinglith Foot. N Yor 7K 47
Golsoncott. Som 2K 7
Golspie. High 4J 79
Gomeldon. Wilts 2K 9
Gomersal. W Yor 5L 41
Gometra House. Arg 3J 63
Gomshall. Surr 1H 11
Gonalston. Notts 5D 36
Gonerby Hill Foot. Linc 6G 37
Gonfirth. Shet 1D 90
Good Easter. Essx 2C 22
Gooderstone. Norf 1D 30
Goodleigh. Devn 2F 6
Goodmanham. E Yor 3F 42
Goodmayes. G Lon 5A 22
Goodnestone. Kent
nr. Aylesham 8J 23
nr. Faversham 7G 23
Goodrich. Here 2D 18
Goodrington. Torb 6L 5
Goodshaw. Lanc 5G 41
Goodshaw Fold. Lanc 5G 41
Goodstone. Devn 8G 7
Goodwick. Pemb 3F 14
Goodworth Clatford. Hants 1A 10
Goole. E Yor 5E 42
Goom's Hill. Worc 6J 27
Goonabarn. Corn 6B 4
Goonbell. Corn 4L 3
Goonhavern. Corn 3L 3
Goonlaze. Corn 5L 3
Goonvrea. Corn 4L 3
Goose Green. Cumb 7D 46
Goose Green. S Glo 5F 18
Gooseham. Corn 4B 6
Goosewell. Plym 6H 5
Goosey. Oxon 4A 20
Goosnargh. Lanc 4D 40
Goostrey. Ches E 2F 34
Gorcott Hill. Warw 5J 27
Gord. Shet 5E 90
Gordon. Bord 5D 60
Gordonbush. High 3J 79
Gordonstown. Abers
nr. Cornhill 8E 80
nr. Fyvie 2G 73
Gorebridge. Midl 3M 59
Gorefield. Cambs 8M 37
Gores. Wilts 8K 19
Gorgie. Edin 2L 59
Goring. Oxon 5D 20
Goring-by-Sea. W Sus 5J 11
Goring Heath. Oxon 6D 20
Gorleston-on-Sea. Norf 1M 31
Gornalwood. W Mid 2H 27
Gorran Churchtown. Corn 7B 4
Gorran Haven. Corn 7C 4
Gorran High Lanes. Corn 7B 4
Gors. Cdgn 5F 24
Gorsedd. Flin 3L 33
Gorseinon. Swan 5E 16
Gorseness. Orkn 8D 88
Gorseybank. Derbs 4L 35
Gorsgoch. Cdgn 1L 15
Gorslas. Carm 3E 16
Gorsley. Glos 1E 18
Gorsley Common. Here 1E 18
Gorstan. High 7D 78
Gorstella. Ches W 3B 34
Gorsty Common. Here 8C 26
Gorsty Hill. Staf 7K 35
Gortantaoid. Arg 2C 56
Gorteneorn. High 1M 63
Gortenfern. High 1M 63
Gortin. Ferm 4D 92
Gortnahey. Caus 3E 92
Gorton. G Man 8G 41
Gosbeck. Suff 6H 31
Gosberton. Linc 6K 37
Gosberton Cheal. Linc 7K 37
Gosberton Clough. Linc 7J 37
Goseley Dale. Derbs 7M 35
Gosfield. Essx 1D 22
Gosford. Oxon 2C 20
Gosforth. Cumb 4K 45
Gosforth. Tyne 5F 54
Gosmore. Herts 1J 21
Gospel End. Staf 2G 27
Gosport. Hants 6D 10
Gossabrough. Shet 5K 91
Gossington. Glos 3F 18
Gossops Green. W Sus 2K 11
Goswick. Nmbd 5H 61
Gotham. Notts 6C 36
Gotherington. Glos 1H 19
Gott. Arg 3F 62
Gott. Shet 3E 90
Goudhurst. Kent 2D 12
Goulceby. Linc 2K 37
Gourdon. Abers 8H 73
Gourock. Inv 2M 57
Govan. Glas 3D 58
Govanhill. Glas 3D 58
Goverton. Notts 5E 36
Goveton. Devn 7K 5
Govilon. Mon 2A 18
Gowanhill. Abers 7K 81
Gowdall. E Yor 5D 42
Gowdystown. Arm 6G 93
Gowerton. Swan 5E 16
Gowkhall. Fife 1J 59
Gowthorpe. E Yor 2E 42
Goxhill. E Yor 3J 43
Goxhill. N Lin 5J 43
Goxhill Haven. N Lin 5J 43
Goytre. Neat 6G 17
Grabhair. W Isl 2E 76
Graby. Linc 7H 37
Gracehill. ME Ant 3G 93
Graffham. W Sus 4G 11
Grafham. Cambs 5J 29
Grafham. Surr 1H 11
Grafton. Here 8C 26
Grafton. N Yor 1B 42
Grafton. Oxon 3L 19
Grafton. Shrp 8C 34
Grafton. Worc
nr. Evesham 8H 27
nr. Leominster 5D 26
Grafton Flyford. Worc 6H 27
Grafton Regis. Nptn 7E 28
Grafton Underwood. Nptn 3G 29
Grafty Green. Kent 1E 12
Graianrhyd. Den 5M 33
Graig. Carm 6L 15
Graig. Cnwy 3H 33
Graig. Den 3K 33
Graig-fechan. Den 5L 33
Graig Penllyn. V Glam 7J 17
Grain. Medw 6E 22
Grainsby. Linc 8K 43
Grainthorpe. Linc 8L 43
Grainthorpe Fen. Linc 8L 43
Graiselound. N Lin 8E 42
Gramasdail. W Isl 8K 75
Grampound. Corn 7B 4
Grampound Road. Corn 6B 4
Granborough. Buck 1E 20
Granby. Notts 6E 36
Grandborough. Warw 5B 28
Grandpont. Oxon 3C 20
Grandtully. Per 2C 66
Grange. Cumb 4A 46
Grange. E Ayr 6C 58
Grange. Here 4C 26
Grange. Mers 2M 33
Grange. Per 5F 66
The Grange. N Yor 6C 48
Grange Corner. ME Ant 4G 93
Grange Crossroads. Mor 8D 80
Grange Hill. Essx 4M 21
Grangemill. Derbs 4L 35
Grange Moor. W Yor 6L 41
Grangemouth. Falk 1H 59
Grange of Lindores. Fife 6F 66
Grange-over-Sands. Cumb 8C 46
Grangepans. Falk 1J 59
Grange Park. New M 6J 93
Grangetown. Card 7L 17
Grangetown. Red C 3C 48
Grange Villa. Dur 6F 54
Granish. High 4J 71
Gransmoor. E Yor 2J 43
Granston. Pemb 3E 14
Grantchester. Cambs 6M 29
Grantham. Linc 6G 37
Grantley. N Yor 1L 41
Grantlodge. Abers 4G 73
Granton. Edin 2L 59
Grantown-on-Spey. High 3L 71
Grantshouse. Bord 3F 60
Grappenhall. Warr 1E 34
Grasby. Linc 7H 43
Grasmere. Cumb 5B 46
Grasscroft. G Man 7H 41
Grassendale. Mers 1B 34
Grassgarth. Cumb 7H 53
Grassholme. Dur 3H 47
Grassington. N Yor 1J 41
Grassmoor. Derbs 3B 36
Grassthorpe. Notts 3E 36
Grateley. Hants 1L 9
Gratton. Devn 4C 6
Gratton. Staf 4H 35
Gratwich. Staf 6J 35
Graveley. Cambs 5K 29
Graveley. Herts 1K 21
Gravelhill. Shrp 8C 34
Gravel Hole. G Man 7H 41
Gravelly Hill. W Mid 2K 27
Graven. Shet 6J 91
Graveney. Kent 7G 23
Gravesend. Kent 6C 22
Grayingham. Linc 8G 43
Grayrigg. Cumb 6D 46
Grays. Thur 6C 22
Grayshott. Hants 2F 10
Grayson Green. Cumb 2J 45
Grayswood. Surr 2G 11
Graythorp. Hart 3C 48
Grazeley. Wok 7D 20
Grealin. High 7G 77
Greasbrough. S Yor 8B 42
Greasby. Mers 1A 34
Great Abington. Cambs 7B 30
Great Addington. Nptn 4G 29
Great Alne. Warw 6K 27
Great Altcar. Lanc 7B 40
Great Amwell. Herts 2L 21
Great Asby. Cumb 4E 46
Great Ashfield. Suff 5F 30
Great Ayton. N Yor 4C 48
Great Baddow. Essx 3D 22
Great Bardfield. Essx 8C 30
Great Barford. Bed 6J 29
Great Barr. W Mid 2J 27
Great Barrington. Glos 2L 19
Great Barrow. Ches W 3C 34
Great Barton. Suff 5E 30
Great Barugh. N Yor 8E 48
Great Bavington. Nmbd 3C 54
Great Bealings. Suff 7J 31
Great Bedwyn. Wilts 7L 19
Great Bentley. Essx 1H 23
Great Billing. Nptn 5F 28
Great Bircham. Norf 6D 38
Great Blakenham. Suff 6H 31
Great Blencow. Cumb 8J 53
Great Bolas. Telf 7E 34
Great Bookham. Surr 8J 21
Great Bosullow. Corn 5H 3
Great Bourton. Oxon 7B 28
Great Bowden. Leics 3E 28
Great Bradley. Suff 6C 30
Great Braxted. Essx 2E 22
Great Bricett. Suff 6G 31
Great Brickhill. Buck 8G 29
Great Bridgeford. Staf 7G 35
Great Brington. Nptn 5D 28
Great Bromley. Essx 1G 23
Great Broughton. Cumb 8E 52
Great Broughton. N Yor 5C 48
Great Budworth. Ches W 2E 34
Great Burdon. Darl 4M 47
Great Burstead. Essx 4C 22
Great Busby. N Yor 5C 48
Great Canfield. Essx 2B 22
Great Carlton. Linc 1M 37
Great Casterton. Rut 1G 29
Great Chalfield. Wilts 7G 19
Great Chart. Kent 1F 12
Great Chatwell. Staf 8F 34
Great Chesterford. Essx 7B 30
Great Cheverell. Wilts 8H 19
Great Chilton. Dur 8F 54
Great Chishill. Cambs 8M 29
Great Clacton. Essx 2H 23
Great Cliff. W Yor 6M 41
Great Clifton. Cumb 2K 45
Great Coates. NE Lin 6K 43
Great Comberton. Worc 7H 27
Great Corby. Cumb 6J 53
Great Cornard. Suff 7E 30
Great Cowden. E Yor 3K 43
Great Coxwell. Oxon 4L 19
Great Crakehall. N Yor 6L 47
Great Cransley. Nptn 4F 28
Great Cressingham. Norf 1E 30
Great Crosby. Mers 7B 40
Great Cubley. Derbs 6K 35
Great Dalby. Leics 8E 36
Great Doddington. Nptn 5F 28
Great Doward. Here 2D 18
Great Dunham. Norf 8E 38
Great Dunmow. Essx 1C 22
Great Durnford. Wilts 2K 9
Great Easton. Essx 1C 22
Great Easton. Leics 2F 28
Great Eccleston. Lanc 3C 40
Great Edstone. N Yor 7E 48
Great Ellingham. Norf 2G 31
Great Elm. Som 1F 8
Great Eppleton. Tyne 7G 55
Great Eversden. Cambs 6L 29
Great Fencote. N Yor 6L 47
Great Finborough. Suff 6G 31
Greatford. Linc 8H 37
Great Fransham. Norf 8E 38
Great Gaddesden. Herts 2H 21
Great Gate. Staf 5J 35
Great Gidding. Cambs 3J 29
Great Givendale. E Yor 2F 42
Great Glemham. Suff 5K 31
Great Glen. Leics 2D 28
Great Gonerby. Linc 6F 36
Great Gransden. Cambs 6K 29
Great Green. Norf 3J 31
Great Green. Suff
nr. Lavenham 6F 30
nr. Palgrave 4H 31
Great Habton. N Yor 8E 48
Great Hale. Linc 5J 37
Great Hallingbury. Essx 2B 22
Greatham. Hants 2E 10
Greatham. Hart 3B 48
Greatham. W Sus 4H 11
Great Hampden. Buck 3F 20
Great Harrowden. Nptn 4F 28
Great Harwood. Lanc 4F 40
Great Haseley. Oxon 3D 20
Great Hatfield. E Yor 3J 43
Great Haywood. Staf 7H 35
Great Heath. W Mid 3M 27
Great Heck. N Yor 5C 42
Great Henny. Essx 8E 30
Great Hinton. Wilts 8H 19
Great Hockham. Norf 2F 30

Great Holland – Hendomen

Great Holland. Essx 2J 23
Great Horkesley. Essx 8F 30
Great Hormead. Herts 8M 29
Great Horton. W Yor 4K 41
Great Horwood. Buck 8E 28
Great Houghton. Nptn 6E 28
Great Houghton. S Yor 7B 42
Great Hucklow. Derbs 2K 35
Great Kelk. E Yor 2J 43
Great Kendale. E Yor 1H 43
Great Kimble. Buck 3F 20
Great Kingshill. Buck 4F 20
Great Langdale. Cumb 5A 46
Great Langton. N Yor 6L 47
Great Leighs. Essx 2D 22
Great Limber. Linc 7J 43
Great Linford. Mil 7F 28
Great Livermere. Suff 4E 30
Great Longstone. Derbs 2L 35
Great Lumley. Dur 7F 54
Great Lyth. Shrp 1C 26
Great Malvern. Worc 7F 26
Great Maplestead. Essx 8E 30
Great Marton. Bkpl 4B 40
Great Massingham. Norf 7D 38
Great Melton. Norf 1H 31
Great Milton. Oxon 3D 20
Great Missenden. Buck 3F 20
Great Mitton. Lanc 4F 40
Great Mongeham. Kent 8K 23
Great Moulton. Norf 2H 31
Great Munden. Herts 1L 21
Great Musgrave. Cumb 4F 46
Great Ness. Shrp 8B 34
Great Notley. Essx 1D 22
Great Oak. Mon 3B 18
Great Oakley. Essx 1H 23
Great Oakley. Nptn 3F 28
Great Offley. Herts 1J 21
Great Ormside. Cumb 4F 46
Great Orton. Cumb 6H 53
Great Ouseburn. N Yor 1B 42
Great Oxendon. Nptn 3E 28
Great Oxney Green. Essx 3C 22
Great Parndon. Essx 3M 21
Great Paxton. Cambs 5K 29
Great Plumpton. Lanc 4B 40
Great Plumstead. Norf 8K 39
Great Ponton. Linc 6G 37
Great Potheridge. Devn 4E 6
Great Preston. W Yor 5B 42
Great Raveley. Cambs 3K 29
Great Rissington. Glos 2K 19
Great Rollright. Oxon 8M 27
Great Ryburgh. Norf 7F 38
Great Ryle. Nmbd 8H 61
Great Ryton. Shrp 1C 26
Great Saling. Essx 1D 22
Great Salkeld. Cumb 8K 53
Great Sampford. Essx 8C 30
Great Sankey. Warr 1D 34
Great Saredon. Staf 1H 27
Great Saxham. Suff 5D 30
Great Shefford. W Ber 6A 20
Great Shelford. Cambs 6A 30
Great Shoddesden. Hants 1L 9
Great Smeaton. N Yor 5M 47
Great Snoring. Norf 6F 38
Great Somerford. Wilts 5H 19
Great Stainton. Darl 3M 47
Great Stambridge. Essx 4E 22
Great Staughton. Cambs 5J 29
Great Steeping. Linc 3M 37
Great Stonar. Kent 8K 23
Greatstone-on-Sea. Kent 3G 13
Great Strickland. Cumb 3D 46
Great Stukeley. Cambs 4K 29
Great Sturton. Linc 2K 37
Great Sutton. Ches W 2B 34
Great Sutton. Shrp 3D 26
Great Swinburne. Nmbd 4C 54
Great Tew. Oxon 1A 20
Great Tey. Essx 1E 22
Great Thirkleby. N Yor 8B 48
Great Thorness. IOW 6B 10
Great Thurlow. Suff 6C 30
Great Torr. Devn 7J 5
Great Torrington. Devn 4D 6
Great Tosson. Nmbd 1D 54
Great Totham North. Essx 2E 22
Great Totham South. Essx 2E 22
Great Tows. Linc 8K 43
Great Urswick. Cumb 8A 46
Great Wakering. Essx 5F 22
Great Waldingfield. Suff 7F 30
Great Walsingham. Norf 6F 38
Great Waltham. Essx 2C 22
Great Warley. Essx 4B 22
Great Washbourne. Glos 8H 27
Great Wenham. Suff 8G 31
Great Whelnetham. Suff 6E 30
Great Whittington. Nmbd 4D 54
Great Wigborough. Essx 2F 22
Great Wilbraham. Cambs 6B 30
Great Wilne. Derbs 6B 36
Great Wishford. Wilts 2J 9
Great Witchingham. Norf 7H 39
Great Witcombe. Glos 2H 19
Great Witley. Worc 5F 26
Great Wolford. Warw 8L 27
Greatworth. Nptn 7C 28
Great Wratting. Suff 7C 30
Great Wymondley. Herts 1K 21
Great Wyrley. Staf 1H 27
Great Wytheford. Shrp 8D 34
Great Yarmouth. Norf 1M 31
Great Yeldham. Essx 8D 30
Grebby. Linc 3M 37
Greeba Castle. IOM 6C 44
The Green. Cumb 6L 45
The Green. Wilts 2G 9
Greenbank. Shet 3K 91
Greenbottom. Corn 4L 3
Greenburn. W Lot 3H 59
Greencastle. Ferm 4D 92
Greencroft. Dur 6E 54
Greendown. Som 8D 18
Greendykes. Nmbd 7H 61
Green End. Bed
nr. Bedford 7H 29
nr. Little Staughton 5J 29
Green End. Herts
nr. Buntingford 8L 29
nr. Stevenage 1L 21
Green End. N Yor 5F 48
Green End. Warw 3L 27
Greenfield. Arg 8G 65
Greenfield. C Beds 8H 29
Greenfield. Flin 3L 33
Greenfield. G Man 7H 41
Greenfield. Oxon 4E 20
Greenfoot. N Lan 3F 58
Greenford. G Lon 5J 21
Greengairs. N Lan 2F 58
Greengate. Norf 8G 39
Greengill. Cumb 8F 52
Greenhalgh. Lanc 4C 40
Greenham. Dors 5C 8
Greenham. Som 3K 7
Greenham. W Ber 7B 20
Green Hammerton. N Yor 2B 42
Greenhaugh. Nmbd 3A 54
Greenhead. Nmbd 5L 53
Green Heath. Staf 8H 35
Greenhill. Dum 4F 52
Greenhill. Falk 2G 59
Greenhill. Kent 7H 23
Greenhill. S Yor 1M 35
Greenhill. Worc 4G 27
Greenhills. N Ayr 4B 58
Greenhithe. Kent 6B 22
Greenholm. E Ayr 6D 58
Greenhow Hill. N Yor 1K 41
Greenigoe. Orkn 1F 86
Greenisland. ME Ant 4H 93
Greenland. High 5D 86
Greenland Mains. High 5D 86
Greenlands. Worc 5J 27
Green Lane. Shrp 7E 34
Green Lane. Worc 5J 27
Greenlaw. Bord 5E 60
Greenlea. Dum 4E 52
Greenloaning. Per 7B 66
Greenmount. G Man 6F 40
Greenmow. Shet 5E 90
Greenock. Inv 2A 58
Greenock Mains. E Ayr 7E 58
Greenodd. Cumb 7B 46
Green Ore. Som 8D 18
Greenrow. Cumb 6F 52
Greens. Abers 1H 73
Greensgate. Norf 8H 39
Greenside. Tyne 5E 54
Greensidehill. Nmbd 8G 61
Greens Norton. Nptn 7D 28
Greenstead Green. Essx 1E 22
Greensted Green. Essx 3B 22
Green Street. Herts 4J 21
Green Street. Suff 4H 31
Green Street Green. G Lon 7A 22
Green Street Green. Kent 6B 22
Greenstreet Green. Suff 7G 31
Green Tye. Herts 2M 21
Greenwall. Orkn 1G 87
Greenway. Pemb 3G 15
Greenway. V Glam 7K 17
Greenwell. Cumb 6K 53
Greenwich. G Lon 6L 21
Greet. Glos 8J 27
Greete. Shrp 4D 26
Greetham. Linc 2L 37
Greetham. Rut 8G 37
Greetland. W Yor 5J 41
Gregson Lane. Lanc 5D 40
Grein. W Isl 5C 74
Greinetobht. W Isl 6K 75
Greinton. Som 2C 8
Gremista. Shet 3E 90
Grenaby. IOM 7B 44
Grendon. Nptn 5F 28
Grendon. Warw 2L 27
Grendon Common. Warw 2L 27
Grendon Green. Here 6D 26
Grendon Underwood. Buck 1D 20
Grenofen. Devn 8D 6
Grenoside. S Yor 8M 41
Greosabhagh. W Isl 4C 76
Gresford. Wrex 4B 34
Gresham. Norf 6H 39
Greshornish. High 8E 76
Gressenhall. Norf 8F 38
Gressingham. Lanc 1D 40
Greta Bridge. Dur 4J 47
Gretna. Dum 5H 53
Gretna Green. Dum 5H 53
Gretton. Glos 8J 27
Gretton. Nptn 2G 29
Gretton. Shrp 2D 26
Grewelthorpe. N Yor 8L 47
Greyabbey. Ards 5J 93
Greygarth. N Yor 8K 47
Grey Green. N Lin 7E 42
Greylake. Som 2B 8
Greysouthen. Cumb 2K 45
Greysteel. Caus 2D 92
Greystoke. Cumb 8J 53
Greystoke Gill. Cumb 3C 46
Greystone. Ang 3J 67
Greystones. S Yor 1M 35
Greywell. Hants 8E 20
Griais. W Isl 7H 83
Grianan. W Isl 8H 83
Gribthorpe. E Yor 4E 42
Gribun. Arg 4K 63
Griff. Warw 3A 28
Griffithstown. Torf 4A 18
Griffydam. Leics 8B 36
Griggs Green. Hants 2F 10
Grimbister. Orkn 8C 88
Grimeford Village. Lanc 6E 40
Grimeston. Orkn 8C 88
Grimethorpe. S Yor 7B 42
Griminis. W Isl
on Benbecula 8J 75
on North Uist 6J 75
Grimister. Shet 4J 91
Grimley. Worc 5G 27
Grimness. Orkn 2F 86
Grimoldby. Linc 1L 37
Grimpo. Shrp 7B 34
Grimsargh. Lanc 4D 40
Grimsbury. Oxon 7B 28
Grimsby. NE Lin 7K 43
Grimscote. Nptn 6D 28
Grimscott. Corn 5B 6
Grimshaw. Bkbn 5F 40
Grimshaw Green. Lanc 6C 40
Grimsthorpe. Linc 7H 37
Grimston. E Yor 4K 43
Grimston. Leics 7D 36
Grimston. Norf 7D 38
Grimston. York 2D 42
Grimstone. Dors 6E 8
Grimstone End. Suff 5F 30
Grinacombe Moor. Devn 6D 6
Grindale. E Yor 8J 49
Grindhill. Devn 6D 6
Grindiscol. Shet 4E 90
Grindle. Shrp 1F 26
Grindleford. Derbs 2L 35
Grindleton. Lanc 3F 40
Grindley. Staf 7J 35
Grindley Brook. Shrp 5D 34
Grindlow. Derbs 2K 35
Grindon. Nmbd 5G 61
Grindon. Staf 4J 35
Gringley on the Hill. Notts 8E 42
Grinsdale. Cumb 6H 53
Grinshill. Shrp 7D 34
Grinton. N Yor 6J 47
Griomsidar. W Isl 1F 76
Grishipoll. Arg 2G 63
Grisling Common. E Sus 3M 11
Gristhorpe. N Yor 7H 49
Griston. Norf 2F 30
Gritley. Orkn 1G 87
Grittenham. Wilts 5J 19
Grittleton. Wilts 5G 19
Grizebeck. Cumb 6M 45
Grizedale. Cumb 6B 46
Grobister. Orkn 7F 88
Grobsness. Shet 1D 90
Groby. Leics 1C 28
Groes. Cnwy 4K 33
Groes. Neat 6G 17
Groes-faen. Rhon 6K 17
Groesffordd. Gwyn 7B 32
Groesffordd. Powy 2K 17
Groeslon. Gwyn 5D 32
Groes-lwyd. Powy 1M 25
Groes-wen. Cphy 6L 17
Grogport. Arg 5H 57
Groigearraidh. W Isl 1D 74
Gromford. Suff 6K 31
Gronant. Flin 2K 33
Groombridge. E Sus 2B 12
Groomsport. Ards 4J 93
Grosmont. Mon 1C 18
Grosmont. N Yor 5F 48
Groton. Suff 7F 30
Grove. Dors 8E 8
Grove. Kent 7J 23
Grove. Notts 2E 36
Grove. Oxon 4A 20
The Grove. Dum 4D 52
The Grove. Worc 7G 27
Grovehill. E Yor 4H 43
Grove Park. G Lon 6M 21
Grovesend. Swan 4E 16
Grub Street. Staf 7F 34
Grudie. High 7D 78
Gruids. High 3F 78
Gruinard House. High 4L 77
Gruinart. Arg 3B 56
Grulinbeg. Arg 3B 56
Gruline. Arg 3L 63
Grummore. High 8J 85
Grundisburgh. Suff 6J 31
Gruting. Shet 3C 90
Grutness. Shet 7E 90
Gualachulain. High 3F 64
Gualin House. High 6F 84
Guardbridge. Fife 6H 67
Guarlford. Worc 7G 27
Guay. Per 3D 66
Gubblecote. Herts 2G 21
Guestling Green. E Sus 4E 12
Guestling Thorn. E Sus 4E 12
Guestwick. Norf 7G 39
Guestwick Green. Norf 7G 39
Guide. Bkbn 5F 40
Guide Post. Nmbd 3F 54
Guilden Down. Shrp 3B 26
Guilden Morden. Cambs 7K 29
Guilden Sutton. Ches W 3C 34
Guildford. Surr 109 (1G 11)
Guildtown. Per 4E 66
Guilsborough. Nptn 4D 28
Guilsfield. Powy 1M 25
Guineaford. Devn 2E 6
Guisborough. Red C 4D 48
Guiseley. W Yor 3K 41
Guist. Norf 7F 38
Guiting Power. Glos 1J 19
Gulberwick. Shet 4E 90
Gulladuff. M Ulst 4F 93
Gullane. E Lot 1B 60
Gulling Green. Suff 6E 30
Gulval. Corn 5H 3
Gulworthy. Devn 8D 6
Gumfreston. Pemb 6H 15
Gumley. Leics 2D 28
Gunby. E Yor 4E 42
Gunby. Linc 7G 37
Gundleton. Hants 2D 10
Gun Green. Kent 2D 12
Gun Hill. E Sus 4B 12
Gunn. Devn 2F 6
Gunnerside. N Yor 6H 47
Gunnerton. Nmbd 4C 54
Gunness. N Lin 6F 42
Gunnislake. Corn 8D 6
Gunnista. Shet 3E 90
Gunsgreenhill. Bord 3G 61
Gunstone. Staf 1G 27
Gunthorpe. Norf 6G 39
Gunthorpe. N Lin 8F 42
Gunthorpe. Notts 5D 36
Gunthorpe. Pet 1J 29
Gunville. IOW 7B 10
Gupworthy. Som 2J 7
Gurnard. IOW 6B 10
Gurney Slade. Som 1E 8
Gurnos. Powy 4G 17
Gussage All Saints. Dors 4J 9
Gussage St Andrew. Dors 4H 9
Gussage St Michael. Dors 4H 9
Guston. Kent 1K 13
Gutcher. Shet 4K 91
Guthram Gowt. Linc 7J 37
Guthrie. Ang 2J 67
Guyhirn. Cambs 1M 29
Guyhirn Gull. Cambs 1L 29
Guy's Head. Linc 7A 38
Guy's Marsh. Dors 3G 9
Guyzance. Nmbd 1F 54
Gwaelod-y-garth. Card 6L 17
Gwaenynog Bach. Den 4K 33
Gwaenysgor. Flin 2K 33
Gwalchmai. IOA 3C 32
Gwastad. Pemb 4G 15
Gwaun-Cae-Gurwen. Neat 3G 17
Gwbert. Cdgn 2H 15
Gweek. Corn 6L 3
Gwehelog. Mon 3B 18
Gwenddwr. Powy 8K 25
Gwennap. Corn 4L 3
Gwenter. Corn 7L 3
Gwernaffield. Flin 4M 33
Gwernesney. Mon 3C 18
Gwernogle. Carm 3M 15
Gwern-y-go. Powy 3M 25
Gwernymynydd. Flin 4M 33
Gwersyllt. Wrex 4B 34
Gwespyr. Flin 2L 33
Gwinear. Corn 5J 3
Gwithian. Corn 4J 3
Gwredog. IOA 2D 32
Gwyddelwern. Den 6K 33
Gwyddgrug. Carm 3L 15
Gwynfryn. Wrex 4A 34
Gwystre. Powy 6K 25
Gwytherin. Cnwy 4H 33
Gyfelia. Wrex 5B 34
Gyffin. Cnwy 3G 33

H

Haa of Houlland. Shet 3K 91
Habberley. Shrp 1C 26
Habblesthorpe. Notts 1E 36
Habergham. Lanc 4G 41
Habin. W Sus 3F 10
Habrough. NE Lin 6J 43
Haceby. Linc 6H 37
Hacheston. Suff 6K 31
Hackenthorpe. S Yor 1B 36
Hackford. Norf 1G 31
Hackforth. N Yor 6L 47
Hackland. Orkn 7C 88
Hackleton. Nptn 6F 28
Hackman's Gate. Worc 4G 27
Hackness. N Yor 6G 49
Hackness. Orkn 2E 86
Hackney. G Lon 5L 21
Hackthorn. Linc 1G 37
Hackthorpe. Cumb 3D 46
Haclait. W Isl 1E 74
Haconby. Linc 7J 37
Hadden. Bord 6E 60
Haddenham. Buck 3E 20
Haddenham. Cambs 4A 30
Haddenham End Field.
Cambs 4A 30
Haddington. E Lot 2C 60
Haddington. Linc 3G 37
Haddiscoe. Norf 2L 31
Haddo. Abers 2H 73
Haddon. Cambs 2J 29
Hademore. Staf 1K 27
Hadfield. Derbs 8J 41
Hadham Cross. Herts 2M 21
Hadham Ford. Herts 1M 21
Hadleigh. Essx 5E 22
Hadleigh. Suff 7G 31
Hadleigh Heath. Suff 7F 30
Hadley. Telf 8E 34
Hadley. Worc 5G 27
Hadley End. Staf 7K 35
Hadley Wood. G Lon 4K 21
Hadlow. Kent 1C 12
Hadlow Down. E Sus 3B 12
Hadnall. Shrp 7D 34
Hadstock. Essx 7B 30
Hadston. Nmbd 1F 54
Hady. Derbs 2A 36
Hadzor. Worc 5H 27
Haffenden Quarter. Kent 1E 12
Haggate. Lanc 4G 41
Haggbeck. Cumb 4J 53
Haggersta. Shet 3D 90
Haggerston. Nmbd 5H 61
Haggrister. Shet 6H 91
Hagley. Here 7D 26
Hagley. Worc 3H 27
Hagnaby. Linc 3L 37
Hagworthingham. Linc 3L 37
Haigh. G Man 7E 40
Haigh Moor. W Yor 5L 41
Haighton Green. Lanc 4D 40
Haile. Cumb 4K 45
Hailes. Glos 8J 27
Hailey. Herts 2L 21
Hailey. Oxon 2A 20
Hailsham. E Sus 5B 12
Hail Weston. Cambs 5J 29
Hainault. G Lon 4A 22
Hainford. Norf 8J 39
Hainton. Linc 1J 37
Hainworth. W Yor 4J 41
Haisthorpe. E Yor 1J 43
Hakin. Pemb 6E 14
Halam. Notts 4D 36
Halbeath. Fife 1K 59
Halberton. Devn 4K 7
Halcro. High 5D 86
Hale. Cumb 8D 46
Hale. G Man 1F 34
Hale. Hal 1C 34
Hale. Hants 4K 9
Hale. Surr 1F 10
Hale Bank. Hal 1C 34
Halebarns. G Man 1F 34
Hales. Norf 2K 31
Hales. Staf 6F 34
Halesgate. Linc 7L 37
Hales Green. Derbs 5K 35
Halesowen. W Mid 3H 27
Hale Street. Kent 1C 12
Halesworth. Suff 4K 31
Halewood. Mers 1C 34
Halford. Shrp 3C 26
Halford. Warw 7L 27
Halfpenny. Cumb 7D 46
Halfpenny Furze. Carm 5J 15
Halfpenny Green. Staf 2G 27
Halfway. Carm
nr. Llandeilo 1F 16
nr. Llandovery 1H 17
Halfway. S Yor 1B 36
Halfway. W Ber 7B 20
Halfway House. Shrp 8B 34
Halfway Houses. Kent 6F 22
Halgabron. Corn 3C 4
Halifax. W Yor 5J 41
Halistra. High 8D 76
Halket. E Ayr 4C 58
Halkirk. High 6C 86
Halkyn. Flin 3M 33
Hall. E Ren 4C 58
Hallam Fields. Derbs 5B 36
Halland. E Sus 4B 12
The Hallands. N Lin 5H 43
Hallaton. Leics 2E 28
Hallatrow. Bath 8E 18
Hallbank. Cumb 6E 46
Hallbankgate. Cumb 6K 53
Hall Dunnerdale. Cumb 5M 45
Hallen. S Glo 5D 18
Hall End. Bed 7H 29
Hallgarth. Dur 7G 55
Hall Green. Ches E 4G 35
Hall Green. Norf 3H 31
Hall Green. W Mid 3K 27
Hall Green. W Yor 6M 41
Hall Green. Wrex 5C 34
Halliburton. Bord 5D 60
Hallin. High 8D 76
Halling. Medw 7D 22
Hallington. Linc 1L 37
Hallington. Nmbd 4C 54
Halloughton. Notts 4D 36
Hallow. Worc 6G 27
Hallow Heath. Worc 6G 27
Hallowsgate. Ches W 3D 34
Hallsands. Devn 8L 5
Hall's Green. Herts 1K 21
Hallspill. Devn 3D 6
Hallthwaites. Cumb 6L 45
Hall Waberthwaite. Cumb 5L 45
Hallwood Green. Glos 8E 26
Hallworthy. Corn 7A 6
Hallyne. Bord 5K 59
Halmer End. Staf 5G 35
Halmond's Frome. Here 7E 26
Halmore. Glos 3E 18
Halnaker. W Sus 5G 11
Halsall. Lanc 6B 40
Halse. Nptn 7C 28
Halse. Som 3L 7
Halsetown. Corn 5J 3
Halsham. E Yor 5K 43
Halsinger. Devn 2E 6
Halstead. Essx 8E 30
Halstead. Kent 7A 22
Halstead. Leics 1E 28
Halstock. Dors 5D 8
Halsway. Som 2L 7
Haltcliff Bridge. Cumb 8H 53
Haltham. Linc 3K 37
Haltoft End. Linc 5L 37
Halton. Buck 3F 20
Halton. Hal 1D 34
Halton. Lanc 1D 40
Halton. Nmbd 5C 54
Halton. W Yor 4A 42
Halton. Wrex 6B 34
Halton East. N Yor 2J 41
Halton Fenside. Linc 3M 37
Halton Gill. N Yor 8G 47
Halton Holegate. Linc 3M 37
Halton Lea Gate. Nmbd 6L 53
Halton Moor. W Yor 4M 41
Halton Shields. Nmbd 5D 54
Halton West. N Yor 2G 41
Haltwhistle. Nmbd 5M 53
Halvergate. Norf 1L 31
Halwell. Devn 6K 5
Halwill. Devn 6D 6
Halwill Junction. Devn 6D 6
Ham. Devn 5M 7
Ham. Glos 4E 18
Ham. G Lon 6J 21
Ham. High 4D 86
Ham. Kent 8K 23
Ham. Plym 6G 5
Ham. Shet 4B 90
Ham. Som
nr. Ilminster 4A 8
nr. Taunton 3A 8
nr. Wellington 3L 7
Ham. Wilts 7M 19
Hambleden. Buck 5E 20
Hambledon. Hants 4D 10
Hambledon. Surr 2G 11
Hamble-le-Rice. Hants 5B 10
Hambleton. Lanc 3B 40
Hambleton. N Yor 4C 42
Hambridge. Som 3B 8
Hambrook. S Glo 6E 18
Hambrook. W Sus 5E 10
Ham Common. Dors 3G 9
Hameringham. Linc 3L 37
Hamerton. Cambs 4J 29
Ham Green. Here 7F 26
Ham Green. Kent 7E 22
Ham Green. N Som 6D 18
Ham Green. Worc 5J 27
Ham Hill. Kent 7C 22
Hamilton. Leic 1D 28
Hamilton. S Lan 4F 58
Hamiltonsbawn. Arm 6F 93
Hamister. Shet 1F 90
Hammer. W Sus 2F 10
Hammersmith. G Lon 6K 21
Hammerwich. Staf 1J 27
Hammerwood. E Sus 2M 11
Hammill. Kent 8J 23
Hammond Street. Herts 3L 21
Hammoon. Dors 4G 9
Hamnavoe. Shet
nr. Braehoulland 5G 91
nr. Burland 4D 90
nr. Lunna 6J 91
on Yell 5J 91
Hamp. Som 2B 8
Hampden Park. E Sus 5B 12
Hampen. Glos 2J 19
Hamperden End. Essx 8B 30
Hamperley. Shrp 3C 26
Hampnett. Glos 2J 19
Hampole. S Yor 6C 42
Hampreston. Dors 6J 9
Hampstead. G Lon 5K 21
Hampstead Norreys. W Ber 6C 20
Hampsthwaite. N Yor 2L 41
Hampton. Devn 6A 8
Hampton. G Lon 6J 21
Hampton. Kent 7H 23
Hampton. Shrp 3F 26
Hampton. Swin 4K 19
Hampton. Worc 7J 27
Hampton Bishop. Here 8D 26
Hampton Fields. Glos 4G 19
Hampton Hargate. Pet 2J 29
Hampton Heath. Ches W 5D 34
Hampton in Arden. W Mid 3L 27
Hampton Loade. Shrp 3F 26
Hampton Lovett. Worc 5G 27
Hampton Lucy. Warw 6L 27
Hampton Magna. Warw 5L 27
Hampton on the Hill. Warw 5L 27
Hampton Poyle. Oxon 2C 20
Hampton Wick. G Lon 7J 21
Hamptworth. Wilts 4L 9
Hamrow. Norf 7F 38
Hamsey. E Sus 4M 11
Hamsey Green. Surr 8L 21
Hamstall Ridware. Staf 8K 35
Hamstead. IOW 6B 10
Hamstead. W Mid 2J 27
Hamstead Marshall. W Ber 7B 20
Hamsterley. Dur
nr. Consett 6E 54
nr. Wolsingham 8E 54
Hamsterley Mill. Dur 6E 54
Ham Street. Som 2D 8
Hamstreet. Kent 2G 13
Hamworthy. Pool 6H 9
Hanbury. Staf 7K 35
Hanbury. Worc 5H 27
Hanbury Woodend. Staf 7K 35
Hanby. Linc 6H 37
Hanchurch. Staf 5G 35
Hand and Pen. Devn 6K 7
Handbridge. Ches W 3C 34
Handcross. W Sus 2K 11
Handforth. Ches E 1G 35
Handley. Ches W 4C 34
Handley. Derbs 3A 36
Handsacre. Staf 8J 35
Handsworth. S Yor 1B 36
Handsworth. W Mid 2J 27
Handy Cross. Buck 4F 20
Hanford. Dors 4G 9
Hanford. Stoke 5G 35
Hangersley. Hants 5K 9
Hanging Houghton. Nptn 4E 28
Hanging Langford. Wilts 2J 9
Hangleton. Brig 5K 11
Hangleton. W Sus 5H 11
Hanham. S Glo 6E 18
Hanham Green. S Glo 6E 18
Hankelow. Ches E 5E 34
Hankerton. Wilts 4H 19
Hankham. E Sus 5C 12
Hanley. Stoke Stoke 116 (5G 35)
Hanley Castle. Worc 7G 27
Hanley Childe. Worc 5E 26
Hanley Swan. Worc 7G 27
Hanley William. Worc 5E 26
Hanlith. N Yor 1H 41
Hanmer. Wrex 6C 34
Hannaborough. Devn 5E 6
Hannaford. Devn 3F 6
Hannah. Linc 2B 38
Hannington. Hants 8C 20
Hannington. Nptn 4F 28
Hannington. Swin 4K 19
Hannington Wick. Swin 4K 19
Hanscombe End. C Beds 8J 29
Hanslope. Mil 7F 28
Hanthorpe. Linc 7H 37
Hanwell. G Lon 5J 21
Hanwell. Oxon 7B 28
Hanwood. Shrp 1C 26
Hanworth. G Lon 6J 21
Hanworth. Norf 6H 39
Happas. Ang 3H 67
Happendon. S Lan 6G 59
Happisburgh. Norf 6K 39
Happisburgh Common.
Norf 7K 39
Hapsford. Ches W 2C 34
Hapton. Lanc 4F 40
Hapton. Norf 2H 31
Harberton. Devn 6K 5
Harbertonford. Devn 6K 5
Harbledown. Kent 8H 23
Harborne. W Mid 3J 27
Harborough Magna. Warw 4B 28
Harbottle. Nmbd 1C 54
Harbourneford. Devn 5K 5
Harbours Hill. Worc 5H 27
Harbridge. Hants 4K 9
Harbury. Warw 5A 28
Harby. Leics 6E 36
Harby. Notts 2F 36
Harcombe. Devn 6L 7
Harcombe Bottom. Devn 6B 8
Harcourt. Corn 5M 3
Harden. W Yor 4J 41
Hardenhuish. Wilts 6H 19
Hardgate. Abers 5G 73
Hardgate. Dum 5C 52
Hardham. W Sus 4H 11
Hardingham. Norf 1G 31
Hardingstone. Nptn 6E 28
Hardings Wood. Staf 4G 35
Hardington. Som 8F 18
Hardington Mandeville. Som 4D 8
Hardington Marsh. Som 5D 8
Hardington Moor. Som 4D 8
Hardley. Hants 5B 10
Hardley Street. Norf 1K 31
Hardmead. Mil 7G 29
Hardraw. N Yor 6G 47
Hardstoft. Derbs 3B 36
Hardway. Hants 5D 10
Hardway. Som 2F 8
Hardwick. Buck 2F 20
Hardwick. Cambs 6L 29
Hardwick. Norf 3J 31
Hardwick. Nptn 5F 28
Hardwick. Oxon
nr. Bicester 1C 20
nr. Witney 3A 20
Hardwick. Shrp 2B 26
Hardwick. S Yor 1B 36
Hardwick. Stoc T 3B 48
Hardwick. W Mid 2J 27
Hardwicke. Glos
nr. Cheltenham 1H 19
nr. Gloucester 2F 18
Hardwicke. Here 7A 26
Hardwick Village. Notts 2D 36
Hardy's Green. Essx 1F 22
Hare. Som 4A 8
Hareby. Linc 3L 37
Hareden. Lanc 2E 40
Harefield. G Lon 4H 21
Hare Green. Essx 1G 23
Hare Hatch. Wok 6F 20
Harehill. Derbs 6K 35
Harehills. W Yor 4M 41
Harehope. Nmbd 7H 61
Harelaw. Dum 4J 53
Harelaw. Dur 6E 54
Hareplain. Kent 2E 12
Haresceugh. Cumb 7L 53
Harescombe. Glos 2G 19
Haresfield. Glos 2G 19
Haresfinch. Mers 8D 40
Hareshaw. N Lan 3G 59
Hare Street. Essx 3M 21
Hare Street. Herts 1L 21
Harewood. W Yor 3M 41
Harewood End. Here 1D 18
Harford. Devn 6J 5
Hargate. Norf 2H 31
Hargatewall. Derbs 2K 35
Hargrave. Ches W 3C 34
Hargrave. Nptn 4H 29
Hargrave. Suff 6D 30
Harker. Cumb 5H 53
Harkland. Shet 5J 91
Harkstead. Suff 8H 31
Harlaston. Staf 8L 35
Harlaxton. Linc 6F 36
Harlech. Gwyn 7E 32
Harlequin. Notts 6D 36
Harlescott. Shrp 8D 34
Harleston. Devn 7K 5
Harleston. Norf 3J 31
Harleston. Suff 5G 31
Harlestone. Nptn 5E 28
Harley. Shrp 1D 26
Harley. S Yor 8A 42
Harling Road. Norf 3F 30
Harlington. C Beds 8H 29
Harlington. G Lon 6H 21
Harlington. S Yor 7B 42
Harlosh. High 1D 68
Harlow. Essx 2M 21
Harlow Hill. Nmbd 5D 54
Harlsey Castle. N Yor 6B 48
Harlthorpe. E Yor 4E 42
Harlton. Cambs 6L 29
Harlyn Bay. Corn 4A 4
Harman's Cross. Dors 7H 9
Harmby. N Yor 7K 47
Harmer Green. Herts 2K 21
Harmer Hill. Shrp 7C 34
Harmondsworth. G Lon 6H 21
Harmston. Linc 3G 37
Harnage. Shrp 1D 26
Harnham. Nmbd 3D 54
Harnham. Wilts 3K 9
Harnhill. Glos 3J 19
Harold Hill. G Lon 4B 22
Haroldston West. Pemb 5E 14
Haroldswick. Shet 2L 91
Harold Wood. G Lon 4B 22
Harome. N Yor 7D 48
Harpenden. Herts 2J 21
Harpford. Devn 6K 7
Harpham. E Yor 1H 43
Harpley. Norf 7D 38
Harpley. Worc 5E 26
Harpole. Nptn 5D 28
Harpsdale. High 6C 86
Harpsden. Oxon 5E 20
Harpswell. Linc 1G 37
Harpurhey. G Man 7G 41
Harpur Hill. Derbs 2J 35
Harraby. Cumb 6J 53
Harracott. Devn 3E 6
Harrapool. High 3H 69
Harrapul. High 3H 69
Harrietfield. Per 5C 66
Harrietsham. Kent 8E 22
Harrington. Cumb 2J 45
Harrington. Linc 2L 37
Harrington. Nptn 3E 28
Harringworth. Nptn 2G 29
Harriseahead. Staf 4G 35
Harriston. Cumb 7F 52
Harrogate. N Yor 110 (2M 41)
Harrold. Bed 6G 29
Harrop Dale. G Man 7J 41
Harrow. G Lon 5J 21
Harrowbarrow. Corn 5F 4
Harrowden. Bed 7H 29
Harrowgate Hill. Darl 4L 47
Harrow on the Hill. G Lon 5J 21
Harrow Weald. G Lon 4J 21
Harry Stoke. S Glo 6E 18
Harston. Cambs 6M 29
Harston. Leics 6F 36
Harswell. E Yor 3F 42
Hart. Hart 8H 55
Hartburn. Nmbd 3D 54
Hartburn. Stoc T 4B 48
Hartest. Suff 6E 30
Hartfield. E Sus 2A 12
Hartford. Cambs 4K 29
Hartford. Ches W 2E 34
Hartford. Som 3J 7
Hartford Bridge. Hants 8E 20
Hartford End. Essx 2C 22
Harthill. Ches W 4D 34
Harthill. N Lan 3H 59
Harthill. S Yor 1B 36
Hartington. Derbs 3K 35
Hartland. Devn 3B 6
Hartland Quay. Devn 3B 6
Hartle. Worc 4H 27
Hartlebury. Worc 4G 27
Hartlepool. Hart 8J 55
Hartley. Cumb 5F 46
Hartley. Kent
nr. Cranbrook 2D 12
nr. Dartford 7C 22
Hartley. Nmbd 4G 55
Hartley Green. Staf 7H 35
Hartley Mauditt. Hants 2E 10
Hartley Wespall. Hants 8D 20
Hartley Wintney. Hants 8E 20
Hartlip. Kent 7E 22
Hartmount Holdings. High 6H 79
Hartoft End. N Yor 6E 48
Harton. N Yor 1E 42
Harton. Shrp 3C 26
Harton. Tyne 5G 55
Hartpury. Glos 1G 19
Hartshead. W Yor 5K 41
Hartshill. Warw 2M 27
Hartshorne. Derbs 7M 35
Hartsop. Cumb 4C 46
Hart Station. Hart 8H 55
Hartswell. Som 3K 7
Hartwell. Nptn 6E 28
Hartwood. Lanc 6D 40
Hartwood. N Lan 4G 59
Harvel. Kent 7C 22
Harvington. Worc
nr. Evesham 7J 27
nr. Kidderminster 4G 27
Harwell. Oxon 5B 20
Harwich. Essx 118 (8J 31)
Harwood. Dur 8B 54
Harwood. G Man 6F 40
Harwood Dale. N Yor 6G 49
Harworth. Notts 8D 42
Hascombe. Surr 2G 11
Haselbech. Nptn 4E 28
Haselbury Plucknett. Som 4C 8
Haseley. Warw 5L 27
Hasfield. Glos 1G 19
Hasguard. Pemb 6E 14
Haskayne. Lanc 7B 40
Hasketon. Suff 6J 31
Hasland. Derbs 3A 36
Haslemere. Surr 2G 11
Haslingden. Lanc 5F 40
Haslingfield. Cambs 6M 29
Haslington. Ches E 4F 34
Hassall. Ches E 4F 34
Hassall Green. Ches E 4F 34
Hassell Street. Kent 1G 13
Hassendean. Bord 7C 60
Hassingham. Norf 1K 31
Hassness. Cumb 3L 45
Hassocks. W Sus 4L 11
Hassop. Derbs 2L 35
Haster. High 6E 86
Hasthorpe. Linc 3A 38
Hastigrow. High 5D 86
Hastingleigh. Kent 1G 13
Hastings. E Sus 5E 12
Hastingwood. Essx 3A 22
Hastoe. Herts 3G 21
Haston. Shrp 7D 34
Haswell. Dur 7G 55
Haswell Plough. Dur 7G 55
Hatch. C Beds 7J 29
Hatch Beauchamp. Som 3B 8
Hatch End. G Lon 4J 21
Hatch Green. Som 4B 8
Hatching Green. Herts 2J 21
Hatchmere. Ches W 2D 34
Hatch Warren. Hants 1D 10
Hatcliffe. NE Lin 7K 43
Hatfield. Here 6D 26
Hatfield. Herts 3K 21
Hatfield. S Yor 7D 42
Hatfield. Worc 6G 27
Hatfield Broad Oak. Essx 2B 22
Hatfield Garden Village.
Herts 3K 21
Hatfield Heath. Essx 2B 22
Hatfield Hyde. Herts 2K 21
Hatfield Peverel. Essx 2D 22
Hatfield Woodhouse. S Yor 7D 42
Hatford. Oxon 4M 19
Hatherden. Hants 8M 19
Hatherleigh. Devn 5E 6
Hathern. Leics 7B 36
Hatherop. Glos 3K 19
Hathersage. Derbs 1L 35
Hathersage Booths. Derbs 1L 35
Hatherton. Ches E 5E 34
Hatherton. Staf 8H 35
Hatley St George. Cambs 6K 29
Hatt. Corn 5F 4
Hattersley. G Man 8H 41
Hattingley. Hants 2D 10
Hatton. Abers 2K 73
Hatton. Derbs 6L 35
Hatton. G Lon 6H 21
Hatton. Linc 2J 37
Hatton. Shrp 2C 26
Hatton. Warr 1E 34
Hatton. Warw 5L 27
Hattoncrook. Abers 3H 73
Hatton Heath. Ches W 3C 34
Hatton of Fintray. Abers 4H 73
Haugh. E Ayr 7C 58
Haugh. Linc 2M 37
Haugham. Linc 1L 37
Haugh Head. Nmbd 7H 61
Haughley. Suff 5G 31
Haughley Green. Suff 5G 31
Haugh of Ballechin. Per 2C 66
Haugh of Glass. Mor 2D 72
Haugh of Urr. Dum 5C 52
Haughton. Ches E 4D 34
Haughton. Notts 2D 36
Haughton. Shrp
nr. Bridgnorth 2E 26
nr. Oswestry 7B 34
nr. Shifnal 1F 26
nr. Shrewsbury 8D 34
Haughton. Staf 7G 35
Haughton Green. G Man 8H 41
Haughton le Skerne. Darl 4M 47
Haultwick. Herts 1L 21
Haunn. Arg 3J 63
Haunn. W Isl 4D 74
Haunton. Staf 8L 35
Hauxton. Cambs 6M 29
Havannah. Ches E 3G 35
Havant. Hants 5E 10
Haven. Here 6C 26
The Haven. W Sus 2H 11
Haven Bank. Linc 4K 37
Havenstreet. IOW 6C 10
Havercroft. W Yor 6A 42
Haverfordwest. Pemb 5F 14
Haverhill. Suff 7C 30
Haverigg. Cumb 7L 45
Havering-Atte-Bower.
G Lon 4B 22
Havering's Grove. Essx 4C 22
Haversham. Mil 7F 28
Haverthwaite. Cumb 7B 46
Haverton Hill. Stoc T 3B 48
Havyatt. Som 2D 8
Hawarden. Flin 3B 34
Hawbridge. Worc 7H 27
Hawcoat. Cumb 7M 45
Hawcross. Glos 8F 26
Hawen. Cdgn 2K 15
Hawes. N Yor 7G 47
Hawes Green. Norf 2J 31
Hawick. Bord 8C 60
Hawkchurch. Devn 5B 8
Hawkedon. Suff 6D 30
Hawkenbury. Kent 1E 12
Hawkeridge. Wilts 8G 19
Hawkerland. Devn 7K 7
Hawkesbury. S Glo 5F 18
Hawkesbury. Warw 3A 28
Hawkesbury Upton. S Glo 5F 18
Hawkes End. W Mid 3L 27
Hawk Green. G Man 1H 35
Hawkhurst. Kent 2D 12
Hawkhurst Common. E Sus 4B 12
Hawkinge. Kent 1J 13
Hawkley. Hants 3E 10
Hawkridge. Som 2H 7
Hawksdale. Cumb 7H 53
Hawkshaw. G Man 6F 40
Hawkshead. Cumb 6B 46
Hawkshead Hill. Cumb 6B 46
Hawkswick. N Yor 8H 47
Hawksworth. Notts 5E 36
Hawksworth. W Yor 3K 41
Hawkwell. Essx 4E 22
Hawley. Hants 8F 20
Hawley. Kent 6B 22
Hawling. Glos 1J 19
Hawnby. N Yor 7C 48
Haworth. W Yor 4J 41
Hawstead. Suff 6E 30
Hawthorn. Dur 7H 55
Hawthorn Hill. Brac 6F 20
Hawthorn Hill. Linc 4K 37
Hawthorpe. Linc 7H 37
Hawton. Notts 4E 36
Haxby. York 2D 42
Haxey. N Lin 8E 42
Haybridge. Shrp 4E 26
Haybridge. Som 1D 8
Haydock. Mers 8D 40
Haydon. Bath 8E 18
Haydon. Dors 4E 8
Haydon. Som 3A 8
Haydon Bridge. Nmbd 5B 54
Haydon Wick. Swin 5K 19
Haye. Corn 5F 4
Hayes. G Lon
nr. Bromley 7M 21
Hayes. G Lon
nr. Uxbridge 5H 21
Hayfield. Derbs 1J 35
Hay Green. Norf 8B 38
Hayhill. E Ayr 8C 58
Haylands. IOW 6C 10
Hayle. Corn 5J 3
Hayley Green. W Mid 3H 27
Hayling Island. Hants 6E 10
Hayne. Devn 5H 7
Haynes. C Beds 7H 29
Haynes West End. C Beds 7H 29
Hay-on-Wye. Powy 8M 25
Hayscastle. Pemb 4E 14
Hayscastle Cross. Pemb 4F 14
Hayshead. Ang 3K 67
Hay Street. Herts 1L 21
Hayton. Aber 5J 73
Hayton. Cumb
nr. Aspatria 7F 52
nr. Brampton 6K 53
Hayton. E Yor 3F 42
Hayton. Notts 1E 36
Hayton's Bent. Shrp 3D 26
Haytor Vale. Devn 8G 7
Haytown. Devn 4C 6
Haywards Heath. W Sus 3L 11
Haywood. S Lan 4H 59
Hazelbank. S Lan 5G 59
Hazelbury Bryan. Dors 5F 8
Hazeleigh. Essx 3E 22
Hazeley. Hants 8E 20
Hazel Grove. G Man 1H 35
Hazelhead. S Yor 7K 41
Hazelslade. Staf 8J 35
Hazel Street. Kent 2C 12
Hazelton Walls. Fife 5G 67
Hazelwood. Derbs 5M 35
Hazlemere. Buck 4F 20
Hazler. Shrp 2C 26
Hazlerigg. Tyne 4F 54
Hazles. Staf 5J 35
Hazleton. Glos 2J 19
Hazon. Nmbd 1E 54
Heacham. Norf 6C 38
Headbourne Worthy. Hants 2B 10
Headcorn. Kent 1E 12
Headingley. W Yor 4L 41
Headington. Oxon 3C 20
Headlam. Dur 4K 47
Headless Cross. Worc 5J 27
Headley. Hants
nr. Haslemere 2F 10
nr. Kingsclere 7C 20
Headley. Surr 8K 21
Headley Down. Hants 2F 10
Headley Heath. Worc 4J 27
Headley Park. Bris 7D 18
Head of Muir. Falk 1G 59
Headon. Notts 2E 36
Heads Nook. Cumb 6J 53
Heage. Derbs 4A 36
Healaugh. N Yor
nr. Grinton 6J 47
nr. York 3C 42
Heald Green. G Man 1G 35
Heale. Devn 1F 6
Healey. G Man 6G 41
Healey. Nmbd 6D 54
Healey. N Yor 7K 47
Healeyfield. Dur 7D 54
Healing. NE Lin 6K 43
Heamoor. Corn 5H 3
Heanish. Arg 3F 62
Heanor. Derbs 5B 36
Heanton Punchardon. Devn 2E 6
Heapham. Linc 1F 36
Heartsease. Powy 6L 25
Heasley Mill. Devn 2G 7
Heaste. High 4H 69
Heath. Derbs 3B 36
The Heath. Norf
nr. Buxton 7J 39
nr. Fakenham 7F 38
nr. Hevingham 7H 39
The Heath. Staf 6J 35
The Heath. Suff 8H 31
Heath and Reach. C Beds 1G 21
Heath Common. W Sus 4J 11
Heathcote. Derbs 3K 35
Heath Cross. Devn 6G 7
Heathencote. Nptn 7E 28
Heath End. Hants 7C 20
Heath End. Leics 7A 36
Heath End. W Mid 1J 27
Heather. Leics 8A 36
Heatherfield. High 1F 68
Heatherton. Derb 6M 35
Heathfield. Cambs 7A 30
Heathfield. Cumb 7F 52
Heathfield. Devn 8H 7
Heathfield. E Sus 3B 12
Heathfield. Ren 3B 58
Heathfield. Som
nr. Lydeard St Lawrence 2L 7
nr. Norton Fitzwarren 3L 7
Heath Green. Worc 4J 27
Heathhall. Dum 4D 52
Heath Hayes. Staf 8J 35
Heath Hill. Shrp 8F 34
Heath House. Som 1C 8
Heathrow Airport. G Lon 119 (6H 21)
Heathstock. Devn 5M 7
Heathton. Shrp 2G 27
Heathtop. Derbs 6L 35
Heath Town. W Mid 2H 27
Heatley. Staf 7J 35
Heatley. Warr 1F 34
Heaton. Lanc 1C 40
Heaton. Staf 3H 35
Heaton. Tyne 5F 54
Heaton. W Yor 4K 41
Heaton Moor. G Man 8G 41
Heaton's Bridge. Lanc 6C 40
Heaverham. Kent 8B 22
Heavitree. Devn 6J 7
Hebburn. Tyne 5G 55
Hebden. N Yor 1J 41
Hebden Bridge. W Yor 5H 41
Hebden Green. Ches W 3E 34
Hebing End. Herts 1L 21
Hebron. Carm 4H 15
Hebron. Nmbd 3E 54
Heck. Dum 3E 52
Heckdyke. Notts 8E 42
Heckfield. Hants 7E 20
Heckfield Green. Suff 4H 31
Heckfordbridge. Essx 1F 22
Heckington. Linc 5J 37
Heckmondwike. W Yor 5L 41
Heddington. Wilts 7H 19
Heddle. Orkn 8C 88
Heddon. Devn 3F 6
Heddon-on-the-Wall. Nmbd 5E 54
Hedenham. Norf 2K 31
Hedge End. Hants 4B 10
Hedgerley. Buck 5G 21
Hedging. Som 3B 8
Hedley on the Hill. Nmbd 6D 54
Hednesford. Staf 8J 35
Hedon. E Yor 5J 43
Hegdon Hill. Here 6D 26
Heglibister. Shet 2D 90
Heighington. Darl 3L 47
Heighington. Linc 3H 37
Heightington. Worc 4F 26
Heights of Brae. High 7F 78
Heights of Fodderty. High 7F 78
Heights of Kinlochewe.
High 7A 78
Heiton. Bord 6E 60
Hele. Devn
nr. Exeter 5J 7
nr. Holsworthy 6C 6
nr. Ilfracombe 1E 6
Hele. Torb 5M 5
Helen's Bay. Ards 4J 93
Helensburgh. Arg 1A 58
Helford. Corn 6L 3
Helhoughton. Norf 7E 38
Helions Bumpstead. Essx 7C 30
Helland. Corn 4C 4
Helland. Som 3B 8
Hellandbridge. Corn 4C 4
Hellesdon. Norf 8J 39
Hellesveor. Corn 4J 3
Hellidon. Nptn 6C 28
Hellifield. N Yor 2G 41
Hellingly. E Sus 4B 12
Hellington. Norf 1K 31
Hellister. Shet 3D 90
Helmdon. Nptn 7C 28
Helmingham. Suff 6H 31
Helmington Row. Dur 8E 54
Helmsdale. High 2L 79
Helmshore. Lanc 5F 40
Helmsley. N Yor 7D 48
Helperby. N Yor 1B 42
Helperthorpe. N Yor 8G 49
Helpringham. Linc 5J 37
Helpston. Pet 1J 29
Helsby. Ches W 2C 34
Helsey. Linc 2B 38
Helston. Corn 6K 3
Helstone. Corn 3C 4
Helton. Cumb 3D 46
Helwith. N Yor 5J 47
Helwith Bridge. N Yor 1G 41
Helygain. Flin 3M 33
The Hem. Shrp 1F 26
Hemblington. Norf 8K 39
Hemel Hempstead. Herts 3H 21
Hemerdon. Devn 6H 5
Hemingbrough. N Yor 4D 42
Hemingby. Linc 2K 37
Hemingfield. S Yor 7A 42
Hemingford Abbots.
Cambs 4K 29
Hemingford Grey. Cambs 4K 29
Hemingstone. Suff 6H 31
Hemington. Leics 7B 36
Hemington. Nptn 3H 29
Hemington. Som 8F 18
Hemley. Suff 7J 31
Hemlington. Midd 4B 48
Hempholme. E Yor 2H 43
Hempnall. Norf 2J 31
Hempnall Green. Norf 2J 31
Hempriggs. High 7E 86
Hemp's Green. Essx 1F 22
Hempstead. Essx 8C 30
Hempstead. Medw 7D 22
Hempstead. Norf
nr. Holt 6H 39
nr. Stalham 7L 39
Hempsted. Glos 2G 19
Hempton. Norf 7F 38
Hempton. Oxon 8B 28
Hemsby. Norf 8L 39
Hemswell. Linc 8G 43
Hemswell Cliff. Linc 1G 37
Hemsworth. Dors 5H 9
Hemsworth. W Yor 6B 42
Hemyock. Devn 4L 7
Henallt. Carm 4L 15
Henbury. Bris 6D 18
Henbury. Ches E 2G 35
Hendomen. Powy 3M 25

Hendon – Inchbrook

Hendon. G Lon 5K 21
Hendon. Tyne 6H 55
Hendra. Corn 6B 4
Hendre. B'end 6J 17
Hendreforgan. Rhon 6J 17
Hendy. Carm 4E 16
Heneglwys. IOA 3D 32
Henfeddau Fawr. Pemb 3J 15
Henfield. S Glo 6E 18
Henfield. W Sus 4K 11
Henford. Devn 6C 6
Hengoed. Cphy 5L 17
Hengoed. Shrp 6A 34
Hengrave. Suff 5E 30
Henham. Essx 1B 22
Heniarth. Powy 2L 25
Henlade. Som 3A 8
Henley. Dors 5E 8
Henley. Shrp
nr. Church Stretton 3C 26
nr. Ludlow 4D 26
Henley. Som 2C 8
Henley. Suff 6H 31
Henley. W Sus 3F 10
Henley Down. E Sus 4D 12
Henley-in-Arden. Warw 5K 27
Henley-on-Thames. Oxon 5E 20
Henley Street. Kent 7C 22
Henllan. Cdgn 2K 15
Henllan. Den 4K 33
Henllan. Mon 1A 18
Henllan Amgoed. Carm 5H 15
Henllys. Torf 4A 18
Henlow. C Beds 8J 29
Hennock. Devn 7H 7
Henny Street. Essx 8E 30
Henryd. Cnwy 3G 33
Henry's Moat. Pemb 4G 15
Hensall. N Yor 5C 42
Henshaw. Nmbd 5A 54
Hensingham. Cumb 3J 45
Henstead. Suff 3L 31
Hensting. Hants 3B 10
Henstridge. Som 4F 8
Henstridge Ash. Som 3F 8
Henstridge Bowden. Som 3E 8
Henstridge Marsh. Som 3F 8
Henton. Oxon 3E 20
Henton. Som 1C 8
Henwood. Corn 8B 6
Heogan. Shet 3E 90
Heolgerrig. Mer T 4K 17
Heol Senni. Powy 2J 17
Heol-y-Cyw. B'end 6J 17
Hepburn. Nmbd 7H 61
Hepple. Nmbd 1C 54
Hepscott. Nmbd 3F 54
Heptonstall. W Yor 5H 41
Hepworth. Suff 4F 30
Hepworth. W Yor 7K 41
Herbrandston. Pemb 6E 14
Hereford. Here 8D 26
Heribusta. High 6F 76
Heriot. Bord 4B 60
Hermiston. Edin 2K 59
Hermitage. Dors 5E 8
Hermitage. Bord 2K 53
Hermitage. W Ber 6C 20
Hermitage. W Sus 5E 10
Hermon. Carm
nr. Llandeilo 2F 16
nr. Newcastle Emlyn 3K 15
Hermon. IOA 4C 32
Hermon. Pemb 3J 15
Herne. Kent 7H 23
Herne Bay. Kent 7H 23
Herne Common. Kent 7H 23
Herne Pound. Kent 8C 22
Herner. Devn 3E 6
Hernhill. Kent 7G 23
Herodsfoot. Corn 5E 4
Heronden. Kent 8J 23
Herongate. Essx 4C 22
Heronsford. S Ayr 3G 51
Heronsgate. Herts 4H 21
Heron's Ghyll. E Sus 3A 12
Herra. Shet 4L 91
Herriard. Hants 1D 10
Herringfleet. Suff 2L 31
Herringswell. Suff 5D 30
Herrington. Tyne 6G 55
Hersden. Kent 7J 23
Hersham. Corn 5B 6
Hersham. Surr 7J 21
Herstmonceux. E Sus 4C 12
Herston. Dors 8J 9
Herston. Orkn 2F 86
Hertford. Herts 2L 21
Hertford Heath. Herts 2L 21
Hertingfordbury. Herts 2L 21
Hesketh. Lanc 5C 40
Hesketh Bank. Lanc 5C 40
Hesketh Lane. Lanc 3E 40
Hesket Newmarket. Cumb 8H 53
Heskin Green. Lanc 6D 40
Hesleden. Dur 8H 55
Hesleyside. Nmbd 3B 54
Heslington. York 2D 42
Hessay. York 2C 42
Hessenford. Corn 6F 4
Hessett. Suff 5F 30
Hessilhead. N Ayr 4B 58
Hessle. E Yor 5H 43
Hestaford. Shet 2C 90
Hest Bank. Lanc 1C 40
Hester's Way. Glos 1H 19
Hestinsetter. Shet 3C 90
Heston. G Lon 6J 21
Hestwall. Orkn 8B 88
Heswall. Mers 1A 34
Hethe. Oxon 1C 20
Hethelpit Cross. Glos 1F 18
Hethersett. Norf 1H 31
Hethersgill. Cumb 5J 53
Hetherside. Cumb 5J 53
Hethpool. Nmbd 7F 60
Hett. Dur 8F 54
Hetton. N Yor 2H 41
Hetton-le-Hole. Tyne 7G 55
Hetton Steads. Nmbd 6H 61
Heugh. Nmbd 4D 54
Heugh-head. Abers 4C 72
Heveningham. Suff 4K 31
Hever. Kent 1A 12
Heversham. Cumb 7C 46
Hevingham. Norf 7H 39
Hewas Water. Corn 7B 4
Hewelsfield. Glos 3D 18
Hewish. N Som 7C 18
Hewish. Som 5C 8
Hewood. Dors 5B 8
Heworth. York 2D 42
Hexham. Nmbd 5C 54
Hextable. Kent 6B 22
Hexton. Herts 8J 29
Hexworthy. Devn 8F 6
Heybridge. Essx
nr. Brentwood 4C 22
nr. Maldon 3E 22
Heybridge Basin. Essx 3E 22
Heybrook Bay. Devn 7G 5
Heydon. Cambs 7M 29
Heydon. Norf 7H 39
Heydour. Linc 6H 37
Heylipol. Arg 3E 62
Heyop. Powy 5M 25
Heysham. Lanc 1C 40
Heyshott. W Sus 4F 10
Heytesbury. Wilts 1H 9
Heythrop. Oxon 1A 20
Heywood. G Man 6G 41
Heywood. Wilts 8G 19
Hibaldstow. N Lin 7G 43
Hickleton. S Yor 7B 42
Hickling. Norf 7L 39
Hickling. Notts 7D 36
Hickling Green. Norf 7L 39
Hickling Heath. Norf 7L 39
Hickstead. W Sus 3K 11
Hidcote Bartrim. Glos 7K 27
Hidcote Boyce. Glos 7K 27
Higford. Shrp 1F 26
High Ackworth. W Yor 6B 42
Higham. Derbs 4A 36
Higham. Kent 6D 22
Higham. Lanc 4G 41
Higham. S Yor 7M 41
Higham. Suff
nr. Ipswich 8G 31
nr. Newmarket 5D 30
Higham Dykes. Nmbd 4E 54
Higham Ferrers. Nptn 5G 29
Higham Gobion. C Beds 8J 29
Higham on the Hill. Leics 2A 28
Highampton. Devn 5D 6
High Angerton. Nmbd 3D 54
High Auldgirth. Dum 3D 52
High Bankhill. Cumb 7K 53
High Banton. N Lan 1F 58
High Barnet. G Lon 4K 21
High Beech. Essx 4M 21
High Bentham. N Yor 1E 40
High Bickington. Devn 3F 6
High Biggins. Cumb 8D 46
High Birkwith. N Yor 8F 46
High Blantyre. S Lan 4E 58
High Bonnybridge. Falk 2G 59
High Borrans. Cumb 5C 46
High Bradfield. S Yor 8L 41
High Bray. Devn 2F 6
Highbridge. Cumb 7H 53
Highbridge. High 7C 70
Highbridge. Som 1B 8
Highbrook. W Sus 2L 11
High Brooms. Kent 1B 12
High Bullen. Devn 3E 6
Highburton. W Yor 6K 41
Highbury. Som 1E 8
High Buston. Nmbd 1F 54
High Callerton. Nmbd 4E 54
High Carlingill. Cumb 5E 46
High Catton. E Yor 2E 42
High Church. Nmbd 3E 54
Highclere. Hants 7B 20
Highcliffe. Dors 6L 9
High Cogges. Oxon 3A 20
High Common. Norf 1F 30
High Coniscliffe. Darl 4L 47
High Crosby. Cumb 6J 53
High Cross. Hants 3E 10
High Cross. Herts 2L 21
High Easter. Essx 2C 22
High Eggborough. N Yor 5C 42
High Ellington. N Yor 7K 47
Higher Alham. Som 1E 8
Higher Ansty. Dors 5F 8
Higher Ashton. Devn 7H 7
Higher Ballam. Lanc 4B 40
Higher Bartle. Lanc 4D 40
Higher Bockhampton. Dors 6F 8
Higher Bojewyan. Corn 5G 3
High Ercall. Telf 8D 34
Higher Cheriton. Devn 5L 7
Higher Clovelly. Devn 3C 6
Higher Compton. Plym 6G 5
Higher Dean. Devn 5K 5
Higher Dinting. Derbs 8J 41
Higher Dunstone. Devn 8G 7
Higher End. G Man 7D 40
Higherford. Lanc 3G 41
Higher Gabwell. Devn 5M 5
Higher Halstock Leigh. Dors 5D 8
Higher Heysham. Lanc 1C 40
Higher Hurdsfield. Ches E 2H 35
Higher Kingcombe. Dors 6D 8
Higher Kinnerton. Flin 3B 34
Higher Melcombe. Dors 5F 8
Higher Penwortham. Lanc 5D 40
Higher Porthpean. Corn 6C 4
Higher Poynton. Ches E 1H 35
Higher Shotton. Flin 3B 34
Higher Shurlach. Ches W 2E 34
Higher Slade. Devn 1E 6
Higher Tale. Devn 5K 7
Higher Town. IOS 1H 3
Higher Town. Som 1J 7
Highertown. Corn 4M 3
Higher Vexford. Som 2L 7
Higher Walton. Lanc 5D 40
Higher Walton. Warr 1D 34
Higher Whatcombe. Dors 5G 9
Higher Wheelton. Lanc 5E 40
Higher Whiteleigh. Corn 6B 6
Higher Whitley. Ches W 1E 34
Higher Wincham. Ches W 2E 34
Higher Wraxall. Dors 5D 8
Higher Wych. Ches W 5C 34
Higher Yalberton. Torb 6L 5
High Etherley. Dur 3K 47
High Ferry. Linc 5L 37
Highfield. E Yor 4E 42
Highfield. N Ayr 4B 58
Highfield. Tyne 6E 54
Highfields Caldecote.
Cambs 6L 29
High Gallowhill. E Dun 2E 58
High Garrett. Essx 1D 22
Highgate. G Lon 5K 21
Highgate. N Ayr 4B 58
Highgate. Powy 3L 25
High Grange. Dur 8E 54
High Green. Cumb 5C 46
High Green. Norf 1H 31
High Green. Shrp 3F 26
High Green. S Yor 8M 41
High Green. W Yor 6K 41
High Green. Worc 7G 27
Highgreen Manor. Nmbd 2B 54
High Halden. Kent 2E 12
High Halstow. Medw 6D 22
High Ham. Som 2C 8
High Harrington. Cumb 2K 45
High Haswell. Dur 7G 55
High Hatton. Shrp 7E 34
High Hawsker. N Yor 5G 49
High Hesket. Cumb 7J 53
High Hesleden. Dur 8H 55
High Hoyland. S Yor 6L 41
High Hunsley. E Yor 4G 43
High Hurstwood. E Sus 3A 12
High Hutton. N Yor 1E 42
High Ireby. Cumb 8G 53
High Keil. Arg 1B 50
High Kelling. Norf 6H 39
High Kilburn. N Yor 8C 48
High Knipe. Cumb 4D 46
High Lands. Dur 3K 47
The Highlands. Shrp 3E 26
High Lane. G Man 1H 35
High Lane. Worc 5E 26
Highlane. Ches E 3G 35
Highlane. Derbs 1B 36
High Laver. Essx 3B 22
Highlaws. Cumb 7F 52
Highleadon. Glos 1F 18
High Legh. Ches E 1F 34
Highleigh. W Sus 6F 10
High Leven. Stoc T 4B 48
Highley. Shrp 3F 26
High Littleton. Bath 8E 18
High Longthwaite. Cumb 7G 53
High Lorton. Cumb 2L 45
High Marishes. N Yor 8F 48
High Marnham. Notts 2F 36
High Melton. S Yor 7C 42
High Mickley. Nmbd 5D 54
High Moor. Lanc 6D 40
Highmoor. Cumb 7G 53
Highmoor. Oxon 5E 20
Highmoor Cross. Oxon 5E 20
Highmoor Hill. Mon 5C 18
Highnam. Glos 2F 18
High Newport. Tyne 6G 55
High Newton. Cumb 7C 46
High Newton-by-the-Sea.
Nmbd 7K 61
High Nibthwaite. Cumb 7A 46
High Offley. Staf 7F 34
High Ongar. Essx 3B 22
High Onn. Staf 8G 35
High Orchard. Glos 2G 19
High Park. Mers 6B 40
High Roding. Essx 2C 22
High Row. Cumb 8H 53
High Salvington. W Sus 5J 11
High Scales. Cumb 7F 52
High Shaw. N Yor 6G 47
High Shincliffe. Dur 7F 54
High Side. Cumb 8G 53
High Spen. Tyne 5E 54
Highsted. Kent 7F 22
High Stoop. Dur 7E 54
High Street. Corn 6B 4
High Street. Suff
nr. Aldeburgh 6L 31
nr. Bungay 3K 31
nr. Yoxford 4L 31
High Street Green. Suff 6G 31
Highstreet Green. Essx 8D 30
Highstreet Green. Surr 2G 11
Hightae. Dum 4E 52
High Throston. Hart 8H 55
High Town. Staf 8H 35
Hightown. Ches E 3G 35
Hightown. Mers 7A 40
Hightown Green. Suff 6F 30
High Toynton. Linc 3K 37
High Trewhitt. Nmbd 1D 54
High Valleyfield. Fife 1J 59
Highway. Here 7C 26
Highweek. Devn 8H 7
High Westwood. Dur 6E 54
Highwood. Staf 6J 35
Highwood. Worc 5E 26
High Worsall. N Yor 5A 48
Highworth. Swin 4L 19
High Wray. Cumb 6B 46
High Wych. Herts 2A 22
High Wycombe. Buck 4F 20
Hilborough. Norf 1E 30
Hilcott. Wilts 8K 19
Hildenborough. Kent 1B 12
Hildersham. Cambs 7B 30
Hilderstone. Staf 6H 35
Hilderthorpe. E Yor 1J 43
Hilfield. Dors 5E 8
Hilgay. Norf 2C 30
Hill. S Glo 4E 18
Hill. Warw 5B 28
Hill. Worc 7H 27
The Hill. Cumb 6L 45
Hillam. N Yor 5C 42
Hillbeck. Cumb 4F 46
Hillberry. IOM 7C 44
Hillborough. Kent 7J 23
Hillbourne. Pool 6J 9
Hillbrae. Abers
nr. Aberchirder 1F 72
nr. Inverurie 3G 73
nr. Methlick 2H 73
Hill Brow. Hants 3E 10
Hillbutts. Dors 5H 9
Hillcliffiane. Derbs 5L 35
Hillcommon. Som 3L 7
Hill Deverill. Wilts 1G 9
Hilldyke. Linc 5L 37
Hill End. Dur 8D 54
Hill End. Fife 8D 66
Hill End. N Yor 2J 41
Hillend. Fife 1K 59
Hillend. N Lan 3G 59
Hillend. Shrp 2G 27
Hillend. Swan 7L 15
Hillersland. Glos 2D 18
Hillerton. Devn 6G 7
Hillesden. Buck 1D 20
Hillesley. Glos 5F 18
Hillfarrance. Som 3L 7
Hill Gate. Here 1C 18
Hill Green. Essx 8A 30
Hill Green. W Ber 6B 20
Hillhall. Lis 5H 93
Hill Head. Hants 5C 10
Hillhead. Abers 2E 72
Hillhead. Devn 6M 5
Hillhead. S Ayr 8C 58
Hillhead of Auchentumb.
Abers 8J 81
Hilliard's Cross. Staf 8K 35
Hilliclay. High 5C 86
Hillingdon. G Lon 5H 21
Hillington. Glas 3D 58
Hillington. Norf 7D 38
Hillmorton. Warw 4C 28
Hill of Beath. Fife 8E 66
Hill of Fearn. High 6J 79
Hill of Fiddes. Abers 3J 73
Hill of Keillor. Ang 3F 66
Hill of Overbrae. Abers 7H 81
Hill Ridware. Staf 8J 35
Hillsborough. Lis 6H 93
Hillsborough. S Yor 8M 41
Hill Side. W Yor 6K 41
Hillside. Abers 6J 73
Hillside. Ang 1L 67
Hillside. Devn 5K 5
Hillside. Mers 6B 40
Hillside. Orkn 7C 88
Hillside. Shet 1E 90
Hillside. Shrp 3E 26
Hillside. Worc 5F 26
Hillside of Prieston. Ang 4G 67
Hill Somersal. Derbs 6K 35
Hillstown. Derbs 3B 36
Hillstreet. Hants 4M 9
Hillswick. Shet 6G 91
Hill Top. Dur
nr. Barnard Castle 3H 47
nr. Durham 7F 54
nr. Stanley 6E 54
Hilltown. New M 7H 93
Hill View. Dors 6H 9
Hillwell. Shet 6D 90
Hill Wootton. Warw 5M 27
Hillyland. Per 5D 66
Hilmarton. Wilts 6J 19
Hilperton. Wilts 8G 19
Hilperton Marsh. Wilts 8G 19
Hilsea. Port 5D 10
Hilston. E Yor 4K 43
Hiltingbury. Hants 3B 10
Hilton. Cambs 5K 29
Hilton. Cumb 3F 46
Hilton. Derbs 6L 35
Hilton. Dors 5F 8
Hilton. Dur 3K 47
Hilton. High 5H 79
Hilton. Shrp 2F 26
Hilton. Staf 1J 27
Hilton. Stoc T 4B 48
Hilton of Cadboll. High 6J 79
Himbleton. Worc 6H 27
Himley. Staf 2G 27
Hincaster. Cumb 7D 46
Hinchwick. Glos 1K 19
Hinckley. Leics 2B 28
Hinderclay. Suff 4G 31
Hinderwell. N Yor 4E 48
Hindford. Shrp 6B 34
Hindhead. Surr 2F 10
Hindley. G Man 7E 40
Hindley. Nmbd 6D 54
Hindley Green. G Man 7E 40
Hindlip. Worc 6G 27
Hindolveston. Norf 7G 39
Hindon. Wilts 2H 9
Hindringham. Norf 6F 38
Hingham. Norf 1G 31
Hinksford. Staf 3G 27
Hinstock. Shrp 7E 34
Hintlesham. Suff 7G 31
Hinton. Hants 6L 9
Hinton. Here 8B 26
Hinton. Nptn 6C 28
Hinton. Shrp 1C 26
Hinton. S Glo 6F 18
Hinton Ampner. Hants 3C 10
Hinton Blewett. Bath 8D 18
Hinton Charterhouse. Bath 8F 18
Hinton-in-the-Hedges. Nptn 8C 28
Hinton Martell. Dors 5J 9
Hinton on the Green. Worc 7J 27
Hinton Parva. Swin 5L 19
Hinton St George. Som 4C 8
Hinton St Mary. Dors 4F 8
Hinton Waldrist. Oxon 4A 20
Hints. Shrp 4E 26
Hints. Staf 1K 27
Hinwick. Bed 5G 29
Hinxhill. Kent 1G 13
Hinxton. Cambs 7A 30
Hinxworth. Herts 7K 29
Hipley. Hants 4D 10
Hipperholme. W Yor 5K 41
Hipsburn. Nmbd 8K 61
Hipswell. N Yor 6K 47
Hiraeth. Carm 4H 15
Hirn. Abers 5G 73
Hirnant. Powy 8K 33
Hirst. N Lan 3G 59
Hirst. Nmbd 3F 54
Hirst Courtney. N Yor 5D 42
Hirwaen. Den 4L 33
Hirwaun. Rhon 4J 17
Hiscott. Devn 3E 6
Histon. Cambs 5M 29
Hitcham. Suff 6F 30
Hitchin. Herts 1J 21
Hittisleigh. Devn 6G 7
Hittisleigh Barton. Devn 6G 7
Hive. E Yor 4F 42
Hixon. Staf 7J 35
Hoaden. Kent 8J 23
Hoar Cross. Staf 7K 35
Hoarwithy. Here 1D 18
Hoath. Kent 7J 23
Yr Hôb. Flin 4B 34
Hobarris. Shrp 4B 26
Hobbister. Orkn 1E 86
Hobbles Green. Suff 6D 30
Hobbs Cross. Essx 4A 22
Hobkirk. Bord 8C 60
Hobson. Dur 6E 54
Hoby. Leics 8D 36
Hockering. Norf 8G 39
Hockering Heath. Norf 8G 39
Hockerton. Notts 4E 36
Hockley. Essx 4E 22
Hockley. Staf 1L 27
Hockley. W Mid 4L 27
Hockley Heath. W Mid 4K 27
Hockliffe. C Beds 1G 21
Hockwold cum Wilton.
Norf 3D 30
Hockworthy. Devn 4K 7
Hoddesdon. Herts 3L 21
Hoddlesden. Bkbn 5F 40
Hoddomcross. Dum 4F 52
Hodgeston. Pemb 7G 15
Hodley. Powy 3L 25
Hodnet. Shrp 7E 34
Hodsoll Street. Kent 7C 22
Hodson. Swin 5K 19
Hodthorpe. Derbs 2C 36
Hoe. Norf 8F 38
The Hoe. Plym 6G 5
Hoe Gate. Hants 4D 10
Hoff. Cumb 4E 46
Hoffleet Stow. Linc 6K 37
Hogaland. Shet 6H 91
Hogben's Hill. Kent 8G 23
Hoggard's Green. Suff 6E 30
Hoggeston. Buck 1F 20
Hoggrill's End. Warw 2L 27
Hogha Gearraidh. W Isl 6J 75
Hoghton. Lanc 5E 40
Hoghton Bottoms. Lanc 5E 40
Hognaston. Derbs 4L 35
Hogsthorpe. Linc 2B 38
Hogstock. Dors 5H 9
Holbeach. Linc 7L 37
Holbeach Bank. Linc 7L 37
Holbeach Clough. Linc 7L 37
Holbeach Drove. Linc 8L 37
Holbeach Hurn. Linc 7L 37
Holbeach St Johns. Linc 8L 37
Holbeach St Marks. Linc 6L 37
Holbeach St Matthew. Linc 6M 37
Holbeck. Notts 2C 36
Holbeck. W Yor 4L 41
Holbeck Woodhouse. Notts 2C 36
Holberrow Green. Worc 6J 27
Holbeton. Devn 6J 5
Holborn. G Lon 5L 21
Holbrook. Derbs 5A 36
Holbrook. S Yor 1B 36
Holbrook. Suff 8H 31
Holburn. Nmbd 6H 61
Holbury. Hants 5B 10
Holcombe. Devn 8J 7
Holcombe. G Man 6F 40
Holcombe. Som 1E 8
Holcombe Brook. G Man 6F 40
Holcombe Rogus. Devn 4K 7
Holcot. Nptn 5E 28
Holden. Lanc 3F 40
Holdenby. Nptn 5D 28
Holder's Green. Essx 1C 22
Holdgate. Shrp 3D 26
Holdingham. Linc 5H 37
Holditch. Dors 5B 8
Holemoor. Devn 5D 6
Hole Street. W Sus 4J 11
Holford. Som 1L 7
Holker. Cumb 8B 46
Holkham. Norf 5E 38
Hollacombe. Devn 5C 6
Holland. Orkn
on Papa Westray 4D 88
on Stronsay 7F 88
Holland Fen. Linc 5K 37
Holland Lees. Lanc 7D 40
Holland-on-Sea. Essx 2J 23
Holland Park. W Mid 1J 27
Hollandstoun. Orkn 4G 89
Hollesley. Suff 7K 31
Hollinfare. Warr 8E 40
Hollingbourne. Kent 8E 22
Hollingbury. Brig 5L 11
Hollingdon. Buck 1F 20
Hollingrove. E Sus 3C 12
Hollington. Derbs 6L 35
Hollington. E Sus 4D 12
Hollington. Staf 6J 35
Hollington Grove. Derbs 6L 35
Hollingwood B2 36
Hollingworth. G Man 8J 41
Hollins. Derbs 2M 35
Hollins. G Man
nr. Bury 7G 41
nr. Middleton 7G 41
Hollinsclough. Staf 3J 35
Hollinswood. Telf 1F 26
Hollinthorpe. W Yor 4A 42
Hollinwood. G Man 7H 41
Hollinwood. Shrp 6D 34
Hollocombe. Devn 4F 6
Holloway. Derbs 4M 35
Hollowell. Nptn 4D 28
Hollow Meadows. S Yor 1L 35
Hollows. Dum 4H 53
Hollybush. Cphy 4L 17
Hollybush. E Ayr 8B 58
Hollybush. Worc 8F 26
Holly End. Norf 1A 30
Holly Hill. N Yor 5K 47
Hollyhurst. Shrp 5D 34
Hollym. E Yor 5L 43
Hollywood. Worc 4J 27
Holmacott. Devn 3E 6
Holmbridge. W Yor 7K 41
Holmbury St Mary. Surr 1J 11
Holmbush. Corn 6C 4
Holmcroft. Staf 7H 35
Holme. Cambs 3J 29
Holme. Cumb 8D 46
Holme. N Lin 7G 43
Holme. N Yor 7A 48
Holme. Notts 4F 36
Holme. W Yor 7K 41
Holmebridge. Dors 7G 9
Holme Chapel. Lanc 5G 41
Holme Hale. Norf 1E 30
Holme Lacy. Here 8D 26
Holme Marsh. Here 6B 26
Holmend. Dum 1E 52
Holme next the Sea. Norf 5D 38
Holme-on-Spalding-Moor.
E Yor 4F 42
Holme on the Wolds. E Yor 3G 43
Holme Pierrepont. Notts 6D 36
Holmer. Here 7D 26
Holmer Green. Buck 4G 21
Holmes. Lanc 6C 40
Holme St Cuthbert. Cumb 7F 52
Holmes Chapel. Ches E 3F 34
Holmesfield. Derbs 2M 35
Holmeswood. Lanc 6C 40
Holmewood. Derbs 3B 36
Holmfirth. W Yor 7K 41
Holmhead. E Ayr 7D 58
Holmisdale. High 1C 68
Holm of Drumlanrig. Dum 2C 52
Holmpton. E Yor 5L 43
Holmrook. Cumb 5K 45
Holmsgarth. Shet 3E 90
Holmside. Dur 7F 54
Holmwrangle. Cumb 7K 53
Holne. Devn 5K 5
Holsworthy. Devn 5C 6
Holsworthy Beacon. Devn 5C 6
Holt. Dors 5J 9
Holt. Norf 6G 39
Holt. Wilts 7G 19
Holt. Worc 5G 27
Holt. Wrex 4C 34
Holtby. York 2D 42
Holt End. Hants 2D 10
Holt End. Worc 5J 27
Holt Fleet. Worc 5G 27
Holt Green. Lanc 7B 40
Holt Heath. Dors 5J 9
Holt Heath. Worc 5G 27
Holton. Oxon 3C 20
Holton. Som 3E 8
Holton. Suff 4K 31
Holton cum Beckering. Linc 1J 37
Holton Heath. Dors 6H 9
Holton le Clay. Linc 7K 43
Holton le Moor. Linc 8H 43
Holton St Mary. Suff 8G 31
Holt Pound. Hants 1F 10
Holtsmere End. Herts 2H 21
Holtye. E Sus 2A 12
Holwell. Dors 4F 8
Holwell. Herts 8J 29
Holwell. Leics 7E 36
Holwell. Oxon 3L 19
Holwell. Som 1F 8
Holwick. Dur 3H 47
Holworth. Dors 7F 8
Holybourne. Hants 1E 10
Holy City. Devn 5B 8
Holy Cross. Worc 4H 27
Holyfield. Essx 3L 21
Holyhead. IOA 2B 32
Holy Island. Nmbd 5J 61
Holymoorside. Derbs 3M 35
Holyport. Wind 6F 20
Holystone. Nmbd 1C 54
Holytown. N Lan 3F 58
Holywell. Cambs 4L 29
Holywell. Corn 3L 3
Holywell. Dors 5D 8
Holywell. Flin 3L 33
Holywell. Glos 4F 18
Holywell. Nmbd 4G 55
Holywell. Warw 5K 27
Holywell Green. W Yor 6J 41
Holywell Lake. Som 3L 7
Holywell Row. Suff 4D 30
Holywood. Ards 5J 93
Holywood. Dum 3D 52
Homer. Shrp 1E 26
Homer Green. Mers 7B 40
Homersfield. Suff 3J 31
Hom Green. Here 1D 18
Homington. Wilts 3K 9
Honeyborough. Pemb 6F 14
Honeybourne. Worc 7K 27
Honeychurch. Devn 5F 6
Honeydon. Bed 6J 29
Honey Hill. Kent 7H 23
Honey Street. Wilts 7K 19
Honey Tye. Suff 8F 30
Honeywick. C Beds 1G 21
Honiley. Warw 4L 27
Honing. Norf 7K 39
Honingham. Norf 8H 39
Honington. Linc 5G 37
Honington. Suff 4F 30
Honington. Warw 7L 27
Honiton. Devn 5L 7
Honley. W Yor 6K 41
Honnington. Telf 8F 34
Hoo. Suff 6J 31
Hoobrook. Worc 4G 27
Hood Green. S Yor 7M 41
Hooe. E Sus 5C 12
Hooe. Plym 6H 5
Hooe Common. E Sus 4C 12
Hoo Green. Ches E 1F 34
Hoohill. Bkpl 4B 40
Hook. Cambs 2M 29
Hook. E Yor 5E 42
Hook. G Lon 7J 21
Hook. Hants
nr. Basingstoke 8E 20
nr. Fareham 5C 10
Hook. Pemb 5F 14
Hook. Wilts 5J 19
Hook-a-Gate. Shrp 1C 26
Hook Bank. Worc 7G 27
Hooke. Dors 5D 8
Hooker Gate. Tyne 6E 54
Hookgate. Staf 6F 34
Hook Green. Kent
nr. Lamberhurst 2C 12
nr. Meopham 7C 22
nr. Southfleet 6C 22
Hook Norton. Oxon 8A 28
Hook's Cross. Herts 1K 21
Hook Street. Glos 4E 18
Hookway. Devn 6H 7
Hookwood. Surr 1K 11
Hoole. Ches W 3C 34
Hooley. Surr 8K 21
Hooley Bridge. G Man 6G 41
Hooley Brow. G Man 6G 41
Hoo St Werburgh. Medw 6D 22
Hooton. Ches W 2B 34
Hooton Levitt. S Yor 8C 42
Hooton Pagnell. S Yor 7B 42
Hooton Roberts. S Yor 8B 42
Hoove. Shet 3D 90
Hope. Derbs 1K 35
Hope. Flin 4B 34
Hope. High 5G 85
Hope. Powy 1A 26
Hope. Shrp 1B 26
Hope. Staf 4K 35
Hope Bagot. Shrp 4D 26
Hope Bowdler. Shrp 2C 26
Hopedale. Staf 4K 35
Hope Green. Ches E 1H 35
Hopeman. Mor 7M 79
Hope Mansell. Here 2E 18
Hopesay. Shrp 3B 26
Hope's Green. Essx 5D 22
Hopetown. W Yor 5A 42
Hope under Dinmore. Here 6D 26
Hopley's Green. Here 6B 26
Hopperton. N Yor 2B 42
Hop Pole. Linc 8J 37
Hopstone. Shrp 2F 26
Hopton. Derbs 4L 35
Hopton. Powy 3M 25
Hopton. Shrp
nr. Oswestry 7B 34
nr. Wem 7D 34
Hopton. Staf 7H 35
Hopton. Suff 4F 30
Hopton Cangeford. Shrp 3D 26
Hopton Castle. Shrp 4B 26
Hopton Heath. Staf 7H 35
Hoptonheath. Shrp 4B 26
Hopton on Sea. Norf 1M 31
Hopton Wafers. Shrp 4E 26
Hopwas. Staf 1K 27
Hopwood. Worc 4J 27
Horam. E Sus 4B 12
Horbling. Linc 6J 37
Horbury. W Yor 6L 41
Horcott. Glos 3K 19
Horden. Dur 7H 55
Horderley. Shrp 3C 26
Hordle. Hants 6L 9
Hordley. Shrp 6B 34
Horeb. Carm
nr. Brechfa 4M 15
nr. Llanelli 6L 15
Horeb. Cdgn 2K 15
Horfield. Bris 6D 18
Horgabost. W Isl 4B 76
Horham. Suff 4J 31
Horkstow. N Lin 6G 43
Horley. Oxon 7B 28
Horley. Surr 1K 11
Horn Ash. Dors 5B 8
Hornblotton Green. Som 2D 8
Hornby. Lanc 1D 40
Hornby. N Yor
nr. Appleton Wiske 5A 48
nr. Catterick Garrison 6L 47
Horncastle. Linc 3K 37
Hornchurch. G Lon 5B 22
Horncliffe. Nmbd 5G 61
Horndean. Hants 4E 10
Horndean. Bord 5F 60
Horndon. Devn 7E 6
Horndon on the Hill. Thur 5C 22
Horne. Surr 1L 11
Horner. Som 1J 7
Horning. Norf 8K 39
Horninghold. Leics 2F 28
Horninglow. Staf 7L 35
Horningsea. Cambs 5A 30
Horningsham. Wilts 1G 9
Horningtoft. Norf 7F 38
Hornsbury. Som 4B 8
Hornsby. Cumb 6K 53
Hornsbygate. Cumb 6K 53
Horns Corner. Kent 3D 12
Horns Cross. Devn 3C 6
Hornsea. E Yor 3K 43
Hornsea Burton. E Yor 3K 43
Hornsey. G Lon 5L 21
Hornton. Oxon 7A 28
Horpit. Swin 5L 19
Horrabridge. Devn 5H 5
Horringer. Suff 5E 30
Horringford. IOW 7C 10
Horrocks Fold. G Man 6F 40
Horrocksford. Lanc 3F 40
Horsbrugh Ford. Bord 6L 59
Horsebridge. Devn 8D 6
Horsebridge. Hants 2M 9
Horsebrook. Staf 8G 35
Horsecastle. N Som 7C 18
Horsehay. Telf 1E 26
Horseheath. Cambs 7C 30
Horsehouse. N Yor 7J 47
Horsell. Surr 8G 21
Horseman's Green. Wrex 5C 34
Horsenden. Buck 3E 20
Horseway. Cambs 3M 29
Horsey. Norf 7L 39
Horsey. Som 2B 8
Horsford. Norf 8H 39
Horsforth. W Yor 4L 41
Horsham. W Sus 2J 11
Horsham. Worc 6F 26
Horsham St Faith. Norf 8J 39
Horsington. Linc 3J 37
Horsington. Som 3F 8
Horsley. Derbs 5A 36
Horsley. Glos 4G 19
Horsley. Nmbd
nr. Prudhoe 5D 54
nr. Rochester 2B 54
Horsley Cross. Essx 1H 23
Horsleycross Street. Essx 1H 23
Horsleyhill. Bord 8C 60
Horsleyhope. Dur 7D 54
Horsley Woodhouse. Derbs 5A 36
Horsmonden. Kent 1C 12
Horspath. Oxon 3C 20
Horstead. Norf 8J 39
Horsted Keynes. W Sus 3L 11
Horton. Buck 2G 21
Horton. Dors 5J 9
Horton. Lanc 2G 41
Horton. Nptn 6F 28
Horton. Shrp 6C 34
Horton. Som 4B 8
Horton. S Glo 5F 18
Horton. Staf 4H 35
Horton. Swan 8L 15
Horton. Wilts 7J 19
Horton. Wind 6H 21
Horton Cross. Som 4B 8
Horton-cum-Studley. Oxon 2C 20
Horton Grange. Nmbd 4F 54
Horton Green. Ches W 5C 34
Horton Heath. Hants 4B 10
Horton in Ribblesdale.
N Yor 8G 47
Horton Kirby. Kent 7B 22
Hortonwood. Telf 8E 34
Horwich. G Man 6E 40
Horwich End. Derbs 1J 35
Horwood. Devn 3E 6
Hoscar. Lanc 6C 40
Hose. Leics 7E 36
Hosh. Per 5B 66
Hosta. W Isl 6J 75
Hoswick. Shet 5E 90
Hotham. E Yor 4F 42
Hothfield. Kent 1F 12
Hoton. Leics 7C 36
Houbie. Shet 4L 91
Hough. Arg 3E 62
Hough. Ches E
nr. Crewe 4F 34
nr. Wilmslow 2G 35
Hougham. Linc 5F 36
Hough Green. Hal 1C 34
Hough-on-the-Hill. Linc 5G 37
Houghton. Cambs 4K 29
Houghton. Cumb 6J 53
Houghton. Hants 2M 9
Houghton. Nmbd 5E 54
Houghton. Pemb 6F 14
Houghton. W Sus 4H 11
Houghton Bank. Darl 3L 47
Houghton Conquest.
C Beds 7H 29
Houghton Green. E Sus 3F 12
Houghton-le-Side. Darl 3L 47
Houghton-le-Spring. Tyne 6G 55
Houghton on the Hill. Leics 1D 28
Houghton Regis. C Beds 1H 21
Houghton St Giles. Norf 6F 38
Houlland. Shet
on Mainland 2D 90
on Yell 6K 91
Houlsyke. N Yor 5E 48
Houlton. Warw 4C 28
Hound. Hants 5B 10
Hound Green. Hants 8E 20
Houndslow. Bord 5D 60
Houndsmoor. Som 3L 7
Houndwood. Bord 3F 60
Hounsdown. Hants 4M 9
Hounslow. G Lon 6J 21
Housabister. Shet 2E 90
Housay. Shet 6L 91
Househill. High 8J 79
Housetter. Shet 5H 91
Houss. Shet 4D 90
Houston. Ren 3C 58
Housty. High 8C 86
Houton. Orkn 1E 86
Hove. Brig 106 (5K 11)
Hoveringham. Notts 5D 36
Hoveton. Norf 8K 39
Hovingham. N Yor 8D 48
How. Cumb 6K 53
How Caple. Here 8E 26
Howden. E Yor 5E 42
Howden-le-Wear. Dur 8E 54
Howe. High 5E 86
Howe. Norf 1J 31
Howe. N Yor 7A 48
The Howe. Cumb 7C 46
The Howe. IOM 8A 44
Howe Green. Essx 3D 22
Howe Green. Warw 3M 27
Howegreen. Essx 3E 22
Howell. Linc 5J 37
How End. C Beds 7H 29
Howe of Teuchar. Abers 1G 73
Howes. Dum 5F 52
Howe Street. Essx
nr. Chelmsford 2C 22
nr. Finchingfield 8C 30
Howey. Powy 7K 25
Howgate. Midl 4L 59
Howgill. Lanc 3G 41
Howgill. N Yor 2J 41
How Green. Kent 1A 12
How Hill. Norf 8K 39
Howick. Nmbd 8K 61
Howle. Telf 7E 34
Howle Hill. Here 1E 18
Howleigh. Som 4M 7
Howlett End. Essx 8B 30
Howley. Som 5A 8
Howley. Warr 1E 34
Hownam. Bord 8E 60
Howsham. N Lin 7H 43
Howsham. N Yor 1E 42
Howtel. Nmbd 6F 60
Howt Green. Kent 7E 22
Howton. Here 1C 18
Howwood. Ren 3B 58
Hoxne. Suff 4H 31
Hoylake. Mers 2M 33
Hoyland. S Yor 7A 42
Hoylandswaine. S Yor 7L 41
Hoyle. W Sus 4G 11
Hubberholme. N Yor 8H 47
Hubberston. Pemb 6E 14
Hubbert's Bridge. Linc 5K 37
Huby. N Yor
nr. Harrogate 3L 41
nr. York 1C 42
Hucclecote. Glos 2G 19
Hucking. Kent 8E 22
Hucknall. Notts 5C 36
Huddersfield. W Yor 6K 41
Huddington. Worc 6H 27
Huddlesford. Staf 1K 27
Hudswell. N Yor 5K 47
Huggate. E Yor 2F 42
Hugglescote. Leics 8B 36
Hughenden Valley. Buck 4F 20
Hughley. Shrp 2D 26
Hughton. High 1E 70
Hugh Town. IOS 1H 3
Hugus. Corn 4L 3
Huish. Devn 4E 6
Huish. Wilts 7K 19
Huish Champflower. Som 3K 7
Huish Episcopi. Som 3C 8
Huisinis. W Isl 2A 76
Hulcote. Nptn 7E 28
Hulcott. Buck 2F 20
Hulham. Devn 7K 7
Hull. Hull
Kingston upon Hull 110 (5J 43)
Hulland. Derbs 5L 35
Hulland Moss. Derbs 5L 35
Hulland Ward. Derbs 5L 35
Hullavington. Wilts 5G 19
Hullbridge. Essx 4E 22
Hulme. G Man 8G 41
Hulme. Staf 5H 35
Hulme End. Staf 4K 35
Hulme Walfield. Ches E 3G 35
Hulverstone. IOW 7A 10
Hulver Street. Suff 3L 31
Humber. Devn 8J 7
Humber. Here 6D 26
Humber Bridge. N Lin 5H 43
Humberside Airport. N Lin 6H 43
Humberston. NE Lin 7L 43
Humberstone. Leic 1D 28
Humbie. E Lot 3B 60
Humbleton. E Yor 4K 43
Humbleton. Nmbd 7G 61
Humby. Linc 6H 37
Hume. Bord 5E 60
Humshaugh. Nmbd 4C 54
Huna. High 4E 86
Huncoat. Lanc 4F 40
Huncote. Leics 2C 28
Hundall. Derbs 2A 36
Hunderthwaite. Dur 3H 47
Hundleby. Linc 3L 37
Hundle Houses. Linc 4K 37
Hundleton. Pemb 6F 14
Hundon. Suff 7D 30
The Hundred. Here 5D 26
Hundred Acres. Hants 4C 10
Hundred House. Powy 7L 25
Hungarton. Leics 1D 28
Hungerford. Hants 4K 9
Hungerford. Shrp 3D 26
Hungerford. Som 1K 7
Hungerford. W Ber 7M 19
Hungerford Newtown.
W Ber 6A 20
Hunger Hill. G Man 7E 40
Hungerton. Linc 6F 36
Hungladder. High 6E 76
Hungryhatton. Shrp 7E 34
Hunmanby. N Yor 8H 49
Hunmanby Sands. N Yor 8J 49
Hunningham. Warw 5A 28
Hunnington. Worc 3H 27
Hunny Hill. IOW 7B 10
Hunsdon. Herts 2M 21
Hunsdonbury. Herts 2M 21
Hunsingore. N Yor 2B 42
Hunslet. W Yor 4M 41
Hunslet Carr. W Yor 4M 41
Hunsonby. Cumb 8K 53
Hunspow. High 4D 86
Hunstanton. Norf 5C 38
Hunstanworth. Dur 7C 54
Hunston. Suff 5F 30
Hunston. W Sus 5F 10
Hunstrete. Bath 7E 18
Hunt End. Worc 5J 27
Hunterfield. Midl 3M 59
Hunters Forstal. Kent 7H 23
Hunter's Quay. Arg 2L 57
Huntham. Som 3B 8
Hunthill Lodge. Ang 8D 72
Huntingdon. Cambs 4K 29
Huntingfield. Suff 4K 31
Huntingford. Wilts 3G 9
Huntington. Ches W 3C 34
Huntington. E Lot 2B 60
Huntington. Here 6A 26
Huntington. Staf 8H 35
Huntington. Telf 1E 26
Huntington. York 2D 42
Huntingtower. Per 5D 66
Huntley. Glos 2F 18
Huntley. Staf 5J 35
Huntly. Abers 2E 72
Huntlywood. Bord 5D 60
Hunton. Hants 2B 10
Hunton. Kent 1D 12
Hunton. N Yor 6K 47
Hunton Bridge. Herts 4H 21
Hunt's Corner. Norf 3G 31
Huntscott. Som 1J 7
Hunt's Cross. Mers 1C 34
Hunts Green. Warw 2K 27
Huntsham. Devn 3K 7
Huntshaw. Devn 3E 6
Huntspill. Som 1B 8
Huntstile. Som 2A 8
Huntworth. Som 2B 8
Hunwick. Dur 8E 54
Hunworth. Norf 6G 39
Hurcott. Som
nr. Ilminster 4B 8
nr. Somerton 3D 8
Hurdcott. Wilts 2K 9
Hurdley. Powy 2A 26
Hurdsfield. Ches E 2H 35
Hurlet. Glas 3D 58
Hurley. Warw 2L 27
Hurley. Wind 5F 20
Hurlford. E Ayr 6C 58
Hurliness. Orkn 3D 86
Hurlston Green. Lanc 6C 40
Hurn. Dors 6K 9
Hursey. Dors 5C 8
Hursley. Hants 3B 10
Hurst. G Man 7H 41
Hurst. N Yor 5J 47
Hurst. Som 4C 8
Hurst. Wok 6E 20
Hurstbourne Priors. Hants 1B 10
Hurstbourne Tarrant. Hants 8A 20
Hurst Green. Ches E 5D 34
Hurst Green. E Sus 3D 12
Hurst Green. Essx 2G 23
Hurst Green. Lanc 4E 40
Hurst Green. Surr 8L 21
Hurstley. Here 7B 26
Hurstpierpoint. W Sus 4K 11
Hurstway Common. Here 7B 26
Hurst Wickham. W Sus 4K 11
Hurstwood. Lanc 4G 41
Hurtmore. Surr 1G 11
Hurworth-on-Tees. Darl 4M 47
Hurworth Place. Darl 5L 47
Hury. Dur 4H 47
Husbands Bosworth. Leics 3D 28
Husborne Crawley. C Beds 8G 29
Husthwaite. N Yor 8C 48
Hutcherleigh. Devn 6K 5
Hut Green. N Yor 5C 42
Huthwaite. Notts 4B 36
Huttoft. Linc 2B 38
Hutton. Cumb 3C 46
Hutton. E Yor 2H 43
Hutton. Essx 4C 22
Hutton. Lanc 5C 40
Hutton. N Som 8B 18
Hutton. Bord 4G 61
Hutton Bonville. N Yor 5M 47
Hutton Buscel. N Yor 7G 49
Hutton Conyers. N Yor 8M 47
Hutton Cranswick. E Yor 2H 43
Hutton End. Cumb 8J 53
Hutton Gate. Red C 4C 48
Hutton Henry. Dur 8H 55
Hutton-le-Hole. N Yor 7E 48
Hutton Magna. Dur 4K 47
Hutton Mulgrave. N Yor 5F 48
Hutton Roof. Cumb
nr. Kirkby Lonsdale 8D 46
nr. Penrith 8H 53
Hutton Rudby. N Yor 5B 48
Huttons Ambo. N Yor 1E 42
Hutton Sessay. N Yor 8B 48
Hutton Village. Red C 4D 48
Hutton Wandesley. N Yor 2C 42
Huxham. Devn 6J 7
Huxham Green. Som 2D 8
Huxley. Ches W 3D 34
Huxter. Shet
on Mainland 2B 90
on Whalsay 1F 90
Huyton. Mers 8C 40
Hwlffordd. Pemb 5F 14
Hycemoor. Cumb 6K 45
Hyde. Glos
nr. Stroud 3G 19
nr. Winchcombe 1J 19
Hyde. G Man 8H 41
Hyde Heath. Buck 3G 21
Hyde Lea. Staf 8H 35
Hyde Park. S Yor 7C 42
Hydestile. Surr 1G 11
Hyndford Bridge. S Lan 5H 59
Hynish. Arg 4E 62
Hyssington. Powy 2B 26
Hythe. Hants 5B 10
Hythe. Kent 2H 13
Hythe End. Wind 6H 21
Hythie. Abers 8K 81
Hyton. Cumb 6K 45

I

Ianstown. Mor 7D 80
Iarsiadar. W Isl 8E 82
Ibberton. Dors 5F 8
Ible. Derbs 4L 35
Ibrox. Glas 3D 58
Ibsley. Hants 5K 9
Ibstock. Leics 8B 36
Ibstone. Buck 4E 20
Ibthorpe. Hants 8A 20
Iburndale. N Yor 5F 48
Ibworth. Hants 8C 20
Icelton. N Som 7B 18
Ichrachan. Arg 4E 64
Ickburgh. Norf 2E 30
Ickenham. G Lon 5H 21
Ickenthwaite. Cumb 7B 46
Ickford. Buck 3D 20
Ickham. Kent 8J 23
Ickleford. Herts 8J 29
Icklesham. E Sus 4E 12
Ickleton. Cambs 7A 30
Icklingham. Suff 4D 30
Ickwell. C Beds 7J 29
Icomb. Glos 1L 19
Idbury. Oxon 2L 19
Iddesleigh. Devn 5E 6
Ide. Devn 6H 7
Ideford. Devn 8H 7
Ide Hill. Kent 8A 22
Iden. E Sus 3F 12
Iden Green. Kent
nr. Benenden 2E 12
nr. Goudhurst 2D 12
Idle. W Yor 4K 41
Idless. Corn 4M 3
Idlicote. Warw 7L 27
Idmiston. Wilts 2K 9
Idole. Carm 5L 15
Idridgehay. Derbs 5L 35
Idrigill. High 7E 76
Idstone. Oxon 5L 19
Iffley. Oxon 3C 20
Ifield. W Sus 2K 11
Ifieldwood. W Sus 2K 11
Ifold. W Sus 2H 11
Iford. E Sus 5M 11
Ifton Heath. Shrp 6B 34
Ightfield. Shrp 6D 34
Ightham. Kent 8B 22
Iken. Suff 6L 31
Ilam. Staf 4K 35
Ilchester. Som 3D 8
Ilderton. Nmbd 7H 61
Ilford. G Lon 5M 21
Ilford. Som 4B 8
Ilfracombe. Devn 1E 6
Ilkeston. Derbs 5B 36
Ilketshall St Andrew. Suff 3K 31
Ilketshall St Lawrence. Suff 3K 31
Ilketshall St Margaret. Suff 3K 31
Ilkley. W Yor 3K 41
Illand. Corn 8B 6
Illey. W Mid 3H 27
Illidge Green. Ches E 3F 34
Illington. Norf 3F 30
Illingworth. W Yor 5J 41
Illogan. Corn 4K 3
Illogan Highway. Corn 4K 3
Illston on the Hill. Leics 2E 28
Ilmer. Buck 3E 20
Ilmington. Warw 7L 27
Ilminster. Som 4B 8
Ilsington. Devn 8G 7
Ilsington. Dors 6F 8
Ilston. Swan 5E 16
Ilton. N Yor 8K 47
Ilton. Som 4B 8
Imachar. N Ayr 5H 57
Imber. Wilts 1H 9
Immingham. NE Lin 6J 43
Immingham Dock. NE Lin 6K 43
Impington. Cambs 5M 29
Ince. Ches W 2C 34
Ince Blundell. Mers 7B 40
Ince-in-Makerfield. G Man 7D 40
Inchbae Lodge. High 7E 78
Inchbare. Ang 1K 67
Inchberry. Mor 8C 80
Inchbraoch. Ang 2L 67
Inchbrook. Glos 3G 19

Lanarth – Llansanffraid Glan Conwy

Lanarth. Corn 6L 3
Lancaster. Lanc 1C 40
Lanchester. Dur 7E 54
Lancing. W Sus 5J 11
Landbeach. Cambs 5A 30
Landcross. Devn 3D 6
Landerberry. Abers 5G 73
Landford. Wilts 4L 9
Land Gate. G Man 7D 40
Landhallow. High 8C 86
Landimore. Swan 7L 15
Landkey. Devn 2E 6
Landkey Newland. Devn 2E 6
Landore. Swan 5F 16
Landport. Port 5D 10
Landrake. Corn 5F 4
Landscove. Devn 5K 5
Land's End Airport. Corn 6G 3
Landshipping. Pemb 5G 15
Landulph. Corn 5G 5
Landywood. Staf 1H 27
Lane. Corn 2M 3
Laneast. Corn 7B 6
Lane Bottom. Lanc 4G 41
Lane End. Buck 4F 20
Lane End. Hants 3C 10
Lane End. IOW 7D 10
Lane End. Wilts 1G 9
Lane Ends. Derbs 6L 35
Lane Ends. Dur 8E 54
Lane Ends. Lanc 2F 40
Laneham. Notts 2F 36
Lane Head. Dur
 nr. Hutton Magna 4K 47
 nr. Woodland 3J 47
Lane Head. G Man 8E 40
Lane Head. W Yor 7K 41
Lanehead. Dur 7B 54
Lanehead. Nmbd 3A 54
Lane Heads. Lanc 4C 40
Lanercost. Cumb 5K 53
Laneshaw Bridge. Lanc 3H 41
Laney Green. Staf 1H 27
Langais. W Isl 7K 75
Langal. High 1B 64
Langar. Notts 6E 36
Langbank. Ren 2B 58
Langbar. N Yor 2J 41
Langburnshiels. Bord 1K 53
Langcliffe. N Yor 1G 41
Langdale End. N Yor 6G 49
Langdon. Corn 6B 6
Langdon Beck. Dur 8B 54
Langdon Cross. Corn 7C 6
Langdon Hills. Essx 5C 22
Langdown. Hants 5B 10
Langdyke. Fife 7G 67
Langenhoe. Essx 2G 23
Langford. C Beds 7J 29
Langford. Devn 5K 7
Langford. Essx 3E 22
Langford. Notts 4F 36
Langford. Oxon 3L 19
Langford. Som 3M 7
Langford Budville. Som 3L 7
Langham. Dors 3F 8
Langham. Essx 8G 31
Langham. Norf 5G 39
Langham. Rut 8F 36
Langham. Suff 5F 30
Langho. Lanc 4F 40
Langholm. Dum 3H 53
Langland. Swan 6F 16
Langleeford. Nmbd 7G 61
Langley. Ches E 2H 35
Langley. Derbs 5B 36
Langley. Essx 8M 29
Langley. Glos 1J 19
Langley. Hants 5B 10
Langley. Herts 1K 21
Langley. Kent 8E 22
Langley. Nmbd 5B 54
Langley. Slo 6H 21
Langley. Som 3K 7
Langley. Warw 5K 27
Langley. W Sus 3F 10
Langley Burrell. Wilts 6H 19
Langleybury. Herts 3H 21
Langley Common. Derbs 6L 35
Langley Green. Derbs 6L 35
Langley Green. Norf 1K 31
Langley Green. Warw 5K 27
Langley Green. W Sus 2K 11
Langley Heath. Kent 8E 22
Langley Marsh. Som 3K 7
Langley Moor. Dur 7F 54
Langley Park. Dur 7F 54
Langley Street. Norf 1K 31
Langney. E Sus 5C 12
Langold. Notts 1C 36
Langore. Corn 7B 6
Langport. Som 3C 8
Langrick. Linc 5K 37
Langridge. Bath 7F 18
Langridgeford. Devn 3E 6
Langrigg. Cumb 7F 52
Langrish. Hants 3E 10
Langsett. S Yor 7L 41
Langshaw. Bord 6C 60
Langstone. Hants 5E 10
Langthorne. N Yor 6L 47
Langthorpe. N Yor 1A 42
Langthwaite. N Yor 5J 47
Langtoft. E Yor 1H 43
Langtoft. Linc 8J 37
Langton. Dur 4K 47
Langton. Linc
 nr. Horncastle 3K 37
 nr. Spilsby 2L 37
Langton. N Yor 1E 42
Langton by Wragby. Linc 2J 37
Langton Green. Kent 2B 12
Langton Herring. Dors 7E 8
Langton Long Blandford.
 Dors 5G 9
Langton Matravers. Dors 8H 9
Langtree. Devn 4D 6
Langwathby. Cumb 8K 53
Langwith. Derbs 2C 36
Langworth. Linc 2H 37
Lanivet. Corn 5C 4
Lanjeth. Corn 6B 4
Lank. Corn 4C 4
Lanlivery. Corn 6C 4
Lanner. Corn 5L 3
Lanreath. Corn 6D 4
Lansallos. Corn 6D 4
Lansdown. Bath 7F 18
Lansdown. Glos 1H 19
Lanteglos Highway. Corn 6D 4
Lanton. Nmbd 6G 61
Lanton. Bord 7D 60
Lapford. Devn 5G 7
Lapford Cross. Devn 5G 7
Laphroaig. Arg 5C 56
Lapley. Staf 8G 35
Lapworth. Warw 4K 27
Larachbeg. High 3A 64
Larbert. Falk 1G 59
Larden Green. Ches E 4D 34
Larel. High 6C 86
Largie. Abers 2F 72
Largiemore. Arg 1J 57
Largoward. Fife 7H 67
Largs. N Ayr 4M 57
Largue. Abers 1F 72
Largybeg. N Ayr 7K 57
Largymeanoch. N Ayr 7K 57
Largymore. N Ayr 7K 57
Larkfield. Inv 2M 57
Larkfield. Kent 8D 22
Larkhall. Bath 7F 18
Larkhall. S Lan 4F 58
Larkhill. Wilts 1K 9
Larling. Norf 3F 30
Larne. ME Ant 3J 93
Larport. Here 8D 26
Lartington. Dur 4J 47
Lary. Abers 5C 72
Lasham. Hants 1D 10
Lashenden. Kent 1E 12
Lasswade. Midl 3M 59
Lastingham. N Yor 6E 48
Latchford. Herts 1L 21
Latchford. Oxon 3D 20
Latchingdon. Essx 3E 22
Latchley. Corn 8D 6
Latchmere Green. Hants 8D 20
Lathbury. Mil 7F 28
Latheron. High 8C 86
Latheronwheel. High 8C 86
Lathom. Lanc 7C 40
Lathones. Fife 7H 67
Latimer. Buck 4H 21
Latteridge. S Glo 5E 18
Lattiford. Som 3E 8
Latton. Wilts 4J 19
Laudale House. High 2B 64
Lauder. Bord 5C 60
Laugharne. Carm 5K 15
Laughterton. Linc 2F 36
Laughton. E Sus 4B 12
Laughton. Leics 3D 28
Laughton. Linc
 nr. Gainsborough 8F 42
 nr. Grantham 6H 37
Laughton Common. S Yor 1C 36
Laughton en le Morthen.
 S Yor 1C 36
Launcells. Corn 5B 6
Launceston. Corn 7C 6
Launcherley. Som 1D 8
Launton. Oxon 1D 20
Laurelvale. Arm 6G 93
Laurencekirk. Abers 8G 73
Laurieston. Dum 5A 52
Laurieston. Falk 2H 59
Lavendon. Mil 6G 29
Lavenham. Suff 7F 30
Laverhay. Dum 2F 52
Laversdale. Cumb 5J 53
Laverstock. Wilts 2K 9
Laverstoke. Hants 1B 10
Laverton. Glos 8J 27
Laverton. N Yor 8L 47
Laverton. Som 8F 18
Lavister. Wrex 4B 34
Law. S Lan 4G 59
Lawers. Per 4L 65
Lawford. Essx 8G 31
Lawhitton. Corn 7C 6
Lawkland. N Yor 1F 40
Lawley. Telf 1E 26
Lawnhead. Staf 7G 35
Lawrencetown. Arm 6G 93
Lawrenny. Pemb 6G 15
Lawshall. Suff 6E 30
Lawton. Here 6C 26
Laxey. IOM 6D 44
Laxfield. Suff 4J 31
Laxfirth. Shet 2E 90
Laxo. Shet 1E 90
Laxton. E Yor 5E 42
Laxton. Nptn 2G 29
Laxton. Notts 3E 36
Laycock. W Yor 3J 41
Layer Breton. Essx 2F 22
Layer-de-la-Haye. Essx 1F 22
Layer Marney. Essx 2F 22
Laymore. Dors 5B 8
Laysters Pole. Here 5D 26
Layter's Green. Buck 4G 21
Laytham. E Yor 4E 42
Lazenby. Red C 4C 48
Lazonby. Cumb 8K 53
Lea. Derbs 4M 35
Lea. Here 1E 18
Lea. Linc 1F 36
Lea. Shrp
 nr. Bishop's Castle 3B 26
 nr. Shrewsbury 1C 26
Lea. Wilts 5H 19
Leabrooks. Derbs 4B 36
Leac a Li. W Isl 4C 76
Leachd. Arg 8E 64
Leachkin. High 1G 71
Leachpool. Pemb 5F 14
Leadburn. Midl 4L 59
Leadenham. Linc 4G 37
Leaden Roding. Essx 2B 22
Leaderfoot. Bord 6C 60
Leadgate. Cumb 7M 53
Leadgate. Dur 6E 54
Leadgate. Nmbd 6E 54
Leadhills. S Lan 8G 59
Leadingcross Green. Kent 8E 22
Lea End. Worc 4J 27
Leafield. Oxon 2M 19
Leagrave. Lutn 1H 21
Lea Hall. W Mid 3K 27
Lea Heath. Staf 7J 35
Leake. N Yor 6B 48
Leake Common Side. Linc 4L 37
Leake Fold Hill. Linc 4M 37
Leake Hurn's End. Linc 5M 37
Lealholm. N Yor 5E 48
Lealt. Arg 8A 64
Lealt. High 7G 77
Leam. Derbs 2L 35
Lea Marston. Warw 2L 27
Leamington Hastings.
 Warw 5B 28
Leamington Spa, Royal.
 Warw 5M 27
Leamonsley. Staf 1K 27
Leamside. Dur 7G 55
Leargybreck. Arg 2E 56
Lease Rigg. N Yor 5F 48
Leasgill. Cumb 7C 46
Leasingham. Linc 5H 37
Leasingthorne. Dur 8F 54
Leasowe. Mers 8A 40
Leatherhead. Surr 8J 21
Leathley. N Yor 3L 41
Leaths. Dum 5B 52
Leaton. Shrp 8C 34
Leaton. Telf 8E 34
Lea Town. Lanc 4C 40
Leaveland. Kent 8G 23
Leavenheath. Suff 8F 30
Leavening. N Yor 1E 42
Leaves Green. G Lon 7M 21
Lea Yeat. Cumb 7F 46
Leazes. Dur 6E 54
Lebberston. N Yor 7H 49
Lechlade on Thames. Glos 4L 19
Leck. Lanc 8E 46
Leckford. Hants 2A 10
Leckfurin. High 6K 85
Leckgruinart. Arg 3B 56
Leckhampstead. Buck 8E 28
Leckhampstead. W Ber 6B 20
Leckhampton. Glos 2H 19
Leckmelm. High 4B 78
Leckwith. V Glam 7L 17
Leconfield. E Yor 3H 43
Ledaig. Arg 4D 64
Ledburn. Buck 1G 21
Ledbury. Here 8F 26
Ledgemoor. Here 6C 26
Ledgowan. High 8B 78
Ledicot. Here 5C 26
Ledmore. High 2C 78
Lednabirichen. High 4H 79
Lednagullin. High 5L 85
Ledsham. Ches W 2B 34
Ledsham. W Yor 5B 42
Ledston. W Yor 5B 42
Ledstone. Devn 7K 5
Ledwell. Oxon 1B 20
Lee. Devn
 nr. Ilfracombe 1D 6
 nr. South Molton 3H 7
Lee. G Lon 6L 21
Lee. Hants 4A 10
Lee. Lanc 2D 40
Lee. Shrp 6C 34
The Lee. Buck 3G 21
Leeans. Shet 3D 90
Leebotten. Shet 5E 90
Leebotwood. Shrp 2C 26
Lee Brockhurst. Shrp 7D 34
Leece. Cumb 8M 45
Leechpool. Mon 5D 18
Lee Clump. Buck 3G 21
Leeds. Kent 8E 22
Leeds. W Yor 110 (4L 41)
Leeds Bradford Airport.
 W Yor 3L 41
Leedstown. Corn 5K 3
Leegomery. Telf 8E 34
Lee Head. Derbs 8J 41
Leek. Staf 4H 35
Leekbrook. Staf 4H 35
Leek Wootton. Warw 5L 27
Lee Mill. Devn 6H 5
Leeming. N Yor 7L 47
Leeming Bar. N Yor 6L 47
Lee Moor. Devn 5H 5
Lee Moor. W Yor 5M 41
Lee-on-the-Solent. Hants 5C 10
Lees. Derbs 6L 35
Lees. G Man 7H 41
Lees. W Yor 4J 41
The Lees. Kent 8G 23
Leeswood. Flin 3A 34
Leetown. Per 5F 66
Leftwich. Ches W 2E 34
Legbourne. Linc 1L 37
Legburthwaite. Cumb 4B 46
Legerwood. Bord 5C 60
Legsby. Linc 1J 37
Leicester. Leic 110 (1C 28)
Leicester Forest East. Leics 1C 28
Leigh. Dors 5E 8
Leigh. G Man 7E 40
Leigh. Kent 1B 12
Leigh. Shrp 1B 26
Leigh. Surr 1K 11
Leigh. Wilts 4J 19
Leigh. Worc 6F 26
The Leigh. Glos 1G 19
Leigham. Plym 6H 5
Leigh Beck. Essx 5E 22
Leigh Common. Som 3F 8
Leigh Delamere. Wilts 6G 19
Leigh Green. Kent 2F 12
Leighland Chapel. Som 2K 7
Leigh-on-Sea. S'end 5E 22
Leigh Park. Hants 5E 10
Leigh Sinton. Worc 6F 26
Leighterton. Glos 4G 19
Leighton. N Yor 8K 47
Leighton. Powy 2M 25
Leighton. Shrp 1E 26
Leighton. Som 1F 8
Leighton Bromswold.
 Cambs 4J 29
Leighton Buzzard. C Beds 1G 21
Leigh-upon-Mendip. Som 1E 8
Leinthall Earls. Here 5C 26
Leinthall Starkes. Here 5C 26
Leintwardine. Here 4C 26
Leire. Leics 2C 28
Leirinmore. High 5G 85
Leishmore. High 1E 70
Leiston. Suff 5L 31
Leitfie. Per 3F 66
Leith. Edin 2L 59
Leitholm. Bord 5E 60
Leitrim. New M 7H 93
Lelant. Corn 5J 3
Lelant Downs. Corn 5J 3
Lelley. E Yor 4K 43
Lem Hill. Shrp 4F 26
Lemington. Tyne 5E 54
Lempitlaw. Bord 6E 60
Lemsford. Herts 2K 21
Lenacre. Cumb 7E 46
Lenchie. Abers 2E 72
Lenchwick. Worc 7J 27
Lendalfoot. S Ayr 3G 51
Lendrick. Stir 7K 65
Lenham. Kent 8E 22
Lenham Heath. Kent 1F 12
Lenimore. N Ayr 5H 57
Lennel. Bord 5F 60
Lennoxtown. E Dun 2E 58
Lenton. Linc 6H 37
Lentran. High 1F 70
Lenwade. Norf 8G 39
Lenzie. E Dun 2E 58
Leochel Cushnie. Abers 4E 72
Leogh. Shet 2M 89
Leominster. Here 6C 26
Leonard Stanley. Glos 3G 19
Lepe. Hants 6B 10
Lephenstrath. Arg 1B 50
Lephin. High 1C 68
Lephinchapel. Arg 8D 64
Lephinmore. Arg 8D 64
Leppington. N Yor 1E 42
Lepton. W Yor 6L 41
Lerryn. Corn 6D 4
Lerwick. Shet 3E 90
Lerwick (Tingwall) Airport.
 Shet 3E 90
Lesbury. Nmbd 8K 61
Leslie. Abers 3E 72
Leslie. Fife 7F 66
Lesmahagow. S Lan 6G 59
Lesnewth. Corn 2D 4
Lessingham. Norf 7K 39
Lessonhall. Cumb 6G 53
Leswalt. Dum 5F 50
Letchmore Heath. Herts 4J 21
Letchworth Garden City.
 Herts 8K 29
Letcombe Bassett. Oxon 5A 20
Letcombe Regis. Oxon 5A 20
Letham. Ang 3J 67
Letham. Falk 1G 59
Letham. Fife 6G 67
Lethanhill. E Ayr 8C 58
Lethenty. Abers 1H 73
Letheringham. Suff 6J 31
Letheringsett. Norf 6G 39
Lettaford. Devn 7G 7
Lettan. Orkn 5G 89
Letter. Abers 4G 73
Letterewe. High 6L 77
Letterfearn. High 3K 69
Lettermore. Arg 3K 63
Letters. High 5B 78
Lettershendoney. Derr 3D 92
Letterston. Pemb 4F 14
Letton. Here
 nr. Kington 7B 26
 nr. Leintwardine 4B 26
Letty Green. Herts 2K 21
Letwell. S Yor 1C 36
Leuchars. Fife 5H 67
Leumrabhagh. W Isl 2E 76
Leusdon. Devn 8G 7
Levaneap. Shet 1E 90
Levedale. Staf 8G 35
Leven. E Yor 3J 43
Leven. Fife 7G 67
Levencorroch. N Ayr 7K 57
Levenhall. E Lot 2A 60
Levens. Cumb 7C 46
Levens Green. Herts 1L 21
Levenshulme. G Man 8G 41
Levenwick. Shet 5E 90
Leverburgh. W Isl 5B 76
Leverington. Cambs 8M 37
Leverton. Linc 5L 37
Leverton. W Ber 6M 19
Leverton Lucasgate. Linc 5M 37
Leverton Outgate. Linc 5M 37
Levington. Suff 8J 31
Levisham. N Yor 6F 48
Levishie. High 4E 70
Lew. Oxon 3M 19
Lewaigue. IOM 5D 44
Lewannick. Corn 7B 6
Lewdown. Devn 7D 6
Lewes. E Sus 4M 11
Leweston. Pemb 4F 14
Lewisham. G Lon 6L 21
Lewiston. High 3F 70
Lewistown. B'end 6J 17
Lewknor. Oxon 4E 20
Leworthy. Devn
 nr. Barnstaple 2F 6
 nr. Holsworthy 5C 6
Lewson Street. Kent 7F 22
Lewthorn Cross. Devn 8G 7
Lewtrenchard. Devn 7D 6
Ley. Corn 5D 4
Leybourne. Kent 8C 22
Leyburn. N Yor 6K 47
Leycett. Staf 5F 34
Leyfields. Staf 1L 27
Ley Green. Herts 1J 21
Ley Hill. Buck 3G 21
Leyland. Lanc 5D 40
Leylodge. Abers 4G 73
Leymoor. W Yor 6K 41
Leys. Per 4F 66
Leysdown-on-Sea. Kent 6G 23
Leysmill. Ang 3K 67
Leyton. G Lon 5L 21
Leytonstone. G Lon 5M 21
Lezant. Corn 8C 6
Leziate. Norf 8C 38
Lhanbryde. Mor 7B 80
The Lhen. IOM 4C 44
Liatrie. High 2C 70
Libanus. Powy 2J 17
Libberton. S Lan 5H 59
Libbery. Worc 6H 27
Liberton. Edin 3L 59
Liceasto. W Isl 4C 76
Lichfield. Staf 1K 27
Lickey. Worc 4H 27
Lickey End. Worc 4H 27
Lickfold. W Sus 3G 11
Liddaton. Devn 7D 6
Liddington. Swin 5L 19
Liddle. Orkn 3F 86
Lidgate. Suff 6D 30
Lidgett. Notts 3D 36
Lidham Hill. E Sus 4E 12
Lidlington. C Beds 8G 29
Lidsey. W Sus 5G 11
Lidstone. Oxon 1A 20
Lienassie. High 3L 69
Liff. Ang 4G 67
Lifford. W Mid 3J 27
Lifton. Devn 7C 6
Liftondown. Devn 7C 6
Lighthorne. Warw 6M 27
Light Oaks. Stoke 4H 35
Lightwater. Surr 7G 21
Lightwood. Staf 5J 35
Lightwood. Stoke 5H 35
Lightwood Green. Ches E 5E 34
Lightwood Green. Wrex 5B 34
Lilbourne. Nptn 4C 28
Lilburn Tower. Nmbd 7H 61
Lillesdon. Som 3B 8
Lilleshall. Telf 8F 34
Lilley. Herts 1J 21
Lilliesleaf. Bord 7C 60
Lillingstone Dayrell. Buck 8E 28
Lillingstone Lovell. Buck 7E 28
Lillington. Dors 4E 8
Lilstock. Som 1L 7
Lilybank. Inv 2B 58
Lilyhurst. Shrp 8F 34
Limavady. Caus 2E 92
Limbrick. Lanc 6E 40
Limbury. Lutn 1H 21
Limekilnburn. S Lan 4F 58
Limekilns. Fife 1J 59
Limerigg. Falk 2G 59
Limestone Brae. Nmbd 7A 54
Lime Street. Worc 8G 27
Limington. Som 3D 8
Limpenhoe. Norf 1K 31
Limpley Stoke. Wilts 7F 18
Limpsfield. Surr 8M 21
Limpsfield Chart. Surr 8M 21
Linburn. W Lot 3K 59
Linby. Notts 4C 36
Linchmere. W Sus 2F 10
Lincluden. Dum 4D 52
Lincoln. Linc 111 (2G 37)
Lincomb. Worc 5G 27
Lindale. Cumb 7C 46
Lindal in Furness. Cumb 8A 46
Lindean. Bord 6B 60
Linden. Glos 2G 19
Lindfield. W Sus 3L 11
Lindford. Hants 2F 10
Lindores. Fife 6F 66
Lindridge. Worc 5E 26
Lindsell. Essx 1C 22
Lindsey. Suff 7F 30
Lindsey Tye. Suff 7F 30
Linford. Hants 5K 9
Linford. Thur 6C 22
Lingague. IOM 7B 44
Lingdale. Red C 4D 48
Lingen. Here 5B 26
Lingfield. Surr 1L 11
Lingreabhagh. W Isl 5B 76
Lingwood. Norf 1K 31
Lingy Close. Cumb 6H 53
Linicro. High 7E 76
Linkend. Worc 8G 27
Linkenholt. Hants 8A 20
Linkinhorne. Corn 8C 6
Linklater. Orkn 3F 86
Linksness. Orkn 8E 88
Linktown. Fife 8F 66
Linkwood. Mor 7B 80
Linley. Shrp
 nr. Bishop's Castle 2B 26
 nr. Bridgnorth 2E 26
Linley Green. Here 6E 26
Linlithgow. W Lot 2H 59
Linlithgow Bridge. Falk 2H 59
Linneraineach. High 3B 78
Linshiels. Nmbd 1B 54
Linsiadar. W Isl 8F 82
Linsidemore. High 4F 78
Linslade. C Beds 1G 21
Linstead Parva. Suff 4K 31
Linstock. Cumb 6J 53
Linthwaite. W Yor 6K 41
Lintlaw. Bord 4F 60
Lintmill. Mor 7E 80
Linton. Cambs 7B 30
Linton. Derbs 8L 35
Linton. Here 1E 18
Linton. Kent 1D 12
Linton. N Yor 1H 41
Linton. Bord 7E 60
Linton. W Yor 3A 42
Linton Colliery. Nmbd 2F 54
Linton Hill. Here 1E 18
Linton-on-Ouse. N Yor 1B 42
Lintzford. Dur 6E 54
Lintzgarth. Dur 7C 54
Linwood. Hants 5K 9
Linwood. Linc 1J 37
Linwood. Ren 3C 58
Lionacleit. W Isl 1D 74
Lionacro. High 7E 76
Lionacuidhe. W Isl 1D 74
Lional. W Isl 5J 83
Liphook. Hants 2F 10
Lipley. Shrp 6F 34
Lipyeate. Som 8E 18
Liquo. N Lan 4G 59
Lisbane. Ards 5J 93
Lisbellaw. Ferm 6C 92
Lisburn. Lis 5H 93
Liscard. Mers 8B 40
Liscolman. Caus 2F 93
Liscombe. Som 2H 7
Lishahawley. Derr 2D 92
Liskeard. Corn 5E 4
Lislea. New M 7G 93
Lisle Court. Hants 6M 9
Lisnarick. Ferm 6B 92
Lisnaskea. Ferm 7C 92
Liss. Hants 3E 10
Lissett. E Yor 2J 43
Liss Forest. Hants 3E 10
Lissington. Linc 1J 37
Liston. Essx 7E 30
Listooder. New M 6J 93
Lisvane. Card 6L 17
Liswerry. Newp 5B 18
Litcham. Norf 8E 38
Litchard. B'end 6J 17
Litchborough. Nptn 6D 28
Litchfield. Hants 8B 20
Litherland. Mers 8B 40
Litlington. Cambs 7L 29
Litlington. E Sus 5B 12
Littemill. Nmbd 8K 61
Litterty. Abers 8G 81
Little Abington. Cambs 7B 30
Little Addington. Nptn 4G 29
Little Airmyn. N Yor 5E 42
Little Alne. Warw 5K 27
Little Ardo. Abers 2H 73
Little Asby. Cumb 5E 46
Little Aston. Staf 1J 27
Little Atherfield. IOW 7B 10
Little Ayton. N Yor 4C 48
Little Baddow. Essx 3D 22
Little Badminton. S Glo 5G 19
Little Ballinluig. Per 2C 66
Little Bampton. Cumb 6G 53
Little Bardfield. Essx 8C 30
Little Barford. Bed 6J 29
Little Barningham. Norf 6H 39
Little Barrington. Glos 2L 19
Little Barrow. Ches W 3C 34
Little Barugh. N Yor 8E 48
Little Bavington. Nmbd 4C 54
Little Bealings. Suff 7J 31
Littlebeck. Cumb 4E 46
Little Bedwyn. Wilts 7L 19
Little Bentley. Essx 1H 23
Little Berkhamsted. Herts 3K 21
Little Billing. Nptn 5F 28
Little Billington. C Beds 1G 21
Little Birch. Here 8D 26
Little Bispham. Bkpl 3B 40
Little Blakenham. Suff 7H 31
Little Blencow. Cumb 8J 53
Little Bognor. W Sus 3H 11
Little Bolas. Shrp 7E 34
Little Bollington. Ches E 1F 34
Little Bookham. Surr 8J 21
Littleborough. Devn 4H 7
Littleborough. G Man 6H 41
Littleborough. Notts 1F 36
Littlebourne. Kent 8J 23
Little Bourton. Oxon 7B 28
Little Bowden. Leics 3E 28
Little Bradley. Suff 6C 30
Little Brampton. Shrp 3B 26
Little Brechin. Ang 1J 67
Littlebredy. Dors 7D 8
Little Brickhill. Mil 8G 29
Little Bridgeford. Staf 7G 35
Little Brington. Nptn 5D 28
Little Bromley. Essx 1G 23
Little Broughton. Cumb 8E 52
Little Budworth. Ches W 3D 34
Little Burstead. Essx 4C 22
Little Burton. E Yor 3J 43
Littlebury. Essx 8B 30
Littlebury Green. Essx 8A 30
Little Bytham. Linc 8H 37
Little Canfield. Essx 1B 22
Little Canford. Dors 6J 9
Little Carlton. Linc 1L 37
Little Carlton. Notts 4E 36
Little Casterton. Rut 1H 29
Little Catwick. E Yor 3J 43
Little Catworth. Cambs 4J 29
Little Cawthorpe. Linc 1L 37
Little Chalfont. Buck 4G 21
Little Chart. Kent 1F 12
Little Chesterford. Essx 7B 30
Little Cheverell. Wilts 8H 19
Little Chishill. Cambs 8M 29
Little Clacton. Essx 2H 23
Little Clanfield. Oxon 3L 19
Little Clifton. Cumb 2K 45
Little Coates. NE Lin 7K 43
Little Comberton. Worc 7H 27
Little Common. E Sus 5D 12
Little Compton. Warw 8L 27
Little Cornard. Suff 8E 30
Littlecote. Buck 1F 20
Littlecott. Wilts 8K 19
Little Cowarne. Here 6E 26
Little Coxwell. Oxon 4L 19
Little Crakehall. N Yor 6L 47
Little Crawley. Mil 7G 29
Little Creich. High 5G 79
Little Cressingham. Norf 1E 30
Little Crosby. Mers 7B 40
Little Crosthwaite. Cumb 2M 45
Little Cubley. Derbs 6K 35
Little Dalby. Leics 8E 36
Little Dawley. Telf 1E 26
Littledean. Glos 2E 18
Little Dens. Abers 1K 73
Little Dewchurch. Here 8D 26
Little Ditton. Cambs 6C 30
Little Down. Hants 8A 20
Little Downham. Cambs 3B 30
Little Drayton. Shrp 6E 34
Little Driffield. E Yor 2H 43
Little Dunham. Norf 8E 38
Little Dunkeld. Per 3D 66
Little Dunmow. Essx 1C 22
Little Easton. Essx 1C 22
Little Eaton. Derbs 5A 36
Little Eccleston. Lanc 3C 40
Little Ellingham. Norf 2G 31
Little Elm. Som 1F 8
Little End. Essx 3B 22
Little Everdon. Nptn 6C 28
Little Eversden. Cambs 6L 29
Little Faringdon. Oxon 3L 19
Little Fencote. N Yor 6L 47
Little Fenton. N Yor 4C 42
Littleferry. High 4J 79
Little Fransham. Norf 8F 38
Little Gaddesden. Herts 2G 21
Little Garway. Here 1C 18
Little Gidding. Cambs 3J 29
Little Glemham. Suff 6K 31
Little Glenshee. Per 4C 66
Little Gransden. Cambs 6K 29
Little Green. Suff 4G 31
Little Green. Wrex 5C 34
Little Grimsby. Linc 8L 43
Little Habton. N Yor 8E 48
Little Hadham. Herts 1M 21
Little Hale. Linc 5J 37
Little Hallingbury. Essx 2A 22
Littleham. Devn
 nr. Bideford 3D 6
 nr. Exmouth 7K 7
Little Hampden. Buck 3F 20
Littlehampton. W Sus 5H 11
Little Haresfield. Glos 3G 19
Little Harrowden. Nptn 4F 28
Little Haseley. Oxon 3D 20
Little Hatfield. E Yor 3J 43
Little Hautbois. Norf 7J 39
Little Haven. Pemb 5E 14
Little Hay. Staf 1K 27
Little Hayfield. Derbs 1J 35
Little Haywood. Staf 7J 35
Little Heath. W Mid 3M 27
Little Heck. N Yor 5C 42
Littlehempston. Devn 5L 5
Little Herbert's. Glos 2H 19
Little Hereford. Here 5D 26
Little Horkesley. Essx 8F 30
Little Hormead. Herts 1L 21
Little Horsted. E Sus 4A 12
Little Horton. W Yor 4K 41
Little Horwood. Buck 8E 28
Little Houghton. Nptn 6F 28
Little Houghton. S Yor 7B 42
Littlehoughton. Nmbd 8K 61
Little Hucklow. Derbs 2K 35
Little Hulton. G Man 7F 40
Little Irchester. Nptn 5G 29
Little Kelk. E Yor 1H 43
Little Kimble. Buck 3F 20
Little Kineton. Warw 6M 27
Little Kingshill. Buck 4F 20
Little Langdale. Cumb 5B 46
Little Langford. Wilts 2J 9
Little Laver. Essx 3B 22
Little Lawford. Warw 4B 28
Little Leigh. Ches W 2E 34
Little Leighs. Essx 2D 22
Little Leven. E Yor 3H 43
Little Lever. G Man 7F 40
Little Linford. Mil 7F 28
Little London. Buck 2D 20
Little London. E Sus 4B 12
Little London. Hants
 nr. Andover 1A 10
 nr. Basingstoke 8D 20
Little London. Linc
 nr. Long Sutton 7M 37
 nr. Spalding 7K 37
Little London. Norf
 nr. North Walsham 6J 39
 nr. Northwold 2D 30
 nr. Saxthorpe 6H 39
 nr. Southery 2C 30
Little London. Powy 4K 25
Little Longstone. Derbs 2K 35
Little Malvern. Worc 7F 26
Little Maplestead. Essx 8E 30
Little Marcle. Here 8E 26
Little Marlow. Buck 5F 20
Little Massingham. Norf 7D 38
Little Melton. Norf 1H 31
Little Mill. Mon 3B 18
Littlemill. Abers 6C 72
Littlemill. E Ayr 8C 58
Littlemill. High 1K 71
Little Milton. Oxon 3D 20
Little Missenden. Buck 4G 21
Littlemoor. Derbs 3A 36
Littlemoor. Dors 7E 8
Littlemore. Oxon 3C 20
Little Mountain. Flin 3A 34
Little Musgrave. Cumb 4F 46
Little Ness. Shrp 8C 34
Little Neston. Ches W 2A 34
Little Newcastle. Pemb 4F 14
Little Newsham. Dur 4K 47
Little Oakley. Essx 1J 23
Little Oakley. Nptn 3F 28
Little Onn. Staf 8G 35
Little Ormside. Cumb 4F 46
Little Orton. Cumb 6H 53
Little Orton. Leics 1M 27
Little Ouse. Cambs 3C 30
Little Ouseburn. N Yor 1B 42
Littleover. Derb 6M 35
Little Packington. Warw 3L 27
Little Paxton. Cambs 5J 29
Little Petherick. Corn 4B 4
Little Plumpton. Lanc 4B 40
Little Plumstead. Norf 8K 39
Little Ponton. Linc 6G 37
Littleport. Cambs 3B 30
Little Posbrook. Hants 5C 10
Little Potheridge. Devn 4E 6
Little Preston. Nptn 6C 28
Little Raveley. Cambs 4K 29
Little Reynoldston. Swan 8L 15
Little Ribston. N Yor 2A 42
Little Rissington. Glos 2K 19
Little Rogart. High 3H 79
Little Rollright. Oxon 8L 27
Little Ryburgh. Norf 7F 38
Little Ryle. Nmbd 8H 61
Little Ryton. Shrp 1C 26
Little Salkeld. Cumb 8K 53
Little Sampford. Essx 8C 30
Little Sandhurst. Brac 7F 20
Little Saredon. Staf 1H 27
Little Saxham. Suff 5D 30
Little Scatwell. High 8D 78
Little Shelford. Cambs 6A 30
Little Shoddesden. Hants 1L 9
Little Singleton. Lanc 4B 40
Little Smeaton. N Yor 6C 42
Little Snoring. Norf 6F 38
Little Sodbury. S Glo 5F 18
Little Somborne. Hants 2A 10
Little Somerford. Wilts 5H 19
Little Soudley. Shrp 7F 34
Little Stainforth. N Yor 1G 41
Little Stainton. Darl 4M 47
Little Stanney. Ches W 2C 34
Little Staughton. Bed 5J 29
Little Steeping. Linc 3M 37
Littlester. Shet 5K 91
Little Stoke. Staf 6H 35
Littlestone-on-Sea. Kent 3G 13
Little Stonham. Suff 5H 31
Little Stretton. Leics 1D 28
Little Stretton. Shrp 2C 26
Little Strickland. Cumb 4D 46
Little Stukeley. Cambs 4K 29
Little Sugnall. Staf 6G 35
Little Sutton. Ches W 2B 34
Little Sutton. Linc 7A 38
Little Swinburne. Nmbd 4C 54
Little Tew. Oxon 1A 20
Little Tey. Essx 1E 22
Little Thetford. Cambs 4B 30
Little Thirkleby. N Yor 8B 48
Little Thornage. Norf 6G 39
Little Thornton. Lanc 3B 40
Little Thorpe. W Yor 5K 41
Littlethorpe. Leics 2C 28
Littlethorpe. N Yor 1M 41
Little Thurlow. Suff 6C 30
Little Thurrock. Thur 6C 22
Littleton. Ches W 3C 34
Littleton. Hants 2B 10
Littleton. Som 2C 8
Littleton. Surr
 nr. Guildford 1G 11
 nr. Staines 7H 21
Littleton Drew. Wilts 5G 19
Littleton Pannell. Wilts 8J 19
Littleton-upon-Severn.
 S Glo 5D 18
Little Torboll. High 4H 79
Little Torrington. Devn 4D 6
Little Totham. Essx 2E 22
Little Town. Cumb 3M 45
Little Town. Lanc 4E 40
Littletown. Dur 7G 55
Littletown. High 5H 79
Little Twycross. Leics 1M 27
Little Urswick. Cumb 8A 46
Little Wakering. Essx 5F 22
Little Walden. Essx 7B 30
Little Waldingfield. Suff 7F 30
Little Walsingham. Norf 6F 38
Little Waltham. Essx 2D 22
Little Warley. Essx 4C 22
Little Weighton. E Yor 4G 43
Little Wenham. Suff 8G 31
Little Wenlock. Telf 1E 26
Little Whelnetham. Suff 5E 30
Little Whittingham Green.
 Suff 4J 31
Littlewick Green. Wind 6F 20
Little Wilbraham. Cambs 6B 30
Littlewindsor. Dors 5C 8
Little Wisbeach. Linc 6J 37
Little Witcombe. Glos 2H 19
Little Witley. Worc 5F 26
Little Wittenham. Oxon 4C 20
Little Wolford. Warw 8L 27
Littleworth. Bed 7H 29
Littleworth. Glos 8K 27
Littleworth. Oxon 4M 19
Littleworth. Staf
 nr. Cannock 8J 35
 nr. Eccleshall 7F 34
 nr. Stafford 7H 35
Littleworth. W Sus 3J 11
Littleworth. Worc
 nr. Redditch 5H 27
 nr. Worcester 6G 27
Little Wratting. Suff 7C 30
Little Wymondley. Herts 1K 21
Little Wyrley. Staf 1J 27
Little Yeldham. Essx 8D 30
Littley Green. Essx 2C 22
Litton. Derbs 2K 35
Litton. N Yor 8H 47
Litton. Som 8D 18
Litton Cheney. Dors 6D 8
Liurbost. W Isl 1E 76
Liverpool. Mers 111 (8B 40)
Liverpool John Lennon Airport.
 Mers 1C 34
Liversedge. W Yor 5K 41
Liverton. Devn 8H 7
Liverton. Red C 4E 48
Liverton Mines. Red C 4E 48
Livingston. W Lot 3J 59
Livingston Village. W Lot 3J 59
Lixwm. Flin 3L 33
Lizard. Corn 7L 3
Llaingoch. IOA 2B 32
Llaithddu. Powy 4K 25
Llampha. V Glam 7J 17
Llan. Powy 2H 25
Llanaber. Gwyn 1F 24
Llanaelhaearn. Gwyn 6C 32
Llanaeron. Cdgn 6D 24
Llanafan. Cdgn 5F 24
Llanafan-fawr. Powy 7J 25
Llanafan-fechan. Powy 7J 25
Llanallgo. IOA 2D 32
Llanandras. Powy 5B 26
Llananno. Powy 5K 25
Llanarmon. Gwyn 7D 32
Llanarmon Dyffryn Ceiriog.
 Wrex 7L 33
Llanarmon-yn-Ial. Den 5L 33
Llanarth. Cdgn 1L 15
Llanarth. Mon 2B 18
Llanarthne. Carm 4M 15
Llanasa. Flin 2L 33
Llanbabo. IOA 2C 32
Llanbadarn Fawr. Cdgn 4F 24
Llanbadarn Fynydd. Powy 5L 25
Llanbadarn-y-garreg. Powy 8L 25
Llanbadoc. Mon 3B 18
Llanbadrig. IOA 1C 32
Llanbeder. Newp 4B 18
Llanbedr. Gwyn 8E 32
Llanbedr. Powy
 nr. Crickhowell 2M 17
 nr. Hay-on-Wye 8L 25
Llanbedr-Dyffryn-Clwyd.
 Den 5L 33
Llanbedrgoch. IOA 2E 32
Llanbedrog. Gwyn 7C 32
Llanbedr Pont Steffan.
 Cdgn 8E 24
Llanbedr-y-cennin. Cnwy 4G 33
Llanberis. Gwyn 4E 32
Llanbethery. V Glam 8K 17
Llanbister. Powy 5L 25
Llanblethian. V Glam 7J 17
Llanboidy. Carm 4J 15
Llanbradach. Cphy 5L 17
Llanbrynmair. Powy 2H 25
Llanbydderi. V Glam 8K 17
Llancadle. V Glam 8K 17
Llancarfan. V Glam 7K 17
Llancatal. V Glam 8K 17
Llancayo. Mon 3B 18
Llancloudy. Here 1C 18
Llancoch. Powy 5M 25
Llancynfelyn. Cdgn 3F 24
Llandaff. Card 7L 17
Llandanwg. Gwyn 8E 32
Llandarcy. Neat 5G 17
Llandawke. Carm 5J 15
Llanddaniel Fab. IOA 3D 32
Llanddarog. Carm 5M 15
Llanddeiniol. Cdgn 5E 24
Llanddeiniolen. Gwyn 4E 32
Llandderfel. Gwyn 7J 33
Llanddeusant. Carm 2G 17
Llanddeusant. IOA 2C 32
Llanddew. Powy 1K 17
Llanddewi. Swan 8L 15
Llanddewi Brefi. Cdgn 7F 24
Llanddewi'r Cwm. Powy 8K 25
Llanddewi Rhydderch. Mon 2B 18
Llanddewi Velfrey. Pemb 5H 15
Llanddewi Ystradenni.
 Powy 6L 25
Llanddoged. Cnwy 4H 33
Llanddona. IOA 3E 32
Llanddowror. Carm 5J 15
Llanddulas. Cnwy 3J 33
Llanddwywe. Gwyn 8E 32
Llanddyfnan. IOA 3E 32
Llandecwyn. Gwyn 7F 32
Llandefaelog Fach. Powy 1K 17
Llandefaelog-tre'r-graig.
 Powy 1L 17
Llandefalle. Powy 1L 17
Llandegfan. IOA 3E 32
Llandegla. Den 5L 33
Llandegley. Powy 6L 25
Llandegveth. Mon 4B 18
Llandeilo. Carm 2F 16
Llandeilo Graban. Powy 8K 25
Llandeilo'r Fan. Powy 1H 17
Llandeloy. Pemb 4E 14
Llandenny. Mon 3C 18
Llandevaud. Newp 4C 18
Llandevenny. Mon 5C 18
Llandilo. Pemb 4H 15
Llandinabo. Here 1D 18
Llandinam. Powy 4K 25
Llandissilio. Pemb 4H 15
Llandogo. Mon 3D 18
Llandough. V Glam
 nr. Cowbridge 7J 17
 nr. Penarth 7L 17
Llandovery. Carm 1G 17
Llandow. V Glam 7J 17
Llandre. Cdgn 4F 24
Llandrillo. Den 7K 33
Llandrillo-yn-Rhos. Cnwy 2H 33
Llandrindod. Powy 6K 25
Llandrindod Wells. Powy 6K 25
Llandrinio. Powy 8A 34
Llandudno. Cnwy 2G 33
Llandudno Junction. Cnwy 3G 33
Llandudoch. Pemb 2H 15
Llandw. V Glam 7J 17
Llandwrog. Gwyn 5D 32
Llandybie. Carm 3F 16
Llandyfaelog. Carm 5L 15
Llandyfan. Carm 3F 16
Llandyfriog. Cdgn 2K 15
Llandyfrydog. IOA 2D 32
Llandygai. Gwyn 3F 32
Llandygwydd. Cdgn 2J 15
Llandynan. Den 6L 33
Llandyrnog. Den 4L 33
Llandysilio. Powy 8A 34
Llandyssil. Powy 3L 25
Llandysul. Cdgn 2L 15
Llanedeyrn. Card 6M 17
Llaneglwys. Powy 1K 17
Llanegryn. Gwyn 2F 24
Llanegwad. Carm 4M 15
Llaneilian. IOA 1D 32
Llanelian-yn-Rhos. Cnwy 3H 33
Llanelidan. Den 5L 33
Llanelieu. Powy 1L 17
Llanellen. Mon 2B 18
Llanelli. Carm 7M 15
Llanelltyd. Gwyn 1G 25
Llanelly. Mon 3M 17
Llanelly Hill. Mon 3M 17
Llanelwedd. Powy 7K 25
Llan-Elwy. Den 3K 33
Llanenddwyn. Gwyn 8E 32
Llanengan. Gwyn 8B 32
Llanerch. Powy 2B 26
Llanerchymedd. IOA 2D 32
Llanerfyl. Powy 2K 25
Llaneuddog. IOA 2D 32
Llanfachraeth. IOA 2C 32
Llanfachreth. Gwyn 8G 33
Llanfaelog. IOA 3C 32
Llanfaelrhys. Gwyn 8B 32
Llanfaenor. Mon 2C 18
Llanfaes. IOA 3F 32
Llanfaes. Powy 2K 17
Llanfaethlu. IOA 2C 32
Llanfaglan. Gwyn 4D 32
Llanfair. Gwyn 8E 32
Llanfair. Here 7A 26
Llanfair Caereinion. Powy 2L 25
Llanfair Clydogau. Cdgn 7F 24
Llanfair Dyffryn Clwyd. Den 5L 33
Llanfairfechan. Cnwy 3F 32
Llanfair-Nant-Gwyn. Pemb 3H 15
Llanfair Pwllgwyngyll. IOA 3E 32
Llanfair Talhaiarn. Cnwy 3J 33
Llanfair Waterdine. Shrp 5M 25
Llanfair-ym-Muallt. Powy 7K 25
Llanfairyneubwll. IOA 3C 32
Llanfairynghornwy. IOA 1C 32
Llanfallteg. Carm 5H 15
Llanfallteg West. Carm 5H 15
Llanfaredd. Powy 7K 25
Llanfarian. Cdgn 5E 24
Llanfechain. Powy 8L 33
Llanfechell. IOA 1C 32
Llanfendigaid. Gwyn 2E 24
Llanferres. Den 4L 33
Llan Ffestiniog. Gwyn 6G 33
Llanfflewyn. IOA 2C 32
Llanfihangel-ar-Arth. Carm 3L 15
Llanfihangel Glyn Myfyr.
 Cnwy 6J 33
Llanfihangel Nant Bran.
 Powy 1J 17
Llanfihangel-Nant-Melan.
 Powy 7L 25
Llanfihangel near Rogiet.
 Mon 5C 18
Llanfihangel Rhydithon.
 Powy 6L 25
Llanfihangel Tal-y-llyn.
 Powy 2L 17
Llanfihangel-uwch-Gwili.
 Carm 4L 15
Llanfihangel-y-Creuddyn.
 Cdgn 5F 24
Llanfihangel-yng-Ngwynfa.
 Powy 1K 25
Llanfihangel yn Nhowyn.
 IOA 3C 32
Llanfihangel-y-pennant.
 Gwyn nr. Golan 6E 32
 nr. Tywyn 2F 24
Llanfihangel-y-traethau.
 Gwyn 7E 32
Llanfilo. Powy 1L 17
Llanfleiddan. V Glam 7J 17
Llanfoist. Mon 2A 18
Llanfor. Gwyn 7J 33
Llanfrechfa. Torf 4B 18
Llanfrothen. Gwyn 6F 32
Llanfrynach. Powy 2K 17
Llanfwrog. Den 5L 33
Llanfwrog. IOA 2C 32
Llanfyllin. Powy 1L 25
Llanfynydd. Carm 2E 16
Llanfynydd. Flin 4A 34
Llanfyrnach. Pemb 3J 15
Llangadfan. Powy 1K 25
Llangadog. Carm
 nr. Llandovery 2G 17
 nr. Llanelli 6L 15
Llangadwaladr. IOA 4C 32
Llangadwaladr. Powy 7L 33
Llangaffo. IOA 4D 32
Llangain. Carm 5K 15
Llangammarch Wells. Powy 8J 25
Llangan. V Glam 7J 17
Llangarron. Here 1D 18
Llangasty-Talyllyn. Powy 2L 17
Llangathen. Carm 2E 16
Llangattock. Powy 3M 17
Llangattock Lingoed. Mon 1B 18
Llangattock-Vibon-Avel.
 Mon 2C 18
Llangedwyn. Powy 8L 33
Llangefni. IOA 3D 32
Llangeinor. B'end 6J 17
Llangeitho. Cdgn 7F 24
Llangeler. Carm 3K 15
Llangelynin. Gwyn 2E 24
Llangendeirne. Carm 5L 15
Llangennech. Carm 4E 16
Llangennith. Swan 7L 15
Llangenny. Powy 3M 17
Llangernyw. Cnwy 4H 33
Llangian. Gwyn 8B 32
Llangiwg. Neat 4G 17
Llangloffan. Pemb 3F 14
Llanglydwen. Carm 4H 15
Llangoed. IOA 3F 32
Llangoedmor. Cdgn 2H 15
Llangollen. Den 6M 33
Llangolman. Pemb 4H 15
Llangorse. Powy 2L 17
Llangorwen. Cdgn 4F 24
Llangovan. Mon 3C 18
Llangower. Gwyn 7J 33
Llangranog. Cdgn 1K 15
Llangristiolus. IOA 3D 32
Llangrove. Here 2D 18
Llangua. Mon 1B 18
Llangunllo. Powy 5M 25
Llangunnor. Carm 4L 15
Llangurig. Powy 5J 25
Llangwm. Cnwy 6J 33
Llangwm. Mon 3C 18
Llangwm. Pemb 6F 14
Llangwm-isaf. Mon 3C 18
Llangwnnadl. Gwyn 7B 32
Llangwyfan. Den 4L 33
Llangwyfan-isaf. IOA 4C 32
Llangwyllog. IOA 3D 32
Llangwyryfon. Cdgn 5F 24
Llangybi. Cdgn 7F 24
Llangybi. Gwyn 6D 32
Llangybi. Mon 4B 18
Llangyfelach. Swan 5F 16
Llangynhafal. Den 4L 33
Llangynidr. Powy 3L 17
Llangynin. Carm 5J 15
Llangynog. Carm 5K 15
Llangynog. Powy 8K 33
Llangynwyd. B'end 6H 17
Llanhamlach. Powy 2K 17
Llanharan. Rhon 6K 17
Llanharry. Rhon 6K 17
Llanhennock. Mon 4B 18
Llanhilleth. Blae 4M 17
Llanidloes. Powy 4J 25
Llaniestyn. Gwyn 7B 32
Llanigon. Powy 8M 25
Llanilar. Cdgn 5F 24
Llanilid. Rhon 6J 17
Llanilltud Fawr. V Glam 8J 17
Llanishen. Card 6L 17
Llanishen. Mon 3C 18
Llanllawddog. Carm 4L 15
Llanllechid. Gwyn 4F 32
Llanllowell. Mon 4B 18
Llanllugan. Powy 2K 25
Llanllwch. Carm 5K 15
Llanllwchaiarn. Powy 3L 25
Llanllwni. Carm 3L 15
Llanllyfni. Gwyn 5D 32
Llanmadoc. Swan 7L 15
Llanmaes. V Glam 8J 17
Llanmartin. Newp 5B 18
Llanmerwig. Powy 3L 25
Llanmihangel. V Glam 7J 17
Llan-mill. Pemb 5H 15
Llanmiloe. Carm 6J 15
Llanmorlais. Swan 7M 15
Llannefydd. Cnwy 3J 33
Llan-non. Cdgn 6E 24
Llannon. Carm 6M 15
Llannor. Gwyn 7C 32
Llanover. Mon 3B 18
Llanpumsaint. Carm 4L 15
Llanrhaeadr. Den 4K 33
Llanrhaeadr-ym-Mochnant.
 Powy 8L 33
Llanrhian. Pemb 3E 14
Llanrhidian. Swan 7L 15
Llanrhos. Cnwy 2G 33
Llanrhyddlad. IOA 2C 32
Llanrhystud. Cdgn 6E 24
Llanrothal. Here 2C 18
Llanrug. Gwyn 4E 32
Llanrumney. Card 6M 17
Llanrwst. Cnwy 4G 33
Llansadurnen. Carm 5J 15
Llansadwrn. Carm 1F 16
Llansadwrn. IOA 3E 32
Llansaint. Carm 6K 15
Llansamlet. Swan 5F 16
Llansanffraid Glan Conwy.
 Cnwy 3H 33

Llansannan – Meadgate

Llansannan. *Cnwy* 4J 33
Llansannor. *V Glam* 7J 17
Llansantffraed. *Cdgn* 6E 24
Llansantffraed. *Powy* 2L 17
Llansantffraed Cwmdeuddwr.
Powy 6J 25
Llansantffraed-in-Elwel.
Powy 7K 25
Llansantffraid-ym-Mechain.
Powy 8M 33
Llansawel. *Carm* 1F 16
Llansawel. *Neat* 5G 17
Llansilin. *Powy* 8M 33
Llansoy. *Mon* 3C 18
Llanspyddid. *Powy* 2K 17
Llanstadwell. *Pemb* 6F 14
Llansteffan. *Carm* 5K 15
Llanstephan. *Powy* 8L 25
Llantarnam. *Torf* 4B 18
Llanteg. *Pemb* 5H 15
Llanthony. *Mon* 1A 18
Llantilio Crossenny. *Mon* 2B 18
Llantilio Pertholey. *Mon* 2B 18
Llantood. *Pemb* 2H 15
Llantrisant. *Mon* 4B 18
Llantrisant. *Rhon* 6K 17
Llantrithyd. *V Glam* 7K 17
Llantwit Fardre. *Rhon* 6K 17
Llantwit Major. *V Glam* 8J 17
Llanuwchllyn. *Gwyn* 7H 33
Llanvaches. *Newp* 4C 18
Llanvair Discoed. *Mon* 4C 18
Llanvapley. *Mon* 2B 18
Llanvetherine. *Mon* 2B 18
Llanveynoe. *Here* 8B 26
Llanvihangel Crucorney.
Mon 1B 18
Llanvihangel Gobion. *Mon* 3B 18
Llanvihangel Ystern-Llewern.
Mon 2C 18
Llanwarne. *Here* 1D 18
Llanwddyn. *Powy* 1K 25
Llanwenarth. *Mon* 2A 18
Llanwenog. *Cdgn* 2L 15
Llanwern. *Newp* 5B 18
Llanwinio. *Carm* 4J 15
Llanwnda. *Gwyn* 5D 32
Llanwnda. *Pemb* 3F 14
Llanwnnen. *Cdgn* 2M 15
Llanwnog. *Powy* 3K 25
Llanwrda. *Carm* 1G 17
Llanwrin. *Powy* 2G 25
Llanwrthwl. *Powy* 6J 25
Llanwrtud. *Powy* 8H 25
Llanwrtyd. *Powy* 8H 25
Llanwrtyd Wells. *Powy* 8H 25
Llanwyddelan. *Powy* 2K 25
Llanyblodwel. *Shrp* 8M 33
Llanybri. *Carm* 5K 15
Llanybydder. *Carm* 2M 15
Llanycefn. *Pemb* 4G 15
Llanychaer. *Pemb* 3F 14
Llanycil. *Gwyn* 7J 33
Llanymawddwy. *Gwyn* 1J 25
Llanymddyfri. *Carm* 1G 17
Llanymynech. *Powy* 7A 34
Llanynghenedl. *IOA* 2C 32
Llanynys. *Den* 4L 33
Llan-y-pwll. *Wrex* 4B 34
Llanyrafon. *Torf* 4B 18
Llanyre. *Powy* 6K 25
Llanystumdwy. *Gwyn* 7D 32
Llanywern. *Powy* 2L 17
Llawhaden. *Pemb* 5G 15
Llawndy. *Flin* 2L 33
Llawnt. *Shrp* 6A 34
Llawr Dref. *Gwyn* 8B 32
Llawryglyn. *Powy* 3J 25
Llay. *Wrex* 4B 34
Llechfaen. *Powy* 2K 17
Llechryd. *Cphy* 4L 17
Llechryd. *Cdgn* 2J 15
Llechrydau. *Wrex* 7M 33
Lledrod. *Cdgn* 5F 24
Llethrid. *Swan* 7M 15
Llidiad-Nenog. *Carm* 3M 15
Llidiardau. *Gwyn* 7H 33
Llidiart y Parc. *Den* 6L 33
Llithfaen. *Gwyn* 6C 32
Lloc. *Flin* 3L 33
Llong. *Flin* 3A 34
Llowes. *Powy* 8L 25
Lloyney. *Powy* 5M 25
Llundain-fach. *Cdgn* 7E 24
Llwydcoed. *Rhon* 4J 17
Llwyncelyn. *Cdgn* 1L 15
Llwyncelyn. *Swan* 4F 16
Llwyndafydd. *Cdgn* 1K 15
Llwynderw. *Powy* 2M 25
Llwyn-du. *Mon* 2A 18
Llwyngwril. *Gwyn* 2E 24
Llwynhendy. *Carm* 7M 15
Llwynmawr. *Wrex* 7M 33
Llwyn-on Village. *Mer T* 3K 17
Llwyn-têg. *Carm* 4E 16
Llwyn-y-brain. *Carm* 5H 15
Llwynygog. *Powy* 3H 25
Llwyn-y-groes. *Cdgn* 7E 24
Llwynypia. *Rhon* 5J 17
Llynclys. *Shrp* 7A 34
Llynfaes. *IOA* 3D 32
Llysfaen. *Cnwy* 3H 33
Llyswen. *Powy* 1L 17
Llysworney. *V Glam* 7J 17
Llys-y-fran. *Pemb* 4G 15
Llywel. *Powy* 1H 17
Llywernog. *Cdgn* 4G 25
Loan. *Falk* 2H 59
Loanend. *Nmbd* 4G 61
Loanhead. *Midl* 3L 59
Loaningfoot. *Dum* 6D 52
Loanreoch. *High* 6G 79
Loans. *S Ayr* 6B 58
Loansdean. *Nmbd* 3E 54
Lobb. *Devn* 2D 6
Lobhillcross. *Devn* 7D 6
Lochaber. *Mor* 8L 79
Loch a Charnain. *W Isl* 1E 74
Loch a Ghainmhich. *W Isl* 1D 76
Lochailort. *High* 7J 69
Lochaline. *High* 3A 64
Lochans. *Dum* 6F 50
Locharbriggs. *Dum* 3D 52
Lochardil. *High* 1G 71
Lochassynt Lodge. *High* 1B 78
Lochavich. *Arg* 6D 64
Lochawe. *Arg* 5F 64
Loch Baghasdail. *W Isl* 4D 74
Lochboisdale. *W Isl* 4D 74
Lochbuie. *Arg* 5M 63
Lochcarron. *High* 2K 69
Loch Choire Lodge. *High* 8J 85
Lochdochart House. *Stir* 5J 65
Lochdon. *Arg* 4B 64
Lochearnhead. *Stir* 5K 65
Lochee. *D'dee* 4G 67
Lochend. *High*
nr. Inverness 2F 70
nr. Thurso 5D 86
Locherben. *Dum* 2D 52
Loch Euphort. *W Isl* 7K 75
Lochfoot. *Dum* 4C 52
Lochgair. *Arg* 8D 64
Lochgarthside. *High* 4F 70
Lochgelly. *Fife* 8E 66
Lochgilphead. *Arg* 1H 57
Lochgoilhead. *Arg* 7F 64
Loch Head. *Dum* 7J 51
Lochhill. *Mor* 7B 80
Lochindorb Lodge. *High* 2K 71
Lochinver. *High* 1A 78
Lochlane. *Per* 5B 66
Loch Lomond. *Arg* 7H 65
Loch Loyal Lodge. *High* 7J 85
Lochluichart. *High* 7D 78
Lochmaben. *Dum* 3E 52
Lochmaddy. *W Isl* 7L 75
Loch nam Madadh. *W Isl* 7L 75
Lochore. *Fife* 8E 66
Lochportain. *W Isl* 6L 75
Lochranza. *N Ayr* 4J 57
Loch Sgioport. *W Isl* 2E 74
Lochside. *Abers* 1L 67
Lochside. *High*
nr. Achentoul 8L 85
nr. Nairn 8J 79
Lochslin. *High* 5J 79
Lochstack Lodge. *High* 7E 84
Lochton. *Abers* 6G 73
Lochty. *Fife* 7J 67
Lochuisge. *High* 2B 64
Lochussie. *High* 8E 78
Lochwinnoch. *Ren* 4B 58
Lochyside. *High* 8B 70
Lockengate. *Corn* 5C 4
Lockerbie. *Dum* 3F 52
Lockeridge. *Wilts* 7K 19
Lockerley. *Hants* 3L 9
Lockhills. *Cumb* 7K 53
Locking. *N Som* 8B 18
Lockington. *E Yor* 3G 43
Lockington. *Leics* 7B 36
Lockleywood. *Shrp* 7E 34
Locksgreen. *IOW* 6B 10
Locks Heath. *Hants* 5C 10
Lockton. *N Yor* 6F 48
Loddington. *Leics* 1E 28
Loddington. *Nptn* 4F 28
Loddiswell. *Devn* 7K 5
Loddon. *Norf* 2K 31
Lode. *Cambs* 5B 30
Loders. *Dors* 6C 8
Lodsworth. *W Sus* 3G 11
Lofthouse. *N Yor* 8K 47
Lofthouse. *W Yor* 5M 41
Lofthouse Gate. *W Yor* 5M 41
Loftus. *Red C* 4E 48
Logan. *E Ayr* 7D 58
Loganlea. *W Lot* 3H 59
Logaston. *Here* 6B 26
Loggerheads. *Den* 4L 33
Loggerheads. *Staf* 6F 34
Loggie. *High* 4B 78
Logie. *Ang* 1K 67
Logie. *Fife* 5H 67
Logie. *Mor* 8L 79
Logie Coldstone. *Abers* 5D 72
Logie Pert. *Ang* 1K 67
Logierait. *Per* 2C 66
Login. *Carm* 4H 15
Lolworth. *Cambs* 5L 29
Lonbain. *High* 8H 77
Londesborough. *E Yor* 3F 42
London. *G Lon* 112-113 (5L 21)
London Apprentice. *Corn* 6C 4
London Ashford Airport.
Kent 3G 13
London City Airport. *G Lon* 5M 21
London Colney. *Herts* 3J 21
Londonderry. *Derr* 3D 92
Londonderry. *N Yor* 7M 47
London Gatwick Airport.
W Sus 119 (1K 11)
London Heathrow Airport.
G Lon 119 (6H 21)
London Luton Airport.
Lutn 119 (1J 21)
London Southend Airport.
Essx 5E 22
London Stansted Airport.
Essx 119 (1B 22)
Londonthorpe. *Linc* 6G 37
Londubh. *High* 5K 77
Lone. *High* 7F 84
Lonemore. *High*
nr. Dornoch 5H 79
nr. Gairloch 6J 77
Long Ashton. *N Som* 6D 18
Long Bank. *Worc* 4F 26
Longbar. *N Ayr* 4B 58
Long Bennington. *Linc* 5F 36
Longbenton. *Tyne* 5F 54
Longborough. *Glos* 1K 19
Long Bredy. *Dors* 6D 8
Longbridge. *Warw* 5L 27
Longbridge. *W Mid* 4J 27
Longbridge Deverill. *Wilts* 1G 9
Long Buckby. *Nptn* 5D 28
Long Buckby Wharf. *Nptn* 5D 28
Longburgh. *Cumb* 6H 53
Longburton. *Dors* 4E 8
Long Clawson. *Leics* 7E 36
Longcliffe. *Derbs* 4L 35
Long Common. *Hants* 4C 10
Long Compton. *Staf* 7G 35
Long Compton. *Warw* 8L 27
Longcot. *Oxon* 4L 19
Long Crendon. *Buck* 3D 20
Long Crichel. *Dors* 4H 9
Longcroft. *Cumb* 6G 53
Longcroft. *Falk* 2F 58
Longcross. *Surr* 7G 21
Longdale. *Cumb* 5E 46
Longdales. *Cumb* 7K 53
Longden. *Shrp* 1C 26
Longden Common. *Shrp* 1C 26
Long Ditton. *Surr* 7J 21
Longdon. *Staf* 8J 35
Longdon. *Worc* 8G 27
Longdon Green. *Staf* 8J 35
Longdon on Tern. *Telf* 8E 34
Longdown. *Devn* 6H 7
Longdowns. *Corn* 5L 3
Long Drax. *N Yor* 5D 42
Long Duckmanton. *Derbs* 2B 36
Long Eaton. *Derbs* 6B 36
Longfield. *Kent* 7C 22
Longfield. *Shet* 6D 90
Longfield Hill. *Kent* 7C 22
Longford. *Derbs* 6L 35
Longford. *Glos* 1G 19
Longford. *G Lon* 6H 21
Longford. *Shrp* 6E 34
Longford. *Telf* 8F 34
Longford. *W Mid* 3A 28
Longforgan. *Per* 4G 67
Longformacus. *Bord* 4D 60
Longframlington. *Nmbd* 1E 54
Long Gardens. *Essx* 8E 30
Long Green. *Ches W* 2C 34
Long Green. *Worc* 8G 27
Longham. *Dors* 6J 9
Longham. *Norf* 8F 38
Long Hanborough. *Oxon* 2B 20
Longhedge. *Wilts* 1G 9
Longhill. *Abers* 8K 81
Longhirst. *Nmbd* 3F 54
Longhope. *Glos* 2E 18
Longhope. *Orkn* 2E 86
Longhorsley. *Nmbd* 2E 54
Longhoughton. *Nmbd* 8K 61
Long Itchington. *Warw* 5B 28
Longlands. *Cumb* 8G 53
Long Lane. *Telf* 8E 34
Longlane. *Derbs* 6L 35
Longlane. *W Ber* 6B 20
Long Lawford. *Warw* 4B 28
Long Lease. *N Yor* 5G 49
Longley Green. *Worc* 6F 26
Long Load. *Som* 3C 8
Longmanhill. *Abers* 7G 81
Long Marston. *Herts* 2F 20
Long Marston. *N Yor* 2C 42
Long Marston. *Warw* 7K 27
Long Marton. *Cumb* 3E 46
Long Meadow. *Cambs* 5B 30
Long Meadowend. *Shrp* 3C 26
Long Melford. *Suff* 7E 30
Longmoor Camp. *Hants* 2E 10
Longmorn. *Mor* 8B 80
Longmoss. *Ches E* 2G 35
Long Newnton. *Glos* 4H 19
Long Newton. *Stoc T* 4A 48
Longnewton. *Bord* 7C 60
Longney. *Glos* 2F 18
Longniddry. *E Lot* 2B 60
Longnor. *Shrp* 1C 26
Longnor. *Staf*
nr. Leek 3J 35
nr. Stafford 8G 35
Longparish. *Hants* 1B 10
Longpark. *Cumb* 5J 53
Long Preston. *N Yor* 2G 41
Longridge. *Lanc* 4E 40
Longridge. *Staf* 8H 35
Longridge. *W Lot* 3H 59
Longriggend. *N Lan* 2G 59
Long Riston. *E Yor* 3J 43
Longrock. *Corn* 5J 3
Longsdon. *Staf* 4H 35
Longshaw. *G Man* 7D 40
Longshaw. *Staf* 5J 35
Longside. *Abers* 1K 73
Longslow. *Shrp* 6E 34
Longstanton. *Cambs* 5L 29
Longstock. *Hants* 2A 10
Longstowe. *Cambs* 6L 29
Long Stratton. *Norf* 2H 31
Long Street. *Mil* 7E 28
Longstreet. *Wilts* 8K 19
Long Sutton. *Hants* 1E 10
Long Sutton. *Linc* 7M 37
Long Sutton. *Som* 3C 8
Longthorpe. *Pet* 2J 29
Long Thurlow. *Suff* 5G 31
Longthwaite. *Cumb* 3C 46
Longton. *Lanc* 5C 40
Longton. *Stoke* 5H 35
Longtown. *Cumb* 5H 53
Longtown. *Here* 1B 18
Longville in the Dale. *Shrp* 2D 26
Long Whatton. *Leics* 7B 36
Longwick. *Buck* 3E 20
Long Wittenham. *Oxon* 4C 20
Longwitton. *Nmbd* 3D 54
Longworth. *Oxon* 4A 20
Longyester. *E Lot* 3C 60
Lonmore. *High* 1D 68
Looe. *Corn* 6E 4
Loose. *Kent* 8D 22
Loosegate. *Linc* 7L 37
Loosley Row. *Buck* 3F 20
Lopcombe Corner. *Wilts* 2L 9
Lopen. *Som* 4C 8
Loppington. *Shrp* 7C 34
Lorbottle. *Nmbd* 1D 54
Lordington. *W Sus* 5E 10
Loscoe. *Derbs* 5B 36
Loscombe. *Dors* 6D 8
Losgaintir. *W Isl* 4B 76
Lossiemouth. *Mor* 7B 80
Lossit. *Arg* 4A 56
Lostock Gralam. *Ches W* 2E 34
Lostock Green. *Ches W* 2E 34
Lostock Hall. *Lanc* 5D 40
Lostock Junction. *G Man* 7E 40
Lostwithiel. *Corn* 6D 4
Lothbeg. *High* 2K 79
Lothersdale. *N Yor* 3H 41
Lothianbridge. *Midl* 3M 59
Lothianburn. *Midl* 3L 59
Lothmore. *High* 2K 79
Lottisham. *Som* 2D 8
Loudwater. *Buck* 4G 21
Loughborough. *Leics* 8C 36
Loughbrickland. *Arm* 6G 93
Loughgall. *Arm* 6F 93
Loughguile. *Caus* 2G 93
Loughinisland. *New M* 6J 93
Loughmacrory. *Ferm* 5D 92
Loughor. *Swan* 5E 16
Loughries. *Ards* 5J 93
Loughton. *Essx* 4M 21
Loughton. *Mil* 8F 28
Loughton. *Shrp* 3E 26
Lound. *Linc* 8H 37
Lound. *Notts* 1D 36
Lound. *Suff* 2M 31
Lount. *Leics* 8A 36
The Loup. *M Ulst* 4F 93
Louth. *Linc* 1L 37
Love Clough. *Lanc* 5G 41
Lovedean. *Hants* 4D 10
Lover. *Wilts* 3L 9
Loversall. *S Yor* 8C 42
Loves Green. *Essx* 3C 22
Loveston. *Pemb* 6G 15
Lovington. *Som* 2D 8
Low Ackworth. *W Yor* 6B 42
Low Angerton. *Nmbd* 3D 54
Low Ardwell. *Dum* 7F 50
Low Ballochdowan. *S Ayr* 4F 50
Lowbands. *Glos* 8F 26
Low Barlings. *Linc* 2H 37
Low Bell End. *N Yor* 6E 48
Low Bentham. *N Yor* 1E 40
Low Borrowbridge. *Cumb* 5E 46
Low Bradfield. *S Yor* 8L 41
Low Bradley. *N Yor* 3J 41
Low Braithwaite. *Cumb* 7J 53
Low Brunton. *Nmbd* 4C 54
Low Burnham. *N Lin* 7E 42
Lowca. *Cumb* 2J 45
Low Catton. *E Yor* 2E 42
Low Coniscliffe. *Darl* 4L 47
Low Coylton. *S Ayr* 8C 58
Low Crosby. *Cumb* 6J 53
Low Dalby. *N Yor* 7F 48
Lowdham. *Notts* 5D 36
Low Dinsdale. *Darl* 4M 47
Lowe. *Shrp* 6D 34
Low Ellington. *N Yor* 7L 47
Lower Amble. *Corn* 4B 4
Lower Ansty. *Dors* 5F 8
Lower Arboll. *High* 5J 79
Lower Arncott. *Oxon* 2D 20
Lower Ashton. *Devn* 7H 7
Lower Assendon. *Oxon* 5E 20
Lower Auchenreath. *Mor* 7C 80
Lower Badcall. *High* 7D 84
Lower Ballam. *Lanc* 4B 40
Lower Ballinderry. *Lis* 5G 93
Lower Basildon. *W Ber* 6D 20
Lower Beeding. *W Sus* 3K 11
Lower Benefield. *Nptn* 3G 29
Lower Bentley. *Worc* 5H 27
Lower Beobridge. *Shrp* 2F 26
Lower Bockhampton. *Dors* 6F 8
Lower Boddington. *Nptn* 6B 28
Lower Bordean. *Hants* 3D 10
Lower Brailes. *Warw* 8M 27
Lower Breakish. *High* 3H 69
Lower Broadheath. *Worc* 6G 27
Lower Brynamman. *Neat* 3G 17
Lower Bullingham. *Here* 8D 26
Lower Bullington. *Hants* 1B 10
Lower Burgate. *Hants* 4K 9
Lower Cam. *Glos* 3F 18
Lower Catesby. *Nptn* 6C 28
Lower Chapel. *Powy* 1K 17
Lower Cheriton. *Devn* 5L 7
Lower Chicksgrove. *Wilts* 2H 9
Lower Chute. *Wilts* 8M 19
Lower Clopton. *Warw* 6K 27
Lower Common. *Hants* 1D 10
Lower Crossings. *Derbs* 1J 35
Lower Cumberworth. *W Yor* 7L 41
Lower Darwen. *Bkbn* 5E 40
Lower Dean. *Bed* 5H 29
Lower Dean. *Devn* 5K 5
Lower Diabaig. *High* 7J 77
Lower Dicker. *E Sus* 4B 12
Lower Dounreay. *High* 5A 86
Lower Down. *Shrp* 3B 26
Lower Dunsforth. *N Yor* 1B 42
Lower East Carleton. *Norf* 1H 31
Lower Egleton. *Here* 7E 26
Lower Ellastone. *Staf* 5K 35
Lower End. *Nptn* 5F 28
Lower Everleigh. *Wilts* 8K 19
Lower Eype. *Dors* 6C 8
Lower Failand. *N Som* 6D 18
Lower Faintree. *Shrp* 3E 26
Lower Farringdon. *Hants* 2E 10
Lower Foxdale. *IOM* 7B 44
Lower Frankton. *Shrp* 6B 34
Lower Froyle. *Hants* 1E 10
Lower Gabwell. *Devn* 5M 5
Lower Gledfield. *High* 4F 78
Lower Godney. *Som* 1C 8
Lower Gravenhurst. *C Beds* 8J 29
Lower Green. *Essx* 8M 29
Lower Green. *Norf* 6F 38
Lower Green. *W Ber* 7A 20
Lower Halstow. *Kent* 7E 22
Lower Hardres. *Kent* 8H 23
Lower Hardwick. *Here* 6C 26
Lower Hartshay. *Derbs* 4A 36
Lower Hawthwaite. *Cumb* 6M 45
Lower Haysden. *Kent* 1B 12
Lower Hayton. *Shrp* 3D 26
Lower Hergest. *Here* 6A 26
Lower Heyford. *Oxon* 1B 20
Lower Heysham. *Lanc* 1C 40
Lower Higham. *Kent* 6D 22
Lower Holbrook. *Suff* 8H 31
Lower Holditch. *Dors* 5B 8
Lower Hordley. *Shrp* 7B 34
Lower Horncroft. *W Sus* 4H 11
Lower Horsebridge. *E Sus* 4B 12
Lower Kilcott. *Glos* 5F 18
Lower Killeyan. *Arg* 5B 56
Lower Kingcombe. *Dors* 6D 8
Lower Kingswood. *Surr* 8K 21
Lower Kinnerton. *Ches W* 3B 34
Lower Langford. *N Som* 7C 18
Lower Largo. *Fife* 7H 67
Lower Layham. *Suff* 7G 31
Lower Ledwyche. *Shrp* 4D 26
Lower Leigh. *Staf* 6J 35
Lower Lemington. *Glos* 8L 27
Lower Lenie. *High* 3F 70
Lower Ley. *Glos* 2F 18
Lower Llanfadog. *Powy* 6J 25
Lower Lode. *Glos* 8G 27
Lower Lovacott. *Devn* 3E 6
Lower Loxhore. *Devn* 2F 6
Lower Loxley. *Staf* 6J 35
Lower Lydbrook. *Glos* 2D 18
Lower Lye. *Here* 5C 26
Lower Machen. *Newp* 6M 17
Lower Maes-coed. *Here* 8B 26
Lower Meend. *Glos* 3D 18
Lower Midway. *Derbs* 7M 35
Lower Milovaig. *High* 8C 76
Lower Moor. *Worc* 7H 27
Lower Morton. *S Glo* 4E 18
Lower Mountain. *Flin* 4B 34
Lower Nazeing. *Essx* 3L 21
Lower Netchwood. *Shrp* 2E 26
Lower Nyland. *Dors* 3F 8
Lower Oakfield. *Fife* 8E 66
Lower Oddington. *Glos* 1L 19
Lower Ollach. *High* 2G 69
Lower Penarth. *V Glam* 8L 17
Lower Penn. *Staf* 2G 27
Lower Pennington. *Hants* 6M 9
Lower Peover. *Ches W* 2F 34
Lower Pilsley. *Derbs* 3B 36
Lower Pitkerrie. *High* 6J 79
Lower Place. *G Man* 6H 41
Lower Quinton. *Warw* 7K 27
Lower Rainham. *Medw* 7E 22
Lower Raydon. *Suff* 8G 31
Lower Seagry. *Wilts* 5H 19
Lower Shelton. *C Beds* 7G 29
Lower Shiplake. *Oxon* 6E 20
Lower Shuckburgh. *Warw* 5B 28
Lower Sketty. *Swan* 5F 16
Lower Slade. *Devn* 1E 6
Lower Slaughter. *Glos* 1K 19
Lower Soudley. *Glos* 2E 18
Lower Stanton St Quintin.
Wilts 5H 19
Lower Stoke. *Medw* 6E 22
Lower Stondon. *C Beds* 8J 29
Lower Stonnall. *Staf* 1J 27
Lower Stow Bedon. *Norf* 2F 30
Lower Street. *Norf* 6J 39
Lower Strensham. *Worc* 7H 27
Lower Sundon. *C Beds* 1H 21
Lower Swanwick. *Hants* 5B 10
Lower Swell. *Glos* 1K 19
Lower Tale. *Devn* 5K 7
Lower Tean. *Staf* 6J 35
Lower Thurlton. *Norf* 2L 31
Lower Thurnham. *Lanc* 2C 40
Lower Thurvaston. *Derbs* 6L 35
Lower Town. *Here* 7E 26
Lower Town. *IOS* 1H 3
Lower Town. *Pemb* 3F 14
Lowertown. *Corn* 6K 3
Lowertown. *Orkn* 2F 86
Lower Tysoe. *Warw* 7M 27
Lower Upham. *Hants* 4C 10
Lower Upnor. *Medw* 6D 22
Lower Vexford. *Som* 2L 7
Lower Walton. *Warr* 1E 34
Lower Wear. *Devn* 7J 7
Lower Weare. *Som* 8C 18
Lower Welson. *Here* 6A 26
Lower Whatcombe. *Dors* 5G 9
Lower Whitley. *Ches W* 2E 34
Lower Wield. *Hants* 1D 10
Lower Withington. *Ches E* 3G 35
Lower Woodend. *Buck* 5F 20
Lower Woodford. *Wilts* 2K 9
Lower Wraxall. *Dors* 5D 8
Lower Wych. *Ches W* 5C 34
Lower Wyche. *Worc* 7F 26
Lowesby. *Leics* 1E 28
Lowestoft. *Suff* 2M 31
Loweswater. *Cumb* 2L 45
Low Etherley. *Dur* 3K 47
Lowfield Heath. *W Sus* 1K 11
Lowford. *Hants* 4B 10
Low Fulney. *Linc* 7K 37
Low Gate. *Nmbd* 5C 54
Lowgill. *Cumb* 6E 46
Lowgill. *Lanc* 1E 40
Low Grantley. *N Yor* 8L 47
Low Green. *N Yor* 2L 41
Low Habberley. *Worc* 4G 27
Low Ham. *Som* 3C 8
Low Hameringham. *Linc* 3L 37
Low Hawsker. *N Yor* 5G 49
Low Hesket. *Cumb* 7J 53
Low Hesleyhurst. *Nmbd* 2D 54
Lowick. *Cumb* 7A 46
Lowick. *Nptn* 3G 29
Lowick. *Nmbd* 6H 61
Lowick Bridge. *Cumb* 7A 46
Lowick Green. *Cumb* 7A 46
Low Knipe. *Cumb* 3D 46
Low Leighton. *Derbs* 1J 35
Low Lorton. *Cumb* 2L 45
Low Marishes. *N Yor* 8F 48
Low Marnham. *Notts* 3F 36
Low Mill. *N Yor* 6D 48
Low Moor. *Lanc* 3F 40
Low Moor. *W Yor* 5K 41
Low Moorsley. *Tyne* 7G 55
Low Newton-by-the-Sea.
Nmbd 7K 61
Lownie Moor. *Ang* 3H 67
Lowood. *Bord* 6C 60
Low Row. *Cumb*
nr. Brampton 5K 53
nr. Wigton 7F 52
Low Row. *N Yor* 6H 47
Lowsonford. *Warw* 5K 27
Low Street. *Norf* 1G 31
Lowther. *Cumb* 3D 46
Lowthorpe. *E Yor* 1H 43
Lowton. *Devn* 5F 6
Lowton. *G Man* 8E 40
Lowton. *Som* 4L 7
Lowton Common. *G Man* 8E 40
Low Torry. *Fife* 1J 59
Low Toynton. *Linc* 2K 37
Low Valleyfield. *Fife* 1H 59
Low Westwood. *Dur* 6E 54
Low Whinnow. *Cumb* 6H 53
Low Wood. *Cumb* 7B 46
Low Worsall. *N Yor* 5A 48
Low Wray. *Cumb* 5B 46
Loxbeare. *Devn* 4J 7
Loxhill. *Surr* 2H 11
Loxhore. *Devn* 2F 6
Loxley. *S Yor* 1M 35
Loxley. *Warw* 6L 27
Loxley Green. *Staf* 6J 35
Loxton. *N Som* 8B 18
Loxwood. *W Sus* 2H 11
Lubcroy. *High* 3D 78
Lubenham. *Leics* 3E 28
Lubinvullin. *High* 5H 85
Luccombe. *Som* 1J 7
Luccombe Village. *IOW* 7C 10
Lucker. *Nmbd* 6J 61
Luckett. *Corn* 8C 6
Luckington. *Wilts* 5G 19
Lucklawhill. *Fife* 5H 67
Luckwell Bridge. *Som* 2J 7
Lucton. *Here* 5C 26
Ludag. *W Isl* 4D 74
Ludborough. *Linc* 8K 43
Ludchurch. *Pemb* 5H 15
Luddenden. *W Yor* 5J 41
Luddenden Foot. *W Yor* 5J 41
Luddenham. *Kent* 7F 22
Ludderburn. *Cumb* 6C 46
Luddesdown. *Kent* 7C 22
Luddington. *N Lin* 6F 42
Luddington. *Warw* 6K 27
Luddington in the Brook.
Nptn 3J 29
Ludford. *Linc* 1J 37
Ludford. *Shrp* 4D 26
Ludgershall. *Buck* 2D 20
Ludgershall. *Wilts* 8L 19
Ludgvan. *Corn* 5J 3
Ludham. *Norf* 8K 39
Ludlow. *Shrp* 4D 26
Ludstone. *Shrp* 2G 27
Ludwell. *Wilts* 3H 9
Ludworth. *Dur* 7G 55
Luffenhall. *Herts* 1K 21
Luffincott. *Devn* 6C 6
Lugar. *E Ayr* 7D 58
Luggate Burn. *E Lot* 2D 60
Lugg Green. *Here* 5C 26
Luggiebank. *N Lan* 2F 58
Lugton. *E Ayr* 4C 58
Lugwardine. *Here* 7D 26
Luib. *High* 3G 69
Luib. *Stir* 5J 65
Lulham. *Here* 7C 26
Lullington. *Derbs* 8L 35
Lullington. *E Sus* 5B 12
Lullington. *Som* 8F 18
Lulsgate Bottom. *N Som* 7D 18
Lulsley. *Worc* 6F 26
Lulworth Camp. *Dors* 7G 9
Lumb. *Lanc* 5G 41
Lumby. *N Yor* 4B 42
Lumphanan. *Abers* 5E 72
Lumphinnans. *Fife* 8E 66
Lumsdaine. *Bord* 3F 60
Lumsden. *Abers* 3D 72
Lunan. *Ang* 2K 67
Lunanhead. *Ang* 2H 67
Luncarty. *Per* 5D 66
Lund. *E Yor* 3G 43
Lund. *N Yor* 4D 42
Lundie. *Ang* 4F 66
Lundin Links. *Fife* 7H 67
Lundy Green. *Norf* 2J 31
Lunna. *Shet* 1E 90
Lunning. *Shet* 1F 90
Lunnon. *Swan* 8M 15
Lunsford. *Kent* 8C 22
Lunsford's Cross. *E Sus* 4D 12
Lunt. *Mers* 7B 40
Luppitt. *Devn* 5L 7
Lupridge. *Devn* 6K 5
Lupset. *W Yor* 6M 41
Lupton. *Cumb* 7D 46
Lurgan. *Arm* 6G 93
Lurganare. *New M* 7G 93
Lurgashall. *W Sus* 3G 11
Lurley. *Devn* 4J 7
Lusby. *Linc* 3L 37
Luscombe. *Devn* 6K 5
Luson. *Devn* 7J 5
Luss. *Arg* 8H 65
Lussagiven. *Arg* 1F 56
Lusta. *High* 8D 76
Lustleigh. *Devn* 7G 7
Luston. *Here* 5C 26
Luthermuir. *Abers* 1K 67
Luthrie. *Fife* 6G 67
Lutley. *Staf* 3G 27
Luton. *Devn*
nr. Honiton 5K 7
nr. Teignmouth 8J 7
Luton. *Lutn* 1H 21
Luton Airport. *Lutn* 119 (1J 21)
Lutterworth. *Leics* 3C 28
Lutton. *Devn*
nr. Ivybridge 6H 5
nr. South Brent 5J 5
Lutton. *Linc* 7M 37
Lutton. *Nptn* 3J 29
Lutton Gowts. *Linc* 7M 37
Lutworthy. *Devn* 4G 7
Luxborough. *Som* 2J 7
Luxley. *Glos* 1E 18
Luxulyan. *Corn* 6C 4
Lybster. *High* 8D 86
Lydbury North. *Shrp* 3B 26
Lydcott. *Devn* 2F 6
Lydd. *Kent* 3G 13
Lydd Airport. *Kent* 3G 13
Lydden. *Kent*
nr. Dover 1J 13
nr. Margate 7K 23
Lyddington. *Rut* 2F 28
Lydd-on-Sea. *Kent* 3G 13
Lydeard St Lawrence. *Som* 2L 7
Lyde Green. *Hants* 8E 20
Lydford. *Devn* 7E 6
Lydford Fair Place. *Som* 2D 8
Lydgate. *G Man* 7H 41
Lydgate. *W Yor* 5H 41
Lydham. *Shrp* 2B 26
Lydiard Millicent. *Wilts* 5J 19
Lydiate. *Mers* 7B 40
Lydiate Ash. *Worc* 4H 27
Lydlinch. *Dors* 4F 8
Lydmarsh. *Som* 5B 8
Lydney. *Glos* 3E 18
Lydstep. *Pemb* 7G 15
Lye. *W Mid* 3H 27
The Lye. *Shrp* 2E 26
Lye Green. *Buck* 3G 21
Lye Green. *E Sus* 2B 12
Lye Head. *Worc* 4F 26
Lyford. *Oxon* 4A 20
Lyham. *Nmbd* 6H 61
Lylestone. *N Ayr* 5B 58
Lymbridge Green. *Kent* 1H 13
Lyme Regis. *Dors* 6B 8
Lyminge. *Kent* 1H 13
Lymington. *Hants* 6M 9
Lyminster. *W Sus* 5H 11
Lymm. *Warr* 1E 34
Lymore. *Hants* 6L 9
Lympne. *Kent* 2H 13
Lympsham. *Som* 8B 18
Lympstone. *Devn* 7J 7
Lynaberack Lodge. *High* 6H 71
Lynbridge. *Devn* 1G 7
Lynch. *Som* 1J 7
Lynchat. *High* 5H 71
Lynch Green. *Norf* 1H 31
Lyndhurst. *Hants* 5M 9
Lyndon. *Rut* 1G 29
Lyne. *Bord* 5L 59
Lyne. *Surr* 7H 21
Lyneal. *Shrp* 6C 34
Lyne Down. *Here* 8E 26
Lyneham. *Oxon* 1L 19
Lyneham. *Wilts* 6J 19
Lyneholmeford. *Cumb* 4K 53
Lynemouth. *Nmbd* 2F 54
Lyne of Gorthleck. *High* 3F 70
Lyne of Skene. *Abers* 4G 73
Lynesack. *Dur* 3J 47
Lyness. *Orkn* 2E 86
Lyng. *Norf* 8G 39
Lyngate. *Norf*
nr. North Walsham 6J 39
nr. Worstead 7K 39
Lynmouth. *Devn* 1G 7
Lynn. *Staf* 1J 27
Lynn. *Telf* 8F 34
Lynsted. *Kent* 7F 22
Lynstone. *Corn* 5B 6
Lynton. *Devn* 1G 7
Lynwilg. *High* 4J 71
Lyon's Gate. *Dors* 5E 8
Lyonshall. *Here* 6B 26
Lytchett Matravers. *Dors* 6H 9
Lytchett Minster. *Dors* 6H 9
Lyth. *High* 5D 86
Lytham. *Lanc* 5B 40
Lytham St Anne's. *Lanc* 5B 40
Lythe. *N Yor* 4F 48
Lythes. *Orkn* 3F 86
Lythmore. *High* 5B 86

M

Mabe Burnthouse. *Corn* 5L 3
Mabie. *Dum* 4D 52
Mablethorpe. *Linc* 1B 38
Macbiehill. *Bord* 4K 59
Macclesfield. *Ches E* 2H 35
Macclesfield Forest. *Ches E* 2H 35
Macduff. *Abers* 7G 81
Machan. *S Lan* 4F 58
Macharioch. *Arg* 1C 50
Machen. *Cphy* 6M 17
Machrie. *N Ayr* 6H 57
Machrihanish. *Arg* 7F 56
Machroes. *Gwyn* 8C 32
Machynlleth. *Powy* 2G 25
Mackerye End. *Herts* 2J 21
Mackworth. *Derb* 6M 35
Macmerry. *E Lot* 2B 60
Macosquin. *Caus* 2F 93
Madderty. *Per* 5C 66
Maddington. *Wilts* 1J 9
Maddiston. *Falk* 2H 59
Madehurst. *W Sus* 4G 11
Madeley. *Staf* 5F 34
Madeley. *Telf* 1E 26
Madeley Heath. *Staf* 5F 34
Madeley Heath. *Worc* 4H 27
Madford. *Devn* 4L 7
Madingley. *Cambs* 5L 29
Madley. *Here* 8C 26
Madresfield. *Worc* 7G 27
Madron. *Corn* 5H 3
Maenaddwyn. *IOA* 2D 32
Maenclochog. *Pemb* 4G 15
Maendy. *V Glam* 7K 17
Maenporth. *Corn* 6L 3
Maentwrog. *Gwyn* 6F 32
Maen-y-groes. *Cdgn* 1K 15
Maer. *Staf* 6F 34
Maerdy. *Carm* 2F 16
Maerdy. *Cnwy* 6K 33
Maerdy. *Rhon* 5J 17
Maesbrook. *Shrp* 7B 34
Maesbury. *Shrp* 7B 34
Maesbury Marsh. *Shrp* 7B 34
Maes-glas. *Flin* 3L 33
Maesgwyn-Isaf. *Powy* 1L 25
Maeshafn. *Den* 4M 33
Maes Llyn. *Cdgn* 2K 15
Maesmynis. *Powy* 8K 25
Maesteg. *B'end* 5H 17
Maestir. *Cdgn* 8E 24
Maesybont. *Carm* 3E 16
Maesycrugiau. *Carm* 2L 15
Maesycwmmer. *Cphy* 5L 17
Maesyrhandir. *Powy* 3K 25
Magdalen Laver. *Essx* 3B 22
Maggieknockater. *Mor* 1C 72
Maghaberry. *Lis* 5G 93
Magham Down. *E Sus* 4C 12
Maghera. *M Ulst* 3F 93
Maghera. *New M* 7H 93
Magherafelt. *M Ulst* 4F 93
Magheralin. *Arm* 6G 93
Magheramason. *Derr* 3C 92
Magheraveely. *Ferm* 7D 92
Maghery. *Arm* 5F 93
Maghull. *Mers* 7B 40
Magna Park. *Leics* 3C 28
Magor. *Mon* 5C 18
Magpie Green. *Suff* 4G 31
Maguiresbridge. *Ferm* 7C 92
Magwyr. *Mon* 5C 18
Maidenbower. *W Sus* 2K 11
Maiden Bradley. *Wilts* 2G 9
Maidencombe. *Torb* 5M 5
Maidenhayne. *Devn* 6A 8
Maidenhead. *Wind* 5F 20
Maiden Law. *Dur* 7E 54
Maiden Newton. *Dors* 6D 8
Maidens. *S Ayr* 1H 51
Maiden's Green. *Brac* 6F 20
Maidensgrove. *Oxon* 5E 20
Maidenwell. *Corn* 4D 4
Maidenwell. *Linc* 2L 37
Maiden Wells. *Pemb* 7F 14
Maidford. *Nptn* 6D 28
Maids Moreton. *Buck* 8E 28
Maidstone. *Kent* 8D 22
Maidwell. *Nptn* 4E 28
Mail. *Shet* 5E 90
Maindee. *Newp* 5B 18
Mainsforth. *Dur* 8G 55
Mains of Auchindachy. *Mor* 1D 72
Mains of Auchnagatt. *Abers* 1J 73
Mains of Drum. *Abers* 6H 73
Mains of Edingight. *Mor* 8E 80
Mainsriddle. *Dum* 6D 52
Mainstone. *Shrp* 3A 26
Maisemore. *Glos* 1G 19
Major's Green. *Worc* 4K 27
Makeney. *Derbs* 5A 36
Makerstoun. *Bord* 6D 60
Malacleit. *W Isl* 6J 75
Malaig. *High* 6H 69
Malaig Bheag. *High* 6H 69
Malborough. *Devn* 8K 5
Malcoff. *Derbs* 1J 35
Malcolmburn. *Mor* 8C 80
Malden Rushett. *G Lon* 7J 21
Maldon. *Essx* 3E 22
Malham. *N Yor* 1H 41
Maligar. *High* 7F 76
Malinslee. *Telf* 1E 26
Mallaig. *High* 6H 69
Malleny Mills. *Edin* 3K 59
Mallows Green. *Essx* 1A 22
Malltraeth. *IOA* 4D 32
Mallusk. *Ant* 4H 93
Mallwyd. *Gwyn* 1H 25
Malmesbury. *Wilts* 5H 19
Malmsmead. *Devn* 1G 7
Malpas. *Ches W* 5C 34
Malpas. *Corn* 4M 3
Malpas. *Newp* 4B 18
Malswick. *Glos* 1F 18
Maltby. *S Yor* 8C 42
Maltby. *Stoc T* 4B 48
Maltby le Marsh. *Linc* 1A 38
Malt Lane. *Arg* 7E 64
Maltman's Hill. *Kent* 1F 12
Malton. *N Yor* 8E 48
Malvern Link. *Worc* 7F 26
Malvern Wells. *Worc* 7F 26
Mamble. *Worc* 4E 26
Mamhilad. *Mon* 3B 18
Manaccan. *Corn* 6L 3
Manafon. *Powy* 2L 25
Manais. *W Isl* 5C 76
Manaton. *Devn* 7G 7
Manby. *Linc* 1L 37
Mancetter. *Warw* 2M 27
Manchester. *G Man* 111 (8G 41)
Manchester Airport.
G Man 119 (1G 35)
Mancot. *Flin* 3B 34
Manea. *Cambs* 3A 30
Maney. *W Mid* 2K 27
Manfield. *N Yor* 4L 47
Mangotsfield. *S Glo* 6E 18
Mangurstadh. *W Isl* 8D 82
Mankinholes. *W Yor* 5H 41
Manley. *Ches W* 2D 34
Manmoel. *Cphy* 4L 17
Mannal. *Arg* 3E 62
Mannerston. *Falk* 2J 59
Manningford Bohune. *Wilts* 8K 19
Manningford Bruce. *Wilts* 8K 19
Manningham. *W Yor* 4K 41
Mannings Heath. *W Sus* 3K 11
Mannington. *Dors* 5J 9
Manningtree. *Essx* 8H 31
Mannofield. *Aber* 5J 73
Manorbier. *Pemb* 7G 15
Manorbier Newton. *Pemb* 7G 15
Manordeilo. *Carm* 2F 16
Manorowen. *Pemb* 3F 14
Manor Park. *G Lon* 5M 21
Mansell Gamage. *Here* 7B 26
Mansell Lacy. *Here* 7C 26
Mansergh. *Cumb* 7E 46
Mansewood. *Glas* 3D 58
Mansfield. *E Ayr* 8E 58
Mansfield. *Notts* 3C 36
Mansfield Woodhouse.
Notts 3C 36
Mansriggs. *Cumb* 7A 46
Manston. *Dors* 4G 9
Manston. *Kent* 7K 23
Manston. *W Yor* 4A 42
Manswood. *Dors* 5H 9
Manthorpe. *Linc*
nr. Bourne 8H 37
nr. Grantham 6G 37
Manton. *N Lin* 7G 43
Manton. *Notts* 2C 36
Manton. *Rut* 1F 28
Manton. *Wilts* 7K 19
Manuden. *Essx* 1A 22
Maperton. *Som* 3E 8
Maplebeck. *Notts* 3E 36
Maple Cross. *Herts* 4H 21
Mapledurham. *Oxon* 6D 20
Mapledurwell. *Hants* 8D 20
Maplehurst. *W Sus* 3J 11
Maplescombe. *Kent* 7B 22
Mapleton. *Derbs* 5K 35
Mapperley. *Derbs* 5B 36
Mapperley. *Nott* 5C 36
Mapperley Park. *Nott* 5C 36
Mapperton. *Dors*
nr. Beaminster 6D 8
nr. Poole 6H 9
Mappleborough Green.
Warw 5J 27
Mappleton. *E Yor* 3K 43
Mapplewell. *S Yor* 7M 41
Mappowder. *Dors* 5F 8
Maraig. *W Isl* 3D 76
Marazion. *Corn* 5J 3
Marbhig. *W Isl* 2F 76
Marbury. *Ches E* 5D 34
March. *Cambs* 2M 29
Marcham. *Oxon* 4B 20
Marchamley. *Shrp* 7D 34
Marchington. *Staf* 6K 35
Marchington Woodlands.
Staf 7K 35
Marchwiel. *Wrex* 5B 34
Marchwood. *Hants* 4A 10
Marcross. *V Glam* 8J 17
Marden. *Here* 7D 26
Marden. *Kent* 1D 12
Marden. *Wilts* 8J 19
Marden Beech. *Kent* 1D 12
Marden Thorn. *Kent* 1D 12
Mardu. *Shrp* 3A 26
Mardy. *Mon* 2B 18
Marefield. *Leics* 1E 28
Mareham le Fen. *Linc* 3K 37
Mareham on the Hill. *Linc* 3K 37
Marehay. *Derbs* 5B 36
Marehill. *W Sus* 4H 11
Maresfield. *E Sus* 3A 12
Marfleet. *Hull* 5J 43
Marford. *Wrex* 4B 34
Margam. *Neat* 6G 17
Margaret Marsh. *Dors* 4G 9
Margaret Roding. *Essx* 2B 22
Margaretting. *Essx* 3C 22
Margaretting Tye. *Essx* 3C 22
Margate. *Kent* 6K 23
Margery. *Surr* 8K 21
Margnaheglish. *N Ayr* 6K 57
Marham. *Norf* 1D 30
Marhamchurch. *Corn* 5B 6
Marholm. *Pet* 1J 29
Marian Cwm. *Den* 3K 33
Mariandyrys. *IOA* 2F 32
Marian-glas. *IOA* 2E 32
Mariansleigh. *Devn* 3G 7
Marian-y-de. *Gwyn* 7C 32
Marian-y-mor. *Gwyn* 7C 32
Marine Town. *Kent* 6F 22
Marishader. *High* 7F 76
Marjoriebanks. *Dum* 3E 52
Mark. *Dum* 6G 51
Mark. *Som* 1B 8
Markbeech. *Kent* 1A 12
Markby. *Linc* 2A 38
Mark Causeway. *Som* 1B 8
Mark Cross. *E Sus* 2B 12
Markeaton. *Derb* 6M 35
Market Bosworth. *Leics* 1B 28
Market Deeping. *Linc* 8J 37
Market Drayton. *Shrp* 6E 34
Market End. *Warw* 3M 27
Market Harborough. *Leics* 3E 28
Markethill. *Arm* 7F 93
Markethill. *Per* 4F 66
Market Lavington. *Wilts* 8J 19
Market Overton. *Rut* 8F 36
Market Rasen. *Linc* 1J 37
Market Stainton. *Linc* 1K 37
Market Weighton. *E Yor* 3F 42
Market Weston. *Suff* 4F 30
Markfield. *Leics* 8B 36
Markham. *Cphy* 4L 17
Markinch. *Fife* 7F 66
Markington. *N Yor* 1L 41
Marksbury. *Bath* 7E 18
Mark's Corner. *IOW* 6B 10
Marks Tey. *Essx* 1F 22
Markwell. *Corn* 6F 4
Markyate. *Herts* 2H 21
Marlborough. *Wilts* 7K 19
Marlcliff. *Warw* 6J 27
Marldon. *Devn* 5L 5
Marle Green. *E Sus* 4B 12
Marlesford. *Suff* 6K 31
Marley Green. *Ches E* 5D 34
Marley Hill. *Tyne* 6F 54
Marlingford. *Norf* 1H 31
Mar Lodge. *Abers* 7L 71
Marloes. *Pemb* 6D 14
Marlow. *Buck* 5F 20
Marlow. *Here* 4B 26
Marlow Bottom. *Buck* 5F 20
Marlow Common. *Buck* 5F 20
Marlpit Hill. *Kent* 1M 11
Marlpits. *E Sus* 3M 11
Marlpool. *Derbs* 5B 36
Marnhull. *Dors* 4F 8
Marnoch. *Abers* 8E 80
Marnock. *N Lan* 3F 58
Marple. *G Man* 1H 35
Marr. *S Yor* 7C 42
Marrel. *High* 2L 79
Marrick. *N Yor* 6J 47
Marrister. *Shet* 1F 90
Marros. *Carm* 6J 15
Marsden. *Tyne* 5G 55
Marsden. *W Yor* 6J 41
Marsett. *N Yor* 7H 47
Marsh. *Buck* 3F 20
Marsh. *Devn* 4A 8
The Marsh. *Powy* 2B 26
The Marsh. *Shrp* 7E 34
Marshall Meadows. *Nmbd* 4G 61
Marshalsea. *Dors* 5B 8
Marshalswick. *Herts* 3J 21
Marsham. *Norf* 7H 39
Marshaw. *Lanc* 2D 40
Marsh Baldon. *Oxon* 4C 20
Marsh Benham. *W Ber* 7B 20
Marshborough. *Kent* 8K 23
Marshbrook. *Shrp* 3C 26
Marshchapel. *Linc* 8L 43
Marshfield. *Newp* 5A 18
Marshfield. *S Glo* 6F 18
Marshgate. *Corn* 6A 6
Marsh Gibbon. *Buck* 1D 20
Marsh Green. *Devn* 6K 7
Marsh Green. *Kent* 1M 11
Marsh Green. *Staf* 4G 35
Marsh Green. *Telf* 8E 34
Marsh Lane. *Derbs* 2B 36
Marsh Side. *Norf* 5D 38
Marshside. *Kent* 7J 23
Marshside. *Mers* 6B 40
Marsh Street. *Som* 1J 7
Marshwood. *Dors* 6B 8
Marske. *N Yor* 5K 47
Marske-by-the-Sea. *Red C* 3D 48
Marston. *Ches W* 2E 34
Marston. *Here* 6B 26
Marston. *Linc* 5F 36
Marston. *Oxon* 3C 20
Marston. *Staf*
nr. Stafford 7H 35
nr. Wheaton Aston 8G 35
Marston. *Warw* 2L 27
Marston. *Wilts* 8H 19
Marston Doles. *Warw* 6B 28
Marston Green. *W Mid* 3K 27
Marston Hill. *Glos* 4K 19
Marston Jabbett. *Warw* 3A 28
Marston Magna. *Som* 3D 8
Marston Meysey. *Wilts* 4K 19
Marston Montgomery.
Derbs 6K 35
Marston Moretaine. *C Beds* 7G 29
Marston on Dove. *Derbs* 7L 35
Marston St Lawrence. *Nptn* 7C 28
Marston Stannett. *Here* 6D 26
Marston Trussell. *Nptn* 3D 28
Marstow. *Here* 2D 18
Marsworth. *Buck* 2G 21
Marten. *Wilts* 8L 19
Marthall. *Ches E* 2G 35
Martham. *Norf* 8L 39
Marthwaite. *Cumb* 6E 46
Martin. *Hants* 4J 9
Martin. *Kent* 1K 13
Martin. *Linc*
nr. Horncastle 3K 37
nr. Metheringham 4J 37
Martindale. *Cumb* 4C 46
Martin Dales. *Linc* 3J 37
Martin Drove End. *Hants* 3J 9
Martinhoe. *Devn* 1F 6
Martinhoe Cross. *Devn* 1F 6
Martin Hussingtree. *Worc* 5G 27
Martin Mill. *Kent* 1K 13
Martinscroft. *Warr* 1E 34
Martin's Moss. *Ches E* 3G 35
Martinstown. *Dors* 7E 8
Martinstown. *ME Ant* 3G 93
Martlesham. *Suff* 7J 31
Martlesham Heath. *Suff* 7J 31
Martletwy. *Pemb* 5G 15
Martley. *Worc* 5F 26
Martock. *Som* 4C 8
Marton. *Ches E* 3G 35
Marton. *Cumb* 7M 45
Marton. *E Yor*
nr. Bridlington 1K 43
nr. Hull 4J 43
Marton. *Linc* 1F 36
Marton. *Midd* 4C 48
Marton. *N Yor*
nr. Boroughbridge 1B 42
nr. Pickering 7E 48
Marton. *Shrp*
nr. Myddle 7C 34
nr. Worthen 1A 26
Marton. *Warw* 5B 28
Marton Abbey. *N Yor* 1C 42
Marton-le-Moor. *N Yor* 8A 48
Martyr's Green. *Surr* 8H 21
Martyr Worthy. *Hants* 2C 10
Marwick. *Orkn* 7B 88
Marwood. *Devn* 2E 6
Marybank. *High*
nr. Dingwall 8E 78
nr. Invergordon 6H 79
Maryburgh. *High* 8F 78
Maryfield. *Corn* 6G 5
Maryhill. *Glas* 3D 58
Marykirk. *Abers* 1K 67
Marylebone. *G Lon* 5K 21
Marylebone. *G Man* 7D 40
Marypark. *Mor* 2A 72
Maryport. *Cumb* 8E 52
Maryport. *Dum* 8G 51
Marystow. *Devn* 7D 6
Mary Tavy. *Devn* 8E 6
Maryton. *Ang*
nr. Kirriemuir 2G 67
nr. Montrose 2K 67
Marywell. *Abers* 6E 72
Marywell. *Ang* 3K 67
Masham. *N Yor* 7L 47
Mashbury. *Essx* 2C 22
Masongill. *N Yor* 8E 46
Masons Lodge. *Abers* 5H 73
Mastin Moor. *Derbs* 2B 36
Mastrick. *Aber* 5J 73
Matching. *Essx* 2B 22
Matching Green. *Essx* 2B 22
Matching Tye. *Essx* 2B 22
Matfen. *Nmbd* 4D 54
Matfield. *Kent* 1C 12
Mathern. *Mon* 4D 18
Mathon. *Here* 7F 26
Mathry. *Pemb* 3E 14
Matlaske. *Norf* 6H 39
Matlock. *Derbs* 4L 35
Matlock Bath. *Derbs* 4L 35
Matterdale End. *Cumb* 3B 46
Mattersey. *Notts* 1D 36
Mattersey Thorpe. *Notts* 1D 36
Mattingley. *Hants* 8E 20
Mattishall. *Norf* 8G 39
Mattishall Burgh. *Norf* 8G 39
Mauchline. *E Ayr* 7C 58
Maud. *Abers* 1J 73
Maudlin. *Corn* 5C 4
Maugersbury. *Glos* 1K 19
Maughold. *IOM* 5D 44
Maulden. *C Beds* 8H 29
Maulds Meaburn. *Cumb* 4E 46
Maunby. *N Yor* 7A 48
Maund Bryan. *Here* 6D 26
Mautby. *Norf* 8L 39
Mavesyn Ridware. *Staf* 8J 35
Mavis Enderby. *Linc* 3L 37
Mawbray. *Cumb* 7E 52
Mawdesley. *Lanc* 6C 40
Mawdlam. *B'end* 6H 17
Mawgan. *Corn* 6L 3
Mawgan Porth. *Corn* 2M 3
Maw Green. *Ches E* 4F 34
Mawla. *Corn* 4L 3
Mawnan. *Corn* 6L 3
Mawnan Smith. *Corn* 6L 3
Mawsley Village. *Nptn* 4E 28
Mawthorpe. *Linc* 2A 38
Maxey. *Pet* 1J 29
Maxstoke. *Warw* 3L 27
Maxted Street. *Kent* 1H 13
Maxton. *Kent* 1J 13
Maxton. *Bord* 6D 60
Maxwellheugh. *Bord* 6E 60
Maxwelltown. *Dum* 4D 52
Maxworthy. *Corn* 6B 6
Mayals. *Swan* 6F 16
Maybole. *S Ayr* 8B 58
Maybush. *Sotn* 4A 10
Maydown. *Derr* 3D 92
Mayes Green. *Surr* 2J 11
Mayfield. *E Sus* 3B 12
Mayfield. *Midl* 3A 60
Mayfield. *Per* 5D 66
Mayfield. *Staf* 5K 35
Mayford. *Surr* 8G 21
Mayhill. *Swan* 5F 16
Mayland. *Essx* 3F 22
Maylandsea. *Essx* 3F 22
Maynard's Green. *E Sus* 4B 12
Mayobridge. *New M* 7G 93
Maypole. *IOS* 1H 3
Maypole. *Kent* 7J 23
Maypole. *Mon* 2C 18
Maypole Green. *Norf* 2L 31
Maypole Green. *Suff* 6F 30
Maywick. *Shet* 5D 90
Mazetown. *Lis* 5H 93
Mead. *Devn* 4B 6
Meadgate. *Bath* 8E 18

Meadle – Nether Welton

Meadle. Buck 3F 20
Meadowbank. Ches W 3E 34
Meadowfield. Dur 8F 54
Meadow Green. Here 6F 26
Meadowmill. E Lot 2B 60
Meadows. Nott 6C 36
Meadowtown. Shrp 1B 26
Meadwell. Devn 7D 6
Meaford. Staf 6G 35
Mealabost. W Isl
nr. Borgh 6H 83
nr. Stornoway 8H 83
Mealasta. W Isl 1A 76
Meal Bank. Cumb 6D 46
Mealrigg. Cumb 7F 52
Mealsgate. Cumb 7G 53
Meanwood. W Yor 4L 41
Mearbeck. N Yor 1G 41
Meare. Som 1C 8
Meare Green. Som
nr. Curry Mallet 3A 8
nr. Stoke St Gregory 3B 8
Mears Ashby. Nptn 5F 28
Measham. Leics 8M 35
Meath Green. Surr 1K 11
Meathop. Cumb 7C 46
Meaux. E Yor 4H 43
Meavy. Devn 5H 5
Medbourne. Leics 2E 28
Medburn. Nmbd 4E 54
Meddon. Devn 4B 6
Meden Vale. Notts 3C 36
Medlam. Linc 4L 37
Medlicott. Shrp 2C 26
Medmenham. Buck 5F 20
Medomsley. Dur 6E 54
Medstead. Hants 2D 10
Medway Towns.
Medw 111 (7D 22)
Meerbrook. Staf 3H 35
Meer End. W Mid 4L 27
Meers Bridge. Linc 1A 38
Meesden. Herts 8M 29
Meeson. Telf 7E 34
Meeth. Devn 5E 6
Meeting Green. Suff 6D 30
Meeting House Hill. Norf 7K 39
Meidrim. Carm 4J 15
Meifod. Powy 1L 25
Meigh. New M 7G 93
Meigle. Per 3F 66
Meikle Earnock. S Lan 4F 58
Meikle Kilchattan Butts.
Arg 4K 57
Meikleour. Per 4E 66
Meikle Tarty. Abers 3J 73
Meikle Wartle. Abers 2G 73
Meinciau. Carm 5L 15
Meir. Stoke 5H 35
Meir Heath. Staf 5H 35
Melbourn. Cambs 7L 29
Melbourne. Derbs 7A 36
Melbourne. E Yor 3E 42
Melbury Abbas. Dors 3G 9
Melbury Bubb. Dors 5D 8
Melbury Osmond. Dors 5D 8
Melbury Sampford. Dors 5D 8
Melby. Shet 2B 90
Melchbourne. Bed 5H 29
Melcombe Bingham. Dors 5F 8
Melcombe Regis. Dors 7E 8
Meldon. Devn 6E 6
Meldon. Nmbd 3E 54
Meldreth. Cambs 7L 29
Melfort. Arg 6C 64
Melgarve. High 6E 70
Meliden. Den 2K 33
Melinbyrhedyn. Powy 3H 25
Melincourt. Neat 4H 17
Melin-y-coed. Cnwy 4H 33
Melin-y-ddol. Powy 2K 25
Melin-y-wig. Den 6K 33
Melkington. Nmbd 5F 60
Melkinthorpe. Cumb 3D 46
Melkridge. Nmbd 5M 53
Melksham. Wilts 7H 19
Mellangaun. High 5K 77
Melldalloch. Arg 2J 57
Mellguards. Cumb 7J 53
Melling. Lanc 8D 46
Melling. Mers 7B 40
Melling Mount. Mers 7C 40
Mellis. Suff 4G 31
Mellon Charles. High 4K 77
Mellon Udrigle. High 4K 77
Mellor. G Man 1H 35
Mellor. Lanc 4E 40
Mellor Brook. Lanc 4E 40
Mells. Som 1F 8
Melmerby. Cumb 8L 53
Melmerby. N Yor
nr. Middleham 7J 47
nr. Ripon 8M 47
Melplash. Dors 6C 8
Melrose. Bord 6C 60
Melsetter. Orkn 3D 86
Melsonby. N Yor 5K 47
Meltham. W Yor 6K 41
Meltham Mills. W Yor 6K 41
Melton. E Yor 5G 43
Melton. Suff 6J 31
Meltonby. E Yor 2E 42
Melton Constable. Norf 6G 39
Melton Mowbray. Leics 8E 36
Melton Ross. N Lin 6H 43
Melvaig. High 5J 77
Melverley. Shrp 8B 34
Melverley Green. Shrp 8B 34
Melvich. High 5L 85
Membury. Devn 5A 8
Memsie. Abers 7J 81
Memus. Ang 2H 67
Menabilly. Corn 6C 4
Menai Bridge. IOA 3E 32
Mendham. Suff 3J 31
Mendlesham. Suff 5H 31
Mendlesham Green. Suff 5G 31
Menethorpe. N Yor 1E 42
Menheniot. Corn 5E 4
Menithwood. Worc 5F 26
Menna. Corn 6B 4
Mennock. Dum 1C 52
Menston. W Yor 3K 41
Menstrie. Clac 8B 66
Menthorpe. N Yor 4E 42
Mentmore. Buck 2G 21
Meole Brace. Shrp 8C 34
Meols. Mers 1M 33
Meon. Hants 5C 10
Meonstoke. Hants 3D 10
Meopham. Kent 7C 22
Meopham Green. Kent 7C 22
Meopham Station. Kent 7C 22
Mepal. Cambs 3M 29
Meppershall. C Beds 8J 29
Merbach. Here 7B 26
Mercaston. Derbs 5L 35
Merchiston. Edin 2L 59
Mere. Ches E 1F 34
Mere. Wilts 2G 9
Mere Brow. Lanc 6C 40
Mereclough. Lanc 4G 41
Mere Green. W Mid 2K 27
Mere Green. Worc 5H 27
Mere Heath. Ches W 2E 34
Mereside. Bkpl 4B 40
Meretown. Staf 7F 34
Mereworth. Kent 8C 22
Meriden. W Mid 3L 27
Merkadale. High 2E 68
Merkland. S Ayr 2H 51
Merkland Lodge. High 1D 78
Merley. Pool 6J 9
Merlin's Bridge. Pemb 5F 14
Merridge. Som 2M 7
Merrington. Shrp 7C 34
Merrion. Pemb 7F 14
Merriott. Som 4C 8
Merrivale. Devn 8E 6
Merrow. Surr 8H 21
Merrybent. Darl 4L 47
Merry Lees. Leics 1B 28
Merrymeet. Corn 5E 4
Mersham. Kent 2G 13
Merstham. Surr 8K 21
Merston. W Sus 5F 10
Merstone. IOW 7C 10
Merther. Corn 7A 4
Merthyr. Carm 4K 15
Merthyr Cynog. Powy 1J 17
Merthyr Dyfan. V Glam 7L 17
Merthyr Mawr. B'end 7H 17
Merthyr Tudful. Mer T 4K 17
Merthyr Tydfil. Mer T 4K 17
Merthyr Vale. Mer T 5K 17
Merton. Devn 4E 6
Merton. G Lon 7K 21
Merton. Norf 2F 30
Merton. Oxon 2C 20
Meshaw. Devn 4G 7
Messing. Essx 2E 22
Messingham. N Lin 7F 42
Metcombe. Devn 6K 7
Metfield. Suff 3J 31
Metherell. Corn 5G 5
Metheringham. Linc 3H 37
Methil. Fife 8G 67
Methilhill. Fife 8G 67
Methley. W Yor 5A 42
Methley Junction. W Yor 5A 42
Methlick. Abers 2H 73
Methven. Per 5D 66
Methwold. Norf 2D 30
Methwold Hythe. Norf 2D 30
Mettingham. Suff 3K 31
Metton. Norf 6H 39
Mevagissey. Corn 7C 4
Mexborough. S Yor 7B 42
Mey. High 4D 86
Meysey Hampton. Glos 4K 19
Miabhag. W Isl 4C 76
Miabhaig. W Isl
nr. Cliasmol 3B 76
nr. Timsgearraidh 8D 82
Mial. High 6J 77
Michaelchurch. Here 1D 18
Michaelchurch Escley. Here 8B 26
Michaelchurch-on-Arrow.
Powy 7M 25
Michaelston-le-Pit. V Glam 7L 17
Michaelston-y-Fedw. Newp 6M 17
Michaelstow. Corn 4C 4
Michelcombe. Devn 5J 5
Micheldever. Hants 2C 10
Micheldever Station. Hants 1C 10
Michelmersh. Hants 3M 9
Mickfield. Suff 5H 31
Micklebring. S Yor 8C 42
Mickleby. N Yor 4F 48
Micklefield. W Yor 4B 42
Micklefield Green. Herts 4H 21
Mickleham. Surr 8J 21
Mickleover. Derb 6M 35
Micklethwaite. Cumb 6G 53
Micklethwaite. W Yor 3K 41
Mickleton. Dur 3H 47
Mickleton. Glos 7K 27
Mickletown. W Yor 5A 42
Mickle Trafford. Ches W 3C 34
Mickley. N Yor 8L 47
Mickley Green. Suff 6E 30
Mickley Square. Nmbd 5D 54
Mid Ardlaw. Abers 7J 81
Midbea. Orkn 5D 88
Mid Beltie. Abers 5F 72
Mid Calder. W Lot 3J 59
Mid Clyth. High 8D 86
Middle Assendon. Oxon 5E 20
Middle Aston. Oxon 1B 20
Middle Barton. Oxon 1B 20
Middlebie. Dum 4G 53
Middle Chinnock. Som 4C 8
Middle Claydon. Buck 1E 20
Middlecliffe. S Yor 7B 42
Middlecott. Devn 7G 7
Middle Drums. Ang 2J 67
Middle Duntisbourne. Glos 3H 19
Middle Essie. Abers 8K 81
Middleforth Green. Lanc 5D 40
Middleham. N Yor 7K 47
Middle Handley. Derbs 2B 36
Middle Harling. Norf 3F 30
Middlehope. Shrp 3C 26
Middle Littleton. Worc 7J 27
Middle Maes-coed. Here 8B 26
Middlemarsh. Dors 5E 8
Middle Marwood. Devn 2E 6
Middle Mayfield. Staf 5K 35
Middlemoor. Devn 8D 6
Middlemuir. Abers
nr. New Deer 1H 73
nr. Strichen 8J 81
Middle Rainton. Tyne 7G 55
Middle Rasen. Linc 1H 37
The Middles. Dur 6F 54
Middlesbrough.
Midd 111 (4B 48)
Middlesceugh. Cumb 7H 53
Middleshaw. Cumb 7D 46
Middlesmoor. N Yor 8J 47
Middlestone. Dur 8F 54
Middlestone Moor. Dur 8F 54
Middle Stoughton. Som 1C 8
Middlestown. W Yor 6L 41
Middle Street. Glos 3F 18
Middle Taphouse. Corn 5D 4
Middleton. Ang 3J 67
Middleton. Arg 3E 62
Middleton. Cumb 7E 46
Middleton. Derbs
nr. Bakewell 3K 35
nr. Wirksworth 4L 35
Middleton. Essx 8E 30
Middleton. G Man 7G 41
Middleton. Hants 1B 10
Middleton. Hart 8J 55
Middleton. Here 5D 26
Middleton. IOW 7M 9
Middleton. Lanc 2C 40
Middleton. Midl 4A 60
Middleton. Norf 8C 38
Middleton. Nptn 3F 28
Middleton. Nmbd
nr. Belford 6J 61
nr. Morpeth 3D 54
Middleton. N Yor
nr. Ilkley 3K 41
nr. Pickering 7E 48
Middleton. Per 7E 66
Middleton. Shrp
nr. Ludlow 4D 26
nr. Oswestry 7B 34
Middleton. Suff 5L 31
Middleton. Swan 8L 15
Middleton. Warw 2K 27
Middleton. W Yor 5L 41
Middleton Cheney. Nptn 7C 28
Middleton Green. Staf 6H 35
Middleton-in-Teesdale. Dur 3H 47
Middleton One Row. Darl 4A 48
Middleton-on-Leven. N Yor 5B 48
Middleton-on-Sea. W Sus 5G 11
Middleton on the Hill.
Here 5D 26
Middleton-on-the-Wolds.
E Yor 3G 43
Middleton Priors. Shrp 2E 26
Middleton Quernhow.
N Yor 8M 47
Middleton St George. Darl 4M 47
Middleton Scriven. Shrp 3E 26
Middleton Stoney. Oxon 1C 20
Middleton Tyas. N Yor 5L 47
Middle Town. IOS 1H 3
Middletown. Arm 7E 92
Middletown. Cumb 4J 45
Middletown. Powy 8B 34
Middle Tysoe. Warw 7M 27
Middle Wallop. Hants 2L 9
Middlewich. Ches E 3F 34
Middle Winterslow. Wilts 2L 9
Middlewood. Corn 8B 6
Middlewood. S Yor 8M 41
Middle Woodford. Wilts 2K 9
Middlewood Green. Suff 5G 31
Middleyard. Glos 3G 19
Middlezoy. Som 2B 8
Middridge. Dur 3L 47
Midelney. Som 3C 8
Midfield. High 5H 85
Midford. Bath 7F 18
Mid Garrary. Dum 4L 51
Midge Hall. Lanc 5D 40
Midgeholme. Cumb 6L 53
Midgham. W Ber 7C 20
Midgley. W Yor
nr. Halifax 5J 41
nr. Horbury 6L 41
Mid Ho. Shet 4K 91
Midhopestones. S Yor 8L 41
Midhurst. W Sus 3F 10
Mid Kirkton. N Ayr 4L 57
Mid Lambrook. Som 4C 8
Midland. Orkn 1E 86
Mid Lavant. W Sus 5F 10
Midlem. Bord 7C 60
Midney. Som 3D 8
Midsomer Norton. Bath 8E 18
Midton. Inv 2M 57
Midtown. High
nr. Poolewe 5K 77
nr. Tongue 5H 85
Midville. Linc 4L 37
Mid Walls. Shet 3B 90
Mid Yell. Shet 4K 91
Migdale. High 4G 79
Migvie. Abers 5D 72
Milborne Port. Som 4E 8
Milborne St Andrew. Dors 6G 9
Milborne Wick. Som 3E 8
Milbourne. Nmbd 4E 54
Milbourne. Wilts 5H 19
Milburn. Cumb 3E 46
Milbury Heath. S Glo 4E 18
Milby. N Yor 1B 42
Milcombe. Oxon 8B 28
Milden. Suff 7F 30
Mildenhall. Suff 4D 30
Mildenhall. Wilts 7L 19
Milebrook. Powy 4B 26
Milebush. Kent 1D 12
Mile End. Cambs 3C 30
Mile End. Essx 1F 22
Mileham. Norf 8F 38
Mile Oak. Brig 5K 11
Miles Green. Staf 4G 35
Miles Hope. Here 5D 26
Milesmark. Fife 1J 59
Mile Town. Kent 6F 22
Milfield. Nmbd 6G 61
Milford. Arm 6F 93
Milford. Derbs 5A 36
Milford. Devn 3B 6
Milford. Powy 3K 25
Milford. Staf 7H 35
Milford. Surr 1G 11
Milford Haven. Pemb 6F 14
Milford on Sea. Hants 6L 9
Milkwall. Glos 3D 18
Milkwell. Wilts 3H 9
Milland. W Sus 3F 10
Mill Bank. W Yor 5J 41
Millbank. Ant 4H 93
Millbank. High 5C 86
Millbay. ME Ant 4J 93
Millbeck. Cumb 3A 46
Millbounds. Orkn 6E 88
Millbreck. Abers 1K 73
Millbridge. Surr 1F 10
Millbrook. C Beds 8H 29
Millbrook. Corn 6G 5
Millbrook. G Man 8H 41
Millbrook. ME Ant 3H 93
Millbrook. Sotn 4A 10
Mill Common. Suff 3L 31
Mill Corner. E Sus 3E 12
Milldale. Staf 4K 35
Millden Lodge. Ang 8E 72
Milldens. Ang 2J 67
Millearn. Per 6C 66
Mill End. Buck 5E 20
Mill End. Cambs 6C 30
Mill End. Glos 2K 19
Mill End. Herts 8L 29
Millend. Glos 4F 18
Millerhill. Midl 3M 59
Miller's Dale. Derbs 2K 35
Millers Green. Derbs 4L 35
Millerston. Glas 3E 58
Millfield. Abers 6D 72
Millfield. Pet 1J 29
Millgate. Lanc 6G 41
Mill Green. Essx 3C 22
Mill Green. Norf 3H 31
Mill Green. Shrp 7E 34
Mill Green. Staf 7J 35
Mill Green. Suff 7F 30
Millhalf. Here 7A 26
Millhall. E Ren 4D 58
Millhayes. Devn
nr. Honiton 5M 7
nr. Wellington 4L 7
Millhead. Lanc 8C 46
Millheugh. S Lan 4F 58
Mill Hill. Bkbn 5E 40
Mill Hill. G Lon 4K 21
Millholme. Cumb 6D 46
Millhouse. Arg 2J 57
Millhouse. Cumb 8H 53
Millhousebridge. Dum 3F 52
Millhouses. S Yor 1M 35
Millikenpark. Ren 3C 58
Millington. E Yor 2F 42
Millington Green. Derbs 5L 35
Millisle. Ards 5J 93
Mill Knowe. Arg 7G 57
Mill Lane. Hants 8E 20
Millmeece. Staf 6G 35
Mill of Craigievar. Abers 4E 72
Mill of Fintray. Abers 4H 73
Mill of Haldane. W Dun 1C 58
Millom. Cumb 6L 45
Millow. C Beds 7K 29
Millpool. Corn 4D 4
Millport. N Ayr 4L 57
Mill Side. Cumb 7C 46
Mill Street. Norf
nr. Lyng 8G 39
nr. Swanton Morley 8G 39
Millthorpe. Derbs 2M 35
Millthorpe. Linc 6J 37
Millthrop. Cumb 6E 46
Milltimber. Aber 5H 73
Mill Town. Ant 4G 93
Milltown. Abers
nr. Corgarff 5B 72
nr. Lumsden 4D 72
Milltown. Ant 4G 93
Milltown. Arm
nr. Banbridge 6G 93
nr. Coalisland 5F 93
nr. Richhill 6F 93
Milltown. Corn 6D 4
Milltown. Derbs 3A 36
Milltown. Devn 2E 6
Milltown. Dum 4H 53
Milltown of Aberdalgie.
Per 5D 66
Milltown of Auchindoun.
Mor 1C 72
Milltown of Campfield.
Abers 5F 72
Milltown of Edinvillie. Mor 1B 72
Milltown of Rothiemay.
Mor 1E 72
Milltown of Towie. Abers 4D 72
Milnacraig. Ang 2F 66
Milnathort. Per 7E 66
Milngavie. E Dun 2D 58
Milnholm. Stir 1F 58
Milnrow. G Man 6H 41
Milnthorpe. Cumb 7C 46
Milnthorpe. W Yor 6M 41
Milson. Shrp 4E 26
Milstead. Kent 8F 22
Milston. Wilts 1K 9
Milthorpe. Nptn 7C 28
Milton. Ang 3G 67
Milton. Cambs 5A 30
Milton. Cumb
nr. Brampton 5K 53
nr. Crooklands 7D 46
Milton. Derbs 7M 35
Milton. Dum
nr. Crocketford 4C 52
nr. Glenluce 6H 51
Milton. Glas 3D 58
Milton. High
nr. Achnasheen 8D 78
nr. Applecross 1J 69
nr. Drumnadrochit 2E 70
nr. Invergordon 6H 79
nr. Inverness 1F 70
nr. Wick 6E 86
Milton. Mor
nr. Cullen 7E 80
nr. Tomintoul 4A 72
Milton. N Som 7B 18
Milton. Notts 2E 36
Milton. Oxon
nr. Bloxham 8B 28
nr. Didcot 4B 20
Milton. Pemb 6G 15
Milton. Port 6D 10
Milton. Som 3C 8
Milton. S Ayr 7C 58
Milton. Stir
nr. Aberfoyle 7K 65
nr. Drymen 8J 65
Milton. Stoke 4H 35
Milton. W Dun 2C 58
Milton Abbas. Dors 5G 9
Milton Abbot. Devn 8D 6
Milton Auchlossan. Abers 5E 72
Milton Bridge. Midl 3L 59
Milton Bryan. C Beds 8G 29
Milton Clevedon. Som 2E 8
Milton Coldwells. Abers 2J 73
Milton Combe. Devn 5G 5
Milton Common. Oxon 3D 20
Milton Damerel. Devn 4C 6
Miltonduff. Mor 7A 80
Milton End. Glos 3K 19
Milton Ernest. Bed 6H 29
Milton Green. Ches W 4C 34
Milton Hill. Devn 8J 7
Milton Hill. Oxon 4B 20
Milton Keynes. Mil 114 (8F 28)
Milton Keynes Village. Mil 8F 28
Milton Lilbourne. Wilts 7K 19
Milton Malsor. Nptn 6E 28
Milton Morenish. Per 4L 65
Milton of Auchinhove.
Abers 5E 72
Milton of Balgonie. Fife 7G 67
Milton of Barras. Abers 8H 73
Milton of Campsie. E Dun 2E 58
Milton of Cultoquhey. Per 5B 66
Milton of Cushnie. Abers 4E 72
Milton of Finavon. Ang 2H 67
Milton of Gollanfield. High 8H 79
Milton of Lesmore. Abers 3D 72
Milton of Leys. High 1G 71
Milton of Tullich. Abers 6C 72
Milton on Stour. Dors 3F 8
Milton Regis. Kent 7E 22
Milton Street. E Sus 5B 12
Milton-under-Wychwood.
Oxon 2L 19
Milverton. Som 3L 7
Milverton. Warw 5M 27
Milwich. Staf 6H 35
Mimbridge. Surr 7G 21
Minard. Arg 8D 64
Minchington. Dors 4H 9
Minchinhampton. Glos 3G 19
Mindrum. Nmbd 6F 60
Minehead. Som 1J 7
Minera. Wrex 4A 34
Minerstown. New M 7J 93
Minety. Wilts 4J 19
Minffordd. Gwyn 7E 32
Mingarrypark. High 1A 64
Mingary. High 1L 63
Mingearraidh. W Isl 3D 74
Miningsby. Linc 3L 37
Minions. Corn 8B 6
Minishant. S Ayr 8B 58
Minllyn. Gwyn 1H 25
Minnigaff. Dum 5K 51
Minorca. IOM 6D 44
Minskip. N Yor 1A 42
Minstead. Hants 4L 9
Minsted. W Sus 3F 10
Minster. Kent
nr. Ramsgate 7K 23
Minster. Kent
nr. Sheerness 6F 22
Minsteracres. Nmbd 6D 54
Minsterley. Shrp 1B 26
Minster Lovell. Oxon 2M 19
Minsterworth. Glos 2F 18
Minterne Magna. Dors 5E 8
Minterne Parva. Dors 5E 8
Minting. Linc 2J 37
Mintlaw. Abers 1K 73
Minto. Bord 7C 60
Minton. Shrp 2C 26
Minwear. Pemb 5G 15
Minworth. W Mid 2K 27
Miodar. Arg 3F 62
Mirbister. Orkn 7C 88
Mirehouse. Cumb 3J 45
Mireland. High 5E 86
Mirfield. W Yor 6L 41
Miserden. Glos 3H 19
Miskin. Rhon 6K 17
Misson. Notts 8D 42
Misterton. Leics 3C 28
Misterton. Notts 8E 42
Misterton. Som 5C 8
Mistley. Essx 8H 31
Mistley Heath. Essx 8H 31
Mitcham. G Lon 7K 21
Mitcheldean. Glos 2E 18
Mitchell. Corn 6A 4
Mitchel Troy. Mon 2C 18
Mitcheltroy Common. Mon 3C 18
Mitford. Nmbd 3E 54
Mithian. Corn 3L 3
Mitton. Staf 8G 35
Mixbury. Oxon 8D 28
Mixenden. W Yor 5J 41
Mixon. Staf 4J 35
Moaness. Orkn 1D 86
Moarfield. Shet 3K 91
Moat. Cumb 4J 53
Moats Tye. Suff 6G 31
Mobberley. Ches E 2F 34
Mobberley. Staf 5J 35
Moccas. Here 7B 26
Mochdre. Cnwy 3H 33
Mochdre. Powy 4K 25
Mochrum. Dum 7J 51
Mockbeggar. Hants 5K 9
Mockerkin. Cumb 2K 45
Modbury. Devn 6J 5
Moddershall. Staf 6H 35
Modsarie. High 5J 85
Moelfre. Cnwy 3J 33
Moelfre. IOA 2E 32
Moelfre. Powy 8L 33
Moffat. Dum 1E 52
Moggerhanger. C Beds 7J 29
Mogworthy. Devn 4H 7
Moira. Leics 8M 35
Moira. Lis 5G 93
Molash. Kent 8G 23
Mol-chlach. High 4F 68
Mold. Flin 4M 33
Molehill Green. Essx 1B 22
Molescroft. E Yor 3H 43
Molesden. Nmbd 3E 54
Molesworth. Cambs 4H 29
Moll. High 3G 69
Molland. Devn 3H 7
Mollington. Ches W 2B 34
Mollington. Oxon 7B 28
Mollinsburn. N Lan 2F 58
Monachty. Cdgn 6E 24
Monachyle. Stir 6J 65
Monar Lodge. High 1C 70
Monaughty. Powy 6M 25
Monea. Ferm 6B 92
Monewden. Suff 6J 31
Moneydie. Per 5D 66
Moneyglass. Ant 4G 93
Moneymore. M Ulst 4F 93
Moneyneany. M Ulst 4E 92
Moneyreagh. Lis 5J 93
Moneyrow Green. Wind 6F 20
Moneyslane. Arm 7H 93
Moniaive. Dum 2B 52
Monifieth. Ang 4J 67
Monikie. Ang 4J 67
Monimail. Fife 6F 66
Monington. Pemb 2H 15
Monk Bretton. S Yor 7A 42
Monken Hadley. G Lon 4K 21
Monk Fryston. N Yor 5C 42
Monk Hesleden. Dur 8H 55
Monkhide. Here 7E 26
Monkhill. Cumb 6H 53
Monkhopton. Shrp 2E 26
Monkland. Here 6C 26
Monkleigh. Devn 3D 6
Monknash. V Glam 7J 17
Monkokehampton. Devn 5E 6
Monkseaton. Tyne 4G 55
Monks Eleigh. Suff 7F 30
Monk's Gate. W Sus 3K 11
Monk's Heath. Ches E 2G 35
Monk Sherborne. Hants 8D 20
Monkshill. Abers 1G 73
Monksilver. Som 2K 7
Monks Kirby. Warw 3B 28
Monk Soham. Suff 5J 31
Monk Soham Green. Suff 5J 31
Monkspath. W Mid 4K 27
Monks Risborough. Buck 3F 20
Monksthorpe. Linc 3M 37
Monkstown. Ant 4H 93
Monk Street. Essx 1C 22
Monkswood. Mon 3B 18
Monkton. Devn 5L 7
Monkton. Kent 7J 23
Monkton. Pemb 6F 14
Monkton. S Ayr 7B 58
Monkton Combe. Bath 7F 18
Monkton Deverill. Wilts 2G 9
Monkton Farleigh. Wilts 7G 19
Monkton Heathfield. Som 3A 8
Monktonhill. S Ayr 7B 58
Monkton Up Wimborne.
Dors 4J 9
Monkton Wyld. Dors 6B 8
Monkwearmouth. Tyne 6G 55
Monkwood. Dors 6C 8
Monkwood. Hants 2D 10
Monmarsh. Here 7D 26
Monmouth. Mon 2D 18
Monnington on Wye. Here 7B 26
Monreith. Dum 7J 51
Montacute. Som 4C 8
Monteith. Arm 6G 93
Montford. Arg 3L 57
Montford. Shrp 8C 34
Montford Bridge. Shrp 8C 34
Montgarrie. Abers 4E 72
Montgarswood. E Ayr 7D 58
Montgomery. Powy 3M 25
Montgreenan. N Ayr 5B 58
Montrave. Fife 7G 67
Montrose. Ang 2L 67
Monxton. Hants 1M 9
Monyash. Derbs 3K 35
Monymusk. Abers 4F 72
Monzie. Per 5B 66
Moodiesburn. N Lan 2E 58
Moon's Green. Kent 3E 12
Moonzie. Fife 6G 67
Moor. Som 4C 8
The Moor. Kent 3D 12
Moor Allerton. W Yor 4L 41
Moorbath. Dors 6C 8
Moorbrae. Shet 5J 91
Moorby. Linc 3K 37
Moorcot. Here 6B 26
Moor Crichel. Dors 5H 9
Moor Cross. Devn 6J 5
Moordown. Bour 6J 9
Moore. Hal 1D 34
Moor End. E Yor 4F 42
Moorend. Dum 4G 53
Moorend. Glos
nr. Dursley 3F 18
nr. Gloucester 2G 19
Moorends. S Yor 6D 42
Moorfields. ME Ant 4G 93
Moorgate. S Yor 8B 42
Moor Green. Wilts 7G 19
Moorgreen. Hants 4B 10
Moorgreen. Notts 5B 36
Moorhaigh. Notts 3C 36
Moorhall. Derbs 2M 35
Moorhampton. Here 7B 26
Moorhouse. Cumb
nr. Carlisle 6H 53
nr. Wigton 6G 53
Moorhouse. Notts 3E 36
Moorhouse. Surr 8M 21
Moorhouses. Linc 4K 37
Moorland. Som 2B 8
Moorlinch. Som 2C 8
Moor Monkton. N Yor 2C 42
Moor of Granary. Mor 8L 79
Moor Row. Cumb
nr. Whitehaven 3K 45
nr. Wigton 7G 53
Moorsholm. Red C 4D 48
Moorside. Dors 4F 8
Moorside. G Man 7H 41
Moortown. Devn 6C 6
Moortown. Hants 5K 9
Moortown. IOW 7B 10
Moortown. Linc 8H 43
Moortown. M Ulst 5F 93
Moortown. Telf 8E 34
Moortown. W Yor 4M 41
Morangie. High 5H 79
Morar. High 6H 69
Morborne. Cambs 2J 29
Morchard Bishop. Devn 5G 7
Morcombelake. Dors 6C 8
Morcott. Rut 1G 29
Morda. Shrp 7A 34
Morden. G Lon 7K 21
Mordiford. Here 8D 26
Mordon. Dur 3M 47
More. Shrp 2B 26
Morebath. Devn 3J 7
Morebattle. Bord 7E 60
Morecambe. Lanc 1C 40
Morefield. High 4B 78
Moreleigh. Devn 6K 5
Morenish. Per 4K 65
Moresby Parks. Cumb 3J 45
Morestead. Hants 3C 10
Moreton. Dors 7G 9
Moreton. Essx 3B 22
Moreton. Here 5D 26
Moreton. Mers 8A 40
Moreton. Oxon 3D 20
Moreton. Staf 8F 34
Moreton Corbet. Shrp 7D 34
Moretonhampstead. Devn 7G 7
Moreton-in-Marsh. Glos 8L 27
Moreton Jeffries. Here 7E 26
Moreton Morrell. Warw 6M 27
Moreton on Lugg. Here 7D 26
Moreton Pinkney. Nptn 7C 28
Moreton Say. Shrp 6E 34
Moreton Valence. Glos 3F 18
Morfa. Cdgn 1K 15
Morfa Bach. Carm 5K 15
Morfa Bychan. Gwyn 7E 32
Morfa Glas. Neat 4H 17
Morfa Nefyn. Gwyn 6B 32
Morganstown. Card 6L 17
Morgan's Vale. Wilts 3K 9
Morham. E Lot 2C 60
Moriah. Cdgn 5F 24
Morland. Cumb 3D 46
Morley. Ches E 1G 35
Morley. Derbs 5A 36
Morley. Dur 3K 47
Morley. W Yor 5L 41
Morley St Botolph. Norf 2G 31
Morningside. Edin 2L 59
Morningside. N Lan 4G 59
Morningthorpe. Norf 2J 31
Morpeth. Nmbd 3F 54
Morrey. Staf 8K 35
Morridge Side. Staf 4J 35
Morridge Top. Staf 3J 35
Morrington. Dum 3C 52
Morris Green. Essx 8D 30
Morriston. Swan 5F 16
Morston. Norf 5G 39
Mortehoe. Devn 1D 6
Morthen. S Yor 1B 36
Mortimer. W Ber 7D 20
Mortimer's Cross. Here 5C 26
Mortimer West End. Hants 7D 20
Mortomley. S Yor 8M 41
Morton. Cumb
nr. Calthwaite 8J 53
nr. Carlisle 6H 53
Morton. Derbs 3B 36
Morton. Linc
nr. Bourne 7H 37
nr. Gainsborough 8F 42
nr. Lincoln 3F 36
Morton. Norf 8H 39
Morton. Notts 4E 36
Morton. Shrp 7A 34
Morton. S Glo 4E 18
Morton Bagot. Warw 5K 27
Morton Mill. Shrp 7D 34
Morton-on-Swale. N Yor 6M 47
Morton Tinmouth. Dur 3K 47
Morvah. Corn 5H 3
Morval. Corn 6E 4
Morvich. High
nr. Golspie 3H 79
nr. Shiel Bridge 3L 69
Morvil. Pemb 3G 15
Morville. Shrp 2E 26
Morwenstow. Corn 4B 6
Morwick. Nmbd 1F 54
Mosborough. S Yor 1B 36
Moscow. E Ayr 5C 58
Mose. Shrp 2F 26
Mosedale. Cumb 8H 53
Moseley. W Mid
nr. Birmingham 3J 27
nr. Wolverhampton 1H 27
Moseley. Worc 6G 27
Moss. Arg 3E 62
Moss. High 1A 64
Moss. S Yor 6C 42
Moss. Wrex 4B 34
Mossatt. Abers 4D 72
Moss Bank. Mers 8D 40
Mossbank. Shet 6J 91
Mossblown. S Ayr 7C 58
Mossbrow. G Man 1F 34
Mossburnford. Bord 8D 60
Mossdale. Dum 4A 52
Mossedge. Cumb 5J 53
Mossend. N Lan 3F 58
Mossgate. Staf 6H 35
Moss Lane. Ches E 2H 35
Mossley. Ant 4H 93
Mossley. Ches E 3G 35
Mossley. G Man 7H 41
Mossley Hill. Mers 1B 34
Moss of Barmuckity. Mor 7B 80
Mosspark. Glas 3D 58
Mosspaul. Bord 2J 53
Moss Side. Cumb 6F 52
Moss Side. G Man 8G 41
Moss Side. Lanc
nr. Blackpool 4B 40
nr. Preston 5D 40
Moss Side. Mers 7B 40
Moss-Side. Caus 2G 93
Moss-side. High 8J 79
Moss-side of Cairness.
Abers 7K 81
Mosstodloch. Mor 7C 80
Mosswood. Nmbd 6D 54
Mossy Lea. Lanc 6D 40
Mosterton. Dors 5C 8
Moston. Shrp 7D 34
Moston Green. Ches E 3F 34
Mostyn. Flin 2L 33
Mostyn Quay. Flin 2L 33
Motcombe. Dors 3G 9
Mothecombe. Devn 7J 5
Motherby. Cumb 3C 46
Motherwell. N Lan 4F 58
Mottingham. G Lon 6M 21
Mottisfont. Hants 3M 9
Mottistone. IOW 7B 10
Mottram in Longdendale.
G Man 8H 41
Mottram St Andrew.
Ches E 2G 35
Mott's Mill. E Sus 2B 12
Mouldsworth. Ches W 2D 34
Moulin. Per 2C 66
Moulsecoomb. Brig 5L 11
Moulsford. Oxon 5C 20
Moulsoe. Mil 7G 29
Moulton. Ches W 3E 34
Moulton. Linc 7L 37
Moulton. Nptn 5E 28
Moulton. N Yor 5L 47
Moulton. Suff 5C 30
Moulton. V Glam 7K 17
Moulton Chapel. Linc 8K 37
Moulton Eaugate. Linc 8L 37
Moulton St Mary. Norf 1K 31
Moulton Seas End. Linc 7L 37
Mount. Corn
nr. Bodmin 5D 4
nr. Newquay 3L 3
Mountain Ash. Rhon 5K 17
Mountain Cross. Bord 5K 59
Mountain Street. Kent 8G 23
Mountain Water. Pemb 4F 14
Mount Ambrose. Corn 4L 3
Mountbenger. Bord 7M 59
Mountblow. W Dun 2C 58
Mount Bures. Essx 8F 30
Mountfield. E Sus 3D 12
Mountfield. Ferm 5D 92
Mountgerald. High 7F 78
Mount Hawke. Corn 4L 3
Mount High. High 7G 79
Mountjoy. Corn 5A 4
Mountjoy. Ferm 5D 92
Mount Lothian. Midl 4L 59
Mountnessing. Essx 4C 22
Mountnorris. Arm 7F 93
Mounton. Mon 4D 18
Mount Pleasant. Buck 8D 28
Mount Pleasant. Ches E 4G 35
Mount Pleasant. Derbs
nr. Derby 5M 35
nr. Swadlincote 8L 35
Mount Pleasant. E Sus 4M 11
Mount Pleasant. Hants 6L 9
Mount Pleasant. Norf 2F 30
Mount Skippett. Oxon 2A 20
Mountsorrel. Leics 8C 36
Mount Stuart. Arg 4L 57
Mousehole. Corn 6H 3
Mouswald. Dum 4E 52
Mow Cop. Ches E 4G 35
Mowden. Darl 4L 47
Mowhaugh. Bord 7F 60
Mowmacre Hill. Leic 1C 28
Mowsley. Leics 3D 28
Moy. High 2H 71
Moy. M Ulst 6F 93
Moygashel. M Ulst 5F 93
Moylgrove. Pemb 2H 15
Moy Lodge. High 7E 70
Muasdale. Arg 5F 56
Muchalls. Abers 6J 73
Much Birch. Here 8D 26
Much Cowarne. Here 7E 26
Much Dewchurch. Here 8C 26
Muchelney. Som 3C 8
Muchelney Ham. Som 3C 8
Much Hadham. Herts 2M 21
Much Hoole. Lanc 5C 40
Muchlarnick. Corn 6E 4
Much Marcle. Here 8E 26
Muchrachd. High 2C 70
Much Wenlock. Shrp 1E 26
Mucking. Thur 5C 22
Muckle Breck. Shet 1F 90
Muckleford. Dors 6E 8
Mucklestone. Staf 6F 34
Muckleton. Norf 6E 38
Muckleton. Shrp 7D 34
Muckley. Shrp 2E 26
Muckley Corner. Staf 1J 27
Muckton. Linc 1L 37
Mudale. High 8H 85
Muddiford. Devn 2E 6
Mudeford. Dors 6K 9
Mudford. Som 4D 8
Mudgley. Som 1C 8
Mugdock. Stir 2D 58
Mugeary. High 2F 68
Muggington. Derbs 5L 35
Muggintonlane End. Derbs 5L 35
Muggleswick. Dur 6D 54
Mugswell. Surr 8K 21
Muie. High 3G 79
Muirden. Abers 8G 81
Muirdrum. Ang 4J 67
Muiredge. Per 5F 66
Muirend. Glas 3D 58
Muirhead. Ang 4G 67
Muirhead. Fife 7F 66
Muirhead. N Lan 3E 58
Muirhouses. Falk 1J 59
Muirkirk. E Ayr 7E 58
Muir of Alford. Abers 4E 72
Muir of Fairburn. High 8E 78
Muir of Fowlis. Abers 4E 72
Muir of Miltonduff. Mor 8A 80
Muir of Ord. High 8F 78
Muir of Tarradale. High 8F 78
Muirshearlich. High 7B 70
Muirtack. Abers 2J 73
Muirton. High 7H 79
Muirton. Per 5E 66
Muirton of Ardblair. Per 3E 66
Muirtown. Per 6C 66
Muiryfold. Abers 8G 81
Muker. N Yor 6H 47
Mulbarton. Norf 1H 31
Mulben. Mor 8C 80
Mulindry. Arg 4C 56
Mulla. Shet 1E 90
Mullach Charlabhaigh.
W Isl 7F 82
Mullacott. Devn 1E 6
Mullaghbane. New M 7F 93
Mullaghboy. ME Ant 3J 93
Mullaghglass. New M 7G 93
Mullion. Corn 7K 3
Mullion Cove. Corn 7K 3
Mumbles. Swan 6F 16
Mumby. Linc 2B 38
Munderfield Row. Here 6E 26
Munderfield Stocks. Here 6E 26
Mundesley. Norf 6K 39
Mundford. Norf 2E 30
Mundham. Norf 2K 31
Mundon. Essx 3E 22
Munerigie. High 5C 70
Muness. Shet 3L 91
Mungasdale. High 4L 77
Mungrisdale. Cumb 8H 53
Munlochy. High 8G 79
Munsley. Here 7E 26
Munslow. Shrp 3D 26
Murchington. Devn 7F 6
Murcot. Worc 7J 27
Murcott. Oxon 2C 20
Murdishaw. Hal 1D 34
Murieston. W Lot 3J 59
Murkle. High 5C 86
Murlaggan. High 6M 69
Murra. Orkn 1D 86
The Murray. S Lan 4E 58
Murrayfield. Edin 2L 59
Murrell Green. Hants 8E 20
Murroes. Ang 4H 67
Murrow. Cambs 1L 29
Mursley. Buck 1F 20
Murthly. Per 4D 66
Murton. Cumb 3F 46
Murton. Dur 7G 55
Murton. Nmbd 5G 61
Murton. Swan 6E 16
Murton. York 2D 42
Musbury. Devn 6A 8
Muscoates. N Yor 7D 48
Muscott. Nptn 5D 28
Musselburgh. E Lot 2M 59
Muston. Leics 6F 36
Muston. N Yor 8H 49
Mustow Green. Worc 4G 27
Muswell Hill. G Lon 5K 21
Mutehill. Dum 7A 52
Mutford. Suff 3L 31
Muthill. Per 6B 66
Mutterton. Devn 5K 7
Muxton. Telf 8F 34
Mwmbwls. Swan 6F 16
Mybster. High 6C 86
Myddfai. Carm 1G 17
Myddle. Shrp 7C 34
Mydroilyn. Cdgn 1L 15
Myerscough. Lanc 4C 40
Mylor Bridge. Corn 5M 3
Mylor Churchtown. Corn 5M 3
Mynachlog-ddu. Pemb 3H 15
Mynydd-bach. Mon 4C 18
Mynydd Isa. Flin 3A 34
Mynyddislwyn. Cphy 5L 17
Mynydd Llandegai. Gwyn 4F 32
Mynydd Mechell. IOA 1C 32
Mynydd-y-briw. Powy 8L 33
Mynyddygarreg. Carm 6L 15
Mynytho. Gwyn 7C 32
Myrebird. Abers 6G 73
Myrelandhorn. High 6D 86
Mytchett. Surr 8F 20
The Mythe. Glos 8G 27
Mytholmroyd. W Yor 5J 41
Myton-on-Swale. N Yor 1B 42
Mytton. Shrp 8C 34

N

Naast. High 5K 77
Na Buirgh. W Isl 4B 76
Naburn. York 3C 42
Nab Wood. W Yor 4K 41
Nackington. Kent 8H 23
Nacton. Suff 7J 31
Nafferton. E Yor 2H 43
Na Gearrannan. W Isl 7E 82
Nailbridge. Glos 2E 18
Nailsbourne. Som 3M 7
Nailsea. N Som 6C 18
Nailstone. Leics 1B 28
Nailsworth. Glos 4G 19
Nairn. High 8J 79
Nalderswood. Surr 1K 11
Nancegollan. Corn 5K 3
Nancledra. Corn 5H 3
Nangreaves. G Man 6G 41
Nanhyfer. Pemb 3G 15
Nannerch. Flin 4L 33
Nanpantan. Leics 8C 36
Nanpean. Corn 6B 4
Nansledan M2 3
Nanstallon. Corn 5C 4
Nant-ddu. Powy 3K 17
Nanternis. Cdgn 1K 15
Nantgaredig. Carm 4L 15
Nantgarw. Rhon 6L 17
Nant Glas. Powy 6J 25
Nantglyn. Den 4K 33
Nantgwyn. Powy 5J 25
Nantlle. Gwyn 5E 32
Nantmawr. Shrp 7A 34
Nantmel. Powy 6K 25
Nantmor. Gwyn 6F 32
Nant Peris. Gwyn 5F 32
Nantwich. Ches E 4E 34
Nant-y-bai. Carm 8G 25
Nant-y-bwch. Blae 3L 17
Nant-y-Derry. Mon 3B 18
Nant-y-dugoed. Powy 1J 25
Nant-y-felin. Cnwy 3F 32
Nantyffyllon. B'end 5H 17
Nantyglo. Blae 3L 17
Nant-y-meichiaid. Powy 1L 25
Nant-y-moel. B'end 5J 17
Nant-y-pandy. Cnwy 3F 32
Naphill. Buck 4F 20
Nappa. N Yor 2G 41
Napton on the Hill. Warw 5B 28
Narberth. Pemb 5H 15
Narberth Bridge. Pemb 5H 15
Narborough. Leics 2C 28
Narborough. Norf 8D 38
Narkurs. Corn 6F 4
The Narth. Mon 3D 18
Narthwaite. Cumb 6F 46
Nasareth. Gwyn 5D 32
Naseby. Nptn 4D 28
Nash. Buck 8E 28
Nash. Here 5B 26
Nash. Kent 8J 23
Nash. Newp 5B 18
Nash. Shrp 4E 26
Nash Lee. Buck 3F 20
Nassington. Nptn 2H 29
Nasty. Herts 1L 21
Natcott. Devn 3B 6
Nateby. Cumb 5F 46
Nateby. Lanc 3C 40
Nately Scures. Hants 8E 20
Natland. Cumb 7D 46
Naughton. Suff 7G 31
Naunton. Glos 1K 19
Naunton. Worc 8G 27
Naunton Beauchamp. Worc 6H 27
Navenby. Linc 4G 37
Navestock. Essx 4B 22
Navestock Side. Essx 4B 22
Navidale. High 2L 79
Nawton. N Yor 7D 48
Nayland. Suff 8F 30
Nazeing. Essx 3M 21
Neacroft. Hants 6K 9
Nealhouse. Cumb 6H 53
Neal's Green. Warw 3M 27
Near Sawrey. Cumb 6B 46
Neasden. G Lon 5K 21
Neasham. Darl 4M 47
Neath. Neat 5G 17
Neath Abbey. Neat 5G 17
Neatishead. Norf 7K 39
Neaton. Norf 1F 30
Nebo. Cdgn 6E 24
Nebo. Cnwy 5H 33
Nebo. Gwyn 5D 32
Nebo. IOA 1D 32
Necton. Norf 1E 30
Nedd. High 8D 84
Nedderton. Nmbd 3F 54
Nedging. Suff 7G 31
Nedging Tye. Suff 7G 31
Needham. Norf 3J 31
Needham Market. Suff 6G 31
Needham Street. Suff 5D 30
Needingworth. Cambs 4L 29
Needwood. Staf 7K 35
Neen Savage. Shrp 4E 26
Neen Sollars. Shrp 4E 26
Neenton. Shrp 3E 26
Nefyn. Gwyn 6C 32
Neilston. E Ren 4C 58
Neithrop. Oxon 7B 28
Nelly Andrews Green.
Powy 1A 26
Nelson. Cphy 5L 17
Nelson. Lanc 4G 41
Nelson Village. Nmbd 4F 54
Nemphlar. S Lan 5G 59
Nempnett Thrubwell. Bath 7D 18
Nene Terrace. Linc 1K 29
Nenthall. Cumb 7A 54
Nenthead. Cumb 7A 54
Nenthorn. Bord 6D 60
Nercwys. Flin 4M 33
Neribus. Arg 4B 56
Nerston. S Lan 4E 58
Nesbit. Nmbd 6G 61
Nesfield. N Yor 3J 41
Ness. Ches W 2B 34
Nesscliffe. Shrp 8B 34
Ness of Tenston. Orkn 8B 88
Neston. Ches W 2A 34
Neston. Wilts 7G 19
Nethanfoot. S Lan 5G 59
Nether Alderley. Ches E 2G 35
Netheravon. Wilts 1K 9
Nether Blainslie. Bord 5C 60
Netherbrae. Abers 8G 81
Netherbrough. Orkn 8C 88
Nether Broughton. Leics 7D 36
Netherburn. S Lan 5G 59
Nether Burrow. Lanc 8E 46
Netherbury. Dors 6C 8
Netherby. Cumb 4H 53
Nether Careston. Ang 2J 67
Nether Cerne. Dors 6E 8
Nether Compton. Dors 4D 8
Nethercote. Glos 1K 19
Nethercote. Warw 5C 28
Nethercott. Devn 2D 6
Nethercott. Oxon 1B 20
Nether Dallachy. Mor 7C 80
Nether Durdie. Per 5F 66
Nether End. Derbs 2L 35
Netherend. Glos 3D 18
Nether Exe. Devn 5J 7
Netherfield. E Sus 4D 12
Netherfield. Notts 5D 36
Nethergate. Norf 7G 39
Netherhampton. Wilts 3K 9
Nether Handley. Derbs 2B 36
Nether Haugh. S Yor 8B 42
Nether Heage. Derbs 4A 36
Nether Heyford. Nptn 6D 28
Netherhouses. Cumb 7A 46
Nether Howcleugh. S Lan 8J 59
Nether Kellet. Lanc 1D 40
Nether Kinmundy. Abers 1K 73
Netherland Green. Staf 6K 35
Nether Langwith. Notts 2C 36
Netherlaw. Dum 7B 52
Netherley. Abers 6H 73
Nethermill. Dum 3E 52
Nethermills. Mor 8E 80
Nether Moor. Derbs 3A 36
Nether Padley. Derbs 2L 35
Netherplace. E Ren 4D 58
Nether Poppleton. York 2C 42
Netherseal. Derbs 8L 35
Nether Silton. N Yor 6B 48
Nether Stowey. Som 2L 7
Nether Street. Essx 2B 22
Netherstreet. Wilts 7H 19
Netherthird. E Ayr 8D 58
Netherthong. W Yor 7K 41
Netherton. Ang 2J 67
Netherton. Cumb 8E 52
Netherton. Devn 8H 7
Netherton. Hants 8A 20
Netherton. Here 1D 18
Netherton. Mers 8B 40
Netherton. N Lan 4F 58
Netherton. Nmbd 1C 54
Netherton. Per 2E 66
Netherton. Shrp 3F 26
Netherton. Stir 2D 58
Netherton. W Mid 3H 27
Netherton. W Yor
nr. Armitage Bridge 6K 41
nr. Horbury 6L 41
Netherton. Worc 7H 27
Nethertown. Cumb 4J 45
Nethertown. High 4E 86
Nethertown. Staf 8K 35
Nether Urquhart. Fife 7E 66
Nether Wallop. Hants 2M 9
Nether Wasdale. Cumb 4L 45
Nether Welton. Cumb 7H 53

Nether Westcote – Otherton

Nether Westcote. Glos 1L 19
Nether Whitacre. Warw 2L 27
Nether Winchendon. Buck 2E 20
Netherwitton. Nmbd 2E 54
Nether Worton. Oxon 8B 28
Nethy Bridge. High 3L 71
Netley. Shrp 1C 26
Netley Abbey. Hants 5B 10
Netley Marsh. Hants 4M 9
Nettlebed. Oxon 5E 20
Nettlebridge. Som 1E 8
Nettlecombe. Dors 6D 8
Nettlecombe. IOW 8C 10
Nettleden. Herts 2H 21
Nettleham. Linc 2H 37
Nettlestead. Kent 8C 22
Nettlestead Green. Kent 8C 22
Nettlestone. IOW 6D 10
Nettlesworth. Dur 7F 54
Nettleton. Linc 7J 43
Nettleton. Wilts 6G 19
Netton. Devn 7H 5
Netton. Wilts 2K 9
Neuadd. Powy 2K 25
The Neuk. Abers 6G 73
Nevendon. Essx 4D 22
Nevern. Pemb 3G 15
New Abbey. Dum 5D 52
New Aberdour. Abers 7H 81
New Addington. G Lon 7L 21
Newall. W Yor 3L 41
New Alresford. Hants 2C 10
New Alyth. Per 3F 66
Newark. Orkn 5G 89
Newark. Pet 1K 29
Newark-on-Trent. Notts 4E 36
New Arley. Warw 3L 27
Newarthill. N Lan 4F 58
New Ash Green. Kent 7C 22
New Balderton. Notts 4F 36
New Barn. Kent 7C 22
New Barnetby. N Lin 6H 43
Newbattle. Midl 3M 59
New Bewick. Nmbd 7H 61
Newbie. Dum 5F 52
Newbiggin. Cumb
nr. Appleby 3E 46
nr. Barrow-in-Furness 8M 45
nr. Cumrew 7K 53
nr. Penrith 3C 46
nr. Seascale 5K 45
Newbiggin. Dur
nr. Consett 7E 54
nr. Holwick 3H 47
Newbiggin. Nmbd 7C 54
Newbiggin. N Yor
nr. Askrigg 6H 47
nr. Filey 7J 49
nr. Thoralby 7H 47
Newbiggin-by-the-Sea. Nmbd 3G 55
Newbigging. Ang
nr. Monikie 4H 67
nr. Newtyle 3F 66
nr. Tealing 4H 67
Newbigging. Edin 2K 59
Newbigging. S Lan 5J 59
Newbiggin-on-Lune. Cumb 5F 46
Newbold. Derbs 2A 36
Newbold. Leics 8B 36
Newbold on Avon. Warw 4B 28
Newbold on Stour. Warw 7L 27
Newbold Pacey. Warw 6L 27
Newbold Verdon. Leics 1B 28
New Bolingbroke. Linc 4L 37
Newborough. IOA 4D 32
Newborough. Pet 1K 29
Newborough. Staf 7K 35
Newbottle. Nptn 8C 28
Newbottle. Tyne 6G 55
New Boultham. Linc 2G 37
Newbourne. Suff 7J 31
New Brancepeth. Dur 7F 54
New Bridge. Dum 4D 52
Newbridge. Cphy 5M 17
Newbridge. Cdgn 1M 15
Newbridge. Corn 5H 3
Newbridge. Edin 2K 59
Newbridge. Hants 4L 9
Newbridge. IOW 7B 10
Newbridge. N Yor 7F 48
Newbridge. Pemb 3F 14
Newbridge. Wrex 5A 34
Newbridge Green. Worc 8G 27
Newbridge-on-Usk. Mon 4B 18
Newbridge on Wye. Powy 7K 25
New Brighton. Flin 3A 34
New Brighton. Hants 5E 10
New Brighton. Mers 8B 40
New Brinsley. Notts 4B 36
Newbrough. Nmbd 5B 54
New Broughton. Wrex 4B 34
New Buckenham. Norf 2G 31
New Buildings. Derr 3D 92
Newbuildings. Devn 5G 7
Newburgh. Abers 3J 73
Newburgh. Fife 6F 66
Newburgh. Lanc 6C 40
Newburn. Tyne 5E 54
Newbury. W Ber 7B 20
Newbury. Wilts 1G 9
Newby. Cumb 3D 46
Newby. N Yor
nr. Ingleton 8F 46
nr. Scarborough 7H 49
nr. Stokesley 4C 48
Newby Bridge. Cumb 7B 46
Newby Cote. N Yor 8F 46
Newby East. Cumb 6J 53
Newby Head. Cumb 3D 46
New Byth. Abers 8H 81
Newby West. Cumb 6H 53
Newby Wiske. N Yor 7A 48
Newcastle. Ards 6K 93
Newcastle. B'end 6H 17
Newcastle. Mon 2C 18
Newcastle. New M 7H 93
Newcastle. Shrp 4M 25
Newcastle Emlyn. Carm 2K 15
Newcastle International Airport. Tyne 4E 54
Newcastleton. Bord 3J 53
Newcastle-under-Lyme. Staf 5G 35
Newcastle upon Tyne. Tyne 111 (5F 54)
Newchapel. Pemb 3J 15
Newchapel. Powy 4J 25
Newchapel. Staf 4G 35
Newchapel. Surr 1L 11
New Cheriton. Hants 3C 10
Newchurch. Carm 4K 15
Newchurch. Here 6B 26
Newchurch. IOW 7C 10
Newchurch. Kent 2G 13
Newchurch. Lanc 5G 41
Newchurch. Mon 4C 18
Newchurch. Powy 7M 25
Newchurch. Staf 7K 35
Newchurch in Pendle. Lanc 4G 41
New Costessey. Norf 8H 39
Newcott. Devn 5M 7
New Cowper. Cumb 7F 52
Newcraighall. Edin 2M 59
New Crofton. W Yor 6A 42
New Cross. Cdgn 5F 24
New Cross. Som 4C 8
New Cumnock. E Ayr 8E 58
New Deer. Abers 1H 73
New Denham. Buck 5H 21
Newdigate. Surr 1J 11
New Duston. Nptn 5E 28
New Earswick. York 2D 42
New Edlington. S Yor 8C 42
New Elgin. Mor 7B 80
New Ellerby. E Yor 4J 43
Newell Green. Brac 6F 20
New Eltham. G Lon 6M 21
New End. Warw 5K 27
New End. Worc 6J 27
Newenden. Kent 3E 12
New England. Essx 7D 30
New England. Pet 1J 29
Newent. Glos 1F 18
New Ferry. Mers 1B 34
Newfield. Dur
nr. Chester-le-Street 6F 54
nr. Willington 8F 54
Newfound. Hants 8C 20
New Fryston. W Yor 5B 42
Newgale. Pemb 4E 14
New Galloway. Dum 4M 51
Newgate. Norf 5G 39
Newgate Street. Herts 3L 21
New Greens. Herts 3J 21
New Grimsby. IOS 1G 3
New Hainford. Norf 8J 39
Newhall. Ches E 5E 34
Newhall. Derbs 7L 35
Newham. Nmbd 7J 61
New Hartley. Nmbd 4G 55
Newhaven. Derbs 3K 35
Newhaven. E Sus 118 (5M 11)
Newhaven. Edin 2L 59
New Haw. Surr 7H 21
New Hedges. Pemb 6H 15
New Herrington. Tyne 6G 55
Newhey. G Man 6H 41
New Holkham. Norf 6E 38
New Holland. N Lin 5H 43
Newholm. N Yor 4F 48
New Houghton. Derbs 3C 36
New Houghton. Norf 7D 38
Newhouse. N Lan 3F 58
New Houses. N Yor 8G 47
New Hutton. Cumb 6D 46
New Hythe. Kent 8D 22
Newick. E Sus 3M 11
Newingreen. Kent 2H 13
Newington. Edin 2L 59
Newington. Kent
nr. Folkestone 2H 13
nr. Sittingbourne 7E 22
Newington. Notts 8D 42
Newington. Oxon 4D 20
Newington Bagpath. Glos 4G 19
New Inn. Carm 3L 15
New Inn. Mon 3C 18
New Inn. N Yor 8G 47
New Inn. Torf 4B 18
New Invention. Shrp 4A 26
New Kelso. High 1L 69
New Lanark. S Lan 5G 59
Newland. Glos 3D 18
Newland. Hull 4H 43
Newland. N Yor 5D 42
Newland. Som 2H 7
Newland. Worc 7F 26
Newlandrig. Midl 3A 60
Newlands. Cumb 8H 53
Newlands. High 1H 71
Newlands. Nmbd 6D 54
Newlands. Staf 7J 35
Newlands of Geise. High 5B 86
Newlands of Tynet. Mor 7C 80
Newlands Park. IOA 2B 32
New Lane. Lanc 6C 40
New Lane End. Warr 8E 40
New Langholm. Dum 3H 53
New Leake. Linc 4M 37
New Leeds. Abers 8J 81
New Lenton. Nott 6C 36
New Longton. Lanc 5D 40
Newlot. Orkn 8E 88
New Luce. Dum 5G 51
Newlyn. Corn 6H 3
Newmachar. Abers 4H 73
Newmains. N Lan 4G 59
New Mains of Ury. Abers 7H 73
New Malden. G Lon 7K 21
Newman's Green. Suff 7E 30
Newmarket. Suff 5C 30
Newmarket. W Isl 8H 83
New Marske. Red C 3D 48
New Marton. Shrp 6B 34
New Micklefield. W Yor 4B 42
New Mill. Abers 1G 73
New Mill. Corn 5H 3
New Mill. Herts 2G 21
New Mill. W Yor 7K 41
New Mill. Wilts 7K 19
Newmill. Ant 4H 93
Newmill. Mor 8D 80
Newmill. Bord 8B 60
Newmillerdam. W Yor 6M 41
New Mills. Corn 6A 4
New Mills. Derbs 1J 35
New Mills. Mon 3D 18
New Mills. Powy 2K 25
Newmills. Arm 6G 93
Newmills. Fife 1J 59
Newmills. High 7G 79
Newmills. M Ulst 5F 93
Newmiln. Per 4E 66
Newmilns. E Ayr 6D 58
New Milton. Hants 6L 9
New Mistley. Essx 8H 31
New Moat. Pemb 4G 15
Newmore. High
nr. Dingwall 8F 78
nr. Invergordon 6G 79
Newnham. Cambs 6M 29
Newnham. Glos 2E 18
Newnham. Hants 8E 20
Newnham. Herts 8K 29
Newnham. Kent 8F 22
Newnham. Nptn 6C 28
Newnham. Warw 5K 27
Newnham Bridge. Worc 5E 26
New Ollerton. Notts 3D 36
New Oscott. W Mid 2J 27
New Park. N Yor 2L 41
Newpark. Fife 6H 67
New Pitsligo. Abers 8H 81
New Polzeath. Corn 4B 4
Newport. Corn 7C 6
Newport. Devn 2E 6
Newport. E Yor 4F 42
Newport. Essx 8B 30
Newport. Glos 4E 18
Newport. High 1M 79
Newport. IOW 7C 10
Newport. Newp 114 (5B 18)
Newport. Norf 8M 39
Newport. Pemb 3G 15
Newport. Som 3B 8
Newport. Telf 8F 34
Newport-on-Tay. Fife 5H 67
Newport Pagnell. Mil 7F 28
Newpound Common. W Sus 3H 11
New Prestwick. S Ayr 7B 58
New Quay. Cdgn 1K 15
Newquay. Corn 2M 3
Newquay Cornwall Airport. Corn 5A 4
New Rackheath. Norf 8J 39
New Radnor. Powy 6M 25
New Rent. Cumb 8J 53
New Ridley. Nmbd 6D 54
New Romney. Kent 3G 13
New Rossington. S Yor 8D 42
New Row. Cdgn 5G 25
Newry. New M 7G 93
New Sauchie. Clac 8B 66
Newsbank. Ches E 3G 35
Newseat. Abers 2G 73
Newsham. Lanc 4D 40
Newsham. Nmbd 4G 55
Newsham. N Yor
nr. Richmond 4K 47
nr. Thirsk 7A 48
New Sharlston. W Yor 5A 42
Newsholme. E Yor 5E 42
Newsholme. Lanc 2G 41
New Shoreston. Nmbd 6J 61
New Springs. G Man 7D 40
Newstead. Notts 4C 36
Newstead. Bord 6C 60
New Stevenston. N Lan 4F 58
New Street. Here 6B 26
Newstreet Lane. Shrp 6E 34
New Swanage. Dors 7J 9
New Swannington. Leics 8B 36
Newthorpe. N Yor 4B 42
Newthorpe. Notts 5B 36
Newton. Arg 8E 64
Newton. B'end 7H 17
Newton. Cambs
nr. Cambridge 7M 29
nr. Wisbech 8M 37
Newton. Ches W
nr. Chester 3C 34
nr. Tattenhall 4D 34
Newton. Cumb 7M 45
Newton. Derbs 4B 36
Newton. Dors 4F 8
Newton. Dum
nr. Annan 4G 53
nr. Moffat 2F 52
Newton. G Man 8H 41
Newton. Here
nr. Ewyas Harold 8B 26
nr. Leominster 6D 26
Newton. High
nr. Cromarty 7H 79
nr. Inverness 1H 71
nr. Kylestrome 8E 84
nr. Wick 7E 86
Newton. Lanc
nr. Blackpool 4B 40
nr. Carnforth 8D 46
nr. Clitheroe 2E 40
Newton. Linc 6H 37
Newton. Mers 2M 33
Newton. Mor 7A 80
Newton. Norf 8E 38
Newton. Nptn 3F 28
Newton. Nmbd 5D 54
Newton. Notts 5D 36
Newton. Bord 7D 60
Newton. Shet 4D 90
Newton. Shrp
nr. Bridgnorth 2F 26
nr. Wem 6C 34
Newton. Som 2L 7
Newton. S Lan
nr. Glasgow 3E 58
nr. Lanark 6H 59
Newton. Staf 7J 35
Newton. Suff 7F 30
Newton. Swan 6F 16
Newton. Warw 4C 28
Newton. W Lot 2J 59
Newton. Wilts 3L 9
Newton Abbot. Devn 8H 7
Newtonairds. Dum 3C 52
Newton Arlosh. Cumb 6G 53
Newton Aycliffe. Dur 3L 47
Newton Bewley. Hart 3B 48
Newton Blossomville. Mil 6G 29
Newton Bromswold. Nptn 5G 29
Newton Burgoland. Leics 1A 28
Newton by Toft. Linc 1H 37
Newton Ferrers. Devn 7H 5
Newton Flotman. Norf 2J 31
Newtongrange. Midl 3M 59
Newton Green. Mon 4D 18
Newton Hall. Dur 7F 54
Newton Hall. Nmbd 5D 54
Newton Harcourt. Leics 2D 28
Newton Heath. G Man 7G 41
Newton Hill. W Yor 5M 41
Newtonhill. Abers 6J 73
Newtonhill. High 1F 70
Newton Ketton. Darl 3M 47
Newton Kyme. N Yor 3B 42
Newton-le-Willows. Mers 8D 40
Newton-le-Willows. N Yor 7L 47
Newton Longville. Buck 8F 28
Newton Mearns. E Ren 4D 58
Newtonmore. High 6H 71
Newton Morrell. N Yor 5L 47
Newton Mulgrave. N Yor 4E 48
Newton of Ardtoe. High 8H 69
Newton of Balcanquhal. Per 6E 66
Newton of Beltrees. Ren 4B 58
Newton of Falkland. Fife 7F 66
Newton of Mountblairy. Abers 8F 80
Newton of Pitcairns. Per 6D 66
Newton-on-Ouse. N Yor 2C 42
Newton-on-Rawcliffe. N Yor 6F 48
Newton on the Hill. Shrp 7C 34
Newton-on-the-Moor. Nmbd 1E 54
Newton on Trent. Linc 2F 36
Newton Poppleford. Devn 7K 7
Newton Purcell. Oxon 8D 28
Newton Regis. Warw 1L 27
Newton Reigny. Cumb 8J 53
Newton Rigg. Cumb 8J 53
Newton St Cyres. Devn 6H 7
Newton St Faith. Norf 8J 39
Newton St Loe. Bath 7F 18
Newton St Petrock. Devn 4D 6
Newton Solney. Derbs 7L 35
Newton Stacey. Hants 1B 10
Newton Stewart. Dum 5K 51
Newton Toney. Wilts 1L 9
Newton Tony. Wilts 1L 9
Newton Tracey. Devn 3E 6
Newton under Roseberry. Red C 4C 48
Newton upon Ayr. S Ayr 7B 58
Newton upon Derwent. E Yor 3E 42
Newton Valence. Hants 2E 10
Newton-with-Scales. Lanc 4C 40
New Town. Dors 4H 9
New Town. E Lot 2B 60
New Town. Lutn 1H 21
New Town. W Yor 5B 42
Newtown. Abers 7G 81
Newtown. Cambs 5H 29
Newtown. Corn 8B 6
Newtown. Cumb
nr. Aspatria 7E 52
nr. Brampton 5K 53
nr. Penrith 3D 46
Newtown. Derbs 1H 35
Newtown. Devn 3G 7
Newtown. Dors 5C 8
Newtown. Falk 1H 59
Newtown. Glos
nr. Lydney 3E 18
nr. Tewkesbury 8H 27
Newtown. Hants
nr. Bishop's Waltham 4C 10
nr. Liphook 2F 10
nr. Lyndhurst 4L 9
nr. Newbury 7B 20
nr. Romsey 3M 9
nr. Warsash 5B 10
nr. Wickham 4D 10
Newtown. Here
nr. Little Dewchurch 8D 26
nr. Stretton Grandison 7E 26
Newtown. High 5D 70
Newtown. IOM 7C 44
Newtown. IOW 6B 10
Newtown. Lanc 6D 40
Newtown. Nmbd
nr. Rothbury 1D 54
nr. Wooler 7H 61
Newtown. Pool 6J 9
Newtown. Powy 3L 25
Newtown. Rhon 5K 17
Newtown. Shet 5J 91
Newtown. Shrp 6C 34
Newtown. Som 4A 8
Newtown. Staf
nr. Biddulph 3H 35
nr. Cannock 1H 27
nr. Longnor 3J 35
Newtown. Wilts 3H 9
Newtownabbey. Ant 4H 93
Newtownards. Ards 5J 93
Newtownbutler. Ferm 7D 92
Newtown-Crommelin. ME Ant 3G 93
Newtownhamilton. New M 7F 93
Newtown-in-St Martin. Corn 6L 3
Newtown Linford. Leics 1C 28
Newtown St Boswells. Bord 6C 60
Newtownstewart. Derr 4D 92
Newtown Unthank. Leics 1B 28
New Tredegar. Cphy 4L 17
Newtyle. Ang 3F 66
New Village. E Yor 4H 43
New Village. S Yor 7C 42
New Walsoken. Cambs 1A 30
New Waltham. NE Lin 7K 43
New Winton. E Lot 2B 60
New World. Cambs 2L 29
New Yatt. Oxon 2A 20
Newyears Green. G Lon 5H 21
New York. Linc 4K 37
New York. Tyne 4G 55
Nextend. Here 6B 26
Neyland. Pemb 6F 14
Nib Heath. Shrp 8C 34
Nicholashayne. Devn 4L 7
Nicholaston. Swan 8M 15
Nidd. N Yor 1M 41
Niddrie. Edin 2M 59
Niddry. W Lot 2J 59
Nigg. Aber 5J 73
Nigg. High 6J 79
Nigg Ferry. High 7H 79
Nightcott. Som 3H 7
Nimmer. Som 4B 8
Nine Ashes. Essx 3B 22
Ninebanks. Nmbd 6A 54
Nine Elms. Swin 5K 19
Ninemile Bar. Dum 4C 52
Nine Mile Burn. Midl 4K 59
Ninfield. E Sus 4D 12
Ningwood. IOW 7B 10
Nisbet. Bord 7D 60
Nisbet Hill. Bord 4E 60
Niton. IOW 8C 10
Nitshill. Glas 3D 58
Niwbwrch. IOA 4D 32
Nixon's Corner. Derr 3D 92
Noak Hill. G Lon 4B 22
Nobold. Shrp 8C 34
Nobottle. Nptn 5D 28
Nocton. Linc 3H 37
Nogdam End. Norf 1K 31
Noke. Oxon 2C 20
Nolton. Pemb 5E 14
Nolton Haven. Pemb 5E 14
No Man's Heath. Ches W 5D 34
No Man's Heath. Warw 1L 27
Nomansland. Devn 4H 7
Nomansland. Wilts 4L 9
Noneley. Shrp 7C 34
Noness. Shet 5E 90
Nonikiln. High 6G 79
Nonington. Kent 8J 23
Nook. Cumb
nr. Longtown 4J 53
nr. Milnthorpe 7D 46
Noranside. Ang 1H 67
Norbreck. Bkpl 3B 40
Norbridge. Here 7F 26
Norbury. Ches E 5D 34
Norbury. Derbs 5K 35
Norbury. Shrp 2B 26
Norbury. Staf 7F 34
Norby. N Yor 7B 48
Norby. Shet 2B 90
Norcross. Lanc 3B 40
Nordelph. Norf 1B 30
Norden. G Man 6G 41
Nordley. Shrp 2E 26
Norham. Nmbd 5G 61
Norland Town. W Yor 5J 41
Norley. Ches W 2D 34
Norleywood. Hants 6A 10
Normanby. N Lin 6F 42
Normanby. N Yor 7E 48
Normanby. Red C 4C 48
Normanby-by-Spital. Linc 1H 37
Normanby le Wold. Linc 8J 43
Norman Cross. Cambs 2J 29
Normandy. Surr 8G 21
Norman's Bay. E Sus 5C 12
Norman's Green. Devn 5K 7
Normanton. Derb 6M 35
Normanton. Leics 5F 36
Normanton. Notts 4E 36
Normanton. W Yor 5A 42
Normanton le Heath. Leics 8A 36
Normanton-on-Cliffe. Linc 5G 37
Normanton on Soar. Notts 7C 36
Normanton-on-the-Wolds. Notts 6D 36
Normanton on Trent. Notts 3E 36
Normoss. Lanc 4B 40
Norrington Common. Wilts 7G 19
Norris Green. Mers 8B 40
Norris Hill. Leics 8M 35
Norristhorpe. W Yor 5L 41
Northacre. Norf 2F 30
Northall. Buck 1G 21
Northallerton. N Yor 6A 48
Northam. Devn 3D 6
Northam. Sotn 4B 10
Northampton. Nptn 114 (5E 28)
North Anston. S Yor 1C 36
North Ascot. Brac 7G 21
North Aston. Oxon 1B 20
Northaw. Herts 3K 21
Northay. Som 4A 8
North Baddesley. Hants 3A 10
North Balfern. Dum 6K 51
North Ballachulish. High 1E 64
North Barrow. Som 3E 8
North Barsham. Norf 6F 38
Northbeck. Linc 5H 37
North Benfleet. Essx 5D 22
North Bersted. W Sus 5G 11
North Berwick. E Lot 1C 60
North Bitchburn. Dur 8E 54
North Blyth. Nmbd 3G 55
North Boarhunt. Hants 4D 10
North Bockhampton. Dors 6K 9
Northborough. Pet 1J 29
Northbourne. Kent 8K 23
Northbourne. Oxon 5C 20
North Bovey. Devn 7G 7
North Bowood. Dors 6C 8
North Bradley. Wilts 8G 19
North Brentor. Devn 7D 6
North Brewham. Som 2F 8
Northbrook. Oxon 1B 20
North Brook End. Cambs 7K 29
North Broomhill. Nmbd 1F 54
North Buckland. Devn 1D 6
North Burlingham. Norf 8K 39
North Cadbury. Som 3E 8
North Carlton. Linc 2G 37
North Cave. E Yor 4F 42
North Cerney. Glos 3J 19
North Chailey. E Sus 3L 11
Northchapel. W Sus 3G 11
North Charford. Hants 4K 9
North Charlton. Nmbd 7J 61
North Cheriton. Som 3E 8
North Chideock. Dors 6C 8
Northchurch. Herts 3G 21
North Cliffe. E Yor 4F 42
North Clifton. Notts 2F 36
North Close. Dur 8F 54
North Cockerington. Linc 8L 43
North Coker. Som 4D 8
North Collafirth. Shet 5H 91
North Common. E Sus 3L 11
North Commonty. Abers 1H 73
North Coombe. Devn 4H 7
North Cornelly. B'end 6H 17
North Cotes. Linc 7L 43
Northcott. Devn
nr. Boyton 6C 6
nr. Culmstock 4K 7
Northcourt. Oxon 4C 20
North Cove. Suff 3L 31
North Cowton. N Yor 5L 47
North Craigo. Ang 1K 67
North Crawley. Mil 7G 29
North Cray. G Lon 6A 22
North Creake. Norf 6E 38
North Curry. Som 3B 8
North Dalton. E Yor 2G 43
North Deighton. N Yor 2A 42
North Dronley. Ang 4G 67
North Duffield. N Yor 4D 42
Northdyke. Orkn 7B 88
Northedge. Derbs 3A 36
North Elkington. Linc 8K 43
North Elmham. Norf 7F 38
North Elmsall. W Yor 6B 42
North End. E Yor 4K 43
North End. Essx
nr. Great Dunmow 2C 22
nr. Great Yeldham 8D 30
North End. Hants 7B 20
North End. Leics 8C 36
North End. Linc 5K 37
North End. Norf 2F 30
North End. N Som 7C 18
North End. Port 5D 10
North End. W Sus 5J 11
North End. Wilts 4J 19
Northend. Buck 4E 20
Northend. Warw 6A 28
North Erradale. High 5J 77
North Evington. Leic 1D 28
North Fambridge. Essx 4E 22
North Fearns. High 2G 69
North Featherstone. W Yor 5B 42
North Feorline. N Ayr 7J 57
North Ferriby. E Yor 5G 43
Northfield. Aber 5H 73
Northfield. E Yor 5H 43
Northfield. Som 2A 8
Northfield. W Mid 4J 27
Northfleet. Kent 6C 22
North Frodingham. E Yor 2J 43
Northgate. Linc 7J 37
North Gluss. Shet 6H 91
North Gorley. Hants 4K 9
North Green. Norf 3J 31
North Green. Suff
nr. Framlingham 5K 31
nr. Halesworth 4K 31
nr. Saxmundham 5K 31
North Greetwell. Linc 2H 37
North Grimston. N Yor 1F 42
North Halling. Medw 7D 22
North Hayling. Hants 5E 10
North Hazelrigg. Nmbd 6H 61
North Heasley. Devn 2G 7
North Heath. W Sus 3H 11
North Hill. Corn 8B 6
North Holmwood. Surr 1J 11
North Huish. Devn 6K 5
North Hykeham. Linc 3G 37
Northiam. E Sus 3E 12
Northill. C Beds 7J 29
Northington. Hants 2C 10
North Kelsey. Linc 7H 43
North Kelsey Moor. Linc 7H 43
North Kessock. High 1G 71
North Killingholme. N Lin 6J 43
North Kilvington. N Yor 7B 48
North Kilworth. Leics 3D 28
North Kyme. Linc 4J 37
North Lancing. W Sus 5J 11
Northlands. Linc 4L 37
Northleach. Glos 2K 19
North Lee. Buck 3F 20
North Lees. N Yor 8L 47
North Leigh. Kent 1H 13
North Leigh. Oxon 2A 20
Northleigh. Devn
nr. Barnstaple 2F 6
nr. Honiton 6L 7
North Leverton. Notts 1E 36
Northlew. Devn 6E 6
North Littleton. Worc 7J 27
North Lopham. Norf 3G 31
North Luffenham. Rut 1G 29
North Marden. W Sus 4F 10
North Marston. Buck 1E 20
North Middleton. Midl 4A 60
North Middleton. Nmbd 7H 61
North Molton. Devn 3G 7
North Moor. N Yor 7G 49
Northmoor. Oxon 3B 20
Northmoor Green. Som 2B 8
North Moreton. Oxon 5C 20
Northmuir. Ang 2G 67
North Mundham. W Sus 5F 10
North Murie. Per 5F 66
North Muskham. Notts 4E 36
North Ness. Orkn 2E 86
North Newbald. E Yor 4G 43
North Newington. Oxon 8B 28
North Newnton. Wilts 8K 19
North Newton. Som 2A 8
Northney. Hants 5E 10
North Nibley. Glos 4F 18
North Oakley. Hants 8C 20
North Ockendon. G Lon 5B 22
Northolt. G Lon 5J 21
Northop. Flin 4M 33
Northop Hall. Flin 3A 34
North Ormesby. Midd 4C 48
North Ormsby. Linc 8K 43
Northorpe. Linc
nr. Bourne 8H 37
nr. Donington 6K 37
nr. Gainsborough 8F 42
North Otterington. N Yor 7A 48
Northover. Som
nr. Glastonbury 2C 8
nr. Yeovil 3D 8
North Owersby. Linc 8H 43
Northowram. W Yor 5K 41
North Perrott. Som 5C 8
North Petherton. Som 2A 8
North Petherwin. Corn 7B 6
North Pickenham. Norf 1E 30
North Piddle. Worc 6H 27
North Poorton. Dors 6D 8
North Port. Arg 5E 64
Northport. Dors 7H 9
North Queensferry. Fife 1K 59
North Radworthy. Devn 2G 7
North Rauceby. Linc 5H 37
Northrepps. Norf 6J 39
North Rigton. N Yor 3L 41
North Rode. Ches E 3G 35
North Roe. Shet 5H 91
North Ronaldsay Airport. Orkn 4G 89
North Row. Cumb 8G 53
North Runcton. Norf 8C 38
North Sannox. N Ayr 5K 57
North Scale. Cumb 7L 45
North Scarle. Linc 3F 36
North Seaton. Nmbd 3F 54
North Seaton Colliery. Nmbd 3F 54
North Sheen. G Lon 6J 21
North Shian. Arg 3D 64
North Shields. Tyne 5G 55
North Shoebury. S'end 5F 22
North Shore. Bkpl 4B 40
North Side. Cumb 2K 45
North Skelton. Red C 4D 48
North Somercotes. Linc 8M 43
North Stainley. N Yor 8L 47
North Stainmore. Cumb 4G 47
North Stifford. Thur 5C 22
North Stoke. Bath 7F 18
North Stoke. Oxon 5D 20
North Stoke. W Sus 4H 11
Northstowe. Cambs 5M 29
North Street. Hants 2D 10
North Street. Kent 8G 23
North Street. Medw 6E 22
North Street. W Ber 6D 20
North Sunderland. Nmbd 6K 61
North Tamerton. Corn 6C 6
North Tawton. Devn 5F 6
North Thoresby. Linc 8K 43
North Tidworth. Wilts 1L 9
North Town. Devn 5E 6
North Town. Shet 6D 90
Northtown. Orkn 2F 86
North Tuddenham. Norf 8G 39
North Walbottle. Tyne 5E 54
Northwall. Orkn 5G 89
North Walney. Cumb 8L 45
North Walsham. Norf 6J 39
North Waltham. Hants 1C 10
North Warnborough. Hants 8E 20
North Water Bridge. Ang 1K 67
North Watten. High 6D 86
Northway. Glos 8H 27
Northway. Swan 6E 16
North Weald Bassett. Essx 3B 22
North Weston. N Som 6C 18
North Weston. Oxon 3D 20
North Wheatley. Notts 1E 36
North Whilborough. Devn 5L 5
Northwich. Ches W 2E 34
North Wick. Bath 7D 18
Northwick. Som 1B 8
Northwick. S Glo 5D 18
North Widcombe. Bath 8D 18
North Willingham. Linc 1J 37
North Wingfield. Derbs 3B 36
North Witham. Linc 7G 37
Northwold. Norf 2D 30
Northwood. Derbs 3L 35
Northwood. G Lon 4H 21
Northwood. IOW 6B 10
Northwood. Kent 7K 23
Northwood. Shrp 6C 34
Northwood. Stoke 5G 35
Northwood Green. Glos 2F 18
North Wootton. Dors 4E 8
North Wootton. Norf 7C 38
North Wootton. Som 1D 8
North Wraxall. Wilts 6G 19
North Wroughton. Swin 5K 19
North Yardhope. Nmbd 1C 54
Norton. Devn 6L 5
Norton. Glos 1G 19
Norton. Hal 1D 34
Norton. Herts 8K 29
Norton. IOW 7M 9
Norton. Mon 1C 18
Norton. Nptn 5D 28
Norton. Notts 2C 36
Norton. Powy 5B 26
Norton. Shrp
nr. Ludlow 3C 26
nr. Madeley 1F 26
nr. Shrewsbury 1D 26
Norton. S Yor
nr. Askern 6C 42
nr. Sheffield 1A 36
Norton. Stoc T 3B 48
Norton. Suff 5F 30
Norton. Swan 6F 16
Norton. W Sus
nr. Selsey 6F 10
nr. Westergate 5G 11
Norton. Wilts 5G 19
Norton. Worc
nr. Evesham 7J 27
nr. Worcester 6G 27
Norton Bavant. Wilts 1H 9
Norton Bridge. Staf 6G 35
Norton Canes. Staf 1J 27
Norton Canon. Here 7B 26
Norton Corner. Norf 7G 39
Norton Disney. Linc 4F 36
Norton East. Staf 1J 27
Norton Ferris. Wilts 2F 8
Norton Fitzwarren. Som 3M 7
Norton Green. IOW 7M 9
Norton Green. Stoke 4H 35
Norton Hawkfield. Bath 7D 18
Norton Heath. Essx 3B 22
Norton in Hales. Shrp 6F 34
Norton in the Moors. Stoke 4G 35
Norton-Juxta-Twycross. Leics 1M 27
Norton-le-Clay. N Yor 8B 48
Norton Lindsey. Warw 5L 27
Norton Little Green. Suff 5F 30
Norton Malreward. Bath 7E 18
Norton Mandeville. Essx 3B 22
Norton-on-Derwent. N Yor 8E 48
Norton St Philip. Som 8F 18
Norton Subcourse. Norf 2L 31
Norton sub Hamdon. Som 4C 8
Norton Woodseats. S Yor 1A 36
Norwell. Notts 3E 36
Norwell Woodhouse. Notts 3E 36
Norwich. Norf 114 (1J 31)
Norwich Airport. Norf 8J 39
Norwick. Shet 2L 91
Norwood. Derbs 1B 36
Norwood Green. W Yor 5K 41
Norwood Hill. Surr 1K 11
Norwood Park. Som 2D 8
Norwoodside. Cambs 2M 29
Noseley. Leics 2E 28
Noss. Shet 6D 90
Noss Mayo. Devn 7H 5
Nosterfield. N Yor 7L 47
Nostie. High 3K 69
Notgrove. Glos 1K 19
Nottage. B'end 7H 17
Nottingham. Nott 114 (5C 36)
Nottington. Dors 7E 8
Notton. Dors 6E 8
Notton. W Yor 6M 41
Notton. Wilts 7H 19
Nounsley. Essx 2D 22
Noutard's Green. Worc 5F 26
Nox. Shrp 8C 34
Noyadd Trefawr. Cdgn 2J 15
Nuffield. Oxon 5D 20
Nunburnholme. E Yor 3F 42
Nuncargate. Notts 4C 36
Nunclose. Cumb 7J 53
Nuneaton. Warw 2A 28
Nuneham Courtenay. Oxon 4C 20
Nun Monkton. N Yor 2C 42
Nunnerie. S Lan 8H 59
Nunney. Som 1F 8
Nunnington. N Yor 8D 48
Nunnykirk. Nmbd 2D 54
Nunsthorpe. NE Lin 7K 43
Nunthorpe. Midd 4C 48
Nunthorpe. York 2C 42
Nunton. Wilts 3K 9
Nunwick. Nmbd 4B 54
Nunwick. N Yor 8M 47
Nupend. Glos 3F 18
Nursling. Hants 4A 10
Nursted. Hants 3E 10
Nursteed. Wilts 7J 19
Nurston. V Glam 8K 17
Nutbourne. W Sus
nr. Chichester 5E 10
nr. Pulborough 4H 11
Nutfield. Surr 8L 21
Nuthall. Notts 5C 36
Nuthampstead. Herts 8M 29
Nuthurst. Warw 4K 27
Nuthurst. W Sus 3J 11
Nutley. E Sus 3M 11
Nuttall. G Man 6F 40
Nutwell. S Yor 7D 42
Nybster. High 5E 86
Nyetimber. W Sus 6F 10
Nyewood. W Sus 3F 10
Nymet Rowland. Devn 5G 7
Nymet Tracey. Devn 5G 7
Nympsfield. Glos 3G 19
Nynehead. Som 3L 7
Nyton. W Sus 5G 11

O

Oadby. Leics 1D 28
Oad Street. Kent 7E 22
Oakamoor. Staf 5J 35
Oakbank. Arg 4B 64
Oakbank. W Lot 3J 59
Oakdale. Cphy 5L 17
Oakdale. Pool 6J 9
Oake. Som 3L 7
Oaken. Staf 1G 27
Oakenclough. Lanc 3D 40
Oakengates. Telf 8E 34
Oakenholt. Flin 2A 34
Oakenshaw. Dur 8F 54
Oakenshaw. W Yor 5K 41
Oakerthorpe. Derbs 4A 36
Oakford. Cdgn 1L 15
Oakford. Devn 3J 7
Oakfordbridge. Devn 3J 7
Oakgrove. Ches E 3H 35
Oakham. Rut 1F 28
Oakhanger. Ches E 4F 34
Oakhanger. Hants 2E 10
Oakhill. Som 1E 8
Oakington. Cambs 5M 29
Oaklands. Powy 7K 25
Oakle Street. Glos 2F 18
Oakley. Bed 6H 29
Oakley. Buck 2D 20
Oakley. Fife 1J 59
Oakley. Hants 8C 20
Oakley. Suff 4H 31
Oakley Green. Wind 6G 21
Oakley Park. Powy 4J 25
Oakmere. Ches W 3D 34
Oakridge Lynch. Glos 3H 19
Oaks. Shrp 1C 26
Oaksey. Wilts 4H 19
Oaks Green. Derbs 6K 35
Oakshaw Ford. Cumb 4K 53
Oakshott. Hants 3E 10
Oakthorpe. Leics 8M 35
Oak Tree. Darl 4A 48
Oakwood. Derb 6A 36
Oakwood. W Yor 4M 41
Oakwoodhill. Surr 2J 11
Oakworth. W Yor 4J 41
Oape. High 3E 78
Oare. Kent 7G 23
Oare. Som 1H 7
Oare. W Ber 6C 20
Oare. Wilts 7K 19
Oareford. Som 1H 7
Oasby. Linc 6H 37
Oath. Som 3B 8
Oathlaw. Ang 2H 67
Oatlands. N Yor 2M 41
Oban. Arg 115 (5C 64)
Oban. W Isl 3C 76
Oborne. Dors 4E 8
Obsdale. High 7G 79
Obthorpe. Linc 8H 37
Occlestone Green. Ches W 3E 34
Occold. Suff 4H 31
Ochiltree. E Ayr 7D 58
Ochtermuthill. Per 6B 66
Ochtertyre. Per 5B 66
Ockbrook. Derbs 6B 36
Ockeridge. Worc 5F 26
Ockham. Surr 8H 21
Ockle. High 8G 69
Ockley. Surr 1J 11
Ocle Pychard. Here 7D 26
Octofad. Arg 4B 56
Octomore. Arg 4B 56
Octon. E Yor 1H 43
Odcombe. Som 4D 8
Odd Down. Bath 7F 18
Oddingley. Worc 6H 27
Oddington. Oxon 2C 20
Oddsta. Shet 4K 91
Odell. Bed 6G 29
Odie. Orkn 7F 88
Odiham. Hants 8E 20
Odsey. Cambs 8K 29
Odstock. Wilts 3K 9
Odstone. Leics 1A 28
Offchurch. Warw 5A 28
Offenham. Worc 7J 27
Offenham Cross. Worc 7J 27
Offerton. G Man 1H 35
Offerton. Tyne 6G 55
Offham. E Sus 4L 11
Offham. Kent 8C 22
Offham. W Sus 5H 11
Offleyhay. Staf 7G 35
Offley Hoo. Herts 1J 21
Offleymarsh. Staf 7F 34
Offord Cluny. Cambs 5K 29
Offord D'Arcy. Cambs 5K 29
Offton. Suff 7G 31
Offwell. Devn 6L 7
Ogbourne Maizey. Wilts 6K 19
Ogbourne St Andrew. Wilts 6K 19
Ogbourne St George. Wilts 6L 19
Ogden. G Man 6H 41
Ogle. Nmbd 4E 54
Ogmore. V Glam 7H 17
Ogmore-by-Sea. V Glam 7H 17
Ogmore Vale. B'end 5J 17
Okeford Fitzpaine. Dors 4G 9
Okehampton. Devn 6E 6
Okehampton Camp. Devn 6E 6
Okraquoy. Shet 4E 90
Okus. Swin 5K 19
Old. Nptn 4E 28
Old Aberdeen. Aber 5J 73
Old Alresford. Hants 2C 10
Oldany. High 8D 84
Old Arley. Warw 2L 27
Old Basford. Nott 5C 36
Old Basing. Hants 8D 20
Oldberrow. Warw 5K 27
Old Bewick. Nmbd 7H 61
Old Bexley. G Lon 6A 22
Old Blair. Per 1B 66
Old Bolingbroke. Linc 3L 37
Oldborough. Devn 5G 7
Old Brampton. Derbs 2M 35
Old Bridge of Tilt. Per 1B 66
Old Bridge of Urr. Dum 5B 52
Old Brumby. N Lin 7F 42
Old Buckenham. Norf 2G 31
Old Burghclere. Hants 8B 20
Oldbury. Shrp 2F 26
Oldbury. Warw 2M 27
Oldbury. W Mid 3H 27
Oldbury-on-Severn. S Glo 4E 18
Oldbury on the Hill. Glos 5G 19
Old Byland. N Yor 7C 48
Old Cassop. Dur 8G 55
Oldcastle. Mon 1B 18
Oldcastle Heath. Ches W 5C 34
Old Catton. Norf 8J 39
Old Clee. NE Lin 7K 43
Old Cleeve. Som 1K 7
Old Colwyn. Cnwy 3H 33
Oldcotes. Notts 1C 36
Old Coulsdon. G Lon 8L 21
Old Dailly. S Ayr 2H 51
Old Dalby. Leics 7D 36
Old Dam. Derbs 2K 35
Old Deer. Abers 1J 73
Old Dilton. Wilts 1G 9
Old Down. S Glo 5E 18
Oldeamere. Cambs 2L 29
Old Edlington. S Yor 8C 42
Old Eldon. Dur 3L 47
Old Ellerby. E Yor 4J 43
Old Fallings. W Mid 1H 27
Oldfallow. Staf 8H 35
Old Felixstowe. Suff 8K 31
Oldfield. Shrp 3E 26
Oldfield. Worc 5G 27
Old Fletton. Pet 2J 29
Oldford. Som 8F 18
Old Forge. Here 2D 18
Old Glossop. Derbs 8J 41
Old Goole. E Yor 5E 42
Old Gore. Here 1E 18
Old Graitney. Dum 5H 53
Old Grimsby. IOS 1G 3
Oldhall. High 6D 86
Old Hall Street. Norf 6K 39
Oldham. G Man 7H 41
Oldhamstocks. E Lot 2E 60
Old Heathfield. E Sus 3B 12
Old Hill. W Mid 3H 27
Old Hunstanton. Norf 5C 38
Oldhurst. Cambs 4K 29
Old Hutton. Cumb 7D 46
Old Kea. Corn 4M 3
Old Kilpatrick. W Dun 2C 58
Old Kinnernie. Abers 5G 73
Old Knebworth. Herts 1K 21
Oldland. S Glo 6E 18
Old Laxey. IOM 6D 44
Old Leake. Linc 4M 37
Old Lenton. Nott 6C 36
Old Llanberis. Gwyn 5F 32
Old Malton. N Yor 8E 48
Oldmeldrum. Abers 3H 73
Old Micklefield. W Yor 4B 42
Old Mill. Corn 8C 6
Oldmixon. N Som 8B 18
Old Monkland. N Lan 3F 58
Old Newton. Suff 5G 31
Old Park. Telf 1E 26
Old Pentland. Midl 3L 59
Old Philpstoun. W Lot 2J 59
Old Quarrington. Dur 8G 55
Old Radnor. Powy 6A 26
Old Rayne. Abers 3F 72
Oldridge. Devn 6H 7
Old Romney. Kent 3G 13
Old Scone. Per 5E 66
Oldshore Beg. High 6D 84
Oldshoremore. High 6E 84
Old Snydale. W Yor 5B 42
Old Sodbury. S Glo 5F 18
Old Somerby. Linc 6G 37
Old Spital. Dur 4H 47
Oldstead. N Yor 7C 48
Old Stratford. Nptn 7E 28
Old Swan. Mers 8B 40
Old Swarland. Nmbd 1E 54
Old Tebay. Cumb 5E 46
Old Town. Cumb 7J 53
Old Town. E Sus 6B 12
Old Town. IOS 1H 3
Old Town. Nmbd 2B 54
Oldtown. High 5F 78
Old Trafford. G Man 8G 41
Old Tupton. Derbs 3A 36
Oldwall. Cumb 5J 53
Oldwalls. Swan 7L 15
Old Warden. C Beds 7J 29
Oldways End. Som 3H 7
Old Westhall. Abers 3F 72
Old Weston. Cambs 4H 29
Oldwhat. Abers 8H 81
Old Windsor. Wind 6G 21
Old Wives Lees. Kent 8G 23
Old Woking. Surr 8H 21
Oldwood Common. Worc 5D 26
Old Woodstock. Oxon 2B 20
Olgrinmore. High 6B 86
Oliver's Battery. Hants 3B 10
Ollaberry. Shet 5H 91
Ollerton. Ches E 2F 34
Ollerton. Notts 3D 36
Ollerton. Shrp 7E 34
Olmarch. Cdgn 7F 24
Olmstead Green. Cambs 7C 30
Olney. Mil 6F 28
Olrig. High 5C 86
Olton. W Mid 3K 27
Olveston. S Glo 5E 18
Omagh. Ferm 5D 92
Ombersley. Worc 5G 27
Ompton. Notts 3D 36
Omunsgarth. Shet 3D 90
onchan. IOM 7D 44
onecote. Staf 4J 35
onehouse. Suff 6G 31
onen. Mon 2C 18
ongar Hill. Norf 7B 38
ongar Street. Here 5B 26
onibury. Shrp 4C 26
onich. High 1E 64
onllwyn. Neat 3H 17
onneley. Staf 5F 34
onslow Green. Essx 2C 22
onslow Village. Surr 1G 11
onthank. E Ayr 6C 58
Openwoodgate. Derbs 5A 36
Opinan. High
nr. Gairloch 6J 77
nr. Laide 4K 77
Orasaigh. W Isl 2E 76
Orbost. High 1D 68
Orby. Linc 3A 38
Orchard Hill. Devn 3D 6
Orchard Portman. Som 3M 7
Orcheston. Wilts 1J 9
Orcop. Here 1C 18
Orcop Hill. Here 1C 18
Ord. High 4H 69
Ordale. Shet 3L 91
Ordhead. Abers 4F 72
Ordie. Abers 5D 72
Ordiquish. Mor 8C 80
Ordley. Nmbd 6C 54
Ordsall. Notts 2E 36
Ore. E Sus 4E 12
Oreton. Shrp 3E 26
Orford. Suff 7L 31
Orford. Warr 8E 40
Organford. Dors 6H 9
Orgil. Orkn 1D 86
Orgreave. Staf 8K 35
Oridge Street. Glos 1F 18
Orlestone. Kent 2F 12
Orleton. Here 5C 26
Orleton. Worc 5E 26
Orleton Common. Here 5C 26
Orlingbury. Nptn 4F 28
Ormacleit. W Isl 2D 74
Ormathwaite. Cumb 3A 46
Ormesby. Red C 4C 48
Ormesby St Margaret. Norf 8L 39
Ormesby St Michael. Norf 8L 39
Ormiscaig. High 4K 77
Ormiston. E Lot 3B 60
Ormsaigbeg. High 1K 63
Ormsaigmore. High 1K 63
Ormsary. Arg 2G 57
Ormsgill. Cumb 7L 45
Ormskirk. Lanc 7C 40
Orphir. Orkn 1E 86
Orpington. G Lon 7A 22
Orrell. G Man 7D 40
Orrell. Mers 8B 40
Orrisdale. IOM 5C 44
Orsett. Thur 5C 22
Orslow. Staf 8G 35
Orston. Notts 5E 36
Orthwaite. Cumb 8G 53
Orton. Cumb 5E 46
Orton. Mor 8C 80
Orton. Nptn 4F 28
Orton. Staf 2G 27
Orton Longueville. Pet 2J 29
Orton-on-the-Hill. Leics 1M 27
Orton Waterville. Pet 2J 29
Orton Wistow. Pet 2J 29
Orwell. Cambs 6L 29
Osbaldeston. Lanc 4E 40
Osbaldwick. York 2D 42
Osbaston. Leics 1B 28
Osbaston. Shrp 7B 34
Osbournby. Linc 6H 37
Osclay. High 8D 86
Oscroft. Ches W 3D 34
Ose. High 1E 68
Osgathorpe. Leics 8B 36
Osgodby. Linc 8H 43
Osgodby. N Yor
nr. Scarborough 7H 49
nr. Selby 4D 42
Oskaig. High 2G 69
Oskamull. Arg 4K 63
Osleston. Derbs 6L 35
Osmaston. Derb 6A 36
Osmaston. Derbs 5L 35
Osmington. Dors 7F 8
Osmington Mills. Dors 7F 8
Osmondthorpe. W Yor 4M 41
Osmondwall. Orkn 3E 86
Osmotherley. N Yor 6B 48
Osnaburgh. Fife 6H 67
Ospisdale. High 5H 79
Ospringe. Kent 7G 23
Ossett. W Yor 5L 41
Ossington. Notts 3E 36
Ostend. Essx 4F 22
Ostend. Norf 6K 39
Osterley. G Lon 6J 21
Oswaldkirk. N Yor 8D 48
Oswaldtwistle. Lanc 5F 40
Oswestry. Shrp 7A 34
Otby. Linc 8J 43
Otford. Kent 8B 22
Otham. Kent 8D 22
Otherton. Staf 8H 35

Othery – Pound Hill

Othery. Som 2B 8
Otley. Suff 6J 31
Otley. W Yor 3L 41
Otterbourne. Hants 3B 10
Otterburn. Nmbd 2B 54
Otterburn. N Yor 2G 41
Otterburn Camp. Nmbd 2B 54
Otterburn Hall. Nmbd 2B 54
Otter Ferry. Arg 1J 57
Otterford. Som 4M 7
Otterham. Corn 6A 6
Otterhampton. Som 1M 7
Otterham Quay. Medw 7E 22
Ottershaw. Surr 7H 21
Otterspool. Mers 1B 34
Otterswick. Shet 5K 91
Otterton. Devn 7K 7
Otterwood. Hants 5B 10
Ottery St Mary. Devn 6K 7
Ottinge. Kent 1H 13
Ottringham. E Yor 5K 43
Oughterby. Cumb 6G 53
Oughtershaw. N Yor 7G 47
Oughterside. Cumb 7F 52
Oughtibridge. S Yor 8M 41
Oughtrington. Warr 1E 34
Oulston. N Yor 8C 48
Oulton. Cumb 6G 53
Oulton. Norf 7H 39
Oulton. Staf
nr. Gnosall Heath 7F 34
nr. Stone 6H 35
Oulton. Suff 2M 31
Oulton. W Yor 5A 42
Oulton Broad. Suff 2M 31
Oulton Street. Norf 7H 39
Oundle. Nptn 3H 29
Ousby. Cumb 8L 53
Ousdale. High 2L 79
Ousden. Suff 6D 30
Ousefleet. E Yor 5F 42
Ouston. Dur 6F 54
Ouston. Nmbd
nr. Bearsbridge 6A 54
nr. Stamfordham 4D 54
Outer Hope. Devn 7J 5
Outertown. Orkn 8B 88
Outgate. Cumb 6B 46
Outhgill. Cumb 5F 46
Outlands. Staf 6F 34
Outlane. W Yor 6J 41
Out Newton. E Yor 5L 43
Out Rawcliffe. Lanc 3C 40
Outwell. Norf 1B 30
Outwick. Hants 4K 9
Outwood. Surr 1L 11
Outwood. W Yor 5M 41
Outwood. Worc 4H 27
Outwoods. Leics 8B 36
Outwoods. Staf 8F 34
Ouzlewell Green. W Yor 5M 41
Ovenden. W Yor 5J 41
Over. Cambs 4L 29
Over. Ches W 3E 34
Over. Glos 2G 19
Over. S Glo 5D 18
Overbister. Orkn 5F 88
Over Burrows. Derbs 6L 35
Overbury. Worc 8H 27
Overcombe. Dors 7E 8
Over Compton. Dors 4D 8
Over End. Cambs 2H 29
Over Finlarg. Ang 3H 67
Over Green. Warw 2K 27
Overgreen. Derbs 2M 35
Over Haddon. Derbs 3L 35
Over Hulton. G Man 7E 40
Over Kellet. Lanc 8D 46
Over Kiddington. Oxon 1B 20
Overleigh. Som 2C 8
Overley. Staf 8K 35
Over Monnow. Mon 2D 18
Over Norton. Oxon 1M 19
Over Peover. Ches E 2F 34
Overpool. Ches W 2B 34
Overscaig. High 1E 78
Overseal. Derbs 8L 35
Over Silton. N Yor 6B 48
Oversland. Kent 8G 23
Overstone. Nptn 5F 28
Over Stowey. Som 2L 7
Overstrand. Norf 5J 39
Over Stratton. Som 4C 8
Over Street. Wilts 2J 9
Overthorpe. Nptn 7B 28
Overton. Aber 4H 73
Overton. Ches W 2D 34
Overton. Hants 1C 10
Overton. High 8D 86
Overton. Lanc 2C 40
Overton. N Yor 2C 42
Overton. Shrp
nr. Bridgnorth 3E 26
nr. Ludlow 4D 26
Overton. Swan 8L 15
Overton. W Yor 6L 41
Overton. Wrex 5B 34
Overtown. Lanc 8E 46
Overtown. N Lan 4G 59
Overtown. Swin 6K 19
Over Wallop. Hants 2L 9
Over Whitacre. Warw 2L 27
Over Worton. Oxon 1B 20
Oving. Buck 1E 20
Oving. W Sus 5G 11
Ovingdean. Brig 5L 11
Ovingham. Nmbd 5D 54
Ovington. Dur 4K 47
Ovington. Essx 7D 30
Ovington. Hants 2C 10
Ovington. Norf 1F 30
Ovington. Nmbd 5D 54
Owen's Bank. Staf 7L 35
Ower. Hants
nr. Holbury 5B 10
nr. Totton 4M 9
Owermoigne. Dors 7F 8
Owlbury. Shrp 2B 26
Owler Bar. Derbs 2L 35
Owlerton. S Yor 8M 41
Owlsmoor. Brac 7F 20
Owlswick. Buck 3E 20
Owmby. Linc 7H 43
Owmby-by-Spital. Linc 1H 37
Ownham. W Ber 6B 20
Owrytn. Wrex 5B 34
Owslebury. Hants 3C 10
Owston. Leics 1E 28
Owston. S Yor 6C 42
Owston Ferry. N Lin 7F 42
Owstwick. E Yor 4K 43
Owthorne. E Yor 5L 43
Owthorpe. Notts 6D 36
Owton Manor. Hart 3B 48
Oxborough. Norf 1D 30
Oxbridge. Dors 6C 8
Oxcombe. Linc 2L 37
Oxen End. Essx 1C 22
Oxenhall. Glos 1F 18
Oxenholme. Cumb 6D 46
Oxenhope. W Yor 4J 41
Oxen Park. Cumb 7B 46
Oxenpill. Som 1C 8
Oxenton. Glos 8H 27
Oxenwood. Wilts 8M 19
Oxford. Oxon 114 (3C 20)
Oxgangs. Edin 3L 59
Oxhey. Herts 4J 21
Oxhill. Warw 7M 27
Oxley. W Mid 1H 27
Oxley Green. Essx 2F 22
Oxley's Green. E Sus 3C 12
Oxlode. Cambs 3A 30
Oxnam. Bord 8E 60
Oxshott. Surr 7J 21
Oxspring. S Yor 7L 41
Oxted. Surr 8L 21
Oxton. Mers 1B 34
Oxton. N Yor 3C 42
Oxton. Notts 4D 36
Oxton. Bord 4B 60
Oxwich. Swan 8L 15
Oxwich Green. Swan 8L 15
Oxwick. Norf 7F 38
Oykel Bridge. High 3D 78
Oyne. Abers 3F 72
Oystermouth. Swan 6F 16
Ozleworth. Glos 4F 18

P

Pabail Iarach. W Isl 8J 83
Pabail Uarach. W Isl 8J 83
Pachesham Park. Surr 8J 21
Packers Hill. Dors 4F 8
Packington. Leics 8A 36
Packmoor. Stoke 4G 35
Packmores. Warw 5L 27
Packwood. W Mid 4K 27
Packwood Gullet. W Mid 4K 27
Padanaram. Ang 2H 67
Padbury. Buck 8E 28
Paddington. G Lon 5K 21
Paddington. Warr 1E 34
Paddlesworth. Kent 2H 13
Paddock. Kent 8F 22
Paddockhole. Dum 3G 53
Paddock Wood. Kent 1C 12
Paddolgreen. Shrp 6D 34
Padeswood. Flin 3A 34
Padiham. Lanc 4F 40
Padside. N Yor 2K 41
Padson. Devn 6E 6
Padstow. Corn 4B 4
Padworth. W Ber 7D 20
Page Bank. Dur 8F 54
Pagham. W Sus 6F 10
Paglesham Churchend.
Essx 4F 22
Paglesham Eastend. Essx 4F 22
Paibeil. W Isl
on North Uist 7J 75
on Taransay 4B 76
Paiblesgearraidh. W Isl 7J 75
Paignton. Torb 5L 5
Pailton. Warw 3B 28
Paine's Corner. E Sus 3C 12
Painleyhill. Staf 6J 35
Painscastle. Powy 8L 25
Painshawfield. Nmbd 5D 54
Painsthorpe. E Yor 2F 42
Painswick. Glos 3G 19
Painter's Forstal. Kent 8F 22
Painthorpe. W Yor 6M 41
Pairc Shiaboist. W Isl 7F 82
Paisley. Ren 3C 58
Pakefield. Suff 2M 31
Pakenham. Suff 5F 30
Pale. Gwyn 7J 33
Palehouse Common. E Sus 4A 12
Palestine. Hants 1L 9
Paley Street. Wind 6F 20
Palgowan. Dum 3J 51
Palgrave. Suff 4H 31
Pallington. Dors 6F 8
Palmarsh. Kent 2H 13
Palmer Moor. Derbs 6K 35
Palmers Cross. W Mid 1G 27
Palmerstown. V Glam 8L 17
Palnackie. Dum 6C 52
Palnure. Dum 5K 51
Palterton. Derbs 3B 36
Pamber End. Hants 8D 20
Pamber Green. Hants 8D 20
Pamber Heath. Hants 7D 20
Pamington. Glos 8H 27
Pamphill. Dors 5H 9
Pampisford. Cambs 7A 30
Panborough. Som 1C 8
Panbride. Ang 4J 67
Pancrasweek. Devn 5B 6
Pandy. Gwyn
nr. Bala 7H 33
nr. Tywyn 2F 24
Pandy. Mon 1B 18
Pandy. Powy 2J 25
Pandy. Wrex 7L 33
Pandy Tudur. Cnwy 4H 33
Panfield. Essx 1D 22
Pangbourne. W Ber 6D 20
Pannal. N Yor 2M 41
Pannal Ash. N Yor 2L 41
Pannanich. Abers 6C 72
Pant. Shrp 7A 34
Pant. Wrex 5A 34
Pantasaph. Flin 3L 33
Pant Glas. Gwyn 6D 32
Pant-glas. Shrp 6A 34
Pantgwyn. Carm 2E 16
Pantgwyn. Cdgn 2J 15
Pant-lasau. Swan 4F 16
Panton. Linc 2J 37
Pant-pastynog. Den 4K 33
Pantperthog. Gwyn 2G 25
Pant-teg. Carm 4L 15
Pant-y-Caws. Carm 4H 15
Pant-y-dwr. Powy 5J 25
Pant-y-ffridd. Powy 2L 25
Pantyffynnon. Carm 3F 16
Pantygasseg. Torf 3A 18
Pant-y-llyn. Carm 3F 16
Pant-yr-awel. B'end 6J 17
Pant y Wacco. Flin 3L 33
Panxworth. Norf 8K 39
Papa Stour Airport. Shet 2B 90
Papa Westray Airport. Orkn 4D 88
Papcastle. Cumb 8F 52
Papigoe. High 6E 86
Papil. Shet 4D 90
Papple. E Lot 2C 60
Papplewick. Notts 4C 36
Papworth Everard. Cambs 5K 29
Papworth St Agnes. Cambs 5K 29
Par. Corn 6C 4
Paramour Street. Kent 7J 23
Parbold. Lanc 6C 40
Parbrook. Som 2D 8
Parbrook. W Sus 3H 11
Parc. Gwyn 7H 33
Parcllyn. Cdgn 1J 15
Parc-Seymour. Newp 4C 18
Pardown. Hants 1C 10
Pardshaw. Cumb 2K 45
Parham. Suff 5K 31
Park. Abers 6G 73
Park. Arg 3D 64
Park. Derr 3D 92
Park. Dum 2D 52
Park Bottom. Corn 4K 3
Parkburn. Abers 2G 73
Park Corner. E Sus 2B 12
Park Corner. Oxon 5D 20
Park End. Nmbd 4B 54
Parkend. Glos 3E 18
Parkeston. Essx 8J 31
Parkfield. Corn 5F 4
Park Gate. Hants 5C 10
Park Gate. Worc 4H 27
Parkgate. Ant 4H 93
Parkgate. Ches W 2A 34
Parkgate. Cumb 7G 53
Parkgate. Dum 3E 52
Parkgate. Surr 1K 11
Parkhall. W Dun 2C 58
Parkham. Devn 3C 6
Parkham Ash. Devn 3C 6
Parkhead. Cumb 7H 53
Parkhead. Glas 3E 58
Park Hill. Mers 7C 40
Parkhouse. Mon 3D 18
Parkhurst. IOW 6B 10
Park Lane. G Man 7F 40
Park Lane. Staf 1G 27
Park Mill. W Yor 6L 41
Parkmill. Swan 8M 15
Parkneuk. Abers 8G 73
Parkside. N Lan 4G 59
Parkstone. Pool 6J 9
Park Street. Herts 3J 21
Park Street. W Sus 2J 11
Park Town. Oxon 3C 20
Park Village. Nmbd 5L 53
Parkway. Here 8F 26
Parley Cross. Dors 6J 9
Parmoor. Buck 5E 20
Parr. Mers 8D 40
Parracombe. Devn 1F 6
Parrog. Pemb 3G 15
Parsonage Green. Essx 2D 22
Parsonby. Cumb 8F 52
Parson Cross. S Yor 8M 41
Parson Drove. Cambs 1L 29
Partick. Glas 3D 58
Partington. G Man 8F 40
Partney. Linc 3M 37
Parton. Cumb
nr. Whitehaven 2J 45
nr. Wigton 6G 53
Parton. Dum 4A 52
Partridge Green. W Sus 4J 11
Parwich. Derbs 4K 35
Passenham. Nptn 8E 28
Passfield. Hants 2F 10
Passingford Bridge. Essx 4B 22
Paston. Norf 6K 39
Pasturefields. Staf 7H 35
Patchacott. Devn 6D 6
Patcham. Brig 5L 11
Patchetts Green. Herts 4J 21
Patching. W Sus 5H 11
Patchole. Devn 1F 6
Patchway. S Glo 5E 18
Pateley Bridge. N Yor 1K 41
Pathe. Som 2B 8
Pathfinder Village. Devn 6H 7
Pathhead. Abers 1L 67
Pathhead. E Ayr 8E 58
Pathhead. Fife 8F 66
Pathhead. Midl 3A 60
Pathlow. Warw 6K 27
Path of Condie. Per 6D 66
Pathstruie. Per 6D 66
Patmore Heath. Herts 1M 21
Patna. E Ayr 8C 58
Patney. Wilts 8J 19
Patrick. IOM 6B 44
Patrick Brompton. N Yor 6L 47
Patrington. E Yor 5L 43
Patrington Haven. E Yor 5L 43
Patrixbourne. Kent 8H 23
Patterdale. Cumb 4B 46
Pattiesmuir. Fife 1J 59
Pattingham. Staf 2G 27
Pattishall. Nptn 6D 28
Pattiswick. Essx 1E 22
Patton Bridge. Cumb 6D 46
Paul. Corn 6H 3
Paulerspury. Nptn 7E 28
Paull. E Yor 5J 43
Paulton. Bath 8E 18
Pauperhaugh. Nmbd 2E 54
Pave Lane. Telf 8F 34
Pavenham. Bed 6G 29
Pawlett. Som 1A 8
Pawston. Nmbd 6F 60
Paxford. Glos 8K 27
Paxton. Bord 4G 61
Payhembury. Devn 5K 7
Paythorne. Lanc 2G 41
Payton. Som 3L 7
Peacehaven. E Sus 5M 11
Peak Dale. Derbs 2J 35
Peak Forest. Derbs 2K 35
Peak Hill. Linc 8K 37
Peakirk. Pet 1J 29
Pearsie. Ang 2G 67
Peasedown St John. Bath 8F 18
Peaseland Green. Norf 8G 39
Peasemore. W Ber 6B 20
Peasenhall. Suff 5K 31
Pease Pottage. W Sus 2K 11
Peaslake. Surr 1H 11
Peasley Cross. Mers 8D 40
Peasmarsh. E Sus 3E 12
Peasmarsh. Som 4B 8
Peasmarsh. Surr 1G 11
Peaston. E Lot 3B 60
Peastonbank. E Lot 3B 60
Peathill. Abers 7J 81
Peat Inn. Fife 7H 67
Peatling Magna. Leics 2C 28
Peatling Parva. Leics 3C 28
Peaton. Arg 1M 57
Peaton. Shrp 3D 26
Peats Corner. Suff 5H 31
Pebmarsh. Essx 8E 30
Pebworth. Worc 7K 27
Pecket Well. W Yor 5H 41
Peckforton. Ches E 4D 34
Peckham Bush. Kent 8C 22
Peckleton. Leics 1B 28
Pedair-ffordd. Powy 8L 33
Pedham. Norf 8K 39
Pedlinge. Kent 2H 13
Pedmore. W Mid 3H 27
Pedwell. Som 2C 8
Peebles. Bord 5L 59
Peel. IOM 6B 44
Peel. Bord 6B 60
Peel Common. Hants 5C 10
Peening Quarter. Kent 3E 12
Peggs Green. Leics 8B 36
Pegsdon. C Beds 8J 29
Pegswood. Nmbd 3F 54
Peinchorran. High 2G 69
Peinlich. High 8F 76
Pelaw. Tyne 5F 54
Pelcomb Bridge. Pemb 5F 14
Pelcomb Cross. Pemb 5F 14
Peldon. Essx 2F 22
Pelsall. W Mid 1J 27
Pelton. Dur 6F 54
Pelutho. Cumb 7F 52
Pelynt. Corn 6E 4
Pemberton. Carm 6M 15
Pembrey. Carm 6L 15
Pembridge. Here 6B 26
Pembroke. Pemb 6F 14
Pembroke Dock.
Pemb 118 (6F 14)
Pembroke Ferry. Pemb 6F 14
Pembury. Kent 1C 12
Penallt. Mon 2D 18
Penally. Pemb 7H 15
Penalt. Here 1D 18
Penalum. Pemb 7H 15
Penare. Corn 7B 4
Penarth. V Glam 7L 17
Penbeagle. Corn 5J 3
Penberth. Corn 6H 3
Pen-bont Rhydybeddau.
Cdgn 4F 24
Penbryn. Cdgn 1J 15
Pencader. Carm 3L 15
Pen-cae. Cdgn 1L 15
Pencaenewydd. Gwyn 6D 32
Pencaerau. Neat 5G 17
Pencaitland. E Lot 3B 60
Pencarnisiog. IOA 3C 32
Pencarreg. Carm 2M 15
Pencarrow. Corn 3D 4
Pencelli. Powy 2K 17
Pen-clawdd. Swan 7M 15
Pencoed. B'end 6J 17
Pencombe. Here 6D 26
Pencraig. Here 1D 18
Pencraig. Powy 8K 33
Pendeen. Corn 5G 3
Pendeford. W Mid 1G 27
Penderyn. Rhon 4J 17
Pendine. Carm 6J 15
Pendlebury. G Man 7F 40
Pendleton. G Man 8G 41
Pendleton. Lanc 4F 40
Pendock. Worc 8F 26
Pendoggett. Corn 4C 4
Pendomer. Som 4D 8
Pendoylan. V Glam 7K 17
Pendre. B'end 6J 17
Penegoes. Powy 2G 25
Penelewey. Corn 4M 3
Penffordd. Pemb 4G 15
Penffordd-Lâs. Powy 3H 25
Penfro. Pemb 6F 14
Pengam. Cphy 5L 17
Pengam. Card 7M 17
Penge. G Lon 7L 21
Pengelly. Corn 3C 4
Pengenffordd. Powy 1L 17
Pengersick. Corn 6J 3
Pengorffwysfa. IOA 1D 32
Pengover Green. Corn 5E 4
Pengwern. Den 3K 33
Penhale. Corn
nr. Mullion 7K 3
nr. St Austell 6B 4
Penhale Camp. Corn 3L 3
Penhallow. Corn 3L 3
Penhalvean. Corn 5L 3
Penhelig. Gwyn 3F 24
Penhill. Swin 5K 19
Penhow. Newp 4C 18
Penhurst. E Sus 4C 12
Peniarth. Gwyn 2F 24
Penicuik. Midl 3L 59
Peniel. Carm 4L 15
Penifiler. High 1F 68
Peninver. Arg 7G 57
Penisa'r Waun. Gwyn 4E 32
Penistone. S Yor 7L 41
Penketh. Warr 1D 34
Penkill. S Ayr 2H 51
Penkridge. Staf 8H 35
Penley. Wrex 6C 34
Penllech. Gwyn 7B 32
Penllergaer. Swan 5F 16
Pen-llyn. IOA 2C 32
Penmachno. Cnwy 5G 33
Penmaen. Swan 8M 15
Penmaenmawr. Cnwy 3G 33
Penmaenpool. Gwyn 1F 24
Penmaen Rhos. Cnwy 3H 33
Pen-marc. V Glam 8K 17
Penmark. V Glam 8K 17
Penmarth. Corn 5L 3
Penmon. IOA 2F 32
Penmorfa. Gwyn 6E 32
Penmynydd. IOA 3E 32
Penn. Buck 4G 21
Penn. Dors 6B 8
Penn. W Mid 2G 27
Pennal. Gwyn 2G 25
Pennan. Abers 7H 81
Pennant. Cdgn 6E 24
Pennant. Den 7K 33
Pennant. Gwyn 8J 33
Pennant. Powy 3H 25
Pennant Melangell. Powy 8K 33
Pennar. Pemb 6F 14
Pennard. Swan 6E 16
Pennerley. Shrp 2B 26
Pennington. Cumb 8A 46
Pennington. G Man 8E 40
Pennington. Hants 6M 9
Pennorth. Powy 2L 17
Penn Street. Buck 4G 21
Pennsylvania. Devn 6J 7
Pennsylvania. S Glo 6F 18
Penny Bridge. Cumb 7B 46
Pennycross. Plym 6G 5
Pennygate. Norf 7K 39
Pennyghael. Arg 5L 63
Penny Hill. Linc 7L 37
Pennylands. Lanc 7C 40
Pennymoor. Devn 4H 7
Pennyvenie. E Ayr 1K 51
Pennywell. Tyne 6G 55
Penparc. Cdgn 2J 15
Penparcau. Cdgn 4E 24
Pen-pedair-heol. Cphy 5L 17
Penperlleni. Mon 3B 18
Penpillick. Corn 6C 4
Penpol. Corn 5M 3
Penpoll. Corn 6D 4
Penponds. Corn 5K 3
Penpont. Corn 4C 4
Penpont. Dum 2C 52
Penpont. Powy 2J 17
Penprysg. B'end 6J 17
Penquit. Devn 6J 5
Penrherber. Carm 3J 15
Penrhiw. Pemb 2J 15
Penrhiwceiber. Rhon 5K 17
Pen-Rhiw-fawr. Neat 3G 17
Penrhiw-llan. Cdgn 2K 15
Penrhiw-pal. Cdgn 2K 15
Penrhos. Gwyn 7C 32
Penrhos. Here 6B 26
Penrhos. IOA 2B 32
Penrhos. Mon 2C 18
Penrhos. Powy 3H 17
Penrhos Garnedd. Gwyn 3E 32
Penrhyn. IOA 1C 32
Penrhyn Bay. Cnwy 2H 33
Penrhyn-coch. Cdgn 4F 24
Penrhyndeudraeth. Gwyn 7F 32
Penrhyn-side. Cnwy 2H 33
Penrice. Swan 8L 15
Penrith. Cumb 3D 46
Penrose. Corn 4A 4
Penruddock. Cumb 3C 46
Penryn. Corn 5L 3
Pen-sarn. Carm 5L 15
Pen-sarn. Gwyn 8E 32
Pensax. Worc 5F 26
Pensby. Mers 1A 34
Penselwood. Som 2F 8
Pensford. Bath 7E 18
Pensham. Worc 7H 27
Penshaw. Tyne 6G 55
Penshurst. Kent 1B 12
Pensilva. Corn 5E 4
Pensnett. W Mid 3H 27
Penston. E Lot 2B 60
Penstone. Devn 5G 7
Pentewan. Corn 7C 4
Pentir. Gwyn 4E 32
Pentire. Corn 2L 3
Pentlepoir. Pemb 6H 15
Pentlow. Essx 7E 30
Pentney. Norf 8D 38
Penton Mewsey. Hants 1M 9
Pentraeth. IOA 3E 32
Pentre. Powy
nr. Church Stoke 2A 26
nr. Kerry 4L 25
nr. Mochdre 4K 25
Pentre. Rhon 5J 17
Pentre. Shrp 8B 34
Pentre. Wrex
nr. Chirk 5A 34
nr. Llanarmon Dyffryn Ceiriog 7L 33
Pentre-bach. Cdgn 2M 15
Pentre-bach. Powy 1J 17
Pentrebach. Carm 1H 17
Pentrebach. Mer T 4K 17
Pentrebach. Swan 4F 16
Pentre Berw. IOA 3D 32
Pentre-bont. Cnwy 5G 33
Pentrecagal. Carm 2K 15
Pentre-celyn. Den 5L 33
Pentre-clawdd. Shrp 6A 34
Pentreclwydau. Neat 4H 17
Pentre-cwrt. Carm 3K 15
Pentre Dolau Honddu.
Powy 8J 25
Pentre-dwr. Swan 5F 16
Pentrefelin. Carm 2E 16
Pentrefelin. Cdgn 8F 24
Pentrefelin. Cnwy 3H 33
Pentrefelin. Gwyn 7E 32
Pentrefoelas. Cnwy 5H 33
Pentre Galar. Pemb 3H 15
Pentregat. Cdgn 1K 15
Pentre Gwenlais. Carm 3F 16
Pentre Gwynfryn. Gwyn 8E 32
Pentre Halkyn. Flin 3M 33
Pentre Hodre. Shrp 4B 26
Pentre-Llanrhaeadr. Den 4K 33
Pentre Llifior. Powy 3L 25
Pentrellwyn. IOA 2E 32
Pentre-llwyn-llwyd. Powy 7J 25
Pentre-llyn-cymmer. Cnwy 5J 33
Pentre Meyrick. V Glam 7J 17
Pentre-piod. Gwyn 7H 33
Pentre-poeth. Newp 5A 18
Pentre'r beirdd. Powy 1L 25
Pentre'r-felin. Powy 1J 17
Pentre-tafarn-y-fedw. Cnwy 4H 33
Pentre-ty-gwyn. Carm 1H 17
Pentre-uchaf. Gwyn 7C 32
Pentrich. Derbs 4A 36
Pentridge. Dors 4J 9
Pen-twyn. Cphy 4M 17
Pentwyn. Cphy 4L 17
Pentwyn. Card 6M 17
Pentyrch. Card 6L 17
Pentywyn. Carm 6J 15
Penuwch. Cdgn 6E 24
Penwithick. Corn 6C 4
Penwyllt. Powy 3H 17
Pen-y-banc. Carm 2F 16
Penybanc. Carm 3F 16
Pen-y-bont. Carm 4K 15
Pen-y-bont. Powy 8M 33
Penybont. Powy 6L 25
Pen-y-Bont Ar Ogwr. B'end 6J 17
Penybontfawr. Powy 8K 33
Pen-y-bryn. Pemb 2H 15
Pen-y-bryn. Wrex 5A 34
Penybryn. Cphy 5L 17
Pen-y-cae. Powy 3H 17
Penycae. Wrex 5A 34
Pen-y-cae mawr. Mon 4C 18
Penycaerau. Gwyn 8A 32
Pen-y-cefn. Flin 3L 33
Pen-y-clawdd. Mon 3C 18
Pen-y-coedcae. Rhon 6K 17
Penycwm. Pemb 4E 14
Pen-y-Darren. Mer T 4K 17
Pen-y-fai. B'end 6H 17
Pen-y-ffordd. Flin 2L 33
Penyffordd. Flin 3B 34
Penyffridd. Gwyn 5E 32
Pen-y-garn. Cdgn 4F 24
Pen-y-garnedd. IOA 3E 32
Penygarnedd. Powy 8L 33
Pen-y-graig. Gwyn 7B 32
Penygraig. Rhon 5J 17
Penygraigwen. IOA 2D 32
Pen-y-groes. Carm 3E 16
Penygroes. Gwyn 5D 32
Penygroes. Pemb 3H 15
Pen-y-Mynydd. Carm 6L 15
Penymynydd. Flin 3B 34
Pen-yr-heol. Mon 2C 18
Penyrheol. Cphy 6L 17
Penyrheol. Swan 5E 16
Penysarn. IOA 1D 32
Pen-y-stryt. Den 5L 33
Penywaun. Rhon 4J 17
Penzance. Corn 5H 3
Peopleton. Worc 6H 27
Peover Heath. Ches E 2F 34
Peper Harow. Surr 1G 11
Peplow. Shrp 7E 34
Pepper Arden. N Yor 5L 47
Perceton. N Ayr 5B 58
Percyhorner. Abers 7J 81
Perham Down. Wilts 1L 9
Periton. Som 1J 7
Perkinsville. Dur 6F 54
Perlethorpe. Notts 2D 36
Perranarworthal. Corn 5L 3
Perranporth. Corn 3L 3
Perranuthnoe. Corn 6J 3
Perranwell. Corn 5L 3
Perranzabuloe. Corn 3L 3
Perrott's Brook. Glos 3J 19
Perry. W Mid 2J 27
Perry Barr. W Mid 2J 27
Perry Crofts. Staf 1L 27
Perry Green. Essx 1E 22
Perry Green. Herts 2M 21
Perry Green. Wilts 5H 19
Perry Street. Kent 6C 22
Perry Street. Som 5B 8
Perrywood. Kent 8G 23
Pershall. Staf 7G 35
Pershore. Worc 7H 27
Pertenhall. Bed 5H 29
Perth. Per 115 (5E 66)
Perthy. Shrp 6B 34
Perton. Staf 2G 27
Pertwood. Wilts 2G 9
Peterborough. Pet 115 (2J 29)
Peterburn. High 5J 77
Peterchurch. Here 8B 26
Peterculter. Aber 5H 73
Peterhead. Abers 1L 73
Peterlee. Dur 7H 55
Petersfield. Hants 3E 10
Petersfinger. Wilts 3K 9
Peters Green. Herts 2J 21
Peters Marland. Devn 4D 6
Peterstone Wentlooge.
Newp 5A 18
Peterston-super-Ely.
V Glam 7K 17
Peterstow. Here 1D 18
Peters Village. Kent 7D 22
Peter Tavy. Devn 8E 6
Petertown. Orkn 1E 86
Petham. Kent 8H 23
Petherwin Gate. Corn 7B 6
Petrockstowe. Devn 5E 6
Petsoe End. Mil 7F 28
Pett. E Sus 4E 12
Pettaugh. Suff 6H 31
Pett Bottom. Kent 8H 23
Petteridge. Kent 1C 12
Pettinain. S Lan 5H 59
Pettistree. Suff 6J 31
Petton. Devn 3K 7
Petton. Shrp 7C 34
Petts Wood. G Lon 7M 21
Pettycur. Fife 1L 59
Pettywell. Norf 7G 39
Petworth. W Sus 3G 11
Pevensey. E Sus 5C 12
Pevensey Bay. E Sus 5C 12
Pewsey. Wilts 7K 19
Pheasants Hill. Buck 5E 20
Philadelphia. Tyne 6G 55
Philham. Devn 3B 6
Philiphaugh. Bord 7B 60
Phillack. Corn 5J 3
Philleigh. Corn 8A 4
Philpstoun. W Lot 2J 59
Phocle Green. Here 1E 18
Phoenix Green. Hants 8E 20
Pibsbury. Som 3C 8
Pibwrlwyd. Carm 5L 15
Pica. Cumb 2K 45
Piccadilly. Warw 2L 27
Piccadilly Corner. Norf 3J 31
Piccotts End. Herts 3H 21
Pickering. N Yor 7E 48
Picket Piece. Hants 1A 10
Picket Post. Hants 5K 9
Pickford. W Mid 3L 27
Pickhill. N Yor 7M 47
Picklenash. Glos 1F 18
Picklescott. Shrp 2C 26
Pickletillem. Fife 5H 67
Pickmere. Ches E 2E 34
Pickstock. Telf 7F 34
Pickwell. Devn 1D 6
Pickwell. Leics 8E 36
Pickworth. Linc 6H 37
Pickworth. Rut 8G 37
Picton. Ches W 2C 34
Picton. Flin 2L 33
Picton. N Yor 5B 48
Pict's Hill. Som 3C 8
Piddinghoe. E Sus 5M 11
Piddington. Buck 4F 20
Piddington. Nptn 6F 28
Piddington. Oxon 2D 20
Piddlehinton. Dors 6F 8
Piddletrenthide. Dors 5F 8
Pidley. Cambs 4L 29
Pidney. Dors 5F 8
Pie Corner. Here 5E 26
Piercebridge. Darl 4L 47
Pierowall. Orkn 5D 88
Pigdon. Nmbd 3E 54
Pightley. Som 2M 7
Pikehall. Derbs 4K 35
Pikeshill. Hants 5L 9
Pilford. Dors 5J 9
Pilgrims Hatch. Essx 4B 22
Pilham. Linc 8F 42
Pill. N Som 6D 18
The Pill. Mon 5C 18
Pillaton. Corn 5F 4
Pillaton. Staf 8H 35
Pillerton Hersey. Warw 7M 27
Pillerton Priors. Warw 7L 27
Pilleth. Powy 5A 26
Pilley. Hants 6M 9
Pilley. S Yor 7M 41
Pillgwenlly. Newp 5B 18
Pilling. Lanc 3C 40
Pilling Lane. Lanc 3B 40
Pillowell. Glos 3E 18
Pillwell. Dors 4F 8
Pilning. S Glo 5D 18
Pilsbury. Derbs 3K 35
Pilsdon. Dors 6C 8
Pilsgate. Pet 1H 29
Pilsley. Derbs
nr. Bakewell 2L 35
nr. Clay Cross 3B 36
Pilson Green. Norf 8K 39
Piltdown. E Sus 3M 11
Pilton. Edin 2L 59
Pilton. Nptn 3H 29
Pilton. Rut 1G 29
Pilton. Som 1D 8
Pilton Green. Swan 8L 15
Pimperne. Dors 5H 9
Pinchbeck. Linc 7K 37
Pinchbeck Bars. Linc 7J 37
Pinchbeck West. Linc 7K 37
Pinfold. Lanc 6B 40
Pinford End. Suff 6E 30
Pinged. Carm 6L 15
Pinhoe. Devn 6J 7
Pinkerton. E Lot 2E 60
Pinkneys Green. Wind 5F 20
Pinley. W Mid 4A 28
Pinley Green. Warw 5L 27
Pinmill. Suff 8J 31
Pinmore. S Ayr 2H 51
Pinner. G Lon 5J 21
Pins Green. Worc 7F 26
Pinsley Green. Ches E 5D 34
Pinvin. Worc 7H 27
Pinwherry. S Ayr 3G 51
Pinxton. Derbs 4B 36
Pipe and Lyde. Here 7D 26
Pipe Aston. Here 4C 26
Pipe Gate. Shrp 5F 34
Pipehill. Staf 1J 27
Piperhill. High 8J 79
Pipe Ridware. Staf 8J 35
Pipers Pool. Corn 7B 6
Pipewell. Nptn 3F 28
Pippacott. Devn 2E 6
Pipton. Powy 1L 17
Pirbright. Surr 8G 21
Pirnmill. N Ayr 5H 57
Pirton. Herts 8J 29
Pirton. Worc 7G 27
Pisgah. Stir 7A 66
Pishill. Oxon 5E 20
Pistyll. Gwyn 6C 32
Pitagowan. Per 1B 66
Pitcairn. Per 2B 66
Pitcairngreen. Per 5D 66
Pitcalnie. High 6J 79
Pitcaple. Abers 3G 73
Pitchcombe. Glos 3G 19
Pitchcott. Buck 1E 20
Pitchford. Shrp 1D 26
Pitch Green. Buck 3E 20
Pitch Place. Surr 8G 21
Pitcombe. Som 2E 8
Pitcox. E Lot 2D 60
Pitcur. Per 4F 66
Pitfichie. Abers 4F 72
Pitgrudy. High 4H 79
Pitkennedy. Ang 2J 67
Pitlessie. Fife 7G 67
Pitlochry. Per 2C 66
Pitmachie. Abers 3F 72
Pitmaduthy. High 6H 79
Pitmedden. Abers 3H 73
Pitminster. Som 4M 7
Pitnacree. Per 2C 66
Pitney. Som 3C 8
Pitroddie. Per 5F 66
Pitscottie. Fife 6H 67
Pitsea. Essx 5D 22
Pitsford. Nptn 5E 28
Pitsford Hill. Som 2L 7
Pitsmoor. S Yor 1A 36
Pitstone. Buck 2G 21
Pitt. Hants 3B 10
Pitt Court. Glos 4F 18
Pittentrail. High 3H 79
Pittenweem. Fife 7J 67
Pittington. Dur 7G 55
Pitton. Swan 8L 15
Pitton. Wilts 2L 9
Pittswood. Kent 1C 12
Pittulie. Abers 7J 81
Pittville. Glos 1H 19
Pitversie. Per 6E 66
Pity Me. Dur 7F 54
Pityme. Corn 4B 4
Pixey Green. Suff 4J 31
Pixley. Here 8E 26
Place Newton. N Yor 8F 48
Plaidy. Abers 8G 81
Plaidy. Corn 6E 4
Plain Dealings. Pemb 5G 15
Plains. N Lan 3F 58
Plainsfield. Som 2L 7
Plaish. Shrp 2D 26
Plaistow. Here 8E 26
Plaistow. W Sus 2H 11
Plaitford. Wilts 4L 9
Plastow Green. Hants 7C 20
Plas yn Cefn. Den 3K 33
The Platt. E Sus 2B 12
Platt Bridge. G Man 7E 40
Platt Lane. Shrp 6D 34
Platts Common. S Yor 7A 42
Platt's Heath. Kent 8E 22
Plawsworth. Dur 7F 54
Plaxtol. Kent 8C 22
Playden. E Sus 3F 12
Playford. Suff 7J 31
Play Hatch. Oxon 6E 20
Playing Place. Corn 4M 3
Playley Green. Glos 8F 26
Plealey. Shrp 1C 26
Plean. Stir 1G 59
Pleasington. Bkbn 5E 40
Pleasley. Derbs 3C 36
Pledgdon Green. Essx 1B 22
Plenmeller. Nmbd 5M 53
Pleshey. Essx 2C 22
Plockton. High 2K 69
Plocrapol. W Isl 4C 76
Ploughfield. Here 7B 26
Plowden. Shrp 3B 26
Ploxgreen. Shrp 1B 26
Pluckley. Kent 1F 12
Plucks Gutter. Kent 7J 23
Plumbland. Cumb 8F 52
Plumbridge. Derr 4D 92
Plumgarths. Cumb 6C 46
Plumley. Ches E 2F 34
Plummers Plain. W Sus 3K 11
Plumpton. Cumb 8J 53
Plumpton. E Sus 4L 11
Plumpton. Nptn 7C 28
Plumpton Foot. Cumb 8J 53
Plumpton Green. E Sus 4L 11
Plumpton Head. Cumb 8K 53
Plumstead. G Lon 6M 21
Plumstead. Norf 6H 39
Plumtree. Notts 6D 36
Plumtree Park. Notts 6D 36
Plungar. Leics 6E 36
Plush. Dors 5F 8
Plushabridge. Corn 8C 6
Plwmp. Cdgn 1K 15
Plymouth. Plym 115 (6G 5)
Plympton. Plym 6H 5
Plymstock. Plym 6H 5
Plymtree. Devn 5K 7
Pockley. N Yor 7D 48
Pocklington. E Yor 3F 42
Pode Hole. Linc 7K 37
Podimore. Som 3D 8
Podington. Bed 5G 29
Podmore. Staf 6F 34
Poffley End. Oxon 2A 20
Point Clear. Essx 2G 23
Pointon. Linc 6J 37
Pokesdown. Bour 6K 9
Polbae. Dum 4H 51
Polbain. High 3M 77
Polbathic. Corn 6F 4
Polbeth. W Lot 3J 59
Polbrock. Corn 5C 4
Polchar. High 5J 71
Polebrook. Nptn 3H 29
Pole Elm. Worc 7G 27
Polegate. E Sus 5B 12
Pole Moor. W Yor 6J 41
Poles. High 4H 79
Polesworth. Warw 1L 27
Polglass. High 3M 77
Polgooth. Corn 6B 4
Poling. W Sus 5H 11
Poling Corner. W Sus 5H 11
Polio. High 6H 79
Polkerris. Corn 6C 4
Polla. High 6F 84
Pollard Street. Norf 6K 39
Pollicott. Buck 2E 20
Pollington. E Yor 6D 42
Polloch. High 1B 64
Pollok. Glas 3D 58
Pollokshaws. Glas 3D 58
Pollokshields. Glas 3D 58
Polmaily. High 2E 70
Polmassick. Corn 7B 4
Polmont. Falk 2H 59
Polnessan. E Ayr 8C 58
Polnish. High 7J 69
Polperro. Corn 6E 4
Polruan. Corn 6D 4
Polscoe. Corn 5D 4
Polsham. Som 1D 8
Polskeoch. Dum 1A 52
Polstead. Suff 8F 30
Polstead Heath. Suff 7F 30
Poltesco. Corn 7L 3
Poltimore. Devn 6J 7
Polton. Midl 3L 59
Polwarth. Bord 4E 60
Polyphant. Corn 7B 6
Polzeath. Corn 4B 4
Pomeroy. M Ulst 5E 92
Ponde. Powy 1L 17
Pondersbridge. Cambs 2K 29
Ponders End. G Lon 4L 21
Pond Street. Essx 8A 30
Pondtail. Hants 8F 20
Ponsanooth. Corn 5L 3
Ponsongath. Corn 7L 3
Ponsworthy. Devn 8G 7
Pontamman. Carm 3F 16
Pontantwn. Carm 5L 15
Pontardawe. Neat 4G 17
Pontarddulais. Swan 4E 16
Pontarfynach. Cdgn 5G 25
Pont-ar-gothi. Carm 4M 15
Pont ar Hydfer. Powy 2H 17
Pontarllechau. Carm 2G 17
Pontarsais. Carm 4L 15
Pontblyddyn. Flin 3A 34
Pontbren Llwyd. Rhon 4J 17
Pont-Cyfyng. Cnwy 5G 33
Pontdolgoch. Powy 3K 25
Pontefract. W Yor 5B 42
Ponteland. Nmbd 4E 54
Ponterwyd. Cdgn 4G 25
Pontesbury. Shrp 1C 26
Pontesford. Shrp 1C 26
Pontfadog. Wrex 7M 33
Pont-Faen. Shrp 6A 34
Pont-faen. Powy 1J 17
Pontfaen. Pemb 3G 15
Pontgarreg. Cdgn 1K 15
Pont-Henri. Carm 6L 15
Ponthir. Torf 4B 18
Ponthirwaun. Cdgn 2J 15
Pont-iets. Carm 6L 15
Pontllanfraith. Cphy 5L 17
Pontlliw. Swan 4F 16
Pont Llogel. Powy 1K 25
Pontllyfni. Gwyn 5D 32
Pontlottyn. Cphy 4L 17
Pontneddfechan. Powy 4J 17
Pont-newydd. Carm 6L 15
Pont-newydd. Flin 4L 33
Pontnewydd. Torf 4A 18
Ponton. Shet 2D 90
Pont Pen-y-benglog. Gwyn 4F 32
Pontrhydfendigaid. Cdgn 6G 25
Pont Rhyd-y-cyff. B'end 6H 17
Pontrhydyfen. Neat 5G 17
Pont-rhyd-y-groes. Cdgn 5G 25
Pontrhydyrun. Torf 4A 18
Pont-Rhythallt. Gwyn 4E 32
Pontrilas. Here 1B 18
Pontrilas Road. Here 1B 18
Pontrobert. Powy 1L 25
Pont-rug. Gwyn 4E 32
Ponts Green. E Sus 4C 12
Pontshill. Here 1E 18
Pont-Sian. Cdgn 2L 15
Pontsticill. Mer T 3K 17
Pont-Walby. Neat 4H 17
Pontwelly. Carm 3L 15
Pontwgan. Cnwy 3G 33
Pontyates. Carm 6L 15
Pontyberem. Carm 5M 15
Pontybodkin. Flin 4A 34
Pontyclun. Rhon 6K 17
Pontycymer. B'end 5J 17
Pontyglazier. Pemb 3H 15
Pontygwaith. Rhon 5K 17
Pont-y-pant. Cnwy 5G 33
Pontypool. Torf 4A 18
Pontypridd. Rhon 6K 17
Pontypwl. Torf 4A 18
Pontywaun. Cphy 5M 17
Pooksgreen. Hants 4A 10
Pool. Corn 4K 3
Pool. W Yor 3L 41
Poole. N Yor 5B 42
Poole. Pool 118 (6J 9)
Poole. Som 3L 7
Poole Keynes. Glos 4H 19
Poolend. Staf 4H 35
Poolewe. High 5K 77
Pooley Bridge. Cumb 3C 46
Poolfold. Staf 4G 35
Pool Head. Here 6D 26
Pool Hey. Lanc 6B 40
Poolhill. Glos 1F 18
Poolmill. Here 1D 18
Pool o' Muckhart. Clac 7D 66
Pool Quay. Powy 8A 34
Poolsbrook. Derbs 2B 36
Pool Street. Essx 8D 30
Pootings. Kent 1A 12
Pope Hill. Pemb 5F 14
Pope's Hill. Glos 2E 18
Popeswood. Brac 7F 20
Popham. Hants 1C 10
Poplar. G Lon 5L 21
Popley. Hants 8D 20
Porchfield. IOW 6B 10
Porin. High 8D 78
Poringland. Norf 1J 31
Porkellis. Corn 5K 3
Porlock. Som 1H 7
Porlock Weir. Som 1H 7
Portachoillan. Arg 4G 57
Port Adhair Bheinn na Faoghla.
W Isl 8J 75
Port Adhair Thirlodh. Arg 3F 62
Portadown. Arm 6G 93
Portaferry. Ards 6J 93
Port Ann. Arg 1J 57
Port Appin. Arg 3D 64
Port Asgaig. Arg 3D 56
Port Askaig. Arg 3D 56
Portavadie. Arg 3J 57
Portavogie. Ards 5K 93
Portballintrae. Caus 1F 93
Port Bannatyne. Arg 3K 57
Portbury. N Som 6D 18
Port Carlisle. Cumb 5G 53
Port Charlotte. Arg 4B 56
Portchester. Hants 5D 10
Port Clarence. Stoc T 3B 48
Port Driseach. Arg 2J 57
Port Dundas. Glas 3D 58
Port Ellen. Arg 5C 56
Port Elphinstone. Abers 3G 73
Portencalzie. Dum 4F 50
Portencross. N Ayr 5L 57
Port Erin. IOM 8A 44
Port Erroll. Abers 2K 73
Porter's Fen Corner. Norf 1B 30
Portesham. Dors 7E 8
Portessie. Mor 7D 80
Port e Vullen. IOM 5D 44
Port-Eynon. Swan 8L 15
Portfield. Som 3C 8
Portfield Gate. Pemb 5F 14
Portgate. Devn 7D 6
Port Gaverne. Corn 3C 4
Port Glasgow. Inv 2B 58
Portglenone. ME Ant 3F 93
Portgordon. Mor 7C 80
Portgower. High 2L 79
Porth. Corn 2M 3
Porth. Rhon 5K 17
Porthaethwy. IOA 3E 32
Porthallow. Corn
nr. Looe 6E 4
nr. St Keverne 6L 3
Porthcawl. B'end 7H 17
Porthceri. V Glam 8K 17
Porthcothan. Corn 4A 4
Porthcurno. Corn 6G 3
Port Henderson. High 6J 77
Porthgain. Pemb 3E 14
Porthgwarra. Corn 6G 3
Porthill. Shrp 8C 34
Porthkerry. V Glam 8K 17
Porthleven. Corn 6K 3
Porthllechog. IOA 1D 32
Porthmadog. Gwyn 7E 32
Porthmeor. Corn 5H 3
Porth Navas. Corn 6L 3
Portholland. Corn 7B 4
Porthoustock. Corn 6M 3
Porthtowan. Corn 4K 3
Porth Tywyn. Carm 6L 15
Porth-y-felin. IOA 2B 32
Porthyrhyd. Carm
nr. Carmarthen 5M 15
nr. Llandovery 1G 17
Porth-y-waen. Shrp 7A 34
Portincaple. Arg 8G 65
Portington. E Yor 4E 42
Portinnisherrich. Arg 6D 64
Portinscale. Cumb 3A 46
Port Isaac. Corn 3B 4
Portishead. N Som 6C 18
Portknockie. Mor 7D 80
Port Lamont. Arg 2K 57
Portlethen. Abers 6J 73
Portlethen Village. Abers 6J 73
Portling. Dum 6C 52
Port Lion. Pemb 6F 14
Portloe. Corn 8B 4
Port Logan. Dum 7F 50
Portmahomack. High 5K 79
Portmead. Swan 5F 16
Portmeirion. Gwyn 7E 32
Portmellon. Corn 7C 4
Port Mholair. W Isl 8J 83
Port Mor. High 8F 68
Portmore. Hants 6M 9
Port Mulgrave. N Yor 4E 48
Portnacroish. Arg 3D 64
Portnahaven. Arg 4A 56
Portnalong. High 2E 68
Portnaluchaig. High 7H 69
Portnancon. High 5G 85
Port Nan Giuran. W Isl 8J 83
Port nan Long. W Isl 6K 75
Port Nis. W Isl 5J 83
Portobello. Edin 2M 59
Portobello. W Yor 6M 41
Port of Menteith. Stir 7K 65
Porton. Wilts 2K 9
Portormin. High 1A 80
Portpatrick. Dum 6F 50
Port Quin. Corn 3B 4
Port Ramsay. Arg 3C 64
Portreath. Corn 4K 3
Portree. High 1F 68
Port Righ. High 1F 68
Portrush. Caus 2F 93
Port St Mary. IOM 8B 44
Portscatho. Corn 8A 4
Portsea. Port 5D 10
Port Seton. E Lot 2B 60
Portskerra. High 5L 85
Portskewett. Mon 5D 18
Portslade-by-Sea. Brig 5K 11
Portsmouth. Port 115 (5D 10)
Portsmouth. W Yor 5H 41
Port Soderick. IOM 7C 44
Port Solent. Port 5D 10
Portsonachan. Arg 5E 64
Portsoy. Abers 7E 80
Portstewart. Caus 2F 93
Port Sunlight. Mers 1B 34
Portswood. Sotn 4B 10
Port Talbot. Neat 6G 17
Porttannachy. Mor 7C 80
Port Tennant. Swan 5F 16
Portuairk. High 1K 63
Portway. Here 7C 26
Portway. Worc 4J 27
Port Wemyss. Arg 4A 56
Port William. Dum 7J 51
Portwrinkle. Corn 6F 4
Poslingford. Suff 7D 30
Postbridge. Devn 8F 6
Postcombe. Oxon 4E 20
Post Green. Dors 6H 9
Postling. Kent 2H 13
Postlip. Glos 1J 19
Post-Mawr. Cdgn 1L 15
Postwick. Norf 1J 31
Potarch. Abers 6F 72
Potsgrove. C Beds 1G 21
Potten End. Herts 3H 21
Potter Brompton. N Yor 8G 49
Pottergate Street. Norf 2H 31
Potterhanworth. Linc 3H 37
Potterhanworth Booths.
Linc 3H 37
Potter Heigham. Norf 8L 39
Potter Hill. Leics 7E 36
The Potteries. Stoke 5G 35
Potterne. Wilts 8H 19
Potterne Wick. Wilts 8J 19
Potternewton. W Yor 4M 41
Potters Bar. Herts 3K 21
Potters Brook. Lanc 2C 40
Potter's Cross. Staf 3G 27
Potters Crouch. Herts 3J 21
Potter Somersal. Derbs 6K 35
Potterspury. Nptn 7E 28
Potter Street. Essx 3A 22
Potterton. Abers 4J 73
Potthorpe. Norf 7F 38
Pottle Street. Wilts 1G 9
Potto. N Yor 5B 48
Potton. C Beds 7K 29
Pott Row. Norf 7D 38
Pott Shrigley. Ches E 2H 35
Poughill. Corn 5B 6
Poughill. Devn 5H 7
Poulner. Hants 5K 9
Poulshot. Wilts 8H 19
Poulton. Glos 3K 19
Poulton-le-Fylde. Lanc 4B 40
Pound Bank. Worc 4F 26
Poundbury. Dors 6E 8
Poundfield. E Sus 2B 12
Poundgate. E Sus 3A 12
Pound Green. E Sus 3B 12
Pound Green. Suff 6D 30
Pound Hill. W Sus 2K 11

Poundland – St Agnes

Poundland. S Ayr 3G 51
Poundon. Buck 1D 20
Poundsgate. Devn 8G 7
Poundstock. Corn 6B 6
Pound Street. Hants 7B 20
Pounsley. E Sus 3B 12
Powburn. Nmbd 8H 61
Powderham. Devn 7J 7
Powerstock. Dors 6D 8
Powfoot. Dum 5F 52
Powick. Worc 6G 27
Powmill. Per 8D 66
Poxwell. Dors 7F 8
Poyle. Slo 6H 21
Poynings. W Sus 4K 11
Poyntington. Dors 3E 8
Poynton. Ches E 1H 35
Poynton. Telf 8D 34
Poynton Green. Telf 8D 34
Poyntz Pass. Arm 7G 93
Poystreet Green. Suff 6F 30
Praa Sands. Corn 6J 3
Pratt's Bottom. G Lon 7A 22
Praze-an-Beeble. Corn 5K 3
Prees. Shrp 6D 34
Preesall. Lanc 3B 40
Preesall Park. Lanc 3B 40
Prees Green. Shrp 6D 34
Prees Higher Heath. Shrp 6D 34
Prendergast. Pemb 5F 14
Prendwick. Nmbd 8H 61
Pren-gwyn. Cdgn 2L 15
Prenteg. Gwyn 6E 32
Prenton. Mers 1B 34
Prescot. Mers 8C 40
Prescott. Devn 4K 7
Prescott. Shrp 7C 34
Preshute. Wilts 7K 19
Pressen. Nmbd 6F 60
Prestatyn. Den 2K 33
Prestbury. Ches E 2H 35
Prestbury. Glos 1H 19
Presteigne. Powy 5B 26
Presthope. Shrp 2D 26
Prestleigh. Som 1E 8
Preston. Brig 5L 11
Preston. Devn 8H 7
Preston. Dors 7F 8
Preston. E Lot
nr. East Linton 2C 60
nr. Prestonpans 2A 60
Preston. E Yor 4J 43
Preston. Glos 3J 19
Preston. Herts 1J 21
Preston. Kent
nr. Canterbury 7J 23
nr. Faversham 7G 23
Preston. Lanc 115 (5D 40)
Preston. Nmbd 7J 61
Preston. Rut 1F 28
Preston. Bord 4E 60
Preston. Shrp 8D 34
Preston. Suff 6F 30
Preston. Wilts
nr. Aldbourne 6L 19
nr. Lyneham 6J 19
Preston Bagot. Warw 5K 27
Preston Bissett. Buck 1D 20
Preston Bowyer. Som 3L 7
Preston Brockhurst. Shrp 7D 34
Preston Brook. Hal 1D 34
Preston Candover. Hants 1D 10
Preston Capes. Nptn 6C 28
Preston Cross. Glos 8E 26
Preston Gubbals. Shrp 8C 34
Preston-le-Skerne. Dur 3M 47
Preston Marsh. Here 7D 26
Prestonmill. Dum 6D 52
Preston on Stour. Warw 7L 27
Preston on the Hill. Hal 1D 34
Preston on Wye. Here 7B 26
Prestonpans. E Lot 2A 60
Preston Plucknett. Som 4D 8
Preston-under-Scar. N Yor 6J 47
Preston upon the Weald Moors. Telf 8E 34
Preston Wynne. Here 7D 26
Prestwich. G Man 7G 41
Prestwick. Nmbd 4E 54
Prestwick. S Ayr 7B 58
Prestwold. Leics 7C 36
Prestwood. Buck 3F 20
Prestwood. Staf 5K 35
Price Town. B'end 5J 17
Prickwillow. Cambs 3B 30
Priddy. Som 8D 18
Priestcliffe. Derbs 2K 35
Priesthill. Glas 3D 58
Priest Hutton. Lanc 8D 46
Priestland. E Ayr 6D 58
Priest Weston. Shrp 2A 26
Priestwood. Brac 6F 20
Priestwood. Kent 7C 22
Primethorpe. Leics 2C 28
Primrose Green. Norf 8G 39
Primrose Hill. Glos 3E 18
Primrose Hill. Lanc 7B 40
Primrose Valley. N Yor 8J 49
Primsidemill. Bord 7F 60
Princes Gate. Pemb 5H 15
Princes Risborough. Buck 3F 20
Princethorpe. Warw 4B 28
Princetown. Devn 8E 6
Prinsted. W Sus 5E 10
Prion. Den 4K 33
Prior Muir. Fife 6J 67
Prior's Frome. Here 8D 26
Priors Halton. Shrp 4C 26
Priors Hardwick. Warw 6B 28
Priorslee. Telf 8F 34
Priors Marston. Warw 6B 28
Prior's Norton. Glos 1G 19
The Priory. W Ber 7M 19
Priory Wood. Here 7A 26
Priston. Bath 7E 18
Pristow Green. Norf 3H 31
Prittlewell. S'end 5E 22
Privett. Hants 3D 10
Prixford. Devn 2E 6
Probus. Corn 7A 4
Prospect. Cumb 7F 52
Prospect Village. Staf 8J 35
Provanmill. Glas 3E 58
Prudhoe. Nmbd 5D 54
Publow. Bath 7E 18
Puckeridge. Herts 1L 21
Puckington. Som 4B 8
Pucklechurch. S Glo 6E 18
Puckrup. Glos 8G 27
Puddinglake. Ches W 3F 34
Puddington. Ches W 2B 34
Puddington. Devn 4H 7
Puddlebrook. Glos 2E 18
Puddledock. Norf 2G 31
Puddletown. Dors 6F 8
Pudleston. Here 6D 26
Pudsey. W Yor 4L 41
Pulborough. W Sus 4H 11
Puleston. Telf 7F 34
Pulford. Ches W 4B 34
Pulham. Dors 5F 8
Pulham Market. Norf 3H 31
Pulham St Mary. Norf 3J 31
Pulley. Shrp 1C 26
Pulloxhill. C Beds 8H 29
Pulpit Hill. Arg 5C 64
Pulverbatch. Shrp 1C 26
Pumpherston. W Lot 3J 59
Pumsaint. Carm 8F 24
Puncheston. Pemb 4G 15
Puncknowle. Dors 7D 8
Punnett's Town. E Sus 3C 12
Purbrook. Hants 5D 10
Purfleet-on-Thames. Thur 6B 22
Puriton. Som 1B 8
Purleigh. Essx 3E 22
Purley. G Lon 7L 21
Purley on Thames. W Ber 6D 20
Purlogue. Shrp 4A 26
Purl's Bridge. Cambs 3A 30
Purse Caundle. Dors 4E 8
Purslow. Shrp 3B 26
Purston Jaglin. W Yor 6B 42
Purtington. Som 5B 8
Purton. Glos
nr. Lydney 3E 18
nr. Sharpness 3E 18
Purton. Wilts 5J 19
Purton Stoke. Wilts 4J 19
Pury End. Nptn 7E 28
Pusey. Oxon 4A 20
Putley. Here 8E 26
Putney. G Lon 6K 21
Putsborough. Devn 1D 6
Puttenham. Herts 2F 20
Puttenham. Surr 1G 11
Puttock End. Essx 7E 30
Puttock's End. Essx 2B 22
Puxey. Dors 4F 8
Puxton. N Som 7C 18
Pwll. Carm 6L 15
Pwll. Powy 2L 25
Pwllcrochan. Pemb 6F 14
Pwll-glas. Den 5L 33
Pwllgloyw. Powy 1K 17
Pwllheli. Gwyn 7C 32
Pwllmeyric. Mon 4D 18
Pwlltrap. Carm 5J 15
Pwll-y-glaw. Neat 5G 17
Pyecombe. W Sus 4K 11
Pye Corner. Herts 2M 21
Pye Corner. Newp 5B 18
Pye Green. Staf 8H 35
Pyewipe. NE Lin 6K 43
Pyle. B'end 6H 17
Pyle. IOW 8B 10
Pyle Hill. Surr 8G 21
Pylle. Som 2E 8
Pymoor. Cambs 3A 30
Pymore. Dors 6C 8
Pyrford. Surr 8H 21
Pyrford Village. Surr 8H 21
Pyrton. Oxon 4D 20
Pytchley. Nptn 4F 28
Pyworthy. Devn 5C 6

Q

Quabbs. Shrp 4M 25
Quadring. Linc 6K 37
Quadring Eaudike. Linc 6K 37
Quainton. Buck 1E 20
Quaking Houses. Dur 6E 54
Quarley. Hants 1L 9
Quarndon. Derbs 5M 35
Quarrendon. Buck 2F 20
Quarrier's Village. Inv 3B 58
Quarrington. Linc 5H 37
Quarrington Hill. Dur 8G 55
The Quarry. Glos 4F 18
Quarry Bank. W Mid 3H 27
Quarrywood. Mor 7A 80
Quartalehouse. Abers 1J 73
Quarter. N Ayr 3L 57
Quarter. S Lan 4F 58
Quatford. Shrp 2F 26
Quatt. Shrp 3F 26
Quebec. Dur 7E 54
Quedgeley. Glos 2G 19
Queen Adelaide. Cambs 3B 30
Queenborough. Kent 6F 22
Queen Camel. Som 3D 8
Queen Charlton. Bath 7E 18
Queen Dart. Devn 4H 7
Queenhill. Worc 8G 27
Queen Oak. Dors 2F 8
Queensbury. W Yor 4K 41
Queensferry. Flin 3B 34
Queensferry Crossing. Edin 2K 59
Queenstown. Bkpl 4B 40
Queen Street. Kent 1C 12
Queenzieburn. N Lan 2E 58
Quemerford. Wilts 7J 19
Quendale. Shet 6D 90
Quendon. Essx 8B 30
Queniborough. Leics 8D 36
Quenington. Glos 3K 19
Quernmore. Lanc 1D 40
Quethiock. Corn 5F 4
Quholm. Orkn 8B 88
Quick's Green. W Ber 6C 20
Quidenham. Norf 3G 31
Quidhampton. Hants 8C 20
Quidhampton. Wilts 2K 9
Quilquox. Abers 2J 73
Quina Brook. Shrp 6D 34
Quindry. Orkn 2F 86
Quine's Hill. IOM 7C 44
Quinton. Nptn 6E 28
Quinton. W Mid 3H 27
Quintrell Downs. Corn 2M 3
Quixhill. Staf 5K 35
Quoditch. Devn 6D 6
Quorn. Leics 8C 36
Quorndon. Leics 8C 36
Quothquan. S Lan 6H 59
Quoyloo. Orkn 7B 88
Quoyness. Orkn 1D 86
Quoys. Shet
on Mainland 1E 90
on Unst 2L 91

R

Rableyheath. Herts 2K 21
Raby. Cumb 6F 52
Raby. Mers 2B 34
Rachan Mill. Bord 6K 59
Rachub. Gwyn 4F 32
Rack End. Oxon 3B 20
Rackenford. Devn 4H 7
Rackham. W Sus 4H 11
Rackheath. Norf 8J 39
Racks. Dum 4E 52
Rackwick. Orkn
on Hoy 2D 86
on Westray 5D 88
Radbourne. Derbs 6L 35
Radcliffe. G Man 7F 40
Radcliffe. Nmbd 1F 54
Radcliffe on Trent. Notts 6D 36
Radclive. Buck 8D 28
Radernie. Fife 7H 67
Radfall. Kent 7H 23
Radford. Bath 8E 18
Radford. Nott 5C 36
Radford. Oxon 1B 20
Radford. W Mid 3M 27
Radford. Worc 6J 27
Radford Semele. Warw 5M 27
Radipole. Dors 7E 8
Radlett. Herts 4J 21
Radley. Oxon 4C 20
Radnage. Buck 4E 20
Radstock. Bath 8E 18
Radstone. Nptn 7C 28
Radway. Warw 7A 28
Radway Green. Ches E 4F 34
Radwell. Bed 6H 29
Radwell. Herts 8K 29
Radwinter. Essx 8C 30
Radyr. Card 6L 17
RAF Coltishall. Norf 7J 39
Rafford. Mor 8L 79
Raffrey. New M 6J 93
Ragdale. Leics 8D 36
Ragdon. Shrp 2C 26
Ragged Appleshaw. Hants 1M 9
Raggra. High 7E 86
Raglan. Mon 3C 18
Ragnall. Notts 2F 36
Raholp. New M 6J 93
Raigbeg. High 3J 71
Rainford. Mers 7C 40
Rainford Junction. Mers 7C 40
Rainham. G Lon 5B 22
Rainham. Medw 7E 22
Rainhill. Mers 8C 40
Rainow. Ches E 2H 35
Rainton. N Yor 8A 48
Rainworth. Notts 4C 36
Raisbeck. Cumb 5E 46
Raise. Cumb 7M 53
Rait. Per 5F 66
Raithby. Linc 1L 37
Raithby by Spilsby. Linc 3L 37
Raithwaite. N Yor 4F 48
Rake. W Sus 3F 10
Rake End. Staf 8J 35
Rakeway. Staf 5J 35
Rakewood. G Man 6H 41
Ralia. High 6H 71
Ram Alley. Wilts 7L 19
Ramasaig. High 1C 68
Rame. Corn
nr. Millbrook 7G 5
nr. Penryn 5L 3
Ram Lane. Kent 1F 12
Ramnageo. Shet 3L 91
Rampisham. Dors 5D 8
Rampside. Cumb 8M 45
Rampton. Cambs 5M 29
Rampton. Notts 2E 36
Ramsbottom. G Man 6F 40
Ramsburn. Mor 8E 80
Ramsbury. Wilts 6L 19
Ramscraigs. High 1M 79
Ramsdean. Hants 3E 10
Ramsdell. Hants 8C 20
Ramsden. Oxon 2A 20
Ramsden. Worc 7H 27
Ramsden Bellhouse. Essx 4D 22
Ramsden Heath. Essx 4D 22
Ramsey. Cambs 3K 29
Ramsey. Essx 8J 31
Ramsey. IOM 5D 44
Ramsey Forty Foot. Cambs 3L 29
Ramsey Heights. Cambs 3K 29
Ramsey Island. Essx 3F 22
Ramsey Mereside. Cambs 3K 29
Ramsey St Mary's. Cambs 3K 29
Ramsgate. Kent 7K 23
Ramsgill. N Yor 8K 47
Ramshaw. Dur 7C 54
Ramshorn. Staf 5J 35
Ramsley. Devn 6F 6
Ramsnest Common. Surr 2G 11
Ramstone. Abers 4F 72
Ranais. W Isl 1F 76
Ranby. Linc 2K 37
Ranby. Notts 1D 36
Rand. Linc 2J 37
Randalstown. Ant 4G 93
Randwick. Glos 3G 19
Ranfurly. Ren 3B 58
Rangag. High 7C 86
Rangemore. Staf 7K 35
Rangeworthy. S Glo 5E 18
Rankinston. E Ayr 8C 58
Rank's Green. Essx 2D 22
Ranmore Common. Surr 8J 21
Rannoch Station. Per 2J 65
Ranochan. High 7K 69
Ranskill. Notts 1D 36
Ranton. Staf 7G 35
Ranton Green. Staf 7G 35
Ranworth. Norf 8K 39
Raploch. Stir 8A 66
Rapness. Orkn 5E 88
Rapps. Som 4B 8
Rascal Moor. E Yor 4F 42
Rascarrel. Dum 7B 52
Rasharkin. Caus 3F 93
Rashfield. Arg 1L 57
Rashwood. Worc 5H 27
Raskelf. N Yor 8B 48
Rassau. Blae 3L 17
Rastrick. W Yor 5K 41
Ratagan. High 4L 69
Ratby. Leics 1C 28
Ratcliffe Culey. Leics 2M 27
Ratcliffe on Soar. Notts 7B 36
Ratcliffe on the Wreake. Leics 8D 36
Rathen. Abers 7K 81
Rathfriland. Arm 7G 93
Rathillet. Fife 5G 67
Rathmell. N Yor 1G 41
Ratho. Edin 2K 59
Ratho Station. Edin 2K 59
Rathven. Mor 7D 80
Ratley. Hants 3M 9
Ratley. Warw 7A 28
Ratlinghope. Shrp 2C 26
Rattar. High 4D 86
Ratten Row. Cumb 7H 53
Ratten Row. Lanc 3C 40
Rattery. Devn 5K 5
Rattlesden. Suff 6F 30
Ratton Village. E Sus 5B 12
Rattray. Abers 8K 81
Rattray. Per 3E 66
Raughton. Cumb 7H 53
Raughton Head. Cumb 7H 53
Raunds. Nptn 4G 29
Ravenfield. S Yor 8B 42
Ravenfield Common. S Yor 8B 42
Ravenglass. Cumb 5K 45
Ravenhills Green. Worc 6F 26
Raveningham. Norf 2K 31
Ravenscar. N Yor 5G 49
Ravensdale. IOM 5C 44
Ravensden. Bed 6H 29
Ravenseat. N Yor 5G 47
Ravenshead. Notts 4C 36
Ravensmoor. Ches E 4E 34
Ravensthorpe. Nptn 4D 28
Ravensthorpe. W Yor 5L 41
Ravenstone. Leics 8B 36
Ravenstone. Mil 6F 28
Ravenstonedale. Cumb 5F 46
Ravenstown. Cumb 8B 46
Ravenstruther. S Lan 5H 59
Ravensworth. N Yor 5K 47
Raveret. Lis 5H 93
Raw. N Yor 5G 49
Rawcliffe. E Yor 5D 42
Rawcliffe. York 2C 42
Rawcliffe Bridge. E Yor 5D 42
Rawdon. W Yor 4L 41
Rawgreen. Nmbd 6C 54
Rawmarsh. S Yor 8B 42
Rawnsley. Staf 8J 35
Rawreth. Essx 4D 22
Rawridge. Devn 5M 7
Rawson Green. Derbs 5A 36
Rawtenstall. Lanc 5G 41
Raydon. Suff 8G 31
Raylees. Nmbd 2C 54
Rayleigh. Essx 4E 22
Raymond's Hill. Devn 6B 8
Rayne. Essx 1D 22
Rayners Lane. G Lon 5J 21
Reach. Cambs 5B 30
Read. Lanc 4F 40
Reading. Read 115 (6E 20)
Reading Green. Suff 4H 31
Reading Street. Kent 2F 12
Readymoney. Corn 6D 4
Reagill. Cumb 4E 46
Rearquhar. High 4H 79
Rearsby. Leics 8D 36
Reasby. Linc 2H 37
Reaseheath. Ches E 4E 34
Reaster. High 5D 86
Reawick. Shet 3D 90
Reay. High 5A 86
Rechullin. High 8K 77
Reculver. Kent 7J 23
Redberth. Pemb 6G 15
Redbourn. Herts 2J 21
Redbourne. N Lin 7G 43
Redbrook. Glos 3D 18
Redbrook. Wrex 5D 34
Redburn. High 1K 71
Redburn. Nmbd 5A 54
Redcar. Red C 3D 48
Redcastle. High 1F 70
Redcliffe Bay. N Som 6C 18
Red Dial. Cumb 7G 53
Redding. Falk 2H 59
Reddingmuirhead. Falk 2H 59
The Reddings. Glos 1H 19
Reddish. G Man 8G 41
Redditch. Worc 5J 27
Rede. Suff 6E 30
Redenhall. Norf 3J 31
Redesdale Camp. Nmbd 2B 54
Redesmouth. Nmbd 3B 54
Redford. Ang 3J 67
Redford. Dur 8D 54
Redford. W Sus 3F 10
Redfordgreen. Bord 8A 60
Redgate. Corn 5E 4
Redgrave. Suff 4G 31
Red Hill. Warw 6K 27
Red Hill. W Yor 5B 42
Redhill. Abers 5G 73
Redhill. Herts 8K 29
Redhill. N Som 7D 18
Redhill. Shrp 8F 34
Redhill. Surr 8K 21
Redhouses. Arg 3C 56
Redisham. Suff 3L 31
Redland. Bris 6D 18
Redland. Orkn 7C 88
Redlingfield. Suff 4H 31
Red Lodge. Suff 4C 30
Redlynch. Som 2F 8
Redlynch. Wilts 3L 9
Redmain. Cumb 8F 52
Redmarley. Worc 5F 26
Redmarley D'Abitot. Glos 8F 26
Redmarshall. Stoc T 3A 48
Redmile. Leics 6E 36
Redmire. N Yor 6J 47
Rednal. Shrp 7B 34
Redpath. Bord 6C 60
Redpoint. High 7J 77
Red Post. Corn 5B 6
Red Rock. G Man 7D 40
Red Roses. Carm 5J 15
Red Row. Nmbd 2F 54
Redruth. Corn 4L 3
Red Street. Staf 4G 35
Redvales. G Man 7G 41
Red Wharf Bay. IOA 2E 32
Redwick. Newp 5C 18
Redwick. S Glo 5D 18
Redworth. Darl 3L 47
Reed. Herts 8L 29
Reed End. Herts 8L 29
Reedham. Linc 4K 37
Reedham. Norf 1L 31
Reedness. E Yor 5F 42
Reeds Beck. Linc 3K 37
Reemshill. Abers 1G 73
Reepham. Linc 2H 37
Reepham. Norf 7G 39
Reeth. N Yor 6J 47
Regaby. IOM 5D 44
Regil. N Som 7D 18
Regoul. High 8J 79
Reiff. High 2L 77
Reigate. Surr 8K 21
Reighton. N Yor 8J 49
Reilth. Shrp 3A 26
Reinigeadal. W Isl 3D 76
Reisque. Abers 4H 73
Reiss. High 6E 86
Rejerrah. Corn 3L 3
Releath. Corn 5K 3
Relubbus. Corn 5J 3
Relugas. Mor 1K 71
Remenham. Wok 5E 20
Remenham Hill. Wok 5E 20
Rempstone. Notts 7C 36
Rendcomb. Glos 3J 19
Rendham. Suff 5K 31
Rendlesham. Suff 6K 31
Renfrew. Ren 3D 58
Renhold. Bed 6H 29
Renishaw. Derbs 2B 36
Rennington. Nmbd 8K 61
Renton. W Dun 2B 58
Renwick. Cumb 7K 53
Repps. Norf 8L 39
Repton. Derbs 7M 35
Rescassa. Corn 7B 4
Rescobie. Ang 2J 67
Rescorla. Corn
nr. Penwithick 6C 4
nr. Sticker 7B 4
Resipole. High 1B 64
Resolfen. Neat 4H 17
Resolis. High 7G 79
Resolven. Neat 4H 17
Rest and be thankful. Arg 7G 65
Reston. Bord 3F 60
Restrop. Wilts 5J 19
Retford. Notts 1E 36
Retire. Corn 5C 4
Rettendon. Essx 4D 22
Revesby. Linc 3K 37
Rew. Devn 8K 5
Rewe. Devn 6J 7
Rew Street. IOW 6B 10
Rexon. Devn 7D 6
Reybridge. Wilts 7H 19
Reydon. Suff 4M 31
Reymerston. Norf 1G 31
Reynalton. Pemb 6G 15
Reynoldston. Swan 8L 15
Rezare. Corn 8C 6
Rhadyr. Mon 3B 18
Rhaeadr Gwy. Powy 6J 25
Rhandirmwyn. Carm 8G 25
Rhayader. Powy 6J 25
Rheindown. High 1F 70
Rhemore. High 2L 63
Rhenetra. High 8F 76
Rhewl. Den
nr. Llangollen 6L 33
nr. Ruthin 4L 33
Rhewl. Shrp 6B 34
Rhewl-Mostyn. Flin 2L 33
Rhian. High 2F 78
Rhian Breck. High 3F 78
Rhicarn. High 1A 78
Rhiconich. High 6E 84
Rhicullen. High 6G 79
Rhidorroch. High 4B 78
Rhifail. High 7K 85
Rhigos. Rhon 4J 17
Rhilochan. High 3H 79
Rhiroy. High 5B 78
Rhitongue. High 6J 85
Rhiw. Gwyn 8B 32
Rhiwabon. Wrex 5B 34
Rhiwbina. Card 6L 17
Rhiwbryfdir. Gwyn 6F 32
Rhiwderin. Newp 5A 18
Rhiwlas. Gwyn
nr. Bala 7J 33
nr. Bangor 4E 32
Rhiwlas. Powy 7L 33
Rhodes. G Man 7G 41
Rhodesia. Notts 1C 36
Rhodes Minnis. Kent 1H 13
Rhodiad-y-Brenin. Pemb 4D 14
Rhondda. Rhon 5J 17
Rhonehouse. Dum 6B 52
Rhoose. V Glam 8K 17
Rhos. Carm 3K 15
Rhos. Neat 4G 17
The Rhos. Pemb 5G 15
Rhosaman. Carm 3G 17
Rhoscefnhir. IOA 3E 32
Rhoscolyn. IOA 3B 32
Rhos Common. Powy 8A 34
Rhoscrowther. Pemb 6F 14
Rhos-ddu. Gwyn 7B 32
Rhosdylluan. Gwyn 8H 33
Rhosesmor. Flin 4M 33
Rhos-fawr. Gwyn 7C 32
Rhosgadfan. Gwyn 5E 32
Rhosgoch. IOA 2D 32
Rhosgoch. Powy 8L 25
Rhos Haminiog. Cdgn 6E 24
Rhos-hill. Pemb 2H 15
Rhoshirwaun. Gwyn 8A 32
Rhoslan. Gwyn 6D 32
Rhoslefain. Gwyn 2E 24
Rhosllanerchrugog. Wrex 5A 34
Rhôs Lligwy. IOA 2D 32
Rhosmaen. Carm 2F 16
Rhosmeirch. IOA 3D 32
Rhosneigr. IOA 3C 32
Rhôs-on-Sea. Cnwy 2H 33
Rhossili. Swan 8L 15
Rhosson. Pemb 4D 14
Rhostrenwfa. IOA 3D 32
Rhostryfan. Gwyn 5D 32
Rhostyllen. Wrex 5B 34
Rhoswiel. Shrp 6A 34
Rhosybol. IOA 2D 32
Rhos-y-brithdir. Powy 8L 33
Rhos-y-garth. Cdgn 5F 24
Rhos-y-gwaliau. Gwyn 7J 33
Rhos-y-llan. Gwyn 7B 32
Rhos-y-meirch. Powy 5A 26
Rhu. Arg 1A 58
Rhualt. Den 3K 33
Rhubha Stoer. High 8C 84
Rhubodach. Arg 2K 57
Rhuddall Heath. Ches W 3D 34
Rhuddlan. Cdgn 2L 15
Rhuddlan. Den 3K 33
Rhue. High 4A 78
Rhulen. Powy 8L 25
Rhunahaorine. Arg 5G 57
Rhuthun. Den 5L 33
Rhuvoult. High 6E 84
Y Rhws. V Glam 8K 17
Rhyd. Gwyn 6F 32
Rhydaman. Carm 3F 16
Rhydargaeau. Carm 4L 15
Rhydcymerau. Carm 1E 16
Rhydd. Worc 7G 27
Rhyd-Ddu. Gwyn 5E 32
Rhydding. Neat 5G 17
Rhydfudr. Cdgn 6E 24
Rhydlanfair. Cnwy 5H 33
Rhydlewis. Cdgn 2K 15
Rhydlios. Gwyn 7A 32
Rhydlydan. Cnwy 5H 33
Rhyd-meirionydd. Cdgn 4F 24
Rhydowen. Cdgn 2L 15
Rhyd-Rosser. Cdgn 6E 24
Rhydspence. Here 8M 25
Rhydtalog. Flin 5M 33
Rhyd-uchaf. Gwyn 7J 33
Rhydwyn. IOA 2C 32
Rhyd-y-clafdy. Gwyn 7C 32
Rhydycroesau. Powy 7M 33
Rhydyfelin. Cdgn 5E 24
Rhydyfelin. Rhon 6K 17
Rhyd-y-foel. Cnwy 3J 33
Rhyd-y-fro. Neat 4G 17
Rhydymain. Gwyn 8H 33
Rhyd-y-meudwy. Den 5L 33
Rhydymwyn. Flin 4M 33
Rhyd-yr-onen. Gwyn 2F 24
Rhyd-y-sarn. Gwyn 6F 32
Rhyl. Den 2K 33
Rhymney. Cphy 4L 17
Rhymni. Cphy 4L 17
Rhynd. Per 5E 66
Rhynie. Abers 3D 72
Ribbesford. Worc 4F 26
Ribbleton. Lanc 4D 40
Ribby. Lanc 4C 40
Ribchester. Lanc 4E 40
Riber. Derbs 4M 35
Ribigill. High 6H 85
Riby. Linc 7J 43
Riccall. N Yor 4D 42
Riccarton. E Ayr 6C 58
Richards Castle. Here 5C 26
Richborough Port. Kent 7K 23
Richhill. Arm 6F 93
Richings Park. Buck 6H 21
Richmond. G Lon 6J 21
Richmond. N Yor 5K 47
Rickarton. Abers 7H 73
Rickerby. Cumb 6J 53
Rickerscote. Staf 7H 35
Rickford. N Som 8C 18
Rickham. Devn 8K 5
Rickinghall. Suff 4G 31
Rickleton. Tyne 6F 54
Rickling. Essx 8A 30
Rickling Green. Essx 1B 22
Rickmansworth. Herts 4H 21
Riddings. Derbs 4B 36
Riddlecombe. Devn 4F 6
Riddlesden. W Yor 3J 41
Ridge. Dors 7H 9
Ridge. Herts 3K 21
Ridge. Wilts 2H 9
Ridgebourne. Powy 6K 25
Ridge Lane. Warw 2L 27
Ridgeway. Derbs
nr. Alfreton 4A 36
nr. Sheffield 1B 36
Ridgeway. Staf 4G 35
Ridgeway Cross. Here 7F 26
Ridgeway Moor. Derbs 1B 36
Ridgewell. Essx 7D 30
Ridgewood. E Sus 3A 12
Ridgmont. C Beds 8G 29
Ridgwardine. Shrp 6E 34
Riding Mill. Nmbd 5D 54
Ridley. Kent 7C 22
Ridley. Nmbd 5A 54
Ridlington. Norf 6K 39
Ridlington. Rut 1F 28
Ridsdale. Nmbd 3C 54
Riemore Lodge. Per 3D 66
Rievaulx. N Yor 7C 48
Rift House. Hart 8H 55
Rigg. Dum 5G 53
Riggend. N Lan 2F 58
Rigsby. Linc 2M 37
Rigside. S Lan 6G 59
Riley Green. Lanc 5E 40
Rileyhill. Staf 8K 35
Rilla Mill. Corn 8B 6
Rillington. N Yor 8F 48
Rimington. Lanc 3G 41
Rimpton. Som 3E 8
Rimsdale. High 7K 85
Rimswell. E Yor 5L 43
Ringasta. Shet 6D 90
Ringford. Dum 6A 52
Ringing Hill. Leics 8B 36
Ringinglow. S Yor 1L 35
Ringland. Norf 8H 39
Ringlestone. Kent 8E 22
Ringmer. E Sus 4M 11
Ringmore. Devn
nr. Kingsbridge 7J 5
nr. Teignmouth 8J 7
Ring o' Bells. Lanc 6C 40
Ring's End. Cambs 1L 29
Ringsfield. Suff 3L 31
Ringsfield Corner. Suff 3L 31
Ringshall. Buck 2G 21
Ringshall. Suff 6G 31
Ringshall Stocks. Suff 6G 31
Ringstead. Norf 5D 38
Ringstead. Nptn 4G 29
Ringwood. Hants 5K 9
Ringwould. Kent 1K 13
Rinmore. Abers 4D 72
Rinnigill. Orkn 2E 86
Rinsey. Corn 6J 3
Riof. W Isl 8E 82
Ripe. E Sus 4B 12
Ripley. Derbs 4B 36
Ripley. Hants 6K 9
Ripley. N Yor 1L 41
Ripley. Surr 8H 21
Riplingham. E Yor 4G 43
Ripon. N Yor 8M 47
Rippingale. Linc 7H 37
Ripple. Kent 1K 13
Ripple. Worc 8G 27
Ripponden. W Yor 6J 41
Rireavach. High 4M 77
Risabus. Arg 5C 56
Risbury. Here 6D 26
Risby. E Yor 4H 43
Risby. N Lin 6G 43
Risby. Suff 5D 30
Risca. Cphy 5M 17
Rise. E Yor 3J 43
Riseden. E Sus 2C 12
Riseden. Kent 2D 12
Rise End. Derbs 4L 35
Risegate. Linc 7K 37
Riseholme. Linc 2G 37
Riseley. Bed 5H 29
Riseley. Wok 7E 20
Rishangles. Suff 5H 31
Rishton. Lanc 4F 40
Rishworth. W Yor 6J 41
Risley. Derbs 6B 36
Risley. Warr 8E 40
Risplith. N Yor 1L 41
Rispond. High 5G 85
Rivar. Wilts 7M 19
Rivenhall. Essx 2E 22
Rivenhall End. Essx 2E 22
River. Kent 1J 13
River. W Sus 3G 11
River Bank. Cambs 5B 30
Riverhead. Kent 8B 22
Rivington. Lanc 6E 40
Roach Bridge. Lanc 5D 40
Roachill. Devn 3H 7
Roade. Nptn 6E 28
Road Green. Norf 2J 31
Roadhead. Cumb 4K 53
Roadmeetings. S Lan 5G 59
Roadside. High 5C 86
Roadside of Catterline. Abers 8H 73
Roadside of Kinneff. Abers 8H 73
Roadwater. Som 2K 7
Road Weedon. Nptn 6D 28
Roag. High 1D 68
Roa Island. Cumb 8M 45
Roath. Card 7L 17
Roberton. Bord 8B 60
Roberton. S Lan 7H 59
Robertsbridge. E Sus 3D 12
Robertstown. Mor 1B 72
Robertstown. Rhon 4J 17
Roberttown. W Yor 5K 41
Robeston Back. Pemb 5G 15
Robeston Wathen. Pemb 5G 15
Robeston West. Pemb 6E 14
Robin Hood. Lanc 6D 40
Robin Hood. W Yor 5M 41
Robinhood End. Essx 8D 30
Robin Hood's Bay. N Yor 5G 49
Roborough. Devn
nr. Great Torrington 4E 6
nr. Plymouth 5H 5
Rob Roy's House. Arg 6F 64
Roby Mill. Lanc 7D 40
Rocester. Staf 6K 35
Roch. Pemb 4E 14
Rochdale. G Man 6G 41
Roche. Corn 5B 4
Rochester. Medw
Medway Towns 111 (7D 22)
Rochester. Nmbd 2B 54
Rochford. Essx 4E 22
Rock. Corn 4B 4
Rock. Nmbd 7K 61
Rock. W Sus 4J 11
Rock. Worc 4F 26
The Rock. M Ulst 5E 92
Rockbeare. Devn 6K 7
Rockbourne. Hants 4K 9
Rockcliffe. Cumb 5H 53
Rockcliffe. Dum 6C 52
Rockcliffe Cross. Cumb 5H 53
Rock Ferry. Mers 1B 34
Rockfield. High 5K 79
Rockfield. Mon 2C 18
Rockford. Hants 5K 9
Rockgreen. Shrp 4D 26
Rockhampton. S Glo 4E 18
Rockhead. Corn 3C 4
Rockingham. Nptn 2F 28
Rockland All Saints. Norf 2F 30
Rockland St Mary. Norf 1K 31
Rockland St Peter. Norf 2F 30
Rockley. Wilts 6K 19
Rockwell End. Buck 5E 20
Rockwell Green. Som 4L 7
Rodborough. Glos 3G 19
Rodbourne. Wilts 5H 19
Rodd. Here 5B 26
Roddam. Nmbd 7H 61
Rodden. Dors 7E 8
Roddenloft. E Ayr 7C 58
Roddymoor. Dur 8E 54
Rode. Som 8G 19
Rode Heath. Ches E 4G 35
Rodeheath. Ches E 3G 35
Rodel. W Isl 5B 76
Roden. Telf 8D 34
Rodhuish. Som 2K 7
Rodington. Telf 8D 34
Rodington Heath. Telf 8D 34
Rodley. Glos 2F 18
Rodmarton. Glos 4H 19
Rodmell. E Sus 5M 11
Rodmersham. Kent 7F 22
Rodmersham Green. Kent 7F 22
Rodney Stoke. Som 1C 8
Rodsley. Derbs 5L 35
Rodway. Som 2A 8
Rodway. Telf 8E 34
Rodwell. Dors 8E 8
Roecliffe. N Yor 1A 42
Roe Green. Herts 8L 29
Roehampton. G Lon 6K 21
Roesound. Shet 1D 90
Roffey. W Sus 2J 11
Rogart. High 3H 79
Rogate. W Sus 3F 10
Roger Ground. Cumb 6B 46
Rogerstone. Newp 5A 18
Rogiet. Mon 5C 18
Rogue's Alley. Cambs 1L 29
Roke. Oxon 4D 20
Rokemarsh. Oxon 4D 20
Roker. Tyne 6H 55
Rollesby. Norf 8L 39
Rolleston. Leics 1E 28
Rolleston. Notts 4E 36
Rolleston on Dove. Staf 7L 35
Rolston. E Yor 3K 43
Rolvenden. Kent 2E 12
Rolvenden Layne. Kent 2E 12
Romaldkirk. Dur 3H 47
Roman Bank. Shrp 2D 26
Romanby. N Yor 6A 48
Romannobridge. Bord 5K 59
Romansleigh. Devn 3G 7
Romers Common. Worc 5D 26
Romesdal. High 8F 76
Romford. Dors 5J 9
Romford. G Lon 5B 22
Romiley. G Man 8H 41
Romsey. Hants 3A 10
Romsley. Shrp 3F 26
Romsley. Worc 4H 27
Ronague. IOM 7B 44
Ronaldsvoe. Orkn 2F 86
Rookby. Cumb 4G 47
Rookhope. Dur 7C 54
Rooking. Cumb 4C 46
Rookley. IOW 7C 10
Rooks Bridge. Som 8B 18
Rooksey Green. Suff 6F 31
Rook's Nest. Som 2K 7
Rookwood. W Sus 6E 10
Roos. E Yor 4K 43
Roosebeck. Cumb 8M 45
Roosecote. Cumb 8M 45
Rootfield. High 8F 78
Rootham's Green. Bed 6J 29
Rootpark. S Lan 4H 59
Ropley. Hants 2D 10
Ropley Dean. Hants 2D 10
Ropsley. Linc 6G 37
Rora. Abers 8K 81
Rorandle. Abers 4F 72
Rorrington. Shrp 1B 26
Rose. Corn 3L 3
Roseacre. Lanc 4C 40
Rose Ash. Devn 3G 7
Rosebank. S Lan 5G 59
Rosebush. Pemb 4G 15
Rosedale Abbey. N Yor 6E 48
Roseden. Nmbd 7H 61
Rose Green. Essx 1E 22
Rose Green. Suff 7F 30
Rosehall. High 3E 78
Rosehearty. Abers 7J 81
Rose Hill. E Sus 4A 12
Rose Hill. Lanc 4G 41
Rosehill. Shrp
nr. Market Drayton 6E 34
nr. Shrewsbury 8C 34
Roseisle. Mor 7M 79
Rosemarket. Pemb 6F 14
Rosemarkie. High 8H 79
Rosemary Lane. Devn 4L 7
Rosemount. Per 3E 66
Rosenannon. Corn 5B 4
Roser's Cross. E Sus 3B 12
Rosevean. Corn 6C 4
Rosewell. Midl 3L 59
Roseworth. Stoc T 3B 48
Roseworthy. Corn 5K 3
Rosgill. Cumb 4D 46
Roshven. High 8J 69
Roskhill. High 1D 68
Roskorwell. Corn 6L 3
Rosley. Cumb 7H 53
Roslin. Midl 3L 59
Rosliston. Derbs 8L 35
Rosneath. Arg 1A 58
Ross. Dum 7M 51
Ross. Nmbd 6J 61
Ross. Per 5A 66
Ross. Bord 3G 61
Rossendale. Lanc 5F 40
Rossett. Wrex 4B 34
Rossington. S Yor 8D 42
Rosskeen. High 7G 79
Rossland. Ren 2C 58
Rosslea. Ferm 7D 92
Ross-on-Wye. Here 1E 18
Roster. High 8D 86
Rostherne. Ches E 1F 34
Rostholme. S Yor 7C 42
Rosthwaite. Cumb 4A 46
Roston. Derbs 5K 35
Rostrevor. New M 7G 93
Rosudgeon. Corn 6J 3
Rosyth. Fife 1K 59
Rothbury. Nmbd 1D 54
Rotherby. Leics 8D 36
Rotherfield. E Sus 3B 12
Rotherfield Greys. Oxon 5E 20
Rotherfield Peppard. Oxon 5E 20
Rotherham. S Yor 8B 42
Rothersthorpe. Nptn 6E 28
Rotherwick. Hants 8E 20
Rothes. Mor 1B 72
Rothesay. Arg 3K 57
Rothienorman. Abers 2G 73
Rothiesholm. Orkn 7F 88
Rothley. Leics 8C 36
Rothley. Nmbd 3D 54
Rothwell. Linc 8J 43
Rothwell. Nptn 3F 28
Rothwell. W Yor 5M 41
Rotsea. E Yor 2H 43
Rottal. Ang 1G 67
Rotten End. Suff 5K 31
Rotten Row. Norf 8G 39
Rotten Row. W Ber 6C 20
Rotten Row. W Mid 4K 27
Rottingdean. Brig 5L 11
Rottington. Cumb 3J 45
Roud. IOW 7C 10
Rougham. Norf 7E 38
Rougham. Suff 5F 30
Rough Close. Staf 6H 35
Rough Common. Kent 8H 23
Roughcote. Staf 5H 35
Roughfort. Ant 4H 93
Rough Haugh. High 7K 85
Rough Hay. Staf 7L 35
Roughlee. Lanc 3G 41
Roughley. W Mid 2K 27
Roughsike. Cumb 4K 53
Roughton. Linc 3K 37
Roughton. Norf 6J 39
Roughton. Shrp 2F 26
Roundbush Green. Essx 2B 22
Roundham. Som 5C 8
Roundhay. W Yor 4M 41
Round Hill. Torb 5L 5
Roundhurst. W Sus 2G 11
Round Maple. Suff 7F 30
Round Oak. Shrp 3B 26
Roundstreet Common. W Sus 3H 11
Roundthwaite. Cumb 5E 46
Roundway. Wilts 7J 19
Roundyhill. Ang 2G 67
Rousdon. Devn 6A 8
Rousham. Oxon 1B 20
Rousky. Ferm 4D 92
Rous Lench. Worc 6J 27
Routh. E Yor 3H 43
Rout's Green. Buck 4E 20
Row. Corn 4C 4
Row. Cumb
nr. Kendal 7C 46
nr. Penrith 8L 53
The Row. Lanc 8C 46
Rowanburn. Dum 4J 53
Rowanhill. Abers 8K 81
Rowardennan. Stir 8H 65
Rowarth. Derbs 1J 35
Row Ash. Hants 4C 10
Rowberrow. Som 8C 18
Rowde. Wilts 7H 19
Rowden. Devn 6F 6
Rowen. Cnwy 3G 33
Rowfoot. Nmbd 5L 53
Row Green. Essx 1D 22
Row Heath. Essx 2H 23
Rowhedge. Essx 1G 23
Rowhook. W Sus 2J 11
Rowington. Warw 5L 27
Rowland. Derbs 2L 35
Rowlands Castle. Hants 4E 10
Rowlands Gill. Tyne 6E 54
Rowledge. Hants 1F 10
Rowley. Dur 7D 54
Rowley. E Yor 4G 43
Rowley. Shrp 1B 26
Rowley Hill. W Yor 6K 41
Rowley Regis. W Mid 3H 27
Rowlstone. Here 1B 18
Rowly. Surr 1H 11
Rowner. Hants 5C 10
Rowney Green. Worc 4J 27
Rownhams. Hants 4A 10
Rowrah. Cumb 3K 45
Rowsham. Buck 2F 20
Rowsley. Derbs 3L 35
Rowstock. Oxon 5B 20
Rowston. Linc 4H 37
Rowthorne. Derbs 3B 36
Rowton. Ches W 3C 34
Rowton. Shrp
nr. Ludlow 3C 26
nr. Shrewsbury 8B 34
Rowton. Telf 8E 34
Row Town. Surr 7H 21
Roxburgh. Bord 6E 60
Roxby. N Lin 6G 43
Roxby. N Yor 4E 48
Roxhill. Ant 4G 93
Roxton. Bed 6J 29
Roxwell. Essx 3C 22
Royal Leamington Spa. Warw 5M 27
Royal Oak. Darl 3L 47
Royal Oak. Lanc 7C 40
Royal Oak. N Yor 8J 49
Royal's Green. Ches E 5E 34
Royal Sutton Coldfield. W Mid 2K 27
Royal Tunbridge Wells. Kent 2B 12
Royal Wootton Bassett. Wilts 5J 19
Roybridge. High 7C 70
Roydon. Essx 2M 21
Roydon. Norf
nr. Diss 3G 31
nr. King's Lynn 7D 38
Roydon Hamlet. Essx 3M 21
Royston. Herts 7L 29
Royston. S Yor 6A 42
Royston Water. Som 4M 7
Royton. G Man 7H 41
Ruabon. Wrex 5B 34
Ruaig. Arg 3F 62
Ruan High Lanes. Corn 8B 4
Ruan Lanihorne. Corn 7A 4
Ruan Major. Corn 7L 3
Ruan Minor. Corn 7L 3
Ruarach. High 3L 69
Ruardean. Glos 2E 18
Ruardean Hill. Glos 2E 18
Ruardean Woodside. Glos 2E 18
Rubane. Ards 5K 93
Rubery. Worc 4H 27
Ruchazie. Glas 3E 58
Ruckcroft. Cumb 7K 53
Ruckinge. Kent 2G 13
Ruckland. Linc 2L 37
Rucklers Lane. Herts 3H 21
Ruckley. Shrp 1D 26
Rudbaxton. Pemb 4F 14
Rudby. N Yor 5B 48
Ruddington. Notts 6C 36
Rudford. Glos 1F 18
Rudge. Shrp 2G 27
Rudge. Wilts 8G 19
Rudge Heath. Shrp 2F 26
Rudgeway. S Glo 5E 18
Rudgwick. W Sus 2H 11
Rudhall. Here 1E 18
Rudheath. Ches W 2E 34
Rudley Green. Essx 3E 22
Rudloe. Wilts 6G 19
Rudry. Cphy 6M 17
Rudston. E Yor 1H 43
Rudyard. Staf 4H 35
Rufford. Lanc 6C 40
Rufforth. York 2C 42
Rugby. Warw 4C 28
Rugeley. Staf 8J 35
Ruglen. S Ayr 1H 51
Ruilick. High 1F 70
Ruisaurie. High 1E 70
Ruishton. Som 3A 8
Ruisigearraidh. W Isl 5L 75
Ruislip. G Lon 5H 21
Ruislip Common. G Lon 5H 21
Rumbling Bridge. Per 8D 66
Rumburgh. Suff 3K 31
Rumford. Corn 4A 4
Rumford. Falk 2H 59
Rumney. Card 7M 17
Rumwell. Som 3L 7
Runcorn. Hal 1D 34
Runcton. W Sus 5F 10
Runcton Holme. Norf 1C 30
Rundlestone. Devn 8E 6
Runfold. Surr 1F 10
Runhall. Norf 1G 31
Runham. Norf 8L 39
Runnington. Som 3L 7
Runshaw Moor. Lanc 6D 40
Runswick. N Yor 4F 48
Runtaleave. Ang 1F 66
Runwell. Essx 4D 22
Ruscombe. Wok 6E 20
Rushall. Here 8E 26
Rushall. Norf 3H 31
Rushall. W Mid 1J 27
Rushall. Wilts 8K 19
Rushbrooke. Suff 5E 30
Rushbury. Shrp 2D 26
Rushden. Herts 8L 29
Rushden. Nptn 5G 29
Rushenden. Kent 6F 22
Rushford. Devn 8D 6
Rushford. Suff 3F 30
Rush Green. Herts 1K 21
Rushlake Green. E Sus 4C 12
Rushmere. Suff 3L 31
Rushmere St Andrew. Suff 7J 31
Rushmoor. Surr 1F 10
Rushock. Worc 4G 27
Rusholme. G Man 8G 41
Rushton. Ches W 3D 34
Rushton. Nptn 3F 28
Rushton. Shrp 1E 26
Rushton Spencer. Staf 3H 35
Rushwick. Worc 6G 27
Rushyford. Dur 3L 47
Ruskie. Stir 7L 65
Ruskington. Linc 4H 37
Rusland. Cumb 7B 46
Rusper. W Sus 2K 11
Ruspidge. Glos 2E 18
Russell's Water. Oxon 5E 20
Russel's Green. Suff 4J 31
Russ Hill. Surr 1K 11
Russland. Orkn 8C 88
Rusthall. Kent 2B 12
Rustington. W Sus 5H 11
Ruston. N Yor 7G 49
Ruston Parva. E Yor 1H 43
Ruswarp. N Yor 5F 48
Rutherglen. S Lan 3E 58
Ruthernbridge. Corn 5C 4
Ruthin. Den 5L 33
Ruthin. V Glam 7J 17
Ruthrieston. Aber 5J 73
Ruthven. Abers 1E 72
Ruthven. Ang 3F 66
Ruthven. High
nr. Inverness 2J 71
nr. Kingussie 6H 71
Ruthvoes. Corn 5B 4
Ruthwaite. Cumb 8G 53
Ruthwell. Dum 5F 52
Ruxton Green. Here 2D 18
Ruyton-XI-Towns. Shrp 7B 34
Ryal. Nmbd 4D 54
Ryall. Dors 6C 8
Ryall. Worc 7G 27
Ryarsh. Kent 8C 22
Rychraggan. High 2E 70
Rydal. Cumb 5B 46
Ryde. IOW 6C 10
Rye. E Sus 3F 12
Ryecroft Gate. Staf 3H 35
Ryeford. Here 1E 18
Rye Foreign. E Sus 3F 12
Rye Harbour. E Sus 4F 12
Ryehill. E Yor 5K 43
Rye Street. Worc 8F 26
Ryhall. Rut 8H 37
Ryhill. W Yor 6A 42
Ryhope. Tyne 6H 55
Ryhope Colliery. Tyne 6H 55
Rylands. Notts 6C 36
Rylstone. N Yor 2H 41
Ryme Intrinseca. Dors 4D 8
Ryther. N Yor 4C 42
Ryton. Glos 8F 26
Ryton. N Yor 8E 48
Ryton. Shrp 1F 26
Ryton. Tyne 5E 54
Ryton. Warw 3B 28
Ryton-on-Dunsmore. Warw 4A 28
Ryton Woodside. Tyne 5E 54

S

Saasaig. High 5H 69
Sabden. Lanc 4F 40
Sacombe. Herts 2L 21
Sacriston. Dur 7F 54
Sadberge. Darl 4M 47
Saddell. Arg 6G 57
Saddington. Leics 2D 28
Saddle Bow. Norf 8C 38
Saddlescombe. W Sus 4K 11
Saddleworth. G Man 7H 41
Sadgill. Cumb 5C 46
Saffron Walden. Essx 8B 30
Sageston. Pemb 6G 15
Saham Hills. Norf 1F 30
Saham Toney. Norf 1E 30
Saighdinis. W Isl 7K 75
Saighton. Ches W 3C 34
Sain Dunwyd. V Glam 8J 17
Sain Hilari. V Glam 7K 17
St Abbs. Bord 3G 61
St Agnes. Corn 3L 3

Sudbrook – Tregowris

Sudbrook. *Linc* 5G **37**
Sudbrook. *Mon* 5D **18**
Sudbrooke. *Linc* 2H **37**
Sudbury. *Derbs* 6K **35**
Sudbury. *Suff* 7E **30**
Sudgrove. *Glos* 3H **19**
Suffield. *Norf* 6J **39**
Suffield. *N Yor* 6G **49**
Sugnall. *Staf* 6F **34**
Sugwas Pool. *Here* 7C **26**
Suisnish. *High* 2G **69**
Sulaisiadar. *W Isl* 8J **83**
Sùlaisiadar Mòr. *High* 1F **68**
Sulby. *IOM* 5C **44**
Sulgrave. *Nptn* 7C **28**
Sulham. *W Ber* 6D **20**
Sulhamstead. *W Ber* 7D **20**
Sullington. *W Sus* 4H **11**
Sullom. *Shet* 6H **91**
Sully. *V Glam* 8L **17**
Sumburgh. *Shet* 7E **90**
Sumburgh Airport. *Shet* 6D **90**
Summer Bridge. *N Yor* 1L **41**
Summercourt. *Corn* 6A **4**
Summergangs. *Hull* 4J **43**
Summer Hill. *W Mid* 2H **27**
Summerhill. *Aber* 5J **73**
Summerhill. *Pemb* 6H **15**
Summerhouse. *Darl* 4L **47**
Summersdale. *W Sus* 5F **10**
Summerseat. *G Man* 6F **40**
Summit. *G Man* 6H **41**
Sunbury. *Surr* 7J **21**
Sunderland. *Cumb* 8F **52**
Sunderland. *Lanc* 2C **40**
Sunderland. *Tyne* **116** (6G **55**)
Sunderland Bridge. *Dur* 8F **54**
Sundon Park. *Lutn* 1H **21**
Sundridge. *Kent* 8A **22**
Sunk Island. *E Yor* 6K **43**
Sunningdale. *Wind* 7G **21**
Sunninghill. *Wind* 7G **21**
Sunningwell. *Oxon* 3B **20**
Sunniside. *Dur* 8E **54**
Sunniside. *Tyne* 6F **54**
Sunny Bank. *Cumb* 6A **46**
Sunny Hill. *Derb* 6M **35**
Sunnyhurst. *Bkbn* 5E **40**
Sunnylaw. *Stir* 8A **66**
Sunnymead. *Oxon* 3C **20**
Sunnyside. *S Yor* 8B **42**
Sunnyside. *W Sus* 2L **11**
Sunton. *Wilts* 8L **19**
Surbiton. *G Lon* 7J **21**
Surby. *IOM* 7B **44**
Surfleet. *Linc* 7K **37**
Surfleet Seas End. *Linc* 7K **37**
Surlingham. *Norf* 1K **31**
Surrex. *Essx* 1E **22**
Sustead. *Norf* 6H **39**
Susworth. *Linc* 7F **42**
Sutcombe. *Devn* 4C **6**
Suton. *Norf* 2G **31**
Sutors of Cromarty. *High* 7J **79**
Sutterby. *Linc* 2L **37**
Sutterton. *Linc* 6K **37**
Sutterton Dowdyke. *Linc* 6K **37**
Sutton. *Buck* 6H **21**
Sutton. *Cambs* 4M **29**
Sutton. *C Beds* 7K **29**
Sutton. *E Sus* 6A **12**
Sutton. *G Lon* 7K **21**
Sutton. *Kent* 1K **13**
Sutton. *Norf* 7K **39**
Sutton. *Notts* 6E **36**
Sutton. *Oxon* 3B **20**
Sutton. *Pemb* 5F **14**
Sutton. *Pet* 2H **29**
Sutton. *Shrp*
nr. Bridgnorth 3F **26**
nr. Market Drayton 6E **34**
nr. Oswestry 7B **34**
nr. Shrewsbury 8D **34**
Sutton. *Som* 2E **8**
Sutton. *S Yor* 6C **42**
Sutton. *Staf* 7F **34**
Sutton. *Suff* 7K **31**
Sutton. *W Sus* 4G **11**
Sutton. *Worc* 5E **26**
Sutton Abinger. *Surr* 1J **11**
Sutton at Hone. *Kent* 6B **22**
Sutton Bassett. *Nptn* 2E **28**
Sutton Benger. *Wilts* 6H **19**
Sutton Bingham. *Som* 4D **8**
Sutton Bonington. *Notts* 7C **36**
Sutton Bridge. *Linc* 7A **38**
Sutton Cheney. *Leics* 1B **28**
Sutton Coldfield, Royal.
W Mid 2K **27**
Sutton Corner. *Linc* 7M **37**
Sutton Courtenay. *Oxon* 4C **20**
Sutton Crosses. *Linc* 7M **37**
Sutton cum Lound. *Notts* 1D **36**
Sutton Gault. *Cambs* 4M **29**
Sutton Grange. *N Yor* 8L **47**
Sutton Green. *Surr* 8H **21**
Sutton Howgrave. *N Yor* 8M **47**
Sutton in Ashfield. *Notts* 4B **36**
Sutton-in-Craven. *N Yor* 3J **41**
Sutton Ings. *Hull* 4J **43**
Sutton in the Elms. *Leics* 2C **28**
Sutton Lane Ends. *Ches E* 2H **35**
Sutton Leach. *Mers* 8D **40**
Sutton Maddock. *Shrp* 1F **26**
Sutton Mallet. *Som* 2B **8**
Sutton Mandeville. *Wilts* 3H **9**
Sutton Montis. *Som* 3E **8**
Sutton on Hull. *Hull* 4J **43**
Sutton on Sea. *Linc* 1B **38**
Sutton-on-the-Forest.
N Yor 1C **42**
Sutton on the Hill. *Derbs* 6L **35**
Sutton on Trent. *Notts* 3E **36**
Sutton Poyntz. *Dors* 7F **8**
Sutton St Edmund. *Linc* 8L **37**
Sutton St Edmund's Common.
Linc 1L **29**
Sutton St James. *Linc* 8L **37**
Sutton St Michael. *Here* 7D **26**
Sutton St Nicholas. *Here* 7D **26**
Sutton Scarsdale. *Derbs* 3B **36**
Sutton Scotney. *Hants* 2B **10**
Sutton-under-Brailes.
Warw 8M **27**
Sutton-under-Whitestonecliffe.
N Yor 7B **48**
Sutton upon Derwent.
E Yor 3E **42**
Sutton Valence. *Kent* 1E **12**
Sutton Veny. *Wilts* 1H **9**
Sutton Waldron. *Dors* 4G **9**
Sutton Weaver. *Ches W* 2D **34**
Swaby. *Linc* 2L **37**
Swadlincote. *Derbs* 8L **35**
Swaffham. *Norf* 1E **30**
Swaffham Bulbeck. *Cambs* 5B **30**
Swaffham Prior. *Cambs* 5B **30**
Swafield. *Norf* 6J **39**
Swainby. *N Yor* 5B **48**
Swainshill. *Here* 7C **26**
Swainsthorpe. *Norf* 1J **31**
Swainswick. *Bath* 7F **18**
Swalcliffe. *Oxon* 8A **28**
Swalecliffe. *Kent* 7H **23**
Swallow. *Linc* 7J **43**
Swallow Beck. *Linc* 3G **37**
Swallowcliffe. *Wilts* 3H **9**
Swallowfield. *Wok* 7E **20**
Swallownest. *S Yor* 1B **36**
Swampton. *Hants* 8B **20**
Swanage. *Dors* 8J **9**
Swanbister. *Orkn* 1E **86**
Swanbourne. *Buck* 1F **20**
Swanbridge. *V Glam* 8L **17**
Swan Green. *Ches W* 2F **34**
Swanland. *E Yor* 5G **43**
Swanley. *Kent* 7B **22**
Swanmore. *Hants* 4C **10**
Swannington. *Leics* 8B **36**
Swannington. *Norf* 8H **39**
Swanpool. *Linc* 3G **37**
Swanscombe. *Kent* 6C **22**
Swansea. *Swan* **117** (5F **16**)
Swan Street. *Essx* 1E **22**
Swanton Abbott. *Norf* 7J **39**
Swanton Morley. *Norf* 8G **39**
Swanton Novers. *Norf* 6G **39**
Swanton Street. *Kent* 8E **22**
Swanwick. *Derbs* 4B **36**
Swanwick. *Hants* 5C **10**
Swanwick Green. *Ches E* 5D **34**
Swarby. *Linc* 5H **37**
Swardeston. *Norf* 1J **31**
Swarister. *Shet* 5K **91**
Swarkestone. *Derbs* 7A **36**
Swarland. *Nmbd* 1E **54**
Swarraton. *Hants* 2C **10**
Swartha. *W Yor* 3J **41**
Swarthmoor. *Cumb* 8A **46**
Swaton. *Linc* 6J **37**
Swatragh. *M Ulst* 3F **93**
Swavesey. *Cambs* 5L **29**
Sway. *Hants* 6L **9**
Swayfield. *Linc* 7G **37**
Swaythling. *Sotn* 4B **10**
Sweet Green. *Worc* 5E **26**
Sweetham. *Devn* 6H **7**
Sweetholme. *Cumb* 4D **46**
Sweets. *Corn* 6A **6**
Sweetshouse. *Corn* 5C **4**
Swefling. *Suff* 5K **31**
Swell. *Som* 3B **8**
Swepstone. *Leics* 8A **36**
Swerford. *Oxon* 8A **28**
Swettenham. *Ches E* 3G **35**
Swetton. *N Yor* 8K **47**
Swffryd. *Blae* 5M **17**
Swiftsden. *E Sus* 3D **12**
Swilland. *Suff* 6H **31**
Swillington. *W Yor* 4A **42**
Swimbridge. *Devn* 3F **6**
Swimbridge Newland. *Devn* 2F **6**
Swinbrook. *Oxon* 2L **19**
Swincliffe. *N Yor* 2L **41**
Swincliffe. *W Yor* 5L **41**
Swinderby. *Linc* 3F **36**
Swindon. *Glos* 1H **19**
Swindon. *Nmbd* 2C **54**
Swindon. *Staf* 2G **27**
Swindon. *Swin* **117** (5K **19**)
Swine. *E Yor* 4J **43**
Swinefleet. *E Yor* 5E **42**
Swineford. *S Glo* 7E **18**
Swineshead. *Bed* 5H **29**
Swineshead. *Linc* 5K **37**
Swineshead Bridge. *Linc* 5K **37**
Swiney. *High* 8D **86**
Swinford. *Leics* 4C **28**
Swinford. *Oxon* 3B **20**
Swingate. *Notts* 5C **36**
Swingbrow. *Cambs* 3L **29**
Swingfield Minnis. *Kent* 1J **13**
Swingfield Street. *Kent* 1J **13**
Swingleton Green. *Suff* 7F **30**
Swinhill. *S Lan* 5F **58**
Swinhoe. *Nmbd* 7K **61**
Swinhope. *Linc* 8K **43**
Swinister. *Shet* 5H **91**
Swinithwaite. *N Yor* 7J **47**
Swinmore Common. *Here* 7E **26**
Swinscoe. *Staf* 5K **35**
Swinside Hall. *Bord* 8E **60**
Swinstead. *Linc* 7H **37**
Swinton. *G Man* 7F **40**
Swinton. *N Yor*
nr. Malton 8E **48**
nr. Masham 8L **47**
Swinton. *Bord* 5F **60**
Swinton. *S Yor* 8B **42**
Swithland. *Leics* 8C **36**
Swordale. *High* 7F **78**
Swordly. *High* 5K **85**
Sworton Heath. *Ches E* 1E **34**
Swyddffynnon. *Cdgn* 6F **24**
Swynnerton. *Staf* 6G **35**
Swyre. *Dors* 7D **8**
Sycharth. *Powy* 8M **33**
Sychdyn. *Flin* 4M **33**
Sychnant. *Powy* 5J **25**
Sychtyn. *Powy* 2J **25**
Syde. *Glos* 2H **19**
Sydenham. *G Lon* 6L **21**
Sydenham. *Oxon* 3E **20**
Sydenham. *Som* 2B **8**
Sydenham Damerel. *Devn* 8D **6**
Syderstone. *Norf* 6E **38**
Sydling St Nicholas. *Dors* 6E **8**
Sydmonton. *Hants* 8B **20**
Sydney. *Ches E* 4F **34**
Syerston. *Notts* 5E **36**
Syke. *G Man* 6G **41**
Sykehouse. *S Yor* 6D **42**
Sykes. *Lanc* 2E **40**
Syleham. *Suff* 4J **31**
Sylen. *Carm* 6M **15**
Sylfaen. *Powy* 2L **25**
Symbister. *Shet* 1F **90**
Symington. *S Ayr* 6B **58**
Symington. *S Lan* 6H **59**
Symondsbury. *Dors* 6C **8**
Symonds Yat. *Here* 2D **18**
Synod Inn. *Cdgn* 1L **15**
Syre. *High* 7J **85**
Syreford. *Glos* 1J **19**
Syresham. *Nptn* 7D **28**
Syston. *Leics* 8D **36**
Syston. *Linc* 5G **37**
Sytchampton. *Worc* 5G **27**
Sywell. *Nptn* 5F **28**

T

Tabost. *W Isl*
nr. Cearsiadar 2E **76**
nr. Suainebost 5J **83**
Tachbrook Mallory. *Warw* 5M **27**
Tackley. *Oxon* 1B **20**
Tacleit. *W Isl* 8E **82**
Tacolneston. *Norf* 2H **31**
Tadcaster. *N Yor* 3B **42**
Taddington. *Derbs* 2K **35**
Taddington. *Glos* 8J **27**
Taddiport. *Devn* 4D **6**
Tadley. *Hants* 7D **20**
Tadlow. *Cambs* 7K **29**
Tadmarton. *Oxon* 8A **28**
Tadwick. *Bath* 6F **18**
Tadworth. *Surr* 8K **21**
Tafarnaubach. *Blae* 3L **17**
Tafarn-y-bwlch. *Pemb* 3G **15**
Tafarn-y-Gelyn. *Den* 4L **33**
Taff's Well. *Rhon* 6L **17**
Tafolwern. *Powy* 2H **25**
Tai-bach. *Powy* 8L **33**
Taibach. *Neat* 6G **17**
Taigh a Ghearraidh. *W Isl* 6J **75**
Taigh Bhuirgh. *W Isl* 4B **76**
Tain. *High*
nr. Invergordon 5H **79**
nr. Thurso 5D **86**
Tai-Nant. *Wrex* 5A **34**
Tai'n Lon. *Gwyn* 5D **32**
Tairbeart. *W Isl* 4C **76**
Tairgwaith. *Neat* 3G **17**
Takeley. *Essx* 1B **22**
Takeley Street. *Essx* 1B **22**
Talachddu. *Powy* 1K **17**
Talacre. *Flin* 2L **33**
Talardd. *Gwyn* 8H **33**
Talaton. *Devn* 6K **7**
Talbenny. *Pemb* 5E **14**
Talbot Green. *Rhon* 6K **17**
Taleford. *Devn* 6K **7**
Talerddig. *Powy* 2J **25**
Talgarreg. *Cdgn* 1L **15**
Talgarth. *Powy* 1L **17**
Talisker. *High* 2E **68**
Talke. *Staf* 4G **35**
Talkin. *Cumb* 6K **53**
Talladale. *High* 6L **77**
Talla Linnfoots. *Bord* 7K **59**
Tallaminnock. *S Ayr* 2J **51**
Tallarn Green. *Wrex* 5C **34**
Tallentire. *Cumb* 8F **52**
Talley. *Carm* 1F **16**
Tallington. *Linc* 1H **29**
Talmine. *High* 5H **85**
Talog. *Carm* 4K **15**
Talsarn. *Carm* 2G **17**
Talsarn. *Cdgn* 1M **15**
Talsarnau. *Gwyn* 7F **32**
Talskiddy. *Corn* 5B **4**
Talwrn. *IOA* 3D **32**
Talwrn. *Wrex* 5A **34**
Tal-y-Bont. *Cnwy* 4G **33**
Tal-y-bont. *Cdgn* 4F **24**
Tal-y-bont. *Gwyn*
nr. Bangor 3F **32**
nr. Barmouth 8E **32**
Talybont-on-Usk. *Powy* 2L **17**
Tal-y-cafn. *Cnwy* 3G **33**
Tal-y-coed. *Mon* 2C **18**
Tal-y-llyn. *Gwyn* 2G **25**
Talyllyn. *Powy* 2L **17**
Talysarn. *Gwyn* 5D **32**
Tal-y-waenydd. *Gwyn* 6F **32**
Talywain. *Torf* 3A **18**
Tal-y-Wern. *Powy* 2H **25**
Tamerton Foliot. *Plym* 5G **5**
Tamlaght. *Ferm* 6C **92**
Tamlaght O'Crilly. *M Ulst* 3F **93**
Tamnamore. *M Ulst* 5F **93**
Tamworth. *Staf* 1L **27**
Tamworth Green. *Linc* 5L **37**
Tandlehill. *Ren* 3C **58**
Tandragee. *Arm* 6G **93**
Tandridge. *Surr* 8L **21**
Tanerdy. *Carm* 4L **15**
Tanfield. *Dur* 6E **54**
Tanfield Lea. *Dur* 6E **54**
Tangasdal. *W Isl* 5C **74**
Tang Hall. *York* 2D **42**
Tangiers. *Pemb* 5F **14**
Tangley. *Hants* 8M **19**
Tangmere. *W Sus* 5G **11**
Tangwick. *Shet* 6G **91**
Tankerness. *Orkn* 1G **87**
Tankersley. *S Yor* 8M **41**
Tankerton. *Kent* 7H **23**
Tan-lan. *Cnwy* 4G **33**
Tan-lan. *Gwyn* 6F **32**
Tannach. *High* 7E **86**
Tannadice. *Ang* 2H **67**
Tanner's Green. *Worc* 4J **27**
Tannington. *Suff* 5J **31**
Tannochside. *N Lan* 3F **58**
Tan Office Green. *Suff* 6D **30**
Tansley. *Derbs* 4M **35**
Tansley Knoll. *Derbs* 3M **35**
Tansor. *Nptn* 2H **29**
Tantobie. *Dur* 6E **54**
Tanton. *N Yor* 4C **48**
Tanvats. *Linc* 3J **37**
Tanworth-in-Arden. *Warw* 4K **27**
Tan-y-bwlch. *Gwyn* 6F **32**
Tan-y-fron. *Cnwy* 4J **33**
Tanyfron. *Wrex* 4A **34**
Tanygrisiau. *Gwyn* 6F **32**
Tan-y-groes. *Cdgn* 2J **15**
Tan-y-pistyll. *Powy* 8K **33**
Tan-yr-allt. *Den* 2K **33**
Taobh a Chaolais. *W Isl* 4D **74**
Taobh a Deas Loch Aineort.
W Isl 3D **74**
Taobh a Ghlinne. *W Isl* 2E **76**
Taobh a Tuath Loch Aineort.
W Isl 3D **74**
Taplow. *Buck* 5G **21**
Tapton. *Derbs* 2A **36**
Tarbert. *Arg*
on Jura 1F **56**
on Kintyre 3H **57**
Tarbert. *W Isl* 4C **76**
Tarbet. *Arg* 7H **65**
Tarbet. *High*
nr. Mallaig 6J **69**
nr. Scourie 7D **84**
Tarbock Green. *Mers* 1C **34**
Tarbolton. *S Ayr* 7C **58**
Tarbrax. *S Lan* 4J **59**
Tardebigge. *Worc* 5H **27**
Tarfside. *Ang* 8D **72**
Tarland. *Abers* 5D **72**
Tarleton. *Lanc* 5C **40**
Tarlogie. *High* 5H **79**
Tarlscough. *Lanc* 6C **40**
Tarlton. *Glos* 4H **19**
Tarnbrook. *Lanc* 2D **40**
Tarnock. *Som* 8B **18**
Tarns. *Cumb* 7F **52**
Tarporley. *Ches W* 3D **34**
Tarpots. *Essx* 5D **22**
Tarr. *Som* 2L **7**
Tarrant Crawford. *Dors* 5H **9**
Tarrant Gunville. *Dors* 4H **9**
Tarrant Hinton. *Dors* 4H **9**
Tarrant Keyneston. *Dors* 5H **9**
Tarrant Launceston. *Dors* 5H **9**
Tarrant Monkton. *Dors* 5H **9**
Tarrant Rawston. *Dors* 5H **9**
Tarrant Rushton. *Dors* 5H **9**
Tarrel. *High* 5J **79**
Tarring Neville. *E Sus* 5M **11**
Tarrington. *Here* 7E **26**
Tarsappie. *Per* 5E **66**
Tarscabhaig. *High* 5G **69**
Tarskavaig. *High* 5G **69**
Tarves. *Abers* 2H **73**
Tarvie. *High* 8E **78**
Tarvin. *Ches W* 3C **34**
Tasburgh. *Norf* 2J **31**
Tasley. *Shrp* 2E **26**
Tassagh. *Arm* 7F **93**
Taston. *Oxon* 1A **20**
Tatenhill. *Staf* 7L **35**
Tathall End. *Mil* 7F **28**
Tatham. *Lanc* 1E **40**
Tathwell. *Linc* 1L **37**
Tatling End. *Buck* 5H **21**
Tatsfield. *Surr* 8M **21**
Tattenhall. *Ches W* 4C **34**
Tatterford. *Norf* 7E **38**
Tattersett. *Norf* 6E **38**
Tattershall. *Linc* 4K **37**
Tattershall Bridge. *Linc* 4J **37**
Tattershall Thorpe. *Linc* 4K **37**
Tattingstone. *Suff* 8H **31**
Tattingstone White Horse.
Suff 8H **31**
Tattle Bank. *Warw* 5K **27**
Tatworth. *Som* 5B **8**
Taunton. *Som* **117** (3M **7**)
Taverham. *Norf* 8H **39**
Taverners Green. *Essx* 2B **22**
Tavernspite. *Pemb* 5H **15**
Tavistock. *Devn* 8D **6**
Tavool House. *Arg* 5K **63**
Taw Green. *Devn* 6F **6**
Tawstock. *Devn* 3E **6**
Taxal. *Derbs* 1J **35**
Tayinloan. *Arg* 5F **56**
Taynish. *Arg* 1G **57**
Taynton. *Glos* 1F **18**
Taynton. *Oxon* 2L **19**
Taynuilt. *Arg* 4E **64**
Tayport. *Fife* 5H **67**
Tay Road Bridge. *D'dee* 5H **67**
Tayvallich. *Arg* 1G **57**
Tealby. *Linc* 8J **43**
Tealing. *Ang* 4H **67**
Teams. *Tyne* 5F **54**
Teangue. *High* 5H **69**
Teanna Mhachair. *W Isl* 7J **75**
Tebay. *Cumb* 5E **46**
Tebworth. *C Beds* 1G **21**
Tedburn St Mary. *Devn* 6H **7**
Teddington. *Glos* 8H **27**
Teddington. *G Lon* 6J **21**
Tedsmore. *Shrp* 7B **34**
Tedstone Delamere. *Here* 6E **26**
Tedstone Wafer. *Here* 6E **26**
Teemore. *Ferm* 7C **92**
Teesport. *Red C* 3C **48**
Teesside. *Stoc T* 3C **48**
Teeton. *Nptn* 4D **28**
Teffont Evias. *Wilts* 2H **9**
Teffont Magna. *Wilts* 2H **9**
Tegryn. *Pemb* 3J **15**
Teigh. *Rut* 8F **36**
Teigncombe. *Devn* 7F **6**
Teigngrace. *Devn* 8H **7**
Teignmouth. *Devn* 8J **7**
Telford. *Telf* 8E **34**
Telham. *E Sus* 4D **12**
Tellisford. *Som* 8G **19**
Telscombe. *E Sus* 5M **11**
Telscombe Cliffs. *E Sus* 5L **11**
Tempar. *Per* 2L **65**
Templand. *Dum* 3E **52**
Temple. *Corn* 4D **4**
Temple. *Glas* 3D **58**
Temple. *Midl* 4M **59**
Temple Balsall. *W Mid* 4L **27**
Temple Bar. *Carm* 3E **16**
Temple Bar. *Cdgn* 1M **15**
Temple Cloud. *Bath* 8E **18**
Templecombe. *Som* 3F **8**
Temple Ewell. *Kent* 1J **13**
Temple Grafton. *Warw* 6K **27**
Temple Guiting. *Glos* 1J **19**
Templehall. *Fife* 8F **66**
Temple Hirst. *N Yor* 5D **42**
Temple Normanton. *Derbs* 3B **36**
Templepatrick. *Ant* 4H **93**
Temple Sowerby. *Cumb* 3E **46**
Templeton. *Devn* 4H **7**
Templeton. *Pemb* 5H **15**
Templeton. *W Ber* 7A **20**
Templetown. *Dur* 7E **54**
Tempo. *Ferm* 6C **92**
Tempsford. *C Beds* 6J **29**
Tenandry. *Per* 1C **66**
Tenbury Wells. *Worc* 5D **26**
Tenby. *Pemb* 6H **15**
Tendring. *Essx* 1H **23**
Tendring Green. *Essx* 1H **23**
Tenga. *Arg* 3L **63**
Ten Mile Bank. *Norf* 2C **30**
Tenterden. *Kent* 2E **12**
Terfyn. *Cnwy* 3J **33**
Terhill. *Som* 2L **7**
Terling. *Essx* 2D **22**
Termon Rock. *Ferm* 5E **92**
Ternhill. *Shrp* 6E **34**
Terregles. *Dum* 4D **52**
Terrick. *Buck* 3F **20**
Terrington. *N Yor* 8D **48**
Terrington St Clement. *Norf* 7B **38**
Terrington St John. *Norf* 8B **38**
Terry's Green. *Warw* 4K **27**
Teston. *Kent* 8D **22**
Testwood. *Hants* 4M **9**
Tetbury. *Glos* 4G **19**
Tetbury Upton. *Glos* 4G **19**
Tetchill. *Shrp* 6B **34**
Tetcott. *Devn* 6C **6**
Tetford. *Linc* 2L **37**
Tetney. *Linc* 7L **43**
Tetney Lock. *Linc* 7L **43**
Tetsworth. *Oxon* 3D **20**
Tettenhall. *W Mid* 1G **27**
Teversal. *Notts* 3B **36**
Teversham. *Cambs* 6A **30**
Teviothead. *Bord* 1J **53**
Tewel. *Abers* 7H **73**
Tewin. *Herts* 2K **21**
Tewkesbury. *Glos* 8G **27**
Teynham. *Kent* 7F **22**
Teynham Street. *Kent* 7F **22**
Thackthwaite. *Cumb* 3C **46**
Thakeham. *W Sus* 4J **11**
Thame. *Oxon* 3E **20**
Thames Ditton. *Surr* 7J **21**
Thames Haven. *Thur* 5D **22**
Thamesmead. *G Lon* 5A **22**
Thamesport. *Medw* 6E **22**
Thanington Without. *Kent* 8H **23**
Thankerton. *S Lan* 6H **59**
Tharston. *Norf* 2H **31**
Thatcham. *W Ber* 7C **20**
Thatto Heath. *Mers* 8D **40**
Thaxted. *Essx* 8C **30**
Theakston. *N Yor* 7M **47**
Thealby. *N Lin* 6F **42**
Theale. *Som* 1C **8**
Theale. *W Ber* 6D **20**
Thearne. *E Yor* 4H **43**
Theberton. *Suff* 5L **31**
Theddingworth. *Leics* 3D **28**
Theddlethorpe All Saints.
Linc 1A **38**
Theddlethorpe St Helen.
Linc 1A **38**
Thelbridge Barton. *Devn* 4G **7**
Thelnetham. *Suff* 4G **31**
Thelveton. *Norf* 3H **31**
Thelwall. *Warr* 1E **34**
Themelthorpe. *Norf* 7G **39**
Thenford. *Nptn* 7C **28**
Therfield. *Herts* 8L **29**
Thetford. *Linc* 8J **37**
Thetford. *Norf* 3E **30**
Thethwaite. *Cumb* 7H **53**
Theydon Bois. *Essx* 4M **21**
Thick Hollins. *W Yor* 6K **41**
Thickwood. *Wilts* 6G **19**
Thimbleby. *Linc* 3K **37**
Thimbleby. *N Yor* 6B **48**
Thingwall. *Mers* 1A **34**
Thirlby. *N Yor* 7B **48**
Thirlestane. *Bord* 5C **60**
Thirn. *N Yor* 7L **47**
Thirsk. *N Yor* 7B **48**
Thirtleby. *E Yor* 4J **43**
Thistleton. *Lanc* 4C **40**
Thistleton. *Rut* 8G **37**
Thistley Green. *Suff* 4C **30**
Thixendale. *N Yor* 1F **42**
Thockrington. *Nmbd* 4C **54**
Tholomas Drove. *Cambs* 1M **29**
Tholthorpe. *N Yor* 1B **42**
Thomas Chapel. *Pemb* 6H **15**
Thomas Close. *Cumb* 7J **53**
Thomastown. *Abers* 1G **73**
Thomastown. *Rhon* 6K **17**
Thompson. *Norf* 2F **30**
Thomshill. *Mor* 8B **80**
Thong. *Kent* 6C **22**
Thongsbridge. *W Yor* 7K **41**
Thoralby. *N Yor* 7J **47**
Thoresby. *Notts* 2D **36**
Thoresway. *Linc* 8J **43**
Thorganby. *Linc* 8K **43**
Thorganby. *N Yor* 3D **42**
Thorgill. *N Yor* 6E **48**
Thorington. *Suff* 4L **31**
Thorington Street. *Suff* 8G **31**
Thorlby. *N Yor* 2H **41**
Thorley. *Herts* 2A **22**
Thorley Street. *Herts* 2A **22**
Thorley Street. *IOW* 7A **10**
Thormanby. *N Yor* 8B **48**
Thorn. *Powy* 5A **26**
Thornaby-on-Tees. *Stoc T* 4B **48**
Thornage. *Norf* 6G **39**
Thornborough. *Buck* 8E **28**
Thornborough. *N Yor* 8L **47**
Thornbury. *Devn* 5D **6**
Thornbury. *Here* 6E **26**
Thornbury. *S Glo* 4E **18**
Thornby. *Cumb* 6G **53**
Thornby. *Nptn* 4D **28**
Thorncliffe. *Staf* 4J **35**
Thorncombe. *Dors* 5B **8**
Thorncombe Street. *Surr* 1G **11**
Thorncote Green. *C Beds* 7J **29**
Thorndon. *Suff* 5H **31**
Thorndon Cross. *Devn* 6E **6**
Thorne. *S Yor* 6D **42**
Thornehillhead. *Devn* 4D **6**
Thorner. *W Yor* 3A **42**
Thorne St Margaret. *Som* 3K **7**
Thorney. *Notts* 2F **36**
Thorney. *Pet* 1K **29**
Thorney. *Som* 3C **8**
Thorney Hill. *Hants* 6K **9**
Thorney Toll. *Cambs* 1L **29**
Thornfalcon. *Som* 3A **8**
Thornford. *Dors* 4E **8**
Thorngrafton. *Nmbd* 5A **54**
Thorngrove. *Som* 2B **8**
Thorngumbald. *E Yor* 5K **43**
Thornham. *Norf* 5D **38**
Thornham Magna. *Suff* 4H **31**
Thornham Parva. *Suff* 4H **31**
Thornhaugh. *Pet* 1H **29**
Thornhill. *Cphy* 6L **17**
Thornhill. *Cumb* 4K **45**
Thornhill. *Derbs* 1K **35**
Thornhill. *Dum* 2C **52**
Thornhill. *Sotn* 4B **10**
Thornhill. *Stir* 8L **65**
Thornhill. *W Yor* 6L **41**
Thornhill Lees. *W Yor* 6L **41**
Thornhills. *W Yor* 5K **41**
Thornholme. *E Yor* 1J **43**
Thornicombe. *Dors* 5G **9**
Thornington. *Nmbd* 6F **60**
Thornley. *Dur*
nr. Durham 8G **55**
nr. Tow Law 8E **54**
Thornley Gate. *Nmbd* 6B **54**
Thornliebank. *E Ren* 3D **58**
Thornroan. *Abers* 2H **73**
Thorns. *Suff* 6D **30**
Thornsett. *Derbs* 1J **35**
Thornthwaite. *Cumb* 2M **45**
Thornthwaite. *N Yor* 2K **41**
Thornton. *Ang* 3G **67**
Thornton. *Buck* 8E **28**
Thornton. *E Yor* 3E **42**
Thornton. *Fife* 8F **66**
Thornton. *Lanc* 3B **40**
Thornton. *Leics* 1B **28**
Thornton. *Linc* 3K **37**
Thornton. *Mers* 7B **40**
Thornton. *Midd* 4B **48**
Thornton. *Nmbd* 5G **61**
Thornton. *Pemb* 6F **14**
Thornton. *W Yor* 4J **41**
Thornton Curtis. *N Lin* 6H **43**
Thorntonhall. *S Lan* 4D **58**
Thornton Heath. *G Lon* 7L **21**
Thornton Hough. *Mers* 1B **34**
Thornton-in-Craven. *N Yor* 3H **41**
Thornton in Lonsdale.
N Yor 8E **46**
Thornton-le-Beans. *N Yor* 6A **48**
Thornton-le-Clay. *N Yor* 1D **42**
Thornton-le-Dale. *N Yor* 7F **48**
Thornton le Moor. *Linc* 8H **43**
Thornton-le-Moor. *N Yor* 7A **48**
Thornton-le-Moors.
Ches W 2C **34**
Thornton-le-Street. *N Yor* 7B **48**
Thorntonloch. *E Lot* 2E **60**
Thornton Rust. *N Yor* 7H **47**
Thornton Steward. *N Yor* 7K **47**
Thornton Watlass. *N Yor* 7L **47**
Thornwood Common. *Essx* 3A **22**
Thornythwaite. *Cumb* 3B **46**
Thoroton. *Notts* 5E **36**
Thorp Arch. *W Yor* 3B **42**
Thorpe. *Derbs* 4K **35**
Thorpe. *E Yor* 3G **43**
Thorpe. *Linc* 1A **38**
Thorpe. *Norf* 2L **31**
Thorpe. *N Yor* 1J **41**
Thorpe. *Notts* 5E **36**
Thorpe. *Surr* 7H **21**
Thorpe Abbotts. *Norf* 4H **31**
Thorpe Acre. *Leics* 7C **36**
Thorpe Arnold. *Leics* 7E **36**
Thorpe Audlin. *W Yor* 6B **42**
Thorpe Bassett. *N Yor* 8F **48**
Thorpe Bay. *S'end* 5F **22**
Thorpe by Water. *Rut* 2F **28**
Thorpe Common. *S Yor* 8A **42**
Thorpe Common. *Suff* 8J **31**
Thorpe Constantine. *Staf* 1L **27**
Thorpe End. *Norf* 8J **39**
Thorpe Fendike. *Linc* 3A **38**
Thorpe Green. *Essx* 1H **23**
Thorpe Green. *Suff* 6F **30**
Thorpe Hall. *N Yor* 8C **48**
Thorpe Hamlet. *Norf* 1J **31**
Thorpe Hesley. *S Yor* 8A **42**
Thorpe in Balne. *S Yor* 6C **42**
Thorpe in the Fallows. *Linc* 1G **37**
Thorpe Langton. *Leics* 2E **28**
Thorpe Larches. *Dur* 3A **48**
Thorpe Latimer. *Linc* 5J **37**
Thorpe-le-Soken. *Essx* 1H **23**
Thorpe le Street. *E Yor* 3F **42**
Thorpe Malsor. *Nptn* 4F **28**
Thorpe Mandeville. *Nptn* 7C **28**
Thorpe Market. *Norf* 6J **39**
Thorpe Marriott. *Norf* 8H **39**
Thorpe Morieux. *Suff* 6F **30**
Thorpeness. *Suff* 6L **31**
Thorpe on the Hill. *Linc* 3G **37**
Thorpe on the Hill. *W Yor* 5M **41**
Thorpe St Andrew. *Norf* 1J **31**
Thorpe St Peter. *Linc* 3A **38**
Thorpe Salvin. *S Yor* 1C **36**
Thorpe Satchville. *Leics* 8E **36**
Thorpe Thewles. *Stoc T* 3A **48**
Thorpe Tilney. *Linc* 4J **37**
Thorpe Underwood. *N Yor* 2B **42**
Thorpe Waterville. *Nptn* 3H **29**
Thorpe Willoughby. *N Yor* 4C **42**
Thorpland. *Norf* 1C **30**
Thorrington. *Essx* 1G **23**
Thorverton. *Devn* 5J **7**
Thrandeston. *Suff* 4H **31**
Thrapston. *Nptn* 4G **29**
Thrashbush. *N Lan* 3F **58**
Threapland. *Cumb* 8F **52**
Threapland. *N Yor* 1H **41**
Threapwood. *Ches W* 5C **34**
Threapwood. *Staf* 5J **35**
Three Ashes. *Here* 1D **18**
Three Bridges. *Linc* 1M **37**
Three Bridges. *W Sus* 2K **11**
Three Burrows. *Corn* 4L **3**
Three Chimneys. *Kent* 2E **12**
Three Cocks. *Powy* 1L **17**
Three Crosses. *Swan* 5E **16**
Three Cups Corner. *E Sus* 3C **12**
Threehammer Common.
Norf 7K **39**
Three Holes. *Norf* 1B **30**
Threekingham. *Linc* 6H **37**
Three Leg Cross. *E Sus* 2C **12**
Three Legged Cross. *Dors* 5J **9**
Three Mile Cross. *Wok* 7E **20**
Threemilestone. *Corn* 4L **3**
Three Oaks. *E Sus* 4E **12**
Threlkeld. *Cumb* 3B **46**
Threshfield. *N Yor* 1H **41**
Thrigby. *Norf* 8L **39**
Thringarth. *Dur* 3H **47**
Thringstone. *Leics* 8B **36**
Thrintoft. *N Yor* 6M **47**
Thriplow. *Cambs* 7M **29**
Throckenholt. *Linc* 1L **29**
Throcking. *Herts* 8L **29**
Throckley. *Tyne* 5E **54**
Throckmorton. *Worc* 7H **27**
Throop. *Bour* 6K **9**
Throphill. *Nmbd* 3E **54**
Thropton. *Nmbd* 1D **54**
Throsk. *Stir* 8B **66**
Througham. *Glos* 3H **19**
Throughgate. *Dum* 3C **52**
Throwleigh. *Devn* 6F **6**
Throwley. *Kent* 8F **22**
Throwley Forstal. *Kent* 8F **22**
Throxenby. *N Yor* 7H **49**
Thrumpton. *Notts* 6C **36**
Thrumster. *High* 7E **86**
Thrunton. *Nmbd* 8H **61**
Thrupp. *Glos* 3G **19**
Thrupp. *Oxon* 2B **20**
Thrushelton. *Devn* 7D **6**
Thrushgill. *Lanc* 1E **40**
Thrussington. *Leics* 8D **36**
Thruxton. *Hants* 1L **9**
Thruxton. *Here* 8C **26**
Thrybergh. *S Yor* 8B **42**
Thulston. *Derbs* 6B **36**
Thundergay. *N Ayr* 5H **57**
Thundersley. *Essx* 5D **22**
Thundridge. *Herts* 2L **21**
Thurcaston. *Leics* 8C **36**
Thurcroft. *S Yor* 1B **36**
Thurdon. *Corn* 4B **6**
Thurgarton. *Norf* 6H **39**
Thurgarton. *Notts* 5D **36**
Thurgoland. *S Yor* 7L **41**
Thurlaston. *Leics* 2C **28**
Thurlaston. *Warw* 4B **28**
Thurlbear. *Som* 3A **8**
Thurlby. *Linc*
nr. Alford 2A **38**
nr. Baston 8J **37**
nr. Lincoln 3G **37**
Thurleigh. *Bed* 6H **29**
Thurlestone. *Devn* 7J **5**
Thurloxton. *Som* 2A **8**
Thurlstone. *S Yor* 7L **41**
Thurlton. *Norf* 2L **31**
Thurmaston. *Leics* 1D **28**
Thurnby. *Leics* 1D **28**
Thurne. *Norf* 8L **39**
Thurnham. *Kent* 8E **22**
Thurning. *Norf* 7G **39**
Thurning. *Nptn* 3H **29**
Thurnscoe. *S Yor* 7B **42**
Thursby. *Cumb* 6H **53**
Thursford. *Norf* 6F **38**
Thursford Green. *Norf* 6F **38**
Thursley. *Surr* 2G **11**
Thurso. *High* 5C **86**
Thurso East. *High* 5C **86**
Thurstaston. *Mers* 2M **33**
Thurston. *Suff* 5F **30**
Thurston End. *Suff* 6D **30**
Thurstonfield. *Cumb* 6H **53**
Thurstonland. *W Yor* 6K **41**
Thurton. *Norf* 1K **31**
Thurvaston. *Derbs*
nr. Ashbourne 6K **35**
nr. Derby 6L **35**
Thuxton. *Norf* 1G **31**
Thwaite. *Dur* 4J **47**
Thwaite. *N Yor* 6G **47**
Thwaite. *Suff* 5H **31**
Thwaite Head. *Cumb* 6B **46**
Thwaites. *W Yor* 3J **41**
Thwaite St Mary. *Norf* 2K **31**
Thwing. *E Yor* 8H **49**
Tibbermore. *Per* 5D **66**
Tibberton. *Glos* 1F **18**
Tibberton. *Telf* 7E **34**
Tibberton. *Worc* 6H **27**
Tibenham. *Norf* 3H **31**
Tibshelf. *Derbs* 3B **36**
Tibthorpe. *E Yor* 2G **43**
Ticehurst. *E Sus* 2C **12**
Tichborne. *Hants* 2C **10**
Tickencote. *Rut* 1G **29**
Tickenham. *N Som* 6C **18**
Tickhill. *S Yor* 8C **42**
Ticklerton. *Shrp* 2C **26**
Ticknall. *Derbs* 7A **36**
Tickton. *E Yor* 3H **43**
Tidbury Green. *W Mid* 4K **27**
Tidcombe. *Wilts* 8L **19**
Tiddington. *Oxon* 3D **20**
Tiddington. *Warw* 6L **27**
Tiddleywink. *Wilts* 6G **19**
Tidebrook. *E Sus* 3C **12**
Tideford. *Corn* 6F **4**
Tideford Cross. *Corn* 5F **4**
Tidenham. *Glos* 4D **18**
Tideswell. *Derbs* 2K **35**
Tidmarsh. *W Ber* 6D **20**
Tidmington. *Warw* 8L **27**
Tidpit. *Hants* 4J **9**
Tidworth. *Wilts* 1L **9**
Tidworth Camp. *Wilts* 1L **9**
Tiers Cross. *Pemb* 5F **14**
Tiffield. *Nptn* 6D **28**
Tifty. *Abers* 1G **73**
Tigerton. *Ang* 1J **67**
Tighnabruaich. *Arg* 2J **57**
Tigley. *Devn* 5K **5**
Tilbrook. *Cambs* 5H **29**
Tilbury. *Thur* 6C **22**
Tilbury Green. *Essx* 7D **30**
Tilbury Juxta Clare. *Essx* 7D **30**
Tile Hill. *W Mid* 4L **27**
Tilehurst. *Read* 6D **20**
Tilford. *Surr* 1F **10**
Tilgate Forest Row. *W Sus* 2K **11**
Tillathrowie. *Abers* 2D **72**
Tillers Green. *Glos* 8E **26**
Tillery. *Abers* 3J **73**
Tilley. *Shrp* 7D **34**
Tillicoultry. *Clac* 8C **66**
Tillingham. *Essx* 3F **22**
Tillington. *Here* 7C **26**
Tillington. *W Sus* 3G **11**
Tillington Common. *Here* 7C **26**
Tillybirloch. *Abers* 5F **72**
Tillyfourie. *Abers* 4F **72**
Tilmanstone. *Kent* 8K **23**
Tilney All Saints. *Norf* 8B **38**
Tilney Fen End. *Norf* 8B **38**
Tilney High End. *Norf* 8B **38**
Tilney St Lawrence. *Norf* 8B **38**
Tilshead. *Wilts* 1J **9**
Tilstock. *Shrp* 6D **34**
Tilston. *Ches W* 4C **34**
Tilstone Fearnall. *Ches W* 3D **34**
Tilsworth. *C Beds* 1G **21**
Tilton on the Hill. *Leics* 1E **28**
Tiltups End. *Glos* 4G **19**
Timberland. *Linc* 4J **37**
Timbersbrook. *Ches E* 3G **35**
Timberscombe. *Som* 1J **7**
Timble. *N Yor* 2K **41**
Timperley. *G Man* 1F **34**
Timsbury. *Bath* 8E **18**
Timsbury. *Hants* 3M **9**
Timsgearraidh. *W Isl* 8D **82**
Timworth Green. *Suff* 5E **30**
Tincleton. *Dors* 6F **8**
Tindale. *Cumb* 6L **53**
Tindale Crescent. *Dur* 3L **47**
Tingewick. *Buck* 8D **28**
Tingrith. *C Beds* 8H **29**
Tingwall. *Orkn* 7D **88**
Tinhay. *Devn* 7C **6**
Tinshill. *W Yor* 4L **41**
Tinsley. *S Yor* 8B **42**
Tinsley Green. *W Sus* 2K **11**
Tintagel. *Corn* 3C **4**
Tintern. *Mon* 3D **18**
Tintinhull. *Som* 4C **8**
Tintwistle. *Derbs* 8J **41**
Tinwald. *Dum* 3E **52**
Tinwell. *Rut* 1H **29**
Tippacott. *Devn* 1G **7**
Tipperty. *Abers* 3J **73**
Tipps End. *Cambs* 2B **30**
Tiptoe. *Hants* 6L **9**
Tipton. *W Mid* 2H **27**
Tipton St John. *Devn* 6K **7**
Tiptree. *Essx* 2E **22**
Tiptree Heath. *Essx* 2E **22**
Tirabad. *Powy* 8H **25**
Tircoed Forest Village.
Swan 4F **16**
Tiree Airport. *Arg* 3F **62**
Tirinie. *Per* 1B **66**
Tirley. *Glos* 1G **19**
Tiroran. *Arg* 5K **63**
Tir-Phil. *Cphy* 4L **17**
Tirril. *Cumb* 3D **46**
Tirryside. *High* 2F **78**
Tir-y-dail. *Carm* 3F **16**
Tisbury. *Wilts* 3H **9**
Tisman's Common. *W Sus* 2H **11**
Tissington. *Derbs* 4K **35**
Titchberry. *Devn* 3B **6**
Titchfield. *Hants* 5C **10**
Titchmarsh. *Nptn* 4H **29**
Titchwell. *Norf* 5D **38**
Tithby. *Notts* 6D **36**
Titley. *Here* 6B **26**
Titlington. *Nmbd* 8H **61**
Titsey. *Surr* 8M **21**
Titson. *Corn* 5B **6**
Tittensor. *Staf* 6G **35**
Tittleshall. *Norf* 7E **38**
Titton. *Worc* 5G **27**
Tiverton. *Ches W* 3D **34**
Tiverton. *Devn* 4J **7**
Tivetshall St Margaret.
Norf 3H **31**
Tivetshall St Mary. *Norf* 3H **31**
Tivington. *Som* 1J **7**
Tixall. *Staf* 7H **35**
Tixover. *Rut* 1G **29**
Toab. *Orkn* 1G **87**
Toab. *Shet* 6D **90**
Toadmoor. *Derbs* 4A **36**
Tobermore. *M Ulst* 4F **93**
Tobermory. *Arg* 2L **63**
Toberonochy. *Arg* 7B **64**
Tobha Beag. *W Isl* 2D **74**
Tobha-Beag. *W Isl* 6A **76**
Tobha Mor. *W Isl* 2D **74**
Tobhtarol. *W Isl* 8E **82**
Tobson. *W Isl* 8E **82**
Tocabhaig. *High* 4H **69**
Tocher. *Abers* 2F **72**
Tockenham. *Wilts* 6J **19**
Tockenham Wick. *Wilts* 5J **19**
Tockholes. *Bkbn* 5E **40**
Tockington. *S Glo* 5E **18**
Tockwith. *N Yor* 2B **42**
Todber. *Dors* 3G **9**
Todding. *Here* 4C **26**
Toddington. *C Beds* 1H **21**
Toddington. *Glos* 8J **27**
Todenham. *Glos* 8L **27**
Todhills. *Cumb* 5H **53**
Todmorden. *W Yor* 5H **41**
Todwick. *S Yor* 1B **36**
Toft. *Cambs* 6L **29**
Toft. *Linc* 8H **37**
Toft Hill. *Dur* 3K **47**
Toft Monks. *Norf* 2L **31**
Toft next Newton. *Linc* 1H **37**
Toftrees. *Norf* 7E **38**
Tofts. *High* 5E **86**
Toftwood. *Norf* 8F **38**
Togston. *Nmbd* 1F **54**
Tokavaig. *High* 4H **69**
Tokers Green. *Oxon* 6E **20**
Tolastadh a Chaolais. *W Isl* 8E **82**
Tolladine. *Worc* 6G **27**
Tolland. *Som* 2L **7**
Tollard Farnham. *Dors* 4H **9**
Tollard Royal. *Wilts* 4H **9**
Toll Bar. *S Yor* 7C **42**
Toller Fratrum. *Dors* 6D **8**
Toller Porcorum. *Dors* 6D **8**
Tollerton. *N Yor* 1C **42**
Tollerton. *Notts* 6D **36**
Toller Whelme. *Dors* 5D **8**
Tollesbury. *Essx* 2F **22**
Tolleshunt D'Arcy. *Essx* 2F **22**
Tolleshunt Knights. *Essx* 2F **22**
Tolleshunt Major. *Essx* 2F **22**
Tollie. *High* 8F **78**
Tollie Farm. *High* 6K **77**
Tolm. *W Isl* 8H **83**
Tolpuddle. *Dors* 6F **8**
Tolstadh bho Thuath. *W Isl* 7J **83**
Tolworth. *G Lon* 7J **21**
Tomachlaggan. *Mor* 3A **72**
Tomaknock. *Per* 5B **66**
Tomatin. *High* 3J **71**
Tombuidhe. *Arg* 7E **64**
Tomdoun. *High* 5B **70**
Tomich. *High*
nr. Cannich 3D **70**
nr. Invergordon 6H **79**
nr. Lairg 3G **79**
Tomintoul. *Mor* 4A **72**
Tomnavoulin. *Mor* 3B **72**
Tomsléibhe. *Arg* 4M **63**
Ton. *Mon* 4B **18**
Tonbridge. *Kent* 1B **12**
Tondu. *B'end* 6H **17**
Tonedale. *Som* 3L **7**
Tonfanau. *Gwyn* 2E **24**
Tong. *Shrp* 1F **26**
Tonge. *Leics* 7B **36**
Tong Forge. *Shrp* 1F **26**
Tongham. *Surr* 1F **10**
Tongland. *Dum* 6A **52**
Tong Norton. *Shrp* 1F **26**
Tongue. *High* 6H **85**
Tongue End. *Linc* 8J **37**
Tongwynlais. *Card* 6L **17**
Tonmawr. *Neat* 5H **17**
Tonna. *Neat* 5G **17**
Tonnau. *Neat* 5G **17**
Ton Pentre. *Rhon* 5J **17**
Ton-Teg. *Rhon* 6K **17**
Tonwell. *Herts* 2L **21**
Tonypandy. *Rhon* 5J **17**
Tonyrefail. *Rhon* 6K **17**
Toome. *Ant* 4F **93**
Toot Baldon. *Oxon* 3C **20**
Toot Hill. *Essx* 3B **22**
Toothill. *Hants* 4A **10**
Topcliffe. *N Yor* 8B **48**
Topcliffe. *W Yor* 5L **41**
Topcroft. *Norf* 2J **31**
Topcroft Street. *Norf* 2J **31**
Toppesfield. *Essx* 8D **30**
Toppings. *G Man* 6F **40**
Toprow. *Norf* 2H **31**
Topsham. *Devn* 7J **7**
Torbay. *Torb* 5M **5**
Torbeg. *N Ayr* 7H **57**
Torbothie. *N Lan* 4G **59**
Torbryan. *Devn* 5L **5**
Torcross. *Devn* 7L **5**
Tore. *High* 8G **79**
Torgyle. *High* 4D **70**
Torinturk. *Arg* 3H **57**
Torksey. *Linc* 2F **36**
Torlum. *W Isl* 8J **75**
Torlundy. *High* 8B **70**
Tormarton. *S Glo* 6F **18**
Tormitchell. *S Ayr* 2H **51**
Tormore. *High* 5H **69**
Tormore. *N Ayr* 6H **57**
Tornagrain. *High* 1H **71**
Tornaveen. *Abers* 5F **72**
Torness. *High* 3F **70**
Toronto. *Dur* 8E **54**
Torpenhow. *Cumb* 8G **53**
Torphichen. *W Lot* 2H **59**
Torphins. *Abers* 5F **72**
Torpoint. *Corn* 6G **5**
Torquay. *Torb* 5M **5**
Torr. *Devn* 6H **5**
Torra. *Arg* 4C **56**
Torran. *High* 1G **69**
Torrance. *E Dun* 2E **58**
Torrans. *Arg* 5K **63**
Torranyard. *N Ayr* 5B **58**
Torre. *Som* 2K **7**
Torre. *Torb* 5M **5**
Torridon. *High* 8L **77**
Torrin. *High* 3G **69**
Torrisdale. *Arg* 6G **57**
Torrisdale. *High* 5J **85**
Torrish. *High* 2K **79**
Torrisholme. *Lanc* 1C **40**
Torroble. *High* 3F **78**
Torroy. *High* 4F **78**
Torry. *Aber* 5J **73**
Torryburn. *Fife* 1J **59**
Torthorwald. *Dum* 4E **52**
Tortington. *W Sus* 5H **11**
Tortworth. *S Glo* 4F **18**
Torvaig. *High* 1F **68**
Torver. *Cumb* 6A **46**
Torwood. *Falk* 1G **59**
Torworth. *Notts* 1D **36**
Toscaig. *High* 2J **69**
Toseland. *Cambs* 5K **29**
Tosside. *N Yor* 2F **40**
Tostock. *Suff* 5F **30**
Totaig. *High* 8C **76**
Totardor. *High* 2E **68**
Tote. *High* 1F **68**
Totegan. *High* 5L **85**
Tothill. *Linc* 1M **37**
Totland. *IOW* 7M **9**
Totley. *S Yor* 2M **35**
Totnell. *Dors* 5E **8**
Totnes. *Devn* 5L **5**
Toton. *Notts* 6B **36**
Totronald. *Arg* 2G **63**
Totscore. *High* 7E **76**
Tottenham. *G Lon* 4L **21**
Tottenhill. *Norf* 8C **38**
Tottenhill Row. *Norf* 8C **38**
Totteridge. *G Lon* 4K **21**
Totternhoe. *C Beds* 1G **21**
Tottington. *G Man* 6F **40**
Totton. *Hants* 4A **10**
Touchen-end. *Wind* 6F **20**
Toulvaddie. *High* 5J **79**
The Towans. *Corn* 5J **3**
Toward. *Arg* 3L **57**
Towcester. *Nptn* 7D **28**
Towednack. *Corn* 5H **3**
Tower End. *Norf* 8C **38**
Tower Hill. *Mers* 7C **40**
Tower Hill. *W Sus* 3J **11**
Towersey. *Oxon* 3E **20**
Towie. *Abers* 4D **72**
Towiemore. *Mor* 1C **72**
Tow Law. *Dur* 8E **54**
The Town. *IOS* 1G **3**
Town End. *Cambs* 2M **29**
Town End. *Cumb*
nr. Ambleside 5C **46**
nr. Kirkby Thore 3E **46**
nr. Lindale 7C **46**
nr. Newby Bridge 7B **46**
Town End. *Mers* 1C **34**
Townend. *W Dun* 2C **58**
Townfield. *Dur* 7C **54**
Towngate. *Cumb* 7K **53**
Towngate. *Linc* 8J **37**
Town Green. *Lanc* 7C **40**
Town Head. *Cumb*
nr. Grasmere 5B **46**
nr. Great Asby 4E **46**
Townhead. *Cumb*
nr. Lazonby 8K **53**
nr. Maryport 8E **52**
nr. Ousby 8L **53**
Townhead. *Dum* 7A **52**
Townhead of Greenlaw.
Dum 5B **52**
Townhill. *Fife* 1K **59**
Townhill. *Swan* 5F **16**
Townjoy. *M Ulst* 5F **93**
Town Kelloe. *Dur* 8G **55**
Town Littleworth. *E Sus* 4M **11**
Town Row. *E Sus* 2B **12**
Towns End. *Hants* 8C **20**
Townsend. *Herts* 3J **21**
Townshend. *Corn* 5J **3**
Town Street. *Suff* 3D **30**
Town Yetholm. *Bord* 7F **60**
Towthorpe. *E Yor* 1G **43**
Towthorpe. *York* 2D **42**
Towton. *N Yor* 4B **42**
Towyn. *Cnwy* 3J **33**
Toxteth. *Mers* 1B **34**
Toynton All Saints. *Linc* 3L **37**
Toynton Fen Side. *Linc* 3L **37**
Toynton St Peter. *Linc* 3M **37**
Toy's Hill. *Kent* 8A **22**
Trabboch. *E Ayr* 7C **58**
Traboe. *Corn* 6L **3**
Tradespark. *High* 8J **79**
Tradespark. *Orkn* 1F **86**
Trafford Park. *G Man* 8F **40**
Trallong. *Powy* 2J **17**
Y Trallwng. *Powy* 2M **25**
Tranent. *E Lot* 2B **60**
Tranmere. *Mers* 1B **34**
Trantlebeg. *High* 6L **85**
Trantlemore. *High* 6L **85**
Tranwell. *Nmbd* 3E **54**
Trapp. *Carm* 3F **16**
Traquair. *Bord* 6M **59**
Trash Green. *W Ber* 7D **20**
Trawden. *Lanc* 4H **41**
Trawscoed. *Powy* 1K **17**
Trawsfynydd. *Gwyn* 7G **33**
Trawsgoed. *Cdgn* 5F **24**
Treaddow. *Here* 1D **18**
Trealaw. *Rhon* 5K **17**
Treales. *Lanc* 4C **40**
Trearddur. *IOA* 3B **32**
Treaslane. *High* 8E **76**
Treator. *Corn* 4B **4**
Trebanog. *Rhon* 5K **17**
Trebanos. *Neat* 4G **17**
Trebarber. *Corn* 5A **4**
Trebartha. *Corn* 8B **6**
Trebarwith. *Corn* 3C **4**
Trebetherick. *Corn* 4B **4**
Treborough. *Som* 2K **7**
Trebudannon. *Corn* 5A **4**
Trebullett. *Corn* 8C **6**
Treburley. *Corn* 8C **6**
Treburrick. *Corn* 4A **4**
Trebyan. *Corn* 5C **4**
Trecastle. *Powy* 2H **17**
Trecenydd. *Cphy* 6L **17**
Trecott. *Devn* 5F **6**
Trecwn. *Pemb* 3F **14**
Trecynon. *Rhon* 4J **17**
Tredaule. *Corn* 7B **6**
Tredavoe. *Corn* 6H **3**
Tredegar. *Blae* 4L **17**
Trederwen. *Powy* 8A **34**
Tredington. *Glos* 1H **19**
Tredington. *Warw* 7L **27**
Tredinnick. *Corn*
nr. Bodmin 5D **4**
nr. Looe 6E **4**
nr. Padstow 4B **4**
Tredogan. *V Glam* 8K **17**
Tredomen. *Powy* 1L **17**
Tredunnock. *Mon* 4B **18**
Tredustan. *Powy* 1L **17**
Treen. *Corn*
nr. Land's End 6G **3**
nr. St Ives 5H **3**
Treeton. *S Yor* 1B **36**
Trefaldwyn. *Powy* 3M **25**
Trefasser. *Pemb* 3E **14**
Trefdraeth. *IOA* 3D **32**
Trefdraeth. *Pemb* 3G **15**
Trefecca. *Powy* 1L **17**
Trefechan. *Mer T* 4K **17**
Trefeglwys. *Powy* 3J **25**
Trefenter. *Cdgn* 6F **24**
Treffgarne. *Pemb* 4F **14**
Treffynnon. *Flin* 3L **33**
Treffynnon. *Pemb* 4E **14**
Trefil. *Blae* 3L **17**
Trefilan. *Cdgn* 1M **15**
Trefin. *Pemb* 3E **14**
Treflach. *Shrp* 7A **34**
Trefnant. *Den* 3K **33**
Trefonen. *Shrp* 7A **34**
Trefor. *Gwyn* 6C **32**
Trefor. *IOA* 2C **32**
Treforest. *Rhon* 6K **17**
Trefrew. *Corn* 3D **4**
Trefriw. *Cnwy* 4G **33**
Tref-y-Clawdd. *Powy* 4A **26**
Trefynwy. *Mon* 2D **18**
Tregada. *Corn* 7C **6**
Tregadillett. *Corn* 7B **6**
Tregare. *Mon* 2C **18**
Tregarne. *Corn* 6L **3**
Tregaron. *Cdgn* 7F **24**
Tregarth. *Gwyn* 4F **32**
Tregear. *Corn* 6A **4**
Tregeare. *Corn* 7B **6**
Tregeiriog. *Wrex* 7L **33**
Tregele. *IOA* 1C **32**
Tregeseal. *Corn* 5G **3**
Tregiskey. *Corn* 7C **4**
Tregole. *Corn* 6A **6**
Tregolwyn. *V Glam* 7J **17**
Tregonetha. *Corn* 5B **4**
Tregonhawke. *Corn* 6G **5**
Tregony. *Corn* 7B **4**
Tregoodwell. *Corn* 3D **4**
Tregorrick. *Corn* 6C **4**
Tregoss. *Corn* 5B **4**
Tregowris. *Corn* 6L **3**

Tregoyd – Weldon

Tregoyd. Powy 1L 17
Tregrehan Mills. Corn 6C 4
Tre-groes. Cdgn 2L 15
Tregullon. Corn 5C 4
Tregurrian. Corn 5A 4
Tregynon. Powy 3K 25
Trehafod. Rhon 5K 17
Trehan. Corn 6G 5
Treharris. Mer T 5K 17
Treherbert. Rhon 5J 17
Trehunist. Corn 5F 4
Trekenner. Corn 8C 6
Trekenning. Corn 5B 4
Treknow. Corn 3C 4
Trelales. B'end 6H 17
Trelan. Corn 7L 3
Trelash. Corn 6A 6
Trelassick. Corn 6A 4
Trelawnyd. Flin 3K 33
Trelech. Carm 3J 15
Treleddyd-fawr. Pemb 4D 14
Trelewis. Mer T 5L 17
Treligga. Corn 3C 4
Trelights. Corn 4B 4
Trelill. Corn 4C 4
Trelissick. Corn 5M 3
Trellech. Mon 3D 18
Trelleck Grange. Mon 3C 18
Trelogan. Flin 2L 33
Trelystan. Powy 1A 26
Tremadog. Gwyn 6E 32
Tremail. Corn 7A 6
Tremain. Cdgn 2J 15
Tremaine. Corn 7B 6
Tremar. Corn 5E 4
Trematon. Corn 6F 4
Tremeirchion. Den 3K 33
Tremore. Corn 5C 4
Tremorfa. Card 7M 17
Trenance. Corn
nr. Newquay 5A 4
nr. Padstow 4B 4
Trenarren. Corn 7C 4
Trench. Telf 8E 34
Trencreek. Corn 2M 3
Trendeal. Corn 6A 4
Trenear. Corn 5K 3
Treneglos. Corn 7B 6
Trenewan. Corn 6D 4
Trengune. Corn 6A 6
Trent. Dors 4D 8
Trentham. Stoke 5G 35
Trentishoe. Devn 1F 6
Trentlock. Derbs 6B 36
Treoes. V Glam 7J 17
Treorchy. Rhon 5J 17
Treorci. Rhon 5J 17
Tre'r-ddol. Cdgn 3F 24
Tre'r llai. Powy 2M 25
Trerulefoot. Corn 6F 4
Tresaith. Cdgn 1J 15
Trescott. Staf 2G 27
Trescowe. Corn 5J 3
Tresham. Glos 4F 18
Tresigin. V Glam 7J 17
Tresillian. Corn 7A 4
Tresimwn. V Glam 7K 17
Tresinney. Corn 3D 4
Treskillard. Corn 5K 3
Treskinnick Cross. Corn 6B 6
Tresmeer. Corn 7B 6
Tresparrett. Corn 2D 4
Tresparrett Posts. Corn 6A 6
Tressady. High 3G 79
Tressait. Per 1B 66
Tresta. Shet
on Fetlar 4L 91
on Mainland 2D 90
Treswell. Notts 2E 36
Treswithian. Corn 5K 3
Tre Taliesin. Cdgn 3F 24
Trethomas. Cphy 6L 17
Trethosa. Corn 6B 4
Trethurgy. Corn 6C 4
Tretio. Pemb 4D 14
Tretire. Here 1D 18
Tretower. Powy 2L 17
Treuddyn. Flin 4A 34
Trevadlock. Corn 8B 6
Trevalga. Corn 3C 4
Trevalyn. Wrex 4B 34
Trevance. Corn 4B 4
Trevanger. Corn 4B 4
Trevanson. Corn 4B 4
Trevarrack. Corn 5H 3
Trevarren. Corn 5B 4
Trevarrian. Corn 5A 4
Trevarrick. Corn 7B 4
Trevaughan. Carm
nr. Carmarthen 4L 15
nr. Whitland 5H 15
Treveighan. Corn 4C 4
Trevellas. Corn 3L 3
Trevelmond. Corn 5E 4
Treverva. Corn 5L 3
Trevescan. Corn 6G 3
Trevethin. Torf 3A 18
Trevia. Corn 3C 4
Trevigro. Corn 5F 4
Trevilley. Corn 6G 3
Treviscoe. Corn 6B 4
Trevivian. Corn 7A 6
Trevone. Corn 4A 4
Trevor. Wrex 5A 34
Trevor Uchaf. Den 6M 33
Trew. Corn 6K 3
Trewalder. Corn 3C 4
Trewarlett. Corn 7C 6
Trewarmett. Corn 3C 4
Trewassa. Corn 3D 4
Treween. Corn 7B 6
Trewellard. Corn 5G 3
Trewen. Corn 7B 6
Trewennack. Corn 6K 3
Trewern. Powy 8A 34
Trewetha. Corn 4C 4
Trewidland. Corn 6E 4
Trewint. Corn 6A 6
Trewithian. Corn 8A 4
Trewoofe. Corn 6H 3
Trewoon. Corn 6B 4
Treworthal. Corn 8A 4
Trewyddel. Pemb 2H 15
Treyarnon. Corn 4A 4
Treyford. W Sus 4F 10
Triangle. Staf 1J 27
Triangle. W Yor 5J 41
Trickett's Cross. Dors 5J 9
Trillick. Ferm 6C 92
Trimdon. Dur 8G 55
Trimdon Colliery. Dur 8G 55
Trimdon Grange. Dur 8G 55
Trimingham. Norf 6J 39
Trimley Lower Street.
Suff 8J 31
Trimley St Martin. Suff 8J 31
Trimley St Mary. Suff 8J 31
Trimpley. Worc 4F 26
Trimsaran. Carm 6L 15
Trimstone. Devn 1E 6
Trinafour. Per 1M 65
Trinant. Cphy 5M 17
Tring. Herts 2G 21
Trinity. Ang 1K 67
Trinity. Edin 2L 59
Trisant. Cdgn 5G 25
Triscombe. Som 2L 7
Trislaig. High 8A 70
Trispen. Corn 3M 3
Tritlington. Nmbd 2F 54
Trochry. Per 3C 66
Troedrhiwdalar. Powy 7J 25
Troedrhiwfuwch. Cphy 4L 17
Troedrhiw-gwair. Blae 4L 17
Troedyraur. Cdgn 2K 15
Troedyrhiw. Mer T 4K 17
Trondavoe. Shet 6H 91
Troon. Corn 5K 3
Troon. S Ayr 6B 58
Troqueer. Dum 4D 52
Troston. Suff 4E 30
Trottiscliffe. Kent 7C 22
Trotton. W Sus 3F 10
Troutbeck. Cumb
nr. Ambleside 5C 46
nr. Penrith 3B 46
Troutbeck Bridge. Cumb 5C 46
Troway. Derbs 2A 36
Trowbridge. Wilts 8G 19
Trowell. Notts 6B 36
Trowle Common. Wilts 8G 19
Trowley Bottom. Herts 2H 21
Trowse Newton. Norf 1J 31
Trudoxhill. Som 1F 8
Trull. Som 3M 7
Trumaisgearraidh. W Isl 6K 75
Trumpan. High 7D 76
Trumpet. Here 8E 26
Trumpington. Cambs 6M 29
Trumps Green. Surr 7G 21
Trunch. Norf 6J 39
Trunnah. Lanc 3B 40
Truro. Corn 4M 3
Trusham. Devn 7H 7
Trusley. Derbs 6L 35
Trusthorpe. Linc 1B 38
Tryfil. IOA 2D 32
Trysull. Staf 2G 27
Tubney. Oxon 4B 20
Tuckenhay. Devn 6L 5
Tuckhill. Shrp 3F 26
Tuckingmill. Corn 4K 3
Tuckton. Bour 6K 9
Tuddenham. Suff 4D 30
Tuddenham St Martin.
Suff 7H 31
Tudeley. Kent 1C 12
Tudhoe. Dur 8F 54
Tudhoe Grange. Dur 8F 54
Tudorville. Here 1D 18
Tudweiliog. Gwyn 7B 32
Tuesley. Surr 1G 11
Tufton. Hants 1B 10
Tufton. Pemb 4G 15
Tugby. Leics 1E 28
Tugford. Shrp 3D 26
Tughall. Nmbd 7K 61
Tulchan. Per 5C 66
Tullibardine. Per 6C 66
Tullibody. Clac 8B 66
Tullich. Arg 6E 64
Tullich. High
nr. Lochcarron 1L 69
nr. Tain 6J 79
Tullich. Mor 1C 72
Tullich Muir. High 6H 79
Tulliemet. Per 2C 66
Tulloch. Abers 2H 73
Tulloch. High
nr. Bonar Bridge 4G 79
nr. Fort William 7D 70
nr. Grantown-on-Spey 4K 71
Tulloch. Per 5D 66
Tullochgorm. Arg 8D 64
Tullybeagles Lodge. Per 4D 66
Tullyhogue. M Ulst 5F 93
Tullymurdoch. Per 2F 66
Tullynessle. Abers 4E 72
Tumble. Carm 5M 15
Tumbler's Green. Essx 1E 22
Tumby. Linc 3K 37
Tumby Woodside. Linc 4K 37
Tummel Bridge. Per 2A 66
Tunbridge Wells, Royal.
Kent 2B 12
Tunga. W Isl 8H 83
Tungate. Norf 7J 39
Tunley. Bath 8E 18
Tunstall. E Yor 4L 43
Tunstall. Kent 7E 22
Tunstall. Lanc 8E 46
Tunstall. Norf 1L 31
Tunstall. N Yor 6L 47
Tunstall. Staf 7F 34
Tunstall. Stoke 4G 35
Tunstall. Suff 6K 31
Tunstall. Tyne 6G 55
Tunstead. Derbs 2K 35
Tunstead. Norf 7J 39
Tunstead Milton. Derbs 1J 35
Tunworth. Hants 1D 10
Tupsley. Here 7D 26
Tupton. Derbs 3A 36
Turfholm. S Lan 6G 59
Turfmoor. Devn 5A 8
Turgis Green. Hants 8D 20
Turkdean. Glos 2K 19
Turkey Island. Hants 4C 10
Tur Langton. Leics 2E 28
Turleigh. Wilts 7G 19
Turlin Moor. Pool 6H 9
Turnastone. Here 8B 26
Turnberry. S Ayr 1H 51
Turnchapel. Plym 6G 5
Turnditch. Derbs 5L 35
Turners Hill. W Sus 2L 11
Turners Puddle. Dors 6G 9
Turnford. Herts 3L 21
Turnhouse. Edin 2K 59
Turnworth. Dors 5G 9
Turriff. Abers 1G 73
Tursdale. Dur 8G 55
Turton Bottoms. Bkbn 6F 40
Turtory. Mor 1E 72
Turves Green. W Mid 4J 27
Turvey. Bed 6G 29
Turville. Buck 4E 20
Turville Heath. Buck 4E 20
Turweston. Buck 8D 28
Tushielaw. Bord 8M 59
Tutbury. Staf 7L 35
Tutnall. Worc 4H 27
Tutshill. Glos 4D 18
Tuttington. Norf 7J 39
Tutts Clump. W Ber 6C 20
Tutwell. Corn 8C 6
Tuxford. Notts 2E 36
Twatt. Orkn 7B 88
Twatt. Shet 2D 90
Twechar. E Dun 2E 58
Tweedale. Telf 1F 26
Tweedbank. Bord 6C 60
Tweedmouth. Nmbd 4G 61
Tweedsmuir. Bord 7J 59
Twelveheads. Corn 4L 3
Twemlow Green. Ches E 3F 34
Twenty. Linc 7J 37
Twerton. Bath 7F 18
Twickenham. G Lon 6J 21
Twigworth. Glos 1G 19
Twineham. W Sus 4K 11
Twinhoe. Bath 8F 18
Twinstead. Essx 8E 30
Twinstead Green. Essx 8E 30
Twiss Green. Warr 8E 40
Twiston. Lanc 3G 41
Twitchen. Devn 2G 7
Twitchen. Shrp 4B 26
Two Bridges. Devn 8F 6
Two Bridges. Glos 3E 18
Two Dales. Derbs 3L 35
Two Gates. Staf 1L 27
Two Mile Oak. Devn 5L 5
Twycross. Leics 1M 27
Twyford. Buck 1D 20
Twyford. Derbs 7M 35
Twyford. Dors 4G 9
Twyford. Hants 3B 10
Twyford. Leics 8E 36
Twyford. Norf 7G 39
Twyford. Wok 6E 20
Twyford Common. Here 8D 26
Twynholm. Dum 6A 52
Twyning. Glos 8G 27
Twyning Green. Glos 8H 27
Twynllanan. Carm 2G 17
Twyn-y-Sheriff. Mon 3C 18
Twywell. Nptn 4G 29
Tyberton. Here 8B 26
Tyburn. W Mid 2K 27
Tyby. Norf 7G 39
Tycroes. Carm 3F 16
Tycrwyn. Powy 1L 25
Tyddewi. Pemb 4D 14
Tydd Gote. Linc 8A 38
Tydd St Giles. Cambs 8M 37
Tydd St Mary. Linc 8M 37
Tye. Hants 5E 10
Tye Green. Essx
nr. Bishop's Stortford 1B 22
nr. Braintree 1D 22
nr. Saffron Walden 8B 30
Tyersal. W Yor 4K 41
Ty Issa. Powy 7L 33
Tyldesley. G Man 7E 40
Tyler Hill. Kent 7H 23
Tyler's Green. Essx 3B 22
Tylers Green. Buck 4F 20
Tylorstown. Rhon 5K 17
Tylwch. Powy 4J 25
Y Tymbl. Carm 5M 15
Tynan. Arm 6E 92
Ty-nant. Cnwy 6J 33
Tyndrum. Stir 4H 65
Tyneham. Dors 7G 9
Tynehead. Midl 4A 60
Tynemouth. Tyne 5G 55
Tyneside. Tyne 5F 54
Tyne Tunnel. Tyne 5G 55
Tynewydd. Rhon 5J 17
Tyninghame. E Lot 2D 60
Tynron. Dum 2C 52
Ty'n-y-bryn. Rhon 6K 17
Tyn-y-celyn. Wrex 7L 33
Tyn-y-cwm. Swan 4F 16
Tyn-y-ffridd. Powy 7L 33
Tynygongl. IOA 2E 32
Tynygraig. Cdgn 6F 24
Ty'n-y-groes. Cnwy 3G 33
Ty'n-yr-eithin. Cdgn 6F 24
Tyn-y-rhyd. Powy 1K 25
Tyn-y-wern. Powy 8K 33
Tyrie. Abers 7J 81
Tyringham. Mil 7F 28
Tythecott. Devn 4D 6
Tythegston. B'end 7H 17
Tytherington. Ches E 2H 35
Tytherington. Som 1F 8
Tytherington. S Glo 5E 18
Tytherington. Wilts 1H 9
Tytherleigh. Devn 5B 8
Tywardreath. Corn 6C 4
Tywardreath Highway. Corn 6C 4
Tywyn. Cnwy 3G 33
Tywyn. Gwyn 2E 24

U

Uachdar. W Isl 8K 75
Uags. High 2J 69
Ubbeston Green. Suff 4K 31
Ubley. Bath 8D 18
Uckerby. N Yor 5L 47
Uckfield. E Sus 3A 12
Uckinghall. Worc 8G 27
Uckington. Glos 1H 19
Uckington. Shrp 1D 26
Uddingston. S Lan 3E 58
Uddington. S Lan 6G 59
Udimore. E Sus 4E 12
Udny Green. Abers 3H 73
Udny Station. Abers 3J 73
Udston. S Lan 4E 58
Udstonhead. S Lan 5F 58
Uffcott. Wilts 6K 19
Uffculme. Devn 4K 7
Uffington. Linc 1H 29
Uffington. Oxon 5M 19
Uffington. Shrp 8D 34
Ufford. Pet 1H 29
Ufford. Suff 6J 31
Ufton. Warw 5A 28
Ufton Nervet. W Ber 7D 20
Ugadale. Arg 7G 57
Ugborough. Devn 6J 5
Ugford. Wilts 2J 9
Uggeshall. Suff 3L 31
Ugglebarnby. N Yor 5F 48
Ugley. Essx 1B 22
Ugley Green. Essx 1B 22
Ugthorpe. N Yor 4E 48
Uidh. W Isl 6C 74
Uig. Arg 2G 63
Uig. High
nr. Balgown 7E 76
nr. Dunvegan 8C 76
Uigshader. High 1F 68
Uisken. Arg 6J 63
Ulbster. High 7E 86
Ulcat Row. Cumb 3C 46
Ulceby. Linc 2M 37
Ulceby. N Lin 6J 43
Ulceby Skitter. N Lin 6J 43
Ulcombe. Kent 1E 12
Uldale. Cumb 8G 53
Uley. Glos 4F 18
Ulgham. Nmbd 2F 54
Ullapool. High 4B 78
Ullenhall. Warw 5K 27
Ulleskelf. N Yor 4C 42
Ullesthorpe. Leics 3C 28
Ulley. S Yor 1B 36
Ullingswick. Here 6D 26
Ullinish. High 2E 68
Ullock. Cumb 2K 45
Ulpha. Cumb 5L 45
Ulrome. E Yor 2J 43
Ulsta. Shet 5J 91
Ulting. Essx 3E 22
Ulva House. Arg 4K 63
Ulverston. Cumb 8A 46
Ulwell. Dors 7J 9
Umberleigh. Devn 3F 6
Unapool. High 8E 84
Underbarrow. Cumb 6C 46
Undercliffe. W Yor 4K 41
Underdale. Shrp 8D 34
Underhoull. Shet 3K 91
Underriver. Kent 8B 22
Under Tofts. S Yor 1M 35
Underton. Shrp 2E 26
Underwood. Newp 5B 18
Underwood. Notts 4B 36
Underwood. Plym 6H 5
Undley. Suff 3C 30
Undy. Mon 5C 18
Union Mills. IOM 7C 44
Union Street. E Sus 2D 12
Unstone. Derbs 2A 36
Unstone Green. Derbs 2A 36
Unthank. Cumb
nr. Carlisle 7H 53
nr. Gamblesby 7L 53
nr. Penrith 8J 53
Unthank End. Cumb 8J 53
Upavon. Wilts 8K 19
Up Cerne. Dors 5E 8
Upchurch. Kent 7E 22
Upcott. Devn 5E 6
Upcott. Here 6B 26
Upend. Cambs 6C 30
Up Exe. Devn 5J 7
Upgate. Norf 8H 39
Upgate Street. Norf 2G 31
Uphall. Dors 5D 8
Uphall. W Lot 2J 59
Uphall Station. W Lot 2J 59
Upham. Devn 5H 7
Upham. Hants 3C 10
Uphampton. Here 5B 26
Uphampton. Worc 5G 27
Up Hatherley. Glos 1H 19
Uphill. N Som 8B 18
Up Holland. Lanc 7D 40
Uplawmoor. E Ren 4C 58
Upleadon. Glos 1F 18
Upleatham. Red C 4D 48
Uplees. Kent 7F 22
Uploders. Dors 6D 8
Uplowman. Devn 4K 7
Uplyme. Devn 6B 8
Up Marden. W Sus 4E 10
Upminster. G Lon 5B 22
Up Nately. Hants 8D 20
Upottery. Devn 5M 7
Uppat. High 3J 79
Upper Affcot. Shrp 3C 26
Upper Arley. Worc 3F 26
Upper Armley. W Yor 4L 41
Upper Arncott. Oxon 2D 20
Upper Astrop. Nptn 8C 28
Upper Badcall. High 7D 84
Upper Ballinderry. Lis 5G 93
Upper Bangor. Gwyn 3E 32
Upper Basildon. W Ber 6C 20
Upper Batley. W Yor 5L 41
Upper Beeding. W Sus 4J 11
Upper Benefield. Nptn 3G 29
Upper Bentley. Worc 5H 27
Upper Bighouse. High 6L 85
Upper Boddam. Abers 2F 72
Upper Boddington. Nptn 6B 28
Upper Bogside. Mor 8B 80
Upper Booth. Derbs 1K 35
Upper Borth. Cdgn 4F 24
Upper Boyndlie. Abers 7J 81
Upper Brailes. Warw 7M 27
Upper Breinton. Here 7C 26
Upper Broughton. Notts 7D 36
Upper Brynamman. Carm 3G 17
Upper Bucklebury. W Ber 7C 20
Upper Bullington. Hants 1B 10
Upper Burgate. Hants 4K 9
Upper Caldecote. C Beds 7J 29
Upper Canterton. Hants 4L 9
Upper Catesby. Nptn 6C 28
Upper Chapel. Powy 8K 25
Upper Cheddon. Som 3M 7
Upper Chicksgrove. Wilts 3H 9
Upper Church Village.
Rhon 6K 17
Upper Chute. Wilts 8L 19
Upper Clatford. Hants 1A 10
Upper Coberley. Glos 2H 19
Upper Coedcae. Torf 3A 18
Upper Cound. Shrp 1D 26
Upper Cudworth. S Yor 7A 42
Upper Cumberworth.
W Yor 7L 41
Upper Cuttlehill. Abers 1D 72
Upper Cwmbran. Torf 4A 18
Upper Dallachy. Mor 7C 80
Upper Dean. Bed 5H 29
Upper Denby. W Yor 7L 41
Upper Derraid. High 2L 71
Upper Diabaig. High 7K 77
Upper Dicker. E Sus 5B 12
Upper Dinchope. Shrp 3C 26
Upper Dochcarty. High 7F 78
Upper Dounreay. High 5A 86
Upper Dovercourt. Essx 8J 31
Upper Dunsforth. N Yor 1B 42
Upper Dunsley. Herts 2G 21
Upper Eastern Green.
W Mid 3L 27
Upper Elkstone. Staf 4J 35
Upper Ellastone. Staf 5K 35
Upper End. Derbs 2J 35
Upper Enham. Hants 1A 10
Upper Farmcote. Shrp 2F 26
Upper Farringdon. Hants 2E 10
Upper Framilode. Glos 2F 18
Upper Froyle. Hants 1E 10
Upper Gills. High 4E 86
Upper Glenfintaig. High 7C 70
Upper Godney. Som 1C 8
Upper Gravenhurst. C Beds 8J 29
Upper Green. Essx 8M 29
Upper Green. W Ber 7A 20
Upper Green. W Yor 5L 41
Upper Grove Common.
Here 1D 18
Upper Hackney. Derbs 3L 35
Upper Hale. Surr 1F 10
Upper Halliford. Surr 7H 21
Upper Halling. Medw 7C 22
Upper Hambleton. Rut 1G 29
Upper Hardres Court.
Kent 8H 23
Upper Hardwick. Here 6C 26
Upper Hartfield. E Sus 2A 12
Upper Haugh. S Yor 8B 42
Upper Hayton. Shrp 3D 26
Upper Heath. Shrp 3D 26
Upper Hellesdon. Norf 8J 39
Upper Helmsley. N Yor 2D 42
Upper Hengoed. Shrp 6A 34
Upper Hergest. Here 6A 26
Upper Heyford. Nptn 6D 28
Upper Heyford. Oxon 1B 20
Upper Hill. Here 6C 26
Upper Hindhope. Bord 1A 54
Upper Hopton. W Yor 6K 41
Upper Howsell. Worc 7F 26
Upper Hulme. Staf 3J 35
Upper Inglesham. Swin 4L 19
Upper Kilcott. S Glo 5F 18
Upper Killay. Swan 5E 16
Upper Kirkton. Abers 2G 73
Upper Kirkton. N Ayr 4L 57
Upper Knockando. Mor 1A 72
Upper Knockchoilum.
High 4E 70
Upper Lambourn. W Ber 5M 19
Upperlands. M Ulst 3F 93
Upper Langford. N Som 8C 18
Upper Langwith. Derbs 3C 36
Upper Largo. Fife 7H 67
Upper Latheron. High 8C 86
Upper Layham. Suff 7G 31
Upper Leigh. Staf 6J 35
Upper Lenie. High 3F 70
Upper Lochton. Abers 6F 72
Upper Longdon. Staf 8J 35
Upper Longwood. Shrp 1E 26
Upper Lybster. High 8D 86
Upper Lydbrook. Glos 2E 18
Upper Lye. Here 5B 26
Upper Maes-coed. Here 8B 26
Upper Midway. Derbs 7L 35
Uppermill. G Man 7H 41
Upper Millichope. Shrp 3D 26
Upper Milovaig. High 1C 68
Upper Minety. Wilts 4J 19
Upper Mitton. Worc 4G 27
Upper Nash. Pemb 6G 15
Upper Neepaback. Shet 5K 91
Upper Netchwood. Shrp 2E 26
Upper Nobut. Staf 6J 35
Upper North Dean. Buck 4F 20
Upper Norwood. W Sus 4G 11
Upper Nyland. Dors 3F 8
Upper Oddington. Glos 1L 19
Upper Ollach. High 2G 69
Upper Outwoods. Staf 7L 35
Upper Padley. Derbs 2L 35
Upper Pennington. Hants 6M 9
Upper Poppleton. York 2C 42
Upper Quinton. Warw 7K 27
Upper Rissington. Glos 2L 19
Upper Rochford. Worc 5E 26
Upper Rusko. Dum 5L 51
Upper Sandaig. High 4J 69
Upper Sanday. Orkn 1G 87
Upper Sapey. Here 5E 26
Upper Seagry. Wilts 5H 19
Upper Shelton. C Beds 7G 29
Upper Sheringham. Norf 5H 39
Upper Skelmorlie. N Ayr 3L 57
Upper Slaughter. Glos 1K 19
Upper Sonachan. Arg 5E 64
Upper Soudley. Glos 2E 18
Upper Staploe. Bed 6J 29
Upper Stoke. Norf 1J 31
Upper Stondon. C Beds 8J 29
Upper Stowe. Nptn 6D 28
Upper Street. Hants 4K 9
Upper Street. Norf
nr. Horning 8K 39
nr. Hoveton 8K 39
Upper Street. Suff 8H 31
Upper Strensham. Worc 8H 27
Upper Studley. Wilts 8G 19
Upper Sundon. C Beds 1H 21
Upper Swell. Glos 1K 19
Upper Tankersley. S Yor 8M 41
Upper Tean. Staf 6J 35
Upperthong. W Yor 7K 41
Upperthorpe. N Lin 7E 42
Upper Thurnham. Lanc 2C 40
Upper Tillyrie. Per 7E 66
Upperton. W Sus 3G 11
Upper Tooting. G Lon 6K 21
Upper Town. Derbs
nr. Bonsall 4L 35
nr. Hognaston 4L 35
Upper Town. Here 7D 26
Upper Town. N Som 7D 18
Uppertown. Derbs 3M 35
Uppertown. High 4E 86
Uppertown. Nmbd 4B 54
Uppertown. Orkn 2F 86
Upper Tysoe. Warw 7M 27
Upper Upham. Wilts 6L 19
Upper Upnor. Medw 6D 22
Upper Urquhart. Fife 7E 66
Upper Wardington. Oxon 7B 28
Upper Weald. Mil 8E 28
Upper Weedon. Nptn 6D 28
Upper Wellingham. E Sus 4M 11
Upper Whiston. S Yor 1B 36
Upper Wield. Hants 2D 10
Upper Winchendon.
Buck 2E 20
Upperwood. Derbs 4L 35
Upper Woodford. Wilts 2K 9
Upper Wootton. Hants 8C 20
Upper Wraxall. Wilts 6G 19
Upper Wyche. Worc 7F 26
Uppincott. Devn 5H 7
Uppingham. Rut 2F 28
Uppington. Shrp 1E 26
Upsall. N Yor 7B 48
Upsettlington. Bord 5F 60
Upshire. Essx 3M 21
Up Somborne. Hants 2A 10
Upstreet. Kent 7J 23
Up Sydling. Dors 5E 8
Upthorpe. Suff 4F 30
Upton. Buck 2E 20
Upton. Cambs 4J 29
Upton. Ches W 3C 34
Upton. Corn
nr. Bude 5B 6
nr. Liskeard 8B 6
Upton. Cumb 8H 53
Upton. Devn
nr. Honiton 5K 7
nr. Kingsbridge 7K 5
Upton. Dors
nr. Poole 6H 9
nr. Weymouth 7F 8
Upton. E Yor 2J 43
Upton. Hants
nr. Andover 8A 20
nr. Southampton 4A 10
Upton. IOW 6C 10
Upton. Leics 2A 28
Upton. Linc 1F 36
Upton. Mers 1A 34
Upton. Norf 8K 39
Upton. Nptn 5E 28
Upton. Notts
nr. Retford 2E 36
nr. Southwell 4E 36
Upton. Oxon 5C 20
Upton. Pemb 6G 15
Upton. Pet 1J 29
Upton. Slo 6G 21
Upton. Som
nr. Somerton 3C 8
nr. Wiveliscombe 3J 7
Upton. Warw 6K 27
Upton. W Yor 6B 42
Upton. Wilts 2G 9
Upton Bishop. Here 1E 18
Upton Cheyney. S Glo 7E 18
Upton Cressett. Shrp 2E 26
Upton Crews. Here 1E 18
Upton Cross. Corn 8B 6
Upton End. C Beds 8J 29
Upton Grey. Hants 1D 10
Upton Heath. Ches W 3C 34
Upton Hellions. Devn 5H 7
Upton Lovell. Wilts 1H 9
Upton Magna. Shrp 8D 34
Upton Noble. Som 2F 8
Upton Pyne. Devn 6J 7
Upton St Leonards. Glos 2G 19
Upton Scudamore. Wilts 1G 9
Upton Snodsbury. Worc 6H 27
Upton upon Severn. Worc 7G 27
Upton Warren. Worc 5H 27
Upwaltham. W Sus 4G 11
Upware. Cambs 4B 30
Upwell. Norf 1B 30
Upwey. Dors 7E 8
Upwick Green. Herts 1A 22
Upwood. Cambs 3K 29
Urafirth. Shet 6H 91
Uragaig. Arg 8J 63
Urchany. High 1J 71
Urchfont. Wilts 8J 19
Urdimarsh. Here 7D 26
Ure. Shet 6G 91
Ure Bank. N Yor 8M 47
Urgha. W Isl 4C 76
Urlay Nook. Stoc T 4B 48
Urmston. G Man 8F 40
Urquhart. Mor 7B 80
Urra. N Yor 5C 48
Urray. High 8F 78
Usan. Ang 2L 67
Ushaw Moor. Dur 7F 54
Usk. Mon 3B 18
Usselby. Linc 8H 43
Usworth. Tyne 6G 55
Utkinton. Ches W 3D 34
Uton. Devn 6H 7
Utterby. Linc 8L 43
Uttoxeter. Staf 6J 35
Uwchmynydd. Gwyn 8A 32
Uxbridge. G Lon 5H 21
Uyeasound. Shet 3K 91
Uzmaston. Pemb 5F 14

V

Valley. IOA 3B 32
Valley End. Surr 7G 21
Valley Truckle. Corn 3D 4
Valsgarth. Shet 2L 91
Valtos. High 7G 77
Van. Powy 4J 25
Vange. Essx 5D 22
Varteg. Torf 3A 18
Vatsetter. Shet 5K 91
Vatten. High 1D 68
Vaul. Arg 3F 62
The Vauld. Here 7D 26
Vaynor. Mer T 3K 17
Veensgarth. Shet 3E 90
Velindre. Powy 1L 17
Vellow. Som 2K 7
Velly. Devn 3B 6
Veness. Orkn 7E 88
Venhay. Devn 4G 7
Venn. Devn 7K 5
Venngreen. Devn 4C 6
Vennington. Shrp 1B 26
Venn Ottery. Devn 6K 7
Venn's Green. Here 7D 26
Venny Tedburn. Devn 6H 7
Venterdon. Corn 8C 6
Ventnor. IOW 8C 10
Vernham Dean. Hants 8M 19
Vernham Street. Hants 8M 19
Vernolds Common. Shrp 3C 26
Verwood. Dors 5J 9
Veryan. Corn 8B 4
Veryan Green. Corn 8B 4
Vicarage. Devn 7M 7
Vickerstown. Cumb 8L 45
Victoria. Corn 5B 4
Victoria Bridge. Derr 4C 92
Vidlin. Shet 1E 90
Viewpark. N Lan 3F 58
Vigo. W Mid 1J 27
Vigo Village. Kent 7C 22
Vinehall Street. E Sus 3D 12
Vine's Cross. E Sus 4B 12
Viney Hill. Glos 3E 18
Virginia Water. Surr 7G 21
Virginstow. Devn 6C 6
Vobster. Som 1F 8
Voe. Shet
nr. Hillside 1E 90
nr. Swinister 5H 91
Vole. Som 1B 8
Vowchurch. Here 8B 26
Voxter. Shet 6H 91
Voy. Orkn 8B 88
Vulcan Village. Mers 8D 40

W

Waberthwaite. Cumb 5L 45
Wackerfield. Dur 3K 47
Wacton. Norf 2H 31
Wadbister. Shet 3E 90
Wadborough. Worc 7H 27
Wadbrook. Devn 5B 8
Waddesdon. Buck 2E 20
Waddeton. Devn 6L 5
Waddicar. Mers 8B 40
Waddingham. Linc 8G 43
Waddington. Lanc 3F 40
Waddington. Linc 3G 37
Waddon. Devn 8H 7
Wadebridge. Corn 4B 4
Wadeford. Som 4B 8
Wadenhoe. Nptn 3H 29
Wadesmill. Herts 2L 21
Wadhurst. E Sus 2C 12
Wadshelf. Derbs 2M 35
Wadsley. S Yor 8M 41
Wadsley Bridge. S Yor 8M 41
Wadswick. Wilts 7G 19
Wadwick. Hants 8B 20
Wadworth. S Yor 8C 42
Waen. Den
nr. Llandymog 4L 33
nr. Nantglyn 4J 33
Waen. Powy 3J 25
Waen Fach. Powy 1M 25
Waen Goleugoed. Den 3K 33
Wag. High 1L 79
Wainfleet All Saints. Linc 4A 38
Wainfleet Bank. Linc 4A 38
Wainfleet St Mary. Linc 4A 38
Wainhouse Corner. Corn 6A 6
Wainscott. Medw 6D 22
Wainstalls. W Yor 5J 41
Waitby. Cumb 5F 46
Waithe. Linc 7K 43
Wakefield. W Yor 5M 41
Wakerley. Nptn 2G 29
Wakes Colne. Essx 1E 22
Walberswick. Suff 4L 31
Walberton. W Sus 5G 11
Walbottle. Tyne 5E 54
Walby. Cumb 5J 53
Walcombe. Som 1D 8
Walcot. Linc 6H 37
Walcot. N Lin 5F 42
Walcot. Swin 5K 19
Walcot. Telf 8D 34
Walcot. Warw 6K 27
Walcote. Leics 3C 28
Walcot Green. Norf 3H 31
Walcott. Linc 4J 37
Walcott. Norf 6K 39
Walden. N Yor 7J 47
Walden Head. N Yor 7H 47
Walden Stubbs. N Yor 6C 42
Walderslade. Medw 7D 22
Walderton. W Sus 4E 10
Walditch. Dors 6C 8
Waldley. Derbs 6K 35
Waldridge. Dur 6F 54
Waldringfield. Suff 7J 31
Waldron. E Sus 4B 12
Wales. S Yor 1B 36
Walesby. Linc 8J 43
Walesby. Notts 2D 36
Walford. Here
nr. Leintwardine 4B 26
nr. Ross-on-Wye 1D 18
Walford. Shrp 7C 34
Walford. Staf 6G 35
Walford Heath. Shrp 8C 34
Walgherton. Ches E 5E 34
Walgrave. Nptn 4F 28
Walhampton. Hants 6M 9
Walkden. G Man 7F 40
Walker. Tyne 5F 54
Walkerburn. Bord 6A 60
Walker Fold. Lanc 3E 40
Walkeringham. Notts 8E 42
Walkerith. Linc 8E 42
Walkern. Herts 1K 21
Walker's Green. Here 7D 26
Walkerton. Fife 7F 66
Walkerville. N Yor 6L 47
Walkford. Dors 6L 9
Walkhampton. Devn 5H 5
Walkington. E Yor 4G 43
Walkley. S Yor 1M 35
Walk Mill. Lanc 4G 41
Wall. Corn 5K 3
Wall. Nmbd 5C 54
Wall. Staf 1K 27
Wallaceton. Dum 3C 52
Wallacetown. Shet 2D 90
Wallacetown. S Ayr
nr. Ayr 7B 58
nr. Dailly 1H 51
Wallands Park. E Sus 4M 11
Wallasey. Mers 8A 40
Wallaston Green. Pemb 6F 14
Wallbrook. W Mid 2H 27
Wallcrouch. E Sus 2C 12
Wall End. Cumb 6M 45
Wallend. Medw 6E 22
Wall Heath. W Mid 3G 27
Wallingford. Oxon 5D 20
Wallington. G Lon 7K 21
Wallington. Hants 5C 10
Wallington. Herts 8K 29
Wallis. Pemb 4G 15
Wallisdown. Bour 6J 9
Walliswood. Surr 2J 11
Wall Nook. Dur 7F 54
Walls. Shet 3C 90
Wallsend. Tyne 5G 55
Wallsworth. Glos 1G 19
Wall under Heywood. Shrp 2D 26
Wallyford. E Lot 2A 60
Walmer. Kent 8K 23
Walmer Bridge. Lanc 5C 40
Walmersley. G Man 6G 41
Walmley. W Mid 2K 27
Walnut Grove. Per 5E 66
Walpole. Suff 4K 31
Walpole Cross Keys. Norf 8B 38
Walpole Gate. Norf 8B 38
Walpole Highway. Norf 8B 38
Walpole Marsh. Norf 8A 38
Walpole St Andrew. Norf 8B 38
Walpole St Peter. Norf 8B 38
Walsall. W Mid 2J 27
Walsall Wood. W Mid 1J 27
Walsden. W Yor 5H 41
Walsgrave on Sowe.
W Mid 3A 28
Walsham le Willows. Suff 4G 31
Walshaw. G Man 6F 40
Walshford. N Yor 2B 42
Walsoken. Norf 8A 38
Walston. S Lan 5J 59
Walsworth. Herts 8J 29
Walter's Ash. Buck 4F 20
Walterston. V Glam 7K 17
Walterstone. Here 1B 18
Waltham. Kent 1H 13
Waltham. NE Lin 7K 43
Waltham Abbey. Essx 3L 21
Waltham Chase. Hants 4C 10
Waltham Cross. Herts 3L 21
Waltham on the Wolds.
Leics 7F 36
Waltham St Lawrence.
Wind 6F 20
Waltham's Cross. Essx 8C 30
Walthamstow. G Lon 5L 21
Walton. Cumb 5K 53
Walton. Derbs 3A 36
Walton. Leics 3C 28
Walton. Mers 8B 40
Walton. Mil 8F 28
Walton. Pet 1J 29
Walton. Powy 6A 26
Walton. Som 2C 8
Walton. Staf
nr. Eccleshall 7G 35
nr. Stone 6G 35
Walton. Suff 8J 31
Walton. Telf 8D 34
Walton. Warw 6L 27
Walton. W Yor
nr. Wakefield 6A 42
nr. Wetherby 3B 42
Walton Cardiff. Glos 8H 27
Walton East. Pemb 4G 15
Walton Elm. Dors 4F 8
Walton Highway. Norf 8A 38
Walton in Gordano. N Som 6C 18
Walton-le-Dale. Lanc 5D 40
Walton-on-Thames. Surr 7J 21
Walton on the Hill. Surr 8K 21
Walton-on-the-Hill. Staf 7H 35
Walton-on-the-Naze. Essx 1J 23
Walton on the Wolds. Leics 8C 36
Walton-on-Trent. Derbs 8L 35
Walton West. Pemb 5E 14
Walwick. Nmbd 4C 54
Walworth. Darl 4L 47
Walworth Gate. Darl 3L 47
Walwyn's Castle. Pemb 5E 14
Wambrook. Som 5A 8
Wampool. Cumb 6G 53
Wanborough. Surr 1G 11
Wanborough. Swin 5L 19
Wandel. S Lan 7H 59
Wandsworth. G Lon 6K 21
Wangford. Suff
nr. Lakenheath 3D 30
nr. Southwold 4L 31
Wanlip. Leics 8C 36
Wanlockhead. Dum 8G 59
Wannock. E Sus 5B 12
Wansford. E Yor 2H 43
Wansford. Pet 2H 29
Wanshurst Green. Kent 1D 12
Wanstead. G Lon 5M 21
Wanstrow. Som 1F 8
Wanswell. Glos 3E 18
Wantage. Oxon 5B 20
Wapley. S Glo 6F 18
Wappenbury. Warw 5A 28
Wappenham. Nptn 7D 28
Warbleton. E Sus 4C 12
Warblington. Hants 5E 10
Warborough. Oxon 4C 20
Warboys. Cambs 3L 29
Warbreck. Bkpl 4B 40
Warbstow. Corn 6B 6
Warburton. G Man 1F 34
Warcop. Cumb 4F 46
Warden. Kent 6G 23
Warden. Nmbd 5C 54
Ward End. W Mid 3K 27
Ward Green. Suff 5G 31
Ward Green Cross. Lanc 4E 40
Wardhedges. C Beds 8H 29
Wardhouse. Abers 2E 72
Wardington. Oxon 7B 28
Wardle. Ches E 4E 34
Wardle. G Man 6H 41
Wardley. Rut 1F 28
Wardley. W Sus 3F 10
Wardlow. Derbs 2K 35
Wardsend. Ches E 1H 35
Wardy Hill. Cambs 3A 30
Ware. Herts 2L 21
Ware. Kent 7J 23
Wareham. Dors 7H 9
Warehorne. Kent 2F 12
Warenford. Nmbd 7J 61
Waren Mill. Nmbd 6J 61
Warenton. Nmbd 6J 61
Wareside. Herts 2L 21
Waresley. Cambs 6K 29
Waresley. Worc 5G 27
Warfield. Brac 6F 20
Warfleet. Devn 6L 5
Wargate. Linc 6K 37
Wargrave. Wok 6E 20
Warham. Norf 5F 38
Waringsford. Arm 6H 93
Waringstown. Arm 6G 93
Wark. Nmbd
nr. Coldstream 6F 60
nr. Hexham 4B 54
Warkleigh. Devn 3F 6
Warkton. Nptn 4F 28
Warkworth. Nptn 7B 28
Warkworth. Nmbd 1F 54
Warlaby. N Yor 6M 47
Warland. W Yor 5H 41
Warleggan. Corn 5D 4
Warlingham. Surr 8L 21
Warmanbie. Dum 5F 52
Warmfield. W Yor 5A 42
Warmingham. Ches E 3F 34
Warminghurst. W Sus 4J 11
Warmington. Nptn 2H 29
Warmington. Warw 7B 28
Warminster. Wilts 1G 9
Warmley. S Glo 6E 18
Warmsworth. S Yor 7C 42
Warmwell. Dors 7F 8
Warndon. Worc 6G 27
Warners End. Herts 3H 21
Warnford. Hants 3D 10
Warnham. W Sus 2J 11
Warningcamp. W Sus 5H 11
Warninglid. W Sus 3K 11
Warren. Ches E 2G 35
Warren. Pemb 7F 14
Warrenby. Red C 3C 48
Warren Corner. Hants
nr. Aldershot 1F 10
nr. Petersfield 3E 10
Warrenpoint. New M 7G 93
Warren Row. Wind 5F 20
Warren Street. Kent 8F 22
Warrington. Mil 6F 28
Warrington. Warr 1E 34
Warsash. Hants 5B 10
Warse. High 4E 86
Warslow. Staf 4J 35
Warsop. Notts 3C 36
Warsop Vale. Notts 3C 36
Warter. E Yor 2F 42
Warthermarske. N Yor 8L 47
Warthill. N Yor 2D 42
Wartling. E Sus 5C 12
Wartnaby. Leics 7E 36
Warton. Lanc
nr. Carnforth 8C 46
nr. Freckleton 5C 40
Warton. Nmbd 1D 54
Warton. Warw 1L 27
Warwick. Warw 5L 27
Warwick Bridge. Cumb 6J 53
Warwick-on-Eden. Cumb 6J 53
Warwick Wold. Surr 8L 21
Wasbister. Orkn 6C 88
Wasdale Head. Cumb 4L 45
Wash. Derbs 1J 35
Washaway. Corn 5C 4
Washbourne. Devn 6K 5
Washbrook. Suff 7H 31
Wash Common. W Ber 7B 20
Washerwall. Staf 5H 35
Washfield. Devn 4J 7
Washfold. N Yor 5J 47
Washford. Som 1K 7
Washford Pyne. Devn 4H 7
Washingborough. Linc 2H 37
Washington. Tyne 6G 55
Washington. W Sus 4J 11
Washington Village. Tyne 6G 55
Waskerley. Dur 7D 54
Wasperton. Warw 6L 27
Wasp Green. Surr 1L 11
Wasps Nest. Linc 3H 37
Wass. N Yor 8C 48
Watchet. Som 1K 7
Watchfield. Oxon 4L 19
Watchgate. Cumb 6D 46
Watchhill. Cumb 7F 52
Watcombe. Torb 5M 5
Watendlath. Cumb 4A 46
Water. Devn 7G 7
Water. Lanc 5G 41
Waterbeach. Cambs 5A 30
Waterbeach. W Sus 5F 10
Waterbeck. Dum 4G 53
Waterditch. Hants 6K 9
Water End. C Beds 8H 29
Water End. E Yor 4E 42
Water End. Essx 7B 30
Water End. Herts
nr. Hatfield 3K 21
nr. Hemel Hempstead 2H 21
Waterfall. Staf 4J 35
Waterfoot. Caus 2H 93
Waterfoot. E Ren 4D 58
Waterfoot. Lanc 5G 41
Waterford. Herts 2L 21
Water Fryston. W Yor 5B 42
Waterhead. Cumb 5B 46
Waterhead. E Ayr 8D 58
Waterhead. S Ayr 2J 51
Waterheads. Bord 4L 59
Waterhouses. Dur 7E 54
Waterhouses. Staf 4J 35
Wateringbury. Kent 8C 22
Waterlane. Glos 3H 19
Waterlip. Som 1E 8
Waterloo. Cphy 6L 17
Waterloo. Corn 4D 4
Waterloo. Here 7B 26
Waterloo. High 3H 69
Waterloo. Mers 8B 40
Waterloo. Norf 8J 39
Waterloo. N Lan 4G 59
Waterloo. Pemb 6F 14
Waterloo. Per 4D 66
Waterloo. Pool 6J 9
Waterloo. Shrp 6C 34
Waterlooville. Hants 5D 10
Watermead. Buck 2F 20
Watermillock. Cumb 3C 46
Water Newton. Cambs 2J 29
Water Orton. Warw 2K 27
Waterperry. Oxon 3D 20
Waterrow. Som 3K 7
Watersfield. W Sus 4H 11
Waterside. Buck 3G 21
Waterside. Cambs 4C 30
Waterside. Cumb 7G 53
Waterside. E Ayr
nr. Ayr 1K 51
nr. Kilmarnock 5C 58
Waterside. E Dun 2E 58
Waterstein. High 1C 68
Waterstock. Oxon 3D 20
Waterston. Pemb 6F 14
Water Stratford. Buck 8D 28
Waters Upton. Telf 8E 34
Water Yeat. Cumb 7A 46
Watford. Herts 4J 21
Watford. Nptn 5D 28
Wath. Cumb 5E 46
Wath. N Yor
nr. Pateley Bridge 1K 41
nr. Ripon 8M 47
Wath Brow. Cumb 3K 45
Wath upon Dearne. S Yor 7B 42
Watlington. Norf 8C 38
Watlington. Oxon 4D 20
Watten. High 6D 86
Wattisfield. Suff 4G 31
Wattisham. Suff 6G 31
Wattlesborough Heath.
Shrp 8B 34
Watton. Dors 6C 8
Watton. E Yor 2H 43
Watton. Norf 1F 30
Watton at Stone. Herts 2K 21
Wattston. N Lan 2F 58
Wattstown. Rhon 5K 17
Wattsville. Cphy 5M 17
Wauldby. E Yor 5G 43
Waulkmill. Abers 6F 72
Waun. Powy 1M 25
Y Waun. Wrex 6A 34
Waunarlwydd. Swan 5F 16
Waun Fawr. Cdgn 4F 24
Waunfawr. Gwyn 5E 32
Waungilwen. Carm 3K 15
Waun-Lwyd. Blae 4L 17
Waun y Clyn. Carm 6L 15
Wavendon. Mil 8G 29
Waverbridge. Cumb 7G 53
Waverley. Surr 1F 10
Waverton. Ches W 3C 34
Waverton. Cumb 7G 53
Wavertree. Mers 1B 34
Wawne. E Yor 4H 43
Waxham. Norf 7L 39
Waxholme. E Yor 5L 43
Wayford. Som 5C 8
Way Head. Cambs 3A 30
Waytown. Dors 6C 8
Way Village. Devn 4H 7
Wdig. Pemb 3F 14
Wealdstone. G Lon 5J 21
Weardley. W Yor 3L 41
Weare. Som 8C 18
Weare Giffard. Devn 3D 6
Wearhead. Dur 8B 54
Wearne. Som 3C 8
Weasdale. Cumb 5E 46
Weasenham All Saints.
Norf 7E 38
Weasenham St Peter. Norf 7E 38
Weaverham. Ches W 2E 34
Weaverthorpe. N Yor 8G 49
Webheath. Worc 5J 27
Webton. Here 8C 26
Wedderlairs. Abers 2H 73
Weddington. Warw 2A 28
Wedhampton. Wilts 8J 19
Wedmore. Som 1C 8
Wednesbury. W Mid 2H 27
Wednesfield. W Mid 1H 27
Weecar. Notts 3F 36
Weedon. Buck 2F 20
Weedon Bec. Nptn 6D 28
Weedon Lois. Nptn 7D 28
Weeford. Staf 1K 27
Week. Devn
nr. Barnstaple 3E 6
nr. Okehampton 5F 6
nr. South Molton 4G 7
nr. Totnes 5K 5
Week. Som 2J 7
Weeke. Devn 5G 7
Weeke. Hants 2B 10
Week Green. Corn 6B 6
Weekley. Nptn 3F 28
Week St Mary. Corn 6B 6
Weel. E Yor 4H 43
Weeley. Essx 1H 23
Weeley Heath. Essx 1H 23
Weem. Per 3B 66
Weeping Cross. Staf 7H 35
Weethly. Warw 6J 27
Weeting. Norf 3D 30
Weeton. E Yor 5L 43
Weeton. Lanc 4B 40
Weeton. N Yor 3L 41
Weetwood Hall. Nmbd 7H 61
Weir. Lanc 5G 41
Welborne. Norf 8G 39
Welbourn. Linc 4G 37
Welburn. N Yor
nr. Kirkbymoorside 7D 48
nr. Malton 1E 42
Welbury. N Yor 5A 48
Welby. Linc 6G 37
Welches Dam. Cambs 3A 30
Welcombe. Devn 4B 6
Weld Bank. Lanc 6D 40
Weldon. Nptn 3G 29
Weldon. Nmbd 2E 54

Y

Z

Published by Geographers' A-Z Map Company Limited
An imprint of HarperCollins Publishers
Westerhill Road
Bishopbriggs
Glasgow
G64 2QT

www.az.co.uk
a-z.maps@harpercollins.co.uk

HarperCollinsPublishers
Macken House, 39/40 Mayor Street Upper, Dublin 1, D01 C9W8, Ireland

38th edition 2023

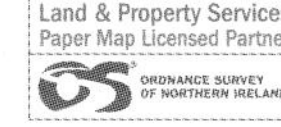

© Collins Bartholomew Ltd 2023

This product uses map data licenced from Ordnance Survey
© Crown copyright and database rights 2022 OS 100018598

AZ, A-Z and AtoZ are registered trademarks of Geographers' A-Z Map Company Limited

Northern Ireland: This is based upon Crown copyright and is reproduced with the permission of Land &
Property Services underdelegated authority from the Controller of Her Majesty's Stationery Office, © Crown
copyright and database right 2020 PMLPA No 100508. The inclusion of parts or all of the Republic of Ireland
is by permission of the Government of Ireland who retain copyright in the data used. © Ordnance Survey
Ireland and Government of Ireland.

Land & Property Services
Paper Map Licensed Partner

INDEX TO SELECTED PLACES OF INTEREST

(1) A strict alphabetical order is used e.g. Benmore Botanic Gdn. follows Ben Macdui but precedes Ben Nevis.

(2) Places of Interest which fall on City and Town Centre maps are referenced first to the detailed map page, followed by the main map page if appropriate. The name of the map is included if it is not clear from the index entry.
e.g. Ashmolean Mus. of Art & Archaeology (OX1 2PH)..........Oxford 114 (3C 20)

(3) Entries in italics are not named on the map but are shown with a symbol only.
e.g. *Aberdour Castle (KY3 0XA)*..........1K 59

SAT NAV POSTCODES
Postcodes are shown to assist Sat Nav users and are included on this basis.
It should be noted that postcodes have been selected by their proximity to the Place of Interest and that they may not form part of the actual postal address. Drivers should follow the Tourist Brown Signs when available.

ABBREVIATIONS USED IN THIS INDEX
Centre : Cen.   Garden : Gdn.   Gardens : Gdns.   Museum : Mus.   National : Nat.   Park : Pk.